Gramophone

Opera

GOOD CD GUIDE

© **Gramophone Publications Ltd 1998**

UK ISBN 0 902470 81 7

USA ISBN 0 902470 82 5

Sales and distribution

North America

Music Sales Corporation
257 Park Avenue South,
New York, NY 10010, USA
Telephone (212) 254 2100
Fax (212) 254 2013

Record Trade (excluding North America)

Gramophone Publications Limited
135 Greenford Road,
Sudbury Hill, Harrow,
Middlesex HA1 3YD, Great Britain
Telephone +44 (0)181-422 4562
Fax +44 (0)181-869 8404

UK and Rest of World Book Trade

Music Sales
8/9 Frith Street,
London W1V 5TZ, Great Britain
Telephone +44 (0)171-434 0066
Fax +44 (0)171-734 2246

Gramophone magazine, founded by the novelist and writer Compton Mackenzie and the broadcaster Christopher Stone, has been published monthly since 1923. As one of the first magazines devoted to the discussion of recorded music, *Gramophone* has maintained its position as the most informed and influential publication of its kind. Calling on the wealth of talent of a panel of the world's leading writers on music, *Gramophone* is the record collector's bible and it is from these writers and in the tradition of *Gramophone* that this book is published. Each month the magazine carries over 200 reviews of music across a wide spectrum, with a special section devoted to new opera recordings, and talks to the leading performers of the day. We are delighted to be publishing this first edition of the *Opera Good CD Guide* in association with BBC Radio 3.

Gramophone

Opera

GOOD CD GUIDE

Published by

**Gramophone Publications Limited,
135 Greenford Road,
Sudbury Hill, Harrow,
Middlesex HA1 3YD,
Great Britain**

Editorial Director	**Christopher Pollard**
Editors	**James Jolly** **Máire Taylor**
Production	**Dermot Jones**
Design	**Isabel Jagoe**

Contributors

**Nicholas Anderson • Alan Blyth
Robert Cowan • Adrian Edwards
Richard Fairman • David Fallows
David Fanning • Iain Fenlon • Hilary Finch
Jonathan Freeman-Attwood
Edward Greenfield • David Gutman
Stephen Johnson • Lindsay Kemp
Tess Knighton • Andrew Lamb
Robert Layton • David Nice
Patrick O'Connor • Michael Oliver
Richard Osborne • Guy Rickards
Stanley Sadie • Lionel Salter
Edward Seckerson • John Steane
Michael Stewart • Jonathan Swain
John Warrack • Arnold Whittall
Richard Wigmore**

Cover illustration Robert Mason
Printed in England by William Clowes Limited,
Beccles, Suffolk, NR34 9QE

Contents

Introduction

James Jolly
Editor, *Gramophone*

Gramophone reviewed *Madam Butterfly*, the first complete opera recording in English, conducted by Eugene Goossens on HMV, in its issue of November 1924. Since then many thousands of complete opera sets have been subjected to the scrutiny of stylus and laser beam, combined with the formidable expertise of a uniquely informed panel of critics as LP succeeded the 78. The advent of digital technology in the late 1970s started the ball rolling all over again. The record companies rushed to the studios to upgrade their opera catalogues: the finest casts available were assembled as A&R directors vied with each other to secure the services of the leading vocal stars of the day; conductors such as Herbert von Karajan took the opportunity to re-record many of the works in their repertoires to take advantage of the latest developments in sound reproduction (the first digital *Magic Flute* or Wagner's *Parsifal*, the first multi-track digital opera recording). But in time the old favourites returned to the catalogue, often sounding better than ever, and proving that once a classic, always a classic. An added bonus for record collectors is that many of these gems were offered at less than full price.

So, curtain up and enter, centre-stage, the ***Gramophone Opera Good CD Guide***, published in association with BBC Radio 3. We have explored our archives and assembled as complete a list of operatic recordings as was possible; the obscure sits alongside the familiar, the classic recording alongside the young pretender. The ***Guide*** will be just that, a companion to exploring the extraordinary variety of music drama on record.

Record stores can be daunting places; row upon row of boxes that all look more or less the same. This ***Guide*** should help unravel some of that mystery. For the popular works we offer a number of recommendations: a version in stereo, often digitally recorded, that has no compromises technically and contains a first-rate performance: these are usually full-price recordings. For the collector on a budget, we suggest a version at less than full price. For the serious opera buff who has maybe 'learnt' the work in a modern, studio recording and wants to get at its heart in a performance from the past (Maria Callas at her peak in the mid-1950s or one of Arturo Toscanini's staggering concert performances), there is a historic or live recommendation. For video collectors – ill-served it must be said by the companies – we have tried to offer a recommendation where the quality of the performance and its filming justifies it but this is not a medium that has been taken seriously enough so there are some lamentable gaps in the catalogue. (We have also, where possible, added any recordings of operas in English translation because, as English National Opera has so triumphantly proved, there is a market for opera in the language of the audience.)

Opera is addictive – the scale, the passions, the spectacle, all combine to make it an enveloping experience in the theatre. On record you can be your own set designer and stage director. With the help of this guide you can be sure that the performance you select will be one to treasure.

Gramophone Opera Good CD Guide

In association with

90-93 FM **BBC** RADIO 3

Welcome to this first edition of the *Gramophone Opera Good CD Guide,* **produced in association with BBC Radio 3. Among the many things that** *Gramophone* **and Radio 3 have in common is a commitment to the highest possible quality and to serving the widest audience of classical music lovers who want to find out more about the music they love. Both are institutions with a long history, and both have changed much in the course of time. Both need to find the best ways to serve their audience in the future.**

Radio 3 matters to its listeners. Its unique offering of the widest repertory of classical music and opera, much of it live and specially recorded, together with drama, documentaries, poetry and features, is highly valued. What the network broadcasts has changed very considerably from the days of the BBC Third Programme (which broadcast only in the evenings), the Music Programme which was introduced during the 1960s, and from the early days of Radio 3. We are now part of a broadcasting world which

has changed radically, offering much more choice to radio listeners, and part of a musical world which has changed too. The CD, too, has totally changed the ease, speed, and quality of sound with which we can access recordings of classical music, and has vastly expanded the recorded repertory. It seems absurd to talk of a crisis in classical music when the record catalogues are bulging with interesting, rare repertory, and where the broadcasting universe has expanded to include a highly successful commercial classical music service based on records, co-existing alongside the BBC's traditional and essential involvement in live music and the broadcasting of concerts from around the country.

The worlds of broadcasting and recording overlap, of course, and one of the many ways in which BBC Radio 3 seeks to be the authoritative voice of classical music in this country is by offering unrivalled comment and discussion of recordings, partly by playing them through the week on our sequence programme such as *In Tune,* which now features new releases

90-93 FM **BBC** RADIO 3

every weeknight at 7pm, and by evaluating them on our favourite and long-running Saturday morning programme, *Record Review*. We are the authoritative voice of opera, bringing you international performances from around Europe, the outstanding *Live from The Met* series of Saturday broadcasts from New York, and all the leading new productions from around the United Kingdom, led by our pioneering agreement with the Royal Opera to relay 12 of their finest performances each year. Leading critics and broadcasters such as Rodney Milnes,

Iain Burnside and most recently Jeremy Sams have had their own series on Radio 3 devoted to exploring the world of opera.

You can read much more about a wealth of opera recordings in this *Guide*: there is material here which will enable you to expand your repertory, find new adventures in the music of the past and present, and grow to love music you never suspected you might like. Exactly what Radio 3, 24 hours a day, 365 days a year, is also about. I hope you will join us regularly.

Nicholas Kenyon
Controller, BBC Radio 3

Travelling with hope

Gone are the days when perfection of execution and reproduction meant an entry into the sacred pantheon of 'great recordings'. Today such things are taken for granted.

So what is it that makes an opera recording great? Is it the glamour of a star singer? Is it the dictatorial conductor whose powerful vision binds the whole thing together? Is it the record producer who assembles an integrated cast and creates stage pictures with all the resources of modern technology? Whatever it is, there is no doubt that there are certain recordings that crop up again and again on everyone's wish-list: recordings which may not display the latest in digital clarity or even a particularly high degree of accuracy. From time to time an artist or group of artists will capture the inner truth and beauty of a piece of music, totally transcending the recorded medium and speaking directly to people of a later generation. Often these recordings aren't the ones which yield their greatness at first hearing. Both the Callas *Normas* can sound excruciating to the untrained ear. And by that I don't mean musically untrained; in fact that great lady's imperfections of pitch and vocal control are especially painful to the highly tuned ear. No, the insights of her performance only emerge on repeated hearings, while the charms of other interpreters come to sound like so much meretricious warbling. And to discover this for ourselves we occasionally need a trusted guide who will lead us into often unfamiliar waters.

And to be a good guide they need to earn our trust.

Radio 3's flagship programme, *Record Review*, proudly celebrated its 40th anniversary last year but we are still young Turks compared to *Gramophone* which, with 75 years of reviewing records behind them, can justly claim to have an Olympian overview of things. However, when it comes to the purchase of opera recordings it's a trusting collector who will act on the advice of just one critic. So *Gramophone* has come together with *Record Review*'s regular *Building a Library* feature to open out a double perspective on this particularly treacherous landscape.

The great thing about *Building a Library* is the fact that listeners can hear snippets of the different versions and make up their own minds about which one they prefer. The reviewers can often be very unorthodox but their judgements have to be backed up with a musical example. Regular listeners love it when someone knocks the standard recommendation off its perch. That happened recently when John Deathridge took as his subject Weber's opera, *Der Freischütz*. Instead of opting for one of the standard recommendations (Kleiber, Kubelík or Keilberth) he made a very strong case for the recent recording from Nikolaus Harnoncourt who has completely rethought the piece and given it a fairly radical reinterpretation. Now, I dare say that had the chattering classes choking on their cornflakes (and personally if I had to grab one version when the library goes up in flames, it would have to be Kleiber for Janowitz singing "Leise, leise") but the point is that the listener is always free to choose. The best critics scatter their reviews with advice such as, "if you want a digital recording go for A", "if you can't bear the sound of the fortepiano go for B", "if you insist on having the score absolutely complete go for C", and so on.

Of the recordings listed in this book 59 have come out as top recommendations both in *Gramophone* and on *Record Review*. Perhaps this level of agreement should not come as that much of a surprise. After all, both have many reviewers in common; both compare new releases with back-catalogue and both insist that budget price only means bargain if the recording is worth listening to more than once.

Collecting opera recordings is always a matter of travelling with hope because, of all musical genres, opera is the most difficult to get right on disc. So often the set with the best cast sounds studio-bound, the set with the most theatrical approach has unbearable sound, the set with the best Figaro has a squally Susanna, and so on. But once in a while all these things come together with that added *frisson* of seeming to discover the work for the first time. If you are in search of these experiences then this book would be an excellent place to start.

Clive Portbury
Producer, Record Review

Alive and Kicking at the Opera

Opera is a strange and mysterious art. It arouses passionate loyalties, passionate likes and dislikes – who was it once called Puccini's *Tosca* a "shabby little shocker"? Not a verdict likely to find much favour among the *aficionados* of Covent Garden! And talking of that particular Home of Opera, it is also true that the great opera-houses themselves sometimes seem to generate stories, myths and legends every bit as dramatic and improbable as the plots of the pieces to be heard within their walls. Not just Floral Street is its own soap opera: La Scala in Milan or La Fenice in Venice or The Met in New York, to name but three, could each provide a cavalcade of juicy scandal if required. Opera, in other words, is News.

Which is surely where broadcasting comes in. Keep your eyes open when attending any of the leading houses in Britain – and I do not just mean Covent Garden and the London Coliseum – and on occasion, discreetly parked in back street, dark back alley or dingy parking lot you'll spot a large grey pantechnicon, with maybe a small trailer in association, and maybe also an untidy labyrinth of cables snaking away from its ungainly rear end. The van is probably showing its age by now – broadcasting hardware does not come cheap, and opera, it must be admitted, is not a high priority on broadcasters' wish-lists – but nevertheless, this is the heart of the action, radiowise. In a nutshell, those warbling voices in the great duet from Bizet's *Pearl Fishers*, or the cavernous roar of the giant Fafner in Wagner's *Siegfried*, or the dulcet tones of newly-arrived diva, Angela Gheorghiu, dying consumptively at the end of Verdi's *La traviata*, all go the same way: down to the footlights, into a microphone, along a pair of wires, into a mixing desk, out again and up into the ether to a satellite, to be fed back down again into the gaping maw of Broadcasting House in London, then to be radiated down a thousand other circuits to hundreds of transmitters into millions of homes. Including, hopefully, yours, and then to you and your wireless set.

Why is the BBC there, and Radio 3 in particular? Could we not simply pluck a CD off the shelf? After all, enter any branch of Tower Records, for example, and the choice of operas alone is today overwhelming. There is, these days, nothing from the mainstream operatic repertoire that has not been recorded, often more than once. Better than that, CDs now offer repertoire that would never see the light of day on stage in 100 years: Salieri's *Falstaff* (eclipsed by Verdi) or Paisiello's *Barber of Seville* (eclipsed by Rossini) or Pizzetti's *Assassinio nella cattedrale* (his version of *Murder in the Cathedral*).

But if you believe that opera is indeed a multi-dimensional experience, involving not just singing, but dramatic action, strong emotion, an essential visual dimension (the character who silently overhears, costume, scenery, lighting), the *frisson* that passes between performers and audience and which makes every night an individual occasion – if you believe in opera as a multimedia event, to use today's terminology – then already you are half-way to accepting the argument for live broadcast opera. That argument says that the best form of broadcasting is live as it happens. That the element of risk, of danger, even if experienced only subliminally, makes all the difference. Will Signor Pavarotti crack on his top C tonight? Will Madam X cancel – again? Dare they risk using the understudy? (Reputations have been made overnight that way.) The broadcasts of the last Covent Garden *Ring* cycle had Brünnhildes too numerous to name!

Yet it seems to be worth all the expense: the days of rehearsal, the complex rigging of the theatre beforehand so voices are never 'off-mike', so microphones don't block sight-lines, so off-stage choruses and trumpets in the gallery (*Lohengrin*) sound just right to the listener in Dumfries or Dungeness. Radio 3 takes a presenter along not just to relate the plot, but specifically charged with giving the flavour of the specific production – Graham Vick's recent *Tales of Hoffmann*, say – the way it looks, the way the singers interpret their roles. Familiar voices such as James Naughtie or Natalie Wheen or even yours truly take their responsibilities in this regard very seriously indeed, often attending productions not once but twice in advance as preparation: it always feels like a race against the clock to cram in the detail.

Radio 3 also takes seriously its responsibilities outside London, and Welsh National Opera, Scottish Opera, Opera North and Glyndebourne are on the lists each year. We try not to ignore the best of the Festivals too. Radio stations from all over Europe offer broadcasts via the European Broadcasting Union: mostly tapes, but just occasionally we are able to go live to La Scala, say, or the Vienna State Opera. Personally I dream of a live Bayreuth *Ring*! But the cream of live opera from overseas has to be the regular Saturday night broadcasts from The Met in New York: a complex financial and technical deal negotiated a few years ago by the BBC with the American broadcast sponsors, Texaco, made The Met Saturday matinées, for long a feature of the American radio scene, at last available in Europe. I sometimes wonder if listeners realize quite how fortunate they are to have them at such a minute cost! Consider the cast-lists for a moment!

And Peter Allen, the regular presenter of those broadcasts, is by now something of an institution in himself – even though the season lasts only 20 weeks, and even though Radio 3 is not his home station! It says something for the pulling power of live opera on the radio that this is so. His measured tones, his artistry, serve one function: to be the listeners' eyes, to fill in the blanks in the imagination and make the experience of live radio opera as close as possible to the real thing. It is not the only way of presenting opera, and the BBC tries many other ways too, from television films, to opera excerpts on radio. And though the costs seem to rise inexorably, and the BBC's income seems permanently static, our determination to rid opera of its élitist image and make it available to all is surely part of what public service broadcasting is all about.

Relax: the sermon has finished: switch on your set: settle into your armchair, exactly placed between your two loudspeakers: unplug the phone, put out the cat: tonight, the magic carpet of radio takes you to: the Opera!

Piers Burton-Page
Executive Producer, Sequences and Talks

90-93 FM BBC RADIO 3

"Vermilion, not yellow!"

Opera at the Proms is always extraordinary. When I think back over recent seasons I still relish the tension and delight, the rapt silence and curious intimacy in the vast spaces of the Royal Albert Hall during an enthralling double-bill of Duke Bluebeard's Castle and L'Enfant et les sortilèges in 1995. Then in 1996 there was an opulent Don Carlo, an incandescent Lulu and a revelatory Leonore from the pre-Fidelio Beethoven. The following year saw London and UK premières of Violanta by the precocious young Korngold, and Henze's glitteringly seductive Venus and Adonis, along with the infectious buffoonery of Rossini's Count Ory. 1998 promises more operatic variety than ever, from The Damnation of Faust to Simon Boccanegra, via Zoroastre, King Roger, Falstaff and Porgy and Bess.

Opera staked a claim at the Proms right from the beginning. The first concert on August 10th, 1895 opened with the Overture to Wagner's *Rienzi* and continued with arias from *Pagliacci*, *Samson and Delilah*, *Philemon and Baucis*, *Carmen* and *The Barber of Seville* – a pretty mixed bag, with five different solo singers! And very soon Monday night at the Proms became Wagner Night. Loved by some, it was the despair of others – notably the hero of A. H. Sidgwick's *The Promenade Ticket*, a 1914 spoof guide to the Proms:

To tell the truth, two and a half hours of Wagner was rather a strain, in this weather too! It is a good deal simply the noise, I think: he does use such a lot of brass. And the singers feel it: the woman who sang the closing scene from *Götterdämmerung* nearly died – which perhaps made it more lifelike! ... That is the worst of Wagner. He had such a lot to say, and said it all!

But not all of *The Promenade Ticket* was tongue-in-cheek:

There is something very special about the Proms ... that electrical moment, the peculiar property of the Promenades, when the music gets over the footlights and the audience are fused in a massive solidarity of appreciation. We thrill together ...

What makes opera at the Proms unique is the immediacy of the purely musical experience. That certainly is what the performances which lodge in my memory have in common. Even when they are semi-staged, even if they sometimes experiment with different locations in the Royal Albert Hall (*Leonore* was set in the Arena), the productions give way to the music – and you can't always say that in the opera-house! Maybe the whole experience is not unlike the sheer concentration on the music you have when listening to opera on CD.

The parallel with CDs is even closer if you tune in to Radio 3 which broadcasts the complete season live. Here we aim to capture the full brightness and vividness of the performance, in all its details, along with a sense of aural perspective – the 3D of 'being there' in that marvellous Hall with its wayward but generous acoustic. On Radio 3 you also get the equivalent of the CD booklet-notes come to life! A presenter guides you through the evening, often with contributions from the conductor and soloists recorded earlier during rehearsal breaks. The whole operation is a huge challenge. However much forward planning, there is rarely more than the one run-through rehearsal on the day of the performance to get everything balanced – soloists, chorus, orchestra, presentation. Every day at the Proms means at least one new event (often two: there are 73 concerts in 58 consecutive days) and the sense of *live* broadcasting is never keener!

Meanwhile, the presentation and broadcasting of the music is just the nucleus of a whole spiralling-outwards of the Proms experience on Radio 3. Each event has an *Interval* feature devised to complement it in some way. Maybe the spotlight is on a visiting orchestra, a major artist, a significant work (new or old), or maybe some general idea behind the concert programming is picked up and developed in an extra-musical context – in 1998, for example, there is a thread of magic and mystery. Selected composers or themes are then focused on in even more depth in a weekly series of *Proms Documentaries*. On weekday mornings the artistry of major Proms performers is explored in *Artist of the Week*, and some of the key composers are celebrated in the broader context of their lives and works in *Composer of the Week*. Topical aspects of the Proms are also featured on the daily drivetime programmes, *On Air*

and *In Tune*, and a weekly magazine programme, *Proms News*, keeps you up-to-the-minute with reports and information about the season as it unfolds. One recent innovation is weekday afternoon repeats of many of the concerts (just in case you missed some of the evening broadcasts, or wanted to enjoy them again) and weekend repeats of the complete lunchtime series of *Proms Chamber Music* which takes place down the road in the Royal Albert Hall's sister building, the Victoria and Albert Museum.

Sir Henry Wood, founding father of the Proms, would have been proud! And he seems to have had an inkling all those decades ago of how significant broadcasting would become. Half serious, half joking, he often used radio as a stick to beat his orchestral musicians with. The story goes that if a passage was clumsily played in rehearsal, the redoubtable Sir Henry would wince and cry:

> It *shows*, it *shows!* If it didn't show it wouldn't matter, but millions of people are listening to the broadcast of this performance, and they've all got the score with them, and they'll be writing in. And all the children who are taught music in the schools are listening in, the little beasts. And they'll say, "It's not in *tune*, Daddy, it's not in *tune!*"

And with a famous twinkle in his eye, Sir Henry would urge his musicians on: "Rhythm in the fingers! More life, more vitality! Vermilion, not yellow!" That's still what opera and everything else at the Proms is all about.

Edward Blakeman
Executive Producer, BBC Proms

90-93 FM **B B C** RADIO 3

The reviews

Using the Guide

For ease of use reviews appear in alphabetical, as opposed to chronological, order

The title for each review contains the following information: composer, work, artists, record company or label, price range and disc number. The text within the brackets indicates the number of discs (if there is more than one), timing, mode of recording and recording date. Period-instrument performances are highlighted by the use of a symbol (see below).

Key to symbols

Ⓕ   Full price £10 and over (per disc)   Ⓜ   Medium price £7 – £9·99
Ⓑ   Bargain price £5 – £6·99   Ⓢ   Super bargain price £4·99 and below

AAD/ADD/DDD denote analogue or digital stages in the recording/editing or mixing/mastering or transcription processes in CD manufacture.

      Recordings where period instruments are used

      Selected by BBC Radio 3 *Building a Library*

      Gramophone Record Award winner

Abbreviations

alto	countertenor/male alto
b.	born
bar	baritone
bass-bar	bass-baritone
c	circa (about)
contr	contralto
cptd	completed
dir	director
fl	flourished
fp	fortepiano
hp	harp
hpd	harpsichord
keybd	keyboard
lte	lute
mez	mezzo-soprano
narr	narrator
Op.	opus
orig.	original
perc	percussion
pf	piano
rev.	revised
sngr	singer
sop	soprano
spkr	speaker
ten	tenor
trans.	transcribed
treb	treble
va	viola
va da gamba	viola da gamba
vars	variations
vc	cello
vn	violin
voc	vocalist

Adolphe Adam

Adam Le toréador.
Michel Trempont *bar* Don Belflor
Sumi Jo *sop* Coraline
John Aler *ten* Tracolin
Welsh National Opera Orchestra / Richard Bonynge.
Decca Ⓕ Ⓛ 455 664-2DHO (77 minutes: DDD). Notes, text and translation included. Recorded 1996.

This is an enchanting performance of Adolphe Adam's three-hander, *Le toréador*, full of sparkling melodies and *opéra comique* fizz. Richard Bonynge's ability to persuade Decca to record out-of-the-way nineteenth-century French stage works has been to our repeated benefit over the past 40 years. Yet few of the results have been more welcome than this delightful operatic soufflé. Not that the music is completely unfamiliar, since a 1963 radio version was briefly available on Musidisc's Gaieté Lyrique label. However, that omitted not only the dialogue but also the overture, some major arias and important incidental music, all of which are included here. Despite the title, there is little specifically Spanish about the piece beyond the Barcelona setting and the cuckolded elderly husband who just happens to have been a toreador. The love interest is between the former opera-singer wife and her flautist admirer, and it is the important contribution of the flute (almost a fourth character, and admirably played by Jonathan Burgess) that accounts for much of the aforementioned incidental music. The admirer identifies himself by means of assorted operatic airs and grades the seriousness of the husband's infidelities by whether he plays a fandango or a cachucha. The score's most familiar number is a set of variations on *Ah, vous dirai-je, maman* (*Twinkle, twinkle, little star*, if you like); but there is much else that brings out Sumi Jo's crystal-clear, effortless coloratura to marvellous effect, as well as showing off John Aler's ardent, elegant tenor and Michel Trempont's well-practised comic baritone. Delicious!

John Adams

Adams The Death of Klinghoffer.
Sanford Sylvan *bar* Leon Klinghoffer
Stephanie Friedman *mez* Omar
James Maddalena *bar* Captain
Thomas Hammons *bar* First Officer
Thomas Young *sngr* Molqi
Eugene Perry *bar* Mamoud
Sheila Nadler *mez* Marilyn Klinghoffer
London Opera Orchestra Chorus; Orchestra of Opéra National de Lyons / Kent Nagano.
Nonesuch Ⓕ Ⓛ 7559-79281-2 (two discs: 135 minutes: DDD). Notes and text included. Recorded 1991.

Rarely before has a composer snatched subjects from yesterday's news and made operas out of them. First *Nixon in China*, here *The Death of Klinghoffer*: They are works for instant consumption, for today rather than tomorrow. Admittedly themes of lasting significance lurk beneath the work's immediate surface: conflict between cultures and ideologies, rival claims to ancestral lands, human rights in general. Specifically, however, it takes us back no further than October 1985, when Palestinian terrorists hijacked the Italian cruise liner Achille Lauro, and murdered wheelchair-bound passenger Leon Klinghoffer. The opera guides us through those events, albeit in an oblique fashion, but its impact is all the greater for the fact that television newsreel and newspaper reportage of the Achille Lauro crisis are still fresh in the mind.

Whatever the long-term fate of the opera, Alice Goodman's libretto certainly deserves to be spared from falling into oblivion. It is eloquent and beautiful, compassionate and humanitarian, rich in imagery and spacious in its sentence-structure. Dialogue is virtually absent; the characters speak in long reflective soliloquies, sometimes as if to a diary, sometimes to a reporter, sometimes to a close friend, but hardly ever to one another. Surprisingly little action is allowed to take place on stage. It must surely rank as one of the least dramatic librettos ever devised, a poem in which everything borders on the confessional. It is marvellous to read, but how can it possibly be the stuff of opera?

John Adams has been hard pressed to come up with a solution. If *The Death of Klinghoffer* doesn't totally succeed, it is because the marriage of words and music is so fragile. True, Adams has a sure sense of how to underpin the mood of the text. Had his music been made to accompany the spoken word, as in a film-score, all might have been well. Instead his setting never seems at ease with the verse. Some of Goodman's most elegant lines simply fail to register their meaning when sung, their structure is too complex, their style too sumptuous, for the medium of opera. For all that the opera's musical language is firmly rooted in tradition, it is doubtful if anyone will come away from *The Death of Klinghoffer* with a single theme or memorable lyric moment lodged in the mind.

The recording uses the cast of the original production, and contains no weak links. As one expects from Adams, the score has been superbly orchestrated, and it is done full justice by the Lyon Opera Orchestra under Kent Nagano. Least satisfactory are the chorus: Goodman entrusts it with her most purple passages, but little colour emerges from singing that is so carefully accurate and lifeless. (Listen to the opening Chorus of Exiled Palestinians and see what you can understand from it without turning to the booklet for help.)

Eugen d'Albert   Scottish/German 1864-1932

d'Albert Tiefland.

Gerd Feldhoff *bar* Sebastiano
Ivan Sardi *bass* Tommaso
Ernst Krukowski *bar* Moruccio
Isabel Strauss *sop* Marta
Martha Musial *sop* Pepa
Alice Oelke *contr* Antonia
Margarete Klose *contr* Rosalia
Angelika Fischer *sop* Nuri
Rudolf Schock *ten* Pedro
Karl-Ernst Mercker *ten* Nando
Berlin RIAS Chorus; Berlin Symphony Orchestra / Hans Zanotelli.
RCA Ⓟ Ⓒ 74321 40574-2 (two discs: 130 minutes: ADD). Notes, text and translation included. Recorded 1963.

Tiefland is German *verismo* with a disconcerting flavour of operetta to it. The plot is melodramatically gamy (evil baritone Sebastiano has been having his wicked way with downtrodden Marta for years; now wishes to marry her off so that he can contract a profitable wedding but still proposes exercising his *droit du seigneur* over her; rustic tenor bumpkin chosen for the role of complaisant husband turns out to be not quite the patsy both Sebastiano and Marta take him for; happy ending, would you believe?), and it is no surprise to learn that Puccini once toyed with it. He dropped it on learning that d'Albert had the rights, but it is likely that he would ultimately have found its mingling of *Cavalleria rusticana* with *The Maid of the Mountains* (with *Rose-Marie*, indeed, one of whose tunes is unnervingly pre-echoed in the nearest thing d'Albert's score has to a love duet) unworkable.

It is of the essence of the plot that Pedro (the noble simpleton; could he have been called anything but Pedro?) is from the highlands, where men are men and emotions are plain but real, whereas Marta and Sebastiano are of the corrupt plain, the Tiefland. The two must be characterized somehow: the highlands (sheep country) by pastoral clarinet and cor anglais and by a would-be lofty (in fact quite decent) lyrical melody, the lowlands by a great deal of peasant picturesqueness (which is where operetta comes in; no doubt d'Albert intended the village women who mock Marta to sound emptily heartless and malign, but they are Rose Maybuds and Little Buttercups, every one of them). To sweeten the pudding still further, there is an *ingénue*-role for a little girl, Nuri, whose function in the drama is to act as everyone's confidante and to reflect upon what she hears with childish naïvety; whenever she appears, with her innocent but slightly sugary pipings (she is played here by a soprano who sounds not a day over 12), the plot stops for five or ten minutes of ersatz-Humperdinck.

These elements lie uncomfortably alongside the fairly rank sex'n'violence which is the real meat of the opera, and for which d'Albert seems rather less well equipped than for evocations of pastures and village greens. He is not bad at basic vehemence, quite good at heightened narrative (the dialogue nips along very briskly and syllabically indeed) and his melodic invention is sometimes appealing. d'Albert is occasionally numbered among Wagner's disciples, but apart from some clever motif-juggling (invariably in the orchestra; the singers are busy narrating) and a flagrant lift from the Johannistag monologue in *Die Meistersinger*, his Wagnerism is skin-deep. Mascagni plus a pinch of Sullivan (d'Albert's first teacher, after all) and a ladle-full of Millöcker or Ziehrer would be a closer definition of his curiously hybrid style.

The best moments are mostly Pedro's: his Act 1 monologue, telling of his life among the flocks (Richard Tauber once recorded it) has a hint ... well, yes, of Wagner in his lighter vein, or of Strauss's Barak reduced to a cameo. His scene at the end of that act, proud and confident in his love though coldly rejected by Marta, is sincere and even touching. Her monologue contains so much quasi-recitative narration that there is little room for sustained lyrical eloquence, but the utterances of the coarsely coloured pasteboard villain strongly suggest that complex or deep emotions were not within d'Albert's range. It is an operetta with pretensions beyond its means, really, but pretty enough and definitely worth a recording, if not a place in the repertory.

This recording derives from a television film from 35 years ago. Schock is on splendid form as Pedro: how good to be reminded that there were once German tenors of charm, forthrightness and security. Strauss is touchingly earnest as Marta and Feldhoff does the vocal equivalent of twirling his moustache and glaring through his monocle with great vigour. No weak links elsewhere in the cast, and Hans Zanotelli sounds as though he has been conducting and loving the work all his life. The recording is dryish, with the voices placed so far in front of the orchestra that they seem to inhabit a different acoustic, but on the whole the case for *Tiefland* is very capably put.

Tomaso Albinoni
Italian 1671-1751

Albinoni Il nascimento dell'Aurora.
June Anderson *sop* Dafne
Margarita Zimmermann *mez* Zeffiro
Susanne Klare *mez* Flora
Sandra Browne *mez* Apollo
Yoshihisa Yamaj *ten* Peneo
I Solisti Veneti / Claudio Scimone.
Erato Ⓑ ① 4509-96374-2 (two discs: 114 minutes: DDD). Text and translation included.
Recorded at a performance in the Teatro Olimpico, Vicenza during June 1983.

This non-dramatic *festa pastorale*, an overblown panegyric on the birth in 1717 of the future Empress Maria Theresa, marks a departure from the purely instrumental works by which Albinoni is currently represented on the *Gramophone* Database, and prompts the speculation that it might well be worth investigating his 50 or so operas. It reveals a lively imagination, not perhaps always very distinctive, but very agreeable; and there is one outstandingly lovely aria, "Questa fronda", for Dafne. The scoring throughout, however, is very individual and full of interest: several arias (mostly florid in style) have solo instrumental obbligatos – Apollo's "Pianta bella" an extensive one for viola d'amore – or dialogue with the violins ("Zeffiretti innamorati" is delightful); Apollo's "Con cetra più sonora" is accompanied only by archlute and cello; and in Peneo's attractive "Se l'alba io scorgerò" the string writing is unusually elaborate.

With the exception of Susanne Klare, all the cast are more than acceptable: Yoshihisa Yamaj's light tenor, indeed, deals cleanly and flexibly with ornate *fioriture*. Something radical seems to have been done to the recording since the LP issue: balance is no longer variable, the singers' words are quite intelligible (and here some appreciation of John Underwood's stylish translation of the libretto is in order), and applause is confined only to the end of each half, except after a spectacularly virtuoso aria from Margarita Zimmermann. What hasn't changed is a jarring *non sequitur* of key between the recitative and Flora's aria, "La rosa per regnar", and Claudio Scimone's direction, which is notable for hectic haste but not for sensitivity, and which shows scant consideration for his singers, with whom ensemble is frequently touch-and-go.

William Alwyn
British 1905-1985

Alwyn Miss Julie.
Jill Gomez *sop* Miss Julie
Benjamin Luxon *bar* Jean
Della Jones *mez* Kristin
John Mitchinson *ten* Ulrik
Philharmonia Orchestra / Vilem Tausky.
Lyrita Ⓔ ① SRCD2218 (two discs: 118 minutes: ADD). Notes and text included. Recorded 1979.

It is good to have this compellingly atmospheric reissue of William Alwyn's colourful and confident adaptation of Strindberg's play. Alwyn, an outstanding film-composer, here consistently demonstrates his mastery of atmosphere and timing to bring out the chilling intensity of this story of Miss Julie's sudden infatuation for her father's man-servant. He adapted the play himself, and understood far more than most librettists the need for economy over text. His principal modification of Strindberg is that to the play's three characters – Miss Julie, Jean the man-servant and Kristin the cook – he adds the gamekeeper, Ulrik, who acts as a commentator. So in his drunken scene of Act 1 he makes explicit what is happening, to the embarrassment of both Miss Julie and Jean. He also shoots (off-stage) the lap-dog which Miss Julie wants to take away with her on her elopement, a convenient but less horrific alternative to the slaughter of the pet finch in the original Strindberg.

Alwyn, with those modifications, presents the developments in the story with Puccinian sureness, and the idiom, harmonically rich and warmly lyrical, grateful for singers and players alike, brings occasional Puccinian echoes which, along with reminiscences of other composers, add to the music's impact rather than making it seem merely derivative. So in Act 2, Miss Julie's growing uncertainty over Jean's love is reflected in a passage (disc 2, track 5) which initially brings an echo of the heroine's last solo in Walton's *Troilus and Cressida*, and builds to a passionate climax which erupts first in echoes of *Fanciulla del West* and then in a direct quotation of the main theme of the trio from Strauss's *Der Rosenkavalier*, a motif repeated later. This is a confidently red-blooded opera.

The performance under Vilem Tausky is strong and forceful with superb singing from all the principals. Jill Gomez is magnificent in the title-role, producing ravishing sounds, not least in the glorious mid-summer night solo, expansively melodic but with wide-leaping intervals, which comes at the end of the first of the two scenes of Act 1. Benjamin Luxon gives a wonderfully swaggering portrait of the unscrupulous man-servant, vocally firmer than on almost any of his other recordings. Della Jones is splendidly characterful too, relishing her venomous cry of "Bitch!" when, at the very end of scene 1, she realizes Julie and Jean have gone off together. John Mitchinson is characterful too, in his drunken scene reminding you of Peter Pears as Albert Herring. The two discs come with a libretto and an excellent essay by Rodney Milnes, together with illuminating quotations from the composer – all, alas, in microscopic print.

Anonymous   c1140

Anonymous The Play of Daniel.
Eric Trémolières *ten* Daniel
Antoine Sicot *bass* Habacuc
Paul Médioni *bass* King Baltassar
Philippe Desandrè *sngr* King Darius
Dominique Thibaudat *sngr* Queen
Samuel Husser *sngr* Noble of the Court
Catherine Ravenne *sngr* Woman of the Court
Philippe Le Chevalier *sngr* First Prince
Bruno Renhold *ten* Second Prince
Adrian Brand *ten* First Counsellor
Richard Costa *sngr* Second Counsellor
Eric Guillermin *sngr* First Wise Man
Alain Brumeau *sngr* Second Wise Man
Jean-Louis Paya *bass-bar* Third Wise Man
Oriane Turblin *sngr* First Angel
Françoise Lévy *sngr* Second Angel
Béatrice de Vigan *sngr* Third Angel
Marie Estève *sngr* Child
Amiens Conservatory Children's Chorus; Ensemble Venance Fortunat / Anne-Marie Deschamps.
L'Empreinte Digitale ℗ ① ED13052 (71 minutes: DDD). Text and translation included.
Recorded *c*1995.

Various features distinguish this version of *The Play of Daniel*. First, the text is more clearly and flexibly sung than in any other recording: while there is a hint of the regular 'modal rhythm' normally applied to the unrhythmized pitch notation of the music, this is treated with considerable freedom, and innumerable shades of meaning come across more clearly. Certainly the result is a loss of the vigour, metre, rhyme and assonance of the poetry, but that seems a price worth paying. Second, the sections of the drama are interspersed with narrative that tells the story (in modern French). This is a good solution to the many points where important details of the action are simply presented as staging descriptions in the single surviving manuscript. It also articulates the drama well, showing how the sections divide up. Third, the Ensemble Venance Fortunat find a very good solution to the perplexing variety of written pitch levels in the drama. Essentially the singers each take the pitches at their own level within the Guidonian hexachord scheme; so quite often separate lines within a single song will sound a fifth or a fourth apart, and if everybody is singing the result is parallel *organum*. (There is also a fair amount of newly composed, and stylistically very good, polyphony devised around the surviving monophonic lines.)

Those are all good features; and the singing is mostly excellent. In particular, Eric Trémolières is quite superb in the title-role: his high tenor voice, firm and clear, gives a marvellous reading of the famous lament, which is rightly the high point of the performance. Listeners may find the dramatic pace less impressive. If you believe that *The Play of Daniel* is a masterpiece of theatre, the repetition of material will seem to get badly in the way of the structure. This leisurely approach softens the impact of the work's great moments. But it is a good and originally conceived performance; and nobody will be disappointed by its quality.

Thomas Arne   British 1710-1778

Arne Artaxerxes.
Christopher Robson *alto* Artaxerxes
Ian Partridge *ten* Artabanes
Patricia Spence *mez* Arbaces

Richard Edgar-Wilson *ten* Rimenes
Catherine Bott *sop* Mandane
Philippa Hyde *sop* Semira
The Parley of Instruments / Roy Goodman.
Hyperion Ⓟ Ⓒ CDA67051/2 (two discs: 140 minutes: DDD). 🖋 Notes and text included.
Recorded 1995.

Artaxerxes is a work of great historical importance and musically fascinating. Thomas Arne, the leading English composer of his time for the theatre, wanted to write serious as well as comic English operas, and decided that Italian *opera seria* should serve, on the literary side, as his model; he chose the most famous of all the Metastasio librettos, *Artaserse*, as the basis for his first (and last) attempt at the genre. It is generally supposed that the translation was his own work. He performed the opera at Covent Garden in 1762 with considerable success and it remained a favourite for many years. He never followed up that success, and nor, regrettably, did anyone else. But perhaps there were reasons for that. Metastasio, when translated into English, provides a libretto in rather elaborate, flowery language which is not really very well suited to the kind of music that English composers traditionally wrote for the theatre – and it would have worked even less well had Arne tried a more Italianate style. Arne did not employ the Italian *da capo* aria but kept, for the most part, to the simpler and more direct forms, even strophic ones, used in the English theatre. English vocal music of this period has quite a distinctive manner, tuneful, rather short-breathed, often with a faintly 'folky' flavour. It does not naturally reflect the exalted emotional manner of an *opera seria* text. This statement possibly has wider implications about the English temperament as well as the English language; but as far as *Artaxerxes* is concerned the result is a curious hybrid.

Nevertheless, the music is enormously enjoyable, full of good melodies, richly orchestrated, never (unlike Italian operas of the time) long-winded. Several of its numbers became popular favourites in Arne's time, and for long after – many readers will know the splendid and very brilliant final air, "The soldier tir'd of war's alarms", which Dame Joan Sutherland recorded for Decca in 1960. The story of *Artaxerxes* is a typical Metastasian one, with 'treasonous designs' and misunderstandings, and plenty of opportunity for the expression of strong and varied emotion. Much of the best and most deeply felt music goes to Arbaces, originally a castrato role written for the famous Tenducci, at mezzo-soprano pitch: here it is very finely and expressively sung by Patricia Spence. She begins with a big D major air demanding considerable agility and continues with a richly accompanied piece, very original in line: then in Act 2 she has a fine two-tempo air and an eloquent farewell piece as Arbaces is taken off in chains (suspected of regicide); and lastly there is the admired "Water parted from the sea", a minuet air, very English in style. Spence uses more vibrato than anyone else in the cast but her warmth of tone and expressive power are ample justification. Mandane, Arbaces's beloved, composed for Arne's mistress Charlotte Brent, is another rewarding part and is finely sung here by Catherine Bott, bright in tone and true in pitch and scrupulous in her verbal articulation, who can encompass both the charming English ditties and the more Italianate virtuoso pieces – the semiquavers in "The soldier tir'd" are dispatched with real brilliance and precision. The opera begins with a duet for these two that hints at (and indeed could have influenced) Mozart's "Ruhe sanft" in *Zaïde*.

Philippa Hyde sings very gracefully and charmingly in the role of Semira but does not always bring sufficient clarity to the words. As the conspiring Artabanes, Ian Partridge sings as clearly and intelligently as always. The role of Artaxerxes, the king, is taken by Christopher Robson, an excellent stylist, though this castrato part is bound to be testing for a countertenor and he is often covered by the orchestra. The smaller part of Rimenes, an insinuating traitor, is neatly sung and characterized by Richard Edgar-Wilson. Arne's orchestral style here is very rich, with much prominent wind writing; sometimes, as indicated above, the singers – given less prominence by the engineers than one might expect – do not ride the full textures very comfortably. Roy Goodman's accompaniments are not generally very subtle or carefully shaded. The original score does not survive complete, a victim (like so many) of the frequent theatre fires of the time; Peter Holman has done a predictably unobtrusive and stylish job of reconstructing some of the lost recitatives for this recording. This is certainly a set that can be recommended to anyone drawn to Arne's very individual and appealing melodic style.

Daniel-François-Esprit Auber
French 1782-1871

Auber Le domino noir.
Sumi Jo *sop* Angèle d'Olivarès
Isabelle Vernet *sop* Brigitte de San Lucar
Bruce Ford *ten* Horace de Massarena
Patrick Power *ten* Count Juliano
Martine Olmeda *mez* Jacinthe
Jules Bastin *bass* Gil Perez
Doris Lamprecht *mez* Ursule
Jocelyne Taillon *mez* La tourière
Gilles Cachemaille *bar* Lord Elfort

Auber Gustav III, ou Le bal masqué – Overture; Ballet Music.

London Voices; English Chamber Orchestra / Richard Bonynge.
Decca Ⓟ Ⓒ 440 646-2DHO2 (two discs: 144 minutes: DDD). Notes, text and translation
included. Recorded 1993.

Le domino noir clocked up 1,200 performances in Paris alone, after its 1837 première, and was soon
seen in London and in New Orleans. This spiffing recording – the only previous one was a much-
abridged affair from French radio – is the surest blow yet to be struck for a revival of Auber's
popularity in our time. The music is tuneful, danceable, constantly surprising in its form, and full of
interesting orchestration. The story is a variation on the usual masked-ball romantic comedy: couple
meet and fall in love without ever quite seeing each other, or finding out each other's names. The twist
to the plot is the fact that the heroine, Angèle, is a novice at the convent of the Annonciades, about
to take her final vows. Since she is out on the town at a masked ball, we must assume that she already
knows that the life of a nun is not really her destiny. The opening scene, when Angèle and her friend
discuss their escapade while the hero is (supposedly) asleep on a sofa, is a delight, as it develops into
a trio, "Le trouble et la frayeur". As Angèle, Sumi Jo sounds even more confident than she did in the
recital of French arias ("Carnival!" – also on Decca), which she and Bonynge recorded at the same
time as this.

The Second Act takes place later the same night, when Angèle finds herself locked out of the
convent, and takes refuge with the servants in a house, where it turns out the hero and his chums
repair for an after-the-ball supper. During the 1860s a visiting company starring the soprano Désiré
Artot planned a production of *Le domino noir* in Moscow, and Artot persuaded Tchaikovsky to
compose recitatives to replace some of the spoken dialogue. Bonynge has used four of these in this
act; it is unlikely that even the most accomplished Tchaikovsky scholar would recognize the master's
hand, but they certainly help this act to go with a bang. As the young man in pursuit of the beautiful
masked stranger, Bruce Ford sings with a good deal of elegance; he takes the high notes in full voice,
rather than the head tone which was more than likely customary in the 1830s. Both he and Sumi Jo
deal pretty well with the French language – most of the rest of the cast consists of distinguished
French singers: Isabelle Vernet as Angèle's confidante, Martine Olmeda splendid as the housekeeper,
Jacinthe, and the veteran Jules Bastin as Gil Perez, porter at the convent. Gilles Cachemaille has a
cameo as one of those satirical English milords who were so much a part of nineteenth-century
Parisian comedy.

Act 2 ends with a splendid build-up as all the disguises make more complications. One assumes that
Rossini was the main influence on Auber's style for such a comic piece, but he has an originality all
his own which in turn was to have an enormous influence, not only on the successors in the Paris
comic-opera business, Offenbach and Hervé, but also on Verdi. One of Auber's most successful tragic
operas was another masked ball – *Gustav III*, the libretto of which, also by Scribe, later served for
Verdi's *Un ballo in maschera*. As a fill-up on the second disc we get the ball scene from that opera,
which is a ballet in itself. Richard Bonynge conducts with his usual flair, keeping everything going at
a sparkling pace and encouraging some really imaginative singing.

Auber Gustav III, ou Le bal masqué.

Laurence Dale *ten* Gustav
Rima Tawil *sop* Amélie
Christian Tréguier *bass-bar* Ankastrom
Brigitte Lafon *mez* Oscar
Valérie Marestin *mez* Arvedson
Roger Pujol *ten* Ribbing
Gilles Dubernet *bar* Dehorn
Patrick Foucher *ten* Christian
Frank Leguérinel *sngr* Kaulbart, Armfelt, Valet, Chamberlain
Intermezzo Vocal Ensemble; French Lyrique Orchestra / Michel Swierczewski.
Arion Ⓟ Ⓒ ARN368220 (three discs: 184 minutes: DDD). Notes, text and translation included.
Recorded at performances in the Théâtre Impérial, Compiègne between September 28th and
October 6th, 1991.

Auber has become one of the forgotten men of music. Textbooks credit him with being the initiator
of the Grand Opera genre that Meyerbeer was to develop, and with being the first to compose an
opera on the subject of Manon Lescaut (nearly 30 years before Massenet), but his once-popular *Fra
Diavolo* has dropped out of the repertoire, and even his *opéra comique* overtures, at one time a staple
of light orchestras, are now seldom heard. What we have here is a forerunner, by a quarter of a
century, of *Un ballo in maschera* that Verdi not only knew but declared "vast, grandiose and
beautiful". Bellini, too, praised it highly, and its first performance in 1833 was followed by hundreds
of others in Paris and London. It would, however, be idle to pretend that it in any way rivals Verdi's
tautly dramatic treatment of basically the same Scribe libretto: Auber's tends to be long-winded, with
much verbal repetition, and despite his effective large ensembles, his facile, tuneful musical invention,
designed for uncommitted and undemanding audiences, could be called (according to taste) either

unpretentious or commonplace. Even at many key points in the plot the music would seem equally apt for light comedy: at really tense moments Auber tends to fall back on chromatic scales. Some of this lack of quality was probably also due to haste, the last three acts having to be completed after rehearsals had already begun.

The best music is undoubtedly to be found in Act 3, with a sinister introduction to the scene in the gallows-field, followed by a long bravura aria for Amelia and a duet between her and Gustav – employing musical material already foreshadowed in the overture. To please the Parisian bourgeoisie there were ballets in both the First and Fifth Acts (the latter more extensive and including an odd march in 3/4 time): in the present performance, recorded before an enthusiastic but well-behaved audience in the excellent acoustics of the theatre in Compiègne, both have been slightly cut – that in Act 5, astonishingly, omitting the famous galop, which originally caused a sensation when performed by 120 dancers.

It is a performance that reflects considerable credit on all concerned. The star of the show, following in the steps of Nourrit, who originally took the title-role, is Laurence Dale (an Englishman with perfect French), who employs his lyrical, freely-produced voice (which also contains the requisite metal) with the greatest intelligence, making every word not only clear but meaningful, and pacing his recitatives admirably: he has two big arias, one in Act 5, the other, at the start of the opera, sailing up twice to a top D. Christian Tréguier brings a fine *voix noble* to the part of the wronged Ankastrom who eventually assassinates Gustav (with a very unconvincing pistol shot, incidentally); there is a suitably dark-voiced sorceress from Valérie Marestin and a flexible, soubrettishly bright Oscar from Brigitte Lafon. Rima Tawil is a dramatic soprano who at times seems to be exerting overmuch pressure, but she is certainly an impressive figure: her Belgian-type rolled 'rs', however, are somewhat obtrusive. Chorus and orchestra are excellent, and Swierczewski judges tempos well and, bearing in mind that the recording is taken from live performances, secures very laudable precision even in the largest-scale ensembles (only once, in the Act 2 finale, is there a momentary lapse). The printed libretto, rather faultily translated, has not been quite fully co-ordinated with what is actually sung.

Johann Christian Bach   German/Italian/British 1735-1782

J. C. Bach Amadis des Gaules (sung in German).
  James Wagner *ten* Amadis
  Ulrike Sonntag *sop* Oriane
  Elfrieda Hobarth *sop* Coryphée
  Ibolya Verebics *sop* Arcabonne
  Wolfgang Schöne *bass* Arcalaus
  Etsuko Matsushita *sop* First Temptress
  Ruth Altrock *mez* Discord, Second Temptress, Urgande
  Reinhard Hagen *bass* Hatred, Voice from the grave
  Stuttgart Gächinger Kantorei; Stuttgart Bach Collegium / Helmuth Rilling.
  Hänssler Classic Ⓕ Ⓘ 98 963 (two discs: 124 minutes: DDD). Text and translation included.
  Recorded 1990.

Johann Christian Bach, the only member of his family to have had any career in the opera-house, began writing for the stage in Italy, continued in London and Mannheim and ended in Paris. This work is the last of his operas, written in 1779 to a revision of the libretto by Quinault that Lully had set almost a century before. It was not a success; there were only seven performances and it was never revived. One can see some of the reasons why it failed to please the French audiences at the time, but there is nevertheless some superlative music here which certainly affects our view of J. C. Bach, whom we tend to regard above all as an elegant, *galant* composer of courtly, Italianate symphonies and chamber music.

Amadis des Gaules (or *de Gaule*, as it is more usually and no less correctly known) is a *tragédie-lyrique*, on a magical medieval theme about a pair of sorcerers, brother and sister, who seek vengeance on Amadis and his beloved Oriane because he earlier killed their brother, Ardan Canale. It is rather a silly plot and one that no music of the late eighteenth century could plausibly support. Bach, however, produces a number of very fine pieces. Some are virtually Italian-style arias, for example the first two, the one for Coryphée near the end of Act 2 and that for the sorcerer Arcalaus in the final act. But there are also some intensely eloquent airs, notably all the solo music for Amadis (the part was composed for the famous *haute-contre*, Legros) including a very Gluckian air at the end of Act 1; there is a powerful invocation for Arcalaus, an astonishing ghost scene for Ardan Canale (recalling with its misty, low-pitched halo of sound Handel's for Samuel in his *Saul*, which Bach must have known) and several duets, among them an impassioned piece for the sorcerers earlier in Act 1 and an appealing one soon after for the lovers, as well as a very warmly written piece (also for the lovers) near the end of the opera.

There are some fine choruses, including a vivid one for the sorcerers' demons, an amorous, languid item for the spirits enchained by the sorcerers and a noble, chromatic piece to open Act 2 for the prisoners and the guards. Being a French opera, *Amadis* of course has no *secco* but rather orchestral recitative throughout, music in the manner of the recitative in *Idomeneo* though not, of course dramatically as dense or as closely worked. But much of it is strong, taut, effective music, often very richly orchestrated: even the string writing seems texturally dense, and there is plenty of imaginative and resourceful writing for the woodwind (which includes clarinets). That for the orchestra is altogether particularly attractive: the highly expressive introduction to Act 3 is like nothing else – it's not much like any other J. C. Bach either, if it comes to that – and with the expressions of grief that follow from the heroine, Oriane, it makes a very remarkable scene. Gluck, of course, is the obvious point of reference in terms of style: his two *Iphigénies*, *Armide* and the French versions of *Alceste* and *Orfeo* had been heard in Paris not long before, though Bach reverts at times to his more Italian manner and lacks the broad dramatic command and concentration that distinguish Gluck's greatest works. Bach had also composed for Mannheim and there is some influence of the reform style favoured in that progressive centre.

A French opera, often Italian in idiom, written by a German who spent most of his working life in England: a real European Community piece, this! And it is made the more so here by being performed in German. That is of course regrettable, because the music takes its rhythms and the shape of its lines from the French language and the mismatch is palpable. The performance is, one imagines, based on those given in 1988 in Stuttgart and Frankfurt. Helmuth Rilling, always a dependable and efficient conductor, directs what is a largely effective and stylish reading, with well-chosen tempos and a real sense of drama where it is called for. And he clearly relishes the variety of orchestral colour in the score. There are a few cuts, notably of some of the ballet music at the ends of acts. Bach made some adjustments during the run of the original performances, which seem to be reflected in different versions of the autograph; in some cases Rilling prefers the changed text.

Of the singers, the American, James Wagner, is particularly impressive; he negotiates the very high-lying music for Amadis without evident strain and with smooth tone and expressive line. Ibolya Verebics is impressive, too, for her dramatic singing of Arcabonne's music. The rest of the cast are also very competent. *Amadis des Gaules* is unlikely to enter the repertory, but there is a lot of very fine, highly original and deeply serious music in this score; it's certainly worth trying.

Francisco Barbieri   Spanish 1823-1894

Barbieri El Barberillo de Lavapiés.

Lola Casariego *mez* Paloma
María Bayo *sop* Marquesita del Bierzo
Manuel Lanza *bar* Lamparilla
José Sempere *ten* Don Luis de Haro
Juan Pons *bass-bar* Don Juan de Peralta
Stefano Palatchi *bass* Don Pedro de Monforte;
La Laguna University Polyphonic Chorus Reyes Bartlet Choir, Puerto de la Cruz;
Tenerife Rondalla and Symphony Orchestra / Victor Pablo Pérez.
Auvidis Valois Ⓔ Ⓘ V4731 (67 minutes: DDD). Notes, text and translation included.
Recorded 1994.

Much of the sparkle in this performance of one of the pillars of the *zarzuela grande* repertoire – which first saw the light three months before both *Carmen* and *Trial by Jury* – is due to the young conductor, Victor Pablo Pérez (who has won praise for previous recordings of works by Gerhard, Falla and de Pablo), who secures orchestral playing of a finesse all too rare in this sphere. Shorn of the raucous and crude sonorities with which many *zarzuela* performances have been fobbed off, this classic work – heard here in Barbieri's original orchestration, not the makeshift reduced version of 1929 – is given a chance to reveal its quality, which, however different in style, bears comparison with the best Viennese operettas (it is exactly contemporaneous with *Die Fledermaus*). Pablo Pérez has the advantage of a well-trained, fresh-voiced chorus and a cast of good singers, all with commendably clear enunciation – which lends point, for example, to the scene where the two women imitate the low-life speech of Madrid *majas* (more or less the equivalent of Cockney sparrows).

Chief vocal honours go to Manuel Lanza in the title-role of the 'little barber' who, like his Rossinian forebear, gets caught up in intrigue, though here a political rather than an amorous nature: the parallel with Figaro is heightened on this occasion by the role being sung by a baritone instead of the usual tenor; and he is well partnered by Lola Casariego as his seamstress sweetheart. Their music, imbued with popular dance flavours, is contrasted with the more Italianate style allotted to the two aristocratic principals, Don Luis and the Marquesita. The former has a fine voice but seems too intent on showing it off: if only the producer had persuaded him to sing less than *forte* occasionally! Rather the same goes for María Bayo, who tends to become shrill and does little in the way of characterization (she makes no effort to modify her tone for asides, for example). Juan Pons has so noble-sounding a voice (bass-baritone rather than baritone) that it is a pity he has to disappear so soon from the action.

The recording is of the music only, without any of the extensive dialogue, but the big gaps in the plot are summarized in synopses, which happily are also translated.

Béla Bártok

Hungarian 1881-1945

Bartók Duke Bluebeard's Castle.
John Tomlinson *bass* Bluebeard
Anne Sofie von Otter *mez* Judith
Sandor Elès *spkr*
Berlin Philharmonic Orchestra / Bernard Haitink.
EMI Ⓟ Ⓒ CDC5 56162-2 (63 minutes: DDD). Notes, text and translation included. Recorded
live in 1995.

Bernard Haitink's poetic axis is vividly anticipated in the rarely recorded spoken prologue where
Sandor Elès bids us search beneath the story's surface. Elès's timing and his sensitivity to word-
colouring and to the rhythmic inflexions of his native language affirm the Gothic imagery of Bartók's
solemn opening bars. The crossover between words and music is skilfully managed while the main
protagonists soon establish very definite personalities, Bluebeard/Tomlinson as commanding,
inscrutable and just a little arrogant, von Otter/Judith as profoundly frightened but filled with
curiosity. When she enquires "Is this really Bluebeard's Castle?" (track 1, 5'53"), you sense the full
measure of her terror; "Why no windows, no sweet daylight?" she asks, and Bluebeard answers with
a menacing, though resolute, "Never".
  Haitink and the Berlin Philharmonic paint a rich aural backdrop that is neither too slow nor overly
lugubrious and that shows due appreciation of Bartók's seamless scoring, especially in terms of the
woodwind. The disembodied sighs that greet Judith's violent hammering on the first door (12'19")
mark a momentary retreat from the Philharmonie's ambient acoustic (or so it seems) and in so doing
suggest – quite appropriately – a chilling 'world beyond'. Judith's shock as she recoils in horror
("What was that? Who was sighing?") is conveyed in clipped, halting tones by von Otter (note too how
seductively she manipulates Bluebeard into opening the first door: "Come, we'll open it together," at
14'25"). Beyond the expansive introduction (the opera's longest single span) come the doors
themselves, and here too Haitink balances the 'outer' and 'inner' aspects of Bartók's score to
perfection – whether in the torture chamber (with its fiercely rattling xylophone), "The Armoury"
(note an almost Tchaikovskian slant to the writing at 1'43"), the glowing textures of "The Secret
Garden"or the Brucknerian expanses of the fifth door, "Bluebeard's Kingdom" (the opera's structural
apex), launched here on a series of epic crescendos. Von Otter's stunned responses suggest lonely
disorientation within a vast space, whereas the sullenness of the "Lake of Tears" prompts an exquisite
blending of instrumental timbres, most particularly between brass and woodwind. Haitink draws an
aching curve to the string writing, but when, at 9'28" (track 7), Judith rushes panic-stricken towards
the seventh door, fearful of Bluebeard's secret murders, he effects a gradual but cumulatively thrilling
accelerando. The internment itself is devastating, while Bluebeard's helpless retreat marks a slow
journey back to the questioning void.
  Recording live can have its pitfalls, but here the atmosphere is electric, the grasp of Bartók's sombre
tone-painting – whether sung or played – absolute. EMI's engineering favours a full sound stage rather
than picking out specific instrumental details, but the overall effect remains satisfying.

Bartók Duke Bluebeard's Castle.
Walter Berry *bass* Bluebeard
Christa Ludwig *mez* Judith
London Symphony Orchestra / Istvan Kertész.
Decca The Classic Sound Ⓜ Ⓒ 443 571-2DCS (59 minutes: ADD). Notes, text and translation
included. Recorded 1965.

This issue must count as one of Decca's great operatic recordings, to be treasured by all who
appreciate this marvellous score. What strikes you most about this production is its sumptuousness,
its warmth and a vivid sense of audio theatre. It is conceived as a dramatic performance, with
changing perspectives as the characters enter the darkness of Bluebeard's castle and move to the
various forbidden doors. If this were all, it would be a question only of individual preference, since
the essential drama of the piece lies not in its external action, which is symbolic, but in the mind –
though whether Bluebeard's or one's own can be argued. But it is by no means all.
  When it comes to the husband-and-wife team of Walter Berry and Christa Ludwig, one senses more
a woman discovering sinister aspects of the man she loves than an inquisitive shrew intent on
plundering Bluebeard's every secret. Here, Judith seems perpetually poised to take Bluebeard's arm
and linger lovingly about him, while Berry's assumption of the title-role – which is beautifully, if not
terribly idiomatically, sung – suggests neither *Angst* nor impatience. Ludwig, too, was in wonderful
voice at the time of this recording, and instances of her eloquence are far too numerous to list
individually. Perhaps the work's spacious introduction provides the best place to sample – there, or
the lead-up to the seventh door. For all that the opera is sung in Hungarian, it is possible to follow
the changing moods of the characters with ease (and in any case a complete translation of the text is
provided) – in fact, it is impossible not to be carried away by the performance. Then there is the
orchestral playing, under Kertész, which can be described only as ravishing: the warmth and beauty

of tone are matched by wonderful finesse of accentuation and dynamics. And finally the recording, which is astonishingly evocative and full of atmosphere, allowing everything to be heard yet without thrusting detail under our noses. This is a thrilling recording of a great work.

Bartók Duke Bluebeard's Castle.

Robert Lloyd *bass* Bluebeard
Elizabeth Laurence *sop* Judith
London Philharmonic Orchestra / Adám Fischer. *Film Director:* **Leslie Megahey.**
Teldec ⚏ 9031-73830-3; ⚊ 9031-73830-6 (64 minutes). Text and translation included. Recorded 1988.

Béla Balász, Bartók's librettist, was a distinguished man of the films, so it's hardly surprising that this opera works so well in cinematic terms, as this video testifies. Its success can be measured by how imaginatively the director meets the exigent demands of the authors. Leslie Megahey's award-winning film succeeds admirably, with touches of pure brilliance, for all that occasional signs of being studio-bound make it less inspired than it might have been. The action is set within the confines of a gloomy, dark-looking Victorian mansion, the setting being firmly defined at the outset by the shot of Bluebeard's eyes opening as a key is turned; the 'castle' is behind the lofty brow of Robert Lloyd, in rich voice. His Bluebeard is initially affable, only later turning nasty, as Judith rattles more insistently at those doors within his mind. Elizabeth Laurence is in fine voice for her role, but her acting lacks fire and real erotic charge. Adám Fischer's conducting is sombre, but still very impressive. The Prologue is included, spoken in English, but there are no subtitles although Teldec credit a translator. The sound on LaserDisc is superior to the VHS version. In many ways more sophisticated than its rival (the currently unavailable 1981 Solti/Decca version), it falls short as a complete interpretation.

Ludwig van Beethoven   German 1770-1827

Beethoven Fidelio.

Christa Ludwig *mez* Leonore
Jon Vickers *ten* Florestan
Walter Berry *bass* Don Pizarro
Gottlob Frick *bass* Rocco
Ingeborg Hallstein *sop* Marzelline
Gerhard Unger *ten* Jacquino
Franz Crass *bass* Don Fernando
Kurt Wehofschitz *ten* First Prisoner
Raymond Wolansky *bar* Second Prisoner
Philharmonia Chorus and Orchestra / Otto Klemperer.
EMI ⓟ ⓞ CDS5 56211-2 (two discs: 128 minutes: ADD). Notes, text and translation included. Recorded 1962.

Klemperer's recording is a magnificent realization of this work. It springs, of course, from his Covent Garden performances of the opera, though only two of the cast (Vickers and Frick) are the same. It can, perhaps, be regarded as an idealization of what Klemperer was seeking to express in those performances, as a more faithful realization of his vision of the work – just as his *St Matthew Passion* recording proved incomparably greater than the Festival Hall performance he gave. There are all sorts of factors to account for this, not only the evident one of a rather better cast.

Klemperer's command of an orchestra was, all would admit today, sometimes far from perfect. Many who heard his *Fidelio* broadcast from Covent Garden were shocked by all kinds of inexactnesses. These can be remedied on disc not only by rejecting the ragged 'takes', but also from the start by seating the orchestra and placing the singers more favourably than an opera-house allows. Then again, in a Klemperer performance there was not a great deal of interplay between performers and conductor, or between audience and conductor. He was said to be unpredictable on occasion – he kindles to the work rather than to 'the occasion' – and is a less spontaneous interpreter than, say, Furtwängler. For that reason his performances lose little or nothing through being captured in the studio rather than the concert-hall or opera-house. It is as if he held steady an inner vision of what the work ought to be and with each rehearsal was able to come closer to its realization, irrespective of the circumstances. In fact it is probably this very steadiness, lack of impulsiveness, that people sometimes object to in his performances. But in the greatest works – in the *Matthew Passion* and *Fidelio* – he seems to create something that one lives with, and lives in, long after the actual sounds have ceased. Superficially, or in excerpts, a listener could find some (but not much) of this *Fidelio* slow, or even 'dull'. Certainly there is little that is excitable about it but as a whole it is a deeply exciting, stirring, noble performance.

What one first notices especially is not so much any detail of the execution, as marvels in the music. It leads one to spend hours examining and analysing such things as Florestan's repetition of the phrase "Süsser Trost in meinem Herzen: meine Pflicht hab' ich getan" ("Sweet consolation in my heart: I have done my duty") – nearly an exact repetition, but expanded by one bar, and with the vocal line subtly varied, and completely new scoring. Rhythmically, *Fidelio* seems here as intricate a score as, say, Stravinsky's *The Rite of Spring*, with the motifs contracted, augmented, redistributed across the metre, in an absorbingly subtle and expressive way. This is the kind of performance which makes one more conscious of the work than of its execution. One of the things that makes *Fidelio* so endlessly enthralling is the tension between what might variously be described as the 'ideal' or the symphonic drama, and the 'operatic' or theatrical one. This tension is here held in perfect balance: with Klemperer as conductor ensuring that nothing in the orchestra is ever mere accompaniment, but that everything is alive and meaningful; and on the other hand a cast who are not only fine musicians, but also vivid characters.

Christa Ludwig – a mezzo, is boldly cast as Leonore – but successfully. Indeed she seems far less severely taxed by the high tessitura of the role than several of the sopranos who sing it, and carries her rich, passionate, well-focused tones up to high B fearlessly and unflinchingly. She sings with warm expression, variety of feeling, and great sensitivity to words and phrase-shapes. There is much emotion in her enunciation of "Komm, Hoffnung": in the little break at the comma she approaches the knife-edge division between high art and exaggeration – without crossing it. Like many a soprano, she does not fully pronounce the consonants of "O namenlose Freude" – but that is easy to forgive. You may not much like her attacking "Doch toben auch wie Meereswogen" *forte* instead of *piano*; but you will like almost everything else she does. Like is too weak a word – it is stirring, moving.

Jon Vickers's Florestan must be well known by now. Such intensity both of tone and of pronunciation, artistry and understanding are rarely united with such magnificent singing. He conveys the character, and the character's physical state, in his voice, but at the same time realizes too all musical values to the full. Gottlob Frick's Rocco is also an example of keen characterization wedded to fine singing. Walter Berry's Pizarro is not quite on this level. Sometimes he seems to be striving too hard after his expressive effects: "Er sterbe", for example, is certainly a fierce explosion, but Berry achieves the fierceness at the expense of exact pitching of the notes. But on the whole he is satisfying – a good voice intelligently used in a role that makes just slightly too heavy a demand on it.

Ingeborg Hallstein is an excellent Marzelline: young-sounding but not soubrettish, fresh but not skittish, with full, clear tones. The runs of the opening duet are admirably clear. There is a slight vibrancy in the sustained notes of the aria which are most attractive. Gerhard Unger starts too emphatically, overinflecting such a phrase as "Wenn du mir nicht freundlicher blickest" as if he were trying to compensate for the lack of the stage: but very quickly he catches the style of the performance, and then is admirable.

Klemperer exaggerates the horn parts in "Ha! welch ein Augenblick", and more seriously in "Er sterbe"; they are not marked to bray out through everything else – this is his only 'obtrusiveness'. The *allegro con brio* of the Pizarro/Rocco duet, even in context (and despite what was said above), continues with each hearing to sound a little sedate. The accompaniment at the end of Florestan's aria is *piano*, not the *fortissimo* which the series of crescendos should eventually lead to. When Leonore gives Florestan the piece of stale bread, the customary tempo slackening is made, almost as if she were being sacramental about it (Florestan may be given wine and bread, but any liturgical symbolism here does not seem to make sense, and was surely not what was intended). Marzelline does not accept Beethoven's implied offer of a brief cadenza in her aria, but on the whole there are more appoggiaturas than are usual today: Leonore closes her aria with one, and Vickers, quite properly, supplies one on "Gottes Wille". Frick omits some that one feels are needed.

But so many other things are especially fine: the differentiation in the accompaniment to the verses of Rocco's aria; the unexaggerated but eloquent realization of the 'heart-beat' accompaniment, just three little figures written in for the violins when in the Trio Leonore sings "Wie heftig pocht dieses Herz"; the quite extraordinary effect of the bare octaves at the close of the Leonore/Rocco Act 2 duet (perfectly judged orchestral balance and phrase-weighting). The stereo recording is extremely natural: not one of those double-perspective sounds where we seem at once to be on-stage close to the singers and at the same time in the stalls so far as the orchestra are concerned. The production appears to be that of Covent Garden, with one slightly puzzling moment when, during the second entry of the Canon Quartet, Leonore and Marzelline appear to cross over one another. It has atmosphere, enough movement to give it life but not so much as to make one gasp at the engineer's skill and fail for a while to be absorbed in the music. The balance of voices and orchestra is ideal. One criticism only: Don Fernando (for once cast at strength, and admirably sung and expressed by Franz Crass) seems to have acquired a disturbing 'edge' around his tone: this faint halo (added resonance? a different kind of solo microphone?) does not affect the other singers in the finale.

One must also remark on how well the dialogue is spoken. One of the most regularly moving passages in the opera is without music at all – the dialogue before the Trio in Act 2, and this is superlatively well delivered and recorded with a skilful, undisturbing use of stereo. Incidentally there is no intrusive *Leonore* No. 3 Overture, and so the finale can make its full effect (Klemperer's handling of this – especially the *sostenuto* 3/4 passage – is sublime). The chorus sing magnificently in both acts; the two solo prisoners are excellent. There will always be other *Fidelio* performances with different virtues: more theatricality, more patent dramatic effects. But one hardly expects ever to hear another *Fidelio* performance so sustainedly fine in detail, generally excellent in casting, and above all, so consistently and steadily inspired.

Beethoven Fidelio.

Birgit Nilsson *sop* Leonore
James McCracken *ten* Florestan
Tom Krause *bar* Don Pizarro
Kurt Böhme *bass* Rocco
Graziella Sciutti *sop* Marzelline
Donald Grobe *ten* Jaquino
Hermann Prey *bar* Don Fernando
Kurt Equiluz *ten* First Prisoner
Gunter Adam *bass* Second Prisoner
Vienna State Opera Concert Choir; Vienna Philharmonic Orchestra / Lorin Maazel.
Double Decca Ⓜ ① 448 104-2DF2 (two discs: 119 minutes: ADD). Recorded 1964.

Although a cordial welcome was given to Maazel's *Fidelio* when it first appeared, it was generally and inevitably given second place to the then all-conquering Klemperer version. Like the 1957 Fricsay on DG, Maazel has a clear-eyed, piercingly vivid view of the work, Toscanini-like in its fierce accents, insistent rhythms, refusal to linger in the cause of sentiment, not as aware of a metaphysical dimension as Sir Colin Davis on his 1995 RCA set. The Vienna Philharmonic's playing faithfully seconds their conductor's view.

In 1964 Decca made one of their most elaborate attempts at 'staging'. Characters can be heard approaching, receding, moving about the spectrum in the Culshaw tradition (Erik Smith was the producer), and, controversially, an echo effect was used to suggest the dungeon, an effect much disliked by some critics. In truth, it is not unduly disturbing since, apart from Florestan's opening "Gott", which sounds artificially contrived, the echo is confined to the dialogue (here greatly foreshortened), but as a whole the sound has little of the warmth found on the Davis set. Nilsson seems something of a paragon in her effortless vocalization, better focused than Voigt (Davis), but there's not only the gleaming voice to admire. Her well thought-through characterization, though not quite as moving as Ludwig's (Klemperer) or Rysanek's (Fricsay), combines heroic resolve with womanly vulnerability. McCracken's Florestan seems to have been underrated. His vibrant, heroic tenor is equal to all the demands placed on it and if he occasionally over-emotes he never sentimentalizes his role as Klemperer's Vickers is inclined to do. Krause is an incisive, boldly sung Pizarro. Böhme is a paragon of a Rocco, on a par with Frick (Klemperer). Sciutti makes an appealing Marzelline but one not always able to sustain a line to the end of a phrase. Grobe is a decent Jaquino. Prey makes much of little as Don Fernando; that is even truer of Kurt Equiluz who offers a touching cameo of the First Prisoner. The Pitz-trained chorus excel themselves. Praise too for the choice of van Gogh's *Exercise Yard* on the booklet cover, but none for the omission of text and translation.

As truthfully conducted as any reading, the Fricsay is also a good mid-price choice, but for anyone wanting a larger-scale reading than Fricsay provides there is no hesitation in recommending the Maazel. At full price, the 1994 Harnoncourt set on Teldec offers a challenging alternative view to Klemperer and Davis. Among the latter two, Davis has much the broader, fresher sound. You may be further swayed by Davis's bonus of *Leonore* No. 2 (played at the 1805 première of the work's first version, *Leonore*), given a typically thoughtful reading.

Beethoven Fidelio.

Kirsten Flagstad *sop* Leonore
Julius Patzak *ten* Florestan
Paul Schöffler *bass-bar* Don Pizarro
Josef Greindl *bass* Rocco
Dame Elisabeth Schwarzkopf *sop* Marzelline
Anton Dermota *ten* Jaquino
Hans Braun *bar* Don Fernando
Hermann Gallos *ten* First Prisoner
Ljubomir Pantscheff *bass* Second Prisoner
Vienna State Opera Chorus; Vienna Philharmonic Orchestra / Wilhelm Furtwängler.
EMI Festspieldokumente mono Ⓜ ① CHS7 64901-2 (two discs: 150 minutes: ADD). Recorded at a performance in the Festspielhaus, Salzburg on August 5th, 1950.

It took many years for this noble document to appear on an 'official' label. Whatever your opinion concerning the interpretation of *Fidelio*, you should hear this version. It is, in a word, memorable; the very epitome of the romantic view of this work, now out of fashion (so much the worse you may say, for fashion). Furtwängler takes very deliberate speeds, indulges in massive rubato and *ritardandos*, yet justifies them all by his trenchant, spiritual, deeply involving view of the music, one derived from a lifetime spent in the service of Beethoven. Wherever you touch down in this reading you will hear considered detail, subtle phrasing pregnant with meaning, eloquent playing and singing. Everything has been carefully prepared with a sense of devotion and sincerity on all sides palpable throughout. If you pick out the phrases underpinning the melodrama near the beginning of Act 2 or, just before, the falling phrases after Florestan comes out of his fevered ecstasy, it is because these show Furtwängler not simply conducting the music, but making them emotionally significant. This is the subjective as against the objective view of the piece and it is overwhelming. The inclusion of the *Leonore* Overture No. 3 is justified here as a summation of Furtwängler's reading, and – as throughout – the Vienna Philharmonic, which in these years owed so much to this conductor, play superbly for him. In every respect this surpasses his later 1954 studio recording, where there is nothing like the tension evinced here.

Three peerless interpretations grace this account. Patzak's searing Florestan has never been equalled, let alone surpassed – except perhaps by Patzak himself, in fresher voice, in the 1948 Salzburg performance available 'unofficially'. Making a virtue of Furtwängler's stretching speeds for Florestan's scene, he ekes out each phrase, each word with aching intensity and then speaks his dialogue (the stifled, desperate "Wie finde ich Ruhe?") like a man genuinely *in extremis*. And who has begun the trio "Euch werde Lohn" with such pathetic accents or indeed with such refined legato? Greindl, in speech and singing, performs with the utmost conviction as Rocco in projecting the paradox of the kindly father and time-serving gaoler. At the beginning of her career Schwarzkopf is a firm, eager Marzelline, while Dermota as Jaquino is almost in her class. Reservations about Flagstad concern only some wear on the voice, hardly surprising in a soprano just turned 55, but she compensates for some unwieldy moments with the firmness and radiance of her tone, and the sincerity of her reading. Certain things, such as the optimistic cry "noch Heute" and the passage in the Act 2 duet with Rocco, beginning "Gewiss!", convey all Leonore's conviction and determination. Schöffler makes up for the occasional moment of out-of-tune singing and strain at the top with the authority and drive he brings to his interpretation of the evil, overbearing Pizarro. He is especially notable in his idiomatic and experienced use of the text. Braun is a noble Minister, the veteran Gallos a touching First Prisoner.

So immediate is the sound that you feel, in an uncanny way, that you are sitting there in the Salzburg house watching the eternal drama being unfolded. You and the performers are part of history. That said, in spite of the booklet's claims, it is hard to believe that it is in every respect an improvement on the already excellent 'unofficial' Hunt CDs. The balance is sometimes cleaner, some but not all distortion has been eliminated, but sometimes the new technology introduces a slight and unwanted edge to the strings, and there are moments of underlay that appear to trouble some EMI reissues using computer technology. Any doubts on this count are as nothing set against the inspiration of the occasion. The audience, generously applauding, is certainly aware of a great evening in the opera-house.

Beethoven Leonore.

Hillevi Martinpelto *sop* Leonore
Kim Begley *ten* Florestan
Matthew Best *bass* Don Pizarro
Franz Hawlata *bass* Rocco
Christiane Oelze *sop* Marzelline
Michael Schade *ten* Jaquino
Alastair Miles *bass* Don Fernando
Robert Burt *ten* First Prisoner
Colin Campbell *bar* Second Prisoner
Monteverdi Choir; Orchestre Révolutionnaire et Romantique / John Eliot Gardiner.
Archiv Produktion ℗ ① 453 461-2AH2 (two discs: 138 minutes: DDD). 🗲 Notes, text and translation included. Recorded 1996.

Romain Rolland, writing specifically of Beethoven's *Leonore*, described the work as "a monument of the anguish of the period, of the oppressed soul and its appeal to liberty". John Eliot Gardiner, in the first complete recording of *Fidelio*'s predecessor for more than two decades, reveals both musically and verbally how the early, more radical opera has worked its spell on him, too. This, he says, is Beethoven struggling to recover the revolutionary fervour of his Bonn years; this is the score where the direct expression of spontaneous emotion, rather than the nobility of philosophical abstraction, is really to be found.

Characteristically, this recording brings in its wake both a reappraisal of all the available source material, and insights aplenty gathered from the touring production which preceded it. Co-editor Nicholas McNair draws a fine-tooth comb through the comparative *Leonore/Fidelio* versions in an absorbing thesis which sees *Leonore* in the broader context of contemporary German philosophy. And, given that the slower musical pace of *Leonore* is counterbalanced by a stronger narrative thrust, the actor Christoph Bantzer contributes a sprightly narration which interleaves, deftly and movingly, brief asides from the likes of Wordsworth, Goethe and Hölderlin.

And then, of course, there is the music. The *Leonore* No. 2 Overture is distinguished by the telling contrasts Gardiner draws between brooding strata of strings and the pearly light of the woodwind; and a reversal of the first two numbers gives Christiane Oelze a head start as a radiant Marzelline. The trio (Rocco, Marzelline and Jaquino) which prepares the Quartet "Mir ist so wunderbar", does tend to impede the momentum but, like the 'extra' Marzelline and Leonore duet, "Um in der Ehe" in

Act 2, it has a telling effect on the beat of the work's human heart, and Gardiner's sensitivity to its pulse throughout makes good any shortfall in dramatic impetus.

The D major March which introduces Act 2 is here restored to its original place for the first time since the première. With period-instrument brass and timpani making menacing circumstance out of what can be mere pomp, it makes the entry of Don Pizarro darker still. Matthew Best is, in articulation if not in range, one of the most blood-curdling Pizarros on disc, just as Alastair Miles is one of the noblest Don Fernandos. "Komm, Hoffnung" reveals the resilience and steady, gleaming core of Hillevi Martinpelto's Leonore. There are times when one craves a fiercer edge of passion; but, with the equally sharply focused tenor of Kim Begley, it is a joy to hear "O namenlose Freude" perfectly paced, and really *sung*. This Florestan sings his great aria without *Fidelio*'s vision of an "Engel Leonore": Begley, no Heldentenor after all, is particularly well suited to the constant, dark minor key of this "Lebens Frühlingstagen", which presages Gardiner's triumphant – and often surprising – finale.

Vincenzo Bellini   Italian 1801-1835

Bellini Beatrice di Tenda.
Dame Joan Sutherland *sop* Beatrice
Luciano Pavarotti *ten* Orombello
Cornelius Opthof *bar* Filippo
Josephine Veasey *mez* Agnese
Joseph Ward *bar* Anichino, Rizzardo
Ambrosian Opera Chorus

Bellini Arias.
Norma – Sediziose voci ... Casta diva ... Ah! bello a me ritorna.
Dame Joan Sutherland *sop*
Richard Cross *bass*
London Symphony Chorus and Orchestra / Richard Bonynge.
I puritani – Son vergin vezzosa; Oh rendetemi la speme ... Qui la voce ... Vien diletto.
Dame Joan Sutherland *sop*
Margreta Elkins *mez*
Pierre Duval *ten*
Ezio Flagello, Renato Capecchi *basses*
La sonnambula – Ah, non credea mirarti ... Ah! non giunge.
Dame Joan Sutherland *sop*
Nicola Monti *ten*
Fernando Corena *bass*
Maggio Musicale Fiorentino Chorus and Orchestra / Richard Bonynge.
Decca Ⓜ ① 433 706-2DMO3 (three discs: 198 minutes: ADD). Texts and translations included.
Recorded 1966.

Beatrice di Tenda has had four recordings, including a notable one on Rizzoli released in 1988. Conducted by Alberto Zedda and having the remarkable Mariana Nicolesco in the title-role, it too was flawed, yet had strengths which helped to define some of the defects in this Bonynge/Sutherland version. The Romanian soprano was uneven, sometimes disconcertingly so, but she also proved herself an artist with fine resources for the coloration of her singing and with a dramatic power that did justice to the heroic qualities of the role. Sutherland by contrast caught the pathos but not the full nobility of this woman, whose defiance takes her out of the line of passive heroines such as Lucia, Amina and the Elvira of *I puritani*. Moreover, Nicolesco was expressive and unfussy: she did not share Sutherland's apparent inability to see a phrase as a whole and sing it in a way that preserved its unity. In the 1992 recording on the Swiss Nightingale label, conducted by Pinchas Steinberg, Edita Gruberová seems to have Sutherland in mind, for despite the difference in their voices (Gruberová's brighter and slimmer and, at a *forte* rather more edgy) there are times when she could be mistaken for her predecessor. As for the conducting, Zedda/Rizzoli often brings a subtler touch to bear, where Bonynge's distinction lies rather more in energy and efficiency. Steinberg has neither Bonynge's crisp sense of purpose nor Zedda's more thoughtful sensitivity here, yet he too captures in the score something which eludes Bonynge and is an essential characteristic of Bellini, as in the start of that sadly swaying melody, "Ah, scomigliato", in the finale of Act 1.

In other respects the Decca recording is distinctly preferable to the modern one on Nightingale: for one thing, the recorded sound itself is better in balance and clarity. The Agnese and Filippo of Steinberg's version have voices of unusually fine material, but the mezzo's incipient tremolo and the baritone's elementary sense of style make them poor substitutes for Josephine Veasey and the admirable Cornelius Opthof. The tenor's role in this opera is not a very fulfilling one, but as Pavarotti sings it in the Decca recording he shares principal billing with Sutherland. In his original review Andrew Porter wrote: "As tenors go today, Luciano Pavarotti is distinctly good. The voice is firm, unstrained, even lustrous. He is not exactly a delicate or imaginative artist, but he is not a brute." The same could be said of Don Bernardini (Nightingale). At the point where Pavarotti is caught out, crying "Oh gioia!" in "almost comically expressionless declamation", Bernardini goes cautiously, with a quiet exclamation suggestive, perhaps, of modified rapture.

An advantage of the Nightingale recording is that it gets substantially the same text on to two discs instead of three, omitting a brief passage between Filippo and confidant in Act 2. A disadvantage is that the change of disc intersects the finale of Act 1, coming only 3'18" before the end. A Bellini recital by Sutherland fills in the remainder of Decca's third disc, taken from her recordings of the complete operas in the early-1960s, all with their share of the glories and faults of her singing in that period.

Bellini I Capuleti e i Montecchi.
Edita Gruberová *sop* Giulietta
Agnes Baltsa *mez* Romeo
Dano Raffanti *ten* Tebaldo
Gwynne Howell *bass* Capellio
John Tomlinson *bass* Lorenzo
Chorus and Orchestra of the Royal Opera House, Covent Garden / Riccardo Muti.
EMI Ⓜ ① CMS7 64846-2 (two discs: 130 minutes: DDD). Text and translation included.
Recorded at performances in the Royal Opera House, Covent Garden during April 1984.

All Berlioz's strictures against Bellini's *Romeo and Juliet* opera ("No Shakespeare, nothing – a wasted opportunity", is the severest) were happily set at naught when Covent Garden revived the work in April 1984, for the first time since 1848. Praise for the opera, Muti's conducting and the singing was almost universal. That enthusiasm was extended to this recording. Muti reveals all the beauty and subtlety of Bellini's scoring, emphasizing the opera's romantic eloquence and giving its tautly shaped scenes, all essentials of the story pared away, the benefit of his understanding of the flow and pulse of a score that is far from conductor-proof – as a succeeding revival indicated (Campanella's 1991 Nuovo Era recording). Being himself wholly committed to the work, Muti was able to convince his singers and the audience of its noble utterance, the vocal lines, so much admired by Wagner and the instrumentation (clarinet, horn and harp in particular) having that peculiarly Bellinian delicacy. Here feeling his way to his later triumphs, the composer also succeeded, as he wished to, in banishing the boredom of the recitatives, giving them their own significant part in the structure, not least in the final scene which has a literally dying fall.

Then the Royal Opera House found the near-ideal singers for the central roles. One cannot imagine Romeo better cast than with Agnes Baltsa. From her determined, urgent first entrance, she discloses an innate sense of how to shape both recitative and cantilena, and she manages to get the intensity and passion of her acted performance into her voice; indeed, the two are as one, the desperate cries of "Giulietta!" being of the essence. Baltsa has a Callas-like ability to print a phrase in her accents indelibly on the mind – or at least she does here. And she is in superb voice – steady, resinous, vibrant, reaching heights of expressive beauty in her Second Act cavatina.

It happens to blend naturally with Edita Gruberová's crystalline soprano, so that the First Act duet for the lovers, so prophetic of those for the ladies in *Norma*, and just as yielding and tender on its own account, is an unalloyed pleasure. Both "Oh, quante volte" and her sinuous aria before she takes the sleeping draught are sung by Gruberová with just the right pathetic accents and they are as securely vocalized as one would expect. With the recording distancing her from the microphone, there is no suggestion of the slight edge that marred her recordings in the studio.

It is as good to hear on record, as it was in the house, Dano Raffanti's open-throated, Italianate singing of the rather one-dimensional tenor role of Tebaldo (Tybalt). Capellio (Capulet) is something of a villain in this non-Shakespearian version, his implacable attitude shown in hard-grained music. Gwynne Howell sounds suitably ferocious. Lorenzo (Laurence) is here family doctor rather than friar; he is ineffectually sympathetic. John Tomlinson does what he can with a negative role. The Covent Garden orchestra always play their best for Muti, and the solos here are well taken. The chorus sing strongly as furious partisans of each side, then as mourners.

The whole performance gains greatly from being recorded direct from the stage. Emotions are heightened, there is no suggestion of the limbo of studio recordings. The sound retains a theatre balance, with the orchestra kept in their proper place. There are very few stage noises, applause only at the end of scenes. This is a live recording that completely eclipses the same company's 1976 set and is both a wonderful reminder of the Covent Garden performances and also gives the work a new definition and standing in the Bellini canon. Reissued at mid price, this should be irresistible to anyone interested in the best in Bellinian interpretation.

Bellini Norma.
Maria Callas *sop* Norma
Christa Ludwig *mez* Adalgisa
Franco Corelli *ten* Pollione
Nicola Zaccaria *bass* Oroveso

BBC RADIO 3
90-93 FM

Piero de Palma *ten* Flavio
Edda Vincenzi *sop* Clotilde
Chorus and Orchestra of La Scala, Milan / Tullio Serafin.
EMI Ⓜ ① CMS5 66428-2 (three discs: 161 minutes: ADD). Notes, text and translation included.
Recorded 1960.

The most accurate vocal score for *Norma* is Boosey's Royal Edition, edited by Sullivan and Pitman but the usual Ricordi score often contains more (by no means all) of the stage and, above all, the *singing* directions in which the autograph abounds *(con voce cupa e terribile,* etc.). The autograph is available in facsimile, and this is what was used for this review. It is a revelation of Bellini's careful artistry – his cuts for dramatic effect, emendations, simplifications, his imaginative and ambitious scoring of such passages as the "Pastoral Symphony" dying away of the Overture, or the introductions to "Ite sul colle" and to the assembly in Act 2. The first character we meet is Oroveso: Zaccaria is nobler, firmer and smoother than Rossi-Lemeni in the old 1954 set (also reissued on EMI), and so his two great scenas carry their proper weight in this carefully proportioned score, and make a great effect; they are not merely interludes to give the diva a break. The choral singing is splendid. "Ah! del Tebro" is now (correctly) accompanied by *pizzicato* triplets, not by the *legato* which Bellini cancelled in the score, but which Serafin used in his earlier recording. Then Pollione's Corelli. He is better than Filippeschi. He bellows a bit in "Meco all'altar"; but whenever he meets Norma, you can sense him striving after style. Bellini is not his music – but who is there better? It's a big, handsome voice and an enjoyable performance.

Norma viene! – and here is the crux of the set. Better or worse than the 1954 recording? The answer cannot be put in a word. But those who heard Callas sing Norma at Covent Garden in 1953-4, and then again, slim, in 1957, will know the difference. The facts are that in 1954 the voice above the stave was fuller, more solid and more certain, but that in 1960 the middle timbres were more beautiful and more expressive; and, further, that an interpretation which was always magnificent had deepened in finesse, flexibility and dramatic poignancy. The emphasis you give to these facts must be a matter of personal opinion. But you cannot help wondering whether those people who so readily declared their preference for the earlier *Lucia* had really listened to both performances right through, or merely compared the showy bits. Certainly Callas's voice lets her down again and again, often when she essays some of her most beautiful effects. The F wobbles when it should crown a heart-rending "Oh rimembranza"; the G wobbles in an exquisitely conceived "Son io" (the unforgettable moment when Norma removes her wreath, declares her own guilt) – and yet how much more moving it is than the simpler, if steadier *messa di voce* of the earlier set. There are people who have a kind of tone-deafness to the timbres of Callas's later voice, who don't respond to one of the most affecting and eloquent of all sounds. They will stick to the earlier set. But ardent Callas collectors will probably find that it is the later one to which they will be listening again and again, not unaware of, not even unflinching from, its faults, but still more keenly responsive to its beauties.

That the phrasing, the pronunciation, the weight and shape and meaning of the music, are peerlessly conceived can go without saying. "Casta Diva", by the way, is sung in F, as in 1954 – not in the original G, as in the Covent Garden performances of June 1953. (There is no point in fussing about Bellini's keys; the composer's favourite Amina, Malibran, used to put "Ah non giunge" down a full fourth.) Both times Callas sings the climactic A with the syncopated attacks, although the Ricordi score, with its unbroken semibreve the second time, correctly represents what Bellini wrote. The big duet with Adalgisa is again down a tone, "Deh! con te" in B flat, "Mira, o Norma" in E flat, and the change is once again effected in the recitative phrase "nel romano campo" (evidently a long-standing transposition, for on a blank stave of the autograph there is sketched, not by Bellini, another way of getting the recitative down a tone). Callas does not decorate the music; Pasta did – some of her embellishments are preserved. Adalgisa, a soprano role, is as usual taken by a mezzo. Given a mezzo, we are given a good one, and one who blends beautifully with Callas in the low-key "Mira, o Norma" (though her downward scales are as ill-defined as her colleague's). She is no veteran Adalgisa, but youthful and impetuous except when (for example in her verse of "Deh! con te") she lets the rhythm get heavy, and Serafin does nothing to correct her.

As before, Serafin restores the beautiful quiet coda to the "Guerra" chorus (found in the Boosey but not the Ricordi score), and as before, Callas disappointingly does not float over the close of that slow rising arpeggio which should be as magical as Leonora's identical one in "La Vergine degli Angeli" from *La forza del destino*. It is a pity that Serafin did not restore the second statement (solo cello and woodwinds) of the *con dolore* melody that opens Act 2 – even though Bellini was right to cut it for the theatre. The conducting is spacious, unhurried, elevated and eloquent. Serafin's *allegro moderato* for the duet "In mia man" may be an *andante sostenuto,* but Callas makes it sound utterly right. Only in his handling of the mounting tension and the two great climaxes and releases of the finale, might you decisively prefer the earlier version. The La Scala playing is superlative, and the recording is excellent; it makes the 1954 one seem curiously faded.

Bellini Norma.
Montserrat Caballé *sop* Norma
Fiorenza Cossotto *mez* Adalgisa

Plácido Domingo *ten* Pollione
Ruggero Raimondi *bass* Oroveso
Kenneth Collins *ten* Flavio
Elizabeth Bainbridge *mez* Clotilde
Ambrosian Opera Chorus; London Philharmonic Orchestra / Carlo Felice Cillario.
RCA Victor Ⓜ ① GD86502 (three discs: 157 minutes: ADD). Text and translation included.
Recorded 1973.

Callas had the vocal-character for the part, as Sutherland and Caballé had not (and Sutherland's recording on Decca, conducted by Richard Bonynge, shows how important voice-character is by casting Caballé in the role which is right for her, that of Adalgisa). Caballé's Norma, heard here, is sometimes moving, sometimes celestial; but it is not the full, tragic, heroic character, the "sublime donna", or the fiercely impassioned woman who sings "Oh, non tremare" and "Tutti! i Romani a cento".

That said, it has to be acknowledged that there will be listeners who prefer not to go back as far in recording history as Callas's time, whether 1954 or 1960, and that some will positively not want Callas's flawed greatness though they will nevertheless want Norma. This, then, is surely the one for them. It is well recorded, well cast and well conducted. Cillario's moderate tempos and steady beat in the Overture might seem to foretell a performance of good sense and good taste but lacking in attack and excitement. Gradually one comes to appreciate his quality, as, for instance, when he shows a feeling for rubato, recognizing that all those dull-looking bars with rows of quavers accompanying the duet "Vieni in Roma" don't at all mean what they say but something far more subtle instead. The LPO certainly play extremely well for him; there's distinguished work by the woodwind, and when the time comes for the trumpets to call all good Druids to come to the aid of the army they do so with neat articulation and plenty of spirit. The Ambrosians also provide good tone and style in the choruses.

Taking the cast in likely order of curtain-calls, we applaud Raimondi for his sonorous upper notes, reserving the observation that a bass who is half-way to baritone is not quite right for father Oroveso. Domingo, his voice half-way from Cavaradossi to Otello, makes a fine Pollione, though we forget him more easily than we do Franco Corelli on Callas's 1960 recording. A great strength in the present set is Cossotto's Adalgisa. Where the voice-character isn't right by nature she makes it so by art, and in the firm, even placing of notes and binding of phrases she is exemplary. She sings with a Norma who loves to spin long phrases, but Cossotto can equal her in this and doesn't jib (as many do) at the note-for-note matching of the soprano line. Much of Caballé's best singing is done in the duets: "Oh, cari accenti", the lead-in to "Ah, si, fa core" and the verse of "Mira, o Norma" are lovely examples. Her "Casta Diva" begins poorly and the cabaletta leaves a certain amount undone, but she can be moving in recitative and provides moments of rare loveliness, as in "Qual cor, tradisti". She deserves her bouquets.

Bellini Il pirata.

Piero Cappuccilli *bar* Ernesto
Montserrat Caballé *sop* Imogene
Bernabé Martí *ten* Gualtiero
Giuseppe Baratti *ten* Itulbo
Ruggero Raimondi *bass* Goffredo
Flora Raffanelli *sop* Adele
Rome RAI Chorus and Orchestra / Gianandrea Gavazzeni.
EMI Ⓜ ① CMS7 64169-2 (two discs: 142 minutes: ADD). Notes, text and translation included.
Recorded 1970.

When Andrew Porter reviewed this in 1971, he wrote of it as "a set that must be acquired both by voice-lovers and (not that the two terms are necessarily exclusive) by music-lovers". All three points can be reiterated, though some caveats might be added. First, the parenthesis. It is good to see that the offensive term 'canary-fancier' has almost dropped out of usage, where in the 1970s it still might have been applied in reference to the appeal of such an opera as this. Then the attraction to 'voice-lovers', that is to lovers of singing, which in turn means the application of the singing voice to musical texts: the recording helped to convince listeners, 28 years ago, that these so-called bel canto operas could find modern singers to make a performance possible, and that modern times could also throw up a prima donna worthy of the tradition we understand to have flourished in the nineteenth century. The third point concerns the music itself. There is a good deal of Rossini in it, not surprisingly so, as six of Rossini's operas were performed at La Scala in the season of 1827 when *Il pirata* had its première. There are also passages of considerable beauty and power that are entirely characteristic of their composer: the duets of Imogene with Gualtiero ("Pietosa il padre") and with Ernesto ("Tu m'apristi"), the trio "Cedo al destin orribile" and the final scene, which goes under the generic title 'mad', are all excellent examples.

The caveats to some extent concern our appreciation of the score. Though Porter (this time in the insert-notes, rather than in his review) wrote that "nothing is carelessly composed", it has to be conceded that (bar-by-bar) some weak repetitions, symmetrical fill-ins, complacent harmonies, tonic-dominant codas and so forth necessarily modify the admiration aroused by the 26-year-old composer's work. Vocally, too, the undoubted distinction of the performance needs some further qualifying. Caballé is in many respects at the height of her powers. Yet even by this time her singing had acquired a characteristic which is surely a pervasive flaw. Just what the technical name for it would be difficult to say, but it could be described as a glottal punctuation of the tone, frequently occurring on consonants, as in the word "tempesta" shortly after Imogene's entrance. It is a habit of production that many may consider an acceptable, even an impressive, part of 'the grand manner', but it now seems to be the sort of thing we would consider ludicrous if a singer in our own native language were to indulge in it. Among the men, Raimondi is indeed impressive in the opening scene, but Cappuccilli, steady and solid as he is, lacks lustre both of timbre and temperament, and Bernabé Martí, coping heroically with his challenging role, produces a rather throaty tone and sings rarely below a *forte*.

This now gets the fault-finding out of balance. To restore perspective, it should be repeated that the welcome given to the original applies just as well to its reissue, that the opera is a vigorous and often beautiful piece of writing, that Caballé is at her finest and Gavazzeni an inspired conductor. The standard of orchestral and choral work is high, recorded sound is vivid, and the booklet retains the valuable notes.

Bellini I puritani.

Dame Joan Sutherland *sop* Elvira
Luciano Pavarotti *ten* Arturo
Piero Cappuccilli *bar* Riccardo
Nicolai Ghiaurov *bass* Giorgio
Anita Caminada *mez* Enrichetta
Gian Carlo Luccardi *bass* Gualtiero
Renato Cazzaniga *ten* Bruno
Chorus of the Royal Opera House, Covent Garden;
London Symphony Orchestra / Richard Bonynge.
Decca Ⓟ Ⓒ 417 588-2DH3 (three discs: 174 minutes: ADD). Notes, text and translation included. Recorded 1973.

Bellini I puritani.

Maria Callas *sop* Elvira
Giuseppe di Stefano *ten* Arturo
Rolando Panerai *bar* Riccardo
Nicola Rossi-Lemeni *bass* Giorgio
Aurora Cattelani *mez* Enrichetta
Carlo Forti *bass* Gualtiero
Angelo Mercuriali *ten* Bruno
Chorus and Orchestra of La Scala, Milan / Tullio Serafin.
EMI mono Ⓟ Ⓒ CDS5 56275-2 (two discs: 142 minutes: ADD). Notes, text and translation included. Recorded 1953.

Were *I puritani* to be produced as frequently as *La bohème*, one could still spend a lifetime of opera-going and not come upon a performance as distinguished as either of these. Obviously both are desirable, and still more obviously, as far as most of us are concerned, *both* cannot be had. It may be simplest and safest to allow personal preferences for one or other of the two great ladies to settle the matter: both are at their characteristic best and each has her own special gift to bring to the role. For those unfortunates who find this only adds to the difficulty, the following notes may help.

I puritani is a tenor's opera as well as a soprano's. Di Stefano, who partnered Callas so well in Puccini, is out of his element here. His untidy approach to notes from below, his uncovered upper register and wide-open vowels cause one again to regret the loss of that elegance imparted to some of his earlier recordings, such as the *Mignon* and *L'arlesiana* solos. He is never merely bland and can often be exciting, but comparison with Pavarotti shows him at a disadvantage. Both of these tenors make a particularly lovely thing of the solo "A una fonte" in Act 3, and they do impressively well in the bel canto test-piece, "A te, o cara". For the baritones, Panerai with Callas has most character in his voice, though Cappuccilli has good solid tone and offers no offence to the vocal line even if he fails to caress or excite it. Ghiaurov with Sutherland sings with immense dignity and admirable evenness and Rossi-Lemeni is in good voice with Callas.

Perhaps the conductors can decide the issue. Both secure good orchestral playing, Bonynge having a little extra liveliness, Serafin a little more weight. So the conductors are unlikely to be the deciding factor after all, and one turns to the question of recorded sound. The Callas version from 1953, by now 'historic', lacks the detailed clarity of the other yet is still remarkably vivid and full-bodied, not obviously 'dated'. The Decca compensates with brighter definition. No, it is back to the two great ladies. Callas constantly amazes. The thrill of the first sound of her voice at the start of the great solo scene, the sadness which underlies the gaiety of the Polonaise, the affection of her verse in the final duet – all have the stamp of greatness. On the other hand there are occasional sour or raw high notes, where in Sutherland's performance these are the crowning glory. She also sings with feeling, phrases broadly, invests her *fioriture* with unequalled brilliance, but commands less dramatic intensity than her rival. Clearly, objectivity is getting us nowhere: time to fall back on pure personal prejudice.

Bellini La sonnambula.
Luba Orgonasova *sop* Amina
Raúl Giménez *ten* Elvino
Francesco Ellero d'Artegna *bass* Rodolfo
Dilbèr *sop* Lisa
Alexandra Papadjiakou *contr* Teresa
Nanco de Vries *bass* Alessio
Ioan Micu *ten* Notary
Netherlands Radio Choir and Chamber Orchestra / Alberto Zedda.
Naxos Ⓢ ① 8 660042/3 (two discs: 135 minutes: DDD). Recorded at a performance in the Concertgebouw, Amsterdam on November 14th, 1992.

At her entrance, Luba Orgonasova's declamation of the recitative preceding "Come per me" is so full and dramatic that it sounds like *Norma* – and the opening phrase is remarkably similar to "Sediziose voci". She sings the aria simply and sweetly, but in "Sovra il sen" some fairly modest embellishments reveal a metallic, edgy quality at the top of her voice. Giménez, one of the most eloquent *bel canto* tenors, is well suited to the high-lying role of Elvino – in its original form as perilous as that of Arturo in *I puritani*. He doesn't risk some of the high options that Pavarotti goes for in the second Bonynge recording. His voice blends surprisingly well with Orgonasova's in the two duets in Act 1 and it is his performance that makes this set particularly attractive.

Zedda conducts a very spirited account of the opera. The crucial finale of Act 1 – the scene in the inn – is given complete and the smaller parts are well taken, with Dilbèr having a big success with the very enthusiastic audience at her Second-Act aria. Any *Sonnambula*, though, is going to be judged initially by the soprano's performance of the sleepwalking scene – by this point in the evening Orgonosova obviously has the audience in the palm of her hand and she sings with style and brilliance. Needless to say, if one compares her with singers of the past – from Patti and Tetrazzini to Sutherland and Callas – she still has quite a way to go before she achieves total command.

This is the only Bellini opera available at super-budget price and as such it deserves a special welcome. It is a thoroughly enjoyable live performance, which devotees of Bellini will find interesting. With the earlier Sutherland and the Callas versions reissued at mid price, competition in the *Sonnambula* stakes is fierce. As an all-round recommendation the Sutherland recording reviewed overleaf is the one to have, but this bargain version is a good introduction to Bellini for the beginner as well as being a fine souvenir of what was obviously an exciting evening.

Bellini La sonnambula.
Maria Callas *sop* Amina
Nicola Monti *ten* Elvino
Nicola Zaccaria *bass* Rodolfo
Eugenia Ratti *sop* Lisa
Fiorenza Cossotto *mez* Teresa
Giuseppi Morresi *bass* Alessio
Franco Ricciardi *ten* Notary
Chorus and Orchestra of La Scala, Milan / Antonino Votto.
EMI mono Ⓜ ① CDS5 56278-2 (two discs: 121 minutes: ADD). Notes, text and translation included. Recorded 1957.

Here we hear the Amina which for two seasons delighted audiences at La Scala, and very wonderful it is. The voice is not perfect. There are once or twice hints of that second note underlying and sullying the proper one. There are sharp, wobbly notes (the final one of "Come per me sereno", for example). But there is also much exquisitely beautiful singing – lovely tone, movingly tender phrasing, gloriously delicate and virtuosic moments such as at some upward arpeggios in "Sovra il sen".

Words such as "spellbinding and sublime art" have been used about Callas's interpretation of the role. It is very intricate, and fired by poetic intellect. To quote Felice Romani, the librettist of the opera, on the subject of his heroine, for all that he says is relevant to Callas's performance: "The role of Amina," he wrote, "although it may seem at first sight easy to play, is perhaps more difficult than many others deemed more important. It calls for an actress who is playful, ingenuous and innocent, and at the same time passionate, impetuous and affectionate; who has one cry for joy and another for sorrow, different timbres for reproof and for pleading; who displays in every movement, in every glance, every sigh, a certain stylization mixed with realism such as we find in some paintings by Albani and certain of Theocritus' idylls".

Thus, said Romani, did Giuditta Pasta create the role … and thus does Maria Callas perform it. It is almost unnecessary to point out how strikingly she colours every phrase, note and word. After a couple of playings almost every line of recitative sticks in the mind with the exact colour and expression that she gives to it: "Compagne, teneri amici", before "Come per me"; "Il cor soltano", the only dowry she brings Elvino; "Qui! perchè?", filled with terror and amazement as she wakes in the Count's bedroom; "Ah! il mio anello", the cry which wrings our hearts as much as Brünnhilde's shriek, and far more affectingly, when the ring is torn from her finger. It is difficult to define why Callas's "Ah, non credea" should strike you as less than satisfying; perhaps the timbre is too strongly coloured for the line of the music. "Ah, non giunge" is relatively unaffecting because simple gaiety is not something that this soprano can easily express. Welling, interior, almost unbearable joy, yes, but not bright, clear happiness.

The concerted numbers go well, especially the two soprano/tenor duets of Act 1, with limpid sixths in the second verse of "Prendi, l'anel" and fascinating phrasing of the lovely " Son geloso del zefiro". Monti's voice has been stepped up a little by the engineers to sound more robust than it did in life. He is a smooth, reliable, well-tuned and tasteful singer. Zaccaria too is reliable. Ratti's Lisa is delightful, and Cossotto brings a lovely firm voice to the part of Teresa, though she tends to sing too loudly. Norberto Mola's Scala choir are outstanding in the chorus describing the *fantasma*, and also in the one where the villagers creep into the Count's bedroom, only to be surprised by finding a girl asleep on the bed. The chorus which opens Act 2 would have sounded better had the important accompaniment been conducted more sensitively.

Votti has mostly fine players under him, in particular a most poetical first horn (important in Elvino's "Tutto è sciolto"). But the flute is rather wretched, pedestrian in "Ah! perchè non posso odiarti". Votto's chugging accompaniment to the recitative before "Come per me" or to the introduction to Act 2, which could sound magical, seems to show that he does not always prize Bellini's beautifully worked orchestral writing nearly as much as he should. The cuts are the same: the usual ones of reprises in strettas, plus a verse of Lisa's opening cavatina (a pity, since Ratti is so charming), a slice of Elvino's "Tutto è sciolto", Lisa's aria in the final scene, and the complete stretta ("Lisa menace anch' essa") of the quartet, "Signor Conte!", which precedes Amina's last entry.

The recording is good but not without those 'difficulties' which seemed to beset many, not all, of the Scala series. It needs a little help if it is to come out smoothly all along, and sometimes Monti must be turned down to preserve a true dynamic level.

Bellini La sonnambula.

Dame Joan Sutherland *sop* Amina
Nicola Monti *ten* Elvino
Fernando Corena *bass* Rodolfo
Sylvia Stahlman *sop* Lisa
Margreta Elkins *mez* Teresa
Giovanni Foiani *bass* Alessio
Angelo Mercuriali *ten* Notary
Chorus and Orchestra of the Maggio Musicale Fiorentino / Richard Bonynge.
Decca Grand Opera Ⓜ ① 448 966-2DMO2 (two discs: 136 minutes: ADD). Notes, text and translation included. Recorded 1962.

Just as today composers occasionally turn to the cinema for subjects on which to base operas, in the 1820s and 1830s librettists looked to the stage – and not just to plays: *La sonnambula* is based on Scribe's story for Hérold's ballet of the same title. The role of Amina was created by Giuditta Pasta who was also Bellini's first Norma and Beatrice di Tenda, and who, in the same season and at the same theatre as she first sang Amina, was also Donizetti's Anna Bolena. Pasta was a great dramatic soprano, but as the nineteenth century wore on Amina became a favourite with light voices, especially Jenny Lind. Only in the 1950s and 1960s did Callas and Sutherland reaffirm its potential for more dramatic treatment. (To add to the confusion it was also done by singers we would today call mezzos – Malibran and Viardot – and this was continued not so long ago by Frederica von Stade.)

The occasion of Dame Joan Sutherland's seventieth birthday in November 1996 prompted Decca to reissue various opera sets from the 1960s, all for the first time on CD. *La sonnambula* was Bonynge's and Sutherland's first Bellini recording, although their second version (also Decca), which has Pavarotti as Elvino, is in better sound. Sutherland's Amina in the early-1960s was sung with such extraordinary freedom and exuberance that this is the set to have, indeed even now many consider it to be the best *Sonnambula* on disc. It's no good comparing Sutherland with Callas at this late stage – but it is inevitable where this is concerned, especially as the Elvino, Nicola Monti, also sings the role with Callas. No Sutherland admirer is going to convert to Callas in this opera, but it is fascinating to find one's remembered reactions sometimes wrong. (Callas does superb things in the coloratura of "Sovra il sen", Sutherland is full of dramatic fire in the scene in the inn.)

Bellini Zaira.

Katia Ricciarelli *sop* Zaira
Ramón Vargas *ten* Corasmino
Simone Alaimo *bar* Orosmane

Alexandra Papadjiakou *contr* Nerestano
Silvana Silbano *mez* Fatima
Roberto de Candia *bar* Meledor
Luigi Roni *bass* Lusignano
Giovanni Battista Palmieri *ten* Castiglione
Chorus and Orchestra of the Teatro Massimo Bellini, Catania / Paolo Olmi.
Nuova Era ℗ ① 698283 (two discs: 152 minutes: DDD). Notes, text and translation included.
Recorded at performances in Catania on September 23rd, 25th and 27th, 1990.

Zaira was Bellini's first failure, written and produced in 1829, and coming shortly after the successes of *Il pirata* and *La straniera*. The composer himself appears to have done nothing to revive the fortunes of his opera either at Parma or elsewhere, though he certainly took its hostile reception to heart. In his introductory essay, the distinguished Bellini scholar Friedrich Lippmann ascribes this uncharacteristic reticence to the fact that Bellini used the score of *Zaira* as a quarry for material later incorporated into *Norma*, *Bianca e Fernando* and, most notably, *I Capuleti ed i Montecchi*. Lippmann examines these 'parodies' (which, incidentally, is such a misleading word that another should surely be found), and discovers much to be said for their original form. For Bellini there was a very natural satisfaction in gaining applause for music first heard in the rejected opera: hence his remark "*Zaira* was avenged in *I Capuleti*".

Revived today, as at Catania, the opera would probably be well received, partly because there is real merit in it, and partly because audiences at a 'classical' revival are usually so docile. The emotional situations and particularly the plight of the heroine provide Bellini with suitable material, but there are points in the story that defy parody (in the more usual sense of the word), one (or more accurately two) of them being of the "Tell me, is there by any chance a strawberry mark to the right of your left elbow?" variety. Still, the melodies rise and fall with the sweetness and sadness expected of them, and sometimes with an almost defiant touch that surprises by some modification of accepted form.

Of the singers, most is demanded from the heroine and least from the tenor. He, a nationalist hardliner and unsympathetic character generally, gets his solos over and done with early on, and in the present performance this is rather a pity, for Ramón Vargas is a good, fine-edged singer of whom one would willingly hear more. The 'trousers' role of Nerestano is sung by the characterful and convincingly male-sounding Alexandra Papadjiakou; and the sorely tried Sultan, Orosmane, gains additional sympathy when Simone Alaimo produces such beautiful tone as he does in the duet "Ma se tu m'ami". Ricciarelli herself sounds perfectly lovely when singing softly, but the wear on her voice is very evident at other points. The droopy portamento used for pathos had become almost automatic at this stage. Even so, she remains impressive in the florid music and would no doubt be a touchingly beautiful presence on stage. The stage, in this recording, is ever with us, prompter and all. The orchestral playing sometimes sounds provincial, yet one feels that Paolo Olmi is securing a good account of the score. 'Feels' because we have no recorded version for comparison, and it may be some time before one appears: meanwhile the opportunity of hearing this 'world première' is well worth taking.

Alban Berg
Austrian 1885-1935

Berg Lulu.
  Teresa Stratas *sop* Lulu
  Franz Mazura *bar* Dr Schön
  Kenneth Riegel *ten* Alwa
  Yvonne Minton *mez* Countess Geschwitz
  Robert Tear *ten* Painter, Negro
  Toni Blankenheim *bar* Schigolch, Professor of Medicine, Police Officer
  Gerd Nienstedt *bass* Animal Tamer, Rodrigo
  Helmut Pampuch *ten* Prince, Manservant, Marquis
  Jules Bastin *bass* Theatre Manager, Banker
  Hanna Schwarz *mez* Wardrobe Mistress, Schoolboy, Groom
  Jane Manning *sop* Girl
  Ursula Boese *mez* Her mother
  Anna Ringart *mez* Lady Artist
  Claude Meloni *bar* Journalist
  Pierre-Yves le Maigat *bass* Manservant
  Paris Opéra Orchestra / Pierre Boulez.
DG ℗ ① 415 489-2GH3 (three discs: 172 minutes: ADD). Notes, text and translation included.
Recorded 1979.

BBC RADIO 3
90-93 FM

1979

It is fair, though arguable, to aver that the première of Alban Berg's *Lulu*, in all its three acts, at the Paris Opéra on February 24th, 1979 was the single most important operatic event of this century's second half, maybe of the past half-century. Here was an acknowledged masterpiece, internationally familiar for some three to four decades as an unfinished torso, now revealed at full stretch, bearing every mark of complete authenticity. For several years Berg scholars had intimated that a complete stage performance was feasible, and greatly desirable if the full impact and significance of *Lulu* were to be appreciated. Erwin Stein must have known as much when he prepared a complete vocal score in the late-1930s, and his work could have been accessible to all ever since, but for the waxing power of the Nazis, the war and, since the 1950s, the determination of Berg's widow that nobody must attempt a complete *Lulu*, not even look at Berg's complete short score.

At first working in secret, the Viennese composer Friedrich Cerha set about finishing the orchestration, and filling out bars incompletely notated by Berg: Cerha's work was known as soon as Helene Berg died in 1977 and it was Paris which won the privilege of the complete unveiling, a splendid social, as well as a great artistic occasion. The production has been seen on British television, and DG made their recording following the first performance with Jane Manning replacing Daniele Chlostawa as the teenage daughter in the Paris gambling-room scene and Toni Blankenheim adding an extra role too.

Berg's *Lulu*, like Frank Wedekind's two plays which were its literary source, is much concerned with symmetry: Lulu's success in the first half of the opera has to be matched with her steady catastrophic downfall in the second half, from the murder of Dr Schön, her only real love, onwards. She is furthermore destroyed, in the closing scene, by three brothel clients who are to be recognized as reflections of the three husbands whom she destroyed earlier. (The Paris production wilfully ignored that point, but not to the detriment of these discs since the Professor, her first client, does not utter anything, so we are not aware that he is not the *alter ego* of Dr Goll.) It is this symmetry, musical as well as dramatic, which makes a full-length *Lulu* so desirable; apart from the musical richness *per se* of the Third Act, the performance benefits from the many ensembles of the gambling scene (the duet for Lulu and the Marquis sounds not quite complete), the witty or pointed reprises, Alwa's solo in the final scene, leading to an eloquent vocal quartet.

For all these reasons, the present recording has significant advantages over Decca's Viennese recording under Christoph von Dohnányi, which offers only the first two acts and fragments from the Third Act as included in Berg's *Lulu* Suite. The careful Decca casting, production and interpretation must not be underestimated: it is, in some ways, a more beautiful, considered performance than the DG, but incomplete and therefore not truly comparable. Meanwhile, we can be grateful that the DG set is so well cast, and the Paris orchestra on such fine form for Boulez – discipline, tone quality, nuance and firmly distinctive characterization of each new section or mood, are all much to be appreciated on these discs. So is the scrupulous balance of the recording, all the voices well forward, but not at the expense of orchestral detail, even if one might occasionally wish for subtler distancing of characters: the recorded sound is close, somewhat dry, especially compared with the Decca.

Main admiration goes to Franz Mazura, for his tough and ruthless but not unfeeling Dr Schön, a magnificent assumption, and to Hanna Schwarz's unusually convincing Schoolboy and Groom. The recording increases enthusiasm for Stratas's Lulu, softer and more feline than Anja Silja on Decca, not so starry but easier on the ear. Stratas, more than Silja, conveys Berg's deep compassion for Lulu who is not just a selfish bitch, but a victim of unscrupulous men. Kenneth Riegel's Alwa commands respect as a dramatic and musical impersonation; the voice is attractive, the singing bold and cogent. Both of them, and several others in the cast, have less than faultless German pronunciation, which may disturb enjoyment of the spoken passages for those sensitive to such things. Yet one would not willingly forgo Robert Tear's ardent Painter, or Yvonne Minton's edgy, thwarted Countess Geschwitz, or Jules Bastin's gloriously pompous Banker. An exception, of course, is Toni Blankenheim, a splendid Schigolch who almost survives comparison with the *non-pareil* Hans Hotter on the Decca set. They are a good cast, and Pierre Boulez deserves much of the credit for the cogency of the set, even if he also perhaps influenced its clinical sound quality.

For getting to know the whole opera, this DG set is indispensable, and in many ways is ideal, just because Boulez made sure that everything (even the backstage jazz band in the cabaret scene) would be as audible as it was to Berg's inner ear when he set *Lulu* on paper. You need to learn a language, even in music, before you can fully enjoy its literature, and what an absorbing, affecting piece of literature Berg's *Lulu* is!

Berg Lulu.
   Christine Schäfer *sop* Lulu
   Wolfgang Schöne *bass* Dr Schön, Jack the Ripper
   David Kuebler *ten* Alwa
   Kathryn Harries *sop* Countess Geschwitz
   Stephan Drakulich *ten* Painter, Negro
   Norman Bailey *bar* Schigolch
   Jonathan Veira *bar* Professor of Medicine, Banker, Theatre Manager
   Donald Maxwell *bar* Animal Trainer, Athlete
   Neil Jenkins *ten* Prince, Manservant, Marquis
   Patricia Bardon *mez* Wardrobe Mistress, Groom, Schoolboy
   London Philharmonic Orchestra / Andrew Davis.
   Stage Director: **Graham Vick.** *Video Director:* **Humphrey Burton.**
   NVC Arts Ⓟ 🔲🔲 0630-15533-3 (182 minutes). Recorded at Glyndebourne during July 1996.

1997

One of Glyndebourne's most daring choices in the summer of 1996 was *Lulu*. In Graham Vick's staging the single set consisted of a curved red-brick wall that looked like an extension of the theatre's own architecture, the idea surely being to draw the audience into the drama, make the wealthy share the experience of the deprived. Its drawback is that the various milieux predicated by the libretto – Vienna studio, artist's salon, theatre dressing-room, Paris gaming-room and London attic – all look the same. However ingenious the lighting may be, that is something of a disadvantage and tends towards visual monotony.

It forms a suitable enough backdrop to Vick's seemingly disengaged attitude to the piece itself. His cool, objective gaze on the characters also detaches us from their predicaments, thus making the work seem even more sleazy than it already is. Of course there may be a case to be made for such a clear-eyed, unsentimental view of Berg's second and last opera, emphasizing the single-minded self-interest of all the characters apart from the lesbian Geschwitz.

Paradoxically one does in the end find some sympathy for Lulu herself as portrayed by Schäfer, more so here on video than in the opera-house, because we more intimately share her feelings as a victim of her own inner erotic yearnings, irresistible to all men, herself drawn to them all in spite of herself. Schäfer conveys this in her body language, even more in her facial expressions portraying her sheer vulnerability. Unlike many previous Lulus, Silja perhaps excepted, Schäfer, being herself young and attractive, doesn't have to engage in the vamping we so often see in the part from older sopranos: her allure is there in her person. All she has to do is 'be'. Similarly, unlike most of her predecessors, she sings the role with apparently effortless ease, also with an accuracy that is truly astonishing. Nor does any sign of wobble or strain affect her tone. It is a compelling portrayal, beautifully caught by Burton in his video direction.

Schöne's strongly sung, worried Dr Schön, slave to Lulu, and his frighteningly mad Jack the Ripper, Kuebler's intense Alwa (made up, deliberately, to look like Berg, who had a secret mistress), Bailey's wheezy, crafty Schigolch, Harries's eloquent Geschwitz are leaders of an excellent ensemble, conducted by Davis with total conviction: the score has never sounded so translucent yet so rich-hued. In terms of both picture and sound this video is faithful to the original in which Vick's command of stagecraft is everywhere evident but never obtrusive. Subtitles are provided and the booklet has a good essay on the opera by Mark Pappenheim.

Berg Wozzeck.

Franz Grundheber *bar* Wozzeck
Hildegard Behrens *sop* Marie
Walter Raffeiner *ten* Drum-Major
Philip Langridge *ten* Andres
Heinz Zednik *ten* Captain
Aage Haugland *bass* Doctor
Anna Gonda *mez* Margret
Alfred Sramek *bar* First Apprentice
Vienna Boys' Choir; Vienna State Opera Chorus;
Vienna Philharmonic Orchestra / Claudio Abbado.
DG Ⓟ Ⓞ 423 587-2GH2 (two discs: 89 minutes: DDD). Notes, text and translation included.
Recorded at performances at the Vienna State Opera during June 1987.

BBC RADIO 3
90-93 FM

The first ever recording of *Wozzeck* was made at a couple of concert performances in New York conducted by Dimitri Mitropoulos (in mono on Philips). It seemed at the time an appallingly risky thing to do, but although it was an untidy performance, with mostly dull singing and fistfuls of wrong notes, it had a fiery eloquence and a fidelity to the spirit of Berg's score that have seldom been approached since. Subsequent recordings have been more accurate, on the whole, and have captured individual performances of great distinction, but they have tended in the grooming process to diminish the opera's pain and ferocity, and few of them have had much sense of the stage.

Abbado's live recording has plenty of this latter quality. We hear it from the front row of the stalls, with a theatrical rather than a studio balance between singers and orchestra, and the sense of a real stage with real action taking place upon it is very strong: the placing and movement of the military band in Act 1 scene 3 is pretty well ideal; so are the two crowded inn-scenes. More important still, one is aware that this is a genuine performance, not a studio replica of one. A tiny example is the way that Behrens's voice momentarily breaks with pity and guilt as Marie thanks Wozzeck for giving her his wages: it is a spur-of-the-moment thing, an even an involuntary one, and certainly not premeditated – it is over in a second but it adds a poignantly graphic stroke to her portrayal. The touch of Viennese *schmalz* that comes over Grundheber's Wozzeck when he says what he would do "if I were a gentleman, with a hat and eye-glasses" is another such moment; it tells you precisely what Wozzeck's image of genteel morality is, and how unbridgeably remote from it he knows himself to be. It is somehow characteristic of this performance that Alfred Sramek, who was soberly staid as the drunken First Apprentice for Dohnányi on his 1979 Decca recording, lets at least some of his hair down for Abbado and even hiccups in the place where Berg has provided him with an obvious cue to do so.

Wozzeck is an expressionist score, not a late romantic one; there is a danger that once the hideous difficulties of playing it have been mastered, an orchestra (especially if that orchestra be the Vienna

Philharmonic, perhaps) will be tempted by the obvious, just-under-the-surface kinships with Mahler to play it as though it were Mahler. Dohnányi's outstandingly beautiful performance falls into this trap once in a while, and it is good to hear Abbado resisting any temptation to gloss over the shocking brutality and savage grotesqueness that are such crucial elements of the opera's manner. His underlining of a blackly sinister waltz element in scenes where you might not expect to find it, the way that the tavern band music has something alarming to it from the very outset are both instances of this. Happily, though, the bad habits of overtly expressionist *Wozzeck* performances (accuracy of pitch and rhythm sacrificed to strenuous histrionics) are met with only rarely here; indeed the emphasis in the *Sprechstimme* passages is very much on *Stimme*, Behrens in particular making a very good case for regarding Berg's precisely notated pitches as proof that he wanted those notes and no others.

Grundheber was the world's first-ranking Wozzeck when this recording was made, and one can easily see why; without either the beauty of tone or the vivid acting of Walter Berry (for Boulez on Sony Classical) he is a scrupulous musician; his voice is unstrained by the role's cruel demands (which one cannot say of Dohnányi's raw and unsteady Eberhard Waechter) and he conveys Wozzeck's pathos and bitterness finely, though missing something of his crazed visionariness. Behrens's voice is perhaps a size too large for Marie, ideally, but her intelligence, her eloquent involvement with the role and the effortless openness of her high notes are ample compensation for an occasional tremulousness when singing quietly. There are no real weaknesses in the rest of the cast, but Haugland's demonstration that in order to characterize the Doctor's vehement monomania you do not need to rewrite a high proportion of his vocal line is a particular strength.

The possible drawback (for some listeners it will not be a drawback at all, for others quite a severe one) is that live recording. The orchestra are very much in the foreground, and instrumental details are apt to protrude simply because of this close proximity. It is difficult to recall having been *that* close to a contra-bassoon ever before (or to the bombardon in the stage band – an artist of consummate virtuosity, by the way), and when the heavy brass are brought into play you may cower before their onslaught. As often as not, though, you will like this impression of sharing the rostrum with Abbado: the harshly protesting dissonances of the D minor interlude emerge with grinding bitterness (no, the piece is *not* a Mahlerian *Adagietto* in disguise!) and the closeness of much of the opera to Berg's phantasmagoric Op. 6 *Orchestral Pieces* has never been more apparent. But the voices are distinctly recessed, even sometimes overwhelmed (you could do with eavesdropping at closer range on the Doctor's conversation with the Captain in Act 2, for example) and the occasional orchestral balance strikes you as being determined more by the exigencies of microphone-placing in a crowded Staatsoper than by Abbado's preference.

Dohnányi's Decca version is more beautiful in orchestral texture, more sophisticated in recording technique, at times more subtle in its pacing than Abbado's rawly urgent account, but both his principal singers sound strained, Waechter severely so. It is easier to listen to than the DG, and many collectors will return to it whenever they want a more comfortable perspective or a more Straussian view of the work (and the inclusion of a decent account of Schoenberg's *Erwartung* makes it better value than its rivals), but compared to the Abbado it is studio-bound, with all the singers in word-enhancing but illusion-shattering close-up. Nowhere near so close as those in Boulez's Sony reading, where practically everything is presented to the listener eyeball-to-eyeball and in a harshly bright light. The voices give very little pleasure, with the solitary, glorious exception of Walter Berry (perhaps the best Wozzeck on record). Boulez's direction veers between the miraculously precise and the fidgety; he is very good at nail-biting suspense and lucid clarification of complex textures but he seems more absorbedly interested in the score than in love with it. First choice rests with Abbado, almost unhesitatingly.

Berg Wozzeck.

Dietrich Fischer-Dieskau *bar* Wozzeck
Evelyn Lear *sop* Marie
Helmut Melchert *ten* Drum-Major
Fritz Wunderlich *ten* Andres
Gerhard Stolze *ten* Captain
Karl Christian Kohn *bass* Doctor
Alice Oelke *mez* Margret
Chorus of the Deutsche Oper, Berlin

Berg Lulu.

Evelyn Lear *sop* Lulu
Dietrich Fischer-Dieskau *bar* Dr Schön
Donald Grobe *ten* Alwa
Patricia Johnson *mez* Countess Geschwitz
Loren Driscoll *ten* Painter
Josef Greindel *bass* Schigolch;
Gerd Feldhoff *bass* Animal Tamer, Rodrigo
Karl-Ernst Mercker *ten* Prince
Leopold Clam *ten* Theatre Manager
Alice Oelke *mez* Wardrobe Mistress

Barbara Scherler *mez* Schoolboy
Walther Dicks *bar* Professor of Medicine.
Orchestra of the Deutsche Oper, Berlin / Karl Böhm.
DG Ⓜ ① 435 705-2GX3 (three discs: 216 minutes: ADD). Recorded in 1968.

Lulu herself is one of the most mercilessly demanding roles in all opera, as well as the reagent without which none of the piece's chemistry would work. A vocal personality of such vivid allure that it rivets the attention despite the absence of any stage picture, *plus* a voice that can untiringly scintillate up on the ledger-lines: few sopranos have ever satisfied both demands to the full, except perhaps Schäfer. Böhm's two-act *Lulu*, now recoupled on three CDs with his *Wozzeck*, is a tempting bargain. For the price you get very beautiful and finely recorded orchestral sound, superb conducting and a pair of principal singers who intriguingly change roles between operas: Lear, the disappointing Lulu, becomes a first-rate Marie in *Wozzeck*, while Fischer-Dieskau, the best Schön ever, is a bit too subtle and poetic an artist for the brutalized and inarticulate Wozzeck.

Böhm's *Lulu* was also recorded live, by the way, but escapes most of the pitfalls. So, on the whole, does Abbado's ferociously dramatic *Wozzeck*, a vivid demonstration that recording in the opera-house can pack a huge theatrical punch. On that account and that of his cast Abbado must remain first choice for *Wozzeck*. For a *Lulu* at full price, Boulez still awaits a real challenger.

Berg Wozzeck.

Franz Grundheber *bar* Wozzeck
Waltraud Meier *mez* Marie
Mark Baker *ten* Drum-Major
Endrik Wottrich *ten* Andres
Graham Clark *ten* Captain
Günter von Kannen *bar* Doctor
Dalia Schaechter *mez* Margret
Siegfried Vogel *bass* First Apprentice
Roman Trekel *bar* Second Apprentice
Peter Menzel *bass* Idiot
Chorus of the Deutsche Oper, Berlin; Staatskapelle Berlin / Daniel Barenboim.
Stage Director: **Patrice Chéreau.**
Teldec Ⓟ 💿 0630-16338-3 (94 minutes). Recorded at performances in the Deutsche Staatsoper, Berlin during April 1994. Also available on Ⓟ ① 0630-14108-2 (two discs: 94 minutes: DDD).

Seeing Patrice Chéreau's riveting production of *Wozzeck* at the Staatsoper, Berlin, where the work had its première in 1925, adds enormously to the pleasure of merely listening to Barenboim's interpretation on CD. In the context of such a closely integrated, finely honed staging, the performance gains in stature. Richard Peduzzi's sets merely suggest the milieu of each scene so that we lose some of that eerie atmosphere created by Caspar Neher's famous décor for the 1925 première later reproduced at Covent Garden and elsewhere, and some stipulated props are absent. That hardly matters, given the superb management of lighting and the subtle, intelligent direction of the singing-actors that is such a hallmark of Chéreau's work. With Barenboim's large-scale, committed and deeply moving interpretation to back it up, this is the kind of *Gesamtkunstwerk* that Barenboim has brought to the house on the Unter den Linden. You feel everyone concerned is utterly dedicated to his or her contribution.

Grundheber's Wozzeck is securely sung and convincingly acted even if here he misses that touch of vulnerability exposed by the greatest interpreters. Meier's Marie, accurately sung, conjures up the anguished contrast between the needs of that character's body and conscience: the look in her eyes tells all even when her singing is a shade squally. Von Kannen's obsessed Doctor and Graham Clark's loony Captain are close cousins, respectively, to their Alberich and Mime. Mark Baker is an adequate Drum-Major, but the role could be made at once more threatening and ludicrous. The support is splendid, notably veteran Siegfried Vogel's rollicking First Apprentice and Peter Menzel's pitiful Idiot.

The quality of video direction, picture and sound is exemplary, and the provision of subtitles a lesson to other companies in this field. Reservations which apply where the recording is concerned seem not to matter when you can actually see the stage action. The Vienna/Abbado/ Dresden version of 1987 was once available on a Pioneer video. In any case one cannot imagine anyone preferring it to this overwhelming achievement particularly as there the cameras move lamely to the conductor and orchestra during the interludes.

Erik Bergman
Finnish 1911-

Bergman The Singing Tree.

Peter Lindroos *ten* King
Charlotte Hellekant *mez* Witch

Kaisa Hannula *sop* Princess
Petteri Salomaa *bass* Prince Hatt
Sauli Tiilikainen *bar* Fool
Martti Wallén *bass* Fruit Seller
Anna-Lisa Jakobsson *mez* First Princess
Marianne Harju *sop* Second Princess
Tuula-Marja Tuomela *sop* First Solo Voice
Eeva-Kaarina Vilke *mez* Second Solo Voice
Tom Nyman *ten* Solo Voice, First Servant
Petri Lindroos *bass* Second Servant
Dominante Choir; Tapiola Chamber Choir; Finnish National Opera Orchestra / Ulf Söderblom.
Ondine Ⓟ Ⓒ ODE794-2D (two discs: 129 minutes: DDD). Notes, text and translation included.
Recorded 1992.

Musically, this issue is a triumph: the *magnum opus* of one of the leading Finnish composers in an excellent and committed performance, captured in all its intricate detail by a remarkably clear and faithful recording. *The Singing Tree* is Erik Bergman's only full-length opera and, as fellow-composer Jouni Kaipainen comments in the booklet, is a "grand synthesis" of his life's work. Often it sounds like a compendium of the vocal and instrumental techniques that Bergman has developed throughout his long career melded together by his vibrant and incisive musicianship.

The fable of the princess who may not see her husband's face is common to many cultures: Bo Carpelan's libretto uses a Swedish version but incorporates elements of many other stories, ancient and more modern. Prince Hatt, imprisoned by his mother, the Witch, is set free by a Princess who first communes with him via the song of the Tree of Life, which they both hear in dreams. Unlike many fairy-tale operas, Bergman and Carpelan lay bare the nightmare that exists at the centre of all fables; and as if to emphasize that this is not kids' stuff, the happy ending is marred by the blinding of the Princess through the Witch's dying curse.

The only reservation about *The Singing Tree* concerns dramatic pacing which, like the musical pulse, is unremittingly slow. A sequence of 22 tableaux divided into two acts (plus Prologue, Interlude and Epilogue), there is often insufficient variety between the scenes which makes the opera seem to be jogging on the spot. Individual tableaux are often effective in themselves but many take not very dissimilar routes to achieve common goals. Only two really dramatic moments alter the relief: at the climax of Act 1, when the Princess is lured by the Witch to look upon the face of the sleeping Prince, and the final denouement itself when the Witch is destroyed by the power of Light. Written in 1986-8, *The Singing Tree* is exactly coeval with Sallinen's *Kullervo* (also available on Ondine, reviewed under Sallinen). This speaks volumes for the commitment, industry and musical culture of Finland and puts most other countries to shame.

Michael Berkeley
British 1948

M. Berkeley Baa Baa Black Sheep.
Malcolm Lorimer *treb* Punch, Mowgli as a child
William Dazeley *bar* Mowgli as a young man
Ann Taylor-Morley *mez* Judy, Grey Wolf
George Mosley *bar* Father, Father Wolf, Messua's Husband
Eileen Hulse *sop* Mother, Mother Wolf, Messua
Henry Newman *bass* The Captain, Akela
Fiona Kimm *mez* Auntirosa, Baldeo
Philip Sheffield *ten* Harry, Sheer Khan
Mark Holland *bar* Bhini-in-the-garden, Baloo
Clive Bayley *bar* Meeta, Bagheera
Paul McCann *ten* Captain Sahib, Ka
Brian Cookson *ten* Priest
Chorus of Opera North; English Northern Philharmonia / Paul Daniel.
Collins Classics Ⓟ Ⓒ 7036-2 (two discs: 115 minutes: DDD). Text provided. Recorded at performances at the Grand Theatre, Leeds on November 13th, 16th, 17th and 19th, 1993.

Michael Berkeley's fascinating opera has a libretto by David Malouf which juxtaposes elements from Kipling's *Jungle Book* with others from an early semi-autobiographical short story in which Kipling described his and his sister's wretched existence in "The House of Desolation", his name for the brutal foster-home in England to which his parents sent him after an early childhood spent entirely in India. From this grey and stifling world of beatings and sanctimony Kipling's imagination transports him to a fantasy world where he can have his revenge by transforming himself into Mowgli and the adults into the animals of the jungle.

Kipling and Malouf together have thus given Berkeley two marvellous cues for musical drama and he seizes both: the transitions from the hateful real world (edgy music, angular and harsh) to the warmth and the magic of the jungle are indeed magical, and the transformation of Kipling's *alter ego*, the boy Punch, firstly into the child Mowgli (sung by a treble voice) and then into Mowgli as a young man, a baritone with vocal lines that reflect his agile strength, is one of the score's most powerful coups. The magic takes its time to register (necessarily: the arid misery of the House of Desolation cannot be sketched in a mere line or two), and the 'matching' of jungle characters with those in Punch's everyday existence is not altogether perfect. His worst adversary, the puritanical Auntirosa, really needs a more formidable jungle equivalent than the cowardly hunter Baldeo, for example. But much more often this pairing works: Auntirosa's husband, the sympathetic but ineffectual Captain, becomes as Akela, the old wolf, all that he cannot be as a human and the odiously bullying Harry is transformed into a chilling mythic prototype of bullies, not only schoolboy ones, in the guise of Sheer Khan the tiger.

Bagheera the panther and Baloo the bear are again not ideally paired with the tiny roles of the Indian servants Meeta and Bhini – as humans they hardly register as characters at all – but as Mowgli's surrogate parents and dearest friends they are crucial to the opera's central theme of a child for whom servants and his own fantasy world take the place of family. It was right that Malouf should make the conclusion of the story a shade harsher than Kipling's own (when his mother begs Punch's forgiveness for her unwitting cruelty he replies "Too late, too late"), not least because Berkeley's music has already so beautifully sketched Mowgli's tender but doomed relationship with Baloo and Bagheera as more loving than anything Punch or Kipling could find with their parents.

It has often been said that Berkeley's once lyrical, broadly conservative style has become harsher and harder. It would be more accurate to say that he has broadened his expressive range. Ample melodic breadth is still there, in Mowgli's own music and that for his mother, in the florid "music of the watching" as Mowgli, observed but unaided by his animal friends saves his human parents from being burned alive, and above all in the eloquent scene of the "Spring Running", Mowgli's realization that he must rejoin mankind and leave the jungle. Earlier on there is almost a Hollywood lushness to the moonlight scene in which he dances with Grey Wolf (the 'double' of Punch/Mowgli's sister Judy). But there is bleakness and harshness as well, largely associated of course with human cruelty. It is almost too successful, this linking of hateful human characters with fiercely angular chromatic declamation, but the implied presence in the sympathetic ones of the subcontinent's alluring warmth smooths the violent contrast. It is a fine opera, and this live recording is very welcome.

A live recording, some of the voices are obviously projecting into a large auditorium, rather than to the kinder and closer ear of a microphone. This is especially noticeable in the case of Eileen Hulse, who inevitably has the least sympathetic, most tortuous vocal lines. It isn't just because William Dazeley has some of the most appealing ones, though, that he stands out from an accomplished cast: his voice has glamour as well as lyrical warmth. There are no weak links, and the tricky business of balance between stage and orchestra in a theatre performance has been well managed. All the same, you will need the libretto provided, though there are numerous small differences between it and what is actually sung.

Hector Berlioz French 1803-1869

Berlioz Béatrice et Bénédict.
Dame Janet Baker *mez* Béatrice
Robert Tear *ten* Bénédict
Christiane Eda-Pierre *sop* Héro
Helen Watts *contr* Ursule
Thomas Allen *bar* Claudio
Jules Bastin *bass* Somarone
Robert Lloyd *bass* Don Pedro
Richard Van Allan *narr* Léonato
London Symphony Orchestra; John Alldis Choir / Sir Colin Davis.
Philips Ⓟ Ⓞ 416 952-2PH2 (two discs: 98 minutes: ADD). Notes, text and translation included. Recorded 1977.

The CD format, so good at strengthening the already firm dramatic outlines of a *Rigoletto* or *Otello*, is merciless in its exposure of a complementary weakness. There is dramatic structure here, with a finely weighted internal balance, yet the total effect is more of a divertissement than of *opéra comique*. This recording was Sir Colin Davis's second (the first is available on a Double Decca mid-price set with Josephine Veasey and John Mitchinson in the leading roles). Its principal competitor (under Barenboim on DG) has a starry cast headed by Yvonne Minton and Plácido Domingo, with Ileana Cotrubas and Dietrich Fischer-Dieskau in the second line: its principal drawback is its use of a sophisticated narrative device substituting for the admittedly not very effective, spoken dialogue which provides the links here.

The present Davis recording has few flaws – Jules Bastin's crudely blustering Somarone is the most tiresome – and many strengths, most notably (among the singers) the vividly characterized, radiantly voiced Béatrice of Dame Janet Baker. Robert Tear copes nimbly with the vocal line and points his satire adroitly. Christiane Eda-Pierre sings Héro's long and demanding solo with lyric warmth and employs an assured technique in the florid finale. The smaller roles are taken by artists big enough to bring the same professional thoroughness to whatever they undertake, and the excellent John Alldis Choir are allowed more presence and immediacy than the chorus generally obtain in many latter-day recordings. Davis and the LSO present the magical score as a humane document as well as a work of wit and undimmed brilliance, the subject of a beautifully written study by David Cairns included in the booklet.

Berlioz Benvenuto Cellini.

Nicolai Gedda *ten* Benvenuto Cellini
Jules Bastin *bass* Giacomo Balducci
Robert Massard *bar* Fieramosca
Roger Soyer *bass* Pope Clément VII
Derek Blackwell *ten* Francesco
Robert Lloyd *bass* Bernardino
Hugues Cuénod *ten* Innkeeper
Raimund Herincx *bar* Pompeo
Christiane Eda-Pierre *sop* Teresa
Jane Berbié *mez* Ascanio
Janine Reiss *spkr*
Chorus of the Royal Opera House, Covent Garden; BBC Symphony Orchestra / Sir Colin Davis.
Philips Ⓔ Ⓛ 416 955-2PH3 (three discs: 161 minutes: ADD). Notes, text and translation included. Recorded 1972.

Even Sir Colin Davis has rarely conducted a more electrifying Berlioz performance on record than here, demonstrating – with the help of singers from the presentation he promoted at Covent Garden – that for all its awkwardness on stage, this can be a thrilling opera on record. He is enormously helped by his cast, and most of all by Nicolai Gedda, here giving one of the very finest, most powerful, most searching performances of his whole career. The Philips transfer engineers have been just as concerned as in the other big opera project in this series, *Les Troyens*, to use the format of CD with maximum benefit. So the First Act is complete on the first two discs, with each of the two tableaux (six scenes in the first, seven in the second) taking up a whole disc each. That leaves the third disc for the whole of the Second Act, over 70 minutes, ensuring no unnecessary breaks anywhere.

The sound too remains very vivid, with the firmness of focus and sense of presence characteristic of Philips engineering of the period all the more apparent on CD. The orchestra are not quite so forward as in some of the Davis/Berlioz series, but that sets the stage picture the more clearly, and even the most complex scenes – notably the final scene of the casting – are sharpened by the separation of voices. What is not so welcome is that there seems to be rather more treble emphasis than usual, occasionally to the point of fierceness, but that is something which will very much depend on individual hi-fi equipment. You might prefer to have had that brightness compensated by more body in the orchestral sound, but that is to be hyper-critical. This is a superb set, which as in the original issue comes with generous essays as well as libretto. David Cairns's essay on the romantic cult of the Artist-hero, is particularly valuable, along with its explanation of Davis's text, which restores cuts enforced in Liszt's Weimar version and presents the piece (as at Covent Garden) as an extended *opéra comique* with dialogue.

Berlioz Les Troyens.

Josephine Veasey *mez* Dido
Jon Vickers *ten* Aeneas
Berit Lindholm *sop* Cassandra
Peter Glossop *bar* Corebus, Corebus's ghost
Heather Begg *sop* Anna
Roger Soyer *bar* Narbal, Spirit of Hector
Anthony Raffell *bass* Panthus
Anne Howells *mez* Ascanius
Ian Partridge *ten* Iopas
Pierre Thau *bass* Priam, Mercury, Trojan Soldier
Elizabeth Bainbridge *mez* Hecuba, Cassandra's ghost
Ryland Davies *ten* Hylas
Raimund Herincx *bar* Priam's ghost, First Sentry
Dennis Wicks *bar* Hector's ghost, Second Sentry
David Lennox *ten* Helenus
Wandsworth School Boys' Choir;
Chorus and Orchestra of the Royal Opera House, Covent Garden / Sir Colin Davis.
Philips Ⓔ Ⓛ 416 432-2PH4 (four discs: 241 minutes: ADD). Notes, text and translation included. Recorded 1969.

Not until 1985 did *Les Troyens* receive its first complete performance in French at Covent Garden, not until 1985 was the full score published, in the New Berlioz Edition's Vols. 2*a* and 2*b*; not until this had the work been recorded, complete. Hitherto one of the masterpieces of nineteenth-century opera has been known only through inaccurate vocal scores and very occasional performances in which the work has suffered the death of the thousand cuts (there have been honourable exceptions: Westrup's Oxford production was a fine effort), while for records one was dependent on the old Ducretet-Thomson of the Carthage acts (with Arda Mandikian, the Oxford Dido), a Régine Crespin digest, Janet Baker in the final scenes, and the usual excerpts. Here the most handsome amends have been made, and the troubled ghost of Hector may rest triumphant.

This is basically the Covent Garden cast and players. But all that was troublesome on that edgy first night has been set true, and Colin Davis here reasserts his eminence as the greatest Berlioz conductor of his day. His command of the score in all its splendour has never seemed more complete. He understands with total instinct how the whole work presents one great imaginative act, from the disaster at Troy through all the Trojans' adventures to the dying Dido's final vision of Rome: this was Berlioz's theme, and to it all the incident falls second. And so the climactic moments are not the diversions nor even the intense lyricism of the Carthage love scenes – which assume an extra poignancy by their sense of transience – but the scenes in which the score is possessed by a sense of urgency as the call to Rome is felt. A splendid rhythmic impetus lies at the heart of Davis's interpretation, matching the nervous intensity of the metres and the constant sense of unrest: as in other works of Berlioz it may be a half-concealed harmonic stress or a carefully marked (but usually neglected) inner part that gives the colour to the music, so here it is characteristically time and again a sudden emphasis on an off-beat (as in the last half-beats of the bar in "Va ma soeur") or rhythmic contrast in the closely succeeding numbers. Davis builds his large structures upon a closely observed rhythmic detail, down to the crisp beat of the *constructeurs* and the witty trudge of the two soldiers and up to the hectic, despairing thrust of Cassandra's "Non, je ne verrai pas" and the inexorable tread of the *Marche et Hymne* (No. 4). For once, the prophetic vision of Rome really does seem to crown the work.

There are few places where this sure touch seems to waver, and they are chiefly in the more reflective moments. Energy characterizes the performance so much, and is such a creative centre of an interpretation bound to a sense of progress, that it is difficult to allow the sections where repose and a sense of stillness fill the score to assume their role without imposing a pull-back. But this is exactly what they must do; and even so simple and touching a song as poor drowsy, homesick Hylas's "Vallon sonore" needs more calm than Davis seems willing to allow, or than Ryland Davies's lucid but very open-eyed singing gives it. Andromache's marvellous scene is oddly tame: the clarinet is too determined, and hardly seems to feel the mourning atmosphere, or the agony that comes over the music at the turn to the major. The Septet and Duet are superbly handled; but you can imagine a greater sense of a poised, timeless lyricism, the threat of war and the call of Mercury far from the lovers' minds, so that when the shield clashes and his voice sounds it is a shattering of happiness.

Dido and Aeneas, as at Covent Garden, are Josephine Veasey and Jon Vickers. Veasey's Dido does not attempt the queenly dignity and tragic passion of Janet Baker's great performance; but if smaller, it is womanly, touching, decided and sung with great musical intelligence. Vickers is at his finest in the heroic scenes: his first irruption into Troy is thrilling, and he never loses his grip on Aeneas's sense of mission. Only in the duet does he slip into the habit of allowing phrases to distort under tonal pressure: but his aria "Ah! quand viendra l'instant" is affectingly done. He pairs Veasey intelligently, though there are times when the balance seems to favour him. Cassandra is new: Berit Lindholm. Not even she, with admirably strong, ardent support from Peter Glossop's Corebus, can make much of their duet; but she characterizes the unhappy priestess superbly, conveying a sense of constant, unremitting tragedy without ever allowing her voice to slip into the lachrymose, and carrying an extraordinary weight of suffering in her bitter phrase, "mon inutile vie". She leads her doomed Trojan women with a fine spirit and a glistening top B. The smaller parts are no less carefully cast. Heather Begg supports Veasey almost too discreetly, though Anna is not an easy role to distinguish without self-assertion; Ian Partridge sings Iopas beautifully, with a ravishing soft A flat and C at the end of his song, where most tenors cannot resist ruining the piece for the sake of their own effect; Roger Soyer descends unruffled to a low F in his noble, sombre performance of Narbal; Anne Howells is a touching Ascanius. The chorus, though not always getting top marks in French Oral, sing magnificently.

The recording itself is worthy of the whole enterprise, with a few exceptions. It is a pity that a certain indistinctness at the start of Cassandra's "Malheureux roi" should risk lending support to the view that Berlioz never wrote any counterpoint, and the woodwind is not ideally balanced in Corebus's cavatina "Reviens à toi". But the great climaxes are both full, powerful and lucid, with the telling detail shining through as it should. Best of all is the handling of the distances, so that a sense of movement and space is felt without any restlessness. The ghost scenes are marvellous – a beautiful balance between the stopped horn and the plucked strings for Priam, and a reversal of what most engineers might do with the Trojan ghosts, when Aeneas is set some way back and sings out strongly while the ghosts sing in soft voices, blanched of expression, close to the microphone. It is a brilliantly eerie effect.

Les Troyens is a masterpiece, but one that demands understanding and dedication of a peculiar intensity if it is to assume its true stature. The old accusations against it were based partly on ignorance, partly on inadequate playing (the Covent Garden orchestra are at their superlative best here) and insensitive conducting. Davis has lived with the score for many years, and clearly believes in every note. With this recording he overtakes all his previous achievements in recording Berlioz.

Leonard Bernstein

Bernstein Candide.

Jerry Hadley *ten* Candide
June Anderson *sop* Cunegonde
Adolph Green *ten* Dr Pangloss, Martin
Christa Ludwig *mez* Old lady
Nicolai Gedda *ten* Governor, Vanderdendur, Ragotski
Della Jones *mez* Paquette
Kurt Ollmann *bar* Maximilian, Captain, Jesuit father
Neil Jenkins *ten* Merchant, Inquisitor, Prince Charles Edward
Richard Suart *bass* Junkman, Inquisitor, King Hermann Augustus
John Treleaven *ten* Alchemist, Inquisitor, Sultan Achmet, Crook
Lindsay Benson *bar* Doctor, Inquisitor, King Stanislaus
Clive Bayley *bar* Bear-keeper, Inquisitor, Tsar Ivan
London Symphony Chorus and Orchestra / Leonard Bernstein.
DG Ⓔ Ⓛ 429 734-2GH2 (two discs: 112 minutes: DDD). Notes and text included. Recorded 1989.

1992

It was an Original Cast highlights LP that first turned *Candide* into a cult musical after what was only modest success for the show on Broadway in the winter of 1956-7. Here – after what seemed like an eternity of revivals and revisions – *Candide* once again seems destined to find a true resting-place, not in the theatre, but on record, with the composer himself directing the salvage team as they dive for musical gold in this wonderful old shipwreck of a show. The trouble with *Candide* as a theatre piece can be traced back to the fact that Bernstein (like many show-biz folk) was a sucker for politics. Tom Wolfe dubbed these political dabblings "radical chic" after the Bernsteins notoriously hosted a 'meeting' for members of the Black Panther group in their New York apartment in January 1970. That was primarily a publicity fiasco for Bernstein. *Candide*, more seriously, was always something of an artistic fiasco, with Bernstein once again suffering, not for his own misdeeds or miscalculations (the score is brilliantly inventive and finely composed) but by association with the political axe-grinding of his friends.

Voltaire's *Candide* is a hair-raisingly vicious *prestissimo* revel at the expense of the apparent fatuousness of some of the eighteenth-century's more optimistic philosophies. In its time and place it was, undoubtedly, the best of all possible books. It might even have become the book for the best of all possible musicals. But despite the brilliance of the Auto-da-fé scene, it was hardly the medium for a satire on anti-Communist witch-hunts in America in the early-1950s. (Senator McCarthy and his friends had already been effectively impaled by Arthur Miller's *The Crucible* in 1953.) Nor was a satire on optimism exactly the ticket in a still chronically anxious age – least of all, with music by Bernstein whose personal and artistic orientation was always itself yearningly optimistic. (The end of *Candide*, for instance, is a clear descendant of the soaring "Auferstehʼn" that concludes Mahler's *Resurrection* Symphony.) Tyrone Guthrie, who produced the original Broadway show, summed it all up in a much-quoted remark when he likened Bernstein's music and Lillian Hellman's book to Rossini and Cole Porter rearranging *Götterdämmerung*.

Generous to a fault, Bernstein was still prepared to defend Hellman's original (and long abandoned) work on *Candide* in an improvised speech, delivered mid-performance during the Barbican concert that preceded the Abbey Road studio sessions in December 1989. You can hear the defence on Humphrey Burton's film of that concert: a slightly shambolic flu-ridden house-party of a performance that further reinforces one's sense of *Candide* as a kind of comic oratorio. Because the music has always been the thing with *Candide*, the drama nugatory, highlights discs have served the piece rather well. First, there was the original cast recording, with Robert Rounseville, Barbara Cook and Max Adrian (on Sony Classical). This is a stylish and sparky performance with the authentic feel of Broadway about it still. Then there is That's Entertainment's selection of highlights from Scottish Opera's 1988 revival and revision, with Nickolas Grace as a Pangloss in the Adrian tradition, Marilyn Hill Smith as rather a good Cunegonde, and Justin Brown (Mauceri's deputy), and then Bernstein's for the DG sessions conducting with a lightness that outflanks Mauceri's leaden efforts and often complements Bernstein's own weight and grandiloquence.

With New World's complete recording, directed by Mauceri, we enter a real minefield. When Hellman's book was finally abandoned in 1973 and replaced with one by Hugh Wheeler for Hal Prince's Chelsea Theater production in Brooklyn, there was a good deal of tut-tutting in critical circles. And there was even sterner disapproval in 1982 when Mauceri and the New York City Opera came out with their two-act opera-house version of the Wheeler edition. There were those, Andrew Porter tells us in his DG booklet essay, who deplored the reduction of this "moving, spirited operetta awaiting rediscovery, to a frivolous romp". In fact, Porter himself had led the charge. Having declared that the City Opera *Candide* deserved no further currency, he subsequently deplored New World's temerity in issuing their recording of the production.

Certainly, the losses and changes were grievous and though Bernstein himself keeps faith with a good deal of what happened in 1973/82 there is no doubt that the New World set is now dead in the water. (Though not Mauceri's work – as Bernstein conceded in an interview with Edward Seckerson in the August 1991 issue of **Gramophone**, "He knows more about this piece than I do!") Among other things, the New World set is 20 minutes shorter than Bernstein's "Final Revised Version, 1989". It omits such things as the all-Bernstein number "Words, Words, Words" and, even more crucially, Bernstein's great 'Puccini' aria for Candide in Act 2, "Nothing More Than This". Bernstein retains one of the numbers for which Stephen Sondheim provided new lyrics in 1973, "Life is Happiness Indeed" (Quartet, Act 1, with distinguished contributions from the American Kurt Ollmann and Della Jones), but other Sondheim revisions are junked. "Candide's Lament" here has La Touche's original words, and we get back the exquisite "Ballad of Eldorado", an original Hellman number, where Sondheim had later been asked to write a "Sheep Song" better suited to *Into The Woods* than *Candide*. The "Ballad of Eldorado", with its purling Bach flutes and Arcadian mood, is here limpidly realized by Bernstein and the LSO, with Jerry Hadley every bit as persuasive as the wonderful Robert Rounseville (Stravinsky's first Rakewell and Beecham's Hoffmann) on the original cast recording. The new edition also spares us a special New York horror where the Governor ends up singing "My Love" to Maximilian in drag. Here we have the Governor (Gedda tolerably comprehensible as the foreign blackguard) and Cunegonde; though the original trio version on Sony Classical with William Olvis, Barbara Cook and Irra Petina as a matchless Old Lady is preferable.

Even if the New World set was editorially acceptable, it would still be ruled out on account of the astonishing blandness of most of the singing and the playing. The DG set is not without its problems, but blandness is not one of them. Jerry Hadley is, throughout, an affecting and eloquent Candide. Rounseville's mellifluously confiding performance of "It Must Be So" is to be preferred, but that is because with Hadley the number is all but ruined by an old Bernstein failing: a fondness for tempos that are slow to the point of complete stasis. People brought up on the original cast recording think Barbara Cook's Cunegonde 'definitive'. She's wonderful as this demure and glitzy tart whose career in *Candide* takes her progressively past her sell-by date and no one does the patter in "Glitter and Be Gay" better than Cook. But the coloratura of June Anderson, Bernstein's Cunegonde, is incomparable (without it "Glitter and Be Gay" is a lot less funny than it should be) and she makes a decent fist of the rest of the characterization. "Oh, Happy We" is a great success, with Anderson and Hadley making Wilbur's lyrics (their evolution fascinatingly documented in Porter's essay) crystal-clear. Words are sometimes a problem with Nicolai Gedda and Christa Ludwig, though Ludwig's diction is legendary and her English is pretty good, albeit with a faint and obviously deliberate touch of exoticism about it. Bernstein supports her superbly, the conducting stylishly pointed in "What's The Use", all snake-hipped sleaze in the tango "I Am Easily Assimilated". Adolph Green's Pangloss is not superior to either of his rivals on the highlights discs but he is a characterful performer and a bit of history in his own right – a friend of Bernstein's way back to 1937 when Green played the Pirate King in one of Lennie's famous G&S shows. The syphilis song "Dear Boy" doesn't wear well; all that ironic nastiness about "love's divine disease" has been rather overtaken by events.

Bernstein conducts the score with power and zest, drawing on the LSO's full symphonic resources. If this, in Guthrie's phrase, is Rossinian, it is the Rossini of a big *semi-seria* piece like *La gazza ladra* rather than the decorous pleasantries of earlier frolics. Bernstein's debt to Mahler is evident in the way he supports and shapes the vocal line in Candide's lament, in the scoring of the "Battle Music", and in the feverish, bitter-sweet strains of the "Paris Waltz". And with Bernstein at the helm, no one is going to miss the eight-second gibe at *Der Rosenkavalier* at the end of "You Were Dead, You Know". This great spoof duet falls entirely flat in Mauceri's New York set, with dull conducting, emasculated diction ("Holland, Portu ... / Ah, what torture"), and dim singing in the great canoodling cadenza. With Bernstein, Hadley and Anderson it is all glorious, even if it seems that it is Ivor Novello who is being sent up rather than Strauss or Puccini.

In the concert-hall, the actors spoke John Wells's revised narration; on record the narrative links are reduced to italicized entries in the printed libretto. It's like *Die Zauberflöte* without the spoken dialogue, and it works well enough, even if we miss the occasional telling piece of melodrama – Candide speaking over the instrumental "Introduction to Eldorado", for example. The recording will knock you out of your seat at the start of the Overture but is remiss in balancing the chorus far too distantly. The Sullivan-esque "Bon Voyage" is a case in point, with Gedda gawkily indistinct alongside, say, That's Entertainment's English-born Bonaventura Bottone. The chorus balance is also a minor blight on Bernstein's realization of the great parody of the McCarthyite trials, "What a day, what a day / For an auto-da-fé" (omitted on both highlights discs). But the rip-roaring exuberance of Bernstein's conducting soon wipes away any misgivings, and the inquisition itself is powerfully characterized with the searing parody Requiem played with terrific panache.

It is good, then, that Bernstein and a host of friends and collaborators managed to sort out *Candide* before he died. And sort it out they did, because – rest assured – this recording gives the same kind of uncomplicated pleasure (and more of it) as did that famous old Sony highlights LP all those years ago. Certainly, this is as good a *Candide* as we are likely to get, on or off record. So it's 'case closed'. And let the great army of scholars, librettists, arrangers and producers now exit stage left and start cultivating someone else's garden.

Bernstein Candide.

Jerry Hadley *ten* Candide
June Anderson *sop* Cunegonde

Adolph Green *ten* Dr Pangloss, Martin
Christa Ludwig *mez* Old lady
Nicolai Gedda *ten* Governor, Vanderdendur, Ragotski
Della Jones *mez* Paquette
Kurt Ollmann *bar* Maximilian, Captain, Jesuit father
Neil Jenkins *ten* Merchant, Inquisitor, Prince Charles Edward
Richard Suart *bass* Junkman, Inquisitor, King Hermann Augustus
John Treleaven *ten* Alchemist, Inquisitor, Sultan Achmet, Crook
Lindsay Benson *bar* Doctor, Inquisitor, King Stanislaus
Clive Bayley *bar* Bear-Keeper, Inquisitor, Tsar Ivan
London Symphony Chorus and Orchestra / Leonard Bernstein. *Film Director*: **Humphrey Burton.**
DG Ⓕ 🔲 072 423-3GH (147 minutes). Filmed at a performance in the Barbican Centre,
London on December 13th, 1989.

Even Bernstein rarely had so great a triumph in London as at the concert performance of *Candide*,
only months before he died, during his last visit to London. He was suffering from the flu which had
afflicted, or was about to hit, most others in the cast as well. Yet Bernstein's electricity, his searchlight
intensity, were at the fullest peak; in every way it was a great and moving event. It is even more
compelling than the superb CD recording. The musical text is the same, but here in concert
performance the numbers are supplemented not only by spoken introductions to each set by Bernstein
himself, talking from the rostrum, but by the witty narration devised by John Wells for linking the
numbers, making wry sense of Voltaire's improbable story. Adolph Green, veteran lyric-writer
himself, as Dr Pangloss, delivers most of them, with a few unscripted asides and extra contributions
from Bernstein, aided at times by Kurt Ollmann, otherwise underemployed as Maximilian.

At the time of this issue it was seriously suggested to DG that an alternative audio CD set might be
issued, as well as this video version, presenting the concert *Candide*. Though it is over 35 minutes
longer, it could still be fitted on two CDs. After all, you could always programme out the narrations,
if you did not want to hear them. As for the performance, it amply makes up in electricity for what it
may lose in polish, and generally the playing of the LSO and the singing of the chorus as well as of
the soloists brings pin-point ensemble. Jerry Hadley as Candide was only just recovering from his flu,
and the top of his voice shows occasional signs of strain as the evening progresses, but it remains a
winning performance.

The gains from actually seeing the performers are many. If Bernstein's philosophical introduction
to Act 1 may seem a trifle heavy, it sets the right confidential atmosphere, while the comparable
introduction to Act 2 is a revelation, deeply moving, explaining the political background of the time.
In addition, it adds greatly to the point of number after number, when you can witness Bernstein's
own response to a passage far more illuminatingly than was possible in the hall – as when he joins in
singing the ensembles or dances a tango on the podium. Those close-ups of Bernstein as conductor
are deftly touched in to supplement the main shots of each performer in Humphrey Burton's excellent
video direction.

It also heightens the Gilbertian quality of music and libretto, the calculated absurdities, to be able
to see the performers acting out their numbers. So June Anderson's instant changes of face in
Cunegonde's big aria, "Glitter and Be Gay", from melodramatic agonizing to carefree joy, are much
funnier when seen. In the duet between Cunegonde and Candide, "Oh, Happy We", one is also made
to register far more amusingly the delicious contradiction between their tone of perfect agreement
and the total incompatibility of their respective wants – "Cows and chickens", "Social whirls", "Peas
and cabbage", "Ropes of pearls". Vision also makes all the difference to a point number like the Old
lady's "I Am Easily Assimilated". If in the studio recording the choice of Christa Ludwig seemed odd,
however characterful the results, she is totally bewitching in concert, what with her wicked smile,
switched on with perfect timing, as well as her seductive dancing.

The sound, drier than in the studio recording, is yet clean and immediate, allowing you to hear the
words better, with voices balanced a little closer. The Laserdisc version (now gone from the catalogue)
was more refined than the VHS both in sound and vision. Unfortunately, the limit of an hour per side
for the Laserdisc meant that it spread to three sides, with both the breaks in the middle of acts.

Bernstein On the Town.
Frederica von Stade *mez* Claire
Tyne Daly *sngr* Hildy
Marie McLaughlin *sop* Ivy
Thomas Hampson *bass* Gabey
Kurt Ollmann *bar* Chip
David Garrison *sngr* Ozzie
Samuel Ramey *bass* Pitkin
Evelyn Lear *sop* Madame Dilly
Dame Cleo Laine *sngr* Nightclub singer
London Voices; London Symphony Orchestra / Michael Tilson Thomas.
DG Ⓕ ① 437 516-2GH (75 minutes: DDD). Recorded 1992.

1994

On the Town is a peach of a show, a show which positively hums along on the heat of its inspiration, a show rejoicing in the race of time, but regretful of its passing, a show which lovingly encapsulates those transitory moments seized and then lost amidst the impatient, pulsating heart and soul of the lonely city – the Big Apple. On two amazing nights in June 1992, Michael Tilson Thomas and this starry cast brought New York City to the Barbican, London, and played out its energy and charms against a fantasy skyline straight out of Broadway stock. Its unique atmosphere was never entirely going to make it 'down the wire' on to disc – does it ever? But it's been swell attempting to relive the occasion. No studio recording could even have come close.

Maybe not close enough. Recording this semi-staged performance live must have been a living nightmare for DG's engineers, but one wonders if they might not have pulled off a more up-front balance for the voices? Was this the balance by choice or necessity? It's a musical, not an opera, you want to be grabbed by the lapels, feel the size of the personalities, the clout of the lyrics. Only Cleo Laine gets to be really intimate with her bluesy nightclub song "Ain't got no tears left", one of three numbers dropped from the original show (Bernstein *aficionados* will know the tune from the "Masque" of Symphony No. 2, *Age of Anxiety*). You'll hang on every breath Laine takes. Many of the notes are threadbare, but who needs the notes when you've got instincts like hers. These tears dried up long ago and it hurts. A slightly sadder (even embarrassing) piece of casting finds Evelyn Lear popping up as Ivy Smith's matriarchal singing coach, Miss Dilly, and you haven't lived till you've heard Adolph Green's Rajah Binney sounding a little as though some middle-eastern voodoo chant has been processed through a ring-modulator. Just keep reminding yourself that this was the show's original Ozzie.

Which brings us to the major roles and, happily, no grave misjudgements in casting such as marred the composer's by now infamous *West Side Story* on this label. Mind you, you know you're in big-league production when you get Samuel Ramey delivering (gloriously) the Brooklyn Navy Yard Workers' ode to morning, "I feel like I'm not out of bed yet". And Ramey was an inspired choice for Claire's monumentally boring boyfriend, Pitkin. His "Song", a masterpiece of arch formality, is very funny indeed. In performance, Tyne Daly's cab-driving Hildy knocked 'em in the aisles with her huggable personality. The voice has really come on since the Broadway revival of *Gypsy*, and in the first of her numbers, with Chip (the excellent Kurt Ollmann, honorary member of the Bernstein Rep), "Come up to my place", she uses what she has to terrifically spunky effect. "I can cook too" is more of a problem. Heard but not seen, you're more aware of her grappling with the technical difficulties – the breathing, the syncopation. Frankly, she's not sufficiently on top of the singing to really sell the song. It's a great lyric: but you have to be a very skilled practitioner to savour the sexual innuendo. "My chickens just *ooze* … my ribs get applause" – you'd like to believe her.

The three sailors, Gabey, Chip, Ozzie – Thomas Hampson, Kurt Ollmann, David Garrison – are just perfect. Not only are they well matched vocally, but you could put them on any stage and never look back. Hampson's two big numbers – "Lonely Town" and "Lucky to be Me" – are handsomely sung with careful avoidance of that peculiarly 'operatic' articulation. The too, too English chorus won't fool you in the latter any more than their well-mannered ladies did in "Gabey's Coming" but you may be taken in by the squeaky Charleston girls of "So Long Baby". Adolph Green must surely have approved of Garrison's Ozzie, and Betty Comden probably felt much the same about Frederica von Stade's super-cool, dusky-voiced Claire. Together, they are the business in "Carried away" with von Stade doing just that with a high C nobody knew she had. She, of course, gets to launch the best number in the show – the bittersweet "Some other time". It makes you wonder if a more perfect little song ever graced a Broadway show.

But finally to the real heroes of this dizzy enterprise: Tilson Thomas and the LSO – every last player a character, an individual. *On the Town* lives and breathes through its dance interludes: it struts and swaggers and bustles and broods; it's this music which gives the score its sassy New York *tinta*. The playing here is stunning, there's no other word.

Bernstein West Side Story.

Tinuke Olafimihan Maria
Paul Manuel Tony
Caroline O'Connor Anita
Sally Burgess Off-stage voice
Nicholas Warnford Riff
Julie Paton Rosalia
Elinor Stephenson Consuela
Nicole Carty Francisca
Kieran Daniels Action
Mark Michaels Diesel
Adrian Sarple Baby John
Adrian Edmeads A-rab
Garry Stevens Snowboy
Nick Ferranti Bernardo
chorus; National Symphony Orchestra / John Owen Edwards.
TER Ⓔ Ⓘ CDTER2 1197 (two discs: 101 minutes: DDD). Notes included. Recorded 1993.

The composer's own DG recording of *West Side Story* had been in the catalogue for the best part of ten years when this recording was made, so it wasn't so surprising that two accounts of his most famous musical play should appear in quick succession, the one from IMG Records (with Barbara Bonney as Maria and Michael Ball as Tony) and this. Unlike the IMG release, there are no reservations in expressing wholehearted admiration here. To cap Bernstein's, even given his controversial casting of opera stars, is something of an achievement. Yet that's the story here, where artistic production and recording values are of a high order. The set starts with the major advantage of being inspired by a production at the Haymarket, Leicester, so many of the cast are really inside their roles. They have youth on their side, too. Paul Manuel from that company may not have a large voice, but his sympathetic portrayal of Tony, both in his solos and duets with Maria that were such a disappointment on the IMG version, makes one feel that he identifies totally with the part.

Moreover, the way in which he can float a high note, as at the end of the alternative film version of "Something's coming" puts him on a par with Carreras (for Bernstein). His Maria, Tinuke Olafimihan, is a gem. Although she wasn't in the Haymarket production, her ability to interact with him and to express the laughter and the tragedy of the heroine is very real. At key moments in the drama, as at the start of the ballet where her bitterness turns to understanding, and later in her reprimand to Anita's taunts ("you were in love, or so you said"), she can touch the heart. Her charming singing of "I feel pretty" is given an added femininity by being preceded by its Act 2 Entr'acte that introduces so gracefully the scene in the bridal shop. At the heart of the "Somewhere" ballet, Sally Burgess voices the lovers' plea for peace with a magnificent rendition of its famous soaring tune. Nicholas Warnford as leader of the Jets gives no less than his rival in the tricky "Cool" sequence and Jet song. Caroline O'Connor's Anita touches a raw note here and there, yet given such a flamboyant personality, no one should mind.

John Owen Edwards directs the score as if he believes in every note of it. Moreover, he has imparted to his players the very pulse that sets this music ticking. In the playing of the Prologue the orchestra capture the indolence of youth and the underlying tension between the gangs that explodes into warfare with such tragic results. Mention should also be made of the fine string playing in the Copland-esque passages to the ballet, and in small yet vital transitions such as the bridge between "A boy like that" and "I have a love", where, in just a couple of bars, a switch from anger to resignation is all in the hands of the conductor. In addition to the Act 2 Entr'acte, this recording also includes the Overture and four alternative versions of the songs as they were heard in the screen adaptation. These changes reflect alterations to the lyrics rather than the music, chiefly in "Gee Officer Krupke", where Sondheim's lines have been given the cleansing treatment.

In his long and interesting booklet Jeffrey Dunn misleadingly implies that *West Side Story* was only given in London following its subsequent return to Broadway in 1960. However, he then adds the opening date of December 1958. In fact, *West Side Story* as given in London's Her Majesty's Theatre was an even greater success than it had been on Broadway, running longer and taking the *Evening Standard* Drama Award from *My Fair Lady!* And indeed, audiences didn't have to wait for the songs to gain popularity from the movie, for "Tonight" and "One hand, one heart" cropped up regularly on request programmes at that time.

Ferdinando Bertoni   Italian 1725-1813

Bertoni Orfeo.
Delores Ziegler *mez* Orfeo
Cecilia Gasdia *sop* Euridice
Bruce Ford *ten* Imeneo
Ambrosian Opera Chorus; I Solisti Veneti / Claudio Scimone.
Arts Ⓢ Ⓘ 47118-2 (65 minutes: DDD). Notes and text included. Recorded 1990.

In 1776, Ferdinando Bertoni wrote a new setting of the Calzabigi *Orfeo* libretto for the castrato Gaetano Guadagni, who had created the title-role for Gluck 14 years before. Gluck's setting was famous and Bertoni made no bones about having had Gluck's score before him as he composed. Some parts of the works are very much alike, above all the confrontation between Orpheus and the Furies that makes up most of Act 2, and then the entry into the Elysian fields; Bertoni's version seems almost like a recomposition of Gluck's. There are plenty of echoes elsewhere too, often in the rhythms (which to some extent are determined by the text, of course) and sometimes in the turn of a phrase – it is impossible to conceive that anyone knowing Gluck's setting could escape from it for long.

Perhaps to a modern audience familiar with Gluck the Bertoni version will often seem rather bland and conventional. But it should not be too readily dismissed. Bertoni was a considerable composer, widely admired (by Mozart among others), holding appointments at St Mark's, Venice, and writing some 50 operas among which his *Orfeo* was highly successful and went on to several revivals. There is some attractive music in it, perhaps particularly in Act 3, where the settings of the duet and Euridice's aria are quite unlike Gluck's and have a good deal of fire and intensity. His version of "Che farò" is quietly eloquent, not at all exalted in the way Gluck's is, although it later becomes impassioned.

The performance here is directed with plenty of spirit by Claudio Scimone and the title-role is splendidly sung by Delores Ziegler, a mezzo-soprano with a particularly warm and firm middle and lower register, a good deal of tonal intensity and a warm and shapely line. The Act 3 dialogue with Euridice is conducted with considerable passion on both sides; and Imeneo (who replaces Gluck's Amore) is sung with much elegance by Bruce Ford. It is likely that many lovers of Gluck's masterpiece will find it very worthwhile to explore this tributary of operatic history.

Heinrich Biber
Bohemian 1644-1704

Biber Arminio.
Barbara Schlick sop Giulia
Gotthold Schwarz bass Arminio
Gerd Türk ten Nerone
Xenia Meijer mez Segesta
Gerd Kenda bass Tiberio
Bernhard Landauer alto Calligola
Markus Forster alto Vitellio
Hermann Oswald ten Germanico
Otto Rastbichler ten Erchino
Irena Troupova sop Claudia
Regina Schwarzer mez Climmia
Florian Mehltretter bar Seiano
Salzburg Hofmusik / Wolfgang Brunner.
CPO Ⓟ Ⓒ CPO999 258-2 (three discs: 197 minutes: DDD). 🖉 Text and translations included.
Recorded at performances in the Aula Academica of the University of Salzburg in April 1994.

Though we recognize Biber nowadays foremost for his colourful instrumental music, he was none the less quite a prolific composer of vocal works for the theatre and the church. His two beautiful Requiem Masses are growing in popularity among audiences but his music for the stage is almost unknown. Well, all that changed overnight, so-to-speak, with this complete recording – some three-and-a-quarter hours of music – of Biber's only surviving opera of *Dramma Musicale*, "Chi la dura la vince" (*Arminio* or "He who endures, triumphs"). The exact date of *Arminio* has not been established but it was probably produced some time between 1690 and 1692. Biber was at that time *Kapellmeister* to Max-Gandolph, Prince-Archbishop of Salzburg, and wrote the piece for the Archbishop's court. The librettist was probably Francesco Maria Raffaelini, about whom there is a little information in the accompanying booklet. The text, with its frequently occurring comic scenes and its focus on a hero of Roman times (Arminius), suggests that his models were the Venetian opera librettos of the time, favoured by Cavalli and others.

There are three acts, each subdivided into as many as 16 scenes made up from alternating unaccompanied recitative and a pleasingly rich variety of strophic arias, simply accompanied by continuo but with effective little instrumental ritornellos. These elements of the opera have been preserved virtually intact but the instrumental introduction, and the ballet music, whose presence is indicated in the text, have not. Sensibly, the director, Wolfgang Brunner has supplied these missing sections from music occurring elsewhere in the opera, and the results are by and large convincing. There are 12 solo vocal parts in all, all of which would presumably have been sung by court musicians. Brass, timpani and recorders feature in scenes calling for special effects; otherwise, an imaginatively assembled continuo group reigns supreme, with two violins providing most of the upper voices of the ritornellos.

The plot, based on an account in the *Annals* of Tacitus, deals with the Roman revenge, led by Germanicus, on the Germans, under their leader Arminius in AD 9. Arminius had massacred three Roman legions under Quintilius Varus in the Rhineland and was himself, according to Raffaelini, murdered, though in fact he committed suicide, but no matter. From these events stem the fictional action of the opera with its disguises, love element, divided loyalties and comic scenes. Biber's music is, as we might expect, wonderfully effective in the way it enlivens the many contrasting images of the text. Calls to arms such as the fanfares for brass and drums which encompass Germanicus's ostinato-based aria, "All' armi, a battaglie" (disc 2, track 6) are but among many such instances of Biber's skill at heightening moments of drama with colourful gestures.

The vocalists range from the excellent to the adequate. Barbara Schlick is, as usual, fluent in matters of style and well cast in the role of Giulia, one of three rivals for the affection of Caligula – her bitterly reflective aria "Sembra veleno" (disc 1, track 4) is beautifully sung – and Xenia Meijer is sensitive as the faithful, captive Segesta, wife of Arminio. Bernhard Landauer as the mixed-up Calligola has a comfortable technique but he fails to convey the disagreeable side of his nature. Gerd Türk and Hermann Oswald respectively project a lyrical Nerone and a heroic Germanico, and Gotthold Schwarz admirably conveys Arminius's strength of character. The large continuo group is excellent for the most part, but the ritornello violinists, though spirited in their playing, sometimes lack finesse. The three trumpets and trombones make fine, if occasional, contributions and the recorder group (descant, treble, tenor and bass), Il Dolcimelo, are first-rate though, alas, they appear once only (disc 2, track 16). The Salzburg Hofmusik are a period-instrument group, incidentally.

Musically, Biber's *Arminio* makes a much stronger and more favourable impression than it does dramatically. The libretto is no masterpiece and the action is long-winded, but the opera is considerably more than a mere curiosity. Biber is skilled not only in achieving vivid characterization by means of tonal colour but also by the effective deployment of varied rhythmic patterns. He handles the comic scenes deftly and with subtle humour. The most notable of these occur at the end of Act 1 where the court jester, Erchino, feigns death, for the love of Climmia, Giulia's nurse. As he affects lifelessness, "Grim Death" approaches, to the accompaniment of a stealthy 'Pink Pantherish' melody on unison violone, viola da gamba and cello. The effect is almost as startling as the sudden introduction of a xylophone to conjure up the rattling of bones in the same scene. All this has been lovingly and meticulously realized by Brunner in this recording, compiled from performances given in Salzburg University in 1994. The sound is clear, with only an occasional discreet cough from members of the audience; and the booklet contains a helpful, informative introduction with full texts in translation. Warmly recommended, especially to enthusiasts of baroque music.

Sir Harrison Birtwistle   British 1934

Birtwistle Gawain.

François Le Roux *bar* Gawain
Marie Angel *sop* Morgan Le Fay
Anne Howells *mez* Lady de Hautdesert
Richard Greager *ten* Arthur
Penelope Walmsley-Clark *sop* Guinevere
Omar Ebrahim *bar* Fool
Alan Ewing *bass* Agravain
John Marsden *ten* Ywain
Kevin Smith *alto* Baldwin
John Tomlinson *bass* Green Knight, Bertilak
Chorus and Orchestra of the Royal Opera House, Covent Garden / Elgar Howarth.
Collins Classics Ⓕ Ⓞ 7041-2 (two discs: 136 minutes: DDD). Notes and text included. Recorded at a performance at the Royal Opera House, Covent Garden on April 20th, 1994.

1996

Gawain marks a climactic point in Sir Harrison Birtwistle's output, combining dramatic strategies from his four earlier stage works with a clearer narrative than any of them and drawing together aspects of his musical language that he had been exploring in concert works for 15 years or more. It is possibly his finest dramatic work, an opera of compelling power and grandeur.

Gawain's magnificent opening gesture immediately promises that it will be an epic opera. The First Act ends with the characteristic Birtwistle device of a fivefold cycle of the seasons, symbolically portraying Gawain's preparation for his confrontation with the Green Knight, while Act 2 turns on a threefold cycle of lullabies, hunting scenes and seductions in which he learns how few of the knightly virtues for which he is famed he in fact possesses. These cyclical structures are not mere machines, nor is the plot a mere pretext for them, as it arguably was in Birtwistle's earlier work, *The Mask of Orpheus*. The "Turning of the Seasons" cycle, each part having a light and a dark phase, day and night, each incorporating both solemn ritual and an only apparently jocular riddle from the Fool, is in fact a powerful cumulative metaphor for the peril of Gawain's quest and its vanity, to which he is as yet blind. Self-realization comes in the second cycle, in which he acts ignobly and is shamed.

Another long-term constituent of Birtwistle's style is those long, sinuous, ranging lines that underlie so much of his music. The very opening gesture, a craggy descent, is one mode that it adopts here; another is the intense, often ornate, wide-spanning lyricism heard soon afterwards as Morgan Le Fay and Lady de Hautdesert begin their plot to subvert King Arthur's court with Gawain as their unwitting instrument. Morgan's lullabies in Act 2, each of them sinking Gawain deeper into enthralment, have a sinister beauty in them that is the very image of witchcraft. Indeed, although none of the characters in this fable is a rounded personality – *Gawain* is no *verismo* opera – each of them is boldly and tellingly portrayed. Morgan is unchanging, venom personified. Arthur, too, does not change: an old soldier, bored with peace but unwilling to emerge from the cosy myth of Camelot. But Gawain matures, from arrogance to bitter self-awareness. Most strikingly of all the Green Knight, the opera's real and profoundly mysterious central character, has music of true lyrical strength and pride at his first challenge, and denunciatory eloquence when he spares Gawain's life at their second encounter, telling him that mere cowardice is too small a sin to die for.

It is an opera whose drama often takes place in the wonderfully rich and strange sounds of Birtwistle's orchestra: massive, striding bass-lines, whooping brass, the prominent cimbalom at times almost as central as it once was in Stravinsky's imagination. The solo singers must achieve extremes of intensity to stand out in relief. Among them John Tomlinson is in outstandingly noble voice as the Green Knight and François Le Roux, when not obliged to force, is moving in the title-role. Marie Angel is fearless though often bitingly shrill as Morgan, Anne Howells a voluptuous Lady de

Hautdesert. The recording brings the voices forward, which helps comprehension of the text, but does not diminish Elgar Howarth's masterly control of the score's burnished splendours. The whole enterprise is a huge achievement, a worthy recording of one of the most powerful operas of the late twentieth century.

Birtwistle The Mask of Orpheus.
Jon Garrison *ten* Orpheus: Man
Peter Bronder *ten* Orpheus: Myth, Hades
Jean Rigby *mez* Euridice: Woman
Anne-Marie Owens *mez* Euridice: Myth, Persephone
Alan Opie *bar* Aristaeus: Man
Omar Ebrahim *bar* Aristaeus: Myth, Charon
Marie Angel *sop* Aristeus: Oracle of the Dead, Hecate
Arwel Huw Morgan *bar* Caller
Stephen Allen *ten* Priest, First Judge
Nicholas Folwell *bar* Priest, Second Judge
Stephen Richardson *bass* Priest, Third Judge
Juliet Booth *sop* Woman, First Fury
Philippa Dames-Longworth *sop* Woman, Second Fury
Elizabeth McCormack *mez* Woman, Third Fury
Ian Dearden (sound diffusion); BBC Singers;
BBC Symphony Orchestra / Andrew Davis, Martyn Brabbins.
NMC Ⓜ ① NMCD050 (three discs: 162 minutes: DDD). Notes and text included. Recorded 1996.

This might seem an odd recommendation, but it is earnestly suggested that, at least for a first hearing of this remarkable work, you do not follow the libretto, nor the synopsis, nor even the track listing. Birtwistle's opera is about the Orpheus myth, but the familiar story has been fragmented, several different versions of its main events being presented, sometimes simultaneously, often non-chronologically. Each of the principal characters is represented by two singers and a (silent) dancer, and much of what happens is not directly described in the libretto.

Listening 'innocently' you will not be able to follow all of what is being sung; at times very little (the text is sometimes broken up; some passages, including much of Act 3, are sung in an invented language). Rituals are often at their most powerful when they appeal to the imagination rather than to reason, and here the sense of ritual is awesomely powerful: solemn and often gravely beautiful in Act 1, much tougher and more complex but at the same time hugely exciting in Act 2 and with a formidable, gathering sense of culmination in Act 3. It is an extraordinarily patterned opera, with many varied repetitions, all meticulously labelled ("First Structure of Decision", "Second Time Shift" and so on) in the score. Again, it is important not to worry too much about these until the sound of the opera has worked its spell. There are, for example, six scenes or interludes (intended to be mimed by a separate cast) which are accompanied by an electronic tape. The music of these scenes is so spectacular and works so strongly on the imagination that it might be more of a hindrance than a help to know in advance what they represent. This is an opera which, to borrow a phrase from Gertrude Stein, "describes things without mentioning them".

And it is an opera in which everything happens in the music. The ritual repetitions, the elaborate patternings and allegorical structures make their own effect. In the boldest of these, the 17 'arches' over which Orpheus passes in his quest for Euridice in Act 2, Birtwistle aids comprehension by quite extensive use of speech. But the music says far more than the sometimes enigmatic words, and the ceremonial retelling of the whole story in Act 3, a sequence of mysteriously dramatic episodes framed by verses of a song, would perhaps have less impact if the words of that song were comprehensible. Birtwistle communicates his refracted but gripping myth with, above all, orchestral colour: an orchestra of wind, percussion and plucked instruments (plus tape, sampler and a small chorus) used with vivid mastery. The sheer sound of this opera is quite haunting and, not least at the end when the myth dissolves, moving.

The Mask of Orpheus is a masterpiece, and this performance is fully worthy of it. There are no weak links at all in the extremely fine cast. Although it is unfair to single out any singer for special mention, Jon Garrison's portrayal of Orpheus the Man is outstanding. The recording, direct and pungent but by no means lacking in atmosphere (the electronic tape is pervasive in the right sense: it is the voice of Apollo), leaves nothing to be desired.

Birtwistle Punch and Judy.
Stephen Roberts *bar* Punch
Jan DeGaetani *mez* Judy, Fortune-teller
Phyllis Bryn-Julson *sop* Pretty Polly, Witch
Philip Langridge *ten* Lawyer
David Wilson-Johnson *bar* Choregos, Jack Ketch

1980

John Tomlinson *bass* Doctor
London Sinfonietta / David Atherton.
Etcetera Ⓟ Ⓘ KTC2014 (two discs: 103 minutes: ADD). Notes and text included. Recorded 1979.

It was very good news when Etcetera licensed one of the most exciting of the late lamented Decca Headline series, devoted to major twentieth-century works. Birtwistle's opera was composed in the mid-1960s, and since this recording first appeared we have had the remarkable Opera Factory production of the work, directed by David Freeman, seen on stage and television. Does the 1980 cast seem rather genteel compared with Freeman's uncompromisingly forceful team of singing actors? As Punch, Stephen Roberts is certainly less consistently menacing and 'over the top' in vocal demeanour than Opera Factory's Omar Ebrahim. But Roberts remains a very satisfying interpreter of a part which is far from uniformly aggressive in character, and in which a kind of crazy vulnerability offsets the ritual violence. The general excellence of the singers on this set is impressive, with a typically spectacular contribution (especially above the stave) from Phyllis Bryn-Julson.

In the light of Birtwistle's finest later works, especially the opera *The Mask of Orpheus* and such pieces as *Secret Theatre* and *Earth Dances*, *Punch and Judy* can seem relatively anonymous in style, at least in those places which offer the kind of brittle, fragmented textures found in many composers at that time. Yet these are only moments, and as a whole the opera loses none of its powerful and sustained impact when compared with Birtwistle's own more mature compositions. If anything, its startling primitivisms stand out more vividly, while its not inconsiderable moments of reflection and lyricism acquire an enhanced poignancy. The performance gains immeasurably from the alert control of David Atherton and the superlative musicianship of the London Sinfonietta. The analogue recording may lack depth, but it is as clear and immediate as this throat-grabbing music demands.

Georges Bizet   French 1838-1875

Bizet Carmen.
Teresa Berganza *sop* Carmen
Plácido Domingo *ten* Don José
Ileana Cotrubas *sop* Micaëla
Sherrill Milnes *bar* Escamillo
Yvonne Kenny *sop* Frasquita
Alicia Nafé *sop* Mercédès
Gordon Sandison *bar* Dancaïre
Geoffrey Pogson *ten* Remendado
Stuart Harling *bar* Moralès
Robert Lloyd *bass* Zuniga
Watson College Boys' Choir; Ambrosian Singers; London Symphony Orchestra / Claudio Abbado.
DG Ⓜ Ⓘ 427 885-2GX3 (three discs: 157 minutes: ADD). Notes, text and translation included.
Recorded 1977.

B B C RADIO 3
90-93 FM

This notable recording followed immediately on from the famous Faggioni production at the 1977 Edinburgh Festival, a staging finely observed enough to remain in the mind of anyone who was there. In it Berganza declared her aim of rescuing the role from bad traditions and from its insults to Spanish womanhood. Her reading was restrained, haughty, but no less attractive and haunting for that. She developed the character, as she does on the discs, from carefree gipsy to tragic woman and, in doing so, is scrupulous in her obedience to Bizet's notes, rhythms and dynamics. Nothing is exaggerated yet nothing is left out in this sensuous yet never overtly sensual portrayal, bewitchingly sung. Maybe you don't feel quite the full engagement of her emotions in her entanglement with José, but better a slight reticence than overacting. Migenes, on the 1982 Maazel/Erato set, is more immediately seductive, and occasionally more varied in tonal colouring, but Berganza is the more subtle artist.

She works in keen rapport with Abbado, who brings clarity of texture, Mediterranean fire, and intense concentration to the score. You may find more elegance, more Gallic wit in, say, Beecham's famous EMI set, but only Maazel of other conductors comes near Abbado's emphasis on close-knit ensemble and histrionic strength – and both their sets come as the result of experience of 'real' performances. Domingo benefits here, as on the Maazel, as distinct from the 1975 Solti set (Decca), in the same way, being more involved in affairs. He sometimes wants variety of colour in his singing, but its sheer musicality and, in the last two acts, power, count for much. Sherrill Milnes, not in the Edinburgh cast, is at once virile and fatuous as Escamillo should be, but he isn't the equal of José van Dam (Solti) in the right sort of voice and diction, i.e. Francophone. Cotrubas makes a vulnerable, touching Micaëla. Robert Lloyd, the Zuniga, speaks and sings in excellent French, and is the most engaging of the supporting cast.

The dialogue is heavily foreshortened as compared with the rival sets. Abbado chooses some of the questionable Oeser alternatives, but – apart from the one in the finale – you should not find them disturbing. The recording is absolutely first-rate, well balanced between voices and the secure LSO, and forward without being in the least confined.

Bizet Carmen.

Leontyne Price *sop* Carmen
Franco Corelli *ten* Don José
Mirella Freni *sop* Micaëla
Robert Merrill *bar* Escamillo
Monique Linval *sop* Frasquita
Geneviève Macaux *mez* Mercédès
Jean-Christophe Benoit *bar* Dancaïre
Maurice Besançon *ten* Remendado
Bernard Demigny *bar* Moralès
Frank Schooten *bass* Zuniga
Vienna Boys' Choir; Vienna State Opera Chorus;
Vienna Philharmonic Orchestra / Herbert von Karajan.
RCA Ⓜ ① 74321 39495-2 (three discs: 160 minutes: ADD). Notes, text and translation included.
Recorded 1963.

If you like and want *Carmen* as the grandest of grand operas this is the set for you without question. Even if you don't, you may find it hard to resist the combined assets of Price's smoky, sensual Carmen, Corelli's virile, exciting José, Freni's marvellously sung Micaëla, Karajan's precisely sensuously, leisurely yet vital conducting (so much more admirable than on his 1982 DG version) and, almost most commendable of all, the spacious, natural Culshaw recording.

John Steane in *The Grand Tradition* (London: 1974), states that Carmen is Price's most important contribution to the gramophone, giving chapter and verse for his view, and one can only agree. Less genteel than los Angeles (Beecham), less tigerish than Callas (Prêtre on his 1964 EMI set), more earthy than Berganza (Abbado), less blatant than Migenes (Maazel), Price's Carmen positively insinuates herself into your listening room, a very real and alluring presence, even if just occasionally she just overdoes the eroticism. As singing, her account of the role marvellously contrasts the light, airy, seductive Carmen of the earlier acts with the fatalistic woman of the last two. Corelli, though his French is distracting (that coach, mentioned amusingly in Culshaw's memoirs, seems to have been employed in vain), gives us one of the most exciting Josés on disc, quite frightening in his agony and frustration in the last two acts, and not without signs of subtlety in the duets with Micaëla and Carmen earlier. The heroic, tragic quality in his singing makes one forgive his occasional liberties over note values. In the finale, Price and Corelli evince an extraordinary animal passion, overwhelming in its intensity. Freni's French can be worrying and she enunciates vaguely, but she sings her aria with a strength and beauty seldom equalled. Merrill is a strong but not very individual Escamillo. The smaller parts are well taken. Of course, we have Guiraud recitatives here, not dialogue.

The playing of the VPO is as excellent as that on any set of this work – listen to the sensuous quality of the postlude to Micaëla's aria. Karajan, even in 1963, leaned towards slowish, slightly stately tempos, but it doesn't suffer from the stiffening of the arteries of the later set. The recording is irreproachable, and it comes up with even more immediacy on CD. This set must have an equal recommendation with Abbado and Beecham, all of which present different and valid views of the work.

Bizet Carmen.

Victoria de los Angeles *sop* Carmen
Nicolai Gedda *ten* Don José
Janine Micheau *sop* Micaëla
Ernest Blanc *bar* Escamillo
Denise Monteil *sop* Frasquita
Marcelle Croisier, Monique Linval *sops* Mercédès
Jean-Christophe Benoit *bar* Dancaïre
Michel Hamel *ten* Remendado
Bernard Plantey *bar* Moralès
Xavier Depraz *bass* Zuniga
Petits Chanteurs de Versailles; French National Radio Maîtrise;
French National Radio Chorus and Orchestra / Sir Thomas Beecham.
EMI Ⓟ ① CDS5 56214-2 (three discs: 161 minutes: ADD). Notes, text and translation included.
Recorded 1958-9.

It has to be said that this Beecham set should be in every collection. It is without doubt, *hors concours* – and that French expression is just the right one for a performance that breathes French elegance, wit and charm in a way still not equalled elsewhere, while not neglecting the passion and tragedy when they are called for. In brief, Beecham is the complete *Carmen* conductor in a way nobody else, not even Abbado, succeeds in emulating – listen to the entr'actes, if nothing else, if you are doubtful. The only way he sins is in preferring the Guiraud recitatives on which he was nurtured rather than the more authentic dialogue. As reported when the set was issued on LP, Philip Hope-Wallace, who loved the score to distraction, greeted it on its first appearance in typical fashion thus: "I send up a loud olé", while Rodney Milnes called it a "milestone in the history of *Carmen* on record" and he admired Victoria de los Angeles inordinately for her sense of humour in Act 1, the élan, the seductiveness of Act 2, the fatal acceptance of the card scene, the proud dignity of the finale. While missing nothing in verbal clarity or of subtle interpretation, she actually sings the role as musically as one would want. Berganza (for Abbado) is her peer in that respect but sounds a little detached by comparison with her Spanish predecessor. Indeed, los Angeles captures virtually every facet of the consistently fascinating part, if she is not quite so immediately alluring as Migenes (Maazel) or obviously so commanding or demanding as Callas, but then Callas had little charm in this role.

Gedda turned in one of his most persuasive performances as José, one full of good singing but wanting only the sense of dark, doomed intensity for the last two acts that Domingo manages (Abbado, Solti and Maazel – where he's at his very best), but nobody achieves the natural flow of the Flower song so easily as Gedda. Blanc is as idiomatic as any Escamillo except van Dam (Solti); Micheau is also authentic in timbre, but somewhat dry of tone at this stage of her career. It is worth noting that Xavier Depraz, Zuniga here, was still singing the role to good effect at Glyndebourne in 1987. A change of Mercédès was needed as the first singer of the role unfortunately died in the 15 months intervening between the two series of sessions. EMI honestly point this out in an accompanying note, which also suggests that on CD the change in recorded quality is marked. It will not detract much from your enjoyment of this admirable set. Even if the range of sound overall is a shade restricted its natural immediacy and perfect balance between voice and orchestra is appealing.

Bizet Carmen.
  Maria Ewing *sop* Carmen
  Barry McCauley *ten* Don José
  Marie McLaughlin *sop* Micaëla
  David Holloway *bar* Escamillo
  Elizabeth Collier *sop* Frasquita
  Jean Rigby *mez* Mercédès
  Gordon Sandison *bar* Dancaïre
  Petros Evangelides *ten* Remendado
  Malcolm Walker *bar* Moralès
  Xavier Depraz *bass* Zuniga
  Federico Davià *bass* Lillas Pastia
  Glyndebourne Festival Chorus; London Philharmonic Orchestra / Bernard Haitink.
  Stage/Video Director: **Sir Peter Hall.**
  NVC Arts 🔲 4509 99494-3 (175 minutes). Recorded 1985.

This video, based on Glyndebourne's 1985 staging, has the inestimable advantage of presenting a virtually complete version of the dialogue, filling in the characters' background and motives, thus presenting the work as its creators intended, a play with music, all thanks to Peter Hall's fidelity to the original (he is in charge of the video as well as the stage direction). He controls the whole, and particularly the speech, with his customary eye for pertinent detail and John Bury's evocative sets help re-create the true tradition of French performances. Movement is at all times natural. Maria Ewing, a lissome *jolie laide* of a Carmen, is wilful, witty, youthfully daring, athletic, sometimes self-indulgent. Some of her singing may be more that of a chansonniere than of an opera singer, but the results justify the approach. Barry McCauley is most convincing, though his singing, for all its conviction, is sometimes wiry. There's a weak Escamillo, but Marie McLaughlin is a demure, pleasing Micaëla. Haitink brings out all the sensuousness of Bizet's familiar score and successfully cleanses it of sentimentality and overblown orchestral sound. The picture and sound are no more than average but there are subtitles.

Bizet Djamileh.
  Lucia Popp *sop* Djamileh
  Franco Bonisolli *ten* Haroun
  Jean-Philippe Lafont *bass* Splendiano
  Jacques Pineau *spkr* Merchant
  Bavarian Radio Chorus; Munich Radio Orchestra / Lamberto Gardelli.
  Orfeo Ⓟ Ⓒ C174881A (65 minutes: DDD). Notes, text and translation included. Recorded 1983.

Were it not for its static action and its uncomfortable length we should surely see and hear Bizet's penultimate opera very often, for it contains some of the best of that sensuous, harmonically subtle, orchestrally delicate music for which he has become famed. There are harbingers here of the most inspired pages of *Carmen*, but also much pseudo-orientalism that wasn't repeated in that masterpiece. Indeed, Winton Dean has commented that it is both musically Bizet's "first really mature work" and that it contains "some of his most striking music", verdicts with which one would entirely concur. From the opening off-stage chorus to the final duet, which has something of both the José/Micaëla and José/Carmen duets in it, the score evokes just the right atmosphere.

The bored Haroun, constantly seeking to renew his amorous appetite with a new slave-girl, is aptly portrayed in his couplets. Djamileh, the girl who really loves him and eventually wins him through a ruse, is charmingly depicted in her first music, a dream song. Her ghazel, where she tells Haroun the tale of a girl whose love is unrequited (its main refrain returns at the end of the piece), has an irregular melody, exquisitely harmonized, creating a very special mood. Her Tristan-esque Lament is even more remarkable. Splendiano, who thinks he'll get Djamileh as one of his master's cast-offs is also nicely characterized in his couplets. The choruses evoke the Middle-Eastern milieu.

This performance is delightful. Popp sings Djamileh's entrancing music in impeccable French and with just the right plangency of tone, the voice floating easily in melismatic passages. Bonisolli seems transformed, as is often the case when he tackles French music, from the beefy tenor known at Covent Garden. Here he sings with attractive tone, refined line and restrained passion. He is about as attuned to the part of Haroun as you could wish. Lafont makes a lively Splendiano. Gardelli unerringly delineates the perfumed charm of the score, and receives warm singing and playing from the Bavarian Radio forces. The recording is unassumingly right, perhaps just a little too recessed for some tastes. The inclusion of text and translation completes one's pleasure in this issue.

Bizet Les pêcheurs de perles.
Barbara Hendricks *sop* Leïla
John Aler *ten* Nadir
Gino Quilico *bar* Zurga
Jean-Philippe Courtis *bass* Nourabad
Chorus and Orchestra of the Capitole, Toulouse / Michel Plasson.
EMI Ⓟ Ⓒ CDS7 49837-2 (two discs: 127 minutes: DDD). Notes, text and translation included. Recorded 1989.

If you don't know the opera, you come away from this recording with a head full of tunes, if you do know it your head is likely to be full of tunes and questions. As provoked here, the questions begin in Act 3 and end in Act 1. After Zurga's aria, the Third Act continues with a duet between him and Leïla where two unfamiliar passages appear (the first at "Quoi? l'innocent" – page 89 in the libretto – extending to "Nadir! Ah!", the second a solo for Zurga, "Tu me demandais sa vie" – page 93). In the Second Tableau the opening chorus is followed (page 101) by a dramatic episode for Nadir and chorus and shortly after that comes a substantial duet for Nadir and Leïla ("Ah, Leïla" to "Nadir, adieu" – page 105). Zurga and Nadir have an additional exchange ("Par ce Dassage" – page 107) and nothing is heard of the final Trio printed in the Choudens score and performed in the Dervaux/EMI recording ("O lumière sainte"). Dervaux also included a short but significant earlier remark by Zurga ("Mon collier") omitted in Choudens and in the Plasson recording, and both recordings contain a reprise of the famous tune originally in the Nadir-Zurga duet of Act 1, now sung by the fleeing lovers, and not given in Choudens. The Plasson version adds, in the form of an appendix, a repeat performance of the Act 1 duet, with a totally different final section ("Amitié sainte"), absent from the original Choudens score and Dervaux. Now on all of this, we (and more particularly the section of the public that knows the opera from different and less complete performances) want information. An editorial footnote tells of "good reasons to believe that the more familiar version [of the duet] is Bizet's", but the assurance of good reasons is not good enough. Would it be too much to ask what they may be? The printed essay by Jean Roy contains a remark or two about posthumous alterations made after the opera's revival in 1893 but has no explanation (for example) of the textural status of Zurga's "collier" phrases or the "lumière sainte" trio. This is an important and texturally valuable recording of the opera, and some solid information on textural matters should have accompanied it – and in the days of LP doubtless would have done.

As for the performance, whatever limitations it may have, it is superior in every way to the 1960 recording under Dervaux. That of course had Gedda, who might have been a great source of strength, but who then settles down like the rest of the cast into dull routine. By comparison Plasson's team have youth on their side and much more than that. Barbara Hendricks has a silvery beauty of voice, charmingly apt in the Brahma Invocation, and she is always imaginatively involved: her "Je frémis, je chancelle" in Act 3 most touchingly embodies the frightened young girl who sees tragedy before her. John Aler, less than ideal in the Romance, sings his off-stage serenade most gracefully and is even better in the Love Duet. The Nourabad, Jean-Philippe Courtis, is authoritative and sonorous, and Gino Quilico invests his role with such splendid qualities that for once Zurga takes his rightful place as the central figure in the drama. The Act 3 solo sung conventionally can seem to be little more than Buggins's turn for the baritone; here it is heard as a reflective, deeply personal soliloquy, which with the subsequent duet constitutes the most moving part of the whole performance.

Plasson favours generally slower speeds than the metronome markings (Bizet's?) in the score but all is in due proportion and kept within well-judged limits. Orchestral playing is fine, and the chorus work particularly neat. If there are disappointments they lie for the most part in the famous numbers where we all have a favourite recording to judge by. In "Au fond du temple saint" Aler does not sing a soft B flat as does Alessandro Bonci on an ancient Fonotipia, and in "Ton coeur n'a pas compris" he has not the poetry of Fernando de Lucia (though both of those sing in Italian which for some might put them out of court). Barbara Hendricks has not Ninon Vallin's fine sense of line in "Comme autrefois", and in "Je crois entendre encore" neither the singer nor the orchestra captures the feeling for the dreamy melody drifting in the warm night air among the forest leaves rustling in the lightest of breezes. Indeed at that point in the opera it is not clear that this is going to be such a worthy recording; it gets better by the act, and ultimately is not to be missed.

Bizet Les pêcheurs de perles.

Martha Angelici *sop* Leïla
Henri Legay *ten* Nadir
Michel Dens *bar* Zurga
Louis Noguera *bass* Nourabad
Chorus and Orchestra of the Opéra-Comique, Paris / André Cluytens.
EMI mono Ⓜ Ⓞ CMS5 65266-2 (two discs: 107 minutes: ADD). Notes and text included.
Recorded 1954.

It is a generally held, received opinion that the decline of true French vocal style set in around the 1940s and that 'French' voices in some way disappeared. The truth is much more complicated – it was the decline in fashion for French opera and song and the long periods of inactivity at both houses in Paris, and the consequent lack of interest shown by recording companies, that denied many French singers of the 1940s, until the 1980s, an international platform. This recording was taped in the Palais de la Mutualité. It is a beautiful performance of this much-recorded, but comparatively rarely staged work. Angelici and Dens as Leïla and Zurga are joined by the stylish and beautifully sung Nadir of Henri Legay. Despite its age, this must still be a strong contender as the first choice for *Les pêcheurs*. What is there to say of André Cluytens, who conducts this historic EMI issue? In a fascinating essay printed in the booklet (which has marvellous recording-session photographs) Michel Beretti outlines the history of the "Réunion des Théâtres Lyriques Nationaux", and the repertory system they operated at the time that Cluytens was Director of the Opéra-Comique, when this recording was made. "Delicate sonorities ... as well as the heady flourish" is how Beretti describes Cluytens's style; it might sum up the essence of French opera.

John Blow   British 1649-1708

Blow Venus and Adonis.

Catherine Bott *sop* Venus
Michael George *bass* Adonis
Libby Crabtree *sop* Cupid
Julia Gooding *sop* Shepherdess, First Grace
Andrew King *ten* First Shepherd
Simon Grant *bass* Second Shepherd, Third Huntsman, Third Grace
Christopher Robson (alto) Third Shepherd, First Huntsman, Second Grace
Paul Agnew *ten* Second Huntsman
Westminster Abbey School Choristers; New London Consort / Philip Pickett.
L'Oiseau-Lyre Ⓟ Ⓞ 440 220-2OH (57 minutes: DDD). 🎵 Notes and text included. Recorded 1992.

Philip Pickett's recordings have reflected an increasing interest in under-represented masterpieces of the seventeenth century, though not, thankfully, at the expense of his acclaimed and colourful renaissance reconstructions. Yet so distinctive has his style become that we can perceive with surprisingly little effort common musical values between, say, Susato and Schmelzer – or any other composers separated by 100 years or so. Far from suggesting that Pickett's approach to all periods and genres is stereotypical or uniform, there is a pervasive and fanatical concern for symbolic coloration, rhythmicality, textural finesse and a clarity of design which is unyieldingly pursued to its logical conclusion. In the case of John Blow's only opera (and lamentably one of only two real 'all-sung' dramas to emerge from England in the Restoration period), Pickett is at his most luminous. Whilst Charles Medlam and London Baroque on Harmonia Mundi take a robust and homespun view of the overture, Pickett has his listener mentally prepared from the outset for the opera's solemn denouement. The noble and eloquent opening (with some minor ensemble infelicities) sets the scene in more ways than one since Pickett is not content to see the Prologue's traditional machinations undermine the cultivated expression he believes this work merits. Consequently, the introduction of *Venus and Adonis* emerges sumptuously from Blow's skilful preparations, notably in the beautifully sung chorus refrain "In these sweet groves" and an ethereal Act Tune of three recorders which delivers the doomed lovers to their first intimate exchanges.

  Catherine Bott is the most telling and sensual Venus imaginable, her singing always captivating in its tonal variety and emotional nuance. Her relationship with Adonis is never mannered but tense and simmering, and in its chilling realism allows the listener to experience the brutal psychology of an anonymous adaptation. (Story line: Venus insists that Adonis goes hunting and the former suffers incessant grief when he meets his match with an Aedalian boar.) Michael George, as Adonis, plays his part thoughtfully in the striking immediacy of the tragedy, elegantly shaping his lines with a prescient tinge of melancholy before he is led in wounded at the start of Act 3. Both he and Bott are aided in their moving valediction by a continuo realization which demonstrates an acute characterization in articulation as much as in the choice of timbre. Despite the charms of Lynne Dawson's Venus and a largely satisfying performance in other respects by Medlam's forces, Pickett's account is the clear leader. For those who think of *Dido* as the only operatic achievement England could offer in the mid-baroque, a rude awakening awaits: this recording reveals Blow's opera to be a work of rare quality and pathos.

Adrien Boïeldieu
French 1775-1834

Boïeldieu Le Calife de Bagdad.

Laurence Dale *ten* Isauun
Lydia Mayo *sop* Zétulbé
Joëlle Michelini *sop* Késie
Claudine Cheriez *mez* Lémaïde
Huw Rhys-Evans *ten* Judge
Camerata de Provence Chorus and Orchestra / Antonio de Almeida.
Sonpact Ⓟ Ⓒ SPT93007 (61 minutes: DDD). Notes, text and translation included. Recorded 1992.

Question: in which nineteenth-century French opera does the heroine sing an aria called "Depuis le jour"? Answer: Boïeldieu's *Le Calife de Bagdad*. (Charpentier's *Louise* is one month into the twentieth century.) This is just one of the pleasures of becoming acquainted with this, Boïeldieu's first resounding success, initially given in Paris in 1800 and popular there for a quarter of a century. The plot is basic: true love triumphs when the heroine discovers that her 'outlaw' lover is none other than the Caliphe. As with all examples of *opéra comique*, there is a lot of dialogue, which although it is delivered in idiomatic fashion, might prove wearisome on repeated hearings.

Laurence Dale sings the Caliphe with a good sense of style – he has only one big aria, "Pour obtenir celle qu'il aime". Although the piece has obvious affinities with late eighteenth-century works with pastiche 'Eastern' effects – especially noticeable in the Overture with more than a hint of *Entführung* about it – this must have sounded very modern to its first, Napoleonic, audience. The form and style set the fashion for *opéra comique* for another 50 years. Of the two sopranos, Joëlle Michelini impresses most and gets the best aria, "De tous les pays", in which the musical quirks of various countries are tried out. The Camerata de Provence Chorus and Orchestra play and sing with conviction, and Antonio de Almeida conducts a generally sprightly performance. He may also have set some kind of precedent, in that he also speaks one of the non-singing roles, namely the newly-appointed Emir.

Boïeldieu La dame blanche.

Adrien Legros *bass* Gaveston
Françoise Louvay *sop* Anna
Michel Sénéchal *ten* Brown
Aimé Doniat *bar* Dickson
Jane Berbié *sop* Jenny
Germaine Baudoz *mez* Marguerite
Pierre Héral *bass* MacIrton
Paris Symphony Chorus and Orchestra / Pierre Stoll.
Accord Ⓟ Ⓒ 22086-2 (two discs: 123 minutes: ADD). Text included. Recorded 1961.

You'd have difficulty finding a stage performance of *La dame blanche* these days, but in the nineteenth century it was a huge success, clocking up 1,000 performances in Paris alone in the 40 years from its première in 1825 and being considered as important in the development of French opera as *Der Freischütz* in that of German. It owed a lot of its original appeal to the romantic era's fascination both with Sir Walter Scott (on whose *Guy Mannering* and *The monastery* Scribe based his libretto) and with tales of the supernatural, which figures in the plot; but the charm and grace of Boïeldieu's music is hard to resist, even if it plumbs few depths.

Weber and Mendelssohn were among its admirers, and Boïeldieu's melodic gift, allied to more advanced harmony, a flair for colourful orchestration and a freer sense of key (as in the auction scene) immediately establishes his superiority over Méhul (his predecessor as professor of composition at the Paris Conservatoire). He was seen as guiding French opera out from under the influence of Rossini, which had swamped Europe: nevertheless, there are typically Rossinian crescendos in the Overture, and some of the florid vocal writing also shows some indebtedness.

Scottish local colour is called upon when the supposedly English lieutenant George Brown remembers the tune of *Robin Adair* from his childhood and thereby (among other things) discovers that he is really the Earl of Avenel, whose castle the scheming steward Gaveston had been intent on securing for himself. The plot is somewhat complicated, but great pains seem to have been taken here to shield listeners from making any attempt to follow it: the 80-word English synopsis is ridiculously inadequate, and the printed French text (untranslated) omits all the dialogue, as does the recording, so that what happens between the musical numbers is only to be guessed at. (When a trio sing "Que viens-je donc d'entendre?" – a key point in the action – we are left wondering what it is that they have heard.) This Official Secrets Act extends even to withholding any indication of who the characters are.

The music, always pleasant and extremely skilfully written (especially in large ensembles such as the extended finale of Act 2), is given a very lively and likeable performance by a conductor who controls his forces well and a cast with no weaknesses and first-class enunciation. Two singers are outstanding: Sénéchal, upholding the best tradition of French lyric tenors and taking the numerous high B flats and Cs with complete confidence and ease, and Louvay, whose excellent coloratura in her Act 3 air leads one to ask why she was not recorded more. Despite some unevennesses in level – the start of Brown's "Viens gentille dame", the chorus in the auction scene overloud – the recording wears well.

Joseph Bodin de Boismortier

French 1689-1755

Boismortier Don Quichotte chez la Duchesse.

Stephan Van Dyck *ten* Don Quichotte
Richard Biren *bar* Sancho Panza
Meredith Hall *sop* Altisidore
Marie-Pierre Wattiez *sop* Peasant girl
Paul Gay *bar* Duke, Merlin, Japanese man
Patrick Ardagh-Walter *bass* Montesinos
Akiko Toda *sop* Lover
Brigitte Le Baron *mez* Lover
Nicole Dubrovitch *sop* Attendant of the Duchess
Paul Médioni *bass* Interpreter
Anne Mopin *sop* Japanese woman
Le Concert Spirituel / Hervé Niquet.
Naxos Ⓢ ① 8 553647 (61 minutes: DDD). Notes, text and translation included. ✍ Recorded 1996.

The French baroque composer Boismortier is chiefly known for his attractive and accommodatingly written sonatas and concertos for a variety of instruments, above all flute, violin and bassoon. Nowadays he is hardly recognizable at all for his vocal music and, though a performance of this three-act *ballet comique* was given in London some 27 years ago it has not, as far as we know, surfaced since then either here, or perhaps anywhere else. That is until Hervé Niquet and his enterprising ensemble, Le Concert Spirituel, recorded the work.

Boismortier's comic ballet, with a libretto by Favart, received its première in 1743 and was his first work for the Paris Opéra. The piece lasts only an hour or so and therefore was given as part of a double-bill; the other work was Mouret's *Les amours de Ragonde ou la soirée de village*. Favart based his libretto on a splendidly mischievous episode recounted in the second book of Cervantes's epic poem. In it, the Knight of the Lions and his squire, Sancho Panza, are subjected to a variety of preposterous and, in one instance, extremely uncomfortable practical jokes. Once read, never forgotten, but it should be added that Boismortier's music, modest in its aim, is very engaging and provides an effective foil to Favart's text with its 'apparent' monster, who gives a ferocious roar at the conclusion of the overture, its sorcery, disguise and diversion. For all this Boismortier, mirroring the simpler rococo taste of the time, provided charming airs, supple choruses and many invigorating dances. What more enticement is needed? The cast is stylish and conveys the spirit of Cervantes and Favart with evident relish. The score is a delight from start to finish and makes one long to hear the composer's pastorale, *Daphnis et Chloé*, first performed four years after *Don Quichotte*, but which shares with the earlier piece several of its most beguiling dances. There is certainly more to Boismortier than all those *morceaux favoris* for flutes, hurdy-gurdys and the like would suggest. Hugely entertaining, with an unexpected reappearance of the monster after the concluding chaconne. It sounds as if the cast was as startled by its roar as you will be. Go and buy it without delay!

Arrigo Boito

Italian 1842-1918

Boito Mefistofele.
Nicolai Ghiaurov *bass* Mefistofele
Luciano Pavarotti *ten* Faust

Mirella Freni *sop* Margherita
Montserrat Caballé *sop* Elena
Nucci Condò *contr* Martha
Della Jones *mez* Pantalis
Piero de Palma *ten* Wagner
Robin Leggate *ten* Nereo
Trinity Boys Choir; National Philharmonic Orchestra London Opera Chorus / Oliviero de Fabritiis.
Decca Ⓟ Ⓓ 410 175-2DH3 (three discs: 147 minutes: DDD). Notes, text and translation
included. Recorded 1981.

Ernest Newman viewed Boito's artistry sourly as a "semi-musical gift that rarely rises above the
mediocre and generally dips a point or two below it". By contrast Kobbé described *Mefistofele* as
"one of the most profound works for the lyric stage, one of the most beautiful scores to come out of
Italy". Listening to this recording makes you inclined to favour Kobbé. Indeed you begin to wonder
why this refined and finely shaped version of the Faust story doesn't replace in public esteem
Gounod's much more meretricious opera. The answer may lie in Gounod's more experienced
dramaturgy and in the greater immediacy of the older composer's melodies. In every other respect,
Boito far surpasses him, not least in his own, imaginative libretto. Shaw had it right as usual:
"Gounod has set music to Faust, Boito has set Faust to music." The late de Fabritiis, in what proved
to be his swan-song for the gramophone (the set is dedicated to his memory), enters fully into the
spirit of the piece, balancing carefully its poetic and dramatic images, emphasizing subtly the quaint
beauty of Boito's scoring, revelling in its opportunities for orchestral brio: he is much more successful
than his older contemporary, Serafin, in keeping the score moving, never allowing us to think about
its *longueurs*, or become bogged down by its occasionally too literary bent.

Although all the soloists may be thought on the mature side for their roles, each appears to be
inspired to give of her or his best by the conductor's demands. There is little of Pavarotti's singing that
is better than his Faust, portraying the ardour and ecstasy of Faust's passions and poetry. "Dai
campi" is elegantly turned; "Giunto sul passo estremo" appropriately plaintive (dynamic marks
observed). "Lontano, lontano", with Freni, is lovingly done in a half-voice. The *mormorato*
(murmured) injunction, at "Pace, pace", when Faust tries to calm the stricken Margherita in Act 3, is
obeyed. The lead into the big ensemble, "Forma ideal", in the Helen scene is properly impassioned,
with its climactic phrase to the high B flat taken in a single breath, even if the ultimate note itself
hardens unduly, as do other top notes throughout the opera, all tighter than they should be.

Freni sounds involved, but a little laboured in "L'altra notte", with an intrusive beat when her tone
comes under pressure (Tebaldi, for Serafin, is much to be preferred here), but once that aria is past,
she sings with both finesse and pathos, the solo "Spunta l'auora pallida" most affecting. It is a luxury
indeed to have Caballé, no less, cast as Elena, and she is very properly in seductive voice, matching
Pavarotti note for note in their moment of rapture. But, in an opera named after him, the Devil rightly
receives the most imposing interpretation. Nicolai Ghiaurov, as with Gounod's Mephisto, has a high
old time portraying the evil/jolly fellow, all his solos delivered with the vocal equivalent of a leering
smile. It is true that the Bulgarian bass had, by this stage, problems at the top of his register, many
high notes sounding strained and/or hollow, but the total effect of the assumption puts that criticism
into perspective.

The choral singing is tremendous, full of bite and vivid accents, excellently 'caught' by the natural
and immediate recording; the orchestral playing deserves equal commendation. All this can be heard
in the work's finale, a true climax to what has gone before. This should make Mefistofele many
friends. Yet, except in terms of sound, the old Decca set isn't superseded. Tebaldi is better equipped
for Margherita than Freni, and shows it in her exquisite phrasing of "L'altra notte". Siepi, not so
obviously histrionic as Ghiaurov, sometimes scores over his rival in his subtle understatement of his
role. And del Monaco turned in one of his most restrained performances as Faust, after a rough "Dai
campi". Serafin's unassuming way with the work shows his affection for it.

Boito Mefistofele.
Cesare Siepi *bass* Mefistofele
Mario del Monaco *ten* Faust
Renata Tebaldi *sop* Margherita
Floriana Cavalli *sop* Elena
Lucia Danieli *mez* Martha, Pantalis
Piero de Palma *ten* Wagner, Nereo
Chorus and Orchestra of the Santa Cecilia Academy / Tullio Serafin.
Decca Grand Opera Ⓜ Ⓓ 440 054-2DMO2 (two discs: 141 minutes: ADD). Notes, text and
translation included. Recorded 1958.

All the currently available recordings of *Mefistofele* have at least one major flaw. De Fabritiis's
sensitive account occupies three CDs and has in the title-role the intelligent and grand-voiced but
fundamentally unidiomatic Nicolai Ghiaurov, gruffly and blackly Slavonic in a part that ideally needs
an Italianate *basso cantante* with elegance and relish as well as malignity. The flaw in this present

reissue is the dated recording. There is a decent impression of space in the difficult opening and closing scenes (cancelled out though it soon is by a forward-placed, valiant but not especially distinguished chorus), while the orchestra take on a rather fizzy top whenever it plays loudly. If you can put up with that, the performance has fewer drawbacks than its more recent rivals.

In particular it has in Siepi a real Italian bass with a fine sense of line and a genuine enjoyment of Boito's words. Phrases that are often merely snarled are here truly sung, and Siepi's is the only devil to suggest in the quartet that he is trying to seduce Martha, and that he will very probably succeed. There is incisiveness and grain there, too, to add menace to his suavity. This was a central role in Siepi's repertory, and we're fortunate that he recorded it while he was still at the height of his powers. From their present-day reputations the other two principals look a bit more problematical: Tebaldi, flawless but chilly, and del Monaco the unsubtle, leather-lunged belter. She, in fact, gives one of the best accounts of "L'altra notte" on record, strongly sung and very touching in its suggestion of grieving guilt; she is more secure than the otherwise touching but slightly overparted Mirella Freni in de Fabritiis's recording. Del Monaco sings "Dai campi, dai prati" without the slightest acknowledgement of its poetry, but the splendour of the sound and his instinctive feeling for legato have their own allure, and they give nobility to his finely phrased "Giunto sul passo estremo". The most poetically sung version of this role is Pavarotti's for de Fabritiis. Cavalli sings Elena strongly, with a dramatic and fearless account of "Notte, cupa, truce", and the secondary parts are characterfully done. The recording doesn't allow Serafin to make a sonic spectacular of the outer scenes, but his care for Boito's often rather old-fashioned *cantabil*e, his quirky rhythms and orchestral colours is scrupulous throughout. If you are buying a *Mefistofele*, this could be your first choice; if you can afford it, buy de Fabritiis as well, on his account and Pavarotti's, but also for the inspired, luxury casting of Montserrat Caballé as Elena.

Alexander Borodin   Russian 1833-1887

Borodin Prince Igor.
Mikhail Kit *bar* Igor
Galina Gorchakova *sop* Yaroslavna
Gegam Grigorian *ten* Vladimir
Vladimir Ognovenko *bass* Prince Galitsky
Bulat Minjelkiev *bass* Khan Konchak
Olga Borodina *mez* Konchakovna
Nikolai Gassiev *ten* Ovlur
Georgy Selezniev *bass* Skula
Konstantin Pluzhnikov *ten* Eroshka
Evgenia Perlasova *mez* Nurse
Tatyana Novikova *sop* Polovtsian Maiden
Kirov Opera Chorus and Orchestra / Valery Gergiev.
Philips Ⓟ Ⓒ 442 537-2PH3 (three discs: 209 minutes: DDD). Notes, text and translation included. Recorded 1993.

Curious things happen long before the official surprises of this vitally fresh *Prince Igor*, not least in the Overture, where Gergiev takes the horn's beautiful melody at a very slow pace. No doubt it would be different in a concert performance, but Gergiev is anxious to prepare us for the weighty events which follow and his particular point with the theme is to relate it to its place in the opera as the heart of Igor's great aria. There, in league with the bass-baritonal timbre of Gergiev's prince, Mikhail Kit, it solemnly underlines the fact that this is an aria of potency frustrated, sung by a hero who spends most of the opera in captivity and that is further emphasized by a second aria which no listener will ever have heard before. It is the most significant of the passages discovered among Borodin's papers, rejected by Rimsky-Korsakov in his otherwise sensitive tribute to Borodin's memory but specially orchestrated for this recording by Yuri Faliek. It may not rank with the most memorable numbers in the score, but like the other 'new' music (inserted to portray Galitsky in a more threatening light in his short-lived rebellion at the end of Act 2) and unlike the greater part of Borodin's score where, in spite of what the insert-note maintains, Borodin's style and orchestration are so close to Rimsky-Korsakov's as to be virtually indistinguishable, it has a Mussorgskyan ruggedness about it. It also helps to give a weighty focus to Act 3, otherwise a phenomenal feat of reconstruction on Glazunov's part, but somehow insubstantial.

The other problem with the *Prince Igor* we already know is the way that Act 3 rather weakly follows its much more imposing Polovtsian predecessor. Gergiev obviates both that, and the problem of too much time initially spent in Igor's home town of Putivl, by referring to a structural outline of Borodin's dating from 1883 which proposes alternating the Russian and Polovtsian acts. In the theatre, we might still want the famous Polovtsian divertissement as a centrepiece, but on the recording the new order works splendidly, not least because Gergiev is at his fluent best in the scenes of Galitsky's dissipation and Yaroslavna's despair, now making up the opera's Second Act and no weak sequel to the exotica of Konchak's entertainment.

If anything, the new Second Act is a more satisfactory achievement than the first Polovtsian act, where Gergiev veers between extremes of languor and vigour. While Borodina executes Konchakovna's seductive chromatics with astonishing breath control and focus of tone, Grigorian as her captive lover should surely have let the Polovtsian air work rather more wonders on his beaten-bronze tenor heroics (too loud too much of the time). Bulat Minjelkiev's Konchak – he would be perfect on stage – is a little too free and easy, at least in comparison with Ognovenko's perfectly gauged Galitsky, a rogue who needs the extra rebellion music of this version to show more threatening colours. There's just the right degree of relaxation, too, about his drunken supporters Skula and Eroshka. It takes two Russian character-singers to make sense of this pair – "with our wine and our cunning we will never die in Russia", they tell us truthfully – and their comical capitulation on Igor's return, so tedious in the Covent Garden production several years back, wins respect for Borodin's daring happy-end transition here. It is beautifully paced by Pluzhnikov (rather strained by the awkward vocal writing, not inappropriately), Selezniev and their conductor, and crowned by a choral cry of joy which brings a marvellous rush of tearful adrenalin.

That leaves us with Gorchakova, so touching in Yaroslavna's first aria, and her way is paved with a wonderful sense of atmosphere from the Kirov strings – but not always projecting the text very vividly and clearly not at her best in the big scena of the last act (another take might have helped both here and at the end of the off-stage chorus that follows – the last F sharp is *very* sharp; Gorchakova's in the aria is flat). Nor is rejoicing Kit's strongest asset in the duet of reunion that follows. The last finale, though, is the best of the four performance-wise, and the only one where the imposing bass of the Kirov's acoustics doesn't overwhelm detail in the treble – still rather cowled, and in any case the Polovtsian clarinet lacks bite throughout the dances.

Still, in terms of long-term vision, orchestral detail and strength of ensemble, Gergiev is ahead of the competition. You can also see the Royal Opera production on video to decide whether the new, sanctioned restructuring isn't a better option but certainly Gergiev's pleading for the Act 2 finale and Act 3 puts this recording of a flawed masterpiece in a league of its own.

Borodin Prince Igor.

Ivan Petrov *bass* Igor
Tatyana Tugarinova *mez* Yaroslavna
Vladimir Atlantov *ten* Vladimir
Artur Eisen *bass* Prince Galitsky
Alexander Vedernikov *bass* Khan Konchak
Elena Obraztsova *mez* Konchakovna
Alexander Laptev *ten* Ovlur
Valery Yaroslavtsev *bass* Skula
Konstantin Baskov *ten* Eroshka
Irina Terpilovskaya *mez* Nurse
Margarita Miglau *sop* Polovtsian Maiden
Chorus and Orchestra of the Bolshoi Theatre, Moscow / Mark Ermler.
Melodiya Ⓜ ① 74321 29346-2 (three discs: 196 minutes: ADD). Notes, text and translation included. Recorded 1969.

As with the opera itself, so with this recording: the defects must be got out of the way if one is to find the rewards that are certainly there. When it was made in Moscow, Russian recording techniques were still laggard, and in many places the sound is acidulated and the acoustic cavernous to the point of approaching obscurity. Ermler drives the orchestra hard, but without regard to recorded effect, so that the hurtling violin figures of the overture are virtually inaudible. The chorus suffer most of all, especially in the massed scenes of acclamation and so on; the more lightly scored Polovtsian Dances come off considerably better.

There are other matters requiring allowances to be made. Some of the smaller parts are not taken with much distinction, and Yaroslavna herself is sung by Tatyana Tugarinova with a shrill tone which a fearsome vibrato does nothing to improve. Konchakovna is very much better sung by Obraztsova. Though her tone is heavy, she charges it with expression, and phrases her graceful lines with meaning and authority. The men are generally excellent. Igor himself is strongly sung by Ivan Petrov, with a degree of vibrato but not at the expense of line and tone. He makes a dignified figure, and some of the best moments in the performance come in Act 2 with the exchanges between him and Alexander Vedernikov's dignified Konchak. This 'noble savage' is given a warmth, a humanity, a manly compassion that are there in the melodic lines, especially in the great aria giving his captive Igor a welcome between warriors. This is superbly done. Vladimir is sung with a good strong ring by Vladimir Atlantov; and Artur Eisen completes a good group of singers, representing the best of the Bolshoi Theatre's style in the 1960s. Since then, there has been some easing in the rigidity which can produce attitudes rather than characterization, in the honouring of a long-held tradition of performance; but there is here, at best, a magnificence which is impressive, even if it is not one to dislodge Gergiev's recording from pride of place.

The orchestral playing is strong, though some of it reflects a style which has since mellowed a little. The horns here sound rather too much in the older French manner, with a shimmering vibrato; some of the string phrasing uses what now sounds like exaggerated portamento, though it has to be said that this is likely to be what Borodin heard and expected. It is a rich score and, for all the improbabilities and awkwardnesses of the plot, not to mention its jerky movement forward and sideways, one that is packed with marvellous music. The booklet has a transliteration and translations into English (reasonable), German and French. There is an introductory note, too brief by far for a work that needs some of the complicated historical and compositional background setting out for the listener's enlightenment. In Act 2 the track listing stops corresponding to that on the disc.

Borodin Prince Igor.

Sergei Leiferkus *bar* Igor
Anna Tomowa-Sintow *sop* Yaroslavna
Alexei Steblianko *ten* Vladimir
Nikola Ghiuselev *bass* Prince Galitsky
Paata Burchuladze *bass* Khan Konchak
Elena Zaremba *mez* Konchakovna
Robin Leggate *ten* Ovlur
Eric Garrett *bar* Skula
Francis Egerton *ten* Eroshka
Gillian Webster *sop* Polovtsian Maiden
Royal Ballet; Chorus and Orchestra of the Royal Opera House, Covent Garden / Bernard Haitink.
Stage Director: **Andrei Serban.** *Video Director:* **Humphrey Burton.**
Decca Ⓟ ⚬⚬ 071 421-3DH2 (two cassettes: 186 minutes). Recorded 1990.

In retrospect this can be seen as the production with which Covent Garden turned the corner, from being a critical whipping-boy to becoming the new darling of reviewers. And deservedly so. In Andrei Serban's panoramic yet economic staging many of the problems said to attend a staging of this lengthy, somewhat sprawling epic (its attractive Act 3 often omitted) virtually disappeared. Serban unerringly depicts in turn the suffering of Mother Russia and the pagan joys and lusts of Konchak's entourage with Galitsky's roistering somewhere in between. Liviu Ciulei's pinewood, unit set and Deirdre Clancy's colour-coded costumes are all of a piece with the ethos of this gratifyingly unified production. There is perhaps too much emphasis on drunkenness, ungovernable desire and brutal killing, or perhaps they are not quite convincingly enough enacted by an army of extras, but the unity of the whole overcomes specific reservations on detail. There can be no doubts about Bernard Haitink's cogently limned conducting, distinguishing with the composer between different moods, different milieux, and bringing out the epic nature of the writing with his chorus and orchestra responding accordingly.

The Royal Opera sensibly chose a cast of Russian speakers for the main roles. Among them Anna Tomowa-Sintow's Yaroslavna stands out for her all-embracing characterization of the sad, dignified, vulnerable heroine. Although close-ups unflatteringly reveal a more motherly figure than that intended by her creators, Tomowa-Sintow overcomes such a drawback by the conviction of her acting and singing – the latter lustrous, long-breathed, eloquently accented, all its qualities fused into a deeply moving account of her Act 4 solo. Leiferkus's determined, proud Igor, sung in those firm, incisively enunciated tones of his, is an apt foil to his wife's eloquence. Burchuladze catches to perfection Khan Konchak's odd blend of generosity and brutality in a roistering, highly-spiced portrayal, sumptuously sung. Nikola Ghiuselev's lecherous, insistent Galitsky is no less impressive.

Elena Zaremba has the vibrant, specifically dark-hued timbre of the best of her kind and ideal for Konchakovna's sensual utterance. That she looks the role to perfection is a bonus. Unfortunately Steblianko's Vladimir looks far too old for such a glamorous lover, older indeed than his father Igor, and his loosely-phrased, poorly-pitched singing does little justice to Vladimir's elegiac cavatina. Of the British contingent, Gillian Webster begins Act 2 with a lovely account of the Polovstian Girl's solo. Robin Leggate is a suitably devious Ovlour. As the two drunken comics, Egerton and Garrett are not convincingly Russian, more English music-hall. Humphrey Burton's video direction is unobtrusively right. The sound is up to Decca's high standard in this field. Subtitles are provided.

Rutland Boughton   British 1878-1960

Boughton Bethlehem.

Helen Field *sop* Virgin Mary
Richard Bryan *alto* Gabriel
Roger Bryson *bar* Joseph
Robert Evans *bass* Jem
John Bowen *ten* Sym
Adrian Peacock *bass* Dave
Alan Opie *bar* Zarathustra
Jamie McDougall *ten* Nubar

Richard Van Allan *bass* Merlin
Claire Seaton *sop* Believer
Colin Campbell *bar* Unbeliever
Ian Boughton *ten* Calchas
Graeme Matheson-Bruce *ten* Herod
Holst Singers; New London Children's Choir; City of London Sinfonia / Alan G. Melville.
Hyperion Ⓟ ① CDA66690 (79 minutes: DDD). Notes and text included. Recorded 1993.

Bethlehem gave great offence in 1926 when in the wake of the General Strike it was produced in modern dress with a capitalist-looking Herod and a miner's cottage for a manger. Generally, it is as inoffensive as any music on earth. The Christmas story is told in an adaptation of one of the medieval Miracle plays, with the Shepherds as jolly characters, the Wise Men (clueless in their dealings with Herod) presenting a more stately trio in the second half. There is no Slaughter of the Innocents and no raging in the streets on the part of Herod, who is here a high reedy tenor instead of Roaring Bill the Blacksmith whose deep bass would affright awestruck babes and tender maids. Well-known carols are incorporated as choral interludes, and the musical idiom is friendly and folky (Vaughan Williams thought that Boughton must have gone round collecting tunes he and Cecil Sharp had missed).

The Choral Drama was written for Boughton's recently instituted Glastonbury Festival in 1915 and makes fairly moderate demands upon its performers. Orchestration is for the most part light and considerate towards the voices, brass being added to give colour and a deliberately tawdry splendour to the royal court. Ballet music, which the composer allowed to have little point unless the dancing could be seen, is omitted in the recording, which also makes a few small cuts so as to prevent it spilling over, which it would do for only a few minutes, on to a second disc. All is finely played, sometimes to quite beautiful effect. The singing is rather more variable, with Helen Field bringing too operatic a vibrato to the essentially unsophisticated music written for Mary, and Richard Bryan being somewhat too pipey a Gabriel (resourceful as he is on the high notes). Roger Bryson is a well-cast Joseph, steady in voice as in character, Alan Opie is gratefully heard among the Wise Men, and Claire Seaton makes an impression in her brief appearance as a Believer. The children's choir contribute distinctively, and the choral passages are among the most delightful: indeed, sometimes inspired, as in the introduction to "The First Noël". Well recorded and well presented (with photographs of early productions, including the scandalous modern-dress of 1926).

Boughton The Immortal Hour.
Roderick Kennedy *bass* Dalua
Anne Dawson *sop* Etain
David Wilson-Johnson *bar* Eochaidh
Maldwyn Davies *ten* Midir
English Chamber Orchestra; Geoffrey Mitchell Choir / Alan G. Melville.
Hyperion Ⓟ ① CDA66101/2 (two discs: 124 minutes: DDD). Notes and text included. Recorded 1983.

The Immortal Hour is part of theatrical folklore: in London in the early-1920s it ran, unprecedentedly, for 216 consecutive performances and, shortly afterwards, for a further 160 at the first of several revivals; within a decade it had been played a thousand times. Many in those audiences returned repeatedly, fascinated by the other-worldly mystery of the plot (it concerns the love of a mortal king, Eochaidh, for the faery princess Etain and the destruction of their happiness by her nostalgic longing for the Land of the Ever Young, removed from her memory though it has been by a magic spell) and by the gentle, lyrical simplicity of its music. In the bleak aftermath of 1918, with civil war in Ireland, political instability at home and the names of Hitler, Mussolini and Stalin already emerging from obscurity into the headlines, what blessed escapism this blend of Celtic myth and folk-tinged pentatonic sweetness must have offered; there are still those who remember it with gratitude and affection as a glimpse of a beautiful world of legend: faeryland and Avalon co-mingled.

Legends cannot always withstand revisiting, but Boughton's score still has the power to evoke that world, immediately and effortlessly. The libretto by "Fiona McLeod" (the *nom de plume* of William Sharp) is post-Rossetti high kitsch, often veering into bathos or becoming embarrassingly overheated, but it does grope towards something uncomfortably deep in the human psyche, the potentially schizoid fracture-zone between physical and spiritual, Apollo and Dionysos, and Boughton unerringly places the conflict in a world where it can be treated as a myth, a world which lies somewhere in the borderland between Wagner's *Forest of the Grail*, Debussy's *Allemonde* and Burne-Jones's grey-green pre-Raphaelite shadows. It is, though, a world that lacks the power and much of the shadow of those. Boughton's charming melodies, cleverly juggled though they are by a simplified version of Wagner's leitmotiv technique, are not capable of pungent characterization or of conveying strong dramatic conflict or urgent narrative. It is quiet, sweet music, muted in colour and softly plaintive in utterance, and whenever the plot demands more than this the opera sags.

Midir, the visitant from the Land of the Ever Young who lures Etain away from the mortal world, really needs music of dangerously heady, Dionysiac incandescence – something like that Strauss gave to Bacchus in *Ariadne auf Naxos*, perhaps – but Boughton's vocabulary can run to nothing more transported than the prettily lilting Faery Song and to some pages of folksy lyricism with a few showy high notes for emphasis. No less seriously, the music has little dramatic grip. This is partly because of its predominant slowness, partly because it lacks rhythmic variety (Eochaidh, for example, has a dispiriting habit of ending his phrases on three accented crotchets), but it has much to do with a failure to focus on the essentials of the plot. There are a pair of picturesquely glum rustics in the First Act ("I am Manus, and this poor woman is Maive, my childless wife") who simply hold up the action by mournfully commenting on the weather and retailing incomprehensible folk myths. Worse, in Act 2 there is a quite superfluous chorus of druids, warriors, maidens and (God help us) bards who, having been got on stage in an interminable sequence of processions, must be got off stage, to a repetition of them, before the plot can proceed.

Despite all this, and the consequent evocation of a mythology that is at times a lot closer to Never-Never-Land than to Tir-na-n'Og, *The Immortal Hour* does have a quality, difficult to define, that is genuinely alluring. This is to be found in the touching purity of Etain's music, as she sings of a beauty she can no longer recall but whose loss is an inassuageable ache (and how movingly Anne Dawson sings the role). It is there in the moments of true darkness that the music achieves: Dalua, the tormented Lord of Shadow conjures up something of the sombre shudder of the supernatural world. And the off-stage choruses of invisible spirits in Act 1, the approaching and retreating hosts of faeryland at the end of that act give an idea of the spell this work could still cast if judiciously cut and staged as Boughton intended, in a woodland setting, with voices echoing through the trees and the audience led to some new grove or clearing for each scene-change.

The performance could hardly speak more eloquently for the opera. Alan G. Melville allows the music to emerge from and retreat into shadowy silences, all the principal singers are accomplished and the excellent chorus have been placed so as to evoke a sense of space. The recording seldom suggests the studio: it is easy to imagine oneself in the "dark and mysterious wood" at the world's end where the drama takes place – or in the Regent Theatre, Euston, where hushed audiences again and again sought refuge from the realities of 1922.

Walter Braunfels

German 1882-1954

Braunfels Verkündigung.

Siegmund Nimsgern *bass-bar* Andreas Gradherz
Claudia Rüggeberg *sngr* The mother
Andrea Trauboth *sop* Violaine
Chieko Shirasaka-Teratani *sop* Mara
John Bröcheler *bass* Jakobäus
Christer Bladin *ten* Peter von Ulm
Christian Brüggemann *sngr* Peter's assistant
Akemi Kajiyama *sngr* Angel
Stefan Sevenich *sngr* Labourer
Barbara Dommer *spkr* A woman
Rolf-Dieter Krüll *spkr* Mayor of Rothenstein
Cologne Symphony Chorus and Orchestra / Dennis Russell Davies.
EMI Ⓟ Ⓒ CDS5 55104-2 (two discs: 132 minutes: DDD). Notes and text included. Recorded at a performance in the Philharmonie, Cologne on March 4th, 1992.

In the period between the two world wars, Braunfels was among the most widely performed of all living opera composers. He fell foul of the Nazis, and little was heard of him again until after their fall from power. *Verkündigung* ("Annunciation") was written between 1934 and 1937, presumably in full knowledge that it had no foreseeable prospect of performance, and it was not staged until 1948. It is not really an opera, but a mystery play, the action proceeding in almost free-standing emblematic tableaux, with few narrative links between them, all the characters being more symbolic than three-dimensional. The libretto is based on a German translation of Paul Claudel's *L'Annonce faite à Marie*, and tells the story of a woman, Violaine, who is moved by pity to kiss a leper. She contracts leprosy herself, heals the leper she had embraced, brings the child born to her cross-grained sister and her own former fiancé back from the dead, and dies forgiving the ex-fiancé who could never quite bring himself to believe that her kiss to the leper was no more than an act of saintly compassion.

The music is as remote as can be from any idea of what a German 'opera' of the 1930s might sound like. Its stylistic affinities are all in the past, with Pfitzner (but a simpler, a pietistic Pfitzner), with Reger (though much less chromatic) and with Strauss (though much less voluptuous). There seems also to be a level at which the music is rooted, though so deep that the roots can hardly be discerned, in German chorale, and in a counterpoint that has more affinities with Bach than with Hindemith (though there is a hint of a kinship there, too). Most difficult of all, for some listeners (though it should be stressed that Braunfels's language is amply melodious and harmonically straightforward), is the fact that the drama proceeds on an almost exclusively spiritual level. Moments of insight and mystical vision are dramatized, more everyday events, such as there are, are not. It places something of a premium on the listener's response to the story.

A note by Frithjof Haas (translated in the booklet, though the libretto is not) explains that all the characters represent earthly reactions to heavenly forces. Thus the evil sister Mara (whose reaction to the resurrection of her child is jealously to fling her by now blind sister into a pit) "lives in a world that excludes God", while her and Violaine's mother, who cannot understand her husband's decision "to overcome mortal needs and failings" by going on a pilgrimage to Jerusalem, "is not part of the mystery". An unsympathetic listener may find Mara's 'wickedness' bafflingly unmotivated, her father's action selfish and may side with the downtrodden and unconsidered mother, may even find the incessant sweetness-and-light of Violaine cloying. When her jealous fiancé curses her for her apparent infidelity she exclaims, radiantly, "I am not accursed, I am the gentle, the gentle Violaine"; when he discovers she has given her engagement ring to the leper as well, to help pay for the cathedral he is building, her response is "I am more than a ring; I am a great treasure".

The music is often radiant, often touching in the sincerity of its belief in tonality and the workings of the Holy Ghost; it is easy to imagine it becoming a sort of cult piece among some listeners, while others are bound to find it, like some really virtuous and spiritual people, a touch boring. A third group, those who simply cannot accept a eulogy of redemptive suffering, may even find it repulsive. What no one can deny is a curious and individual voice, individual even in its Catholic reliance on the sanctified authority of tradition. Nor could anyone claim that this fine performance sells the work short in any way: the singing is admirable throughout, Andrea Trauboth in especially beautiful voice (she would sound wonderful in Strauss!), and Davies conducts with real conviction. The recording, made at a live concert performance, has only a few minor fluffs and some noisy page-turns to mar it.

Braunfels Die Vögel.

Hellen Kwon *sop* Nightingale
Endrik Wottrich *ten* Good Hope
Michael Kraus *ten* Loyal Friend
Marita Posselt *sop* Wren
Wolfgang Holzmair *bar* Hoopoe
Iris Vermillion *mez* First Thrush
Brigitte Wohlfarth *sop* Second Thrush
Matthias Goerne *bar* Prometheus
Johann Werner Prein *bass* Eagle
Martin Petzold *ten* Flamingo
Dirk Schmidt *ten* Raven
Christiane Hossfeld *mez* First Swallow
Romelia Lichtenstein *sop* Second Swallow
Uta Schwabe *mez* Third Swallow
Berlin Radio Chorus; Deutsches Symphony Orchestra, Berlin / Lothar Zagrosek.
Decca Entartete Musik Ⓟ Ⓒ 448 679-2DHO2 (two discs: 139 minutes: DDD). Notes, text and translation included. Recorded 1994.

Bruno Walter conducted the first performance of *Die Vögel* ("The Birds") in Munich in 1920, with Maria Ivogün as a charmingly plump Nightingale and Karl Erb and Alfred Jerger as the two human visitors to the kingdom of the birds, Loyal Friend and Good Hope. Many years later he still remembered this "noble and lovely work" as one of those things which had "given value to life". It was very successful (50 performances in Munich alone in its first two years, numerous other productions including one at the Vienna State Opera), and one can readily understand its appeal to Germans of that period. Its more conversational scenes are rooted in the reassuring, comfortable world of German light opera, but in the Nightingale's florid song (she is rather like a cross between two Strauss heroines, Zerbinetta and Daphne) and the noble theme that introduces the birds' ruler, the Hoopoe (once a human himself: Wolfgang Holzmair in splendid voice) it is immediately obvious that this is no mere light comedy.

It is in fact a lightly touched allegory loosely based on Aristophanes: Loyal Friend and Good Hope persuade the birds to build an aerial fortress between heaven and earth to intercept and tax the smoke from altar fires upon which the gods depend for sustenance. But at the centre of the drama, occupying the first half-hour of Act 2, is a quite gorgeous love duet for the Nightingale and Good Hope, or rather a duet between his idealism and the uncomplicated natural world that she represents. It is so warmly beautiful, this duet, that the author of the accompanying booklet compares it to Act 3 of *Tristan und Isolde*. Understandable, but missing the point: Braunfels's language is post-*Meistersinger*, not post-*Tristan*. It is quite devoid of death wish or narcissism: it is innocent, as innocent as the childlike charm of the wedding ceremony for two pigeons that consecrates the soon-to-be-destroyed fortress, as joyously innocent as the ensemble (for no fewer than 25 different birds plus chorus) that greets Loyal Friend and Good Hope on their arrival in the avian kingdom.

And it is the innocent freshness of Braunfels's imagination that saves his fable from being merely coy or saccharine. There is a magic to the Nightingale's music, alongside her stratospheric coloratura: she has a beautiful hovering theme, heard on unaccompanied violins at the outset, that gives its colour to the entire opera. Nor is the drama without darkness: Prometheus arrives in Act 2 (an impressive appearance from the young German baritone, Matthias Goerne) to warn the birds that they have underestimated the power of Zeus, and his music has something of grandeur to it; something, indeed, of Hugo Wolf's portrayal of the same character. And Good Hope's return to the human world, somehow transfigured by the Nightingale's song and her innocent kiss, is obstinately memorable. The opera could hardly be better sung; apart from those already mentioned, Kwon is a vivid Nightingale and Wottrich an ardent Good Hope. Zagrosek directs a performance in which everyone seems to be delightfully discovering ... well, not a masterpiece, perhaps, but, as Walter said, a work that had "given value to life". The recording is admirable.

Tomás Bretón   Spanish 1850-1923

Bretón La Verbena de la Paloma.
   María Bayo *sop* Susana
   Plácido Domingo *ten* Julián
   Raquel Pierotti *mez* Seña Rita
   Silvia Tro *sop* Casta
   Rafael Castejón *sngr* Don Hilarión
   Jesús Castejón *bass-bar* Don Sebastián
   Ana Maria Amengual *sngr* Tia Antonia
   Milagros Martin *folk sngr* Cantaora
   Enrique Baquerizo *bass* Watchman
   Madrid Comunidad Chorus; Madrid Symphony Orchestra / Antoni Ros Marbà.
   Auvidis Valois Ⓕ ① V4725 (46 minutes: DDD). Recorded 1994.

Entering the orchestra pit to conduct the first performance of his light-hearted one-acter *La Verbena de la Paloma* in 1894, Tomás Bretón, a highly cultured musician with his heart set on writing serious operas (his *Los amantes de Teruel* the previous year had had a very mixed reception), leant over to his first violin and murmured, "I think I've made a terrible mistake this time". He could not have been more wrong. The piece was not only immediately acclaimed with the utmost enthusiasm, but has become a classic at the core of the *género chico* zarzuela repertoire: its habanera *¿Dónde vas con mantón de Manila?* is familiar from birth to every single Spaniard. The plot, slight as it is but skilfully developed, concerns the young typesetter Julián's jealousy when he sees his beloved, Susana, and her sister taken by the randy old chemist Don Hilarión to the fair on the eve of the festival of Our Lady of the Dove (August 14th).

   Like the earlier recording under Moreno Torroba on Hispavox, this version omits the dialogue connecting the musical numbers (but includes the watchman's scene, mostly spoken over strings), and there is an attempt to create a theatrical atmosphere by crowd noises and the like. The orchestral playing and the choral singing (particularly in the famous *seguidillas*) show a polish and sensitivity that are unfortunately far from usual in zarzuela performances; and to capture the authentic scenic setting the producer has reverted to the original score and presented the *soleá* with piano and the *mazurka* on piano and violin, as would have been the practice in the cafés. Domingo is in excellent voice in his only solo; María Bayo has little to do except in the quintet (an unusual feature in such pieces); the biggest part, that of Don Hilarión, is as usual taken by a character actor who sings after a fashion. It is all very engaging and cheery. (By the way, when Auvidis's hapless translator more than once writes, in idiosyncratic English, of a "cut for voice and piano", she actually means a vocal score.)

Benjamin Britten (Lord Britten of Aldeburgh)   British 1913-1976

Britten Albert Herring.
   Sir Peter Pears *ten* Albert Herring
   Sylvia Fisher *sop* Lady Billows
   Johanna Peters *contr* Florence Pike
   April Cantelo *sop* Miss Wordsworth
   John Noble *bar* Mr Gedge
   Edgar Evans *ten* Mr Upfold
   Owen Brannigan *bass* Mr Budd
   Joseph Ward *ten* Sid
   Catherine Wilson *mez* Nancy
   Sheila Rex *mez* Mrs Herring
   Sheila Amit *sop* Emmie
   Anne Pashley *sop* Cis
   Stephen Terry *treb* Harry
   English Chamber Orchestra / Benjamin Britten.
   Decca London Ⓕ ① 421 849-2LH2 (two discs: 138 minutes: ADD). Notes and text included. Recorded 1964.

Britten Albert Herring.

Christopher Gillett *ten* Albert Herring
Dame Josephine Barstow *sop* Lady Billows
Felicity Palmer *mez* Florence Pike
Susan Gritton *sop* Miss Wordsworth
Peter Savidge *bar* Mr Gedge
Stuart Kale *ten* Mr Upford
Robert Lloyd *bass* Mr Budd
Gerald Finley *bar* Sid
Ann Taylor *mez* Nancy
Della Jones *mez* Mrs Herring
Yvette Bonner *sop* Emmie
Témimé Bowling *sop* Cis
Matthew Long *treb* Harry
Northern Sinfonia / Steuart Bedford.
Collins Classics Ⓔ Ⓘ 7042-2 (two discs: 142 minutes: DDD). Text included. Recorded 1996.

Having shown us the grim and nasty side of Aldeburgh life at the beginning of the nineteenth century in *Peter Grimes*, Britten had fun with its parochial aspects at the end of the century in his comic opera *Albert Herring*. For some tastes, it has proved too parochial, almost cosy. This tale of the mother-dominated shop assistant who is elected May King because of his virtue, is slipped a laced drink at his crowning and goes off for a night on the tiles, after which he asserts himself, repels some who otherwise admire the composer, because of its self-regarding whimsicality. The possible cure for these people is to listen to Britten's own recording, here marvellously transferred to CD and showing once again what a genius John Culshaw was at making records of opera. Britten finds all the humour in the piece, but he gives it a cutting-edge and he is totally successful in conveying the proximity of comedy to tragedy in the remarkable ensemble where Albert is thought to have been killed.

As in all his recordings, Britten is a hard act to follow. Yet when his version of *Albert Herring* appeared in 1964 (17 years after the première; no chance of reassembling the original cast) there were plenty who found Sylvia Fisher's classic portrayal of Lady Billows not really up to their memories of Joan Cross, nor April Cantelo as deliciously funny a Miss Wordsworth as her creator, Margaret Ritchie, or her peerless successor Jennifer Vyvyan. Cantelo's is an enchanting portrayal, and those who have grown up with it may find Susan Gritton (Collins) not *quite* her equal ... and so on. Its superbly varied and resourceful recitative and its innumerable, pungent, thumbnail-sketch 'arias' provide resourceful singer-actors with the juiciest chances imaginable to become totally memorable.

Gritton seizes those chances with both hands, sounding at times uncannily like Vyvyan and bringing so much of Joyce Grenfell to the role that you expect her at any moment to tell Emmie, Cis and Harry about all the acceptable gifts one can make from nut-husk clusters. Felicity Palmer is a splendid Florence, relishing gossip, moral outrage and her authority as Lady Billows's ADC. Of course Christopher Gillett cannot erase memories of Peter Pears in the title-role; who could? But there is more sense of a worm turning in his performance, less of a feeling that no one so irredeemably daft and downtrodden could possibly escape from Mum's apron-strings. Ann Taylor and Gerald Finley are admirable, believable both as lovers and as baker's girl and butcher's boy respectively. The village worthies are all sharply done, with Robert Lloyd especially good as an irascible Superintendent Budd.

The one reservation on the Collins set concerns Josephine Barstow's Lady Billows. She is formidably authoritative, every inch the *grande dame*, at her best when she loses her notes in mid-speech but improvises with magnificent clichés ("Cleanliness is next to ... God for England and Saint ... Keep your powder dry and leave the rest to nature!") until wild applause allows her to regain her gist. But, at least on the close, clear recording, her voice has a very sharp edge to it, all the more apparent since she almost never sings quietly. Still, she has the power to disconcert you, and one of the great pleasures of this set is its demonstration of how much of the earlier Britten is recalled in it and how much of the later prefigured. It is largely Steuart Bedford's doing (and his instrumentalists: as good as Britten's ensemble) that Nancy's rueful Act 3 aria ("What would Mrs Herring say?") so startlingly recalls Ellen Orford's "Were we mistaken when we planned?" and that Sid's "Churchyard's agog!" is so obviously an ancestor of "The Choirmaster's burial" from the Hardy cycle, *Winter Words*.

Of course the Collins recording cannot supersede Britten's own, but when the next version arrives there will be many who ruefully decide that Miss X cannot measure up to Gritton nor Mr Y to Gillett. There will probably be some who sigh that no other Lady Billows has Barstow's vocal equivalent of an imperious basilisk glare. Bedford's version is worthy of the opera, in short, and as good as its rival at making clear that *Albert Herring* is as central to the Britten canon as any of his operas.

Britten Billy Budd.

Peter Glossop *bar* Billy Budd
Sir Peter Pears *ten* Captain Vere
Michael Langdon *bass* John Claggart
John Shirley-Quirk *bar* Mr Redburn
Bryan Drake *bar* Mr Flint

David Kelly *bass* Mr Ratcliffe
Gregory Dempsey *ten* Red Whiskers
David Bowman *bar* Donald
Owen Brannigan *bass* Dansker
Robert Tear *ten* Novice
Robert Bowman *ten* Squeak
Delme Bryn-Jones *bar* Bosun
Eric Garrett *bar* First Mate
Nigel Rogers *ten* Maintop
Benjamin Luxon *bar* Novice's Friend
Geoffrey Coleby *bar* Arthur Jones
Wandsworth School Boys' Choir; Ambrosian Opera Chorus;
London Symphony Orchestra / Benjamin Britten.

Britten The Holy Sonnets of John Donne, Op. 35a. Songs and Proverbs of William Blake, Op. 74b.
aSir Peter Pears *ten*
bDietrich Fischer-Dieskau *bar*
Benjamin Britten *pf*
Decca Ⓟ Ⓞ 417 428-2LH3 (three discs: 205 minutes: ADD). Notes and text included. Recorded 1967.

Many people claim this to be the greatest of Britten's operas, although perhaps *The Turn of the Screw* claims that accolade. *Billy Budd* is remarkable in having been composed for male voices, yet not once is there any lack of colour or variety. Britten marvellously supports the tenor, baritone and bass protagonists with extraordinary flair in the use of brass and woodwind.

This was the last operatic recording John Culshaw produced for Decca and he again showed himself unsurpassed at creating a theatrical atmosphere in the studio. His use of stereo effects and his inspired balancing of voices and orchestra ensure that listeners at home feel that they are not merely observers of but participators in events aboard *Indomitable* in 1797. There have been several striking and brilliant stage productions of this opera, two having been built around Thomas Allen's outstanding performance of the title-role, and the modern Erato recording was long overdue. But having said that, it must also be said that both technically and interpretatively this Britten/Culshaw collaboration represents the touchstone for any that follows it, particularly in the matter of Britten's conducting. Where Britten is superb is in the dramatic tautness with which he unfolds the score and his unobtrusive highlighting of such poignant detail as the use of the saxophone after the flogging. His conducting of the choral scenes, particularly when the crew are heard singing below decks while Captain Vere and his officers are talking in his cabin, is profoundly satisfying and moving. Most of all, he focuses with absolute clarity on the intimate human drama against the background of life aboard the ship.

And what a cast he had, headed by Peter Pears as Vere, conveying a natural authoritarianism which makes his unwilling but dutiful role as "the messenger of death" more understandable, if no more agreeable. Peter Glossop's Billy Budd is a virile performance, with nothing of the 'goody-goody' about him; instead, a rough honesty in keeping with Melville's conception of the character. Nor does one feel any particular homo-eroticism about his relationship with Michael Langdon's black-voiced Claggart: it is a straight conflict between good and evil, and all the more horrifying for its stark simplicity. Add to these principals John Shirley-Quirk, Bryan Drake and David Kelly as the officers, Owen Brannigan as Dansker and Robert Tear and Benjamin Luxon in the small roles of the novice and his friend, and one can apply the adjective 'classic' to this recording, with a clear conscience.

Also on the discs are two of Britten's most sombre song-cycles, the *Donne Sonnets* and the *Blake Songs and Proverbs*, the former with Pears, the latter with Fischer-Dieskau, and both incomparably accompanied by Britten. One can understand why neither has achieved the popularity of the *Serenade* and the Hardy settings – not because the music is in any way inferior, but because the dark mood is unrelieved. They make ideal complements to *Billy Budd*. This is a vintage set.

Britten Billy Budd (four-act version).
Thomas Hampson *bar* Billy Budd
Anthony Rolfe Johnson *ten* Captain Vere
Eric Halfvarson *bass-bar* John Claggart
Russell Smythe *bar* Mr Redburn
Gidon Saks *bass* Mr Flint
Simon Wilding *bass* Mr Ratcliffe
Martyn Hill *ten* Red Whiskers
Christopher Maltman *bar* Donald
Richard Van Allan *bass* Dansker
Andrew Burden *ten* Novice
Christopher Gillett *ten* Squeak

Matthew Hargreaves *bass* Bosun
Ashley Holland *bass* First Mate
Simon Thorpe *bar* Second Mate, Arthur Jones
Robert Johnston *ten* Maintop
William Dazeley *bar* Novice's Friend
Manchester Boys' Choir; Northern Voices; Hallé Choir and Orchestra / Kent Nagano.
Erato Ⓟ Ⓒ 3984-21631-2 (two discs: 148 minutes: DDD). Notes and text included. Recorded at performances in Bridgewater Hall, Manchester during May 1997.

This is an exciting achievement. Based on concert performances given in Manchester in 1997, it restores to circulation the original, four-act version of the score (coincidentally set exactly 200 years earlier in the troubled summer of 1797). The main and crucial difference between this and Britten's two-act revision is a scene at the close of what is here Act 1, in which 'Starry' Vere addresses his crew and is hailed by them as the sailors' and particularly Billy's champion, thus establishing the relationship between captain and foretopman (something, by the way, that doesn't exist in Melville's novel). It is thus an important scene though musically not particularly distinguished. One can quite see why Britten wanted a tauter two-act drama. There are also minor restorations in the scenes between Vere and Claggart before and after the aborted attempt to engage the French in battle.

In Manchester's Bridgewater Hall, where the recording was made (though, to judge by the absence of background noise, there must have been sessions without an audience), the orchestral contribution was apparently heard with exceptional clarity. That has been carried over into what is an amazingly wide spectrum of sound on the recording: indeed sometimes the orchestra is simply too loud. Nagano's Hallé is now very much his own orchestra, fashioned to suit his ideas, and he gives us a wonderfully full-bodied, accurate and detailed account of the many-faceted score. There are electrifying moments, not least the battle scene, where the listener feels very much in the middle of things, and the end of Act 3 where those tremendous and ominous series of chords represent Vere telling Budd of the sentence of death. Britten, in his studio recording, prefers a leaner sound and a slightly tauter approach all-round – in his hands you feel the tension of the personal relationships even more sharply than with Nagano.

Britten, of course, is conducting his preferred, revised edition. In 1993, however, there came to light an off-the-air recording of the première production, issued by VAI, using the 1951 original and, fascinatingly, made on a tape recorder by the wife of Theodor Uppman, the original Billy. It is a riveting document in very tolerable sound, though a few bars are missing where tapes were changed. The young Britten in the theatre gives even greater tension to his interpretation though inevitably the orchestral sound leaves much to be desired. This recording is more revelatory in letting us make comparisons with the first cast and that of the new set. A close comparison favours Uppman's Budd over Hampson's, or Glossop's on Decca, or even Thomas Allen's on the arresting PolyGram video of Tim Albery's ENO staging. Uppman catches better than any the sheer, simple, unsophisticated, natural goodness of the man, a smile in his tone, a lightness in his heart. Hampson, like Uppman an American baritone, is, by any other standard, very good, singing with all his customary beauty of voice and intelligence of style, but he isn't so evidently 'in' the role as are Uppman and Allen, imparting a touch of self-consciousness that goes against the grain of the writing. For instance, Hampson makes too much of Billy of the Darbies, singing it as a set piece; Uppman sings it to himself as a folk-song in a reflective, plangent tone, which is exactly as it should be.

Halfvarson, as Budd's antagonist, the evil Claggart – how unerringly Britten depicts his malevolent nature! – gives us a mighty presence, singing with tremendous power and bite, but by the same token he gives us almost too much, and not always steady, tone. His slightly generalized projection of nastiness might do as well for Hagen as for the master-at-arms. Michael Langdon in 1967, even more Frederic Dalberg (quite horribly sinister on stage) in 1951, are much more specific, varying tone more subtly, voicing the text more pointedly. Where Vere is concerned, Rolfe Johnson sings his heart out as he presents Vere's tormented soul, but vocally he hasn't the cutting edge and heroic touch of Pears in 1967, even more in 1951 where he was nearer the right age for the part than either his later self or Rolfe Johnson, whose tone these days sounds uncomfortably strained under pressure. Pears's cries of "It's not his trial, it's mine, mine. It is I whom the devil awaits", a quite crucial passage after Budd has struck Claggart dead, is simply soul-searing in 1951. For the rest, Gidon Saks makes a dominant Mr Flint, the sailing-master, but he, like Halfvarson, tends to let voice take over from interpretation in the modern manner. Richard Van Allan (a really implacable Claggart on the video) is here, predictably, a characterful Dansker, and Andrew Burden stands out as a properly scared Novice, far preferable to Tear's placid reading on Decca.

In spite of any reservations about individual interpretations, the sum here is greater than the parts, and this version is heartily recommended; in almost every respect, it is equal to the demands of a technically difficult piece, not least as regards the choirs taking part. The harrowing drama is brought into the home with almost unbearable immediacy. It is also the first recording to contain the opera on two discs. Of course, if you want the two-act version, the Decca is still there as a satisfying record, in every sense, of the composer's revised thoughts (by a small margin, the changes were for the better), and the VAI issue is an invaluable piece of documentation with some superb portrayals to commend it. And the video version, superbly conducted by David Atherton with Langridge as the most tortured Vere of all, is a riveting experience.

Britten Billy Budd.

Thomas Allen *bar* Billy Budd
Philip Langridge *ten* Captain Vere
Richard Van Allan *bass* John Claggart
Neil Howlett *bar* Mr Redburn
Phillip Guy-Bromley *bass* Mr Flint
Clive Bayley *bass* Mr Ratcliffe
Edward Byles *ten* Red Whiskers
Mark Richardson *bass* Donald
John Connell *bass* Dansker
Barry Banks *ten* Novice
Howard Milner *ten* Squeak
Malcolm Rivers *bass-bar* Bosun
Anthony Cunningham *bar* First Mate
Christopher Ross *bass* Second Mate
Richard Reaville *ten* Maintop, Arthur Jones
Christopher Booth-Jones *bar* Novice's Friend
English National Opera Chorus and Orchestra / David Atherton.
Stage Director: **Tim Albery.** *Video Director:* **Barry Gavin.**
Polygram RM Collection Ⓟ 🎦 079 221-3 (157 minutes). Recorded 1988.

Tim Albery's staging for ENO is non-representational, emphasizing the darkest side of the work through a dour, harsh setting on a tilted stage with little feeling of sea or ship. It derives its inspiration from modern practice on German stages. Sharp spotlights concentrate the eye on key actions. Only in the scene when the crew prepares for battle are colour and movement employed, appropriately so as this is the one moment when the crew and its masters are united in a cause, hatred of the French. The ENO forces give the work such a convincing interpretation that the production's sometimes perverse ideas proves their own justification. Albery directs with a strong eye for essentials, most of all in depicting the still, baleful presence of Claggart as a man who uses his hold over men to force them into betrayals and worse. When he finds the handsomeness of Budd too much for his repressed homosexuality he sets out to destroy him with single-minded purpose as portrayed in masterly fashion by Richard Van Allan.

Captain Vere is, first and last, shown as a shambling, Forster-like figure, in the action more conventionally. Langridge acts and sings to perfection, another of this versatile tenor's perceptive and involving performances. Allen, singing Billy for the last time, may look a shade mature for the part but conveys ideally the straightforward, forthright nature of the youth, the very soul of fidelity and truth and thus horribly and fatally shocked by Claggart's false witness. His final solos are given with deep pathos. All the subsidiary roles are sung with conviction. The chorus, superbly directed, sing magnificently. The piece has had no better interpreter than Atherton, who paces it unerringly, finds just the right weight and balance, and revels in the consistent inspiration of the writing. Barrie Gavin directs the video sympathetically but is sometimes defeated by the dark surroundings.

Britten The Burning Fiery Furnace.

Sir Peter Pears *ten* Nebuchadnezzar
Bryan Drake *bar* Astrologer
John Shirley-Quirk *bar* Shadrach (Ananias)
Robert Tear *ten* Meshach (Misael)
Stafford Dean *bass* Abednego (Azarias)
Peter Leeming *bass* Herald
English Opera Group / Benjamin Britten.
Decca London Ⓜ ① 414 663-2LM (64 minutes: ADD). Text included. Recorded 1967.

If *Curlew River* is the best and most moving of Britten's three church parables, *The Burning Fiery Furnace* is the most colourful and exotic. It also has humour; and Nebuchadnezzar gave Pears a role which ideally suited him vocally and histrionically. The remarkable East-West orchestration which Britten adopted for the parables, with its mixture of gamelan and chamber ensemble, and the mesmerizing soloistic use of viola, double-bass, alto trombone, flute and harp are at their peak in the *Furnace*. It is curious, too, now that the idiom is familiar, how one notices that while it points forward to *Death in Venice*, the echoes of earlier works strike us today more forcefully – Puck from *A Midsummer Night's Dream* in the Acolytes' music, for example, and reminiscences of Claggart and Vere in *Billy Budd* when Nebuchadnezzar grows irritable with the Astrologer. This John Culshaw recording was made in Orford Church, the birthplace and inspiration of the parables. It conveys with the utmost fidelity the extraordinary atmosphere that a Britten performance created in this milieu, with the cast carefully chosen and rehearsed. Hopefully, another recording will be made one day, but this one will remain definitive and, in a very real sense, irreplaceable. Performances like those of Bryan Drake and John Shirley-Quirk encapsulate the Aldeburgh style of the 1960s.

Britten Curlew River.

Sir Peter Pears *ten* Madwoman
John Shirley-Quirk *bar* Ferryman
Harold Blackburn *bass* Abbot
Bryan Drake *bar* Traveller
Bruce Webb *treb* Voice of the Spirit
English Opera Group / Benjamin Britten, Viola Tunnard.
Decca London Ⓜ ① 421 858 2LM (69 minutes: ADD). Text included. Recorded 1965.

Here's another historic Britten recording successfully transferred to CD. *Curlew River* captured completely the composer's fascination with the Japanese Noh play on which it was based. It was an inspired idea to locate the action in East Anglia, so one has the clash and intermingling of East and West with an immediacy that reflects the keenness of Britten's response to both. The recording was also produced by John Culshaw in Orford Church (is there an aircraft overhead near the start?). The atmosphere of this unforgettable occasion is preserved. The procession of monks at the beginning and end comes towards us and recedes, just as if we were sitting in a pew. Peter Pears's performance as the Madwoman is one of his finest and most touching, while John Shirley-Quirk and Bryan Drake are equally authoritative as the Ferryman and Traveller. The voice of the Madwoman's dead son is devoid of the sentimentality that might have been a peril if any treble other than Bruce Webb had sung it, and the inventive and beguiling orchestral score is marvellously played by such names as Cecil Aronowitz, Richard Adeney and James Blades. With the composer and Viola Tunnard directing the performance, it is in a class of its own.

Britten Death in Venice.

Sir Peter Pears *ten* Gustav von Aschenbach
John Shirley-Quirk *bar* Traveller, Elderly Fop, Old Gondolier, Hotel Manager, Hotel Barber,
    Leader of the Players, Voice of Dionysus
James Bowman *alto* Voice of Apollo
Kenneth Bowen *ten* Hotel Porter
Peter Leeming *bass* Travel Clerk
Neville Williams *bass-bar* Strolling Player
Penelope MacKay *sop* Strolling Player
Iris Saunders *sop* Strawberry-seller
English Opera Group Chorus; English Chamber Orchestra / Steuart Bedford.
Decca London Ⓟ ① 425 669-2LH2 (two discs: 145 minutes: ADD). Notes and text included.
Recorded 1973.

Without exception, Decca have transferred to CD all their recordings of Britten's stage works, most of them conducted by the composer with hand-picked casts. All were superb recordings in the first place and CD has given them extra clarity. As Sir Colin Davis (among others) has shown on Philips with two examples (*Peter Grimes* and *The Turn of the Screw*), there is room for alternative interpretations of these remarkable works, but the first recordings will remain as documentary/historical evidence of the highest importance and value. Christopher Palmer also has pertinent things to say about the sexual climate of Britten's last opera, *Death in Venice*; but again these seem to become of less consequence as one listens to the music. Its potency and inventiveness create this opera's disturbing and intense atmosphere, each episode heightened dramatically by instrumental colouring. Steuart Bedford's conducting avoids any tendency towards the episodic as a result of the quick succession of scenes: under his direction each scene is fully integrated into a fluent and convincing whole. This recording was made while Britten was very ill and, as Donald Mitchell has related in an essay in the Cambridge University Press handbook on the opera, it omits Aschenbach's first recitative ("I have always kept a close watch over my development as a writer ... "), given as an optional cut in the vocal score, which was published *after* the recording was made, by which time Britten had changed his mind about this cut and wished it had been included in the recording. Pears's Aschenbach, a very English conception, is a masterly performance, matched by Shirley-Quirk's assumption of the six characters who are Aschenbach's messengers of death and the Voice of Dionysus.

Britten Gloriana.

Josephine Barstow *sop* Queen Elizabeth I
Philip Langridge *ten* Earl of Essex
Della Jones *mez* Lady Essex
Jonathan Summers *bar* Lord Mountjoy
Alan Opie *bar* Sir Robert Cecil
Yvonne Kenny *sop* Penelope
Richard Van Allan *bass* Sir Walter Raleigh
Bryn Terfel *bass-bar* Henry Cuffe

1994

Janice Watson *sop* Lady-in-waiting
Willard White *bass* Blind ballad-singer
John Shirley-Quirk *bar* Recorder of Norwich
John Mark Ainsley *ten* Spirit of the Masque
Peter Hoare *ten* Master of Ceremonies
Welsh National Opera Chorus and Orchestra / Sir Charles Mackerras.
Argo Ⓟ Ⓒ 440 213-2ZHO2 (two discs: 148 minutes: DDD). Notes and text included. Recorded
1992.

It is 45 years since the ill-fated première of Britten's Coronation opera. In his introductory essay to
this set, Donald Mitchell vividly recalls the furore it caused. Instead of the staid pageant expected by
the bejewelled and stiff audience assembled for a royal gala they were given an intimate study of the
ageing Queen's torment as she copes with the conflict of private emotions in the midst of public
pomp, both unerringly depicted in the score. Recognition of the work's importance in the Britten
oeuvre only came about when it was given by Sadler's Wells Opera in 1966 in Colin Graham's
sympathetic production, which survived in the repertory well into the 1980s and was video-recorded
in 1984 by Virgin Classics (not currently in the catalogue). By then Sarah Walker had succeeded to
the role of Elizabeth, and Rolfe Johnson was the Essex. Unforgotten in the title-role are Sylvia Fisher,
in 1966, followed by Ava June, who sang the part when the company visited Vienna with the work in
1975. Hopes of a complete recording back in the 1970s with Dame Janet Baker were never fulfilled
and we had to wait until 1992 for the full panoply of this recording by Argo.

Sir Charles Mackerras had long been an admirer of the piece, conducting the revival that went to
Vienna. He presents it here with the utmost conviction, drawing together the motivic strands of the
score into a unified, coherent whole (not an altogether easy task), appreciating the contrast of the
public and private scenes, exposing the raw sinews of the writing for the two principal characters, and
drawing superb playing from his own WNO Orchestra – although it must be said that the chorus
aren't always as confident in execution as one might wish and at the start of the opera, observing the
duel, they are too backwardly recorded. Above all, Mackerras is obviously convinced of the work's
stature and – as a longtime interpreter of the composer's music – places it, as it were, in the context
of his whole output. How delicately he etches in the exquisite detail of the riverside, Act 2 scene 2,
underpinning the illicit love of Penelope Rich and Mountjoy, how unerringly he realizes the two
central encounters between the Queen and Essex, what Mitchell in *The Britten Companion* (Faber:
1984) describes as "a brilliant study of the ambiguities that can surround a grand passion".

Josephine Barstow crowns her career with her Gloriana. Sounding uncannily similar to Sylvia
Fisher in the part, she follows that underrated but unforgotten soprano in commanding the opera by
her vocal presence, her imposing, vibrant tone, her vital treatment of the text, and her attention to
detail. She conveys the Queen's dilemma in the superb solo at the end of Act 1, her petulance, in the
dancing scene where she changes dresses with Lady Essex (to the latter's embarrassment), and, in the
later of the two scenes with Essex, her sadness at passing time – "But the years pursue us ...". Just
before that Barstow – and Britten, of course – reveal the monarch's vulnerability when Essex bursts
in on her and catches her "unadorned". And here is an appropriate point to praise William Plomer's
poetic libretto, one of the best Britten set as he implicitly acknowledges in contemporary correspondence. In the theatre, too, much of it is lost; here we can enjoy its strong and original flavour.

Philip Langridge projects all the vehement impetuosity of Essex but also, in the famous lute songs,
the poetic ardour of the handsome if unruly Earl. Like his Queen, he is adept at making the most of
the words, but he can't quite match the mellifluousness called for here and heard in the performances
of Pears (on a Covent Garden tape) and Rolfe Johnson. As with all Langridge's many portrayals of
the Pears roles, he sets his own parameters and convinces the listener of the validity of his reading.
There is much discerning interpretation elsewhere and, as ever, Britten provides brief vignettes in
which character is revealed. Della Jones is, as expected, a vivid Lady Essex, Yvonne Kenny a proud
Penelope Rich, Jonathan Summers a forthright Mountjoy. Even better are the wily Cecil of Alan Opie
and the subtle Raleigh of Richard Van Allan, and what a sensitive touch to have cast John Shirley-
Quirk, always a Britten singer *par excellence*, as the Recorder of Norwich. If worn tone sometimes
reveals that some of these singers are no longer in their prime, we are consoled by their understanding
of their parts. Bryn Terfel's rotund tones are rather wasted on Henry Cuffe. John Mark Ainsley makes
a sweet-voiced Spirit of the Masque and Willard White is cleverly cast as the Ballad-singer.

By and large, the recording is worthy of the performance, but you may occasionally be troubled by
an unnaturally overemphatic bass, and the spoken passages near the end don't quite come off. These
small reservations are as nothing before the triumph of the achievement as a whole, with particular
praise due to Barstow and Mackerras.

Britten The Little Sweep.
David Hemmings *treb* Sam
Jennifer Vyvyan *sop* Rowan
Nancy Evans *contr* Miss Baggott
April Cantelo *sop* Juliet Brook
Trevor Anthony *bass* Black Bob, Tom

Sir Peter Pears *ten* Clem, Alford
Michael Ingram *treb* Gay Brook
Marilyn Baker *sop* Sophie Brook
Robin Fairhurst *treb* John Crome
Lyn Vaughan *treb* Hugh Crome
Gabrielle Soskin *sop* Tina Crome
Alleyn's School Choir; English Opera Group Orchestra / Benjamin Britten.

Britten Gemini Variations, Op. 73.

Gabriel Jeney *vn/pf*
Zoltán Jeney *fl/pf*

Britten Children's Crusade, Op. 82.

Mark Emney *treb* Leader
John Wojciechowski *treb* Little Jew, Second Lover
Daymond Hares, Stephen Daniels *trebs* Two Brothers
Adrian Thompson *treb* Boy from Nazi legation
Colin Morris *treb* Drummer-boy
Graham Preston *treb* Dog
Barnaby Jago *treb* First Lover
Wandsworth School Boys' Choir; chamber ensemble / Russell Burgess, Benjamin Britten.
Decca London mono/stereo Ⓜ ① 436 393-2LM (78 minutes: ADD). Texts included. *The Little Sweep* recorded 1955, *Gemini Variations* and *Children's Crusade* recorded 1966.

Britten wrote much music for children, yet one must not imagine that they are cosy and (in the pejorative sense) childish. Many of Britten's friends thought that there remained much of the child in him, and this clearly comes out in the boisterous high spirits of some of his music. By and large, the (purely instrumental) *Gemini Variations* is a happy work. Yet even here there are troubled elements. For all its nursery jollity, *The Little Sweep* portrays the ill-treatment of the pre-pubertal sweep boy Sam and one notices the comment of the good-hearted nursemaid Rowan, "Cruel men will soil and blacken / Childish heart and childish mind!". Sammy is saved (principally by children, be it noted), but the children in *Children's Crusade* die in a wild winter of wartime Poland. In this shattering work by a lifelong pacifist, the children's search for peace is the central theme.

The Little Sweep gets a vivid performance in this, its first recording. It hasn't worn as well as other Britten works, partly because the libretto is middle class and the language twee, as when the children sing of Sammy "Poor young boy! He's just a baby! / Weak with toil and wan with strain". Yet one can forget that when listening to music that mostly remains delightfully fresh, and even join in the audience songs if one has a mind. The *Gemini Variations*, written for two Hungarian boys whose charming request won Britten over, and using flute and violin as well as piano duet, is less striking. None the less, these works still make invigorating listening. The boys of the Wandsworth School Boys' Choir and their conductor Russell Burgess (with Britten as second conductor) also perform *Children's Crusade*. Britten himself was known to have said how powerful he thought this latter performance was and that he had had difficulty in notating the piece because of its rhythmic freedom.

Britten A Midsummer Night's Dream.

Brian Asawa *alto* Oberon
Sylvia McNair *sop* Tytania
John Mark Ainsley *ten* Lysander
Paul Whelan *bar* Demetrius
Ruby Philogene *mez* Hermia
Janice Watson *sop* Helena
Brian Bannatyne-Scott *bass* Theseus
Hilary Summers *contr* Hippolyta
Robert Lloyd *bass* Bottom
Gwynne Howell *bass* Quince
Ian Bostridge *ten* Flute
Stephen Richardson *bar* Snug
Mark Tucker *ten* Snout
Neal Davies *bar* Starveling
David Newman *treb* Cobweb
Claudia Conway *sop* Peaseblossom
Sara Rey *sop* Mustardseed
Matthew Long *treb* Moth
Carl Ferguson *spkr* Puck
New London Children's Choir; London Symphony Orchestra / Sir Colin Davis.
Philips Ⓟ ① 454 122-2PH2 (two discs: 148 minutes: DDD). Notes and text included. Recorded 1995.

To coin a phrase: new version, new perceptions. It is strange how listening in quick succession to the same passage can arrestingly highlight differences of approach. The Philips set is in almost every respect immediate and present, almost to a fault. As compared with the 1990 Virgin Classics set for Hickox, the voices are advantageously forward, yet there are few if any attempts at suggesting the perspectives you hear on the Virgin recording, even more on the 32-year-old Decca for the composer, so evocatively directed by John Culshaw. For instance, on Decca, Puck seems to be everywhere, on Virgin he tends to stay in one place. On this version you are in the front stalls listening to an enjoyable concert – this recording was made in conjunction with a performance at London's Barbican Hall – with little attempt to simulate a stage.

That may have in some way influenced the often leisurely pacing of Davis's reading. Everything is heard with great clarity, the sensuousness of Britten's ravishing score, with all its mysterious harmonies and sonorities, is fully realized, action and reaction among the singers are keenly heard, yet something of the midsummer magic so naturally conjured up under Britten's direction eludes Davis and his team. On Decca we hear this music fresh-minted, unadorned; in Davis's hands the work is viewed through a tougher, more modern prism, something that those who know the original set will need to become accustomed to.

One wonders if any members of the LSO today were in the orchestra under the composer back in 1966: they are certainly as acute if not more so in their playing than their predecessors. As for pacing, if you try either Oberon's "I know a bank" or Tytania's solo "Come, now a roundel and a fairy song" you will immediately hear how much tauter is Britten's approach, Davis allowing his singers more licence. In the case of McNair this gives her space to develop what is a knowingly sophisticated approach to her role, even more evident in her sensual account of the Act 2 solo "Hail, mortal, hail". Her singing is in itself lovely, portamento used to suggest sensuality, but it is an earthly reading where Elizabeth Harwood for Britten suggests a more other-worldly Queen of the Fairies. Similarly the luscious, vibrant voice of the American countertenor Brian Asawa is very different from Bowman's more acerbic tone (Hickox), or Deller's ethereal delicacies (Britten). Like McNair's singing, Asawa's, taken on its own terms, is most seductive, certainly a new look at the familiar, but disconcerting at first hearing. Puck is also upfront, not so much puckish as rough-hewn.

With Bottom we meet another thought-provoking interpretation. Lloyd makes the weaver sound more high-born than his predecessors. This is almost a noble craftsman, with no hint of the rustic portrayed by Donald Maxwell (Hickox), or – unforgettably – by Owen Brannigan, the role's creator (Britten), who savours the text so lovingly. Lloyd scores with his splendidly resonant account of "O grin-look'd night" in the play. One thing is sure: there has never been a more amusing Flute than Ian Bostridge (hilarious as Thisbe) or a better sung Quince than Gwynne Howell. Another plus for the Philips set is the casting of the lovers with young singers in their early prime, a great advance on the Hickox set, a smaller one on the Britten. In particular, Philogene's ripe mezzo as Hermia and Ainsley's ardent tenor as Lysander stand out as ideal interpretations. The Quarrel and Reconciliation Quartets are done with total conviction on all sides. Neither Hippolyta nor Theseus matches the regal authority of Helen Watts and Shirley-Quirk on the composer's set.

You will derive a great deal of pleasure from this set with its exemplary recording, in terms of forward, full-toned sound, and careful preparation on all sides. It is the prime recommendation for a modern set. But the Decca, one of the most successful opera recordings of all time, remains as fresh and inspired as the day it was made; Britten's taut, disciplined yet magical reading is a must.

Britten A Midsummer Night's Dream.

Alfred Deller *alto* Oberon
Elizabeth Harwood *sop* Tytania
Sir Peter Pears *ten* Lysander
Thomas Hemsley *bar* Demetrius
Josephine Veasey *mez* Hermia
Heather Harper *sop* Helena
John Shirley-Quirk *bar* Theseus
Helen Watts *contr* Hippolyta
Owen Brannigan *bass* Bottom
Norman Lumsden *bass* Quince
Kenneth MacDonald *ten* Flute
David Kelly *bass* Snug
Robert Tear *ten* Snout
Keith Raggett *ten* Starveling
Richard Dakin *treb* Cobweb
John Prior *treb* Peaseblossom
Ian Wodehouse *treb* Mustardseed
Gordon Clark *treb* Moth
Stephen Terry *spkr* Puck
Choirs of Downside and Emanuel Schools; London Symphony Orchestra / Benjamin Britten.
Decca London Ⓟ Ⓓ 425 663-2LH2 (two discs: 144 minutes: ADD). Notes and text included. Recorded 1966.

As a successful operatic version of Shakespeare *A Midsummer Night's Dream* ranks with Verdi. Britten's own performance, recorded in 1966, is sheer delight. His conducting, more than anyone else's conveys the sinister strata in the score which underlie the comic and fantastic. Alfred Deller's unmatched Oberon, Owen Brannigan's Bottom, Thomas Hemsley's Demetrius, Norman Lumsden's Quince and David Kelly's Snug are the only survivors on record from the 1960 first performances. Sir Peter Pears sang Flute then but moved to Lysander on record, a pity, for his comic impersonations were at once subtle and funny. Elizabeth Harwood's Tytania is a lovely performance, both warm and unearthly. The transfer to CD is triumphant.

Britten A Midsummer Night's Dream.

James Bowman *alto* Oberon
Ileana Cotrubas *sop* Tytania
Ryland Davies *ten* Lysander
Dale Duesing *bar* Demetrius
Cynthia Buchan *mez* Hermia
Dame Felicity Lott *sop* Helena
Lieuwe Visser *bass* Theseus
Claire Powell *mez* Hippolyta
Curt Appelgren *bass* Bottom
Roger Bryson *bar* Quince
Patrick Power *ten* Flute
Andrew Gallacher *bass* Snug
Adrian Thompson *ten* Snout
Donald Bell *bar* Starveling
Martin Warr *treb* Cobweb
Stephen Jones *treb* Peaseblossom
Jonathan Whiting *treb* Mustardseed
Stuart King *treb* Moth
Damien Nash *spkr* Puck
Glyndebourne Festival Chorus; London Philharmonic Orchestra / Bernard Haitink.
Stage Director: **Sir Peter Hall.**
NVC Arts ⊙⊙ 0630-16911-3 (160 minutes). Recorded at a performance at Glyndebourne Festival Opera on August 24th, 1981.

This is not only a fine video interpretation of Sir Peter Hall's brilliant Glyndebourne staging, but a striking performance musically – interestingly, due in large part to a Dutch conductor and two non-English stars. Hall and designer Bury's masterstroke is to take the opera's nightbound woodland setting, so often relegated to cardboardy backdrop or decorative abstraction, and bring it into the action as a living participant. The trees and bushes are literally alive, foliage-bedecked, vaguely human shapes moving almost imperceptibly among mist and shadow to Britten's eerily sonorous scales, changing the scene constantly as the mortal and immortal worlds collide among and around them, heightening both the aura of enchantment and the sense of mounting confusion and frustration. As daylight dawns, with dazzling effect, they revert to solid trunk and branch. The original's moonlit magic suffers a little under the harsher lighting then required by cameras, but TV director Dave Heather recaptures it pretty well, although the electronic enhancements during the interludes look rather dated now.

Among these sentient tangles stalks the fairy court, conceived (rather as in Hall's legendary RSC production of the play) as fantastical Elizabethan grandees in rich black and silver court costumes, with upswept hair and pointed ears to make Mr Spock green(er) with envy. James Bowman, in secure and reasonably fresh voice, is a haughtily moustachio'd, coldly regal Oberon, towering over the sexy spitfire Tytania of Ileana Cotrubas. Her excellent acting, despite some slight pitch problems, lends the role an unusual intensity; she articulates English with the clarity of someone who has taken the trouble to learn it properly, and the faint exotic tang remaining sounds no more than appropriate. Equally unconventional is Damian Nash's Puck, utterly and mercifully uncute, a carrot-headed, snake-eyed, pasty-faced imp, soaring in and out on an airborne branch. The child fairies sing rather well, and manage not to be too embarrassing.

The mortals, nobles and Mechanicals alike, are much drabber and Jacobean in appearance, but not so vocally or dramatically. The lovers are very strongly cast – Ryland Davies and Cynthia Buchan against Dale Duesing and Felicity Lott, no less. Beautifully as they sing, though, they don't generate many sparks. Contemporary strictures about Britten's 'stiff' love music have largely been demolished, not least by Hall's *Albert Herring,* but Buchan and Duesing don't seem to have heard. Duesing in particular misses Demetrius's Jack-the-lad arrogance, and its comic possibilities (well caught by Paul Whelan on stage and in the Davis recording). The unflattering costuming doesn't help, and on camera, of course, they don't look quite young enough. Lott is a delight, though, and when she and Buchan suddenly revert to schoolgirls respectively soppy and snappy, the comedy comes alive. The Mechanicals are better yet. Curt Appelgren is a rich-voiced Bottom, genial rather than bumptious, and catching the trace of true dreamer beneath the clownish surface. His English sounds still more idiomatic than Cotrubas, even through his ass's head – is there even a hint of a Sussex accent? His fellow Mechanicals are no less well sung and meatily characterized, notably Roger Bryson's pompous Quince. Patrick Power isn't as subtle a Flute as some, but his Italianate voice suits the *bel canto* parody very well, and the play is hilarious – thanks not least to Haitink's light touch.

His conducting is a major asset throughout. With his penchant for clear textures, and the LPO on fine form, he captures the score's translucent colours and timeless atmosphere beautifully, without making them overly lush and wallowing, as some conductors tend to; there is a pleasingly sinewy, slightly astringent strength about this reading, recalling Britten's own. The picture quality and stereo sound were excellent on the original release and the quality remains very acceptable, even through a hi-fi system.

Britten Noye's Fludde.
  Owen Brannigan *bass* Noye
  Sheila Rex *mez* Mrs Noye
  David Pinto *treb* Sem
  Darien Angadi *treb* Ham
  Stephen Alexander *treb* Jaffett
  Trevor Anthony *spkr* The Voice of God
  Caroline Clack *sop* Mrs Sem
  Marie Thérèse Pinto *sop* Mrs Ham
  Eileen O'Donovan *sop* Mrs Jaffett
  Patricia Garrod, Margaret Hawes, Kathleen Petch, Gillian Saunders *sops* Mrs Noye's Gossips
  chorus; English Chamber Orchestra; East Suffolk Children's Orchestra / Norman Del Mar.

Britten The Golden Vanity.
  Mark Emney *treb* Captain
  John Wojciechowski *treb* Bosun
  Barnaby Jago *treb* Cabin-boy
  Adrian Thompson *treb* Captain
  Terry Lovell *treb* Bosun
  Benjamin Britten *pf*
  Wandsworth Boys' Choir / Russell Burgess.
  Decca London Ⓜ ① 436 397-2LM (66 minutes: ADD). Texts included. *Noye's Fludde* recorded at a performance in Orford Parish Church during the 1961 Aldeburgh Festival; *The Golden Vanity* recorded 1969.

This recording of *Noye's Fludde* is entrancing. The sheer exuberant ingenuity of the piece; that multi-layered storm passacaglia, for example, has a superbly cumulative theatrical impact, a conjuring-trick cleverness about the way its disparate elements fit together just so, a powerful emotional charge as the congregation's hymn crowns the structure (and is then equipped with a descant!) and it contrives to find something characterful and rewarding for every child and adult in the ensemble to do. The sense of space and of taking part in a real performance, thrillingly reinforced on CD, that the recording gives (as the animals cross the stage into the ark you crick your neck trying to see whether next door's Jennifer has got her tail on straight), is unforgettable. It is also good to be reminded of what an openheartedly sincere as well as generously open-throated artist Owen Brannigan was, of how hugely the East Suffolk Boys' Brigade, or whoever they were, enjoyed belting out their bugle-calls (and how satisfying to have lots of bugles echoing round the church), of the magnificent space-fillingness of the final hymn, and of what cunning use, throughout the work, Britten made of what he had learned of multiple ostinato technique from the gamelan music of Bali.

The Golden Vanity, a virtuoso party-piece written for the Vienna Boys' Choir, is lesser Britten but what a number of crucial threads from his other works meet in it. Its plot is a sort of prepubertal *Billy Budd* (which it acknowledges by quoting from that opera), or an appendix to *Peter Grimes* (if the surname-less John had not been sold as Grimes's apprentice, what might have become of him?) and it provides the pretext for one of Britten's most concise explorations of his theme of destroyed innocence, as well as a great deal of (vocally very tricky) letting off steam for the singers, and a degree of innocent enjoyment for whoever was in charge of the solitary but hilarious sound effect (a bucket of water). A richly enjoyable coupling. *The Golden Vanity*, a very bright-textured piece, has acquired an extra touch of dazzle on CD, but *Noye's Fludde* has gained nothing but still greater immediacy.

Britten Peter Grimes.
  Sir Peter Pears *ten* Grimes
  Claire Watson *sop* Ellen Orford
  James Pease *bass* Balstrode
  Jean Watson *contr* Auntie
  Raymond Nilsson *ten* Bob Boles

Owen Brannigan *bass* Swallow
Lauris Elms *mez* Mrs Sedley
Geraint Evans *bar* Ned Keene
John Lanigan *ten* Rector
David Kelly *bass* Hobson
Marion Studholme *sop* First Niece
Iris Kells *sop* Second Niece
Chorus and Orchestra of the Royal Opera House, Covent Garden / Benjamin Britten.
Decca Ⓟ Ⓓ 414 577-2DH3 (three discs: 132 minutes: ADD). Recorded 1958.

1986

The curtain rose for the first time on *Peter Grimes* in 1945, the first English opera on the grand scale which at once proclaimed itself a masterpiece, and which was soon to enter the repertoire of opera-houses all over the world. It is astonishing how freshly this 40-year-old recording comes up on this remastered transfer. The advance is particularly marked on this occasion because Erik Smith, the producer, attempted to suggest a live, stage performance. Now, the movement involved is much more in evidence than on LP, even to the extent of some score-rustling and floor squeaks being heard. What is more important is to have the composer's unsurpassed account of the score so vividly conveyed. You may hear a greater range of sound on the Sir Colin Davis/Philips recording but it doesn't surpass this issue in sheer theatrical excitement.

Britten is more faithful than Davis to the written note in matters of tempo and articulation, and generally moves with a leaner gait to remind us just what a stroke of genius the whole work is. Maybe Davis plumbs even greater depth of feeling, but often at the cost of forward movement. As for the singers, the Borough's characters as delineated here are delightful, most of all perhaps James Pease's hugely sympathetic Balstrode and Sir Geraint Evans's perky Ned Keene. Claire Watson isn't quite so moving an Ellen as Heather Harper (for Davis), but her reading is finely sung and more than adequate so far as showing sympathy is concerned. It is good to meet again Owen Brannigan's Swallow, as he created the part in 1945. And, of course, Sir Peter Pears was the first Grimes. His interpretation is worlds apart from that of the equally fine but quite different portrayal by Vickers (for Davis), to which we have grown accustomed in recent years on stage. Here is a more poetic, less tortured Peter, but in terms of accurate phrasing and attention to musical detail, there is only one tenor in this role, and he is Pears. You feel willing to sacrifice some of Vickers's involvement and rude vigour for Pears's subtler approach, which is also easier to live with in the home.

Returning to the transfer, the natural balance achieved here between voice and orchestra should be emphasized, the fact that each of the three CDs holds a single act – and mention should also be made of the perceptive booklet-essay, by Philip Brett, especially strong on the genesis of the libretto.

Britten Peter Grimes.
Jon Vickers *ten* Grimes
Heather Harper *sop* Ellen Orford
Jonathan Summers *bar* Balstrode
Elizabeth Bainbridge *mez* Auntie
John Dobson *ten* Bob Boles
Forbes Robinson *bass* Swallow
Patricia Payne *mez* Mrs Sedley
Thomas Allen *bar* Ned Keene
John Lanigan *ten* Rector
Richard Van Allan *bass* Hobson
Teresa Cahill *sop* First Niece
Anne Pashley *sop* Second Niece
Chorus and Orchestra of the Royal Opera House, Covent Garden / Sir Colin Davis.
Philips Ⓜ Ⓓ 432 578-2PM2 (two discs: 146 minutes: ADD). Notes and text included. Recorded 1978.

Jon Vickers as Grimes is one of the most exciting and riveting operatic performances on disc, the occasionally rasping tone suggesting the man's violent and repressed nature far more truthfully than Pears's more restrained and gentlemanly performance on Britten's classic recording. The scorn in Vickers's voice in the Prologue when he sings "Somebody brought the parson" sets the tone for this vivid characterization. Yet he also conveys the visionary side of the 'sadistic fisherman', with a ravishingly beautiful account of the "Great Bear and Pleiades" aria in the pub scene.

But it is not all Vickers. There is also Heather Harper's perceptive and sympathetic vocal portrayal of Ellen Orford, more matronly than Claire Watson on the Decca set and also more dramatic in the Sunday Morning scene when she discovers the apprentice's bruises. Watson's softer conception of the role is, of course, superb in the context of Britten's interpretation, which is generally more romantic than Sir Colin's. From Davis we get a tenser, more neurotic approach to the music, with the Interludes superbly played by the Royal Opera House orchestra. There is little to choose between the performances of the smaller roles. Both Davis and Britten draw sharply etched vignettes from their singers, with Jonathan Summers a splendidly bluff Balstrode on the Philips set. The chorus is in fine voice on both sets. Decca gave Britten a very full and detailed recording; the Philips set is more atmospheric, but some may find the off-stage church service in Act 2 a fraction too distant.

A choice between these two classic recordings must depend on whether one prefers Britten-Pears to Davis-Vickers. There is probably no choice – have both, for both have outstanding merits. Remember, though, the Vickers plays about with the text, sometimes omitting lines altogether. But if you want only one *Peter Grimes*, the fact that the Philips set is on two mid-price discs against Decca's three full-price could tempt you to opt for the former instead of the received wisdom of the incomparable original.

Britten Peter Grimes.

Philip Langridge *ten* Grimes
Janice Cairns *sop* Ellen Orford
Alan Opie *bar* Balstrode
Ann Howard *contr* Auntie
Alan Woodrow *ten* Bob Bowles
Andrew Greenan *bass* Swallow
Susan Gorton *contr* Mrs Sedley
Robert Poulton *bar* Ned Keene
Edward Byles *ten* Rector
Mark Richardson *bar* Hobson
Maria Bovino *sop* First Niece
Sarah Pring *sop* Second Niece
English National Opera Chorus and Orchestra / David Atherton.
Stage Producer: **Tim Albery.** *Video Director:* **Barry Gavin.**
Decca ℗ 🔲 071 428-3DH (144 minutes). Recorded at a performance at the Coliseum, London during 1994.

In this ENO production we move even further from the Suffolk coast than on the NVC Arts Moshinsky version from Covent Garden under Sir Colin Davis, indeed from any sense of the sea. A basically dour, abstract set and timeless costumes lend Albery's staging in Hildegard Bechtler's scenery, dominated by concrete sea-walls and swathes of sailcloth, an expressionist, almost Brechtian atmosphere, with the Nieces' bright boots and blouses the only touch of colour on stage. All the fishy props are highly stylized. Within this forbidding, arresting décor, the characters are no longer recognizable as English eccentrics, however prejudiced, but louring figures of a universal bigotry out to destroy Grimes as an outsider, an outcast. That makes the message of the work even more frightening in its implications and, like Tim Albery's *Budd*, at times almost too terrible to watch.

But human feelings are there aplenty in the central roles. As directed by Albery, Langridge presents at once a pitiful and paradoxically heroic figure, searing in anger as in madness and in-between catching the poetry of his two great monologues. He admirably conveys, from the start, a violent man on the edge of madness, a fanatical visionary and fisherman, eyes gleaming with an inner fire. It is an utterly riveting portrayal, and Langridge sings the role as well as any interpreter past or present. On screen it is more credible, more achingly eloquent than that of Vickers on the rival set, and more accurately, more keenly articulated.

Cairns makes a profoundly sympathetic Ellen, a younger woman than Harper's, more obviously in love with Peter and desperately eager to comfort and abet him, thus making his rebuttal of her affection that much more moving. She sings with a sincere dignity and a refined attention to verbal detail. For the rest Covent Garden tends to have the stronger cast. Opie sounds too strenuous as Balstrode, missing Bailey's worldly-wise warmth, but as usual he is very much 'in' the given production, loyal to an ensemble performance. Mrs Sedley, a particularly vicious busybody in this reading, is given a forceful performance by Gorton, and Howard is a formidable Auntie. The rest haven't either the voice or the character evinced by their Royal Opera counterparts, but the sum here is definitely greater than the parts. Atherton's interpretation matches Albery's in elemental force and in uncovering the bare bones of the music. While allowing full play to the more reflective passages, especially the later interludes, he also can unleash a fury of biting sound in the set pieces, gaining an answering charge from chorus and orchestra. The sound is first-rate. Gavin's video direction is always prompt, in the right place at the right time. In the interludes he superimposes characters miming or in repose as appropriate to the moment and indulges in effective, impressionist glosses, something that can be attempted in a filmed version of the production without an audience in attendance. Both this and the Covent Garden staging are profound experiences, well worth seeing and hearing. Langridge's overwhelming performance and the more amenable sound incline one by a hair's breadth to the ENO, not least because sound and picture are decidedly superior.

Britten The Rape of Lucretia.

Dame Janet Baker *mez* Lucretia
Sir Peter Pears *ten* Male Chorus
Heather Harper *sop* Female Chorus

Benjamin Luxon *bar* Tarquinius
John Shirley-Quirk *bar* Collatinus
Bryan Drake *bar* Junius
Jenny Hill *sop* Lucia
Elizabeth Bainbridge *mez* Bianca
English Chamber Orchestra / Benjamin Britten.

Britten Phaedra, Op. 937.

Dame Janet Baker *mez*
English Chamber Orchestra / Steuart Bedford.
Decca London Ⓟ Ⓓ 425 666-2LH2 (two discs: 124 minutes: ADD). Notes and texts included.
The Rape of Lucretia recorded 1970; *Phaedra* recorded 1976.

This recording of *The Rape of Lucretia* was not made until 1970, nearly 25 years after the first performances at Glyndebourne, so that apart from Pears as the Male Chorus none of the original cast sings in it. But archival 'off-the-air' recordings do exist in which the first Lucretias, Kathleen Ferrier and Nancy Evans, may be heard (Ferrier's anguished performance being particularly emotive). This was Britten's first chamber opera, and it is his orchestral scoring, particularly the use of harp and low woodwind, that is its principal virtue. Listening to a recording, without the visual element, tends to expose the self-consciously 'poetic' parts of Ronald Duncan's libretto and the fact that Lucretia herself never really stirs our emotions, not even in so sympathetic a performance as Dame Janet Baker's. The male singers – Shirley-Quirk, Luxon, Bryan Drake and, of course, Pears – are all trusted Brittenites. As a fill-up, the cantata Britten wrote for Dame Janet in 1975, the unlovable *Phaedra*, is an intelligent choice.

Britten The Rape of Lucretia (abridged).

Nancy Evans *mez* Lucretia
Sir Peter Pears *ten* Male Chorus
Joan Cross *sop* Female Chorus
Frederick Sharp *bar* Tarquinius
Norman Lumsden *bass* Collatinus
Denis Dowling *bar* Junius
Margaret Ritchie *sop* Lucia
Flora Nielsen *contr* Bianca
English Opera Group Chamber Orchestra / Sir Reginald Goodall.

1994

Britten Peter Grimes – Whatever you say ... Let her among you without fault; Now the Great Bear and Pleiades; Interlude III ... Glitter of waves ... Wherefore I pray and beseech you ... O all ye works of the Lord; In dreams I've built myself some kindlier home; Embroidery in childhood; Interlude VI ... Grimes! ... Steady! There you are!

Joan Cross *sop*
Sir Peter Pears *sop*
Tom Culbert *ten*
BBC Theatre Chorus; Orchestra of the Royal Opera House, Covent Garden / Sir Reginald Goodall.

Britten Folk-song Arrangements.

Voici le printemps; Fileuse; Quand j'étais chez mon père; Le roi s'en va-t'en chasse;
La belle est au jardin d'amour.
Sophie Wyss *sop*
The Salley Gardens; Little Sir William; Oliver Cromwell; The Bonny Earl o' Moray; The ash grove; Quand j'étais chez mon père; There's none to soothe; Sweet Polly Oliver; Le roi s'en va-t'en chasse; The plough boy; The foggy foggy dew; Come you not from Newcastle?; O waly waly.
Sir Peter Pears *sop*
Benjamin Britten *pf*
EMI British Composers mono Ⓜ Ⓓ CMS7 64727-2 (two discs: 156 minutes: ADD). Recorded 1943-53.

Richard Abram of EMI is to be congratulated on assembling this fascinating and historically essential document. Andrew Walter and Paul Baily are to be thanked for the loving care they have shown in transferring these performances by creator artists. They are obviously of the utmost importance. Then the booklet contains invaluable essays by Eric Crozier, Nancy Evans, John Lucas (Goodall's biographer) and Philip Reed (leading Britten archivist) on the genesis of the operas and recordings. We learn from Lucas that Walton, on the British Council committee which sponsored the *Lucretia* discs, wanted to record only four sides of the work, while Bliss thought about half the score should be recorded. In the event, about two-thirds was committed to disc. One side has remained unpublished until now; the others have long been unavailable (they were briefly reissued on an unsatisfactory Music for Pleasure LP).

Ferrier and Evans shared the title-role in the first run of performances at Glyndebourne in 1946. Lucas now reveals that Goodall preferred Evans in the part. However that may be, the two singers – who Evans tells us here were boon companions, both being "Lancashire lasses" – presented complementary interpretations. Evans is infinitely moving, both in the timbre of her lovely mezzo and in her verbal accents – the simplicity of her Orchid aria would melt the hardest heart. That sterling artist Frederick Sharp (he was a superb Onegin at Sadler's Wells Opera) is a fiery, priapic Tarquinius. Maybe the refined vowels of Ritchie and Nielsen now sound anachronistic for servant roles, but both sing finely. Best of all are the Choruses of Cross and Pears, still unrivalled in their roles, revelling in the colourful imagery of Ronald Duncan's libretto. Pears is magnificent both in the Ride to Rome and the *Sprechgesang* of Tarquinius's stealthy approach to Lucretia's chamber.

The sad story of how the attempt to record the première of *Grimes* in 1945 was bungled is retold here by Lucas, but in 1948, after the first performances at Covent Garden, EMI made some amends by recording Pears and Cross in substantial portions of their original roles. Britten vetoed their issue at the time, for unknown reasons, but relented in 1972 to allow eight (of 11) sides to be included in HMV's three-LP "Stars of the Old Vic and Sadler's Wells" (a much-prized album).

Here the three unissued sides appear for the first time, allowing us to hear Cross in Ellen's "Let her among you" solo from the opera's opening scene, Pears in Grimes's "Great Bear and Pleiades" monologue of Act 1 scene 2 and the visionary solo from the hut scene in Act 2. Needless to say, these are revelatory additions to what we already have. Nobody, not even Pears in the complete Decca set, has sung these arias with such beauty of tone and such consummate mastery in welding voice to words, every accentuation subtly placed, to achieve a searingly truthful portrayal. It is wonderful to hear again, and in much cleaner sound, the rest of the extracts, most of all the Ellen/Grimes confrontation in Act 2 and Grimes's mad scene in Act 3, both quite heart-rendingly done. These excerpts represent the work at white heat, straight off the stage. Goodall shows his empathy with and command of both scores. The orchestral playing isn't always as exact as one might wish, but the spirit of the orchestral contribution is all it should be.

As a substantial bonus on these generously filled discs, we have all the folk-song arrangements that Pears and Britten recorded on 78s for both Decca and EMI, including three originally issued only in the USA, and three French songs made by Wyss and Britten in 1943 (previously unpublished – they are a delight). Some of these, such as *The Salley Gardens*, *There's none to soothe* and *The foggy foggy dew* long ago became classics; so surely now will the infinitely moving account of *The ash grove*. As throughout this issue, Pears is in glorious voice and these performances surpass the repetitions set down for LP. This is a 'must' for any lover of Britten's music, a reissue that shows as much care and dedication in preparation as is evinced by the performers themselves. An exhilarating, pioneering period in British music is here suitably chronicled.

Britten The Turn of the Screw.
Philip Langridge *ten* Prologue, Quint
Dame Felicity Lott *sop* Governess
Sam Pay *treb* Miles
Eileen Hulse *sop* Flora
Phyllis Cannan *mez* Mrs Grose
Nadine Secunde *sop* Miss Jessel
Aldeburgh Festival Ensemble / Steuart Bedford.
Collins Classics Ⓟ Ⓓ 7030-2 (two discs: 106 minutes: DDD). Notes and text included. Recorded 1993.

This is a well-prepared and exciting version of what's probably the tautest, most compact of all Britten's scores for the stage. It was the first of the operas to be recorded complete following the highly successful première and, as outlined below, will obviously remain an essential document. Britten never got round to re-recording it in stereo with the second generation of interpreters: perhaps he thought he couldn't improve on the original cast, so we have been deprived of, among others, Heather Harper's and Jill Gomez's memorable readings of the Governess's role. There had only been one stereo recording – the excellent 1981 Philips/Sir Colin Davis soundtrack (now available on CD only) of a dubbed film of the work (with Helen Donath, Heather Harper and Robert Tear singing but not acting, the Governess, Mrs Grose and Quint). The Davis issue provides strong competition to the creators' Decca set and this one, each version being wholly worthy of this extraordinary score.

The Collins version comes with a fascinating essay by Donald Mitchell, a close musical analysis by him and Philip Reed and letters from the composer relating to the work. Astonishingly these reveal that, as a youth in 1932, Britten heard a dramatized version of James's story on the wireless and described it as "eerie and scary", adjectives that apply even more strongly to his own setting of 22 years later. At the time of composition he wrote frequently to his chosen librettist, Myfanwy Piper: these letters reveal once again his meticulous care for word setting. After the première Britten agreed with Desmond Shawe-Taylor's assessment that the subject was the nearest to the composer that he had yet chosen, adding revealingly "although what that indicates of my own character I shouldn't like to say". Undoubtedly it adumbrates what Tippett might have called the 'dark side' of Britten of which he was himself acutely conscious. A description of the conflicting views of *The Turn of the Screw* is to be found in CUP's handbook on the work by Patricia Howard. Mitchell here gives as his opinion that the music discloses the Governess and Quint as two sides of the same character (rather like the Donington view of Wotan and Alberich): "The Governess/Quint symbiosis (and its musical realization) has its roots precisely in the pursuit of power, power to possess Miles ...".

Consciously or not, that struggle, once you are aware of it, is very much present in the forceful, histrionic portrayal of the roles here by Felicity Lott and Philip Langridge (who sings only the Prologue on the film soundtrack), coming to a climax in the final confrontation where the tension is almost unbearable in such a lifelike, big-scale recording. Both bring all their long stage experience to bear on giving character and verbal enlightenment to their roles; both are in excellent voice.

They are at the centre of this performance's success, they and Steuart Bedford (who paces the work to within a minute of Britten's own timing). He and his players have the advantage over the composer and his hand-picked ensemble in the ability of modern recording to open up the score and also subject it to the minutest scrutiny so that one is amazed again not only at the intricate skill with which it is woven but also by its extraordinary aptness in fitting individual instruments to evoke a mood, a situation, a place. But it has a possible drawback: the old mono recording has an intimacy, a claustrophobic feeling appropriate to the work that the sometimes reverberant acoustic here is bound to dissipate. Then you may not always be happy about where the voices were placed. At his first appearance, Quint is certainly supposed to be distant, but not so much so as to be almost inaudible and, in her letter-writing scene, the Governess seems further away than is natural. But these are small drawbacks to what is by and large a vivid representation of the piece.

With a single, important exception the supporting singers offer arresting interpretations. Phyllis Cannan, that grievously underused soprano (what a superb Elizabeth I in *Gloriana* she would make), is a vital, rounded Mrs Grose, surpassing even Joan Cross (Decca) in vocal assurance and attention to detail, always following to the letter Britten's injunctions. Nadine Secunde brings another kind of soprano timbre, more incisive and high-flying, to Miss Jessel – just right – and she's rather moving in her eventual defeat. Eileen Hulse makes a lively and cleverly naughty Flora. What a pity then that the Miles is disappointing. You may think that Sam Pay's totally innocent-sounding, pure choirboy sound makes the whole story just that much more horrifying, but David Hemmings's trail-blazing performance (Decca), knowing and devilish, is closer to the story's and opera's intentions.

Those of us who have lived with and loved the original version over the years are not going to let our affection for it dim, but this set is happily in the true tradition of the piece, and deserves a high placing among all the other recent performances of Britten's operas. The work itself will surely capture the imagination of any newcomer who hasn't yet been made aware of its greatness.

Britten The Turn of the Screw.
Sir Peter Pears *ten* Prologue, Quint
Jennifer Vyvyan *sop* Governess
David Hemmings *treb* Miles
Olive Dyer *sop* Flora
Joan Cross *sop* Mrs Grose
Arda Mandikian *sop* Miss Jessel
English Opera Group Orchestra / Benjamin Britten.
Decca London mono Ⓔ Ⓓ 425 672-2LH2 (two discs: 105 minutes: ADD). Notes and text included. Recorded 1955.

Will there ever be a better performance, let alone recording, of *The Turn of the Screw* than this by the original cast, recorded less than four months after the 1954 Venice première? Christopher Palmer contributes a stimulating essay to the booklet with this reissue, in which he faces squarely all the implications of this choice of subject by Britten as far as what Palmer calls his "intellectual paedophilia" is concerned. It is a valid and provocative comment, a useful contribution to the ever-growing body of Britten criticism. This score is Britten at his greatest, expressing good and evil with equal ambivalence, evoking the tense and sinister atmosphere of Bly by inspired use of the chamber orchestra and imparting vivid and truthful life to every character in the story. As one listens, transfixed, all that matters is Britten's genius as a composer.

Jennifer Vyvyan's portrayal of the Governess is a classic characterization, her vocal subtleties illuminating every facet of the role and she has the perfect foil in Joan Cross's motherly and uncomplicated Mrs Grose. The glittering malevolence of Pears's Quint, luring David Hemmings's incomparable Miles to destruction; the tragic tones of Arda Mandikian's Miss Jessel; Olive Dyer's spiteful Flora – how fortunate we are that these performances are preserved.

Ferruccio Busoni
Italian/German 1866-1924

Busoni Arlecchino.
Robert Wörle *ten* Arlecchino, Leandro
Marcia Bellamy *mez* Colombin

René Pape *bass* Ser Matteo del Sarto
Siegfried Lorenz *bar* Abbate Cospicuo
Peter Lika *bass* Dottore Bombasto
Berlin Radio Symphony Orchestra / Gerd Albrecht.
Capriccio Ⓟ Ⓓ 60 038 (67 minutes: DDD). Notes and synopsis included. Recorded 1992.

Capriccio's Complete Busoni Edition is a very impressive series indeed. Musically *Arlecchino* is far superior and more evenly inspired than *Turandot*. It also demands a good deal more from the listener both musically and intellectually. Though superficially a simple and straightforward tale of the rakish exploits of the hero/rogue Arlecchino, the opera contains a good deal of philosophical debate on the human condition – particularly the less attractive side of human nature. In Arlecchino's own words: "'Tis not for children, nor for gods, this play; for understanding people 'tis designed. The sense of what the characters may say may well escape an all too literal mind." An interesting feature of the opera is the purely spoken role of Arlecchino, which serves the two-fold purpose of creating a bridge between audience and action as well as emphasizing his vital, disruptive force over the other characters. A blow-by-blow account of the plot is unnecessary; what is important to know, however, is that *Arlecchino* was a product of the First World War and (perhaps more specifically) of the emotions that the war had aroused in Busoni's mind. It also establishes Busoni's principles of theatrical poetry and his own attitude toward opera as an art form, that is, that a musical drama should "create a pretend world in such a way that life is reflected in either a magic or a comic mirror, presenting consciously that which is not to be found in real life" – hence Busoni's lifelong admiration for Mozart's *The Magic Flute*. Although Busoni himself described his *Arlecchino* as "less than a challenge and more than a jest" it must surely take its place as a major landmark in his output. Musically (and indeed philosophically) there is much that foreshadows his crowning achievement – begun around the same time but unfinished at his death in 1924 – *Doktor Faust*.

Gerd Albrecht's performance of *Arlecchino* is even more impressive than his recording of *Turandot* and certainly one of the finest readings of a Busoni opera yet committed to disc. As fine as Kent Nagano's Virgin Classics reading is (reviewed below with *Turandot*), Albrecht projects a greater feeling of drama and dramatic pace (as well as the *commedia dell'arte* aspects of the opera) and he seems to have absorbed the Busoni spirit far more successfully; the presence of *Doktor Faust*, is exceptionally strong. Another exceptional feature of this version is Albrecht's excellent cast. Marcia Bellamy is a shade more suited to the role of Colombina than Susanne Mentzer (Nagano), and there are some exceptionally fine performances from René Pape, Siegfried Lorenz and Peter Lika in the roles of Matteo, Abbate Cospicuo and Dottor Bombasto. The master-stroke, however, is the casting of Robert Wörle in both the Arlecchino and Leandro roles, an inspired idea and one which is delivered with great aplomb and panache – his Leandro is more sharply characterized than Stephan Dahlberg's for Nagano. As usual, Albrecht draws some superb orchestral playing from the Berlin Radio Symphony Orchestra (especially in the wind and brass departments) and the recording is well balanced and atmospheric.

Busoni Doktor Faust.

Dietrich Fischer-Dieskau *bar* Doktor Faust
William Cochran *ten* Mephistopheles
Anton de Ridder *ten* Duke of Parma
Hildegard Hillebrecht *sop* Duchess of Parma
Karl Christian Kohn *bass* Wagner, Master of Ceremonies
Franz Grundheber *bar* Soldier, Natural Philosopher
Manfred Schmidt *ten* Lieutenant
Marius Rintzler *bass* Jurist
Hans Sotin *bass* Theologian
Bavarian Radio Chorus and Symphony Orchestra / Ferdinand Leitner.
DG 20th Century Classics Ⓜ Ⓓ 427 413-2GC3 (three discs: 156 minutes: ADD). Notes text and translation included. Recorded 1969.

Sooner or later there must be a new recording of *Doktor Faust*: it is an opera great enough to need the varying perspectives of different interpretations. And besides, Antony Beaumont has demonstrated that Philipp Jarnach's completion of the final scene is, at the very least, an incomplete realization of Busoni's intentions – Beaumont's own solution deserves the currency of a recording. No less urgently, Leitner's DG account, pioneering though it was and eloquent advocacy though it remains, is quite extensively cut: 12 passages are excised, 700 bars in all, including most of the church scene and its organ prelude, three fine orchestral passages (including the very beautiful transformation music before the vision of Helen of Troy) and the first three sections of the students' serenade. These trimmings were made necessary, no doubt, by a prudent desire to get the opera on to three LPs; it is tough luck on DG that the resultant timing makes it just marginally too long for two CDs.

Until someone takes the risk of a new version, though, this one will remain an essential document, and although recent productions in London and elsewhere have demonstrated that the casting of

Doktor Faust is not insuperably difficult any future recording will be hard put to it to match Fischer-Dieskau's magnificently authoritative interpretation of the title-role or DG's luxurious casting of the 'secondary' parts (Sotin, Rintzler, Grundheber, Schmidt and de Ridder as the five 'spirit voices'!). Cochran is not the most ingratiating Mephistopheles imaginable, but his intelligence and his fearless scaling of the cruelly high tessitura ensure that he is malignancy incarnate. Intelligent, too, is Hillebrecht's Duchess, but her voice is worn and imperfectly controlled. This is the only real vocal disappointment, however, and there are none in Leitner's direction of Busoni's score, that magic-box of lucidly complex invention and mysterious sonorities. The recording sounds very well for its age, too, with a good sense of space and with on-stage, off-stage and in-the-orchestra choruses (very well sung) carefully distinguished; only the usual forward placing of the solo voices detracting from the impression of a real performance. Does it sound too much of a back-hander to say that we earnestly recommend this set despite urgently looking forward, not to its successor but to its first rival?

Busoni Turandot.
Mechthild Gessendorf *sop* Turandot
Stefan Dahlberg *ten* Kalaf
Franz-Josef Selig *bass* Altoum
Gabriele Sima *sop* Adelma
Falk Struckmann *bar* Barak
Anne-Marie Rodde *sop* Queen Mother
Markus Schäfer *ten* Truffaldino
Michael Kraus *ten* Pantalone
Wolfgang Holzmair *bar* Tartaglia

Busoni Arlecchino.
Ernst Theo Richter *bar* Arlecchino
Susanne Mentzer *mez* Colombina
Thomas Mohr *bar* Ser Matteo del Sarto
Wolfgang Holzmair *bar* Abbate Cospicuo
Philippe Huttenlocher *bar* Dottore Bombasto
Stefan Dahlberg *ten* Leandro
Chorus and Orchestra of the Opéra de Lyon / Kent Nagano.
Virgin Classics Ⓟ Ⓒ VCD7 59313-2 (two discs: 137 minutes: DDD). Notes, texts and translations included. Recorded 1991.

Just when we'd given up hope of hearing a recording of *Turandot* on disc, what happens? – two come along at the same time (the other being Gerd Albrecht's on Capriccio). It happened with the Piano Concerto as well – to the point where we ended up with a veritable traffic-jam of recordings! Choice is made easier, of course, by Kent Nagano's logical coupling (*Arlecchino* and *Turandot* were intended as an evening's double-bill).

Turandot contains a good deal of fine music (perhaps among the finest that Busoni composed for the stage) but in truth does not attain the same degree of theatrical completeness as *Arlecchino*. As a representation of Carlo Gozzi's original fable, however, it is much more faithful (and closer in spirit) than Puccini's masterpiece. With Busoni the fable remains a fable, with Puccini fable is transformed into powerful symbolism and emotions of transcendental heights. Puccini's selfless, sacrificing Liù, for instance, is here replaced by Busoni's pragmatic, opportunist Adelma, whilst the former's cruel and terrifying Princess is seen here as a highly subtle character driven to inhumane ends in a quest for her equal. Busoni's eclectic style produces some curious (though undoubtedly highly effective) musical moments: the wailing lament of the Queen of Samarkand's female retinue sounding for all the world like a Red Indian chant, and a bizarre appearance at the beginning of Act 2 of the English melody *Greensleeves* (a symbolic clue as to Busoni's interpretation of the tale?). Much of the finest music is to be found in the opening and closing stages of the opera.

The Capriccio recording also has much to commend it (though the lack of a printed libretto is not one of them), not least a particularly fine and formidable Kalaf in the shape of Josef Protschka (sample the opening "Peking! Stadt der Wunder!" and a superb trio of performances from Robert Wörle, Johannes Werner Prein and Gotthold Schwarz as Truffaldino, Pantalone and Tartaglia (the equivalent of Puccini's Ping, Pang and Pong). Less convincing, however, is Linda Plech's interpretation of the title-role, which is weak beside Mechthild Gessendorf's magnificent performance for Virgin. Albrecht (so persuasive in unusual repertoire) conducts a spirited account of the work, attentive to both its smaller detail and its more majestic moments, and his Berlin Radio Symphony Orchestra respond with some stunningly inspired playing.

Nagano's reading, however, has equal stature, and, as indicated, a much stronger Turandot in Mechthild Gessendorf, whose darker voice seems to be more appropriate to the role. Stefan Dahlberg's Kalaf is very fine too. Although the orchestral playing is not as sharply or vividly executed as the RSO Berlin for Albrecht, Nagano's players are not far behind in their involvement and commitment to the score. The recording, as in *Arlecchino*, is well balanced and spacious and the set is crowned with an informative and lavish booklet.

As for Nagano's *Arlecchino*, his is a persuasive recording (a 1954 Glyndebourne performance lays claim to the première recording of the opera). Ernst Theo Richter's spoken Arlecchino is outstanding – a performance of irresistible magnetism – and Thomas Mohr provides a fine account of the much put upon Matteo, but the opera is strongly cast throughout, with exceptionally committed supporting performances from Suzanne Mentzer, Stefan Dahlberg, Wolfgang Holzmair and Philippe Huttenlocher. The orchestral playing from the Lyon Opéra Orchestra, is, as we have come to expect, quite superb, with Kent Nagano once again displaying his skill at finding the perfect dramatic pace whilst eliciting exceptionally elegant performances from his players.

André Campra   French 1660-1744

Campra Idoménée.
Bernard Delétré *bass* Idoménée
Sandrine Piau *sop* Electre
Monique Zanetti *sop* Ilione
Jean-Paul Fouchécourt *bass* Idamante
Marie Boyer *mez* Venus
Jérôme Corréas *bass* Eole, Neptune, Jealousy, Nemesis
Richard Dugay *ten* Arcas
Jean-Claude Sarragosse *bass* Arbas, Protée
Mary Saint-Palais *sop* Cretan Girl
Anne Pichard *sop* First Shepherd
Anne Mopin *sop* Second Shepherd, Trojan Girl
Les Arts Florissants Chorus and Orchestra / William Christie.
Harmonia Mundi ℗ ① HMC90 1396/8 (three discs: 166 minutes: DDD). 🖉 Notes, text and translation included. Recorded 1992.

André Campra was one of the leading figures on the French musical stage between Lully's death in 1687 and Rameau's operatic début in 1733. He made a pioneering contribution to *opéra-ballet*, and wrote several *tragédies en musiques* and a significant corpus of sacred music in his capacity as Maître de musique at Notre-Dame in Paris. Campra's best-known *tragédie en musique*, and one of his most successful, was *Tancrède*, first performed in 1702 and revived at frequent intervals between then and 1764 when, following Rameau's death, the Académie Royale de Musique staged it in place of the latter's *Les Boréades*. The reasons behind this last minute change of plan have never been fully explained but it might well have been that the Académie Royale, preferring to be safe than sorry, decided to produce a piece which had proved popular over many years rather than one which was entirely new to the repertory.

Idoménée, like *Tancrède*, is a *tragédie* in five acts and a prologue. The librettist in both cases was Campra's frequent collaborator, Antoine Danchet. *Idoménée* was first staged on January 12th, 1712 and ran for 12 performances that month. Then it was dropped until 1731 when, in a reworked version, it was revived; this later version has been chosen by William Christie for his recording. As Antonia Banducci remarks in her introductory essay, much of the story will be familiar to readers acquainted with Mozart's *Idomeneo*. Mozart's librettist, Varesco, in fact used Danchet's text as a prime source for his own, Danchet himself turning to Crébillon's play *Idoménée* which had been performed at the beginning of the eighteenth century. But whereas Varesco changed the ending to ensure the *lieto fine*, Danchet remained faithful to Crébillon in preserving a tragic conclusion to the opera.

Unlike the majority of French opera prologues of the period, that belonging to *Idoménée* is not a royal encomium but one concerning the power of love over forces of nature which is later paralleled, to some extent, in the opera itself. The action takes place in and around Crete. Ilione, daughter of the Trojan King Priam, has rejected Idoménée, King of Crete, in favour of his son Idamante whom she secretly loves. It is announced that Idoménée has drowned in a storm at sea, whereupon Ilione and Idamante openly declare their love for one another. Agamemnon's daughter Electre also loves Idamante and burns with jealous rage. But Idoménée has been rescued by Neptune, who makes him promise that he will sacrifice the first person he meets on returning to *terra firma*. That person is his son Idamante. Idoménée warns him to be fearful of his father's presence while Electre and Venus plot to destroy both of them. Idoménée attempts to protect Idamante by making him escort Electre from Crete back to Argos. But he receives a message from the gods to keep his promise to Neptune or else play host to a sea-monster which will wreak havoc in Crete. The gods are as good as their word, the monster appears, sets to work but is slain by Idamante. Believing that all is now well, Idoménée, reconciled to the Ilione-Idamante situation, prepares for appropriate celebrations. But all is far from well. In the midst of festivities Nemesis appears. The gods are not appeased. Idoménée, in a moment of insanity, kills his son and, when his senses return, attempts suicide. But he is restrained by his subjects. Ilione is distraught: "To punish him, leave him alive; it is I alone who must die".

Here we have not only a complete version of *Idoménée* but one that does justice to the music. The casting is strong with outstanding contributions from Monique Zanetti, Sandrine Piau and Bernard Delétré. Jean-Paul Fouchécourt is hardly behind them in his often touching portrayal of Idamante and Jérôme Corréas makes both a resonant Neptune and an awesome Nemesis. Campra's score is an attractive one but, while never perhaps reaching the imaginative heights scaled by his contemporary Marais in the oft-cited storm "symphonie" and chorus of his opera *Alcyone* (Act 4), has few if any *longueurs*. Campra is skilful in his instrumental writing, which plays a prominent part in the texture throughout the opera; the Third Act, for instance, contains a captivating "air des matelots" for piccolos, drums and strings while the Fourth, in its opening instrumental prelude, reveals the composer's feeling for string textures, as well as containing an affecting little musette later on. The Second Act storm scene is effective, though Campra's weather conditions are less ferocious than those of Marais. The arrival of Nemesis in Act 5, however, is very powerfully conveyed, as are the remaining darkly shaded moments of the drama. Generally speaking the music underlines the lighter, lyrical gifts for which Campra has been justly praised and the closing passages of the opera confirm a fluency in an altogether different affective range.

In his vocal writing Campra shows greater understanding of, or at least sympathy for, singers' requirements than many of his contemporaries. By and large the parts lie within a comfortable tessitura though in no other sense is virtuosity confined. As well as lively, technically athletic ariettes, though not so called by Campra, there are vividly characterized scenes such as those in which Venus, Jealousy and his attendants plot their assault on Idoménée (Act 2 scenes 7 and 8), and passages of finely sustained dialogue, above all one between Idoménée and Idamante (Act 2 scene 4). And their bitter, tormented duet for (Act 3 scene 2) is striking both for its intensity and the clarity of its declamation.

To sum up, here is an opera which proves itself well deserving of the attention paid it by William Christie and Les Arts Florissants. This is not one of those recordings which once heard, gather dust thereafter. If not in the end a great opera, it at least has the virtue of being consistently effective and the best things in it are well above the jottings of a *petit-maître*. Supple choruses, mostly very well sung, colourful divertissements and a profusion of beguiling airs make this a tempting proposition.

Alfredo Catalani
Italian 1854-1893

Catalani La Wally.
Renata Tebaldi *sop* Wally
Justino Diaz *bass* Stromminger
Piero Cappuccilli *bar* Vincenzo
Mario del Monaco *ten* Giuseppe
Lydia Marimpietri *sop* Walter
Stefania Malagù *mez* Afra
Alfredo Mariotti *bass* Soldier
Turin Lyric Chorus, Monte Carlo National Opera Orchestra / Fausto Cleva.
Decca Grand Opera Ⓜ ① 425 417-2DM2 (two discs: 124 minutes: ADD). Notes, text and translation included. Recorded 1968.

Catalani was by instinct and temperament a post-Verdian (even an anti-Verdian) composer whose short life ended just as the post-Verdian age began. It brought him not triumph but despair: Mascagni's *Cavalleria rusticana* (first performed just as Catalani began work on *La Wally*, his last opera), Puccini's *Manon Lescaut* (whose success put *La Wally* into the shade and embittered the final months of Catalani's life), even Verdi's own *Falstaff* seemed more convincing models for the future than the one he had been labouring to perfect over 20 years and five previous operas.

A century later we don't have to be too hard on him for proposing a path that wasn't taken. He was abused for writing 'German operas' (four of his six stage works have romanticized Teutonic or Nordic settings) and he does have moments of atmospheric scoring that recall Weber but in *La Wally*, his maturest score, he is obviously and fundamentally an Italian who knew more about French opera than most of his compatriot contemporaries. He had, after all, spent perhaps as much as a year in Paris before going to the Milan Conservatoire, a year during which he could have heard most of Meyerbeer's grander operas, one of Massenet's, two by Ambroise Thomas and Weber's *Der Freischütz*.

Think of a blend of those influences (fairly well digested) plus long-lined Italian lyricism and a sort of hectic, driven vigour (is it too fanciful to attribute part of this to Catalani's by now galloping consumption?) and you will have a pretty good idea of the style of *La Wally*. Plenty of local colour, both in the obvious operatic sense (a huntsmen's chorus, a recurrent yodelling song – the work is set in the Austrian Alps) and, more impressively, in the evocations of cold in Act 4: piccolo and double-bass four octaves apart in the prelude, icily thin scoring in the opening scene on the snow-bound mountain peak, strangely Shostakovich-like chords in the soprano's despairing scena – Catalani's orchestral writing, though coarse now and then, has vitality and sometimes real poetry to it. Despite efforts not to be, *La Wally* is basically a number opera, and inevitably the big solo scenes stick most obstinately in the memory: the heroine's famous "Ebben? ne andrò lontana", of course, but she has arias of similar melodic appeal in each of the other three acts (her baritone suitor and the tenor who first scornfully spurns her then learns to love her too late have their most characterful moments in duet with her); the melodic language is generous, with here and there a brusque, striking angularity. And in moments like the quite ingeniously complex ensemble in Act 2 (quartet and chorus) and above all in the sequence of not-quite-arias and not-quite-declamatory-recitatives of the Fourth Act an individual voice begins to assert itself.

An immature voice, a crude and awkward one at times, and Catalani's characters are mere emblems with no depth or roundness to them. But the music of Wally herself can be filled out by a voice with Tebaldi's thrilling heft into a larger-than-life emblem of wild, proud independence, and when that happens you suddenly notice the skill with which the mood of her Act 1 aria is carried over into the following scene: she has cast her spell, and the act ends magically. Indeed, in Tebaldi's performance, in Cappuccilli's as the decent but out-of-his-depth-in-waters-as-murky-as-these suitor (Wally has fallen for the tenor who ignored and then humiliated her) and in Cleva's lapel-seizing urgency Catalani's alternative route to post-Verdian opera looks as though it might have been worth developing: what a pity he didn't live to do so. Stentorian belting from del Monaco, decent support from the others and an excellent if rather bright recording with some endearing period sound effects.

Francesco Cavalli   Italian 1602-1676

Cavalli Calisto (realized Jacobs)

María Bayo *sop* Calisto, Eternità
Marcello Lippi *bass* Giove
Simon Keenlyside *bass* Mercurio
Graham Pushee *alto* Endimione
Alessandra Mantovani *sop* Diana, Destino
Sonia Theodoridou *sop* Giunone
Gilles Ragon *ten* Linfea
Barry Banks *ten* Pane, Natura
Dominique Visse *alto* Satirino, Furia
David Pittsinger *bass* Silvano
Judith Vindevogel *sop* Furia
Concerto Vocale / René Jacobs.
Harmonia Mundi Ⓟ Ⓒ HMC90 1515/7 (three discs: 165 minutes: DDD). ✎ Notes, text and translation included. Recorded 1994.

It was originally Raymond Leppard who, more than any other conductor, introduced Cavalli's operas into the repertory and got them accepted as front-line theatre music for the first time since the seventeenth century. Working at Glyndebourne with Sir Peter Hall, Leppard was instrumental in producing a series of revivals, beginning in 1962 with Monteverdi's *L'incoronazione di Poppea*, of then forgotten masterpieces from the first decades of Venetian public opera. One of the more permanent results of this immensely successful venture was a series of recordings and editions, based on the Glyndebourne experiences, which brought two works in particular, *L'Ormindo* and *La Calisto*, to an even wider public.

But there were problems too. Leppard's approach, as scholars and critics were quick to note, was essentially empirical, and his 'realizations' (or, better, performing editions), took an extremely free and interventionist attitude towards Cavalli's texts. In the interests of making these operas more approachable to audiences unfamiliar with both the music and the theatrical conventions of the period, Leppard had no compunction in transposing voice parts, cutting sections or even whole scenes, adding others and remodelling the librettos. Criticized as these procedures were at the time, it is easy to see how Leppard might have thought that it was necessary for him to adopt a Mendelssohn-like posture in order to gain new friends for Cavalli. Thirty-five years on, with Cavalli's stature fully established, it is extremely hard to see quite so much value in the decision to reissue Leppard's recordings of these severely mutilated and rewritten versions.

With René Jacobs we are clearly on different ground. His version of *Calisto* is clearly the product of much careful and informed thought, even if the results also sometimes fly in the face of what is known about performance conditions in at least some seventeenth-century Venetian houses. The real difficulty here is the paucity of information. From two sets of damp-stained accounts dating from around 1660 we learn that the standard opera orchestra in the city consisted of single strings together with a continuo group comprising harpsichord and theorbo. In other words, the whole weight of the audience's experience was, and should be in any reconstruction, upon the voice, which was supported by a skeletal underpinning. Exceptions there may have been, but this was clearly the norm. And as far as the voices are concerned, there is much to enjoy in this recording.

María Bayo, an artist who has recorded both older and contemporary works, has a good sense of Cavalli's vocal manner, which for much of the time ranges from the declamatory to the arioso, with occasional flowerings into those short arias that are the forebears of later, more structured operas. This mellifluous language she handles with real understanding, accommodating each textural nuance, each shift of emotional condition with ease and conviction. Among the other major roles Marcello Lippi sings with an attractively rich and tightly focused tone, while Alessandra Mantovani has a light, clear but firm voice. As for the rest of this largish cast (another highly characteristic feature of early Venetian opera), there is a very high level of achievement. So far so good if not excellent. More controversial is Jacobs's approach to the instrumental aspects of the score; against the historical evidence, the orchestra has been expanded to include cornetts, recorders and violas while the continuo group also contains an organ, a lirone and a harp. Some of these instruments have been encouraged to improvise at various points, and in general there is a great deal by way of added counter-melodies and other intrusions much in the manner of Harnoncourt's Monteverdi recordings. The result will not be liked by everyone, for all that the musicianship on display is of a high order. Certainly there is room for a leaner approach that more accurately reflects what is known about performance conditions and conventions in the Venetian houses in which Cavalli worked, and for which *Calisto* was written.

Cavalli L'Ormindo.

John Wakefield *ten* Ormindo
Peter-Christoph Runge *bar* Amida
Isabel Garcisanz *mez* Nerillo
Hanneke van Bork *sop* Sicle
Jean Allister *mez* Melide
Hugues Cuénod *ten* Erice
Anne Howells *mez* Erisbe
Jane Berbié *mez* Mirinda
Federico Davià *bass* Ariadeno
Richard Van Allan *bass* Osmano
London Philharmonic Orchestra / Raymond Leppard.
Decca Serenata Ⓜ Ⓓ 444 529-2DMO2 (two discs: 134 minutes: ADD). Notes, text and translation included. Recorded 1968.

As explained above, Leppard took a very free attitude towards Cavalli's texts (it has been estimated, for example, that his *L'Ormindo* contains between a half and two-thirds of Cavalli's score). This is not to deny that there is some fine singing here, especially among the women. It is never dull (though occasionally it is irritatingly mannered): Anne Howells's characterization of Erisbe is highly convincing and brings out the full dramatic range of Cavalli's writing, and Isabel Garcisanz as the page Nerillo extracts every last ounce of humour from the role. The men are less impressive, perhaps, while the continuo realizations are overcrowded and inappropriately exhibitionist, and the unmistakably modern sonority and articulation with which the string section of the LPO (or of any standard modern orchestra) is bound to play by training and habit creates a totally false sound world. This reissue of Leppard's *L'Ormindo* is a fascinating document of taste and is, moreover, its only recording.

Emmanuel Chabrier

French 1841-1894

Chabrier Briséïs.

Joan Rodgers *sop* Briséïs
Mark Padmore *ten* Hylas
Simon Keenlyside *bar* Le Catéchiste
Michael George *bass* Stratoclès
Kathryn Harries *mez* Thanastô
Scottish Opera Chorus; BBC Scottish Symphony Orchestra / Jean Yves Ossonce.
Hyperion Ⓕ Ⓓ CDA66803 (74 minutes: DDD). Notes, text and translation included. Recorded at a performance at the Edinburgh Festival on August 18th, 1994.

The name of Chabrier is so associated with vivacious, gaily extrovert music and with comic operas (*L'étoile, Le roi malgré lui, Une éducation manquée*) that we are apt to forget that he was a fervent admirer of Wagner, whose influence is patent in his opera *Gwendoline* and, to a rather lesser extent, in *Briséïs*, which preoccupied him for six years but was left with only its First Act complete. The story is based on Goethe's ballad *The Bride of Corinth*, but the original vampire heroine is replaced by a bride who returns from the dead to claim her promised husband. The rift between paganism and Christianity is bridged by her when she is converted to the new faith to save her dying mother, but at the bitter price of taking a vow of chastity. What is Wagnerian in the opera is the overblown libretto (by Catulle Mendès, the librettist of *Gwendoline*), Chabrier's ingeniously elaborate use of leitmotivs (though he rejected Wagnerian declamation as boring), some of the harmonies and modulations, and the very full orchestration at rapturous moments in the action. Nevertheless the basic language remains French, notably at the very start, with the young sailor Hylas on his galley, yearning for his beloved, and later when he sails away – a lovely passage sensitively handled here by the BBC's recording engineer (for this performance comes from a BBC Radio 3 relay). The last scene of the act is very fine, with a lyrical orchestral prelude, a combination of the quasi-ecclesiastical pleas of the catechist with the grandiose gestures of the pagans, led by old Stratocles, Briséïs's struggle between her vow to Hylas and her desire to save her mother, and a big triumphal conclusion.

The performance was rightly hailed with acclamation by the Edinburgh Festival audience. Joan Rodgers, who as the heroine is on stage throughout the act, copes brilliantly with her cruelly exacting, high-lying part, in which she shows no sign of tiring. The initial scene between her and the fresh-voiced Mark Padmore is overlong by dramaturgical criteria, but both artists convincingly convey the two lovers' ecstasy. Kathryn Harries as the mother and Simon Keenlyside as the catechist are both excellent in their demanding roles (Chabrier certainly did not spare his singers). Except for Michael George, whose vibrato becomes disturbing, the whole cast's enunciation (in very good French) is admirably clear; and the orchestral playing is both eloquent and full of nuance. This is a decisive first British performance of this hitherto little-known work – which, however, Richard Strauss conducted in 1899 – which modifies our overall view of Chabrier.

Chabrier Une éducation manquée.

Christiane Castelli *sop* Gontran
Claudine Collart *sop* Hélène
Xavier Depraz *bass* Pausanias
orchestra / Charles Bruck.

Chabrier Mélodies.

Le Roi malgré lui – Hélas, à l'esclavage. Chanson pour Jeanne. L'île heureuse. Gwendoline – Blonde aux yeux de pervenche. Ballade des gros dindons. Pastorale des cochons roses.
Christiane Castelli *sop*
Hélène Boschi *pf*.
Le Chant du Monde mono Ⓟ Ⓓ LDC278 1068 (55 minutes: AAD). Texts included. Recorded 1953-4.

Anyone who enjoyed Chabrier's sparkling style will certainly relish this entertaining pocket opera that he produced to entertain the Press. (Now there's something for our Critics' Circle to emulate!) *Une éducation manquée* ("A defective education") is no more than a sketch, set in the time of Louis XVI, about two very young aristocrats who have just been married but are totally innocent of the facts of life: the tutor to whom the young Count turns for advice has spent his whole life amid books and out of the world and is equally ignorant and it is only when the disappointed bride, frightened by a thunderstorm, seeks refuge in her husband's arms that the problem solves itself. The libretto is witty – one *buffo* duet in which the tutor catalogues the subjects he has taught is a riot – and the music is not only fresh and charming but beautifully crafted and scored. The three participants here act out their roles admirably and the whole performance, given just the right amount of production, has a vivacity and forward impulse that sweeps the listener along with it. The orchestral sound is somewhat withdrawn, but the acoustics of the spoken and sung sections match up fairly well: no translation of the text is supplied, but the diction of all the singers is exemplary, and even those with no French should be able to follow the action easily.

To fill the disc, Christiane Castelli (who was a member of the Paris Opéra in the 1950s, but who seems to have made almost no recordings) adds half a dozen varied Chabrier songs. Her bright, typically French voice has charm and poise – why, one wonders, was nothing more heard of her? – and her enunciation is among the clearest ever encountered. She sounds completely at ease in all the songs' moods except in the spinning song from *Gwendoline*, where, exceptionally, her high notes are less well placed. Both she and her very able pianist are closely recorded, and there is some tape background.

Gustave Charpentier   French 1860-1950

G. Charpentier Louise.

Berthe Monmart *sop* Louise
André Laroze *ten* Julien
Louis Musy *bar* Father
Solange Michel *mez* Mother
Paris Opéra-Comique Chorus and Orchestra / Jean Fournet.
Philips mono Ⓜ Ⓓ 442 082-2PM3 (three discs: 163 minutes: ADD). Notes, text and translation included. Recorded 1956.

The charms of *La vie parisienne*, *Manon* and *La bohème* notwithstanding, *Louise* is the essential opera set in, and about, Paris. Anyone who has seen the room furnished with Charpentier's belongings and looked out through the vine-planted terraced garden of the Musée de Montmartre, must recognize how faithfully he depicted his milieu in the opera. This recording has the air of authority and authenticity throughout. All the principals were members of the company at the Opéra-Comique during the 1950s, when Jean Fournet was its Music Director. For the 50th anniversary of its première, Louis Musy, who sings the Father, staged a new production of *Louise*, with décor by Utrillo, in February 1950.

Berthe Monmart who sings the title-role may not be the soprano of one's dreams, but she fulfils all the role's requirements, and on the evidence of this had quite a big voice (her other roles in the early-1950s included Ariadne and Santuzza). She is the only French singer to have recorded the role since Ninon Vallin, in the abridged version supervised by the composer in the 1930s (conducted by Eugène Bigot, available on Nimbus). Her singing is full of charm, and she manages moments such as the leap to a soft high G at "des pétales de roses" in the opening love duet without apparent strain. Of course, every prima donna has recorded "Depuis le jour" (Melba, Callas, Price, Caballé, Sutherland, the list is endless) and it is useless to suggest that Monmart has such vocal allure, but she achieves complete conviction. All the singers have well-nigh perfect diction – essential in this supreme example of French *verismo*. What genius Charpentier mustered for this one work. When the Father makes his entrance in Act 1, to his 'tired' music and asks if the soup is ready, the psychological portrait is completed – mother/father/daughter, caught in this early picture of youth in rebellion. Musy's career had begun in the 1920s, and he had sung the entire baritone repertory at the Opéra-Comique before becoming its director of productions.

André Laroze does not have the reserves of stentorian tone that Georges Thill brought to Julien's music on disc and film (Abel Gance, director, with Grace Moore, in 1938), but he is the real thing – a French tenor. In the duet that follows "Depuis le jour" he and Monmart get up steam in fine ecstatic fashion. The rather ungrateful role of the Mother, whom Charpentier does not mock in his music, is also a sympathetic character in her way despite all the nagging, and is taken by Solange Michel, another veteran of the rue Favart. In the many small roles are several well-known names, among them Andrea Guiot and Jacques Mars. Fournet's pacing of the score achieves excitement at the climactic moments, the lovers' duets, Louise's almost hysterical apostrophe to Paris in the closing scene, while making the faintly mystical opening of Act 2 a miniature poem, with its street cries and little ripples of *chanson*.

Praise for the Prêtre performance with Cotrubas and Domingo in 1976 was rather reserved, and there was even less enthusiasm for Cambreling on Erato in 1983; in between came the Rudel version with Beverly Sills and Nicolai Gedda (EMI), which has two major drawbacks (by the time the set was recorded in 1977, cruel time has made the tremolo in Sill's voice perilous) and too often she seems to be unable to sustain even notes in the middle of the voice. Gedda is more secure but the voice still sounds dry and tight. It is, however, in the orchestral and choral singing, and above all in the performance of José van Dam as Louise's father, this this recording scores. However, it still seems fair to say that Fournet's 42-year-old recording is the one to have. The mono sound is amazingly vivid – you will be completely swept along by its fresh sense of theatricality and by the true *opéra comique* style of all concerned.

Marc-Antoine Charpentier French 1643-1704

M-A. Charpentier La descente d'Orphée aux enfers.
Sophie Daneman *sop* Euridice
Paul Agnew *ten* Orphée
Jean-François Gardeil *bar* Apollon, Titye
Patricia Petibon *sop* Daphné, Enone
Monique Zanetti *sop* Proserpine
Katalin Károlyi *mez* Aréthuze
Steve Dugardin *alto* Ixion
François Piolino *ten* Tantale
Fernand Bernadi *bass-bar* Pluton
Les Arts Florissants / William Christie.
Erato Ⓔ Ⓞ 0630-11913-2 (56 minutes: DDD). 🖊 Notes, text and translation included.
Recorded 1995.

La descente d'Orphée aux enfers may not be a work on the scale of *Médée* but the familiar tale of Orpheus entering the Underworld to retrieve his lost love Euridice provides Charpentier (like so many others) with plenty on which to exercise his considerable dramatic skills. That is true, even without the customary denouement, for this two-act piece (composed in the mid-1680s for private performance at the residence of the Duchesse de Guise) ends with the triumph of Orpheus's music over the powers of the Underworld, and thus misses out the moment when he loses Euridice for a second time. In his insert-notes, H. Wiley Hitchcock suggests that a third act may at least have been intended, and certainly there are some prophetic lines in Act 2 which would make more sense if that were true. The existing ending works quite well, however, and it is at least worth noting that in 1710 Clérambault's famous cantata, *Orphée*, ended at the same point in the story.

As it is, Charpentier provides us with a chillingly sudden death for Euridice, an interesting scene in which three shades are charmed by some relatively minor examples of Orpheus's art, and a hero with all the desperation and impetuosity one would need to undertake as reckless a task as his. These last qualities are excellently conveyed by the unrestrained, dramatic singing of Paul Agnew, who is also equal to the task of characterizing Orpheus's musical entreaty to the Underworld, by turns artful and impassioned (and accompanied with great tenderness by two bass viols). Agnew's heart-on-sleeve approach is not always beautiful, but it never leaves good taste behind, and in this he is well matched by his colleagues. William Christie's direction shows its customary sure dramatic touch, and the result – as usual from these artists – is a performance which seems unlikely to be bettered.

M-A. Charpentier Médée.

Lorraine Hunt *sop* Médée
Bernard Delétré *bass* Créon
Monique Zanetti *sop* Créuse
Mark Padmore *ten* Jason
Jean-Marc Salzmann *bar* Oronte
Noémi Rime *sop* Nérine
Les Arts Florissants / William Christie.
Erato Ⓕ Ⓓ 4509-96558-2 (three discs: 195 minutes: DDD). 🖋 Texts and translations included.
Recorded 1994.

William Christie himself answered the question that everyone was bound to ask: why did he choose to make a new recording of this splendid (but still little-known) early opera – Charpentier's only *tragédie lyrique* – ten years after his previous (Harmonia Mundi) version, when other fine works are still waiting their turn? For a start, the Erato issue is of the complete work (to fit on to the three-LP format cuts had been necessary) and the experience of staging the opera had changed Christie's view of its pacing and sharpened the response of the orchestra (an unusually large one for its period) and continuo. When reviewing the earlier version Nicholas Anderson, though understandably bowled over by Charpentier's music and dramatic sense and finding much to praise in the performance, expressed some reservations about the soloists and about the intonation of the chorus.

Here we have an entirely new cast, though the Medea, by far the most important role, is again an American. Lorraine Hunt is fuller-voiced than was Jill Feldman, and her performance is something of a *tour de force*. She invests every word with meaning and produces the widest range of colour to express all the emotional nuances in Medea's complex character – jealousy, indignation, tenderness, sorrow, fury, malignity and outright barbarism: she is especially outstanding in Act 3, one of the most superb acts in all baroque opera, in which she has no fewer than four great monologues, the first with affecting chromatic harmonies, the second accompanied by feverish rushing strings, the third the sombre "Noires filles du Styx" with its eerie modulations, the fourth with dark orchestral colours. Charpentier's orchestration and texture, indeed, are wonderfully effective: string writing varies between extreme delicacy (beautifully played here) and savage agitation; the cool sound of the recorders is refreshing (as in Jason's arioso where this irresolute anti-hero complains, "How happy I should be if I were loved less!"); and the many dances featuring recorders and oboes – for of course the work had to create substantial opportunities for ballet, as well as spectacular stage effects – are enchanting. Among the instrumental highlights is the inventive chaconne near the end of Act 2 (which also includes an arioso in Italian style and in the Italian language, which upset Charpentier's original audience in 1693).

The Jason in Christie's earlier recording was occasionally not quite high enough: no such charge can be levelled against Mark Padmore, a real *haute-contre*, who sings with admirable ease and intelligence, subtly characterizing the one-time hero of the Golden Fleece, now faithless to the sorceress who had made his exploit possible. As the tragic Creusa, poisoned by the vengeful Medea, the light-voiced Monique Zanetti is the very embodiment of youthful innocence and charm: her death scene, still protesting her love for Jason, is most moving. A notable detail in all the principals, incidentally, is their absorption of *agréments,* with Hunt showing special mastery in this regard. Jean-Marc Salzmann makes a virile Oronte, alert in verbal nuance: only the Créon – curiously enough, rather a weakness in the previous recording too – is undercharacterized, though he makes more of an effort for the scene where Medea robs him of his senses prior to destroying him. There is a large cast for the numerous minor roles, all well taken; and the chorus sing cleanly and with evident commitment (though the chorus of demons in Act 3 starts too mildly). All told, a considerable achievement, and a triumph for Christie, whose decision to re-record the work is amply justified by the result.

Francesco Cilea   Italian 1866-1950

Cilea Adriana Lecouvreur.

Renata Scotto *sop* Adriana Lecouvreur
Plácido Domingo *ten* Maurizio
Sherrill Milnes *bar* Michonnet
Elena Obraztsova *mez* Princesse de Bouillon
Giancarlo Luccardi *bass* Prince de Bouillon

Florindo Andreolli *ten* Abbé de Chazeuil
Lillian Watson *sop* Jouvenot
Ann Murray *mez* Dangeville
Paul Crook *ten* Poisson, Major-domo
Paul Hudson *bass* Quinault
Ambrosian Opera Chorus; Philharmonia Orchestra / James Levine.
Sony Classical ℗ ① M2K79310 (two discs: 135 minutes: ADD). Notes, text and translation
included. Recorded 1977.

If Maurizio Arena's lively and sympathetic account of *Adriana Lecouvreur* for RCA demonstrated
that the opera still had stageworthy potential, and not just as a vehicle for an old-fashioned prima
donna (for to tell the truth his donna, Raina Kabaivanska, is a rather small-scale Adriana, the voice
not always under perfect control), James Levine's sumptuous Sony reading makes an even stronger
case for it, and his donna is decidedly prima. It is Levine's *Adriana Lecouvreur* as much as Renata
Scotto's, indeed, and some listeners may find his affectionate moulding of the score, his underlining
of its every expressive detail and his leisurely speeds (he adds a full 15 minutes to Arena's timing)
rather overdone. His approach generally strikes you as an admirable one, rooted in a real love for the
score (he has a distinct talent for making you think again about supposedly second-rate Italian
operas; he is a first-rate conductor of Zandonai, for example) and in great consideration for his
singers. Scotto certainly responds to this, and makes a part that might have seemed a size too large for
her (there are one or two brief moments of strain) thoroughly her own, with a range that extends from
caressed murmur to splendidly melodramatic hauteur.

Domingo is in ardent voice and fills out the rather thinly sketched Maurizio admirably (Arena's
elegant tenor, Alberto Cupido, is rather overparted) and Milnes makes a sympathetic figure of the
soft-hearted Michonnet. Obraztsova's fans will not mind too much that she makes the haughty
Princesse de Bouillon sound like Azucena or Ulrica (one quite expects her to offer balefully to tell
Adriana's fortune). But this opera stands or falls on whether the soprano can convince you that she
is both a *grande dame* and touchingly vulnerable (as evidenced by Renata Tebaldi on the old Decca
reissue), and on whether the conductor realizes how much more than an accompanist he needs to be
(Cilea was a cunning builder of dramatic tension, and an imaginative orchestrator). On both counts
this set succeeds finely, and it is beautifully recorded.

Cilea Adriana Lecouvreur.

Renata Tebaldi *sop* Adriana Lecouvreur
Mario del Monaco *ten* Maurizio
Giulio Fioravanti *bar* Michonnet
Giulietta Simionato *mez* Princesse de Bouillon
Silvio Maionica *bass* Prince de Bouillon
Franco Ricciardi *ten* Abbé de Chazeuil
Dora Carral *sop* Jouvenot
Fernanda Cadoni *mez* Dangeville
Angelo Mercuriali *ten* Poisson, Major-domo
Giovanni Foiani *bass* Quinault
Santa Cecilia Academy Chorus and Orchestra, Rome / Franco Capuana.
Decca Grand Opera Ⓜ ① 430 256-2DM2 (two discs: 126 minutes: ADD). Notes, text and
translation included. Recorded 1961.

All that was best in the singing to be heard in post-war Italy seemed to be represented by Renata
Tebaldi. She was that essential centrepiece of an opera company, the well-tutored lyric-dramatic
soprano with a beautiful voice and a gracious stage presence, having the power and stamina to make
an effective Tosca and the serenity and elegance of a fine Desdemona. There were things she could
not do, or at least things that were accepted as being not part of her equipment (trills, thrills on the
very highest notes, flashes of unexpected colouring or temperament). Still, she was sound: firm, even,
ample, sensitive, well controlled. Indeed, there was more to her than that, as a return to this recording
shows.

But of course then came Callas and, with her, the excitements of danger in the singing and the
personality, the compulsiveness of listening and watching because you never quite knew what the next
moment would bring; and the operatic recordings of which she was the centre made even the most
distinguished rivals look second-elevenish: which is largely how many rival sets appeared when they
were current in the 1950s and early-1960s. So what of them now, when the heady rivalries and
partisanships of those days are past? Tebaldi herself: does she survive with estimation enhanced or
does she perhaps emerge as one of those singers whose style and production seem dated, the freshness
lost through familiarity, the vocal manner quaint, like the style of speech in some old film? Those last
questions can have an immediate answer. To hear Tebaldi in Adriana's "Io son l'umile ancella" is to
be reminded that hers are the classic virtues (that is, the values we generally accept as permanent):
those of beautiful tone, musical feeling, sincere utterance. And if for these qualities she was supreme
among her contemporary Italian sopranos, she surely stands head and shoulders above any of the

present generation. Tebaldi is superb, and in the last act sings her "Poveri fiori" movingly and with some touches that are exquisite. Simionato as the Princess is a great strength, and so is the singing of Giulio Fioravanti as Michonnet (though neither of them has the way of making sung words come to life). Maurizio is a part that suits del Monaco relatively well (once he has done his ungainliest with the start of "La dolcissima effigie"). The recording is vivid.

Domenico Cimarosa
Italian 1749-1801

Cimarosa Il matrimonio segreto.
Arleen Auger *sop* Carolina
Julia Varady *sop* Elisetta
Dietrich Fischer-Dieskau *bar* Geronimo
Júlia Hamari *contr* Fidalma
Ryland Davies *ten* Paolino
Alberto Rinaldi *bar* Count Robinson
English Chamber Orchestra / Daniel Barenboim.
DG Ⓜ Ⓒ 437 696-2GX3 (three discs: 165 minutes: ADD). Text and translation included. Recorded 1975-6.

Consider the stamina shown just over 200 years ago in Vienna, when after listening to a three-hour opera (presumably plus a pause between the two acts) Leopold II ordered the work to be repeated in its entirety after an interval for supper. Assuming at least an hour for this (probably longer), the evening's entertainment must have extended over about nine hours – almost awe-inspiring in this sound-bite era of ours. It is understandable, at any rate, that Leopold was delighted with his new Kapellmeister Cimarosa's *Matrimonio segreto* (his 53rd stage work), for, as Hanslick was later to remark, it is "full of sunshine". Its melodic invention and rhythmic vitality seem inexhaustible, its scoring is colourful, and the plot is not too involved to be followed with ease. The music may not have the more adventurous harmony or contrapuntal dexterity of Mozart (whose opening of the *Zauberflöte* Overture only four months earlier Cimarosa must almost certainly have cribbed), but it abounds in delightfully fresh melodic invention and rhythmic vitality – its bubbling patter-work too is worthy of Rossini at his best; together with its construction, with as many ensembles as solo arias and with skilfully planned finales, and its scoring, primarily aimed at supporting the singers but giving the orchestra some independent interest (there are occasional interventions by a solo clarinet, for example), it marks not merely an expert craftsman but a composer of distinction whose wide popularity at the time is understandable. (Only one other of his operas has been recorded – *Il maestro di cappella*, coupled with an unsatisfactory performance of Donizetti's *Don Pasquale* on Decca – surely an opening here for an enterprising company?)

Barenboim makes the music dance along with the utmost sparkle, and he is fortunate in having a splendid cast, in whom it is almost invidious to praise Ryland Davies (with free tone-production, fine breath-control and native-sounding Italian) and the silver-voiced Arleen Auger as the young couple at the centre of the plot. But Alberto Rinaldi also brings a real sense of character to the blustering Count Robinson (was this personage intended as a dig at the British?), who sets his heart on the clandestinely married Carolina and ends up, most improbably, marrying her shrewish elder sister whom he had previously declared he would rather die than wed; and Julia Varady gives a stunning performance of that character's big florid aria in the last act. This is an issue not to be missed. It is a pity that room was not found in the CD format for Stanley Sadie's introductory essay which was included with the original LP release.

Cimarosa Il matrimonio segreto.
Susan Patterson *sop* Carolina
Janet Williams *sop* Elisetta
Alfonso Antoniozzi *bar* Geronimo
Gloria Banditelli *contr* Fidalma
William Matteuzzi *ten* Paolino
Petteri Salomaa *bass* Count Robinson
Orchestra of Eastern Netherlands / Gabriele Bellini.
Arts Ⓢ Ⓒ 47117-2 (three discs: 192 minutes: DDD). Italian text included. Recorded 1991.

Although enthusiasm for the now 23-year-old Barenboim set remains undiminished, this 1991 issue has much to commend it. Gabriele Bellini paces the work admirably and secures alert playing from his orchestra, whose response to dynamic shadings and readiness to point *forte-piano* accents are most laudable: as a result, the music trips along with vivacity and sparkle. The cast, mostly experienced Rossinians, show a good understanding of the post-Mozartian style required, and enter wholeheartedly into their characters. Susan Patterson is an appealing heroine, affectionate-sounding with her clandestine husband, and truly affecting in the accompanied recitative in which she contemplates being forced to enter a convent. As her elder sister, whom the Count has contracted to marry but rejects at his first sight of the embarrassed Carolina (yet whom, in the story's one improbability, he ends up reluctantly accepting – though what Elisetta thinks of this humiliating position is left unsaid), Janet Williams is brilliant, especially in her big bravura aria "Se son vendicata": the unseemly squabble between the sisters in Act 1 is acted out with spirit. Gloria Banditelli makes less of her characterization, and isn't entirely at ease at the repeated Fs in her one aria. Alfonso Antoniozzi displays a talent for patter-technique in the role of the grasping social-climbing father, and Petteri Salomaa is excellent as the Count – aristocratic at his entry, convincingly self-accusatory when trying his utmost to deter Elisetta: the dispute between the two at the start of Act 2 was a show-stopper at the original performance. Which leaves only William Matteuzzi, and here it has to be said that he is far outshone by Ryland Davies on the Barenboim set: for all the firmness and metal in his voice, his initial exchanges with his secret wife do not sound tender, as marked and expected; and in the duet with the Count, "Signor, deh concedete" his tone, already rather edgy, becomes tight.

The one real blot on this issue is the dreadfully fussy continuo (played on fortepiano) in the recitatives, not only irritatingly intrusive but at times actually submerging the words to which it is supposed to offer discreet minimal support. However, at super-bargain price this is worth putting up with for the sake of the rest, although it is a great pity that no translation is provided.

Azio Corghi   Italian 1937

Corghi Divara – Wasser und Blut.

Susanna von der Burg *sop* Divara
Christopher Krieg *spkr* Jan van Leiden
Hanslutz Hildmann *spkr* Jan Matthys
Michael Holm *spkr* Bernhard Rothmann
Heinz Fitz *spkr* Bernd Knipperdollinck
Robert Schwarts *ten* Lame Man
Eva Lillian Thingboe *mez* Hille Feiken
Suzanne McLeod *mez* Else Wandscherer
Gabriele Wunderer *sop* Mother
David Midboe *bar* Bishop Waldeck
Michael Baba *ten* Catholic Theologian
Günter Kiefer *bar* Mayor
Mark Coles *bass* Biblical Voice
Münster City Theatre Chorus; Münster Symphony Orchestra / Will Humburg.
Marco Polo Ⓟ Ⓒ 8 223706/7 (two discs: 111 minutes: DDD). Notes and text included. Recorded live in 1993.

Azio Corghi obviously knows about dramatic timing and how music may be used to build suspense and intensify conflict. An operatic scholar as well as a composer (the critical editions of Rossini's *L'italiana in Algeri* and Puccini's *Tosca* are his work), his own first full-length opera (*Gargantua*, 1984) was so well received that his next (*Blimunda*, 1990) was commissioned by La Scala, Milan. *Divara* was another commission, from the city of Münster to celebrate its 1,200th anniversary. Münster was the town that the Anabaptist John of Leyden declared the City of God, the New Jerusalem, but the idealistic, theocratic republic degenerated into a dictatorship under his fanatical and megalomaniac rule. John's downfall came shortly after he proclaimed himself King and decreed enforced polygamy (he to have the first choice of wives), ostensibly in order to increase Münster's population to the total of the 'chosen' predicted in the Book of Revelation.

The plot of Corghi's opera is thus roughly the same as that of Meyerbeer's *Le Prophète*, but told from a radically different point of view. Hence its title: Divara was the name which John of Leyden's wife (by then, so to speak, his senior wife) took at her 'coronation'. She is the central character of the opera, a submissive wife and a devout believer in the Anabaptists' Utopianism but also a proto-feminist Cassandra, crying out against the cruelty of her husband's regime and at the end beseeching God to reveal his purposes to women. It was apparently Corghi's original intention that she should be the only singing character in the drama, wordless (because her warnings are never heeded), with the plot played out by actors and narrated by a 'madrigal choir'. In the event he introduced several other singing roles, and gave Divara words to sing, but enough of the original intention remains for his opera to sound very often, and we do mean very often indeed, like a spoken play with incidental music.

In an odd sort of way the original idea was better; it would have dramatized Divara effectively as a 'lone voice'. As it is, four of the seven principal roles are spoken, while all the minor ones are sung. Still more strangely, at the end of the opera, where Divara is condemned to death and addresses her last words to God, those words are spoken not sung; a disappointing end to the otherwise dramatic final scene, a sort of chorale-fantasy (it helps that by this time only characters who sing are left on stage). Though her earlier interjections are effective, not least because they are lyrical amid so much speech, Divara has nothing approaching an 'aria', and she has less presence than the avenging Bishop Waldeck or the striking figure of the Lame Man, John of Leyden's malign, sarcastic *alter ego* and betrayer. The characterization of the other major roles, therefore, is largely entrusted to the orchestra that underlies them, and here Corghi has been ingenious, equipping each of them with adaptable leitmotivs. These range from a preoccupation with particular intervals (descending fourths for John) to the familiar *Ad nos, ad salutarem undam* chorale from Meyerbeer's opera (and Liszt's organ Fantasy and Fugue) and to 'diabolical' fanfares quoted from Stravinsky's *The Soldier's Tale*; the trumpet is placed on stage, derisively pointing up John's hypocrisy.

These quotations and simple interval-patterns add tonal reference and irony to Corghi's accomplished but not very individual middle-of-the-road modernism. The choral scenes, often rooted in the *Ad nos* chorale or in simple ostinatos, are effective; so is what remains (not much) of the narrative 'madrigal chorus'. The use of pre-recorded tape at one or two crucial points is imaginative, and Corghi is good at musical scenery (the shimmering snowscape and distant conflict at the beginning of Act 2, for example). For the rest, speech (amplified speech, at times) is at war with music, and speech generally wins. The text is in German and no translation is provided, but the English plot summary is very detailed. Susanna von der Burg makes the most of Divara's moments of lyricism, but Robert Schwarts's strongly sung Lame Man (somewhere between Busoni's Mephistopheles and Schoenberg's Aaron) makes a greater impression by far. The performance was recorded in the Civic Theatre at Münster, apparently at a live performance (there is lots of audible action); if an audience was present it was a remarkably quiet one.

Peter Cornelius
German 1824-1874

Cornelius Der Cid.
Robert Schunk *ten* Fernando
Ronnie Johansen *bass* Luyn Calvo
Gertrud Ottenthal *sop* Chimene
Albert Dohmen *bar* Ruy Diaz
Endrik Wottrich *ten* Alvar Fanez
Michael Schopper *bass* Herald
Georg Taube *ten* First Mayor, Third Messenger;
Klaus Silber *sngr* Second Mayor
Jörg Schneider *sngr* Third Mayor, Second Messenger
Michael Timm *sngr* Fourth Mayor, First Messenger
Berlin Radio Chorus and Symphony Orchestra / Gustav Kuhn.
Koch Schwann Ⓟ Ⓓ 31522-2 (two discs: 127 minutes: DDD). Notes, text and translation included. Recorded 1993.

Peter Cornelius was one of the most sympathetic of all the Wagner circle, from which he was able to detach himself without incurring too much in the way of Wahnfried's thunder. Having fallen under the spell of *Lohengrin* and then made a success with *The Barber of Bagdad* in 1858, even though this led to his champion Liszt being forced out of Weimar, he sought to emancipate himself by proving that with *Der Cid* he could write a major 'lyric drama' in which Wagner's influence should be absorbed and his ideas renewed. It is easy to say that the task was beyond his creative powers, and to point to the weaknesses in this ambitious opera: they include awkward dramatic pacing, especially a too ready acceptance of the static nature of Act 1 of *Lohengrin*. Still, if this is not a record for the general collector, those with a particular interest in German romantic opera – and Wagnerians who, like Cornelius himself, are prepared to venture beyond the Meister's immediate circle – should find enjoyment here.

The libretto, Cornelius's own, has distinguished sources in Corneille and Herder. The hero is Ruy Diaz, known as the Cid, who in Act 1 has drawn Chimene's vengeful hostility for his slaying of her father. After a *Euryanthe*-influenced overture, which has the measured melodic style if not the firm stride of Wagner, there are long, static exchanges in which Albert Dohmen delivers himself of the Cid's exculpation strongly while Gertrud Ottenthal tries to suggest more emotional confusion than is really allowed for by Cornelius's music. The Bishop attempts reconciliation: Ronnie Johansen sounds as if this tessitura lies low for him, and indeed the bottom F ending one aria disappears completely. A recording which obscures too much does not help. The Cid then has to set off for the Moorish wars. With Act 2 it becomes clear that beneath Chimene's blazing hostility another emotion is smouldering, and there builds up a hate/love duet that draws them passionately together in a scene clearly reflecting Tristan and Isolde dramatically though scarcely in musical intensity. Nevertheless, the scene is strongly written, and the whole act is much better paced; moreover, Cornelius's expert orchestration can draw the lovers together from her high *Lohengrin* violins and his deep brass sonorities until there is unity between them. Act 3 brings the Cid's triumph over the Moors, and, impelled by a somewhat token tenor rival for her love, Chimene's disclosure of their passion. There is much parading and fanfaring and processing, and some agreeable use of conventions such as the women's chorus opening Act 2 and the Bishop's prayer opening Act 3.

The work is a curiosity, in fact. Though it was a success in Weimar in 1865 (three weeks before *Tristan* in Munich), it has never had many champions, with the notable exception of Hermann Levi, who made a new arrangement. The last performance of the original seems to have been in 1938. Whatever the reservations about the work, and regrets that the recording can be less than ideally clear, it is easy to feel indulgent towards Cornelius, and to this set.

Luigi Dallapiccola   Italian 1904-1975

Dallapiccola Il Prigioniero.
Jorma Hynninen *bar* Prisoner
Phyllis Bryn-Julson *sop* Mother
Howard Haskin *ten* Jailer/Grand Inquisitor
Sven-Erik Alexandersson *ten* First Priest
Lage Wedin *bass* Second Priest

Dallapiccola Canti di Prigonia.
Eric Ericson Chamber Choir;
Swedish Radio Chorus and Symphony Orchestra / Esa-Pekka Salonen.
Sony Classical Ⓟ ① SK68323 (69 minutes: DDD). Texts and translations included. Recorded live in 1995.

Dallapiccola's short opera, *Il Prigioniero*, completed in 1948, is a troubling work, its eternally relevant political message set to music that seems increasingly problematic in its bold attempt to create a post-war 'mainstream' style, synthesizing tonal and serial techniques. Glib though it is to talk of a '12-note *Tosca*', this work's eroticization of torture (most explicitly in the final encounter between prisoner and grand inquisitor), as well as the associations it creates between sacred and secular musical genres, makes comparisons with Puccini irresistible. The music, and the drama, are weakest when the rhetoric is overblown, the expression reduced to hammered-out repetitions of dissonant chords. The opera is at its best when least insistent, and when Dallapiccola's sinuous counterpoint resists inflation into overheated climaxes. Some of the opera's more explicitly expressionistic moments pack an undeniable punch, but when the central character is so brutally exploited and so cruelly misled, the best thing the music can do is to observe a complementary restraint.
  This is a performance of many virtues, and a more than adequate replacement for the old Decca Headline account under Antál Dorati from 1975. Phyllis Bryn-Julson is cooler than the music requires in the opening scene, but once Jorma Hynninen appears the temperature rises and stays suitably high. Hynninen doesn't always observe the quieter dynamics requested by Dallapiccola, but this is no vice in a finely sung as well as dramatically persuasive account, well supported by Salonen's alert pacing of the score. The live recording sacrifices orchestral presence and detail, so that Dallapiccola's writing sounds even more opaque at certain points than it actually is. The *Canti di Prigonia* makes a logical coupling, but there are *longueurs* in this early composition in which Dallapiccola was still feeling his way forward from a relatively Stravinskian style into the world of Berg and Webern. These performances sustain the rather static textures efficiently, although as in the opera the recording seems to be seeking atmosphere in preference to maximum textural clarity.

Claude Debussy   French 1862-1918

Debussy Pelléas et Mélisande.
Claude Dormoy *ten* Pelléas
Michèle Command *sop* Mélisande
Gabriel Bacquier *bar* Golaud
Roger Soyer *bass* Arkel
Jocelyne Taillon *mez* Geneviève
Monique Pouradier-Duteil *sop* Yniold
Xavier Tamalet *bass* Doctor, Shepherd
Bourgogne Chorus; Orchestra of the Opéra de Lyon / Serge Baudo.
RCA Opera Ⓑ ① 74321 32225-2 (two discs: 147 minutes: ADD). Synopsis and text included. Recorded 1978.

Of few operas have there been so many fine historic recordings as of *Pelléas et Mélisande*: reissues have included Desormière's from 1941, Ansermet's (1952), Fournet's (1953), Cluytens's (1956), Inghelbrecht's (1962) – and here is yet another, from Baudo, a conductor with a great reputation as an interpreter of French music and closely associated with this particular work. The excellence of this performance leaves one wondering why it took the best part of 20 years to emerge. Baudo, whom Karajan recommended to take over *Pelléas* from him at La Scala, isn't as Wagnerian in his treatment as the latter, but he produces a warm sound from the Lyon orchestra, knows how to shape Debussy's subtle phrases, and is notably good at making use of silences.

He is fortunate to have a cast without a single weak member. It is often the case that the central figure of Golaud, tortured by blind jealousy, steals the show, but Gabriel Bacquier is superb, capturing every nuance from tenderness to abrupt anger (at the news of the loss of the ring) or agonized frustration beside Mélisande's deathbed. Michèle Command, here at an early stage of her career, and entirely free from the undue weightiness that has sometimes characterized her work since, makes a shy, fey Mélisande who remains an enigmatic figure; she invests with a sense of melancholy the famous solo about her long hair. The big surprise of this set is the Pelléas, a sensitive singer who seems, inexplicably, to have appeared in only one other recording (*The Merry Wives of Windsor*), made in the year before this – in a bass role! Listed here as a tenor, he is more a high baritone (which is appropriate for the part), just occasionally sounding a trifle stretched on a high note. The part of Arkel, sometimes sung insufficiently exactly, is given nobility by Roger Soyer; and the Yniold sounds convincingly childlike.

Care has been taken in the production, as can be heard in the hollower acoustic of the scene in the vaults; only the perspective of the sailors on the unseen ship – always a problem in recordings – is a little uncertain. Make no mistake: this is a very rewarding version of this masterpiece, and as a two-disc bargain-price issue is a real snip.

Debussy Pelléas et Mélisande.

Gérard Théruel *bar* Pelléas
Mireille Delunsch *sop* Mélisande
Armand Arapian *bar* Golaud
Gabriel Bacquier *bar* Arkel
Hélène Jossoud *mez* Geneviève
Françoise Golfier *sop* Yniold
Jean-Jacques Doumène *bass* Doctor, Shepherd
Choeur Régional Nord, Pas de Calais; Lille National Orchestra / Jean-Claude Casadesus.
Naxos Ⓢ ① 8 660047/9 (three discs: 157 minutes: DDD). Notes, synopsis and text included.
Recorded at performances at the Opéra de Lille on March 15th-23rd, 1996.

This performance has the advantage of particularly fine singers throughout the cast, and a conductor who clearly loves this magical score (in which, incredibly, Richard Strauss declared he could find no music), conveys this to his orchestra, and understands the value of the silences on which the composer set such store.

Debussy was insistent that every word of the libretto should tell, and certainly the enunciation of the present cast is exemplary; but because the recording is taken from stage performances, the singers often project too much or are too close to the stage microphones to convey the requisite atmosphere. For example, not until the last act does Mireille Delunsch suggest the fey, timid creature Golaud finds cowering in the forest, and later, when she confesses that she loves Pelléas, it is not in a "voice that comes from the world's end"; and Gérard Théruel (a splendidly free-toned *baryton-martin*), overloud on his first entrance, throughout the opera seems too intense, too determined that his voice should reach the back row of the theatre audience. The expression of urgency is all very well, but when, in Act 4, he seeks a clandestine rendezvous with Mélisande, he speaks to her in a manner for which Queen Victoria is said to have reproved Mr Gladstone. (There is a very audible tape edit around here.) The almost conversational tone and the nuances of meaning made possible in a studio production are rarely attained here, so that little is created of Maeterlinck's atmosphere of strangeness and mystery. There is little feeling for character or imaginative insight in Delunsch's words, pure though her singing voice is. The other parts are well taken. The veteran Gabriel Bacquier, a distinguished Golaud on the Baudo set, is perfectly in character as the kindly and understanding old Arkel; Hélène Jossoud is a firm-voiced, sympathetic Geneviève; and Françoise Golfier, vocally amazingly childlike, is an ideal little Yniold.

But despite its title the opera really revolves round Golaud, who, in capable hands, can usually steal the show. He emphatically does so here. Armand Arapian enters into the role with a sensitivity and thoroughness born of considerable experience (he has also sung it at the Deutsche Staatsoper and throughout Europe in Peter Brook's adaptation): whether baffled by the mysteriously vague creature he meets while lost, frenzied at her loss of his wedding ring, menacing in the scene with Pelléas in the vaults (where an effective perspective is achieved), tormented by jealousy when he forces his little son to spy on the two young people, or, finally, racked with remorse but still tortured by doubts, he becomes the focus of the listener's attention.

There are some less than skilful edits (one sudden rise in level comes, ironically, as Arkel says "Ne parlez pas trop fort") and a fair amount of stage noise, which makes one regret that this performance could not all have been made in the studio, when the admirable voices also might have been able to adopt a more intimate style. The French booklet-note (much the best of the three language essays) is exceptionally interesting and informative. At super-bargain price this is an issue well worth investigating, though the Baudo set (working out in the same price range, being on only two discs) better captures the work's elusive atmosphere.

Debussy Pelléas et Mélisande.

Jacques Jansen *bar* Pelléas
Irène Joachim *sop* Mélisande
Henri Etcheverry *bar* Golaud
Paul Cabanel *bass* Arkel
Germaine Cernay *mez* Geneviève
Leila ben Sedira *sop* Yniold
Emile Rousseau *bass* Shepherd
Armand Narçon *bass* Doctor
Yvonne Gouverné Choir; symphony orchestra / Roger Desormière.
EMI Références mono Ⓜ Ⓞ CHS7 61038-2 (three discs: 196 minutes: ADD). Booklet with
translation included. Recorded 1941.

BBC RADIO 3
90-93 FM

Record collectors who may perhaps have been tempted to smile indulgently at the frequency with which
older critics have evoked this classic recording of Debussy's masterpiece now have the opportunity to
hear for themselves why we treasured the 20 78s (an almost inconceivable format in today's high-tech
world!) on which it was originally issued. Keith Hardwick's alchemy in transforming these into sound
of improved quality (and with only minimal vestiges of the 78rpm surfaces) is nothing short of
amazing. He has not, of course, been able to correct the thin 1941 recording of the woodwind, but one
soon comes to terms with the dated instrumental sound because of Desormière's inspired pacing and
moulding of the score, the committed orchestral playing, and the well-nigh perfect casting. In this
recording, which was produced by that tasteful light-music composer Louis Beydts, the placing of the
voices is such that every single word is crystal-clear. More important, every word is invested with
meaning by a native French cast – in other versions allowances sometimes need to be made for
non-French singers – which had immersed itself totally in the emotional nuances and overtones of the
text. Every shade of expression is caught, but nevertheless the overall feeling is of subtle Gallic understatement (very different from the hothouse overplaying by some conductors) – with Golaud's
self-tormenting jealousy and Pelléas's final inability to resist declaring his love for his brother's
mysterious, fey wife creating the great emotional climaxes.

The strength of the performance owed much to the fact that Irène Joachim, Jacques Jansen and
Henri Etcheverry had already sung the work many times under Desormière at the Opéra-Comique; yet
meticulous piano rehearsals preceded each recording session, the wax for which (it being wartime) was
far too scarce to be wasted on any error. Irène Joachim had studied the role of Mélisande with its
creator, Mary Garden; and both she and Jansen had been coached by Georges Viseur, who with
Messager had been the *répétiteur* for the opera's first performance. Jansen with his free, youthful-toned
production and Joachim with her silvery voice and intelligent response to every verbal nuance, set
standards for the doomed lovers that, though nearly equalled, have never been surpassed; but even
more impressive is Etcheverry's interpretation of Golaud, a role in which, arguably, he has yet to be
rivalled. Leila ben Sedira gives one of the most convincing portrayals ever heard of the child Yniold
(not forgetting Marjorie Westbury at the BBC); and Germaine Cernay and Paul Cabanel (who alone is
just a trifle free with the text in places) fill the parts of the older characters with distinction. We should
be grateful to EMI for this reissue – and sparing us having to change sides 39 times, as we once did!

Debussy Pelléas et Mélisande.

François Le Roux *bar* Pelléas
Colette Alliot-Lugaz *sop* Mélisande
José van Dam *bass-bar* Golaud
Roger Soyer *bass* Arkel
Jocelyne Taillon *mez* Geneviève
Françoise Golfier *sop* Yniold
René Schirrer *bar* Doctor
Chorus and Orchestra of Opéra National de Lyons / John Eliot Gardiner.
Stage Director: **Pierre Strosser.**
PolyGram Video Ⓕ ▣ 079 211-3 (147 minutes). Recorded 1987.

This Lyon Opera staging was presented at the 1985 Edinburgh Festival, when Gardiner said that he
had spotted 470 errors (!) in the 'traditional' score and established the fact that the composer wanted
the orchestra laid out in a specific configuration. As a result of these emendments, the score sounded
sharper, more iridescent, more chamber-like in texture, as it does again on this video recording, in
spite of indifferent sound. Gardiner also eliminated the longer interludes Debussy wrote for the
original production to cover extensive scene changes, which helps tauten a work that can seem
somewhat prolonged in its usual form. Though recorded by Erato the performance has never appeared
on CD in the UK, so this video is also welcome in musical terms, particularly as it is so well cast.

The staging is much more problematic. For all the dedication of the singers, Strosser's concept
seems to accord ill with Maeterlinck and Debussy. His set proposes the large salon of a château seen
at about the time of the work's composition, an idea that had already become a cliché 12 years ago.

There is no change of venue and therefore no tower, no sea-shore, no vault, no grotto, all specifically demanded by the libretto. Instead, sepia colours, subtle lighting and stylized movement have to suffice.

In the first scene, Golaud is seen decrepit in a dressing-gown, recalling the events of the past, possibly in an inebriated dream though that isn't made explicit. Mélisande's voice is here disembodied. When she does appear it is in a prim, everyday dress, though since Edinburgh at least she has had her long hair restored. Like so much that is relevant to text and music, the loss of her ring has to be contrived by throwing it out of the window. The sense of forest, water and the marvellous idea of emerging into light out of the vault are further casualties of Strosser's strait-jacket, and the absence of a baby in Act 5 seems perverse.

The gains are in part impressive. The inner tensions of the characters in a confined space are ever-present, as we have to concentrate on their motivation. This domestic, Ibsen-like tragedy has Mélisande as something of a *femme fatale*, able to destroy both brothers by just being herself, so that Golaud's embracing of Pelléas as she stabs his half-brother may be intended to indicate that they have a greater affinity with each other than either has with Mélisande, particularly as the young lovers seldom establish physical contact even at their final and fatal meeting. Mélisande's singular behaviour is further indicated by the fact that she walks off casually from her sick-chair, perhaps to commit suicide rather than dying in a bed. Although too often what we see simply runs counter to what we hear, Strosser's rethink is undoubtedly thought-provoking. Van Dam's tortured, unstable landowner is a powerful presence throughout, and he sings the role, as ever, with magnificent élan. Le Roux is a touchingly vulnerable Pelléas, delivering the text in the classic mould. Alliot-Lugaz's strange, seductive, mysterious yet almost austere Mélisande is beautifully sung and articulated, an unforgettable performance that itself justifies the whole project. Golfier is a convincing soprano Yniold, Soyer a grave Arkel who never bores, Taillon a dignified Geneviève.

This version's only video rival, the 1992 Stein/Boulez production for Welsh National Opera, could hardly be a bigger contrast. That boasts precise and particular changes of décor for each scene, and obeys the libretto pretty literally. As a whole it is a convincing act of re-creation, realistically acted, well but not as idiomatically sung, of course, as the Lyon performance. It has a far superior quality of picture and sound and also subtitles, sadly omitted on the newer version – it's a pity PolyGram didn't get their act together on this front. Even if the WNO set is the safer recommendation, Gardiner (who is preferable to Boulez), Strosser and the Lyon cast offer a mightily persuasive alternative.

Debussy Rodrigue et Chimène (recons. Langham Smith and orch. Denisov).

Laurence Dale *ten* Rodrigue
Donna Brown *sop* Chimène
Hélène Jossoud *mez* Iñez
Gilles Ragon *ten* Hernan
Jean-Paul Fouchécourt *ten* Bermudo
José van Dam *bass-bar* Don Diègue
Jules Bastin *bass* Don Gomez
Vincent le Texier *bass-bar* King
Jean-Louis Meunier *ten* Don Juan d'Arcos
Jean Delescluse *ten* Don Pèdre de Terruel
Chorus and Orchestra of the Opéra de Lyon / Kent Nagano.
Erato Ⓟ Ⓒ 4509-98508-2 (two discs: 109 minutes: DDD). Notes, text and translation included.
Recorded 1993-4.

It may come as a surprise to many who treasure the unique magic of *Pelléas et Mélisande* that Debussy toyed with some 30 other plans for operas, and two years before his masterpiece had all but completed his first operatic venture. Catulle Mendès, a scheming writer of Wagnerian tastes, having been unsuccessful in interesting established composers in a stilted, third-rate libretto he had written on the subject of El Cid, inveigled the impecunious and still obscure young Debussy, with a false promise of performance at the Opéra, into composing a work to his text. Debussy very soon realized that its blustering tone was alien to his ideals of half-hinted action in short scenes, and became increasingly restive, finally abandoning it and claiming that it had been accidentally destroyed. In reality it survived complete in a sketch in short score (some parts extremely detailed, some with alternative suggestions, some mere outlines, and in general with only casual indications of accidentals), though some pages have since been lost. Richard Langham Smith reconstructed the work from the manuscripts in the Piermont Morgan Library in New York, it was completed and orchestrated, with a remarkable insight into Debussian style, by Edison Denisov, and in 1993 it was presented by the Opéra de Lyon to mark the opening of its new house.

Inconsistencies of style reveal something of Debussy's uncertainties and doubts over a subject inappropriate for him. There is little in Act 3 that would lead anyone to identify him as the composer, and virtually the only sections of the work with a harmonic idiom that was later to become characteristic of him are Rodrigue's and Chimène's mutual declaration of love at the start of Act 1 (after a reflective modal prelude with a tinge of Russian influence), the orchestral prelude to Act 2 and the unexpected quiet interlude that precedes Rodrigue's mortal challenge to his beloved's father, Don Gomez, who had shamed his own father. Debussy is less at home with the choral scene leading up to the angry conflict between the two initially friendly houses, the heroic and warlike atmosphere of much of Act 2, and the bombastic assembling of the royal court; but all these are tackled, if not with individuality, at least with vigour. Don Gomez's death scene is affecting, and the unaccompanied choral requiem for him makes an effective close to Act 2. Unlike *Pelléas*, there are a number of extended set pieces for the singers, including Rodrigue's dutiful dilemma, Don Diègue's hymn to the concept of honour, Chimène's lament for her father and her final anguish as she is torn between love and hate for Rodrigue.

As a performance and recording, this is in the highest class. Nagano's orchestra play for him with finesse, and the work is cast from strength. Laurence Dale is a near-perfect Rodrigue – youthful, ardent, sensitive to changes of mood, and with a free vocal production that is a constant pleasure to hear; Donna Brown makes a passionate Chimène, though occasionally just too close to the microphone for sudden outbursts; José van Dam is his always reliable self, with nobility in his voice; and Jules Bastin is on excellent form. Debussy was perhaps asking for trouble in casting all three of Don Diègue's sons as tenors, but by subtle coloration it is made clear that Bermudo is the youngest. Clarity of enunciation throughout (except, at times, from the chorus) is particularly to be applauded. Altogether an intriguing addition to our knowledge of Debussy at an early stage of his career.

Léo Delibes
French 1836-1891

Delibes Lakmé.
  Dame Joan Sutherland *sop* Lakmé
  Alain Vanzo *ten* Gérald
  Gabriel Bacquier *bar* Nilakantha
  Jane Berbié *sop* Mallika
  Claud Calès *bar* Fréderic
  Gwenyth Annear *sop* Ellen
  Josephte Clément *sop* Rose
  Monica Sinclair *contr* Miss Benson
  Emile Belcourt *ten* Hadji
  Monte Carlo Opera Chorus; Monte Carlo National Opera Orchestra / Richard Bonynge.
  Decca Grand Opera Ⓜ ① 425 485-2DM2 (two discs: 138 minutes: ADD). Synopsis, text and translation included. Recorded 1967.

This recording of Delibes's Indian opera – just one example of French authors' and musicians' fascination, in the late nineteenth century, with all things Oriental – firmly held its place in the catalogue, unchallenged until the appearance of the version conducted by Alain Lombard with Mady Mesplé in the title-role and an acceptable supporting cast (EMI) – which in fact had been made only a year later than the present set. Despite the many good qualities of the EMI, this one still wins on points. For one thing, it has the inestimable advantage of Alain Vanzo, the French lyric tenor *par excellence*, in the role of Gérald, another of those servicemen (though not a cad like Pinkerton) who fall victim to the exotic glamour of the East. Gabriel Bacquier is his usual dependable self as Lakmé's father, and Monica Sinclair contributes a capital study of the prim-and-proper governess which (unlike that of her rival in the other recording) cleverly avoids becoming too ridiculous; the other minor characters are very well taken, the orchestral playing is stylish, and the production is intelligent and lively.

It is only on considering the title-role that some difficult weighing-up becomes necessary. Mady Mesplé's very French, light girlish tone admirably suggests the virginal character and innocence of the heroine: her intonation is impeccable, her coloratura seemingly effortless, and the clarity of her enunciation could stand as a model for all singers. In contrast, it is next to impossible to guess what Sutherland is singing about, and even with the libretto in front of one it is often hard to recognize the text as she sings it: consonants are sacrificed to the production of a striking beauty of tone, limpid and even throughout the compass (though, if one is to be purist about it, more Italian than French in character). A consideration in choosing between the two versions must be the recording quality, here still fresh and clean, the EMI having to contend with the over-resonant acoustics of the Salle Wagram in Paris, which among other things leaves the chorus in mid distance. And one final point to clinch matters: this is a medium-price issue.

Frederick Delius
British 1862-1934

Delius Fennimore and Gerda (sung in German).
  Randi Stene *mez* Fennimore
  Judith Howarth *sop* Gerda
  Peter Coleman-Wright *bar* Niels Lyhne
  Mark Tucker *ten* Erik Refstrup

Aage Haugland *bass* Consul Claudi
Annette Simonsen *mez* Mrs Claudi
Gert Henning-Jensen *ten* Voice across the water
Helle Charlotte Pedersen *sop* Marit
Michael W. Hansen *bar* Sportsman
Bo Anker Hansen *bar* Town Councillor
Peter Fog *bar* Distiller
Finn Bielenberg *bar* Tutor
Stefan Cushion *bar* Councillor Skinnerup
Susse Lillesoe *sop* Ingrid
Marianne Lund *sop* Lila
Danish National Radio Choir and Symphony Orchestra / Richard Hickox.
Chandos Ⓕ Ⓓ CHAN9589 (80 minutes: DDD). Notes, text and translation included. Recorded 1996.

There is a strong kinship between this recording and Davies's 22-year-old account. Both cast a Scandinavian soprano as Fennimore, with British singers in the two principal male parts (Tear and Rayner Cook in Davies's recording) and Danes in all the others. Both versions use the same chorus and orchestra; both were recorded in the same hall, in association with Danish Radio and under the auspices of the Delius Trust. Three singers from the 1976 cast reappear in this one.

There are important differences, too. For Davies, Söderström sang both Fennimore and Gerda, the naïve schoolgirl with whom Niels eventually finds not altogether credible happiness. The older account was sung in Heseltine's English translation, this new one uses Delius's original German text. Now that we can compare the two, Heseltine's translation strikes you as pretty faithful. The problem remains: that Erik can seem tiresomely self-pitying, Niels ineffective and Gerda so confused and contrary that one loses patience with her.

As far as the men are concerned Tear and Rayner Cook are a shade or two more believable and involving than Tucker and Coleman-Wright, well though the latter pair both sing. Between Stene's and Söderström's accounts of Fennimore the differences are more interesting. Söderström suggests the vulnerability of a woman both driven by her emotions and rather afraid of them. Stene's voice has an attractive mezzo quality which adds a touch of mystery to the character: we can well understand that neither Niels nor Erik can really fathom her. Delius subtitled his opera "Two episodes from the life of Niels Lyhne". Stene sings so beautifully and projects the allure and the predicament of Fennimore so strongly that it might be renamed 'Fennimore: a tragedy': both her lovers seem rather pallid beside her. For all Söderström's distinction, Tear and Rayner Cook are less readily upstaged.

As mentioned below, although Delius was no doubt fascinated by all three central characters, this is a drama that really takes place in the orchestra, in which some of Delius's richest and strongest music powerfully evokes not only nature and the changing seasons but those emotions that his words only haltingly suggest. Davies's reading is admirable, and it is not suggested that anyone who already owns it should acquire Hickox's as well, but this account does have a rather more ample richness of texture and at times an agreeably urgent impulsiveness. It also, however, has sound effects – wind, waves, clinking of glasses – and for some listeners these may grow tedious on repeated hearing.

Judith Howarth makes as much as can be made of Gerda; so does Söderström. In both versions the smaller parts – some of them are *very* small – are well taken, but Anthony Rolfe Johnson's is a more lyrically evocative Voice across the water than Gert Henning-Jensen's. It will be Randi Stene's Fennimore more than anything else which will draw you back to Hickox's version.

Delius Fennimore and Gerda.
Elisabeth Söderström *sop* Fennimore, Gerda
Brian Rayner Cook *bar* Niels Lyhne
Robert Tear *ten* Erik Refstrup
Birger Brandt *bass* Consul Claudi
Hedvig Rummel *mez* Mrs Claudi
Anthony Rolfe Johnson *ten* Voice across the water
Kirsten Buhl-Møller *sop* Marit, Lady
Mogens Berg *bass* Sportsman
Peter Fog *bar* Town Councillor, Distiller
Michael W. Hansen *ten* Tutor
Hans Christian Hansen *bar* Councillor Skinnerup
Bodil Kongsted *sop* Ingrid
Ingeborg Junghans *sop* Lila
Chorus and Symphony Orchestra of Danish Radio / Meredith Davies.
EMI British Composers Ⓜ Ⓓ CDM5 66314-2 (78 minutes: ADD). Notes and text included. Recorded 1976.

Fennimore and Gerda is Delius's last opera, and his most problematical: "three rather dreary people who have nothing to sing" was Beecham's judgement (four, of course, if you count Gerda, who appears only briefly, in a happy ending awkwardly quarried from what in the original book was a grimly tragic, pessimistic conclusion). And indeed it is hard to like or care much about any of them: Fennimore, who marries Erik but loves Niels – and then angrily rejects him when her husband dies; Erik, weakly subsiding into drunkenness because life seems pointless; Niels, who ineffectively loves both of them but eventually finds unbelievable happiness with the schoolgirl Gerda.

The dismal libretto, however (rendered still worse, according to Beecham, by Philip Heseltine's English translation – Delius wrote and set it in German), accompanies some of Delius's strongest as well as some of his most sensuous music, and it articulates an attempt to rethink opera to suit his by now mature gifts. It is an orchestral opera, in short (the vocal lines are neither especially characterful nor especially grateful), its 11 scenes and four interludes carefully balanced in colour, pace and duration. One might even say that the intervals form part of the design: although the opera is very short, Delius envisaged it being divided into three acts.

The work's beauties are more obvious and its weaknesses more tolerable when it is as strongly sung and played as it is here. Söderström, in fine voice, does all that can be done for Fennimore, and gives even Gerda a touch of character. Tear makes Erik a believably Ibsenish Erik, and Rayner Cook is a poetic, sensitive Niels. We even have a fleeting appearance by Anthony Rolfe Johnson as the Voice across the water. Davies's direction was criticized when this recording was new for not measuring up to Beecham's subtlety. Pish tush; he paces finely and draws wonderful colours from an orchestra who sound as though they are enjoying themselves greatly. The recording is exemplary.

Gaetano Donizetti   Italian 1797-1848

Donizetti L'Ajo nell'imbarazzo.
Alessandro Corbelli *bar* Don Giulio
Paolo Barbacini *ten* Enrico
Luciana Serra *sop* Gilda
Vito Gobbi *ten* Pippetto
Enzo Dara *bar* Don Gregorio
Aracelly Haengel *mez* Leonarda
Delfo Menicucci *sngr* Simone
Orchestra of the Teatro Regio, Turin / Bruno Campanella.
Fonitcetra Italia Ⓟ Ⓒ CDC81 (two discs: 128 minutes: ADD). Notes included. Recorded at performances in the Teatro Regio, Turin during April 1984.

Literally "The Tutor in Embarrassment" (but "The Embarrassed Tutor" will do), the comedy has a familiar basis in an old man who makes life difficult for the young ones but is eventually brought to see sense. The plot has nevertheless some original variations. Don Giulio is a kind of Mr Barrett (of Wimpole Street) who wishes his children to remain chaste and single till they have reached at least the age of 40. This proves tricky as the elder son (romantic lyric tenor), being of an amorous disposition, is already the father of a child and has secretly married. The younger (*buffo* tenor) is such a ninny that he is likely prey for anything in a skirt, and has in fact fallen for the ancient housemaid. At the centre of the plot is the resident tutor, Don Gregorio, whose name served as the opera's title in some nineteenth-century productions. Written in 1824, it was Donizetti's 50th opera and his first lasting success. Three years later it reached Vienna (where Lablache, the future Don Pasquale, sang Don Giulio), and by 1829 arrived in Rio de Janeiro. In modern times Wexford gave the lead, reviving it successfully in 1973; Berne and Vienna followed, and then Turin, where this recording was made.

The audience seem to have enjoyed themselves, especially as the action gradually warms up: the applause then sounds spontaneous and there is even some genuine-sounding laughter. It is indeed a charming score. The Overture is well constructed and fertile in ideas, even if it does not go for long without the influence of Rossini becoming apparent. Throughout the opera, melodies are abundant, fresh and graceful, with the mood occasionally deepening a little, and everything kept on sound guidelines by the skilful librettist, Jacopo Ferretti. This production seems also to have been wisely handled, with no obvious buffoonery, and the central roles of father and tutor played 'straight'.

Vocally, its star is Luciana Serra, who is well suited and in the final solo achieves a genuine brilliance of effect. Paolo Barbacini, the leading tenor, copes with a high-lying vocal part, making his listeners sympathize but not rejoice. Alessandro Corbelli and Enzo Dara share a laudable determination to sing and not to clown, and the secondary couple have at any rate some character in their voices. The orchestra sound thin, and the singers sometimes take up a remote position on the stage. Even so, it makes agreeable entertainment. The absence of an English translation of the libretto is not too serious given the provision of a synopsis in English and the average opera-goer's smattering of Italian.

Donizetti Anna Bolena.
Edita Gruberová *sop* Anna Bolena
Stefano Palatchi *bass* Enrico VIII
Delores Ziegler *mez* Giovanna Seymour

José Bros *ten* Riccardo Percy
Igor Morozov *bar* Rochefort
Helene Schneiderman *mez* Smeton
José Guadalupe Reyes *ten* Hervey
Chorus and Orchestra of Hungarian Radio and Television / Elio Boncompagni.
Nightingale Classics Ⓟ Ⓓ NC070565-2 (three discs: 167 minutes: DDD). Notes, text and translation included. Recorded 1994.

Edita Gruberová is a superlative artist, one of the most accomplished singers of the age, heard in a repertoire to which she is one of the few sopranos who can do justice, and to which she would have been lost on records had not Nightingale Classics, so closely associated with her name, been at hand to present her. She is here on shining form. The brilliant tone seems as pure as ever, the fluency unimpeded, the *altissimi* still at command even if with a second or two more of preparation and with the glimpse of a limbering-up exercise on the spring-board an octave below. Recording has never been entirely kind to her, showing up patches of uneven production such as has scarcely been audible 'in the flesh'. In this, she resembles Sutherland at a comparable age (she was 48 when this recording was made), and Sutherland's is a name that comes to mind repeatedly when listening to her on record.

Perhaps it is simply the repertoire that accounts for it, but in the very first phrases sung by the heroine of this opera it is hard to banish the notion that Gruberová herself has a sound picture of her eminent predecessor in mind. It is through certain points of style rather than a similarity of timbre that the connection becomes so insistent. Like Sutherland, Gruberová favours an expressively inflected style, which secures recognition of the character's pathos, roguishness or whatever, but loosens the melody's cohesiveness. The effect is less marked than it was with Sutherland, partly because Gruberová's brighter tone is less relaxing, and partly because her vowel-sounds have more vitality. But the influence is still potent – as it is not when she sings Mozart and Strauss.

Then there is the question of the supporting cast. On the whole, they have a habit of offering the unobjectionable while avoiding any suggestion of overcharged excitement. None of the secondary roles is so well sung as to tip the balance of any comparative reviewing in favour of this recording. However, as far as competition is concerned, the timing is auspicious. The Sutherland/Bonynge version (on Decca) has gone from the catalogue and only the Callas-Gavazzeni version presents a genuine challenge. The recording was made in two days for Hungarian Radio. Some kind of audience seems to have been present (fervent applause at the end), but generally they are not much in evidence. Clarity and balance are well cared-for. Recording catches a rather hard, worn quality on Delores Ziegler's top notes. Among the less familiar names, José Bros shows unusual sweetness in some quieter passages. The Henry, Stefano Palatchi, carries formidable weight and the best singing is done by the Smeton, Helene Schneiderman.

The performance is imaginatively conducted, Elio Boncompagni bringing to it an uncommonly refined touch. For those who insist on a modern recording, this version on Nightingale is the obvious choice. However, the Callas (despite obvious faults, including cuts) is in a different class altogether – even, for instance, where Gruberová makes a particularly fine effect in the hushed opening of the Act 2 Quintet, Callas, simpler but more idiomatic in approach, freshly heard, is thrilling.

Donizetti Anna Bolena.
Maria Callas *sop* Anna Bolena
Nicola Rossi-Lemeni *bass* Enrico VIII
Giulietta Simionato *mez* Giovanna Seymour
Gianni Raimondi *ten* Riccardo Percy
Plinio Clabassi *bass* Rochefort
Gabriella Carturan *mez* Smeton
Luigi Rumbo *ten* Hervey
Chorus and Orchestra of La Scala, Milan / Gianandrea Gavazzeni.
EMI mono Ⓜ Ⓓ CMS5 66471-2 (two discs: 140 minutes: ADD). Notes, text and translation included. Recorded at a performance in La Scala, Milan on April 14th, 1957.

EMI have for some years been supplementing their Callas library, the essential volumes of complete operas in inspired studio performances mostly produced by Walter Legge, with live events known to us previously either in 'pirated' editions or vicariously through the pages of John Ardoin's *The Callas Legacy* (Duckworth: 1983). Of *Anna Bolena* we already know Callas's way with some of the principal solos, but of course what Callas had most characteristically to offer was quite likely not to be found in those so much as in some turning-points in the drama or some apparently incidental phrase of recitative, and so it proves here. Another of her qualities was to inspire an audience with the sense of a great occasion, and to key-up a sympathetic conductor into the production of something to match her own intensity and the public's expectations.

Callas indeed gives one of her finest performances. The first impression is essentially a vocal one, in the sense of the sheer beauty of sound, for recording reveals it to be so much better focused than Simionato's. Then, in the first solo, "Come innocente giovane", addressing Jane Seymour, she is so clean in the cut of the voice and the style of its usage, delicate in her *fioriture*, often exquisite in her shading, that anyone, ignorant of the Callas legend, would know immediately that this is an artist of patrician status. There are marvellous incidental moments, and magnificent crescendos, into, for instance, "per pietà delmio spavento" and "segnata è la mia sorte", culminating in the Tower scene.

Again, the singers at her side hardly measure up. Simionato was reported, on excellent authority, to have given a splendid performance, but what we hear in this recording is a splendid voice that nevertheless bumps as it goes into the low register and is not reliably steady in many passages, while the manner is too imperious and unresponsive in expression. The tenor role, of the ineffectual lover Percy, has been reduced by Gavazzeni's cuts (of which there are several), but Gianni Raimondi makes limited impression in what remains; and, as the King, Rossi-Lemeni produces that big but somewhat woolly tone that became increasingly characteristic. Even so, the great ensembles still prove worthy of the event, and the recording, which is clear without harshness or other distortion, conveys the special quality of this memorable evening at the opera with remarkable vividness and fidelity.

Donizetti L'Assedio di Calais.
Christian du Plessis *bar* Eustachio de Saint-Pierre
Della Jones *mez* Aurelio
Russell Smythe *bar* Edward III
Eiddwen Harrhy *sop* Isabella
John Treleaven *ten* Edmondo
Norman Bailey *bar* A Spy
Nuccia Focile *sop* Elenora
Geoffrey Mitchell Choir; Philharmonia Orchestra / David Parry.
Opera Rara Ⓟ Ⓓ ORC009 (two discs: 124 minutes: DDD). Notes, text and translation included.
Recorded 1988.

For his 49th opera Donizetti lacked a tenor, so he gave the part of the hero to a woman, thereby condemning the work to a long sleep of nearly a century and a half. Perhaps the absence of a love-story, in the conventional sense of the term, is equally responsible. Perhaps it is simply an accident of history, for when an artist is as prolific as Donizetti it cannot be wondered at if some of his children get lost. Wherever the fault lay, it could not have been with the music or libretto. A thoroughly well-made opera, it impresses as the invention and masterly work of a composer fully involved in his subject; and the subject is one which arouses emotions of a broader humanity than usual.

The story of the burghers of Calais is good operatic material; for one thing, it provides opportunity for a powerful ensemble when the heroic decisions are made, and another when the farewells are taken, taken so movingly, moreover, that even the beastly English feel pity. The opera begins with the escape of the Mayor's son from the English soldiers, whose frustration and promise of revenge form the opening chorus. Then we meet the Mayor himself, a noble character who at this stage believes his son to be dead, and when the daughter-in-law arrives confirming the bad news there is a fine duet of just the sort that was such a favourite with Verdi. Good tidings of the young man's survival prompt the second half of the duet, which the rules of opera at this time required to be of a faster, more exciting type, and again the demands of form act not as a shackle upon the imagination but as a stimulus. Donizetti's 49th would be an excellent example to use in any contention that this was the great period of opera as an art-form, and that the disintegration of form throughout the second half of the century in the interests of realism was not the pure progress it is normally taken to be.

Another of the conventions is that the separate numbers come to a definite end which is the cue for applause. There is more of a case than usual for live recordings of opera of this type, as applause is almost part of the score. Here the conductor sensibly leaves a few seconds' gap, and there is certainly no lack of material for us to applaud mentally. The performance has that unostentatious reliability which characterizes British singing at its best. That best is well represented by Della Jones in her *travesto* role of the hero-son. The firm compactness of her voice, the strength of character, clean pacing of notes and fluent passagework are a delight throughout. As the Mayor, Christian du Plessis gives a deeply moving performance, his voice having acquired an extra depth of tone that fits him for this role which lies somewhere between the bass and baritone tessitura. The high baritone of the cast is Russell Smythe, splendidly even and accomplished in the *fioriture* of his solos, making Edward III a perfect English gentleman who cannot refuse a lady and who is much more in his element granting pardons than chopping off heads (the French are gentlemen, too, and in the translation thank the King for sparing their lives with the courtly statement "You give us enormous happiness"). Nuccia Focile sings in a clear bright soprano of the type that all but disappeared with Lina Pagliughi.

Chorus and orchestra are alert and sensitive throughout, and David Parry sees that justice delayed is not justice denied: in every way, including the exemplary booklet, this first recording of the opera (indeed, the first performance since 1840) is an achievement of which all can be proud.

Donizetti Il campanello di notte.
Agnes Baltsa *mez* Serafina
Enzo Dara *bass* Don Annibale Pistacchio
Carlo Gaifa *ten* Spiridione

Biancamaria Casoni *mez* Madame Rosa
Angelo Romero *bar* Enrico
Vienna State Opera Chorus; Vienna Symphony Orchestra / Gary Bertini.
Sony Classical Ⓕ Ⓒ MK38450 (56 minutes: DDD). Notes, text and translation included.
Recorded 1981.

Il campanello, though not among Donizetti's most inspired works, often turns up in a double-bill with one or other comic one-acter. The nightbell of the title is the one that constantly disturbs the old apothecary Don Annibale on his bridal night, the culprit being Enrico, the successful suitor for the hand of Serafina, the young bride. Pre-echoes of *Don Pasquale* in every sense except on this occasion the girl seems quite satisfied with her lot. There are a couple of superb *buffo*-patter duets for the baritone and bass, a great deal of recitative, but not much of a chance for Serafina to shine. The role lies a little high for Baltsa but she manages to do much with the little offered her. The two *buffo* parts could not be better done than by Dara and Romero, who not only engage themselves accurately and brilliantly with all their words and notes in the duets, but also manage to enliven the acres of recitative by dint of their pointed diction. When Enrico pretends to be an old man, desiring to have filled a prescription which is so long that Donizetti put a note in the score advising the singer to have the words to hand, Romero fulfils the composer's inordinate demands with ease. Gary Bertini and the Vienna Symphony seem fully transported into the *ottocento* idiom.

Donizetti Don Pasquale.

Renato Bruson *bar* Don Pasquale
Eva Mei *sop* Norina
Frank Lopardo *ten* Ernesto
Thomas Allen *bar* Malatesta
Alfredo Giacomotti *bass* Notary
Bavarian Radio Chorus; Munich Radio Orchestra / Roberto Abbado.
RCA Victor Red Seal Ⓕ Ⓒ 09026 61924-2 (two discs: 120 minutes: DDD). Notes, text and translation included. Recorded 1993.

This is a most attractive set, presenting a serious challenge to the excellent Gabriele Ferro version on Erato from 1990 (currently out of the catalogue), and the slightly po-faced Riccardo Muti on the 1982 EMI version. Roberto Abbado balances equably the witty and more serious sides of the score. If he and his orchestra don't quite achieve the brio of Ferro – for instance, the lighter, faster Ferro touch in the famous "Cheti, cheti immatinente" duet is better at suggesting *sotto voce* plotting – Abbado finds a gratifying lightness in the "A quel vecchio" section of the Act 1 finale and creates a delightful sense of expectancy as Pasquale preens himself while awaiting his intended bride. All three versions play the score complete, banishing the traditional emendations added by his interpreters over the years.

Abbado's cast has many strengths and few weaknesses: indeed it would be hard to cast the piece more successfully. Pasquale is usually assigned to a veteran singer. In the case of Bruscantini (Muti) and Bacquier (Ferro), allowances definitely have to be made for the singer's age: both men cleverly compensate with the vocal equivalent of guying for failing voices. With Bruson you hear a voice hardly touched by time and a technique still in perfect repair. Apart from weak low notes (not surprising as this is a bass rather than a baritone part), he sings and acts the part with real face, and his vital diction, particularly in recitative (listen to this Pasquale reciting his chapter of complaints about "Sofronia" to Malatesta in the final scene), is a pleasure to hear. His portrayal is ripely and intelligently sung. He works well with Thomas Allen's nimble, wily Malatesta, an unexpected piece of casting that proves to be inspired. Like Bruson, Allen sings every note truly and relishes his words, evincing a sense of comedy as he prepares, cruel to be kind, to gull his friend. Allen sings "Bella siccome" as suavely as Nucci (Muti) and acts with his voice just as keenly.

Eva Mei's Norina is an ebullient creature with a smile in her tone, much more pointed and pert than the accurate but lacklustre Hendricks (Ferro) or the admittedly warmer-voiced Freni (Muti). The edge to Mei's voice seems to be just right for Norina, though others may find it tends towards the acerbic under pressure. Her skills in coloratura are as exemplary as you would expect from a reigning Queen of Night. She is at her very best in "Tornami a dir", her pure line and refined phrasing ideally matching those of Lopardo as Ernesto. Lopardo is that rare thing, a tenor who can sing in an exquisite half-voice, as in "Com' è gentil", yet has the metal in his tone to suggest something heroic in "E se fia", the cabaletta to "Cercherò lantern terra", which in turn is sung in a plangent loving way, just right: the *pp* cadenza into the second verse is wonderful. Not even Schipa had all these accomplishments. Perhaps Canonici's timbre (Ferro) is the more Italianate, but Lopardo is the more accomplished singer, indeed is here a great one. As the recording here is exemplary as compared with the EMI (too reverberant) and the Erato (singers often too backward), this version is the one to have.

Donizetti Don Pasquale.

Italo Tajo *bass* Don Pasquale
Alda Noni *sop* Norina

Cesare Valletti *ten* Ernesto
Sesto Bruscantini *bar* Malatesta
Renato Ercolani *ten* Notary
Chorus and Orchestra of RAI, Milan / Alberto Erede. *Director:* **Alessandro Brisson.**
Bel Canto Society Ⓟ 🔲 BCS0686 (109 minutes). Filmed in 1954.

As with previous Bel Canto Society issues, the films made in the studio for television have to be distinguished from those made, sometimes on location, for the cinema. This splendid 1954 RAI production falls into the latter category, marred only by Italo Tajo's overdone mugging in the title-part. Alda Noni, remembered affectionately by older opera-goers in the same part at London's Cambridge Theatre in the late-1940s, remains a charming, minxish though now more buxom Norina. Sesto Bruscantini is a model of a Malatesta, Cesare Valletti even better as an Ernesto in the class of his teacher, Tito Schipa. Erede's seasoned conducting and a resourceful staging makes this a delightful experience.

Donizetti L'elisir d'amore.
Angela Gheorghiu *sop* Adina
Roberto Alagna *ten* Nemorino
Roberto Scaltriti *bar* Belcore
Simone Alaimo *bar* Dulcamara
Elena Dan *sop* Giannetta
Chorus and Orchestra of the Opéra National de Lyon / Evelino Pidò.
Decca Ⓟ ① 455 691-2DHO2 (two discs: 123 minutes: DDD). Notes, text and translation included. Recorded 1996.

The bicentenary of Donizetti's birth was virtually overlooked in 1997 in favour of the Schubert, Brahms and Mendelssohn commemorations, but near the end of it came this delightful set to put things partly to rights. As Philip Gossett suggests in his thoughtful booklet-essay, in this work the composer ideally combined the needs of comedy and sentiment, and that is the reason it has always been so loved by opera-goers. The set catches these contrasting moods to perfection under Pidò's alert and affectionate conducting, not least because the recording is based on live performances at the Lyon Opera. Everyone, chorus and orchestra as much as the principals, enters enthusiastically into the mood of the piece so that you sense it being enacted before your eyes. To complete one's pleasure Decca have provided an ideally balanced sound picture which has plenty of natural presence.

But main interest will undoubtedly be on how our most sought-after operatic pairing fares in the central roles. Gheorghiu presented her credentials as Adina at Covent Garden in 1996. Some found her dramatically a shade shrewish in the part, but Adina is a feisty, temperamental girl, and a touch of steel doesn't seem inappropriate. It makes her capitulation when she realizes the true depth of Nemorino's feelings that much more moving. And so it is on disc. She provides plenty of flirtatious fire in the early scenes and turns Nemorino away with determination, making her intentions clear in pointed attack in the recitative, but her concern for him is never far below the surface and comes to the fore in her colloquy with Dulcamara. All this is conveyed in singing that matches warmth with pointed diction and fleet technique, something essential at Pidò's sometimes racy speeds (Adina's final cabaletta is a little fast for comfort). The contrast in her approach can be illustrated by the whizzing projection of "Una tenera occhiatina" and the sensuous, palpitating tone she gives to "Prendi, per me sei libero". Listen to the single word "resta", plaintively expressing her real love for Nemorino. Then the line "Sempre scontento e mesto" has an even, limpid cut precisely in accord with the illuminating moment in the drama. It's a winning interpretation on all fronts.

Alagna's Nemorino is almost on the same level. For those who have yet to hear him, Alagna is a French tenor of Sicilian parents who won the 1988 Pavarotti Prize and bids fair to succeed the big man if he is given space to develop in his own time. Since he recorded the role under Viotti for Erato, he has evidently given it more thought, his singing having added life and variety, though he eschews a few *piano* touches he found appropriate there. He obviously enjoys himself greatly as the lovelorn yokel, one with a vulnerable soul as he shows at his moment of greatest heartbreak, "Adina, credimi" in the Act 1 finale. His sense of fun is obvious in the bottle-shaking episode when he thinks he has found the elixir of the title. There were moments when this style was just a shade strenuous for the part; a little more caressing would have been welcome, but he does find that missing element in "Una furtiva lagrima". And here comes the surprise of the performance: he sings a version which the composer composed for revival in which the music is transposed down to G to accommodate a gently ornamented second strophe. You may not be convinced that it is as effective as the original but it makes an interesting alternative.

The two Italians in the lower roles are admirable. Scaltriti may not be as preening as some Belcores but he sings the part with a firmness (though too many aspirates) that older singers miss and he is fully in character. Alaimo is a naturally witty Dulcamara and never indulges in unwanted *buffo* mugging though he lacks the ripe, rich timbre of Taddei on the *c*1958 Serafin/Classics for Pleasure version and of Panerai on the unavailable Ferro/DG version. As with all the singers on Pidò's set he is very much part of a team. The score is, of course, given absolutely complete.

The Erato set presents formidable opposition and anyone who possesses it may not want the new set. Devia is a less wilful, less vivid Adina than Gheorghiu, but her style is, if possible, even more idiomatic. There's not much to choose between the Belcores and Dulcamaras, but as a whole the Decca sounds, not surprisingly, the more lifelike reading. The now historic recordings, Serafin at budget price and the mid-price Molinari-Pradelli/Decca set with di Stefano, are both vivid performances, but both are cut. The super-budget Naxos has much to commend it including the same Dulcamara as here, but neither performance nor recording is in the same class as the new version, which thus becomes a clear and welcome choice for this work, worth every penny of the asking price.

Donizetti L'elisir d'amore.

Mariella Devia *sop* Adina
Roberto Alagna *ten* Nemorino
Pietro Spagnoli *bar* Belcore
Bruno Praticò *bass* Dulcamara
Francesca Provvisionato *mez* Giannetta
Tallis Chamber Choir; English Chamber Orchestra / Marcello Viotti.
Erato Ⓜ ① 0630-17787-2 (two discs: 129 minutes: DDD). Notes, text and translation included.
Recorded 1992.

This is something very special; indeed, a delight from start to finish, making one fall in love again with this delightful comedy of pastoral life. If you can, take tracks 7 and 8 on the first CD and listen to how Alagna gently caresses the phrase "O di fame o d'amor, per me è tutto uno" and Devia's gentle reply "Odimi. Tu sei buono, modesto sei ..." and you'll hear the heart of Nemorino and Adina – and *L'elisir* – exposed, singers wholly engrossed in their roles. Then Devia sings "Chiedi all'aura lusinghiera", possibly the score's most liquidly eloquent solo (among so many), with the tone finely balanced, the legato pure, the expression soulful. In the duet's second section from Adina's "Per guarir di tal pazzia", the pair again find the art that conceals art, addressing and answering each other in a stylish yet 'felt' manner that charms the ear and warms the heart.

Alagna's singing reminds one inevitably of the younger Pavarotti on the 1971 Bonynge/Decca set, except that Alagna sounds even younger, even more vulnerable, certainly more so than Pavarotti's elder self (for Levine on DG in 1989). Occasionally the microphone seems to catch some hardness in his voice that is definitely not there in live performance, but by and large it is a youthful, ardent reading sung in authentically Italianate tones, the words forward, on the tone, culminating in a nicely poised and shaded "Una furtiva lagrima", sung inwardly, not at an audience.

Devia is even better. She sings almost all her rivals off the stage, securer than Ricciarelli (Scimone on his 1984 Philips set), more fleet than Cotrubas (Pritchard on his 1976 Sony Classical set), warmer than Battle (Levine), less mannered than Sutherland (Bonynge). If you are sceptical, listen to her in either "Una tenera occhiatina" (second CD, track 10) or in "Prendi, per me sei libero" (track 13) and compare her with any or all of the above, and you will have to agree with this verdict. The line is consistently steady, the tone full, the *fioriture* clean, the characterization alert because it comes from a full understanding of what she sings.

Italian speakers also fill the other roles, to their advantage. Praticò is a Dulcamara in the Bruscantini mould; a shade short in voice but lively with the text, quite avoiding the *buffo* tricks of Sir Geraint Evans (Pritchard), although not as rich or as lovable as Panerai (on the Ferro/DG version) or Taddei on the admirable Serafin set, where Panerai is an ideal Belcore; here Spagnoli is 'correct', as the Italians say, no more. But both singers are well into the lively ensemble, led with limpidity and sparkle by Viotti who – like Scimone on the Philips set – allows them room to manoeuvre while keeping his rhythms effervescent. No band plays quite so lightly and elegantly as the ECO, certainly not the Metropolitan orchestra on the overblown and unauthentic Levine set. The ECO benefit from Erato's well-aired but never reverberant recording. The Tallis Choir may betray one or two signs of unidiomatic accent, but are firmer in tone than most Italian choruses.

A note by the ever-industrious Alberto Zedda speaks of authenticated discoveries about the score and its editions – but then a note, somewhat ambivalently, suggests that traditional practice had been married with new research. In the event listeners won't notice much difference, at least from the Scimone account, until almost the end when Adina is allotted a second more ornate verse to her quasi-cabaletta. A fortepiano accompanies the recitatives.

It is not suggested that collectors should scrap all the old versions – many listeners wouldn't be without Carreras's peculiarly plaintive Nemorino on the Scimone version (though he vocalizes with more effort than Alagna), or Pavarotti's endearing portrait for Bonynge – but as a whole, for performance and recording this must be at the top of the list with Pidò, a little ahead of the Scimone on account of a superior Adina and the generally youthful, artless fervour all round.

Donizetti L'elisir d'amore.

Hilde Gueden *sop* Adina
Giuseppe di Stefano *ten* Nemorino
Renato Capecchi *bar* Belcore

Fernando Corena *bass* Dulcamara
Luisa Mandelli *sop* Giannetta
Chorus and Orchestra of the Maggio Musicale Fiorentino / Francesco Molinari-Pradelli.
Double Decca Ⓜ ① 443 542-2LF2 (two discs: 108 minutes: ADD). Recorded 1955.

This set certainly proves itself to be a survivor. On first appearance it was welcomed by Philip Hope-Wallace as "delightful entertainment: I don't wish to overstate the case for it, but I think if you are disposed to like Donizetti at all, then this performance of the opera with its high spirits, rustic romps and sentiments will give you real pleasure." The mono version was replaced by the previously unissued stereo in 1969, the LP by the CD, and all the time the competition grew. Its most recent reissue prior to this present one was in 1991. There are cuts in this version, of course, but the restoration of defective texts had not then become the big business it is today.

Attractions include the Adina of Hilde Gueden. Far more than most German-trained sopranos she sounds at home in Italian opera: there is even a little touch of Toti Dal Monte girlishness about her, and the later hint of Viennese sophistication does not come amiss when the tone is fresh and sharply flavoured, the line firm, the manner unaffected. Di Stefano is at the very top of his form. His "Una furtiva lagrima" is often touchingly beautiful, and throughout he presents a live, likeable character. Corena is an effective Dulcamara, Capecchi an unstylish Belcore. Molinari-Pradelli conducts ably, and the recorded sound is brighter and more spacious than remembered. This is one of those neat little CD packages which at first you think will have to be prised open in order to get at the second disc; very welcome nevertheless to those with a storage problem.

Donizetti L'elisir d'amore.
Angela Gheorghiu *sop* Adina
Roberto Alagna *ten* Nemorino
Roberto Scaltriti *bar* Belcore
Simone Alaimo *bar* Dulcamara
Elena Dan *sop* Giannetta
Chorus and Orchestra of Opéra National de Lyons / Evelino Pidò.
Stage Director: **Frank Dunlop.**
Decca Ⓕ ⚏ 074 103-3DH (125 minutes). Recorded live in 1996.

This recording was made live at the Lyon Opera in September 1996 and is therefore different from that heard on its CD counterpart. Frank Dunlop's production sets the piece in a rather fanciful 1930s setting. Adina at first appears in riding gear, Dulcamara's caravanserai is brought in by a sleek saloon of the era and he purveys patent medicines and cosmetics appropriate to the period; Belcore might be one of Mussolini's military officers. An air of slight sophistication hangs over the whole affair that doesn't quite march with Donizetti's intentions. Although there's a deal of slapstick, nothing is taken to excess apart from the unsavoury way Dunlop makes fun of a frisky old lady among the peasants. A suitable mode for playing comedy of the Rossini era and beyond is hard to find today. This one is at the least well executed and, by and large, there to be enjoyed.

It houses one great performance, Gheorghiu's Adina, sung with all the flair she showed in the role at Covent Garden and on CD, and acted with a new face and expression for every change of Adina's mood. Here she is by turns, haughty, flighty, concerned (her look of dismay when Nemorino begins "Adina, credimi" indicates that she knows she has gone too far in teasing him), annoyed when the other girls appear to fall for him, and eventually tender when love at last triumphs. These moods are individually delineated in her vibrant tone, finely etched phrasing and deft coloratura. And she looks a treat in four different costumes, a stage being to her fingertips. Alagna makes an attractively naïve, clown-like yet emotionally vulnerable Nemorino, his inner misery at Adina's harsh treatment palpable. As on CD, his singing is verbally vivid, purposefully shaped but a shade monochrome. Scaltriti is less appealing than before. His or Dunlop's idea of the character, when you see him, is unsympathetic and he works too hard for his effects. Then Scaltriti seems to be pushing his tone unnecessarily hard, leading to a slightly overblown sound. Dulcamara is also nastier than usual, not the *buffo* of tradition but a rogue on the make, yet Alaimo's natural geniality keeps on breaking through and his fleet singing is admirable. Pidò conducts a trim reading, his fast speeds justified by the way his singers obviously enjoy them in terms of athletic delivery.

The youthfulness of this cast gives the set an obvious advantage over its rivals, but the Levine/Copley Metropolitan staging (DG) is better to look at and Pavarotti is, of course, *hors concours* as Nemorino – as are Taddei's Dulcamara and Capecchi's Belcore on the Belcanto issue, which also has Valletti's beautifully, subtly sung Nemorino to commend it, but of course in terms of staging it leaves a lot to be desired. The Decca version is the one that will be preferred by most buyers today.

Donizetti Emilia di Liverpool.
Yvonne Kenny *sop* Emilia
Anne Mason *sop* Candida
Bronwen Mills *sop* Luigia

Chris Merritt *ten* Federico
Sesto Bruscantini *bar* Don Romualdo
Geoffrey Dolton *bar* Claudio di Liverpool
Christopher Thornton-Holmes *bar* Count

Donizetti L'eremitaggio di Liwerpool.

Yvonne Kenny *sop* Emilia
Anne Mason *sop* Candida
Bronwen Mills *sop* Bettina
Chris Merritt *ten* Colonel Villars
Sesto Bruscantini *bar* Count Asdrubale
Geoffrey Dolton *bar* Claudio di Liverpool
Christopher Thornton-Holmes *bar* Giacomo
Geoffrey Mitchell Choir; Philharmonia Orchestra / David Parry.
Opera Rara Ⓔ Ⓓ ORC008 (three discs: 199 minutes: DDD). Notes, texts and translations
included. Recorded 1986.

Emilia di Liverpool having failed to impress the Neapolitans in 1824, Donizetti obtained the services
of a different librettist and reworked the whole opera pretty thoroughly in 1828, eventually producing
L'eremitaggio di Liverpool, which fared no better. An upturn in the luckless Emilia's fortunes came
eventually not from ungrateful Naples but from her native city of Liverpool where a concert
performance was given in 1957. A broadcast with Joan Sutherland in the leading role later that same
year earned currency for the title as an esoteric joke, and the recently acquired habit of taking
Donizetti seriously led to this scholarly production by Opera Rara. Both versions are recorded,
introduced in an admirable essay by Jeremy Commons, and, though the CD format does not allow
space for parallel texts, such as graced the original issue on LP, an outline is provided which makes it
possible to compare versions quite conveniently.

And it is a thoroughly delightful addition to the operatic library. The two versions have a certain
amount in common but there is enough that is new in the 1828 score to justify the presence of both;
and of course they provide a fascinating opportunity to observe a composer at work. The
performance is delightful too. This is music that assumes a high degree of accomplishment in its
singers, and listening to the practised skill of Yvonne Kenny and Geoffrey Dolton in their *fioriture*,
the range of Chris Merritt's tenor, the flair of the veteran Bruscantini, one might well wonder whether
it would be reasonable to ask for anything more. Chorus and orchestra do fine work, and David Parry
conducts with a sure feeling for the life and elegance of the piece. All gratitude to the Peter Moores
Foundation for making it possible.

Donizetti La favorita.

Fiorenza Cossotto *mez* Leonora
Luciano Pavarotti *ten* Fernando
Gabriel Bacquier *bar* Alfonso
Nicolai Ghiaurov *bass* Baldassarre
Ileana Cotrubas *sop* Ines
Piero de Palma *ten* Don Gasparo
Chorus and Orchestra of the Teatro Comunale, Bologna / Richard Bonynge.
Decca Grand Opera Ⓜ Ⓓ 430 038-2DM3 (three discs: 168 minutes: ADD). Text and translation
included. Recorded 1974.

La favorita has not been in favour at Covent Garden since 1896. Regretting the opera's lack of
popularity in America, Kobbé observed that it contains some of Donizetti's finest music, and added
"Pity 'tis not heard more frequently". He put it down to the lack of an important soprano role, for
nobody wants a mere mezzo for heroine. "'Tis true 'tis pity and pity 'tis 'tis true" we respond, doing
our best imitations of Polonius. But after hearing (or returning to) this recording we probably say it
with a bit more conviction, for it really is a very fine opera indeed. At least (for perhaps that is going
a little too far), Kobbé was right about the music. Though there are passages where it fails to rise to
the situation, and unfortunately the final duet is one of them, it has much in it that goes to the heart
within the drama, and it is richly supplied with melody and opportunities for fine singing.

The opportunities are well taken here. The recording has Pavarotti in freshest voice. That
understates it: his singing is phenomenal. Wherever you care to test it, it responds. Of the two best-
known solos, "Una vergine" in Act 1 is sung with graceful feeling for line and the shape of the verses
(a fine rounding off of the first half of the second verse, for instance); the voice is evenly produced,
of beautifully pure quality and with an excitingly resonant top C sharp; moreover, the aria is
presented imaginatively as a narration. In "Spirto gentil" the quiet start, poised and well phrased,
works towards intensified but unexaggerated emotion, a beautifully even descent on "ahimè" (no
aspirates) to the reprise of the melody, and though the lack of traditional cadenza is regrettable the
finely controlled quiet ending has its own beauty. Throughout the opera he gives himself sincerely to
the role dramatically as well as vocally.

Cossotto, who in her absolute prime was one of the most exciting singers ever heard, is just fractionally on the other side of it here; she still gives a magnificent performance, gentle as well as powerful, in a part she made very much her own at La Scala. The role of Alfonso attracted all the great baritones in the time when the opera was heard regularly. Here, Gabriel Bacquier provides a tasteful reminder of the French connection (first performance at Paris, 1840), singing with a somewhat colourless tone – there's no spread of the fantail as with Battistini in "mai del don si pentirà". Yet Alfonso emerges as a credible character, a man of feeling, whose "A tanto amor" has, in context, a moving generosity of spirit and refinement of style. Ghiaurov brings sonority, Cotrubas sweetness, Piero de Palma character. The chorus are poorly recorded but that may be to their advantage. The orchestra do well under Bonynge, especially in the 20-minute stretch of ballet music which would be ten too many if less well played. Recorded sound is fine; the booklet contains a brief note, synopsis and text with a not unamusing translation.

Donizetti La fille du régiment.

Dame Joan Sutherland *sop* Marie
Luciano Pavarotti *ten* Tonio
Spiro Malas *bass* Sulpice
Monica Sinclair *contr* Marquise
Edith Coates *contr* Duchess
Jules Bruyère *bass* Hortensius
Eric Garrett *bar* Corporal
Alan Jones *ten* Peasant
Chorus and Orchestra of the Royal Opera House, Covent Garden / Richard Bonynge.
Decca Ⓟ Ⓞ 414 520-2DH2 (two discs: 107 minutes: ADD). Notes, text and translation included. Recorded 1968.

Even Dame Joan Sutherland has rarely if ever made an opera recording so totally enjoyable and involving as this. With the same cast (including chorus and orchestra) as at Covent Garden, it was recorded immediately after a series of live performances in the Royal Opera House, and both the comedy and the pathos come over with an intensity born of communication with live audiences. That impression is the more vivid on this superb CD transfer, for with spoken dialogue used in this original French version of the opera the absence of background noise is a special benefit, and the production vividly captures the developments in the story.

Where on LP the first of the two acts spread on to the second record, here the two acts are each contained complete on one disc, an obvious convenience, though the booklet gets the timings reversed for each, the First Act being much the longer. As with some of Decca's early CD transfers, you could do with more bands to separate items and it strikes one as odd not to indicate separately the most spectacular of Luciano Pavarotti's contributions, his brief but important solo in the finale to Act 1, which was the specific piece which prompted the much-advertised boast "King of the High Cs". For those who want to find it, it comes at 2'58" in band 13 of the first disc, but you should have been able to find it at the touch of a button. Dazzling as the young Pavarotti's singing is, it is Sutherland's performance which, above all, gives glamour to the set, for here in the tomboy, Marie, she found a character through whom she could at once display her vocal brilliance, her ability to convey pathos and equally her sense of fun. The reunion of Marie with the men of her regiment and later with Tonio makes one of the most heartwarming operatic scenes on record, at once a moment for laughing and crying, magically captured here.

The recording is one of Decca's most brilliant, not perhaps quite so clear on inner detail as some, but equivalently more atmospheric. Though there are one or two deliberately comic touches – such as Edith Coates's last cry of "Quelle scandale" – that get near the limit of vulgarity, the production is generally admirable. The sound at once takes one to the theatre, without any feeling of a cold, empty studio. To quote Richard Bonynge in the notes he wrote before the first Covent Garden presentation of this production: "The great point about *La fille du régiment* is that it must be a 'fun' evening for everyone. It is charming musically, and, although it is a mixture of gaiety and real pathos, it must sparkle. It is not my business to educate but to entertain the public. They have a right to be dramatically satisfied and vocally stunned, and it is up to us not to disappoint them". Thanks to the whole cast and to Decca, he certainly hasn't.

Donizetti Linda di Chamounix.

Edita Gruberová *sop* Linda
Don Bernardini *ten* Carlo
Anders Melander *bass* Marquis de Boisfleury
Ettore Kim *bar* Antonio
Monica Groop *mez* Pierotto
Stefano Palatchi *bass* Prefect
Ulrika Precht *sop* Maddalena
Klas Hedlund *ten* Intendant

Mikaeli Chamber Choir; Swedish Radio Symphony Orchestra / Friedrich Haider.
Nightingale Classics Ⓟ Ⓓ NC070561-2 (three discs: 168 minutes: DDD). Notes, texts and translation included. Recorded at a concert performance in the Berwald Hall, Stockholm during September 1993.

This was released at the same time as the 1956 mid-price Serafin reissue on Philips. Given a choice between a two-disc set at medium price and three discs at full, one sincerely hopes to prefer the former. When the difference in playing-time amounts to no more than 13 minutes, it becomes almost a duty to do so. But however well prepared one may be to lean over backwards till it hurts, in this instance it really cannot be done. The Nightingale recording will give pleasure; the old one would bring at best a doubtful enjoyment tempered by regret.

In its own time, the Philips set did indeed afford something of a revelation concerning the opera itself. In 1960 few opera-goers in the UK had seen *Linda di Chamounix*. It was new apart from the famous aria "O luce di quest' anima" and a couple of excerpts recorded long ago by Battistini. Critics were agreeably surprised: "consistently elegant and beguiling" was one description, and another concluded that his previous notion "that it was a somewhat empty piece ... turns out to be completely wrong". Partly why it had seemed to be a thin, insipid entertainment was that it was not helped by the fact that "O luce di quest' anima" comes early in Act 1 and is unmatched in tunefulness by anything that follows, partly the familiar want of harmonic exploration and the relapse into a facile prettiness. But there is much more than that. The opera has its distinctive identity, and each of the numbers has its own strength: familiarity breeds respect.

The Swedish orchestra bring a refinement to the Overture which does justice to its origins in chamber music (Donizetti adapted one of his string quartets when he found that in Vienna, where the opera had its première, they expected more than a brief prelude). Then the chorus enter, raggedly and with uncertain intonation in the San Carlo ranks for Serafin, admirably precise, well balanced and sensitive in Stockholm. In both performances, the supporting soloists have their merits, but this is one of those operas named after its heroine, and she is crucial to its success. In the Philips recording Antonietta Stella is simply and seriously miscast: she has not the shine, the vivacity, the technical ease, for the part. Of Gruberová it may be true that her voice would have been still more apt a few years earlier, but she gives a magnificent performance. The tone still has an almost Tetrazzini-like radiance for her introductory aria, and her triumph is also in the creation, through purely vocal means, of a real character. It is an extremely demanding role – in Act 2 she is never off-stage, as one solo or duet follows another, culminating with a Mad scene at the end of which the audience will be disappointed if there is no crowning high E flat. This is a live concert performance, and Gruberová impresses with her stamina, as she does with her vocal skill and dramatic vividness.

In the Philips set, there are stalwart performances by some of the leading Italian singers of the time, and it is particularly good to hear Barbieri again, her strong Italianate lower register rather more appropriate to the 'trousers' role than Monica Groop's more maternal mezzo. The Nightingale version has less resounding names, but all do well, the tenor, Don Bernardini, having sufficient grace and elegance to reconcile us at least partially to the loss of Cesare Valletti. The set comes with a mildly amusing English translation, and 40 pages in densely printed Japanese!

Donizetti Linda di Chamounix.

Mariella Devia *sop* Linda
Luca Canonici *ten* Carlo
Alfonso Antoniozzi *bar* Marquis de Boisfleury
Petteri Salomaa *bass* Antonio
Sonia Ganassi *mez* Pierotto
Donato di Stefano *bar* Prefect
Francesca Provvisionato *mez* Maddalena
Boguslaw Fiksinski *ten* Intendant
Koor van de Nationale Reisopera; Orchestra of Eastern Netherlands / Gabriele Bellini.
Arts Ⓢ Ⓓ 47151-2 (three discs: 177 minutes: DDD). Italian text included. Recorded 1992.

For a newcomer to *Linda di Chamounix* (or one who is hovering on the brink, or, having not been impressed by a first hearing, wonders whether it might be time to try again), it may be helpful to think of it as Donizetti's *Luisa Miller*. There are similarities in subject – a strong father-and-daughter relationship, a simple family and communal life threatened by the high-and-mighty. More than that, both operas evoke a strong sense of compassion. Donizetti's is lighter, with a comic element, a happy ending, and reassurance from the start in that the 'villain' is only the *buffo* bass-baritone whom operatic convention will not allow to win. Still, tragedy looms and the situations involve heartache of various kinds, of which the separation of soprano-and-tenor lovers is not the only one. There is a homeliness about the melodies and their harmonies that makes it seem all rather tame. Yet the proof, or at any rate evidence, that this is far from the whole story lies in the way that this opera has of deepening its impression on each encounter over the years.

As indicated above, the Serafin recording has to be dismissed, in spite of its being on two discs. The Nightingale set is in almost every way a delight. Readers who have that version would not find it worth their while to replace it with this one, but for those who have to choose this is certainly a viable alternative and in certain respects to be preferred.

Mariella Devia sings with purity of tone and brilliancy of range and technique; just occasionally it sounds like a voice that needs a rest (the same is true of the tenor Canonici), yet much is beautiful as well as skilful. Though Gruberová leaves a stronger impression of the character, Devia too presents a fully human Linda and no mere coloratura-singing doll. In the main supporting roles, the two recordings each have an advantage, the Haider performance gaining from the livelier Carlo of Don Bernardini, this one from the outstanding bass of Petteri Salomaa. The 'trousers' role of Pierotto (whose hurdy-gurdy and plaintive folk-song theme contribute so distinctively) is sung here by the rather fruitily vibrant Sonia Ganassi, and Monica Groop, though somewhat maternal, is perhaps preferable. Both versions offer a suitably authoritative Prefect and a discreetly *buffo*-ish Marquis.

Both are fine in ensemble, chorus work and orchestral playing. Friedrich Haider in Stockholm moves it along at a livelier pace; Gabriele Bellini is more contemplative. Haider's live recording has the singers further forward; this one brings more orchestral detail to notice. One clear advantage lies with its predecessor – it includes an English translation of the libretto – but it also costs about twice as much.

Donizetti Lucia di Lammermoor.
Maria Callas *sop* Lucia
Giuseppe di Stefano *ten* Edgardo
Rolando Panerai *bar* Enrico
Nicola Zaccaria *bass* Raimondo
Giuseppe Zampieri *ten* Arturo
Luisa Villa *mez* Alisa
Mario Carlin *ten* Normanno
Chorus of La Scala, Milan; Berlin RIAS Symphony Orchestra / Herbert von Karajan.
EMI mono Ⓟ Ⓞ CMS7 63631-2 (two discs: 119 minutes: ADD). Notes, text and translation included. Recorded at a performance in the Berlin State Opera on September 29th, 1955.

For many years this live performance of *Lucia di Lammermoor*, recorded on tour in Berlin in 1955 with Callas, Karajan and members of La Scala company, was one of the most prized of all unauthorized sets, offering those of us who weren't there a chance to sample a sensation and discover why some normally robust critics were robbed of sleep for a week by the experience. EMI subsequently obtained the rights to this recording and in many respects it is a set that can lay claim to being the most representative – the most vivid and searching – of all extant recordings of Callas in this, one of her most famous roles.

The fact that the performance is live, rather than studio-bound, is crucial in a single key respect. Callas is herself transformed by the experience. In the very act of playing Lucia on stage she completely becomes her in mind and spirit. And she does this in a way that was never quite the case in her two EMI studio recordings. The live version brings with it some technical limitations which are mentioned below, but it is not without its advantages, not least in the crucial matter of perspective. In this Berlin recording, Callas herself is often more naturally 'placed' than is the case in the 1953 Florence set, where the close microphoning favoured by EMI's Italian production team tends to rob the singing of mystery and allure. (Walter Legge, who had signed Callas for Columbia but who didn't supervise the recording, later described the Florence hall as "antimusical and inimical", and insisted on delaying the *Lucia* until the better produced and more 'revelatory' *I puritani* was recorded and released.)

It must be said that the engineers, whose tapes are here digitally remastered by EMI, were enormously helped in all this by Karajan's production. Franco Zeffirelli recalls: "He arranged everything round her. She did the Mad scene with a follow-spot, like a ballerina, against black. Nothing else. He let her be music, absolute music." It was, Zeffirelli argued, the only way to produce Callas, whose musical command and command of gesture obviated all need for fabricated play-acting. Callas's was not a Lucia that needed to flutter about the stage like a demented dove. Musically and dramatically, the relationship between Callas and Karajan was symbiotic, as it was later to be in their 1955 recording of *Madama Butterfly* (reviewed under Puccini). As a result, Callas's portrayal of Lucia is here deeper than ever it was. In this performance, the depth of her love for Edgardo, and her trust in him, are so overwhelming that when she is shown the fabricated letter of betrayal the shock is monstrous. We hear this not only in her enunciation of the words "Me infelice! Ahi! La folgore piombò" but in the *Larghetto* that follows where she seems already to have passed beyond this world. The Mad scene is not so much presaged at this moment; spiritually, this is where it begins, just as with Callas's Medea where we know, psychologically, the precise moment when she resolves to sacrifice her children's lives.

In the Mad scene itself, the lines are longer than in the Florence recording, the phrasing subtler, the gradations of tone more unerringly placed. And the voice is in generally excellent shape. Reviewing the performance in *Opera* in December 1955, Desmond Shawe-Taylor wrote: "I dare say she will never sing better than she does now; there is Greek resin in her voice which will never be quite strained away; she will never charm us with the full round ductile tone of Muzio or [Rosa] Raisa or Ponselle. But she has sudden flights, dramatic outbursts of rocketing virtuosity, of which even those more richly endowed singers were hardly capable." In the opening scene by the fountain, in fact, it is the grain in Callas's tone – the Greek resin – that helps give the performance its disturbing visionary power: more Graham Sutherland than Joan.

As a study of Lucia herself this performance is well-nigh unsurpassable. As an account of Donizetti's *Lucia di Lammermoor* it has its dated elements, of course. In the first place, it is heavily cut. Not quite as heavily cut as the 1953 recording conducted by Serafin (Karajan gives us more of the Act 2 finale) but pretty much an old-style 'Lucy Lammermoor Show'. And this is exacerbated by Karajan's impatience with the music for the *comprimario* roles. Poor Luisa Villa, singing the role of Lucia's confidante Alisa, is rushed off her feet, and the hapless Arturo sounds more than usually uptight. Nor does Karajan always accompany the co-principals, Panerai and di Stefano, with the kind of sympathy he so obviously lavishes on Callas. With Callas the tempos are just, the lines are long, and the rubatos are infinitely subtle and intense. Edgardo, by contrast, is confronted by some exceptionally slow tempos. Even more than usual, he is treated as a figure straight out of Victorian melodrama, with Karajan and di Stefano treating the final scene among the tombs as pure Grand Guignol. But di Stefano copes. Panerai, by contrast, is strained by some of the tempos, though it has to be said that the role of Enrico seems to lie awkwardly for him. That being the case, one wonders why on earth Karajan allowed him to launch into a roughly taken and vulgarly sustained high G at the end of the first section of "Cruda, funesta". Gobbi (1953) is grander and altogether more assured, but he is also blander than Panerai (Cappuccilli, 1959, is blander still). Judged purely as singing, Panerai's Enrico is something of a nightmare, but as a dramatic performance – Enrico as a devilish spur to the tragedy of Callas's Lucia – it is something of a *tour de force*. It is also worth noting how Karajan manages to invest Donizetti's apparently innocuous accompanying figures with a tremendous viciousness and feline power in many of Enrico's exchanges with Lucia.

EMI have done the performance proud both in their packaging and in the physical brilliance of the remastering of the tapes for CD. These are the cleanest, brightest and most articulate transfers we have yet had. But there is a rather large snag. On the original tapes there is a good deal of residual distortion where Lucia, Edgardo, or the solo flautist are both close and at the very top of their registers. Transfer to LP tended to mop up this high-frequency distortion, and the somewhat attenuated CD transfers from one of the unauthorized issues achieve the same effect. Initially, you may think this is a disaster from the EMI set, particularly as the worst example of all comes in the big cadenza at the height of the Mad scene. In fact, one gets used to it. But it must be a case of *caveat emptor*; there are collectors who may prefer the more dimly transferred, and poorly packaged, rival sets.

The other quibble with EMI, and it is a tiny one, is their rather parsimonious way with the applause. Mostly this makes excellent sense, but one of the performance's most remarkable features is the encoring of the great Sextet in Act 2. To judge by rival transfers, the encore is a clear concession to the need to retain public order in the opera-house and in the streets of Berlin beyond. EMI, though, fillet the applause to a 15-second dribble, making the reprise sound like an act of gross self-indulgence on the part of the artists. Many would agree that there are times in a live recording when the sideshow should be retained, though only video would convey the evening's most astonishing sideshow – Callas's consummate art in remaining half in character whilst she took ten minutes of solo curtain calls after the Mad scene. With or without visuals, though, this is the Lucia of a lifetime.

Donizetti Lucia di Lammermoor.
Maria Callas *sop* Lucia
Ferrucio Tagliavini *ten* Edgardo
Piero Cappuccilli *bar* Enrico
Bernard Ladysz *bass* Raimondo
Leonard del Ferro *ten* Arturo
Margreta Elkins *mez* Alisa
Renzo Casellato *ten* Normanno
Philharmonia Chorus and Orchestra / Tullio Serafin.
EMI Ⓔ Ⓓ CDS5 56284-2 (two discs: 142 minutes). Notes, text and translation included.
Recorded 1959.

Callas was certainly more fallible here than in her first Lucia for Serafin in 1953, but the subtleties of interpretation are much greater; she is the very epitome of Scott's gentle, yet ardently intense heroine, and the special way she inflects words and notes lifts every passage in which she is concerned out of the ordinary gamut of soprano singing. In that sense she is unique, and this is certainly one of the first offerings to give to an innocent ear or a doubter in convincing them of Callas's greatness. The earlier part of the Mad scene provides the most convincing evidence of all. Then the pathos of "Alfin son tua", even more that of "Del ciel clemente" are here incredibly eloquent, and the coloratura is finer than it was in 1953, if not always so secure at the top. Tagliavini, after a rocky start, offers a secure, pleasing, involving Edgardo. Cappuccilli, then in his early prime, is a forceful but not insensitive Enrico, Bernard Ladysz a sound Raimondo. Serafin is a far more thoughtful, expressive Donizettian than his rivals on other sets. Of course, this isn't the truly complete Lucia; for that you must look to the 1971 Sutherland/Bonynge/Decca recording (reissued on CD in 1985), but the set does have the most complete, in another sense, Lucia, and that puts it among the most persuasive accounts of the opera ever recorded.

Donizetti Lucia di Lammermoor.

Montserrat Caballé *sop* Lucia
José Carreras *ten* Edgardo
Vicente Sardinero *bar* Enrico
Samuel Ramey *bass* Raimondo
Claes Hakon Ahnsjö *ten* Arturo
Ann Murray *mez* Alisa
Vincenzo Bello *ten* Normanno
Ambrosian Opera Chorus; New Philharmonia Orchestra / Jesús López-Cobos.
Philips Ⓜ ⓓ 446 551-2PM2 (two discs: 143 minutes: ADD). Recorded 1976.

Lucia di Lammermoor is a role for a coloratura soprano, and one who (like Sutherland in her prime) can throw off the upper tessitura with creamy tone and consummate ease. The more surprising that Montserrat Caballé, essentially a dramatic soprano, copes so well with the vocal intricacies of the Mad scene, bringing an added dimension of drama which all but compensates for the moments of fierceness. She is well partnered by José Carreras as Edgardo and the rest of the cast, which includes Claes Hakon Ahnsjö, Vicente Sardinero and Samuel Ramey, is more than adequate. The lively contribution of the Ambrosian Opera Chorus is well projected in a recording which is atmospheric and vivid. Jesús López-Cobos could display more zest at times, yet in spite of this the performance has certainly got considerable impetus. Very good value, especially for Caballé fans.

Donizetti Lucrezia Borgia.

Montserrat Caballé *sop* Lucrezia
Alfredo Kraus *ten* Gennaro
Ezio Flagello *bass* Alfonso
Shirley Verrett *mez* Orsini
Franco Ricciardi *ten* Liverotto
Fernando Iacopucci *ten* Vitellozzo
Franzo Romano *bass* Gazella
Ferruccio Mazzoli *bass* Petrucci
Giuseppe Baratti *ten* Rustighello
Vito Maria Brunetti *bass* Gubetta
Robert El Hage *bass* Astolfo
RCA Italiana Opera Chorus and Orchestra / Jonel Perlea.
RCA Victor Gold Seal Ⓜ ⓓ GD86642 (two discs: 125 minutes: ADD). Notes, text and translation included. Recorded 1966.

Neither this, or the Sutherland/Bonynge set on Decca met with a really enthusiastic reception when first released on LP: Andrew Porter found Caballé undramatic, Perlea dull and the recording underproduced ("not a *performance* of the opera in the way that Walter Legge's Angel or John Culshaw's Decca sets are; rather, a collection of good singers in a studio going through the score"), while in 1979, Lionel Salter thought Decca's Sutherland variable ("at her swoopiest and swooniest" in her appreciation of the sleeping Gennaro but snapping out of it later) and Bonynge inclined to confuse "full-bloodedness with blood-and-thunder". These two critics shared a liking for the opera itself.

This time round Perlea's conducting seems to carry more conviction and Caballé's singing more dramatic involvement than the review (and memory) suggested. Her alternations of tenderness and regal authority bring the woman to a more interesting kind of life than Sutherland manages to do, and when she is playing opposite Alfredo Kraus a genuinely mutual responsiveness does much to counteract the sense of a concert performance or merely "going through the score". With the proviso that there aren't any trills worth speaking of (and they are not a luxury in this role), Caballé sings the part beautifully, her voice at its loveliest, the tone completely steady (contrasting with Sutherland) and the breadth of phrasing a delight. Kraus is splendid (but Aragall, with Sutherland, is also very fine); Flagello sonorous and preferable in the part to the baritone Ingvar Wixell; and as Orsini, Verrett has exactly the freshness that makes it just possible to think of her as Gennaro's young friend, which Horne, for all the sumptuousness of her voice, did not. On balance, then, this recording is preferable as far as the singing is concerned – and that is much. The orchestra is less of a presence than in the Decca version, and there is less pointed attention to detail. Texturally, Bonynge is preferable, certainly in the inclusion of the fine aria for Gennaro recovered by Bonynge and originally performed in St Petersburg. As to the musical value of the opera, if it were all up to the standard of the Prologue, with its intensely moving ensemble, it would be great indeed; as it is, you will find it yielding more, rather than less, as time goes by.

Donizetti Maria Padilla.

Lois McDonall *sop* Maria
Della Jones *mez* Inès
Graham Clark *ten* Don Ruiz
Christian du Plessis *bar* Don Pedro
Roderick Earle *bass* Ramiro
Ian Caley *ten* Don Luigi
Roderick Kennedy *bass* Don Alfonso
Joan Davies *mez* Francisca
Geoffrey Mitchell Choir; London Symphony Orchestra / Alun Francis.
Opera Rara Ⓕ ① ORC006 (three discs: 151 minutes: DDD). Notes, text and translation included.
Recorded 1980.

We tend to assume that unfamiliar operas by famous composers must have been either juvenilia or failures in their own time. *Maria Padilla* was neither: it had its première in 1841, late in Donizetti's career, and though its initial reception appears to have been tepid, it went on to enjoy considerable success in Italy and as far abroad as Rio de Janeiro and Odessa. London first heard it in 1973, when it was given a concert performance by Opera Rara at the Queen Elizabeth Hall; the first stage production took place 15 years later, by Dorset Opera at Sherborne. By that time the present recording had been issued, causing widespread astonishment at the opera's non-performance over such a long span of time.

It has to be said that there are other Donizetti operas whose neglect is more astonishing (*L'assedio di Calais*, also an Opera Rara rediscovery, reviewed above, is one). The score becomes remarkable only with the Second Act, and the ending, over which Donizetti and his commentators have taken such pains, makes unsatisfactory drama whether in the surviving 'happy' version or the original death-by-joy. At several places there is a curious feeling of near-miss. The long duet for father and daughter in Act 3 is unable, because of the scenario, to come to the moment of recognition and reconciliation which might have been at the heart of the opera. Then in the finale of that act, starting with the solemn "Giurata innanzi a Dio", and clearly written with the corresponding point in *Norma* somewhere at the back of Donizetti's mind, the ensemble grows steadily with the sad swell of sound, so much the glory of Italian opera, till, with the climax in sight just a few bars away, inspiration seems to fail and we drop earthwards. Yet that finale remains one of the best numbers. Finer still, and again reminiscent of *Norma*, is the Prelude to Act 3 and the continuation of its mood into the passage where the demented old father sings off-stage while Maria is urged by her sister to go to him. There are in fact many fine passages, and not all are in the tragic part of the opera, but it is too uneven for sustained satisfaction, dramatically and musically too much in the condition of potentiality rather than achievement.

The performance itself is an undoubted achievement, as is the recording, again helped by the Peter Moores Foundation. Alun Francis conducts with conviction, the Geoffrey Mitchell Choir make an excellent contribution and the soloists put heart and soul into their work. The part of Maria needs a soprano with "a voice like a cannon", as Donizetti said of his favourite, Tadolini. Lois McDonall hardly answers to that description, her voice sounding as though, at least above the middle notes and at medium volume, it has at some point suffered a loss of quality: even so, there is impressive technical mastery and a generous emotional involvement. Christian du Plessis is overparted: best in the most dramatic moments, vocally uncomfortable and prone to stylistic exaggerations elsewhere. An inspired piece of casting is that of Graham Clark as the aged father (conventionally a bass, but here a tenor role), and the most thoroughly enjoyable singing comes from Della Jones.

Donizetti Maria Stuarda.

Edita Gruberová *sop* Maria Stuarda
Agnes Baltsa *mez* Elisabetta
Francisco Araiza *ten* Leicester
Francesco Ellero d'Artegna *bass* Talbot
Simone Alaimo *bar* Cecil
Iris Vermillion *mez* Anna
Bavarian Radio Chorus; Munich Radio Orchestra / Giuseppe Patanè.
Philips Ⓕ ① 426 233-2PH2 (two discs: 133 minutes: DDD). Notes, text and translation included.
Recorded 1989.

How this opera grows in the affections. And how it strengthens the larger, ever-deepening appreciation not merely of Donizetti's work but of operatic conventions as such, meaning that the frequently derided forms of opera (the set-pieces, aria-and-cabaletta and so forth) can increasingly be a source of pleasure and of perceived power in the writing. Here, for instance, part of the exhilaration arises out of the composer's skill in suiting the conventions to his dramatic and musical purposes. Elizabeth's first aria, meditatively hopeful yet anxious, fits the lyric-*cantabile* form; then the arrival of Talbot and Cecil with their opposing influences provokes the intensified turbulence of irresolution that makes dramatic sense out of the cabaletta. It is so with the duets and ensembles: they look like conventional set-pieces, but established form and specific material have been so well fitted that, with the musical inspiration working strongly (as it is here), you have opera not in its naïve stage awaiting development towards freedom from form but, on the contrary, opera at the confident height of a period in its history when it was entirely true to itself.

This recording fortifies such conviction, partly for the very reason that the opera survives a lack of some of the drama so vividly presented by its immediate predecessor in the catalogues. Indeed the work has sufficient dramatic power inherent in it to be able to do much more than merely survive. A loss is incurred essentially because Elizabeth is undercharacterized by the singer: Baltsa's performance is by no means devoid of feeling, but she is curiously selective in the emotions she chooses or manages to convey. Thus, we are given a sense of strong will-power through the characteristic thrust of her lower register, in the Queen's determination to settle the destinies of England and France, but when it comes to the aria, though tenderness is evident, the more tense and anxious tones required in its development are not. When she then turns to the hateful thought that Mary Stuart may have stolen the heart of her lover, Baltsa fails to mirror the change of mood. Then, in the scene with Leicester, she is not good at the angry or regretful asides or in fully expressing the harsh determination behind the references to her rival. The greater completeness and vividness of Gruberová's presentation of Mary throw this into relief, yet when it comes to the confrontation of the two Queens, both singers are somewhat underpowered, Baltsa in the bite of her "No", Gruberová in the venom of her "Bastarda". Plowright and Baker made more out of this on their Mackerras/EMI recording (currently out of the catalogue), as indeed did their predecessors, Sutherland and Tourangeau with Bonynge on Decca.

All the same, this is opera as opera (not 'opera as drama' or any other such silly concept), and in opera much of the drama comes through the singing ('as such'). Baltsa's is a glorious voice beautifully produced; she has feeling for the music, which is enabled to communicate through delighted ears to what we call the heart. At Covent Garden the performance of Baltsa and Gruberová together in Bellini's *I Capuleti e i Montecchi* produced the truest, most moving evening of *bel canto* opera that opera-goers had known in many years. When they sing together it is an occasion, and though Gruberová's voice does not always sound completely steady in recording it is still an instrument of exceptional purity. The accomplishment at work in its usage is matched here by an imaginative and intellectual grasp of the part. Hers is a most lovely performance throughout. Araiza also sings well, especially in Act 3 (earlier there are some small points, but telling ones, where score-markings go unobserved). Alaimo as Cecil makes little impression till his duet ("duettino") with Elizabeth, Francesco Ellero d'Artegna makes a firm-voiced dull old stick out of Talbot (which is perhaps what he is).

The Munich Chorus are excellent, both musically and dramatically. Orchestral playing is fine too, and Patanè's direction both spirited and flexible: rather more than the other recordings that have appeared since his death, this one serves as a worthy memorial. Recorded sound compares well with the Mackerras, and the relevance of further comparisons is reduced because Sutherland and Bonynge use a different score while the Baker and Mackerras version is in English with a mezzo-soprano Mary. The present recording makes some small cuts in the Gérard score, all of coda material apart from the second verse of Elizabeth's cabaletta in Act 1.

Donizetti Poliuto.

José Carreras *ten* Poliuto
Katia Ricciarelli *sop* Paolina
Juan Pons *bar* Severo
László Polgár *bass* Callistene
Paolo Gavanelli *bass* Nearco
Harry Peeters *bass* Felice
Jorge Pita *ten* A Christian
Vienna Singakademie Chorus; Vienna Symphony Orchestra / Oleg Caetani.
Sony Classical Ⓟ Ⓒ M2K44821 (two discs: 106 minutes: DDD). Notes, text and translation included. Recorded at concert performances in the Konzerthaus, Vienna in 1986.

The *Poliuto* set by Latham-König on Nuova Era from 1988 has certain textural advantages over this one, most notably the inclusion of Poliuto's solo "Fu macchiato" following the recitative "Veleno è l'aura" in Act 2, where for the first time the hero's character has some musical life. In other respects this version, recorded in the Vienna Konzerthaus in 1986, is distinctly preferable. Even in textural matters, such as the inclusion of the fine trio for Poliuto, Paolina and Nearco, it can offer reasonable competition.

Apart from cheers and applause at the end of acts, one would not know it was a live recording. The sound is clear and well balanced, orchestral and choral work have refinement and the soloists vary from adequate to distinguished – the best is Ricciarelli. She softens her role, turns it inward, imparts an anxious tenderness. Notes that are loud and high are fewer than remembered. Passages such as the Act 1 aria ("Di quai soavi lagrime") and "Ah! fuggi da morte" in the Prison scene become exceptionally beautiful. The baritone and bass, too, are remarkably good, Juan Pons and the noteworthy Lászlo Polgár both singing with finely concentrated tone and plenty of authority. As for Carreras (this was before his illness), the performance is interesting principally as it shows, still more clearly than other recordings did, the direction his career was taking. Characterization seems not to go much beyond a generalized sincerity, but that may also be a limitation of the role itself: it is difficult to see why tenors have found it so attractive.

On the other hand, it becomes ever more easy to see why the opera survives. Despite some banalities, it's a seminal score: Verdi, for instance, must have known it and had it working inside him from (at least) *Il trovatore* to *Aida*. There are many fine things in it, and the Act 2 finale is quite simply one of the best sustained ensemble passages in Italian opera.

Donizetti Poliuto.

Franco Corelli *ten* Poliuto
Maria Callas *sop* Paolina
Ettore Bastianini *bar* Severo
Nicola Zaccaria *bass* Callistene
Piero de Palma *ten* Nearco
Rinaldo Pelizzoni *ten* Felice
Virgilio Carbonari, Giuseppe Morresi *basses* Christians
Chorus and Orchestra of La Scala, Milan / Antonino Votto.
EMI mono Ⓜ ① CMS5 65448-2 (two discs: 111 minutes: ADD). Notes, text and translation included. Recorded live on December 7th, 1960.

The book on Franco Corelli by Marina Boagno (published in English by Baskerville, USA; 1996) lists no less than nine 'unofficial' labels through which this recording had already been made available. Only here has it been received into the official canon, by incorporation into the release-list of EMI's Callas Edition; and the quality is certainly an improvement on the Rodolphe LPs by which many previously knew the work. The sound is clear and faithful to the timbre of the voices, which are slightly favoured in the balance at the expense of the orchestra. The theatre's acoustic tends to sound boxy on record, but that at least helps definition and does nothing to disguise the raw edge that in some of her more strenuous passages was likely by then to have become notable in Callas's voice. With it comes unforgettable testimony to what was clearly a great night at La Scala.

Its place in the Callas history owes less to the importance of this new role in her repertory than to the triumph of her return to the house she had left in high dudgeon in 1958. The part of Paolina in this Roman tragedy is restricted in opportunities and leaves the centre of the stage to the tenor. In other ways it suits her remarkably well, the Second Act in particular involving the heroine in grievous emotional stress with music that here runs deep enough to give it validity. In the first scene of that act she has a duet with the baritone in which her solo ("Ei non vegga il pianto mio") has a tenderness she knew so well to depend on the right, instinctively judicious use of portamento. Later, in the Temple scene, her every utterance has its beauty or intensity or both, and the whole company rises with her to the inspired climax of Donizetti's score.

For this is, to a surprising extent, a company-opera. There is a big part for the chorus, who sing with fine Italian sonority. Nicola Zaccaria, La Scala's leading *basso cantabile*, has not quite the sumptuous quality of his predecessors, Pasero and Pinza, but is still in their tradition, singing with authority in his number with chorus in Act 3. Ettore Bastianini is rapturously received and, though wanting in polish and variety of expression, uses his firm and resonant voice to exciting effect. The tenor *comprimario* Piero de Palma cuts a by no means inadequate vocal figure by the side of Corelli, who, for the most part, is stupendous. It is not just the ring and range of voice that impress, but a genuinely responsive art, his aria "Lasciando la terra" in Act 3 providing a fine example. It is for his part in the opera, quite as much as for Callas's, that the recording will be valued.

Donizetti Rosmonda d'Inghilterra.

Renée Fleming *sop* Rosmonda
Bruce Ford *ten* Enrico II
Nelly Miricioiu *sop* Leonora di Guienna
Alastair Miles *bass* Gualtiero Clifford
Diana Montague *mez* Arturo
Geoffrey Mitchell Choir; Philharmonia Orchestra / David Parry.
Opera Rara Ⓔ ① ORC13 (two discs: 150 minutes: DDD). Notes, text and translation included. Recorded 1994.

With the persistence of the *bel canto* revival, or more specifically the unearthing, editing and performance of forgotten early nineteenth-century operas, it becomes ever more difficult to make out the line which has separated survival from extinction. By the criteria appropriate to its kind, *Rosmonda d'Inghilterra* is a very good opera, inferior to *Lucia di Lammermoor* but not annihilatingly so. To say that score and libretto are highly workmanlike may register as a kind of belittlement, though it should not do so, and it needs saying since we know that Donizetti worked fast and turned out operas by the dozen and so are inclined to assume that he must have been slipshod. In fact, this, his 41st, shows the confident mastery of form that can make useful, unselfconscious innovations, and there is scarcely more than a single item in which he seems not to be writing with genuine creativity. The answer must lie with the absence of the really Big Tune (though the gift for melody never falters). Or possibly it is as a matter of state or opera-house politics (a King shown letting his heart rule his head, and a finale in which the principal soprano lies dead upon the floor while her rival sings the last solo, which she naturally regards as her rightful own). Whatever the cause, over the period of roughly a century-and-a-half audiences have been missing out on an opera that is a credit to its genre, which in turn is far more of a credit to the art-form than has been generally conceded.

The performance could hardly be improved. David Parry conducts with what any listener who presumes to judge is likely to feel a natural rightness: one is not, from the armchair, forever calling out 'Slow down!', 'Put some life into it!' or the other familiar cries of encouragement. More than that, the playing of the Philharmonia is of unvaryingly high quality, and they have plenty to play – the Overture is one of Donizetti's best, and the orchestral score shares interest on equable terms with the voice-parts. These include two virtuoso roles for sopranos, who in the final scene confront each other in duet. As Rosmonda, the immured and misled mistress, Renée Fleming shows once again that not only has she one of the most lovely voices to be heard in our time but that she is also a highly accomplished technician and a sympathetic stylist. Nelly Miricioiu is the older woman, the Queen (originally Eleanor of Aquitaine) whose music encompasses a wide range of emotions with an adaptable vocal character to match. Whether by design or by the condition of her voice in the different recording sessions, she fits the Second Act more happily than the First, where for much of the time the tone appears to have lost its familiar incisive thrust. Bruce Ford is an excellent Enrico (plenty of incisiveness there), and Alastair Miles makes an authoritative father and councillor in the person of Clifford. The *travesto* role of Arturo is taken by the ever welcome Diana Montague, and it is good to find that a solo has been dutifully included for 'him' in Act 2, even if it is a less than inspired piece of music.

As always with Opera Rara's productions, the booklet adds substantially to the value of the set and contains a first-rate introduction by Jeremy Commons. The only complaint with the recording concerns balance, which sometimes accords prominence and recession in a somewhat arbitrary way. The opera and performance, however, are strong enough to take that on board, and the set is keenly recommended.

Donizetti Ugo, Conte di Parigi.

Maurice Arthur *ten* Ugo
Della Jones *mez* Luigi V
Eiddwen Harrhy *sop* Emma
Janet Price *sop* Bianca
Yvonne Kenny *sop* Adelia
Christian du Plessis *bar* Folco di Angiò
Geoffrey Mitchell Choir; New Philharmonia Orchestra / Alun Francis.
Opera Rara Ⓟ Ⓓ ORC001 (three discs: 157 minutes: AAD). Notes, text and translation included. Recorded 1977.

This was the first in Opera Rara's invaluable series of Donizetti rarities, and its reissue on CD is justified by both the quality of the work itself and that of the highly creditable performance. Though given at La Scala, Milan in 1832 with Pasta and Grisi fresh from their triumphs in *Norma*, the opera failed to gain more than five performances. Donizetti used bits of it for other operas, and the manuscript was bundled away, tied up with string, and left forgotten on the shelves of the Naples Conservatory. When prepared for this recording, the score required orchestral parts to be reconstructed. More had to be done on the text and, according to Jeremy Commons's essay (considerably more than a mere 'note'), the heroine's final aria "is here performed, probably for the first time ever, in its original form".

As with so many of its successors in the Opera Rara series, *Ugo* is likely to impress the present-day listener as being by no means a world distant in merit from others that are far better remembered. The libretto and the original censor's mangling of it are said to be principally responsible for the failure, but in fact the story holds together quite well, the drama centering on four characters (quite enough), and the residual interest in past events is not likely to trouble anyone who has grappled with similar problems in, say, *Il trovatore* or *Simon Boccanegra*. Arias, duets and concerted pieces arise naturally, are of good (not superlative) quality, and take their places in a genuinely assured musical-dramatic construction.

The provision of singers in our own time may seem more problematic, but Janet Price, Yvonne Kenny and Della Jones are gifted and accomplished artists and prove a great source of strength. When in fighting mood, the name-part requires a more heroic, full-bodied tone than Maurice Arthur has to offer, but the quieter lyrical passages are often beautifully done. Good, crisp singing by the chorus and admirably alert playing by the orchestra, are further attractions. Alun Francis conducts in such a way that everything sounds right (comparisons not being available); recorded sound is clear and well balanced; presentation is excellent.

Paul Dukas

Dukas Ariane et Barbe-bleue.
Katherine Ciesinski *sop* Ariane
Gabriel Bacquier *bar* Barbe-bleue
Mariana Paunova *contr* La Nourrice
Hanna Schaer *mez* Sélysette
Anne-Marie Blanzat *sop* Ygraine
Jocelyne Chamonin *sop* Mélisande
Michèlle Command *sop* Bellangère
French Radio Chorus; New Philharmonic Orchestra / Armin Jordan.
Erato Libretto Ⓜ Ⓓ 2292-45663-2 (two discs: 117 minutes: DDD). Notes, text and translation included. Recorded 1983.

Listening to this recording of *Ariane et Barbe-bleue* at least obviates the need to suffer the idiocies of stage productions such as the notorious one in Paris, where the action was set, unbelievably, on a rooftop. On the other hand, without any visual aid and from the sound alone, it is often impossible, except by following the score or the libretto (fortunately provided) to know who is singing at any given moment or even to understand what is going on – quite apart from the fact that Ariane's companion, the Nurse, who occupies much of Act 1, is all but unintelligible because of her plummy production and obscure vowels. For surely no opera ever was so perversely planned from the dramaturgical point of view: six female principals (aurally very difficult to distinguish one from another) and one male who, despite being one of the title-roles, has precisely 20 bars to sing in the entire work. In contrast Ariane, a militant feminist and determined liberalist (almost her opening words are "First one must disobey") with suspiciously erotic reactions to the physical beauties of Bluebeard's previous wives, is on stage throughout the opera's nearly two hours, and singing most of the time. Hers is a hugely demanding part, basically for a mezzo but dipping down to low G sharp and in places, such as her "Diamonds" aria in Act 1, her urging of the other wives in Act 2, and her shattering of the glass panel shutting out the light, calling for the impact of a dramatic soprano. The American-born Katherine Ciesinski is to be admired not only for her stamina and technical assurance but for the colorations of her tone according to Ariane's changing moods, now aggressive, now tender.

Ariane, like the five-years-earlier *Pelléas*, is based on a Maeterlinck play, but is more symbolical, nothing like as fragile, more symphonic in structure and considerably more opulent, even Wagnerian, in its scoring. Armin Jordan secures orchestral playing of fine intensity from the New Philharmonic Orchestra, though the passionate surges of the music are sometimes in danger of swamping the voices. Not that it matters so much: in its emotional lyricism this performance does full justice to Dukas's powerful and impressive score. Moreover, this is its only available recording.

Edouard Dupuy

Dupuy Youth and Folly.
Ulrik Cold *bass* Grøndal
Djina Mai-Mai *sop* Vilhelmine
Peter Grønlund *ten* Rose
Guido Paëvatalu *bar* Johan
Poul Elming *ten* Poul
Erik Harbo *ten* Mikkel Madsen

Dupuy Flute Concerto in D minor.
Toke Lund Christiansen *fl*
Collegium Musicum Copenhagen / Michael Schønwandt.
Da Capo Ⓕ Ⓓ 8 224066/7 (two discs: 111 minutes: DDD). Notes, text and translation included. Recorded 1996/7.

If Edouard Dupuy hadn't written an opera somebody would have had to write an opera about him. Of obscure parentage and unknown date of birth he was trained in Paris (by, among others, Dussek), making a career as composer, violinist, singer and conductor. He was expelled from Prussia for neglect of his duties (other sources say for riding into church on horseback), from Sweden for revolutionary sympathies and from Denmark for a not very clandestine relationship with the wife of the Crown Prince. His amatory adventures were so notorious that his most recent biography is entitled *The Don Juan of the North* (Copenhagen: 1952), a reference also to his most famous operatic role, Mozart's Don Giovanni, though he also sang as a tenor, creating the leading role in his own *Youth and Folly* ("Ungdom og Galskab"). The libretto is a Danish version of Bouilly's *Une folie*, already set by Méhul, and the story goes that after the translation had been prepared, with the intention of Dupuy singing in the Danish première of Méhul's work, he refused and the aggrieved translator suggested that he set it himself. He did so, relocating the plot in Copenhagen and adding several numbers including a couple of comedy turns in broad Jutland dialect. The opera was evidently a success at its première in 1806 and it remained in the Danish repertory for many years.

The plot is simple – debonair Hussar Captain outwits tyrannical guardian of girl he loves – only slightly complicated by the need to provide roles for a couple of the Copenhagen company's popular comedians. The style is somewhere between Mozart (minor Mozart usually, but with an occasional hint of the real thing, especially in ensembles) and the French contemporaries of Beethoven, with a glint of Rossini every now and then. The music for the two principals is often charmingly lyrical, showing off the tenor's high notes and the soprano's florid coloratura. The comic roles, especially the servant Johan, are engaging, and throughout the opera both the vocal writing and the scoring are accomplished. Dupuy had a talent for obstinately memorable tunes: it's no surprise that Vilhelmine's Act 1 romance was a favourite in Danish drawing-rooms for many years, or that the march-tempo drinking song in Act 2 was sung by generations of students. A thoroughly likeable piece, and in such numbers as the Act 1 finale and the trio and quartet in Act 2, the work of a shrewd musical dramatist.

The performance could hardly show the work off in a better light. Mai-Mai has a pretty, slightly pale soprano but the agility of a soubrette in coloratura. In Dupuy's own role of Captain Rose Grønlund is an accomplished lyric tenor and Paevatalu's Mozartian baritone is well suited to the Figaro- or Leporello-like Johan. Cold barks a little as the heavy father; Elming and Harbo enjoy themselves a good deal in the slighter roles of Poul and Mikkel Madsen, and Schønwandt conducts with a real feeling for period style. The opera is sensibly performed without spoken dialogue and therefore plays for not much more than 80 minutes. The fill-up is a Flute Concerto with some pretty ideas in it, and a lot of showy passagework for the (very fine) soloist, but it is hopelessly overextended. The opera, though, is a charming discovery, performed with infectious enthusiasm and wit.

Antonín Dvořák
Bohemian 1841-1904

Dvořák The Cunning Peasant.
Václav Zítek *bar* Prince
Eva Děpoltová *sop* Princess
Karel Berman, Karel Průša *basses* Martin
Jitka Soběhartová *sop* Bětuška
Marie Veselá *sop* Veruna
Leo Marian Vodička *ten* Václav
Jozef Kundlák *ten* Jeník
Božena Effenberková *sop* Berta
Miroslav Kopp *ten* Jean
Prague Radio Chorus and Symphony Orchestra / František Vajnar.
Supraphon Ⓟ Ⓓ SU0019-2 (two discs: 118 minutes: DDD). Notes, text and translation included. Recorded 1985-6.

The Cunning Peasant was the first of Dvořák's operas to be performed abroad (Dresden in 1882, four years after the première), and it had a success at home in the years that followed Smetana's *Bartered bride*. Much in it is owed to that work, with a plot of peasant marital confusions, but more markedly with an idiom that takes its cue from the bouncy rhythms and the often very affecting lyrical flowerings that can make for a charming aria. The comparisons also sometimes made with *The Marriage of Figaro* have little in them apart from a plot that includes a Princess changing clothes with her maid so as to expose her husband's philandering. Josef Veselý, the amateur and amateurish librettist, had little command over the complications, and he set the not yet wholly expert Dvořák some tricky problems. Not surprisingly, it is the minor characters who come off best, in that they are simple types who give their composer some fairly obvious opportunities which he takes interestingly. A jolly duet in Act 1 might well fall very flat indeed; Dvořák makes it one of the most entertaining numbers in the score. This is sung in lively fashion by Leo Marian Vodička, as Václav, one of Bětuška's rich suitors, and Karel Berman as her father Martin, all in favour of the match (later, Karel Průša sings some of this part, perhaps because of session problems).

Bětuška herself really needs a more lyrical line, and a greater warmth of voice, than is managed by Jitka Soběhartová, but she is not helped by the less than lively characterization given her by Veselý (and hence, in this case, Dvořák), as she clings to the somewhat wimpish Jeník. But on the whole the singers rise to the challenge, as does the conductor, František Vajnar, with some music that looks well forward from Smetana to Dvořák's own more mature operatic manner. There are very few opportunities of hearing this uneven but engaging score, and this is its only recording, so collectors of Czech operatic rarities would do well to acquire it. They will find much to enjoy.

Dvořák Dimitrij.
Leo Marian Vodička *ten* Dimitri Ivanovich
Drahomíra Drobková *contr* Marfa Ivanovna
Magdaléna Hajóssyová *sop* Marina Mníshkova

Lívia Aghová *sop* Xenia Borisnova
Peter Mikuláš *bass* Pyotr Fyodorovich Basmanov
Ivan Kusnjer *bar* Prince Shuisky
Luděk Vele *bass* Iov
Prague Radio Chorus; Czech Philharmonic Chorus and Orchestra / Gerd Albrecht.
Supraphon Ⓟ Ⓒ 11 1259-2 (three discs: 190 minutes: DDD). Notes, text and translation included.
Recorded 1989.

Dimitrij is a work to challenge the view that Dvořák was (*Rusalka* notwithstanding) no opera composer. The stage did not really come very easily to him, despite his persistent attempts to master its demands, but here the subject seems to have awoken particular responses. It continues the story of *Boris Godunov* where Mussorgsky left off. Dmitrij enters Moscow at the head of his Polish army. Marfa, mother of the murdered Dmitrij, claims to recognize him as her son, seeing here a possible means of vengeance for the wrongs she has suffered. Dmitrij marries Marina, but later, encountering Boris's daughter Xenia hiding from the revelling Poles, falls in love with her. Marina now jealously discloses Dmitrij's true origin, and succeeds in having Xenia killed. Eventually the truth is forced out of Marfa, and Dimitrij is shot by Shuisky.
    A crucial difference from Mussorgsky lies in the characterization of Dmitrij. Deriving not from Pushkin, but partly from Schiller and from the Czech writer Ferdinand Mikovec, the plot here has Dmitrij convinced of his legitimacy, and only gradually realizing that he has been used by the Poles; he is a character of considerable nobility, destroyed by his sense of honour as much as by Shuisky's bullet. The work is to some extent a product of the Czech Russophilia of the 1880s and shares with many a Russian opera, from Glinka's *A Life for the Tsar* onwards, the casting of the Poles as nasty, decadent, Roman Catholic creeps who can only conduct their affairs through a haze of alcohol and to the rhythm of the polonaise. However, the opportunity for antiphonal choruses pitting them against the tough Russian folk is splendidly seized by Dvořák, and he has a good ear for alternating these public scenes with the more private moments of lyricism or emotional tension. These take place mostly between Dmitrij and the three women surrounding him. Leo Marian Vodička shoulders the title-role bravely and though his voice is considerably tested by a very demanding part, he makes much of his exchanges, especially with Marfa. She is well sung by Drahomíra Drobková, who gives a powerful interpretation to set against the two rivals for Dmitrij's love, Lívia Aghová a slightly tense strained Xenia to Magdaléna Hajóssyová's expertly handled Marina. Ivan Kusnjer spins his web craftily as Shuisky. The performance is vigorously conducted by Gerd Albrecht.
    The work has featured from time to time in Czech repertories, especially at Brno; but the only production in this country has been one put together from the various possible versions by John Tyrrell for the Nottingham University Opera Group in the heyday of its enterprise back in 1979. Milan Popíšil sets out the issues, and his own solution of them for this recording, in the booklet, which includes French, German and Tyrrell's English translations of the libretto. This is a fine, convincing recording of a rarity that is well worth investigating.

Dvořák The Jacobin.
Václav Zítek *bar* Bohuš
Vilém Přibyl *ten* Jiří
Daniela Sounová-Brouková *sop* Terinka
Karel Průša *bass* Count Vilém
René Tuček *bar* Adolf
Marcela Machotková *sop* Julie
Karel Berman *bass* Filip
Beno Blachut *ten* Benda
Ivana Mixová *mez* Lotinka
Kantiléna Children's Chorus; Kühn Chorus; Brno State Philharmonic Orchestra / Jiří Pinkas.
Supraphon Ⓟ Ⓒ 11 2190-2 (two discs: 155 minutes: ADD). Notes, text and translation included.
Recorded 1977.

This was the first (and, so far, only) recording of Dvořák's charming village comedy – for the Jacobin of the title is not here a political activist but a young man, Bohuš, returning from exile in Paris to his stuffy old father, Count Vilém. The sub-plots include all manner of misunderstandings, and set in the middle of them is the touching figure of Benda, the fussy, rather pedantic but wholly moving music-master. Dvořák is known to have had in mind his own boyhood teacher Antonín Liehmann, whose daughter gives her name, Terinka, to Benda's daughter. Beno Blachut celebrated his 64th birthday during the making of this set. His was a long career, as well as one of great distinction; he is still well able to get round the lines of this part, and gives an affecting picture of the old musician, never more so than in the rehearsing of the welcome ode. This is an idea that has cropped up in opera before, but it is charmingly handled here. Václav Zítek sings Bohuš pleasantly and Marcela Machotková trips away lightly as Julie. Vilém Přibyl is less energetic than usual, but his voice is in good fettle; and there is some lack of drive from Jiří Pinkas, who might have done more to relish the often witty touches in Dvořák's scoring. Never mind: this revived version of a delightful piece can be safely recommended.

Dvořák Kate and the Devil.

Anna Barová *contr* Kate
Richard Novák *bass* Devil Marbuel
Miloš Ježil *ten* Shepherd Jirka
Daniela Suryová *contr* Kate's mother
Jaroslav Horáček *bass* Lucifer
Jan Hladík *bass* Devil the Gate-keeper
Aleš Sťáva *bass* Devil the Guard
Brigita Sulcová *sop* Princess
Natália Romanová *sop* Chambermaid
Pavel Kamas *bass* Marshall
Oldřich Polášek *ten* Musician
Brno Janáček Opera Chorus and Orchestra / Jiří Pinkas.
Supraphon ℗ ① 11 1800-2 (two discs: 119 minutes: AAD). Notes, text and translation included.
Recorded 1979.

Kate and the Devil has never fared very well outside Czech lands, where after a slow start it has been steadily popular. Even England, where Dvořák won such early popularity, did not see the work until an Oxford production in 1932, and the first professional performance in these islands was at enterprising Wexford in 1988. Record collectors have fared better, and it was high time to welcome back this version. Though this was never one of the best Supraphon recordings, it is perfectly serviceable. The plot is complicated, and broadly speaking concerns the bossy Kate who, finding herself a wallflower at the village hop, angrily declares that she would dance with the Devil himself. Up there duly pops a junior devil, Marbuel, who carries her off to hell, where her ceaseless chatter wearies Lucifer himself. The diabolical company is only too happy to allow the shepherd Jirka to remove her again. Jirka, attractively sung by Miloš Ježil, also manages to help the wicked but later repentant Princess to escape the Devil's clutches, and all ends well.

It is, unfortunately, not only Kate who is garrulous. Adolf Wenig's libretto does not compensate for static situations with its wordiness; but it did serve to turn Dvořák in an interesting direction. The rapid exchanges and succinct phrases of some of the conversations suggest a composer he had begun to admire, Janáček, though in 1897 he cannot have known much beyond *Amarus*. The influence hurled at Dvořák's head at the time was, as so often at Czech composers in these years, that of Wagner; but really it is very superficial, resting on a few similarities of texture (the opening of Act 3 of *Tristan* puts in a brief appearance, for instance) and a misapprehension of the nature of Wagner's handling of motif. Marbuel's seductive account of his (non-existent) castle was one passage that caused critics to see Wagner under the bed. The work has a proper coherence, and much good humour besides.

Anna Barová's Kate is strong and full of character, but manages not to exclude the charm that should underlie her rantings at Marbuel, who is handsomely sung by Richard Novák. Brigita Sulcová similarly makes much of the not very sympathetic Princess. Jaroslav Horáček enjoys himself hugely as Lucifer. Jiří Pinkas accompanies them well. The insert-notes contain a brief introductory essay, singer biographies (with pictures), and full text with English, French and German translations.

Dvořák King and Charcoal Burner.

René Tuček *bar* King Matyáš
Viktor Kočí *ten* Jindřich
Dalibor Jedlička *bass* Matěj
Drahomíra Drobková *contr* Anna
Jitka Svobodová *sop* Liduška
Miroslav Kopp *ten* Jeník
Stěpán Buršík *ten* First Cavalier
Jaroslav Prodělal *bass* Second Cavalier
Chorus and Orchestra of the National Theatre, Prague / Josef Chaloupka.
Supraphon ℗ ① SU3078-2 (70 minutes: ADD). Notes, text and translation included. Recorded 1989.

Dvořák's second opera, his first in Czech, tells the tale of King Matyáš taking refuge incognito in the hut of the charcoal-burner Matěj and causing a misunderstanding when he tries to further the love of his host's daughter Liduška; her angry lover Jeník storms off and becomes a soldier, later turning up at court and through a series of ruses on the part of the King becoming reconciled to Liduška. It is a slender tale, in its first version (1871) apparently being so overloaded with difficulties that it was rejected in rehearsal when the performers found it all too much for them. It was then completely recomposed in a lighter vein in 1874, with further revisions in 1887. Yet another revision was made by Karel Kovařovic in 1914, and that forms the basis of the present recording, originally made for television and much cut (the four-language libretto in the booklet very sensibly prints the missing passages, in a different colour). It is a remarkably enjoyable work. Dvořák's grasp of what he was doing dramatically is not always entirely secure, even after all that revision, and there is no great depth of characterization, but he has a nice feeling for a given situation and a tuneful way of expressing it. This is nowhere more so than with Liduška, an affecting heroine with a spark of spirit, touchingly sung by Jitka Svobodová. Miroslav Kopp sings Jeník with a lyrical enthusiasm, and stands up well to the King he does not recognize (René Tuček on good form). Josef Chaloupka directs his forces with a lively feeling for the work's qualities. The recording is not ideal, but neither this, nor the problems as regards versions, should deter anyone curious about an almost unknown Dvořák opera. If no great discovery, it is a very engaging one.

Dvořák Rusalka.

Gabriela Beňačková-Cápová *sop* Rusalka
Richard Novák *bass* Watergnome
Věra Soukupová *contr* Witch
Wiesław Ochman *ten* Prince
Drahomíra Drobková *mez* Foreign Princess
Jana Jonášová *sop* First Woodsprite
Daniela Sounová-Brouková *sop* Second Woodsprite
Anna Barová *contr* Third Woodsprite
Jiřina Marková *sop* Turnspit
René Tuček *bar* Hunter
Prague Philharmonic Chorus; Czech Philharmonic Orchestra / Václav Neumann.
Supraphon Ⓟ Ⓒ 10 3641-2 (three discs: 158 minutes: DDD). Notes, text and translation included. Recorded 1982-3.

It is not the least of the pleasures of this fine set of Dvořák's most popular opera that the orchestral playing (and the recording of it) is of such high quality. An essential element, in all senses, of the work is its woodland setting, with the feeling of Nature and a mysterious, untroubled world in which a sudden magical contact is made between the water nymph and her Prince, between the forces of nature and the kingdom of reason. Unless there is a real sense of the beauty of the natural world, in which Rusalka belongs, a crucial part of the opera is gone. The subtlety and range and tenderness of the playing here under Václav Neumann give a more complete account of the score than ever heard before: it has the simplicity and directness of music with which conductor and players have long familiarity, yet at the same time a cunning and skill in realizing this which is a constant delight. One aspect which must be singled out is the particular tone of the wind instruments. It is a characteristic of the finest Czech orchestras that their woodwind have a naturalness, a kind of sylvan freshness, which is ideal for this music and which no other nation seems quite able to match. The recording engineers are, as good Czechs, sensitive to this quality: the result is a constant joy.

The singers enter into the spirit of the work no less warmly. Gabriela Beňačková-Cápová sings the title-role with a skilful understanding of where the voice must lie in the orchestral texture, and of how Dvořák's melodic lines have their tensions and relaxations, but also with a directness and above all, a touching quality which is crucial to the part. Few Rusalkas have combined these qualities so fully into a most beautiful performance. There is splendid support for her. Wiesław Ochman is a heroic Prince, who earns our sympathy while remaining the agent of Rusalka's grief. Richard Novák sings fiercely and ruggedly as the Watergnome, and Věra Soukupová is a vivid Witch. The other parts are well taken, with a lively vignette of the Turnspit from Jiřina Marková.

The booklet includes an essay in English, German and French by Ladislav Sip (it is something of a feat for one of the music examples to be printed upside down in all three versions). There is also a synopsis, and a libretto with three-language translations. That into English is the old one by Jindřich Elbl, which really does need an eye cast over it by a friendly English-speaker. The moon breaks into a room "burglar-wise", the Watergnome does not fish by moonlight but has "fishnettings in moonrays", the Prince feels "strange nostalgy", and so on. Not much is needed to make the translation perfectly acceptable; it is a pity this has not been done. But no matter, or not much: of the three versions of the opera which Supraphon have recorded, this is by far the best, and a splendid account of a delightful work.

Dvořák Rusalka.

Milada Subrtová *sop* Rusalka
Eduard Haken *bass* Watergnome
Marie Ovčačíková *contr* Witch
Ivo Zídek *ten* Prince
Alena Míková *mez* Foreign Princess
Jadwiga Wysoczanská *sop* First Woodsprite
Eva Hlobilová *sop* Second Woodsprite
Věra Krilová *contr* Third Woodsprite
Ivana Mixová *sop* Turnspit
Václav Bednář *bar* Hunter

Prague National Theatre Chorus and Orchestra / Zdeněk Chalabala.
Supraphon Ⓟ Ⓒ SU0013-2 (two discs: 149 minutes: ADD). Notes, text and translation included.
Recorded 1961.

This excellent set replaced for many people its predecessor, made in the mid-1950s under Jaroslav Krombholc on Supraphon. With the exception of Věra Krilová in the small part of the Third Woodsprite, the only survivor on to the new version is Eduard Haken, one of the great interpreters of the Watergnome and in robust voice, infusing the somewhat enigmatic character with a rueful gentleness as well as a firmness of utterance. Ivo Zídek takes over from Beno Blachut as the Prince, and in his mid-thirties he was in his prime, singing ardently and tenderly and with a grace of phrasing that matches him well to Milada Subrtová's Rusalka (her predecessor was Lída Cervinková). Hers is a beautiful performance, sensitive to the character's charm as well as to her fragility and pathos. The Slavonic tradition of the old watersprite legend places her in the line of the suffering heroine, one in complete contrast to the livelier Undine of Hoffmann or Lortzing; it is a measure of Dvořák's success that her delicate appeal holds throughout quite a long opera, and her sinuous but never oversensual lines and the piercing harmony associated with her give her a unique appeal. Subrtová sings the part with unfaltering sensitivity.

Of the other parts, Marie Ovčačíková takes over from Marta Krásová, and makes the Witch the more alarming by singing her with at times an almost sinister lightness of touch, while Alena Míková is now the Princess in place of Marie Podvalová. Zdeněk Chalabala, who died only a couple of months after completing this recording, handles the score with great tenderness and an affection that shines through every bar. He was sometimes underrated as a conductor: this is a beautiful performance. The recording comes up remarkably well; and the booklet includes full text and translations into French, German, and – one or two unfortunate turns of phrase apart – quite reasonable English.

George Enescu   Bohemian 1881-1955

Enescu Oedipe.

José van Dam *bass-bar* Oedipus
Barbara Hendricks *sop* Antigone
Brigitte Fassbaender *mez* Jocasta
Marjana Lipovšek *contr* The Sphinx
Gabriel Bacquier *bar* Tirésias
Nicolai Gedda *ten* Shepherd
Jean-Philippe Courtis *bass* Watchman
Cornelius Hauptmann *bass* High Priest
Gino Quilico *bar* Theseus
John Aler *ten* Laius
Marcel Vanaud *bar* Créon
Laurence Albert *bass* Phorbas
Jocelyne Taillon *mez* Mérope
Les Petits Chanteurs de Monaco; Orféon Donostiarra;
Monte Carlo Philharmonic Orchestra / Lawrence Foster.
EMI Ⓟ Ⓒ CDS7 54011-2 (two discs: 157 minutes: DDD). Notes, text and translation included.
Recorded 1989.

Enescu worked on his masterpiece, *Oedipe*, for more than 15 years (even keeping the score by his bedside at night for additions and revisions, as his pupil Menuhin testifies) before it was finally produced in Paris in 1926. It was universally acclaimed by the critics, but after a revival the following year the work was not heard again until 1955, in a concert version by French radio in memory of the composer, who had just died. The Monnaie in Brussels gave it a new production in 1956, but after that, apart from a few performances in German theatres, it has remained in the repertoire only of the Bucharest Opera. (It was their production – sung in Romanian, though the work was written to a French libretto – which appeared on Electrecord in 1968.) Possible reasons for its neglect are its immense difficulties for the orchestra and the extremely demanding title-role – Oedipus is on stage throughout except for Act 1, which is in the nature of a prologue in which Tiresias tells the appalled Laius that, since he has disregarded Apollo's warning to stay childless, the new-born Oedipus will kill his father and marry his mother.

Let it be said straight away that both these problems, and indeed all the others posed by the elaborate score, have been triumphantly overcome in this excellent recording. Lawrence Foster, who has done so much for Enescu's music, secures most impressive playing from the Monte Carlo orchestra, never allowing the complex texture to become matted or turgid, and bringing out the score's delicacy (e.g. in the delicious Act 1 dance) as well as its violent climaxes; and the always admirable José van Dam is at the height of his considerable form. Investing the words with expressive meaning throughout, he covers the whole range from *Sprechstimme* to both lyrical and dramatic singing – passionate in his tormented soliloquy in Act 2 (before the fateful encounter at the crossroads), his interchanges with Tiresias (taken with distinction by Gabriel Bacquier) in Act 3 and the altercation with Creon (who has a rather wide vibrato) in Act 4, deeply affecting in his long self-disculpation in that last act, as he goes peacefully to his transfiguration.

Great care has obviously been taken in the production (special effects such as the thunder-sheet, wind-machine, nightingale song and musical saw handled with discretion) and engineering; and whoever was responsible for casting assembled a quite remarkable constellation of stars, even for minor roles (Barbara Hendricks tender as Antigone, Gino Quilico with only 18 bars to sing as Theseus, John Aler – perhaps a bit lightweight as Laius – with a mere 14 bars). Brigitte Fassbaender shows that she fully merits the many encomiums showered on her; and Marjana Lipovšek is bloodcurdlingly sinister in the part of the Sphinx whose riddle Oedipus dismissively answers. Special mention should also be made of Cornelius Hauptmann's authoritative High Priest and of the beautiful voice of Jean-Philippe Courtis as the Watchman who tries to dissuade Oedipus from challenging the Sphinx. It is of interest that it was apparently felt necessary to call in a Spanish choir, but its contributions (in impeccable French) are first-rate.

What of the work itself? Stylistically it is highly individual, with an ultra-sophisticated harmonic idiom, very free, complex and elusive rhythms, and instrumentation of the utmost subtlety. There are occasional passages – like the pastoral choral celebrations at the opening of Act 1 and the peaceful introduction to Act 4 – that are in a vein similar to that in *Pénélope* by Enescu's teacher Fauré; but there are also exotic elements (notably the Shepherd's flutings, which clearly derive from Romanian *doinas*), including occasional quarter-tones (though these are scarcely detectable), and in some places, such as the awakening of the Sphinx, the ecstatically deliquescent quality of the writing is reminiscent of Enescu's near-contemporary Szymanowski.

If you want to sample this powerful opera, it is suggested that you start with Act 2, with, orchestrally, its lovely reflective introduction, the foreboding first interlude and the extraordinary, mysterious interlude before the scene with the Sphinx, dramatically with several key scenes, and chorally with the exultant finale of rejoicing.

Manuel de Falla   Spanish 1876-1946

Falla Atlántida (scenic cantata; arr. E. Halffter).
Enriqueta Tarrés *sop*
Anna Ricci *mez*
Eduardo Giménez *ten*
Vincente Sardinero *bar*
Children's Chorus of Our Lady of Remembrance;
Spanish National Chorus and Orchestra / Rafael Frühbeck de Burgos.

Falla El sombrero de tres picos.
Victoria de los Angeles *sop*
Philharmonia Orchestra / Rafael Frühbeck de Burgos.
EMI Matrix Ⓜ Ⓓ CMS5 65997-2 (two discs: 146 minutes: DDD). Texts and translations included. *Atlántida* recorded 1977; *El sombrero de tres picos* recorded 1963/4.

Not even the devoted efforts of Falla's pupil Ernesto Halffter could succeed – despite putting together two distinct versions – in making a convincing whole of the oratorio his master left in a jumble of disorganized fragments. Both textually and musically it remains a disparate collection of ideas that the composer, through ill-health and the depression caused by the cumulative effects of the Spanish civil war, an unhappy refuge in Argentina and then the great European war, was for over two decades unable to muster into order. Yet it was conceived with the most elevated of aims – a mystic 're-emergence' of submerged Atlantis signifying a celebration of Spain's extending the bounds of Christianity. It recalls classical legends of the country's formation and dramatizes Columbus's fulfilment of the Senecan prophecy of a new world. There is much splendid music in the widest diversity of styles, particularly for the chorus who, with a baritone narrator, carry the main weight of the work – curiously, neither Hercules nor Columbus, key figures in the story, has a solo. (The present version has a fuller Part 2 – the section left in the greatest chaos, full of unfinished sketches and alternate jottings – than that in Colomer's version for Auvidis in 1993.)

Sardinero is a noble-voiced narrator, Ricci brings pathos to her solo as the dying Queen Pyrene; in the charmingly folk-like "Isabella's dream" a steadier line than Tarrés produces would have been preferable. The chorus, who have some of the most impressive sections – such as the hymn to Barcelona, the hymn of Columbus's expedition at sea, and the final "supreme night" – are mostly good, though once or twice (as in "Herald voices") showing signs of tiredness; and the orchestra provide useful support. Balance is a bit variable. In view of its troubled genesis, the work is inevitably flawed, and some people might prefer merely a suite of its finest sections; but the full Halffter reconstruction, now accepted as definitive, gives us a glimpse of the masterpiece *Atlántida* might have been. The booklet contains a first-class note by Enrique Franco.

There have been many other excellent performances of the ever-fresh *Three-cornered hat*, but none better than this imaginative and scintillating reading by Frühbeck de Burgos and the Philharmonia. So vivacious and idiomatic is the playing, so flexible and alive to all the score's sly, witty allusions, and so subtle are the nuances, that the stage-pictures seem to be conjured up before our eyes. Some of the tempos are unusual: a faster fandango for the miller's wife, a steadier final jota, and most strikingly, a slower but marvellously taut and incisive farruca for the miller's dance. The recording, now over 35 years old, is as vivid as the performance. Terrific!

Falla La vida breve.

Teresa Berganza *mez* Salud
Paloma Perez Iñigo *sop* Carmela, First and Third Street Vendors
Alicia Nafé *mez* Grandmother, Second Street Vendor
José Carreras *ten* Paco
Juan Pons *bar* Uncle Salvador
Manuel Mairena *voc* Flamenco singer
Ramon Contreras *voc* Manuel
Manuel Cid *ten* Voice in the smithy, Voice in the distance, Voice of a hawker
Ambrosian Opera Chorus; London Symphony Orchestra / Garcia Navarro.
DG Ⓔ ① 435 851-2GH (60 minutes: ADD). Notes, text and translation included. Recorded 1978.

In the long operatic chronicle of fine musical scores handicapped by dramatically naïve, feebly structured plots and badly written librettos, *La vida breve* unfortunately ranks high – all the more surprisingly as Carlos Fernández Shaw was an immensely experienced playwright and poet. But Falla's atmospheric and colourfully orchestrated score, even with its evident glances over its shoulder at Massenet and Italian *verismo*, is full of striking things – even magical, like its evocation of Granada (which, astonishingly enough, Falla had at that time never seen). Little wonder that Dukas, to whom the frustrated 29-year-old played through the score after arriving in Paris, immediately recommended its performance – though another six years were to pass before that materialized. *La vida breve* is all but a one-woman opera for the wronged Salud, the other characters, besides being the merest pasteboard, having very little to do; but in this passionate, high-flying role Berganza, who in 1978 was in her prime, is splendid. She projects a real sense of character, adopting where necessary the hard timbre indicated by the composer ("to be sung in the style of Andalusian songs") and generally riveting the attention. Within the limited scope of the part of the faithless and caddish lover, Carreras is lyrical; the other main protagonists here are the LSO, who play superbly. The famous first dance at the wedding party in Act 2, which follows the solo by the *cantaor* (flamenco singer), is wildly exciting, permeated as it is with highly idiomatic castanets, heeltaps, and stamping, and encouraging interjections by the admirable Ambrosian Opera Chorus (which is first-class throughout). Apart from some inconsistency in the placing of off-stage voices (and some momentary break-up of the sound on track 15, in the second dance), the work is very well recorded.

Gabriel Fauré   French 1845-1924

Fauré Pénélope.

Jessye Norman *sop* Pénélope
Jocelyne Taillon *mez* Euryclée
Colette Alliot-Lugaz *sop* Alkandre
Christine Barbaux *sop* Phylo
Danièle Borst *sop* Lydie
Michèle Command *sop* Mélantho
Norma Lerer *sop* Cléone
Alain Vanzo *ten* Ulysses
Jean Dupouy *ten* Antinoüs
Paul Guigue *bar* Ctésippe
Gérard Friedmann *ten* Léodès
Philippe Huttenlocher *bar* Eurymaque
José van Dam *bass-bar* Eumée
François Le Roux *bar* Pisandre
Jean Laforge Vocal Ensemble; Monte Carlo Philharmonic Orchestra / Charles Dutoit.
Erato Libretto Ⓜ ① 2292-45405-2 (124 minutes: ADD). Notes, text and translation included. Recorded 1980.

Informed French opinion rates *Pénélope* as a high point in the history of its native opera, not far behind Debussy's *Pelléas et Mélisande*; but opportunities of seeing it on the stage are few and far between – there is, in any case, little action until the climactic ending when Ulysses triumphantly draws the great bow that had defeated the parasitic suitors, whom he drives out and slaughters – and so it is fortunate that this fine performance has reappeared. *Pénélope* is essentially a lyrical work, though there are almost no arias as such; it employs Wagner's leitmotiv technique (although in an individual way) but is not at all Wagnerian in idiom; it is basically intimate and restrained, though there are also powerful emotional scenes; and it was scored (most of it by Fauré himself, though his responsibilities as director of the Conservatoire left him little time) for a large orchestra, but his interest lay in the musical substance rather than colourful timbre. Jessye Norman is on splendid form, both regal and tender, as the patient wife who nightly unpicks her spinning in order to foil her suitors as she waits and waits for Ulysses to return; Alain Vanzo, that most intelligent French tenor, is a mellifluous Ulysses, even if he does sound too youthful and healthy to deceive his wife when he comes in disguised as a feeble old beggar; José van Dam is his usual admirable self, phrasing beautifully as the faithful shepherd Eumée; and Dutoit makes the Monte Carlo orchestra glow.

Some problems of variable levels noted in the LP set have not been corrected: the initial servants' chorus in Act 1 is still too faint, Ulysses's outburst at the end of Act 1 is still overpowering; but these are minor flaws in a most welcome reissue. A special word is merited by Jean-Michel Nectoux's excellent long commentary.

Zdeněk Fibich   Bohemian 1850-1900

Fibich The Bride of Messina.
  Libuše Márová *contr* Donna Isabella
  Václav Zítek *bar* Don Manuel
  Ivo Zídek *ten* Don Cesar
  Gabriela Beňačková *sop* Beatrice
  Karel Hanuš *bass* Diego
  Jaroslav Horáček *bass* Cayetan
  Miroslav Svejda *ten* Bohemund
  Naďa Sormová *sop* Page
  Prague Radio Chorus; Prague National Theatre Chorus and Orchestra / František Jílek.
  Supraphon Ⓟ Ⓞ 11 1492-2 (two discs: 136 minutes: AAD). Notes, text and translation included. Recorded 1975.

The Bride of Messina is an opera that, especially in a fine performance such as this, triumphs over severe disadvantages. For a start, the plot (from Schiller) is gloomy and static. The quarrelling brothers Cesar and Manuel are reconciled by their mother Princess Isabella, who has meanwhile hidden their sister Beatrice in a convent; for their father once had a dream that Beatrice would cause their deaths. Manuel abducts a beautiful nun, but Cesar also falls in love with her. Before Manuel can explain he has discovered that she is in fact Beatrice, Cesar kills him, then stabs himself in remorse. The libretto sets this out in a series of monologues, virtually without ensembles but with an important role for commenting choruses: Schiller was consciously trying to reconstruct Greek practice, as he says in his preface. This imposes severe demands on a composer. Fibich was certainly influenced to some extent by Wagner, though this is mostly after the ceremonial fashion of *Lohengrin* together with a feeling for the more mature Wagner's command of musical declamation. His use of motive is very much his own; and his lyrical declamatory lines are closely derived from Czech speech-rhythms, offering splendid opportunities to the quartet of leading singers (quintet, if one includes the significant part for the servant Diego, finely sung here by Karel Hanuš). Libuše Márová leads matters off with that risky operatic device, a long opening narration explaining the story so far; but she has a commanding presence and a dignified voice, and certainly the attention is immediately held. The brothers are well contrasted, Ivo Zídek elegant and heroic as Cesar, Václav Zítek pronouncing his reconciliation to his brother in their duet gravely and sombrely but with the resources in his voice for a tender declaration of love. Beatrice is beautifully sung by Gabriela Beňačková, nowhere better than in her own opening soliloquy to Act 2 as she is torn between her passion for her mysterious knightly abductor and her fear and remorse at having abandoned the cloister.

Much falls, obviously, on chorus and orchestra. Fibich writes beautifully for massed voices, and the care lavished on the singing here goes a long way towards justifying the quasi-Greek device. He was also a fine orchestrator, with this opera in a style more Germanic than elsewhere or among his compatriots, but with a warmth and fluency that are well realized in the hands of František Jílek. The recording, though elderly, does well by all concerned. Text and translations are provided though there are misprints and the English version, generally fair, occasionally slips up through misuse of the dictionary. "Mind the ends", the brothers are admonished, for "Consider the consequences" and the excited Beatrice observes of her lover, "He stood before me in his virile handsomeness"!

Fibich Sárka.
  Václav Zítek *bar* Prince Přemysl
  Vilém Přibyl *ten* Ctirad
  Josef Klán *bass* Vitoraz

Eva Děpoltová *sop* Sárka
Eva Randová *mez* Vlasta
Jaroslava Janská *sop* Libina
Božena Effenberková *sop* Svatava
Jitka Pavlová *sop* Mlada
Anna Barová *contr* Radka
Věra Bakalová *contr* Hosta
Daniela Survoyá *contr* Castava
Brno Janáček Opera Chorus; Brno State Philharmonic Orchestra / Jan Stych.
Supraphon Ⓟ ① SU0036-2 (two discs: 131 minutes: AAD). Notes, text and translation included.
Recorded 1978.

Sárka was the Bohemian warrior maiden expelled from the court of Prince Přemysl after the death of Libuše, together with her female companions. They take arms against the men to try to recover power. The central scene of the opera comes when the women plot to lure Ctirad to his doom by the ancient huntsman's ploy of a live decoy, in this case tying Sárka to a tree. Ctirad duly falls for it, but also falls for Sárka: before anything else can happen, his fascination with this powerful figure begins to stir other emotions; and she in turn discovers that her blazing hatred for him is becoming charged with an erotic force. Like some tragic Beatrice and Benedict, they fall into each other's arms; for after a love scene that Fibich clearly hoped would become something of a Czech *Tristan* duet, violence is resumed, and the guilt-ridden Sárka, tormented by apparitions of her dead maiden comrades, hurls herself over a cliff (in Janáček's opera, Ctirad dies and she joins him on his funeral pyre).

There is plenty here for feminist critics; but anyone can enjoy a well-written, passionate opera which may owe much to Wagner, but also anticipates a good deal in Smetana and Dvořák. It is good to have the work back in the catalogue, especially in a performance that understands it so thoroughly and does it such splendid justice. Eva Randová, in the person of Vlasta, the actual leader of the women, detonates a splendid opening aria, to which Václav Zítek retorts with a vehement aria from Přemysl. Vilém Přibyl sings Ctirad with great energy and passion, and Eva Děpoltová, though sometimes a trifle shrill – it is a feature of epic nationalist operas for the characters to address one another at the tops of their voices – handles the long love scene magnificently. Jan Stych leads his forces with great spirit. The text is included, with translations into English, German and French.

Benjamin Fleischmann

USSR *c*1919-*c*1942

Fleischmann Rothschild's Violin (orch. Shostakovich).
Marina Shaguch *sop*
Konstantin Pluzhnikov *ten*
Ilya Levinsky *ten*
Sergei Leiferkus *bar*

Shostakovich From Jewish Folk Poetry, Op. 79.
Marina Shaguch *sop*
Larissa Diadkova *mez*
Konstantin Pluzhnikov *ten*
Rotterdam Philharmonic Orchestra / Gennadi Rozhdestvensky.
RCA Victor Red Seal Ⓟ ① 09026 68434-2 (66 minutes: DDD). Notes, texts and translations included. Recorded 1995.

This is something of an event for followers of Shostakovich and Soviet music. Venyamin Fleyshman (or, in less scholarly form, Benjamin Fleischmann) was among the most talented of Shostakovich's first tranche of pupils from the time of the latter's official rehabilitation in 1937. His opera on Chekhov's short story was completely composed but only two-thirds orchestrated by June 1941 when he was conscripted, and he apparently died soon afterwards at the battlefront. Shostakovich thought so highly of *Rothschild's Violin* that he took the manuscript with him on his evacuation from Leningrad, and in February 1944 he completed the orchestration. Ten days later he began work on his Second Piano Trio, the first of his works to include Jewish themes with their thinly veiled symbolism of solidarity with the oppressed.

The strongest parts of Fleischmann's score are the interludes and the postlude. These fully bear out his teacher's faith in him, and parts of them would not be out of place in Shostakovich's own *Lady Macbeth*. There are also hints of Stravinsky's *Symphony of Psalms*, which Shostakovich had been demonstrating to his pupils at the time. But the influence went both ways. Fleischmann's conclusion finds an echo in the final pages of Shostakovich's *Leningrad* Symphony, and the latter's own incomplete wartime opera *The Gamblers* occasionally comes to mind.

Performances of *Rothschild's Violin* have been few and far between. Solomon Volkov, of *Testimony* notoriety, was involved in putting it on in Leningrad in 1968, and there was a British première in May 1997 by Mecklenburgh Opera with the LPO. There was a Melodiya LP recording in 1982 which enjoyed wider circulation than many discs from that source. Rozhdestvensky was the conductor there as here, and differences between his two performances are negligible. For the RCA issue the Rotterdam Philharmonic are on excellent form, and Leiferkus is in superb voice as the village coffin-maker/violinist nicknamed Bronze, who on his deathbed passes his instrument to his fellow amateur musician and former rival Rothschild. Yet there are more nuances in the role than Leiferkus finds. He does not rise fully to the challenge of Bronze's long deathbed aria, culminating in the cry "Why can't people live and let live?", and the world-weariness of his concluding words is only half-registered.

RCA's well-balanced recording is a plus, but the main advantage of this issue is simply that it gives us for the first time the complete libretto (in Cyrillic) and translation. The booklet-essay is short but to the point; curiously it is uncredited. Even more curiously, no synopsis is provided. The CD is at the same time the soundtrack of a French film which builds a pseudo-documentary around the opera. The post-history of *Rothschild's Violin* includes Shostakovich's 1949 song-cycle *From Jewish Folk Poetry*. This work has proved a minefield for commentators. The essay in the booklet rightly reminds us that at the time it was composed it seemed to fulfil all the demands for Shostakovich's rehabilitation into the Socialist Realist fold. Yet you only have to read some of the texts ("I am happy on my kolkhoz") and compare them with the musical setting to realize that there is an element of *inoskazaniye* ('other-speaking', i.e. allegory) at work.

This isn't the place to get into ideological brawls (the fur flew over this piece in the *New York Times* and elsewhere). Suffice it to say that this is one of Shostakovich's most consistently fine song-cycles and that the performance here is first-rate. The three voices are admittedly better individually than as an ensemble; heard together their blend and intonation are not ideal. The main point is that *Rothschild's Violin* is a worthwhile piece in its own right. Shostakovich's restoration was far more than a tribute to a tragically curtailed talent. It was a phenomenon without which the picture of his own development is seriously incomplete, and its first appearance on CD is a noteworthy event.

Friedrich Flotow
German 1812-1883

Flotow Martha.
Anneliese Rothenberger *sop* Lady Harriet Durham
Brigitte Fassbaender *mez* Nancy
Nicolai Gedda *ten* Lionel
Hermann Prey *bar* Plunkett
Dieter Weller *bass* Lord Tristram Mickelford
Hans Georg Knoblich *bass* Sheriff of Richmond
Bavarian State Opera Chorus; Bavarian State Orchestra / Robert Heger.
EMI Ⓜ ① CMS7 69339-2 (two discs: 131 minutes: ADD). Notes and German text included. Recorded 1968.

Let those who acquired the 1977 Wallberg/Eurodisc/RCA reissue of Flotow's *Martha* not fret unduly, but on balance this EMI recording is preferable. It's a livelier production, with happy crowd-noises helping to set the scene, and a fuller-bodied sound throughout. The second couple, Nancy and Plunkett, make a great deal of difference when played with the verve and freshness of Fassbaender and Prey; Doris Soffel and Karl Ridderbusch, on the Wallberg set, are staid and flavourless by comparison. Gedda also has more life about him than Siegfried Jerusalem (Wallberg) though not everything is in his favour (for instance, he makes a poor, lumpy thing out of his solo in the Act 1 duet, where Jerusalem, if without Carusan caress, is more pleasingly lyrical). With Harriet the charm and vivacity of Lucia Popp score strongly for the Wallberg version, Rothenberger on the EMI set being very competent vocally but almost totally inexpressive.

In short, neither recording is without some drawback and both will give pleasure. On the whole, there's a more generous, fun-loving kind of life in this EMI one. What they have not been so generous about is the text, translated in the Eurodisc but here given in German only with an English synopsis.

Flotow Martha.
Erna Berger *sop* Lady Harriet Durham
Else Tegetthoff *mez* Nancy
Peter Anders *ten* Lionel
Josef Greindl *bass* Plunkett
Eugen Fuchs *bass* Lord Tristram Mickelford
Franz Sauer *bass* Sheriff of Richmond
Berlin State Opera Chorus; Staatskapelle Berlin / Johannes Schüler.
Berlin Classics mono Ⓔ ① 0021 632BC (two discs: 103 minutes: ADD). Notes, text and translation included. Recorded from a broadcast performance in the Funkhaus an der Masurenallee, Berlin in 1944.

A remark or two on the insert-notes and presentation in general concludes these reviews, if indeed it finds any place in them at all. Here it deserves priority. With a 'historical' recording what one wants is something which puts the performance into the context of its times, with information about the circumstances of recording, the association of the singers with their roles, their reception by the critics, and a little light on those supporting artists who are now no more than names but were once the lifeblood of the company seen night after night by a faithful public for whom probably nothing is so evocative of those days as the characteristic sound of their voices. Einhard Luther's essay, "A Martha to savour", does this admirably. He writes with the knowledge of one to whom these things have been an inseparable part of life, and whose words also carry the warmth of affection. It should be added that Berlin Classics find room in their 96-page booklet for synopsis, libretto and translation, matters that can by no means be taken for granted in the 'historical' department.

The recording, which was first issued in Germany as an LP set on DG, was made over a three-day period in the Berlin Radio building on Masurenallee. October 1944, in the grim period of 'total war', might seem a strange month for the performance of such a brightly lit story-book opera: perhaps the contrast with the times is one reason why everyone here seems to give themselves with such spirit to the charming make-believe. Certainly this is a real performance – no 'going-through-the-motions', but a devoted preservation of standards and of a world in which gaiety and lyrical charm are not extinct.

The recording itself may originally have been something of a triumph for the new tape-recording process. In its present form, there is an over-reverberance, a tendency to distort and an over-insistent recording of consonants, which makes you wonder how judicious the transfer engineers have been. As for the singers, the main point is that individually they give sharply characterized performances that fit like magic into the ensemble. A very Germanic flavour is imparted by the casting of Josef Greindl as Plunkett. One feels his hearty geniality spreading and in 1944 it was that, and not the voice itself, that 'spread'. His opposite number, too, is splendidly played by Else Tegetthoff (remembered over here as Else Ruziczka). Berger's 'Lady' is invariably sweet (but Lucia Popp, with her characteristic squeeze of lemon juice is preferable on Eurodisc/RCA), but there is plenty of accomplishment in her singing and an unmistakable vocal identity. Keenest expectation is probably aroused by Peter Anders as Lionel. Less of a character than the others, he makes little of his embittered solos in Act 3, but is at his best in the sublime opening of the Quintet.

The insert-notes make a special point about the conductor, Johannes Schüler, the centenary of whose birth fell in 1994. Precious little else of him remains in the current catalogue and as the notes make very clear his life and work deserve at least this memorial.

Baron Alberto Franchetti   Italian 1860-1942

Franchetti Cristoforo Colombo.
Renato Bruson *bar* Cristoforo Colombo
Roberto Scandiuzzi *bass* Don Roldano Ximenes
Rosella Ragatzu *sop* Isabella, Iguamota
Marco Berti *ten* Don Fernan Guevara
Gisella Pasino *mez* Anacoana
Vicente Ombuena *ten* Matheos
Andrea Ulbrich *contr* Yanika
Enrico Turco *bass* Bobadilla
Pierre Lefebvre *ten* Diaz
Fabio Previati *bar* Marguerite
Dalibor Jenis *bar* Old man
Hungarian Radio Chorus; Frankfurt Radio Symphony Orchestra / Marcello Viotti.
Koch Schwann Ⓜ ① 310302 (three discs: 159 minutes: DDD). Notes, text and translation included. Recorded at performances in the Alte Oper, Frankfurt on August 30th and September 2nd, 1991.

As the historian of the *Monte Carlo Opera* says: "Like most operas composed to celebrate special occasions, its success faded with the occurrence that had created it" (T. J. Walsh, *Monte Carlo Opera 1879-1909*; Gill and Macmillan). Apparently it gained no particular renown there in 1909, even though the title-role was taken by the mighty Titta Ruffo. Revivals have been sparse, and it has not previously established itself as one of those cult-operas that the *cognoscenti* wrap in their bated breath till it becomes part of general knowledge, when they lose interest.

Its merit lies in its middle. That is: while the First Act is colourful, it is also commonplace, and the Epilogue, which might possibly be affecting on stage, is too drawn-out, the musical substance spread too thin. But Act 2 is something of a masterpiece, and Act 3 is pretty good also. The structure of the opera goes as follows: Act 1, Columbus wins permission to sail; Act 2, he is on the high seas and sights land just in time to avert mutiny on the Santa Maria; Act 3, the Indians suffer under the dastardly Spaniards who have Columbus shipped back to Spain as a prisoner, and in the Epilogue he dies. It is a good, purposeful libretto by Luigi Illica, who has thought of everything including a way to introduce some love-interest for the tenor, and who had the foresight to present Columbus himself as a respecter of Indians and almost Politically Correct. Franchetti was an eclectic composer, with a lot of Wagner in his head, even a little Mendelssohn, as well as Italian scores such as *La Gioconda* and (perhaps) *Mefistofele*. He does a thoroughly dutiful job in Act 1, but something far richer and more creative arrives with Act 2.

Here a great broad sweep of double-octaves suggests the limitless ocean and its power (rather extraordinarily, it is the Vaughan Williams of the *Sinfonia antartica* that comes to mind here). Then follows a sequence of choruses, finely expressive of the sailors' acute discomfort tinged with superstitious dread. There is some highly evocative atmospheric writing with the use of off-stage voices. When Columbus enters, the solos have a new depth of character, and everything is skilfully calculated to rise to the double climax of mutiny and the sighting of land. To a very large extent a comparable inspiration is sustained in Act 3, and even when conventions are being appeased, as by the inclusion of some dances, a special flavour and more serious point is given to them by the sighing chorus of Indians.

The performance under Marcello Viotti is fine where it matters most, that is in the orchestral, choral and ensemble work. Renato Bruson has the authority, power and roundness of voice that are right for the part of Columbus, but he is not vivid as a character, and at climaxes the beat on sustained notes is quite insistent. The tenor, Marco Berti, is well defined and often graceful, but some of the writing seems to call for a more heroic voice. The abominable Don Roldano is sung by an impressively sonorous bass, Roberto Scandiuzzi. The women are so-so. The recorded sound is big and generous, having the voices well forward, and the booklet gives all appropriate assistance.

John Gay   British 1685-1732

Gay The Beggar's Opera (arr. Britten).
Ann Murray *mez* Polly
Philip Langridge *ten* Macheath
Yvonne Kenny *sop* Lucy
John Rawnsley *bar* Lockit
Robert Lloyd *bass* Peachum
Anne Collins *contr* Mrs Peachum
Nuala Willis *mez* Mrs Trapes
Christopher Gillett *ten* Filch
Declan Mulholland *sngr* Beggar
Aldeburgh Festival Choir and Orchestra / Steuart Bedford.
Argo Ⓟ Ⓒ 436 850-2ZHO2 (two discs: 108 minutes: DDD). Notes and text included. Recorded 1992.

"Not a 'sport' among Britten's operas but an integral part of the totality of theatrical work, from *Paul Bunyan* to *Death in Venice*": Donald Mitchell puts the claim well, and this first recording supports it all the way. *The Beggar's Opera* was Britten's new work for the English Opera Group in 1948 and had its première at the Arts Theatre, Cambridge. There were joyful performances in subsequent years at Sadler's Wells but revivals have been comparatively rare. Whether on doctrinal grounds (a preference for Gay-without-gloss, the folk opera naked and unashamed), or whether out of a notion that being an arrangement, it hardly constitutes a 'work', Op. 43 has had less than its due.

Everything here is well set-up to make amends. The 12 players forming the chamber orchestra are excellent individually (and each is provided with special opportunities) and they respond sensitively to Steuart Bedford's direction. With Harry Christophers as chorus master and Michael Geliot in charge of dialogue, the singer-actors are expertly assisted, and Michael Woolcock's production is vivid without being obtrusive. There is always a problem over the matching of speaking voices with the singing, and another over the accents ('common', 'posh', 'mummerset' or whatever). Occasional anomalies persist here. Mrs Peachum's singing voice is splendidly forthcoming, her speaking a trifle reticent, and Lucy clearly has been brought up 'posh' though her dad is decidedly 'common'. At the very least, the speech causes no embarrassment; at best it is spirited, and the full-fathom-five depth of Robert Lloyd's Peachum gives profound pleasure. The singing is probably as good as it should be; in many of the numbers, character matters more than beauty of tone, though a more consistent steadiness of voice-production would not come amiss.

"All scores have a reckoning" as the Beggar remarks, and finally it is to Britten's score that one has to return when making a recommendation. *The Beggar's Opera* can also be obtained on disc in very different forms. There is the 'authentic' version with the Broadside Band under Jeremy Barlow (Hyperion), and highly unattractive and curiously unentertaining it is too. The starry version under Richard Bonynge (Decca) is entertaining, but there the gloss is thick and the enrichment of musical interest scarcely stretches the imagination. Britten's work is of a different order altogether. It is not mere cleverness, though the sheer ingenuities of rhythm, counterpoint, harmony and orchestration keep the ear fully occupied and delighted. Much more, the process is one of absorption and re-creation, sometimes fierce or poignant, sometimes magical in its loveliness (the use of the chorus in "Cease your funning", for example). The marvel is that the tunes themselves, so far from rejecting Britten's treatment as the body might reject a transplant, seem to find themselves in their element. The recording fills a gap in respect of Gay's masterpiece as surely as it fills another in the Britten *oeuvre*.

Gay The Beggar's Opera (arr. Bonynge/Gamley).
Dame Kiri Te Kanawa *sop* Polly
James Morris *bass* Macheath
Dame Joan Sutherland *sop* Lucy
Stafford Dean *bass* Lockit
Alfred Marks *bar* Peachum
Angela Lansbury *mez* Mrs Peachum
Regina Resnik *mez* Mrs Trapes
Anthony Rolfe Johnson *ten* Filch
Graham Clark *ten* Matt of the Mint
Ann Murray *mez* Jenny Diver
Anne Wilkens *mez* Dolly Trull
John Gibbs *bar* Jemmy Twitcher
Warren Mitchell *spkr* Beggar
Michael Hordern *spkr* Player
London Voices; National Philharmonic Orchestra / Richard Bonynge.
Decca Ⓕ ① 430 066-2DH2 (two discs: 125 minutes: ADD). Notes and text included. Recorded 1981.

Since the musical content of *The Beggar's Opera* has always been a movable feast, Richard Bonynge and Douglas Gamley moved it as much as their predecessors. The most familiar of the traditional airs that Gay used are all there, but, as Bonynge and Gamley state in their introductory note, "a number of the original melodies have been rejected ... and some new ones incorporated". The whole has been adapted for singers and full-size symphony orchestra, "with at least some of the satirical element of the original retained by gentle parodying of a wide-range of eighteenth, nineteenth and twentieth-century musical styles".

Those committed to period-style performance may thus read no further, and yet it would be a pity to miss something that really works remarkably well. The dialogue has been tastefully pruned and modified and, for recording purposes, it was surely sensible to upgrade the singing ability above what might be tolerated in the theatre. At the same time, it is the musical theatre performers and the lighter singers who come off best. The likes of Angela Lansbury and Alfred Marks know how to put the text across in a musical context, and it is around them that the performance really revolves.

Of the more serious singers, James Morris sings superbly as Macheath, but he is less at home with the dialogue, while the two Dames seem to be too heavily operatic for a work that was conceived as an antidote to opera proper. Yet it is difficult to fault numbers such as the Polly/Macheath duet, "Pretty Polly, say". In supporting roles Anthony Rolfe Johnson makes an excellent Filch, and Regina Resnik a formidable Mrs Trapes. At the end of the day the result is undeniably a successful and highly enjoyable modern realization of Gay's classic work.

Gay The Beggar's Opera (arr. F. Austin).
Elsie Morison *sop* Polly /Zena Walker
John Cameron *bar* Macheath/John Neville
Monica Sinclair *contr* Lucy/Rachel Roberts
Ian Wallace *bass* Lockit/Eric Porter
Owen Brannigan *bass* Peachum/Paul Rogers
Constance Shacklock *mez* Mrs Peachum, Mrs Trapes/Daphne Heard
Alexander Young *ten* Filch/Robert Hardy
Anna Pollak *mez* Jenny Diver/Jane Jacobs
Pro Arte Chorus and Orchestra / Sir Malcolm Sargent.
Classics for Pleasure Silver Doubles Ⓢ ① CD-CFPSD4778 (two discs: 88 minutes: ADD). Recorded 1955.

It's a wise beggar that knows his own opera, so many guises has it been through on stage and on record. Here it comes in the version which everybody used to know best: the one adapted for 'a nice class of person' on 'a good night out' at the theatre. Arranged by the baritone Frederic Austin (who also played Macheath) and produced by Nigel Playfair, it ran for more than three years at the Lyric, Hammersmith, opening in 1920 and priding itself on marking a return to the original version of 1728. To us now, it is no more an 'authentic' performance than (what shall we say?) the old Mass in B minor under Albert Coates was 'authentic' Bach. Its orchestration and to some extent its harmonies have less in common with, say, Handel's *Tolomeo* (written in the same year as the first *Beggar's Opera*) than they have with Edward German's *Merrie England*. None of which means that we are not allowed to enjoy it.

At the start of this recording, enjoyment on the part of those who are willing to enjoy seems guaranteed. A lively crowd applauds the announcement ("Ladies and gentlemen, I have great pleasure ..."), the beggar speaks his introduction in good style (ending "So, conductor, play away the overture"), and a fine stately tune gives way to a jig and curtain-up on the opera itself. The trouble is one that plagues many recordings which have double casts of actors and singers – the voices don't match. There is no way in which Paul Rogers's reedy speaking voice could turn into Owen Brannigan's ripe *basso*. In this instance it is a matter of 'How happy could I be with either', but it is not always so: Constance Shacklock is no Mrs Peachum or Mrs Trapes (she sings both), and John Cameron is no Macheath. Both come straight out of oratorio, and excellently as they sing they are not remotely in character. Nor are some of the speaking voices: Polly and Lucy play their scenes together as though they were in *The Importance of Being Earnest*.

Still, the spirit of enjoyment is sufficiently robust not to wilt over details of this sort, and there remain the good tunes, the good voices, the wit, the high professionalism of the actors and of Sir Malcolm's orchestra – as well as the new-fangled thing called 'stereo', for that is what it was when the recording was made, in stereo, in 1955. It came out in mono, and the reissue in 1963 restored the stereo original, which has Peachum walking around the room while talking, and the bells ting-a-linging stage-left. It was the first opera EMI recorded in stereo, and so has its place in history.

Roberto Gerhard Spanish/British 1896-1970

Gerhard The Duenna (ed. Drew).
Claire Powell *mez* The Duenna
Neill Archer *ten* Don Antonio
Richard Van Allan *bass* Don Jerome
Adrian Clarke *bar* Don Ferdinand
Eric Roberts *bar* Don Isaac
Susannah Glanville *sop* Donna Luisa
Ann Taylor *mez* Donna Clara d'Almanza
Paul Wade *ten* Father Paul
Jeremy Peaker *spkr* López
David Owen-Lewis *spkr* Servant
Deborah Pearce *spkr* Maid
Denise Mulholland *sop* Gipsy
Opera North Chorus; English Northern Philharmonia / Antoni Ros Marbà.
Chandos Ⓟ ① CHAN9520 (two discs: 148 minutes: DDD). Notes, text and translation included. Recorded 1996.

Stanford Robinson, who conducted the first performance of Roberto Gerhard's *The Duenna* (a studio broadcast) in 1949, is said to have told the composer that he loved the work but wished that he hadn't mingled its sprightly comic opera elements and Spanish rhythms with atonality. What he was probably thinking of was a scene in Act 2 where three characters drink together to a vivacious quodlibet of Spanish folk melodies. This is followed by a spoken scene in which the young Don Ferdinand pleads with his father Don Jerome to allow Ferdinand's sister Luisa to marry the man she loves. Jerome refuses, telling his son that he himself married for money, and such loveless but companionable marriages are not to be despised. The music, Spanish no longer – indeed atonal – darkens under this, refusing to allow us to laugh at Jerome's "We were never fond enough to quarrel", and a solo violin most movingly tells us what he cannot say himself, that the widowed old man misses his wife terribly. Gerhard was intent on creating that apparently impossible paradox, an English zarzuela or tonadilla, but he could not have achieved the depth and poignancy of that involuntary self-confession with folk music references alone. *The Duenna* gains its strength from this hybrid status, but it was that quality, no doubt, that kept it off the stage for so long. Absurdly enough – but it wounded Gerhard deeply – when it was heard by an audience unlikely to be put off by its occasional modernisms, at the ISCM Festival in Wiesbaden in 1951, it was coolly received because Gerhard, the pupil of Schoenberg, seemed to be wasting his time on light music.

It mingles not only modernism with copious references to Spanish vernacular music but also broad comedy with meltingly lyrical arias (try Luisa's monologue in Act 2 scene 2) and with something deeper and occasionally more disturbing. One of the most touching moments is towards the end, where Don Isaac, the rich but plain suitor whom Jerome intended for Luisa, is married off by a trick to the elderly duenna of the title. Despite themselves they feel happy in each other's company, and they briefly sing some of the sincerest love music in the opera. The mostly jubilant final scene, three pairs of lovers finally united, is repeatedly undercut, by a chorus of beggars outside and by references to an austere penitential chant heard at the beginning of the opera. Like the Sheridan play that was its source it is a comedy that touches on the mercenary and the moral aspects of marriage, and reflects that happiness is a very chancy thing indeed.

It wasn't until 1992 that *The Duenna* finally reached the stage, 22 years after Gerhard's death. That production (sung in English) was seen in Madrid and Barcelona; it was splendidly cast (Felicity

Palmer, David Rendall, Anthony Michaels-Moore, Enrique Baquerizo, Richard Van Allan) but, deplorably and unaccountably, was not recorded. Nor was the Opera North production, mounted very soon afterwards with much the same cast. This recording is of a recent revival, with Van Allan and the conductor the only remaining links with those 1992 performances. With mostly young voices that will not take pressure, it is a creditable but slightly small-scale reading. Claire Powell is accomplished but does not quite make the title-role as central as it should be; Van Allan is vivid and touching as Don Jerome, but his voice is now rather worn. Susannah Glanville is effective in her Act 2 aria and elsewhere. All the other principals are more than competent, and their very clear diction and way of suggesting the pace and pungency of a stage production make up for a feeling that the opera has been slightly under-cast. Antoni Ros Marbà conducts with a fine ear for Gerhard's strange and magical sonorities as well as the obvious local colour; the recording is clean but pleasantly atmospheric, again strongly evoking the stage.

Sheridan's play contains rather more plot than an opera of reasonable length can handle, and there are some awkwardnesses of timing – and rather too many scenes of speech over music – that David Drew's performing edition has not been able wholly to eradicate. Yet John Gardner's judgement ("The greatest of all Spanish operas – and one of the greatest English ones, too") seems not too much of an exaggeration.

Sir Edward German   British 1862-1936

German Merrie England.
Monica Sinclair *contr* Queen Elizabeth
William McAlpine *ten* Sir Walter Raleigh
Peter Glossop *bar* Earl of Essex
June Bronhill *sop* Bessie Throckmorton
Patricia Kern *mez* Jill-All-Alone
Howell Glynne *bass* Walter Wilkins
Rita Williams Singers; Michael Collins Orchestra / Michael Collins.
Classics for Pleasure Silver Doubles Ⓢ Ⓘ CD-CFPSD4796 (two discs: 97 minutes: ADD).
Recorded 1959-60.

Perhaps the chief downside of the success of the Gilbert and Sullivan comic operas is that all other British light operas are judged adversely against them. On any appreciation of its positive virtues, a work such as Edward German's *Merrie England* deserves our attention. Of course it's old-fashioned; but it has great charm, with some delightful melodies and fluent vocal and orchestral writing. Numbers such as "Love is meant to make us glad", "The Yeomen of England", "O peaceful England", "Dan Cupid hath a garden" and "Who shall say that love is cruel?" are just some of its more obvious attractions. Though not actually a stage-cast recording, this virtually complete version dates from the time of the 1960 Sadler's Wells revival and features several members of that company.

Patricia Kern, William McAlpine, Peter Glossop and Howell Glynne were among the company's leading lights, and here they sing the rewarding numbers with great distinction and commendably straight. In the leading role June Bronhill has one of those distinctive voices that one either likes or doesn't – a little inclined to squeakiness – but she is always extremely characterful and produces beautiful phrasing and enunciation. Curiously the supporting roles are swapped around between singers, which does not help for continuity of characterization. Yet on any count this is a most welcome reissue of the only recording of this work, and at bargain price and economically packaged it should be snapped up.

George Gershwin   American 1898-1937

Gershwin Blue Monday.
Amy Burton *sop* Vi
Gregory Hopkins *ten* Joe
William Sharp *bar* Tom, Sweet Pea
Arthur Woodley *bass-bar* Sam
Jamie J. Offenbach *bass-bar* Mike

Gershwin Piano Concerto in F major.
Leslie Stifelman *pf*

Levant Caprice.
Concordia / Marin Alsop.
EMI Ⓔ Ⓘ CDC7 54851-2 (64 minutes: DDD). Notes included. Recorded 1992/3.

For those who do not already know it (which will be nearly everyone, although there was a previous recording in 1977) this will be an astonishing discovery. Gershwin's first opera was written as part of George White's 1922 *Scandals* and although one or two critics recognized its importance, it was generally derided and the impresario had it removed from the bill. The libretto by B. G. DeSylva is little more than a bar-room parody of the worst operatic clichés – which include an aria "Vi, I'm expecting a telegram". The 23-year-old Gershwin's music, however, exhibits all the qualities that later grew into his mastery of total American music and which, to a large extent, laid down the rules and the technique for future generations of American opera composers.

The Overture leaps forward with all the vigour of later Gershwin essays in similar jazz-oriented style and the main song, "Blue Monday Blues", is as strong a parody of the blues style as anyone had created up to that time. One needs to try and imagine the impact of this piece on an audience in 1922 – when even ragtime had yet to be heard as anything but an aberration. Five years before *Showboat* and 13 before *Porgy, Blue Monday* seems to be really the first true 'jazz opera'. Its brevity does not lend itself to much interpretation but all the soloists throw themselves into their roles with feeling – happily there is no sense of condescending parody. It makes one realize how little we still know of Gershwin's total theatrical *oeuvre* – when will we ever hear *Treasure Girl, Show Girl* or *Song of the Flame*?

Marin Alsop conducts her own Concordia orchestra, which she founded in 1984, in Oscar Levant's *Caprice* for orchestra, an agreeable interlude originally conceived for a radio show in 1940, and which Joseph Smith's informative notes tell us was once featured by Beecham. Leslie Stifelman plays the Gershwin Concerto with clarity and strength – there have been more subtle performances of it, but it is the perfect companion piece to the opera, showing the progress the composer was making in his quest for the American sound.

Gershwin Porgy and Bess.

Willard White *bass* Porgy
Cynthia Haymon *sop* Bess
Harolyn Blackwell *sop* Clara
Cynthia Clarey *sop* Serena
Damon Evans *ten* Sportin' Life
Marietta Simpson *mez* Maria
Gregg Baker *bar* Crown
Bruce Hubbard *bar* Jake
Barrington Coleman *ten* Mingo
Johnny Worthy *ten* Robbins
Curtis Watson *bass* Jim
Mervyn Wallace *ten* Peter
Maureen Brathwaite *mez* Lily
Autris Paige *ten* Undertaker
William Johnson *bar* Frazier
Paula Ingram *mez* Annie
Linda Thompson *sop* Scipio
Colenton Freeman *ten* Nelson, Crab Man
Camelia Johnson *mez* Strawberry Woman
Alan Tilvern *spkr* Detective
Billy J. Mitchell *spkr* Coroner
Ted Maynard *spkr* Mr Archdale
Ron Travis *spkr* Policeman
Wayne Marshall *pf* Jasbo Brown
Glyndebourne Festival Chorus; **London Philharmonic Orchestra / Sir Simon Rattle.**
Stage/Video Director. **Trevor Nunn.**
EMI Ⓔ Ⓛ CDS5 56220-2 (three discs: 189 minutes: DDD). Recorded 1988.
EMI Ⓔ 📼 MVD49 1131-3; 📀 LDB49 1131-4 (two cassettes/discs: 189 minutes). Filmed 1992.

1989

In an ideal world, operatic recordings would always evolve in this way. Catfish Row came to Abbey Road Studio No. 1 two-and-a-half years after a Glyndebourne first-night that people still talk about and with the added benefits of two London concert performances to prime everyone for the occasion. We've a real sense here of Gershwin's community, a feeling of oneness with the piece from singers who've not only lived with, but through, their characters. It is doubtful if we'll ever hear the score in a better light. And what a score it is.

Irving Berlin once wrote: "the rest of us were songwriters. George was a composer." There you have it. This remarkable opera is a constant reminder of Gershwin's astonishing facility – his ability to rejoice in so many musical cultures and somehow absorb them into his own distinctive style. In *Porgy and Bess* we have the spirituals, the gospel chants and impulsive rhythms of the Negro culture (witness the wild syncopated drumming which transports us to Kittiwah Island), the jazz and burlesque origins of Sportin' Life's music, the ache of the blues which finds its way into all the great lyric melodies, not least the two celebrated love duets, the Hebraic strains of Gershwin's own roots (Act 1 scene 2 – the Wake for Robbins), and everywhere, evidence too of the harmonic lessons learned from composers like Ravel and Debussy who were among the idols of his youth.

Gershwin takes to the opera medium like a past master; the musical techniques are exceptionally well developed (we should, of course, remember that he had already experimented extensively with 'through-composition' in his ambitious Broadway shows *Of Thee I Sing* and *Let 'em at Cake*), the motivic use of themes (his leitmotivs) especially effective: note the way in which Porgy's theme (first heard in the strings on his entrance – Act 1 scene 1, track 5 – later an integral part of "I loves you Porgy") gradually achieves a kind of sublimation through the opera, or Porgy's first important solo (again Act 1 scene 1) where the words "Night time, day time" offer us a fleeting premonition of "Bess, you is my woman now". And so on. All of which does wonders, of course, for the dramatic cogency of the piece. Gershwin's theatrical instincts are always spot-on. Take the Storm scene (Act 2 scene 4) which puts one in mind of Act 1 scene 2 of Britten's *Peter Grimes*, but which of course came ten years later. Gershwin symmetrically frames his scene with an extraordinary sextet of voices each chanting his or her own prayer (Ivesian overtones here); the inner tensions generated in that one simple gesture set up the mood for the whole sequence.

It helps of course that Simon Rattle's terrific Glyndebourne company, with every support from producer David Murray and his engineer Mark Vigars – the production sounds quite superb – manage to turn Abbey Road into such a theatrical environment. We might just as easily be back on the Glyndebourne stage: you can positively smell the drama in such scenes as the fight and killing of Robbins in Act 1 and the scene on Kittiwah Island. Which brings us back to the performers. First, a word or two for the LPO who so wholeheartedly give everything they have to this difficult and sometimes awkward score (Gershwin was still, in some respects, feeling his way as an orchestrator). If you doubt for a moment the benefits of familiarity, just listen to the Paganinian brilliance of the violins as Rattle pitches into his scorching tempo for the introduction (and what a marvellous touch on Gershwin's part to have Jasbo Brown's bar-room piano – atmospherically recorded here some way off – take up the repeated brass riff of that introduction). The strings, of course, can deliver at will the high Broadway gloss of the big lyric moments (not least those love duets, here given a truly operatic breadth of line), while the melodramatic high spots – i.e. the strenuous fugal writing for brass in the fight sequence of Act 1 – are tough and primitive. Most creditable of all, though, is the way in which these players have gamely loosened their belts where Gershwin asks them to swing. The brass have a field-day – no holds barred in their final chorus, "There's a boat dat's leavin' soon for New York".

And behind it all is Rattle himself, so attuned and so alive to every aspect of the score. Mention has already been made of his expansiveness and of the impulsive energy (the juxtaposing of "Bess, you is my woman now" and "I can't sit down" – I need hardly tell you what Rattle makes of that), but somehow it's the subtler poetic nuances that linger longest in the mind: Bess's farewell to Porgy as she leaves for the picnic – solo horn over a simple shimmering ostinato in the strings – is but one such instance.

The cast are so *right*, so much a part of their roles, and so well integrated into the whole, that one almost takes the excellence of their contributions for granted. The singing is most beautiful – one fine voice after another, beginning in style with Harolyn Blackwell's radiant Clara whose "Summertime", at Rattle's gorgeously lazy tempo, is just about as beguiling as one could wish for. In the title-roles, Willard White (the Porgy on Maazel's pioneering 1975 Decca set) and Cynthia Haymon seem ideal. Through his dark, warm-centred voice, White conveys both the simple honesty and inner strength of this decent, proud man ("plain old Adam, the simple genuine self against the whole world", as Ralph Waldo Emerson put it), and he does so without milking the sentiment. Haymon's passionately sung Bess will go wherever a little flattery and encouragement take her. We shed tears for her too. Both are victims.

As Sportin' Life, the good-time viper, Damon Evans not only relishes the burlesque elements of the role (you can feel the razzle-dazzle of his stage presence in both his big numbers – especially of course, "It ain't necessarily so") but he really sings what's written – or a lot more than is customary; and there are sonorous assumptions of Crown and Jake from Gregg Baker and Bruce Hubbard. Maria's brief tirade is treasurable – 'spoken', not sung, with a swing – against Sportin' Life – "I hates yo' struttin' style" – and, in marked contrast, the Strawberry Woman's haunting chant in Act 2 scene 3 – a brief but unforgettable snatch of Camellia Johnson's extraordinary voice. But then, remember we've a chorus (if you can call them that), a 'community', here full of such voices and they deliver throughout with all the unstinted fervour of a Sunday revivalist meeting. Sample for yourself the final moments of the piece – "Oh Lawd, I'm on my way". If that doesn't stir you – nothing will.

For the film, shortly after the Glyndebourne production was given at Covent Garden, Trevor Nunn opened out his Glyndebourne stage production into a film studio, the principals miming to their EMI recording of three years earlier, a not altogether happy procedure. Nunn's attempt to turn the work into the equivalent of an MGM musical, *c*1945, risks losing some of the intense *frisson* of his own Glyndebourne original. John Gunter's clapboard décor for Catfish Row has been unobtrusively enlarged, but the outdoor scenes lack conviction with, for instance, a few palm-fronds making do for the picnic scene on Kittowah Island. Even with these drawbacks, the work's impact is for the most part conveyed. Apart from some haphazard lip-synch, the cast performs impeccably. Haymon and White repeat their rounded, eloquent assumptions of the title-roles. Evans is an insouciant, plausible

Sportin' Life, Baker a powerful presence as Crown, with a voice to match, Clarey a trenchant Serena. For no very good reason some of the original cast have been replaced with other artists and they are obviously the ones who have difficulty miming to the singing of their recorded counterparts. The choral singing is superb. Camera work is occasionally restless, but by and large Nunn achieves what he may have wanted, a reincarnation of the period of the work's conception. Most of the electrifying sound of the CD recording has been preserved. But unaccountably the Buzzard Song has gone missing.

Umberto Giordano   Italian 1867-1948

Giordano Andrea Chénier.
Luciano Pavarotti *ten* Andrea Chénier
Montserrat Caballé *sop* Maddalena
Leo Nucci *bar* Carlo Gérard
Piero De Palma *ten* Incredible
Kathleen Kuhlmann *mez* Bersi
Christa Ludwig *mez* Madelon
Astrid Varnay *sop* Countess
Tom Krause *bar* Roucher
Hugues Cuénod *ten* Fléville
Neil Howlett *bar* Fouquier-Tinville, Maestro di casa
Giuseppe Morresi *bass* Schmidt
Ralph Hamer *bass* Dumas
Florindo Andreolli *ten* Abate
Giorgio Tadeo *bass* Mathieu
Welsh National Opera Chorus; National Philharmonic Orchestra / Riccardo Chailly.
Decca Ⓟ Ⓓ 410 117-2DH2 (two discs: 107 minutes: DDD). Notes, text and translation included. Recorded 1982-4.

Whatever else, this is undoubtedly the best-recorded and probably the best-conducted *Chénier* we've yet had (not forgetting the Levine/RCA set). Ray Minshull, the Decca producer, has achieved a theatre balance between voices and orchestra. There is presence but nothing is exaggerated. As for Chailly, sometimes he overconducts the score, drawing attention to himself rather than to Giordano, but by and large he is sympathetic to both the score and his singers. *Chénier* isn't easy to interpret; it bustles along busily all the time, but not always with much distinction or to any very strong purpose as we learnt from its Covent Garden revival. Chailly almost convinces us that the story and the music, especially where Gérard is concerned, is about something more than merely contrivance and cardboard, and he and the National Philharmonic bring out the work's colour and melodrama, both vividly presented.

For the many and important small roles, Decca have assembled half a dozen old faithfuls in various states of vocal health, all enjoying their moments of character performing. Varnay goes rather over the top as the old Countess in Act 1. The three *comprimario* tenors, whose combined ages must be more than 200, all make the mark with Piero De Palma the most potent as the spy Incredible, an object-lesson in acting with the voice. Giorgio Tadeo, a *buffo* bass of distinction, here turns himself into the nasty Mathieu. Krause is an honourable Roucher. But Christa Ludwig is better than any, making old Madelon's brief appearance into a moving vignette. Of the younger singers, Kathleen Kuhlmann is a rather anonymous Bersi, Neil Howlett a snarling Fouquier-Tinville. But *Chénier* stands or falls by its three principals. All three here perform eloquently. Pavarotti tends to rasp his way through the Improvviso, but improves no end in his first love duet with Maddalena, and defies the court in Act 3 with real heroism. But it is in the final act that his tone recaptures its old refulgence in his poetic musings and his death-going duet. Pavarotti may never quite suggest, as Corelli does on the 1964 Santini/EMI set (now available on a mid-price CD set), that he is the revolutionary poet of youthful ardour, but he is much the more musical singer.

Similar comparisons might be made between Caballé and Stella (Santini). The Italian soprano shows none of the strain under pressure as does the Spanish, but time and again a phrase will set Caballé apart as the more subtle artist, as at the forlorn passage sung to Gérard after "La mamma morta" – "Corpo di moribunda e il corpo mio!". There are occasionally those self-regarding mannerisms that Caballé indulges in, also a want of sheer tonal weight (that is to be found ideally in Tebaldi's singing in the earlier Gavazzeni/Decca set, also available at mid price), but you will warm to her portrayal. Nucci's Gérard is excellent, delivered with a nice balance between line and punch. His voice never seems individual, but his schooling is sound, and he is faithful to the score. Neither so forceful as Bastianini (Gavazzeni) nor as biting as Sereni (Santini), Nucci is as convincing as either in suggesting Gérard's equivocal, finally heroic character.

Pavarotti and Caballé enthusiasts will need to have this set; others should perhaps endeavour to hear the pros and cons of Levine (RCA) and even the other available sets, not forgetting the Gavazzeni (rudely powerful with Tebaldi at her best).

Giordano Andrea Chénier.

Plácido Domingo *ten* Andrea Chénier
Renata Scotto *ten* Maddalena
Sherrill Milnes *bar* Carlo Gérard
Michael Sénéchal *ten* Incredible
Maria Ewing *mez* Bersi
Gwendolyn Killebrew *mez* Madelon
Jean Kraft *mez* Countess
Allan Monk *bar* Roucher
Terence Sharpe *bar* Fléville
Stuart Harling *bass* Fouquier-Tinville
Isser Bushkin *bass* Schmidt
Malcolm King *bass* Dumas
Piero De Palma *ten* Abate
Nigel Beavan *bass-bar* Maestro di casa
Enzo Dara *bar* Mathieu
John Alldis Choir; National Philharmonic Orchestra / James Levine.
RCA Ⓜ ① 74321 39499-2 (two discs: 114 minutes: ADD). Notes, text and translation included.
Recorded 1976.

It really is a problem, choosing between these two recordings. It might seem sensible to start with the tenor in the title-role, and here a strong inclination would be to plump for RCA and Domingo: he is in splendid voice, with a touch of nobility to his manner that makes for a convincing portrayal of a poet. Pavarotti (Chailly) begins with a rather leather-lunged Improvviso, but he later finds poetry in the role as well, especially when responding to his soprano, Caballé,f who is rather stretched by the more exhausting reaches of her role and sounds audibly grateful for the occasional opportunities he gives her to float rather than belt a high-lying phrase. However, Pavarotti is an *Italian* tenor, and his Italianate sense of line adds one per cent or so of elegance to some phrases that even Domingo cannot match. Caballé does many things beautifully, and her fine-spun *pianissimos* and subtle shadings only occasionally sound mannered, but the role is undeniably half-a-size too big for her. So it is for Scotto, you might say, and a hint of strain is audible once or twice, in her timbre rather than her phrasing. It is her phrasing, indeed, that tips the balance back to RCA: Scotto is as subtle a vocalist as Caballé, but she gives meaning and eloquence to every phrase without ever breaking the long line, which one cannot always say of the Spanish soprano.

Matters are about even as far as the baritones are concerned: Milnes acts admirably, but refrains from over-acting, and the voice is rich and characterful. Nucci for Chailly is a bit less compelling dramatically, but the voice strikes you as more integrated, more even, than Milnes's, and thus, again, is more Italianate in its line. Decca field a sumptuous supporting cast (Astrid Varnay, worn of voice but full of character as the Countess, Christa Ludwig, no less, in the ten lines of Madelon's part, Tom Krause as a fine Roucher, Giorgio Tadeo an implacable Mathieu), but RCA's striking Bersi, vividly characterized Incredibile, and their Roucher, too, are not outmatched (only their Madelon, both fruity and acid – a grapefruit of a voice – is disappointing). A lot of people will enjoy the huge energy and bustle of Levine's direction. It is vividly characterful, but a shade exhausting and overassertive. The flow of the music seems more natural in Chailly's hands, and orchestral detail is clearer. The Decca recording, too, is warmer than the RCA, which has a slight edge to it. Even so, for Scotto's sake and to a slightly lesser extent for Domingo's, Levine just nudges ahead, but that would mean rejecting Chailly, Pavarotti and the Decca recording … it really is a problem.

Giordano Andrea Chénier.

Mario Del Monaco *ten* Andrea Chénier
Antonietta Stella *sop* Maddalena
Giuseppe Taddei *bar* Carlo Gérard
Athos Cesarini *ten* Incredibile
Luisa Mandelli *sop* Bersi
Ortensia Beggiato *mez* Madelon
Maria Amadini *mez* Countess
Franco Calabrese *bass* Roucher
Antonio Sacchetti *bass* Fléville
Leonardo Monreale *bass* Fouquier-Tinville
Bruno Cioni *bass* Schmidt
Arrigo Cattelani *bass* Dumas
Salvatore de Tommaso *ten* Abate
Egidio Casolari *bass* Maestro di casa
Leo Pudis *bass* Mathieu
Chorus and Orchestra of RAI, Milan / Angelo Questa. *Director:* **Mario Landi.**
Bel Canto Society Ⓔ ◾◽ BCS0003 (115 minutes). From a film made in 1958.

This is a hugely enjoyable *Chénier*, another of the 1950s films made expressly for Italian television. In what we can now hear and see as a golden era for the performance of Italian opera, an almost ideal cast was assembled under the well-routined baton of Angelo Questa. The staging is conventional in the best sense, catching much of the *frisson* of the French revolutionary drama while concentrating rightly on the principals – and what principals! Del Monaco, in his prime, is perfect casting for the title-role and conveys Chénier's ardent, fiery nature in his acting and singing. In spite of his reputation for unremittingly *forte* delivery, he here tempers his stentorian outbursts – the best of which is "Sì, fui soldato" before the revolution's tribunal – with singing of a subtler hue in the romantic passages in which the part abounds. As his beloved Maddalena, Stella was also at the height of her appreciable, underrated powers, equal to all the considerable demands of her role and deeply moving in "La mamma morta", her explanation of her plight to the complex character (most interesting in the work) of Gérard.

Their scene in Act 3 is the heart of the piece and Taddei is superb in his part of it. He gives ample profile to "Nemico della patria" and thereafter explores every facet of the role as his lust for Maddalena is sublimated into platonic affection. His warm, pliant voice is ideally employed throughout and he acts with patent sincerity – a great assumption. There's no weakness, and many strengths in the all-Italian support, with special praise due to the blind Madelon whose beseeching solo is movingly done. Sound and picture, albeit black and white, are more than adequate, apart from a couple of moments of sonic fall-out.

Giordano Fedora.

Eva Marton *sop* Fedora Romazoff
José Carreras *ten* Loris Ipanov
János Martin *bar* Giovanni de Siriex
Veronika Kincses *sop* Olga Sukarev
József Gregor *bass* Grech
István Rozsos *ten* Desire
Kolos Kováts *bar* Cirillo
Jutta Bokor *contr* Dmitri
Hungarian Radio and Television Symphony Chorus and Orchestra / Giuseppe Patanè.
Sony Classical Ⓟ Ⓒ M2K42181 (two discs: 95 minutes). Notes, text and translation included.
Recorded 1986.

Almost as often as Giordano is written off as a one-opera composer (if that), *Fedora* is dismissed as a one-tune opera, the tune in question being the tenor Loris's "Amor ti vieta". Pish-tush, it is a three-tune opera. Loris is the second man in Fedora's life; the first, Count Vladimir, is murdered (by Loris) half-way through Act 1 and before he has had a chance to sing a note, but not before a wide-spanned lyrical melody has become associated with him, or rather with Fedora's illusory image of him as noble, virtuous and worthy of her love: he turns out later to have been a thoroughly unpleasant character and he casts a long shadow, symbolized by references to 'his' melody, over the remainder of the opera. Fedora, who has not yet met Loris nor learned the truth, desires revenge and vows that she will have it in a solemn, chorale-like phrase that is intended to recall Orthodox chant. Vows of vengeance (and the melodies accompanying them) have a way of coming home to roost and that tune, too, becomes something of a leitmotiv.

Three tunes do not an opera make, of course, and there are lengthy passages between the pretexts for their recurrence during which Giordano can find little for his singers to do but declaim at each other. He therefore sends the entire cast, in search of local colour, firstly to Paris (cue for a frothy waltz, for a lively song in praise of Russian women – the tune here, to be sure, is not by Giordano, who pinched it from Alabiev – and, less expectedly, for a polacca and two piano solos – a nocturne and a bravura study – the latest lover of one of Fedora's friends being a Polish pianist, "the nephew and successor of Chopin"), and then to Switzerland. The drama by now is moving faster than the music, and there is a dispiriting *quart d'heure* during which Giordano absently writes a mock-folk-song for a chorus of female peasants, two or three largely irrelevant and not very interesting solo numbers, a tea-drinking ensemble and even, heaven help us, a bicycle aria before getting on with the plot (*Fedora* has some Trivial Pursuits claim to be the first opera to feature bikes in the plot!). And when he does get back to the story his invention is not always up to it: the potentially heart-rending scene, in which Loris receives news of his mother's and brother's deaths and Fedora realizes that she is responsible for them, is sketched with no more than a couple of anonymous vocal phrases and a scrap of would-be pathetic violin obbligato.

Those three tunes, in short, are stretched well beyond breaking-point, and the rents are often patched (when they are not left gaping) with threadbare material, but *Fedora*, for all that, is more than three tunes and a lot of padding. The timing of "Amor ti vieta", to begin with, is quite stunning, and tells you immediately that Giordano is something more than a tunesmith: it arrives with almost appalling abruptness, like a bolt of lightning (or like love at first sight, indeed), and its impact keeps one listening through the *longueurs* of Act 3 in the confidence that at the crucial moment Giordano will produce the goods. And he does: his recipe for Fedora's death-scene sounds appallingly artificial and no doubt is so, but goodness, how satisfyingly sad it is! As her life ebbs away in broken phrases we hear firstly a recollection of the Orthodox chant theme, then from off-stage the voice of a child (first cousin to the shepherd-boy in Puccini's *Tosca*) playing a concerto concertina, lastly the pathetic ghost of "Amor ti vieta". Enough: you will know by now whether this is the sort of thing that you will like. You may sneer at it in your severer moments, but then you will probably find yourself playing that *sotto voce* duet in which Fedora learns the truth about Vladimir (no accompaniment save ersatz Chopin from off-stage) or the ensuing wordless scene of her indecision (a wandering string line suggesting that Giordano had heard the Pimen scene in Mussorgsky's *Boris Godunov*; then Loris's and Vladimir's themes weighed against each other) and you might say "Crude, undeniably crude, and vastly inferior to Puccini, but what a reek of the stage!"

And it is the stage and its over-life-size gestures that Eva Marton's performance of the title-role immediately evokes. She is not an especially subtle artist and hers is the voice of a Turandot rather than the Tosca that one suspects Giordano had in mind, but she has the declamatory fearlessness and the flamboyance that the character demands. Carreras, too, enjoys every opportunity for full-throated 'can belto' that the opera offers, and he is in burnished, Italianate, risk-taking voice. The supporting roles are only so-so (an Olga who manages to be both plummy and shrill; a de Siriex who sings "La donna russa" loudly, very fast and with not a trace of charm), but Giuseppe Patanè expertly plays up such subtleties as the score contains and the recording is lively and reasonably spacious.

Giordano Fedora.

Magda Olivero *sop* Fedora Romazoff
Mario del Monaco *ten* Loris Ipanov
Tito Gobbi *bar* Giovanni de Siriex
Lucia Cappellino *sop* Olga Sukarev
Silvio Maionica *bass* Grech
Riccardo Cassinelli *ten* Desire
Peter Binder *bar* Cirillo
Dame Kiri Te Kanawa *sop* Dmitri
Monte Carlo Opera Chorus and Orchestra / Lamberto Gardelli.

Zandonai Francesca di Rimini – excerpts.

Act 2 – E ancora sgombro il campo del comune? ... Date il segno, Paolo, date ... Un'erba io m'avea, per sanare ... Onta et orrore sopra. Act 3 – No, Smadragedi, no! ... Paolo, datemi pace! ... Ah la parola chi i miei occhi incontrano. Act 4 – Ora andate ... E così, vada s'è pur mio destino.
Magda Olivero *sop* Francesca
Mario del Monaco *ten* Paolo
Annamaria Gasparini *mez* Biancofiore
Virgilio Carbonari *bass* Man-at-arms
Athos Cesarini *ten* Archer
Monte Carlo Opera Orchestra / Nicola Rescigno.
Decca Grand Opera Ⓜ ① 433 033-2DM2 (two discs: 132 minutes: ADD). Notes, texts and translations included. Recorded 1969.

There was real excitement surrounding the release of these recordings in 1970. A few months after they were recorded, in Monte Carlo in April and May 1969, Magda Olivero returned to the Edinburgh Festival (she had made a highly acclaimed appearance there in 1963 as Adriana Lecouvreur in the San Carlo Opera, Naples production of Cilea's opera) as the deranged mother in Malipiero's *Sette Canzoni*. Although she was on stage for less than ten minutes, her searing dramatic commitment, the individuality of her phrasing, the high notes and spine-tingling *diminuendos*, summoned by visibly steely will-power, will stay in the memory of anyone who saw her on that occasion, or in the long series of performances she gave during the blazing Indian summer of her career which lasted well into the 1980s.

Fedora is a mishmash of Czarist spies, noble Nihilists drowned in cellars (the news arriving by cable), the heroine swallowing poison. Giordano took his lessons from *Tosca* seriously; while one could not wish his opera on any sensible theatre manager, it resides perfectly in this enthralling performance. Del Monaco was by this stage in his career even less subtle about the relentless *forte* at which he sang, but although he occasionally strays off-pitch the positive elements, the roaring tone, crystal-clear diction and phrasing worthy of a prize-fighter, make him a superb match for Olivero. If in doubt, try track 5 on the second disc, the scene in which Fedora extracts a murder-confession from the noble Loris. Their intense conversation, backed by the playing of Pascal Rogé as the Polish pianist-spy, "a nephew of Chopin", is one of the supreme examples of *verismo* acting on record.

Gobbi doesn't get a lot to sing, except the adaptation of Alabiev's *Nightingale* song, "La Donna Russa", but his conversation with Olivero at the beginning of Act 3, in which he relates the series of disasters that have been triggered off by her vengeance, is another terrific example of Giordano's craftsmanship, their whispered exchanges sung against a marvellous Wagnerian obbligato on the basses. Dame Kiri Te Kanawa takes the tiny role of a groom, and the Monte Carlo opera chorus and orchestra play the piece for all its worth under the always reliable Gardelli. *Fedora* really is one of the most satisfying examples of recorded opera from this already far-off age, with three great stars, each of them in their later fifties, showing just how and why a career dedicated to the correct repertory, not chopping and changing, can become, well, monumental.

The three scenes from Zandonai's *Francesca*, an opera that del Monaco and Olivero had appeared in together at La Scala a few years before the recording, are equally convincing, a real wallow: Olivero's aria in the extract from Act 3, "Paolo, datemi pace!" is one of those nagging tunes that once heard is difficult to banish. The recordings are as clear and fresh-sounding, with no gimmicks, as they were on the original releases. A pity about the booklet for *Fedora*; in the LP issue it contained an excellent essay by William Weaver as well as set designs by Benois and a stunning photograph of Gobbi as de Siriex in plus-fours, Argyle socks and waxed moustache, wheeling in his bicycle in Act 3.

Philip Glass American 1937

Glass Akhnaten.

Paul Esswood *alto* Akhnaten
Milagro Vargas *mez* Nefertiti
Melinda Liebermann *sop* Queen Tye
Tero Hannula *bar* Horemhab
Helmut Holzapfel *ten* Amon High Priest
Cornelius Hauptmann *bass* Aye
Victoria Schnieder, Lynne Wilhelm-Königer, Maria Koupilová-Ticha *sops* Daughters of Akhnaten
Christina Wahtler, Geraldine Rose, Angelika Schwarz *mezzos* Daughters of Akhnaten
David Warrilow *narr* Scribe
Stuttgart State Opera Chorus and Orchestra / Dennis Russell Davies.
Sony Classical Ⓔ Ⓓ M2K42457 (two discs: 129 minutes: DDD). Notes, text and translation included. Recorded 1987.

Akhnaten, Philip Glass's third opera, is a work of relatively compact dimensions but with all the qualities of epic about it. More a history than a story, it tells in Glass's characteristically elliptical fashion of the rise and fall of Akhnaten, sun-worshipper and monotheist, the 'man of religion' who complements in Glass's opera-trilogy the 'man of science' in *Einstein on the Beach*, and Gandhi, the 'man of politics' in *Satyagraha*. Instead of a libretto there are texts and documents recovered by the Egyptologists, sung or spoken against an endlessly flowing line of orchestral background that symbolizes the passage of time.

Characters as such barely exist, indeed the very notion of 'characterization' is quite inapplicable to the elusive figures who pass through the music like ghosts or shadows. Religious fervour always excepted, everything is drained of human detail and emotion. Even the Act 2 duet between Akhnaten and Nefertiti has all the passion of a pair of scarab beetles mating, indeed, it comes as no surprise to find that the words of this domestic exchange are the same ones used just minutes earlier to address the sun-god Aten. Such is the manner of this solemn, ritualistic work. Decades pass; religions are set up and topple; always the orchestra, the ultimate protagonist, throbs underneath with its almost seamless weft of minor-mode arpeggios. Like Satie's *Socrate*, another piece of 'white music' and a score to which *Akhnaten* owes a great deal, this is a statuesque work of such earnestness that the term 'opera', with its implication of drama, fails to communicate the nature of the conception.

Akhnaten contains some of Glass's very best music. The Act 1 funeral scene, almost anthropologically observed with its terrifying drumming and the wild trumpet that accompanies the male chorus at the climax of the procession, strikes a chilling note from which the atmosphere never recovers. The final scene, sung wordlessly by the ghosts of Akhnaten, his wife and his mother in the ruins of their city, haunts the mind long after the music has ceased to play. Strangest and most wonderful of all is the "Hymn to the Sun", sung by Akhnaten himself at the centre of the opera, and addressed to the audience in its own language – English was chosen for the recording. It is one of the very few moments when we are invited to participate in Akhnaten's private world of belief, and with Glass's mesmeric music it's difficult not to be drawn in completely and utterly.

Success in the performance of *Akhnaten* relies more upon the orchestra than on voices, and here the Stuttgart State Opera (which commissioned the work) do a superb job. With relatively limited scope for interpretation, the soloists are to be judged more for the nature of their voices than for what they put into the playing of their parts, and in this regard you will be slightly disappointed only by Paul Esswood, whose tense, tight-toned singing of the title-role turns Akhnaten into a colder, more remote figure than he need have been. The chorus are marvellous. Documentation, vital for an understanding of the story, is more than adequate, with full texts and translations from the Egyptian and Hebrew.

Glass La Belle et la Bête.

Janice Felty *mez* La Belle
Gregory Purnhagen *bar* La Bête, Avenant, Ardent, Port Official
John Kuether *bass* Father, Usurer

Ana Maria Martinez *sop* Félicie
Hallie Neill *sop* Adélaïde
Zheng Zhou *bar* Ludovic
Philip Glass Ensemble / Michael Riesman.
Nonesuch Ⓟ Ⓓ 7559-79347-2 (two discs: 89 minutes: DDD). Notes, text and translation
included. Recorded 1994.

This is one of Philip Glass's most innovative and impressive works. It isn't exactly an opera, nor is it
film music; cantata is the nearest term, but even that won't really convey the idea. What Glass has
done is to make a setting of the script for Jean Cocteau's 1946 film *La Belle et la Bête*, using every
word as it is spoken in the film, but having it sung, the whole thing designed to be performed in
concert, with a print of the film being projected silently. Of all Cocteau's movies, *La Belle et la Bête*
is visually the most stylized, with its images of the Beast's castle, and the Vermeeresque settings for
the family home of the merchant whose search for a rose to give to his youngest daughter sets off the
nightmarish story. For all its surreal photography and extravagant décor by Christian Bérard (the
apparently living, arms-bearing candelabra, poking out from the wall, have influenced hundreds of
interior decorators), the dialogue in the film is delivered in a naturalistic way. Georges Auric's music
is typical of the time, slightly jokey, but there are a surprising number of moments in the film where
there is no music or dialogue: it is almost like a silent movie in places.

   Glass has changed all this. Now the words are sung in an ethereal, other-worldly way, and the music
trembles with typical Glass motifs. Without the visual images to go with it, *La Belle et la Bête* hovers
somewhere between genteel beat music and Messiaen-influenced *mélodie*. This is the most enjoyable
of Glass's music-theatre pieces since *1,000 Airplanes on the Roof*, another work which defies
categorization. As Beauty, Janice Felty's voice matches the image of Josette Day in the film, but
Gregory Purnhagen's light baritone would never suggest Jean Marais, whose smoky tones were such
an inspiration to Cocteau. Most people prefer the Beast with his hairy face and claws to the rather
effete-looking Prince Charming who emerges at the end, and Glass's music seems to make an ironic
commentary on this transformation. Even for those devoted to the film, this is well worth investigating.

Glass Satyagraha.
Douglas Perry *ten* Gandhi
Claudia Cummings *sop* Miss Schlesen
Rhonda Liss *mez* Kasturbai, Mrs Alexander
Robert McFarland *bar* Mr Kallenbach, Prince Arjuna
Scott Reeve *bass* Parsi Rustomji, Lord Krishna
Sheryl Woods *sop* Mrs Naidoo
Chorus and Orchestra of New York City Opera / Christopher Keene.
Sony Classical Ⓟ Ⓓ M3K39672 (three discs: 123 minutes: DDD). Notes, text and translation
included. Recorded 1985.

Unlike the dreamlike fantasy of *Einstein on the beach* (also on Sony, currently out of the catalogue)
or the historical epic of *Akhnaten*, Glass's second opera, *Satyagraha*, has a strong flavour of
documentary about it. The subject here is the early career of Mahatma Gandhi and his involvement
with the Indian community of South Africa in its movement of passive resistance to white oppression
during the first two decades of this century. A more conventionally minded composer might have
exploited the story's potential for dramatic action and sharp characterization to make something fast-
moving and overtly theatrical. Glass, on the other hand, chooses the subtler option of treating the
subject as a sequence of sharply contrasted and monumental tableaux, in which events crucial to the
progress of the struggle are acted out on stage against words and music of a more distanced,
impersonal nature – a commentary that seems to direct our attention away from the particular and
towards the universal.

   Glass's libretto for *Satyagraha* is a selection of verses from the *Bhagavad-Gita*, chosen and
rearranged by Constance DeJong, and set not in translation but in the original Sanskrit. As in
Akhnaten, this releases Glass from the problem of composing what would be essentially non-
rhetorical, meditative music to texts that retain the vocabulary, syntax and ready comprehensibility of
a Western language. Neutralized and yet still symbolic, the Sanskrit words instead break down into a
string of syllables that become absorbed into Glass's brightly coruscating sound world: clean, lean
music, which as ever possesses its own logic and drive. This is not to say that the score lacks drama
and pathos, however. On the contrary, Glass once again proves himself capable of reflecting mood
and prevailing action on stage, using the 'process' means of his characteristically modular style to
heighten the sense of ritual. At its most potent, this extraordinary mix of action and repetition give
rise to a powerful sense of energy, as in the first scene of Act 2, where Gandhi, molested in the streets
of Durban, is protected from the crowd by the wife of the superintendent of police, Mrs Alexander.
It should be added that in this scene Glass has also given us what is surely one of the greatest choruses
in modern opera.

   The cast of *Satyagraha* is small, and in a sense less conspicuous than the orchestra. Many of the
roles are understandably statuesque, and they require stamina as much as an ability to convey states

of mind. In this regard, Douglas Perry makes an imposing Gandhi, authoritative and yet slightly glazed and inaccessible. At the opposite extreme is the emotive part of Mrs Alexander, vividly communicated by Rhonda Liss (who also takes the ensemble role of Kasturbai, Gandhi's wife). The remaining principals have perhaps fewer openings for characterization; it was not Glass's intention to bring them beyond the middle ground, and they tend to merge into the prevailing musical flow. Both chorus and orchestra (the latter comprising only woodwind, strings and keyboards) sound most impressive throughout.

The recording itself is unusual by normal classical-music standards in that it has been made entirely by the overdubbing process. Astonishingly, the result is far more suggestive of the opera-house than of the studio, with the orchestra naturalistically balanced and the voices located as though on the stage. *Satyagraha* is an extraordinary and often moving score, and it demands immediate attention.

Mikhail Glinka   USSR 1804-1857

Glinka A Life for the Tsar.

Boris Martinovich *bass* Ivan Susanin
Alexandrina Pendachanska *sop* Antonida
Chris Merritt *ten* Sobinin
Stefania Toczyska *contr* Vanya
Stoil Georgiev *bass* Polish Commander
Mincho Popov *ten* Messenger
Konstantin Videv *bass* Russian Commander
Sofia National Opera Chorus and Festival Orchestra / Emil Tchakarov.
Sony Classical Ⓕ Ⓓ S3K46487 (three discs: 210 minutes: DDD). Notes, text and translation included. Recorded 1989.

This is indeed *A Life for the Tsar*, not *Ivan Susanin*. An opera glorifying the establishment of the Romanov dynasty was an awkward one for the Communists, the more so as the work is with some reason honoured in its own land as the first great Russian opera. The censors found various ways round the problem, and all modern scores (such as the 1978 Muzyka vocal score) contain the version by Sergey Gorodetsky, which gets off to a characteristic start by making the peasants sing "I'll die for Holy Russia" instead of "I'll die for the Tsar, for Rus". They do it rather tentatively here; perhaps that particular kind of folk polyphony, the so-called *podgolosok*, comes more easily to Russians than to Bulgarians. They are much better in the splendid rowing chorus, as the men round the bend in the thawing river to be greeted by the excited villagers: no wonder the first orchestra applauded Glinka's brilliant balalaika pizzicato as they recognized a composer who could write not just imitations, but compose from within Russian idioms. The beautiful 5/4 wedding chorus is charmingly sung, and the final "Slavsya" is properly jubilant as the people hail the Tsar whose throne has been saved by Susanin's sacrifice.

Earlier, deep in the frozen forest where he has deliberately misled the invading Poles, he has sung his great farewell to the last dawn he will see. Boris Martinovich rises well to the occasion of this famous aria; before, he is reflective but not always as firm as the music suggests. His daughter Antonida is sung by Alexandrina Pendachanska. She has a clear, acute voice, with a slight edge to it and under pressure the familiar Slavonic vibrato, but she phrases well and sings with character. Her betrothed, Sobinin, is well taken by Chris Merritt; he has a good sense of line and, like Pendachanska, the ability to make a single expressive gesture in those arias where Glinka's initial Russian enthusiasms dissolve into Italian gestures as he slightly loses his way. Stefania Toczyska sings Vanya's charming song about the little bird affectingly, and also has the character to make a strong dramatic gesture of the scena when he arrives, unhorsed and freezing, to warn of the Poles' seizure of Susanin.

The orchestra play well for Emil Tchakarov, making much of all the Polish glitter and stamp, and the recording is fair if not outstanding: the voices come across well, but the various effects of space and distance, of arrivals and departures, are not as atmospheric as they might be. No matter: it is splendid to have on disc a good version of Glinka's seminal masterpiece of Russian opera in its true form.

Glinka A Life for the Tsar.

Evgeny Nesterenko *bass* Ivan Susanin
Marina Mescheriakova *sop* Antonida
Aleksandr Lomonosov *ten* Sobinin
Eléna Zaremba *mez* Vanya
Boris Bezhko *bar* Polish Commander
Bolshoi Theatre Chorus; Bolshoi Symphony Orchestra / Alexander Lazarev.
Stage Director: **Nicolai Kuznetsov.**
Teldec Ⓕ ⏺ 4509-92051-3; ▶ 4509-92051-6 (175 minutes). Recorded 1992.

This became one of the great national works, the invariable opening-night opera for any new season in Moscow or St Petersburg. In 1917 its title was changed to *Ivan Susanin* (which had been Glinka's own) and a way round the embarrassing enthusiasm for the first of the Romanovs was found for its revival in 1939. With Glasnost, the official title and libretto became possible again, and this is what the video presents, a performance at the Bolshoi, the scene of the opera's première, of the production closely associated with the Gorbachev era and first given in 1989. One wonders what the next stage in its history will be.

Such a production as this is already a curiosity, almost an anachronism. We all know about 'the modern producer' (lumping them all, good and bad, conveniently together), but here is an old-style production, probably not greatly changed since the nineteenth century. The chorus lines up or stands in a semicircle. Occasionally somebody within the ranks raises an arm or smiles, but generally they don their costumes, take up their appointed places and just sing. The chorus, moreover, are on-stage more often than not; more than usually, it is their opera. With this dramatically inert element, and with a ballet that is merely pretty and expert occupying most of Act 2, it is for a long time difficult to accept the opera as being more than an expensive, old-fashioned 'show'. Only with Act 4, and the lengthy solos for Susanin and son, does the performance really begin to matter.

Here, in this act, the singers are fine, and Eléna Zaremba as the boy Vanya is indeed magnificent. Nesterenko may be now a little past his best and, like the others, inclined to sing loudly throughout, yet the method is sound, the tone more than agreeable and his stage-presence noble. The tenor, Aleksandr Lomonosov, faces up manfully to the ardours of his role and is the best actor among them. Musically, the performance holds together well (its effect not enhanced by the camera's tour of the orchestra during Preludes). Visually, we tend to feel cheated too often of the full stage; probably the most effective filming is of the Epilogue, presenting a richly coloured panorama, closing in finally on the newly-crowned, 16-year-old Tsar.

Glinka Ruslan and Lyudmila.

Vladimir Ognovienko *bass-bar* Ruslan
Anna Netrebko *sop* Lyudmila
Mikhail Kit *bar* Svetozar
Larissa Diadkova *mez* Ratmir
Gennadi Bezzubenkov *bass* Farlaf
Galina Gorchakova *sop* Gorislava
Konstantin Pluzhnikov *ten* Finn
Irina Bogachova *mez* Naina
Yuri Marusin *ten* Bayan
Chorus and Orchestra of the Kirov Theatre / Valery Gergiev.
Philips Ⓟ Ⓒ 446 746-2PH3 (three discs: 202 minutes: DDD). Notes, text and translation included. Recorded at performances in the Maryinsky Theatre, St Petersburg during February 1995.

Let's get things completely out of proportion, in the way for which we canary-fanciers are notorious, and draw attention first to a marvellous soprano. She is delightfully pure in tone, even and steady in production, highly accomplished and at her ease in florid passages, ranging widely and 'taking' cleanly, expressive as well (though perhaps less strikingly so). It would no doubt be rash to call her a new Nezhdanova, but listening in suitable company one might risk it, at least as an observation with question-mark.

But of course "The play's the thing", or here the opera – 'the father of Russian opera', a famous paternity – and it certainly was time for a new recording. The other one (on a 1978 Melodiya, reissued in BMG's Russian opera series) has an excellent, and superior, Ruslan in Nesterenko but a needly Lyudmila in Bela Rudenko. Still, it is not so much in the solo singing as in recorded sound and the spark running through the orchestra that the distinction of the Philips version lies. With Gergiev, the playing rises well above the reliability of long-practised routine; indeed, the Overture, always a winner, has quite exceptional brilliance and exhilaration. Later, the performance is just as remarkable for its refinement of detail and for sensitivity in the meditative, tender passages which enrich the musical score as they do the humanity of this operatic fairy-tale.

There was a video available, and it here begins to press its claims, in the Deluxe Edition which housed both discs and film (described as 'limited edition only' when it was released – it's no longer in the catalogue) . This is a rather curious business, since, for much of the time, there is not really a great deal to watch. Good story-book sets and magnificent costumes satisfy the eye for a while, but soon the sight of those serried ranks of chorus, doing nothing, incites the producer *manqué* in us, and we fret to take hold and move them about – not so as to distract, for heaven's sake, but because music and drama provide both opportunity and need. *Ruslan* should, one feels, be a strongly visual opera, and the Russians should know how to produce it: yet they are really not very clever. Big dramatic moments such as the great darkness and Lyudmila's abduction in Act 1, or the Head's appearance (pure pantomime – "He's *behind* you!") in Act 2, have far less effect when seen than one had imagined when merely listening. And yet there is the magical Fourth Act with Chernamor's garden, the processions and dances, veiled women and pantalooned warriors, not to mention the great white beard which requires attendants preceding its owner, almost as numerous as those who elsewhere tend the silken train following in the wake of the Princess Turandot.

The principals act with the professionalism of those brought up in a rigid school; they know their job and proceed accordingly. Essentially, they are singers, the Ruslan (Ognovienko) an ample bass-baritone, the Farlaf (Bezzubenkov) a sturdy bass with a neat capacity for patter, Bayan (Marusin) a tenor with tense tone, slightly flat intonation, especially memorable when seen as the white-haired bardic figure who holds in thrall an audience with a longer attention-span than might be counted on today. Larissa Diadkova's Ratmir made a strong impression in the 1995 Edinburgh Festival and is good to see as well as hear. Gorchakova brings glamour of voice as of appearance to her role of Gorislava, and the Lyudmila of Netrebko is outstanding. The recording (thinking now of cost and conscience) might almost be justified as essential, the Deluxe Edition (if it can be found) as one of those luxuries that are essential too, once in a way, every now and then.

Christoph Gluck   Bohemian 1714-1787

Gluck Alceste.

Jessye Norman *sop* Alceste
Nicolai Gedda *ten* Admète
Tom Krause *bar* High Priest
Robert Gambill *ten* Evandre
Peter Lika *bass* Herald
Siegmund Nimsgern *bass* Hercule
Bernd Weikl *bar* Apollon
Roland Bracht *bass* The Oracle
Kurt Rydl *bass* Thanatos (God of the Underworld)
Bavarian Radio Chorus and Symphony Orchestra / Serge Baudo.
Orfeo Ⓔ Ⓓ C027823F (three discs: 151 minutes: ADD). Notes, text and translation included. Recorded 1982.

The dithering and debating which normally accompany record-buying can be happily dispensed with here. The opera is a masterpiece, the recording admirable, and the alternative is abstinence. Like other works on classical subjects, *Alceste* suffers from a reputation for respectable dullness or from the kind of critical veneration which never suggests that one is actually going to enjoy it. In the late Spike Hughes's history of Glyndebourne (David and Charles: 1981) he remarks that it was "not everybody's cup of tea", and Alan Blyth reviewing the original issue of this set quoted complaints about its monotony when produced at Covent Garden in 1981. When praised, it gathers solemn abstractions like dust on a monument: 'sublimity', 'profundity', 'nobility', 'restraint'. All of them are apt, but they fail to lay the ghost of a suspicion that we are going to find it a sublime bore. Some criticism can be dealt with, for instance Ernest Newman's that the mood is one of sustained sorrow and lamentation: true of Act 1 but not of the rejoicing which opens Act 2; true of the end of Act 2 but then belied by Hercules, Apollo and the general rejoicing with which the opera ends. A more valid criticism can be levelled at Act 3 and particularly the figure of Hercules, introduced (like the ballet, not included here) for the Paris production: his aria, "C'est en vain que l'enfer", is taken from an earlier opera, *Ezio*, and it would seem that Gluck's heart was not in it. Even so, *Alceste* is an opera that delights the ears, moves the emotions and is emphatically not a bore.

Jessye Norman rises to greatness in the aria "Ah, malgré moi", and whenever she is singing there is likely to come a moment (as in the contralto "ministres de la mort") in which the sheer glory of the sound stands out in gold. Alan Blyth is no doubt right in wishing for more inwardness and eloquence; still, there is much to be thankful for. With Gedda, too, one has to take the rough (that is, the vocal style) not so much with the smooth, for there is not a great deal of that, but the heartfelt involvement that distinguishes his performance. Krause is always heard with gratitude, Nimsgern less so. The chorus, so important in this opera, are consistently pleasing, and Baudo is both firm and sensitive in his handling of the score. The acoustic is clear, the balance fine, the booklet informative, the print tiny.

Gluck Le Cinesi.

Kaaren Erickson *sop* Sivene
Alexandrina Milcheva *contr* Lisinga
Marga Schiml *contr* Tangia
Thomas Moser *ten* Silango
Munich Radio Orchestra / Lamberto Gardelli.
Orfeo Ⓔ Ⓓ C178891A (66 minutes: DDD). Notes, text and translation included. Recorded 1983.

In the hands of Gluck, the all-powerful Viennese court poet Metastasio's *Le cinesi* ("The Chinese ladies") is a delightful work. How very interesting it would be to compare it with Caldara's original 1735 setting for the young Maria Theresa to perform with two friends. Gluck's version was also composed for the Habsburg Empress, though by 1754 she no longer took part in theatrical productions. Within a single act the text and music of the opera-serenade brightly illuminates the relationships between the three women and the man in a series of contrasting vignettes. Using a single exotic set, the characters are left to devise an afternoon's entertainment; each of them has a different idea and after essaying scenes from a hypothetical heroic opera, a pastorale and a comedy (in which the romantic undercurrents between the man and two of the women are explored), they resolve instead to dance, thereby requiring yet a different kind of music.

In contrast with the Deutsche Harmonia Mundi recording by René Jacobs and the orchestra of the Schola Cantorum Basiliensis playing on period instruments (never reissued on CD), this is a thoroughly modern performance (replete with 'resonant' harpsichord). Most listeners will favour the mature sound of the Munich Radio Orchestra over the less experienced conservatory players, but it is harder to choose between the singers, who almost all deliver polished performances; Alexandrina Milcheva as Lisinga and Thomas Moser as Silango stand out. However, it is René Jacobs who tips the balance by generating far more dramatic intensity than Lamberto Gardelli who, for example, tends to allow the introductions to the arias to become sticky and sag. However, having been roused from a 200-year sleep, Gluck's jewel-like *Cinesi* seems set to attract and survive a wide spectrum of amateur and professional performances.

Gluck La corona.
 Alicja Slowakiewicz *sop* Atalanta
 Halina Górzyńska *sop* Meleagro
 Lidia Juranek *sop* Climene
 Barbara Nowicka *mez* Asteria
 Bavarian Radio Chorus

Gluck La danza.
 Ewa Ignatowicz *sop* Nice
 Kazimierz Myrlak *ten* Tirsi
 Maria Jurasz *hpd*
 Warsaw Chamber Opera Orchestra / Tomasz Bugaj.
 Orfeo ℗ ① C135872H (two discs: 110 minutes: DDD). Notes, texts and translations included.
 Recorded 1983.

Though Gluck's major Italian operas – *Orfeo, Alceste* and *Paride ed Elena* – were to librettos by his exact contemporary Calzabigi, he also composed no fewer than 17 others (including a *Clemenza di Tito* all but 40 years before Mozart's) on texts by Metastasio. *La corona*, the last of these, was intended for the Emperor Franz I's birthday in 1765, but owing to his sudden death it was never performed (in fact it remained unheard until 1937). As the present recording shows, it was well worth disinterring, even if the 'action' of this *azione teatrale* is of the slightest – an argument between Atalanta, her sister and a friend about joining in the hunt for a huge boar ravaging Calydon, followed by another with the prince Meleagro as to who should be given the credit for killing it. The music consists of a three-movement *sinfonia* (including a number of hunting-calls), six arias and a duet (mostly extremely florid), and a brief final quartet; particularly striking are Atalanta's first aria, where the word "palpitar" sparks off elaborate *fioriture*, Meleagro's second (with oboe obbligato) and their one duet. The Polish singers here make a valiant and quite creditable showing at their very difficult parts, which cast an intriguing light on the evidently considerable virtuosity of the young archduchesses who were to have given the first performance; only a hooty mezzo (who, one has to be ungallant enough to say, does not convey the impression of being "of so tender an age", as in the text) is disappointing. The orchestral playing is neat and fresh, and the recording clean: the gaps between recitatives and arias could with advantage have been shortened.

La danza, written ten years previously as a curtain-raiser to a "grand ballet de bergers", rather belies its description as a "dramatic pastoral composition" by being totally static: we find only a lover endlessly agonizing over the fidelity of his inamorata (despite her repeated assurances), who is going to dance at a local festivity. Gluck thought well enough of the music to use it again in revised form for his *Echo et Narcisse* a quarter of a century later: the *sinfonia* is charming, but the four arias and final duet somewhat overstay their welcome. This may, however, be due to a decidedly undistinguished performance: the soprano sounds cautious and lacking in confidence, the tight-throated tenor produces an unpleasing dusty tone, and the apparently dispirited orchestra stolidly chug through the all-too-many repeated chords of the accompaniments without the least trace of nuance.

Beware of the English translations: besides perpetrating grotesqueries like "I bethink that I am …", "He deposes the arrow" and "May whoever remain who can!" they are often wildly inaccurate.

Gluck Iphigénie en Aulide.
 Lynne Dawson *sop* Iphigénie
 José van Dam *bass* Agamemnon
 Anne Sofie von Otter *mez* Clytemnestra

John Aler *ten* Achille
Bernard Delétré *bass* Patrocle
Gilles Cachemaille *bass* Calchas
René Schirrer *bass* Arcas
Guillemette Laurens *mez* Diane
Ann Monoyios *sop* First Greek woman, Slave
Isabelle Eschenbrenner *sop* Second Greek woman
Monteverdi Choir; Orchestra of Opéra National de Lyons / John Eliot Gardiner.
Erato Ⓟ ① 2292-45003-2 (two discs: 132 minutes: DDD). Notes, text and translation included.
Recorded 1987.

Iphigénie en Aulide was the opera with which the mature Gluck made his Paris début, in 1774, and though flawed by an oddly unbalanced plot – which keeps dramatic interest at a low level in the first half of the opera, and because of the need for a happy ending offers a 'cop-out', *dea ex machina* solution of the (admittedly insoluble) dilemma at the end – it has some superlative scenes at the close of the Second Act and throughout the Third for all the principals: scenes which draw on the traditions of French opera and indeed French theatre to enlarge Gluck's expressive palette. Its neglect is understandable, as compared with *Orfeo* or *Alceste* or the other *Iphigénie*, but the loss is ours. Just like *Il trovatore*, it is an easy opera to bring off as long as you happen to have the four best singers in the world in your cast (though the criteria here are decidedly different from those applicable to Verdi). This performance may not quite do that, but it is certainly good enough to help rehabilitate the opera.

It is regrettable, however, that – especially with such a conductor as John Eliot Gardiner – this is not a period-instrument performance. The Lyon Opéra band is a perfectly good one, but the smooth and bland sound of modern strings and wind does little to help animate the music of the First Act. There would be more vitality with a sharper-edged period sound. Gardiner directs a finely poised and balanced account of the Overture, which, however, is a little unexciting and perhaps wanting something of the sense of foreboding that is surely intended. There are one or two unexpected ornaments here. Nor does the drama much quicken in the opening scene, where José van Dam – perhaps husbanding his resources – seems unduly calm in facing the possibility of sacrificing his daughter. Hints of stronger feeling come with Clytemnestre's offended pride (at the rumour that Achille is planning to jilt Iphigénie) and with Achille's declarations of his passion. It is only with the disclosure that Iphigénie is going to the altar not for marriage but to be sacrificed, with her father's consent, that the emotional temperature rises, especially in the trio where her mother and her lover express their rage but she, like those other proposed sacrificial victims in eastern Mediterranean mythology, Iphis and Idamantes, is reconciled to what she sees as filial and national duty, to an extent that she and Achille practically quarrel over it.

From this point the performance becomes steadily more intense, as the singers rise to the challenge of the increasingly powerful music. Anne Sofie von Otter, vocally the most sophisticated member of the cast, sings her pathetic "Par un père cruel" with some depth of feeling and brings real force to her great outburst, "Ma fille!", as she imagines her daughter on the sacrificial altar and then calls on the gods, in strongly focused, passionate tones. Lynne Dawson does some fine things as Iphigénie, her slightly grainy and intense sound carrying much emotional weight, especially in the two airs of farewell, quite different in character, to Achille and to Clytemnestre. Both are very movingly done. Yet you are not quite convinced that her voice is really ideal for French music; it is a large one, less than ideally flexible for these supple lines. Her air at the beginning of Act 2 seems, at a quickish tempo, a little hectic. John Aler's Achille seems to be an unqualified success, with just the right blend of the heroic and the graceful, as well as ardent in the scenes with Iphigénie. He has a fine warlike air, delivered with splendid energy, in Act 3. Of all the principals, he is the surest stylist. As indicated above, José van Dam starts off at a rather low voltage, but certainly rises to his magnificent monologue at the end of Act 2 as he tussles with himself, contemplating his daughter's death and the screams of the Eumenides, and resolves to flout the gods' decree and face the consequences. Van Dam uses a wide range of tone and does not fail to convey the agonies Agamemnon undergoes. There are some excellent performances in the smaller parts, Anne Monoyios in particular singing with charm and feeling as a Greek girl and as a slave, and Gilles Cachemaille doing well as Calchas.

Here and there you may find yourself wondering whether John Eliot Gardiner is not pressing the score forward a shade too much when a more deliberate tempo would convey more of its gravity. Some of the choruses (done by the admirable Monteverdi Choir) seem unduly cheerful, and a slightly less polished sound might serve better when the Greeks, impatient to embark for Troy, are baying for Iphigénie's blood. The dances too might occasionally have profited from rather steadier tempos; but of course the direction is always carefully executed and tellingly detailed, notably in the big Passacailles in the Second and Third Acts. Not all of the cast's French pronunciation sounds quite assured. In sum, then, this may not be the last word on *Iphigénie en Aulide*, but it has many fine things and it will undoubtedly be the standard version in the catalogue for a good time to come.

Gluck Iphigénie en Tauride.
Diana Montague *mez* Iphigénie
John Aler *ten* Pylade

Thomas Allen *bar* Oreste
Nancy Argenta *sop* First Priestess
Sophie Boulton *mez* Second Priestess
Colette Alliot-Lugaz *sop* Diana
René Massis *bass-bar* Thoas
Monteverdi Choir; Orchestra of Opéra National de Lyons / John Eliot Gardiner.
Philips Ⓟ Ⓒ 416 148-2PH2 (two discs: 102 minutes: DDD). Notes, text and translation included.
Recorded 1985.

The praises of Gluck's *Iphigénie en Tauride* are sung a good deal more often than the opera itself. Written for the Paris Opéra in 1779, it represents the consummation of his 'reformist' ideals through the marriage with the traditions of the French *tragédie lyrique*. No other work of Gluck's is planned and executed with such breadth or such purposefulness. But it is a difficult work to carry off in performances – or indeed recording.

It was in this opera that John Eliot Gardiner made his Covent Garden début in 1973 – his dramatic concentration and his powerful intellectual control make him an ideal interpreter of the score, and evidence of this comes speedily in the present recording with the storm that breaks – equally in Iphigénie's soul and in the seas off the Scythian coast – at the beginning of the First Act. The effect is formidable. Gardiner's direction is impressive too in the impassioned recitative that is so strong a feature throughout this opera, and in the accompaniments to the arias, so rich in emotional suggestion; the dances too are done with grace and, for the Scythians in Act 1, great spirit. The orchestra is not a period one, which is a pity, because it cannot articulate the music quite as Gluck intended. But it is an efficient and responsive group.

There has long been a tradition of casting Iphigénie as a high mezzo, although the part is in true soprano range. Diana Montague does many fine things. Her voice has nobility and intensity, and in the middle registers one could hardly ask for a truer, cleaner sound, particularly at *mezzo forte* and above. Possibly the top of the voice does not have quite the support it needs to sustain her great Act 1 monologue, nor indeed to lend true grandeur – which surely is what Gluck wanted – to the "O malheureuse Iphigénie" in Act 2. A singer here needs to be able to make an expressive virtue of the difficulty, and Montague does not quite do that. There is plenty of feeling in the last-act "Je t'implore, je tremble" (a Bach parody), but not much of vocally expressed urgency. The tone quality is apt to falter in soft music, and in the top register the vibrato is sometimes obtrusive. In short, a brave and musicianly performance, but not quite on the scale this exceptionally testing role ideally needs.

Of the men, Thomas Allen as Oreste is outstanding, a thrillingly alive and passionate performance of a part that seems too small. "Dieux qui me poursuivez" is duly intense, while the darkening of tone in "Le calme rentre dans mon coeur" (with the quietly agitated violas telling us that his reassurance is false) drives its point home. And every word of his French can be heard and understood. John Aler sings his air at the beginning of Act 2 a trifle stiffly, without quite the expressive freedom it ought to have; but he seems to warm, and with his easy and natural delivery, and with his sweet, flexible tone, he makes a persuasive Pylade. René Massis's Thoas is somewhat unsubtle, even for a barbarian tyrant, though the blustery delivery and occasionally rather hollow tone serve reasonably well. All the parts are capably done. The sound is good, if a shade string-heavy and blended as modern orchestras are liable to be; generally the balance tends to favour the voices.

There is a serious rival to Gardiner in the live 1992 Muti/Sony Classical recording. Although the former is the more disciplined and more refined, and rationally is the one to prefer, it has to be said that the sustained intensity and excitement, the sense of vision, about the Muti set makes it something quite out of the ordinary and lovers of Gluck's music will not fail to find it uplifting and illuminating. Carol Vaness makes a formidable Iphigénie, Gösta Winberg an impressive Pylade; Orestes is again sung by Thomas Allen and you could scarcely imagine a finer, more truthful or more impassioned reading. Thoas is capably sung by Giorgio Surian but the smaller parts are not all done with much style. There are aspects of Muti's interpretation that some, and not just stylists or purists, may find exceptionable: heavily slow tempos here and there, spongy textures, a few flaws in the orchestral ensemble and rather a lot of general hum, or ambient noise, from the La Scala audience.

Gluck Orfeo ed Euridice.
Derek Lee Ragin *alto* Orfeo
Sylvia McNair *sop* Euridice
Cyndia Sieden *sop* Amor
Monteverdi Choir; English Baroque Soloists / John Eliot Gardiner.
Philips Ⓟ Ⓒ 434 093-2PH2 (two discs: 89 minutes: DDD). 🎧 Notes, text and translation included. Recorded 1991.

BBC RADIO 3
90-93 FM

There have been a number of recordings of *Orfeo ed Euridice* issued in recent times, in one or other of its incarnations, among them a version under John Eliot Gardiner on EMI in 1989, of a compromise nineteenth-century text (a compromise, that is, between the Italian original of 1762 and the 1774 *Orphée et Eurydice*) and a very fine recording of the original version under Frieder Bernius with Michael Chance in the title-role on Sony Classical. That version, the prime recommendation at least until this one, has more the aura of an 'early music' performance than does the present one, with quicker tempos, a more detached string playing style and a cooler, purer Orpheus at the centre of it. This version, however, also played on period instruments and following the original text, has a degree of spiritual force to which the earlier scarcely aspires, and that is to the credit primarily of the conductor, again John Eliot Gardiner.

It begins with a taut, almost explosive account of the overture, moves to a deeply sombre opening chorus and then a *ballo* of intense expressiveness, finely and carefully moulded phrases (but plenty of air between them) and a lovely translucent orchestral sound. Every one of the numerous dances in this set, in fact, is the subject of thoughtful musical characterization, shapely execution and refined timing of detail. This is of course the essence of what Gluck was seeking, music that conveys something strong and specific in terms of drama and character; you feel sure he would have relished such a performance, although he probably would have found some of the tempos a little slower than he himself would have chosen. The Second Act too starts very powerfully, again with an intensely characterized *ballo* – and then with a huge unleashing of energy as the Furies let fly at the docilely lute-playing Orpheus. Exaggerated? – well, it is certainly wonderfully effective, and a reminder that this is no mere rococo entertainment and we are dealing with issues of life and death. Dynamics throughout are given full value, if not more. The choruses during this act are again very carefully weighted so that the sense of the Furies' fading resolution in the face of Orpheus's grief is progressively felt. And then, as we enter the Elysian Fields, the orchestral fabric assumes a glorious richness, sweetness and light, with gorgeously florid detail, for "Che puro ciel!". The 'heavenly' ambience of the remainder of the act is movingly and joyously conveyed. And the tension and violence of the first part of Act 3 is no less faithfully captured.

Derek Lee Ragin excels himself as Orpheus; the sound is often very beautiful, the phrasing quite extraordinarily supple and responsive for a countertenor voice. The arguments for a woman's voice in this role need to be taken seriously, the most important of them residing in the 'sexlessness' of the countertenor; but the more disembodied quality here (or equally in Chance's performance) has its own justification and appeal. Ragin, in any case, sings with passionate involvement – listen to the drama of the recitative at the end of Act 1, or the ardour of his pleas to the Furies, or his fervour in the duet with Eurydice at the beginning of the final act. Ragin ornaments Orpheus's part a good deal, taking his cue, and his notes, from the text alleged to have been sung by the original Orpheus, Guadagni. Whether Guadagni ornamented his part under Gluck, who was so eager to rid opera of the abuses of singers, we do not know, but he certainly did when he sang the role (in J. C. Bach's revised version, incidentally) in London. The *strophe* at the beginning of Act 1 is ornamented progressively, to good effect (the unusual orchestral colours are highly evocative here, too, by the way), and "Che farò senza Euridice" is considerably elaborated. It does not necessarily gain in force from that, but we are all creatures of habit and after repeated listening it will perhaps seem more natural. Eurydice is sung clearly and truly, and with due passion, by Sylvia McNair – she delivers "Che fiero momento" and some of the recitative with considerable force – and the casting of Cyndia Sieden, with her rather pert, forward voice, as Amor is very successful. There are those who will slightly prefer Chance's poised and refined artistry in Orpheus's music, but in general this is, as a total interpretation of the work, more penetrating than any other in the catalogue.

Gluck Orfeo ed Euridice.
Dame Janet Baker *mez* Orfeo
Elisabeth Speiser *sop* Euridice
Elizabeth Gale *sop* Amor
Glyndebourne Chorus; London Philharmonic Orchestra / Raymond Leppard.
Erato Libretto Ⓜ ① 2292-45864-2 (two discs: 127 minutes: DDD). Notes, text and translation included. Recorded 1982.

B B C RADIO 3
90-93 FM

This reissue at mid price was a most welcome addition to the catalogue. The Glyndebourne cast recording is technically superb, coupled with excellent orchestral playing from the LPO, first-rate choral singing, and conducting of a very high order from Raymond Leppard, whose sense of the drama is strong and whose management of the ballet music, beautifully timed and shaped, is a constant delight. The text is the traditional Italian-French one, using the best of everything, a policy that on the whole one could deprecate while understanding why it is a temptation. Orpheus is wonderfully sung by Dame Janet Baker, with characteristic emotional force and concentration, even though it was never one of her greatest roles and she isn't in fact in her very best voice here. The Amor is only adequate; the Euridice is musical and accomplished but not outstanding. The whole performance bears the marks of its theatrical origins, and among the traditional versions it certainly ranks very high.

Gluck Orfeo ed Euridice (abridged recording).
Kathleen Ferrier *contr* Orfeo
Ann Ayars *sop* Euridice
Zoë Vlachopoulos *sop* Amor

Glyndebourne Festival Chorus; Southern Philharmonic Orchestra / Fritz Stiedry.
Dutton Laboratories Essential Archive mono ⑧ ① CDEA5015 (63 minutes: ADD). Recorded
1947.

Dutton improve on the 1992 reissue in Decca's Ovation series by including everything in the original
set. Missing on Ovation are the dance at the start of Act 2, the flute solo ("Dance of the Blessed
Spirits"), Euridice's "Quest'asilo dolce e beato", and the first, concerted, "Trionfi, amore" passage in
the finale. The omissions are pointless and the restorations entirely to be welcomed. The text is the
hybrid Ricordi version that was most commonly in use at the time and which is now usually disowned
in favour of either Vienna, Paris or Berlioz. In these excerpts it coheres, and the effect of the
abridgement is concentrated and moving. Stiedry's speeds, especially the urgent "Che farò", are likely
(as Alan Blyth says in his notes) now to seem 'right', far more than they did at the time. The beauty
of Ferrier's singing will often go straight to the heart – in "Euridice non è più ed io respiro ancor" for
instance. Her lovely singing of "Che puro ciel", in the scene in the Elysian Fields, and her touching
rendering of the words "Euridice dov'è?" in the same scene, alone makes the disc memorable. Her
Italian is clear and serviceable but unmistakably English, with a slight tendency ("Millay paynay")
towards diphthong. Her colleagues are better in this respect and indeed sing very agreeably
throughout. The chorus have a less impersonal sound than is usual nowadays, but are not all that well
recorded.
   Nothing like comparisons for putting things in perspective. "What a horrible sound!" one is inclined
to think at the beginning of this, and then, taking the Decca Ovation reissue into consideration, you
decide that it is relatively Elysian after all. The Decca is edgy, acid and crackly. Dutton have
eliminated the crackles and to some extent rounded the edginess; the acid tone of the violins is
presumably beyond remedy unless through a top-cut of the kind that would draw scandalized
condemnation from most music critics. The sound remains unpleasing though it is certainly a great
deal better than its predecessor.
   These of course are minor matters. The set goes into the library, and stays there, for its noble and
intensely human Orfeo.

Gluck Orphée et Eurydice.

Jennifer Larmore *mez* Orphée
Dawn Upshaw *sop* Eurydice
Alison Hagley *sop* Amour
Chorus and Orchestra of the San Francisco Opera / Donald Runnicles.
Teldec ⑤ ① 4509-98418-2 (two discs: 109 minutes: DDD). Notes, texts and translations included.
Recorded 1995.

This latest version of Gluck's masterpiece is something of a double hybrid: its starting point is the
Berlioz version, which combines what Berlioz regarded as the best of the Italian original and the
French revision (and using a contralto Orpheus), and then it is modified further, with a number of
reorderings and some music restored, as well as revised orchestration. It isn't very 'authentic', in
terms of Gluck No. 1, Gluck No. 2 or Berlioz, but that of course doesn't much matter as long as it
works. Some readers may not be wholly persuaded, especially by the structure of Act 3 as it is
here, with the weak chorus from *Echo et Narcisse* and without the vaudeville finale (which seems to
be necessary).
   On its own terms, however, the recording has much in its favour. Donald Runnicles begins
splendidly, with an account of the Overture as dramatic and pregnant as any. When the chorus enter,
sounding large, distant and impersonal, the immediacy and poignancy of the drama and of Orpheus's
plight fade somewhat, in spite of the passionate "Eurydice" calls that strike through the texture; and
the romantic direction of the ballet that ensues does not help, for it cuts against the elegiac simplicity
that is at the heart of the score. Yet Jennifer Larmore's voice is very full and beautiful, unashamedly
womanly in sound and manner, but amply and intensely conveying Orpheus's agony. The singing of
the three-verse *strofe* (only two verses in the Berlioz version and here) is particularly expressive and
the recitative that follows is highly impassioned. Alison Hagley's singing of Amour is fresh,
characterful and alert. Act 1 ends with the virtuoso aria, either by Gluck or Bertoni, that was used in
the Paris version, and Larmore throws it off in forthright, heroic fashion against a very unGluckian
orchestration. She uses the terrible cadenza allegedly put together by Berlioz, Saint-Saëns and
Viardot herself.
   There is more of well-disciplined and vigorous choral singing in Act 2, as Orpheus is at first denied
admission to Hades. This famous scene is grandly and impressively done but not particularly moving:
again it seemed rather impersonal in spite of the appealing quality of Larmore's firm and rounded
yet finely focused voice. The Furies' dances are done with some ferocity, those of the Blessed Spirits
quite gracefully, if coolly. The end of the act, however, is telling, with a soft, veiled quality in the
Blessed Spirits' chorus, and Dawn Upshaw's lovely, open, almost girlish sound in Eurydice's music.
The final dance has a proper hint of sublimity and the effect of this scene as a whole is in its way
exalted. Upshaw continues to delight in the final act with her unaffected singing and her natural
conformity to Gluck's marking *tendrement*: even when Eurydice is being fatally disputatious her

manner is appealing. Larmore gives a direct, firm-toned account of "J'ai perdu mon Eurydice", better known as "Che farò", at a nicely moving tempo. Hers is by no means an undistinguished reading of the role but nor is it a very individual one.

In sum, then, this is a good modern version of the score. Admirers of Larmore's singing and musicianship – and they should be numerous – will be eager to hear it, and the other two cast members are hardly less admirable. Runnicles's direction is alive and efficient and large in scale, more Berliozian than Gluckian. The recorded sound is warm and well blended. In terms of style this set isn't superior to that of John Eliot Gardiner's 1989 DG recording of a similar version, but there is much to enjoy here.

Gluck Orphée et Eurydice.

Léopold Simoneau *ten* Orphée
Suzanne Danco *sop* Eurydice
Pierrette Alarie *sop* Amour
Roger Blanchard Vocal Ensemble; Lamoureux Orchestra / Hans Rosbaud.
Philips Opera Collector mono Ⓜ Ⓞ 434 784-2PM2 (two discs: 115 minutes: ADD). Notes, text and translation included. Recorded 1956.

The Simoneau reissue was welcomed back to the catalogue with particular warmth. The central role is of course appallingly difficult for a modern tenor, with its strenuously high tessitura; it had also been recorded by Gedda (on Columbia in 1958), but this version is generally and rightly regarded as a classic because of the beautifully even-toned, poised singing of Léopold Simoneau, who negotiates the high music with almost nonchalant ease and shows throughout a refinement of style that is very much his own – he is ardent, to be sure, but in a controlled way that clearly defines the opera's framework as he sees it. He is supported by admirable performances from Pierrette Alarie, a charming and tender Amour, and Suzanne Danco, graceful and at times urgent as Eurydice. The support of conductor and choir is rather less satisfactory by today's standards. Rosbaud's tempos are mostly rather deliberate and there is not much of drama or vitality; and the 1956 orchestra often sounds heavy in texture. The text is claimed as the complete 1774 one, but that is not quite correct; the virtuoso ariette that Gluck used to end Act 1 is omitted (it may not be Gluck's own composition, but he used it just the same), and several of the dances are omitted, notably the final chaconne. Still, the recording has many virtues of style, and of uniqueness.

Gluck Paride ed Elena.

Roberta Alexander *sop* Paride
Claron McFadden *sop* Elena
Dorothea Frey *sop* Amore
Kerstin Ganninger *sop* Pallade
La Stagione Vocal Ensemble; La Stagione / Michael Schneider.
Capriccio Ⓟ Ⓞ 60 027-2 (two discs: 132 minutes: DDD). ✍ Notes, text and translation included. Recorded at performances in the Alte Oper, Frankfurt during September 1991.

Among Gluck's three Italian 'reform' operas, *Paride ed Elena* (1770) comes, in every respect, third. Gluck's reformist notion, of concentrating in each opera on a single dramatic theme, is followed here as in *Orfeo ed Euridice* and *Alceste*, but in this case the theme – certainly to us, but seemingly to Gluck's own audiences too – is less momentous. We cannot be as excited as we are by the grand, all-embracing love-death themes of the other two by what Gluck himself described as the portrayal in music of the different characters of two nations, the Phrygians and the Spartans, "contrasting the rude and savage nature of the one with all that is delicate and soft in the other" (Spartan austerity, that is, against Trojan voluptuousness). It was originally criticized as of "strange and unequal taste", and it is hard to disagree with that. It avoids, as Gluck said, "the strong passions suitable to tragedy"; he must have thought of it as something of an experiment. He did not adapt it, as he did the other two, for Paris, and clearly never intended to, for he borrowed some of its music for the Paris *Orphée* (1774).

The story isn't quite as it is in familiar versions of the myth. Galzabigi no doubt adapted it to meet Gluck's special requirements. Helen is betrothed to Menelaus of Sparta, not married to him, and Paris arrives to woo her with the help of Amore, who disguises himself as a Spartan adviser to Helen. Paris is assigned 'exotic', amorous and eventually passionate music; Helen's is cool and restrained and for a long time she resists his pleas apparently with little difficulty and it is only by duplicity – angering Helen by pretending to go away after an impassioned declaration, then returning – that Paris ultimately secures his prize. The first of the five acts is in fact for Paris and his followers alone, just with Amore, a series of sensuous songs of which the first, "O del mio dolce amor", is the most enchanting, indeed ravishing, along with ballets; it is not until Act 3 that the work really begins to take fire with his "Quegli occhi belli", a response to her invitation to sing to the Spartans that alarmingly (to Helen) raises the sexual temperature. At the end of the opera, when Helen has capitulated, Athene utters (to the music of the overture) dire warnings about the consequences: but they are undeterred.

The role of Paris was written for a soprano castrato, Giuseppe Millico, who was admired for the seductive beauty of his voice. It is sung here, with a good deal of passion, by Roberta Alexander, with considerable sensuousness of tone though a more womanly timbre than is perhaps ideal. But there is no want of intensity in her singing: listen to the third short aria in Act 1, for example, "Spiage amate", or the lovely "Le belle imagini" in Act 2, or the moving pleas in Act 4 before her aria "Di te scordarmi", and indeed that aria itself. Sometimes the singing becomes a shade gusty and near-frenetic, but that is at least partly a matter of characterization. Claron McFadden's Helen is sung well and intelligently, in a voice that has a touch of the Spartan austerity that Gluck asks for and in a manner that conveys both her sense of propriety and, at least in some degree, her final surrender to anger and then passion. The increasing anger in Act 3 at Paris's effrontery, the sense of her dilemma, is all admirably conveyed, and so too is the agitation in at the end of Act 4. Dorothea Frey provides a well-sung Amore but her Italian falls heavily on the ear; it is all too plain that the cast includes no native Italian speaker (though Roberta Alexander does make real efforts to use the words to good effect).

Michael Schneider's conducting is sound and sensible but undercharacterized. He does not seem to have quite the measure of Gluck's idiom with its unique blend of the flowing and the statuesque. Several numbers, for example the pizzicato dance at the very beginning, are taken too quickly to have the grace and poise that properly belong to them; these are not qualities in which the performance is strong. There are touches of roughness too: the recording was made at the Alte Oper, Frankfurt (there are a few coughs). Still, the performance has a good deal of life, and far surpasses a previous recording on Orfeo, with its odd casting and its transpositions. Admirers of Gluck need not hesitate; this may not be one of his greatest works but there is much that is original and compelling.

Gluck La rencontre imprévue.

Julie Kaufman *sop* Rezia
Iris Vermillion *mez* Balkis
Annegeer Stumphius *sop* Dardané
Anne-Marie Rodde *sop* Amine
Robert Gambill *ten* Ali
Claes Hakon Ahnsjö *ten* Osmin
Ulrich Ress *ten* Sultan
Malcolm Walker *bar* Vertigo
Jan-Hendrick Rootering *bar* Calender
Paolo Orecchia *bass* Chef de Caravane
Munich Radio Orchestra / Leopold Hager.
Orfeo Ⓟ Ⓒ C242912H (two discs: 101 minutes: DDD). Notes, text and translation included. Recorded 1990.

La rencontre imprévue belongs, along with works by Haydn and Mozart, to an eighteenth-century tradition of 'Turkish' works in which a Sultan or Pasha, after threatening all kinds of tortures, magnanimously frees the beautiful Western lady and her lover who were trying to escape from his harem. Of these, Mozart's is the latest and the most serious; Gluck's little *opéra-comique*, written in 1764 at the end of the Viennese vogue for that genre, is an altogether slighter piece, with several comic characters singing lines like "Castagno, castagna, pistafanache" (here 'translated' as "Conker, bonker, treacly trail") or "Coui, coui, coui, tri, tri, tri", and short airs in a very direct and simple style: this, two years after *Orfeo*! Only the central character, Ali, gets music on a higher plane, with some very eloquent little arias that give scope for graceful legato at the top of the tenor compass. Ali, believing his beloved Rezia dead, resists the amorous blandishments of three beauties she sends to test him; then Rezia and he, escaping, are betrayed by the Calender, but of course spared along with most of the secondary characters.

Leopold Hager conducts a lively performance here, with brisker tempos and sharper articulation than he generally provides in his Mozart recordings. Here and there, however, the manner is a little lush for this kind of music, which would have benefited from performance by the acute-toned strings of a period-instrument group in place of the rather sumptuous sound of these Müncheners. Still, it is by the singing that the performance stands or falls, and this one stands pretty well. The tenor Robert Gambill, though sometimes tested by the high tessitura – he can't easily sing quietly and gracefully up there – produces some very beguiling sounds and appealing phrasing; there is one really delectable air, very French in manner, in Act 1 with cor anglais and bassoon and solo violin passages too, and in the next act "Ah, que vos plaintes" is uncommonly lovely. Julie Kaufman sings very touchingly in "Maître de coeurs", the most appealing of her airs, but she could have done with bringing a little more expressive weight to the role, setting it apart from the lesser ones. Malcolm Walker makes a resonant Vertigo, without sounding too convincing in French; Jan-Hendrick Rootering sings with some distinction in the Calender's role.

There used to be an Erato set in the catalogue, rather more idiomatically conducted by John Eliot Gardiner; he had the advantage of a superior Rezia in Lynne Dawson but Guy de Mey is a less persuasive Ali. There is little to choose in the lesser roles.

Berthold Goldschmidt

German/British 1903-1996

Goldschmidt Beatrice Cenci.

Simon Estes *bass* Cenci
Della Jones *mez* Lucretia
Roberta Alexander *sop* Beatrice
Fiona Kimm *mez* Bernardo
Peter Rose *bass* Cardinal Camillo
Endrick Wottrich *ten* Orsino
Siegfried Lorenz *bar* Marzio
Reinhard Beyer *bass* Olimpio
Stefan Stoll *sngr* Colonna
John David de Haan *ten* Judge
Ian Bostridge *ten* Tenor Solo
Berlin Radio Chorus; Deutsches Symphony Orchestra, Berlin / Lothar Zagrosek.

Goldschmidt Clouds. Ein Rosenzweig. Nebelweben. Time.

Iris Vermillion *mez*
Berthold Goldschmidt *pf*
Sony Classical Ⓟ Ⓒ S2K66836 (two discs: 129 minutes: DDD). Notes, texts and translations included. Recorded 1994.

Beatrice Cenci was one of five operas commissioned by the Arts Council for the Festival of Britain. Only one of them (George Lloyd's *John Socman*) was staged at the time; none has ever been produced by a major British opera company (and Karl Rankl's *Deirdre and the Sorrows* remains in limbo to this day). Two (Alan Bush's *Wat Tyler* and Arthur Benjamin's *A Tale of Two Cities*) were later demonstrated by *ad hoc* productions to be amply stageworthy, but Berthold Goldschmidt's work had to wait until 1988 before a concert performance in London strongly suggested that it might well be the finest of them; not much doubt is left by this splendid new recording.

With *Der gewaltige Hahnrei*, written while Goldschmidt was in his twenties, he had demonstrated a remarkable gift for the stage and a musical language already both compelling and individual. *Beatrice Cenci* is as pithy and swift-moving as its predecessor, and no less dramatic, but its melodic sweep and urgent eloquence are a distinct advance. It is based on Shelley's play, in which Beatrice is portrayed not as a murderess but as the victim of a vile father and of a corrupt and immoral society. Goldschmidt had recent experience of such a society; his portrayal of this one, and his sympathy for Beatrice and her mother Lucretia, give the opera an emotional force made all the more powerful by masterful restraint. A strong vein of generous lyricism is present throughout, but until the final act its flowerings are beautiful but brief; they are hastened along by the grim pace of the drama. Thus an elegantly tuneful song at a grand feast in Count Cenci's palace has but one verse: the purpose of the feast is Cenci's malignly joyous announcement that two of his hated sons have been killed. In Act 2 Beatrice's aria "Rough wind that moaneth loud" is heartfelt and touching but again brief; she is trying to tell her mother, but cannot find the words, that her father has raped her.

The whole of that act has ferocious pace and grip. It is only in the third, after Beatrice has been condemned to death, that we see how shrewdly Goldschmidt has paced the opera and at the same time made it clear that the daughter and wife of such a man, in a society that pardons his crimes, can achieve long-breathed lyricism not in an aria or a duet of love or hope but only in a dream of paradise or a lament at their fate. The destination of all those earlier lyrical moments is here, above all in Beatrice's beautiful final aria, a melody of haunting memorability. In this almost incident-less final act Goldschmidt has the leisure to repeat that melody, most poignantly, as Beatrice and Lucretia go to their deaths – even to cap it with a solemn threnody.

Roberta Alexander is very moving in the title-role; more might have been made of her implacably evil father by a singer less stolid, more careful with words than Simon Estes, but his voice is big, authoritative and quite unbothered by the vocal demands of the part. Della Jones's sympathetic Lucretia and the excellent Siegfried Lorenz as the evil priest who sets up the murder but then leaves Beatrice and Lucretia to take the blame for it stand out in a cast which has no weak links. Lothar Zagrosek expertly clarifies Goldschmidt's baleful orchestral colours and the remorseless turnings of the screw of his thematic development; the recording gives a strong impression of how powerful this remarkable opera would be on stage.

The four songs are no mere makeweights: the gravity of *Clouds* (Rupert Brooke) and the dark vehemence of Shelley's *Time* (a setting also used in the opera) are especially impressive. The composer had obviously kept up his piano practice, and Iris Vermillion sings expressively.

Goldschmidt Der gewaltige Hahnrei.

Roberta Alexander *sop* Stella
Robert Wörle *ten* Bruno
Michael Kraus *ten* Petrus
Claudio Otelli *bar* Ochsenhirt

Helen Lawrence *sop* Mémé
Martin Petzold *ten* Estrugo
Erich Wottrich *ten* Young Man
Marita Posselt *sop* Cornelie
Christiane Berggold *mez* Florence
Franz-Josef Kapellmann *bass* Gendarme
Berlin Radio Chorus; Berlin Deutsches Symphony Orchestra / Lothar Zagrosek.

Goldschmidt Mediterranean Songs.

John Mark Ainsley *ten*
Leipzig Gewandhaus Orchestra / Lothar Zagrosek.
Decca Entartete Musik Ⓔ Ⓓ 440 850-2DHO2 (two discs: 125 minutes: DDD). Notes, texts and translations included. Recorded 1992.

Der gewaltige Hahnrei ("The magnificent cuckold") was successfully premièred in Mannheim in 1932, scheduled for a prestige production in Berlin the year after, but it and its composer's career were victims of the rise of the Nazis. Goldschmidt, after his emigration to Britain, earned the respect and the affection of many musicians in this country, but along with most of his other compositions this opera was ignored and forgotten. It is a masterly work. In its vivid characterization, its dramatic use of pungent orchestral colour and sinewy counterpoint and its gripping narrative thrust it is an achievement all the more remarkable for a first opera by a composer then in his twenties.

The central character, Bruno, is an obsessive as repellent yet compulsively fascinating as Hindemith's Cardillac. He is a man so jealous of his submissive, adoring wife that he suspects every available man of being her secret lover, is so tormented by doubt that he compels her to commit adultery so that he will at least be certain of that, and ends by forcing her into the arms of a would-be rapist. His obsession is portrayed by a powerfully cumulative use of, as one might expect, ostinato figures, but this grim portrayal of mounting monomania is given poignant context by the tenderly lyrical, indeed chaste music of Bruno's wife, Stella, and by the ardour (including a noble entrance theme) associated with his sympathetic friend Petrus. The secondary characters are just as sharply defined; so is the chorus of neighbours, maliciously enjoying the scandal, righteously demanding punishment. Goldschmidt's language is tonal but bony; those who know the music of his teacher Schreker may hear echoes of it; others may detect an occasional kinship (scarcely attributable to influence) with Weill, Shostakovich or Prokofiev. But it is undoubtedly a personal voice, the voice of one acquainted with atonality (Goldschmidt had coached some of the singers and played the celeste in the first performance of *Wozzeck*) but no more inclined to adopt it than the exotic, over-rich late romanticism still in vogue in many circles in Germany at the time. In fact the assurance of his style is almost as impressive a feature of this opera as its swift-moving, murderously ironic dramaturgy.

So often when a work of real quality is rediscovered one has to make a few apologies for the performance. Not in this case. Alexander sings her heart out as the cruelly treated Stella, and as a result quite avoids the risk that she will appear a mere faceless victim. Wörle, very properly a Loge rather than a Siegfried, acts shrewdly as well as singing incisively; so does the more lyrical Petzold, grateful for Goldschmidt's differentiation of the two quite dissimilar tenor roles. Kraus seizes all the many opportunities to make Petrus a rounded character as well as a gift of a part for a lyric baritone. It is a tribute as much to Goldschmidt as to the singers to say that even in quite brief roles Lawrence, Otelli, Wottrich and Kapellmann all make very positive contributions to the drama. Each of them is there for a purpose, and so is the pithily characterful music given to each of them. The concise economy of this opera is one of the reasons for its power.

The *Mediterranean Songs* date from nearly 30 years later, and for those encountering Goldschmidt's music for the first time they will be an encouraging indication that three decades of neglect had not soured his lyricism. They are rich and delicate; eloquent evocations of the Mediterranean world, scored with great refinement and with vocal lines of a grateful amplitude. Ainsley sings them beautifully, with care for words (Goldschmidt sets English as eloquently as he does German) as well as smoothness of line. Zagrosek is throughout a powerful advocate for Goldschmidt's music, sensitive to its poignancy (the end of the opera is quite haunting) as well as its formidable strength. An important addition to Decca's imaginative Entartete Musik series, this is a major rediscovery, and all those involved seem urgently convinced of it.

Carlos Gomes

Brazilian 1836-1896

Gomes Il Guarany.

Hao Jiang Tian *bass* Don Antonio de Mariz
Verónica Villarroel *sop* Cecilia
Plácido Domingo *ten* Pery
Marcus Haddock *ten* Don Alvaro
Carlos Alvarez *bass* Gonzales
Graham Sanders *ten* Ruy-Bento

John Paul Bogart *bass* Alonso
Boris Martinovic *bass-bar* Indian chief
Bonn Opera Chorus; Orchestra of the Beethovenhalle, Bonn / John Neschling.
Sony Classical Ⓕ Ⓓ S2K66273 (two discs: 147 minutes: DDD). Recorded at performances in the Oper der Stadt Bonn, Germany during June 1994. Notes, text and translation included. Recorded 1994.

The most internationally acclaimed opera composer of Brazil, hailed by Verdi as a "real musical genius", Antonio Gomes is today all but forgotten outside his native country (where the brilliant overture to *Il Guarany* is regarded as a national artistic treasure). The opera itself is known largely from books and from a recording by Caruso and Destinn of the love duet at the end of Act 1. After the enthusiastic reception in Rio of a couple of his operas, Gomes, who came from a family of modest musicians, was awarded a grant enabling him to study in Milan. There he wrote *Il Guarany*, which was produced at La Scala in 1870 with huge success.
   The story is set in sixteenth-century Brazil and deals with the love of Cecilia, daughter of the Portuguese nobleman Don Antonio, and the 'noble savage' Pery, chieftain of the Indian tribe of Guarany (who eventually accepts baptism). They are threatened both by the hostility of the cannibal Aimorè tribe and by Spanish adventurers led by Gonzales, who has designs on the silver mine owned by Antonio and on Cecilia. The opera ends spectacularly *à la* Meyerbeer when Antonio, to save his daughter, blows up his castle with himself and his enemies in it. The work is categorized as an 'opera-ballet', but, at least in this performance, there is no music for dancing.
   So Italianized was Gomes that except for a very few bars there is no real local colour: indeed Cecilia's first aria, rich in coloratura, is a *polacca*! Overall the music, for Indians and whites alike, is purely Italian, similar to middle-period Verdi, but the atmospheric orchestration is far more adventurous and inventive – one example being the sinister opening to Act 2. Highlights other than the duet mentioned are Pery's aria at the start of Act 2, a jaunty adventurer's song by Gonzales, Cecilia's Act 2 soliloquy (which however leads to a rather conventional ballad with quasi-guitar accompaniment), and the duet scene for the lovers in the savages' camp. The stars of this performance, given before an excited but discriminating audience, are Domingo himself in the title-role – ardent and committed (though, as elsewhere, he will not alter the intensity of his projection for asides), Villarroel on the most brilliantly stunning form, and the capable and intelligent Alvarez; too many of the others are afflicted with tiresome wobbles. Both chorus and orchestra are excellent, and John Neschling invests the whole with a real dramatic sense. Those who like full-blooded romantic opera should not miss this.

Charles Gounod   French 1818-1893

Gounod Faust.
   Richard Leech *ten* Faust
   Cheryl Studer *sop* Marguérite
   José van Dam *bass-bar* Méphistophélès
   Thomas Hampson *bass* Valentin
   Martine Mahé *mez* Siébel
   Nadine Denize *sop* Marthe
   Marc Barrard *bar* Wagner
French Army Chorus; Toulouse Capitole Choir and Orchestra / Michel Plasson.
EMI Ⓕ Ⓓ CDS5 46224-2 (three discs: 204 minutes: DDD). Notes, text and translation included. Recorded 1991.

BBC RADIO 3
90-93 FM

"Salut Faust!"; indeed, to a large extent, "Salut *Faust*!". Richard Leech as the eponymous hero sings his part with the fresh, eager tone, the easy legato, the sense of French style that it has so badly been wanting all these years, certainly since Nicolai Gedda essayed the role on the now rather aged Cluytens/EMI set. Gedda's voice may be more lyrical, more liquid in the role, but Leech encompasses it with less effort, and creates a real character. From the beginning, as the old, weary Faust in his study, he seems to have thought himself into the part. That magical moment when he first greets Marguérite in the Kermesse scene is full of anticipatory feeling, the cavatina is redolent of true ardour, as is the whole Garden scene, where Leech's phrasing is at once disciplined and eloquent; then he brings increasing desperation to the later stages of the work without ever becoming mawkish. This is an extremely distinguished piece of singing.
   Beside him he has an equally impressive loved one in Studer and antagonist van Dam. Studer, incredibly enough, finds herself another amenable *métier* in Gounod; her Marguérite is not only sung with her customary attributes of innate musicality, firm tone and expressive phrasing but also with a deep understanding of this style of French music in terms of nuance and the lighter touch. The Jewel song is a treasure; the King of Thulé, even more the sad solo in Marguérite's chamber are touching. In the latter this Marguérite really captures the sense of hopelessness combined with longing for the absent lover. Later Studer rises to the more dramatic demands of the finale. She is particularly moving

here in the recollections of past happiness – the first encounter with Faust, his solos in the Garden scene. To add to one's satisfaction her French seems faultless.

Leech and Studer are to an extent unexpected pleasures: van Dam's success as Méphistophélès is more predictable. He achieves so much more by subtlety of accent and by care over note values than have basses, mostly from eastern Europe in modern times, by over-egging the pudding. Here is a resolute, implacable Devil with a firm, even tone to second the insinuating characterization. Maybe that element of elegance found on records of interpreters in the first half of the century is missing in this more rugged reading; little else. Van Dam's voice may have dried out a little, but he remains a paragon of a stylist in all he attempts.

Three French-speaking singers excel in subsidiary roles. Martine Mahé is no less well suited to Siébel, and she is granted her second and better aria "Si la bonheur", at one time regularly excised in theatre performance. Nadine Denize makes much of little as Dame Marthe; ditto Marc Barrard as Wagner whose role is somewhat lengthened by a trio, included in an Appendix, of which more below. Thomas Hampson is in places overextended as Valentin, a role that needs experience and perfect French. Plasson almost but not quite kills the score with kindness. He so loves the piece that his tempos, especially in the more reflective moments, such as the start of the Garden scene, become much slower than the score predicates and demands. Against that must be set his respect for the minutiae of Gounod's often inspired writing for orchestra and a general warmth that lights the score from within. In his hands the work seems the very epitome of French nineteenth-century opera and never for a moment as conventional as its detractors would have us believe. Here Plasson is immeasurably helped by having his own Toulouse forces, well versed in this kind of music. It was an inspired stroke to invite the French Army Chorus to sing the Soldiers' Chorus, delivered with such verve as to make it seem unhackneyed.

Plasson here restores three passages in an appendix, which were cut by Gounod before the première, two because they appeared awkward where they stood in the score, the third because he had second thoughts. The first is a trio for Faust, Wagner and Siébel placed uncomfortably halfway through Faust's Act 1 soliloquy, pleasing enough but eminently disposable. The second is a substantial duet for Marguérite and Valentin as he goes off to war. It tells us why he wears the "sainte médaille", but included in its place it quite spoils that first and magical appearance of the heroine at the Kermesse. The third item is the song of Maître Scarabée, a racy, Offenbachian conceit, which originally stood instead of the much more sinister Calf of Gold. It's good to have these pieces recorded, in both senses, even if they don't warrant inclusion in the opera as we now have it. They have been gleaned from the American edition of the score in the Bibliothèque Nationale. While authenticity was in the air Plasson might have returned to the original *opéra-comique* version and thus used dialogue in place of the recitatives. All the rival versions are fatally flawed in casting and/or conducting. Although one may occasionally want to recall the attributes of Gedda and los Angeles (Cluytens/EMI), Colin Davis's affectionate conducting (Philips), Freni's appealing Marguérite (Prêtre/EMI), or Massard's unforgettable Valentin on the reissued Decca, there is no hesitation in preferring Plasson and the all-round excellence of his team, who restore the work to something near its idiomatic best.

Gounod Faust.

Jerry Hadley *ten* Faust
Cecilia Gasdia *sop* Marguérite
Samuel Ramey *bass* Méphistophélès
Alexander Agache *bar* Valentin
Susanne Mentzer *mez* Siébel
Brigitte Fassbaender *mez* Marthe
Philippe Fourcade *bass* Wagner
Welsh National Opera Chorus and Orchestra / Carlo Rizzi.
Teldec Ⓟ Ⓒ 4509-90872-2 (three discs: 211 minutes: DDD). Notes, text and translation included. Recorded 1993.

Where Gounod is at his most inspired this newer version of his most popular work is more than commendable. One thinks particularly of the solos for Marguérite and Faust, the Garden scene, the vignette in Marguérite's room that used to be regularly cut, and the Prison scene (considerably extended by the restoration of passages cut – presumably – before the première: we are in controversial Oeser territory). Here the tender, sweet-toned and idiomatically French singing and style of Gasdia and Hadley quite exceed expectations in these days of homogenized and uniform interpretation. These two principals step outside those predictable parameters to give us readings of high individuality, favouring their grateful music with delicately etched line, varied dynamics and real involvement in their characters' predicaments – Faust's vain search for the elixir of renewal, Marguérite for the ideal man. Both their happiness and later remorse are eloquently expressed.

After somewhat dragging the King of Thulé solo (we'll come to the often lax conducting in a minute) Gasdia gives a well-nigh faultless performance – light-hearted, elated in the Jewel song, ardent in the Garden duet, ecstatic in the bedtime solo that follows, ineffably sad in her "Il ne revient pas". How can this exquisite solo have ever been omitted we think when Gasdia moves us so deeply?

She is no less touching when she has lost her reason. Subtle timbres, poised high notes inform all her singing. She hasn't quite the technical accomplishment of Studer (Plasson), but surpasses even Studer's lovely portrayal through her extra colouring of tone and words. Hadley, with the ideal weight of voice for Faust, has done nothing better. "Je t'aime" at the first meeting with Marguérite is whispered in wonder. The cavatina is suitably intimate, not projected as a show-piece but as a love song closing with a high C taken in the head in place of an ugly *ut de poitrine*. In the love duet he sings to his Marguérite as a gentle lover, never bawling, caressing his music, and Gasdia replies in kind. Hadley is marginally preferable to Plasson's Leech by virtue of his greater variety of expression.

The good news continues with Mentzer. She sings both Siébel's regular solos with vibrant, properly virile tone, the quick vibrato attractive. Another piece, "Versez vos chagrins", cut before the première, is given what must be its first recording, in an appendix, and offers further evidence of the American mezzo's suitability for the role. You may prefer Agache's manly, full-voiced Valentin to Hampson's more self-conscious reading on the Plasson set, and it's a real coup to have Fassbaender as Marthe, making so much of little. Ramey is the one singer to give a standardized performance. His Méphistophélès is as soundly and resolutely sung as one would expect from this sturdy bass, but it doesn't have the Francophone smoothness and subtlety of van Dam (Plasson) and quite misses the individual touches of basses from the distant past, such as Journet on the 1930 HMV 78 set available on Pearl.

As implied above, Rizzi conducts an often alarmingly slow account of the score, even more tardy than Plasson, himself noted for his moderate tempos. In compensation the more exciting passages are given rather too much verve. The recent reissue of the old 1928 Beecham set reminds us that there is no substitute for stage experience in knowing how to pace a work. Where Rizzi goes slow, Beecham keeps the score moving and buoyant. Excellent as are the WNO Chorus and Orchestra they don't quite match the authentic sound provided by their Toulouse counterparts for Plasson, but Rizzi is always aware of the sensuous nature of Gounod's scoring.

Following the Oeser Edition means unusual variants and an alteration in the placing (later) of the Church scene. These are questionable decisions but not serious enough to cause a problem when making a choice of versions. As with Plasson, the ballet music is rightly consigned to an appendix. The recording, made in Cardiff's Brangwyn Hall, is by and large open, full of presence and well balanced, but once or twice Ramey's voice seems to be in another acoustic. Both this and the Plasson have much in their favour. A choice between them must, on this occasion, rest on a preference for one or other singer.

Gounod Faust.

Nicolai Gedda *ten* Faust
Victoria de los Angeles *sop* Marguérite
Boris Christoff *bass* Méphistophélès
Ernest Blanc *bar* Valentin
Liliane Berton *sop* Siébel
Rita Gorr *mez* Marthe
Victor Autran *bar* Wagner
Paris Opéra Chorus and Orchestra / André Cluytens.
EMI Ⓜ ① CMS7 69983-2 (three discs: 171 minutes: ADD). Notes, text and translation included. Recorded 1958.

BBC RADIO 3
90-93 FM

Méphistophélès is in his kingdom here. From "Me voici" to "Jugée" Boris Christoff occupies the centre of the stage, incomparably vivid, and, as recorded, invincibly powerful. With Victoria de los Angeles as an adorable Marguérite it is not surprising that the Church scene becomes the focal point of the opera, pathos and menace intensely contrasted. Between these two, poor old-and-young Faust has the title-role in name only, though Nicolai Gedda's eager style and mellifluous tone earn gratitude throughout. The other two principals are French, and for that, too, one is grateful, though Liliane Berton's Siébel, light and graceful enough, lacks something in impulsiveness and ardour, while Ernest Blanc makes a dull, stock figure out of the brother Valentin.

Other sets have a better Valentin; Thomas Allen excellent with Prêtre as is Andreas Schmidt with Colin Davis. But if those sets have an overall advantage it is not in the matter of casting but rather in the more spacious and detailed recorded sound, and (certainly where Davis is concerned) in the more thoughtful conducting. They also include the scene of Marguérite at the spinning-wheel, beautifully sung by both Freni (Prêtre) and Te Kanawa (Davis), and it is followed by Siébel's "Si le bonheur" which we used to know as "When all was young". What these two cannot offer is a Méphistophélès with the presence of Christoff and a Marguérite with the charm and pathos of los Angeles. Her solo scene is most beautiful as pure singing and vividly characterized in changes of mood; in the love duet, too, her "O silence" and the reply to Faust's "O nuit d'amour" are lovely passages. In the Church scene her terror is pitiable: sympathies can rarely have been as fully engaged as in this recording. But then, with Christoff singing into the ear (but really of course unashamedly into the microphone) it is very easy to share her alarm: a treasurable collaboration between two great singers here, comparable to that of Callas and Gobbi in the Nile scene from *Aida*. This alone makes the recording worth the purchase.

Gounod Faust.

Nicolai Gedda *ten* Faust
Victoria de los Angeles *sop* Marguérite
Boris Christoff *bass* Méphistophélès
Jean Borthayre *bass* Valentin
Martha Angelici *sop* Siébel
Solange Michel *mez* Marthe
Robert Jeantet *bar* Wagner
Paris Opéra Chorus and Orchestra / André Cluytens.
EMI mono Ⓜ Ⓛ CMS5 65256-2 (three discs: 176 minutes: ADD). Notes and text included.
Recorded 1953.

Here again are the much admired trio of Gedda, los Angeles and Christoff. The recording was made in the Palais de la Mutualité in Paris, and the sound is a lot clearer than that on earlier Champs-Elysées productions. There is not a lot to choose between this and the stereo recording reviewed above: Christoff is slightly more restrained in the later version, Gedda and los Angeles in marginally fresher voice on the mono set. Michel, taking a break from her endless Carmens, is Marthe on the 1953 recording, Rita Gorr on the 1958 – the main gain in the latter is the charming Siébel of Liliane Berton. Finally, what is there to say of André Cluytens? In a fascinating essay in the booklet (which has marvellous recording-session photographs) Michel Beretti outlines the history of the "Réunion des Théâtres Lyriques Nationaux", and the repertory system they operated at the time that Cluytens was Director of the Opéra-Comique. "Delicate sonorities ... as well as the heady flourish" is how Beretti describes Cluytens's style: it might sum up the essence of French opera.

Gounod Mireille.

Janette Vivalda *sop* Mireille
Nicolai Gedda *ten* Vincent
Christiane Gayraud *contr* Taven
Michel Dens *bar* Ourrias
Madeleine Ignal *sop* Vincenette
Andre Vessières *bass* Ramon
Christiane Jacquin *sop* Clémence
Marcello Cortis *bar* Ambroisè
Aix-en-Provence Festival Chorus; Paris Conservatoire Orchestra / André Cluytens.
EMI mono Ⓜ Ⓛ CMS7 64382-2 (two discs: 134 minutes: ADD). Notes and text included.
Recorded 1954.

Mireille was composed four years after *Faust*, and three years before *Roméo et Juliette*. The middle of Gounod's trio of enduring successes, it has always been a problem piece and something of a poor relation of the others. The most famous number, the waltz-song "O légères hirondelles", beloved of Lily Pons and many other coloratura sopranos, was written to order for the prima donna of the Théâtre Lyrique a year after the première. It is included here as a bonus, a souvenir of what sounds to have been one of the most magical productions ever put on under the auspices of the Aix Festival – in a production by Jean-Pierre Grenier, designed by Wakhevich, it was a one-off.

The version used is that prepared in the 1930s by Gounod's pupil, Henri Busser, and Reynaldo Hahn, who conducted it at the Opéra-Comique. This restored the opera to its original tragic five acts (the 'waltz-song' revision had been performed in various two- and three-act editions, with a happy ending). Although the mono sound is fairly restricted by modern standards, the performance could hardly be better. In the title-role, Janette Vivalda has one of those typical French voices, the effect of which can be like drinking undiluted *citron-pressé* without sugar, but she is completely inside the part, her diction is crystal-clear, and she rises to the delirious Crau desert scene with surprising conviction.

Gedda was at the very beginning of his recording career; his account of "Anges du Paradis" is completely without that sense of strain that so often infects these high tenor parts, and he joins Vivalda in the other famous moment, the duet "O Magali", with honeyed charm. The star of the recording, though, is Michel Dens as the bully Ourrias. His Second Act celebration of the charms of the Arles girls and the strength of the Camargue boys, is an attempt by Gounod to repeat the impact of the "Veau d'or" from *Faust*. In Act 3, his duet with Gedda and then the marvellous scene in which he is drawn to a watery grave by some *Giselle*-type phantoms are the highlights of this set. Cluytens conducts an exemplary performance; there are some orchestral effects where one yearns for a more spacious recording, but it is unlikely that this version can easily be replaced for authentic atmosphere.

Gounod Roméo et Juliette.

Roberto Alagna *ten* Roméo
Angela Gheorghiu *sop* Juliette
José van Dam *bass-bar* Frère Laurent

Simon Keenlyside *bar* Mercutio
Marie-Ange Todorovitch *sop* Stéphano
Alain Fondary *bar* Capulet
Claire Larcher *mez* Gertrude
Daniel Galvez Vallejo *ten* Tybalt
Didier Henry *bar* Paris
Till Fechner *bass* Gregorio
Alain Vernhes *bar* Duke of Verona
Toulouse Capitole Chorus and Orchestra / Michel Plasson.
EMI ℗ ① CDS5 56123-2 (three discs: 180 minutes: DDD). Notes, text and translation included.
Recorded 1997.

Assuming for a moment that the reader does not have to be persuaded that the work itself deserves a place in the collection, then the question is simply: is this 1977 recording better than its two nearest full-price rivals, and if so is the superiority such as will merit the additional expenditure that is (presumably) involved in the purchase of three discs rather than two. The most recent alternative version is the RCA set under Leonard Slatkin, with Ruth Ann Swenson and Plácido Domingo as the lovers, appreciatively greeted by the critics, as indeed was its predecessor, with Catherine Malfitano and Alfredo Kraus and conducted by Michel Plasson (EMI). Certainly if the opera's brief Prologue is representative, this present set is the best of the three. Compared with his earlier self, Plasson is more assuredly his own man, taking a broader view of the turbulent, dramatic opening, and especially of the fugato which introduces its second section. This now has the unhurried, confident thrust of an expert duellist, and in place of a rather generalized picture, a much more specific and vivid one forms in the mind. The contrast is stronger with Slatkin, who urges forward, piles on the brass, and achieves an arresting but altogether cruder effect. Then comes the chorus's introductory narration which the Munich choir under Slatkin sing like oratorio. Plasson's 1983 recording from Toulouse puts greater emphasis on story-telling, but that too is not nearly so imaginative as the quieter, more intimate style he favours now, the chorus having more light-and-shade, better rhythmic pointing, more 'face'.

At curtain-up for Capulet's ball, Plasson now leads a subtly textured waltz where Slatkin's is a thick-soled, heavy-downbeat sort of thing, and when his chorus, supposedly seeing Juliette, exclaim "Ah! qu'elle est belle", they are really seeing little more than their copies. Plasson's people catch the vision with their subdued exclamation of wonder. In all of this, and so on throughout the performance, the newest version marks a sure improvement, almost a breakthrough. But *Roméo et Juliette* means Roméo and Juliette, and here the preference may be slightly less clear-cut. Catherine Malfitano, Plasson's earlier Juliette, had a fresh, girlish quality which, rather doll-like at first, gains tenderness and sensitivity. Swenson, for Slatkin, makes less of the character and sings the famous Waltz song without pace or gaiety, or dreaminess either. Gheorghiu, here, immediately makes her listeners echo the chorus's "Ah! qu'elle est belle", for the sound matches the imagined sight. Its beauty is more mature than Malfitano's, and to that extent perhaps less appropriate, but as the part develops towards tragedy so her warmer, richer tone is better able to embody the depth of feeling, and she brings a fine conviction to the despairing scene with Frère Laurent and then to the scene of the potion.

Alagna's Roméo has, of course, youth on his side if he is similarly to have the rivals brought up for comparison. Domingo performs magnificently in what now seems an unlikely role, while Kraus, a 56-year-old Roméo at the time of the recording, is still clear-toned and has no problems on high. Alagna does not sound too happy with the B flats of "Ah, lève-toi, soleil", and sometimes the voice appears to have added weight in a way that makes him less suited to the part than he was when we first admired him at Covent Garden. Yet there are many, many things to enjoy as one listens, and still more as one compares.

Actually, Roméo and Juliette are *not* all: the opera abounds in rewarding secondary roles. In one of these, that of Stéphano the page, the present recording loses to Slatkin. Marie-Ange Todorovitch has some sense of style but not the voice for this, and especially not when compared with the delightful Susan Graham. The Friar is still José van Dam ('still' because he sang it with Plasson nearly 15 years ago), and is gravely firm and fine as ever. The Capulet, Alain Fondary, is a bluff father-figure not unlike his predecessor, Bacquier. As Mercutio, Simon Keenlyside is excellent, though not better than Gino Quilico, outstanding in the 1983 set. The others even out reasonably well, but it is not these on whom the choice depends. On the merits of the cast, and perhaps still more on those of the choral singing, orchestral playing and recorded sound, we would certainly recommend the present version above its rivals. But there remains the question of that third disc, essentially there to accommodate the ballet music. This is pleasant, tuneful and well orchestrated, but the opera is better off without it. As a statutory requirement of the Paris Opéra, it was placed between the night of Juliette's agony and her awakening for the proposed marriage to Count Paris, destroying the dramatic tension at a crucial moment. Although you might not buy the recording for that; you would for almost everything else.

Gounod Roméo et Juliette.
Raoul Jobin *ten* Roméo
Janine Micheau *sop* Juliette
Heinz Rehfuss *bar* Frère Laurent

Pierre Mollet *bar* Mercutio
Claudine Collart *sop* Stéphano
Charles Cambon *bass* Capulet
Odette Ricquier *sop* Gertrude
Louis Rialland *ten* Tybalt
Camille Roquetty *bar* Paris
André Philippe *bass* Gregorio, Duke of Verona
Chorus and Orchestra of the Paris Opéra / Alberto Erede.
Double Decca mono Ⓜ Ⓓ 443 539-2LF2 (two discs: 143 minutes: ADD). Recorded 1953.

Of the recordings of this piece which have been made in recent times the second EMI set, conducted by Plasson, is probably the best but although this rather dimly recorded mono version is not ideal, it certainly has its merits. Alberto Erede provides plenty of élan, in a slim, most acute reading. Micheau's Juliette sounds uninvolved at the beginning but improves as the work progresses – and, of course, she has the text in her bones. The same is true of Jobin as Roméo. However much we may long for more subtle, delicate phrasing and a less strenuous attack, we are consoled by a French timbre that is in itself so right for the role. The support here is close to the true tradition in singing Gounod of the previous 50 or so years, all the singers phrasing with a real feeling for the words – Rehfuss in particular, as Frère Laurent, although he does lack a low G. In spite of the drawbacks of the dated though still tolerable recording, and an occasional hint of distortion, you will probably derive much pleasure from this version which makes many of the traditional cuts, all restored on the Plasson set. If you can find it, an LP of highlights made in 1965, under Lombard's baton (Columbia), with Carteri (a lovely, underrated soprano) and Gedda, will please; even better, there is an 'unofficial' live Metropolitan Opera recording with Sayão and Björling. Various versions from the 78rpm era of the duets, some available on CD, are even better.

Gounod Sapho.
Michèle Command *sop* Sapho
Sharon Coste *sop* Glycère
Christian Papis *ten* Phaon
Eric Faury *ten* Alcée
Lionel Sarrazin *bass* Pythéas
Philippe Georges *ten* Cygénire, High Priest
Sébastien Martinez *sngr* Goat-herd
Saint-Etienne Lyric Chorus and Nouvel Orchestra / Patrick Fournillier.
Koch Schwann Ⓕ Ⓓ 313112 (two discs: 124 minutes: DDD). Notes, text and translation included. Recorded 1992.

Sapho was Gounod's first opera, composed in 1850 at the behest of Pauline Viardot, who took the title-role when it was performed at the Paris Opéra the following year. It is a fascinating piece, above all because one can hear the composer gain confidence from the ceremonial First Act, through the intrigue and rivals' quarrel of the Second, to achieve a really tragic and individual form in the last. This recording originates in a production at St Etienne in 1992. There is consequently a fair amount of stage noise and applause. The libretto, by Emile d'Augier, concerns a fictional Sapho, partly inspired by the poetess, partly by another classical heroine, who threw herself from the cliffs for love of Phaon. In this version the story is reduced to a simple love triangle – Phaon is loved by Glycère, whom he scorns in favour of Sapho. His involvement in a plot to overthrow the tyrant Pittacus (who does not appear, although he is much sung about) is discovered by Glycère, who uses the information to blackmail Sapho, so that she lets Phaon go.

The First Act has a fine declamatory aria for Sapho – part of an Olympic poetry contest – this must have been the kind of thing Viardot did supremely well. When she spots her rival, and utters "Quelle est cette femme hardie?" one can hear an echo of Fidès's "Qui je suis?" from *Le Prophète* – the role in which Viardot had triumphed a couple of years before. Similarly, in Act 2, there is a conspirators' ensemble that bears more than a passing resemblance to the blessing of the daggers in *Les Huguenots*. It is the role of Glycère that seems to have got Gounod going; she dominates the Second Act with a dramatic recitative and duet with Pythéas – Phaon's confidant, a sort of precursor of Méphisto – followed by a slanging match with Sapho, in which she gets the better of her, and then a really beautiful trio-finale in which Sapho urges Phaon to flee, and he agrees to take Glycère instead ("O douleur qui m'oppresse!").

Phaon's Act 3 lament, "O jours heureux où j'entendais ta voix!" must have provided a triumph for Louis Gueymard; the whole scene is infused with a superb sense of doom, with a prelude in which the strings suggest the lapping waves against the ship on which the hero must depart. As he goes, in the distance a sad chorus of exiles fades away, to leave a lone goat-herd with a flute to sing a little song to the distraught Sapho, before she launches her famous *stances*, "O ma lyre immortelle". This, the one famous number from the score, has been recorded by many great singers from Litvinne (the very first 12-inch French G&T of a female soloist), and Schumann-Heink down to Bumbry, Verrett and Horne in our own time. Michèle Command who sings the title-role is hardly in that league, but she makes a positive impression with good diction and full-bodied tone; her voice is inclined to wobble a bit more than one wants whenever pressure is applied. The same goes for Christian Papis as Phaon, who rather unwisely attempts a couple of high notes in head-tone – stylistically correct, of course, but not a pleasure on the ear. Both of them gain considerably in confidence and control as the performance progresses. The Canadian soprano Sharon Coste makes a most convincing Glycère; her big scenes in Act 2 reinforce its quality. Lionel Sarrazin is most effective as Pythéas. Gounod later reshaped the opera twice, as a two-act piece in 1858, then in four in 1884. Patrick Fournillier has reconstructed the original three-act version and he conducts with vigour and obvious relish. The recording favours the voices on the whole – if we lived in an age of great French singing one would say that one day it would be nice to see this on the stage, or to have a full-scale studio recording. As both these things seem extremely unlikely, this set is most welcome and a valuable addition to any collection of nineteenth-century opera, French or otherwise.

Enrique Granados   Spanish 1867-1916

Granados Goyescas.
   María Bayo *sop* Rosario
   Ramón Vargas *ten* Fernando
   Enrique Baquerizo *bass* Paquiro
   Lola Casariego *mez* Pepa
   Milagros Martín *mez* A voice
   Orfeón Donostiarra; Madrid Symphony Orchestra / Antoni Ros Marbà.
   Auvidis Valois Ⓟ Ⓒ V4791 (60 minutes: DDD). Notes, text and translation included. Recorded 1996.

Never has there been a more literal illustration of the tag *Prima la musica, poi le parole* ("The music first, then the words") than the opera *Goyescas*. Granados worked the music up orchestrally from the two books of his piano *Goyescas* composed three years earlier, and Fernando Periquet, who had written the texts for his *tonadillas*, was given the unenviable task of adding a libretto to fit it (more or less), on the basis of a creaking plot cobbled together by the composer. Periquet is scarcely to be blamed for weak dramaturgy, stilted language, lack of continuity and absence of characterization in the result, which is a series of tableaux rather than a properly conceived opera. (It received five performances at the New York Met in 1916 but has rarely tempted anyone else to stage it since.) However, the picturesque, if inconsequential, charm of the music is undeniable, and the nature of the work makes it particularly suitable for gramophone listening.

It is certainly given nearly every chance in the present performance, which is notable above all for its superior and sensitive orchestral playing, both when accompanying and on its own, as in the famous "Intermedio" (which Granados reluctantly added at the last moment) and a later interlude before Rosario's big solo scene in the garden ("The maiden and the nightingale"). Incidentally, although at the start of the "Ball by lamplight" the libretto states that a couple are dancing to the sound of the guitar, there is no guitar in the score. The chorus, who are worked very hard for the first half hour and then dispensed with, sing with fervour, though their words can rarely be made out. There is a good *majo* in Enrique Baquerizo, even if he sounds rather too noble for such a low-life role; but the main burden of the solo singing falls on Ramón Vargas and María Bayo as the upper-class lovers, who have the last two scenes of the opera to themselves. She sings with great passion and tenderness (though we cannot but remember the ineffable Victoria de los Angeles in the opera's one aria): he is as excellent and intelligent as we already know him to be from previous recordings of Italian opera – he really *is* a tenor to cherish. First-rate recording quality adds to the disc's attraction.

Carl Graun   German 1703/4-1759

Graun Cesare e Cleopatra.
   Iris Vermillion *mez* Cesare
   Janet Williams *sop* Cleopatra
   Lynne Dawson *sop* Cornelia
   Robert Gambill *ten* Tolomeo
   Ralf Popken *alto* Arsace
   Jeffrey Francis *ten* Lentulo
   Klaus Häger *bass* Achilla
   Elisabeth Scholl *sop* Cneo
   Maria-Cristina Kiehr *sop* Sesto
   RIAS Chamber Choir; Berlin Concerto Köln / René Jacobs.
   Harmonia Mundi Ⓟ Ⓒ HMC90 1561/3 (three discs: 198 minutes: DDD). ✎ Notes, text and translation included. Recorded 1995.

Within weeks of his accession to the Prussian throne in 1740 Frederick the Great had appointed Carl Heinrich Graun as his court Kapellmeister, before dispatching him to Italy to talent-scout for singers. Well before ascending the throne Frederick had made plans for a new opera-house in Berlin but until such plans came to fruition operas were presented in a large upstairs drawing-room in the palace. Though not Graun's first opera for Berlin, *Cesare e Cleopatra* – for some reason the title is given back to front in this recording – was that which inaugurated the new Royal Berlin Opera House, the Linden Opera, in December 1742. Between then and 1756 Graun was closely associated with the Berlin Opera, providing it with almost all the works staged within that period.

  Cesare e Cleopatra is loosely based on Corneille's *La mort de Poupée* but, like Handel's *Giulio Cesare* which had first been staged in London 18 years earlier, places emphasis on the love-affair between Caesar and Cleopatra rather than on Pompey's death at the hands of Cleopatra's brother Ptolemy. Giovanni Bottarelli's libretto would doubtless have appealed to Frederick who probably saw in Caesar's military and political prowess an appealing image of himself. Graun was no Handel, but while there is nothing here to match the older composer's psychological insight and therefore his depth and constancy of character portrayal, there is a wealth of music which, at its best – and it often is – beguiles the senses with its profusion of fine melodies and imaginative instrumental colouring.

  One of the first of several outstandingly affective arias is given to Cornelia, in the second scene of Act 1. She has just witnessed the treacherous murder of husband Pompey at Ptolemy's hands and expresses her grief in an F minor aria, noble, tender and deeply sorrowful. Lynne Dawson brings intensity and a tragic presence to the role. Caesar's horror at Pompey's death is genuine if, as here, short-lived. His mind is soon caught up with thoughts of Cleopatra as his aria, "Quel che lontano" (first disc, track 10) reveals. This role was originally a castrato one but is very well sung here by mezzo-soprano Iris Vermillion. Janet Williams's Cleopatra is wonderfully athletic. Graun has given her some exacting coloratura and Williams delivers it with effortless finesse. Her dazzling virtuosity in "Tra la procelle assorto" is not only splendidly dramatic but also musically satisfying. Robert Gambill's Tolomeo is robust and agile, though his vocal timbre is sometimes a little hard and unyielding. He, too, has some splendid music, for instance in "Sopportar non devo in pace" in Act 1. Klaus Häger is commanding as the Egyptian prince Achilla and Ralf Popken makes a plausible Arab prince, Arsace, though some readers may find his vocal timbre takes a little getting used to. The remaining roles are very well sung indeed.

  What sets the seal on this performance of Graun's opera is the consistent excellence of Concerto Köln who make the music spring to life from the printed page. And all is directed with energy and dramatic insight by René Jacobs. As implied earlier, you will look almost in vain for anything approaching the subtlety or sustained dramatic development that characterizes Handelian opera. But Graun's straightforward music, which adopts almost throughout the *galant* idiom, the fluency of his writing, and the sheer amiability of his style make the opera far from a disappointment from a purely musical standpoint. Only the overture, one of the last he wrote in the by then old-fashioned 'French ouverture' mould, harks back, at least in its ceremonial opening, to the baroque. An altogether stimulating release that should have wide appeal.

Johann Haeffner   German/Swedish 1759-1833

Haeffner Electra.
  Hillevi Martinpelto *sop* Electra
  Peter Mattei *bar* Orest
  Helle Hinz *sop* Klytemnestra
  Mikael Samuelson *bar* Aegisth
  Klas Hedlund *ten* Pilad
  Stig Tysklind *bass* Arcas
  Alf Häggstam *bass* High Priest
  Christina Högman *sop* Ismene
  Stockholm Radio Chorus; Drottningholm Baroque Ensemble / Thomas Schuback.
  Caprice Ⓕ ① CAP22030 (two discs: 88 minutes: DDD). Notes, text and translation included.
  Recorded 1992.

Perhaps most famous as founder of the great musical traditions of Uppsala University, Johann Christian Friedrich Haeffner was a German (born a month before Handel's death) who studied in Leipzig, and after conducting in Frankfurt and Hamburg moved to Stockholm, where he eventually rose from singing coach and occasional viola player in the Royal Opera to become (still aged only 36) its Musical Director. Eight years earlier, he had been commissioned to write his first opera for the queen's nameday. This was *Electra*, given in Drottningholm in July 1787; it was written to a Swedish translation of a French libretto after Sophocles that had already been used by Jean-Baptiste Lemoyne. Haeffner was even more heavily influenced by Gluck (whom he idolized) than his slightly older French contemporary; and the colourful orchestration (especially his use of trombones), the declamatory recitative, and indeed the shaping of some scenes, clearly reveal that admiration. Of special interest, too, is his employment of leitmotivs, which begins with the programmatic overture depicting Electra's thirst for Orest to avenge their father's murder, and the intervention of the Furies. (The similarity of key, mood and repeated cadential figures with the start of Mozart's *Don Giovanni*, premièred the same year, is interesting.)

For the 1991 production in Drottningholm, here recorded in the studios of the Swedish Radio a year later, various cuts were made, particularly of choruses, and Act 3 was compressed. Except in that part there is little stage action, so that all emphasis falls on the music itself; and from the very outset, where the Furies are urging Orest on (only to pursue him at the end of the opera) Haeffner shows a powerful dramatic sense. Much of the plot is played in a continually inventive, highly expressive orchestrally accompanied recitative that constantly flowers into arioso; and there are effective homophonic choruses, orchestral processionals and, at the close, an exciting mime for the Furies. Conspicuously rare, though, is any concerted singing (apart from the choruses) except for two duets, one in Act 1 in the scene between Electra and her mother, the other in Act 3, after Electra's thrilling cry of recognition, "Orest!", between sister and brother; but there are a few striking arias, mostly for Electra ("Come, grim troop" and "Yes, know that Electra's heart" in Act 1, "Tyrant, your cruelty" in Act 2) but also one each for Klytemnestra and Aegisth in Act 2.

Thomas Schuback drives the work along with an unremitting instinct for its tension, securing crisp playing from the orchestra and well-drilled vigorous singing from the chorus; and he is fortunate in having at his disposal a cast so uniformly excellent, bringing clarity and meaning to every word and expressive nuance to every phrase, that it would be invidious to single out any one member. The whole adds up to the most stimulating operatic discovery of recent times. Gluck repudiated Lemoyne's claim, in his *Electre*, to be his pupil: you get the impression he would have been proud to acknowledge Haeffner's *Electra*.

Fromental Halévy
French 1799-1862

Halévy La juive.
José Carreras *ten* Eléazar
Julia Varady *sop* Rachel
June Anderson *sop* La Princesse Eudoxia
Ferruccio Furlanetto *bass* Le Cardinal de Brogni
Dalmacio Gonzalez *ten* Le Prince Léopold
René Massis *bass-bar* Ruggiero
René Schirrer *bar* Albert
Ambrosian Opera Chorus; Philharmonia Orchestra / Antonio de Almeida.
Philips Ⓟ Ⓒ 420 190-2PH3 (three discs: 183 minutes: DDD). Notes, text and translation included. Recorded 1986/9.

This recording of a once-popular opera, now neglected, is a landmark on several fronts. No commercial recording of the complete opera has ever been available in this country, let alone one with so starry a cast as this. It also marked the return of José Carreras to the recording studio after his recovery from leukaemia, taking the title-role long coveted by great tenors of the past, most notably of all Enrico Caruso. *La juive* ("The jewess") was the last opera Caruso added to his repertory right at the end of his career, and his very last appearance in public, at the old Metropolitan in New York on Christmas Eve in 1920, was as the Jew, Eléazar. The principal solos became regular recording items before the age of LP, and in 1973 the same conductor as here, Antonio de Almeida, with the then New Philharmonia Orchestra and Ambrosian Opera Chorus, recorded for RCA a well-chosen if dully performed collection of excerpts.

Almeida's conducting this time is altogether tauter and more dramatic, helped by an atmospheric, well-balanced recording, which undistractingly presents a convincing stage picture in a plot which for all the splendour of the setting in the French grand opera tradition is relatively simple in human terms, involving only five principal characters. Eléazar the Jew and his adopted daughter, Rachel, are set against Prince Léopold (who loves Rachel) and his wife, Princess Eudoxia. The fifth character is the Cardinal de Brogni, who has two superb bass arias, including one where he vehemently pronounces anathema. Musically it is not a help that the roles of the Jew and of Léopold are both for tenor, the one weightily heroic, the other much lighter and involving a very high tessitura. Similarly flouting convention, Halévy made both Rachel and Eudoxia sopranos, and though Julia Varady as Rachel and June Anderson as Eudoxia have very different voices, they are not so sharply contrasted as to avoid confusion entirely.

With Carreras already ill, there were problems over the original schedule of sessions. The main recording was done in an intensive period of nine days in the summer of 1986, and plainly that speed helped to intensify the performance's dramatic thrust, with fine playing from the Philharmonia and powerful singing from the Ambrosian Opera Chorus. But it was a case of Hamlet without the prince. Then in 1989, taking a whole week over the task, the Spanish tenor recorded his part in what must be the most ambitious exercise yet in 'overdubbing', with the singer's voice superimposed on the original tape. If that sounds a dubious exercise, the results are astonishingly convincing. From the clear placing of Carreras on the stereo stage, not to mention the sense of presence, you would never know that there had been any such engineering trickery. Even knowing the deception you will be readily able to sit back and enjoy a vividly recorded opera, with the co-ordination between Carreras and the others in the many ensembles astonishingly exact.

Given first in 1835, the same year as Donizetti's *Lucia di Lammermoor*, Halévy's *La juive* very much represents a Parisian look towards the future. In five acts, its scale is vast, and the grand choral climaxes are pivotal in the well-crafted libretto of Eugene Scribe. But Halévy, far less than his more prominent colleague, Meyerbeer, used the grandeur not as an end in itself but to underpin and intensify the central, personal drama. Even the opening prelude is lyrical and unassuming, predominantly gentle, and the key solos regularly lead almost at once into duets and ensembles, in which they are developed both musically and dramatically. Small wonder that Wagner – who was in Paris around the time of the first performance – was a firm admirer of the piece, suppressing his usual anti-semitism both over the subject and over the composer himself, Halévy, *né* Levy. As Almeida notes, Wagner in *Die Meistersinger* barefacedly cribbed Halévy's idea for the opening of Act 1: as the curtain rises you hear off-stage organ and chorus in church, as vividly atmospheric here as at the start of *Die Meistersinger*.

There are many other anticipations, both musical and dramatic. When at the close of the opera Eléazar, at the moment of Rachel's execution (thrown into a cauldron of boiling oil), reveals to the Cardinal that she is the long-lost daughter he has been looking for, the parallel with Verdi's *Il trovatore* could hardly be closer. It is to Halévy's credit that he brings the curtain down on the coup just as briskly as Verdi. It is striking, too, that Halévy's imaginative instrumentation sometimes anticipates mature Verdi, most strikingly in the darkness of timbre from heavy woodwind associated with Eléazar himself. That will make you think above all of *Don Carlos* – one of Verdi's own essays in French 'grand opera' – and no one will miss the parallel in the famous passage introducing Eléazar's big final aria, "Rachel, quand du Seigneur", where Halévy has two cor anglais playing in thirds and sounding very different from the chains of thirds favoured by Donizetti.

As to the text used, the conductor and the recording producer, Erik Smith, have opted for an expanded version of the score published by Schlesinger after the première in 1835. That had many cuts, but rather than resurrecting every single note that Halévy had written – the whole probably never performed on a single evening – Almeida and Smith have aimed "to woo the opera public to this remarkable work with a dedicated performance of manageable length", actually well over three hours. The main cuts are of crowd scenes, drinking choruses and the like, some of which, as at the start of Act 5 seriously hold up the action. On the other hand, the whole of the grand finale to Act 3, culminating in the Cardinal's Malediction solo, is included as the opera's centrepiece. Among the solo items preserved, but omitted by Schlesinger, is Eudoxia's delightful *Boléro*, first recorded on Almeida's previously mentioned RCA record. Balancing that, another of her arias, "Je l'ai revu", is omitted. The ballet scene of Act 3 is included "not only for its real charm but because ballet was such an indispensable element in Grand Opera". In other words, the tailoring of the text has been done, not with savagery, but with concern for the opera's effectiveness on record.

Hearing this fine performance will fill you with admiration for the finesse and technical mastery of Halévy and his librettist. There are occasional absurdities of a kind inevitable in romantic opera but characterization, mood and motivation are strongly drawn to convey instant conviction, with the basic simplicity of the plot to help. Handling of musical structure and texture is masterly, and the one serious doubt – which probably explains the failure of the work latterly to hold the stage – is over the melodic writing, free and uninhibited, but rarely distinctive enough to be really haunting, even in the big solos. Halévy also tends to let down his big moments by allowing ensembles to lapse into jaunty 'oom-pah' rhythm, too close for comfort to French operetta.

None the less, there is much to enjoy in this well-made opera. The most involving singer is Julia Varady, who gives a tender yet positive portrait of Rachel, moving and convincing in all her confrontations, whether loving or defiant as a daughter to Eleàzar, whether loving or accusing in her devotion to Léopold, or whether simply responding to the pleas of Eudoxia, Léopold's wife. The voice has all its usual distinctiveness and beauty, to make June Anderson as Eudoxia sound a little raw by comparison, agile as she is in the dramatic coloratura passages. Her *Boléro* in the opening scene of Act 3 is delightfully pointed. The bass, Ferruccio Furlanetto, makes a splendid Cardinal de Brogni, relishing above all his two big solos, "Si la rigueur", the most striking arioso in Act 1, as well as the anathema solo of Act 3, not to mention the final confrontation with Eléazar. Like most Italians singing French he rolls his 'rs, but no French bass today begins to match him in a role once associated with Ezio Pinza.

The two tenors are well contrasted by timbre. Dalmacio Gonzalez has a slightly throaty production, not unpleasing except when under strain as he is in parts of his opening serenade with its stratospheric high notes. Carreras as Eleàzar, not surprisingly, shows signs of strain too, and the exposed unaccompanied solos which alternate with the chorus in the lovely Passover service music of Act 2 show that the voice, still distinctive, has lost much of its honeyed tone. Production and tone are not so firm as they once were, but the wonder is that Carreras copes with the big outbursts with such heroic weight. One imagines that Caruso drew the portrait of this rather unsympathetic character, obsessive in anti-Christian hatreds, more distinctively than Carreras, but even the element of vulnerability in the voice is apt for a mature character under extreme stress.

As with so many complete recordings of French opera there are few French singers in the cast. In the two *comprimario* bass-baritone roles, René Massis as Ruggiero, the city provost of Constance where the opera is set, and René Schirrer as Albert, sergeant in Léopold's regiment, are both first-rate exceptions here, but no one would envy a record producer today intent on casting entirely from French sources. Far better to put up with the occasional rolled 'r' or odd vowel. The layout on three discs is generous, and involved only one break within an act – in the middle of Act 2 before the meeting of Rachel and Léopold.

George Frideric Handel   German/British 1685-1759

Handel Agrippina.
 Della Jones *mez* Agrippina
 Derek Lee Ragin *alto* Nero
 Donna Brown *sop* Poppea
 Alastair Miles *bass* Claudius
 Michael Chance *alto* Otho
 George Mosley *bar* Pallas
 Jonathan Peter Kenny *alto* Narcissus
 Julian Clarkson *bass* Lesbo
 Anne Sofie von Otter *mez* Juno
 English Baroque Soloists / John Eliot Gardiner.
 Philips Ⓟ Ⓒ 438 009-2PH3 (three discs: 217 minutes: DDD). 🖉 Notes, text and translation included. Recorded 1991-2.

B B C RADIO 3
90-93 FM

Agrippina is Handel's Venetian opera, composed in 1709 for the S. Giovanni Grisostomo theatre, where it was evidently and deservedly a great success; according to Handel's first biographer, the audience were struck with the "grandeur and sublimity of its style". Handel drew on its music, but he never revived it: its scheme, with a large number of short and lightly accompanied arias (often with only continuo until the final orchestral ritornello), is very much of its time and its place – that amplitude of phrase and structure and indeed emotion, what we regard today as his "grandeur and sublimity", that distinguishes Handel's operas from those of his contemporaries, had yet to come. Yet *Agrippina* is a very effective piece, if directed with due vitality (as it certainly is here), and it is full of appealing music in a wide variety of moods.

The plot is a typically Venetian, and largely fictional, account of an episode in Roman history, chiefly referring to the Empress Agrippina's intrigues to see her son, Nero, on the imperial throne in succession to her husband, Claudius. There is a marked comic element as the two women, Agrippina and Poppea, manipulate the largely guileless men unfortunate enough to cross their paths; the characters, save the emperor and Otho, are unprincipled and self-seeking, which rather limits the opportunities for grandeur or sublimity. The big, near-tragic moment comes in Act 2, where Otho, in spite of his loyalty to the emperor and his devotion to Poppea, is universally betrayed, and left isolated on the stage as in turn the lesser characters denounce or dismiss him in brief *ariettas* and walk off: he then sings a passionate and poignant F minor lament ("Voi che udite il mio lamento") which, in any good performance of the opera, is its high point. It certainly is that here. Michael Chance sings it magnificently, with great depth of feeling and beauty and evenness of tone. Chance is no less impressive in his other arias, for example the lively one that opens Act 2 (beautifully clear articulation), or the first of the pair that soon follows the lament – an exquisite piece with recorders, "Vaghe fonti" – or the gentle D minor miniature with which he opens the last act. The role of Otho was originally sung by a woman, and in principle should be sung by one today, but such a performance as this disarms criticism.

Any admirer of countertenor singing should be prepared to buy the set for Michael Chance's singing alone. But in fact there are two other countertenors here who are well worth hearing, especially Derek Lee Ragin, whose high-lying voice and sensitive, thoughtful phrasing serve Nero's music admirably. His last aria, a brilliant piece with colourful instrumental writing, as he renounces Poppea in expectation of the imperial crown (Monteverdians, of course, know that he gets both in the end), is breathtakingly done; fiery singing with very precise execution of the divisions. The third of the countertenors is Jonathan Peter Kenny as Narcissus, rather softer in tone and line, who provides some particularly musical singing in his aria near the end of Act 2.

Della Jones gives a masterful performance in the title-role. Her music is very varied in mood: there are several brief and catchy little pieces, which she throws off with spirit, but also some larger-scale numbers, such as the marvellous C minor aria near the end of Act 1 (although totally insincere in sentiment), which is done with great vigour, and the noble, invocation-like "Pensieri, voi mi tormentate", another of the opera's high points, to which she brings much intensity. Her commanding singing is ideal for Agrippina, and her occasional exuberant ornamentation (most of the cast are quite sparing of embellishment) is not out of place. Also enjoyable are the spirit and the charm of Donna Brown's singing of Poppea; she makes the most of a role with much lively and appealing music. Alastair Miles's full and resonant bass – the part goes down to cello C – brings due weight of authority to the emperor Claudius; Pallas is done by a clean, lightish but nicely firm baritone, George Mosley, and Julian Clarkson contributes some very neat singing in the role of Lesbo. Not to mention

Anne Sofie von Otter, who comes in as a *dea ex machina* at the very end, not to rescue the situation but to honour the marriage of Poppea and Otho – which of course she does in style.

John Eliot Gardiner is a fine and very experienced conductor of Handel and he has a sure feeling for tempo and for the character of each movement. He keeps the *secco* recitative, of which there is a great deal, moving along pretty quickly while allowing the singers opportunity to convey its meaning – at one point in the middle of Act 2, for example, there is a stretch of very tense dialogue, done with considerable urgency and drama. The orchestral playing is beyond reproach. The text followed is that of the Chrysander edition which probably doesn't correspond too closely to Handel's own. This recording is comfortably among the finest recordings of Handel operas.

Handel Alcina.

Arleen Auger *sop* Alcina
Eiddwen Harrhy *sop* Morgana
Kathleen Kuhlmann *mez* Bradamante
Della Jones *mez* Ruggiero
Patrizia Kwella *sop* Oberto
Maldwyn Davies *ten* Oronte
John Tomlinson *bass* Melisso
City of London Baroque Sinfonia; Opera Stage Chorus / Richard Hickox.
EMI Ⓔ ① CDS7 49771-2 (three discs: 217 minutes: DDD). ✍ Notes, text and translation included. Recorded 1985.

Though twice recorded before (a 1959 Melodrama under Leitner – never available in the UK – and a 1962 Decca under Bonynge), *Alcina*, musically and dramatically among the finest of Handel's operas, has been in need of a modern version, taking advantage of contemporary thinking on Handel performance. The recording is complete, indeed more than that: the entire original 1735 score is given, as done by Handel at Covent Garden, with two extra items not used by Handel at the first performances as an appendix. There are no cuts; and much care has gone into the provision of an accurate, dependable text (prepared by Clifford Bartlett).

This set must certainly have a strong claim to be reckoned one of the best sung of Handel opera recordings. There is no member of the cast who is not a Handelian of high quality and natural sense of style. In the title-role Arleen Auger has little to fear from comparison with Dame Joan Sutherland on both the previous versions; what she loses in sheer brilliance of tone or technique she makes up by the sweetness and musicality of her voice. The very first of her arias, "Di, cor mio", is lightly done, beautifully controlled, with phrase-endings delicately tapered, and the ornamentation is restrained and aptly pretty. Though the tempo is slow for her next, at risk of sentimentalization, it too is sung with refined nuance. Her big central aria in Act 2, "Ah! mio cor!", is best of all, for its intensely musical singing and purity of tone; but here again the tempos are extreme and the effect is rather romantic to the ears in the slow music, while not all the ornamentation seems natural or stylish. Auger is at her best in the early part of the opera, lacking in the later part the edge that can give full force to the scorned sorceress's angry music. The scene leading to "Ombre pallide", with its unaccompanied passage, is not done at quite high enough voltage, though the quickish tempo for the aria itself works well. But in Act 3 both arias suffer at some point from excessively slow speeds which make stylish expressive singing impossible.

Della Jones in the *primo uomo* role of Ruggiero, excels in the incisive music, like her two arias in Act 1 and the one in Act 3, though this last is rushed and becomes a shade hectic in feeling (and there is some wild ornamentation). She gives a fine performance too of the lovely "Mi lusinga", well focused in tone, strongly expressed yet always stylish. But the sensuous beauty of castrato tone needed for the finest of her arias, the incomparable "Verdi prati", perhaps understandably, eludes her; it is, however, well done, if marred at the end by the solecism of a large, romantic *rallentando*. For Kathleen Kuhlmann, the Bradamante, there can be nothing but warm praise. She has a splendid natural sense of how to give direction to the music, she throws off the semiquaver passages with clarity and fire, and conveys the character's qualities admirably with her firm line and heroic manner.

The smaller roles are taken by established British Handel singers of the middle generation. Patrizia Kwella's singing of Oberto is particularly enjoyable in a part sometimes omitted in performances; she sings with a clean line, glittering tone and a natural sense of style. The role was intended for a boy singer, and it might have been an attractive idea to have had a boy record it; but Kwella's tone and manner do have a certain direct, boyish quality. Eiddwen Harrhy's sharp and brilliant tone is well suited to the character of Alcina's sister, Morgana; she shines less, perhaps, in the energetic music of the First Act, some of which is rather languid and wanting in attack, than in the fine detail of her later ones – the exquisite Act 3 aria is particularly compelling, with her gleaming, almost instrumental tone (and a finely controlled *pp* ending) and the solo cello part done with much refinement and sensitivity. Lastly we have pleasant and graceful singing from Maldwyn Davies as Oronte, always shapely, quite assured in the rapid passagework, and a confident, resonant if perhaps rather heavy reading from John Tomlinson of Melisso's small role.

The singing, then, is on a high level; the choral numbers are also well done, if with what sounds like a larger group than is appropriate for the music. The orchestral playing is generally very capable.

There are, however, reservations about the direction, as some of the remarks above, especially on matters of tempo, might imply. One sometimes feels that Richard Hickox hasn't got a very dependable instinct for tempo in Handel – the slower music is often exaggeratedly slow, the fast sometimes driven – or that he characterizes the music very effectively. There is a certain soft-grained quality to the attack, and a want of variety in mood, partly a consequence of a style of phrasing broader than is suitable to the music. The use of a double-bass in the solo items seems seriously misguided: the music is often weighed down by it. And often the recitatives need to move more rapidly. Most of the ornamentation, which one presumes is Clifford Bartlett's work, is stylish if just occasionally too strenuous to be properly ornamental (though this nowhere approaches the hectic ornamentation on the old Decca set). Bartlett includes some, but not all, the obligatory appoggiaturas in the recitatives, omitting them at points where he feels that they may become monotonous. This surely is beside the point: either the convention of inserting them did exist, or it didn't – one is not at liberty to choose arbitrarily whether to observe them or to ignore them.

In sum, then, a recording with many merits, principally vocal ones. The recorded quality is a little variable: sometimes the acoustic seems hugely spacious, at other times more conventional. There is an excellent supporting booklet, with valuable, informative essays. As a whole there can be little doubt that this *Alcina*, in its style and its completeness, comfortably surpasses its predecessors.

Handel Alessandro.

René Jacobs *alto* Alessandro
Sophie Boulin *sop* Rossane
Isabelle Poulenard *sop* Lisaura
Jean Nirouët *alto* Tassile
Stephen Varcoe *bar* Clito
Guy de Mey *ten* Leonato
Ria Bollen *contr* Cleone
La Petite Bande / Sigiswald Kuijken.
Deutsche Harmonia Mundi Editio Classica Ⓜ ① GD77110 (three discs: 207 minutes: ADD). ✍
Notes, text and translation included. Recorded 1985.

Handel completed *Alessandro* in April 1726 and performed it at the Haymarket Theatre in the following month. It was the first of five operas in which he wrote for the rival prima donnas, Faustina Bordoni and Francesca Cuzzoni, spreading their work with diplomatic evenness. The cast also included the great castrato, Senesino. The libretto was the work of Paolo Rolli who may have adapted his text from Ortensia Mauro's *La superbia d'Alessandro* which had been set by Steffani some 35 years earlier. In common with every Handel opera, it contains an abundance of musical riches. The story of Alexander the Great's Macedonian invasion is treated more or less heroically but there is an element of irony, too, in his amorous vacillation between a Scythian princess and a Persian slave-girl. War and love are the principal themes, though the latter, as Winton Dean has remarked, brought the hero singularly little success.

The music of the First Act includes some splendidly colourful 'symphonies' and choruses, while that of the Second is often affecting at a deeper level. The solo cast is a strong one, though not, perhaps, outstanding. René Jacobs makes an imposing and authoritative Alexander and he can be lyrical too, as and when the situation requires. The two sopranos, Sophie Boulin and Isabelle Poulenard, jealous rivals for the love of the Greek hero, have light and youthful-sounding voices; but Handel's admittedly often considerable demands are not always comfortably met and the techniques of both singers are evidently stretched on occasion. The recording is excellent, affording the listener plenty of detail within a pleasantly spacious ambience. The booklet is informative, with texts and translations, the English faithfully reproduced from the word book printed for the first performance.

Handel Almira.

Ann Monoyios *sop* Almira
Patricia Rozario *sop* Edilia
Linda Gerrard *sop* Bellante
David Thomas *bass* Consalvo
Douglas Nasrawi *ten* Osman
Jamie MacDougall *ten* Fernando
Olaf Haye *bass* Raymondo
Christian Elsner *ten* Tabarco
Fiori Musicali / Andrew Lawrence-King.
CPO Ⓟ ① CPO999 275-2 (three discs: 224 minutes: DDD). ✍ Notes, text and translation included. Recorded 1994.

Handel composed *Almira*, his first opera, in 1704, when he was a violinist in the opera orchestra at Hamburg; it was performed at the beginning of 1705, six weeks before his 20th birthday. The models were, of course, the Hamburg operas of the time, in particular those of Reinhard Keiser; indeed the

Almira libretto is derived from a text by F. C. Feustking, partly a translation from an Italian original by Pancieri, that Keiser had earlier set. It is of course a German opera, although for 15 of the arias the original Italian is retained (the effect of this isn't as odd as you might expect; in fact it is hardly noticeable). The most obvious difference between Handel's Hamburg operas and his later ones is that the arias are much more numerous and mostly much shorter.

Almira has a plot about a young Spanish queen and her marital affairs, with the usual complications of deceptions and misunderstandings, stray would-be suitors, and the rediscovery of a long-lost heir; but there is also a comic, earthy servant, in the old Venetian manner, which leads to a mixture of styles and moods. The music itself is very short-breathed for Handel; he had yet to acquire the full amplitude and resource of his later vocal style – that, of course, was to happen in Italy, although Johann Mattheson later claimed that he was largely responsible for Handel's mastery of vocal writing through the instruction he gave him in Hamburg. There is a good deal of variety, however, about the arias (of which a high proportion are in minor keys). Many are simple continuo-accompanied arias, especially the very brief ones; often they have much-repeated bass figures. Several have light accompaniment and then a full orchestral ritornello at the end, a type he occasionally used later. There are a few with unusual scoring, for example one with flutes and viola, and there are several effective ones with oboe (sometimes oboe and continuo only), including what is surely the finest in the opera, Almira's "Geloso tormento", a poignant and powerful outburst, rivalled only by the music of the Act 3 Prison scene where Fernando (her beloved) thinks himself about to die (he had been falsely charged with infidelity, evidently a capital offence): an impassioned F minor aria, and a deeply felt accompanied recitative gliding into arioso as he reconciles himself to death, watched and commented on by Almira, his true lover, who will of course spare him – a worthy precursor of many later scenes of this kind.

There are the usual stirring, military numbers in C major, with triadic themes, some fine pathetic ones, and a couple of arias where the characters' boasting is neatly conveyed in the music. Many arias, of course, provided Handel with material he used later, in Italy and in London (you will hear among the Act 3 dances the very first – as far as we know – incarnation of what was to be "Lascia ch'io pianga"): *Almira*, you might say, is full of quotations. Ultimately, however, it has to be said that the musical level in this long work is variable, more so than in the mature operas, because there is some trivial music here; and often the short phrases, with too many cadences, dissipate the vitality the music promises to generate. Mattheson's and Keiser's operas are similar; but *Almira* does embody many ideas that hint at the later Handel – indeed already bear his fingerprints unmistakably – and show a brilliance and depth far beyond those men.

So Handelians are urged to give *Almira* a hearing. The performance, based on a staging given in Bremen and Halle in 1994, gives a very fair idea of the work. Andrew Lawrence-King, who took over the direction of the recording when the original conductor (Thomas Albert) withdrew through illness, paces it well and generally keeps the recitative moving. Where it is allowed to slow down, one is sometimes reminded of the world of German Passion music. The continuo instrumentation is varied a good deal; often a bassoon alone is used, and sometimes violone alone, both of which seem unsatisfactory, and the effect is not infrequently rather bass-heavy. The dance pieces that survive only as melody and bass are played that way when they should surely have inner parts added. There is a certain amount of ornamentation, mostly quite discreet though here and there extravagant (as in Bellante's Act 3 aria).

Among the singers, Ann Monoyios makes a generally sympathetic Almira, light and bright in tone, and often phrasing her music gracefully; she does well in her demanding Act 3 aria although it really calls for a higher level of virtuosity. Patricia Rozario sometimes seems under strain in Edilia's music, which perhaps lies high for her. There are three tenor roles (no castratos in Hamburg!), of which Fernando's is particularly attractively sung by Jamie MacDougall, a tenor of some depth of tone and capable of expressive phrasing. David Thomas sings with directness and particular authority in the role of Consalvo and Olaf Haye supplies warm singing in Raymondo's music.

Handel Amadigi di Gaula.
Nathalie Stutzmann *contr* Amadigi
Jennifer Smith *sop* Oriana
Eiddwen Harrhy *sop* Melissa
Bernarda Fink *mez* Dardano
Pascal Bertin *alto* Orgando
Musiciens du Louvre / Marc Minkowski.
Erato Ⓟ Ⓒ 2292-45490-2 (two discs: 149 minutes: DDD). ✒ Notes, text and translation included. Recorded 1989.

Dating from Handel's early years in London (1715), this opera proved once more the composer's early command in creating drama within the formalities of *opera seria* as it was then practised. It is the second of Handel's magical operas; set in Gaul, it describes how the scheming sorceress Melissa tries to entice Amadigi away from the lovely Oriana, who is also hopelessly desired by Dardano, Prince of Thrace. Although there are only four principal characters, all originally taken by high voices (the hero by an alto castrato), Handel wholly avoids monotony through his skill in giving their emotions true expression in a wonderfully varied succession of numbers, every one appropriate to the situation in hand. Such pieces as Amadigi's aria alternating a *presto* section for anger with an *adagio* for sorrow, Melissa's brilliant outburst of triumph that closes Act 2 in a blaze of striking invention, Oriana's "Dolce vita" at the start of Act 3, or Melissa's Death scene, a solemn sarabande enclosing a lamenting arioso, evince Handel's burgeoning genius, also his ability – like that of all the most telling composers of opera – to sympathize with the baddies as well as the goodies (cf. Mozart and Wagner). Throughout, Melissa's frustrations are as aptly delineated as the simple happiness of Oriana, whose B flat *largo* "O caro mio tesor" is perhaps the work's most sensuous delight. But that is to overlook Dardano's "Pena tiranna" (a sarabande that is the basis of Melissa's Death scene) – have the pangs of unrequited love ever been expressed with such languorous beauty, the sinuous vocal line underpinned by five-part strings and a languishing oboe and bassoon? At the same time, the recitative, when treated as boldly as it is here, carries forward the drama in succinct fashion. Indeed, in that respect, and its spare orchestration, it demonstrates Handel's early, Italianate style at its most attractive.

The merits of the piece might not be so obvious were not this performance so convincing, at once sensitive and spirited. Wholly eschewing the British fashion for performing Handel without vibrato, in a 'hoot and tweet' manner, Minkowski and his team treat it as a very present drama. Minkowski's direction, lithe, direct yet always responsive to the emotional turbulence voiced by the principals, is consistently admirable, avoiding the Scylla of over-accentuation and the Charybdis of dullness, and his Musiciens du Louvre play with an ease and character that sound right and natural.

His singers have been chosen with an ear for their aptness to the characters. Nathalie Stutzmann confirms her deserved reputation with her palpitating, eager Amadigi. She sings Handel's divisions securely and uses her grave, peculiarly dark voice to arresting effect throughout. She is a true contralto, well contrasted with the mezzo of Bernarda Fink, and Amadigi's friend and rival, Dardano. Her voice has just the right colour and timbre for Handel's special demands: she is particularly suited to the aforementioned "Pena tiranna" and to Dardano's highly original scene as a Ghost in Act 3, intoned against staccato strings. Similarly, Jennifer Smith's soft-grained, somewhat languid singing as Oriana is nicely contrasted with Eiddwen Harrhy's more incisive, fiery style as Melissa – listen to her deft handling of the awkward runs of "Vanne lungi" in Act 3 – and yet Harrhy draws out all the pathos from Melissa's dying words. Occasionally both sopranos show a suspicion of strain in their topmost notes, but you will be willing to bear with that slight drawback in order to gain and enjoy the warmth of their performances. Orgando's role is tiny, but in his few phrases Pascal Bertin reveals a pleasing countertenor.

To add to one's pleasure the recording is wellnigh ideal, forward and realistically balanced with no hint of the current preference for the cavernous, that gives the drama just that much more sense of immediacy. Erato, quite cleverly, print the Italian libretto and its English translation as it must have appeared originally, with a delightful précis of each aria. Thus, Melissa's aria of fury, superbly delivered by Harrhy, with trumpet obbligato that ends Act 2, is described: "She says she'll raise every Fury to make war against Amadis and Oriana, whom she calls cruel and perfidious, and commands the blackest Ghosts to ascend from their Dungeons to torment those who slight her." Altogether a set to convert the most obstinate anti-Handelian.

Handel Ariodante.

Lorraine Hunt *sop* Ariodante
Juliana Gondek *sop* Ginevra
Lisa Saffer *sop* Dalinda
Jennifer Lane *mez* Polinesso
Rufus Müller *ten* Lurcanio
Nicolas Cavallier *bass* King of Scotland
Jörn Lindemann *ten* Odoardo
Wilhelmshaven Vocal Ensemble; Freiburg Baroque Orchestra / Nicholas McGegan.
Harmonia Mundi Ⓟ Ⓒ HMU90 7146/8 (three discs: 202 minutes: DDD). Notes, text and translation included. Recorded 1995.

1996

Many Handelians will probably already have a recording of *Ariodante*, either the original LPs or the CD set issued at the end of 1994 of the Leppard performance on Philips of 1978 with Dame Janet Baker in the title-role. Baker was in superb voice, and for her commanding singing alone the set is more than worth having; but this version under Nicholas McGegan certainly surpasses it in almost every other way. This recording, made with the cast from the 1994 Göttingen Festival (largely American singers who have collaborated with McGegan in his Californian performances), seems to be at least the equal of the best he has done before. The quality of the music is of course a factor: *Ariodante* is one of the richest of the Handel operas. It begins with a flood of fine numbers, just like *Giulio Cesare*, mostly love music for the betrothed pair, Ariodante and the Scottish princess Ginevra – she is introduced in a wonderfully carefree aria, he in a gentle, exquisite slow arietta; then they have a very individual and beautiful love duet, and each goes on to a more jubilant aria. But the plot thickens and the music darkens with Polinesso's machinations, designed to impugn her fidelity: so that Act 2 contains music of vengeance and grief (above all the magnificent "Scherza infida!" for Ariodante, a G minor aria with muted upper and pizzicato lower strings, and soft bassoons), while the final act shows all the characters *in extremis*, until the plot is uncovered and equilibrium is restored. This is also one of Handel's few operas with extensive ballet; each act includes some splendid and ingeniously tuneful dance music.

McGegan directs in his usual spirited style. There is a real theatrical sense to his conducting: this is one of those opera sets where, after the overture, you find your spine tingling in expectation of the drama, which isn't surprising for a performance that originated in the theatre, though it doesn't always happen. At any rate, his tempos are wide-ranging – quicker ones move pretty smartly, but the slower ones are given ample time for the import of the music to make itself felt. He does not shirk the tragic grandeur that has a place in this score: listen for example to the opening music of Act 3. The dances are done with springy rhythms and often with considerable vigour. The recitatives are sung at a good pace but with full dramatic weight. Some people may not quite like some of the dapper staccatos and unshaped cadences, but they don't offend; nor, on the whole, does the singers' ornamentation on those occasions when it goes beyond the ornamental and departs too radically from the lines of the music. The orchestra, modest in size (the strings are only 4.4.2.3.2: more violins might have been preferable), are efficient and precise.

Lorraine Hunt's soprano seems warm and full for a castrato part, but her line is always well defined and she has a delightfully musical voice which she uses gracefully and expressively. Her virtuoso A major aria in Act 1 is masterly in style and control and so are the rapid semiquaver runs in the aria that opens Act 2. And there is great intensity in her singing of the two minor key arias that begin the final act. "Scherza infida!" seems curiously balanced, the voice excessively forward or the orchestra subdued. As Ginevra, Juliana Gondek, even with a touch more vibrato than might be ideal, sings with a natural musicianship – to be heard in her phrasing and her way of shaping the music – and a wide range of expression: best of all perhaps in the virtuoso aria in Act 1 and the magnificent tragic scene at the end of Act 2, though the poignant D minor farewell to her father in Act 3 is deeply touching too. Lisa Saffer provides a charming and spirited Dalinda and Nicolas Cavallier a King with suitable warmth and depth of tone. Rufus Müller's voice is a shade baritonal for the tenor role of Lurcanio and his Italian sounds a little awkward but he sings capably and sympathetically. The role of Polinesso, intended for a contralto rather than a castrato, is projected by Jennifer Lane with style and some passion, the latter particularly in the final aria where he looks forward to his triumph. A fine set.

Handel Berenice.

Julianne Baird *sop* Berenice
D'Anna Fortunato *mez* Selene
Jennifer Lane *mez* Demetrio
Andrea Matthews *sop* Alessandro
Drew Minter *alto* Arsace
John McMaster *ten* Fabio
Jan Opalach *bass* Aristobolo
Brewer Chamber Orchestra / Rudolph Palmer.
Newport Classic Ⓕ Ⓘ NPD85620/3 (three discs: 149 minutes: DDD). Notes, text and translation included. Recorded 1994.

Commentators have tended to be dismissive of *Berenice*, one of Handel's last operas. It is understandable that it should have failed (achieving only four performances) in 1737 before a London audience, already tiring of conventional Italian *opera seria*, that was faced with yet another stilted complex plot of amorous and political intrigues (between Egypt and Rome, if anyone cared), and, through financial constraints, with an orchestra largely reduced to strings only and lacking Handel's usual subtleties of instrumental colour. But that it should have remained totally ignored, save for a German version six years later, until the University of Keele revived it in 1985 is rather shameful (and the current recorded catalogue contains almost nothing of it except the overture, which includes the famous Minuet): so all the more thanks are due to this attractive first recording, by all-American forces, which may help to redress the balance.

Though it is true that the level of invention in *Berenice* is uneven, not always equal to Handel at his best (the aria that concludes Act 2, for example, is a disappointment, and the only well-known solo, "Sì, tra i ceppi" – which was in fact merely an alternative aria – is an inappropriately cheerful setting of the words), there is a striking final ensemble, virtuoso florid arias (notably Demetrio's "Sù, Megera", Arsace's "Senza nudrisce", Alessandro's "Che sarà?" and Selene's impassioned "Gelo, avvampo") and a fine accompanied recitative for Demetrio. The producer, John Ostendorf (who provides an extremely free translation), has assembled an exceptionally good cast without a single weak member, mostly from stalwarts of his previous Handel recordings for Newport Classic. Recitatives, often the weak point in performances of baroque operas, are handled meaningfully throughout, with intelligent timing and asides given proper perspective; and all the singers decorate *da capo* sections of arias (often with very free final cadenzas). Julianne Baird produces a lovely pure sound (she might have appeared more indignant in her very first aria, though later she is properly spirited), and at the risk of seeming invidious, mention must be made of the sterling contributions of Jennifer Lane.

Few reservations need to be made: Andrea Matthews, in the castrato part of Alessandro, sounds unmistakably female; the admirable John McMaster's angry "Guerra e pace" would have been better taken faster; and the reverberant acoustic of the church where the opera was recorded sometimes forces itself on the attention. The 30-piece Brewer Chamber Orchestra have drawn criticism in the past, but here they are on far better form and give no cause for concern. All in all, then, a most welcome addition to the catalogue.

Handel Flavio.

Jeffrey Gall *alto* Flavio
Derek Lee Ragin *alto* Guido
Lena Lootens *sop* Emilia
Bernarda Fink *contr* Teodata
Christina Högman *sop* Vitige
Gianpaolo Fagotto *ten* Ugone
Ulrich Messthaler *bass* Lotario
Ensemble 415 / René Jacobs.
Harmonia Mundi Ⓟ Ⓒ HMC90 1312/3 (two discs: 156 minutes: DDD). 🖊 Notes, text and translation included. Recorded 1989.

Flavio is possibly the most delectable of all Handel's operas. Although many writers are tempted (but decline) to make comparisons between Handel and Mozart, because the two composers' operatic and expressive worlds are so far apart, *Flavio* demands it, through its charming mixture of humour and seriousness, of delicately drawn amorous feeling and passionate grief. Its situations are half-jocular, at least to start with, but they soon begin to involve emotion of real depth, and the music matches it. The plot is about Flavio, King of Lombardy, whose unruly passion for Teodata interferes with the lives of all around him, imperilling the loves of two couples and leading to the dishonour of one of his counsellors and the death of the other. Although the opera dates from Handel's 'heroic' period, the high days of the Royal Academy of Music in London (it immediately precedes *Giulio Cesare*, in fact), its prevailing mood is lightish, with slender textures, dance rhythms and short-phrased yet graceful melodies, a sensitive response to the character of the Venetian libretto on which the opera is based. *Flavio* was never much of a success, probably for this very reason; English taste was more for the grand, serious style. It had a run of eight performances and was only once revived. Its first modern revival in the UK was at Abingdon in 1969; since then it has also been seen in London and Cambridge.

This recording ranks with those of *Partenope* and *Alessandro* as among the finest ever made of Handel operas and it can be recommended almost unreservedly. The casting is not spectacular – there are no really eye-catching names in the cast-list – but there is not a weak voice to be heard and the singing is beautifully unified in approach and style. The voices are light ones, as indeed the opera calls for. There is a general sense, not always common in this repertory, of a performance carefully thought out and thoroughly prepared. Of course, there is room for disagreement over some aspects of it, and while one has to respect René Jacobs's direction he is, arguably, sometimes misguided over ornamentation (especially where he allows it in the orchestra) and is slightly too preoccupied with detailed shaping (the little *rallentando*, the hesitation before the critical chord and the like), possibly at the expense of broader rhythm. But his pacing of the whole is lively and dramatically motivated. His addition to the score of a handful of orchestral sinfonias at various junctures in the plot is a little puzzling – Handel supplied nothing of the kind – and at one point an arioso for Flavio. But the orchestral playing by Chiara Banchini's admirable Ensemble 415 is so shapely and so refined, and so alert, that it is a constant pleasure to listen to.

The opera begins beguilingly, with a love-duet for the secondary couple, Teodata and Vitige, as he slips away from her room at night after an assignation: the singing of Bernarda Fink and Christina Högman is not only tender and graceful but perfectly disciplined in its details of phrasing and the like. Fink distinguishes herself again in her later numbers, most of all in the delicious "Con un' vezzo, con un' riso", in Act 2, which is done very lightly, with charm and humour and excellent control. Högman, as the royal attendant who is deputed to press Flavio's importunities on the girl he himself loves, also rises splendidly to her Act 2 aria, a finely written aria originally intended for the experienced Durastanti, which she handles subtly and with some exquisite detail. Her Act 1 aria is taken curiously quickly by Jacobs, but it works, and she carries off her angry outburst in the last act in fine fashion.

The *prima donna* and *primo uomo* roles were written for two of Handel's greatest singers, Cuzzoni and Senesino. Emilia is taken here by Lena Lootens, a clean, true singer who is always good to listen to (try the brilliant A major aria ending Act 1) and sometimes much more than that – as in her aria near the beginning of Act 2, "Parto, sì, mà non sò poi", one of the great moments in all Handel operas where suddenly real emotion floods to the surface: this, the first really slow aria in the opera, will inevitably recall "Comfort ye", in the same key of E major (Cuzzoni is said to have had a remarkable E, and Handel often exploited it, usually setting her music in a sharp key for the purpose). Later in the act, too, she has a deeply poignant *siciliano*-style aria, this time in F sharp minor. Lootens's expressive and natural singing is a real joy. Her partner here, as Guido, is the countertenor Derek Lee Ragin, a flexible and well-controlled singer who does pretty well at a fiendish pace in his brilliant "Rompo i lacci" in Act 2 (the contrast with the slow middle section is arguably overdone), but rises particularly to his very last aria, a B flat minor expression of passion. The final duet for these two has some lovely, meltingly musical singing; at a tempo nearer to the specified *andante* it would, happily, have gone on for longer.

The other countertenor role, that of Flavio himself, is sung by Jeffrey Gall, who has a slightly firmer edge to the voice: a capable and rhythmic singer, pleasing in his opening gavotte aria, though he is required to sing too slowly in his aria in Act 2, which seems oddly interpreted. The two male parts are both quite modest: Gianpaolo Fagotto dispatches the demanding semiquavers of Ugone's single aria very accurately and with no shortage of passion, while Lotario (who is murdered by his intended son-in-law) is done in duly fiery fashion by Ulrich Messthaler. The recitative is kept moving at a good pace, and sometimes a lute is used in the continuo team, to good effect on the whole. Appoggiaturas, of course, are properly in place. There are no cuts, in what is one of Handel's shortest operas; *au contraire*, in fact. The recording leaves nothing to be desired and there is an excellent booklet.

Handel Floridante (abridged).
Catherine Robbin *mez* Floridante
Ingrid Attrot *sop* Timante
Nancy Argenta *sop* Rossane
Linda Maguire *contr* Elmira
Mel Braun *bar* Oronte
Tafelmusik Baroque Orchestra / Alan Curtis.
CBC Records Ⓜ ① SMCD5110 (76 minutes: DDD). 🗩 Text and translation included.

It's probably not going too far to say that this excerpt disc of *Floridante* sets new standards in the presentation of Handel as a dramatic composer. No one who hears it will be able to be condescending about Handel's operas again. The combination of Alan Curtis's full-blooded direction, which takes the music simply for what it is, a cast who show a real grasp of how to convey powerful emotion through this idiom, and a good deal of music of supremely high quality, makes it as exciting an issue in its way as the **Gramophone** Award-winning *Giulio Cesare* under Jacobs (reviewed further on). *Floridante* is not musically quite on that level, or certainly not consistently so; but it does have several superb numbers and a lot of music in a vivacious and appealing style for the secondary characters, Rossane and Timante.

The disc concentrates on the music for Floridante himself, offering five of his seven arias and his duet. There is a wonderfully simple first aria, typical of the way Handel had his star castrato capture his audience's attention at the start of an evening, with just continuo accompaniment (and a closing orchestral ritornello), then a *Larghetto* in 12/8, a fiery G minor piece from Act 2, with great urgency in the orchestral playing providing the singer with real support, and all three of his arias from the last act, including another deeply felt 12/8 one, in C minor, a serene farewell to life, and a spirited final one. Catherine Robbin's firm, beautifully formed tone and her wide emotional range make her the ideal interpreter of these alto castrato parts written for the great Senesino. She sings finely too in the very moving duet that ends Act 1, a piece with echoes of *Esther*, where she is joined by Linda Maguire, who makes no less accomplished a heroine in Elmira's music – listen to her powerful, ringing mezzo in the vigorous "Ma pria vedrò le stelle" (a furious protestation of fidelity), or her outburst of rage ("Barbaro!") in Act 2, or above all her second aria in that act, sung with a Verdian intensity yet without a hint of infringing the limits of Handelian style: this is a remarkable piece, in the very special key of B flat minor, a clear precursor with its noble descending theme of the most moving chorus in *Judas Maccabaeus* (still more than 20 years off).

There are also three arias, much lighter in style, for Rossane, sung in spirited fashion by Nancy Argenta, and a dulcet duet for her and Ingrid Attrot. All the arias are preceded by recitatives, sung with considerable vitality and drama; the performance sounds as if these artists had given the work theatrically. There is some generally appropriate ornamentation (and one horribly inappropriate bit, by Robbin at the beginning of the *da capo* of her last aria, creating a harmonic and contrapuntal solecism). The disc is one that no Handelian should miss; and it provides an object lesson in baroque operatic style under Alan Curtis's alert and knowledgeable direction.

Handel Giulio Cesare.
Jennifer Larmore *mez* Giulio Cesare
Barbara Schlick *sop* Cleopatra
Bernarda Fink *mez* Cornelia
Marianne Rørholm *mez* Sextus
Derek Lee Ragin *alto* Ptolemy
Furio Zanasi *bass* Achillas
Olivier Lallouette *bar* Curio
Dominique Visse *alto* Nirenus
Concerto Cologne / René Jacobs.
Harmonia Mundi Ⓟ ① HMC90 1385/7 (four discs: 244 minutes: DDD). 🗩
Notes, text and translation included. Recorded 1991.

90-93 FM

1992

If this isn't the greatest of all baroque operas, indeed the greatest opera before Mozart, then goodness knows what is. More than any other Handel opera, *Giulio Cesare* goes from one superb number to another, covering a vast range of emotion – the triumphant, the amorous, the vengeful, the deeply pathetic, almost anything you can name. Further, the character of Cleopatra, which seems to develop in a way that characters in baroque opera normally do not, is perhaps the fullest and most fascinatingly drawn of all Handel's stage women: and the characterization of women habitually drew from Handel his most penetrating insights.

The great strength of this recording is that it treats the work as a live piece of musical drama, in which everyone is involved at an intense level from beginning to end. René Jacobs, whose conducting sometimes seemed a shade tentative in his early recordings, seems totally in command and with a clear view of the piece and how it functions. You may not always agree with the view, but it is a powerful and persuasive one. It leads him to splendidly sturdy rhythms and lively tempos, to recitatives that, if occasionally too slow, often come as near as can be to the ideal of 'musicalized' conversation and sometimes are very dramatic – listen for example to the group near the opening of Act 3 – and to a real concentration of feeling in the numbers where that is appropriate: that is, in the elegiac music for Cornelia, for Cleopatra in her pathetic situations, and perhaps above all for Caesar himself in the two great accompanied recitatives, one over the tomb of his late rival Pompey, done to death by the treacherous Ptolemy, the other on his survival after his leap into the sea when cornered. What one may be slightly less happy about is the handling of the orchestra, and especially the lower instruments. It may only be a trick of the rather boomy acoustic, but the cellos and basses often seem to be playing roughly and crudely. Their accents are sometimes absurdly heavy, and this represents a real (and sometimes disconcerting) lapse of judgement and a real flaw. The continuo lines are never really as well, as sensitively or as functionally shaped as they ought to be. Sometimes, too, Jacobs writes in extra music for them, for example an intrusive series of interjections when Caesar finally comes to rescue Cleopatra in the last act. (It is unlikely that these are in the authoritative edition by Winton Dean and Sarah Fuller that, very properly, forms the basis of this performance; the faithfully reproduced harmonic error in "Aure, deh, per pietà" probably originates in the Chrysander text.)

The cast has no weaknesses and many strengths. Foremost among them is the Julius Caesar of Jennifer Larmore. With her firm, focused and beautifully formed voice, she does much better in this alto castrato part than any countertenor could. Burney once wrote of the original singer, the famous Senesino, "thundering out his divisions", and this is the nearest to "thundering out" that you will hear from a singer at this pitch; in the final aria of triumph, "Qual torrente", the semiquaver runs are as brilliant, as exact and as powerfully rhythmic as one could imagine – a real *tour de force*. Going back to the beginning of the opera, you may find her vibrato a shade too marked in the opening aria, but here and in "Non è si vaga", later in the act, the full and rich lower register particularly compels admiration. It is a pity the 'hunting' aria, "Va tacito", had not been done a little quicker; but the horn playing is splendid. Another mistake, surely, is the vast *rallentando* in "Al lampo dell' armi", which rather seems to contradict Caesar's eagerly belligerent sentiments. Larmore excels in the grave music of the accompanied recitatives, to which she brings considerable weight and a real sense of the Roman honour and integrity that Handel and his librettist were clearly so intent on, and successful in, conveying.

Barbara Schlick's Cleopatra is a success, too. She possibly lacks the sensuous warmth that can so effectively irradiate this role, for example in "V'adoro, pupille" and "Piangerò" (which, however, is beautifully phrased), but the quick numbers demanding agility and spirit go especially well – the trills in "Tu la mia stelle" have a delightful glitter, "Venere bella" is graceful and spirited – and it would be greedy to ask for more. There is a sterling Cornelia from Bernarda Fink, firmly and evenly sung, with due depth of tone and feeling in "Priva son" (taken very slowly) and the noble "Nel tuo seno". Sextus is rightly taken by a soprano (as in the original; Handel later adapted and rewrote it for tenor), the very capable Marianne Rørholm, aptly boyish in tone, suitably fiery in "Svegliatevi", vigorous and brilliant in "L'aure che spira". Ptolemy, the villain of the piece, is well done by the countertenor Derek Lee Ragin, who is particularly admirable in his recitative near the end of Act 2 and in the marvellous last-act aria, with its wilful violin line, "Domerò la tua fierezza"; he manages to convey the character's malice without using unmusical means. Furio Zanasi sings the two bass arias very ably and Dominique Visse does an aria for Nirenus, Cleopatra's eunuch, as an appendix (it was written for a revival; no text or translation is provided). Most of the singers provide occasional ornamentation, and most but not all of it is tasteful, restrained and musical.

There have been several previous recordings of this opera, but none of this quality, consistency or style. It is wonderful music, and in spite of minor imperfections René Jacobs and his musicians give a compelling account of it.

Handel Giulio Cesare (sung in English).
Dame Janet Baker *mez* Julius Caesar
Valerie Masterson *sop* Cleopatra
Sarah Walker *mez* Cornelia
Delia Jones *mez* Sextus
James Bowman *alto* Ptolemy
John Tomlinson *bass* Achillas

Christopher Booth-Jones *bar* Curio
David James *alto* Nirenus
English National Opera Chorus and Orchestra / Sir Charles Mackerras.
Stage Director: **John Copley.** *Video Director:* **John Michael Philips.**
EMI Ⓜ Ⓓ CMS7 69760-2 (three discs: 183 minutes: DDD).
PolyGram RM Collection Ⓕ 🔲 079 246-3 (183 minutes). Notes and English text included with
the CD. Recorded 1984.

This production, deriving from the opera-house, is utterly faithful to Handel, a pleasure to see and
hear. No doubt because it depicts events well documented in history, this was the first piece to restore
Handel's reputation in the house-house. It shows the ardent, wilful nature of the eponymous hero and
the voluptuous, minxish character of the seductive, scheming Cleopatra in a number of varied and
wonderfully apt arias. The supporting characters are similarly favoured. John Copley's long-running
production has Janet Baker as Julius Caesar. All in all this is an invaluable souvenir of Dame Janet's
work in Handel and she handles this trousers role as to the manner born and learnt. This emperor is,
as Handel predicates, at once commanding, amorous and self-willed. Baker's singing is vibrant, fleet
and, where needed, as in the touching recitative mourning Pompey's ashes, deeply eloquent.
Masterson is an apt Cleopatra for this Caesar, voluptuous, flighty, pleasing to the eye, and her singing
of Cleopatra's many arias conveys the differing moods of each unerringly. Della Jones is a properly
concerned and impetuous Sextus; as his grieving mother Cornelia, Sarah Walker sings and acts with
noble dignity. Bowman is as imperious and nasty as Ptolemy should be (in the clear light of CD, his
aggressive alto sounds just a little fulsome) and John Tomlinson is a rightly vicious Achillas.
  Sir Charles's conducting is full of verve and sensitivity with tempos ideally judged and the
instrumental textures made plain within keenly-sprung rhythms. The CD is enhanced by a recording
with a good deal of presence and a booklet that is a model of what such things should be. Copley's
staging may by now seem a little dated but it is never less than in sympathy with the music and keeps
well within the bounds of Handelian style. Several arias are omitted, modern instruments are used,
but neither matters much in the context of such an enjoyable interpretation. The video direction is
sensitive, the sound excellent.

Handel Giustino.

Michael Chance *alto* Giustino
Dorothea Röschmann *sop* Arianna
Dawn Kotoski *sop* Anastasio
Juliana Gondek *sop* Fortuna
Dean Ely *sngr* Polidarte
Jennifer Lane *mez* Leocasta
Mark Padmore *ten* Vitaliano
Drew Minter *alto* Amanzio
Cantamus Chamber Choir, Halle; Freiburg Baroque Orchestra / Nicholas McGegan.
Harmonia Mundi Ⓕ Ⓓ HMU90 7130/2 (three discs: 173 minutes: DDD). 🎺 Notes, text and
translation included. Recorded 1994.

Giustino, none too successful in Handel's own day, has had an unjustifiably poor press from Handel
biographers. Taken on its own terms – which are considerably removed from those of traditional
heroic *opera seria* – it strikes one as a thoroughly delightful work: consistent in style but very varied
in manner, run through with lively touches of wit and irony, and at its best moments serious and
genuinely moving. First given in 1737, and not revived in Handel's time, indeed not until 1967, it tells
a tale based very loosely on history, about the early days of Justin, the country lad who became
Byzantine emperor. The shifts of allegiance and the slender motivation sometimes make it hard to be
sure where our sympathies are meant to lie, but the story clearly isn't intended to be taken over-
seriously. The work happens to be particularly well suited to Nicholas McGegan's interpretative
approach: the light textures, the faintly quizzical, abrupt phrase-ends, the quickish tempos, the crisp
rhythms and the general reluctance to dawdle or luxuriate or aggrandize – all these seem to capture
the special qualities of *Giustino* very neatly and make the set highly agreeable entertainment.
  The opera has an unusual overture, virtually an oboe concerto, with long and virtuoso oboe solos
in the fugue and a solo *Adagio* to follow: it is outstandingly well played here by Katharina Arfken,
under McGegan's spruce direction. The singing, by the cast McGegan conducted at the Göttingen
Festival in 1994, is stylish and assured though vocally not consistently distinguished. It is slightly
regrettable, in a recording, that the voices of the royal couple, Anastasio and Arianna, should sound
rather alike. Anastasio was originally a soprano castrato role (it was written for the famous Conti).
Dawn Kotoski has the right firmness of focus and concentration of tone, with considerable delicacy
and rhythmic life, but the narrow, quick vibrato sometimes makes the intonation seem a shade
suspect. The Arianna, Dorothea Röschmann, is also a light and quite graceful singer, firm in line. She
distinguishes herself, and raises the level of intensity of the whole performance, with her singing of
the last aria of Act 1, a highly chromatic D minor aria of considerable pathos, and her big virtuoso
piece, a triumphant D major duet with the oboe at the end of Act 2, is equally splendid in quite a

different way. Her first Act 3 aria, a very individual F minor expression of grief and the emotional high point of the opera, is also quite outstanding.

The other castrato role is Giustino's, superbly sung here by Michael Chance. Handel characteristically introduced his singer with a light and simple piece, a minuet accompanied only by three recorders, oboe and viola; it is followed by a C minor 'sleep song'. Chance does the first charmingly, the second very expressively with many subtle details of timing and shading. He has an unusually generous allocation of arias; these include the finely virile and agile singing of "Se parla nel mio cor" later in Act 1, the noble "Sull' altar" in Act 2 (perhaps best of all) and the shapely performance of his first Act 3 aria. The steady and beautiful tone and controlled singing should subdue the objections that many people feel to countertenors in castrato roles. In that context it seems misguided to use a countertenor where another option is offered, or indeed chosen, by the composer: the role of Amanzio, originally taken by a contralto, is here assigned to Drew Minter – a very musical and intelligent singer but the voice seems soft-edged and does not come over with much life or definition, so that the character, scheming and villainous, is not very effectively conveyed. Jennifer Lane makes a strong and precise Leocasta and Mark Padmore shows plenty of vitality as Vitaliano.

Recitatives are briskly done, as they should be. There is a good deal of ornamentation in the *da capo* sections, occasionally too like rewriting for some tastes. McGegan characterizes the orchestral slurring and staccatos very markedly, often without evident justification in the text; it sounds well enough but sometimes it represents editorial decisions that are not easy to understand. Still, it does bring life to the music and that is what matters most. He also tends to stress the top and bottom of the texture and keep the middle (whether strings or continuo filling) very light. The set is well presented, with a useful note by Duncan Chisholm though there is neither a synopsis nor a list of the original cast. However, Handelians must not miss this addition to the recorded repertory of the operas.

Handel Orlando.

Patricia Bardon *mez* Orlando
Rosemary Joshua *sop* Angelica
Hilary Summers *contr* Medoro
Rosa Mannion *sop* Dorinda
Harry van der Kamp *bass* Zoroastro
Les Arts Florissants / William Christie.
Erato Ⓟ Ⓒ 0630-14636-2 (three discs: 168 minutes: DDD). ✍ Notes, text and translation included. Recorded 1996.

There is already an excellent *Orlando* recording (Christopher Hogwood on L'Oiseau-Lyre), but of course there is always room for more than one version and the present recording is rather different in character from Hogwood's. Christie is very much concerned with a smooth and generally rich texture and with delicacy of rhythmic shaping. His management of the recitative could hardly be bettered. True, he doesn't always elide the cadences with the final vocal phrase, as we know with fair certainty was done in Handel's time, but he paces it in a natural manner, making it properly representative of conversation, but of course heightened dramatic conversation, with the musical lines effectively declaimed. Moments of urgency or of other kinds of emotional stress are tellingly handled. One might feel less happy with the rather sustained style Christie favours in the arias. Sometimes the textures seem airless and heavy, and the lines within them too smooth; and this is apt to make the music seem unduly uniform in temper. This is most striking in Act 2. But to set against it there is Christie's exceptional delicacy of timing, his careful but always natural-sounding moulding of cadences and other critical moments in the score. Not many Handel interpreters show this kind of regard for such matters, and some might argue that it is more a modern than a baroque way of handling the music. But it is certainly a delight to hear Handel's music so lovingly nurtured and of course it helps the singers to convey meaning.

The cast is very strong, as is Hogwood's. While the older recording has a countertenor (James Bowman) in the title-role, this one has a mezzo, Patricia Bardon, who draws a very firm and often slender line, with that gleam in her tone that can so enliven the impact of a lowish mezzo. Here and there she lets herself use more vibrato than some might like, but there is great vitality to the splendid "Fammi combattere", and considerable brilliance in "Cielo! se tu il consenti", and the famous Mad scene is magnificent, with a wide range of tone (though slightly too hectic, surely, at the very end: this is stylized Handel, not *verismo*). The Sleep scene, with very sweet, soft-toned playing of the *violette marine*, is lovely. The other high male role was in fact originally sung by a woman: here Hilary Summers offers a very sensitively sung Medoro, pure and shapely in line, duly touching in her aria at the end of Act 1, quite impassioned at the opening of Act 3. Harry van der Kamp makes a finely weighty Zoroastro, with plenty of resonance in his bottom register; the last aria in particular is done in rousing fashion.

As Angelica, Rosemary Joshua shows a big, mettlesome voice with a bright top; her musicianship comes through in some attractive phrasing and timing. In the G minor aria in Act 2, "Verdi pianta", her voice floats beguilingly above the orchestral textures (which seem rather heavy here); "Così giusta" in Act 3 draws some powerfully elegiac singing from her. Rosa Mannion's Dorinda is no less full of delights – spirited, beautifully graceful and poised in her exquisite arietta that opens Act 2, attractively free and relaxed in her Act 3 aria. This very talented singer catches the character of Dorinda to perfection. The Hogwood set was always one of the finest available of a Handel opera and it too has superlative singing from the sopranos, Arleen Auger and Emma Kirkby. There is really nothing to choose between these two sets vocally unless one has a decided preference for a mezzo as opposed to a countertenor. We are lucky to have so many accomplished Handelians, both on the rostrum and on the stage: amazing, on the abundant evidence here, that only a few years ago people were still saying that Handel operas were unsingable.

Handel Ottone.

James Bowman *alto* Ottone
Claron McFadden *sop* Teofane
Michael George *bass* Emireno
Jennifer Smith *sop* Gismonda
Dominique Visse *alto* Adelberto
Catherine Denley *mez* Matilda
King's Consort / Robert King.
Hyperion Ⓟ Ⓒ CDA66751/3 (three discs: 175 minutes: DDD). ✒ Notes, text and translation included. Recorded 1993.

Ottone was one of Handel's most successful operas in his own time, and in our own time it seems to have achieved the distinction of being the first to appear on rival period-style recordings. This one was made in 1993, hard on the heels of Harmonia Mundi's with Nicholas McGegan, after performances in Japan and in London. Robert King comes to it with plenty of experience in Handel but little in opera, and that is often evident in his direction. The performance is not strong in dramatic vitality; a number of times, events in this creaky plot demand a stronger, more firmly characterized reaction than he provides, and in particular there is no keen sense of when the music needs, because of the situation on stage, to be more energetically paced. The recitative mostly goes at quite a sensible speed, steady enough for the words to come across but never ponderous, though here too one sometimes wishes for more urgency. He also signally fails to use ornamentation to heighten the drama: indeed, he scarcely uses it at all. A few of the singers add the odd flourish or piece of embellishment, but there is no consistency and none uses it expressively or to strengthen the impact of the words. Exaggerated, wild ornamentation (there is some of that on the McGegan set) is worse than none at all; but it misses the whole point of the *da capo* aria if one simply repeats the main section without doing anything to make it different from what has gone before.

There is not a lot to choose between the two versions as far as the cast is concerned. Claron McFadden, in the *prima donna* role of Teofane (the role sung by the famous Cuzzoni on her London début), is something of a disappointment: too light and shallow-toned a voice, too girlish in sound, to bear the emotional weight of this music. She sings tastefully but not interestingly and never with much hint of passion, even in the lovely Act 1 *siciliana*, "Affanni del pensier". In James Bowman, who takes the *primo uomo* part originally composed for Senesino, King has an experienced Handelian and indeed an experienced opera singer, but the voice is neither as rich nor as even as it can be and the top is occasionally a little hooty. King spoils his big aria that brings down the Act 1 curtain (well, they didn't actually use curtains in Handel's time) by taking it too fast; it needs more weight than he allows, and Bowman is forced to snatch at the music. He is at his best here in the two great mournful arias at the opening of Act 3, the finest part of the opera.

The secondary roles fare better. Jennifer Smith brings plenty of life and a real sense of how to shape a Handelian line to the music of the villain of the piece, Gismonda; villain or no, Handel was obviously sympathetic to her love of her son as expressed in the beautiful aria near the beginning of Act 2, "Vieni, o figlio!", and her defiant G minor outburst in Act 3 goes splendidly too. Catherine Denley rises to the part of Matilda with some shapely and expressive singing; and Dominique Visse's even, controlled countertenor shines in Adelberto's music – he does the first aria in an appropriately languid style, the second with tremendous attack and vitality, though his Act 3 aria is vitiated by a want of rhythmic drive in the direction. Michael George, too, provides shapely and rhythmic singing and clarity of articulation in the bass part of Emireno.

Taken all round, the cast here is marginally preferable to McGegan's; the men are stronger, the women perhaps slightly weaker. Neither conductor seems fully idiomatic; McGegan is the more dramatic but his set is the more flawed by sins of commission than King's is by those of omission. The orchestra here are rather modest in size, much smaller than Handel himself used, but is over-resonantly recorded in what sounds like a church acoustic.

Handel Partenope.

Krisztina Laki *sop* Partenope
René Jacobs *alto* Arsace
John York Skinner *alto* Armindo
Stephen Varcoe *bar* Ormonte

Helga Müller-Molinari *mez* Rosmira
Martyn Hill *ten* Emilio
La Petite Bande / Sigiswald Kuijken.
Deutsche Harmonia Mundi Editio Classica Ⓜ Ⓘ GD77109 (three discs: 192 minutes: ADD). 🖉
Notes, text and translation included. Recorded 1979.

This recording of *Partenope* was first issued in 1979 and briefly reissued on CD in 1988 by EMI before appearing once more on this latest reissue. Neither the success of *The Beggar's Opera* nor the collapse of the Royal Academy in 1728 deflected Handel from the pursuance of his operatic career. In 1729 he rented the King's Theatre in the Haymarket and in partnership with Heidegger began a second 'new Academy' on a subscription basis. He presented two new operas for the 1729-30 season; one of them was *Lotario*, the other *Partenope*, which was first performed on February 24th, 1730.

Though indifferently received *Partenope* is an enchanting opera whose libretto, by Silvio Stampiglio, has a rich vein of comic irony running through it. The plot, as in so many Italian operas of the period, centres round a woman disguising herself as a man; but here the conventions and several of the characters typifying heroic opera are held in ridicule, allowing Handel to respond with music which is beguiling, light-hearted and subtly imbued with parody. Among the many lovely arias are "Dimmi pietoso Ciel" and Partenope's "Io ti levo", both from Act 1, "Ma quai note" and a captivating quartet, "Non è incanto", from Act 3, momentarily recalling the "Quia fecit" from Bach's *Magnificat*.

The cast is a strong one. Krisztina Laki makes a charming Partenope – hers is the only soprano role in the opera – and there are dazzling contributions from Helga Müller-Molinari as Rosmira who, in pursuit of Arsace, assumes male disguise (Eurimenes) almost to the end of the opera. The orchestra of La Petite Bande is hardly less impressive in its sympathetic playing and graceful gestures; its accompaniment of Partenope's arias "Cara Mura" (Act 2) and the beautiful "Voglio amara" (Act 2) are just two particularly affecting instances of it. Recorded sound is clear and presentation informative with full texts provided.

Handel Poro, Re dell'Indie.
Gloria Banditelli *contr* Poro
Rossana Bertini *sop* Cleofide
Bernarda Fink *contr* Erissena
Gérard Lesne *alto* Gandarte
Sandro Naglia *ten* Alessandro il Grande
Roberto Abbondanza *bar* Timagene
L'Europa Galante / Fabio Biondi.
Opus 111 Ⓔ Ⓘ OPS30-113/5 (three discs: 167 minutes: DDD). 🖉 Notes, text and translation included. Recorded 1994.

Poro is the second, and certainly the best, of the three Handel operas based on texts by the young Metastasio – suitably doctored, of course, for English audiences, with shortened recitatives and generally a greater focus on the music than on the elegant Italian verse as the prime expressive force. It was a fair success and was twice revived. Metastasio's *Alessandro nell'Indie*, influenced by Racine, was to become one of the most popular of his librettos (Handel was the second to set it, within months of the Vinci original; the third was Hasse, whose very different version, *Cleofide*, is available on CD from Capriccio). Handel's setting still, however, explores the different kinds of heroic virtue of Alexander the Great, the conquering but unfailingly magnanimous invader of India, and the local king Poro, proud and unswervingly regal in defeat and also driven by his fierce love for Cleofide (whom Alessandro also admires, to the point of inviting marriage). Of course, everyone wins in the end, even the traitorous general Timagene, who repents and is duly forgiven; both loving couples are allowed to marry and Alessandro goes off to fresh conquests of another kind.

Handel had a strong cast, on the whole, for his première, at the beginning of 1731: the great castrato Senesino had now come back, to sing Poro, with Strada as Cleofide and (exceptionally) a tenor, Fabri, as Alessandro; there were two good contraltos, Bertolli and Merighi, and the only weakness was the bass, to whom Handel allowed only recitative (later, for a revival with a better singer, he put in some arias borrowed from other operas). Until near the end of Act 1, one would rate it as not more than a bit above average in quality among Handel's operas; then it rises, as the drama thickens, to a fine Act 2 and an Act 3 with some very distinguished music.

Poro has been recorded before, a quite terrible Eterna (East German) set of the 1950s, gloomy, slow and earnest, reflecting the Hallé performances on which it was based. This Opus 111 set is certainly one that lovers of Handel will want to buy, even though there are a few reservations. The cast is headed by that very capable musician Gloria Banditelli in the title-role, with confident manner and clear, disciplined singing – very expressively sustained in the slow Act 1 aria, "Se possono tanto", fiery in the passagework, but somewhat undermined by the direction (of which more later) in the grandly mournful F minor final aria in which he thinks himself betrayed by Cleofide. The relationship between these two is central to the opera: in Act 1 they swear mutual fidelity, but Poro is later tortured by her apparent interest in Alexander and that Act ends with a duet in which they tauntingly fling each other's vows in their faces, making a new duet out of two arias already heard – a brilliant and thrilling stroke of musical drama (on Metastasio's part as well, one must say, but Handel makes the most of it). Rossana Bertini is not without charm in Cleofide's music, and she sings it with care and accuracy, but the tone is oddly constricted and this seems to narrow the whole scope of the performance: her expression of profound desolation in the aria at the end of Act 2 (A minor, with a finely detailed solo violin obbligato) seems shallow, and earlier in that act the mood of "Digli, che son fedele" is surely misjudged and its force lost.

Alessandro's music is sung, on the whole rather blandly, by Sandro Naglia, with a smooth, slightly grainy tenor of modest weight, but fluent enough and with a touch here and there of rather self-conscious eloquence. The vigorous manner and demanding passagework of his final, triumphant aria, however, defeat him. An Alexander the Great ought really to be more strongly projected and emerge larger. The role of Poro's sister Erissena is neatly and precisely sung in a lightish mezzo voice by Bernarda Fink; it is a pity that her charming "Son confusa pastorella", a show-stopper in Handel's day which ought to be now too, is done so slowly as to forfeit much of its gentle pastoral character. It is difficult to see the logic of engaging a countertenor to sing a part composed for a contralto, but Gérard Lesne is certainly a useful recruit to the limited number of good countertenors, clear and light with firm tone and excellent articulation.

Fabio Biondi is clearly a conductor who knows what he wants, but one is not always convinced that this is the same as what Handel wants. Tempos, with only a few exceptions, are generally well judged. But Biondi is not well attuned to the Handelian idiom and seems reluctant to let the music speak for itself. One wishes for more functional shape to the bass line. He often accents notes in a curiously arbitrary way. Listen for example to Poro's F minor aria in Act 3. Here the accompaniment, with no dynamic markings, moves in pairs of steady crotchets, the second usually an octave below the first (a favourite Handel device): by making the general level *piano* with an occasional *fortissimo*, the sombre breadth of the utterance is destroyed and false emphases introduced. The effect, here and elsewhere, is often uncomfortably choppy with many 'pecked' notes from the strings. Sometimes Biondi alters Handel's phrasing without reason: put slurs into regular quavers and you cannot but adjust their sense. He also has a rather romantic mannerism of pausing before cadences (and sometimes in full flow too). The changes he permits in the arias often involve a simple rewriting which is in no true sense embellishment and several times makes nonsense of Handel's elaborate imitative writing. Alexander's arias are sometimes simpler in the *da capo* than first time round.

One doesn't want to be too hard on a set that has many fine things in it; but it might so easily have been much better! Still, it's a fine opera, now available in complete form with a very capable cast, decently recorded and with a good note by Ivan Alexandre and full libretto, and all admirers of Handel will surely want it.

Handel Radamisto.

Ralf Popken *alto* Radamisto
Juliana Gondek *sop* Zenobia
Lisa Saffer *sop* Polissena
Dana Hanchard *sop* Tigrane
Monika Frimmer *sop* Fraarte
Michael Dean *bass-bar* Tiridate
Nicolas Cavallier *bass* Farasmane
Freiburg Baroque Orchestra / Nicholas McGegan *hpd*.
Harmonia Mundi Ⓟ Ⓞ HMU90 7111/3 (three discs: 190 minutes: DDD). 🖉 Notes, text and translation included. Recorded 1993.

Radamisto was Handel's first opera for the Royal Academy of Music, the company set up in 1719 under his musical directorship to put London opera on a secure basis (as optimistic a notion then as now). It had its première in the spring of 1720 and Handel revived it the following winter, in a heavily revised and substantially improved version, which provides the basis of the text used here. Senesino, the great alto castrato who created most of his heroic roles, made his Handelian début in the name part, originally sung by a soprano, Durastanti, who now moved over to become the heroine, Zenobia; while the fine bass Boschi took on the part of the villainous Tiridate, previously assigned to a tenor (the Scot Alexander Gordon, chiefly remembered for his threat to jump on the harpsichord – encouraged by Handel: "I will advertise it ... more people will come to see you jump than to hear you sing").

In modern times *Radamisto* has often been heard in Germany, but only twice, both times by the lamented Handel Opera Society, in England. It is a tale of dynastic doings in post-classical Thrace, with King Tiridate of Armenia forsaking his wife Polissena because he becomes enamoured of Zenobia, Radamisto's queen; Radamisto and Zenobia go through various trials, but "after various Accidents, it comes to pass, that he recovers both Her and his Kingdom". It is easy enough to poke fun at plots such as these, but the score of *Radamisto*, one of Handel's richest, is its justification. Handel certainly knew how to 'wow' the London audiences on these big occasions. In the Second Act particularly, one arresting number follows another; Radamisto's "Ombra cara", which has been claimed (not without justice) as the finest aria Handel ever wrote, falls early in the act, and towards the end there is a wonderful sequence, chiefly of minor-key numbers, as the emotional tensions mount, culminating in a duet for the apparently doomed lovers. The Third Act, although dramatically less powerful, is also full of colourful and characterful music, including a noble quartet which Handel clearly remembered 30 years later when composing *Jephtha* (here Tiridate, there Jephtha, refuses three people's pleas for mercy, to similar music).

This performance is the best by far we have had from Nicholas McGegan. It begins a shade unpromisingly, with a light, rather hurried account of the overture, and sometimes in Act 1 you might feel McGegan is underplaying the music – Tiridate's first aria is somehow energetic but not vigorous, Zenobia's diminished by too brisk a tempo and snatched notes from the strings. But once Act 2 begins, with a slow aria for Zenobia that foreshadows "Ombra mai fù" (*Adagio*, not *Largo*), we are on a new level of intensity, and McGegan clearly recognizes that and rises to it. There are a few perfunctory endings, and one or two places where violent emotion is too graphically represented; but any Handelian will relish the constantly alert playing, the strong dramatic pacing and the weight given to the orchestral textures (*Radamisto* is unusually resourceful in its scoring). The result is as compelling as any Handel opera performance on record. McGegan takes the recitative a little slower than he generally does, which may be explained by the fact that this performance originated at the Göttingen Festival – by German standards in Handelian recitative this is decidedly on the speedy side.

He has the benefit of an excellent cast. The Senesino role is taken by a countertenor, Ralf Popken, very secure, clean and resonant in tone and sensitive in phrasing, just occasionally a little plummy-sounding as if the voice is produced too far back. The tessitura isn't quite ideal for a Senesino part: his voice lies higher and some of the low-lying passages don't quite get full value, but the top notes are superb (he goes up to G with evidently something to spare). "Ombra cara" is done with great feeling and the ornamentation in the *da capo* enhances the expression. Juliana Gondek, with her full and ringing soprano, makes much of Zenobia's music, especially the passionate grief she is most called upon to express (the *siciliano,* "Fatemi, oh cieli, almen", for example, and the 'mock-*Largo*', are movingly done; perhaps finest of all is her climactic aria in Act 3, with cello obbligato, which combines grief and furious outburst). Lisa Saffer's Polissena is attractively light-toned but often dramatic and always musically sung, and the very fluent and spirited Tigrane of Dana Hanchard (originally for a soprano, then given to a castrato) is also a delight, with *fioritura* that is a model of clarity and precision. The two delightful arias left for Fraarte, a role reduced by Handel in the revisions, are happily done by Monika Frimmer. Both the lower voices, Nicolas Cavallier's warm Farasmane and Michael Dean's more vigorous Tiridate, are strong and secure and in fact, in the recording, seem a shade larger than life. The playing of the Freiburg orchestra is first-rate, though one might have wished for a rather larger body of strings.

Handel Riccardo Primo, Rè d'Inghilterra.

Sara Mingardo *contr* Riccardo Primo
Sandrine Piau *sop* Costanza
Olivier Lallouette *bass* Berardo
Roberto Scaltriti *bar* Isacio
Claire Brua *sop* Pulcheria
Pascal Bertin *alto* Oronte
Les Talens Lyriques / Christophe Rousset.
L'Oiseau-Lyre Ⓔ Ⓓ 452 201-2OHO3 (three discs: 197 minutes: DDD). 🖉 Notes, text and translation included. Recorded 1995.

This is the world première release of the opening opera of the Royal Academy season for 1727-8. Rescue operas are not what one is used to associating with Handel, yet that, in a sense, is what this is. Costanza, a princess of Navarre, has been shipwrecked on Cyprus, where she now awaits the arrival of her betrothed, Richard the Lionheart – yes, the same). The island's tyrannical ruler, Isacio, fancies her for himself, however, and spends the entire opera trying to prevent the intended union from going ahead, first by sending Riccardo his daughter Pulcheria instead, and, when that has failed, thanks to Pulcheria's brave entreaties, by imprisoning Costanza and declaring war. Only with his final defeat by Riccardo's army, aided by Pulcheria's own fiancé Oronte, do things finally turn out happily.

As plots go this is not a great one and it certainly has problems in sustaining itself, even with a conspicuously short First Act. There is some fairly pointless stuff at the beginning involving assumed identities, and the whole business is effectively wrapped up by the end of Act 2, so that Act 3 is only made possible by Isacio going back on his word and abducting Costanza, thereby starting everything up again. Furthermore, Riccardo and Costanza have never met before, and while the libretto makes it clear that an unimpeachable sense of honour is what drives the English king, we are nevertheless asked to believe that their love is already a deep and unbreakable one. Little evidence is given why this should be: Riccardo himself is a standard *opera seria* hero, a stern but valorous military leader who wins his battles yet is magnanimous in victory; while Costanza seems a hopeless wet who mopes around waiting for other people to sort things out for her. Of greater interest are the more proactive figures of Pulcheria, who functions as a go-between for the two camps, and Isacio, a typically complex Handelian villain whose actions (prompted by desire for Costanza) are understood if not exactly condoned. Ultimately though, these characters hold little fascination, though they are at least consistent, and are drawn with all Handel's usual skill.

On the other hand, you can never expect to listen to over three hours of this composer's work without hearing enjoyable music of extremely high quality, and in that respect few listeners will be disappointed here. The performance, too, has many things in its favour. When the opera was written, Handel and his librettists were having to wrestle with the problem of accommodating the two star sopranos – Cuzzoni and Bordoni – in distinct but equal roles. Cuzzoni is known to have had a simple but affecting voice, which presumably explains why she laments so much, whilst Bordoni had a strong sound and was thus perhaps better suited to the no-nonsense Pulcheria. Christophe Rousset's casting takes account of this most effectively: as Costanza, Sandrine Piau mixes virtuosity with vocal beauty, while Claire Brua's no less virtuosic Pulcheria has a darker, more firmly mezzo-like sound. The part of Riccardo himself was written for the great alto castrato Senesino, and Rousset follows recent trends in allocating the part to a mezzo-soprano with a background in nineteenth-century opera. Like Jennifer Larmore in René Jacobs's *Giulio Cesare* (reviewed above), Sara Mingardo is a complete success, showing great vocal dexterity and strength in the low-lying passagework that was Senesino's trademark, and communicating all that one could wish for in the character of Riccardo. This Roberto Scaltriti, the Isacio, is not noted for Handel singing either, but his experience in Verdi and Puccini also pays dividends in his loudly villainous arias and recitatives. Olivier Lallouette, as Costanza's guardian Berardo, and Pascal Bertin, as Oronte, have less to get their teeth into, but both acquit themselves well. This is not a starry cast, but it is well chosen and not one of its members lacks the ability to deal with Handel's thrilling vocal demands.

The instrumentalists of Les Talens Lyriques, here making their L'Oiseau-Lyre début, are also well up to the job. The acoustic of the refectory at the Royal Abbey at Fontevraud (where Richard I has one of his three tombs) is a dry one, a little closed in and thus appropriately reminiscent of a theatre, though by the same token the sound is not always a smooth one. Rousset's direction is sure and idiomatic without being quite as on the ball dramatically as that of a Christie, a McGegan or a Gardiner. Many of the recitatives are well acted at a local level, but had a staged production preceded this recording, instead of a single concert performance, there might have been more dramatic flow and coherence than there is here. There is also a feeling that some of the silences between items were a bit long, but many may not agree. In general, though, this is an extremely well-sung performance of a Handel opera that few people can have heard; for that we should be pleased, although this is not Handel at his best.

Handel Serse.

Judith Malafronte *mez* Serse
Jennifer Smith *sop* Romilda
Brian Asawa *alto* Arsamene
Susan Bickley *mez* Amastre
Lisa Milne *sop* Atalanta
Dean Ely *bar* Ariodate
David Thomas *bass* Elviro
Hanover Band and Chorus / Nicholas McGegan.
Conifer Classics Ⓟ Ⓒ 75605 51312-2 (three discs: 177 minutes: DDD). 🖊 Notes, text and translation included. Recorded 1997.

Handel's *Serse* has proved to be one of the most popular of his operas over recent years – certainly in England, where the witty production by Nicholas Hytner for the ENO, put on in the tercentenary year of 1985, still continues to draw full houses. Wit may not be a part of most people's image of Handel's operas, and rightly: but from time to time, and especially when he was using a libretto of Venetian origins, Handel and his London librettists permitted themselves touches of ironic humour and sometimes rather more than that – *Serse* has one truly comic character, a servant, and King Xerxes himself is in some degree made a figure of fun by his unruly amorous whims. But as in all the best comedy, the situations give rise to serious emotion too, and in Act 2 of *Serse*, when events provoke first Xerxes, then Romilda (whom he thinks he loves) and then Amastre (who loves him) into forceful expressions of passion, touchingly followed by a gentle aria from Xerxes's brother Arsamene (Romilda's true lover), the music springs into real life and enters more than a purely entertaining plane. Otherwise, however, it is inclined to be elegant, thin-textured, short-breathed: quite unlike the great heroic operas of the Royal Academy period or even the finest of the works of the early or middle 1730s. *Serse* dates from 1738, just after the time of the Nobility Opera rivalries; Handel composed only two more operas before turning his back finally on the form.

This recording is welcome, and although the cast here isn't obviously starry it is evenly accomplished and the performance holds together very well under Nicholas McGegan's assured direction. His own personal touch is unmistakable – the light textures, the quickish tempos, the spruce rhythms, the dapper cadences, the generally faintly ironic tone – and it works well for this opera, perhaps better than it does for a big heroic piece. Sometimes you wish for a little more weight, and the slurring patterns McGegan often applies in the violin ritornellos do not always seem justified; but in general the accompaniment textures are sympathetically handled. Judith Malafronte starts off with a very beautiful account of "Ombra mai fu", smooth, focused in tone, delicately phrased and shaped, and not without hints of vibrato, and she finds a good swagger for Xerxes's second aria. Best of all is the serious, C minor aria in Act 2, "Il core spera e teme", done with some depth of expression. This, of course, was originally a castrato part; while the role of Xerxes's brother Arsamene was originally composed for a woman but is sung here by a countertenor – which would be regrettable if it weren't so well done, by Brian Asawa who has a steady, warm, slightly throaty tone and a capacity for refined shading. His pathetic F minor aria in Act 2 is done with much intensity, and his ensuing fast one too is very exact and indeed elegant. Romilda is sung in assured style by Jennifer Smith, with a good ring to her voice; she too is at her best in the dramatic music in Act 2. Lisa Milne's Atalanta catches neatly the rather frivolous character of the *seconda donna*, heard at her best in the brilliant "Un cenno leggiadretto" which ends Act 1 – it is thrown off very spiritedly, with wit and abandon (and rather abrupt phrase-endings). The Amastre is Susan Bickley, clean, careful and direct singing, but with ample power in her F sharp minor outburst in Act 2. Dean Ely brings due weight and athleticism to the bass part of Ariodate; Elviro is spiritedly done by David Thomas.

This set comfortably outclasses the Malgoire recording of 1979 in both its direction and its singing and must surely be the choice for anyone wanting a stylish version of this lively and appealing work.

Handel Serse (ed Mackerras and N. Davies; sung in English).
Ann Murray *mez* Serse
Valerie Masterson *sop* Romilda
Christopher Robson *alto* Arsamene
Jean Rigby *mez* Amastre
Lesley Garrett *sop* Atalanta
Rodney McCann *bass* Ariodate
Christopher Booth-Jones *bar* Elviro
English National Opera Chorus and Orchestra / Sir Charles Mackerras.
Video Director: **John Michael Phillips.** *Stage Director:* **Nicholas Hytner.**
PolyGram RM Collection ℗ 💿💿 079 293-3. Recorded at a performance in the London Coliseum in 1988.

As a performance of a Handel opera, this is also near-perfect, justifying it as a winner of the Laurence Olivier Opera Award. As a piece it represents Handel at the peak of his achievement. It is a comic opera with more than an underlay of emotional seriousness where the passions of the principals are concerned – the central character, King Xerxes, lover of a plane tree (the so-called Largo, so often recorded on its own, is a paean to the tree at the beginning of the work) and a bridge over the Hellespont, here represented in miniature. As outlined in the review above, there is plenty of scope for deception, scheming and misunderstanding, although all ends happily. Under the musical direction of such an experienced Handelian as Sir Charles Mackerras, the score is lovingly sung and played, and the members of the original cast are without exception perfect in their roles. Ann Murray provides an authoritative portrait of the preening, self-willed monarch, her singing in the bravura class. Masterson projects Romilda's many feelings with clear, steady tone and flexible line, and she acts superbly. Countertenor Christopher Robson makes Arsamene into a man of many emotions, all keenly expressed. As Atalanta, Lesley Garrett is all wheedling charm. Jean Rigby portrays the faithful, distressed Amastre in firm alto tones. McCann's portrayal of Ariodate is properly ridiculous.

All are directed by Hytner with loving care within a highly ingenious framework, featuring deckchairs, a statue of the composer and a vista of ancient Persepolis, in the décor of David Fielding. The translation, Hytner's own, is impeccable and the performance draws much applause from the audience. We are, in fact, sharing a most enjoyable evening at the London Coliseum. The picture and sound quality are excellent.

Johann Hasse   German 1699-1783

Hasse Piramo e Tisbe.
Barbara Schlick *sop* Piramo
Suzanne Gari *sop* Tisbe
Michel Lecocq *ten* Father
Capella Clementina / Helmut Müller-Brühl.
Koch Schwann ℗ ① 310882 (two discs: 109 minutes: DDD). 📁 Recorded 1984.

When Hasse (who had been a pupil of Alessandro Scarlatti) wrote *Piramo e Tisbe* in 1768, he already had over 70 stage works to his credit and had long been the most famous opera composer in Europe, with a whole string of successes in his various sojourns in Dresden, Vienna and Venice. So when he called this "one of the best things I have ever done ... with this work I shall round off my theatrical career" (in fact he didn't, but wrote one more opera), his words deserve to be taken seriously. This two-act *intermezzo tragico* – on the pattern of *opera seria* but enriched by characterization and an advanced technique of continuity – is indeed an outstandingly fine work, of which we are fortunate to have here a most rewarding performance and recording.

The story (from *Ovid*) is familiar from its parody in Shakespeare's *A Midsummer Night's Dream*, though besides the two ill-starred lovers there is a part for Thisbe's father, who because of an old feud (like Capulet in *Romeo and Juliet*) is bitterly opposed to Pyramus, and who at the end, discovering that they have both (in fatal misunderstandings) taken their own lives, also stabs himself, believing himself to be responsible. In Hasse's setting a number of features at once capture the attention – the vigour of his melodic invention, the richness of the harmony, the very prominent role allotted to the orchestral wind (which includes, besides horns and bassoons, both flutes *and* oboes, who don't merely alternate), the strongly contrasting middle sections of *da capo* arias, the expressive, characterful and dramatic accompanied recitatives, and particularly the fluid continuity, so unlike the closed forms of the older *opera seria*. Here the spirited Overture leads straight into the first aria, thence into an accompanied recitative which in turn is linked with a duet (of great charm); and this kind of approach is constant, arias often being attached to *secco* recitatives which then become accompanied, or to ariosos; Act 2 begins with a sequence lasting nearly 18 minutes, made up of diverse elements.

The role of Pyramus was cast by Hasse as a breeches part (not for a castrato), and it is not always easy to distinguish between the two soprano voices in the regrettable absence of a printed libretto (for which a précis of individual numbers is not an adequate substitute, for example in the first recitative, which lasts four minutes). Both ladies, however, are admirable. The purity of Barbara Schlick's voice is well known, and her breath control in her first aria is awesome: she has a particularly delightful aria in Act 1 when, aided by wind soloists, Pyramus dreams of a happy existence for the pair far from the pressures of their present life. Suzanne Gari, too, has a seductive tone (a trifle weak in the low notes of a very wide-compass part) and is adept at the baroque style: she has a fine aria, "Perderò l'amato bene", in which Thisbe tearfully promises her father to give up Pyramus if only she is not forced to marry another. Michel Lecocq is not quite their equal in vocal quality: he has splendidly clear enunciation, but in Act 1 does not convey the necessary paternal sternness: only at the end of Act 2, when he reappears, does he make the father's initial fury and then remorse convincing. The Capella Clementina give first-rate partnership to the singers – their oboes and horns call for special praise – and Müller-Brühl not only seems unerring in his choice of tempos but keeps the work flowing forward with a well-judged sense of its drama. This is a most distinguished issue.

Joseph Haydn
Austrian 1732-1809

Haydn L'anima del filosofo, ossia Orfeo et Euridice.
Uwe Heilmann *ten* Orfeo
Cecilia Bartoli *mez* Euridice, Genio
Ildebrando d'Arcangelo *bass* Creonte
Andrea Silvestrelli *bass* Pluto
Angela Kazimierczuk *sop* Baccante
Roberto Scaltriti *bar* First Chorus
Jose Fardilha *bass* Second Chorus
Colin Campbell *bar* Third Chorus
James Oxley *ten* Fourth Chorus
Chorus and Orchestra of the Academy of Ancient Music / Christopher Hogwood.
L'Oiseau-Lyre Ⓔ ① 452 668-2OHO2 (two discs: 124 minutes: DDD). ✍ Notes, text and translation included. Recorded 1996.

When Haydn was finally released from his duties at Esterházy by the death of Prince Nicolaus in 1790, he arrived in Vienna where he met Salomon who immediately poached him for England with a commission which included the "London" Symphonies – and an opera. Political and theatrical intrigues (*plus ça change*) prevented *L'anima del filosofo* from being staged, and it was not until 1951 in Florence that Haydn's Orpheus opera ever confronted the greasepaint. It was recorded a year later by the Vienna State Opera (Haydn Society), and then not again until 1992, when Leopold Hager and his Munich forces took it on. After such a long wait, it was all the more disappointing when, despite a promising cast led by Robert Swenson and Helen Donath, a 1995 release (on Orfeo) asked so few questions of Haydn's unique approach to the Orpheus myth, offering an affectionate but anodyne reading of a vividly distinctive score.

At last, we have a truly searching performance. Christopher Hogwood builds his band on the model of those prevalent in late-eighteenth-century London theatres. Not only does his phrasing and articulation discover no end of both witty and poignant nuances which Hager's blander, more *svelte* direction ignores, but the grave austerity of the string playing, and the plangency of the early woodwind instruments are eloquent advocates of an opera whose uncompromisingly tragic ending (even the seductive Bacchantes perish) owes more to Ovid and Milton than to operatic tradition.

Hogwood also remembers that Haydn was writing for a Handelian London choral tradition: his chorus, be they cast as Cupids, Shades or Furies, have robust presence (in Munich they could be in an adjacent studio), and sculpt their lines with firm muscle. Cecilia Bartoli takes the role of Euridice. In her very first aria, "Filomena abbandonata", she understands and eagerly re-creates the type of coloratura writing which simultaneously fleshes out the central nightingale simile and incarnates the single word "crudeltà". Her unmistakable, melting half-voice comes into its own as emotion first clouds reason, only to create the fatal emotional extremes to which she gives voice so thrillingly.

Not for nothing is this *Orfeo ed Euridice* first called *L'anima del filosofo*. Its typically eighteenth-century aspect and temper is focused in Bartoli's *alter ego*, Genio, the sibyl who is Orfeo's own second self and spiritual guide. She offers, with disarming simplicity, the "herb of philosophy" and reason, then gives feisty and unfaltering coloratura urging to constancy and valour. Uwe Heilmann is just the tenor of rare agility and wide vocal range vital for this particular Orfeo. A more spacious tone than Swenson's gives room for *soave accenti* as well as heroism; though in slower, more sustained passages one craves a leaner approach.

The minor parts are more strongly profiled than in Hager's recording: Ildebrando d'Arcangelo is a stern, noble Creonte, Andrea Silvestrelli a fearsome, stentorian Pluto – and there's even a convincing *strepito ostile* off-stage as Euridice's abduction is attempted in Act 2. Beyond the detail, it is above all the unique poignancy of the musical drama at the heart of this strange, grave *Orfeo* which Hogwood discovers, not before time, and reveals with such sympathetic and compelling imaginative insight.

Haydn Esterházy opera cycle.
Various artists. Lausanne Chamber Orchestra / Antál Dorati.
Philips Ⓟ Ⓓ 438 167-2PH20 (20 discs, also available separately: 19 hours 51 minutes: ADD). Notes, texts and translations included.

Haydn L'infedeltà delusa.
Edith Mathis *sop* Vespina
Barbara Hendricks *sop* Sandrina
Claes Hakon Ahnsjö *ten* Nencio
Aldo Baldin *ten* Filippo
Michael Devlin *bass-bar* Nanni.
Philips Ⓟ Ⓓ 432 413-2PH2 (two discs: 111 minutes). Recorded 1980.

Haydn L'incontro improvviso.
Claes Hakon Ahnsjö *ten* Ali
Linda Zoghby *sop* Rezia
Margaret Marshall *sop* Balkis
Della Jones *mez* Dardane
Domenico Trimarchi *bar* Osmin
Benjamin Luxon *bar* Calandro
Jonathan Prescott *bass* Sultan, Dervish
James Hooper *bar* Official, Dervish
Nicolas Scarpinati *bass* Dervish

Haydn Arias – Ah, tu non senti ... Qual destra omicidia. Se tu mi sprezzi. Tergi i vezzosi rai.
La Circe – Lavatevi presto.
Claes Hakon Ahnsjö *ten*
Aldo Baldin *ten*
Michael Devlin *bass*.
Philips Ⓟ Ⓓ 432 416-2PH3 (three discs: 188 minutes). Recorded 1979.

Haydn Il mondo della luna.
Domenico Trimarchi *bar* Buonafede
Luigi Alva *ten* Ecclitico
Frederica von Stade *mez* Lisetta
Arleen Auger *sop* Flaminia
Lucia Valentini-Terrani *mez* Ernesto
Anthony Rolfe Johnson *ten* Cecco
Suisse Romande Radio Chorus

Haydn Arias – Vada adagio, signorina, HobXXIV*b*/12. Infelice sventurata, HobXXIV*b*/15.
Miseri noi! misera patria, HobXXIV*a*/7. Son pietosa, son bonina, HobXXXII/*1b*. D'una sposa meschinella, HobXXIV*b*/2. Sono Alcina e sono ancora, HobXXIV*b*/9. Che vive amante, HobXXIV*b*/13. Solo e pensoso, HobXXIV*b*/20.
Edith Mathis *sop*
Lausanne Chamber Orchestra / Armin Jordan.
Philips Ⓟ Ⓓ 432 420-2PH3 (three discs: 212 minutes). Recorded 1977.

Haydn La vera costanza.
Jessye Norman *sop* Rosina
Helen Donath *sop* Lisetta
Claes Hakon Ahnsjö *ten* Count Errico

Wladimiro Ganzarolli *bar* Villotto
Domenico Trimarchi *bar* Masino
Kari Lövaas *sop* Baroness Irene
Anthony Rolfe Johnson *ten* Marquis Ernesto.
Philips Ⓕ Ⓛ 432 424-2PH2 (two discs: 123 minutes). Recorded 1976.

Haydn L'isola disabitata.
Norma Lerer *sop* Costanza
Linda Zoghby *sop* Silvia
Luigi Alva *ten* Gernando
Renato Bruson *bar* Enrico.
Philips Ⓕ Ⓛ 432 427-2PH2 (two discs: 88 minutes). Recorded 1977.

Haydn La fedeltà premiata.
Lucia Valentini-Terrani *mez* Celia
Tonny Landy *ten* Fileno
Frederica von Stade *mez* Amaranta
Alan Titus *bar* Perrucchetto
Ileana Cotrubas *sop* Nerina
Luigi Alva *ten* Lindoro
Maurizio Mazzieri *bass* Melibeo
Kari Lövaas *sop* Diana
Suisse Romande Radio Chorus
Philips Ⓕ Ⓛ 432 430-2PH3 (three discs: 162 minutes). Recorded 1975.

Haydn Orlando Paladino.
Arleen Auger *sop* Angelica
Elly Ameling *sop* Eurilla
Gwendoline Killebrew *mez* Alcina
George Shirley *ten* Orlando
Claes Hakon Ahnsjö *ten* Medoro
Benjamin Luxon *bar* Rodomonte
Domenico Trimarchi *bar* Pasquale
Maurizio Mazzieri *bass* Caronte
Gabor Carelli *ten* Licone.
Philips Ⓕ Ⓛ 432 434-2PH3 (three discs: 167 minutes). Recorded 1976.

Haydn Armida.
Jessye Norman *sop* Armida
Claes Hakon Ahnsjö *ten* Rinaldo
Norma Burrowes *sop* Zelmira
Samuel Ramey *bass* Idreno
Robin Leggate *ten* Ubaldo
Anthony Rolfe Johnson *ten* Clotarco.
Philips Ⓕ Ⓛ 432 438-2PH2 (two discs: 140 minutes). Recorded 1978.

These are reissues of the splendid late-1970s initiative by Dorati, the European Broadcasting Union and Philips – a pioneering achievement of huge magnitude. All these eight operas were written in a single decade from 1773 (when Haydn was also busy revising, preparing and directing for Esterházy a mass of operas by other composers): they range from farce to *opera seria*. If the just criticism is made that, for the most part (though not entirely) characterization is superficial and dramatic structure slack, blame should fall on the conventional (when not downright silly) plots: Haydn did not have Mozart's huge advantage of a da Ponte as librettist, and comparison between the two composers fails to take into account that most of Haydn's operas were written before Mozart's first masterpiece, *Idomeneo*. On the other hand, what Haydn did provide, in plenty, were superb opportunities for first-class singers and a great strength of this batch is the very high standard of performance of music that is not only immensely demanding of the artists but extremely attractive to the listener. Another strength is the alert orchestral playing; and special praise must go to the exemplary presentation.

L'infedeltà delusa, the earliest of these eight operas and, by tradition, the one which occasioned Maria Theresa's famous tribute, "If I want to hear good opera I go to Esterházy", was legitimately labelled "endearing if not profound" by its original *Gramophone* reviewer, Stanley Sadie. The Overture begins brightly and breezily, but a slower section leads directly into a fine vocal quartet, which in turn is interrupted by a scene for the four characters – an anything but conventional opening to an opera. Highlights of the work are the finales to the acts (this is the only two-act opera apart from *L'isola disabitata*) and a vengeance duet in Act 1. Vocal honours are taken by Mathis, who as the vivacious Vespina (a forerunner by 17 years of Mozart's Despina) does not overdo caricature when adopting various disguises (including that of a notary) to further her intrigues to capture the man she wants: Hendricks, fluent in ornate passages, does not avoid some shrillness.

That work deals with peasant folk; *L'incontro improvviso* (on a plot previously used by Gluck) is a comic abduction opera exotically set in Turkey, though unlike Mozart's *Entführung* six years later it is the lady who is the chief engineer of her escape. There is a lot of very funny comedy – a gibberish begging scene and a patter-song in praise of the dervish life (Trimarchi on boisterous form, as he is in all the comedy parts he takes in these operas, though Luxon here, as his foil, is equally good) – but Haydn also lavishes some wonderful music on the serious characters. The heroine has a big bravura showpiece in Act 2 that became famous in the eighteenth century (Zoghby is impressive in this, but not so exact in her intonation in a florid Act 1 aria as her lover, Ahnsjö, who has a number of plums, the most spectacular of which is a martial aria with trumpets and drums in which he negotiates huge leaps and a heroic top D; Della Jones also shows great agility; and Marshall's clean *fioriture* in two exacting arias are delicious. But the gem of the work is the women's trio (with two cors anglais adding colour to the orchestra) in Act 1, touching heights of Mozartian sublimity. A virtuoso aria for Devlin from *Acide e Galatea* is included in a supplement to this disc, and Haydn's comic male trio for Cimarosa's *Circe* is another delight, though goodness knows what it has to do with the Circe story as we know it.

Several composers had set Goldoni's *Il mondo della luna* before Haydn, whose perfunctory Third Act, however, departs from the original. There had been problems with the casting, for the ranges of three roles had been changed more than once, but he obviously thought well of the music, since no fewer than eight numbers were reused (as the first movement of Symphony No. 63, as the *Benedictus* of the Mariazell Mass, and in the flute trios). It is the ladies who are given most of the best music here: Auger in particular shines in her tremendous coloratura, "Ragion nell'alma", but Mathis and von Stade also contribute valuably. Terrani in almost the last of Haydn's castrato roles, however, is less than ideally steady. A special feature of the score is its delicate and unusual instrumentation. This disc comes with an addition which Philips had so far kept from us: eight Haydn arias beautifully sung by Mathis with the orchestra under Armin Jordan. In some, the singer is indignant or cynical about the deception of men, and of these the lovely "D'una sposa meschinella" is of particular interest for its oboe obbligato; but also here are the 1790 dramatic *opera seria* aria *Miseri noi!* about the sack of (presumably) Troy, and the 1798 setting of Petrarch's Sonnet No. 28.

For *La vera costanza*, a remarkably fine *dramma giocosa* (an appellation shared with *Don Giovanni*), Jessye Norman was enlisted as the much-tried fisher-girl Rosina. Too grand a voice? Not really: she brings out the character's essential nobility, is especially fine in her despairing Act 2 accompanied recitative and aria, and holds the too-involved story together. As to other parts, Donath is captivatingly pert, Rolfe Johnson stylishly elegant, Lövaas suitably imperious as the scheming baroness, and Ahnsjö assured in an exceptionally varied and demanding scene in Act 1. But the opera is notable for its ensembles: it indeed begins with a sextet as a small boat battered by a tempest limps in to shore; and the finales to the first two acts are the most developed and complex Haydn had yet written. The one real weakness in the performance lies in the recitatives: as in the other operas too, they have been somewhat cut down (which is no great loss) but are taken too deliberately, and unfortunately Dorati, who insisted on playing the harpsichord continuo himself, is impossibly ponderous and heavy-handed.

That particular problem is avoided in the briefest of these works, with just four characters and a single set, Haydn's only Metastasio opera, *L'isola disabitata*, for all its recitatives are accompanied, not *secco*. Described as an *azione teatrale*, it is entirely serious, without any comic element: the mood is set by the Overture, which in style resembles Haydn's *Sturm und Drang* symphonies. The arias, generally shorter, include no display pieces but depend on their emotional content and are deeper than usual in their description of character – the apparently deserted and embittered woman, the noble lover whose absence was due to his having been captured by pirates, his faithful companion, and an artlessly prattling young girl who has never seen a man. Haydn's use of wind instruments here is very striking, and the final quartet has *concertante* interludes for violin, cello, flute and bassoon, respectively symbolizing the four characters. Zoghby comes out of this well, with neat, graceful singing; Lerer's arias do not offer her warm voice much opportunity for variety of colour; Alva's *fioriture* in "Non turbar" are not as exact as they might have been; and Bruson is charmless.

Haydn's last and most successful comic opera – again with a sizeable serious element – was *La fedeltà premiata*, written for the magnificent new opera-house in Esterházy (the earlier one having been burnt down, with the loss of valuable instruments, scenery and music just before *L'isola disabitata*). Its plot is convoluted and its motivation poor, but Haydn was unusually, and justifiably, proud of its music and of his delineation of character. The cast here is exceptionally starry, with Alva (back on top form), Cotrubas (enchantingly frivolous) and von Stade (pungent and brilliant): only Landy might have brought more meaning to his words, and the pronounced throb in Valentini-Terrani's voice begins to be distracting, though she rises to the occasion in her Act 1 aria that includes a virtuoso solo for a horn. The emotional core of the opera is in two long scenas in Act 2, culminating in a beautiful and heartfelt lament for von Stade: from the constructional point of view the key-sequence in the finales – which Robbins Landon calls "miraculous and intricate" but Stanley Sadie felt to lack logical forward propulsion – are of special interest.

Orlando Paladino enjoyed an immense success during the composer's lifetime, and after a longish run in Esterházy was taken up in some 20 other Central European centres. It is a 'heroic-comic' opera with a score of exceptional brilliance written for an aborted gala occasion, and centres not on the eponymous Orlando – who in fact doesn't appear until 45 minutes in to the opera – but on a queen of Cathay in love with a faint-hearted Saracen who is being furiously pursued by Orlando, himself literally out of his mind for love of her: he is finally deterred not by a blustering king of Barbary but by the intervention of the sorceress Alcina. There are some parallels with *Don Giovanni* five years later (da Ponte certainly saw *Orlando* in Vienna) – an ineffectual lover, and particularly a comic squire not only always hungry and terrified in the presence of the supernatural but given a patter catalogue-song (of places that have witnessed his pretended valour). In this latter role Trimarchi is in his element, not only richly comic, savouring every syllable, but also displaying a ringing high G; Shirley effectively conveys Orlando's dazed infatuation and madness; there is a splendidly powerful sorceress from Killebrew, who is stunning in what must be one of the most sensational entry arias (with braying horns) any character ever had; but it is the heroine who dominates the action, and the melting beauty (and technical virtuosity) of Auger's singing in a whole range of expressive solos is memorable.

What is widely considered Haydn's finest opera is *Armida*, his last for Esterházy, where it received over 50 performances. Like *Orlando*, it was based on a familiar literary classic adopted for opera by numerous other composers: what is surprising is that in his setting Haydn reverted to *opera seria* style, with no *buffo* characters, very few ensembles and extensive *secco* recitatives. Dramatic action is minimal: for three acts Rinaldo lingers under the spell of the enchantress Armida despite all the efforts of fellow-Crusaders to recall him to his mission. The work's static nature, however, casts the emphasis on its musical qualities, and in this regard *Armida* is of the highest standard. The enchantress herself, personified by the redoubtable Jessye Norman, has the widest range of emotions to portray, from tenderness to rage; Ahnsjö as Rinaldo produces a fine legato and very accurate florid passagework (as he does elsewhere in this Haydn series too), but his low register rather lets him down; Ramey shows laudable firmness and flexibility; and Burrowes's fresh, youthful charm is very appealing. The most notable features of the opera are three long, through-composed sequences and imaginative scoring: the scene in the magic forest, where Rinaldo at last, to Armida's fury, breaks free from her spell, is masterly, and in itself is sufficient to compel a revision of the too common neglect of Haydn as an operatic composer.

Peter Heise

Danish 1830-1879

Heise Drot og Marsk.
Poul Elming *ten* King Erik
Bent Norup *bar* Stig Andersen
Eva Johansson *sop* Ingeborg
Kurt Westi *ten* Rane Johnsen
Christian Christiansen *bass* Count Jakob
Aage Haugland *bass* Jens Grand
Ole Hedegaard *ten* Arved Bengtsen
Inge Nielsen *sop* Aase
Ronnie Johansen *bass* Herald
Danish National Radio Choir; Danish National Radio Symphony Orchestra / Michael Schønwandt.
Chandos Ⓟ Ⓓ CHAN9143/5 (three discs: 158 minutes: DDD). Notes, text and translation included. Recorded 1992.

There is a lot to be said for Nordic charm and *Drot og Marsk* ("King and Marshall"), despite its tragic plot, possesses this in abundance. As with so much Scandinavian painting of the period, suffused by that crystal-clear light so redolent of Northern Europe, this opera (completed in 1877) breathes that special air made familiar by the scores of Grieg, Svendsen and Nielsen. Peter Heise is an important figure in Danish music, forming the essential link between Niels Gade and Carl Nielsen (despite the fact that Gade outlived Heise by 11 years). Listening to *Drot og Marsk* one can hear in many passages the manner from which sprang the Nielsen of *Maskarade* and *Springtime in Funen* (though towards the end of Heise's final act there is one brief, astonishing pre-echo of the Hindemith of *Mathis der Maler*). Heise remained relatively free of Wagner's influence, learning rather from Verdi, and his conflation of song-like lyricism within large-scale structures is most impressive. If Heise's music does not possess quite the punch of a Verdi, Wagner or Mussorgsky, it none the less has its moments – quite a few in fact – and unsurprisingly has come to be seen as something of a watershed in Danish opera. Its status is not unakin to that in Finland of Leevi Madetoja's *The Ostrobothnians*.

The plot of *Drot og Marsk* concerns the events leading up to the murder (not assassination; there was no political motive) in 1286 of the Danish king, Erik V Glipping. As with Rimsky-Korsakov's *Mozart and Salieri*, though, the libretto's machinations are fanciful and the central role of the Marshall, Stig Andersen, as main protagonist in the King's murder (allegedly in revenge for his wife's seduction and eventual suicide) is historically without foundation – although he was banished for the crime. Chandos are to be congratulated on their enterprise in producing *Drot og Marsk*, their version superseding that conducted by John Frandsen available ten years ago on Unicorn-Kanchana. The present all-Danish cast all distinguish themselves, particularly Poul Elming and Bent Norup in the title-roles (despite one or two raw patches in Elming's upper range), and conductor Michael Schønwandt proves to be in complete command of this wonderful score.

The death in 1890 of Heise's mentor, Niels Gade, was widely mourned in Denmark but that of Heise himself, at the untimely age of 49, was arguably the greater loss. Not until Nielsen arrived on the scene was a comparable figure active.

Hans Werner Henze

German 1926

Henze Die Bassariden.

Kenneth Riegel *ten* Dionysus, Voice, Stranger
Andreas Schmidt *bar* Pentheus
Michael Burt *bass* Cadmus
Robert Tear *ten* Tiresias
William B. Murray *bass* Captain of the Guard
Karan Armstrong *sop* Agave
Celina Lindsley *sop* Autonoe
Otrun Wenkel *alto* Beroe
Berlin Radio Chamber Choir; South German Radio Choir;
Berlin Radio Symphony Orchestra / Gerd Albrecht.
Koch Schwann Musica Mundi ℗ Ⓓ 314 006 (two discs: 120 minutes: DDD). Notes, text and translations included. Recorded 1986.

This was an excellent present for Henze, who celebrated his 65th birthday in 1991, and was a start, at least, at making available a small part of the operatic output of this outstanding composer. *The Bassarids* dates from 1965 and lies chronologically midway between the Fifth and Sixth Symphonies of 1962 and 1969. It is mentioned in relation to the symphonies because in many ways *The Bassarids* represents the perfect synthesis of Henze's symphonic and operatic writing. He even goes so far as to divide its single act into four distinct movements; a first movement sonata form, a *Scherzo*, an *Adagio* (which also includes an Intermezzo entitled *The Judgement of Calliope*; though unfortunately this is omitted in this recording) and a *passacaglia* finale.

Musically it represents the culmination of Henze's lyrical Italian period, and not only embodies many of the precepts that dominated his musical thought during those years but also looks forward to the revolutionary works initiated by the Sixth Symphony. The plot (after Euripides's play *The Bacchae*) has definite Wagnerian resonances, and one can understand why W. H. Auden and Chester Kalman, the opera's librettists, were so insistent that Henze should attend a performance of *Götterdämmerung* before commencing work on the opera.

The plot of *The Bassarids* is too complex for a full summary here, but concerns the conflict between Pentheus, the newly appointed king of Thebes and the god Dionysus, and Pentheus's subsequent murder at the hands of Dionysus's intoxicated followers (who incidentally include Pentheus's mother Agave) – the Bassarids. Essentially it's a drama of extremes; Dionysus, the god of wine and fertility on the one hand and Pentheus, the ascetic and monotheist on the other. Wine can warm and cheer; it's also capable of making people drunk, causing them to commit atrocious crimes. Conversely, Pentheus's noble aspirations of asceticism and orderliness amount to nothing if carried out with autonomy, dogmatism and an unawareness of the nature of man's duality. The parallels with our time are plain, of course – the bacchanalia of the hippie revolution in the 1960s immediately springs to mind. Henze himself makes an interesting statement when he says "I understand *The Bassarids* better nowadays, and like it much more than when I wrote it – which was at top speed, in less than year, in a spirit of protest and with no properly reasoned basis". At a time when the musical world was either preoccupied with the libertarianism of, say, Stockhausen and Cage, or the order and totalitarianism of the serialists, Henze's balanced approach to tradition and modernity makes a lot of sense.

Written in a spirit of protest or not, *The Bassarids* contains some of Henze's most imaginative and compelling music. This is lyrical music too, and superbly written for the voice as the committed performances from the soloists on this disc so persuasively reveal; those who have doubts about the approachability of contemporary music would do well to explore this opera. The principal roles include some stunning performances headed by Andreas Schmidt, who gives a thoroughly convincing and human portrayal of the arrogant but voyeuristic Pentheus, and Kenneth Riegel as the somewhat sinister Dionysus. Karan Armstrong's lyrical Agave deserves special mention too. Praise must also go to Gerd Albrecht and the Berlin Radio Symphony Orchestra who bring Henze's gloriously colourful orchestration to life. The superb booklet-notes and libretto put the finishing touches to a very commendable issue.

Henze The English Cat.

Richard Berkeley Steele *ten* Lord Puff
Mark Coles *bass* Arnold
Alan Watt *bass* Jones
Ian Platt *bar* Tom
Julian Pike *ten* Peter

Louisa Kennedy *sop* Minette
Gunvor Nilsson *mez* Babette
Donna Bennett *sop* Louise
Carol Court *sop* Miss Crisp
Jacqueline Bremar *sop* Mrs Gomfit
Rachael Hallawell *mez* Lady Toodle
Glyn Davenport *bass-bar* Mr Plunkett
Parnassus Orchestra / Markus Stenz.
Wergo Ⓟ Ⓒ WER6204-2 (two discs: 125 minutes: DDD). Notes, text and translation included.
Recorded 1989.

A gap of some 20 years separates *Boulevard Solitude* from *The English Cat*, but despite definite stylistic differences between the two (musical language here, whilst still eclectic, is leaner and orientated more toward the stylistic element of Italian and German comic opera of the eighteenth century), they comment on the same moral issues of greed, manipulation and money. The libretto is a freely adapted version of Balzac's short story, *Peines de coeur d'une chatte anglaise* by the English dramatist Edward Bond, with whom Henze had collaborated on the operas, *We come to the River* (1974-6) and *Orpheus* (1978). The action of *The English Cat* takes place in London at the turn of the century, and features a number of characters (they could be ladies and gentlemen or cats and tom-cats – a deliberate ambiguity is implied) who spend their time in charitable pursuits for the Royal Society for the Protection of Rats (yes, rats!). However, with the exception of a few characters (notably the lovers Minette and Tom) all are motivated exclusively by the greed for money, and as the booklet-note so succinctly puts it: "doubts remain as to whether the characters are animals who behave like evil and hypocritical human beings – or human beings who behave worse than animals".

The production heard here (described by Henze as 'experimental') followed an intensive period of study and rehearsal by the cast and orchestra at Henze's own Summer Academy in Gutersloh, in order, the composer says, that the artists involved should aim to be "so well acquainted with the content, the symbolism and the psychology in *The English Cat* that a deeper understanding of the piece can be reached ... which in turn is imparted to the audience, enabling them to become part of the action in a deeper and more effectual way than is usually possible". It certainly pays off in regard to this recording which is exemplary in every aspect and a worthy addition not only to recordings of Henze's music, but to recordings of contemporary music in general.

Henze Der junge Lord.
Barry McDaniel *bar* Sir Edgar's Secretary
Loren Driscoll *ten* Lord Barrat
Vera Little *mez* Begonia
Manfred Röhrl *bass-bar* Bürgermeister;
Ivan Sardi *bass* Magistrate Hasentreffer
Ernst Krukowski *bar* Comptroller Scharf
Helmut Krebs *ten* Professor von Mucker
Patricia Johnson *mez* Baroness Grünwiesel
Ruth Hesse *mez* Frau von Hufnagel
Lisa Otto *sop* Frau Hasentreffer
Edith Mathis *sop* Luise
Bella Jasper *sop* Ida
Marina Türke *sop* Chambermaid
Donald Grobe *ten* Wilhelm
Günther Treptow *ten* Amintore
Fritz Hoppe *bar* Lamplighter
Schönberg Boys' Choir;
Chorus and Orchestra of the Deutsche Oper, Berlin / Christoph von Dohnányi.
DG 20th Century Classics Ⓜ Ⓒ 445 248-2GC2 (two discs: 138 minutes: ADD). Notes, text and translation included. Recorded 1967.

The 'young Lord' is an ape, disguised as an English aristocrat and introduced into a smug early-nineteenth-century German community to teach it a few basic lessons about the difference between acceptable and unacceptable social behaviour. This ape is no holy fool; but nor does the plot permit Henze to treat him like the monosyllabic cretin of Schnittke's parable of Marxist fellow-travelling, *Life with an Idiot*. This ape ultimately regresses from artificial human eloquence to crude animal violence, and the inherent ambiguity is neatly encapsulated in the fact that the ape's first utterances, marked in the score as "screams", come across in this performance as a conventional, melancholy vocalise. Even before he starts singing in words this is a very musical ape, but it is his misery at being forced to assume human attributes that comes to the fore, even more than his ability to make social conventions look hollow.

It is the slightness rather than the implausibility of the parable that makes the enterprise so risky. Henze is a natural elaborator, capable of burying any story's broad satire under a welter of allusion and overcomposition. His score is certainly uneven, with the pretty, bland love music of Act 1 a low point. But the coda of that act (for percussion) foreshadows the menace of the politicized Henze (the ending of *The Raft of the Medusa*; 1968) and the entire final scene, starting with an expansive aria for the soprano lead, and building into a complex ensemble of crisis and explanation, generates the powerful symphonic depth of Henze at his considerable best. The moment where the ape interrupts Luise's meditation is genuinely frightening, and even the cardboard cut-out civic dignitaries come to life in the ensuing mayhem.

Henze is impressively served here by the young Christoph von Dohnányi, who keeps the climaxes in view without starving local details of musical point. The recording sounds dry, with a light bass and narrow dynamic range, but the singers profit from their experience of the opera on stage to give full weight to the expressive shape of Henze's long lines. In a performance a fraction less exuberant than this, *Der junge Lord* could seem the most leaden of moralities, a misguided attempt to provide a modern but not merely neo-classical equivalent to Donizetti and Rossini. Maybe Brecht and Weill would have done it better; but even when one longs for Henze to get a move on, one can respect the energy and richness of his invention. This, then, is a classic reissue, and DG deserve particular credit for offering it at medium price while including full notes and Lionel Salter's translation of the libretto.

Paul Hindemith German 1895-1963

Hindemith Cardillac (1926 version).
Siegmund Nimsgern *bar* Cardillac
Verena Schweizer *sop* Cardillac's daughter
Robert Schunk *ten* Officer
Harald Stamm *bass* Gold dealer
Jozsef Protschka *ten* Cavalier
Gabriele Schnaut *sop* Lady
Andreas Schmidt *bar* Chief of Military Police
Berlin Radio Chamber Choir and Symphony Orchestra / Gerd Albrecht.
Wergo Ⓔ Ⓓ WER60148/9-50 (two discs: 90 minutes: DDD: 7/89). Notes and text included.
Recorded 1988.

Cardillac is one of the most provoking and fascinating operas of its time; it is ferociously inventive and packs a dramatic punch that knocks the breath out of you, yet it inhabits only the outer suburbs of the 'standard repertory'. Hindemith's youthful reputation as an irritatingly clever *enfant terrible* has something to do with it, no doubt; so has his own later disowning of the work. A wholesale emasculation of the opera appeared in 1952, and the original version (recorded here) was not heard again during Hindemith's lifetime. This recording makes an imperatively eloquent case for its reassessment (if the English National Opera could play Shostakovich's *Lady Macbeth of Mtsensk* to packed houses they would have queues round the block for *Cardillac*).

The rediscovery of its three one-act predecessors (the recording reviewed further on of the 'Burmese marionette-play,' *Das Nusch-Nuschi*, completes the trilogy, Gerd Albrecht's accounts of its companion-pieces having already appeared on Wergo) puts *Cardillac* into focus as the culmination of a process. In the three one-acters Hindemith, in effect, boxes the compass of how music may 'accompany' violent or lurid action: in brutal ritual, as in *Mörder, Hoffnung, der Frauen*, in *Sancta Susanna*'s dismaying counterpoint of chaste lyricism and abnormal psychopathology or in the cheerfully riotous burlesque of *Das Nusch-Nuschi*. Elements of all these are present in *Cardillac*, but in the service of a difficult and deeply serious objective: the portrayal of a monster who is also a hero, an archetype of the creative artist, even in some sense a self-portrait.

Cardillac is a goldsmith so obsessed with the inviolable perfection of his creations that he murders to regain them; when he dies, his last loving glance is directed not at his pitying daughter kneeling by his side, but at the gold chain round her neck, his handiwork. That his love for his golden creatures has a bleak lyrical nobility, that his death scene is moving, even, are striking achievements, and most cunningly contrived. Cardillac himself is depicted not so much in arias (he has only one, in which, like a Verdian father he surveys his 'children' and resolves to defend them) but in a sequence of duets with the other, significantly unnamed, characters. They may be cyphers by comparison, but they are carefully differentiated in order to cast varying lights on the protagonist who, daringly but no less significantly, does not appear until Act 2. The music for Cardillac's daughter, including a florid Handelian aria complete with instrumental obbligatos, marks her off very clearly from the lyrically seductive but heartless Lady, just as the officer (the daughter's lover) has an ardour quite lacking in the Lady's posturing paramour, the Cavalier. In the portrayal of these characters (even the silent role of the King) the stylized neo-baroque forms that give this opera its apparent 'artificiality' are in fact expressively functional.

So is Gerd Albrecht: the cogs and springs of Hindemith's precisely dimensioned chamber orchestra could not be more clearly displayed (a pity, then, that the engineers adopt the usual voices-to-the-fore balance; it would have been preferable for the orchestra to dominate more) and the *coups de théâtre* (the *coups contre théâtre*, really: the bedroom scene and murder presented in dumb-show to the elegantly antiseptic accompaniment of two flutes, the decidedly 1926-style tavern music that echoes through the streets of seventeenth-century Paris) are pungently characterized. The cast is very accomplished, though close recording gives a touch of squalliness to both sopranos. Schunk is a ringingly full-voiced Officer and Nimsgern an expressive Cardillac whose voice sounds a bit smaller in this focus than it does on stage: he therefore lacks a shade or two of implacable authority. If DG were to reissue their old recording on CD it would be welcome for the sake of Dietrich Fischer-Dieskau's balefully over-life-size Cardillac and Elisabeth Söderström's brief appearance as the Lady, but in most other respects this Wergo issue equals or surpasses it.

Hindemith Mathis der Maler.

Dietrich Fischer-Dieskau *bar* Mathis
James King *ten* Albrecht
Gerd Feldhoff *bass* Lorenz von Pommersfelden
Manfred Schmidt *ten* Capito
Peter Meven *bass* Riedinger
William Cochran *ten* Schwalb
Alexander Malta *bass* Truchsess von Waldburg
Donald Grobe *ten* Sylvester von Schaumberg
Rose Wagemann *mez* Ursula
Urszula Koszut *sop* Regina
Trudeliese Schmidt *mez* Countess Helfenstein
Bavarian Radio Chorus and Symphony Orchestra / Rafael Kubelík.
EMI Ⓟ Ⓒ CDS5 55237-2 (three discs: 183 minutes: ADD). Notes, text and translation included. Recorded 1977.

The CD unavailability of this, one of the pinnacles of twentieth-century German opera, was unfortunate, not only in keeping a masterpiece hidden from view but because Gerd Albrecht on Wergo eventually beat EMI to the first CD issue. Modern critical opinion generally regards the original three-act *Cardillac* (not the composer's misconceived four-act revision) more highly than *Mathis der Maler* and in some respects *Cardillac* is the most consistently successful of Hindemith's operas; but *Mathis* has the greater depth of vision, albeit not always realized with optimum clarity.

One suspects that the *Mathis* Symphony's enduring success has been at the expense of the opera's reputation, likewise the overemphasis of the Third Reich context. One has to disagree with Dieter Rexroth's assertion in his essay for EMI that the opera's "genesis is closely connected with the political changes due to National Socialism", or that without "the developments of the time, the opera would be inconceivable in its present form". The notion that Hindemith withdrew purposefully into "internal emigration" is also wide of the mark, and something of an insult to the memory of those who really did so, such as Karl Amadeus Hartmann, whose *Simplicius Simplicissimus* is precisely the work of protest Rexroth would have us believe (erroneously) *Mathis der Maler* is.

But enough of the soapbox – what matters is the music. There is little to choose between the two versions – neither is perfect, but both are very fine. Albrecht, who makes one or two minor but noticeable cuts, has the benefit of more modern sound, but EMI's for Kubelík has transferred well. The choruses in particular are excellent, although Albrecht's seem tame in the famous "Temptation of St Antony" scene when set next to Kubelík's devilish-sounding Bavarians. Comparison of the casts yields a mixed picture. Fischer-Dieskau as Mathis is preferable to the rather raw-voiced Roland Hermann (except in the final tableau); for many this will be the crucial criterion, but Wergo do have the better of some other principals. The roles of Schwalb and his daughter encapsulate the predicament: for EMI, William Cochran is more imposing than Heinz Kruse as the peasant leader but Wergo's Gabriele Rossmanith is sweeter and younger-toned as Regina. For Albrecht, their first appearance seems to be a mid-afternoon stroll and not the convincing escape from pursuit that Kubelík effects here (first disc, track 4).

Despite the urgings of sentiment, neither set outclasses the other. For most, choice will rest on preferences for specific cast members.

Hindemith Das Nusch-Nuschi.

Harald Stamm *bass* Mung Tha Bya, Bettler, First Herald, Second Writer
Marten Schumacher *spkr* Ragweng
Victor von Halem *bass* Field-Marshall Kyce-Waing, Master of Ceremonies
Josef Becker *bass* Henker
David Knutson *alto* Susulu
Wilfrid Gahmlich *ten* Tum Tum
Peter Maus *ten* Kamadewa, First Writer
Alejandro Ramirez *ten* Second Herald
Verena Schweizer *sop* Bangsa, First Maiden
Celina Lindsley *sop* Osasa

Gabriele Schreckenbach *contr* Twaise, Second Maiden
Gudrun Sieber *sop* Ratasata, Third Maiden
Georgine Resick *sop* First Bajadere
Gisela Pohl *contr* Second Bajadere
Werner Marschall *ten* First training monkey
Manfred Kleber *ten* Second training monkey
Berlin Radio Symphony Orchestra / Gerd Albrecht.
Wergo Ⓟ ⓘ WER60146-50 (60 minutes: DDD). Notes and text included. Recorded 1987.

Das Nusch-Nuschi (you won't ask about the plot, will you?) is the most inventive and musically substantial of the pre-*Cardillac* trilogy. (You insist? Well, you have only yourself to blame: Field-Marshall Kyce-Waing is accused of enjoying all four of the King of Burma's wives during a single night; he is sentenced to 'the usual' – castration: cue for rib-nudging quotation from *Tristan*; he isn't guilty, actually, and there's an unexpected last-minute impediment to the execution of the sentence; there are also these singing apes – what do apes sing? "Rrrai, rrrai", of course – and four dancing girls and a couple of poets and a comic servant and in any case the *real* principal character doesn't sing – he would hardly have time to in a 60-minute opera with a cast list of 25 – and besides there's the Nusch-Nuschi, half rat, half alligator, quite possibly a symbol of the destructiveness of desire – enough? you were warned.) Despite the plot the score is an alluringly vivid kaleidoscope of orientalisms, lyrical arabesque, languorous allure and brilliant colour. In its orchestral mastery alone it demonstrates that Hindemith was ready for *Cardillac*; that he later suppressed this music-packed score entirely is breathtakingly inexplicable.

The performance is very fine, the recording – close focus on the voices apart – is excellent. As with *Cardillac* the libretto is printed in German only. *Cardillac* is a 'number opera', and has cueing bands for each number; *Das Nusch-Nuschi* has none, which is a pity, since you'll probably want to play the interludes and dance-music to friends who think they don't like Hindemith.

Gustav Holst   British 1874-1934

Holst At the Boar's Head.
Philip Langridge *ten* Prince Hal
John Tomlinson *bass* Falstaff
Elise Ross *sop* Mistress Quickly
Felicity Palmer *mez* Doll Tearsheet
David Wilson-Johnson *bar* Pistol
Peter Hall *ten* Peto
Richard Suart *bass* Bardolph
Michael George *bass* Poins
Women's voices of the Royal Liverpool Philharmonic Orchestra / David Atherton.

Holst The Wandering Scholar.
Michael Rippon *bass* Louis
Norma Burrowes *sop* Alison
Michael Langdon *bass* Father Philippe
Robert Tear *ten* Pierre
English Chamber Orchestra / Steuart Bedford.
EMI British Composers Ⓜ ⓘ CDM5 65127-2 (76 minutes: ADD). Texts included. *At the Boar's Head* recorded 1981; *The Wandering Scholar* recorded 1974.

A most valuable Holst double-bill. With not one wasted note during its mere 24-minute duration, *The Wandering Scholar* (Holst's last opera, composed in 1929-30 to a libretto by Clifford Bax) makes marvellously entertaining listening. Holst was too ill to attend the 1934 première and the manuscript remained unrevised until 1968, when Benjamin Britten and Imogen Holst edited the score for its first publication. Steuart Bedford directs what sounds like an ideal performance, drawing splendidly characterful contributions from singers and instrumentalists alike, and John Willan's 1974 Abbey Road production continues to sound extremely vivid.

At the Boar's Head, Holst's Falstaff opera (or "musical interlude in one act" as he called it), dates from 1924, and is an ambitious amalgamation of texts from the fat knight's scenes in *Henry IV*, Parts 1 and 2, and tunes drawn mainly from Playford's *English Dancing Master* of 1651 (Colin Matthews's note informs us that only three of the melodies in the work are actually Holst's own). Even in a realization as enjoyable as this one, Holst's inspiration perhaps tends to outstay its welcome, the overall effect tending toward a certain unrelieved 'wordiness' (the opera is, in fact, over twice the length of its sparkling companion here). There are no complaints, though, about the largely admirable assembled cast (with Tomlinson and Palmer outstanding) or the RLPO's lively playing under David Atherton's watchful lead. The slightly dry recording (made in Liverpool's Philharmonic Hall) captures every detail with crystal clarity.

Holst Sávitri.
Felicity Palmer *mez* Sávitri
Philip Langridge *ten* Satyaván
Stephen Varcoe *bar* Death
Richard Hickox Singers; City of London Sinfonia / Richard Hickox.

Holst Dream City – song cycle, H174 (arr. and orch. C. Matthews).
Patricia Kwella *sop*
Richard Hickox Singers; City of London Sinfonia / Richard Hickox.
Hyperion Ⓕ Ⓞ CDA66099 (58 minutes: DDD). Texts included. Recorded 1983.

The reissue on Argo of Imogen Holst's own classic performance of *Sávitri*, with Janet Baker, Robert Tear and Thomas Hemsley, got in ahead of this version, but does not thereby rob it of interest. Indeed, Imogen Holst herself has lent it her implicit blessing by arranging for the Holst Foundation to sponsor it. Richard Hickox conducts a most vivid and sensitive performance that, if it is much in the mould of Imogen Holst's own performance, is none the less freshly thought out again. The opera is an amazing little masterpiece: it deserves all Hickox's care with the subtle bitonal contrapuntal lines and the spare yet sonorous textures. Only very seldom have the latter gone wrong; it is, for instance, not easy to hear the flutes' sixths and thirds figure as Death approaches, where it should colour the texture distinctively, and once or twice the basses are perhaps a little powerful. There is inevitably little feeling of the open air at the start and finish as Death advances from the forest and recedes back into it, but the sense of a large hall is too vivid.

These are not important points. Interest attaches more to the performances, about which there is only one reservation. This concerns Stephen Varcoe's performance of Death. Beautifully as he sings it, with a firm yet flexible line and a proper understanding of the part, the timbre of his voice is, especially in the upper register, too close to a tenor sound for the essential contrast. When Death finally stands before Sávitri, or grants her the boon with which she tricks him, there is too great a sense of him being some *alter ego* of Satyaván – and it is hard to believe that there is a subtle eschatological point being made here. Philip Langridge is a superb Satyaván: singing here with stronger timbre and greater range of colour in a voice that was always fine and true. As always, it is an immensely intelligent performance. Felicity Palmer, established as a mezzo-soprano when this recording was made, is no less admirable. She is responsive to the wonderful opening dialogue between Sávitri and the slowly approaching figure of Death, when her vocal line seems to be propelled by Death's melody in another key without being attached to it; she is rich and tender with Satyaván; she has all the strength and the ringing tone for her triumph over Death.

There is extra interest in this record in Colin Matthews's orchestration of the little-known and grossly undervalued set of Humbert Wolfe songs. Possibly the poetry has kept them out of the public eye, but they are truly remarkable songs, among the most original pieces Holst ever wrote. Matthews will indeed have done the composer a service if this loving enterprise helps to put them into renewed and wider circulation. His orchestration would undoubtedly have satisfied Holst, which is high praise.

Engelbert Humperdinck German 1854-1921

Humperdinck Hänsel und Gretel.
Anne Sofie von Otter *mez* Hänsel
Barbara Bonney *sop* Gretel
Hanna Schwarz *mez* Mother
Andreas Schmidt *bar* Father
Barbara Hendricks *sop* Sandman
Eva Lind *sop* Dew Fairy
Marjana Lipovšek *contr* Witch
Tölz Boys' Choir; Bavarian Radio Symphony Orchestra / Jeffrey Tate.
EMI Ⓕ Ⓞ CDS7 54022-2 (two discs: 103 minutes: DDD). Notes, text and translation included. Recorded 1989.

There is a Brucknerian glow to the sound in the opening of the Prelude, giving a reminder that the orchestra was for long associated with Eugen Jochum. Tate's warm moulding of phrase has something Jochum-like about it too, but if that seems to promise a heavyweight reading of Humperdinck's magical children's opera, it is a misleading impression. Tate's crisp and delicate pointing of the Witch's spell theme in the Prelude then leads on to a reading of exceptional warmth and sympathy which yet adopts speeds generally faster than those in rival versions. In the complete opera an overall difference in timing of five minutes between Tate and the others may seem small, but it is enough to give an extra tautness, when rhythms are sprung so resiliently, and moulded phrasing leads on with such persuasiveness and refinement. Karajan may be more rapt, giving more mystery at slower speeds to such passages as the Evening Hymn and Dream Pantomine, but the freshness of Tate avoids any hint of sentimentality, giving the Evening Hymn the touching simplicity of a children's prayer. Tate, like Pritchard in his fine Cologne version, does not bring Wagnerian power to the Witch's Ride as Solti does, but his still weighty approach matches the way that, like Pritchard, he relates the opera more to the Wagner of Act 2 of *Die Meistersinger*.

In any case, the Witch of Marjana Lipovšek is the finest of all, firm and fierce, using the widest range of expression and tone without any of the embarrassing exaggerations that mar, for example, Elisabeth Söderström's strong but controversial reading for Pritchard, and without any of the fruitiness of the other conventional readings. Lipovšek's change of voice between the hocus-pocus spell (given extra horror with echo-chamber resonance) and her insinuating address to the children is a model of characterization. That is typical, and the chill she conveys down to a mere whisper makes one wish, more than usual, that the part is not longer.

The rest of the casting matches that in finesse, with no weak link. Barbara Bonney as Gretel and Anne Sofie von Otter as Hänsel are no less fine than the exceptionally strong duos on the rival sets, notably Schwarzkopf and Grümmer on the Karajan set and Cotrubas and von Stade on the Pritchard. The main difference is that Bonney and von Otter have younger, fresher voices, so that they have to use fewer operatic wiles in their characterizations, yet with timbre ideally contrasted. In a note with the booklet, the EMI executive producer, Peter Alward says, "young children should have young parents", and he chose Andreas Schmidt and Hanna Schwarz accordingly. Both of them, like Lipovšek, characterize vocally with a wide range of expression and tone, but without the underlining and 'funny-voice' exaggeration you often get. Barbara Hendricks is warm and distinctive as the Sandman, pure and sweet of tone, if not always ideally clean in attack. The one slight reservation about the casting is over Eva Lind as the Dew Fairy, not quite pure enough in her topmost register and not ideally hushed, but that is a role which regularly tends to bring disappointments in the casting, as rather more markedly with Ruth Welting in the Pritchard set. There is a slight question-mark, too, over the use of the Tölz Boys' Choir for the ginger-bread children at the end. Inevitably they sound what they are, a beautifully matched team of trebles, and curiously the heart-tug is not quite so intense as with the more childish-sounding voices in the rival choirs.

Those are minimal reservations, when the breadth and warmth of the recording add to the compulsion of the performance, giving extra perspectives in focus and dynamic. For all the brilliance of the Decca recording, Solti's set lacks real warmth. The Karajan will never be superseded for the magic and intensity of the performance, and the 1953 mono recording is astonishingly clear, but the modern sound cocoons the ear in quite a different way. The merits of the Pritchard set on CBS follow closely those of Tate, but the playing of the Gurzenich Orchestra rarely, if ever, quite matches that of the Bavarian Radio Symphony Orchestra in refinement and point, and on balance the EMI casting is preferable. EMI are also more generous with the number of tracks provided.

Humperdinck Hänsel und Gretel.

Brigitte Fassbaender *mez* Hänsel
Lucia Popp *sop* Gretel
Júlia Hamari *contr* Mother
Walter Berry *bass* Father
Norma Burrowes *sop* Sandman
Edita Gruberová *sop* Dew Fairy
Anny Schlemm *mez* Witch
Vienna Boys' Choir; Vienna Philharmonic Orchestra / Sir Georg Solti.
Decca Ⓜ Ⓞ 455 063-2DMO2 (two discs: 108 minutes: ADD). Notes, text and translation included. Recorded 1978.

Humperdinck Hänsel und Gretel.

Frederica von Stade *mez* Hänsel
Ileana Cotrubas *sop* Gretel
Christa Ludwig *mez* Mother
Siegmund Nimsgern *bass-bar* Father
Dame Kiri Te Kanawa *sop* Sandman
Ruth Welting *sop* Dew Fairy
Elisabeth Söderström *sop* Witch
Cologne Opera Children's Chorus; Cologne Gurzenich Orchestra / Sir John Pritchard.
Sony Classical Ⓕ M2K79217 (two discs: 108 minutes: ADD). Notes, text and translation included. Recorded 1978.

When Solti and Pritchard appeared in the late-1970s, the Decca issue in sound quality had a slight edge over its Sony rival in presenting the opera with all the sonic trappings that were the glory of Solti's Wagner series. However, with the onset of CD, any discrepancy in sound quality was cancelled out, with the less spectacular Cologne recording bringing more warmth, more bloom and a very natural balance, mirroring the performance itself.

The Wagnerian bite and power of Solti's reading is remarkable, but the warmth of Pritchard's is more apt for this lovely work. Conveying the impression of performers who know the piece in the theatre, Pritchard is the one who consistently conjures up a more genial, more winning tone of voice. Some may even prefer his relatively relaxed reading of the Witch's Ride over Solti's fierceness. Karajan in his classic reading might be counted to have the best of both worlds here, but the mono recording of the orchestra, if not of the voices, inevitably sounds thin next to good modern stereo. In the casting, too, some readers may prefer the CBS set to the Decca, strong as both are. Ileana Cotrubas and Frederica von Stade (Pritchard) delicately characterize the two children, conveying freshness and childish innocence, while in fact exercising the most sophisticated vocal control. Well-chosen as Lucia Popp and Brigitte Fassbaender are for Solti, it is hard to imagine them as children, with their voices sounding more womanly. Elisabeth Schwarzköpf's portrait of Gretel for Karajan is the most positive of all but you may find the detail overdone.

There is not a weak link in the Pritchard cast, with the Witch from Söderström, strongly characterized, even caricatured, but without some of the grotesqueries of such a traditional mezzo as Anny Schlemm for Solti. The element of rawness in Christa Ludwig's singing as the Mother gives an apt bite to the character, while Nimsgern is an upstanding Father, firmer, less middle-aged than most, though Walter Berry on the Solti set is equally fine. Some of the most ravishing singing of all comes from Dame Kiri Te Kanawa as the Sandman (Pritchard), warmer, richer and purer than the Dew Fairy, Ruth Welting. Edith Gruberová as the Dew Fairy on the Solti set is made to sound edgy.

EMI's transfer of the Karajan has rather more generous tracking than Solti, but both use CD to avoid breaks within acts, getting the first two on disc one, the third on disc two.

Humperdinck Hänsel und Gretel.

Elisabeth Grümmer *sop* Hänsel
Dame Elisabeth Schwarzköpf *sop* Gretel
Maria von Ilosvay *mez* Mother
Josef Metternich *bar* Father
Anny Felbermayer *sop* Sandman, Dew Fairy
Else Schürhoff *mez* Witch
Loughton High School for Girls and Bancroft's School Choirs;
Philharmonia Orchestra / Herbert von Karajan.
EMI mono Ⓜ ① CMS7 69293-2 (two discs: 108 minutes: ADD). Notes and text included.
Recorded 1953.

This classic recording has never been surpassed. The producer, Walter Legge, remained sceptical of the advantages of stereo, and he regularly cited his placing of the off-stage sound of the cuckoo in the wood in this recording to show that you could get a vivid sense of space and distance without stereo. With the extra clarity of CD sharpening the sense of presence, at that point you would indeed have registered the recording as in stereo, had you not known otherwise, and similarly the arrival of the father from afar singing his jolly song has a multi-dimensional effect. In no way do you feel a lack of atmosphere in this highly atmospheric piece. What you may be less happy about is the balancing of treble and bass in the remastering. For all its extra inner clarity, it lacks something in body. You can boost it with the volume control, but that brings up the hiss, which is relatively high but not objectionable.

Whatever the reservations over the transfer, this remains a gorgeous performance, masterfully paced by Karajan, Schwarzköpf delightfully partnered by Grümmer and with the firm-toned Metternich in particular, making one regret that he did not record a great deal more.

Humperdinck Königskinder.

Thomas Moser *ten* King's Son
Dagmar Schellenberger *sop* Goose-girl
Dietrich Henschel *bar* Fiddler
Marilyn Schmiege *mez* Witch
Andreas Kohn *bass* Woodcutter
Heinrich Weber *ten* Broom-maker
Gabriele Weinfurter-Zwink *sop* Broom-maker's Daughter
Dankwart Siegele *bass* Innkeeper
Hanne Weber *sop* Innkeeper's Daughter
Andreas Schulist *ten* Tailor
Jutta Bethsold *mez* Stable Maid
Gerald Häussler *bar* Senior Councillor
Bavarian Radio Chorus; Munich Boys' Choir and Radio Orchestra / Fabio Luisi.
Calig Ⓔ ① CAL50968/70 (three discs: 167 minutes: DDD). Notes and text included. Recorded 1996.

It is easy to see why *Königskinder*, for all its many beauties, has never begun to match Humperdinck's masterpiece, *Hänsel und Gretel*, in popularity. One appreciated the work's problems all the more when English National Opera boldly staged it five years ago. Not only is the story of the Prince and the

Goose-girl less involving, more disorganized than that of *Hänsel*, but Humperdinck runs the risk of seeming long-winded, when the outer acts in this recorded performance are each over an hour long, with the central act a full 40 minutes, and with minor characters and incidents holding up the plot. The score is as lyrical as you could wish, but time and time again what in *Hänsel* would have developed into a big tune peters out far too soon.

That said, it is good to have this modern recording of a rich score, well sung and warmly conducted by Fabio Luisi. He captures the buoyancy of much of the writing as well as the lyrical flow. Curiously, this version uses the same choir and orchestra as the Wallberg/EMI set recorded in 1976. The venue this time is the Herkulessaal in Munich instead of the radio studio used by EMI, with sound that is rather more spacious but not so immediate. The glow of Humperdinck's scoring is more ripely caught this time, but the focus is less sharp than on EMI.

None the less, a digital recording of this score is most welcome, and though the voices are not specially characterful, there is no serious weakness. The tenor of Thomas Moser, taking the central role of the Prince, is more heroic than that of his EMI rival, Adolf Dallapozza, and the recording captures it cleanly, with the voice often shaded down beautifully. Though Dagmar Schellenberger as the Goose-girl cannot match Helen Donath in sweetness of tone, with the voice getting a little raw above the stave, hers is a feeling, well-characterized performance, and she finds a delicate *mezza voce* for the prayer to her parents, which the Goose-girl sings at the end of Act 1.

If Schellenberger sounds on the mature side for the Goose-girl, Marilyn Schmiege with her warm, firm mezzo makes rather a young Witch, a more equivocal character, not nearly so clearly defined as the Witch in *Hänsel*. There is no danger in this performance of caricature, when Hanne Weber, singing well as the Innkeeper's daughter who in Act 2 tries to seduce the Prince, makes it sound rather like Eva's approach to Sachs in Act 3 of Wagner's *Die Meistersinger*. Most important among the others are the Fiddler and the Woodcutter, with both Dietrich Henschel and Andreas Kohn singing freshly and clearly in their key roles. All told, this is a performance marked by good teamwork, with the chorus bringing energetic echoes of Smetana's *The bartered bride* in their all-too-brief contributions in Act 2.

Leoš Janáček   Moravian 1854-1928

Janáček The Cunning Little Vixen.

Lucia Popp *sop* Vixen, Young vixen
Dalibor Jedlička *bass* Forester
Eva Randová *mez* Fox
Eva Zikmundová *mez* Forester's wife, Owl
Vladimir Krejčik *ten* Schoolmaster, Gnat
Richard Novák *ten* Priest, Badger
Václav Zítek *bar* Harašta
Beno Blachut *ten* Pásek
Ivana Mixová *mez* Pásek's wife, Woodpecker, Hen
Libuše Márová *contr* Dog
Gertrude Jahn *mez* Cock, Jay
Eva Hríbiková *sop* Frantik
Zuzana Hudecová *sop* Pepik
Peter Saray *treb* Frog, Grasshopper
Miriam Ondrášková *sop* Cricket
Vienna State Opera Chorus; Bratislava Children's Choir;

1982

Janáček The Cunning Little Vixen – orchestral suite (arr. V. Talich).

Vienna Philharmonic Orchestra / Sir Charles Mackerras.
Decca Ⓟ Ⓓ 417 129-2DH2 (two discs: 109 minutes: ADD). Notes, text and translation included. Recorded 1981.

Sir Charles Mackerras's Janáček opera cycle lost little time in attaining classic status. The gains of this CD reissue are the expected ones, with the extra clarity and depth in the woodland music, especially that for the animal's wedding feast, giving the score, in more ways than one, a new dimension. This does also, to some extent, help to redress the balance between voices and orchestra: it is the orchestra which plays for much of the work the prime expressive role, but there were instances (for instance with some of the Forester's music, sung by Dalibor Jedlička) where a slight sense of strain showed. Lucia Popp's Vixen is sheer delight; she is exquisitely matched to Eva Randová as the Fox. The menfolk are well characterized; they include Beno Blachut, who was nearly 70 when the record was made, in the tiny role of the Innkeeper – a pleasant tribute to a veteran singer who has done so much for Czech opera.

Dr John Tyrell's invaluable booklet-essay (invaluable as a commentary on the work, not only as introduction to the recording) is included in full. So is Deryck Viney's racy translation. It will be a long time before performance and recording are superseded.

Janáček From the House of the Dead.
  Dalibor Jedlička *bar* Goryanchikov
  Jaroslava Janská *sop* Alyeya
  Jiří Zahradníček *ten* Luka (Morosov)
  Vladimir Krejčík *ten* Tall Prisoner
  Richard Novák *bass* Short Prisoner
  Antonín Svorc *bass-bar* Commandant
  Beno Blachut *ten* Old Prisoner
  Ivo Žídek *ten* Skuratov
  Jaroslav Soušek *bar* Chekunov, Prisoner acting Don Juan
  Eva Zigmundová *mez* Whore
  Zdeněk Soušek *ten* Shapkin, Kedril
  Václav Zítek *bar* Shishkov
  Zdeněk Svehla *ten* Cherevin, A Voice
  Vienna State Opera Chorus; Vienna Philharmonic Orchestra / Sir Charles Mackerras.

1980

Janáček Mládi.
  London Sinfonietta / David Atherton.

Janáček Nursery rhymes.
  London Sinfonietta Chorus; London Sinfonietta / David Atherton.
  Decca Ⓟ Ⓓ 430 375-2DH2 (two discs: 123 minutes: ADD/DDD). Notes, texts and translations included. Recorded 1980.

Sir Charles Mackerras's Janáček opera series has been one of the major recording events of recent years. *From the House of the Dead* (the 1980 **Gramophone** Record of the Year) was here recorded for the first time in its proper, original version; and this, the fruit of brilliant musicological work by Dr John Tyrrell, revealed it as even more of a masterpiece – a work, indeed, to count among the handful of masterpieces produced by twentieth-century opera. The loss of the final chorus, a sentimental addition, is but the most striking of the clarifications: throughout, the sound is sharper, the textures are sparer, and this serves both to sharpen the effect and to give the singers more clearly differentiated support. They are led, nominally, by Goryanchikov; but though Dalibor Jedlička sings him warmly and well, the character is not really the hero of an opera that has no heroes and in which all are heroes. The prisoners are skilfully contrasted in Janáček's writing so as to make an apparently random yet actually well-structured group, and there is not a weak performance among them.

  The extra space available on CD allows some generous fill-ups: *Mládi* and the *Nursery rhymes* come from David Atherton's splendid 1981 set of five LPs devoted to Janáček.

Janáček From the House of the Dead.
  Nicolai Ghiaurov *bass* Goryanchikov
  Elzbieta Szmytka *sop* Alyeya
  Barry McCauley *ten* Luka
  Bojidar Nickolov *ten* Tall Prisoner
  Richard Novák *bass* Short Prisoner
  Harry Peeters *bass* Commandant
  Josef Veverka *ten* Old Prisoner
  Philip Langridge *ten* Skuratov
  Pavel Kamas *bass* Chekunov
  Richard Haan *bass* Don Juan
  Christiane Young *mez* Whore
  Alexander Oliver *ten* Kedril
  Heinz Zednik *ten* Shapkin
  Monte Pederson *bass-bar* Shishkov
  Miroslav Kopp *ten* Cherevin
  Andrea Rost *sop* A Voice
  Vienna State Opera Chorus; Vienna Philharmonic Orchestra / Claudio Abbado.
  Stage Director: **Klaus Michael Grüber.** *Video Director:* **Brian Large.**
  DG Ⓟ ⚏ 072 139-3GH (93 minutes:). Recorded at performances in the Grosses Festspielhaus, Salzburg in summer 1992.

This Salzburg production of 1992, taken from the Grosses Festspielhaus, although at times insufficiently focused, does in the end convey the unremitting harshness of the milieu, the uselessness of life in prison, and the individuality and feeling that can arise even in such circumstances. Eduardo Arroyo's décor was castigated as being a 'designer-gulag' by one hostile critic, but its clean lines and evocation of mood have the advantage of filling the vast stage effectively and forming a suitable setting for several riveting performances. It is wondrously seconded by Abbado's forceful yet subtle reading of the score, which is played by the Vienna Philharmonic with incisiveness allied to an inner warmth, thus reflecting exactly the feeling of the music. Pain and compassion are held in fine balance.

The chief narratives are enacted by three characters. Langridge adds another eccentric to his repertory as the pitiful, slightly crazed Skuratov, who has committed a crime of passion. McCauley's Luka is a more aggressive, bitter inmate who has murdered a prison officer under extreme provocation. These are both tenor roles; bass-baritone Pederson takes the part of Shishkov, who has killed his unfaithful wife, and is haunted by the memory of her and her lover. His is by far the longest autobiography and Pederson sustains it magnificently. Veteran Ghiaurov movingly plays the elderly aristocrat Goryanchikov, the most sympathetic character, who befriends the vulnerable youth Alyeya, a role given to a soprano to provide vocal contrast; it is here sung without sentiment by Szmytka. Zednik's Shapkin is a well-observed addition to his gallery of *comprimario* parts. The many others make their mark in smaller roles. Large's direction for video is as sensitive as ever, giving vivid close-ups of the principals while never neglecting the larger canvas. The picture quality is good, but the sound is a trifle too backward. Subtitles, essential here, are thankfully provided.

Janáček Jenůfa.

Elisabeth Söderström *sop* Jenůfa
Wieslaw Ochman *ten* Laca
Eva Randová *mez* Kostelnička
Petr Dvorský *ten* Steva
1984
Lucia Popp *sop* Karolka
Marie Mrazová *contr* Stařenka
Václav Zitek *bar* Stárek
Dalibor Jedlička *bass* Rychtar
Ivana Mixová *mez* Rychtarka
Vera Soukupová *mez* Pastuchyňa, Tetka
Jindra Pokorná *mez* Barena
Jana Janášová *sop* Jano
Vienna State Opera Chorus; Vienna Philharmonic Orchestra / Sir Charles Mackerras.
Decca Ⓟ Ⓓ 414 483-2DH2 (two discs: 130 minutes: DDD). Notes, text and translations included. Recorded 1982.

The appearance of each opera in the Decca Janáček cycle under Sir Charles Mackerras was a major gramophone event, for a number of reasons. Not only are the casts well chosen, and the recordings of great technical sophistication, often 'solving' virtually intractable problems posed by Janáček's idiosyncratic scoring: Sir Charles combines a scholarly assessment of the problems with the understanding and freshness of a major Janáček interpreter, certainly one of the greatest of the day; and he has at his elbow Dr John Tyrrell to prepare correct performing versions that often take us back, for the first time, to Janáček's intentions.

This *Jenůfa* is no exception. To the cast, first. It is led by Elisabeth Söderström, a Jenůfa of great tenderness and strength, one in whom the sense of threatening despair is held at bay by a glowing simplicity and strength of character. She phrases Janáček's soaring melodic lines with a full understanding of their romantic passion without ever allowing them to loosen into sentimentality; she has a sharp appreciation of the cut of his often difficult rhythms; her voice is flexible in expression, ranging from a sorrowful warmth in the scenes over the loss of the baby to a pride of utterance in the confrontations with Steva and a moving dignity in the closing reconciliation with the Kostelnička. Eva Randová sings the latter role very responsively to Söderström, and makes the character less of a termagant than is usual. In this, she is encouraged by a restoration in the score, the so-called 'explanation' aria in Act 1 in which the Kostelnička tells of her own unhappy past. The piece might perhaps hold up the drama on the stage, if it were to be included: on the gramophone, it is a valuable inclusion, apart from returning to us a fine piece of music. So although the frightened Steva calls her "divná, strasná" – "strange, frightful" – it is the misery he also sees in her which is a key to her complicated character, and which Randová brings out. The final confrontation with the forgiving Jenůfa is most movingly done.

The two men are well contrasted. Peter Dvorský sings a lively, attractive Steva, self-regarding and of course essentially weak, so that at the climax he is found still posturing so as to lay a claim on everyone's attentions, and getting pretty short shrift from Karolka: he does this cleverly, and is well matched by Lucia Popps's sprightly Karolka. Wieslaw Ochman, as the more serious Laca, sings soberly but with considerable passion contained within his utterances, and he handles very well indeed both the dreadful scene when he slashes Jenůfa's cheek and his dignified acceptance of her past relationship with Steva. The smaller parts are well handled, and the bustle and confusion of the climax keeps them well separated both in characterization and in recorded presentation without exaggeration. Under Sir Charles, the orchestra play marvellously, with power and warmth but also, as at the start of Act 3, with a delightful freshness that is an essential part of the opera's nature.

The two discs on which this short but immensely full opera is fitted find room for two bonuses. The original Overture, now usually separated and known as Zarlivost ("Jealousy"), is included. Secondly, there is a 'new' ending – actually the old one. All these years, *Jenůfa* has been given in the version prepared by Karl Kovařovic, which modifies the closing pages by taking Janáček's melodic figures and making of them a series of instrumental imitations in a kind of canon. It is glowing and effective; but trying now to rid one's ears of it, one does as usual find that the sparer, more understated Janáček original in fact says more. Both are here recorded, the original as part of the opera, Kovařovic as a separately banded appendix. Apart from this, the entire score has been revised and restored to its original form by Dr Tyrrell. He has also provided a masterly introduction which takes us through the whole story of the work, from an appreciation of the original author, Gabriela Preissová, and the reception of her work to a consideration of the libretto's formation and of the score itself in a detail that is wholly fascinating. He is very perceptive, and independent-minded, about Janáček's approach to the text, particularly about his handling of the Kostelnička.

Finally, there is a complete text with a translation by Deryck Viney. This is fresh and lively, if sometimes rather too free in its praiseworthy attempt to make the language colloquial. All in all, this set, combining as it does high interpretative artistry, scrupulous and original scholarship and technical excellence, does credit to all.

Janáček Jenůfa.

Libuše Domanínská *sop* Jenůfa
Vilém Přibyl *ten* Laca
Naděža Kniplová *sop* Kostelnička
Ivo Zídek *ten* Steva
Marta Boháčšová *sop* Karolka
Marie Mrázová *contr* Stařenka
Jindřich Jindrák *bar* Stárek
Zdeněk Kroupa *bar* Rychtar
Slávka Procházková *mez* Rychtarka
Eva Hlobilová *mez* Pastuchyna
Božena Effenberková *sop* Barena
Anna Rousková *contr* Tetka, A woman
Helena Tattermuschová *sop* Jano
Prague National Theatre Chorus and Orchestra / Bohumil Gregor.
EMI Ⓜ ① CMS5 65476-2 (two discs: 118 minutes: ADD). Notes, texts and translation included. Recorded 1969.

In the 29 years since this recording was issued, appreciation of Janáček has come far. This was the first stereo *Jenůfa*, produced as a joint recording between HMV and Supraphon; it pioneered the way for many more Janáček recordings to come from Czechoslovakia, and perhaps served to encourage Decca to their superb series under Sir Charles Mackerras. This set is now something of a period piece, and that unfortunately extends to a less than distinguished recording, with a good deal of the detail obscure. The recording reviewed above must remain, for the foreseeable future, the version to recommend. But it should not be overlooked that the HMV/Supraphon did much to draw attention to Janáček's greatness as an opera composer, for many who had had little opportunity to discover this masterpiece in any other way. It was also a fine performance that included some of the greatest Czech singers of the day in roles they knew and loved deeply.

Naděža Kniplová is a strong but by no means inflexible Kostelnička, stern in her adherence to her moral code until she feels impelled to break it for the deepest human reasons. Her voice is strong and resonant; it is a heroic performance. Libuše Domanínská is a tender Jenůfa, vulnerable near the start but also in her own way deepening in human understanding as the drama develops; and her response to the music at the end, as she forgives the Kostelnička and takes Laca, is true to Janáček's soaring melodic phrases. Steva is sung with light cheerfulness by Ivo Zídek, Laca with fervour and, again, a deepening sense of understanding, by Vilém Přibyl. Tarty little Karolka gets nowhere in understanding, as Marta Boháčšová suggests: Steva deserves her. The smaller parts are taken with no less care and effectiveness. Newcomers to the work will do well to head for Mackerras; but old Janáček hands treasure this set, and its return to the catalogue is very welcome.

Janáček Káta Kabanová.

Elisabeth Söderström *sop* Káta
Petr Dvorský *ten* Boris
Naděžda Kniplová *contr* Kabanicha
Vladimír Krejčík *ten* Tichon
Libuše Márová *mez* Varvara
Dalibor Jedlička *bass* Dikoj
Zdeněk Svehla *ten* Kudrjáš
Jaroslav Souček *bar* Kuligin
Jitka Pavlová *sop* Glaša
Gertrude Jahn *mez* Fekluša
Vienna State Opera Chorus; Vienna Philharmonic Orchestra / Sir Charles Mackerras.

1977

Janáček Capriccio. Concerto Concertino.
Paul Crossley *pf*
London Sinfonietta / David Atherton.
Decca Ⓕ 421 852-2DH2 (two discs: 140 minutes: ADD). Notes, text and translation included.
Recorded 1976-8.

This splendid set of *Káta Kabanová* led the way in Decca's classic series in 1977, when it won a *Gramophone* Record Award. The actual sound is somewhat enhanced by CD, and this lends extra clarity to some of the very difficult problems which Janáček set conductors in the theatre. Among the most unusual is his use of the viola d'amore, an instrument to which he was devoted principally, it seems, for its name: he was at the height of his devotion to Kamila Stösslová, and wanted originally also to include the instrument in 'her' quartet, *Intimate Letters*. Thanks to sensitive sound engineering, "the plaintive tone of the viola d'amore", as Sir Charles writes, "can be heard at many poignant moments, lending 'amore' in both name and sound".

Sir Charles's superlative performance hardly needs further recommendation nor does the wonderfully moving interpretation of the title-role by Elisabeth Söderström establishing by an infinity of subtle touches and discreet, sensitive singing the picture of Káta as the richest and most human character in the drama. It is a performance that moves with the greatest intelligence between the public and the private drama of Káta's sad life, and the release into death which she sees as her only possible fulfilment. Most of the rest of the cast are Czech: they include Naděžda Kniplová as a Kabanicha the more formidable in her repressive morality for the suggestion of banked-up reserves of passion of her own. Libuše Márová and Zdeněk Svehla make a lively pair of secondary lovers, and there is a sympathetic performance of Tichon from Vladimír Krejčík, an elegant Boris from Petr Dvorský, and a strong Dikoj from Dalibor Jedlička.

The booklet retains John Tyrrell's invaluable synopsis and essay, now slightly revised, together with Sir Charles's more personal note; these are now translated into French, German and Italian, though the libretto is printed only in Czech and in Deryck Viney's serviceable English translation (and without his useful note on Czech pronunciation). There is also a pleasant bonus in the shape of the excellent performances of the *Concerto Concertino* and *Capriccio* extracted from the original five-record LP set of Janáček's piano and chamber works.

Janáček Káta Kabanová.
Drahomíra Tikalová *sop* Káta
Beno Blachut *ten* Boris
Ludmila Komancová *contr* Kabanicha
Bohumír Vích *ten* Tichon
Ivana Mixová *mez* Varvara
Zdenck Kroupa *bass* Dikoj
Viktor Kočí *ten* Kudrjáš
Rudolf Jedlička *bar* Kuligin
Eva Hlobilová *sop* Glaša
Marcela Lemariová *mez* Fekluša
Prague National Theatre Chorus and Orchestra / Jaroslav Krombholc.
Supraphon Ⓕ Ⓓ 10 8016-2 (two discs: 90 minutes: AAD). Notes, text and translation included.
Recorded 1959.

This, the first recording of *Káta Kabanová*, was made in Prague in 1959. It must have been treasured by many lovers of Janáček's music. To return to it after some years will be no disappointment. Much, of course, has happened since then. The sound now cannot help seeming thin, notably in the strings, and the balance with the voices is not always favourable to them, so that Drahomíra Tikalová can strain her fresh, charming but not very powerful voice. She sings so perceptively as to make light of these problems. But setting the recording beside Mackerras's version puts it at a number of other disadvantages. The newer set not only helps the notoriously difficult internal orchestral balance, but it corrects a lot of errors and includes the two interludes which were composed for a 1928 production so as to help the scene changes. It also has the incomparable performance from Elisabeth Söderström.

Yet while one cannot possibly recommend this set in preference to Mackerras's, it holds its own place in the catalogue. It captures performances by some of the great generation of Czech singers who were developing careers in a country few of them could leave, so that records were a tantalizing glimpse of, for instance, the great Beno Blachut. Here, at 46, his voice still has a heroic quality, and he sings Boris with the easy, natural musicianship that marked all his work. Zdenek Kroupa, one of the finest of all Foresters in *The Cunning Little Vixen*, is in firm voice as Dikoj. Ludmila Komancová, a year older than Blachut, makes up in strength of character and skill of declamation what she lacks in power of tone. Bohumír Vích characterizes skilfully the pathetic Tichon. And Jaroslav Krombholc gives a lyrical performance of the score, one that may yield to Mackerras's in character and intensity but that has its own touching quality in its freshness and sincerity of phrasing. The set is accompanied by a full synopsis, with text and new English, French and German translations; the original essay has had to go, for along with some helpful commentary there went in it the obligatory socialist realist special pleading. For newcomers, then, Mackerras is unquestionably the first choice; but Janáček collectors who missed Krombholc first time round will find much to move them in this vintage reissue.

Janáček The Makropulos Affair.

Elisabeth Söderström *sop* Emilia Marty
Peter Dvorský *ten* Albert Gregor
Vladimir Krejčik *ten* Vítek
Anna Czaková *mez* Kristina
Václav Zítek *bar* Jaroslav Prus
Zdeněk Svehla *ten* Janek
Dalibor Jedlička *bass* Kolenatý
Jirí Joran *bass* Stage technician
Ivana Mixová *contr* Cleaning Woman
Beno Blachut *ten* Hauk-Sendorf
Blanka Vitková *contr* Chambermaid
Vienna State Opera Chorus; Vienna Philharmonic Orchestra / Sir Charles Mackerras.

Janáček Lachian Dances.

London Philharmonic Orchestra / François Huybrechts.
Decca Ⓕ ① 430 372-2DH2 (two discs: 118 minutes: ADD). Notes, text and translation included. Recorded 1978.

The Makropulos Affair has, of course, very much a heroine, in the tragic figure of Emilia Marty; and Elisabeth Söderström gives one of her greatest recorded performances. She succeeds amazingly in conveying the complexity of the character, the elegance yet flinty cynicism, the aloofness yet vulnerability, the latent warmth that can flower into such rich expressive phrases and then be reined in with a sense of nervy panic. She is only really alarmed by Prus, the most formidable of the men around her, powerfully sung by Václav Zítek; she has amused tenderness for poor silly Hauk-Sendorf, a captivating little vignette from Beno Blachut. Mackerras is masterly: the opera operates in many ways at a much swifter pace, with the narrative speeding by in a series of graphic strokes whose sharpness of characterization can need familiarity for its full impact. A recording is an excellent way of really getting to know such a work; but this is a recording to set among great performances of it.

As with *From the House of the Dead*, there is an essay by John Tyrrell that not only gives the listener the best possible introduction to the opera but is also a contribution to scholarship. These essays are repeated to all intents and purposes unaltered from the original issues, complete with music examples. There is also a Czech-English libretto. The fill-up of the *Lachian Dances* set is a rather less successful companion to *Makropulos*. Nevertheless, the opera is what counts.

Janáček The Makropoulos Affair.

Anja Silja *sop* Emilia Marty
Kim Begley *ten* Albert Gregor
Anthony Roden *ten* Vítek
Manuela Kriscak *mez* Kristina
Victor Braun *bar* Jaroslav Prus
Christopher Ventris *ten* Janek
Andrew Shore *bar* Kolenatý
Henry Waddington *bass* Stage Technician
Menai Davies *mez* Cleaning Woman
Robert Tear *ten* Hauk-Sendorf
Susan Gorton *mez* Chambermaid
London Philharmonic Orchestra / Andrew Davis.
Stage Producer: **Nikolaus Lehnhoff.** *Video Director:* **Brian Large.**
Warner Vision Ⓕ ▣ 0630 14016-3 (95 minutes). Recorded at a performance during the Glyndebourne Festival in August 1995.

Treated as a vehicle for the admittedly wonderful Anja Silja, Nikolaus Lehnhoff's production of *The Makropoulos Affair*, in Tobias Hoheisel's subtly mobile set, catches all the surreal, yet strangely moving mood of this story of a woman who has lived more than 300 years and is finally weary of life and love. However, he made a mistake in treating the final scene as a solo turn, banishing the subsidiary characters from the stage. The ever-energetic Andrew Davis catches all the work's empathy with Emilia Marty's plight, and Brian Large conveys as much in his video direction. This was recorded in studio conditions, allowing Large, during the Prelude, to show a wall of legal documents and the many travelling bags of Emilia Marty in her various incarnations, a most evocative start to the opera. Davis's conducting evinces a deep feeling for the long survivor's conflict of feelings. As a whole this subtitled production worked even better on film than it did in the house. The London Philharmonic are on top form and play splendidly.

Scott Joplin
American 1868-1917

Joplin Treemonisha.

Carmen Balthrop *sop* Treemonisha
Betty Allen *mez* Monisha
Curtis Rayam *ten* Remus
Willard White *bass* Ned
Ben Harney *bar* Zodzetrick
Cora Johnson *sop* Lucy
Kenneth Hicks *voc* Andy
Dorceal Duckens *voc* Luddud
Dwight Ransom *voc* Cephus
Raymond Bazemore *voc* Simon
Edward Pierson *voc* Parson Alltalk
Houston Grand Opera Chorus and Orchestra / Gunther Schuller.
DG Ⓜ ① 435 709-2GX2 (two discs: 90 minutes: ADD). Text included. Recorded 1975.

There is a tragic side to Joplin's only surviving opera, *Treemonisha*, in spite of its sparkling tunes and, partly, ragtime rhythms. He spent the last years of his life obsessed with getting the opera staged and his experience of rejection led to his decline and early death. Fortunately he published the vocal score at his own expense in 1911. Even though the run-through performance in 1915 was a flop, this printed score enabled Gunther Schuller to orchestrate the work and obtain recognition for Joplin as more than just a composer of rags, excellent though those classics are, through the Houston Grand Opera production in 1975.

It is impossible to imagine anyone better qualified than Schuller to bring *Treemonisha* back to life. His orchestrations show complete sympathy and idiomatic expertise, even if some decisions may still raise queries. For example, "Aunt Dinah has blowed de horn" (track 17), is marked *Assai moderato con espressione* but Schuller really dashes it off against all Joplin's instructions elsewhere about his rags. One can see why – the opera is starved of events and some of the straightforward narration quickly palls. *Treemonisha*, to Joplin's own libretto, urges education as the solution to the downtrodden Blacks' predicament. Lacking this benefit himself, Joplin could not command the theatrical skills and experience needed to make his story more than a naïve curiosity. But this matters little in a recording where mellifluous arias in the mainstream nineteenth-century Italian tradition make their effect interspersed with delightful Americanisms – the barber-shop group in "We will rest awhile" (track 6 on the second CD) and the fully-fledged delicate rag which forms the Prelude to Act 3 (track 10). Above all, perhaps, the "Real Slow Drag" at the end.

The cast is well balanced and convincing – interesting to hear Willard White, as Ned, well before his later triumphs – the recording, showing its age slightly, is adequate and the whole production much to be welcomed.

Erich Korngold
Austro-Hungarian/American 1897-1957

Korngold Der Ring des Polykrates.

Endrik Wottrich *ten* Arndt
Beate Bilandzija *sop* Laura
Jürgen Sacher *ten* Döblinger
Kirsten Blanck *sop* Lieschen
Dietrich Henschel *bar* Vogel
Deutsches Symphony Orchestra, Berlin / Klauspeter Siebel.
CPO Ⓔ ① CPO999 402-2 (70 minutes: DDD). Notes, text and translation included. Recorded 1995.

The fact that so many distinguished recordings of Korngold's works have appeared in recent years must surely be an indication of the sheer quality of this music. It certainly inspires some exceptionally fine performances from both soloists and orchestras alike, and CPO's world première recording of Korngold's first opera, *Der Ring des Polykrates*, one of the first issues of his centenary year, is no exception.

The thing that will astound most listeners approaching this opera for the first time (or indeed this period in Korngold's career in general) will be the extraordinary mastery of both orchestration and vocal writing – not to mention the sheer melodic inventiveness – of a mere 17-year-old. The rather slight, though elegantly simple, plot (the libretto was freely adapted from a comic drama of the same name by Heinrich Teweles by Korngold himself) is a classic case of mischief-making. Wilhelm Arndt, celebrating his supreme good fortune at landing the lucrative and prestigious post of court music director, a large monetary inheritance, and reflecting on a blissfully happy marriage, is visited by a long-lost friend, Peter Vogel, who, envious of his friend's good fortune (especially his marital bliss), goads Wilhelm into questioning his wife about any previous loves; Vogel's premise being that a sacrifice to the gods of good fortune is necessary in order to avert the bad luck that must surely follow in the wake of the good. To cut a short story even shorter, Vogel's plan fails, and he himself becomes the sacrifice as Wilhelm hands him his luggage and sends him on his way. In short *Der Ring des Polykrates* is a kind of comedic *Otello* with a happy ending.

As for the music, the opera is extremely beautiful throughout but one or two moments are especially worth mentioning for their Straussian, even Mahlerian, beauty – notably the declaration of the couple's love ("Gab's dir Mut ...") toward the end of scene 2 (track 2) and Wilhelm's wife Laura's rapturous "Schatz, jetzt muss ich dich küssen" (scene 7; track 7). But it's not just the beauty of the melodic and harmonic palette that impresses; Korngold shows us his superb grasp of pacing, plot control and structural cohesion too – as the booklet-notes point out, one would normally only expect such skill from a more mature composer of operas. The performances from Endrik Wottrich (Arndt) and Beate Bilandzija (Laura) are quite exceptional – everything one could wish for in a première recording – as indeed are the performances from the rest of the cast, and the Berlin orchestra under the direction of Klauspeter Siebel play as though this music were in their blood.

Korngold Die tote Stadt.

René Kollo *ten* Paul
Carol Neblett *sop* Marietta, The apparition of Marie
Benjamin Luxon *bar* Frank
Rose Wagemann *mez* Brigitta
Hermann Prey *bar* Fritz
Gabriele Fuchs *sop* Juliette
Patricia Clark *sop* Lucienne
Anton de Ridder *ten* Gaston, Victorin
Willi Brokmeier *ten* Count Albert
Tölz Boys' Choir; Bavarian Radio Chorus; Munich Radio Orchestra / Erich Leinsdorf.
RCA Opera Series Ⓜ ① GD87767 (two discs: 137 minutes: ADD). Notes, text and translation included. Recorded 1975.

The aria (eventually becoming a duet) "Glück, das mir verblieb", which kept the name of this opera and its composer alive during their long eclipse, is a stunner, there's no other word for it: obstinately memorable, moving in its lovely reprise at the very end of the opera. And of course if it's opulence you're after, big melodramatic gestures stunningly scored, strikingly stage-evocative images, gratefully curving and beautifully supported vocal lines, Korngold provides it in abundance.

The quality of "Glück, das mir verblieb", in its simplicity, its directly touching, almost folk-like plainness, is, however, sometimes at war with Korngold's amazingly sophisticated resource. Several times in the opera he hints at that quality again: early on, in a little exchange between the hero Paul and his devoted old servant Brigitta, again in Act 2 when Brigitta almost wordlessly reproaches him for his relationship, to her a blasphemy, with an actress who is the double of his dead wife. There is just a shadow of that directness to Paul's infatuated duet, later in the same act, with the double herself, Marietta, and it fleetingly but more strongly returns in the last act, where shadow and substance, living Marietta and ghostly Marie, are in direct confrontation. But time and again it is buried in strenuously melodramatic declamation, in orchestral overkill, and in a plethora of far more trivial ideas which Korngold seems unable to distinguish from the real thing. The opera's 'big scenes' (the interruption of a wild masquerade by an apparition of ghostly nuns; a half-real, half-nightmarish religious procession) are splendiferously noisy but can seem insubstantial.

Still, in a performance like this the undoubted allure of Korngold's surfaces is maximized. Kollo neighs a bit in his declamatory passages, and Neblett has a touch of squalliness in hers, but both can float the high phrases of the tune quite beautifully. Prey is in honeyed voice for the other song that survived independently, a toothsome little Viennese bon-bon of a Serenade in Act 2; Wagemann and Luxon add touches of distinction to their roles. Leinsdorf brings a great deal of energy to Korngold's noisier pages and yards and yards of multi-coloured plush to the luxuriant ones. The recording is bright and clear.

Korngold Die tote Stadt.

Thomas Sunnegårdh *ten* Paul
Katarina Dalayman *sop* Marietta, The apparition of Marie
Anders Bergström *bar* Frank
Ingrid Tobiasson *mez* Brigitta
Per-Arne Wahlgren *bar* Fritz
Hilde Leidland *sop* Juliette
Anna Tomson *mez* Lucienne
Lars-Erik Jonsson *ten* Gaston, Victorin
Ulrik Qvale *ten* Count Albert
Tomtberga School Children's Choir;
Chorus and Orchestra of the Royal Opera, Stockholm / Leif Segerstam.

Naxos ⑤ ① 8 660060/1 (two discs: 125 minutes: DDD). Notes and German text included. Recorded at performances in the Royal Swedish Opera House, Stockholm on August 31st, September 5th and 13th, 1996.

This is only the second commercial recording of Korngold's most famous work for the theatre. Die-hard Korngoldians will already have treasured copies of Leinsdorf's sumptuous world première recording, so any contender arriving on the scene faces a hard task from the start.

For this recording Naxos have acquired a Swedish Broadcasting Corporation recording of a production given at the Royal Swedish Opera House, Stockholm. The soloists give committed and acceptable performances, especially Thomas Sunnegårdh whose tormented Paul is particularly commendable, and on the whole the Stockholm Royal Opera Orchestra project Korngold's lavish and colourful orchestration well. But there are some niggles. For those familiar with the RCA recording, a glance at the overall timing of the Naxos set suggests that Segerstam is the faster of the two, but this version actually has numerous small, and sometimes not so small, cuts – primarily in Acts 1 and 2. These are cuts that were made for the Swedish Opera House production, and so were beyond Naxos's control, but when the rival recording is so strong these are a significant factor in choosing between different readings. However, even with the omission, Segerstam is slow and this hinders the flow and pacing of the opening act. Other negative points include some particularly intrusive stage noise towards the end of the opera and, at the other extreme, occasional moments when voices are not as well projected and clear as they could be.

Returning to Leinsdorf's superb recording immediately after listening to Segerstam's, the opera moves on to an altogether higher plane due to the luxuriously vivid recording and exceptionally fine performances. However, there will be many who, unfamiliar with the opera, and noting Naxos's super-bargain price-tag, will take the plunge and discover this remarkable piece, and that has to be for the good; but for a little extra outlay the RCA recording really is the one to go for.

Korngold Violanta.
Eva Marton *sop* Violanta
Siegfried Jerusalem *ten* Alfonso
Walter Berry *bass* Sirnone Trovai
Horst R. Laubenthal *ten* Giovanni Bracca
Gertraut Stoklassa *sop* Bice
Ruth Hesse *mez* Barbara
Manfred Schmidt *ten* Matteo
Heinrich Weber *ten* First Soldier
Paul Hansen *bass* Second Soldier
Karin Hautermann *mez* First Maid
Renate Freyer *mez* Second Maid
Bavarian Radio Chorus; Munich Radio Orchestra / Marek Janowski.
Sony Classical ⑤ ① MK79229 (74 minutes: ADD). Notes, text and translation included. Recorded 1979.

The producer of this recording is the composer's son, and a splendid job he has made of it. Janowski must take most of the credit for the combination of clarity and luxuriousness with which Korngold's richly embroidered orchestral textures are presented, but the balancing of voices against orchestra, much more natural than in many modern recordings, is the producer's doing and it subtly underlines his father's brilliantly skilful way of placing vocal lines in cunningly contrived glamorous relief. You can hear the singers responding to this, and to the shrewd building of those lines towards satisfying releases of vocal and emotional energy. Conductor and players respond, too, to Korngold's vivid sense of orchestral colour and the precision of his teeming imagination; for all the effects to come off in an opera by an 18-year-old is astonishing. Korngold's timing is no less sure; every entrance expertly prepared, the action daringly halted (and the suspense thereby intensified) for a motionless scene in which the all-too-chaste Violanta waits (and we wait too, on tenterhooks) for the arrival of the libertine she has lured to her Venetian palace so that she may kill him for having seduced her sister. In his arms she discovers that she has loved him since she first saw and hated him: strong stuff, indeed, from an 18-year-old!

It is amazing that the soft-featured youth who cockily grins at us on the back cover of the libretto booklet should have known so much so young (young for his years: by the look of him: his rakish trilby would fool no one). And in a performance as whole-hearted and full-voiced as this one (Marton in her Turandot voice, Jerusalem ardently heroic, Berry bleakly authoritative as Violanta's husband), one can readily understand the excitement aroused at the opera's early performances by the extent of what young Korngold knew. One has to remark on the lack of melodic distinction that lies beneath the score's fertile motivic working, on its awkward word-setting, its coarsely sensational purple patches or the cold falsity of its feigned emotionalism. How much can one expect from a child prodigy (assiduously trained for prodigy-hood and head-turningly praised since the age of nine) but gratifyingly prodigious cleverness? *Violanta* is a remarkable document in the abnormal psychology of precocity, absorbing yet dismaying.

Korngold Das Wunder der Heliane.

Anna Tomowa-Sintow *sop* Heliane
Hartmut Welker *bar* Ruler
John David de Haan *ten* Stranger
Reinhild Runkel *contr* Messenger
René Pape *bass* Porter
Nicolai Gedda *ten* Blind Judge
Martin Petzold *ten* Young Man
Berlin Radio Chorus; Berlin Radio Symphony Orchestra / John Mauceri.
Decca Ⓟ Ⓓ 436 636-2DH3 (three discs: 168 minutes: DDD). Notes, text and translation
included. Recorded 1992.

Korngold thought *Das Wunder der Heliane* his masterpiece. All that most people know of it is the
emotional "Ich ging zu ihm", recorded by Lotte Lehmann, the first Vienna Heliane. The opera
appeared in 1927 and made the rounds for a while, but not as widely as *Die tote Stadt*. Korngold – no
longer the wonder-child praised by Mahler, Strauss, Puccini and Ernest Newman; conducted by
Nikisch, Weingartner and Walter – turned to the adaptation and conducting of operettas. Later, in
Hollywood, he composed scores for the Errol Flynn epics and, in 1945, a concerto for Heifetz. *Heliane*
itself was a very late fruit of ripe, erotic romanticism in the line of d'Albert, Zemlinsky and Schreker.

A Stranger from the south – a version of Dionysus – is imprisoned in a harsh, bleak country.
Heliane, the wife of the tyrant Ruler, visits him; at his request she lets down her long golden hair;
bares her little white feet so that he can kiss them; then grants his request to reveal her body. ("It was
done very discreetly," Lehmann says; the soprano has seven pages of score in the buff, not just the
moments assigned to Thaïs and Salome.) But the Ruler appears and, seeing his wife naked (which he
has not done before, since he's never known her love), orders her arrest. Act 2 is her trial for adultery,
and "Ich ging zu ihm" her defence: she recounts the events of Act 1 and declares that only mentally,
not physically, did she give herself to the Stranger. The lovers are allowed a last moment together, and
at the close of their duet the Stranger stabs himself. In Act 3 Heliane must prove her innocence by
bringing him to life. She does so: he rises from his bier, but the jealous Ruler stabs her. The scene
changes: "the air is transparent, a snow of flower-petals falls", and Heliane has also returned to life.
After a last, tender duet the lovers again expire, into Eternal Love.

An expanded Adonis rite, a Resurrection allegory? (At the start a mystic chorus, accompanied by
organ and harps, sings "Blessed are they that love, for death shall not claim them".) The music is
sonically rich – Korngold has absorbed techniques of Mahler, Strauss and Puccini. He composes
fluently, copiously, on tonal bases with lush harmonies of bitonality and added notes, and he scores
exuberantly for a very large orchestra (with off-stage brass and bells and a heavenly choir). Korngold's
inspiration is uneven and some listeners may think the ecstatic, and even the angry scenes, somewhat
protracted. In the theatre, cuts might be welcome; on record we want the whole thing, and that is what
we are given here.

Decca have done the piece proud. The recording is wide-ranging. John Mauceri conducts with
conviction and with enthusiasm. Choral sopranos sail fearlessly to high C sharp. Anna Tomowa-
Sintow is a delicate, touching heroine, lacking only full, easy radiance of tone for soaring climaxes.
John David de Haan does well as the ardent, lyric-heroic Stranger. Hartmut Welker, the Ruler, is firm
and strong but inclined to bluster: though violence is implicit in the role, he tends to overdo it, and
his loving aria in Act 2 comes as relief. So does the gentler music of the Porter, warmly sung by René
Pape. The small parts are taken with distinction. A bold, interesting issue.

Hans Krása   Czechoslovakian 1899-1944

Krása Brundibár (ed. Karas).

Petra Krištofová *treb* Brundibár
Vít Ondračka *treb* Little Joe
Gabriela Přibilová *sop* Annette
Tomáš Staněk *treb* Ice-cream man
Michal Alexandridis *treb* Baker
Klára Tichá *sop* Milkman
Dora Horáčková *sop* Policeman
Jana Kratěnová *sop* Sparrow
Barbora Drofová *sop* Cat
Jan Flegl *treb* Dog Fido

Domažlický Eight Czech Songs, Op. 17.

Disman Radio Children's Choir and Orchestra / Joža Karas.
Channel Classics Ⓟ Ⓓ CCS5193 (42 minutes: DDD). Notes, opera text and translation included.
Recorded 1992.

The successful launch of Decca's Entartete Musik project should not obscure the dedicated work of smaller companies working in a similar field. For some time, Channel Classics have been disinterring much worthwhile music composed or performed in Theresienstadt, the notorious ghetto city established by the Nazis from 1941 and used in the main as a transit camp for Auschwitz. It is hard to be objective about what is after all an essentially lightweight children's opera. Composed in 1938, *Brundibár* ("The Bumble Bee") was subsequently reconstituted for performance by the musicians available in Theresienstadt. There it received as many as 55 performances and acquired unlikely resonances as it entered the group consciousness of the incarcerated deportees. Thousands of children passed through. How many who perished in the camps must have hummed Krása's hit tunes? – the notes assure us that the score used here is very much the one they would have heard.

The much-praised Czech TV recording, once available on Romantic Robot (conducted by Mario Klemens), involves a larger complement of strings and creates a rather different effect: close-miked, bold, romanticized and 'commercial' in a way that is less than affecting. Under Karas, cool, literal and idiomatic, the purely musical qualities of the score are more readily apparent. The genre is an inventive amalgam of popular Czech elements from Janáček, Martinů and Weill, and it is perhaps the veiled allusions to the famous Dvořák *Humoresque* (track 1), *Petrushka* (track 6) and *Verklärte Nacht* (track 9) which most clearly point up Krása's own subversive pre-war personality. The only real drawback comes with the opulent packaging. To provide full librettos in (American) English, French and German without correlating them with the original Czech seems like a missed opportunity, and the inaccurate track listing for the Second Act makes it difficult to get your bearings in any language. The Czech song arrangements by František Domažlický are an ungenerous bonus (no texts), executed without the high polish accorded the main work though not without their own quiet charm.

Ernst Krenek   Austrian/American 1900-1991

Krenek Jonny spielt auf.

Krister St Hill *bar* Jonny
Heinz Kruse *ten* Max
Alessandra Marc *sop* Anita
Michael Kraus *bar* Daniello
Martina Posselt *sop* Yvonne
Dieter Scholz *bass* Manager
Dieter Schwartner *ten* Hotel Manager
Martin Petzold *sngr* Station Announcer, First Policeman
Matthias Weichert *sngr* Second Policeman
Erwin Noack *sngr* Third Policeman
Leipzig Opera Chorus; Chinchilla; Leipzig Gewandhaus Orchestra / Lothar Zagrosek.
Decca Ⓟ Ⓓ 436 631-2DH2 (two discs: 131 minutes: DDD). Notes, text and translation included. Recorded 1991.

Krenek always resisted the description of *Jonny spielt auf* as a 'jazz opera'. In part, no doubt, he was reacting against the charges of opportunism already being levelled against him as he changed, seemingly as rapidly as he changed his clothes, from atonality to neo-classicism, through *Jonny* to a seemingly neo-romantic phase and on to serialism, post-serialism and a late involvement with electronic music. The reasons for these changes have been insufficiently studied. The serial phase, for example, coincides with the rise of Nazism and Krenek's despairing realization that he had no future in Europe. To arrive in America with a suitcase full of 12-tone scores and a reputation as the author of *Jonny spielt auf*, an opera that New York had found distasteful and almost unstageable because its title-role is black and amoral, hardly looks like opportunism.

And *Jonny* is something far more interesting than a cynical ride to success (50 productions in its first year!) on the band-wagon, set rolling by Milhaud's *La création du monde*. It uses jazz, but does not try to absorb it into a unified language. Indeed it's quite important for the plot that jazz should be treated as an exotic import, however liberating, since the opera's real central character, as Krenek insisted, is not the jazz fiddler Jonny but the archetypally middle-European composer Max, at least a partial self-portrait. Max, who feels at home only amid glaciers (Ibsen would have recognized the symbolism), is partially thawed by his love for a singer, Anita, but only achieves real wholeness when he emerges from his ivory (or ice) tower and takes control of his own future. Jonny's theft of a valuable violin from the worldly virtuoso Daniello, a symbolic theft from a dying culture by a vital one, is the secondary plot, for all that it provides the pretext for most of the opera's more sensational scenes.

The great merit of this recording, derived from a revival at the Leipzig Opera House where *Jonny* had its triumphant première, is that it devotes as much care to Max's music as to Jonny's. Treat the work as a 'jazz opera' and its non-jazz scenes (the majority) risk sounding thin by comparison. In fact Krenek's own idiom is a curious but effective blend of lyricism, sounding pre- rather than post-Wagnerian, with harmonies that often render that lyricism ambiguous. But it is the lyrical quality that unifies the opera's two worlds, that and a crisp use of rhythmic motif. The famous blues, the tango-duet, the uproarious final scene (heralded, as the score stipulated, by all the alarm bells in the theatre going off), with its culminating image of Jonny astride a station clock that has turned into a revolving globe, leading the entire Old World to the New with his irresistible dance – all these have immense vigour under Zagrosek's alert direction. But the song from Max's opera, mocked as it is in the notorious scene on the glacier where he hears his own music booming from the public address system of a hotel in the valley below 'vanquished' by Jonny's: that, too (Alessandra Marc's voluptuous singing of it withstands even the distortion of the loudspeaker), has its own memorability and allure; so does the long duet scene in which Anita teaches Max what is missing from his philosophy ("at every moment be yourself, be wholly yourself"), with its finely arching melodies.

The cast is uniformly excellent though Kruse lacks the Tauberish glamour that Krenek no doubt had in mind for Max. St Hill is an immensely likeable Pied Piper of a Jonny, Posselt a pretty, soubrettish Yvonne (the Despina of the piece) and Kraus an ample-voiced, overbearing Daniello. The recording ensures that you won't miss the swanee whistle and the flexatone, and provides enjoyable sound effects to stand in for the car-chase and the steam locomotive that were as much a part of the opera's newsworthiness as its jazz elements. If you are expecting period fun, you will find that *Jonny spielt auf* is a good deal more than that, and the case for investigating the music of Krenek's subsequent six decades of creative life seems compelling.

John Lampe
British c1703-1751

Lampe Pyramus and Thisbe.
Mark Padmore *ten* Pyramus
Susan Bisatt *sop* Thisbe
Michael Sanderson *ten* Wall, Master
Arwel Treharne *ten* Moon, Prompter
Andrew Knight *bass* Lion, Prologue
Peter Milne *spkr* Mr Semibrief
Alan McMahon *spkr* First Gentleman
Jack Edwards *spkr* Second Gentleman

Lampe Flute Concerto in G major, "The Cuckoo".
Rachel Brown *fl*
Opera Restor'd / Peter Holman.
Hyperion Ⓔ Ⓞ CDA66759 (64 minutes: DDD). Notes and text included. Recorded 1994.

John Lampe, for a time, played the bassoon in Handel's opera orchestra; then in the early-1730s he was one of the group of musicians who put on English operas at the theatre opposite Handel's in the Haymarket and he wrote several pieces for the company before turning to burlesque, enjoying particular success with *The Dragon of Wantley* (1737). *Pyramus and Thisbe* (1745) was his last opera; later he went to Dublin and to Edinburgh, where he died in 1751. None of his operas survives complete; publications of the time usually reproduced the airs but not the recitatives or choruses, and the scores of most operas perished in the numerous theatre fires of the time.

For *Pyramus* Peter Holman has had to supply recitatives, which he does with style and a touch more imagination than Lampe himself might have managed. Yet Lampe's airs are deftly written. The text is based on Shakespeare's 'lamentable play' in *A Midsummer Night's Dream*, with Wall, Moon and Lion among the characters as well as Pyramus and Thisbe. Lampe's music has a good deal of wit – listen for example to the Wall's Song, with the lovers' groans and moans represented by harsh open violin Gs, its pseudo-pathetic G minor tonality, its amusing setting of "whisp'ring whisp'ring [17 times] hole"; or the duet as the lovers depart 'without delay', in typical operatic haste, with much repetition and many pauses; or the Lion's song with its rhythmic growls.

No one would suggest that it is high-quality music, but it is resourceful and entertaining. And it is excellently presented here, in unpretentious style – this kind of music fares far better with modest-sized voices and careful diction than if more self-consciously sung. The two principals sing with due charm and tenderness: Mark Padmore offers a pleasantly relaxed and fresh-sounding tenor and Susan Bisatt some shapely lines and well-focused tone. Peter Holman's conducting is direct and idiomatic.

Franz Lehár
Hungarian/Austrian 1870-1948

Lehár Friederike.
Helen Donath *sop* Friederike
Adolf Dallapozza *ten* Goethe
Martin Finke *ten* Lenz
Gabriele Fuchs *sop* Salomea

Helene Grabenhorst *sop* Hortense
Erika Rüggeberg *sop* Liselotte
Gudrun Greindl-Rosner *contr* Dorothée
Harry Kalenberg *spkr* Grand Duke
Gustl Datz *spkr* Brion
Maria Stadler *spkr* Magdalena
Christian Wolff *spkr* Weyland
Jürgen von Pawels *spkr* Knebel
Bavarian Radio Chorus; Munich Radio Orchestra / Heinz Wallberg.
EMI Ⓜ ① CMS5 65369-2 (two discs: 95 minutes: ADD). Recorded 1980.

To listen to this reissue is to revisit what seems like a golden age, when the recording of Viennese operetta in more or less complete versions actually went beyond *Die Fledermaus* and *Die lustige Witwe*. *Friederike*, a romanticized story of Goethe's love for an Alsatian pastor's daughter, is strictly speaking not an operetta at all but a Singspiel or 'play with music'. Much dialogue intersperses solos and duets divided between two couples of lovers, with just a few choral contributions. Since the voices of the two couples are not too greatly contrasted in this recording, there is not the variety of sound one might expect from a Lehár score. On the other hand, there are typically glorious Lehár songs – "O Mädchen, mein Mädchen", "Warum hast du mich wachgekusst?", as well as his setting of Goethe's "Sah' ein Knab' ein Roslein steh'n" – and some typically glorious Lehár orchestration. There is unlikely to be another opportunity to hear it complete so this should be welcomed and snapped up.

Lehár Giuditta (sung in English).
Deborah Riedel *sop* Giuditta
Jerry Hadley *ten* Octavio
Jeffrey Carl *bar* Manuele Biffi, Antonio
Andrew Busher *spkr* The Duke
Naomi Itami *sop* Anita
Lynton Atkinson *ten* Pierrino
William Dieghan *ten* Sebastiano
English Chamber Orchestra / Richard Bonynge.
Telarc Ⓕ ① CD80436 (78 minutes: DDD). Text included. Recorded 1996.

Giuditta was Lehár's last stage work and the peak of his compositional development. Written for the Vienna State Opera, it is a highly ambitious score, containing some fiendishly difficult vocal writing and using a large orchestra featuring mandolin and other exotic instruments. For this recording some two hours of music have been compressed into 78 minutes by means of snips here and there and the omission of a couple of subsidiary numbers (which incidentally may be heard in the excerpts from the 1958 Decca recording on London). The piece has a *Carmen*-like story, about the disenchanted wife of an innkeeper who persuades a soldier to desert, before eventually abandoning and ruining him as she goes from lover to lover. The best-known number is Giuditta's "On my lips every kiss is like wine", here gloriously sung by Deborah Riedel; but the leading male role was written for Tauber, and there are some marvellous and demanding tenor solos, equally superbly sung by the ever impressive Jerry Hadley. Despite writing for the opera-house, Lehár remained faithful to his formula of interspersing the music for the principal couple with sprightly dance numbers for a comedy pair, here in the hands of Naomi Itami and Lynton Atkinson. Assisted by Richard Bonynge's lilting conducting, these contribute richly to the appeal of the recording. One hopes that such an adventurous and generously filled CD will succeed in spreading the appeal of this ravishing score.

Lehár Giuditta.
Edda Moser *sop* Giuditta
Nicolai Gedda *ten* Octavio
Klaus Hirte *bar* Manuele Biffi
Ludwig Baumann *bass* Antonio
Jürgen Jung *spkr* Lord Barrymore
Thomas Wiedenhofer *spkr* The Duke
Brigitte Lindner *sop* Anita
Martin Finke *ten* Pierrino
Friedrich Lenz *ten* Sebastiano
Munich Concert Chorus; Munich Radio Orchestra / Willi Boskovsky.
EMI Ⓜ ① CMS5 65378-2 (two discs: 129 minutes: DDD). Recorded 1983-4.

Though Nicolai Gedda takes the Tauber role on this mid-price EMI reissue, his voice had by this time lost some of its earlier glories, and the part is in any case a fiendishly difficult one. For all its much better sound quality, this recording does not altogether surpass Decca's early stereo version, referred to above, from which extended excerpts have been reissued. There Hilde Gueden was a far more alluring Giuditta than Edda Moser here. Yet this is a shimmeringly beautiful score, full of glorious full-blooded melody and like *Das Land des Lächelns*, it should be in every Viennese operetta collection.

Lehár Das Land des Lächelns (sung in English).
Nancy Gustafson *sop* Lisa
Lynton Atkinson *ten* Gustl
Jerry Hadley *ten* Sou-Chong
Naomi Itami *sop* Mi
London Voices; English Chamber Orchestra / Richard Bonynge.
Telarc Ⓕ Ⓞ CD80419 (79 minutes: DDD). Text included. Recorded 1995.

English-language studio performances of late Lehár operettas make a welcome novelty at a time when such works are increasingly neglected in favour of revivals of jazz-age musical comedy. This recording offers distinguished principals and a conductor whose affection for such music is second to none. Moreover, it makes full use of the capacity of the CD format, with only minor snips necessary to accommodate the whole work on a single CD.
Das Land des Lächelns ("The Land of Smiles") will be the more likely to appeal to an English-speaking audience as it is the one already established on English-language stages. Jerry Hadley is a fine singing actor, but he is also a superb tenor who brings out the full romantic appeal of the big Act 2 aria. Here this becomes "My heart belongs to you!" in a new translation of the libretto which is by none other than Hadley himself. A fine one it is too, with some beautifully poetic images. As Lisa, Nancy Gustafson applies her clear soprano to Lehár's exquisite vocal writing, and her duet with Hadley, "Ah, who has given us our dream come true?", shows off the pair to perfection. In the *buffo* numbers, Naomi Itami and Lynton Atkinson provide the necessary contrast, whilst giving full value to the musical demands. The text is sufficiently complete to include not only the large-scale Overture but also the Chinese Wedding Procession – here recorded for the first time.

Lehár Das Land des Lächelns.
Anneliese Rothenberger *sop* Lisa
Harry Friedauer *ten* Gustl
Nicolai Gedda *ten* Sou-Chong
Renate Holm *sop* Mi
Jobst Moeller *bar* Tschang
Bavarian Radio Chorus; Graunke Symphony Orchestra / Willy Mattes.
EMI Ⓜ Ⓞ CMS5 65372-2 (two discs: 87 minutes: ADD). Recorded 1967.

EMI's second version of *Das Land des Lächelns*, Lehár's portrayal of the clash of Western and Eastern cultures, is far more complete and in richer sound than the version here. However, it does not overshadow this 1967 recording in terms of performance. The great glory of this earlier version is the singing of Nicolai Gedda, who brings off "Dein ist mein ganzes Herz" and the other Tauber favourites to splendid effect. With a distinguished supporting cast, including a secondary pair of singers who contrast well with the more serious leading pair, it's a recording to savour.

Lehár Die lustige Witwe.
Cheryl Studer *sop* Hanna
Boje Skovhus *bar* Danilo
Bryn Terfel *bass-bar* Zeta
Rainer Trost *ten* Camille
Barbara Bonney *sop* Valencienne
Uwe Peper *ten* Raoul
Karl-Magnus Fredriksson *bar* Cascada
Heinz Zednik *ten* Njegus
Richard Savage *bar* Bogdanowitsch
Lynette Alcantara *sop* Sylviane
Philip Salmon *ten* Kromow
Constanze Backes *mez* Olga
Julian Clarkson *bass* Pritschitsch
Angela Kazimierczuk *sop* Praškowia
Wiener Tschuschenkapelle; Vienna Philharmonic Orchestra / John Eliot Gardiner.
DG Ⓕ Ⓞ 439 911-2GH (80 minutes: DDD). Notes, text and translation included. Recorded 1994.

First the cliché. You wait 14 years for a new *Merry Widow* and then two come along at once! Only five months before this came EMI's recording of the 1993 Royal Festival Hall concert performance conducted by Franz Welser-Möst, followed by this star-studded studio version from DG. Next the blurb. Surprisingly, perhaps, this is the Vienna Philharmonic's first recording of *The Merry Widow*. It is also apparently the first time the orchestra have worked with John Eliot Gardiner. Characteristically, he consulted the composer's autograph score and corrected a whole series of errors in the orchestral parts. We are told that, far from resenting the intrusion of an outsider, the Vienna Philharmonic players were throughout amazed at the sensitivity and humour that Gardiner brought to the piece.

Well, there is no promise that anyone will notice the results of Gardiner's work on the orchestral parts. But you can certainly believe the utter sincerity of the VPO's assessment of his conducting. This is one of those great operetta interpretations that is committed to record once in a generation if one is lucky. No wonder the orchestra booked Gardiner to conduct not only for further recordings but at the Vienna Philharmonic Ball itself. Where Welser-Möst's conducting for EMI was welcome for its *echt-wienerisch* approach, Gardiner's is on an altogether more inspired plane. In the Viennese rhythms, Gardiner shows himself utterly at home – as in the Act 2 Dance scene (omitted from the EMI recording), where he eases the orchestra irresistibly into the famous waltz. But there are also countless instances where Gardiner provides a deliciously fresh inflexion to the score, perhaps the most obvious example being in the delightful but oft-neglected "Zauber der Häuslichkeit" duet. Gardiner takes its first section at something closer to a galop than the usual polka, thereby capturing all the more vividly the sheer elation of Valencienne's and Camille's relationship.

The cast of singers is uniformly impressive. If Cheryl Studer's Hannah isn't quite as assured as Lott's for EMI, her captivatingly playful "Dummer, dummer Reitersmann" is typical of a well-characterized performance. As Danilo, Boje Skovhus may never challenge the sheer polish of Thomas Hampson's almost superhuman Danilo, but he offers a much more natural, more human characterization. No less beautifully sung in its different way, his lighter baritone takes us nearer to the tenor *buffo* Lehár had in mind. For the secondary couple, Rainer Trost proves an excellent alternative to EMI's impressive John Aler, while Barbara Bonney easily outshines EMI's Elzbieta Szmytka. Not the least inspired piece of casting comes with Bryn Terfel, who transforms himself outstandingly well into the bluff Pontevedrin ambassador. As for Gardiner's personally selected chorus, they make Monteverdi to Montenegro and Pontevedro seem the most natural transition in the world.

DG's recorded sound has an astonishing clarity and immediacy, as in the way the piccolos shriek out at the Widow's Act 1 entrance or in the beautiful *pianissimo* accompaniment to the "Vilja-Lied". The DG version outstrips the EMI in offering a fully integrated version with linking dialogue, rather than EMI's musical numbers linked by audience applause or a Dirk Bogarde narration.

Lehár Die lustige Witwe.
Dame Elisabeth Schwarzköpf *sop* Hanna
Erich Kunz *bar* Danilo
Anton Niessner *bar* Zeta
Nicolai Gedda *ten* Camille
Emmy Loose *sop* Valencienne
Josef Schmidinger *bass* Raoul
Ottakar Kraus *bar* Cascada
Philharmonia Orchestra and Chorus / Otto Ackermann.
EMI mono Ⓟ Ⓘ CDH7 69520-2 (72 minute: ADD). Recorded 1953.

BBC RADIO 3
90-93 FM

In this star-studded performance from the previous generation to Gardiner's, the music emerged as one of the great classics of light opera. The one thing in the score below standard is the lengthy Overture Lehár wrote for a special performance in Vienna in 1940; but it is played, like everything else, in such style that even Lehár's attempts at counterpoint (the famous waltz is used as a counter-melody) sound convincing. In the English score this waltz comes into Act 2, hummed by Hanna (Sonia in the English version) and Danilo as they dance, and placed between "Oh the women" and the duet for Valencienne (Natalie to us) and Camille. In the present recording we have it only in the last act and there truncated, for Hanna begins it half-way through.

Emmy Loose has exactly the right appealing kind of voice for the 'dutiful wife' who plays with fire, and Nicolai Gedda is a superb Camille, sounding extraordinarily like Tito Schipa at his best. His high notes ring out finely and his caressing lyrical tones would upset a far better-balanced woman than the susceptible Valencienne. These two sing their duets beautifully, both excelling in the second act duet, in which Gedda has the lion's share. Nothing in this recording, except Schwarzköpf's Vilia, is so ravishing as his soft tone in the second half of the duet ("Love in my heart is waking"), which begins "Sich dort den keinen Pavillon" ("See, there's a little about there") which is perhaps the loveliest in the score.

Erich Kunz has not the charm but more voice and a perfect command of the style the music requires; and he is very taking in the celebrated Maxim's song. He speaks the middle section of the little song about the Königskinder possibly because the vocal part lies uncomfortably high for him; and perhaps his rich laughter would not be considered quite the thing in the diplomatic service. But his is, in most ways, a very attractive and lively performance. The Baron's part was probably much written up for George Graves (it will be remembered he was called Popoff, to conform to the English conviction that most foreigners are rather funny), but here what little he has to do is done well by Anton Niessner. Elisabeth Schwarzköpf sings Hanna radiantly and exquisitely. She commands the ensembles in no uncertain manner and makes it clear that the 20-million-francs widow would be a personage even if she had only 20 centimes. It is a grand performance, crowned with the sensuous, tender singing of the celebrated waltz in Act 3.

The chorus singing is first-rate and its Viennese abandon sounds absolutely authentic, whatever its address. Otto Ackermann conducts with complete understanding, and notable sympathy for the singers, and the Philharmonia Orchestra play like angels for him. We have here the happy marriage of a perfect performance with a recording as perfect as one can reasonably expect and, very important in such a score, the string tone is lovely throughout. The balance between orchestra and voices, also, could not be better.

Ruggiero Leoncavallo   Italian 1858-1919

Leoncavallo Pagliacci.
Joan Carlyle *sop* Nedda
Carlo Bergonzi *ten* Canio
Giuseppe Taddei *bar* Tonio
Ugo Benelli *ten* Beppe
Rolando Panerai *bar* Silvio.

Mascagni Cavalleria rusticana.
Fiorenza Cossotto *mez* Santuzza
Carlo Bergonzi *ten* Turiddu
Adriane Martino *mez* Lola
Giangiacomo Guelfi *bar* Alfio
Maria Gracia Allegri *contr* Lucia
Chorus and Orchestra of La Scala, Milan / Herbert von Karajan.

Opera Intermezzos
Cilea Adriana Lecouvreur – Intermezzo.
Giordano Fedora – Intermezzo.
Mascagni L'amico Fritz – Intermezzo.
Massenet Thaïs – Méditation.
Puccini Manon Lescaut – Intermezzo. Suor Angelica – Intermezzo.
Schmidt Notre Dame – Intermezzo.
Verdi La traviata – Prelude, Act 3.
Wolf-Ferrari I Gioiello della Madonna – Intermezzo.
Michel Schwalbé *vn.*
Berlin Philharmonic Orchestra / Herbert von Karajan.
DG Ⓕ ① 419 257-2GH3 (three discs: 198 minutes: ADD). Notes, texts and translations included where appropriate. Recorded 1965.
Pagliacci is available separately on DG The Originals Ⓜ ① 449 727-2GOR (78 minutes: ADD).

Leoncavallo Pagliacci.
Maria Callas *sop* Nedda
Giuseppe di Stefano *ten* Canio
Tito Gobbi *bar* Tonio
Nicola Monti *ten* Beppe
Rolando Panerai *bar* Silvio

Mascagni Cavalleria rusticana.
Maria Callas *sop* Santuzza
Giuseppe di Stefano *ten* Turiddu
Anna Maria Canali *mez* Lola
Rolando Panerai *bar* Alfio
Ebe Ticozzi *contr* Lucia
Chorus and Orchestra of La Scala, Milan / Tullio Serafin.
EMI mono Ⓕ ① CDS5 56287-2 (two discs: 141 minutes): ADD. Notes, texts and translations included. Recorded 1954.

These two sets place us in a quandary; both have so much to offer that choice between them is extremely difficult. Of the famous Karajan set, opulent in sound, big in scale, one might comment, "manipulated but magnificent" or perhaps "magnificent but manipulated". At the time of listening, one is quite carried away by the grandeur and passion of the readings. It is only later that one begins to call into question the extremely slow tempos and the almost too effusive orchestra. Don't the dramas then tend to become ponderous and Germanic rather than Italianate, even if the presence of the Scala chorus and orchestra lend them authenticity? They are also present on the EMI performances of some ten years earlier. Here the sound is much more confined, though rather more immediate, and mono. Serafin conducts swifter-moving performances, yet ones quite as notable as Karajan's for pointing up relevant detail. All four interpretations carry with them a real sense of the theatre and are quite free from studio routine.

It is just as difficult to choose between the casts. Callas sang Santuzza only as a 15-year-old (in her native Greece), Nedda not at all on stage. Yet, as is her way, she lives the characters more vividly than anyone. The sadness and anguish she brings to Santuzza's unhappy plight are at their most compelling at "io piango" in "Voi lo sapete" and at "Turiddu mi tolse" in her encounter with Alfio, where the pain in Santuzza's heart is expressed in almost unbearable terms. As Nedda, she differentiates marvellously between the pensiveness of her aria, the passion of her duet with Silvio, and the playfulness of her *commedia dell'arte* acting. One unforgettable moment among many is when her tone shivers on the word "lurido" as she sees Tonio leaving, then becomes all smiling a moment later as she greets her love with "Silvio!"

Her partner in both operas is di Stefano. They work up a huge lather of passion in the big *Cavalleria* duet, and the tenor is wholly believable as the caddish Turiddu. In the immediacy of emotion of his Canio, it is the tenor's turn to evoke pity and display anguish. Di Stefano does it as well as any Canio on record without quite having the heroic tone for the latter part of the opera. The same can be said of Bergonzi on the Karajan version, but he carries all before him by the nobility and dignity of his singing here. He is a little too upstanding for Turiddu; one cannot believe this nice guy would betray Santuzza, but again the singing is a model of style, and there is no lack of feeling in Bergonzi's reading of the role. His Santuzza is Fiorenza Cossotto; famous in the part over a long period and justifiably so. She hasn't Callas's subtlety of inflexion, but the big wodges of secure tone and the sheer emotional content of her singing carry all before them. Nedda on DG is sung by Joan Carlyle, at the peak of her form in the mid-1960s. She catches precisely the airy nature of her ballad and sings with Italianate timbre in the duet with Silvio. That role is ideally taken in both performances by Rolando Panerai, vibrant and sensuous of voice, suitably impassioned in manner.

Panerai is also a strong Alfio on the Serafin set, but Guelfi, with his huge voice, is possibly even better suited to this macho part. It is impossible to choose between the two Tonios, both pertinently cast. Taddei plays the part a little more comically, Gobbi more menacingly; both sing the Prologue with that bite on the consonants that drives home the message about art aping life. Monti and Benelli are attractive Beppes. So both sets have casts that would be hard to equal today though the 1983 Prêtre *Pagliacci* (Philips) comes near to doing so.

We cannot recommend the Karajan above the Serafin or the other way round. Callas or Karajan enthusiasts will have no difficulty making their choice – for admirers of the latter DG generously include a selection of opera intermezzos played with verve if not very tidily by the Berlin Philharmonic. Others may be guided by quality of sound. With either you will be ensured hours of memorable listening.

Leoncavallo Pagliacci.
   Renata Scotto *sop* Nedda
   José Carreras *ten* Canio
   Kari Nurmela *bar* Tonio
   Ugo Benelli *ten* Beppe
   Thomas Allen *bar* Silvio

Mascagni Cavalleria rusticana.
   Montserrat Caballé *sop* Santuzza
   José Carreras *ten* Turiddu
   Júlia Hamari *contr* Lola
   Matteo Manuguerra *bar* Alfio
   Astrid Varnay *sop* Lucia
   Southend Boys' Choir; Ambrosian Opera Chorus; Philharmonia Orchestra / Riccardo Muti.
   EMI Ⓜ ① CMS7 63650-2 (two discs: 150 minutes: ADD). Notes, texts and translations included. Recorded 1979.

BBC RADIO 3
90-93 FM

When these recordings first appeared, their didactic pretensions stimulated resistance. In *Cavalleria rusticana* it was as though the conductor had been through the orchestral parts, doubly underlining every expression mark, while in *Pagliacci* he had censored all those naughty high notes not to be found in the composer's autograph score. Fortunately, both operations seem less obtrusive now than they did in 1979. The overinsistence of conductors is something we have lived with long enough for this instance to appear relatively mild, and the traditional high notes have persisted in subsequent performances of *Pagliacci* simply because experience has found them to be more effective. Nor has it become general practice to have Tonio sing "La commedia è finita" as indicated in the score, the ineffectiveness of a monotone being amply demonstrated in this recording. However, it is a curious anomaly that the Prologue to *Pagliacci* should be so revered in theory that the traditional A flat and

G are banished from its presence and yet so little cared for in practice that it is given one of the dullest, least imaginative performances in its history on records.

This is by Kari Nurmela, of whom at one time great things were expected. Instead, among the baritones, it is Thomas Allen, the Silvio, who has made the progress and who carries the distinction here. His singing of "E allor perchè" in the love duet is one of the finest things of all. The baritone in *Cavalleria rusticana*, Matteo Manuguerra, has impressive power and quality but a somewhat inexpressive style (and in his song is upstaged by the whip which cracks ferociously at no more than an arm's length in front of its owner). The two sopranos, Caballé and Scotto, have some lovely moments and both are strong in dramatic commitment: not ideally cast, even so, for Santuzza needs more body in the middle register and more steel at the top, while Nedda should have a more girlish quality, less of the mature prima donna, and much greater firmness on the louder high notes.

Carreras gives generously of voice and emotion in both of his roles – they are among his best achievements on disc. More could be done with solos such as the *Siciliana* and "No, Pagliaccio non son". Muti himself is best with orchestral work and choruses: outstanding, for instance, are all of the choruses in *Pagliacci*. It is in such passages that he presents an interesting and viable alternative to Karajan's spacious manner and refined style.

Leoncavallo Pagliacci.
Teresa Stratas *sop* Nedda
Plácido Domingo *ten* Canio
Juan Pons *bar* Tonio
Florindo Andreolli *ten* Beppe
Alberto Rinaldi *bar* Silvio
Chorus and Orchestra of La Scala, Milan / Georges Prêtre.
Stage/Video Director: **Franco Zeffirelli.**
Philips Video Classics ▣▣ 070 104-3PH (70 minutes). Recorded 1982.

This Zeffirelli film was made cheek by jowl with *Cavalleria rusticana* in 1982 (reviewed under Mascagni). The two performances, although on sale separately, show how the genre of video can excel itself away from the opera-house when an inspired hand such as Zeffirelli is involved. *Pagliacci* was shot on a large studio set in Milan, although an outdoor milieu is cleverly suggested. Zeffirelli moves the action forward credibly to the inter-war years and his nicely flowing direction always leads the eye to the appropriate spot or face. When that concerns Stratas's vulnerable Nedda, torn between young lover and older husband, the results are moving. She is an eloquent singing actress even if her singing as such leaves something to be desired. The look of sheer misery as she makes up for the play during the Intermezzo is unforgettable. Domingo gives one of the most notable performances of all his many on video, conveying all the pathos of this big-hearted man overcome by jealousy and inner torment. Pons is a properly gross, mean Tonio, Rinaldi a sensuous Silvio. The dubbing is convincing and the sound and picture are beyond reproach.

Franco Leoni   Italian 1864-1949

Leoni L'Oracolo.
Richard Van Allan *bass* Uin-Sci
Tito Gobbi *bar* Cim-Fen
Clifford Grant *bass* Hu-Tsin
Dame Joan Sutherland *sop* Ah-Joe
Ian Caley *ten* L'indovino
Ryland Davies *ten* Uin-San-Lui
Huguette Tourangeau *mez* Hua-Qui
Finchley Children's Music Group; John Alldis Choir;
National Philharmonic Orchestra / Richard Bonynge.
Decca Ⓟ Ⓓ 444 396-2DHO (65 minutes: ADD). Notes, text and translation included. Recorded 1975.

Hokum, but any opera that begins with three crashes, a very loud cock-crow, a chorus shouting in fake-Chinese and then launches into a vehement unaccompanied solo for Tito Gobbi has clearly got something going for it. So, if it comes to that, has any opera that ends with the villain (Gobbi, of course) being strangled with his own pigtail. And between? Well, there's abundant evidence that Franco Leoni was a contemporary of Puccini and, like him, a pupil of Ponchielli. Not as good as Puccini, mind, not nearly, but not to be contemptuously dismissed, either. Yes, *L'Oracolo* is often crude, often tawdry, but Leoni knew enough about voices to give them long and singable lines that Gobbi, Davies and Sutherland are properly grateful for. He knows, too, that simple effects are often more direct than lavish ones. When Sutherland's heroine, desired by the evil Cim-Fen, discovers that he has murdered the young man she loves, her lament has an underlying simplicity (and it is, besides, accompanied by beautiful divided strings) that ... well, one can't quite paraphrase Shakespeare's Hippolyta and exclaim "Beshrew my heart, but I pity the woman!", but nor can one snigger at her patronizingly.

It is an excellent performance, the chorus obviously rather enjoying all that gibberish they have to sing ("Wufet; tanhae fulu; samciau, ha ha ha!"), and Gobbi, in only slightly worn voice, can make even "Hai-la!" sound by turns malign and sinisterly jovial. Davies is in admirably Italianate voice and Sutherland's control of vocal colour gives a trace of reality even to the paper-thin role of Ah-Joe (pronounced "Ah-Yoeh", thank goodness). Lively conducting, a decent sense of stage atmosphere and a clean, unexaggerated recording.

Gyorgy Ligeti Hungarian/Austrian 1923

Ligeti Le grand macabre.
Eirian Davies *sop* Chief of the Secret Police (Gepopo), Venus
Penelope Walmsley-Clark *sop* Amanda
Olive Fredericks *mez* Amando
Kevin Smith *alto* Prince Go-Go
Christa Puhlmann-Richter *mez* Mescalina
Peter Haage *ten* Piet the Pot
Dieter Weller *bar* Nekrotzar
Ude Krekow *bass* Astradamors
Johann Leutgeb *bar* Ruffiak
Ernst Salzer *bar* Schobiak
Laszlo Modos *bar* Schabernack
Herbert Prikopa *spkr* White Minister
Ernst Leopold Strachwitz *spkr* Black Minister.
**Austrian Radio Chorus; Arnold Schönberg Choir; Gumpoldskirchner Spatzen;
Austrian Radio Symphony Orchestra / Elgar Howarth.**
Wergo Ⓟ Ⓒ WER6170-2 (two discs: 116 minutes: ADD). Notes, text and translations included. Recorded 1987.

This is a most welcome (and long-awaited) addition to Ligeti's music on disc. Dating from 1974-7 *Le grand macabre* acts as a kind of bonding agent between the avant-garde tendencies of Ligeti's early works (the Requiem and the two anti-operas, *Aventures* and *Nouvelles aventures*, for instance) and his subsequent transition towards a more traditional, though no less experimental style that had its beginnings in works like the Double Concerto and *San Francisco Polyphony*. The evolution of *Le grand macabre* is long and complex. It was first commissioned in 1965 by Göran Gentele (director of the Stockholm Opera) and was originally going to follow the same crazy style and sound world as the two surrealistic anti-operas mentioned above.

However, by 1969 Ligeti was beginning to move away from the idea of an anti-opera, and in collaboration with Gentele, began work on a comic-strip version of the Oedipus legend. The project, however, was abandoned in 1972 following the sudden and tragic death of Gentele, and once again Ligeti found himself in search of a suitable subject. He had been considering an Ubu drama by Alfred Jarry when he stumbled upon the play, *La balade du grande macabre* by the Belgian writer, Michel de Ghelderode. Here was a subject that had all the ingredients and potential that he had been searching for, and together with Aliute Meczies and Michael Meschke they began the process of 'Jarrifying' it and transforming it into a usable libretto.

The opera is set in the imaginary country of Breughelland: a dilapidated and shabby principality under the rulership of the childish glutton Prince Go-Go. It opens with a Toccata for 12 motor car horns (vintage variety) in the manner of Monteverdi's Toccata from *Orfeo* – a kind of 'Monteverdi meets the Marx Brothers meet Ligeti'. To this the sinister character Nekrotzar (the Tsar of death) makes his entrance announcing the imminent destruction of the world. Enlisting the services of the local inebriate Piet the Pot (as his horse), he rides off to spread the terrible news. Also introduced in the first scene are the lovers Spermando and Clitoria (though prudishly renamed Amando and Amanda for the recording) who are so absorbed in each other they remain oblivious of the arrival of Nekrotzar. They retreat to a tomb to enjoy the pleasures of the flesh.

The second scene takes place in the house of the royal astrologer, Astradamors, where we find him, and his wife Mescalina, engaged in some very peculiar practices involving leather gear, whip and – a saucepan lid? After a while Mescalina orders her husband back to his telescope. Enter Nekrotzar and Piet. Nekrotzar ravages Mescalina whilst she is experiencing an erotic vision involving the goddess Venus: Mescalina dies in mid-orgasm. Nekrotzar, Piet and Astradamors proceed to the royal palace.

Act 2 continues with more slapstick capers and *risqué* banter; this time involving Prince Go-Go, his two ministers and his Chief of the Secret Police – Gepopo. Gepopo announces the arrival of Nekrotzar, who duly appears and pronounces the end of the world and ... and nothing happens. Overcome with embarrassment, Nekrotzar shrivels and dies, leaving the principal characters (including a resurrected Mescalina) to ponder the moral of the tale.

The moral, of course, is open to many interpretations and has no doubt gathered a few more since its first performance in 1978), but that is Ligeti's intention – to pose more questions than answers. Is Nekrotzar really Death, or is he just a pretentious charlatan? Do they really survive, or is death just a continuation of life? Unanswered questions are the only certainty you'll encounter in this opera, that and two hours of immensely enjoyable entertainment.

Musically *Le grand macabre* represents a pinnacle of Ligeti's output. There are many passages that recall the earlier works, and a few, though only a few, that point to the rhythmic complexity of his recent scores. But there is also a great deal that is entirely unique to the opera. Ligeti cites as his models Monteverdi's *L'incoronazione di Poppea* and Verdi's *Falstaff* – in so much as the opera follows more or less the same episodic structure with orchestral intermezzos alternating with very short independent musical units. There are also numerous 'half' quotations and allusions, which Ligeti describes as signals to the real world (outside the surrealistic world of the opera). When all is said and done, *Le grand macabre* remains an opera of ambiguities – a movable feast open to numerous interpretations. The one thing we can be certain of, however, is that since its first performance 20 years ago it has rightfully earned a place as one of the classic operas of contemporary music.

Elgar Howarth's superlative performance hardly needs any recommendation (it was he, after all, who conducted the first performance in Stockholm); nor do the committed and sharply drawn performances from the excellent line-up of singers. Dieter Weller's Nekrotzar and Peter Haage's Piet are particularly fine. A superb recording (made in the Konzerthaus, Vienna) sets the seal on this magnificent recording.

Jean-Baptiste Lully   Italian/French 1632-1687

Lully Alceste.
 Collete Alliot-Lugaz *sop* Alceste
 Jean-Philippe Lafont *bar* Alcides (Hercules)
 Howard Crook *ten* Admète
 Sophie Marin-Degor *sop* Céphise, Glory
 Giles Ragon *ten* Lychas
 Jean-François Gerdeil *bar* Straton
 François Loup *bar* Lycomède, Pluto
 Gregory Reinhart *bass* Caron
 Michel Dens *ten* Phérès
 Véronique Gens *sop* Prosperine, Nymph of the Tuilieries, Nymph of the Marne
 Claudine Le Coz *sop* Thetis, Diana, Nymph of the Sea
 Miriam Ruggeri *sop* Nymph of the Seine
 Olivier Lallouette *bar* Eole, Cléante
 Douglas Nasrawi *ten* Alecton, Apollo
 Sagittarius Vocal Ensemble; La Grande Ecurie et La Chambre du Roy / Jean-Claude Malgoire.
 Auvidis Astrée Ⓟ Ⓒ E8527 (three discs: 159 minutes: DDD). 📻 Notes, text and translation included. Recorded at performances in the Théâtre des Champs-Elysées, Paris between January 4th and 8th, 1991.

Alceste was Lully's second opera in the form of which he was architect, the *tragédie en musique*. It was first performed in Paris early in 1674 and was, according to Madame de Sévigné, loved both by Louis XIV and his court. As in his first opera, *Cadmus et Hermione*, Lully drew from his experience as a composer of ballets, introducing scenes whose comic element was not, however, universally applauded. *Alceste* in fact contains one of the finest comic scenes ever to have been penned by Lully, that between Caron and the poverty-stricken Shades who jostle for a place on his boat. Those who can pay embark but others are sent packing. Lully and his regular librettist, Quinault, richly endowed this scene with both comedy and satire and its well-contrasted airs, interspersed with recitative, choral episodes and instrumental *ritournelles* provide a high-water-mark in the opera.

This recording from Jean-Claude Malgoire is his second version of the opera on disc. The earlier one on CBS has long been deleted but, while its cast which included Felicity Palmer, Bruce Brewer, John Elwes and Max van Egmond was a strong one, the performance was weakened by indifferent instrumental playing and stylistic hesitancy. These and other shortcomings have been largely overcome in this later recording, which was made during live performances in Paris. Malgoire has chosen his cast well on the whole, with Colette Alliot-Lugaz in the title-role, Howard Crook as Admète, her preferred suitor, François Loup as the scheming Lycomède – he sang the role in Malgoire's earlier version and is the only singer common to both – Jean-Philippe Lafont as the noble and heroic Alcides (Hercules) – he also loves Alceste as it turns out – and Gregory Reinhart as the ferryman, Caron. Alliot-Lugaz does not achieve a strength of characterization comparable with that of Palmer in the other version but hers is an attractive voice even if she is inclined to understate her role; but her exchanges with Admete are touching and well sustained.

The wonderfully entertaining Fourth Act comes across well. Alcides, whose offer of rescuing Alceste from Hades has been accepted, leaps into Caron's barge which almost capsizes with unaccustomed mortal bodily weight. On arrival he finds that Pluto already has his eye on Alceste; the king of the Underworld, displeased at this untimely intrusion, orders his retinue to set loose the three-headed monster watchdog, Cerberus. But Alcides soon deals with him: "I was born to tame the fury of the most insane monsters," he boasts and Pluto, recognizing that in Alcides he has met his match, allows the intruder to lead Alceste away. Malgoire handles all this with an admirably light touch and supple rhythmic sense. The Shades, puny-sounding and pitiful, are effectively contrasted with Caron's resonantly projected and reiterated terms of passage. But the *Symphonie* prefacing the scene at Pluto's court is lacking in awe. The problem here and elsewhere, too, is that which so often besets live recordings where an ideal sound balance is less easily achieved. Nevertheless there are many affecting moments in this act which are vividly realized, above all in the choruses which are incisively sung by the Sagittarius Vocal Ensemble and the dances of Pluto's retinue which Malgoire brings to life imaginatively and with rhythmic precision.

All in all, then, this is a lively, stylish and entertaining account of one of Lully's most immediately attractive operas. As noted above, the principal roles are well cast and they are matched by some excellent performances by lesser dramatis personae; from among these one could single out Véronique Gens whose vocal technique and feeling for shapely melodic gesture are a constant pleasure. Olivier Lallouette, on the other hand, shares little of Gens's assurance though his allotted roles are, admittedly, small ones. Only towards the end of the Fifth Act do you detect any fatigue in Malgoire's performance, mainly evident in the choral singing and in the otherwise clean-sounding string section of 24 players. As implied earlier on, a greater disappointment lies in the sound quality of the recording itself which is too dry and confined to serve the best interests either of singers or instruments. But that will not prevent you from enjoying a performance whose strengths should assist in rehabilitating Malgoire's somewhat chequered career on disc. The booklet is a model of its kind with full texts and translations, clear layout, readable print, and documentation which is both interesting and informative.

Lully Atys.

Prologue:
Bernard Deletré *bass* Le temps
Monique Zanetti *sop* Flore
Jean-Paul Fouchécourt *bass* Zephir
Gilles Ragon *ten* Zephir
Arlette Steyer *sop* Melpomene
Agnès Mellon *sop* Iris
Tragédie lyrique:
Guy de Mey *ten* Atys
Agnès Mellon *sop* Sangaride
Guillemette Laurens *mez* Cybèle
Françoise Semellaz *sop* Doris
Jacques Bona *bass* Idas
Noémi Rime *sop* Mélisse
Jean-François Gardeil *bass* Célénus
Gilles Ragon *ten* Le sommeil
Jean-Paul Fouchécourt *ten* Morphée, Trio
Bernard Deletré *bass* Phobétor, Sangar
Michel Laplénie *ten* Phantase
Stephan Maciejewski *bass* Un songe funeste
Isabelle Desrochers *sop* Trio
Véronique Gens *sop* Trio
Les Arts Florissants Chorus and Orchestra / William Christie.
Harmonia Mundi Ⓟ Ⓒ HMC90 1257/9 (three discs: 170 minutes). ✒ Notes, text and translation included. Recorded 1987.

Atys was Lully's fourth *tragédie-lyrique* and it was first staged in 1676 by the "Académie Royale de Musique" at the King's residence at Saint-Germain-en-Laye. Louis XIV is said to have preferred *Atys* to all other of Lully's operas and his opinion seems to have been widely shared, up to a point, both in and perhaps outside France. Telemann, in a letter to Carl Heinrich Graun, once remarked that French airs had replaced the previous vogue for Italian cantatas in Germany. Indeed, Telemann claimed, "I have known Germans, Englishmen, Russians, Poles and even Jews who knew by heart entire passages from Lully's operas, *Bellerophon* and *Atys*". Five recently discovered letters, all relating to a greater or lesser extent to the preparation and performance of *Atys*, and reproduced in the accompanying booklet to this recording, add further witness to the evident esteem in which the work was held. "But *Atys* will not be an opera, any more than *Thésée* was," reads a letter of August 1675; "Imagine, rather, a stage with machinery, dances and obbligato music: almost a copy of the antique. The prologue is the introduction, a preamble. The rest is a story, a play, which we leave for a moment from time to time, for an ephemeral landscape, an enchanted or terrifying divertissement ... Lully claims that he is able to do without the orchestra and choir during the entire main body of the drama, in order to obtain a contrast, lighting effects, breaks during the divertissements where there will be a debauch, an orgy of voices and instruments. The entire drama will evolve in this way, in half-tints; no impressive showpieces for the singers, no big airs; but small *airs de cour* and recitatives, with continuo ... ".

Lully's librettist, Quinault, turned to Ovid's *Fasti* for his subject matter. Ovid's design was to interpret the calendar in the light of ancient annals, to record events commemorated on each day and examine the origins of the various rites. There was to have been one book of elegiacs for each month of the year but Ovid only got halfway. The story of *Atys* is contained in the fourth book; he was a Phrygian deity who, in this version of the story, loves Sangaride. Sangaride loves Atys, in return, yet is all set to marry Célénus, King of Phrygia. But Atys, very unfortunately for him, as it turns out, is secretly loved by the goddess Cybèle; her arrival for the forthcoming marriage of Célénus and Sangaride is but a pretext for seeing Atys and revealing to him her love. Courtly or godly propriety, however, prevents her from openly declaring her feelings so, instead, she causes Atys to fall into a deep sleep, intending to let him know of her love in a dream. The dream turns into something of a nightmare and when he wakes from it Cybèle learns that Atys and Sangaride love one another. The two lovers swear eternal faith while Cybèle and Célénus are left licking their wounds. Cybèle determines upon a terrible revenge. By application of her magic she makes Atys believe that he sees a horrible monster; he stabs it to death only then to discover that it is his beloved Sangaride. Broken-hearted, Atys stabs himself but is prevented from a normal death by Cybèle who turns him into a pine tree. Deeply regretting her immortality, which gives her no respite from her suffering, Cybèle is left mourning over a love that has for ever been snatched away from her. The work is unusual amongst Lully's operas, therefore, in not having a happy ending.

In this recording from Harmonia Mundi William Christie has used the same musical resources that he drew upon for his highly successful and illuminating performances at the Salle Favart in Paris in 1987. His orchestra is a large one, roughly corresponding with the size and disposition of the kind of ensemble which Lully, himself, had at his disposal; and the continuo group, the Petit Choeur, separate from the main body of the orchestra in functional terms, consist of nine players roughly but not precisely corresponding with documentary evidence of the early eighteenth century. The exact nature and augmentation of the instrumentation of Lully's scores, however, remains a complex problem to the modern performer. What exactly did Lully mean, for example, when he referred to *instruments champestres* in the *livret* of *Atys*? The *livrets*, which contained a mixture of text and specific performance information, often gave details of the instrumentalists appearing on stage; in that produced for *Atys* in 1676, for example, three crumhorns are listed along with five oboes for the "Entrée des Zéphirs" (Act 2 scene 4). Christie's orchestra provide a full complement of the latter instruments but omits crumhorns altogether, an understandable omission perhaps since the word may have embraced a variety of reed instruments including larger members of the oboe family. An absence here of a musette, too, is something of a surprise, for this would almost certainly have been included amongst the *instruments champestres*. Thirty-three voices make up the chorus in addition to a cast of 16 soloists.

Few lovers of baroque opera will be disappointed with this recording by William Christie and Les Arts Florissants. The orchestral playing and the choral singing have moved towards greater technical sophistication since their first recording of Charpentier's *Médée*, released in 1984 on Harmonia Mundi; and whilst there is little in the solo singing that is outstanding, the general level of accomplishment, both declamatory and musical, is high. Guy de Mey, who takes the high tenor role of Atys, is excellent for most of the time, as is Agnès Mellon as the hapless Sangaride. There are several occasions here where she affectingly captures the pathos in Lully's airs. The mezzo-soprano role of Cybèle is sung by Guillemette Laurens; her strong, clear voice suits the part though her intonation is weak in places. Jean-François Gardeil makes an authoritative Célénus and his resonant voice has an appropriately commanding ring to it. Amongst several smaller roles the soprano voice of Noémi Rime as Mélisse, confidante of Cybèle, and the soprano, Françoise Semellaz are particularly striking.

Whilst there is nothing musically as memorable in *Atys* as, for instance, in *Médée*, or indeed perhaps in Lully's own *Armide*, there is no shortage of affecting airs and ensembles of varying sizes. From amongst them you could single out a duet of Atys and Sangaride (Act 4 scene 4) and an animated scene between them (Act 1 scene 6). Duets are the most frequently occurring small ensembles in Lully's operas but *Atys* has some delightful trios and quartets too, such as the quartet with Atys, Sangaride and their respective confidantes, Idas, a bass role, and Doris, a soprano one (Act 1 scene 3); and the trio of Sangaride, Doris and Idas, "Qu'une première amour est belle!" (Act 4 scene 1). The most striking and original music of the opera occurs in the Third Act where Lully treats his audience to one of his undoubted specialities, a sleep scene of the kind that he introduced so effectively into *Armide*, ten years later. The music is full of nuances, and contrast between the drowsy utterances of Sommeil, Morphée, and Phobétor, on the one hand, and the harsh, strident warnings of the "Songes funestes" on the other. Here, too, there is a suggestion of the comic element which had played a larger part in Lully's earlier operas, above all, in *Alceste* but which virtually disappeared in the later ones. Christie uses an organ as an accompanying instrument in this scene but no mention is made of it in the otherwise detailed list of instruments included in the booklet.

What ensures the success of this performance as much as anything is Christie's lively rhythmic sense, and his informed handling of French music of this period. He keeps the recitative moving with admirable flexibility and vitality and makes the frequent shifts between three and four time, often within the same musical phrase, so much a part of Lully's style, with ease and conviction. Much of the recitative is expressive and it requires sensitive treatment both from singers and players alike. The success with which Christie and his ensemble interpret it may be measured by the high level of interest which they generate in scenes of extended recitative such as that at the beginning of Act 2. The many little orchestral *ritournelles* are brought to life with vitality and brilliance by Christie's colourful orchestral forces.

To sum up, this is a major achievement which will do much to improve Lully's somewhat lacklustre reputation as a composer. There will doubtless be sceptics, but only adversely prejudiced hearts will remain unsoftened by a scene such as that where Atys murders his beloved Sangaride (Act 5 scene 3), observed by the chorus, which comment in a poignant refrain, somewhat in the manner of Greek tragedy. Fine, clear, resonant recording and full texts in French, English and German.

Lully Phaëton.

Howard Crook *ten* Phaëton
Rachel Yakar *sop* Clymène
Jennifer Smith *sop* Théone
Véronique Gens *sop* Libye
Gérard Thervel *bar* Epaphus
Jean-Paul Fouchécourt *ten* Triton, Sun, Earth, Goddess
Philippe Huttenlocher *bar* Mérops
Laurent Naouri *bar* Saturn, Protée
Virginie Pochon *mez* Astrée, Hour of the Day
Jérôme Varnier *sop* Autumn, Jupiter
Florence Couderc *sop* Shepherdess, Hour of the Day
Sagittarius Vocal Ensemble; Les Musiciens du Louvre / Marc Minkowski.
Erato Ⓟ Ⓒ 4509-91737-2 (two discs: 144 minutes: DDD). Notes, text and translation included. Recorded 1993.

Marc Minkowski here adds the *tragédie en musique*, *Phaëton*, to the discography of Lully's operas (of which only three are represented in the current catalogue). *Phaëton* was first produced, not at the Palais-Royal Théâtre in Paris, but modestly at Versailles in January 1683. In the spring of that year it transferred to the Palais-Royal and was well enough thought of to enjoy revivals at regular intervals into the early 1740s. Indeed, rather as *Atys* became known as the "King's opera" and *Isis* as the musicians', *Phaëton* acquired its sobriquet, "the opera of the people". Among the many attractive airs "Hélas! Une chaîne si belle" (Act 5) was apparently a favourite duet of Parisian audiences, while "Que mon sort serait doux" (Act 2), another duet, was highly rated by Lully himself. In 1688 *Phaëton* was chosen to inaugurate the new Royal Academy of Music at Lyon where, as Jérôme de la Gorce remarks in his excellent introduction, it was so successful "that people came to see it from forty leagues around". The present recording is a co-production between Erato and Radio France, set up to mark the occasion of the opening of the new Opera House at Lyon.

The libretto is by Lully's regular collaborator, Philippe Quinault, who based his version of the famous legend on the account in Ovid's *Metamorphoses*. That is, of course, after the customary adulatory Prologue in which a return to the Golden Age is envisaged, with the promise of peace and pleasure. Phaëton is loved by Théone, daughter of the god, Protée. But Phaëton is ambitious, with his eye on the Egyptian throne; and the quickest, surest path to that is to marry Libye, daughter of the Egyptian king, Mérops. Mérops not only offers Libye in marriage to Phaëton but announces his abdication in favour of his proposed son-in-law. But Phaëton has reckoned without the intervention of Epaphus, the disappointed lover of Libya. He questions Phaëton's pedigree, obliging Phaëton to pay a visit to the Palace of the Sun so that his father, the Sun God, can declare his legitimacy. That is still not enough for Phaëton who wants to *prove* his father's identity by driving his chariot. The remainder of the story is indeed, legendary. Phaëton loses control of the Chariot of the Sun and Jupiter, seeing that his lack of horsemanship could set the Earth on fire, strikes him with a thunderbolt. Phaëton plunges to the ground and is killed.

All this afforded composer and librettist ample opportunity for evocative and colourful writing and the score is generously endowed with divertissements, an invigorating overture and a supple, swiftly moving chaconne. The casting is effective, by and large, and notably for the stylish, alluring and impassioned singing of Véronique Gens. Hers is one of the finest voices engaged in French baroque music and she goes from strength to strength. This much is apparent right from the start where her melancholy air, "Heureuse une âme indifférente" ("Happy the soul that is indifferent") strikes an affectingly sombre note. Jennifer Smith is authoritative as the hapless Princess Théone; her diction is excellent and her careful placing of notes comparably so. The exchanges with Phaëton are passionately sung, with Howard Crook in the title-role engaging vigorously in the dialogue. Only occasionally, as in her touching Act 2 monologue, "Il me fait, l'inconstant", is there the slightest hint of vocal strain. Third in this impressive triumvirate of princesses is Rachel Yakar who, as Clymène, Phaëton's mother, is affectionate yet forceful. Her Act 1 air, "D'une amoureuse ardeur un grand coeur peut brûler" ("A mighty heart can burn with amorous ardour"), with its fleeting resemblance to

Henry Lawes's "Sufferance", is beautifully done with the dual emphasis on heroism and love skilfully balanced. There are fine contributions from the remaining dramatis personae, too. Jean-Paul Fouchécourt's Triton is crystal-clear, with an ease of delivery which has not always been the case in some of his earlier recordings; and baritone Laurent Naouri makes a commanding Protée, notably in his revelation of Phaëton's impending fate (Act 1 scene 8). Philippe Huttenlocher brings lively characterization to the ageing King Mérops; he is among the most experienced singers in the cast and his declamation is both fluent and stylistically convincing. Gérard Thervel takes the baritone role of Epaphus, musically a rewarding one, in which he shares the two once celebrated duets, mentioned earlier on, with Libye. His voice blends well in this context though it seems to lack any of the individual character present in several others of the singers.

Last, but in French opera certainly not least, are the choral and instrumental contributions; both make a strong impression, the orchestra especially so with a resonant basso continuo team affording constant pleasure. Minkowski sets a cracking pace for the drama and there are few if any flagging moments. Readers who feel that one Lully opera is much like another may perhaps be conceded a point or two but it cannot be emphasized strongly enough that early appearances are deceptive. Lully's airs are full of charm and variety and, conforming to various types as they do, are far from repetitive. ("Hélas! Une chaîne si belle" is a ravishing example.) Likewise, the many dances at which Lully excelled are most beguiling. In addition to the overture and chaconne already mentioned are several other splendid movements including a robust March (Act 3), an Air with a bell illustrating The Hours of the Day at the court of the Sun (Act 4) – this one marvellously enlivened by the presence of a baroque guitar – and a Bourrée with two deliciously scored Airs (Act 5). In short, all this is engaging music, imaginatively performed and thoroughly entertaining.

Recorded sound is excellent and the booklet, give or take a few small errors, all that one could wish for. Strongly recommended; the cover illustration alone, one of a group of seventeenth-century wooden panels depicting Phaëton, horses and chariot plunging headlong to earth, invites further investigation.

Leevi Madetoja
Finnish 1887-1947

Madetoja Juha.
Jorma Hynninen *bar* Juha
Maija Lokka *sop* Marja
Eero Erkkilä *ten* Shemeikka
Anita Välkki *sop* Mother-in-law
Margareta Haverinen *sop* Kaisa
Tapani Valtasaari *bass* Vicar
Merja Wirkkala *sop* Anja
Maaria Metsomäki *sop* First Maiden
Kristina Haartti *mez* Second Maiden
Kai Airinen *ten* First Man
Kalevi Olli *bass* Second Man
Finnish Radio Youth Choir and Symphony Orchestra / Jussi Jalas.
Ondine Ⓟ Ⓒ ODE714-2 (two discs: 99 minutes: ADD). Notes, text and translation included. Recorded 1977.

If Juhani Aho's tale of misplaced love leading to tragedy was a landmark for the Finnish novel, its operatic potential has proved scarcely less and was spotted early by the singer Aino Ackté. She created a libretto which was offered first to Sibelius (he prevaricated for a couple of years before finally declining), then to Aarre Merikanto who completed his setting, one of the great operas of the century, in 1921 (also recorded by Ondine and reviewed under Merikanto). Merikanto's style was too radical for Finland in the 1920s and his opera was not staged until 1963.

Ackté eventually took her libretto back and offered it to Leevi Madetoja, who duly completed his version in 1934. Yet even the most cursory glance at the texts as printed in the booklets accompanying the Merikanto and Madetoja sets reveals that the librettos are utterly different. There are concurrences, but consistent only with both librettos having been derived from a common source. Even the cast lists vary. Madetoja radically simplified the action, concentrating on the three principals (Juha, his errant wife, Marja, and the itinerant Karelian pedlar, Shemeikka). In doing so, many of the subtler motivations present in Merikanto's score were lost, most crucially at the climax with the role of Shemeikka in Juha's discovery that Marja had left him of her own accord. What saves Madetoja's version is the music.

If Merikanto's opera now seems the more impressive achievement that is no reflection on Madetoja's, which is as finely conceived as his earlier *The Ostrobothnians* and hugely enjoyable. Although Madetoja never apes Sibelius's manner, now and again one gets a hint of what a mature Sibelian opera might have sounded like. With so natural a talent for opera it is a shame that Madetoja completed only two. The two acts of *Juha* are divided one per disc, although at 58 and 41 minutes respectively the second is somewhat short measure. Given that this is not a new recording a suitable coupling could have been found in one of the suites from his ballet, *Okon Fuoko*, or even *The Ostrobothnians*. This is the only quibble about this set; the performance, built around the peerless Jorma Hynninen, is splendid. Even if one has the Merikanto *Juha*, Madetoja's is still well worth investigating on its own merits, let alone as an alternative treatment.

Gian Malipiero   Italian 1882-1973

Malipiero L'Orfeide.

Alvinio Misciano *ten* Orfeo
Giorgio Giorgetti *bar* Brighella
Mario Carlin *ten* Arlecchino
Renato Capecchi *bar* Doctor Balanzon, Drunken man
Paolo Pedani *bar* Captain Spaventa
Claudio Giombi *bar* Pantalon
Enzo Guagni *ten* Tartaglia
Mario Ferrara *ten* Pulcinella
Alberto Rinaldi *bar* Ballad-singer, Nerone
Magda Olivero *sop* Old Mother
Dino Formichini *ten* Lover
Gino Orlandini *bar* Bell-ringer
Manlio Micheli *sngr* Lamp-lighter
Ottavio Taddei *ten* Knight
Valiano Natali *ten* Drinks-seller
Antonietta Daviso *sop* Agrippina
Chorus and Orchestra of the Maggio Musicale Fiorentino / Hermann Scherchen.
Tahra mono Ⓜ ① TAH190/1 (two discs: 106 minutes: ADD). Notes, text and translation included. Recorded at a performance in the Teatro della Pergola, Florence on June 7th, 1966.

L'Orfeide is one of the strangest operas of the century, though some listeners will have difficulty in accepting Malipiero's assurance that it *is* an opera at all. Its central act (entitled "Seven Songs") is a sort of dramatic song-cycle, its seven independent scenes linked only by the fact that each contains an element of bizarre or ironic contradiction: a mad old woman grieving over her lost son does not recognize him when he returns; a bell-ringer sings a cheerful song while his bells peal, apparently oblivious of the fact that the town is burning down, and so on. All the characters who appear in this act are introduced, in dumb-show, towards the end of its predecessor, in which the characters of the ancient *commedia dell'arte* step forward one by one, only to be rejected by Orpheus, who announces "The Death of the Masks" (the title of this act) and their replacement by characters drawn from real life. Act 3, finally (entitled "Orpheus" but also "Epilogue: The Eighth Song") is set in a theatre within a theatre. We see not only a marionette show representing the cruelty of Nero but the reactions to this of three separate audiences: a King and his aristocratic court (unmoved and immobile), old fogeys (outraged) and children (gleefully applauding all the carnage). At the end, Orpheus appears as a clown, lyrically praises the aristocratic audience for their impassivity, and leaves with the Queen on his arm.

The action is still further dislocated by a curious and deliberate mismatch between text and action. For example, although each of the 'seven songs' has a contemporary setting, the texts are all chosen from early Renaissance poetry: the mad mother's lament is from a poem by Jacopone da Todi (author of the *Stabat mater*), describing the Virgin Mary contemplating the dead Christ; the bell-ringer sings a learnedly classicizing but disgusting catalogue of the deformities of old age by Angelo Poliziano. The music, too, in underlining these scenes, veers oddly but effectively from pungent neo-classicism via lyrical expressiveness to a style that somehow suggests archaic folk theatre. It is a tribute to the queer strength of Malipiero's eclecticism that the great *verista*, Magda Olivero, in the very brief role of the Mother, seems perfectly at home at the centre of this Pirandellian extravaganza.

The outer wings of the triptych are more perplexing, especially the 'epilogue'. But somehow Malipiero was right: yes, these three disparate miniature dramas *are* a trilogy, chapters from an essay on the nature of musical drama. Other chapters would include Stravinsky's *L'histoire du soldat*, all the operas of Busoni and (perhaps especially: there are distinct similarities of idiom), Falla's *El retablo de Maese Pedro*. The 'seven songs' are at times moving, always impressive, but *L'Orfeide* as a whole is compulsively fascinating even when its illogicalities seem most irritating.

The performance is a fine one, the chamber orchestra lucidly directed by Scherchen, the singing of pretty well uniformly high standard. The recording is close and a shade harsh, with stage noises and the prompter quite prominent. But as an introduction to Malipiero's huge, uneven but absorbing output for the stage (he wrote 46 operas, some of them, like *L'Orfeide*, trilogies of one-acters) this is invaluable. As the last performance Hermann Scherchen ever gave (he collapsed during it and died a few days later), it is also a moving tribute to him. The recording is supplemented by interviews with Olivero and the stage director of these performances, Gianfranco de Bosio (both in Italian, but translated in the accompanying booklet).

Bohuslav Martinů   Bohemian 1890-1959

Martinů The Greek Passion.
John Mitchinson *ten* Manolios
Helen Field *sop* Katerina
John Tomlinson *bass* Grigoris
Phillip Joll *ten* Kostandis
Geoffrey Moses *bass* Fotis
Arthur Davies *ten* Yannakos
Rita Cullis *sop* Lenio
Catherine Savory *sop* Nikolios, Old woman
Jeffrey Lawton *ten* Panait, Andonis
John Harris *ten* Michelis
David Gwynne *bass* Old man, Patriarcheas
Jana Jonášová *sop* Despinio
Michael Geliot *spkr* Ladas
**Kühn Children's Chorus; Czech Philharmonic Chorus;
Brno State Philharmonic Orchestra / Sir Charles Mackerras.**
Supraphon Ⓟ Ⓓ 10 3611-2 (two discs: 115 minutes: DDD). Notes and text included. Recorded 1981.

No, not a great opera, not even Martinů's finest, but it contains moments, pages, whole scenes of such archetypal Martinů that no admirer of his should be without it. And on repeated hearings its indubitable flaws do lessen, or rather you begin to realize that you simply have to take the piece as a whole, that it really would be diminished if its barer or more halting pages were cut. It stammers in its utterance, but one can grasp what the stammerer is trying to say; at times even the effort can be moving.

For his last opera Martinů set himself an almost impossible task: to reduce Nikos Kazantzakis's sprawling novel, *Christ Recrucified*, to a scenario of four brief acts, to set it in a language not his own (his English prosody is sometimes awkward) and, most difficult of all, to discuss matters that his characters themselves could hardly put into words. The shepherd Manolios, chosen to play Christ in the passion-play of a poor Greek village under Turkish rule, is moved to preach Christ's message in simple earnestness. He preaches charity towards those who are even poorer than he and his fellow-villagers, to a starving group of refugees. "The light shineth in darkness and the darkness comprehended it not"; he is ostracized, excommunicated, then killed.

It is of Manolios's essence that he is not a silver-tongued Aaron: in his one extended solo he is audibly struggling to find words to express the inexpressible; even the scene in which he is overtly identified with Christ is unassertively still. So the eloquence of Martinů's score is often confided to the supra-personal voice of the chorus or to the orchestra. Manolios has no 'aria' to express his unworthiness of the role of Christ; no more than four hesitant words, indeed. We must await the noble melody that closes Act 1, still more for that which serves as prelude to Act 2, to hear musical images of the goodness of heart that underlies Manolios's perplexity and of the change his election has wrought in him.

The scenes of the opera are more likely to be dramatic or moving as entities than in detail. One of the most tragic of them, in which the exhausted refugee villagers make the hopeless gesture of founding a new village on the aridly inhospitable slopes of a mountain, and in which an old man volunteers to be buried in its foundations to ensure the community's survival, is very plain in its word-setting and is denied a satisfyingly climactic conclusion. Yet in its stoic monody and memories of ancient chant (memories as much of Martinů's Moravia as of Greece), it is moving in its depiction of those who have no choice but to be brave. Moving also are the increasingly luminous scenes between Manolios and Katerina, the play's and the village's Magdalen, the utter simplicity (image of redemptive sacrifice?) that follows Manolios's murder and, more and more, the tellingly bare strokes with which the two communities' austere lives are sketched. Perhaps, then, not just for the shelves of Martinů's admirers after all.

Fittingly, this is an ensemble performance in the best sense of the word, the three principals standing out as much for the truthfulness of their performances as for vocal distinction: Mitchinson's troubled sincerity, Field's sense of self-awakening and Tomlinson's rigid authority are compelling. Choral singing and orchestral playing are very fine under Mackerras's committed direction. The splendid recording has not, as is sometimes the disappointing case, been acidified by transfer to CD, and its spaciousness has if anything been intensified. Despite its flaws *The Greek Passion* seems more and more like one of the century's essential operas.

Martinů Julietta.
Maria Tauberová *sop* Julietta
Ivo Zídek *ten* Michel
Antonín Zlesák *ten* Police Officer, Postman, Forest Warden
Zdenek Otava *bar* Man with the Helmet

Václav Bednář *bass* Man in the Window
Ivana Mixová *mez* Small Arab
Vladimír Jedenáctík *bass* Old Arab
Jaroslava Procházková *mez* Bird-seller
Ludmila Hanzalíková *mez* Fishmonger
Jaroslav Horáček *bass* Old Man, Youth
Karel Kalaš *bass* Grandfather
Milada Cadikovičová *contr* Grandmother
Stepánka Jelínková *sngr* Old Lady
Vera Soukupová *mez* Fortune-teller
Jindřich Jindrák *bar* Souvenir seller
Jaroslav Veverka *bass* Old Sailor
Zdenek Svehla *ten* Young Sailor
Marcela Lemariová *mez* Errand-boy
Karel Berman *bass* Beggar
Dalibor Jedlička *bass* Convict
Jaroslav Stříška *ten* Engine driver
Bohumír Lalák *bass* Night Watchman
Prague National Theatre Chorus and Orchestra / Jaroslav Krombholc.
Supraphon Ⓔ Ⓓ 10 8176-2 (three discs: 145 minutes: ADD). Notes, text and translation included.
Recorded 1964.

How could one describe the fascination of Martinů's *Julietta* to someone who has never heard it? One could begin, perhaps, with that scene in the Second Act where an old couple visit a bar in a wood. They are charmed when the proprietor recognizes them, even to describing the dress that she was wearing when they first came there many years ago, and the flattering remarks that another customer made about it. He is lying and they know it. They, like him and everyone else in this nameless country, can remember nothing that happened more than a few minutes ago, but they are as grateful for false, comforting memories as a blind man would be for the gift of sight, and the music of the scene, warmly nostalgic and mainly for solo piano, treats those memories as genuine and touching.

The subject, centred around a young man's search for a girl that he may once have met in this dream-country, struck a chord in Martinů. Some of his most moving works are evocations of folk rituals and peasant customs which it is rather unlikely that he genuinely 'remembered'; they are idealized visions, rather, of an unrecapturable past. George Neveux's play (Martinů said that he one day "discovered that he had set its First Act without knowing quite how") tapped a rich vein of nostalgia, of the borderland between memory and fantasy and of dreams that are somehow more real than reality. It drew from Martinů the most haunting and poetic of all his operas (there is something of a self-portrait in the central character, the troubled dreamer, Michel), with a sense, akin to that in the paintings of René Magritte, that these dreamlike and improbable places and events are real.

Martinů's admirers have long been wearing out copies of the LP version of this outstanding recording; its transfer to CD is an event of major importance. The very large cast is without a weak link, with Ivo Zídek as a flawless exponent of the youthful, perplexed, ardent Michel. Krombholc had the mysterious poetry of this lovely score in his bones. The subtitle of the opera, by the way, is "A dream-book". Is there any language but Czech in which such a surely recondite concept can be expressed by a matter-of-fact word of a mere four letters: snář?

Martinů The Miracles of Mary.
Anna Barová *contr* Archangel Gabriel, Sister Marta
Jiřina Marková *sop* Mariken
Václav Zítek *ten* The Devil
Dalibor Jedlička *bass* Blacksmith
Eva Děpoltová *sop* Sister Paskalina
Anna Kratochvílová *sop* Maria, Maiden
Marie Mrázová *contr* Foolish Virgin, Mother of God
Jindřich Jindrák *bar* First Dealer in Oils
Bohumil Maršík *bass* Second Dealer in Oils
Vojtech Kocián *ten* Mascaron
Ivan Kusnjer *bar* God the Son
Jaromír Vavruška *bass* Drunkard
Blanka Vítková *contr* Blacksmith's Daughter, Girl
Karel Průša *bass* Innkeeper
Prague Children's Choir; Prague Radio Chorus; Prague Symphony Orchestra / Jiří Bělohlávek.
Supraphon Ⓔ Ⓓ 11 1802-2 (two discs: 151 minutes: ADD). Notes, text and translation included.
Recorded 1982-3.

Martinů's enchanting tetralogy of miracle plays (or rather a diptych, each part with its own extensive prologue; and incidentally "The Plays of Mary" or even "The Games of Mary" would be a better translation) is very near the centre of his output. It owes its appeal partly to its rootedness in Martinů's nostalgia for his homeland, his childhood and an ancient way of life from which he felt himself uprooted, partly to its status as a 'research laboratory' into those areas where music theatre could be enriched by contact with ritual, popular drama, games and folk-song. Each of the constituent parts proposes a different, 'non-operatic' solution to the problem of setting a dramatic text. Thus "The Wise and Foolish Virgins" is a solemn, almost static tableau. "Mariken of Nijmegen" incorporates dance and mime (the title-role is shared between singer and dancer) and a crucial 'play within a play', complete with its own orchestra. "The Nativity" leaps joyously back and forth in time, as folk ballads often do, from the Nativity to the Annunciation, from the baptism of Christ to the shepherds in the fields. "Sister Paskalina", lastly, includes extensive dance scenes, others in which the distinction between narrative and dialogue is blurred, but also the nearest in any of these four dramas to a true aria.

In other words the work is centred on those areas which are the very source of that luminous quality, at times rather close to Copland's wide-open harmonies and arching melodies, that any admirer of Martinů's music will recognize as his most personal vein. It is related to folk music, most obviously in some of the choral scenes, which strongly recall folk dance or danced games. Memories of Eastern European church music may be there also (there are chorales, hints of the folk-song-based Mass settings once popular in Czechoslovakia). But a nostalgic idealization of all this is as much part of the style as any identifiable component. We hear it most clearly when simple, peasant emotions are being expressed. When, at the Nativity, an armless child is made whole by the Virgin, it is there not in her innocent joy, but in her father's shamed realization of whom he has denied hospitality: "If I had known, I would have given her the new bed and entertained her in the best room". And when Mariken, dragged from her nunnery by a personification of her own unruly desires, appeals for help: "Is there no one here from Moravia?" – at moments like this Martinů's homesickness becomes more than mere sentiment; it taps very deep wells of lucid, radiant eloquence.

Anyone caught by the almost (but never quite) naïve solemnity of the style will not mind much that "Sister Paskalina" is perhaps a shade too long. Or perhaps it isn't; perhaps the concluding scene (in which Paskalina, miraculously rescued from the stake, returns to her nunnery to find that no one has noticed her absence: the Virgin, confident of her eventual repentance, had taken her place) needs leisured story-telling to build to its perilous but intensely moving fusion of sentiment, piety and peasant exuberance. Even a few flaws in the performance (one or two raw voices; the principals and Bělohlávek's direction are thoroughly reliable) hint at another of the work's central qualities: it is a true folk-drama, pageant-like and crying out for amateur involvement, audibly related both to Honegger's *Le roi David* and to Britten's *Noye's Fludde*. Enough: you will have gathered that you won't get any dry-as-dust critical reservations about this lovely work here. As further inducement, there's even a vintage piece of Supraphon translator-ese: the deformed girl, showing her stumps to the Virgin, apologizes for having "only these hooklets to hold my booklets"!

Pietro Mascagni
Italian 1863-1945

Mascagni L'amico Fritz.

Mirella Freni *sop* Suzel
Luciano Pavarotti *ten* Fritz Kobus
Vincenzo Sardinero *bar* David
Laura Didier Gambardella *mez* Beppe
Benito di Bella *bass* Hanezò
Luigi Pontiggia *ten* Federico
Malvina Major *sop* Caterina
Chorus and Orchestra of the Royal Opera House, Covent Garden / Gianandrea Gavazzeni.
EMI Ⓔ Ⓞ CDS7 47905-8 (two discs: 92 minutes). Notes, text and translation included. Recorded 1968.

With pleasure in this work and admiration for this performance even further enhanced by its reissue on CD, Shaw's dictum that it is an opera which will "pass the evening pleasantly enough for you but which you need not regret missing if you happen to have business elsewhere" seems all that more unkind. When given as lovingly as it is here it has its own validity; the score consistently charming, elegiac, unassuming and well made, and these are qualities to be cherished in an age that has tended to overlook or ignore them in its own contributions to the genre.

What makes the reading so recommendable now is that one is very unlikely to hear the work today in the theatre and even less likely to hear it sung with such affection. At the point in their careers when Freni sang Suzel and Pavarotti sang Fritz, they were ideally suited to these roles. From her opening solo, throughout her ballad, the inspired Cherry duet and her Third Act solo of sorrow, Freni sings with such warmth of tone and expression as to melt any heart doubting the worth of the music. She sounds at once vulnerable and wistful. Pavarotti strikes just the right note of eager ardour as he gradually falls in love with Suzel after averring that he is impervious to the emotion. He shades his part with elegiac accent and winning *pianissimos*. These Modenese neighbours obviously enjoyed singing together, and their contributions, not least their Third Act duet where they fall into each other's arms, alone make the recording worthwhile. But there are also Vicenzo Sardinero's firm, vibrant tones to turn the role of the matchmaking rabbi David into something positive and Gavazzeni's affectionate way with the orchestra to indicate Mascagni's care over instrumentation.

Less appealing is the blustery Beppe, a too fulsome mezzo for a travesti part. But as a whole the pastoral-passionate mood of the piece is wonderfully caught – and recorded: if only more producers today could imitate this kind of natural, forward sound. Only the range of the orchestra shows the age of the recording – but that may have something to do with the dry tone of the Covent Garden strings. Any enterprising opera-lover should own this pleasing work, when it is so charmingly done.

Mascagni Cavalleria rusticana.

Renata Scotta *sop* Santuzza
Plácido Domingo *ten* Turiddu
Isola Jones *mez* Lola
Pablo Elvira *bar* Alfio
Jean Kraft *mez* Mamma Lucia
Ambrosian Opera Chorus; National Philharmonic Orchestra / James Levine.
RCA ℗ Ⓓ 74321 39500-2 (71 minutes: ADD). Notes, text and translation included. Recorded 1978.

BBC RADIO 3
90-93 FM

This was a strong contender in an overcrowded field when it was first released and this welcome reissue confirms this opinion. You would be hard put to find a more positive or a more intelligent Turiddu or Santuzza than Domingo or Scotto. Scotto manages to steer a precise course between being too ladylike or too melodramatic. She suggests all the remorse and sorrow of Santuzza's situation without self-pity. Her appeals to Turiddu to reform could hardly be more sincere and heartfelt, her throbbing delivery to Alfio, "Turiddi mi tolse l'honore", expresses all her desperation when forced to betray her erstwhile lover, and her curse on Turiddu, "A te la mala pasqua", while not resorting to the lowdown vigour of some of her rivals, is filled with venom. Not since Callas (for Serafin on EMI, reviewed under Leoncavallo), have so many aspects of the character been so vividly encompassed.

Domingo proved how committed he was to his role when the part was first given to him at Covent Garden in the mid-1970s. He gives an almost Caruso-like bite and attack to Turiddu's defiance and (later) remorse, and finds a more appropriate timbre than Bergonzi (for Karajan on DG, also reviewed under Leoncavallo). He also delivers the Brindisi with an appropriately carefree manner, oblivious of the challenge awaiting him. Pablo Elvira's Alfio is no more than adequate, and the other American support is indifferent. Levine's direction, as positive as Karajan's, is yet quite different. He goes much faster, and time and again catches the passion if not always the delicacy of Mascagni's score. He is well supported by the superb National Philharmonic Orchestra. With a recording that is bright and forward, there is altogether a theatrical dimension to this reading that is wholly arresting. For anyone wanting *Cavalleria* on a single disc, or for those with a *Pagliacci* but no *Cavalleria* in their collection, this set is a definite recommendation. Others who already have the famous Karajan may like to consider this as an addition on an altogether different and equally valid plane of interpretation.

Mascagni Cavalleria rusticana (sung in English).

Nelly Miricioiu *sop* Santuzza
Dennis O'Neill *ten* Turiddu
Diana Montague *mez* Lola
Phillip Joll *bar* Alfio
Elizabeth Bainbridge *mez* Lucia
Geoffrey Mitchell Choir; London Philharmonic Orchestra / David Parry.
Chandos Opera in English ℗ Ⓓ CHAN3004 (79 minutes: DDD). Notes and text included. Recorded 1997.

From the first "O Lola, pretty one" to the last "They have killed neighbour Turiddu" we used to relish *Cav* in that special language known as opera-in-English. There was "Mother, you know the story" and "So thou see'st what thou hast done me", "My heart, my heart is broken; his doom, his doom is spoken", "Now homeward returning sing we a merry lay" and "Mother, the red wine". It went with the heroic make-do-and-mend scenery, with *Pag* to follow and perhaps three more nights of the great week in the year when Carl Rosa came to town in wartime. Later the act was spruced up but there was never anything again like those nights of delight and absurdity. Sensible translations have long replaced the loved fustian, singers (by and large) no longer resort to the system of pronunciation the first rule of which was to roll every 'r' in sight, and the orchestra have improved out of recognition. But it all comes back now as dawn breaks yet again over the Sicilian village on that fateful Easter Sunday of long ago.

It is one of the most magical beginnings in opera, beautifully played here, and at this early stage one is not getting restive over the slow speeds. Dennis O'Neill sings his *siciliana* like a lover, with touches of an imaginative tenderness that are rare if not unique in this music. His voice distances effectively, and very effective too is the mingling of the church bells with the singing of the off-stage chorus. Santuzza, Nelly Miricioiu, must have been born in another village, but that doesn't matter; her voice has some raw patches but that also troubles less than it might as she brings such concentrated feeling to the part. On the other hand, when the Alfio arrives one can't go on saying it doesn't matter: it does. We want a vibrant Italianate voice if possible, and a firm one at least. Elizabeth Bainbridge is a vivid Mamma Lucia, but Diana Montague, immensely welcome as a singer, has quite the wrong voice-character for Lola, who should be either the local Carmen or a shallow, pert flirt. But it is also by about the time of her entry that one is consciously willing it to go faster. The speeds are consistent, and we know from his recording that Mascagni liked it slow ... many don't.

Still, for those collecting the Opera in English series this is certainly not one to miss. The drama keeps its hold, the grand old melodies surge, the score reveals more of its inspired detail, and the English language (in Edmund Tracey's translation) does itself credit.

Mascagni Cavalleria rusticana.

Elena Obraztsova *mez* Santuzza
Plácido Domingo *ten* Turiddu
Axelle Goll *sop* Lola
Renato Bruson *bar* Alfio
Fedora Barbieri *mez* Lucia
Chorus and Orchestra of La Scala, Milan / Georges Prêtre.
Stage/Video Director: **Franco Zeffirelli.**
Philips Video Classics 📀 070 103-3PH (70 minutes). Recorded 1982.

Cavalleria rusticana and Leoncavalli's *Pagliacci* (*Cav* and *Pag*) have virtually been inseparable partners almost since their creation. The pieces are obvious companions in that they both deal with passion, jealousy and murderous revenge in close-knit Italian communities: the first in a Sicilian village, the second in a Calabrian town. The action here is opened out into the Sicilian landscape with richly coloured results merging imperceptibly on to a set of La Scala for certain of the intimate colloquys. Zeffirelli also takes the opportunity given by film to make the motives explicit. In the prelude we see Turiddu leaving Lola's house at dawn, spied upon by Santuzza, thus setting up the plot. Turiddu sings his opening serenade while riding off happily into the countryside, having just left Lola. Stopping to turn his horse, he catches sight of the returning Alfio. During the famous Intermezzo Santuzza wanders round the fields filled with remorse. We see an aerial view of the combat in which Alfio knifes Turiddu, which usually takes place off-stage. Zeffirelli shows us shots of the beautiful Sicilian countryside, peasants labouring in the fields with their livestock beside them, and we glimpse the baroque church, built of grey lava stone, dominating everything. Domingo sings a suitably insouciant yet paradoxically intense Turiddu. Obraztsova may not have the most pleasing of timbres, but her Santuzza is a portrayal of a woman driven to extremes by Turiddu's infidelity, a black-clothed figure of wronged womanhood, even if this sometimes shades over into harshness and misses something of the role's pathos. Bruson's Alfio, lean and eagle-eyed, is sung in biting tones. The veteran Fedora Barbieri makes a significant contribution as Turiddu's mother, Mamma Lucia, conveying all her fear of the inevitable outcome. Prêtre's somewhat erratic conducting is the only drawback. The dubbing is convincingly managed and the sound and picture are first-rate.

Mascagni Iris.

Ilona Tokody *sop* Iris
Plácido Domingo *ten* Osaka
Juan Pons *bar* Kyoto
Bonaldo Giaiotti *bass* The Blind Man
Gabriella Ferroni *sop* Dhia
Conchita Antuñano *sop* Geisha
Sergio Tedesco *ten* First Ragpicker
Heinrich Weber *ten* Second Ragpicker, Pedlar
Bavarian Radio Chorus; Munich Radio Orchestra / Giuseppe Patanè.
Sony Classical Ⓔ Ⓓ M2K45526 (two discs: 124 minutes: DDD). Notes, text and translation included. Recorded 1988.

In the words of a survey of nineteenth-century Italian opera, published by the Corriere della sera to mark the turning of the century, Mascagni was "condemned to a masterpiece": after the triumph of *Cavalleria rusticana* nothing less would do. He lived for another 55 years, and although some of his 14 subsequent operas were immensely successful for a while (he claimed that *Iris* was better received than *Cavalleria*, and there was a near-riot of enthusiasm at the première of *Il piccolo Marat*) none was judged by the critics to be the awaited 'masterpiece', and nearly all had fallen from the repertory by the end of his life. It would be a sad enough story if all that he had done was to attempt, vainly, to repeat his first success. The evidence (of *Il piccolo Marat*, of *L'amico Fritz*, of *Iris* – to name but three) suggests that he did no such thing, that he had the capacity to develop, and the scruple and the skill to strike out on new paths, and that his very reluctance to repeat himself contributed to the long decline of his career.

Iris is an extremely interesting opera, even (in the context of late nineteenth-century Italy) an 'experimental' one. It contains an elaborate 'play within a play', both triggering the main event of the drama (the abduction of the innocent child Iris by a libertine and his procurer) and foreshadowing its outcome (her father curses her, believing that she has voluntarily become a prostitute) with pathetic irony. There is a duet in which one character speaks while the other sings, and a crucial, wordless scene where 'light' music darkens to accompany sinister action. The rich orchestration is filled with cunningly contrived local colour (the opera is set in Japan) from which Puccini clearly learned a thing or two when writing *Madama Butterfly* six years later (there is an off-stage humming chorus in *Iris*, too …). Each act has a quasi-symphonic, atmospheric orchestral prelude, and each scene has at least one strong *coup de théâtre*: the puppet-play itself in Act 1 (Iris is so caught up with the sad story that she is at one point heard in a touchingly sympathetic duet with her puppet *alter ego* in Act 2, the paper walls of Iris's oppressively luxurious prison slide away to reveal the brothel quarter of Tokyo, with a noisy crowd of eager customers clamouring for her; and the Act 3 curtain rises, not, as we half expect, on Iris's longed for but now desolate home, but on an open sewer, with scavengers rooting among the filth, eventually discovering a body wrapped in mud-spattered silken rags.

And is the music up to it? It is, and it is quite unlike *Cavalleria*, save in its melodiousness. The once famous "Hymn to the Sun", which opens and closes the opera, has a brazen, only slightly over-the-top splendour. Iris has four solo scenes, each with its own curiously still, passive pathos, rising to heart-warming Italianate eloquence at the end, as she dies, welcoming the rising sun as her deliverer. The odious Osaka has at least the elegant (and also once famous) serenade, "Apri la tua finestra" and several other pages of warm and ample ardour (true, he ought to have been the tenor equivalent of Peter Lorre, but would you have written such a part for Fernando de Lucia?), and most of Mascagni's 'experiments' actually work: the 'play within a play' is oddly, grippingly effective, the wordless dance scene is salon music, really, but with a queer dramatic power to it; the three 'visions' that appear to Iris in her degradation, ghosts of those whose egoism has destroyed her, are simple (plain vocal lines over dark solo strings) but telling.

Oh, yes, if you insist, one has to admit that Mascagni is Mascagni (which is to say 'like Puccini but not quite so good'); that Illica's vaporous and mystical libretto is something of a liability, and yes, all the characters save Iris are two-dimensional. But the quality of the opera's best pages suggests that Mascagni was the victim of the unkindest injustice of all: condemned for not living up to *Cavalleria* when he had, if intermittently, surpassed it.

A fine performance and an excellent recording (not the first, as Sony claim; there were at least two others, one of which at least seems not to have been pirated – taken from a Dutch radio tape – both featuring that riveting artist Magda Olivero in the title-role). Tokody's exciting, rather Callas-like voice has a slight wobble under pressure on high notes, but she makes a touching and full-voiced Iris. Domingo is in full, burnished voice as well (a bit too full in the serenade, perhaps, but rising splendidly to the wild ardour of the scene in which Osaka realizes what he has lost by his contemptuous dismissal of Iris as a mere unresponsive doll). Pons and Giaiotti bring vocal distinction and something like a third dimension of real character to the cynical whore-monger and the stern, blind father; Patanè lavishes affectionate care on Mascagni's polychrome orchestra; only a woefully inadequate First Ragpicker lowers the standard of the supporting cast. The whole enterprise is let down rather by the provision of a florid and often ludicrously inaccurate English translation of the libretto, but don't let that put you off. *Iris*, as Mascagni said, is an opera with almost too much music in it.

Mascagni Lodoletta.

Maria Spacagna *sop* Lodoletta
Péter Kelen *ten* Flammen
Károly Szilágyi *bar* Giannotto
László Polgár *bass* Antonio
Zsuzsanna Bazsinka *sop* Maud
Andrea Ulbrich *contr* Mad Woman
Jolán Sánta *mez* La Vanard
Mihály Kálmándi *bar* Franz
Hungarian State Opera Children's Chorus; Hungarian Radio and Television Chorus;
Hungarian State Orchestra / Charles Rosekrans.
Hungaroton Ⓟ Ⓓ HCD31307/8 (two discs: 103 minutes: DDD). Notes, text and translation included. Recorded *c*1989.

As a whole it doesn't suffice, and in the end it repels, the story developing towards a conclusion of more than usually heart-hardening sentimentality. But fragments remain: the memory can't quite sweep it all away, for a few sections of the opera and quite a number of individual moments cling teasingly and send one back to try again. Right at the start, for instance, a melodic phrase blossoms with a happy freshness, full of promise. Throughout, there is a scattering of short, incidental choruses, each of them a distinct pleasure. Occasionally the musical ideas are less fleeting, as with the long winding path of elegiac melody in the woodwind after the father's death in Act 1. When we move for the Third Act from the Dutch village to Paris, on New Year's Eve, again there are some fascinating and memorable touches (a waltz, an off-stage tenor, some discordant noises indicative, presumably, of city hubbub). In the music for the main characters, too, a tenderness or a sudden surge of emotion will breathe life into responses that have languished and nearly expired. The score is badly weakened by the failure, among so much that is melodious, to produce sustained melody and by a lack of instinct for the crucial dramatic moment. None the less, imagination is at work and its individuality is unmistakable.

As with the score, so with the performance: it would be easy to conceive of a better one, but ungrateful not to recognize achievement. Here is a Hungarian company dealing with a very Italian opera (the Dutch and French elements being necessary only to provide clogs and snow). The chorus, particularly the children, haven't the right Italianate edge and vibrancy but are unfailingly musical and efficient. The secondary roles, notably the father, Antonio, and the village lover, Giannotto, are decently sung but lack impulse and temperament. The heroine, Maria Spacagna, is a young American lyric soprano attractively pure in timbre much of the time but showing little ability to fashion her voice into an expressive instrument. The tenor, Péter Kelen, is quite another matter: he sings splendidly and is the only member of the cast to act convincingly with the voice.

Charles Rosekrans does good work with the orchestra but must share some responsibility with the record producer for the extent to which, Kelen apart, the singers are so studio-bound. Production has not set a high enough standard, for instance, in the important matter of off-stage music. The booklet also needed more critical supervision: the translation often goes astray and the historical note is ill-informed on the opera's origin. Something on the performing history would have been welcome (New Yorkers seem to have viewed with indifference "the spectacle of Flammen [Caruso] in full evening dress and without a hat singing on his doorstep in a snowstorm", as the *Tribune* critic noted). Still, the opera is a rarity worth collecting, and of present-day 'Italian' tenors there are few (if any) one would prefer to hear in it than the excellent Kelen.

Jules Massenet
French 1842-1912

Massenet Amadis

Hélène Perraguin *sop* Amadis
Danièle Streiff *sop* Floriane
Didier Henry *bar* Galaor
Antoine Garcin *bar* King Raimbert
Nadyne Chabrier *spkr* Fairy
Paul Descombes *spkr* Huntsman
Maîtrise des Hauts-de-Seine; Paris Opéra Chorus and Orchestra / Patrick Fournillier.
Forlane Ⓔ ① UCD16578/9 (two discs: 99 minutes: DDD). Text and translation included.
Recorded 1988.

Connoisseurs of operatic curiosities will here find another strange piece to add to a list that includes Rimsky-Korsakov's *Mlada* (where the heroine, dead before the work starts, appears as a silent ghost), Auber's *La muette de Portici* (where the heroine is dumb), Holst's *The Perfect Fool* (in which the hero speaks only a single word) and Blacher's *Abstract Opera* (where none of the characters has any words to sing): in this posthumous opera of Massenet's – begun shortly before *Werther*, in 1890, but put aside for 20 years, and then not produced for another 12 – Act 1 is purely orchestral, with a spoken narration super-imposed, and in Act 3, though the fairies sing, their leader only speaks. However, *Amadis* is not to be dismissed as a mere curiosity: on the contrary, it shows the composer at his most inventive and unusually robust (with only one brief descent into salon style where the fairies dance seductively around Amadis).

The story, set in a Burne-Jones world of medieval chivalry (his name is actually invoked in the stage directions), tells of twin infant brothers entrusted by their dying mother (a fugitive princess) to the care of fairies, who nevertheless foretell suffering for both. Brought up apart and not knowing each other, they meet as rival knights in the lists for the hand of the princess Floriane, whom her father has promised to the victor. Amadis (with whom she is romantically in love) is defeated by Galaor and shamefacedly goes into exile as a hermit, but he cannot banish Floriane from his mind and returns at Christmas as the royal wedding is about to be celebrated: he challenges Galaor and in the ensuing combat kills him. Only then does he discover that he has killed his brother.

The two are strongly cast, Amadis (a travesti role for soprano, for some reason) by an admirably firm-voiced, heroic-sounding singer, Hélène Perraguin, Galaor by the splendid Didier Henry: both artists make the most of their parts, though the libretto allows little opportunity for either character to be drawn in the round. Danièle Streiff is an acceptable princess, but Antoine Garcin as her royal father is altogether too wobbly even if he is supposed to be old. The part of the Fairy is well spoken, that of the narrating Hunt in Act 1 too self-consciously and portentously. There are unfortunately virtually no set-piece arias that could be extracted to illustrate and publicize the opera (Amadis's soliloquy, "O Madone du ciel" consists largely of recitative): much of the musical interest is carried by the orchestra; and in the present performance the Paris Opéra players acquit themselves with distinction under a young conductor, Patrick Fournillier, whose grip on the work is impressive.

The recording is rich and full (with splendidly warm, unblatant brass in the joust scene), the voices a trifle set back but mostly well balanced (though Amadis's spoken words at the end of Act 2 get lost under a viola solo). There are some effective sound perspectives, but why did the producer fail to organize any crowd acclamations, cries of distress or cheers called for in Act 2? All in all, though, a distinctive acquisition to the recorded repertoire which should enhance Massenet's standing.

Massenet Cendrillon.

Frederica von Stade *mez* Cendrillon
Nicolai Gedda *ten* Prince Charmant
Jane Berbié *sop* Madame de la Haltière
Jules Bastin *bass* Pandolfe
Ruth Welting *sop* La Fée
Teresa Cahill *sop* Noémie
Elizabeth Bainbridge *mez* Dorothée
Claude Méloni *ten* Le Roi, La Voix du Héraut
Paul Crook *ten* Le Doyen de la Faculté
Christian du Plessis *bar* Le Surintendant des Plaisirs
John Noble *bar* Le Premier Ministre
Ambrosian Opera Chorus; Philharmonia Orchestra / Julius Rudel.
Sony Classical Ⓕ Ⓞ M2K79323 (two discs: 137 minutes: ADD). Notes, text and translation included. Recorded 1978.

A most delightful web of moonshine choruses, pastoral woodwind, coloratura filigree, wistful sentiment, tender concern and neat comedy is this opera, and on no account to be missed is this recording. Julius Rudel conducts a sensitively played and on the whole a winningly sung performance. Once again the Ambrosian Chorus are a great asset, with their sure musicianship and sense of how to turn sound into visual effect, similarly the Philharmonia are at their best, repeatedly allowing one to relish the imaginative scoring and rhythms.

Frederica von Stade makes a touchingly beautiful Cendrillon. The sadness that her voice expresses so well has its place in some of the most exquisite of Massenet's solos, and many of her phrases ("Les étoiles ont l'air de me sourire, aux cieux", for instance, or "Qui me berçaient d'espoirs menteurs") have a specially memorable loveliness. The part suits her almost to perfection, the limitation being felt in louder high passages which bring a reminder that this is properly a soprano role. So, of course, is that of the Prince and the casting of Nicolai Gedda, particularly at this late stage of his career, was a mistake. Nor has Jules Bastin the finesse and vocal elegance called for by the sympathetic role of Pandolfe, originally sung by that most polished of singers, Lucien Fugère. The remainder of the cast, headed by the accomplished Ruth Welting, do well, and the criticisms, such as they are, should not deter a hesitating purchaser from making the acquaintance of so enchanting a work.

Massenet Chérubin.

Frederica von Stade *mez* Chérubin
Samuel Ramey *bass* Jacoppo
June Anderson *sop* L'Ensoleillad
Dawn Upshaw *sop* Nina
Jean-Marc Ivaldi *bar* Count
Hélène Garetti *sop* Countess
Michel Trempont *ten* Baron
Brigitte Balleys *contr* Baroness
Michel Sénéchal *ten* Duke
Claes Hakon Ahnsjö *ten* Ricardo
Armand Arapian *ten* Innkeeper
Rainer Scholze *bass* Officer
Bavarian State Opera Chorus; Munich Radio Orchestra / Pinchas Steinberg.
RCA Victor Red Seal Ⓕ Ⓞ 09026 60593-2 (two discs: 115 minutes: DDD). Notes, text and translation included. Recorded 1991.

Chérubin was given its première at Monte Carlo in 1903 by a cast that included Mary Garden, Lina Cavalieri and Maurice Renaud. The opera gets a basically good performance in this studio recording, with the advantage of spacious and clear sound: anybody who wishes to investigate one of Massenet's most appealing lighter operatic scores need have no reason to hesitate.

The story concerns the further amorous exploits of Chérubin, better known to opera audiences as Cherubino, who is now 17 and still more helplessly smitten by an insatiable desire for women than before. There is no other connection with Mozart's opera in the play by Francis de Croisset, from which the libretto was drawn, and it would seem that Massenet's interest was taken more by the period of the story and its openly erotic nature. The rococo spirit is nicely caught, as it was in *Manon*, by scenes of the well-to-do at play, using pastiche dance music. At one point Chérubin even fights a duel to the accompaniment of a gavotte, a weak passage sometimes cut in performance, though not here. The aim was to create a light and bubbling theatrical entertainment, for which Massenet coined the term *comédie chantée*. One of the few extracts to have been recorded during the LP era, Nina's delectable Act 1 Air, was included by Dame Joan Sutherland in her Decca set "Long Live Forever", devoted to musical comedy.

It would be too much to claim that Massenet's *Chérubin* is anything like as vivid a portrait as Mozart's *Cherubino*, although it has its own attractions. Frederica von Stade makes the young lad a sensitive soul. She is marvellously touching, for example, in the nocturnal love duet, where Massenet conjures some of the score's most enchanting pages, but has less success at portraying the hot-headed, lustful youth, always quick to draw his sword. When von Stade sang the opera in concert in the early-1980s, she was more outgoing and in firmer voice. The top notes sound strained here.

As in so many of his operas, such as *Manon* and *Thaïs*, Massenet is fascinated with the two sides of the eternal feminine, the innocent and the temptress, but in *Chérubin* they actually become two separate characters. The pure Nina is very affectingly taken by Dawn Upshaw, though she is neither quite fresh and spontaneous, nor entirely idiomatic. The dazzling L'Ensoleillad is sung with glamorous, but not consistent tone by June Anderson, who might sound really brilliant if she did not lift up to notes from below. (This is the role which includes the Act 3 Aubade, once recorded by Emma Eames on an acoustic Victor.) Samuel Ramey sings with an appropriate air of mature wisdom as the philosopher, Jacoppo, Chérubin's moral tutor, evidently a full-time job. The smaller roles are mostly filled by first-rate French singers, including Michel Sénéchal, whose self-important Duke is predictably engaging.

The score has been recorded without the small cuts used in some of the few modern performances the opera has received. Pinchas Steinberg leads the Munich Radio Orchestra in an ebullient performance, although he allows a couple of slow speeds in the more sentimental numbers (compare Upshaw's inward "Air de Nina" with Sutherland's rollicking account). In the last 15 minutes, however, the space he gives the music is fully justified. This is where the adolescent Chérubin faces up to the realities of love for the first time and Massenet, unrivalled man of the theatre that he was, touches upon deeper feelings at just the right moment. In this heartfelt closing scene *Chérubin* grows into a fully fledged opera after all.

Massenet Le Cid.

Plácido Domingo *ten* Rodrigue
Grace Bumbry *sop* Chimène
Eleanor Bergquist *sop* Infanta
Paul Plishka *bass* Don Diegue
Jake Gardner *bar* King
Clinton Ingram *ten* Don Arias
Theodore Hodges *bass* Don Alonzo
Arnold Voketaitis *bar* Count de Gormas
Peter Lightfoot *bass-bar* Moorish Envoy
John Adams *bar* St Jacques
Byrne Camp Chorale; New York Opera Orchestra / Eve Queler.
Sony Classical Ⓟ Ⓒ M2K79300 (two discs: 146 minutes: ADD). Recorded at a performance in Carnegie Hall, New York on March 8th, 1976. Notes, text and translation included.

Massenet or Meyerbeer? You may have to think twice. It's not altogether surprising, for here is Massenet broadening his canvas, brightening his colours, strengthening his outlines. There is a love story, to be sure, but it is swept up in the grand movement of nations, the throne, the power-struggle. To an extent, the composer is out of his element, and his score often resorts to empty gestures: there's a ready-made musical language, as in a film score, in which a certain kind of chord or orchestration indicates a moment of high tension, and so forth. Yet for all that, it does survive as an opera worth reviving from time to time as a whole, that is, and not just in the famous (or once famous) 'bits'. The acts are notably well structured, there is quite a skilful play of light and shade in the handling (influenced, possibly, by *Don Carlos*), and, in the scenes before battle, in Act 3, an effective evocation of the stir and stillness of the field at night. As for the 'bits', they include the highly colourful ballet music, Chimène's "Pleurez, mes yeux" and Rodrigue's "O Souverain, ô juge", which are among the finest and most deeply felt of all Massenet's arias.

Gratitude, then, is due to this "World Première Recording" and to all responsible for it. At the head of the list stands Eve Queler, who has done so much to bring just such operas into the light of day and who conducts an animated, sympathetic performance. Bumbry is exciting and firm on *fortissimo* high notes and in the rich contralto depths, but in between few of her notes are really steady. Domingo comes out with more incisiveness in the CD transfer: "O noble lame" perhaps wants still more edge, but his call "Paraissez, Navarrais" has a thrilling heroic ring to it, as has his phrasing up to the B flat in "O Souverain". The other roles might be better and could well be worse; so might (and could) the French pronunciation. Though recorded in New York's Carnegie Hall, the performance shows no sign of having an audience till the end, when they duly raise the roof.

Massenet Cléopâtre.

Kathryn Harries *sop* Cléopâtre
Didier Henry *bar* Marc-Antoine
Jean-Luc Maurette *ten* Spakos
Daniele Streiff *sop* Octavie
Martine Olmeda *sop* Charmion
Mario Hacquard *bar* Ennius
Claude Massoz *bass* Amnhès, Sévérus
Philippe Georges *ten* Slave
Massenet Festival Chorus; Nouvel Orchestre de Saint-Etienne / Patrick Fournillier.
Koch Schwann Ⓕ ① 310322 (two discs: 117 minutes: DDD). Recorded at performances at the Massenet Festival, Saint-Etienne, France during October 1990.

Massenet's last opera enjoyed scarcely more than a *succès d'estime* at Monte Carlo on its première in 1914, and subsequently it has had less than that. The score was completed only a few weeks before his death in June 1912, and there was until now probably, at least, little disposition to quarrel with the verdict of T. J. Walsh in his history of the Monte Carlo Opera that "it was the composition of an old man whose inspiration had left him". Though the Paris première in 1919 had a cast headed by Garden, Renaud and Friant, it again aroused little interest, and the opera has only the briefest mention in *Mary Garden's Story* (Michael Joseph: 1952). J. W. Harding's study of Massenet (1970) is scarcely more enthusiastic, describing it as "a paler shade of Thaïs" with "episodes of sub-Debussyan pastiche". Its revival at Saint-Etienne, Massenet's birthplace, in October 1990 should have provided the opportunity for a re-evaluation, but according to *Opera*'s critic the production ("framing the work as if a silent film were being made") made it difficult to form a judgement as "Massenet was almost obliterated". Fortunately in the recording of this Saint-Etienne revival it is the producer who is obliterated, and Massenet comes out rather well.

It is a tightly constructed opera, the librettist being much less concerned about history than with giving the composer opportunities of the kind that suited him best. Octavius Caesar, an unoperatic character if ever there was one, is eliminated. Mark Antony being a baritone, a role has to be found for the tenor, so an amorous slave called Spakos is invented. As in Dryden, but certainly not in Shakespeare, Octavia meets Cleopatra: a good operatic confrontation there, with Antony put on the spot between the two of them. The Cleopatra who in North's Plutarch "would be also in a chambermaid's array and amble up and down the streets" is discovered in an Alexandrian tavern, where dances and choruses are in progress, and which is neatly capped with news of Antony's return from Rome. The six dances which comprise the obligatory ballet are introduced into Act 3, conveniently set as a feast in Cleopatra's gardens. Actium is mentioned near the start of Act 4 (there is at least that much history), and when the dying Antony arrives, circumstances are ideal for one of those sweet-sad duets in which Massenet had had plenty of practice.

Musically, it is true that there are important moments when Massenet's energy for sustained invention seems to have failed him. Yet much remains to admire and enjoy. The musical characterization of Cleopatra herself is interesting. Her charm, her magic, are communicated through restraint – singing softly so that the gentle richness of the middle register can be exploited, while the orchestra provide a sumptuous cushion, rich but subdued in colouring. The contrast between Egypt and Rome is well made. Octavia's aria ("Par vous, j'ai tout perdu") has something of classical nobility about it, almost an overt allusion to Gluck; and the wedding march is a stately melody, like the 'B' section of a ceremonial piece by Elgar or Walton. The last act is probably the weakest; Cleopatra's death certainly never suggests the glint or substantiality of Berlioz. Yet when the lovers' voices join ("C'est l'heure la plus douce") there is a feeling that this is Massenet's swansong too.

And certainly, as recorded, the performance does not disgrace its position as a première recording. It carries conviction, can claim consistently good work by chorus and orchestra, and is well sung by the soloists. Didier Henry compares creditably with Vanni Marcoux in the one solo familiar from early records. Kathryn Harries sings many of the best passages with the beauty of tone which *Opera*'s critic feared she had lost, and the secondary parts are very adequately taken, though the tenor needs more body in his big moments in the tavern scene. Some stage-resonance surrounds the voices, and there is an occasional creak; some slightly dubious applause too, at the very end. None the less, a recording and an opportunity to welcome.

Massenet Don Quichotte.

José van Dam *bass-bar* Don Quichotte
Alain Fondary *bar* Sancho Panza
Teresa Berganza *mez* Dulcinée
Isabelle Vernet *sop* Pedro
Marie-Ange Todorovitch *sop* Garcias

Christian Papis *ten* Rodriguez
Nicolas Rivenq *bar* Juan
Toulouse Capitole Chorus and Orchestra / Michel Plasson.
EMI Ⓕ Ⓞ CDS7 54767-2 (two discs: 115 minutes: DDD). Notes, text and translation included.
Recorded 1992.

Together with the magical *Chérubin*, Massenet's *Don Quichotte* marks the ripe maturity of his art. The final scene, of Quichotte's death, still seems to be a weakening both musically and dramatically, yet, with time, it gets less so; certainly it is all the better for being, as here, played with restraint. Even in Ghiaurov's recording (reviewed below), which is the necessary comparison here, there is just a touch of the Boris Godunovs, and of course the more of that from the master, the more the servant is encouraged to respond in kind. Van Dam and Fondary put their trust in the sympathies induced throughout the opera: if the rest has gone well and these two characters have become endeared to us, we shall feel the pathos at the end without sobs and exclamations from the stage in the last five or ten minutes.

And no doubt about it, this performance has gone well, and sympathy is secure. Van Dam has sung beautifully throughout. The greying of his voice, here a very gentle instrument, lovingly preserved and used scrupulously for purposes of genuine singing, suits the role admirably except perhaps in the few moments of challenge, whether to the brigands or the windmills, when a more outgoing power is needed. His Sancho, Alain Fondary, sounds almost like an *alter ego*, for he too produces well-rounded genuine singing-tone and indulges in no untoward comic-business. Berganza as Dulcinée has the appropriate maturity of tone, more luscious than Crespin's in the Decca recording, and she too sings on the understanding that the whole idiom of the opera cries out against the cheap glamour which a Carmen of yesteryear might be tempted to infuse. The supporting roles are well taken, while chorus and orchestra do good work under an able conductor.

But choice is involved, and that is not so simple. The Decca recording (reviewed below), for one thing, is far more imaginatively and vividly produced. The opera opens with crowds of Spaniards in festive mood, during which they are not noted for their silence, and in the Decca recording we hear, and therefore, see them, whereas on EMI there is not so much as the odd "Olé". In addition, the Decca chorus are further forward, more part of the scene. Plasson's drive in this opening act is energetic enough, but it is the Decca conductor, Kazimierz Kord, who has the surer rhythmic touch. On balance, too, the principals are better on Decca – not as singers but as singers in their roles. Bacquier, for instance, addresses his defence of the hapless Quixote against the detractors with much more point than Fondary can summon. The more distant sound of Dulcinée's voice as heard in the Decca recording at the end of the opera is also preferable. Add to this the *Scènes Alsaciennes*, Massenet's four orchestral pictures aptly brought in to fill up the short second disc, together with the mid price of the Decca reissue, and one might settle for that as providing better value. Yet it would be a pity to miss this more recent one entirely. Mention it encouragingly, perhaps, to a less well-informed friend.

Massenet Don Quichotte.
Nicolai Ghiaurov *bass* Don Quichotte
Gabriel Bacquier *bar* Sancho Panza
Régine Crespin *sop* Dulcinée
Michèle Command *sop* Pedro
Annick Duterte *sop* Garcias
Peyo Garazzi *ten* Rodriguez
Jean-Marie Frémeau *ten* Juan
Suisse Romande Chorus and Orchestra / Kazimierz Kord.

Massenet Scènes Alsaciennes.
National Philharmonic Orchestra / Richard Bonynge.
Decca Ⓜ Ⓞ 430 636-2DM2 (two discs: 133 minutes: ADD). Notes, text and translation included.
Recorded 1978.

At the beginning *Don Quichotte* looks all set to be Massenet's *Falstaff*. It was not his final opera, but it was his last great success; and if at the time of composition he was a mere lad of 67 compared with Verdi in his 80th year when writing his comic masterpiece, Massenet had nevertheless plenty to contend with and to dampen the spirits. The opera opens in a brilliance of Spanish sunlight, reflected in music which dances and exults, youthful in its rhythmic vitality as in the sheer fecundity of invention. For four delightful acts the freshness is maintained, while at appropriate times (as with *Falstaff*) the mood deepens or simply quietens down. The trouble is that there is still an act to come, a death-scene which adds little to the characterization (the apotheosis of *Quichotte* having been movingly achieved in Act 4) or to what is valuable in the music. It can be played with restraint, as here, but it remains thin and sugary, a dilution at the end of this otherwise finely concentrated score.

Nicolai Ghiaurov gives one of his finest performances on records: less touching and idiomatic than Vanni Marcoux (the first Paris Don Quichotte) in his recorded extracts, but none the less sincere, with clear, well-schooled enunciation, and a sonorous beauty of tone which he disciplines so that it establishes authority without belying the saintly absurdity of the old knight. Bacquier, too, creates a character that comes to inspire respect and affection, and all the minor parts are well taken. Crespin, whose Dulcinée has been widely praised, seems miscast: the sound is too mature and gutsy. Fine orchestral playing and choral work under Kazimierz Kord are supported by the excellent production of Christopher Raeburn and his team, and all that is missing is the essay by Rodney Milnes which graced the booklet of the LP album. It was a good idea to use the orchestral suite, *Scènes Alsaciennes*, as a fill-up: four colourful pieces, some having an affinity with the open-air scenes of *Werther* but also with the festival spirit of *Don Quichotte*, admirably caught in this recording under Richard Bonynge.

Massenet Esclarmonde.

Dame Joan Sutherland *sop* Esclarmonde
Giacomo Aragall *ten* Roland
Huguette Tourangeau *mez* Parséis
Ryland Davies *ten* Enéas
Louis Quilico *bar* Bishop of Blois
Robert Lloyd *bass* King Cléomer
Ian Caley *ten* Saracen Envoy
Graham Clark *ten* Byzantine Herald
Clifford Grant *bass* Emperor Phorcas
Finchley Children's Music Group; John Alldis Choir;
National Philharmonic Orchestra / Richard Bonynge.
Decca Grand Opera Ⓜ ① 425 651-2DM3 (three discs: 156 minutes: ADD). Synopsis, text and translation included. Recorded 1975.

"To have heard *Manon* is to have heard the whole of Massenet," wrote an imprudent contributor to the fifth edition of *Grove* who obviously had never heard *Esclarmonde*, which owes more to Meyerbeer and Wagner than any other of his two dozen or so operas. "His orchestration, often piquant, was unambitious and varied little from scene to scene," claimed the same writer – an unfortunate comment, as can be heard from the contrast between the exquisite writing at the start of Act 2 and the violent prelude to the next act, the grandiosity of the prologue or some almost Puccinian lyricism. *Esclarmonde*, proclaimed Empress with magic powers, on condition that she veil her face from men until the age of 20 (though how old she is to start with is not divulged), falls madly in love with the knight, Roland, who, after yielding to her magic arts, has to return home to fight the Saracens. (Esclarmonde's cry as she buckles on his sword, "Moi, je t'en armerai!", recalls Sieglinde's great cry "Siegmund, so nenn' ich dich!".) The ensuing action becomes more and more involved, with an invincible sword that will shatter if a vow of secrecy is broken, Roland refusing the hand of the daughter of the king whose lands he has saved (by a victory that takes him all of three minutes!), rites of exorcism and of renunciation, and finally a happy ending at a tournament.

   Meaty stuff, and Bonynge, on his best form, procures a full-blooded performance from a well-chosen cast, aided by a suitably vivid recording that shows no sign at all of its age. It is as well to have the libretto before one's eyes while listening, however, as Sutherland's words are not easy to understand, even though her enunciation is better than usual; but the precision, brilliance and sweetness of her voice in the prominently featured upper register (rather less steady lower down) compensates for much. Equally, Aragall's French is the least idiomatic of all the cast, with too many false vowels; but after a poor start, missing his very first note and being distinctly flat on his first entry, he sings with a passion and heroic ringing tone that are hard to resist. The performances by Quilico and Grant are splendid (both with exemplary enunciation), and the chorus are excellent.

Massenet Grisélidis.

Michèle Command *sop* Grisélidis
Claire Larcher *mez* Fiamina
Brigitte Desnoues *sop* Bertrade
Jean-Philippe Courtis *bass* Le Diable
Jean-Luc Viala *ten* Alain
Didier Henry *bar* Le Marquis
Christian Treguier *bar* Le Prieur
Maurice Sieyès *bar* Gondebaud
Lyon National Choir; Chorus of Opéra National de Lyons;
Franz Liszt Symphony Orchestra, Budapest / Patrick Fournillier.
Koch Schwann Ⓕ ① 312702 (two discs: 121 minutes: DDD). Text and translation included. Recorded at a performance at the Massenet Festival, Saint-Etienne during 1992.

For a composer of Massenet's known predilections, *Grisélidis* addresses an unexpected subject. The tale, related by Petrarch, Boccaccio and Perrault concerns itself with a woman's unswerving fidelity. Various composers have set about making an opera of it, including Vivaldi and Bononcini, but

Massenet's *Grisélidis* probably just has the edge in public awareness today. It has been staged both at Wexford and Saint-Etienne, from where this generally acceptable live performance was taken in 1992. A complete recording of the opera comes fairly late in the day. As we tick off the rare Massenet operas in the record catalogue, *Grisélidis* has more musical substance to it than the frothy *Chérubin* and a stronger score than *Cléopâtre*, each of which has received a warm welcome on disc. The fact that he is dealing with constancy as the central issue does not restrain Massenet from indulging his most languorously romantic vein: the music for Grisélidis is barely less sensual than that for Manon or Thaïs, two ladies who were not exactly known for their monogamy.

The weakest aspect of the opera is its dabbling with the supernatural, since Massenet introduces the Devil into the story as a laughably mundane figure, henpecked by his nagging wife. Although that provides scope to lighten the opera's stern moral atmosphere, the music fails to uncork the requisite hellish fizz. Jean-Philippe Courtis invests the role with some character, but could do more; it needs the lip-smacking relish that Chaliapin might have brought to it. Claire Larcher is more lively as his wife, Fiamina. By contrast, the scenes between Grisélidis and her husband, the Marquis, are written with deeply touching seriousness. The most original scene is the close of Act 1, when the Marquis leaves for war: he bids a heart-rending farewell and then a lady-in-waiting reads from the story of *Penelope and Odysseus*, while warlike trumpets fade into the distance. All this is expertly handled (the leitmotiv of their child throbs in the mind for hours afterwards) and in the theatre has seemed very moving. It does not quite have that effect here. The recorded sound is drab, robbing orchestra and voices alike of vibrancy and colour.

For Grisélidis herself, one wants a lyric soprano to fill out those long, Massenet vocal lines. Michèle Command is not a light, warbling French soprano in the old style, but a singer with real body to her tone. Unfortunately, her style is apt to be gutsy; there are moments in the score which look as though they should make a beautiful effect, but in the event do not. Didier Henry starts in dry voice, but rises to better form for the closing scene where husband and wife affirm their trust. It is a shame – but hardly unexpected – that their duet fails to dispel memories of the seductive music in the Second Act, when Grisélidis is tempted by the shepherd Alain, a well-written tenor role sung with a fine balance of strength and poetry by Jean-Luc Viala. It is a bonus that the cast was entirely French-speaking, even if it did not equal Wexford's for vocal quality and panache. The orchestra in residence was the Franz Liszt Symphony Orchestra, Budapest, a modest band conducted here with appreciable feeling for the Massenet style by Patrick Fournillier. For those who have had no chance to see the opera in the theatre, this recording should fit the bill well enough.

Massenet Hérodiade.
Nadine Denize *mez* Hérodiade
Cheryl Studer *sop* Salomé
Ben Heppner *ten* Jean
Thomas Hampson *bar* Hérode
José van Dam *bass-bar* Phanuel
Marcel Vanaud *bar* Vitellius
Jean-Philippe Courtis *bass* High Priest
Martine Olmeda *mez* Young Babylonian
Jean-Paul Fouchécourt *ten* Voice in the Temple
Toulouse Capitole Chorus and Orchestra / Michel Plasson.
EMI Ⓔ Ⓞ CDS5 55378-2 (three discs: 166 minutes: DDD). Notes, text and translation included. Recorded 1994.

As Sony's recording team were packing away their master tapes in San Francisco, the EMI engineers were setting out their microphones in Toulouse. After waiting years for a complete commercial recording, Massenet's *Hérodiade* suddenly found itself being recorded twice within a matter of days in November 1994 – a coincidence that is worthy of the most contorted opera librettos, including this one. The surprise is that the opera had to wait so long. Written in 1880, *Hérodiade* is typical of the early grand operas with which Massenet courted popularity. In its final version, which is basically the one used for these recordings, it offers five magnificent roles to singers who have the wherewithal to make the most of them. It is no wonder that sopranos like Studer and Fleming (Sony), tenors like Domingo (Sony) and Heppner, want to sing the opera, when their solo scenes are such glorious show-pieces and – as always with Massenet – gratefully written for the voice.

There is little point in making biblical comparisons. Forget Strauss's *Salome* for a moment and think instead of Verdi and *Aida*. It is impossible to say whether Massenet consciously took Verdi's masterpiece as a model, but we do know that he put in his request for tickets to see the first performance of *Aida* at the Palais Garnier while he was orchestrating *Hérodiade*. The similarities are inevitable, as both operas are descendants of Meyerbeer. There are copious ballets, mystic off-stage chanting, grand choral finales and exotic settings of Eastern promise. It would seem difficult for EMI on their rival set to equal Domingo's Jean for Sony, but in choosing Ben Heppner they almost do. Gifted with a voice of enviable capacity, Heppner phrases the music with remarkable breadth and seems to have heroic top notes to spare (a dream Aeneas for *Les Troyens* in the making?). All his voice lacks is Domingo's in-built passion.

In all other respects the EMI set is a fairly clear winner. Michel Plasson conducts the opera uncut, as it is printed in the Heugel score, and has the advantage of a good studio recording. Ironically, this is the set that feels the more theatrical. Plasson is not one for taking an objective view of the music and there are times when he rushes frenetically ahead, as if he is as possessed by the lurid goings-on in the drama as the characters on stage. The sense of atmosphere is palpable. In Plasson's hands the heavy chords at the opening of Act 3 resound with a potent mysticism that presages Klingsor's castle (Massenet knew his Wagner too). In fact, we are at the dwelling of Phanuel the sorcerer, a less threatening proposition. José van Dam is marvellous in this big solo, leaning on the opening words of "Dors, ô cité perverse" with a sinister gleam in his voice that sends shivers down one's spine. The sturdy Kenneth Cox on the Sony set has none of his imagination.

Having enjoyed a success with Strauss's Salome, Cheryl Studer dons her veils a second time and proves no less seductive for EMI in Massenet's version. Some people may complain that Studer has a 'recording voice', but when she sounds as good as she does here, that seems a compliment rather than an insult. Silvery pure in tone, her Salomé throws herself into the drama with lustful abandon. For all her virtues Renée Fleming works harder for the same effects in Sony's San Francisco set and is not helped by a live recording that often places her at a disadvantage. Being in front of a microphone helps all the singers on the EMI set make the most of the words and especially Hampson, whose French has never come across more vividly. The best-known aria from the opera is Hérode's "Vision fugitive", which Hampson sings with the proudly handsome tone and virile beauty of a matinée idol. The character of drooling, incestuous old Herod really demands something else, but it is impossible not to capitulate to him. By comparison, Sony's Juan Pons is rather dry-voiced and workaday.

It may seem strange to leave the title-role till last, but Hérodiade only makes a passing impact on the opera that bears her name. This is Massenet's Amneris and Dolora Zajick for Sony knows it, tearing on to the stage with a fearsome energy that must have made the rest of the cast run for cover. Nadine Denize, though welcome as the only French principal on either set, does not have her attack or such a settled voice. What we ideally need is a present-day Rita Gorr, who took the role on EMI's pioneering disc of excerpts with the unsurpassed Régine Crespin as Salomé back in the 1960s. It is a great shame that the opportunity was missed to record *Hérodiade* complete with that 1960s cast, but the company has made amends with this recording. Lovers of Massenet need not worry if it takes as long for the opera to come round on disc again. This EMI set will do very nicely, thank you.

Massenet Manon.

Ileana Cotrubas *sop* Manon
Alfredo Kraus *ten* Des Grieux
Gino Quilico *bar* Lescaut
José van Dam *bass-bar* Comte des Grieux
Jean-Marie Frémeau *bar* De Bretigny
Charles Burles *ten* Guillot
Ghyslaine Raphanel *sop* Pousette
Colette Alliot-Lugaz *sop* Javotte
Martine Mahé *mez* Rosette
Jacques Loreau *bar* Innkeeper
Toulouse Capitole Chorus and Orchestra / Michel Plasson.
EMI Ⓟ Ⓓ CDS7 49610-2 (three discs: 154 minutes: DDD). Notes, text and translation included.
Recorded 1982.

"Well worth waiting for" was the verdict on the original LP issue, and as much can be said again for the CD reissue. The performance carries dramatic conviction and is musically more than acceptable. The Manon and Des Grieux are memorable and distinctive, but probably a more decisive factor in the success of the recording is the strength of the whole company, typified by the elegantly sung Guillot of Charles Burles and the perfect ensemble of his three lady-friends. The roles of Lescaut and the Count are here taken, as rarely in the opera-house, by singers of the front rank (there are few baritones who surpass Gino Quilico in bright, well-defined tone, and for even-textured sound and noble authority José van Dam stands in special eminence). These two have indeed a quality which one could wish to find more reliably in the protagonists, particularly the Manon herself, namely vocal firmness. Cotrubas is admirable in other respects; she lets the character grow and mature, she avoids excesses either of winsome charm or sugary pathos, and she sings beautifully in certain passages such as "Voyons, Manon" and the "Adieu". But all too often the vibrations loosen and obtrude, so that one is rather sadly aware of a singer whose best days seem to have passed. If this thought occurs when Kraus is singing, it does so less frequently and is then countered by the wonder that he still sings so well: the clarity of his tone, its individuality and stylistic control are still quite exceptional.

Massenet Le roi de Lahore.
Luis Lima *ten* Alim
Dame Joan Sutherland *sop* Sitâ
Sherrill Milnes *bar* Scindia

Nicolai Ghiaurov *bass* Indra
James Morris *bass* Timour
Huguette Tourangeau *mez* Kaled
London Voices; National Philharmonic Orchestra / Richard Bonynge.
Decca Grand Opera Ⓜ Ⓓ 433 851-2DMO2 (two discs: 146 minutes: DDD). Text and translation
included. Recorded *c*1980.

It is hardly surprising that *Le roi de Lahore* should have swept its early audiences off their feet. The
work is pure escapism, transporting the listener away to exotic locales on the Indian subcontinent,
even – in the central tableau – to the paradise of Indra, which is the cue for celestial beings to dance
around to some rather delectable ballet music. It is difficult to see why the opera cannot revive that
popularity today, at least on disc. Massenet's score is overflowing with the sensuous melodic material
that seems to have come to him so easily in his earlier years. A heady atmosphere, steeped in Gallic
eroticism, drenches the orchestral writing, while the solo voice parts are written to show off the
singers to maximum effect. The cast on this Decca reissue from 1980 is generally a strong one. Dame
Joan Sutherland enjoys soaring aloft vocally as Sitâ: it is possible to admire her impressive high notes,
while wishing those further down were a bit firmer. The young Luis Lima makes a hard-working
Alim. Sherrill Milnes gives the treacherous Scindia plenty of red corpuscles and Nicolai Ghiaurov is
duly noble as the god Indra, James Morris's Timour is majestically sung, but has a suspect American
drawl. The orchestra under Richard Bonynge captures the opera's luxuriant beauty to good effect,
although this CD transfer benefits from a little taming in the treble. Not to be missed.

Massenet Werther.
José Carreras *ten* Werther
Frederica von Stade *mez* Charlotte
Thomas Allen *bar* Albert
Isobel Buchanan *sop* Sophie
Robert Lloyd *bass* Bailli
Paul Crook *ten* Schmidt
Malcolm King *bass* Johann
Children's Choir; Orchestra of the Royal Opera House, Covent Garden / Sir Colin Davis.
Philips Ⓟ Ⓓ 416 654-2PH2 (two discs: 131 minutes). Notes, text and translation included.
Recorded 1980.

1981

The only small criticism of this CD reissue of Sir Colin Davis's admirable *Werther* is the break point
between the two discs. It comes just as Charlotte and Werther are knuckling down to their first serious
confrontation in Act 2, and it annoyingly breaks the tension just before Werther's "Ah! qu'il est loin
ce jour!". One only minds this so much, of course, because the ebb and flow of word and music, the
warm, tremulous life of the string playing, and the pacing of each *tableau vivant* is handled so
superbly by Sir Colin that there is not a single moment of *longueur*. The Royal Opera House orchestra
play at their very best: the solo detail and the velocity of their every response to Massenet's flickering
orchestral palette operates as if with heightened awareness under the scrutiny of the laser beam.
    The casting polarizes this *Werther* and this Charlotte. José Carreras is very much a Werther of
action rather than of dream, of impetuous self-destruction rather than of brooding lyricism. The real
élan he brings to lines like "Rêve! Extase! Bonheur!" is more impressive than the conjuring of "l'air
d'un paradis", where the voice can be overdriven at the top. So far as style, line and inflection are
concerned, Frederica von Stade's performance can hardly be faulted. Her voice is the very incarnation
of Charlotte's essential simplicity of character; but there are times when one could wish for a darker
tinta to find the shadows in the role, and to bring a greater sense of the undercurrent of emotional
conflict as it grows towards the last two acts.
    Thomas Allen finds unusual breadth in this Albert, noting the slightest giveaway flutter in the line:
when he sings "J'en ai tant au fond du coeur" one does actually begin to believe there may be depths
there of which one is too often kept ignorant. Isobel Buchanan's is a small-scale, straightforward
Sophie, a real "oiseau d'aurore", ready to fly away into the emotion of each changing moment.

Massenet Werther.
Nicolai Gedda *ten* Werther
Victoria de los Angeles *sop* Charlotte
Roger Soyer *bass* Albert
Mady Mesplé *sop* Sophie
Jean-Christophe Benoit *bar* Bailli
André Mallabrera *ten* Schmidt
Christos Grigoriou *bar* Johann
Children's voices of the French National Maîtrise; Orchestre de Paris / Georges Prêtre.
EMI Ⓜ Ⓓ CMS7 63973-2 (two discs: 122 minutes: ADD). Notes, text and translation included.
Recorded 1968/9.

What a power it has, after all, this old piece with its contrived poignancies of merriment and tragedy, its facile reminiscences, its domesticated heroine and self-absorbed poet-hero. The proof of the power lies quite simply in the experience: you think you are by now impervious to its effects, and then suddenly out comes a melody or a phrase or a forgotten detail of orchestration, and your whole immune system is invaded. With a gulp, as likely as not. This time it attacked not in the early scenes which quite commonly take the emotions as by a charm, but in the scene in Act 3 where the sisters are together – the melody which enters almost casually as Sophie perceives Charlotte's unhappiness, and then of course the "larmes", always moving but here doubly so as it is meltingly sung by Victoria de los Angeles.

She is very nearly the ideal Charlotte, just a trifle overtaxed by the strenuous lines at the end of that act but otherwise adorable, both in character and in the sheer beauty of sound. Gedda's Werther is often finely sung, and it is preferable to Alfredo Kraus's famous portrayal (Plasson/EMI): there's more sweetness, less self-pity, and something closer than all the other post-war Werthers to a natural French elegance. The secondary roles are all well taken, though Mady Mesplé's Sophie is perhaps excessively French in its brightness. About Prêtre's conducting some overtly critical things have been said, and it does sometimes run to extremes; even so, there is life and feeling in it, and there is more conviction, attention to detail too, than in Plasson, and more straightforward passion than in Chailly (DG).

In fact the principal weaknesses in the set have to do with recorded sound, which first strikes the ear as somewhat harsh and gritty (though either it or the ear settles down after a while). Balance is not always satisfactory or consistent, and there are some noticeable tape-joins. If you don't let these little things worry you, you will probably enjoy it hugely: a reminder, though, that as well as the many rivals, including Sir Colin's, the *Gramophone* Award-winning reissue of the 1931 version with Vallin and Thill is also available.

Massenet Werther.
Georges Thill *ten* Werther
Ninon Vallin *mez* Charlotte
Marcel Roque *bar* Albert
Germaine Féraldy *sop* Sophie
Armand Narçon *bass* Bailli
Henri Niel *ten* Schmidt
Louis Guénot *bass* Johann

B B C RADIO 3
90-93 FM

1990

Cantoria Children's Choir; Chorus and Orchestra of the Opéra-Comique, Paris / Elie Cohen.
EMI Références mono Ⓜ ① CHS7 63195-2 (two discs: 121 minutes: ADD). Notes, texts and translation included. Recorded 1931.

If you want to hear just how thoroughly prepared, technically secure, idiomatic and deeply felt French singing could be between the wars, you need only listen to this wonderful performance, brought to new life on this excellent EMI transfer. The reading shows the benefits of singers sticking to their own language and singing repertory they knew through and through. When we have listened to more recent recordings, there has always been a moment, as John Steane puts it in his note, "when the mind jumps back half a century to recall the pure singing line of Vallin and Thill so finely drawn, even in texture and rich in natural grace".

Now one can hear these singers again in such good sound, the merits of their performances can be marvelled at anew. Vallin develops her portrayal unerringly from a comparatively cool and contained start to the emotional outpouring of the *Air des lettres* (where the single line "Mon âme est plein de lui!" exemplifies her perfect placing of words on the tone with meaning but no overemphasis), the *Air des larmes* and Prayer, where all the desperate emotions of Charlotte pour out of her in sympathy with Massenet's impassioned writing. The placing of her tone, the way she moves naturally with the music and the consistently warm and steady tone – these are things to treasure. Thill's tone is just as glorious and true as his partner's, his enunciation of the text pleasing and unaffected. Each of Werther's many solos receives a near-ideal reading, with the voice at once plangent and virile. Perhaps what one marvels at more than anything is the way both singers scrupulously follow Massenet's copious markings of feeling and dynamics, and how rewarding are the results. Nowhere is this more significant than in the final scene. In lesser hands it can seem an anti-climax: here it is infinitely moving. Listen just to Thill at "Je meurs en te disant que je t'adore!" – all Werther's happiness at being close to Charlotte as he lies dying is there expressed.

The singers surrounding this sovereign pair are no less pleasing. Roque provides a mellow baritone and just the right amount of concern as the solid Albert. Narçon starts off the opera splendidly as a jovial Bailli. Féraldy is pert and lively as Sophie, with the light, airy soprano the role calls for but so seldom gets. Elie Cohen's conducting has elegance, balance and passion – but passion that never becomes overheated as it does in some modern interpretations (the Prelude to Act 3 shows this as well as any passage). Tempos are all perfectly judged and Cohen avoids the heavy-handed lingering that doesn't allow Massenet to speak for himself. So, all in all, a classic set that, it can safely be said, will never be surpassed and is unlikely to be equalled. The sound for 1931 is more than adequate. The libretto includes passages for the minor characters that are cut here.

Nicholas Méhul French 1763-1817

Méhul Stratonice.
  Patricia Petibon *sop* Stratonice
  Yann Beuron *ten* Antiochus
  Etienne Lescroart *ten* Séleucus
  Karl Daymond *bar* Erasistrate
  Cappella Coloniensus; Corona Coloniensis / William Christie.
  Erato Ⓟ Ⓒ 0630-12714-2 (65 minutes: DDD). Notes, text and translation included. Recorded 1995.

Those who revere Donald Francis Tovey's writings as almost the musical equivalent of Holy Writ will remember that the sage was dismissive of Méhul ("His chief misfortune is that his field of musical activity was opera, though I am not sure that he could have done better in other fields") – a verdict undermined by a hearing of his symphonies (Nimbus). In fact Méhul was the most famous French composer in the time of the Revolution, Consulate and Empire, praised by Mendelssohn, Schumann, Weber and Berlioz, and lauded to the skies by Cherubini, who called *Stratonice* (the fifth of his 35 operas) "a work of genius, Méhul's masterpiece". Nor was he alone in this opinion, since in Paris alone it was performed over 200 times during the next quarter of a century, though withdrawn during the Reign of Terror because of the finale praising royal compassion. The opera – *comique* only in the sense of including spoken dialogue – is serious in tone (as the grave and dramatic overture presages): based on a classical subject, it tells how Séleucus, King of Syria, engages a doctor (Erasistrate) to cure his son Antiochus's suicidal depression, which is in fact caused by his love for his father's fiancée, the Princess Stratonice. (You can guess the rest.)

  The opening chorus, with its classical poise, seems to forecast a work in Gluckian style; but an individual personality soon makes itself apparent, both in an altogether freer and more independent orchestral texture – to take only one instance, the featured cellos in a trio (of which more in a moment) – and in a richer harmonic vocabulary, as in Antiochus's big aria at the start of the work. In this splendid movement, more a scena than an aria, Méhul displays a powerful talent in the delineation of strong passions ("the Michelangelo rather than the Raphael of music", in Cherubini's words) and in the flexibility with which he follows the rhythm of the words. He could also write with fine lyricism, as in Séleucus's aria of concern for his son. Very striking, too, is his flair for structure, with *ariosas* developing from initial recitative-like passages, though the most impressive example of this sense of theatrical effect occurs half-way through the work, when, in notable diversity of texture, a duet leads to a trio which in turn leads to a quartet. Curiously, the title-role of Stratonice has extremely little to sing, the solos being allotted to the three men (one each). Vocal honours conspicuously go to Yann Beuron, a stylish and mellifluous tenor who illuminates Antiochus's mood of despair, with its subtle changes, by his meaningful treatment of words. Karl Daymond, as the doctor, shows an enviable ease in his high register, but the insistent throb in his voice becomes distracting. Christie brings out all the nuances in Méhul's score; and the dialogue (which is plentiful) is admirably spoken and paced by all – obviously well produced and intelligently performed.

Felix Mendelssohn German 1809-1847

Mendelssohn Die Hochzeit des Camacho.
  Rosmarie Hofmann *sop* Quiteria
  Andrea Ulbrich *mez* Lucinda
  Scot Weir *ten* Basilio
  Huw Rhys-Evans *ten* Vivaldo
  Nico van der Meel *ten* Camacho
  Waldemar Wild *bass* Carrasco
  Urban Malmberg *bar* Sancho Panza
  Ulrik Cold *bass* Don Quixote
  Aachen Youth Choir; Modus Novus Choir; Anima Eterna Orchestra / Jos van Immerseel.
  Channel Classics Ⓟ Ⓒ CCS5593 (two discs: 110 minutes: DDD). ✎ Notes, text and translation included. Recorded in association with Royale Belge in 1992.

One revival of a little-known opera makes another twice as likely, and here we are with a second recording just a little more than two years after the first (Bernhard Klee on Koch Schwann). If only the second were twice as good, or even half as good, that would make this newly created choice a blessing. Instead, it is better in one respect, worse in another, and altogether makes rather a nuisance of itself. Jos van Immerseel puts the case for the newer recording in his introductory note: a performance "with the instruments as Mendelssohn would have known them, shows the orchestration in an even more remarkable light". And 'light' is the word, for not only is there a greater clarity, with a shifting of balance away from the strings, but the 'weight' is lightened too, and even more than in Klee's recording we feel the affinity with Mozart. This is only 1827 after all, or earlier still, back to 1824, if we go not by the date of the opera's première but of its conception. The trouble is that this interest in the orchestration has subordinated the singers. In orchestral passages a normal volume level of playing is perfectly adequate, but the voices have one fidgeting to turn it up. They are (appropriately) lightweight voices and they needed good forward placing if they were to establish their dramatic characters with any vividness.

The Klee is certainly better in that respect, and in one instance, that of Camacho (he whose wedding this turns out not to be), Klee has the more effective casting. Otherwise Immerseel has singers whose voices are rather more firmly placed than Klee's, including a particularly good Sancho Panza in Urban Malmberg. In the matter of their Don Quixote they are fairly even – which is exactly what the voice-production of the two singers is not. Klee's William Murray and Immerseel's Ulrik Cold have it as an assumption in common that the character of the doleful knight can be established by the infirmity with which he sings a sustained note, as on the word "Halt!".

So choice is uncertain. The point to hold on to is that the opera itself is well worth hearing. That understates. Orchestrally, this is a magical score, alight with the joy in composition which we know in the young Mendelssohn of the Octet and *A Midsummer Night's Dream* Overture. Dramatically it is less sure, but there are some highly effective atmospheric touches, and the ensembles show remarkable skill in construction. Immerseel describes it as possibly "the most brilliant opera ever written by a youthful composer". Mendelssohn was 16, and it is true that we have to look to Mozart to rival that. As to the recordings, they have far more in common than they have of difference: preference will depend on the relative value the listener places upon period instruments and stage presence. In both, the accompanying booklet leaves much unnoted: neither mentions that the original had spoken dialogue. For that matter, neither makes any attempt to solve obvious problems, such as the start of the ensemble in Act 2 (No. 17) where everybody exclaims about a voice which nobody has heard.

Gian Carlo Menotti   Italian/American 1911

Menotti Amahl and the Night Visitors.
   James Rainbird *treb* Amahl
   Lorna Haywood *sop* Mother
   John Dobson *ten* King Kaspar
   Donald Maxwell *bar* King Melchior
   Curtis Watson *bass* King Balthazar
   Christopher Painter *bar* Page
   Chorus and Orchestra of the Royal Opera House, Covent Garden / David Syrus.
   That's Entertainment ℗ ① CDTER1124 (49 minutes: DDD). Text included. Recorded 1986.

A modern recording of this perennially popular nativity play for children (it has almost certainly been heard by more people than any other opera written this century) has been long overdue; this one will fill the bill nicely. It was made during a run of performances at Sadler's Wells theatre in London around Christmas 1986, and the recording has preserved a good sense of theatre, with audible exits, entrances and movement about an imaginary stage. The performance carries the composer's imprimatur, and one can well understand his approval of Lorna Haywood as the Mother: she is in full, fine voice and projects the character most sympathetically. The Amahl himself, James Rainbird, sings from the throat with a plaintive, tremulous reediness that will not please the starched-ruffs-and-red-cassocks brigade, but his diction is admirable and he genuinely acts (a real snap of defensive fury when the Page to the Three Kings accuses Amahl's mother of theft; believable jubilation after his lameness is miraculously cured). There is a good trio of Kings (John Dobson enjoying himself a great deal as the aged and deaf-as-a-post Kaspar) and the chorus, who have pretty well the best music in the whole piece, are first-class. So are the instrumental playing and the recording.

Oh, of course the work's musical weaknesses are pointed up by gramophone listening: that the infallibly moving conclusion is not really a musical denouement at all, that the tunes are short-breathed and over-reliant on ostinato and sequence, that the songs for Melchior and for the Mother don't have melodies strong enough for their function. They work, that's the point, and what one also notices on a revisit to Menotti's amazingly durable and undated little classic are his enviable gift for story-telling (how obvious that the Kings should arrive one by one, increasing the Mother's anger at what she believes to be Amahl's mendacious make-believe but how irresistible to an audience of children!), his talent for evocative musical gesture (Amahl's rustic piping, the pretty orientalism of the shepherds' dance; again quite obvious, both of them, but could they have been done better?) and the charming, never patronizing wit and sincerity of his text. *Amahl* certainly deserves its popularity.

Aarre Merikanto   Finnish 1893-1958

Merikanto Juha.
   Jorma Hynninen *bar* Juha
   Eeva-Liisa Saarinen *sop* Marja

Raimo Sirkiä *ten* Shemeikka
Ritva-Liisa Korhonen *sop* Anja
Päivi Nisula *contr* Mother-in-law
Merja Wirkkala *sop* Kaisa
Matti Lehtinen *bar* Kalamatti
Hannu Ilmolahti *bar* First Tar-maker
Hannu Forsberg *bass* Second Tar-maker
Mia Huhta *sop* First Girl
Elina Laakkonen *sop* Second Girl
Tapiola Chamber Choir; Finnish Chamber Singers;
Finnish Radio Symphony Orchestra / Jukka-Pekka Saraste.
Ondine Ⓕ Ⓘ ODE872-2D (two discs: 148 minutes: DDD). Notes, text and translation included.
Recorded 1995.

The Finnish soprano Aino Ackté, an enthusiastic promoter of her country's music (she founded the Savonlinna Festival to foster a national operatic repertoire), was so struck by Juhani Aho's novel *Juha* that she wrote a libretto based on it and offered it to Sibelius. When after long consideration he rejected it, the next composer she turned to was Aarre Merikanto. It was an imaginative choice: in 1920 he was a promising young composer, from an operatic background (his father Oskar Merikanto was the most successful Finnish opera composer of the period), and had already written one opera himself. That student one-acter, however, had been condemned as excessively modern, and Merikanto destroyed it. Almost a worse fate awaited *Juha*. The Finnish Opera demanded various changes and then, without actually rejecting the piece, shelved it. With remarkable insensitivity Ackté later offered the libretto to yet another composer, Leevi Madetoja, thus making it even less likely that Merikanto's work, with its rumoured reputation as a difficult piece, would ever be performed. It was not heard until a broadcast performance after the composer's death, and was unstaged for another five years.

Since then, however, despite the continuing popularity of Madetoja's 'rival' setting, Merikanto's work has come to be seen as something of a classic in the Finnish operatic repertoire. It is late- or post-romantic in style, the richly sonorous orchestration owing something to the nineteenth-century Russians and to Scriabin, something to Debussy (at times, therefore, it sounds faintly Delian or Baxian). The very word-responsive vocal lines recall Janáček; so does Merikanto's way of ending some scenes with dramatic abruptness. But the melodic lines have a strength that is his own; it is easier to trace their influence on his pupil Aulis Sallinen than to find any obvious model for them. The plot, too, is one that Sallinen might have taken to instinctively had two other composers not already set it: an eternal triangle of a loving but elderly, crippled husband, dissatisfied young wife and glamorous but brutal stranger. Marja leaves Juha for the wealthy merchant Shemeikka (in fact much of his income is from robbery and extortion) but soon discovers that she is but the latest of his annual 'summer girls', who become unpaid servants once he has finished with them. She returns to Juha, who forgives her, forgives even the child she has had by Shemeikka, but on learning that she was not abducted by him but followed him of her own free will he despairs and kills himself.

The music is at its strongest when it touches the rawest emotions: Juha's passive suffering and his blind animal rage when he at last confronts Shemeikka and cripples him; Marja's adoration of Shemeikka and her pain at his abandonment of her; the moving sincerity of Juha's forgiveness; perhaps most of all the touching lyricism of Anja, an earlier 'summer girl' who still loves Shemeikka despite everything. The music is saved from austerity by its often rich colour (when for example Shemeikka tempts Marja with gifts of a silk scarf, a golden brooch) and the use of folk (or folk-like) music: Shemeikka, at times a jovial Hunding or a jesting Scarpia, turns into a Finnish Khan Kontchak when he welcomes his newest temporary consort with music and dancing. The performance is splendid, Hynninen dark-voiced and vehemently eloquent, Saarinen capable both of long-lined lyricism and a touch of edgy shrewishness, Sirkiä suggesting Shemeikka's allure in broad lyrical lines delivered with a heroic ring. There are no weak links in the supporting cast, and Saraste obviously loves the score's opulence and its big gestures. The recording is first-rate.

Giacomo Meyerbeer
German 1791-1864

Meyerbeer Dinorah.
Deborah Cook *sop* Dinorah
Christian du Plessis *bar* Hoël
Alexander Oliver *ten* Corentin
Della Jones *mez* Goatherd
Marilyn Hill Smith *sop* Goatgirl
Roderick Earle *bass* Huntsman
Ian Caley *ten* Reaper
Geoffrey Mitchell Choir; Philharmonia Orchestra / James Judd.
Opera Rara Ⓕ Ⓘ ORC005 (three discs: 151 minutes: ADD). Notes, text and translation included.
Recorded 1979.

The day after its première at the Opéra-Comique, Meyerbeer wrote to his wife to say that everybody, including the Emperor and Empress, seemed to have liked his opera but that with a Paris first-night you could never really be sure. In the event, success pursued it till the taste for such things lapsed. As far as the gramophone is concerned, and, one imagines, most listeners too, many repetitions of the Shadow song and a few of a couple of the other arias have sufficed, but for the rest it has had to wait for our own age, eager to have revivals of everything, however unpromising the material, and here it is, texturally sound, decently performed and ready for re-evaluation.

I suppose one could say that better singing might induce more enthusiasm. Not that there is anything bad about the singing here, simply that it lacks star-quality (which does not necessarily mean big names). Deborah Cook is fluent and likeable in the title-role; Christian du Plessis competent in his (the grief-stricken ending of his aria having fine effect); and Alexander Oliver, an excellent comedian, brings a happy touch to the simple but not entirely witless Corentin. Della Jones does admirably in her supporting role, and the Geoffrey Mitchell Choir sing well, as ever. The orchestral playing is of a quality that makes appreciation of Meyerbeer's scoring no problem at all, and James Judd conducts without too much of the modern maestro's rigidity. As always in Opera Rara's record productions, the presentation is exemplary, and recorded sound, if afflicted in this outdoor opera with distinctly indoor resonance, is clear and well balanced.

The opera itself is, of course, hampered by an awkward plot (involving, for one thing, almost as much retrospective narration as *The Ring*), but the music has a genuine lyric charm. More than that, its strands are skilfully interwoven, with a delightful tail-in-mouth ending. Meyerbeer and his librettists planned originally a short opera in three scenes; if they had had their way it might have been a masterpiece.

Meyerbeer Le prophète.

Marilyn Horne *mez* Fidès
James McCracken *ten* Jean de Leyden
Renata Scotto *sop* Berthe
Jules Bastin *bass* Comte d'Oberthal
Jerome Hines *bass* Zacharie
Jean Dupouy *ten* Jonas
Christian du Plessis *bar* Mathisen
Boys' Choir of Haberdashers' Aske's School, Elstree; Ambrosian Opera Chorus;
Royal Philharmonic Orchestra / Henry Lewis.
Sony Classical Ⓟ Ⓒ M3K79400 (three discs: 202 minutes: ADD). Notes, text and translation included. Recorded 1976.

"The grandest and most wonderful production of the great composer", claimed Covent Garden's prospectus in 1849. The nineteenth century came to outgrow such grandeur, and the twentieth has hardly had time for it at all. Yet if *Le prophète* does ever come to be revived at the Royal Opera House the opening performance, on a quick calculation, will be the 118th. However, a modern production might be too hideous to contemplate: small-town boy with girl-friend problem and Oedipus complex joins wild religious cult and becomes its guru, till seeing the error of his ways he tricks the terrorist arm into exploding a device which blows up the whole caboodle mother and self included. The opera was originally set in sixteenth-century Germany, but only the naïve would suppose that that matters.

And indeed it does not matter to any great extent, for though there are a few musical and dramatic gestures towards 'history' the opera is firmly in the grand manner of the 1840s, endowed with set-pieces and tableaux, made for great voices and a long night out. Of great voices the present recording can offer at least one. Marilyn Horne, even at this date, was no longer singing with the firmness of earlier years, as is clear if this performance of "Ah, mon fils" and the Prison scene is compared with that included in her magnificent first LP recitals on Decca. Even so, much of the richness remains and the majestic virtuosity is unimpaired. She needs to be partnered by an equally impressive tenor (Tamagno in the last Covent Garden revival), but while James McCracken has the fervour, he lacks vocal resource for the part. Nor is Scotto happily cast in a role which knows no mercy for either singer or listener. The Royal Philharmonic under Henry Lewis play well, colourful orchestration being among the score's most attractive features. It also suffers relatively little in a recording production which has a way of banishing soloists to an echo-ridden recess and playing tricks with sound levels in a manner that is bad for the blood-pressure, as it repeatedly creates the impression that one's equipment is going wrong.

Jean-Joseph de Mondonville　　　　　　French 1711-1772

Mondonville Les fêtes de Paphos.

Sandrine Piau *sop* Aglaé, Erigone, L'Amour
Véronique Gens *sop* Vénus
Agnès Mellon *sop* Psyché

Jean-Paul Fouchécourt *ten* Adonis, Mercure
Olivier Lallouette *bass* Mars, Bacchus
Peter Harvey *bass* Comus, Tisiphone
James Oxley *ten* A voice
Accentus Chamber Choir; Les Talens Lyriques / Christophe Rousset.
L'Oiseau-Lyre Ⓟ Ⓒ 455 084-2OHO3 (three discs: 167 minutes: DDD). Notes, text and translation included. Recorded 1996.

It was said of Mondonville's operas that "though nothing may astound, everything pleases". Certainly, with his seemingly inexhaustible graceful melodic gift (even the recitatives, metrically more regular than in the usual flexible tradition, approximate more to ariosos) and his combination of coloratura ariettes, simple Lully-style arias, Italian influences and brilliant orchestral colouring, Mondonville aimed at, and succeeded in, pleasing the diverse tastes of his time; and to us today the results, as exemplified in this 1758 work, are altogether delightful. *Les fêtes de Paphos*, it is true, has little of the depth of his older contemporary, Rameau (whom he rivalled, if not surpassed, in popularity but then, this is not a *tragédie en musique* but an *opéra-ballet* in three dramatically independent acts. The first two – "Vénus et Adonis" and "Bacchus et Erigone" – had begun life in the previous decade as entertainments for Madame de Pompadour, who herself took the leading role in each: their success led Mondonville to add a third action, "Amour et Psyché", and to make some modifications to the existing *entrées*. In accordance with French tastes, the work is liberally interspersed, and concluded, with dance movements, many of which possess great inventiveness and charm; and prominent features of the score are the colourful instrumentation and the independence of the orchestra from the vocal line.

Yet, if nothing 'astounds', there is no lack of telling harmonies, striking virtuosity, or, especially in Act 3, of descriptive dramatic writing. Even from the outset the high-spirited overture – in a single movement, departing from the Lullian pattern – holds out a promise of vitality, which is amply fulfilled in later vigorous Tambourins and in the agitated introductory *ritournelle* to Act 3; and "Amour et Psyché" is notable for a tempest sequence (already a century-old tradition in French opera) and a remarkable scene in Hades, where the implacable cries of demons seem to foreshadow Gluck's *Orfeo* (written only four years later in Vienna, where French plays and light operas were much in vogue). But there are also three very touching slow arias, one in each act: "Qu'en ce bois s'élève une fleur", Venus's lament for Adonis, killed by a monster summoned up by jealous Mars (though he is later restored to life); Erigone's "Dieu des amans", a plea for divine aid in her love for Bacchus; and Psyché's "J'ai perdu mes attraits", her grief when her beauty is brutally destroyed by one of the Furies (though Cupid's continued devotion wins its restitution).

Christophe Rousset directs an extremely enjoyable performance, with well-judged pacing. He secures spirited, flawlessly neat playing from his orchestra and excellent singing from his chorus (whose Act 2 "La victoire vole à ta voix" is especially fine); and he has a team of stylistically experienced soloists. Chief honours among these go to Véronique Gens, radiant as Venus, whose florid Act 1 "Régne à jamais sur nos coeurs" is a high spot, and the outstanding Olivier Lallouette, a redoubtable Mars and, as Bacchus, given "Vous enchantez mon coeur" with its seductive instrumental obbligatos. Sandrine Piau shines in the Act 3 coloratura ariette "Quand je vole" and in the work's most famous number, the stunning Act 2 duet "Amour, lance tes traits" with Lallouette, but in her big "Cessez, guerriers" aria and elsewhere she becomes slightly shrill on higher notes. Agnès Mellon is an affecting Psyché, there is a vigorous "Cher Bacchus" from Peter Harvey as Comus (but he perhaps overdoes tonal harshness in portraying Tisiphone), and Jean-Paul Fouchécourt is stylish as Adonis and Mercure, though there is a somewhat disconcerting whining quality in his voice.

A welcome addition to the catalogue, and a decided success as a recording. The discs come with four distinct commentaries, of which that in German is the most comprehensive.

Italo Montemezzi
Italian 1875-1952

Montemezzi L'amore dei tre re.
Anna Moffo *sop* Fiora
Cesare Siepi *bass* Archibaldo
Plácido Domingo *ten* Avito
Pablo Elvira *bar* Manfredo
Ryland Davies *ten* Flaminio
Elaine Tomkinson *sop* Young Woman
Alan Byers *ten* Youth
Alison MacGregor *sop* Handmaiden
Elizabeth Bainbridge *mez* Old Woman
Michael Sanderson (treb) Off-stage voice
Ambrosian Opera Chorus; London Symphony Orchestra / Nello Santi.
RCA Victor Red Seal Ⓜ Ⓒ 74321 50166-2 (two discs: 98 minutes: ADD). Recorded 1976.

L'amore dei tre re ("The love of three kings") was greeted as a masterpiece when it was first heard at La Scala in 1913, and it remained in the repertory, though more popular in America than in Europe, until fairly recently. This splendid performance suggests that it could be successfully revived if a cast of this quality could be assembled. The opera's date might suggest that it is another example of the, by then, rather tired genre of *verismo*, but the music confirms what the plot (a cross between *Pelléas* and *Tristan*) implies: that it's no such thing. It is a voluptuous mix of Italian lyricism, on the whole closer to Respighi and Zandonai than to the *veristi*, with harmony owing something to Debussy and something to Franck, together with richly post-Wagnerian motivic working. The score is luscious, but never indulgently so: the orchestral writing has symphonic sinew as well as brilliant or shimmering colour. Montemezzi keeps the music moving with skilfully used ostinatos, often of a martial or 'riding' character, and the three brief acts are so pithily concentrated that they could easily be played without a break.

The three 'kings' of the title are the old, blind Archibaldo, who has ruled his province of Northern Italy since conquering it 40 years before, his son Manfredo and the heir, Avito, of the former ruling house. To ensure the succession, Archibaldo has insisted that Fiora, betrothed to Avito, marry Manfredo instead. A conventional 'eternal triangle', in short, but with the difference that Archibaldo, unseeing but hearing, sensing or suspecting everything, is omnipresent, and that Manfredo's love for Fiora is no less sincere than Avito's. Forcing her to confess her adultery, Archibaldo kills Fiora and, suspecting that her still unnamed lover will come to kiss her farewell, smears her lips with poison. Manfredo, having watched his rival die, unable to hate him or to live without Fiora, kisses her himself.

The plot and the thematic material are established in Act 1, Act 2 is essentially an impassioned and tragically interrupted love duet, while Act 3 represents Fiora's funeral (choral writing at times close to Mussorgsky) and the very brief denouement. Only the two lovers and the implacable Archibaldo are fully characterized, though Manfredo's brief solo in Act 1 is touching (Pablo Elvira is very effective here). With Domingo in ardent voice, Moffo at her most sultry and Siepi the personification of dignity and inflexibility, the central drama is very satisfyingly conveyed, and Nello Santi directs a reading of some subtlety as well as splendour; the recording sounds very well. *L'amore dei tre re* is one of the most distinguished Italian operas of its period, and its return to the catalogue is welcome.

Claudio Monteverdi   Italian 1567-1643

Monteverdi L'incoronazione di Poppea.

Sylvia McNair *sop* Poppea
Dana Hanchard *sop* Nerone
Anne Sofie von Otter *mez* Ottavia, Fortune, Venus
Michael Chance *alto* Ottone
Francesco Ellero d'Artegna *bass* Seneca
Catherine Bott *sop* Drusilla, Virtue, Pallas Athene
Roberto Balconi *alto* Nurse
Bernarda Fink *contr* Arnalta
Mark Tucker *ten* Lucano, First Soldier
Julian Clarkson *bass* Lictor, Mercury
Marinella Pennicchi *sop* Love
Constanze Backes *sop* Valletto
Nigel Robson *ten* Liberto, Second Soldier
English Baroque Soloists / John Eliot Gardiner.
Archiv Produktion Ⓟ Ⓒ 447 088-2AH3 (three discs: 191 minutes: DDD). 🏷 Notes, text and translation included. Recorded at performances in the Queen Elizabeth Hall, London in December 1993.

Poppea has a strange history of recordings, ranging from the luscious and enticing arrangement of Raymond Leppard's fascinating video (reviewed below), via the more restrained versions of Harnoncourt (on a four-disc set on Teldec from 1973) and Jacobs (Harmonia Mundi) through to this, the most thoroughly slimmed-down version of all. The central question was always about how much needs to be added to the surviving notes in order to make the work viable on stage; a related question was whether it is realistic to imagine commercial theatres paying a substantial group of musicians to play for only ten or 15 minutes in the course of the opera's three hours. Gardiner and his advisers believe that nothing needs adding and that the 'orchestra' indeed played only when explicitly notated in the score but that it was a very small group. To some ears this will have a fairly ascetic effect, not without its *longueurs* despite some prudent cuts. But it is firmly in line with current scholarly thinking about the opera, with the focus on the words, the vocal lines and the constantly changing emotions of the characters.

To compensate for that asceticism Gardiner has a rich group of continuo players, including two on harps, two on keyboard and four on plucked instruments; and they play with wonderful flexibility. Moreover the performers clearly underline every passing dissonance in the music; that is, they find a new lusciousness to replace the old. And Gardiner's spacious reading of the score bursts with the variety of pace that one might expect from a seasoned conductor of early opera.

Another novelty is to base the performance not on the more famous Venice manuscript but on that in Naples, including several sections that are not usually heard. (Much of this material is thought not to be by Monteverdi, but that is another story, one that concerns much of the opera's most attractive music.) Not content with that, Gardiner has tackled the problem of the strange counterpoint in the instrumental passages by commissioning new ones from Peter Holman, based on only the bass-lines of the Naples manuscript. Such a radical approach may seem almost to come out of the other end of the 'authenticity' debate in a way that makes the two extremes meet round the back; but Holman's new compositions for five solo string instruments do seem well conceived and stylistically apposite.

Sylvia McNair is a gloriously sensuous Poppea: from her sleepy first words to the final duet she is always a thoroughly devious character, with her breathy, come-hither tones. Complementing this is Dana Hanchard's angry-brat Nerone, less even in voice than one might hope, but dramatically powerful. Whether they quite challenge Helen Donath and Elisabeth Söderström for Harnoncourt must remain a matter of opinion, but they certainly offer a viable alternative.

The strongest performances here, though, come from Michael Chance and Anne Sofie von Otter as Ottone and Ottavia, both of them offering superbly rounded portrayals. Again they face severe challenges from Harnoncourt's unforgettable Paul Esswood and Cathy Berberian, but here the challenge is more equal, being on roughly the same grounds. Francesco Ellero d'Artegna is perhaps the most vocally skilled Seneca to date, with a resonant low C (not in the score, but who cares?), though Michael Schopper for René Jacobs comes closer to the character of the oddball philosopher with clear political views for which he is happy to die. Catherine Bott is a wonderfully lively Drusilla; and the remainder of the cast are, as one might expect from Gardiner, consistently strong. If they are not always very good at presenting the work's humorous moments that may be because this was recorded at a public concert (noticeable only from occasional superfluous noises).

Monteverdi L'incoronazione di Poppea.

Maria Ewing *sop* Poppea
Dennis Bailey *ten* Nerone
Cynthia Clarey *sop* Ottavia
Dale Duesing *bar* Ottone
Robert Lloyd *bass* Seneca
Helen Walker *sop* Virtue
Patricia Kern *mez* Fortune
Elizabeth Gale *sop* Drusilla
Anne-Marie Owens *mez* Arnalta
Keith Lewis *ten* Lucano
Roger Bryson *bar* Lictor
Jenny Miller *sop* Pallas
Linda Kitchen *sop* Love
Petros Evangelides *ten* Valletto
Lesley Garrett *sop* Damigella
Glyndebourne Festival Chorus and Orchestra / Raymond Leppard. *Video Director:* **Sir Peter Hall.**
NVC Arts Ⓕ 🔳 0630-16914-3 (155 minutes: DDD). Recorded 1984.

As noted above, since two copies of the score survive, both containing emendations, conductors have to make their own choices regarding instrumentation and voice parts. For Glyndebourne, Leppard opts for a luscious sound and enticing arrangement with, arguably, an unsuitably large number of strings; he is spare in his scoring while allowing a varied palette of sound. Peter Hall's staging is predominantly naturalistic. He places the pieces in the Renaissance period of the work's composition, setting it in simple décor and clothing, and concentrating on the inner emotions of the characters. Maria Ewing conveys both Poppea's sensuality and vulnerability and her compelling interpretation is undoubtedly the highlight of this video. However, Dennis Bailey is a cipher as Nerone, not the almost psychotic emperor of other versions. Cynthia Clarey is a deeply moving, dignified Ottavia. Robert Lloyd's Seneca is a placid, philosophical figure but Dale Duesing portrayal strikes you as being too modern. The sound is acceptable and subtitles are provided.

Monteverdi L'Orfeo.

John Mark Ainsley *ten* Orfeo
Julia Gooding *sop* Euridice
Catherine Bott *sop* Music, Messenger, Proserpina
Tessa Bonner *sop* Nymph
Christopher Robson *alto* Hope, Second Shepherd
Andrew King *ten* First Shepherd, First Spirit, Echo, Apollo
Michael George *bass* Plutone, Fourth Shepherd
Simon Grant *bass* Caronte, Third Spirit

Robert Evans *bass* Third Shepherd, Second Spirit
New London Consort / Philip Pickett.
L'Oiseau-Lyre Ⓔ Ⓓ 433 545-2OH2 (two discs: 108 minutes: DDD). ✐ Notes, text and
translation included. Recorded 1991.

We know little enough about the circumstances in which Monteverdi's first opera was first given in
Mantua in 1607, but that little is highly suggestive and already carries some interesting implications
for anyone concerned with interpreting the work. The first performance took place before the
members of the Accademia degli Invaghiti, one of whose members, Francesco Gonzaga, had
commissioned it. It was probably played in a small room in the Ducal Palace in Mantua with a
minimum of staging and scenery, the title-role being taken by the distinguished Francesco Rasi, and
three roles (including those of Music and Proserpina) being sung by a visiting castrato from Florence.
Prevailing nineteenth-century notions of opera, together with the list of instruments printed at the
front of the score, have often combined to produce rather grand performances, in opera-houses on
large stages and with large choruses and instrumental ensembles. But it is clear from the evidence that
it was conceived as what we would now call a chamber opera, albeit one that calls for a large group
of instruments specified in the score itself.

Philip Pickett's recording takes what might be called an imaginatively minimalist view of how the
score, often imprecise or even totally unhelpful in its indications, should be brought to life. At the
centre of his thinking is an approach to the opera, deeply rooted in Renaissance, humanistic and neo-
platonic thought; this in turn leads to an interpretation of many of the details of the score in which
symbolic meanings are attached to them. In "Possente spirto" one example must serve for many.
Pickett takes the chitarrone as a representation of Orfeo's lyre, and the violins, cornets and harp as
the magical sounds emanating from it; this leads him in turn to silence the chitarrone during the
ritornellos played by these instruments, so also avoiding the practical problems of combining harp
and chitarrone. The practical results of this carefully thought-out approach, often convincing in many
of its consequences, is a colouristic attitude towards questions of instrumentation in which certain
sounds and combinations are associated with particular ambiences and characters. This is not in itself
new, and there is considerable external and internal evidence that shows that Monteverdi thought in
these terms; it is simply that Pickett has thought more carefully about the problem than any previous
interpreter. There are some doubts about the extent to which we should consider the composer a
genuine intellectual in touch with neo-platonic thought, and sometimes what Pickett is talking about
in his lengthy note in the accompanying booklet has more to do with Striggio's libretto than with
Monteverdi's score. Nevertheless, it is in the detail that the argument is won.

If all this sounds a little too abstract, it should be said that in its clear, coherent view of the score,
attention to the historical issues, and in its musicality, this account provides some fierce competition
to the existing recordings. In *Orfeo*, the recitative sections, which really constitute the novelty in the
writing, are often framed within certain set pieces most of which are based on theatrical conventions
that pre-date opera (above all those of the *intermedio*) and many of which are cast in established
musical forms and styles. The first chorus in Act 1, for example ("Vieni, Imeneo") is a homophonic
madrigal which achieves its effect through sensitive declamation of the text allied to a wide-ranging
harmonic palette capable of underscoring affective words by carefully calculated shifts in tension,
while the second chorus ("Lasciate i monti") described in the score as a "balletto", is reminiscent of
the general tone of any number of light canzonettas written in the 1580s and 1590s. And it does seem
that, under Pickett's direction, the performers of the New London Consort have a clear view of the
mosaic-like nature of the opera, made up of (stylistically speaking) *objets-trouvés*, carefully assembled
to provide a dramatic narrative. A strong sense of style and characterization, inevitably reinforced by
Pickett's sensitive approach to instrumentation, leads to a performance which shows flair and
imagination combined with a very high degree of accuracy and technical achievement.

An important test of any performance of *Orfeo* is the prayer, "Possente spirto", the spiritual,
dramatic and literal centre of the work. It is a major challenge to the hero's powers as a great singer,
and as such his aria is a display in the style of early seventeenth-century virtuoso song, with the
virtuosity carried over to the instrumental passages that separate each verse. Here the approach is
leisurely and spacious, allowing plenty of room for the music to speak clearly, and John Mark Ainsley
turns in a strongly mellifluous reading, sensitively shaped and phrased and, above all, stylish and
expressive. The other major soloist, Catherine Bott, who has recorded before with Pickett, displays a
characteristic grasp of that crucial bond between words and music that lies at the heart of the style.
The performer of all three roles originally designed for the Florentine castrato, she draws upon her
remarkable tonal range to characterize each, and executes difficult passagework with bravura. While
one can still harbour an enthusiasm for some aspects of the old Harnoncourt recording on Teldec, on
balance the overall preference must be for this line-up of soloists allied to Pickett's inspired vision.

Monteverdi L'Orfeo.

Nigel Rogers *ten* Orfeo
Patrizia Kwella *sop* Euridice
Emma Kirkby *sop* Music
Jennifer Smith *sop* Proserpina

Helena Afonso *sop* Nymph
Catherine Denley *mez* Hope
Guillemette Laurens *mez* Messenger
Mario Bolognesi *ten* Apollo, First Shepherd
Rogers Covey-Crump *ten* Second Shepherd
John Potter *ten* Third Shepherd
Stephen Varcoe *bar* Fourth Shepherd, Pluto
David Thomas *bass* Charon
Terry Edwards *bass* First Spirit
Geoffrey Shaw *bass* Second Spirit
**Chiaroscuro; London Cornett and Sackbutt Ensemble / Theresa Caudle;
London Baroque / Charles Medlam.**
EMI Ⓜ Ⓞ CMS7 64947-2 (two discs: 104 minutes: DDD). Notes, text and translation included.
Recorded 1983.

Time has not dimmed the appeal or achievement of this recording. Medlam's innovatory and minimalist approach, which essentially saw the work as a chamber opera, has been highly influential, not least on Philip Pickett whose own full-price recording starts from the same position, but reaches rather different conclusions about how instruments should be deployed. In this respect, Medlam's interpretation is less interested in the possibility of there being a symbolic system at work, and throws the weight more comprehensively on the voices. And, despite some roughness of intonation from David Thomas, there is some splendid singing on this version, notably from Emma Kirkby, lyrically rhetorical in the Prologue, and above all, from Nigel Rogers. In the end it is "Possente spirto" that makes or breaks a performance and Rogers, here at the top of his form, produces an unforgettable reading, beautifully paced and with breathtaking control of the passagework. For that alone this set is worth having, but there are many other good things too, all subsumed in a dramatically effective approach, marked by a strong sense of style and characterization. This is a serious contender for the prize of best-available recording.

Monteverdi Il ritorno d'Ulisse in patria.

Christophe Prégardien *ten* Ulisse
Bernarda Fink *contr* Penelope
Christina Högman *sop* Telemaco, Siren
Martyn Hill *ten* Eumete
Jocelyne Taillon *mez* Ericlea
Dominique Visse *alto* Pisandro, Human Fragility
Mark Tucker *ten* Anfinomo
David Thomas *bass* Antinoo
Guy de Mey *ten* Iro
Faridah Subrata *mez* Melanto
Jörg Dürmüller *ten* Eurimaco
Lorraine Hunt *sop* Minerva, Fortune
Michael Schopper *bass* Nettuno, Time
Olivier Lallouette *bass* Giove
Claron McFadden *sop* Giunone
Martina Bovet *sop* Siren, Love
Concerto Vocale / René Jacobs.
Harmonia Mundi Ⓜ Ⓞ HMC90 1427/9 (three discs: 179 minutes: DDD). Notes, text and translation included. Recorded 1992.

In comparison to Monteverdi's other late opera, *L'incoronazione di Poppea*, the meaning of *Il ritorno d'Ulisse* seems comfortingly straightforward. Right from the start we are left in no doubt about the moral message of the work; its main theme, the rewards of constancy and virtue, is foreshadowed in the prologue and then immediately and firmly set into place in the opening of the work proper, Penelope's powerful lament, "Di misera Regina". And although it is not as dissonant as Monteverdi's better-known "Lamento d'Arianna", Penelope's anguish at Ulysses's long absence achieves its effect through similar means: frequent changes in tempo, subtle variations of phrase lengths and rhetorically-motivated phrase repetitions.

Because of the placing, function and sheer length of "Di misera Regina", failure or even miscalculation here is critical. But with Bernarda Fink, a contralto of sustained power and subtlety who has recorded with René Jacobs before, notably as Teodata in his fine account of Handel's *Flavio*, also on Harmonia Mundi (reviewed under Handel), the extremes of Monteverdi's emotional range, as Penelope moves from anguish to near-suicidal despair, are convincingly etched. This involves taking a very flexible view of the beat, a position with which not all purists would agree, but the result is a coherent interpretation which not only pays attention to the details but also shows a firm grasp of the overall architecture. It is a fine start to what turns out to be a performance with many fine qualities.

Jacobs's carefully thought-out version of *Ritorno* is, as the accompanying booklet makes clear, a "réalisation musicale" originally worked out for a production of the opera at Montpellier in 1992. Using the following surviving librettos rather than the single, clearly incomplete manuscript score now in Vienna, Jacobs has arranged the music into five acts rather than the Vienna manuscript's three, and has added extra music (both by Monteverdi and by other composers) when necessary. This certainly has the effect of making the sequence of events dramatically smoother, and the additions are very much in the patchwork spirit of seventeenth-century opera composition, often the assembled work of a number of hands. More controversial, though, is Jacobs's decision to use a comparatively rich palette of instrumental colours including trombones, recorders and cornetts, and to involve a varied continuo grouping which contains lute, guitar, harp and theorbo in addition to keyboards, cello and lirone, a wealth of resources that the Venetian opera-houses seem not to have had. With these to hand, Jacobs has imaginatively orchestrated the sparse indications of the Vienna score, which for much of the time presents little more than a figured bass and vocal lines, and has added written obbligato parts. Inevitably this increases the percentage of music that is not by Monteverdi, and for purists at least will disfigure a good deal of the music that is; in this Jacobs is spiritually very much at one with Harnoncourt's earlier recording on Teldec.

It is something of a commonplace to say that *Ritorno* shows Monteverdi's extraordinary creative power in his last years; certainly it illuminates almost every aspect of human experience in a way that was without precedent. A good example of the idea in practice, and one of the most magical moments in the entire score, is the depiction of Ulysses awakening. It is a moment which Christoph Prégardien exploits to the full, in a beautifully-controlled and sensitive reading which is one of the finest things on this set. Here, and elsewhere, Prégardien shows himself to be a singer with considerable insight into the very particular qualities of Monteverdi's late operatic language, and above all into that highly-charged arioso-recitative through which he explores the complexities of a rich variety of emotional states.

In addition, the score also conveys some sense of a rough, emerging idea of characterization in music. The gods, occasional intruders from an earlier mythological tradition, maintain their dignity in a style of writing familiar from the earlier operas. In this sense Neptune is the natural successor of Charon and Pluto in *Orfeo*, a deep authoritative bass whose words are rather ponderously painted in conventional musical images; the mood is perfectly captured by Michael Schopper, one of the most accomplished performers of the minor roles, and well versed in the style. For the characters whose function is to provide light relief unrelated to the plot, there is another type of music; the character of Iro is, in fact, the prototype for a whole series of *buffo* types (drunkards, simpletons and other unfortunates) who were to populate later Venetian operas. What Iro provides, at least initially, is an opportunity for a detailed essay in comic realism complete with laughs, stutters and sighs, a neat piece of characterization that Guy de Mey, also no stranger to the style, brings off with style.

In the end it is Monteverdi's mellifluous and flexible recitative style, capable of easy movement between declamation and arioso, which remains in the memory as the dominant language of the work. Paradoxically, nowhere in the course of *Ritorno* are the possibilities of this style of writing more extensively explored than in the final appearance of Iro, now transformed by Badoaro and Monteverdi from *commedia dell'arte* to a figure of stature, capable of transcending the limitations of his comic status. As his mood gradually becomes increasingly frenetic, comedy slides towards madness and then, shockingly, towards death. This defeated beggar, the butt of jokes, a low specimen of humanity, becomes, in his decision to commit suicide, a genuinely tragic figure. De Mey exploits the full range of this complex delineation with understanding, authority and taste. The result is a highly memorable *tour de force*, one of a number of high points which combine to make this recording something of a milestone in the history of the interpretation of the work. Certainly there is room for a different view of Monteverdi's intentions as indicated in the score, but the sheer musicality and informed imagination of this version carries the music across the footlights in a way which brings it richly alive. This is a recording to which all serious Monteverdians will wish to return frequently.

Federico Moreno Torroba
Spanish 1891-1982

Moreno Torroba Luisa Fernanda.
Verónica Villarroel *sop* Luisa Fernanda
Ana Rodrigo *sop* Carolina
Juan Pons *bar* Vidal
Plácido Domingo *ten* Javier
Isabel Monar *mez* Rosita
Rosa Maria Ysás *contr* Mariana
Pedro Farrés *bass-bar* Nogales
Enrique R. del Portal *ten* Aníbal
Santiago S. Jerico *bar* Savoyard
Chorus of the Polytechnic University, Madrid; Madrid Symphony Orchestra / Antoni Ros Marbà.
Auvidis Valois Ⓟ Ⓒ V4759 (two discs: 81 minutes: DDD). Notes, text and translation included. Recorded 1995.

A first thought might be that the existence of a performance conducted by the composer (a highly accomplished practical musician) would obviate the need for an alternative recording. But in fact there is no contest. The previous recording of this 1932 zarzuela – one of the last flashes of brilliance in a now defunct genre – was made about 33 years ago by Hispavox, runs for only 57 minutes, and though generally well cast has, in the part of the dashing but fickle army officer Javier, a wooden tenor who lets the side down. This version was made in 1995, has a 30 per cent longer duration – though on two discs instead of one – and has in the part mentioned Plácido Domingo (in splendid voice), who says that he has known every note of the score since childhood and that his parents, whom he heard over 100 times in the work, were regarded by the composer as its ideal interpreters. But he is in excellent company.

Outstanding is the dark-voiced Juan Pons as the solid Extremaduran landowner Vidal, who is Javier's rival for the hand of the eponymous heroine. Wounded by Javier's flirtation with the Duchess Carolina (delightfully sung by Ana Rodrigo), Luisa Fernanda agrees to marry Vidal, who however, realizing her true feelings, magnanimously cedes her to the handsome officer. There is a sense of involvement by all in this performance, both in its gaiety and its pathos, and it is well produced – with a single exception; in the quarrel scene in Act 2, Vidal's demand that Javier and Luisa speak out instead of in asides to each other makes no sense if they have both in fact been singing at full voice.

This is a fine score, exceptional in the zarzuela repertory for the freshness of its invention and the notable sophistication of its orchestration: several of its numbers, such as the "parasols' mazurka", have won a secure place in the hearts of the Spanish public. Especially in this extremely good performance, it can be cordially recommended – particularly to those who have yet to make the acquaintance of this special genre.

Jean-Joseph Mouret
French 1682-1738

Mouret Les amours de Ragonde.
Michel Verschaeve *ten* Ragonde
Jean-Paul Fouchécourt *ten* Colin
Sophie Marin-Degor *sop* Colette
Jean-Louis Bindi *bass* Lucas
Noémi Rime *sop* Mathurine
Gilles Ragon *ten* Thibault
Jean-Louis Serre *bar* Blaise
Les Musiciens du Louvre / Marc Minkowski.
Erato MusiFrance Ⓔ Ⓓ 2292-45823-2 (56 minutes: DDD). ✐ Notes, text and translation included. Recorded 1991.

Here's a rarity, a true *comédie-lyrique* preceding Rameau's *Platée* by over a quarter of a century. Jean-Joseph Mouret was one of the handful of notably gifted but, until comparatively recently, underrated composers who bridged the period of French stage music between Lully and Rameau. During a comparatively short but successful career Mouret directed the Paris Opéra orchestra, was director of the Concert Spirituel and held a court appointment as a singer. But it was in his capacity of Surintendant de la musique at the Duchess of Maine's court at Sceaux that he composed several divertissements including *Le mariage de Ragonde et de Colin ou la veillée de village* (1714). The Duchess was evidently quite a character who, as Ivan Alexandre remarks in an interesting essay accompanying the disc, "though small in stature ... was a highly ambitious woman with a lively temperament and an insatiable love of entertainment". She was also an insomniac and it was this which led to the Grandes Nuits de Sceaux, entertainments which gradually developed into fêtes of great splendour.

In 1742, four years after Mouret's death, the Opéra staged a revised version of *Le mariage de Ragonde* under the title *Les amours de Ragonde ou la soirée de village* which remained in the repertory until 1773. Of the 1714 score there is not a trace and the present recording is largely based on the 1742 printed version with additional material drawn from a later manuscript source. Minkowski and his exuberant team have brought this delightful piece to life with vigour and humour. The libretto in three *intermèdes* by Néricault Destouches is simple enough. Ragonde is an elderly and almost toothless widow who sets her sights on a young, handsome village lad, Colin; but Colin loves Ragonde's daughter Colette and wants to marry her, which Ragonde regards as a personal insult. In the second *intermède* we learn that Lucas, another village lad, also loves Colette. The four-sided intrigue is developed by a ruse in which Colette falsely promises to meet Colin secretly at night. Instead of Colette, however, Colin is confronted by villagers disguised as demons uttering death threats unless he marries Ragonde. A double wedding takes place in the third *intermède*: Colette and Lucas, Ragonde and Colin. Poor Colin is jealous of Lucas's happiness and miserable at his own plight. But Ragonde is merciless and threatens him with a reappearance of the nocturnal demons. That does the trick, for at once Colin replies "mon amour pour Colette expire à vos genoux". The little opera ends with an elaborate divertissement and a very rowdy charivaria.

Mouret's score is diverting. His melodies are attractive and varied – not for nothing was he dubbed "musicien des grâces" – ranging from lively Italianate ariettes ("Accourez, jeunes garçons") to more extended, affecting airs ("L'amour chérit nos paisibles boccages"). Minkowski has assembled an experienced group of singers who not only sing well but bring character to their roles. Michel Verschaeve gives a deliciously mischievous performance as the toothless Ragonde, getting the show off to an entertaining start with his lisping "Allons, allons, mes enfants". Jean-Paul Fouchécourt is lyrical and affecting as the hapless Colin and Sophie Marin-Degor and Noémi Rime are both excellent. Plentifully interspersed among the vocal numbers are numerous enchanting dances in sharply contrasting measures which are tautly and effectively handled by Minkowski and his polished ensemble; the Air (track 24) and Menuet (track 29) are, perhaps, especially beguiling. Alluring though the instrumental pieces are, however, it is the eloquence of Mouret's vocal writing, and that for Colin, in particular, which makes the deeper impression. Unlike Platée, Ragonde gets her way and it is Colin who is ridiculed. And Mouret, like Rameau, lavishes his most affecting melodies on the character for whom we feel pity.

In summary, this is a delightful score, realized with affection, an assured sense of style and imaginative flair. Recorded sound is first-rate and the booklet, with the text in French, English and German, all that one could wish for. Strongly recommended and don't be put off by the alarmingly hideous portrait after Quentin Massys of an old crone which, with contextural, if not historical propriety, adorns both box and booklet covers.

Wolfgang Amadeus Mozart   Austrian 1756-1791

Mozart Apollo et Hyacinthus.
Christian Günther *alto* Apollo
Sébastien Pratschke *treb* Hyacinthus
Markus Schäfer *ten* Oebalus
Christian Fliegner *treb* Melia
Philippe Cieslewicz *alto* Zephyrus
Nice Baroque Ensemble / Gerhard Schmidt-Gaden.
Pavane Prestige Ⓟ Ⓒ ADW7236/7 (two discs: 81 minutes: DDD). ✒ Notes, text and translation included. Recorded *c*1990.

Mozart Apollo et Hyacinthus.
Cornelia Wulkopf *mez* Apollo
Edith Mathis *sop* Hyacinthus
Anthony Rolfe Johnson *ten* Oebalus
Arleen Auger *sop* Melia
Hanna Schwarz *mez* Zephyrus
Salzburg Chamber Choir; Salzburg Mozarteum Orchestra / Leopold Hager.
Philips Mozart Edition Ⓜ Ⓒ 422 526-2PME2 (two discs: 82 minutes: AAD). Notes, text and translation included. Recorded 1981.

Mozart was just 11 when this first of his stage works had its première at Salzburg University on May 13th, 1767. It was designed as an *intermedio* to complement the progress of a Latin tragedy on "The Clemency of Croesus", a worthy moral drama especially written for the occasion by a Benedictine monk (and professor of philosophy) called Rufinus Widl, and since the play had five acts plus this 'comedy intermezzo', that itself lasts 80 minutes, we can only reflect ruefully on times more leisurely than our own, and audiences with more patience and stamina as well.

Save for the tenor role of the Laconian King Oebalus, all the parts in this wunderkind's opera were taken at the first performance by choirboys, and a 12-year-old called Christian Enzinger played Hyacinthus – with whom Apollo falls in love in the original Greek legend, although the worthy Dom Rufinus tactfully modified the tale by providing him with a sister called Melia who attracts the god's attention instead. In the Pavane Prestige account of this work (conducted by Gerhard Schmidt-Gaden), billed as a recording première of the original version, boys of 12 and 13 from the Tölz Boys' Choir play Hyacinthus, Melia, Apollo and Zephyrus. But in the version from Philips we have adult singers.

Here is a case of roundabouts and swings, for while such artists as Arleen Auger and Edith Mathis bring the skill and refinement of long experience to their roles, the boys' voices for which Mozart wrote (with altos as Apollo and Zephyrus) also give something especially fresh to the music. But you pays your money and you takes your choice, and the pluses and minuses continue. Thus, while Anthony Rolfe Johnson does fine justice to the 'adult' role of King Oebalus who is the father of Hyacinthus and Melia (but so does the young German tenor, Markus Schäfer), one can regret Philips's use of female voices for Apollo and Zephyrus, for, skilful though the singers are in these roles, they are not sufficiently masculine-sounding, nor very dissimilar tonally, and Hanna Schwarz has a marked vibrato. But in an ideal world one might hope to possess both of these recordings, for either will give pleasure. Although the music itself is inevitably often conventional, it is more interesting and vocally ambitious than the circumstances of its composition might suggest – those Salzburg boys were certainly good singers! It holds the attention when done as well as this and there are moments that are genuinely touching and exciting. Clearly, too, here was a born opera composer revealing himself for the first time both to himself and to the musical world: some of his own youthful excitement in this discovery comes across clearly.

The Pavane Prestige recording, made in Grasse near Nice (which city also provides the small-sounding but effective orchestra), has a natural and pleasing acoustic and balance. However, while its booklet gives the text in Latin, French and English, these versions are not together, so that one has to skip 18 pages from the opening recitative to follow both the sung Latin and one's native English. Philips do better here by giving us a parallel translation into these languages and German as well. For anyone not fluent in Latin, the many lengthy recitatives will probably seem too much of a good thing: the one telling of Hyacinthus's 'accident' from a thrown discus, that begins the second disc in both versions, lasts nearly six minutes. The French recording has more tracks and access to the various numbers is thus somewhat easier. One can't help adding that it's a pity, when discs lasting 80 minutes are now possible, that both these recordings of *Apollo et Hyacinthus* require two, while noting that the Philips issue is at mid price.

In conclusion, anyone in the process of acquiring Philips's Complete Mozart Edition need not hesitate to purchase their highly professional issue, which was well recorded, though not digitally, by DG in Salzburg in 1981. Since the Salzburg Chamber Choir are good too (though they have little to do), this would be the first choice in terms of cultivated vocal quality. Yet it will be a shame if in consequence the fresher alternative version from France, but with German singers, does not receive attention, for it, too, has much to commend it in that it is closer to what Mozart would have imagined.

Mozart Ascanio in Alba.

Agnes Baltsa *mez* Ascanio
Edith Mathis *sop* Silvia
Peter Schreier *ten* Aceste
Lilian Sukis *sop* Venere
Arleen Auger *sop* Fauno
Salzburg Chamber Choir and Mozarteum Orchestra / Leopold Hager *hpd*.
Philips Mozart Edition Ⓜ Ⓓ 422 530-2PME3 (three discs: 164 minutes: AAD). Notes, text and translation included. Recorded 1976.

Mozart must have cursed *Mitridate*. Thanks to its success, he was landed with two more commissions for Milan, one of which, *Ascanio in Alba*, is revealed in all its circumstantial contrivance as yet another instalment in Philips Complete Mozart Edition. This must have been a particularly tedious chore: the Archduke Ferdinand was to wed and Mozart was hired to cast a musical veil over the political manoeuvring behind the marriage, and to gild the bride with more beauty than could, by all accounts, be properly attributed to her.

So, Venus brings together Ascanio and Silvia in a courtly pastoral, but has to keep them apart long enough to facilitate the creation of a *festa teatrale* substantial enough for a full-blown allegorical intermezzo. If the lovers are not hiding from each other, spying on their respective virtues, then they are becoming sidetracked by the miraculous building of a new city; if they are not flattering each other or the gods in endless *secco* recitative, then they are awaiting destiny – and the waiting is long. Meanwhile a proliferation of nymphs and shepherds are on hand to sing and dance the hours away.

Given the number of undermotivated choruses (most of the ballet music is cut here) it is small wonder that the over-recessed Salzburg Chamber Choir sound weary and disbelieving. But this, and the trim, dutiful playing of the Mozarteum Orchestra under Leopold Hager certainly tries the patience of the listener every bit as much as that of the lovers. Venus's "Ancor per poco soffri" ("You'll have to endure a little longer") seems to be the motto of the day.

But this is Mozart; and, sure enough, just as one is about to sneak off for another coffee, the ear is arrested by the sudden vibrancy of an unexpected accompanied recitative, illuminating a moment's silence, or by an aria, from the 15-year-old's pen, which suddenly flowers from the tight buds of its surrounding growth. Ascanio, for instance, when left alone to question his vow of silence, has his words propelled by a sonorous choir of divided violas, and is granted a wonderful aria of slow-moving harmonies and metrical cross-currents with which to sympathize with Silvia's torments. Agnes Baltsa catches nicely the tremulous ardour and inner turmoil within the lower register of Ascanio's writing, but the brilliance and power of the legendary Florentine male soprano for whom the part was written tends to elude her. Silvia, radiantly sung by Edith Mathis, purls out her "Infelici affetti miei" to an accompaniment which all but pre-echoes *Così*'s "Soave sia il vento". The single terzetto here, though, shows Mozart far from prepared for ensemble writing.

Even Fauno (Arleen Auger as a personable, flighty shepherd) has a little blockbuster all his/her own in "Dal tuo gentil sembiante" which nevertheless tests Auger to the limits. Peter Schreier is the benevolent guardian/prophet/priest Aceste, though a younger, more agile and Italianate tenor might have been a better choice. A pity about the English translation: even Silvia's coy, bewildered innocence deserves better than "Whither doth it compel thee this imprudent foot?".

Mozart La clemenza di Tito.

Anthony Rolfe Johnson *ten* Tito
Julia Varady *sop* Vitellia
Anne Sofie von Otter *mez* Sesto
Catherine Robbin *mez* Annio
Sylvia McNair *sop* Servilia
Cornelius Hauptmann *bass* Publio
Monteverdi Choir; English Baroque Soloists / John Eliot Gardiner.
Archiv Produktion Ⓟ Ⓓ 431 806-2AH2 (two discs: 118 minutes: DDD). 🖋 Notes, text and translation included. Recorded at performances in the Queen Elizabeth Hall, London in June 1991.

Comparing *Clemenza* with *Zauberflöte* one is amazed anew that Mozart could write two such totally contrasted pieces within months of each other. Here, in the composer's last *opera seria*, we are in another world, one of formality tempered by the deep emotions engendered by love and jealousy. Instead of bird-catchers and Masonic rights, we are dealing with historic figures in a supposedly historic context, with down-to-earth feelings. For each Mozart finds precisely the appropriate music.

As anyone who was present at the Queen Elizabeth Hall on the evenings from which these discs derive can testify, the sense of dedication and a taut drama unfolding was palpable. That has been carried over in the CDs. As with his Award-winning *Idomeneo* (reviewed further on) Gardiner favours brisk rhythms, alert, prominent wind and brass, swift tempos. Yet in the great set-pieces there is more than enough time for expressive phrasing and licence for the singers to use rubato when they wish. Above all, there is an overriding sense of a true ensemble with chorus, orchestra and soloists in complete harmony.

Comparisons are hardly relevant when the whole approach here is so much lighter, more period-orientated than in the rival versions. They are all convincingly cast – the piece seems to draw the best from its interpreters – but none is superior, though one or other is in some respects the equal of the one assembled here. Schreier for Böhm is as affecting and, in Act 2, as mentally tormented as Rolfe Johnson, who completes a double with his other anguished ruler, Idomeneo. He makes a convincingly clement Emperor and one rightly amazed at his best friend's treachery – listen to the accompanied recitative near the beginning of Act 2 to judge how sympathetically he accents notes and words. His account of "Se all'impero", that properly trenchant exposition of Tito's *credo*, is technically assured. As in *Idomeneo*, Rolfe Johnson is more than worthily partnered by Anne Sofie von Otter as Sesto. The rapport between them is heartening. Von Otter also scores strongly in accompanied recitative: the passage after Sesto has set the Capitol alight and becomes full of doubt and terror. Sesto's arias have had some splendid performances in previous sets, notably from Teresa Berganza on the Kertész (Decca) and Böhm(DG) versions, but nobody seems as fleet in her runs, so subtle in using them for emotional expression as von Otter. She is also a wonderful purveyor of the text's meaning. Her voice is nicely contrasted with the rather slimmer tones of Catherine Robbin as Annio, who is another Mozartian stylist of substance.

Julia Varady, who is also Böhm's Vitellia, is even more enthralling here. She manages to be at once bitingly jealous, manipulative, sensual and in the end remorseful, her very individual soprano used to create a rounded, complex character. As with Rolfe Johnson and von Otter, her treatment of dry recitative is arrestingly vital. Her reading culminates in an accomplished account of "Non più di fiori", untroubled by its low-lying phrases. Sylvia McNair, singing with her customary sweetness as Servilia, sacrifices character to purity of tone; in a word her singing is bland. The admittedly dull role of Publio is not helped by Cornelius Hauptmann's woolly singing.

Gardiner cuts much more recitative than Sir Colin Davis (Philips) who offers the fullest text recorded. As it isn't by Mozart that's of small consequence except where we are here thrust too suddenly into the trio, "Quello di Tito" in Act 2. The Monteverdi Choir offer just the right urgency and compact sound. One or two slightly ill-kempt passages apart, the playing is as disciplined as it is attentive to keenness of phrasing. The obbligato players are all masterly. We have execution on period instruments that surely must banish all doubts about their use in Mozart. To compound pleasure and satisfaction, Mozart's music-drama, once considered marmoreal, here sounds worthy to stand alongside *Idomeneo* in the *opera seria* canon. It should win even more friends for the piece.

Mozart La clemenza di Tito.

Peter Schreier *ten* Tito
Julia Varady *sop* Vitellia
Teresa Berganza *mez* Sesto
Marga Schiml *sop* Annio
Edith Mathis *sop* Servilia
Theo Adam *bass-bar* Publio
Leipzig Radio Choir; Staatskapelle Dresden / Karl Böhm.
DG Ⓜ Ⓓ 429 878-2GX2 (two discs: 140 minutes: ADD). Notes, text and translations included. Recorded 1979.

Many people find little to admire in Böhm's Mozart and Beethoven. Yet a sustained course in listening to his recordings of Mozart's operas discloses what a lifetime's communion with the composer can produce in terms of a deep understanding of his music. Even at a time when Mozart on period instruments is all the fashion, Böhm can hold his own. Just take the Overture to *La clemenza*: at once one discovers it isn't only the current generation of Mozartians with authenticity in mind who understand how sharp accents, a balance that favours the winds, alert, pointed phrasing, rhythmic buoyancy and a generally lean sound can enhance the dramatic profile of these operas. And listening to this work, as played by the Staatskapelle Dresden, does make one pause to think twice about period-instrument performances, however much one may admire them. Should a newcomer to these works consider now investing in Böhm? In the case of *La clemenza* the answer would be unhesitatingly in the affirmative.

While never pressing the histrionic pace too forcefully, Böhm imparts a kind of Olympian stature to the score, each movement finely judged in tempo, beautifully shaped in texture and ideally balanced in sound, while also realizing its interior drama. These attributes support a virtually ideal cast, led by Schreier's distinguished Tito, sung with mellifluous tone, unerring finesse, regal demeanour, and in the astonishing accompanied recitative of indecision over Sesto's fate (second disc, track 10), wonderful variety of expression. His singing is a consistent pleasure throughout. Julia Varady is properly dominating, spiteful, wheedling, dispatching her recitatives and arias with fiery conviction, only once or twice marred by untidy runs. As Sesto, Teresa Berganza suggests the soul of loyalty in her smooth, cleanly articulated yet characterful singing: "Deh per questo istante solo" is a glorious piece of Mozartian singing, at once full-toned, technically secure, gracious, impassioned. The exchanges between Vitellia and Sesto are vibrant with erotic tension – just right – in spite of the plonking harpsichord.

Edith Mathis is luxury casting as Servilia, Theo Adam an authoritative Publio. The sound is ideal: it is such a pleasure to hear the voices perfectly balanced with the orchestra and the whole having presence and just enough reverberance. If you want to hear each element of this lovely recording at its best try the Sesto/Tito/Publio trio in Act 2 (second disc, track 11), where everything is perfectly executed and recorded. It will certainly persuade you to hear the whole of what is a superb account of an opera that seems to grow in stature at every hearing.

Mozart Così fan tutte.
Amanda Roocroft *sop* Fiordiligi
Rosa Mannion *sop* Dorabella
Eirian James *mez* Despina
Rainer Trost *ten* Ferrando
Rodney Gilfry *bar* Guglielmo
Carlos Feller *bass* Don Alfonso
Monteverdi Choir; English Baroque Soloists / John Eliot Gardiner.
Archiv Produktion Ⓟ Ⓒ 437 829-2AH3 (three discs: 194 minutes: DDD). Recorded at a performance in the Teatro Comunale, Ferrara during June, 1992.

BBC RADIO 3
90-93 FM

Mozart Così fan tutte.
Cast as above with
Claudio Nicolai *bar* Don Alfonso.
Stage Director: **John Eliot Gardiner.** *Video Director:* **Peter Mumford.**
Archiv Produktion Ⓟ ◨ 072 436-3AH2; ◗ 072 436-1AH2 (two sides: 193 minutes). Filmed during performances at the Châtelet, Paris during August 1992.

Of the numerous recordings of *Così fan tutte* in the catalogue, many of them are excellent. However, it is doubtful if anything will move you as intensely at the work's ultimate climax, the Act 2 finale, as this one of John Eliot Gardiner's. Nowadays we recognize, of course, that *Così* is not the frivolous frolic at the expense of womankind that it was long supposed to be, but something much more serious and (in many views) deeply sympathetic to women. Gardiner takes much of the finale at a rather steady pace, allowing plenty of time in the canon-toast for a gorgeous sensuous interplay of these lovely young voices, then carefully pacing the E major music that follows, pointing up the alarmed G minor music after the march is heard and sustaining the tension artfully at a high level during the denouement scene: so that, when their vow of undying love and loyalty, "Idol mio, se questo è vero", is finally reached, it carries great pathos and emotional weight, and the sense too that all are chastened by the experience is evident in the ensemble that ensues.

So this is certainly a *Così* with a heart, and a heart in the right place. It comes from a stage performance at Ferrara – the city from which, of course, the sisters in the story hail – in 1992, and it is also available on video (of which more in a moment). It suffers from the usual disadvantages and advantages of live performance: on the one hand applause, seemingly a little arbitrarily apportioned, after several of the arias and at the ends of the acts, laughter at certain points (more often at the stage action than the text) and some ambient noise (including a lot of shouting after the overture, as the singers enter through the auditorium), and on the other hand some sense that the singers are actually going through the opera's emotional world, not merely feigning it in numerous studio takes. The disadvantages are the greater, especially when laughter intervenes inaptly – as for example between sections of "Come scoglio", where Dorabella (witness the video) is flirting wildly (in spite of Gardiner's very proper animadversions in his perceptive note about the differentiation between the sisters coming too early in most productions today). The vitality and the communicativeness of the recitative is one result of recording a live performance; it is flexible, conversational and lively, as it ought to be, and the Italian pronunciation is remarkably good especially considering that there isn't a single Italian in the cast.

Live performance and video recording do of course place certain constraints on the casting, but the results, vocally speaking, of choosing a plausibly young and handsome cast are very positive. Amanda Roocroft makes a capable Fiordiligi, with a big, spacious "Come scoglio", firm in attack if not specially refined in detail, and showing real depth of feeling in what is a very beautiful account of "Per pietà"; her tone is bright and forward, occasionally apt to harden. But you do miss something of the urgency and passion that belong to her capitulation duet with Ferrando, "Fra gli amplessi"; Gardiner's steady tempo here, no doubt designed to give due weight to the work's emotional climax, seems to be self-defeating, as the piece doesn't quite catch fire. Rainer Trost is a most elegant singer, with a finely focused tenor sound that is most appealing. He doesn't quite pass the stringent test, technical and poetic, posed by "Un' aura amorosa", but sings with charming grace in "Ah lo veggio" (omitted in the video, incidentally) and lyrically in "Tradito! schernito!".

Rosa Mannion, as Dorabella, acts effectively with her voice in "Smanie implacabili" and is full of life in her Act 2 aria. The Guglielmo, Rodney Gilfry, is quite outstanding for his light, warm and flexible baritone, gently seductive in Act 1, showing real brilliance and precision of articulation in "Donne mie". Eirian James's Despina is another delight, spirited, sexy and rich-toned, and full of charm without any of the silliness some Despinas show. It is curious that most of her music as the notary is apparently assigned to a tenor, contrary to what is in the score (or is she faking it down there herself?); Carlos Feller's singing seems initially a shade chubby and gruff-toned – in the first production the Alfonso's voice was higher in pitch than the Guglielmo's – but he is adept in timing, urbane in style and an accomplished vocal actor.

In many ways, the period instruments notwithstanding, this is a fairly traditional performance. There are appoggiaturas, but applied very inconsistently (sometimes you hear the same phrase from two singers, one with and one without). Gardiner often uses quite generous rubato to highlight the shape of a phrase, for example in the girls' first duet, at the expense of pulse; and he is alert, as always, to how the orchestral writing can underline the sense – listen to the sensual phrasing in "Il core vi dono" or the delicate timing in "Non siate ritrosi". He curiously highlights the sustained viola parts in "Di scrivermi ogni giorno" and "Soave sia il vento"; it's good to hear it, but it shouldn't be a viola concerto. Perhaps this is misguided engineering. Gardiner deliberately keeps Act 1, where the characters are, as it were, models rather than their true selves (to be liberated by the disguises), rather cool; but you do miss some of the sensuous warmth that belongs to the quintets in the farewell scene, and find some of the finale too leisured in pace.

In spite of a number of drawbacks, Gardiner's certainly a connoisseur's performance, subtle and sophisticated, and communicating important things about the opera. The video, once past an unimaginatively filmed overture, shows the production, Gardiner's own, to be attractively set in eighteenth-century style coastal views, domestic settings and costumes, and in its staging in some ways a prey to fashionable notions of involving the audience (cast marching through the house, sexuality a lot more explicit than it would have been in Mozart's day), but responsive to the music and what it is saying in a way that is welcome in these days when apparently tone-deaf producers are permitted to impose their own ideas in stark contradiction of the music.

Mozart Così fan tutte.
Dame Elisabeth Schwarzkopf *sop* Fiordiligi
Christa Ludwig *mez* Dorabella
Hanny Steffek *sop* Despina
Alfredo Kraus *ten* Ferrando
Giuseppe Taddei *bar* Guglielmo
Walter Berry *bass* Don Alfonso
Philharmonia Chorus and Orchestra / Karl Böhm.
EMI Ⓜ Ⓞ CMS7 69330-2 (three discs: 165 minutes: ADD). Notes, text and translation included. Recorded 1962.

Other times, other styles. This, and Haitink's set (also on EMI and recorded in 1986) are different in so many ways; the comparisons are fascinating and instructive. Böhm's and Haitink's approaches to the work are very alike – measured in tempo (Haitink just occasionally the faster), refined and pertinent in detail, rather serious, often big in scale. Both command good orchestras, but in matters of exact phrasing the old Philharmonia are superior to the new LPO, but not by a great deal and in any case that verdict may have something to do with the respective recordings. They could not be more different. Walter Legge for Böhm favoured a close, intimate acoustic, which brings the singers and the orchestra near to us at home (some residual tape hiss is apparent but it is hardly disturbing). Haitink, in the modern way, prefers a more distant, more theatrical sound, with space round both voices and instruments. The result on Haitink's set is a less rather than more atmospheric result, which also seems somewhat to hamper the singers in projecting character.

And character is undoubtedly the hallmark of the Böhm set. Legge must have been literally and metaphorically behind the singers, urging them to enunciate their words ever more clearly and pointedly in both recitative and aria; by their side their 1980s counterparts sound just a little penny plain and generalized in that respect. Of course Schwarzkopf and Ludwig had sung their roles many times on stage together at Salzburg and their rapport is close. Then Kraus and Taddei were adept in giving idiomatic accent to their Italian. With Alfonso, however, the balance moves the other way: Desderi for Haitink finds more character (maybe, though, you won't like his disaffected interpretation) in his words than does Berry, excellent though he is in many ways. Steffek, as Despina, has both a warmer voice and a more incisive style than Watson for Haitink: their accounts of their first arias are as good a touchstone as any in defining the contrasts of the sets: Watson sounds lively and pert enough until you hear what Steffek does with words and music – more precise in attack, better defined in mood.

But the argument doesn't go all one way. Vaness's more straightforward and more generously sung Fiordiligi has much to commend it (Schwarzkopf can occasionally sound thin beside her, though her "Per pietà" is an object-lesson in varied, meaningful singing): this is more strictly a Fiordiligi voice, and she is more natural in expression than her predecessor. Ziegler is a younger-sounding, more girlish Dorabella than Ludwig (though also a less interesting one).

The Haitink version is absolutely complete and John Aler has the skills to make "Ah, lo veggio", excluded by Böhm, for once a pleasure to hear. The First Act duettino for Ferrando and Guglielmo is also missing in Böhm's set, and there are a couple of tiny cuts in the finales. Reprehensibly, the booklet of the Böhm issue has only the original text. For all that, one knows it will be this Böhm set, at mid price, that will come down more often from the shelves. It contains a lifetime's enjoyment in warm, experienced Mozartian interpretation from everyone concerned. Listen to Ludwig and Taddei in "Il core vi dono", all smiles and seductive tones, or Schwarzkopf and Kraus in the succeeding recitative – all pent-up emotion. Masterminded by Böhm and Legge, one is in a world of ideal *Così fan tutte* interpretation that may never return.

Mozart Così fan tutte.

Ina Souez *sop* Fiordiligi
Luise Helletsgruber *sop* Dorabella
Irene Eisinger *sop* Despina
Heddle Nash *ten* Ferrando
Willi Domgraf-Fassbaender *bar* Guglielmo
John Brownlee *bar* Don Alfonso
Glyndebourne Festival Chorus and Orchestra / Fritz Busch.
EMI Références mono Ⓜ ① CHS7 63864-2 (two discs: 153 minutes: ADD). Notes and text included. Recorded 1935.

It is sometimes forgotten by younger opera-goers today that until Glyndebourne revived *Così fan tutte* in 1934, the score had very seldom been performed at all in this country, and hardly ever on the Continent in the original language. So the pioneering effort of Busch was a landmark in the restoration of Mozart's operas to the repertory. That it was done at all was remarkable; that it was done so well was truly amazing. Here was a standard of ensemble unheard almost anywhere in those days. Even in the years since, with innumerable performances here, in continental Europe and on disc, there have been few accounts to rival this one in refined execution and dramatic truth. Although on record the EMI/Karajan version may have been more suave, the famous Böhm reading of 1962 was the first version to rival Busch's, followed more recently by several others. None of these invalidates the achievement on this early Busch version from the Sussex Downs.

There can be nothing but praise for Busch's natural, crisp, freely flowing direction and the refined playing of his orchestra. Just as remarkable is the sense of ensemble among the voices. The six soloists have been honed by Busch into such a unity that comparison with a sextet of instruments is not far-fetched. Yet the singers manage to retain their own identity, very much so in fact. The Fiordiligi of Ina Souez is a commanding, confident character, but one eventually susceptible to the charms of Heddle Nash's sweet-voiced, elegant and lively Ferrando (sadly deprived of "Tradito schernito"). Luise Helletsgruber's Dorabella is soft of voice, charming of manner and very feminine: listen to her second "Io burlo" before her capitulation to Guglielmo in "Il core vi dono". In that role Domgraf-Fassbaender's smiling, cheery tone blends well with that of Nash and Helletsgruber. Eisinger is a vivacious, silvery Despina, acting like the others with her voice. John Brownlee may be a shade too gentlemanly for Alfonso but he, too, acts vividly through vocal means alone, and sings with complete security.

The sound here is even more arrestingly excellent than the Pearl reissue of the same set, conveying the impression that the performance had been recorded in good mono a few months, rather than 63 years ago, with a pleasing balance between voices and instruments. It is a natural style of recording without striving for effects (although this clear CD transfer does reveal a few simulations of stage action previously obscured): the method still has something to teach producers today in its absence of electronic tricks and blown-up effects. EMI score further over Pearl's release of this set by squeezing the whole work on to two CDs (helped by Busch's cutting of four numbers and excisions in a few others).

Mozart Don Giovanni.
Eberhard Waechter *bar* Don Giovanni
Dame Joan Sutherland *sop* Donna Anna
Luigi Alva *ten* Don Ottavio
Dame Elisabeth Schwarzkopf *mez* Donna Elvira
Graziella Sciutti *sop* Zerlina
Giuseppe Taddei *bar* Leporello
Piero Cappuccilli *bar* Masetto
Gottlob Frick *bass* Commendatore
Philharmonia Chorus and Orchestra / Carlo Maria Giulini.
EMI Ⓟ Ⓓ CDS5 56232-2 (three discs: 162 minutes: ADD). Notes, texts and translation included.
Recorded 1959.

BBC RADIO 3
90-93 FM

It is extremely difficult to choose between this and the Davis performance on Philips for non-stop momentum born of deep understanding of the musical expression of character and dramatic motivation. There is no doubt that the orchestral playing here is unsurpassed. From the depth and precision of the opening chords to the fugitive spirit of dance which no one else quite captures, the Philharmonia under Giulini become a second cast on their own. So often the tiniest detail – the weight of a chord, the length of a silence, the linking curve of a phrase, the parting of the inner voices of the strings – stage-manages the drama more shrewdly than a good many theatre directors ever do. That having been said, Davis's pacing is marginally more exciting. Giulini does, one feels, occasionally hold back to allow a voice its moment of glory; and the Act 1 finale hasn't quite that thrilling inexorability as the dance hurtles from form to chaos.

The presence of Dame Joan Sutherland does have its drawbacks as well as its glory. Her Donna Anna is never quite a "furia disperata"; the comparative weakness of her lower register and her lack of real impulse in phrasing make her as weak match for Schwarzkopf's Elvira as Te Kanawa's Elvira is for Arroyo's superb Anna for Davis. Only Haitink on his 1984 EMI set, it seems, with Vaness and Ewing, has a pair equally matched, at least in dramatic credibility: Glyndebourne's team casting is, of course, its great strength.

Schwarzkopf's Elvira, together with the orchestral playing, is the glory of this *Don Giovanni*. Listen to their relationship in "In quali eccessi": it could hardly be more potent, more intensely Mozartian. She understands the rhythmic and melodic psychology of her every second on stage. So does this Don Giovanni: though Waechter's thrusting physicality and diabolic laughter leave us just short of the sheer fascination of Wixell's hunter (Davis) or Allen's chilling seducer (Haitink). The casting of the smaller parts doesn't make for such vibrant theatre as in either Davis or Haitink; but the care originally lavished on the production by Walter Legge is celebrated in remastering which cuts out glare and distortion, while losing none of the depth and perspective which belong uniquely to Giulini's reading.

Mozart Don Giovanni.
Ingvar Wixell *bar* Don Giovanni
Martina Arroyo *sop* Donna Anna
Dame Kiri Te Kanawa *sop* Donna Elvira
Mirella Freni *sop* Zerlina
Stuart Burrows *ten* Don Ottavio
Wladimiro Ganzarolli *bar* Leporello
Richard Van Allan *bass* Masetto
Luigi Roni *bass* Commendatore
Chorus and Orchestra of the Royal Opera House, Covent Garden / Sir Colin Davis.
Philips Mozart Edition Ⓜ Ⓓ 422 541-2PME3 (three discs: 164 minutes: ADD). Notes, text and translation included. Recorded 1973.

With this reissue Philips shot themselves in the foot. They issued their full-price Marriner set and the Davis, part of their mid-price Complete Mozart Edition, at roughly the same time; and when it turns out that the older set beats the newer one in almost every respect, the decision looks misguided indeed. In fact, were the Davis, or indeed the Haitink and Giulini (both EMI), not available one would find much to enjoy in Marriner's version of *Don Giovanni*, not least the mostly excellent soloists. Then if you start to make comparisons with the Davis set, you find Arroyo singing securely and with understanding of the role's needs. Dame Kiri, having at the time just undertaken her first Elvira for Davis at Covent Garden, is naturally right inside the part, depicting a distraught, almost demented creature, as she did on stage, and sings with fresh attack and technical assurance. With Freni a delightful and warm Zerlina, there is no contest here with their Marriner counterparts.

Wixell's Giovanni, too, is admirable: more dominating, less subtle or mercurial perhaps than Allen for Marriner, but an interpretation of equal validity, and as well sung. Compare them at the start of "Là ci darem" and you'll appreciate the differences. Ganzarolli exhibits more strength, more of a 'face' than Alaimo, and so is just preferable as Leporello, though Giulini's Taddei is superior to either. With the two tenors, it is a matter of which voice you prefer – Burrows has the more mellifluous tone, Araiza is a shade steadier: both are excellent and sing the long run in "Il mio tesoro" in one breath. Roni is an even more imposing Commendatore than Lloyd.

But then the older cast is singing under one of the great Mozart conductors of our age, who has the full measure of the score. Compare Davis anywhere with Marriner and you hear a grander, tauter, more impassioned reading. Marriner's idea of bumping up the tension is to adopt a faster speed or a more fiercely articulated detail; in Davis's case the fires come from within, and from an acquaintance with the work that, even in 1973, stretched back more than 20 years.

In many numbers it is Davis who chooses the right tempo, just that much slower or faster than Marriner; Davis who captures the underlying fires that drive both *donne*; Davis who realizes the tremendous originality of Giovanni's defiance of the stone guest. And it is Davis who receives the more appropriate recording. Marriner's has presence and an admirable balance, but Davis's has more immediacy and – just – the better distribution of voices over the stereo image.

Those collecting the Marriner versions of Mozart's operas will probably know and appreciate his approach, and may not share these reservations. However, the Davis should stand alongside Haitink and Giulini as a recommended account of the conventional versions – especially as his is available at mid price. Those wanting something different and arrestingly enjoyable will want to investigate the Oestman (L'Oiseau-Lyre) too.

Mozart Don Giovanni.
John Brownlee *bar* Don Giovanni
Inna Souez *sop* Donna Anna
Luise Helletsgruber *sop* Donna Elvira
Audrey Mildmay *sop* Zerlina
Koloman von Pataky *ten* Don Ottavio
Salvatore Baccaloni *bass* Leporello
Roy Henderson *bar* Masetto
David Franklin *bass* Commendatore
Glyndebourne Festival Chorus and Orchestra / Fritz Busch.
EMI Références mono Ⓜ Ⓓ CHS7 61030-2 (three discs: 172 minutes: ADD). Notes, text and translation included. Recorded 1936.

Listening to this set in its clear CD transfer (very little surface noise) confirms the opinion that it is one of the three classic versions of this opera in existence on disc. The other two are the Giulini and the Haitink, the latter also originating from Glyndebourne but not, like this one, recorded there. It shares with them a sense of a true ensemble, a conductor who balances finely between dramatic pulse and sensuous warmth, and a cast that has many strengths and few weaknesses. As with the modern sets, the recitative was produced with a lively sense of situation and with the quickness of repartee particularly important in this of all Mozart's operas.

If you have tended to take this set's merits on memory or reputation, you may begin listening with some fear that the passing of time might have dimmed its merits. The contrary is the case, especially in the case of Busch's conducting, at once so lithe and sensuous, and of at least four members of the cast. Baccaloni still has no superior as Leporello. His swiftness of reaction, his variety of tone and dynamic in the recitatives, his acute and idiomatic way with the text in the musical numbers remains unsurpassed. Taddei (Giulini) runs him very close, but there is an even greater earthiness and relish in Baccaloni's performance. Souez is a paragon among Annas, both in vocal execution and stamina, matched only by Vaness for Haitink. Although that rules out a number of very effective Annas, among them Jurinac, Margaret Price and Sutherland, it does seem that Souez and Vaness have just the poise, drive and vocal calibre needed for the part (although Rethberg on the 'unofficial' 1937 Walter recording from Salzburg is another candidate for the Anna crown).

More controversially, perhaps, Helletsgruber should be put in the Schwarzkopf (Giulini), della Casa and Jurinac class as Elvira, simply because her sensuous and vibrant tone is ideal for the role as was theirs: her phrasing of the recitative before "Mi tradì", even without the appoggiaturas she is allowed on the Walter recording, perfectly mirrors Elvira's feeling and the short arias in Act 1, helped by Busch's alert conducting, have the right thrust. It is a most sensuous, seductive portrayal. Then Koloman von Pataky must have the most sheerly beautiful tenor ever to attempt Ottavio's music. "Dalla sua pace" is particularly warm and suave. In "Il mio tesoro" he breaks his long run twice, as he has to, at Busch's slow tempo (obviously the accepted one at the time as you can hear, with Dino Borgioli, on the contemporaneous Walter and some 78rpm versions by famous tenors of the day).

The other singers, though excellent, aren't on quite that level of achievement. Brownlee sings Giovanni's music as well as anyone so far as voice is concerned, his baritone well set off from Baccaloni's bass, but he is a little too stolid and unimaginative in expression – though the iron sometimes shows through the jovial exterior, as at his order to Leporello, "Leggi, dico", in the

Graveyard scene. Audrey Mildmay is quick-witted enough as Zerlina, but without her appealing presence her singing sounds a little unvaried. Roy Henderson conveys a real presence as Masetto, but is inclined to overact with his voice. David Franklin's Commendatore is lightish in timbre but imposing in utterance. None impairs the sense of a team working together to create the kind of Mozartian style then – and now – rather rare in the opera world.

Busch preferred a piano to a harpsichord, which may disturb some ears today. So may the close recording of the voices, but again, for some, that will be an advantage and the orchestra in no way sound in the background. A few stage effects are unobtrusively added. Text and translation (even of some passages of recitative here omitted) are included. At mid price, this remains a competitive version and, more important, a constantly vivid and enjoyable one. It is a worthy memorial to the late David Bicknell, who was the producer.

Mozart Don Giovanni.

Cesare Siepi *bass* Don Giovanni
Elisabeth Grümmer *sop* Donna Anna
Lisa della Casa *sop* Donna Elvira
Erna Berger *sop* Zerlina
Anton Dermota *ten* Don Ottavio
Otto Edelmann *bass* Leporello
Walter Berry *bass-bar* Masetto
Deszö Ernster *bass* Commendatore
Vienna State Opera Chorus; Vienna Philharmonic Orchestra / Wilhelm Furtwängler.
Stage Director: **Herbert Graf.** *Film Director:* **Paul Czinner.**
DG mono Ⓕ 🎞 072 440-3GH (177 minutes: two cassettes). Filmed in 1954.

This is the famous Paul Czinner film issued in 1955, based on the 1954 Salzburg Festival staging by Herbert Graf but not recorded at a live performance. It is certainly a historic document of some importance, and DG's refurbishment does it proud. The picture now looks in its pristine state: it might almost have been filmed yesterday rather than 44 years ago. The sound is as amenable as it is ever going to be. Though it is a vast improvement on earlier issues, there is still some distortion of the higher voices, della Casa's being the worst affected.

That is particularly regrettable as della Casa's Elvira, convincingly sung and acted, is the most compelling interpretation, the least affected by changes in acting style in opera. Her smooth, positive, natural singing in her arias remains an object-lesson in Mozartian style, absence of appoggiaturas apart. Grümmer is also well caught, dispensing Anna's arias with gloriously firm tone and magnificent delivery of the text. She acts the wronged woman with reasonable conviction. Dermota's Ottavio is conventional but aristocratically phrased, though he is deprived of "Dalla sua pace" and Furtwängler's very leisurely tempo for "Il mio tesoro" means several extra breaks in line for breath.

About the rest there have to be considerable reservations. For today's tastes Siepi's Giovanni is too much like Errol Flynn strayed into opera, hardly a sign of the darker side of Giovanni's character, and his bass sounds heavy for Mozart. Edelmann is far too Germanic for Leporello in both his singing and acting. Berger looks too old and sedate for Zerlina, though she still has sweet tone at her command. Berry is a cipher as Masetto, Ernster a middling Commendatore. Furtwängler's reading sounds laborious, with predominantly slow tempos and a want of forward-moving impulse. As ever with him, he was better heard in a live performance. Inevitably Graf's staging looks old-fashioned, though some detail is well observed – Elvira's face at her first entry is hidden by a veil, making Giovanni's inability to recognize her more plausible. Other more recent videos give a more vital, vivid view of music and action, but this one will always be there as a reminder of the greatness of Grümmer and della Casa.

Mozart Die Entführung aus dem Serail.

Lynne Dawson *sop* Konstanze
Marianne Hirsti *sop* Blonde
Uwe Heilmann *ten* Belmonte
Wilfrid Gahmlich *ten* Pedrillo
Gunther von Kannen *bass* Osmin
Wolfgang Hinze *spkr* Bassa Selim
Academy of Ancient Music Chorus and Orchestra / Christopher Hogwood.
L'Oiseau-Lyre Ⓕ ① 430 339-2OH2 (two discs: 144 minutes: DDD). 🖉 Notes, text and translation included. Recorded 1990.

"Too many notes, my dear Mozart", said the Emperor Joseph II – well, he probably didn't in reality, but the apocryphal story could have been true, for *Die Entführung aus dem Serail* does have a lot more notes than any of the other Singspiels given at the Vienna Burgtheater about that time. It must have seemed difficult and bewildering to the early audiences, who went in expectation of something much simpler. But, like most of Mozart's music, it grew on them, and indeed it widened Mozart's reputation more than did any other of his operas during the 1780s; and its thicker musical fabric has certainly proved a lot more durable than the shoddy cloth of the Umlaufs and the others who supplied the repertory of the German National Singspiel.

Such thoughts on this familiar, lovable and wonderfully spirited work are provoked by hearing it, for the first time on record, in something close to its original colours (the Harnoncourt version on Teldec does not truly offer that). It makes a difference, but not a critical difference: that is, the distinction is instantly discernible but does not of itself determine whether this recording is to be preferred to others. The size of the orchestra and the way it is balanced ensure that the woodwind writing makes its points; even after numerous hearings of the opera, in the theatre and on records, one has never been quite as aware of the richness, variety and allusiveness of the score as this time. Christopher Hogwood uses a string band of 7.6.4.3.3, and favours a fairly slender, pared-down tone from the violins, leaving plenty of room for the wind (and in this he is much helped by the characteristically creative contribution of the late Decca producer, Peter Wadland – the presence of his keen ear, as in the Da Ponte triptych he recorded with Oestman, is always telling). The score comes over with much stronger, more individual character here than it does in a 'modern' performance, where, when the chief emphasis tends to be on the expressiveness of the first violin line, the quirkiness of the scoring of individual numbers accordingly tends to become ironed out.

If you are expecting here the rapid tempos that distinguish the Oestman recordings you may be disappointed. Hogwood's speeds are mostly quite conventional, livelier, to be sure, than you would expect from a conductor of the last generation, but at times quite measured and allowing the soloists the room they need. The first number, Belmonte's "Hier soll ich dich denn sehen", is decidedly leisurely, and Uwe Heilmann takes full advantage of it, especially in his delicate singing at the end – his is a fresh, young-sounding voice, handled very surely and attractively, and with the proper Mozartian blend of the lyrical with a hint of the heroic: there is some lovely hushed singing in "O wie ängstlich", done with a feeling of spontaneity and altogether an unusual and moving interpretation, while the difficult later arias, which can floor quite accomplished tenors, have no fears for him: "Wenn der Freude Tränen fliessen" is airy yet ardent; "Ich baue ganz" elegantly sung at a relaxed pace (and how delectably it is scored).

Opposite Heilmann is that appealing artist Lynne Dawson. There is a real glow to the voice, and a natural fullness and warmth; she has the necessary "flexible throat" (to quote Mozart) for "Ach, ich liebte", suggests real depths of desolation in her spacious account of "Traurigkeit", and sings fearlessly and grandly in "Martern aller Arten" (reservations here, however, about the paucity of appoggiaturas and about Hogwood's interpretation, as *rallentandos*, of the admittedly enigmatic *ad libitum* markings in the orchestral ritornellos). The spirited and shapely singing of the Blonde, Marianne Hirsti, is also enjoyable. There are good things too in the Pedrillo of Wilfrid Gahmlich, notably some graceful phrasing in "Frisch zum Kampfe!", but you may find the Romance, "Im Mohrenland", disappointing because his intonation seems fallible, especially on the higher notes, which often flatten. Then there is the fine Osmin of Gunther von Kannen, the bottom register fine, full and clear, the rhythms and the articulation beautifully spruce, the words well used; he manages to relish the music and the text without ever resorting to empty clowning, as Osmins are apt to do.

A few general points. The dialogue is included, of course, but reduced by about half; the cutting is carefully done and the result seems to be perfectly satisfactory for a recording. There is piano continuo, adding a certain colour, wholly convincingly, to the sound of the orchestra. The recently rediscovered march is included; one can understand why Mozart might have dropped it. The piccolo pierces the orchestral texture in the 'Turkish' music in splendid fashion. The expressive climax of the whole work, the beginning of the supposed farewell scene for the lovers, seems to be slightly wanting in warmth from the orchestra; Hogwood places the accents sharply and the playing is very precise, but the moment's depth is not quite realized. Yet this is soon forgotten in the duet that ensues, where Dawson especially conveys the rapt blend of visionary joy and tragic feeling as the lovers look forward to death together.

This is, probably, the *Entführung* to choose above all. The opera has been only moderately served on records in the past, – Sir Colin Davis's Philips version being the most enjoyable, but the singing is by no means consistently distinguished. Harnoncourt's Teldec version is arresting but contrived and mannered and ultimately not very musical. Hogwood's is a fine achievement which enlarges our understanding of the work and our affection for it.

Mozart Die Entführung aus dem Serail.
Christiane Eda-Pierre *sop* Konstanze
Norma Burrowes *sop* Blonde
Stuart Burrows *ten* Belmonte
Robert Tear *ten* Pedrillo
Robert Lloyd *bass* Osmin
Curd Jürgens *narr* Bassa Selim
John Alldis Choir; Academy of St Martin in the Fields / Sir Colin Davis.
Philips Mozart Edition Ⓜ Ⓓ 422 538-2PME2 (two discs: 128 minutes: DDD). Notes, text and translation included. Recorded 1978.

Even if the Hogwood *Entführung* is more to the liking of period-instrument *aficionados*, the easy authority and loving warmth of Davis's interpretation has stood a reasonable test of time. This is an attractive, naturally paced reading, well, though not outstandingly, cast. Burrowes and Burrows are both undoubted assets, she lively but not too pert as Blonde, he agile and mellifluous as Belmonte. Lloyd is an alert, resourceful Osmin, badly matched by his speaking counterpart, and not quite as rotund as Moll for Böhm, and Tear is a somewhat strenuous Pedrillo. Eda-Pierre's Konstanze is pleasing in voice when not overstretched, and sympathetic in character. Davis persuades the best from the Academy of St Martin's. All said, this set attests to Davis's appreciable and appreciated contribution to the Mozart discography in the opera department and worthily represents *Entführung* in the Mozart Edition. It also shows Philips's consistency in the matter of sound quality.

Mozart Die Entführung aus dem Serail.
Ingrid Habermann *sop* Konstanze
Donna Ellen *sop* Blonde
Piotr Bezcala *ten* Belmonte
Oliver Ringelhahn *ten* Pedrillo
Franz Kalchmair *bass* Osmin
Harald Pfeiffer *spkr* Bassa Selim
Linz Landestheater Choir; Linz Bruckner Orchestra / Martin Sieghart.
Arte Nova Classics Ⓢ Ⓘ 74321 49701-2 (two discs: 115 minutes: DDD). Notes, text and translation included. Recorded live in 1996-7.

If you are strapped for cash, or even if you are not, this is a real bargain, just about as enjoyable as any performance given by more prominent artists on better-known labels. The recording was made at the time of live performances of the piece at the Linz Opera, so it is not surprising to find such a natural sense of ensemble among the principals or such a well-integrated account of the score from Sieghart, who is also aware of the latest research on this score in terms of orchestration, appoggiaturas and small embellishments. His reading is a shade strict and unsmiling, but it has the virtue of keeping the drama on the move in a work that can outstay its welcome in more self-indulgent performances, and the playing of what sounds to be a small band is exemplary. Dialogue is included but kept to the minimum essential to clarify the action.

The young cast boasts several welcome discoveries. Habermann has the dramatic coloratura, the technique and all the notes to encompass the fearful demands of Konstanze's role and shows the dramatic resolution it requires. The Polish tenor, Piotr Bezcala, has also been judiciously cast for his part: his voice is firm and sappy, and he discloses an ability to make his four taxing arias sound relatively simple. One or two unwanted lachrymose moments apart, he is a model of Mozartian style. The Canadian soprano, Donna Ellen, is a mettlesome Blonde, happy in the dizzy heights reached in her first aria. Her Pedrillo is a lively singer but one prone to questionable pitch, particularly in his Serenade. Best of all is the native Austrian, Franz Kalchmair as an Osmin with a rotund, pleasing bass, as happy at the bottom as at the top of his range and he is obviously a formidable actor: he would adorn any performance of this opera. The Bassa Selim's role has been severely curtailed; what remains of it is spoken with the appropriate blend of menace and authority by Harald Pfeiffer.

The recording is reasonably good, but there is a disturbing discrepancy between the acoustic used for respectively the sung and spoken sections of the piece. However, that drawback is not serious enough to prevent this version receiving a strong recommendation.

Mozart Die Entführung aus dem Serail.
Arleen Auger *sop* Konstanze
Reri Grist *sop* Blonde
Peter Schreier *ten* Belmonte
Harald Neukirch *ten* Pedrillo
Kurt Moll *bass* Osmin
Otto Mellies *spkr* Pasha Selim
Leipzig Radio Choir; Staatskapelle Dresden / Karl Böhm.
DG Ⓜ Ⓘ 429 868-2GX2 (two discs: 131 minutes: ADD). Notes, text and translation included. Recorded 1973.

Even at a time when Mozart on period instruments is all the fashion, Böhm can hold his own. *Die Entführung* is the oldest of Böhm's Dresden-made Mozart sets. It remains among the safest, though not the most exciting, recommendation for this opera among the many versions in the catalogue, and is particularly distinguished by Arleen Auger's Konstanze, possibly the most impressive performance on disc, Peter Schreier's stylish Belmonte and Kurt Moll's classic Osmin. There's more tension in the Harnoncourt version, more sense of the danger in the situation, more menace in Salminien's Osmin. Compared with this, Böhm can seem relatively staid, but his virtues aren't to be denied nor the musicality of the Staatskapelle's playing. What a pity, though, that actors rather than the singers speak the dialogue.

Mozart Die Entführung aus dem Serail.

Inga Nielsen *sop* Konstanze
Lilian Watson *sop* Blonde
Deon van der Walt *ten* Belmonte
Lars Magnusson *ten* Pedrillo
Kurt Moll *bass* Osmin
Oliver Tobias *spkr* Bassa Selim
Chorus and Orchestra of the Royal Opera House, Covent Garden / Sir Georg Solti.
Stage Director: **Elijah Moshinsky.**
NVC Arts Ⓕ 🔲 0630-18773-3 (140 minutes). Filmed at a performance in the Royal Opera
House, Covent Garden during 1988.

Sir Georg Solti was an excellent, if slightly bombastic, Mozartian; and if any opera suited his style, it
was *Die Entführung aus dem Serail*. This video is a faithful record of the 1988 run of performances he
gave at Covent Garden and in some respects it could hardly be bettered. First of all, it has Kurt Moll,
one of the few singers today who can stand comparison with those of any other era: Vilem Heš,
Robert Radford, Alexander Kipnis, Gottlob Frick ... none of them sang Osmin better or made him
funnier. And it is doubtful if any of them could match Moll's trick of falling down and getting up
again without spilling a drop from his wineglass. Lars Magnusson is a marvellous Pedrillo and Lilian
Watson is as pert a Blonde as any; both of them sing extremely well. So the comic element is
plentifully supplied. Sadly the two serious singers, Deon van der Walt and Inga Nielsen, lack the
charisma to make their roles come alive; and their singing is pallid, though they get round the notes
pleasantly enough. The designs by Sidney Nolan and Timothy O'Brien are fun and Elijah
Moshinsky's production is enjoyable. It is not unclear as to why the Pasha wears Western garb,
however – and Oliver Tobias speaks very Home Counties German. There are English subtitles.

Mozart La finta giardiniera.

Julia Cornwell *sop* Sandrina
Ezio di Cesare *ten* Podestà
Thomas Moser *ten* Belfiore
Lilian Sukis *sop* Arminda
Brigitte Fassbaender *mez* Ramiro
Jutta-Renate Ihloff *sop* Serpetta
Barry McDaniel *bar* Nardo
Salzburg Mozarteum Orchestra / Leopold Hager.
Philips Mozart Edition Ⓜ ① 422 533-2PME3 (three discs: 205 minutes: ADD). Notes, text and
translation included. Recorded 1980.

La finta giardiniera is moderately amusing and immoderately long. One recording in normal times
would be quite enough. But of course 1991 was not normal times as far as Mozart (and much else)
was concerned, so in Philips's Complete Mozart Edition *La finta giardiniera* comprises Vol. 33. The
other Philips performance under Hans Schmidt-Isserstedt is both talented and devoted, but it lacks
pace. Perhaps one should be cautious here, for with repeated playings over a number of years the
slower speeds and more thoughtful style may prove endearing, while the breezy liveliness of Leopold
Hager's might possibly not wear so well. Still, the feeling that the youthful spirit of the music is
somewhat at odds with Schmidt-Isserstedt's elderly style of performance arises as early on as the
Overture, and not as a result of direct comparisons.

Honours are about even in respect of the casts, though, again, the livelier conducting of Hager
affects the singers, who on the whole establish their characters rather better than their predecessors,
even if they do not improve on the singing. One who does both is Brigitte Fassbaender; the sense of
inner excitement is always there with her, and when she sings "Perfida donna ingrata!" she means it.
In this opera of paired lovers, the singing of Hager's principal couple, Julia Cornwell and Thomas
Moser, is not outstanding. The other recording does, of course, have what looks like a glittering cast,
including Jessye Norman, incomparably the finest voice among them; even so, Hager's people
generally do well. Another factor, and more decisive, is the quality of recorded sound. Schmidt-
Isserstedt's recording has no bloom to it, while Hager's is clearer and less confined.

Mozart La finta semplice.

Barbara Hendricks *sop* Rosina
Siegfried Lorenz *bar* Don Cassandro
Douglas Johnson *sngr* Don Polidoro
Ann Murray *mez* Giacanta
Eva Lind *sop* Ninetta
Hans-Peter Blochwitz *ten* Fracasso
Andreas Schmidt *bar* Simone

C. P. E. Bach Chamber Orchestra / Peter Schreier.
Philips Mozart Edition Ⓜ Ⓞ 422 528-2PME2 (two discs: 147 minutes: DDD). Notes, text and translation included. Recorded 1988.

At first *La finta semplice* may seem to be no less than a miracle, or at least a Very Remarkable Phenomenon. That a 12-year-old could have the creativity and technical skill to write such music defies the normal limits of credulity. Still, that does not necessarily testify to its value. Ignore or forget the biographical fact and listen to it on its own merits (if one can ever do simply that), and then on the first, second or perhaps even third encounter one might smile and pass on. The boy, after all, was responsible for only the musical part of the entertainment, prestigious elders (Goldoni among them) having supplied the play, which at best is trivial and at worst heartless.

The feigned or pretending simpleton of the title is an attractive woman who agrees to help two pairs of lovers by freeing them from the opposition of two bachelor brothers, one a bully and a coward, the other a nincompoop. Both are absurd and objectionable, but the ninny has at least some faintly endearing qualities and sings some likeable music. It is the coarse, bullying, selfish buffoon that she chooses to marry and with whom she joins in mockery of the other. So it is an additional marvel that the 12-year-old's genius can not merely persuade his listeners to tolerate the silly play but to come back for that further encounter which begins to touch the soul with a sense of what by any standards is a refined and exquisite beauty.

Sample Rosina's 'echo' aria ("Senti l'eco", No. 9). This is a fairly slow aria (*Andante un poco adagio*) in E flat, with something of "Porgi, amor" about it. The obbligato instruments are an oboe and two horns. The third phrase ("sussurrar tra fiori e fronde") introduces a delicious murmuring of strings, not remote in effect from the 'breezes' trio in *Così fan tutte*. A B-section (*allegro grazioso*) renews charmingly the comic idiom native to the opera. But then with the return of the 'echo' melody, now at a lower pitch, its melodic and harmonic development has a new depth and poignancy, and the soul is touched. There are many such points – a lovely one, for instance, in the finale of Act 3 where a penitent interpolation by one of the girls ("Fu colpo d'amore") is almost as moving as "Contessa, perdona" in *Le nozze di Figaro*. The longer one were to stay with this apprentice-work, the more apparent would be the master's hand throughout.

The recording improves on its acceptable predecessor (Leopold Hager on Orfeo) in nearly every respect. The recorded sound does more justice to the orchestral texture. Schreier and his players show a livelier appreciation of detail, particularly in rhythm and phrasing. Hendricks is a fresher, firmer voiced Rosina than Helen Donath, and Ann Murray, the Giacinta, has more humanity and humour than Teresa Berganza in the Hager recording. Blochwitz is a more mellifluous Fracasso than Thomas Moser, and Andreas Schmidt is more aptly cast than was Robert Lloyd. Douglas Johnson matches Anthony Rolfe Johnson as the 'wet' brother, and if Siegfried Lorenz hardly sounds like a born comedian in this recording, neither did Robert Holl in the earlier one. The only solo part in which the Hager recording is somewhat better cast is the soubrette, Ninetta, sung here by Eva Lind and previously by Jutta-Renate Ihloff. The recitatives are now better characterized and more sensitively paced, and they are also shortened, by about a quarter, beneficial in several ways but most particularly in reducing the number of discs from three (Hager) to two (and offered at mid price).

Mozart Idomeneo.
Anthony Rolfe Johnson *ten* Idomeneo
Anne Sofie von Otter *mez* Idamante
Sylvia McNair *sop* Ilia
Hillevi Martinpelto *sop* Elettra
Nigel Robson *ten* Arbace
Glenn Winslade *ten* High Priest
Cornelius Hauptmann *bass* Oracle
Monteverdi Choir; English Baroque Soloists / John Eliot Gardiner.
Archiv Produktion Ⓕ Ⓞ 431 674-2AH3 (three discs: 211 minutes: DDD). ✍ Notes, text and translation included. Recorded at performances in the Queen Elizabeth Hall, London in June 1990.

1991

Unless and until further research proves otherwise, this version will remain the definitive recording of Mozart's early masterpiece for a long time to come. That is not to say a bonfire should be made of its rival versions, each of which has special features to commend it, merely that Gardiner – who has written of how much he owes to Mackerras and Harnoncourt in finding the right route to interpreting the work – has given us a reading that seems to accord as closely as can at present be discerned with both a performance of Mozart's time (of which he gives ample evidence in his accompanying notes though nothing is conclusively proved) and one that sounds thoroughly authentic in the best sense. Those who attended any of the three live performances from which this set has been made will confirm that they were evenings of thrilling music-drama. On those occasions Gardiner experimented with mixtures of the various plausible arrangements of the existing music. Then at a further concert, he performed alone the fullest version possible of the opera's final scenes, a fascinating experience, though one that in context of a stage performance might tire both singers and audience alike.

Here we have the best of all worlds. In the main recording we have a composite version of the surviving music for Munich 1981. In practice Gardiner's choices seem the right ones. Thus we have the longer, more elaborate "Fuor del mar", the shorter of the sacrificial scenes, the briefer of the two brass versions of Neptune's pronouncement and the ballet music. Included are Arbace's second aria, Elettra's "D'Oreste e d'Aiace" and Idomeneo's "Torna la pace". All were cut by Mozart before the première but make sense in the context of a recording. In the appendices (on the end of the second disc) are bits of recitative from Act 2, the longer of the sacrificial scenes, the longer of the brass versions of Neptune's pronouncement (plus the setting with wind – marvellous), and the scene in Act 3 for Elettra that replaced her aria. This complete recording (minus only the simpler versions of "Fuor del mar" and the shortest version of Neptune's music) offers the intending buyer three, very well-filled discs.

So much for the (quite important) nuts and bolts. All this thoroughness of approach would be of little avail were the performance in any way inadequate, but Gardiner's reading is in almost every respect profoundly satisfying. As he avers, he came to the piece having traversed on disc this work's two great progenitors, *Jephtha* and *Iphigénie en Tauride*, both operas about parental sacrifice and obviously influential on *Idomeneo*. Then he brings to the work, as does his orchestra, the experience and knowledge gained through recording the Mozart concertos and late symphonies on period instruments. In matters of phrasing, articulation, melodic shaping, they here benefit from their previous achievement: this is a taut, raw, dramatic reading, yet one that fully allows for tenderness and warmth. You can judge these things as well as anywhere in the March before "Plácido è il mar", then in that chorus itself, the one clean in texture, brisk in articulation, the other suave and appealing in its 6/8 rhythm. You can also hear there the advantage of the right-sized band and choir. Listen, too, to the control of dynamics in the great Act 3 Quartet.

Throughout Gardiner and his team recognize what he indicates in another note, the fact that Mozart conceived the work as through-written without any breaks in the piece's forward movement. As at the Queen Elizabeth Hall this creates the correct sense of internal tensions within external formality. Once or twice in Act 1 one felt that Gardiner's penchant for fierce accentuation was getting the better of him and calling attention to the podium rather than to the music, but the impression soon passed and one listened to the new revelations of the reading without let or hindrance. Tempos are admirably judged.

Although some roles have been as well or better sung on rival sets, none is so consistently cast. Sylvia McNair sings Ilia's grateful, sensuous music with eager, fresh tone and impeccable phrasing even if she can't claim the warm appeal of Jurinac (Pritchard/EMI). Hillevi Martinpelto is a properly impetuous Elettra who has no trouble with either the eloquent ("Idol mio") or crazed side of the character and whose vocal allure is impressive. Even so, the interpretative honours go to Anthony Rolfe Johnson's deeply felt, mellifluously sung and technically assured Idomeneo and to Anne Sofie von Otter's ardent, impetuous, and in the end touching, Idamante: the sacrificial scene between father and son is rightly the moving centrepiece of the whole opera, where the two singers' skill in recitative is finely exemplified. Nigel Robson copes splendidly with the concerned Arbace, most touching in his recitative before his second aria (usually omitted) and then sure-voiced in the difficult divisions in that aria itself. Glenn Winslade is a firm High Priest but Cornelius Hauptmann's bass is too woolly for the *deus ex machina*.

As implied, the playing of the English Baroque Soloists is as accomplished and fluent as ever and the balance of the very immediate recording between them and the soloists is just right. Some edits are just audible and one had the feeling that some of the set numbers were recorded without an audience present, but that doesn't detract from the sense of unity and vividness. This set emphatically replaces the startlingly innovative but sometimes eccentric Harnoncourt (Teldec). The Böhm (DG, reviewed below), in no way authentic, remains the work of a great Mozartian, and the Pritchard (EMI) is a historic document, recalling the early days of rediscovery in this field. But those who want the full *Idomeneo* story and a profoundly satisfying musical experience must have this 1990 set.

Mozart Idomeneo.
Wieslaw Ochman *ten* Idomeneo
Peter Schreier *ten* Idamante
Edith Mathis *sop* Ilia
Julia Varady *sop* Elettra
Hermann Winkler *ten* Arbace
Eberhard Büchner *ten* High Priest
Siegfried Vogel *bass* Oracle
Leipzig Radio Choir; Staatskapelle Dresden / Karl Böhm.
DG Ⓜ ① 429 864-2GX3 (three discs: 170 minutes: ADD). Notes, text and translation included. Recorded 1977.

Listening to *Idomeneo*, as played by the Staatskapelle Dresden, does make one pause to think twice about period-instrument performances, however much one may admire them. With the availability of the revelatory Gardiner, should a newcomer to these works also consider investing in Böhm? His overview of the work is convincing, but his editorial choice here gives cause for concern, most notably the foreshortening of some numbers and of the recitatives. His choice of a tenor Idamante is unfashionable, but one has to say that Schreier sings the role so eloquently that criticism is almost silenced on this count – it also allows us to hear some of the alternative Vienna revisions Mozart wrote for a tenor in this work. One or two speeds are questionable at first hearing – the swift one for the last act quartet for instance – but Böhm always seems to justify them. This performance benefits from the same qualities displayed by conductor and orchestra in *Clemenza di Tito* (reviewed earlier) and also from the rewarding contribution of the Leipzig Radio Choir.

Mozart Lucio Silla.

Peter Schreier *ten* Lucio Silla
Arleen Auger *sop* Giunia
Julia Varady *sop* Cecilio
Helen Donath *sop* Celia
Edith Mathis *sop* Cinna
Werner Krenn *ten* Aufidio
Salzburg Radio Chorus; Salzburg Mozarteum Chorus and Orchestra / Leopold Hager.
Philips Mozart Edition Ⓜ ① 422 532-2PME3 (three discs: 212 minutes: ADD). Notes, text and translation included. Recorded 1975.

Verdicts such as "mediocre" (Dent) and "a highly unfortunate and uneven piece of work" (Einstein) do not encourage investment, but it is still rather a pity that one, just one, of the numerous recordings of *Figaro*, *Die Zauberflöte* and so forth could not have been abandoned in favour of a new *Lucio Silla*. It is a genuine need, for this reissue does not really do the 16-year-old Mozart justice.

The role of Giunia is sung by Arleen Auger, and hers is a lovely performance, especially in the gentler passages such as the opening of the final solo, "Fra i pensier". Her opposite number, the Cecilio, is Julia Varady. They certainly made an impression and, though Varady's intonation comes occasionally into question (perhaps affected by the 'tubular' production she sometimes uses), there is real distinction in her singing at almost every point. Mathis and Donath are strong names to have in the secondary roles. Schreier and Krenn hardly present the more ruthless sides of the characters they portray, but at least they have their music intact. Hager also preserves the full load of recitative. As for the conductor, Hager does a conscientious job and he has a natural Mozartian style.

Mozart Mitridate, rè di Ponto.

Werner Hollweg *ten* Mitridate
Arleen Auger *sop* Aspasia
Edita Gruberová *sop* Sifare
Agnes Baltsa *mez* Farnace
Ileana Cotrubas *sop* Ismene
David Kübler *ten* Marzio
Christine Weidinger *sop* Arbate
Salzburg Mozarteum Orchestra / Leopold Hager *hpd.*
Philips Mozart Edition Ⓜ ① 422 529-2PME3 (three discs: 194 minutes: ADD). Notes, text and translation included. Recorded 1977.

The Philips Complete Mozart Edition arrived at Mozart's first great *opera seria* and made a brave enough showing with this 1977 Salzburg recording, originally made for DG. Here is the start of the unfurling of the great themes of loyalty and mercy which reach their apotheosis in *Idomeneo* and *La clemenza di Tito*. Here, too, are the embryos of the highly-charged accompanied recitatives which are their glory. Here there are simply yards of the most *secco* of recitative before a single aria appears. Yet such is the skill in casting that it matters little. As Arbate (Christine Weidinger), Sifare (Edita Gruberová) and Aspasia (Arleen Auger) sort out just who fancies whom, their complementary qualities are revealed, qualities which are later to combine richly in the single duet and the final quintet with which Mozart cautiously approaches ensemble writing.

To Weidinger's bright vigour of enunciation, Gruberová, as the good son Sifare, responds with a flicker of something else besides: a sense of both steadfastness and yearning which hovers in the very first moments of her wonderfully sentient recitative. The smooth sheen which clothes the flames at the core of her voice shows itself beautifully in one of Mozart's first great "Parto" arias, "Parto, nel gran cimento". Gruberová enjoys, too, her "Lungi date, mio bene", the highest register of the voice the more affecting for being played off against the solo horn over the aria's wide spaces and slow-changing harmonies. Agnes Baltsa re-creates scarcely less powerfully the agility and range of the other castrato role, that of the baddie (initially) Farnace. She uses her distinctive, grapey low register to give a dark, glowering patina to Farnace's penchant for deceit and ambition, redoubling her energies as his conscience wins the day in a triumphant final aria, "Già degli occhi".

As for Mitridate himself, Mozart wrote the role bearing in mind both the strengths and limitations of the singer on hand. What the part lacks in athletic *fioritura* it makes up for in tortuous leaps which test the tenor's range to the very limits. Werner Hollweg's voice is not at its most attractive in its extremes, and there are times when the larynx aches vicariously as notes are hurled up to vault over the stave. And he is rather more tremulous here than either his son's or his fiancée's disloyalty warrants. He fares better, though, in recitative, especially in what was one of Mozart's finest accompanied ones to date. It is in these recitatives, by the way, as much as in the arias, that one could wish for a little more from the Salzburg Mozarteum. Their playing, under Leopold Hager, is true, alert and musicianly, but just a little dull: one longs at times for more ventilation of the wind writing, sharper attack, more penetrating phrasing.

There is nothing but pleasure for the listener when Ismene appears, in the melting tones of Ileana Cotrubas; but her arias rarely exploit the expressive qualities of her voice to the full. She is something of a passive exemplar in this libretto, and Mozart knew it. He wrote a lively ditty or two, though, for the Roman tribune, Marzio, and David Kübler rises to his brief moments of heroism with strength and sensitivity.

Mozart Le nozze di Figaro.

Samuel Ramey *bass* Figaro
Lucia Popp *sop* Susanna
Thomas Allen *bar* Count Almaviva
Dame Kiri Te Kanawa *sop* Countess Almaviva
Frederica von Stade *mez* Cherubino
Jane Berbié *sop* Marcellina
Kurt Moll *bass* Bartolo
Robert Tear *ten* Don Basilio
Philip Langridge *ten* Don Curzio
Giorgio Tadeo *bass* Antonio
Yvonne Kenny *sop* Barbarina
London Philharmonic Orchestra; London Opera Chorus / Sir Georg Solti.
Decca Ⓟ Ⓓ 410 150-2DH3 (three discs: 169 minutes: DDD). Notes, text and translation included. Recorded 1981.

Solti's *Figaro* has one of the finest casts of singers that one could contemplate and at the recording session in June of 1981 they were all in fine voice. Listening to this latest manifestation of this complex tale is undeniably an enjoyable Mozartian experience, but there are equally undeniable anomalies which disturb the mind's picture and in the end you may find yourself content to remain with Sir Colin Davis's mid-price version on Philips because of Jessye Norman who is superb as the Countess. The later Decca set has one principal in common, for Robert Tear sings the small role of Basilio, the music-master, on both recordings. However, the LPO's approach under Solti is racily forced and often sounds tired when compared to the BBC SO and Davis. It seems odd too that this Decca recording, made in the familiar territory of London's Kingsway Hall, should feature a degree of its ambience on all the voices which is far removed from the opera's comparatively intimate settings of bedrooms and the Count's garden shrubbery. No real attempt seems to have been made to match the acoustic to the scene and although this may have been a deliberate decision to present a 'performance', it is unconvincing in the event. However, the star cast will make this version a 'must' for many collectors and in that it does not disappoint.

Mozart Le nozze di Figaro.

Hermann Prey *bar* Figaro
Edith Mathis *sop* Susanna
Dietrich Fischer-Dieskau *bar* Count Almaviva
Gundula Janowitz *sop* Countess Almaviva
Tatiana Troyanos *mez* Cherubino
Patricia Johnson *mez* Marcellina
Peter Lagger *bass* Bartolo
Erwin Wohlfahrt *ten* Don Basilio
Martin Vantin *ten* Don Curzio
Klaus Hirte *bar* Antonio
Barbara Vogel *sop* Barbarina
Chorus and Orchestra of the Deutsche Oper, Berlin / Karl Böhm.
DG The Originals Ⓜ Ⓓ 449 728-2GOR3 (three discs: 172 minutes: ADD). Notes, text and translation included. Recorded 1968.

Whatever the merits of sets made since, this one is ensured a revered place in the pantheon of *Figaro* recordings, which also includes Giulini's 1959 EMI set and Erich Kleiber's 1955 Decca set (both available at mid price). Made when Böhm was enjoying an Indian summer, it was based on a production by Sellner at the Deutsche Oper in Berlin and indeed the production was supervised by Sellner. Since its première under Böhm in 1963, he had led many revivals including some performances with this cast, around the time the recording was made, which surely accounts for this sense of a true ensemble felt all round and of a thought-through interpretation. The crisp, clear, yet spacious recording, seldom matched on more recent versions, only enhances the authority and warmth of the reading.

Böhm radiates the wisdom of his years of attendance on the score without any slackening of his rhythmic grip or his demand for precision of execution; indeed this recording is superior to his two previous ones (on Preiser and Philips) in those respects. His choice of speeds always seems right, allowing firm articulation of note and text yet never at the expense of forward movement. Nowhere is his command of a large structure more evident than in his control of the finales to Acts 2 and 4. It was also part of Böhm's genius to weld a heterogenous cast into a convincing whole. No need at this stretch of time to commend the singers individually; each has complete command vocally and dramatically of his or her role though one must just mention Janowitz's dignified yet lively Countess and Mathis's animated, alluring Susanna.

The Kleiber and Giulini versions are also classics in their own right, also notable for close-knit ensembles, dynamically conducted and just as individually cast. They are slightly cut, but that allows them to be contained on two CDs as against DG's three.

Mozart Le nozze di Figaro.
Sesto Bruscantini *bar* Figaro
Graziella Sciutti *sop* Susanna
Franco Calabrese *bass* Count Almaviva
Sena Jurinac *sop* Countess Almaviva
Risë Stevens *mez* Cherubino
Monica Sinclair *contr* Marcellina
Ian Wallace *bass* Bartolo
Hugues Cuénod *ten* Don Basilio
Daniel McCoshan *ten* Don Curzio
Gwyn Griffiths *bar* Antonio
Jeanette Sinclair *sop* Barbarina
Glyndebourne Festival Chorus and Orchestra / Vittorio Gui.
Classics for Pleasure Ⓢ Ⓘ CD-CFPD4724 (two discs: 158 minutes: ADD). Recorded 1955.

This is an exceptional bargain. For about £10·00 you get some 158 minutes of music. The virtues of the set were and are those of a well-schooled ensemble under a mercurial conductor. The work was recorded at the Abbey Road Studio No. 1 in July 1955, not long after performances at Glyndebourne with the same cast, apart from the Susanna, Sciutti replacing Elena Rizzieri. So, not surprisingly, you enjoy – as in a more recent Glyndebourne recording (Haitink on EMI) – an easy sense of singers naturally reacting to each other in a staging originally prepared by that master of Mozart ensemble, Carl Ebert.

The cast is headed by Jurinac's warm, appealing Countess, as rewarding as any on record, sung in golden tone and responsive to the emotions of the moment – listen to "Dove sono" and its recitative (second CD, track 10). Her husband at that time, Sesto Bruscantini, is a light-voiced, eager Figaro, much in the vein of Desderi (Haitink). Indeed, the Italianate bite and diction of his performance and that of Sciutti, a nimble Susanna (enchanting in her Act 4 aria), and Calabrese, an imposing if sometimes slightly rough Almaviva, is another of the set's advantages. The small parts are well taken, a special delight being Cuénod's Basilio (although his aria, included on LP, has here been left out, presumably to get the performance on to two CDs; a pity yet understandable). A drawback is Risë Stevens's tired-sounding and unidiomatic Cherubino, but even she fits well enough into the ensemble. Gui's matching of tempos is laudable and he draws playing from the RPO, then doubling as the Glyndebourne orchestra, that is at once disciplined and full of character. On the transfers, some of the warmth of the original may have drained away, but the difference is marginal. This was one of EMI's earliest stereo efforts, and the placings are well managed, with the sense of intimacy you get in the theatre at Glyndebourne and which so often eludes modern recordings. The impecunious newcomer should hurry to catch this set while it's available.

Mozart Le nozze di Figaro.
Bryn Terfel *bass-bar* Figaro
Alison Hagley *sop* Susanna
Rodney Gilfry *bar* Count Almaviva
Hillevi Martinpelto *sop* Countess Almaviva
Pamela Helen Stephen *mez* Cherubino
Susan McCulloch *sop* Marcellina
Carlos Feller *bass* Bartolo
Francis Egerton *ten* Don Basilio, Don Curzio
Julian Clarkson *bass* Antonio
Constanze Backes *sop* Barbarina
Monteverdi Choir; English Baroque Soloists / John Eliot Gardiner.

Stage director: **Jean-Louis Thamin.** *Video director:* **Olivier Mille.**
Archiv Produktion Ⓕ ⦿ 072 439-3AH; 🔆 072 439-1AH (two sides: 170 minutes). 🖎
Recorded 1993.

This is not the same performance as the CD version, which derived from a semi-staging in London. Here we have the full-scale production from the Châtelet in Paris, although 'full-scale' may not be the right description, given the spare scenery for the Count's mansion set against a cyclorama which variously shows castle and park in silhouette. Jean-Louis Thamin's direction emphasizes both the revolutionary and sexual aspects of the plot as is common these days, the former rather blatantly, with peasants and servants far too rebellious.

Thamin's *Personenregie* and Olivier Mille's direction of it for video bring out the erotic vibes passing from both Figaro and the Count to Susanna, and Cherubino to the Countess. This works well when you have a Figaro as potent and mercurial as Terfel, a Susanna as personable and so expressive in her face as Hagley and a Count as obviously lecherous and dominating as Gilfry, less well when the Cherubino is so obviously a girl play-acting and the Countess somewhat puddingy. Where Cherubino is concerned one can feel as unhappy as with the CD version with the blatant guying of "Voi che sapete" to no good purpose, nor are Egerton's exaggerations as Basilio any more welcome when you see them, but McCulloch and Feller make a witty pair as Marcellina and Bartolo, and move with admirable confidence and finesse.

Gardiner's conducting is much as it is on CD; direct, swift, alive to every nuance of the score and action. Abbado (on Sony) offers a valid alternative for those who oppose period instruments, and a reading just as valid, while Jonathan Miller's direction and the décor there are generally preferable to what we have here. Vocally, both casts are excellent, although their strengths and weaknesses are rather different. Gardiner here excludes the arias for Marcellina and Basilio (as does Abbado) and, of course, all the alternatives available on CD.

LaserDisc has the advantage of better sound and subtitles, but the difference, given PolyGram's hi-fi methods on tape, is marginal. However, one grows increasingly impatient with the black spaces at the top and bottom of the picture in both mediums, which show that the films are actually being made for High Definition Vision.

Mozart Il rè pastore.

Ann Murray *mez* Aminta
Eva Mei *sop* Elisa
Inga Nielsen *sop* Tamiri
Roberto Saccà *ten* Alessandro
Markus Schäfer *ten* Agenore
Vienna Concentus Musicus / Nikolaus Harnoncourt.
Teldec Ⓕ ① 4509-98419-2 (two discs: 108 minutes: DDD). 🖎 Notes, text and translation included. Recorded at a performance in the Musikverein, Vienna during May 1995.

It may be a silly story, but that isn't the point: which is that the pastoral convention that lies behind Metastasio's libretto for *Il rè pastore* allows for a wide range of expression; amorous, tragic, wistful, comical, martial – anything you like. So it gives a composer plenty of working space, which suited the young Mozart in 1775 when his archbishop commissioned him to write an occasional piece, a *serenata*, for the visit to Salzburg of a Hapsburg Archduke. There are a couple of lively arias with trumpets to distinguish the majesty of Alexander the Great (Alessandro), whose benignity enables the right couples to pair off in the end; Aminta, the *rè pastore*, the heir to the throne of Sidon who (Marie-Antoinette-like) prefers his disguise as a simple shepherd, has two outstanding numbers, the fine "Aer tranquillo" and the famous and hauntingly lovely "L'amerò, sarò costante", as well as a fine duet finale with his beloved Elisa; and the secondary couple each have a lightly scored aria to provide contrast, while Agenore is also assigned a fiery C minor piece at the dramatic juncture in his role. And there is a third aria for Alessandro, ingeniously scored with prominent flutes and supporting oboes, for a virtuoso flautist who happened to be in Salzburg at the time. Not all the music is first-rate Mozart; early in the work, before the characters come to life, the tone is sometimes apt to seem bland. But clearly he had fun composing it, and performed with style and energy it's an entertaining piece.

It certainly has plenty of energy here (one is less sure about style). Nikolaus Harnoncourt, in his usual way, gives the music very sharp profiles. Dynamics are unambiguous, accents are vigorous. The colourful orchestration is strongly brought out. The pulse is often quite elastic. It would be surprising if it sounded much like this in Mozart's time, the use of period instruments here notwithstanding, but the music does on the whole benefit from this very incisive characterization and comes over more interestingly and more strikingly than it generally does in more conventionally stylish readings. There are as usual with Harnoncourt some arbitrary adjustments to Mozart's articulation but not really damaging ones. You may be sorry to note that the use of appoggiaturas is so casual and inconsistent (even when two singers have the same phrase); the helpful suggestions in the Neue Mozart-Ausgabe text are mostly ignored. There are some cuts, understandably, in the simple recitative.

Ann Murray, in the title-role, heads the cast in every sense: a big and masterly performance, the words clear, the tone ample and varied, the phrasing graceful, the *fioritura* perfectly defined.

"L'amerò" is taken extremely slowly, nothing like a Mozart *andantino*; the effect is a bit self-indulgent but it is breathtakingly beautiful, the orchestral playing (with solo violin, flutes and cor anglais) sounding as good as the singing. The voice, a bright, well-defined soprano, of Eva Mei as Aminta's beloved Elisa is rather closer to Murray's than might be ideal, but hers is a capable performance and especially persuasive in the noble aria opening Act 2, a big two-tempo piece where she alternately grieves and spits out her defiance. Near the end of the duet there are a couple of notes (in bars 131 and 138) that seem to be flat or misconstrued. Inga Nielsen's Tamiri shows some capacity for warm, rounded tone but is mostly somewhat constricted in sound, and her words are rarely clear. Her final aria has some delicate details of timing. Both tenors – again, rather similar voices – are firm and focused rather than warm or lyrical; Roberto Saccà as Alessandro brings a suitable touch of grandeur to his opening aria (the voice is reminiscent of the young Peter Schreier), while Markus Schäfer does well in his last aria, the C minor outburst, even if the voice lacks the desirable depth.

There is virtually no sign, in terms of noises off, that this is a live recording. The recorded quality, as usual with Harnoncourt, is rather bright and reverberant; loud entries of the bass instruments often seem to cloud the textures. Woodwind and brass are well forward. In spite of any reservations, there is no doubt that this set breathes real life into a work that is often apt to seem static and conventional.

Mozart Il sogno di Scipione.

Peter Schreier *ten* Scipione
Lucia Popp *sop* Costanza
Edita Gruberová *sop* Fortuna
Claes Hakon Ahnsjö *ten* Publio
Thomas Moser *ten* Emilio
Edith Mathis *sop* Licenza
Salzburg Chamber Choir and Mozarteum Orchestra / Leopold Hager *hpd*.
Philips Mozart Edition Ⓜ Ⓛ 422 531-2PME2 (two discs: 112 minutes: ADD). Notes, text and translation included. Recorded 1979.

Leopold Mozart thought of *Il sogno di Scipione* as a mere preparation for the *Ascanio* commission, but everyone, including his son, seems committed to the task in hand in this *azione teatrale*. It may be somewhat less than action-packed and hardly theatrical, but this excuse for an hour or so of Metastasian philosophical and metaphysical speculation in the mouths of Scipio and his two temptresses, Fortuna and Costanza, certainly drew longer-breathed, more sharply characterized writing from Mozart's pen than Parini's courtly pastoral.

Peter Schreier as the dreamer on trial fleshes out Mozart's highly sentient use of vocal register to express his gradual awakening into consciousness, as much as his ardent, if less than agile, rejection of Fortuna. Fortuna puts forward her claim in gleaming, Vitellia-esque arias, robustly trilled and ornamented by Edita Gruberová. Lucia Popp, as her rival, sings with less high glaze but radiantly enough and with apt tenacity. In the celestial and ancestral corridors of power, Publio (Claes Hakon Ahnsjö) puts forward a compelling claim for immortality in his ringing, horn-accompanied aria, while Thomas Moser's incisive and authoritative Emilio brings out the paternal benevolence of Mozart's little two-note phrases. Edith Mathis, though, has the last and the best word. She is granted both the original, concise Licenza ending, and the later, wonderfully expansive aria in the final Homage cantata for the enthronement of Archbishop Colloredo.

Mozart Zaïde.

Lynne Dawson *sop* Zaïde
Hans-Peter Blochwitz *ten* Gomatz
Olaf Bär *bar* Allazim
Herbert Lippert *ten* Sultan Soliman
Christopher Purves *bass* Osmin
Academy of Ancient Music / Paul Goodwin.
Harmonia Mundi Ⓕ Ⓛ HMU90 7205 (75 minutes: DDD). 🎵 Notes, text and translation included. Recorded 1997.

Mozart began composing the work known as *Zaïde* in 1779-80, but left it unfinished, ostensibly because no performance was in prospect, but perhaps also because, very soon after he broke off, he came to see that this rather static kind of musical drama – essentially a play with songs, and rather longish, self-contained ones, with little sense of continuity – was not the sort of piece he wanted to write. Moreover, the character relationships are difficult to deal with: the libretto and the music (as far as it goes) imply a powerful attraction at the beginning of the opera between Zaïde and Gomatz, but ultimately, in the final scene, which Mozart never reached, they turn out to be brother and sister: very touching, and well attuned to the sensibilities of the time, but cramping to the composer. Nevertheless, the music of *Zaïde* is full of fine things, often foreshadowing not only the similar *Entführung* but also *Idomeneo*.

This version captures its beauties and its depth of feeling as no recording has done before. This is partly because of the sympathetic conducting of Paul Goodwin, who paces it with excellent judgement, bringing to it just the right degree of flexibility, and achieves orchestral textures that are both clear and warm – much more so than usual from period-instrument groups. The melodramas, tellingly shaped, perfectly catch the tone of passion. The AAM play at their best for him (notably, and understandably, the principal oboist). It is hard to imagine a better cast. In the title-role Lynne Dawson sings the lovely "Ruhe sanft" with a frail beauty that is very appealing, does her pathetic aria in Act 2 gracefully and then lets things rip in the furious "Tiger! wetze nur die Klauen" (a counterpart to "Martern aller Arten" in *Entführung*). Hans-Peter Blochwitz's shapely lines and full, eloquent tone make Gomatz's arias a delight, too; and Herbert Lippert, the second tenor, as the Sultan (in love, or lust, with Zaïde), is almost his match in evenness and lyrical quality. It is indeed a luxury to have Olaf Bär as Allazim: the music is sung with a refinement of tone and ease of articulation that you don't imagine it has often had before. Christopher Purves sings Osmin cleanly without perhaps quite fully realizing the comedy. In sum, this far excels any previous recording.

Mozart Die Zauberflöte.

Ruth Ziesak *sop* Pamina
Sumi Jo *sop* Queen of Night
Uwe Heilmann *ten* Tamino
Michael Kraus *bar* Papageno
Kurt Moll *bass* Sarastro
Andreas Schmidt *bar* Speaker
Heinz Zednik *ten* Monostatos
Lotte Leitner *sop* Papagena
Adrianne Pieczonka *sop* First Lady
Annette Kuettenbaum *mez* Second Lady
Jard van Nes *mez* Third Lady
Max Emanuel Cencic *treb* First Boy
Michael Rausch *treb* Second Boy
Markus Leitner *treb* Third Boy
Wolfgang Schmidt *ten* First Armed Man
Hans Franzen *bass* Second Armed Man
Clemens Bieber *ten* First Priest
Hans Joachim Porcher *bar* Second Priest
Vienna Boys' Choir; Vienna State Opera Concert Choir;
Vienna Philharmonic Orchestra / Sir Georg Solti.
Decca Ⓟ Ⓒ 433 210-2DH2 (two discs: 152 minutes: DDD). Notes, text and translation included. Recorded 1990.

BBC RADIO 3
90-93 FM

Sir Georg Solti's relationship with *Die Zauberflöte* is long and illustrious. When, in 1937, he was musical assistant to Toscanini in Salzburg, it was Solti's fingers which conjured the sound from Papageno's glockenspiel. In 1990 in Salzburg, Solti turned from rostrum to celesta and duetted with Papageno once again. Thus this recording is a fitting celebration of Solti's own long Mozartian journey. His 1969 Decca recording was praised for its "feeling for excitement ... where a very slight excess of solemnity or relaxation can be deadly". It is exactly that quality which epitomizes this 1990 recording: if anything, tempos are even more finely judged, more intuitively moulded to the shape of the score's harmonic dramas and emotional breathing. Solti's tempos and pacing are in fact the inspiration of this *Flute*. Marginally faster than in 1969, the Overture here springs rather than stings on its way. Sarastro's crew are a merry, totally unpompous lot: there is no more joyful entry than for this Sarastro, truly *mit Freuden* in the finale of Act 1. Solti, like Sir Colin Davis (whose mid-price set is reviewed below), also pays tribute to the *Flute* as fairy-tale. Solti, largely by pacing, Davis by the lightest of orchestral textures, never allow Schikaneder's little motto couplets (Ladies, Boys, Speaker) to become ponderous moralistic asides: each one bounces into its natural place in the dramatic scheme of things.

Solti gives time and space enough, though, for melodically or harmonically self-isolating lines such as Tamino's response to the Speaker, "Der Lieb' und Tugend Eigentum"; for the vibrancy of the inner string parts for Isis and Osiris and the Armed Men; to Pamina's cry of "Die Wahrheit!". This cry is one of the most moving on disc. At Salzburg, and already on this recording, Ruth Ziesak's fresh, highly intelligent performance restored to Pamina that fusion of innocence and strength, vulnerability and courage which the character and her music demand. With Solti's tempo, and sprung orchestral chords pulsing like a heartbeat, her first pure phrase of "Bei Männern" catches the breath with delight; her genuflecting cry of pain to Sarastro pierces the heart; her "Ach, ich fühl's" is shaped by deep desperation, not mere melancholy. Beside Ziesak, Pilar Lorengar (1969) is a comparatively pale characterization, and even Margaret Price for Davis, is more a fairy-tale princess, and not a spirited creature of human flesh and blood.

The casting of Tamino epitomizes another major difference between the two Solti versions. Uwe Heilmann, raw, penetrating and a little Schreier-like of timbre, is a livelier dramatic presence than

Stuart Burrows (1969), if not as aristocratic and well-groomed a voice. The 1969 version is singerly: this newer recording primarily dramatic. By the same token, Hermann Prey's Papageno (1969) is easier to listen to than that of Michael Kraus, who tends to bounce clean off the end of a phrase, and whose chattering quality can be sometimes less purely musical but often more plausible than Prey. Few Papagenos inspire the affection of Mikael Melbye's for Davis; few are so consistently satisfying as Olaf Bär's for Sir Neville Marriner on Philips.

This Queen of Night is a real *sternflammende Königin*, not merely an Olympia with a crown. Although few can compare in sheer other-worldly glimmer and subtly expressive *pianissimo* with Luciana Serra for Davis, Sumi Jo is truly in her ascendant here. A truly rhythmic brightness and glow of melodic phrasing suffuses her singing, and offers considerable relief from the muscular gymnastics of a Christina Deutekom (1969) or the tightrope terror of a Cheryl Studer (Marriner).

Her lunar beauty seems to take its strength, as it surely must, from Sarastro himself. Kurt Moll, appropriately, sings on an entirely other vocal plane: the authority he brought to Davis's recording is renewed here. Unlike Talvela (1969) or Ramey (Marriner), the depth of his voice is fully equal to the breadth of his music. His *heil'gen Hallen* have the longest corridors of all: in his musical temple there are indeed many mansions.

His slaves and his Monostatos (Heinz Zednik) are ably aided and abetted by the natural, well-paced dialogue, often whispering and wondering, sometimes crackling with tension; never, as in Joachim Herz's version for Davis, overdirected. Effects, too, both meteorological and avian, surpass those on previous recordings. Only with Marriner is the dialogue (directed by August Everding) so powerfully edited and felicitously paced: Solti's director is Klaus Gmeiner. In other aspects, Marriner's recording cannot be placed in the same class as Solti's or Davis's, simply because of its uneven casting.

In short, then, Solti's earlier recording bears up well musically, but is eclipsed dramatically by the live presence and meticulous recording balance of this latest version. After Solti, Davis's deeply affectionate and still magnificent *Flute* has something of an 'Are you sitting comfortably?' quality about it. No bad thing in itself, and with Schreier's Tamino and a particularly potent stereo 'staging', it is difficult indeed to live without both.

Mozart Die Zauberflöte.
Margaret Price *sop* Pamina
Luciana Serra *sop* Queen of Night
Peter Schreier *ten* Tamino
Mikael Melbye *bar* Papageno
Kurt Moll *bass* Sarastro
Theo Adam *bass-bar* Speaker, Second Priest
Robert Tear *ten* Monostatos
Maria Venuti *sop* Papagena
Marie McLaughlin *sop* First Lady
Ann Murray *mez* Second Lady
Hanna Schwarz *mez* Third Lady
Frank Höher *treb* First Boy
Michael Diedrich *treb* Second Boy
Friedemann Klos *treb* Third Boy
Reiner Goldberg *ten* First Armed Man
Horst Reeh *bass* Second Armed Man
Armin Ude *ten* First Priest
Dresden Kreuzchor; Leipzig Radio Chorus; Staatskapelle Dresden / Sir Colin Davis.
Philips Mozart Edition Ⓜ ① 422 543-2PME3 (three discs: 162 minutes: DDD). Notes, text and translation included. Recorded 1984.

The easy authority and loving warmth of this interpretation has stood a reasonable test of time. Davis's *Zauberflöte* is already something of a classic. As discussed above, only Solti among rival versions offers as excellent and authoritative a cast. From Moll's epitome of age-old wisdom as Sarastro to Serra's glinting Queen of Night, every part seems cast to near-perfection with Price's stylishly correct, perfectly articulated yet emotionally concerned Pamina, Schreier's nonpareil of a Tamino, Melbye's appealing yet never too arch Papageno, an excellent trio of Ladies, Adam's authoritative Speaker and Tear's nasty Monostatos. Then there is the glorious playing of the Dresden orchestra and the well-balanced recording. The only drawback, and here the Solti scores, is in having the dialogue, Melbye apart, spoken by actors. All said, this set worthily represents *Die Zauberflöte* in the Mozart Edition.

Mozart Die Zauberflöte.
Tiana Lemnitz *sop* Pamina
Erna Berger *sop* Queen of Night
Helge Roswaenge *ten* Tamino
Gerhard Hüsch *bar* Papageno

Wilhelm Strienz *bass* Sarasto
Walter Grossmann *bass* Speaker, Second Armed Man
Heinrich Tessmer *ten* Monostatos, First Armed Man
Irma Beilke *sop* Papagena, First Boy
Hilde Scheppan *sop* First Lady
Elfriede Marherr-Wagner *sop* Second Lady
Rut Berglund *contr* Third Lady, Third Boy
Carla Spletter *sop* Second Boy
Ernest Fabbry *ten* Priest
Favres Solisten Vereinigung; Berlin Philharmonic Orchestra / Sir Thomas Beecham.
EMI Références mono Ⓜ Ⓘ CHS7 61034-2 (two discs: 130 minutes: ADD). Notes, texts and translation included. Recorded 1937-8.
Also available on Pearl mono Ⓟ Ⓘ GEMMCDS9371 (two discs: 130 minutes: ADD).

First thing to report is the last thing discovered, namely that the Pearl transfer provided the greater enjoyment. It is true that some surface sound is always present and that EMI have all but eliminated it; true also that the EMI transfer has greater sharpness of sibilants and 't's with all that may imply about frequency range. But comparisons confirmed a feeling which had persisted in varying degrees during a straight play-through of the EMI, that the sound was not altogether agreeable. On the whole, that feeling did not arise with the Pearl, and, though juxtaposition of the two would not always yield the same result, it did so with sufficient consistency to make it clear that for pleasure in the future it is to the Pearl that you may well turn.

A certain 'grating' quality in the orchestral sound, sometimes extending to the singing, encroached on the pleasure of listening to the EMI; perhaps that puts it too strongly (for the play-through was not a negative experience), but it was enough of a presence to cause relief at its absence in the Pearl. On more precise ground, a comparison of the trio "Soll ich dich, Teurer" in Act 2 provides a clear example. Another curious factor is that whereas Pearl's reduced and steady but clearly audible surface affected enjoyment very little, the intermittent reminders on EMI of the 78rpm origins (a subdued swish in the quiet towards the end of "Ach, ich fühl's", for instance) drew attention to themselves and proved a genuine distraction.

As for the performance, that also yields some mixed findings. Beecham's feeling for both the grandeur and the delicacy, and the evident command he has of his forces, ensure attentiveness and delight. Every appearance of Gerhard Hüsch is a joy: we have had good Papagenos since this, the first of all complete recordings of *Die Zauberflöte*, but he surely remains the best. Tiana Lemnitz sings with such surpassing beauty for so much of the time that the occasional scoop (for instance) is forgiven. Erna Berger's Queen of Night is firm and technically accomplished (though she drops a semiquaver or two in the runs of her first aria), and there are splendid performances by the Three Ladies (Hilde Scheppan, the First, sang Eva at Salzburg and that is something one would like to have heard). The Tamino is not well cast: Roswaenge lacks finesse though he is a positive enough character. Wilhelm Strienz is literally out of his depth, producing nasty, unresonant low notes and generally sounding more like a Hans Sachs than a Sarastro. Walter Grossmann is a woolly Speaker, and Heinrich Tessmer, perfect as Monostatos, is no use as First Armed Man. The absence of dialogue, as the anonymous writer of EMI's admirable sleeve-note says, "turns music-drama into a sort of song-cycle". Altogether a set to pick one's way through, essential though it is to have it at hand. And this also applies to the Pearl, warily recommending it over its rival with the caution that there is surface-sound (however reduced) and, alas, no text and translation. One correction to the Pearl booklet: the aria conducted by Bruno Seidler-Winkler is not Tamino's "Die Bildnis" but the Queen's "O zittre nicht".

Mozart Die Zauberflöte.
Christiane Oelze *sop* Pamina
Cyndia Sieden *sop* Queen of Night
Michael Schade *ten* Tamino
Gerald Finley *bar* Papageno
Harry Peeters *bass* Sarastro
Detlef Roth *bar* Speaker
Uwe Peper *ten* Monostatos
Constanze Backes *sop* Papagena
Susan Roberts *sop* First Lady
Carola Guber *contr* Second Lady
Maria Jonas *sop* Third Lady
Andreas Dieterich *treb* First Boy
Jan Andreas Mendel *treb* Second Boy
Florian Wöller *treb* Third Boy
Paul Tindall *ten* First Armed Man
Richard Savage *bass* Second Armed Man
Monteverdi Choir; English Baroque Soloists / John Eliot Gardiner.

Stage Producers: **John Eliot Gardiner, Stephen Metcalf.** *Video Director:* **Pim Marks.**
Archiv Produktion Ⓟ ⚌ 072 447-3AH (160 minutes). ✎ Notes and synopsis included.
Recorded at performances in the Concertgebouw, Amsterdam during November 1995.

This was taken at a live performance at the Concertgebouw, recorded four months after the CD version. With the support of the semi-staging the experience is more involving. By this time everyone taking part seemed just that much more relaxed, undoubtedly benefiting from the rapt response of the Dutch audience. The staging by Gardiner and Metcalf is at its very best in dealing with the close relationships of the principals. The sense of true love between Schade's Tamino and Oelze's Pamina is palpable in their wondering eyes and body language. They seem the very embodiment of Mozart's and Schikaneder's imagining. In a similar way, Finley's Papageno has a winning spontaneity, and his connections with Tamino, Pamina and ultimately Papagena are unerringly delineated, nowhere more so than at the moment just before Papagena changes from old hag to nubile girl: Papageno places his hand in the old woman's and swears eternal love. Here the mime, as in so many other places, ideally matches the spirit of the piece.

The staging, though fairly spare, misses little that is essential to understanding the work. We are mercifully spared the ugliness of much modern décor, and the costumes of Romeo Gigli, though possibly a mite chic for Mozart's fairy-tale, are neatly evocative of character. The principals move both above and in front of the orchestra, and flow down two large staircases on either side of the platform, a clever use of the available space. One is less certain about the contribution of the Pilobolus Dance Theatre. In the absence of props they busy themselves rather self-consciously, becoming in turn dragon, beasts, water, fire, etc., an economic but not wholly convincing idea. The producers often let the principals use imaginary props. The famous portrait is mainly an empty frame: through it Papageno ingeniously describes Pamina's features. But Tamino has a real flute. Gardiner gives a freshly imagined, engaging, disciplined performance, over which he presides with benign pleasure as the cameras frequently show.

The Concertgebouw's excellent acoustics are well caught by the sound engineers. The video director does his work unobtrusively most of the time, though the cameras miss one gag that delights those in the auditorium and on a couple of occasions heads are disconcertingly cut off. There is at least one sighting of a microphone. No subtitles are provided.

Modest Mussorgsky

USSR 1839-1881

Mussorgsky Boris Godunov.
  Anatoly Kocherga *bass* Boris Godunov
  Sergei Larin *ten* Grigory
  Marjana Lipovšek *mez* Marina
  Samuel Ramey *bass* Pimen
  Gleb Nikolsky *bass* Varlaam
  Philip Langridge *ten* Shuisky
  Helmut Wildhaber *ten* Missail
  Sergei Leiferkus *bar* Rangoni
  Liliana Nichiteanu *mez* Feodor
  Valentina Valente *sop* Xenia
  Yevgenia Gorokhovskaya *mez* Nurse
  Eléna Zaremba *mez* Hostess
  Alexander Fedin *ten* Simpleton
  Albert Shagidullin *bar* Shchelkalov
  Wojciech Drabowicz *ten* Mityukha, Khrushchov, Lavitsky
  Mikhail Krutikov *bass* Nikitich, Chemikovsky, Police Officer
  Slovak Philharmonic Chorus; Berlin Radio Chorus; Tölz Boys' Choir;
  Berlin Philharmonic Orchestra / Claudio Abbado.
Sony Classical Ⓟ ① S3K58977 (three discs: 200 minutes: DDD). Notes, text and translation included. Recorded 1993.

B B C RADIO 3
90-93 FM

Where opera is concerned, our generation will undoubtedly be remembered for its emphasis on restoring scores to their pristine state, or at least attempting to divine and then execute the original intentions of the composer. Whether it be Gluck, Mozart, Verdi or Mussorgsky, authenticity and completeness have been the order of the day, perhaps going even beyond the composer's own wishes. In the case of *Boris* nobody has been more diligent than Abbado over the past 15 years, since he first presented the epic at La Scala, in seeking the truth about this vast canvas. Now we have the latest fruits of his efforts. Incidentally, this work forcibly reminds us how little has changed in Russia regarding conflicts of power: fanaticism and religion competing for attention with cruelty and intrigue. *Plus ça change ...*

As happens most often today, Abbado plays the definitive 1872-4 version, adding scenes, including the complete one in Pimen's cell and the St Basil's scene from 1869. To avoid the Simpleton losing his kopek twice he omits the repetition of this episode, cutting from fig. 20-25 (in the OUP full score) in the Kromy Forest scene; a sensible solution.

This recording took place in 1993, around the same time similar forces presented two concert performances in the Berlin Philharmonie, where the set was also recorded. It preceded stage performances in Salzburg (Easter and summer of 1993) with similar forces. As when Abbado conducted the work at Covent Garden in 1983 and at the Vienna State Opera in 1991, his is a taut, tense reading. With the Berlin Philharmonic at his call, it became grander, more virtuosic, at times hard-driven, favouring extremes of speed. The orchestra are very much in the foreground, sounding more emphatic than would ever be the case in the opera-house. The total effect, for all its magnificence, is a shade unrelenting and the extremes of dynamics, recalling Karajan, are very marked. The precision and clarity are undoubted: whether or not Mussorgsky might not have preferred Gergiev's more understated, equally incisive Kirov reading on the Decca video version (see below) is a matter of conjecture.

What cannot be doubted is that Michael Haas's first opera recording as producer for Sony Classical is of demonstration standard: most potent in the way it captures the wonderfully incisive and pointed singing of the combined choruses in their various guises, best heard through the most wide-ranging loudspeakers. Here all is vividly brought before us by conductor and producer in the wide panorama predicated by Mussorgsky's all-enveloping vision.

Kocherga, the Russian bass, has a superb voice, firmly produced throughout an extensive register. You will be astonished and delighted at the accuracy of his reading and at its complete avoidance of conventional melodrama. He is concerned to show the loving father and his scene with Boris's children is here among the most rewarding. Given the velvety, soft grain of his timbre, it may not be surprising that the inner torment is not always much in evidence as it is with Ghiaurov for Tchakarov (on his Sony Classical recording). But these may seem like quibbles when set beside the beauty and musicality of Kocherga's concept.

The ambitious lovers are well represented. Indeed, Larin is quite the best Grigory yet on disc, sounding at once youthful, heroic and ardent, and quite free of tenor mannerisms. Lipovšek characterizes Marina forcefully: we are well aware of the scheming Princess's powers of wheeler-dealing and of erotic persuasion. A certain hardness that had by now come into her tone is not inappropriate. Even so, one would like to have heard the lovely Eléna Zaremba in the role: here she makes a lively Hostess, a part so often consigned to superannuated mezzos. Marina's scene with the Rangoni of Leiferkus is one of the set's best, accompanied with a sure feeling for its many undercurrents of religious bigotry, voluptuousness and cant. The baritone repeats his pointed portrayal for Gergiev.

Ramey is classy casting for Pimen, but – for all his fine singing – he doesn't quite convince you that he is inside the part. Ghiuselev (Tchakarov) shows just how much more subtlety can be read into the old monk's narration through variations of colour, tone and phrase deriving from long experience in the genre (Tchakarov is also gentler, more yielding here than Abbado). Langridge certainly knows everything there is to know about Shuisky, a role he has often sung with Abbado and though his tone hasn't true Russian character, his range of colour is arresting.

There seems no end to the new talent coming out of Russia. Here we have Albert Shagidullin as Shchelkalov, the Boyar's Secretary, disclosing a baritone of infinite possibilities and Alexander Fedin, a Covent Garden Rodolfo, singing the Simpleton with plaintive beauty (though Tchakarov's Popov is even more touching). Nichiteanu has too fruity a voice for Feodor but Valente is ideal for Xenia. The Missail and Varlaam are nothing special although more than adequate.

There is real competition for Abbado from Tchakarov. Not nearly as high-powered as an orchestral performance or recording as Abbado's, the older Sony is more natural in its sound and balance. Confusingly it is complementary in casting to Abbado's. As the Tsar, Ghiaurov displays an authority and anguish beyond Kocherga's ability: in brief, he is compellingly intense throughout. Mineva's commanding, smoky-voiced Marina is partnered by Svetlev's overstretched Grigory. Ghiuselev is a superb Pimen, and Martinovich is a Rangoni almost in the Leiferkus class. The smaller roles are variably taken. Neither of the Sony versions quite rivals the Decca Kirov video performance, which has the advantage of being recorded live and with an engrossing production to match.

Mussorgsky Boris Godunov.

Ivan Petrov *bass* Boris Godunov
Vladimir Ivanovsky *ten* Grigory
Irina Arkhipova *mez* Marina
Mark Reshetin *bass* Pimen
Alexey Geleva *bass* Varlaam
Georgy Shulpin *ten* Shuisky
Nikolay Zakharov *ten* Missail
Yevgeny Kibkalo *bass* Rangoni
Valentina Klepatskaya *mez* Feodor
Tamara Sorokina *sop* Xenia
Yevgeniya Verbitskaya *mez* Nurse
Veronika Borisenko *mez* Hostess

Anton Grigoryev *bass* Simpleton, Nikitich
Alexey Ivanov *bar* Shchelkolov
Vladimir Valaitis *bar* Lavitsky
Yury Galkin *bass* Chernikovsky
Leonid Ktitorov *bass* Mityukha
Anatoly Mishutin *ten* Khrushchov, Boyar
Chorus and Orchestra of the Bolshoi Theatre, Moscow / Alexander Melik-Pashayev.
Melodiya Ⓜ ① 74321 29349-2 (three discs: 175 minutes: ADD). Notes, text and translation
included. Recorded 1962.

The release of this set was the first time this desirable performance had been generally available in the
UK and it was well worth the wait. It is certainly the most authentic-sounding version of the Rimsky
arrangement so far recorded. Under Melik-Pashayev's conducting, which combines discipline, an
innate understanding of the score's rhythmic and melodic requirements and sheer experience in
directing the work, it flows onwards in a steady stream of musical and dramatic consistency.

Nowhere among versions at present available, or perhaps anywhere else, will you hear such a cast of
singers, steeped in the best tradition of performing the work at the Bolshoi, and at the same time so
apt for their given roles. Petrov isn't at all in the Chaliapin or Christoff mould of performing the work
(for Dobrowen on EMI): his performance is entirely free of melodrama and is sung with all the vocal
verities observed in a rounded, warm bass. In his more modest way, Petrov invests his role with just
as much feeling and drama as his more histrionic rivals – and in that has much in common with
Ghiaurov on the Karajan version (Decca) while being rather more involving. Petrov's is a richly
rewarding portrayal on all counts.

Even better is the Marina of the young Arkhipova. In her case, one can assert with certainty that
she has no peer, let alone a better on any other set. The proud carriage of her voice and the finely
nuanced character of her loud and soft singing are just what one wants from the ambitious Polish
Princess. Her Grigory, Ivanovsky, isn't vocally quite in her class – the voice sounds strained under
pressure – but, like everyone else in the cast, he is very much inside his role and declaims it with real
passion. In the Polish act Kibkalo makes an ideally insinuating Rangoni.

Reshetin is perfectly cast as grave old Pimen; he is another bass whose tone is well supported and
easily produced. Shulpin has one of those sharp-edged tenors that many people abhor, but it seems
absolutely the right voice for that crepuscular, two-faced boyar. Grigoryev is a plangent, touching
Simpleton. Most of the supporting cast is in the same mould, peculiarly Russian, and therefore
idiomatic in timbre.

Some may balk at the backward recording of the orchestra, but at least it is a pleasure to hear the
full tone of the soloists. The excellent singing of the chorus is also vividly caught. The stereo spread
is a trifle too marked. Compared with the resplendent Karajan the sound is inevitably disappointing,
but Karajan's effort is as a whole too glamorous for the piece. The Dobrowen has conducting in the
class of Melik-Pashayev, and the great Christoff, but the sound is mono and the version cut. If you
enjoy Rimsky's admittedly inauthentic scoring, you should make every effort to hear this well-
remastered Melodiya set.

Mussorgsky Boris Godunov.
Robert Lloyd *bass* Boris Godunov
Alexei Steblianko *ten* Grigory
Olga Borodina *mez* Marina
Alexandr Morozov *bass* Pimen
Vladimir Ognovienko *bass* Varlaam
Yevgeny Boitsov *ten* Shuisky
Igor Yan *ten* Missail
Sergei Leiferkus *bar* Rangoni
Larissa Dyadkova *mez* Feodor
Olga Kondina *sop* Xenia
Yeugenia Perlasova *mez* Nurse
Ludmila Filatova *mez* Hostess
Vladimir Solodovnikov *bass* Simpleton
Mikhail Kit *bar* Shchelkolov
Yevgeny Fedotov *bass* Nikitich
Grigory Karasyov *bass* Mityukha
Kirov Theatre Chorus and Orchestra / Valery Gergiev.
Stage Directors: **Andrei Tarkovsky, Stephen Lawless.** *Video Director:* **Humphrey Burton.**
Decca Ⓟ 📹 071 409-3DH2; 🔆 071 409-1DH2 (two sides: 221 minutes). Recorded 1990.

This is masterly on almost every count, musical and visual, and would now be the outright choice for
this work in all the media. It is based on Tarkovsky's original production for Covent Garden which
was transferred, after his untimely death, to the Kirov Theatre, where it was restaged – much to its
benefit – by Stephen Lawless. That in turn was directed for television by Humphrey Burton, and seen

on BBC 2 in 1990, when it was lavishly and rightly praised. Thank goodness it is now generally available in superb vision and sound. The biggest advantage this performance has over the original, 1983 effort at Covent Garden is the predominantly Russian cast, orchestra and chorus. There before our eyes is a whole gallery of boyars, princes, rogues, miscreants, ordinary, downtrodden people, each face almost a painting in itself. Front-stage, as it were, are some of the best of the current generation of Russian singers, not a dud among them. If just one scene should be singled out, that between Marina and Rangoni in the Polish (Third) Act, that is because Borodina's Marina, sensual, wilful, wheedling, and Sergei Leiferkus's Jesuit, sly, repressed, scheming, are portrayals that could not be bettered. Besides, both sing their roles magnificently, Borodina even surpassing her great, unforgotten predecessor Arkhipova (under Fedoseyev on Philips). This encounter is what singing and acting are all about. But it would not be quite as gripping without Lawless's subtle, detailed direction of his principals and Burton's illuminating (literally) video direction.

Hardly less rewarding, among others, are the virile, heroic Grigory of Steblianko, Alexandr Morozov's grave, moving Pimen (although he looks and is too young for the part), Dyadkova's attractive Feodor, Ognovienko's rip-roaring Varlaam, and Boitsov's inveigling Shuisky. All are caught on the wing, giving spontaneous, dedicated performances as part of a well-rehearsed ensemble. At their head is the sole outsider, Robert Lloyd, in the title-role as he was in 1983 at Covent Garden, presenting a figure of inner torment and histrionic power while never upsetting the rules of secure tone and keen line. Everything he does is thought through and outwardly convincing, yet he cannot quite hide his British figure and features which are not quite right for the part. Nor does his tone have all the richness of the most notable of his Russian predecessors in the role. These are minor quibbles before a notable and well-received reading.

Gergiev is another of the recording's heroes. Seldom if ever, not even in Abbado's hands, has the score sounded so hauntingly beautiful and apt for this huge panorama of seventeenth-century Russia, and his orchestra respond to his definite beat with playing of point and precision. Similarly the chorus sound confident and idiomatic, seconding their looks under his firmly controlled direction.

Nicholas Dvigoubsky's décor is full of atmosphere, contrasting the squalor of the public scenes with the grandeur of the private palaces, and much of its quality has been caught for video. Decca provide subtitles and reprint John Warrack's original note. Don't miss this riveting experience.

Mussorgsky Khovanshchina.
Aage Haugland bass Ivan Khovansky
Vladimir Atlantov ten Andrey Khovansky
Vladimir Popov ten Golitsin
Anatoly Kocherga bar Shaklovity
Paata Burchuladze bass Dosifey
Marjana Lipovšek contr Marfa
Brigitte Poschner-Klebel sop Susanna
Heinz Zednik ten Scribe
Joanna Borowska sop Emma
Wilfried Gahmlich ten Kuzka
Vienna Boys' Choir; Slovak Philharmonic Choir;
Vienna State Opera Chorus and Orchestra / Claudio Abbado.
DG Ⓟ Ⓓ 429 758-2GH3 (three discs: 171 minutes: DDD). Notes, text and translation included.
Recorded at performances in the Vienna State Opera during September 1989.

"To Russians, Mussorgsky's music is an integral part of their cultural awareness and, like the novels of Dostoevsky, plagues them with agonizing questions: what are the causes of Russia's continuing calamities ...?" Victor Borovsky's question, in his fine essay in the programme book, is as timely as the opera remains; and it is perhaps no coincidence that, just as Dostoevsky used to be hard to find on Soviet book shelves, so *Khovanshchina* was almost throughout its history misrepresented in Russia. The performances under Claudio Abbado in Vienna in 1989 were in many ways an act of rehabilitation, one that is taken further by the publication of this remarkable set.

In the first place, the version of this tangled, difficult score which has been prepared is essentially that of Shostakovich, based on Pavel Lamm's edition, with Stravinsky's ending. The implications of this are discussed in another authoritative accompanying essay, by Richard Taruskin. In brief, Rimsky-Korsakov is rejected for reasons now very familiar: his orchestration was too glossy, his 'corrections' of Mussorgsky's harmony too conventional. No less importantly, Shostakovich is in part accepted, though some of the brass emphasis that has long troubled admirers of his work is lightened, but rejected with regard to his final 'triumphant' ending with the return of the Preobrazhensky March. The point is crucial. At the centre of the opera is a confrontation of essential Russian characteristics that were to divide into the enduring Slavophile-Westernizer debates; and in Soviet times the view taken by Stasov and then Rimsky-Korsakov, that the Old Believers represented all that was regressive and obscurantist in Russia, was underlined in contrast to the automatic state optimism here associated with Peter the Great. With the beautiful, tragic music of the restored ending, here most beautifully played, the strength, the dignity, the Christian endurance and tolerance of the Old Believers is set back in place as a vital ingredient of the work.

So we have here a *Khovanshchina* which may not present a complete solution to the work – its history is too uncertain and complex for that – but which does come closer than ever before to what seems to have been Mussorgsky's vision. It is very much a collaborative enterprise. Above all, honour must go to Abbado for his lead. His belief in the work and understanding of its issues is evident at every turn, from the exquisite playing of the opening Dawn scene, and the other purely orchestral passages, to his sensitive support of the singers in their contrasting roles and his capacity to articulate the opposing factions by characterizing their music so perceptively. The orchestra are excellently recorded, on the whole, rather better so than some of the singers; the recording is based on several evenings in the Vienna Opera, and not only are the voices sometimes set at rather a distance, but there is a measure of tramping and coughing. But none of this matters much.

The cast mostly rise to the interpretation presented to them by this version and Abbado's intentions. There is, at the start, a vivid scene between Anatoly Kocherga's bullish Shaklovity and the angry, frightened little Scribe of Heinz Zednik. Marfa is superbly sung by Marjana Lipovšek, calm and possessed in her divination scene, maintaining a steady warmth against the frantic assaults of Brigitte Poschner-Klebel's Susanna. There is a lively, colourful, desperate account of Emma from Joanna Borowska, well matched against Vladimir Atlantov's fierce Andrey Khovansky. Aage Haugland is splendid as old Ivan Khovansky; but there is a slightly disappointing performance of Golitsin from Vladimir Popov, who must, especially in the circumstances of this version of the work, carry the burden of the Westernizer ideal in his Act 2 narrative, and does not underline the complexities of the character as fully as others in the role have done. One also has to admit to some disappointment with Paata Burchuladze. Perhaps longer acquaintance with the set will reveal more subtleties in a performance lacking in the towering authority and visionary fervour the part must possess. His interventions, first in Act 1 and then to silence the quarrel between Marfa and Susanna, do not seem to carry enough conviction, and his actual tone is too often disturbed by a low, heavy vibrato.

A vital contribution in this whole collaboration has been that of scholarship; and it is a pleasure to welcome this set's booklet. Outstanding essays include Dr Borovsky's on Chaliapin and the work's theatrical history, Richard Taruskin's magisterial survey of the historical background to the work and changing attitudes to it, and valuable German essays by Michael Stegemann on the history by way of Mussorgsky's letters and by Sigrid Neef on the music (especially the dramatic associations of contrasting sound worlds and tonalities). There is also a contribution by Abbado himself, and a careful table of the manuscript sources and how they have been assembled into this version, together with the original·Russian libretto, a transliteration, and English, French and German translations. The whole provides not only fascinating reading to help and deepen enjoyment of the work, but is the fullest assemblage of the scholarly material ever assembled. This release came hard on the heels of the Tchakarov recording for Sony Classical, presenting a perhaps unfortunately timed choice to collectors; but certainly no one with an admiration for Mussorgsky, or indeed with any feeling for Russia, should miss this set.

Mussorgsky Khovanshchina.
Bulat Minzhilkiev *bass* Ivan Khovansky
Yuri Marusin *ten* Andrey Khovansky
Konstantin Pluzhnikov *ten* Golitsin, Scribe
Viacheslav Trofimov *bar* Shaklovity
Nikolai Okhotnikov *bass* Dosifey
Olga Borodina *mez* Marfa
Evgenia Tselovalnik *sop* Susanna
Tatiana Kravtsova *sop* Emma
Nikolai Gassiev *ten* Kuzka
Valery Lebed *bass* Pastor
Mikhail Chernozhukov *bass* Varsonofiev
Vassili Gerelo *bar* Streshniev
Yevgeny Fedotov *bass* First Strelets
Andrei Khramtsov *bass* Second Strelets
Kirov Ballet; Kirov Theatre Chorus and Orchestra / Valery Gergiev.
Stage Producer: **Leonid Baratov.** *Video Director:* **Brian Large.**
Philips Ⓟ Ⓞ Ⓓ 070 433-3PH2 (two cassettes: 205 minutes). Recorded 1992.

This engrossing performance, recorded at the Kirov, preserves, in the best sense, a tradition of performing the work only possible to see and hear in Russia. As you watch this authentic staging in realistic sets you have to wonder if modern concepts of this or any work can really improve on creating, in the country of origin, a production that conforms to the given libretto and score. This magnificently lit and designed (Fyodor Fedorovsky) production holds the attention from first to last and that through three hours and 25 minutes' music, for Gergiev plays the score absolutely complete, including the scene between Golitsin and the Lutheran pastor in Act 2 almost always excluded.

His is a splendid reading, energetic or ruminative as the work demands, and it makes the very most of Shostakovich's orchestration. His players dig deep into the wells of their collective knowledge of Mussorgsky's particular idiom and psyche. The Kirov Chorus are no less admirable, a multitude of interesting faces making up a convincing whole, and of course properly Russian in timbre as is the sound of every soloist.

Right from the start we catch the note of authenticity in Pluzhnikov's Scribe, a portrait of special significance, a wily, frightened, scheming eccentric with an unforgettable face. Can this be the same tenor who presents Golitsin with equal aplomb, a eupeptic, wilful yet forward-looking aristocrat? Both parts are sung in that peculiarly incisive timbre only Russian tenors possess. Marusin, who here transfers from Golitsin, his role with Abbado (on the currently unavailable Pioneer LaserDisc version recorded at Vienna in 1989), to the selfish, libidinous Andrey Khovansky, is another in the same mould. As his commanding father, Ivan Khovansky, Minzhilkiev is a formidable figure, his sense of power projected in a strong, if not very appealing bass. Viacheslav Trofimov makes the most of Shaklovity's aria, sorrowing over the fate of Russia. Okhotnikov, a noted Boris, is here a resolute and imposing Dosifey who uses his resonant bass and piercing eyes to convey the man's religious conviction, though you can well imagine this man as a formidable boyar in his previous incarnation.

But the performance of the set is Borodina's overwhelming Marfa. For once you believe that this beautiful, sad-looking woman is yearning to be restored to Andrey Khovansky's arms, her earthly, womanly passions vying with her religious faith. Borodina sings her two solos with the glorious tone and lovely phrasing for which she is noted: her scene in Act 3 with Dosifey is infinitely moving.

The video direction by Brian Large is exemplary, giving us the true flavour of the piece, and the sound is good to excellent. Subtitles here are a great help in sorting out the various strands of plot and argument in this panoramic masterpiece. None were provided on the Pioneer version. In any case Gergiev's set is preferable because beside it the modern production at the State Opera looks contrived and arty. By and large Gergiev also has the better singers, even if on occasion Abbado's swifter speeds are preferable to Gergiev's more deliberate ones in keeping the action on the go.

Otto Nicolai
German 1810-1849

Nicolai Die lustigen Weiber von Windsor
Ruth-Margret Pütz *sop* Mistress Ford
Gisela Litz *mez* Mistress Page
Edith Mathis *sop* Ann Page
Gottlob Frick *bass* Sir John Falstaff
Ernst Gutstein *bar* Ford
Kieth Engen *bass* Page
Fritz Wunderlich *ten* Fenton
Friedrich Lenz *ten* Slender
Carl Hoppe *bass* Dr Caius
Bavarian State Opera Chorus; Bavarian State Orchestra / Robert Heger.
EMI Ⓜ ① CMS7 69348-2 (two discs: 145 minutes: ADD). Notes and text included. Recorded 1963.

It is probably no longer so true as it once would have been that everyone knows the Overture to Nicolai's *Die lustigen Weiber von Windsor*. Those who do will know it as not merely a sparkling, melodic piece of music but, more particularly, the product of an obviously highly cultured musician. What is remarkable for an opera so little known outside Germany is the extent to which this is sustained throughout the whole work. Nicolai has an incredible fund of inventiveness – almost as though Mendelssohn had written an opera. It is, quite simply, one musical treat after another, and, arguably, preferable to Verdi's later treatment of the same story.

With this recording it is difficult to find fault. The men are uniformly superb – Gottlob Frick an unmatched, massive-voiced Falstaff, Fritz Wunderlich an ardent, god-like Fenton, and Ernst Gutstein, Kieth Engen, Friedrich Lenz and Carl Hoppe provide uniformly rich support. Ruth-Margret Pütz and Gisela Litz are sprightly-voiced, dependable and enjoyable, and one must pay tribute to Edith Mathis in an early appearance as a sweet, confident and characterful Ann Page. When first released in the UK, the original three-LP set was abridged to fit on to two LPs. Here we are offered it in its entirety on two generously-filled CDs. It comes up with sparkling clarity, with a perfect balance between singers and orchestra, and tape hiss is minimal. Although there have been more recent recordings under Klee (DG) and Kubelík (Decca) – both currently unavailable – it is this version that still receives the highest recommendation.

Carl Nielsen
Danish 1865-1931

Nielsen Maskarade.
Ib Hansen *bass-bar* Jeronimus
Gurli Plesner *contr* Magdelone
Tonny Landy *ten* Leander

Mogens Schmidt Johansen *bar* Henrik
Christian Sørensen *ten* Arv
Gert Bastian *bar* Leonard
Edith Brodersen *sop* Leonora
Tove Hyldgaard *sop* Pernille
Jørgen Klint *bass* Night Watchman
Ove Verner Hansen *bar* Tutor
Aage Haugland *bass* Master of the Masquerade
Danish Radio Symphony Chorus and Orchestra / John Frandsen.
Unicorn-Kanchana Ⓟ Ⓓ DKPCD9073-4 (two disc: 140 minutes: ADD). Notes, text and
translation included. Recorded 1978.

Nearly 100 years on and only one professional staging in Britain (a tremendous and very funny
performance from Opera North in 1990) for this freshest, wisest, most ebullient and humane of
twentieth-century comic operas. How much longer before deprived citizens storm the opera-houses
and demand their rights? Impresarios and managers take heed, before you find yourselves rolling
doomwards in the tumbrils. Don't tell us that a fine modern recording is an adequate substitute – it
is a joy to listen to, but that only makes your timidity the more incomprehensible. Don't tell us we
haven't got the singers – the recording shows that characterful, unaffected voices and a sense of fun
are the only requirements. Don't tell us the critics never alerted you and just look at the quotes in
Unicorn-Kanchana's publicity.

When this recording first appeared in 1978 it was new to the gramophone; until then only the
sparkling and extrovert Overture and the familiar orchestral interludes ("Magdelone's Dance", the
evocative Prelude to the second act, and the "Hanedans" from Act 3) had been available on records.
Considering his lifelong interest both in the stage and the human voice, it is perhaps surprising that
Nielsen composed only two operas, and that after *Maskarade* he never returned to the medium, even
though he still continued to write incidental music for stage productions. He spent many years as a
member of the Kongelige Kapel, the Royal Theatre Orchestra in Copenhagen, and was still in the
second violins in 1905, the year in which he began working on *Maskarade*. Of course, there are more
obstacles in the way of a Scandinavian opera composer than a German or Italian since only
Stockholm could boast a permanent opera-house at the period. Not that this in itself would have been
much of a deterrent to Nielsen. It seems much more likely that he came to realize that his dramatic
genius lay in the direction of the symphonic drama, with its enormous concentration of incident
rather than the operatic stage.

The libretto derives from Holberg's comedy, *Maskarade*, of 1724 which Nielsen himself shaped into
an operatic form in collaboration with the literary historian, Vilhelm Andersen, who adapted the text.
Nielsen was drawn to the subject by the element of masque comedy. To quote the composer from an
article in *Politiken*: "If anything, it was the intermezzo, the element of masque comedy that interested
me, I think. And then, Henrik in *Maskarade*. I think he is great, and then he is quite modern in his
feeling, after all: he even says socialistic things". But Henrik is no Figaro, any more than Holberg was
a Beaumarchais. The basic plot could hardly be simpler. Two young people, Leander and Leonora,
meet at a masque and fall in love. Their parents have promised them both in marriages that they have
arranged. They rebel and go off in search of each other at the next evening's masquerade at which
their parents are also in attendance. When they are unmasked, it transpires that it is to each other that
their respective parents have pledged them.

But the bare bones of the story do scant justice to the charm and interest of the opera. According
to Jürgen Balzer in his essay on the operas published in the *Nielsen Centenary Essays* he edited
(Dobson: London; 1965), the adaptation of the Holberg comedy weakened the characterization of
Leonora and also reduced Leander's father, Jeronimus, to a conventional stock figure. Both fathers
are in fact coarsened by comparison with the Holberg. But as he himself put it, Nielsen was more
interested right from the beginning "in situation comedy rather than in character drama". There is
none of the oratorio-like flavour that some critics have found in the choral writing of *Saul and David*;
nor is there the delineation of character that one finds in Saul himself. *Maskarade* is a buoyant, high-
spirited score full of strophic songs and choruses, making considerable use of dance and dance
rhythms and having the unmistakable lightness of the *buffo* opera. It is a delightful score and works
superbly as a dramatic entertainment.

Among its other merits, *Maskarade* is excellently proportioned in that no act outstays its welcome:
one is always left wanting more. Only one of the acts, the third and last, exceeds 50 minutes, while the
second is less than 40. If the Danes described their language as "a throat disease", their modesty
should be restrained as far as sung Danish is concerned. Danish can sound appealing and often
beautiful, so the decision to record in the original and not attempt an English version is welcome. In
any event every word comes across in this well-focused recording.

The performance offers every evidence of fine teamwork: Ib Hansen makes a vivid Jeronimus and
both he and Tonny Landy, the Leander in this performance, bring plenty of vocal colour to their
parts. In fact nearly all of these roles are well characterized vocally and special mention should be
made of Mogens Schmidt Johansen's Henrik and Christian Sørensen's Arv. Only the Magdelone of
Gurli Plesner is likely to enjoy limited appeal: her first entry in Act 1 sounds uncomfortably like the
falsetto that Schmidt Johansen has given us shortly before. But both the singing and the orchestral

playing have admirable spirit and (predictably) an idiomatic flavour. John Frandsen secures good results from the Danish Radio Symphony Orchestra. There is some good ensemble and the wind playing is particularly fine; only the upper strings leave something to be desired. They sound a little undernourished, wanting in lustre and timbre. This apart, there are no grumbles on this count.

Only one thing to implore of you – please don't throw away the LPs if you've still got them. The sound on CD has a fizzy quality which is inferior to the original. There was no need for any reservations about the recording quality of the LPs. The sound was well focused, the orchestra and singers well blended though the latter are somewhat forward but not obtrusively so. Above all the sound is musical, the images well located and firm, and there are no production effects that are initially successful but prove tiresome on repetition; this is a straight concert-hall performance, and the skills of the singers, the artists and Nielsen himself are left to speak for themselves. Reservations about the sound on the CD transfer is no excuse for you not to get to know an opera which if you give it the chance, should enjoy a popularity somewhere between *The bartered bride* and *Die Fledermaus*. Unicorn-Kanchana are to be thanked for making it available again and thus filling an important gap in the catalogue.

Nielsen Saul and David.

Aage Haugland *bass* Saul
Peter Lindroos *ten* David
Tina Kiberg *sop* Mikal
Kurt Westi *ten* Jonathan
Anne Gjevang *contr* Witch of Endor
Christian Christiansen *bass* Samuel
Jørgen Klint *bass* Abner
Danish National Radio Choir and Symphony Orchestra / Neeme Järvi.
Chandos Ⓟ Ⓓ CHAN8911/2 (two discs: 124 minutes: DDD). Notes, text and translation included. Recorded 1990.

While Scandinavia can boast a roster of world famous singers from Jenny Lind and Christina Nilsson in the last century down to Bjørling, Flagstad and Melchior in our own, it has produced few great operas. But in *Saul and David* we have one of them. As noted above, from 1889 to 1905 Nielsen played in the second violins of the Orchestra of the Royal Theatre in Copenhagen, where he learned his operatic repertoire: he would have played in the first Danish performances of *Falstaff* and *Otello*, and his admiration for *Siegfried* and *Die Meistersinger* are well documented. Admittedly his relationship to Wagner was a little ambivalent but the years when he became the Royal Orchestra's conductor (1908-14) found him expressing eagerness to get to work on *Tristan*! Dating from the period immediately preceding the Second Symphony, *Saul and David* inhabits much the same world. It still remains unstaged at Covent Garden or ENO. Mind you, *Maskarade* took more than 80 years to reach us in the UK and one can never wholly set aside fears nowadays that when *Saul and David* does reach us, it will be set in Salford or Bradford and updated to the 1930s. So far, record collectors have known it only in the 1972 English-language broadcast conducted by Jascha Horenstein with Boris Christoff as Saul, Alexander Young as David and Elisabeth Söderström as Mikal. Unicorn-Kanchana issued this in 1976 and transferred it to CD in 1990. There was also a fine Danish broadcast made in 1960 under Thomas Jensen, no less, with Frans Andersson as Saul (on Danacord) but the present version supersedes both.

In *Nielsen Centenary Essays* the late Jürgen Balzer quoted a diary entry Nielsen made about opera some years before he began work on *Saul*: "The plot must be the 'pole' that goes through a dramatic work; the plot is the trunk; words and sentences are fruits and leaves, but if the trunk is not strong and healthy, it is no use that the fruits look beautiful". His librettist, Einar Christiansen, certainly provided a strong 'pole', and in this splendid Chandos version we are at least able to hear it as both author and composer intended. However intelligent and sensitive the translation, something valuable is lost when we abandon the original language whether it be in *Boris*, *Pelléas*, *L'enfant et les sortilèges* or for that matter, any of the Janáček operas – and the same goes for the two Nielsen operas.

It is on Saul that the opera really focuses: his is the classic tragedy of the downfall of a great man through some flaw of character and it is for him that Nielsen (and the splendid Aage Haugland) mobilizes our sympathy. Haugland's portrayal is thoroughly full-blooded and three-dimensional, and he builds up the character with impressive conviction. Peter Lindroos will strike you as every bit as well cast as Alexander Young's David and finer than Otte Svendsen (Danacord), and Tina Kiberg need not fear comparison with her distinguished rival on Unicorn-Kanchana or, for that matter, Ruth Guldbaek on Danacord. There is some powerful choral writing, some of it strongly polyphonic (in particular, the passage in Act 3 celebrating Saul's repentance: track 5 of disc 2), which has prompted some people to speak of it being like an oratorio. (A penny-in-the-slot reaction prompted as much by the subject matter as anything else.) What is, of course, so striking about this piece is the sheer quality and freshness of its invention, its unfailing sense of line and purpose. No attempt is made at 'stage production' but thanks to the committed performers under Neeme Järvi, the music fully carries the drama on its flow. Järvi paces the work to admirable effect and the recording made in collaboration with the Danish Radio is well balanced and vivid in its detail.

Luigi Nono
Italian 1924-1990

Nono Intolleranza 1960.
David Rampy *ten* An Emigrant
Ursula Koszut *sop* His Companion
Kathryn Harries *sop* A Woman
Jerrold van der Schaaf *ten* An Algerian
Wolfgang Probst *bar* A Tortured Prisoner
Joseph Dieken *spkr* First Policeman
Christian Hoening *spkr* Second Policeman
Carsten Otto *spkr* Third Policeman
Hermann Wenning *spkr* Fourth Policeman
Stuttgart Opera Chorus and Orchestra / Bernhard Kontarsky.
Teldec Ⓟ ① 4509-97304-2 (55 minutes: DDD). Recorded at a performance in the Staatsoper,
Stuttgart during March 1993.

Intolleranza 1960 was a political firecracker flung down by Luigi Nono to shake up complacent
Venetian opera-goers. The controversies that attended its early productions (and, indeed, its
composition) lead one to expect a Problem Piece, but the main problem, 38 years on, lies in deciding
how seriously to take it. *Intolleranza* remains short and (fairly) sharp; it can still make an impact in
the theatre. Yet purely musically, on disc, it is not particularly substantial, and there seems to be a
serious mismatch between the subject-matter, which is no more subtly presented than it might be on
the front page of a tabloid, and the music, which aspires to embody all the qualities of High Modern
Art.

    The lack of musical expansion and development is the more apparent given the lyric power of
Nono's post-Schoenbergian style at the time. His father-in-law's *Moses und Aron* comes to mind, as
does Dallapiccola's *Il prigioniero*. By comparison *Intolleranza* gives too little space for the main
character – an emigrant who suffers intolerance and returns home only to perish in an environmental
disaster – to acquire a true dramatic, psychological identity. In addition, Nono's rejection of vocal
understatement reinforces the impression of ideological overkill, even though the strenuous high
tenor writing is confidently handled – though with little dynamic light and shade – by David Rampy.
All the solo singers strain to some extent to project their angular lines, but the extensive, difficult
choral writing is performed with commendable refinement under Bernhard Kontarsky's taut yet never
brusque direction. The recording, of a stage performance, is not always well balanced, but it
compensates in strength of atmosphere. In the interests of completeness it is a pity that Teldec did not
include the spoken scene that begins Act 2, but at least this can be found in the excellent booklet of
essays and texts.

Per Nørgård
Danish 1932

Nørgård Gilgamesh.
Björn Haugan *ten* Gilgamesh
Helge Lannerbäck *bass-bar* Enkido
Britt-Marie Aruhn *sop* Aruru
Jørgen Hviid *ten* Huwawa
Ranveig Eckhoff *sop* Siduri
Merete Baekkelund *sop* Ishtar
Birger Eriksson *bass* Utnapishtim
Solwig Grippe *sop* Utnapishtims mage
Annika Bartler *mez* Ishara
Rolf Leanderson *bar* Priest
Swedish Radio Symphony Chorus and Orchestra / Tamás Vetö.

Nørgård Voyage into the Golden Screen.
Danish Radio Symphony Orchestra / Oliver Knussen.
Da Capo Ⓟ ① DCCD9001 (two discs: 116 minutes: ADD). Notes, texts and translations
included. Recorded 1973; *Voyage* recorded 1986.

If the archaeologists are correct, it was in the city of Uruk five millennia ago that men first led a
recognizably urban existence. Not inappropriately then, for an opera to be based on the legend of
Uruk's famous king. There is a pioneering, leap-in-the-dark quality about Per Nørgård's music for
Gilgamesh to match the epic of the first city; certainly nothing could be further removed from
Martinů's treatment of the story. There is an alienness about the whole work, not least in its ritualistic
atmosphere, that captures both the essence of the epic and the people that created it. Time and again
one has the feeling of characters from some great carved frieze drawing breath as if for the first time.
Heard in isolation on disc Nørgård's conception is deprived of its visual and spatial elements, with

audience and performers intermingled and the conductor required to transit between 'northern' and 'southern' rostra. The recording, of a 1973 Swedish Radio performance, manages with its shifting focus to realize something of the aural experience of a live *Gilgamesh*, so it is unfortunate that both the Danish and English notes omit the diagrammatic layout.

Although there is no Danish antecedent for this opera "in six days and seven nights", *Gilgamesh* was not created in a vacuum. Nørgård's music resonates both backwards in time through Blomdahl's *Aniara* to *Les noces* and in its soft, dream-like sonorities forwards to Nordheim's Shakespearean ballet *The Tempest*. The syllabic setting of the text is unusual for so inherently theatrical a work, yet there is no lack of dramatic tension. This arises from the inexorable momentum of the story itself, culminating in an ecstatic "Creation Symphony" in the sixth day, when Gilgamesh strives in vain to achieve immortality. *Gilgamesh* was completed in 1972; two years later it deservedly received the Nordic Council's Music Prize. The work receives powerful advocacy from Tamás Vetö and his well-balanced cast.

Precursors of the purely musical elements of *Gilgamesh* can, of course, be found in Nørgård's own works, one of the most vital being *Voyage into the Golden Screen* (1968). This luminous work for chamber orchestra falls into two movements: the first unsettled, the second filled by the emergence of Nørgård's 'infinity' series. *Voyage into the Golden Screen* marks therefore the point of transition between the final works of Nørgård's early period and his familiar mature style. The performance by the Danish RSO under Oliver Knussen is exemplary. All in all, a fine and thought-provoking issue.

Nørgård Siddhartha.

Stig Fogh Andersen *ten* Siddhartha Gotama
Aage Haugland *bass* Suddhodana
Edith Guillaume *mez* Prajapati
Erik Harbo *ten* Asita
Kim Janken *ten* First Counsellor
Christian Christiansen *bass* Second Counsellor
Poul Elming *ten* Messenger
Tina Kiberg *sop* Yasodhara
Anne Frellesvig *sngr* Kamala
Minna Nyhus *contr* Gandarva
Danish National Radio Choir; Danish National Radio Childrens' Choir

Nørgård Percussion Concerto, "For a Change".

Gert Mørtensen *perc*
Danish National Radio Symphony Orchestra / Jan Latham-König.
Da Capo Ⓟ Ⓓ 8 224031/2 (two discs: 137 minutes: ADD). Notes, text and translation included. Recorded 1984.

As in his second opera, *Gilgamesh*, Per Nørgård chose an ancient, legendary figure as the central character of his third, the Indian prince who ultimately became the Buddha. *Siddhartha* (1974-9) opens at the court of the childless King Suddhodana, where his doleful queen, Maya, dances in order to conceive a child – Siddhartha. The birth has dire consequences: the Queen dies, and a ritual horoscope predicts that the prince will abandon the kingdom. Against the protests of Maya's sister, Prajapati, Suddhodana decides to protect his son from life so that he will never be tempted to leave. Only the young, the healthy and the beautiful may see Siddhartha; the rest are interned. Only in Act 3 is the deception revealed, when a dancer falls dead at the prince's feet. Prajapati then reveals the horde of aged, infirm and ugly whose rebellion is duly – and brutally – suppressed. In a mixture of trauma and disgust, Siddhartha leaves home, wife and family to set out on the painful road to enlightenment.

The story of a prince so shielded from real life is an intriguing one, especially given the disturbing resonances of mid-twentieth-century Central European history in the King's 'cleansing' of undesirable elements. Yet the tragedy of the First Act finds no real expression in the music, nor does any tension accumulate in the Second Act: while it could be argued that this reflects the unreality of Siddhartha's existence, Henze would have made of this a much more compelling, if less mystical, experience. Nørgård's music itself is partly to blame, the thematic material being derived (as with *Gilgamesh*) from the 'infinity' series, the inexhaustible, self-perpetuating stream from which themes are extracted by choosing every, say, third, fifteenth, or even seventy-fifth, note. In *Gilgamesh* the series's euphony acted as a correlative of the action; in *Siddhartha* it is at odds with it.

Ironically, the most satisfyingly dramatic music on these discs occurs in the percussion concerto *For a Change* (1982-3, inspired by the Chinese *I Ching* and an arrangement of a solo percussion work of that name, recorded by Mørtensen on BIS), the four movements of which take up where *Siddhartha* left off. Nor is this just a testament to the blistering account by Mørtensen, since the performance of the opera is a fine one; rather, it is that the innately abstract drama of the concerto elicited the more cogent response from the composer.

Michael Nyman   British 1948

Nyman The Man Who Mistook His Wife for a Hat.
Emile Belcourt *ten* Dr S, the Neurologist
Sarah Leonard *sop* Mrs P
Frederick Westcott *bar* Dr P
Alexander Balaneacu, Jonathan Carney *vns*
Kate Musker *va*
Moray Welsh, Anthony Hinnigan *vcs*
Helen Tunstall *hp*
Michael Nyman *pf*
Sony Classical Ⓟ Ⓒ MK44669 (57 minutes: DDD). Notes and text included. Recorded 1987.

The Man Who Mistook His Wife for a Hat is a chamber opera based on Oliver Sacks's book of the same name. A true story, it takes the form of a neurological case-study; Dr P, a professional singer, suffers from visual agnosia – an inability to recognize or make sense of what he sees – and the opera describes in simple, unpretentious dialogue two consultation sessions during which the other two characters, the neurologist (Dr S) and the patient's wife (Mrs P), by way of a sequence of tests and conversations, gradually penetrate the mystery of the symptoms. Beyond that, the opera possesses no story as such, reaches no great climax or conclusion. But drama there is in quantity, supplied largely by the protagonists' reactions and responses to one another. In its wistful way it is also, inevitably, often hilariously funny.

If there had ever been any doubt about the matter, *The Man Who Mistook His Wife for a Hat* firmly secures Michael Nyman as a composer of substance and significance. Although the score blatantly revels in its prosaic ordinariness, the effect has been calculated to avoid superficial theatricality, to underline the ridiculousness of the situation, to instil into the action a tension, a nervous energy, that sustain interest through an hour of what is virtually uninterrupted recitative. (The dialogue is broken only by moments of reflection as the neurologist Dr S steps forward and thinks aloud to the audience.) Ludicrously simple as Nyman's means appear at first, there is never any doubt that he is absolutely in control; by the end, one has the impression rather of a score of unusual power and pathos.

The performances are equally impressive. Pitched at a conversational rather than a conventionally operatic level, the three principals put as much into their acting as they do into their singing, and thus they are able to avoid caricature. Sarah Leonard's playing of Mrs P as the highly strung, solicitous and overprotective wife, blind to the reality of her husband's condition, is nothing less than brilliant. Frederick Westcott as Dr P is cool, composed and bemused throughout. Dr S, proceeding through his deductions with efficiency and tact, is played by Emile Belcourt with quite uncanny realism. Beneath the dialogue a small ensemble directed by Michael Nyman himself provide solid support in the form of a series of intriguing rhythmic, melodic and harmonic patterns – some of them derived, more or less identifiably, from Schumann songs, which also have a place in the libretto. The full text together with useful essays by composer, librettist and Oliver Sacks himself, comes boxed with the CD in a generously fat booklet. Altogether this is an issue not to be missed; utterly engrossing from start to finish.

Jacques Offenbach   German/French 1819-1880

Offenbach La belle Hélène.
Jessye Norman *sop* Hélène
John Aler *ten* Paris
Charles Burles *ten* Menelaus
Gabriel Bacquier *bar* Agamemnon
Jean-Philippe Lafont *bar* Calchas
Colette Alliot-Lugaz *mez* Orestes
Jacques Loreau *bar* Achilles
Roger Trentin *ten* First Ajax
Gérard Desroches *ten* Second Ajax
Nicole Carreras *sop* Bacchis
Adam Levallier *narr* Slave
Toulouse Capitole Chorus and Orchestra / Michel Plasson.
EMI Ⓟ Ⓒ CDS7 47157-8 (two discs: 99 minutes: DDD). Notes, text and translation included. Recorded 1984.

BBC RADIO 3
90-93 FM

If you are familiar with the Lombard set on Barclay from the late-1970s, you may approach this *Belle Hélène* with doubts as to whether Jessye Norman could oust from your affections Jane Rhodes, who sang the title-role and who has been the supreme Hélène of our time. And, to be sure, Jessye Norman does not manage that essentially French way of delivering a phrase that can achieve so much in the parts that Offenbach created for Hortense Schneider. At times, indeed, she is too operatic in her approach. And yet she sings with a vocal clarity and dexterity that was quite beyond Jane Rhodes, and her glorious vocal climb of a ninth on the words "Quel plaisir trouves tu?" in the Invocation to Venus is quite overwhelming.

The Paris is John Aler, who is a little lacking in vocal grace in the Judgement of Paris; but then this is a notoriously difficult number. His particular glory lies in the high notes he brings off so thrillingly well there and in Paris's yodelling at the end of Act 3. The overall effect is certainly way beyond that of Rémy Corazza in the Barclay set. The presence of Gabriel Bacquier and Jean-Philippe Lafont ensures strength, too, in the important baritone roles and enables the Patriotic Trio to make its due effect. There is also a most agreeably sprightly Orestes in Colette Alliot-Lugaz.

Altogether this *Belle Hélène* zips along more agreeably than the Barclay set, which at some points verged on sluggishness. It would have been better, though, if EMI had not achieved this greater sense of movement partly through the device of allowing dialogue to be spoken while the musical numbers are being played and by omitting the Act 3 entr'acte. What really makes this *Belle Hélène* a joy, however, is the utterly exhilarating sparkle that is generated in such numbers as the March of the Kings and the Act 2 finale. The credit for this must go above all, of course, to Michel Plasson, who has learned to such good effect how to treat Offenbach with a much lighter hand than when he gave us *La vie parisienne* in the late-1970s. But this delicious sparkle is also a tribute to a warm, clear recording that has a good stereo movement effect and for which the Barclay is again no match. You may treasure the Barclay set as a souvenir of Jane Rhodes; but there is no doubt at all that this later set is the one to have.

Offenbach Les brigands.

Tibère Raffalli *ten* Falsacappa
Ghislaine Raphanel *sop* Fiorella
Colette Alliot-Lugaz *sop* Fragoletto
Michel Trempont *bar* Piétro
Christian Jean *ten* Carmagnola
Francis Dudziak *ten* Domino
Pierre-Yves le Maigat *bass-bar* Barbavano
Valérie Millot *sop* Princess of Granada
Michel Fockenoy *ten* Adolphe de Valladolid, A Page
Jean-Luc Viala *ten* Comte de Gloria-Cassis
Thierry Dran *ten* Duke of Mantua
François le Roux *bar* Baron de Campotasso
Bernard Pisani *ten* Antonio
René Schirrer *bar* Captain of the Carabinieri
Jacques Loreau *bar* Pipo
Chorus and Orchestra of Opéra National de Lyons / John Eliot Gardiner.
EMI Ⓟ Ⓒ CDS7 49830-2 (two discs: 105 minutes: DDD). Notes, text and translation included. Recorded 1988.

BBC RADIO 3
90-93 FM

Les brigands does not count amongst the best known of Offenbach's works – at any rate in the UK. Perhaps this is due as much as anything to the lack of any of the big numbers that Offenbach wrote for his most effective interpreter, Hortense Schneider, whose absence from the original cast was apparently due to an attack of wounded pride. On the other hand, it is a consistently attractive score, with outstanding individual numbers in Fiorella's rondo "Après avoir pris à droit", Fragoletto's saltarello "Falsacappa voici ma prise", the treasurer's hilarious "O mes amours, ô mes maîtresses", and many more. The work has one of the wittiest of the librettos supplied by the masters Meilhac and Halévy and repays study. The comment that "one should steal according to the position that one occupies in society" is as valid a comment on corruption today as it was in the final throes of Second Empire Paris. And who could resist the zany goings-on of the Second Act, which is set on the border of Italy and Spain, and in which even the characters lose track of their disguises? As for anyone interested in influences on Gilbert and Sullivan (specifically *The Pirates of Penzance*), they might note not only the comic carabinieri who always arrive too late to capture their prey but also the beautiful double chorus in Act 3.

W. S. Gilbert in fact wrote an English version of the work, which was staged to considerable effect in London in the late-1980s. The piece has generally remained much better known on the Continent, though, and not least in Germany. There was an almost complete LP recording in German a few years back on RCA, and there were at least two previous LPs of excerpts in French. This complete version is a great deal better than any of those, though. It is based upon the version staged in Lyon in 1988 and amply shows the benefits of stage preparation. John Eliot Gardiner directs with an attractive lightness of touch, allowing Offenbach's scoring and tempo markings to whip up the excitement as required. He amply shows that one does not need to be French to conduct Offenbach, but rather to have the right 'feel' for the music.

Of the singers, the light tenor Tibère Raffalli leads the way as he does the band of brigands in the part created by Offenbach's favourite male lead, Dupuis (the original Paris in *La belle Hélène*). Ghislaine Raphanel is no less attractively sweet-voiced as his daughter Fiorella, and Bernard Pisani pulls off the treasurer's *tour de force* with splendid aplomb. There is also the usual fine bunch of supporting characters. The one disappointment is with Colette Alliot-Lugaz's Fragoletto, a 'trousers' role to which she brings a voice that at times has a somewhat unpleasant edge to it. The recording is clear and natural, contributing to the lightness of touch of the performance, and with some excellent action effects. Altogether a most worthy addition to EMI's admirable sequence of complete Offenbach recordings.

Offenbach Christopher Columbus.

Maurice Arthur *ten* Christopher Columbus
Joy Roberts *sop* Beatriz
Johanna Peters *mez* Rosa Columbus
Lissa Gray *sop* Fleurette Columbus
Marilyn Hill Smith *sop* Gretel Columbus
Christian du Plessis *bar* Luis de Torres
Alan Opie *bar* Chief of Police
Anna Dawson *sop* Queen Isabella
Alec Bregonzi *ten* King Ferdinand
Clive Harré *bar* Tourist
John Duxbury *ten* Waiter
Rosemary Ashe *sop* Princess Minnehaha Columbus, Esperanza
Celia Kite *sop* Carmelita
Kathleen Smales *mez* Manuela
Amilia Dixey *mez* Valencia
Geoffrey Mitchell Choir; London Mozart Players / Alun Francis.
Opera Rara Ⓟ ① ORC002 (two discs: 124 minutes: ADD). Notes and text included. Recorded 1977.

You will look in vain for *Christopher Columbus* in lists of Offenbach's works. It was put together by Opera Rara for the 1976 American bicentenary celebrations, using a totally new book allied to music from a variety of Offenbach pieces. But not without reason did the *Daily Mail* call it "the best Offenbach opera Offenbach never wrote". It is an absolutely hilarious piece, right from the opening chorus in which the young ladies of Cordóba express their boredom at having nothing to do but snap their castanets and shout "Olé!". The lyrics are quite brilliant and, if the whole doesn't sound quite like an authentic Offenbach piece, it is only for the very good reason that it largely forswears dialogue and the lead-ins to numbers in favour of the juicy central bits. With singers and singing actors of the quality of Marilyn Hill Smith, Johanna Peters, Anna Dawson and Alec Bregonzi supporting Maurice Arthur, it would be difficult to imagine the piece performed with greater skill or relish. If you want a CD set for sheer uninhibited enjoyment, this should be it.

Offenbach Les contes d'Hoffmann.

Plácido Domingo *ten* Hoffmann
Dame Joan Sutherland *sop* Olympia, Giulietta, Antonia, Stella
Gabriel Bacquier *bar* Lindorf, Coppélius, Dapertutto, Dr Miracle
Huguette Tourangeau *mez* La Muse, Nicklausse
Jacques Charon *ten* Spalanzani
Hugues Cuénod *ten* Andrès, Cochenille, Pitichinaccio, Frantz
André Neury *bar* Schlemil
Paul Plishka *bass* Crespel
Margarita Lilowa *mez* Voice of Antonia's Mother
Roland Jacques *bar* Luther
Lausanne Pro Arte Chorus; Du Brassus Chorus;
Suisse Romande Chorus and Orchestra / Richard Bonynge.
Decca Ⓟ ① 417 363-2DH2 (two discs: 143 minutes). Notes, text and translation included. Recorded 1968.

This is a wonderfully refreshing set, made the more sparkling in the CD transfer, which enhances the sense of presence and immediacy in the often-complicated action. The story emerges crystal-clear, even the black ending to the Giulietta scene in Venice, which in Bonynge's text restores the original idea of the heroine dying from a draught of poison, while the dwarf, Pitichinaccio shrieks in delight. As Bonynge says in his explanation of his chosen text (in the insert-booklet), the original ending is "far more in the spirit of Offenbach". One also has to applaud his rather more controversial decision to put the Giulietta scene in the middle and leave the dramatically weighty Antonia scene till last. The epilogue is then the more effective when Bonynge uses the unauthentic septet of the Giulietta scene as the missing quartet, bringing a climactic ensemble reprise of the Barcarolle.

That also makes the role of Stella the more significant, giving extra point to the decision to have the same singer take all four heroine roles. With Dame Joan available it was a natural decision, and though in spoken dialogue she is less comfortable in the Giulietta scene than the rest, the contrasting portraits in each scene are all very convincing, with the voice brilliant in the doll scene, warmly sensuous in the Giulietta scene and powerfully dramatic as well as tender in the Antonia scene. Gabriel Bacquier gives sharply intense performances, firm and dark vocally, in the four villain roles, Hugues Cuénod contributes delightful vignettes in the four *comprimario* tenor roles, while Domingo establishes at the very start the distinctive bite in his portrait of Hoffmann himself. He may at times lack a honeyed French half-tone, but this is both a powerful and a perceptive assumption of the role, pointing forward to his later stage performances in Salzburg, at Covent Garden and elsewhere.

Banding in Acts 2 and 3 could usefully be more generous, but with the acoustic of the much-lamented Victoria Hall in Geneva vividly captured, and with Bonynge drawing consistently lively playing from the Suisse Romande Orchestra this will, arguably, always be first choice for this opera. But read on ...!

Offenbach Les contes d'Hoffmann.

Nicolai Gedda *ten* Hoffmann
Gianna d'Angelo *sop* Olympia
Dame Elisabeth Schwarzkopf *sop* Giulietta
Victoria de los Angeles *sop* Antonia
Renée Faure *spkr* Stella, La Muse
Jean-Christophe Benoit *bar* Nicklausse
Nikola Ghiuselev *bass* Lindorf
George London *bass* Coppélius, Dr Miracle
Ernest Blanc *bar* Dapertutto
Michel Sénéchal *ten* Spalanzani
Jacques Loreau *ten* Andrès, Cochenille, Pitichinaccio, Frantz
Jean-Pierre Laffage *bar* Schlemil, Luther
Robert Geay *bass* Crespel
Christiane Gayraud *mez* Voice of Antonia's Mother
Jeannine Collard *mez* Second voice in the Barcarolle
René Duclos Choir; Paris Conservatoire Orchestra / André Cluytens.
EMI Ⓜ ① CMS7 63222-2 (two discs: 152 minutes: ADD). Notes, text and translation included. Recorded 1964-5.

If there is one thing certain about a comparative review of *Les contes d'Hoffmann*, it must be that it will end in no clear recommendation. Every recording seems to bring a different idea as to the text to use and whether to use the same singers for the principal roles in the central acts. This set opts for the 1907 Choudens score that was very much the standard at the time, as it has been for most of this century. Its casting represents an obvious attempt to use the opera as a star-vehicle, with contrasted singers for the principal soprano roles as well as for the four villain roles. The particular curiosity of the recording, though, comes by way of the use of a baritone rather than a mezzo-soprano, Nicklausse, necessitating the use of a mezzo-soprano just to take the second vocal part in the Barcarolle.

That the result is a considerable disappointment has nothing to do with textural matters and everything to do with the performance itself. Most particularly, there is a curious lack of overall continuity of style. Could it be, one wonders, that the conductor, André Cluytens, panders too much to the three soprano heroines? With the spotlight thus thrown upon the three ladies, their weaknesses are all the more highlighted. Gianna d'Angelo is no more than routine as the doll Olympia and Victoria de los Angeles sounds uncharacteristically insecure. Elisabeth Schwarzkopf is ... well Elisabeth Schwarzkopf – a singer who can do no wrong, but undoubtedly a curiously aristocratic courtesan. As for the villains, the two imported basses, Nikola Ghiuselev and George London both have a decidedly gruff, unattractive tone to add to insecure French.

The other curious lack of continuity lies between the leading roles and the subsidiary ones. The latter, it may be noticed, are sung by native French singers, in contrast to the internationalism of the principals. And how it shows! There is such a feeling of the true French style coming through when the principals briefly leave the stage to Michel Sénéchal's Spalanzani, Jacques Loreau's four servants, Ernest Blanc's splendid Dapertutto and indeed, Jean-Christophe Benoit in his charming performance of Nicklausse's "Une fille aux yeux d'émail". Nicolai Gedda is the one principal singer with sufficient of a feel for the French style to bridge these inconsistencies – a *tour de force* from him indeed. Ultimately that may not be enough to make a compelling case for this recording beyond the undoubted historical value of hearing what this celebrated cast of singers make of the work.

Offenbach Les contes d'Hoffmann.

Raoul Jobin *ten* Hoffmann
Renée Doria *sop* Olympia
Vina Bovy *sop* Giulietta
Géori Boué *sop* Antonia

Fanély Revoil *mez* Nicklausse
Louis Musy *bar* Lindorf
André Pernet *bass* Coppélius
Charles Soix *bass* Dapertutto
Roger Bourdin *bar* Dr Miracle
René Lapelletrie *ten* Spalanzani
Camille Maurane *bar* Hermann
Chorus and Orchestra of the Opéra-Comique, Paris / André Cluytens.
EMI mono Ⓜ ① CMS5 65260-2 (two discs: 130 minutes: ADD). Notes and text included.
Recorded 1948.

It is a generally held, received opinion that the decline of true French vocal style set in around the 1940s and that 'French' voices in some way disappeared. The truth is much more complicated – it was the decline in fashion for French opera and song and the long periods of inactivity at both houses in Paris, and the consequent lack of interest shown by recording companies, that denied many French singers of the 1940s, until the 1980s, an international platform.

In the 1930s in Paris, Raoul Jobin and José Luccioni were the two great opera matinée-idols. Jobin was a French Canadian, made his début in 1930 and was soon singing at both the Opéra, as Faust, Lohengrin and Raoul in *Les Huguenots*, and at the Opéra-Comique, where he was a favourite Hoffmann and Don José. This recording may perhaps find him just a little late in his career. His years at the Metropolitan (throughout the German occupation) obviously took their toll, when he sang roles that were too heavy for him in such a huge theatre. However, the splendour of this earlier Cluytens version is the authenticity of the vocal style and the diction of such stalwarts of the Opéra-Comique ensemble as Louis Musy, Roger Bourdin, Fanély Revoil (better known as an operetta singer) and, luxurious casting, Camille Maurane in the small part of Hermann.

The three heroines are well inside their roles, but are afflicted with a little strain in the higher-lying passages. Renée Doria sang all these parts later in her career – when this recording was made she was just at the outset, having made her début in Paris in 1944. Her Olympia is strong on the *staccato* notes but a bit fragile in the long phrases – this doll broke quite easily, one imagines. In the same act, André Pernet, a great figure from pre-war Paris (he created Shylock in Hahn's *Le marchand de Venise* and the title-role in Enescu's *Oedipe*), is a superb Coppélius. In the Venice act, Vina Bovy is dramatically convincing as Giulietta, but hasn't much vocal sheen left (she made her début in 1919). Géori Boué, the Antonia, is one of the great figures from French post-war opera, but one feels that Giulietta would have been her role ideally. As for Jobin, despite some strain, he makes a convincing poet. Although there is such strong competition on CD where *Hoffmann* is concerned, this historic version is really essential listening for a sense of style if the work absorbs you.

Offenbach Les contes d'Hoffmann.
Plácido Domingo *ten* Hoffmann
Luciana Serra *sop* Olympia
Agnes Baltsa *mez* Giulietta
Ileana Cotrubas *sop* Antonia
Claire Powell *mez* Nicklausse, La Muse
Robert Lloyd *bass* Lindorf
Sir Geraint Evans *bar* Coppélius
Siegmund Nimsgern *bass-bar* Dapertutto
Nikola Ghiuselev *bass* Dr Miracle
Robert Tear *ten* Spalanzani
Philip Gelling *bass* Schlémil
Gwynne Howell *bass* Crespel
Phyllis Cannan *mez* Voice of Antonia's Mother
Paul Crook *ten* Andrès, Cochenille
Francis Egerton *ten* Pitichinaccio
Bernard Dickerson *ten* Frantz
Eric Garrett *bar* Luther
Robin Leggate *ten* Nathanaël
John Rawnsley *bar* Hermann
Deanne Bergsma *mute* Stella
Chorus and Orchestra of the Royal Opera House, Covent Garden / Georges Prêtre.
Stage Director: **John Schlesinger.**
NVC Arts Ⓟ ⚏ 0630-19392-3 (150 minutes). Filmed at a performance in the Royal Opera House, Covent Garden in January 1981.

This is John Schlesinger's award-winning production of *Hoffmann*. Obliged to use the old Choudens edition by Carlos Kleiber, who promptly ducked out, he made brilliant use of it – for example, by having the three villains metamorphose into Lloyd's Lindorf, a demonic Offenbach lookalike. The cast is a Covent Garden roll of honour, but, more important, an excellent ensemble. If some performances – Evans, Gelling – suffer a little from age or youth, they remain splendidly vital; and there are some notable débuts. Serra and Baltsa make, respectively, a hilariously convincing, beautifully sung Olympia, and magnetically cold, vampiric courtesan; Powell is an ideally vibrant Nicklausse/Muse – for once the doubling makes sense. Domingo crowns it all with a superbly sung, galvanic performance, both as the Prologue's dreadfully convincing poetic loser and a naïve, dashing younger self. A shame that at the end he loses the pen with which he's supposed to start scribbling! Prêtre may be less dynamic than Kleiber, but he's very much there, with a warm, romantic reading. Sound and vision are excellent.

Offenbach Orphée aux Enfers.

Michel Sénéchal *ten* Orpheus
Mady Mesplé *sop* Eurydice
Charles Burles *ten* Aristeus-Pluto
Michel Trempont *bar* Jupiter
Danièle Castaing *sop* Juno
Jane Rhodes *mez* Public Opinion
Bruce Brewer *ten* John Styx
Michèle Command *sop* Venus
Jane Berbié *mez* Cupid
Michèle Pena *sop* Diana
Jean-Philippe Lafont *bar* Mars
André Mallabrera *ten* Mercury
Yan -Pascal Tortelier *vn*
Les Petits Chanteurs à la Croix Potencée;
Toulouse Capitole Chorus and Orchestra / Michel Plasson.
EMI Ⓟ Ⓒ CDS7 49647-2 (two discs: 140 minutes: ADD). Notes, text and translation included. Recorded 1978.

BBC RADIO 3
90-93 FM

When this complete *Orpheus in the Underworld* in the original French appeared, its first recording in almost 30 years, it was welcomed not merely as a gap filler but as a very considerable success in its own right and indeed a veritable Offenbach landmark. Although Michel Plasson has sometimes seemed to adopt excessively fast speeds with Offenbach scores, here he seems far more relaxed, caressing the tender moments delectably (Eurydice's "Invocation to Death", for instance), whilst capturing admirably the natural high spirits and lilt of much of the score. Most significantly, perhaps, he makes much more effective use of the changes of tempo that are such an important part of Offenbach's technique. He has the benefit, too, of a first-rate chorus and orchestra, a truly delightful children's chorus and a team of soloists of largely exemplary quality. Mady Mesplé is sweet enough in the unforced range of her voice but shows a decidedly thin and unpleasantly squeaky tone at the top end. Otherwise it is hardly possible to have any serious complaints. Michel Sénéchal is a thoroughly dependable Orpheus, and to mention just a few of the many supporting singers, Charles Burles is a polished Pluto, Jane Berbié a honey-toned Cupid and Jane Rhodes, Offenbach interpreter *par excellence*, has an important contribution to the Act 1 finale which is really superbly done.

The accompanying notes remain curiously reticent about the fact that Plasson follows the revised 1874 version of the operetta. The original *Orphée aux enfers* of 1858 was a relatively modest two-act affair, but in 1874 Offenbach expanded the four scenes into four full acts, with additional characters, songs and ballet numbers. For the expanded version Offenbach provided a new prelude (once available on an old Concert Hall LP). Plasson understandably abridges this curiously rambling affair, but otherwise he gives a very full version of the 1874 score. Only Offenbach's 1874 Overture is in abridged form. The two well-filled discs contain a minimum of dialogue. Though the additional numbers (mostly in the third act, in Pluto's palace) are hardly germane to the plot and thus tend to be omitted in stage productions, they are undeniably attractive. Indeed the very unfamiliarity and charms of such numbers as Mercury's witty rondo, the policemen's chorus and the "Couplets des Baisers" which Miss Berbié sings so fetchingly, will for many be a particular attraction of this recording. The sound is well balanced with a good sense of perspective. A sparkling recording, and a joyful achievement still.

Offenbach Orphée aux Enfers (sung in English).

David Fieldsend *ten* Orpheus
Mary Hegarty *sop* Eurydice
Barry Patterson *ten* Aristeus-Pluto
Richard Suart *bar* Jupiter
Frances McCafferty *sop* Juno
Jill Pert *contr* Public Opinion
Gareth Jones *bar* John Styx
Sian Wyn Gibson *sop* Venus
Rosemarie Arthars *mez* Cupid

Joanne Pullen *sop* Diana
Carl Donohoe *bar* Mars
David Cavendish *ten* Mercury
D'Oyly Carte Opera Chorus; D'Oyly Carte Opera Orchestra / John Owen Edwards.
Sony Classical ℗ ① S2K66616 (two discs: 99 minutes: DDD). Recorded 1994.

The D'Oyly Carte Opera does the CD collector a great service in alighting upon Offenbach's *Orphée aux enfers*. The work has been surprisingly neglected on record with only two complete recordings and a single disc of excerpts in French since the advent of LP. In English, meanwhile, we have had just two excerpt recordings – the classic 1960 Sadler's Wells version with June Bronhill on EMI and the rather less satisfactory ENO account of 1987 on TER Classics.

Offenbach created the work in two versions. Here, apart from the addition of Mercury's number from the later 1874 concept, the D'Oyly Carte have settled for the simple original of 1858. Thus no large-scale Overture (composed by Carl Binder for Vienna) but, instead, Offenbach's small-scale introduction, which more aptly sets the atmosphere of antiquity against which the satire of the Orpheus legend was presented to the 1858 audience. Hearing the work complete in English, and with the benefit of a helpful amount of dialogue, the English-speaking armchair listener has a unique opportunity to understand just what Offenbach was all about – not least with regard to the character of Public Opinion. The whole of the original concept has been followed with uncommon and commendable fidelity – right down to Aristeus's falsetto passage in his Act 1 solo. At the same time, the straightness of presentation against the background of 136 years of cultural and musical development can readily enough leave one wondering what the fuss was all about in 1858. Indeed, that was already the case by 1874 when Offenbach felt moved to re-cast the work as a large-scale spectacular with extra numbers and large forces.

The singing on this recording is of the high standard that one would expect from a team of leading British musical-theatre performers. The contributions of Jill Pert as Public Opinion, Richard Suart as Jupiter and Gareth Jones as John Styx are particularly likeable. On the other hand, the use of regional accents becomes a little wearing at times, and the somewhat clinical recorded sound tends to heighten an impression that this is an *Orpheus* with some sparkle missing. There is a primness about Mary Hegarty's Euridice, for instance, that one doesn't find in the mischief-in-the-voice singing of June Bronhill in the old Sadler's Wells recording. Still, as a means of hearing Offenbach's marvellous melodies in their full context, this Sony Classical recording does the English listener undeniably good service.

Offenbach La Périchole.

Régine Crespin *sop* La Périchole
Alain Vanzo *ten* Piquillo
Jules Bastin *bass* Don Andrès
Gérard Friedmann *ten* Miguel de Panatellas
Jacques Trigeau *bar* Don Pedro
Aimé Besançon *ten* First Notary
Paul Guigue *ten* Second Notary
Rebecca Roberts *sop* Guadalena, Manuelita
Eva Saurova *sop* Berginella, Ninetta
Geneviève Baudoz *mez* Mastrilla, Frasquinella
Ine Meister *mez* Bramdilla
Rhine Opera Chorus; Strasbourg Philharmonic Orchestra / Alain Lombard.
Erato Libretto Ⓜ ① 2292-45686-2 (two discs: 86 minutes: ADD). Notes, text and translation included. Recorded 1976.

BBC RADIO 3
90-93 FM

Of all Offenbach's major collaborations with Meilhac and Halévy, *La Périchole* is the one that oozes charm. The satirical touch is there, but the edge is less sharp, and one detects a vein of genuine feeling for the fate of the Peruvian street-singer heroine that one never does with Eurydice, Helen, Boulotte or the Grand-Duchess of Gerolstein.

The splendid songs of Offenbach composed for Hortense Schneider (the Letter song, "Ah! quel dîner", "Ah! que les hommes sont bêtes" and "Je t'adore, brigand") head up a richly melodic score. Régine Crespin is a somewhat matronly Périchole, but she knows how to tease the textural and melodic phrases in a way that brings the best out of them. Her Piquillo, Alain Vanzo, is the ideal light Offenbach tenor, while Jules Bastin brings experience to the role of the Viceroy, without quite capturing all its comic possibilities. Overall, the performance succeeds better than the more recent Plasson/EMI version, in which Berganza and Carreras never quite sound at home. Alain Lombard directs sympathetically, if not managing the finesse that Igor Markevitch brought to EMI's classic 1958 recording.

The Plasson set scores over this Erato in having the CD-change between acts and in having linking dialogue. On the original LP issue, Erato provided a linking narration by Alain Decaux, which survives in the libretto but has here been edited out of the performance. This presumably explains why, though the box claims a playing time of 100 minutes, neither CD lasts more than a few seconds over 43 minutes. But even if the CD transfer has been somewhat thoughtlessly carried out, Erato are to be praised for providing a complete libretto at mid price. Those who do not know the score should not miss this chance to fall under its spell.

Offenbach Pomme d'Api.

Jean-Philppe Lafont *bar* Rabastene
Léonard Pezzino *ten* Gustave
Mady Mesplé *sop* Catherine
Monte Carlo Philharmonic Orchestra / Manuel Rosenthal.

Offenbach M. Choufleuri restera chez lui.

Jean-Philppe Lafont *bar* Choufleuri
Mady Mesplé *sop* Ernestine
Charles Burles *ten* Babylas
Michel Trempont *bar* Petermann
Michel Hamel *ten* Balandard
Emmy Greger *mez* Mme Balandard
Jean Laforge Choral Ensemble; Monte Carlo Philharmonic Orchestra / Manuel Rosenthal.

Offenbach Mesdames de la Halle.

Michel Hamel *ten* Madame Poiretapée
Jean-Philippe Lafont *bar* Madame Beurrefondu
Michel Trempont *bar* Madame Madou
Monique Pouradier-Duteil *sop* La Marchand de Plaisir
Olympe Dumaine *sop* Marchande de Légumes
Marcel Quillevéré *ten* Le Marchande d'Habits
Charles Burles *ten* Raflafla
Jean-Marie Freméau *bar* Le Commissaire
Léonard Pezzino *ten* Croûte-au-pôt
Mady Mesplé *sop* Ciboulette
Jean Laforge Choral Ensemble; Monte Carlo Philharmonic Orchestra / Manuel Rosenthal.
EMI Ⓜ ① CDS7 49361-2 (two discs: 137 minutes: DDD). Notes, texts and translations included. Recorded 1982.

This Offenbach triple bill presents three different sides of the composer. The charming three-character domestic comedy *Pomme d'Api* is a late work with some especially rewarding soprano solos. *M. Choufleuri* is a more typically zany piece of Offenbach with operatic parodies provoked by the need to impersonate the singers Sontag, Rubini and Tamburini to avoid the host of a soirée losing face before his guests. *Mesdames de la Halle* is a work written on a larger scale, with a full chorus and a group of female market vendors sung by men. It hardly needs saying that there are attractively piquant melodies throughout.

Mady Mesplé, if a little squeaky at the top of the voice, is generally accomplished and agile in the three soprano roles. What really makes the recording, though, is the excellent team of male singers who are so much at home in this repertoire. The humour of the pieces is all there, though the importance of the dialogue means that English listeners will probably need to make good use of the libretto. The recording is well balanced and clear, and the results are altogether delicious. But is one being ungenerous in wishing that EMI had packaged these works a CD apiece rather than splitting *M. Choufleuri* across discs?

Offenbach Robinson Crusoe (sung in English).

John Brecknock *ten* Robinson Crusoe
Yvonne Kenny *sop* Edwige
Roderick Kennedy *bass* Sir William Crusoe
Enid Hartle *mez* Lady Deborah Crusoe
Marilyn Hill Smith *sop* Suzanne
Alexander Oliver *ten* Toby
Sandra Browne *mez* Man Friday
Alan Opie *bar* Jim Cocks
Wyndham Parfitt *bar* Will Atkins
Geoffrey Mitchell Choir; Royal Philharmonic Orchestra / Alun Francis.
Opera Rara Ⓟ ① ORC007 (three discs: 164 minutes: ADD). Notes and English text included. Recorded 1980.

Opera Rara's recording of Offenbach's *Robinson Crusoe* may lack the unremitting high spirits of the same company's *Christopher Columbus* (reviewed above), but at least the Defoe adaptation is a genuine Offenbach work, more obviously constructed as an integral *opéra-comique* score, rather than a pastiche piece compiled from Offenbach plums, as is the case with Opera Rara's American bicentennial celebration. Perhaps surprisingly, *Robinson Crusoe* was composed not for one of Offenbach's operetta theatres but for the Opéra-Comique, so that it displays some more exalted, more symphonic writing than was often Offenbach's wont. The First Act, in the Crusoes' home in Bristol, is perhaps overlong; but the other two, set on the desert island on which the major characters congregate, are constantly diverting. A symphonic entr'acte, a *rêverie* for Robinson, Man Friday's marvellous solo, Edwige's waltz song (recorded by Dame Joan Sutherland for Decca in the 1970s and since reissued on CD) and a splendid quarrelling duet (familiar from the ballet, *Gaîté parisienne*) are just some of the magnificent musical numbers in Act 2.

Don White's English version may have taken liberties with the original libretto; but that is all in the interest of improving the entertainment value for an English-language audience. With a fine cast of singers performing the musical score absolutely complete and unaltered, the recording should be of interest to students of French *opéra-comique* almost as much as to lovers of Offenbach, to whom it should give unbounded joy.

Carl Orff   German 1895-1982

Orff Antigonae.

Inge Borkh *sop* Antigonae
Claudia Hellmann *mez* Ismene
Carlos Alexander *bar* Kreon
Gerhard Stolze *ten* A Guard
Fritz Uhl *ten* Hämon
Ernst Haefliger *ten* Tiresias
Kim Borg *bass* A Messenger
Hetty Plümacher *contr* Eurydike
Kieth Engen *bass* Chorus leader
Bavarian Radio Chorus and Symphony Orchestra / Ferdinand Leitner.
DG 20th Century Classics Ⓜ Ⓓ 437 721-2GC3 (three discs: 160 minutes: ADD). Recorded 1961.

Not many operas take such painstaking care as Orff's *Antigonae* to communicate their chosen text with maximum clarity. Hölderlin's translation of Sophocles (almost uncut, so far as one can tell) is set for the most part syllabically, often in monotone, accompanied and punctuated by simple ostinato figures. There are many passages of unaccompanied recitative on one or two notes; vocal lines expand to melody only for crucially dramatic or expressive phrases. The orchestra (much percussion including five types of xylophone, six each of pianos, flutes, oboes and muted trumpets, four harps and a string section of double basses only) have chosen to combine maximum impact at climaxes and minimum interference with the voices.

The deliberate, even brutal bareness of Orff's language (more minimal than the minimalists) is an effective way of emphasizing the mythic implacability of the plot, at the price of underplaying Sophocles's often poignant lyricism: the beautiful choral invocation to Bacchus, for example ("O Thou the many-named, son of the Thunderer"), here placed at the opening of Act 5, is belted out ferociously with massive onslaughts from the percussion section. You may find the price worth paying as melodic formulae insistently hinted at earlier crystallize into the starkly eloquent phrases of Antigonae's farewell to life (heroically and rivetingly sung by Inge Borkh) or, soon after, as pounding rhythms pointed by six skirling flutes give a genuine impression of ritual dance to the chorus's grave meditations on human destiny. But it does take three acts of (albeit resourcefully) heightened speech and of monotone chanting (much of it very closely derived from the opening scene of Stravinsky's *Oedipus Rex*) to reach that high point.

Since DG do not provide the text to which Orff so austerely deferred, you will need, unless your German is fluent, to acquire a copy of Sophocles's play; or you will find the opera quite easy to follow using E. F. Watling's translation for Penguin Classics. The performance is a devoted one, sumptuously cast; only a slight edge on some of Borkh's more luridly intense utterances suggests the recording's age.

Orff Die Kluge.

Marcel Cordes *bar* The King
Gottlob Frick *bass* The Peasant
Dame Elisabeth Schwarzkopf *sop* The Peasant's Daughter
Georg Wieter *bass* Jailer
Rudolf Christ *ten* Man with the donkey
Benno Kusche *bar* Man with the mule
Paul Kuen *ten* First Vagabond
Hermann Prey *bar* Second Vagabond
Gustav Neidlinger *bass-bar* Third Vagabond

Orff Der Mond.

Rudolf Christ *ten* Narrator
Karl Schmitt-Walter *bar* First Young Man
Helmut Graml *bar* Second Young Man
Paul Kuen *ten* Third Young Man
Peter Lagger *bass* Fourth Young Man
Albrecht Peter *bar* A Peasant
Hans Hotter *bass-bar* An Old Man
Children's choir; Philharmonia Chorus and Orchestra / Wolfgang Sawallisch.
EMI Ⓜ Ⓒ CMS7 63712-2 (two discs: 147 minutes: ADD). Notes included. Recorded 1956-7.

On the surface it would seem that *Die Kluge* and *Der Mond* make ideal bedfellows – both are allegorical fairy-tale operas using as their primary source tales collected by the brothers Grimm, both are scored for similar forces, and both fit neatly on to one CD each of a two-disc set. And yet it is a strangely unsatisfying and uneven experience listening to these as a pair. The earlier of the two, *Der Mond* ("The Moon"), is by far the most interesting, both musically and dramatically. Chronologically it follows hard on the heels of *Carmina Burana*, and those who know and love that work will not be disappointed with what *Der Mond* has to offer: colour, energy, inventiveness and a liberal sprinkling of the same bawdy lasciviousness found in the earlier score – "we're going to drink and fornicate and booze and – if we can – commit adultery" announce the four resurrected youths in the underworld scenes! The structure is musically pleasing, and the dramatic content has both pace and substance enough to fill out its 75-minute duration.

Die Kluge ("The Wise Woman") on the other hand seems to be far too long for its rather paltry content, there's far too much *sprech* and not enough music, and the little there is pales in comparison to *Carmina* or *Der Mond*. It may be successful on stage, but heard on disc it becomes repetitive and tedious in the extreme (a problem confounded even more in both of these recordings, as we are denied English translations of the texts). Sawallisch's recordings have worn the test of time extremely well. There's plenty of refinement and attention to detail, with a wonderful complement of soloists: Elisabeth Schwarzkopf gives a convincing portrayal of the peasant's daughter in *Die Kluge* with a beautifully pure non-operatic tone, and the Three Vagabonds give admirably characterful performances. In *Der Mond*, Hans Hotter's Old Man has a tendency to wobble somewhat in the more dramatic moments, though it must be said that he achieves the right blend of God-like retribution and joviality required of this part. Despite any reservations, the performance can be recommended for its fairy-tale atmosphere, its production qualities and its authoritative performance. If it's more of *Carmina Burana* you want, then these operas are the next logical step in exploring Orff's music.

Giovanni Pacini
Italian 1796-1867

Pacini Saffo.

Francesca Pedaci *sop* Saffo
Carlo Ventre *ten* Faone
Roberto de Candia *bar* Alcandro
Mariana Pentcheva *mez* Climene
Gemma Bertagnolli *sop* Dirce
Aled Hall *ten* Ippia
Davide Baronchelli *bass* Lisimaco
Wexford Festival Chorus; National Symphony Orchestra of Ireland / Maurizio Benini.
Marco Polo Ⓟ Ⓒ 8 223883/4 (two discs: 138 minutes: DDD). Notes, text and translation included. Recorded 1995.

Wexford has long been the home of lost operatic causes that speedily become winners. Giovanni Pacini's *Saffo* is a good example. Widely acclaimed in its time (establishing itself as a favourite in North as well as South America), the opera gradually disappeared from view, as did the composer himself. Yet he wrote over 80 operas, and *Saffo* is generally considered his masterpiece: the first fully ripened fruit of a period, nearly five years long, of retirement from composition, during which he studied, thought and prepared. It appeared in 1840, the year of Donizetti's *La fille du régiment* and *La favorite*, both of them written for the opera in Paris. With Bellini dead and Rossini retired, Pacini may have felt that the way was open before him; a young fellow called Verdi, whose first opera had enjoyed a modest success in Milan the previous year, would scarcely have caused him sleepless nights.

What we now think of the opera, for the first time on a commercial recording, must depend partly on our ability or willingness to hear it as within its period. Without this adjustment it will certainly sound naïve at first, its eventual achievement appearing largely to be of a magpie nature, drawing most obviously on Bellini's *Norma*. Put into context, it offers considerably more. Like the best of its kind, it represents the art-form of Italian opera at its height. Before 'progress' had nibbled away in the interests of dramatic realism, it sought and found its own scope for creativity within the evolved form in which the art became most distinctively and uncompromisingly itself. So, cabaletta duly follows aria or cavatina, ensemble follows solo or duet, but all is skilfully managed; the characters become real through their music, and the emotional climaxes gain force from the fine surge of singing-voices in ensemble, unique to opera among all art-forms.

Another of its merits is the workmanship of the orchestral score; but essentially it calls for real singing. At Wexford, the outstanding success was that of the Climene, Mariana Pentcheva, while Francesca Pedaci's Saffo was rated as rather tame by comparison. On record, a strong preference is less likely to suggest itself: if the Bulgarian mezzo has the more opulent voice, Pedaci's has refreshing purity and a clean focus. With both, there is a slight consciousness of role and voice not quite matching, Pentcheva's tone a trifle too grand and noble (Stignani-like) for the maiden, and Pedaci's too much of the young lyric soprano for a part which, of its kind, is rather low-lying, written for Francilla Pixis, who is usually described as a contralto. The tenor part is hardly a sympathetic one, and Carlo Ventre does little to make it more so, though he sings out sturdily enough. Of Alcandro, whose vindictive pursuit of Saffo takes on a different aspect when he learns she is his daughter, it is probable that more could be made than is evident in de Candia's singing, conscientious as it is.

Recorded from the stage, the performance sometimes has the singers less than ideally placed, and the orchestral sound is somewhat boxed. Still, the catalogue début is a worthy one, and worthy of note too. Congratulations are due to the record company as well as the Festival, and to scholar-advocates such as Philip Gossett and Tom Kaufman as well as the more-than-able conductor, Maurizio Benini.

Krzysztof Penderecki Polish 1933

Penderecki Das Teufel von Loudun.
   Tatiana Troyanos *mez* Jeanne
   Andrzej Hiolski *bar* Urbain Grandier
   Bernard Ladysz *bass* Father Barré
   Hans Sotin *bass* Father Rangier
   Horst Wilhelm *ten* Father Mignon
   Kurt Marschner *ten* Adam
   Heinz Blankenburg *bar* Mannoury
   Helmut Melchert *ten* Baron de Laubardemont
   Chorus and Orchestra of the Hamburg State Opera / Marek Janowski.
   Philips Ⓟ Ⓒ 446 328-2PH2 (two discs: 106 minutes: ADD). Notes, text and translation included. Recorded 1969.

"The Devils" – for many this title will evoke, not the Aldous Huxley novel or the John Whiting play – but the Ken Russell film of 1971, with its pungently parodistic Maxwell Davies score. Penderecki got there first – his opera was premièred in 1969 – but his music has worn far less well than that of Maxwell Davies. Even in a performance that radiates competence and commitment, the experience can sometimes be dispiriting. Penderecki's retreat from his early expressionism is signalled in his first opera's rejection of complexity, especially in the vocal writing, and the occasional accumulations of dense choral and orchestral textures (so effective in the *St Luke Passion*) seem like mere sound effects grafted on for the sake of a little variety. Given the extravagantly harrowing subject-matter – madness, torture and many other manifestations of human behaviour at its worst – we can be grateful that the drama unfolds with such alacrity, and that the performance spares us several of the screams and other noises called for in the text. Yet there's an air of the perfunctory in the way Penderecki so often falls back on normal or heightened speech, even at such crucial moments as the pronouncing of the death sentence on the wayward yet honourable priest, Grandier, and his response.

This is not the only first opera one could name in which a long, incident-packed libretto makes difficulties for the inexperienced composer, and it's a pity that Penderecki didn't spread himself more in the processions, and the various episodes of pandemonium. One is glad that the final, fateful encounter between Grandier and the deluded nun, who is the cause of his doom, is so delicately understated, but that understatement would be still more effective if the earlier music possessed more dramatic weight and substance. This recording was made around the time of the première, though as far as one can tell (the booklet is reticent) it is not of an actual stage performance. The principal singers are given strong forward placement: by contrast the chorus sound improbably distant, even perhaps pre-recorded. The stalwart cast, including such admirably characterful singers as Tatiana Troyanos, Hans Sotin and Helmut Melchert, help to ensure that the experience of listening is not unrewarding, and Philips deserve praise for providing a complete libretto.

Giovanni Pergolesi Italian 1710-1736

Pergolesi Livietta e Tracollo.
   Nancy Argenta *sop* Livietta
   Werner van Mechelen *bass* Tracollo

Pergolesi La serva padrona.

Patricia Biccire *sop* Serpina
Donato di Stefano *bass* Uberto
La Petite Bande / Sigiswald Kuijken *vn*.
Accent Ⓕ ① ACC96123D (80 minutes: DDD: 11/97). ✏ Notes and text included. Recorded
during performances at the Luna Theatre, Brussels on November 21st and 22nd, 1996.

La serva padrona, most famous of *intermezzi*, is given here with a rare but comparable companion-piece. *Livietta e Tracollo* was written a year later and had its première in the same theatre, the San Bartolomeo at Naples, in 1734. It also is for two characters, light soprano and *buffo* bass, with two sections, originally to be played in the intervals of the evening's *opera seria*. Rather more complicated and improbable than *La serva padrona*, it tells of a girl disguised as a French peasant (male) seeking vengeance on a robber who in turn appears disguised as a pregnant Pole. She succeeds in the first half, while in the second the man, now disguised as an astrologer, has more luck and they agree to get married. Musically it is not so very inferior to the *Serva*. Both have more wit in the music than in the libretto, with deft parodies of *opera seria* and a popular appeal in the repeated phrases of their arias, catchy without being coarse. In an interview for the booklet, the conductor Sigiswald Kuijken "dares", as he says, to suggest a parallel with "our purely recreational television-films". One is unsure quite how helpful that is, though it may explain why one wonders from time to time whether one should not be doing something more useful and yet still doesn't switch off.

For *Livietta e Tracollo* there is no other recording currently available in the catalogue (a version from 1961 was recorded on Cetra), and the performance here is a lively one with Nancy Argenta as a resourceful and not too pertly soubrettish Livietta. *La serva padrona* had two previous recordings (Maier on Deutsche Harmonia Mundi and Gilbert Bezzina on Pierre Verany), though neither had the extra attraction of such a coupling. Kuijken's Petite Bande are numerically and stylistically comparable to the Ensemble Baroque de Nice (Pierre Verany) and the Collegium Aureum (Deutsche Harmonia Mundi), but play with a more distinctively 'period' tone. The speeds are sprightly and the rhythms light-footed. In both works, the women are better than the men, who (on this showing) lack the comic touch. Patricia Biccire sings attractively, especially in her 'sincere' aria, "A Serpina penserate", and she paces her recitatives artfully. A lower baroque pitch is used and the final number is the short duet "Per te io ho nel core" as in the original score (the Pierre Verany has a longer, later version). The booklet contains both librettos (in Italian) and summaries of the plots, as well as Kuijken's thoughts on the project.

Hans Pfitzner

German 1869-1949

Pfitzner Palestrina.

Karl Ridderbusch *bass* Pope Pius IV, Cardinal Christoph Madruscht
Bernd Weikl *bar* Giovanni Morone
Herbert Steinbach *ten* Bernardo Novagerio
Dietrich Fischer-Dieskau *bar* Carlo Borromeo
Victor von Halem *bass* Cardinal of Lorraine
John van Kesteren *ten* Abdisu
Peter Meven *bass* Anton Brus von Müglitz
Hermann Prey *bar* Count Luna
Friedrich Lenz *ten* Bishop of Budoja
Adalbert Kraus *ten* Theophilus
Franz Mazura *bass* Avosmediano
Gerd Nienstedt *bass* Master of Ceremonies
Nicolai Gedda *ten* Palestrina
Helen Donath *sop* Ighino
Brigitte Fassenbaender *mez* Silla
Renate Freyer *contr* Lukrezia
Tölz Boys' Choir; Bavarian Radio Chorus and Symphony Orchestra / Rafael Kubelík.
DG 20th Century Classics Ⓜ ① 427 417-2GC3 (three discs: 206 minutes: ADD). Notes, text and
translation included. Recorded in the 1970s.

Approached as an essay in words and music on a particularly resonant historic moment, when music, church and international politics stood at the same crossroads, *Palestrina* is an inspiring and often inspired work. It has at its heart one of the most visionary scenes in all opera, the apparition to Palestrina of the ghosts of his musical ancestors, urging him to save the art of polyphony by composing a Mass that will confound counter-reformation zealotry; it is followed by a still more moving tableau in which the heavens open to reveal a choir of angels from whose dictation Palestrina writes the *Missa Papae Marcelli*. Judged by conventional operatic criteria, however, the work is awkward and gravely flawed. The main line of its plot is furthered hardly at all by the Second Act, which is a lengthy, albeit brilliantly dramatized, résumé of ecclesiastical politics at the Council of

Trent, in which the composer's name is mentioned briefly, almost in passing, twice. The proportions of the opera are ungainly, too (the acts last roughly 100, 75 and a bare 30 minutes respectively), and to make matters apparently worse, the music and the text seem at times to be out-of-phase.

Perhaps the most affecting scene in Act 3 is the reunion of Palestrina and Cardinal Borromeo. Moved to tears by literally heavenly music, the Prince of the Church (who had commissioned the Mass and imprisoned Palestrina when he failed to deliver it) throws himself at the composer's feet and begs his forgiveness. Pfitzner's orchestra, as Borromeo falls to his knees and as Palestrina gently raises and embraces him, says all that is in both men's hearts and says it most movingly, but the rather plain lines of dialogue between those two orchestral passages add very little to them. At other times plainness of dialogue is just what you feel you need: Pfitzner's orchestral writing is so richly eventful, his counterpoint so cunningly wrought (and yes, one must admit, at times so unremitting) that you long either for a moment or two of thinly accompanied simple recitative or for the words to get out of the music's way. And yet you would not wish to have the libretto (Pfitzner's own) a line shorter. Complex though it is, it is of remarkable quality, full of incident and beautiful imagery; it would work well as a spoken play.

In the opera-house this sense of a play and a sequence of orchestral meditations upon it being performed simultaneously could be a problem; so could the long and densely populated scenes that seem to come from another opera (called *Borromeo*, perhaps). But in a fine recorded performance it is easier to accept that this is, so to speak, an opera with footnotes and appendices. The great passages (apart from the apparition scenes they include the eloquent preludes to all three acts, the culminatory pages of Borromeo's and Palestrina's monologues in Act 1, two impressive addresses in Act 2 and the beautiful end of the opera as Palestrina, left alone, returns to his music) are in an odd sort of way justified by what only a severe critic would dismiss as the pages of finicking detail between them. They are no more tiresome than those *quarts-d'heure* in which Wagner's characters remind the audience of what has been happening so far, and once you have allowed them to set the nobler moments in context, you can always skip them on later hearings (DG have provided plentiful cueing bands).

You will probably not want to when even the minor character roles are as strongly cast as they are here. There is not a weak link among them, and *primus* though Gedda's stalwartly eloquent Palestrina and Fischer-Dieskau's grandly authoritative Borromeo are they are very much *inter pares* with the likes of Ridderbusch, Weikl, Steinbach and Nienstedt around. Donath is bright and touching as Palestrina's young son, Fassbaender an impulsively eager pupil. Some of the real urgency that all these singers bring to their parts must be due to the inspired choice of a conductor in whom passion and intellect are ideally balanced; it sounds as though this opera was very close to Kubelík's heart and head, and he directs with noble eloquence. The recording copes with Pfitzner's vast resources very well, with an excellent sense of a space having depth as well as breadth. The sound is a little bright at times (Donath's purity is slightly edged), but for the most part both clear and sumptuous. An exceptionally welcome CD reissue.

Amilcare Ponchielli Italian 1834-1886

Ponchielli La Gioconda.
Montserrat Caballé *sop* La Gioconda
Agnes Baltsa *mez* Laura Adorno
Luciano Pavarotti *ten* Enzo Grimaldo
Sherrill Milnes *bar* Barnaba
Nicolai Ghiaurov *bass* Alvise Badoero
Alfreda Hodgson *contr* La Cieca
John del Carlo *bass* Zuàne
Regolo Romani *ten* Isèpo
Neil Jenkins *ten* Pilot, Distant Voice
Rodney Macann *bass* Barnabatto
Stephen Varcoe *bar* Cantor
London Opera Chorus; Finchley Children's Music Group;
National Philharmonic Orchestra / Bruno Bartoletti.
Decca Ⓟ Ⓒ 414 349-2DH3 (three discs: 151 minutes: DDD). Notes, text and translation included. Recorded 1980.

This admirable performance sounds as immediate and forward as one would expect on a transfer to CD, and it emphasizes the presence of voices and orchestra which were admired on the LP equivalent. The performance has much to commend it: Pavarotti's typically fervent account of Enzo's part, Milnes's splendidly characterized but unexaggerated Barnaba, Baltsa's vivid, lightish Laura, Ghiaurov's powerful Alvise. Reservations concern Caballé's Gioconda. You can enjoy the subtlety of her portrayal, while wishing it was a little less mannered at certain points, sung with rather fuller timbre, and less forced in the chest-register. The orchestra and chorus respond willingly to Bartoletti's vital conducting. The Callas/EMI version is one of that artist's best stereo recordings and provides stiff competition in terms of interpretation, though it can't possibly rival the exciting immediate sound of the Decca, and all-round Decca's cast has much to offer. And let's have no nonsense of this being a second-rate work! It is brim full of melody, skilful scoring, and has a novel and effective form, with at least four characters swept away by their passions.

Ponchielli La Gioconda.

Maria Callas *sop* La Gioconda
Fiorenza Cossotto *mez* Laura Adorno
Pier Miranda Ferraro *ten* Enzo Grimaldo
Piero Cappuccilli *bar* Barnaba
Ivo Vinco *bass* Alvise Badoero
Irene Companeez *contr* La Cieca
Leonardo Monreale *bass* Zuane
Renato Ercolani *ten* Isepo, First Distant Voice
Aldo Biffi *bass* Second Distant Voice
Bonaldo Giaiotti *bass* Barnabotto
Carlo Forte *bass* Cantor, Pilot
Chorus and Orchestra of La Scala, Milan / Antonino Votto.
EMI mono Ⓜ Ⓘ CDS5 56291-2 (three discs: 167 minutes: AAD). Notes, text and translation included. Recorded 1959.

"Nobody could fail to be caught up in its conviction" was one of the comments made about this set when it was first released and now, with the advantage of excellent CD transfers, that can be stated all the more strongly. This was perhaps the most successful of Callas's remakes. She seems to have been in good and fearless voice, and the role's emotions were obviously enhanced by the traumas of her own life at the time. She herself is said to have commented of her part in the last act; "It's all there for anyone who cares to understand or wishes to know what I was about". Here her strengths in recitative, her moulding of line, her response to text, are at their most arresting. Indeed, she turns what can be a maudlin act into real tragedy; that is the alchemy of a great artist. The whole of the beginning of the scene is a magnificent and heart-rending soliloquy in which soul, verbal acting, and tone are bound together into a totally convincing whole. Then, near the close, the final benediction on Laura and Enzo, "Quest' ultimo bacio", is movingly and tenderly phrased.

She completely identifies herself with Gioconda's fate throughout, depicting the unhappy ballad-singer's love, hate, jealousy and eventual magnanimity with absolute conviction and without a trace of artifice. She is just as successful earlier in the piece, throwing insults at Laura, a part sung here by the young Cossotto with a true *spinto* strength not seemingly available to any of her successors, but also with a deal of refinement as in the "Stella del marinar" solo in Act 2. Cossotto's husband, Ivo Vinco, hasn't the most pleasing voice but he makes a suitably implacable Alvise.

Ferraro has the kind of Pertile-like tenor that we hear all too seldom today. He has little of the poetry needed for "Cielo e mar", but his stentorian ebullience is useful elsewhere. Cappuccilli gives the odious spy and lecher, Barnaba, a threatening profile whenever he appears. Votto, though he makes a few unnecessary cuts in the score, did nothing better for the gramophone than this set, bringing out the subtlety of the Verdi-inspired orchestration and the charm of the "Dance of the Hours".

The Bartoletti set has the advantage of modern recording, a superbly snarling Barnaba in Milnes, and Pavarotti as an ardent Enzo, better-mannered but not quite so exciting as Ferraro. Baltsa is appealing but not quite so effective as Cossotto. As for Caballé, as discussed above, she is mightily persuasive, very much inside the role like Callas, but sounds underpowered beside her older rival. As a whole the set hasn't quite the immediacy or excitement of the EMI, which has got to be first preference unless you *must* have up-to-date sound.

Francis Poulenc   French 1899-1963

Poulenc Les Dialogues des Carmélites.

Catherine Dubosc *sop* Blanche de la Force
Rachel Yakar *sop* Madame Lidoine
Rita Gorr *mez* Madame de Croissy
Brigitte Fournier *sop* Soeur Constance
1993
Martine Dupuy *mez* Mère Marie
José van Dam *bass-bar* Marquis de la Force
Jean-Luc Viala *ten* Chevalier de la Force
Michel Sénéchal *ten* L'aumônier
François Le Roux *bar* Le geôlier
Chorus and Orchestra of Opéra National de Lyons / Kent Nagano.
Virgin Classics Ⓕ Ⓘ VCD7 59227-2 (two discs: 152 minutes DDD). Notes, text and translation included. Recorded 1990.

Kent Nagano and his Lyon forces followed their *Gramophone* Award-winning success of 1990 – *The Love for Three Oranges* – with the 1993 Award for this dedicated achievement. Once more the recording was made after a stage production in their home house. In this case they are performing one of only half a dozen or so great operas written since the war (most of the rest are by Britten or Tippett). Poulenc's masterpiece has already stood the test of 41 years; if it continues to be interpreted as lovingly as here, it may well become a repertory piece in the future. Its only previous recording (reviewed below) followed the first performances in France. Pierre Dervaux, who died in 1992, was the conductor there and Nagano has very sensibly followed his predecessor's authoritative reading, one that discloses the piece's interior beauty and exterior skill in depicting the world of the Carmelite order as it faces up to the trials and tribulations of the French Revolution. As Roger Nichols writes in his comprehensive introduction to this set, the composer succeeded in articulating the predicament of "fairly ordinary women caught up in an extraordinary destiny". He did so in music that depends for its unity on recurring motifs and on a setting of the text that leans heavily on Debussy's and his own song-writing idioms: some of the solos could almost be abstracted as songs in themselves. Over and above the technical achievement, Poulenc evokes a convincing sound world of its own (a *sine qua non* for any great opera) and makes his audience believe, as he obviously did, in its characters, in their everyday martyrdom and what leads to it.

Nagano has unerringly responded to its sombre, elevated mood, and also realized the useful contrast provided, in just the right places, of male voices. Only once or twice, as for instance in the scene where Blanche's brother tries to persuade her to leave her retreat for the sake of her own safety, does one feel that Nagano missed an extra touch of urgency achieved by Dervaux, but that may have something to do with the old bugbear among modern producers of putting too much space around voices and instruments, thus losing the immediacy that used to be achieved by less sophisticated means. The Francophone singers here are virtually on a par with their renowned predecessors. As is a tradition in this piece, a former interpreter of one of the younger characters here becomes the Old Prioress; thus Rita Gorr, Dervaux's Mère Marie, is here Madame de Croissy, and she projects the ailing woman's final agonies with superb intensity and a voice little touched by time, except at the top. The unyielding Mère Marie is here taken by that underrated, unfailingly musical mezzo, Martine Dupuy, singing with firm tone and magisterial authority rightly tempered by a good heart. Crespin was Dervaux's Madame Lidoine, the new Prioress. For Nagano, Yakar almost but not quite equals her predecessor's exceptionally eloquent assumption, singing her two extended solos with refined and unaffected diction.

More important than any of these is Sister Blanche. The opera is as much about her personal torments and eventual saving as anything else. A neurotic, fantasizing girl, she seeks comfort in the convent but never quite comes to terms with its rigours of mind and body. Poulenc wrote it for Denise Duval, who took the role for Dervaux. Happily Catherine Dubosc matches Duval in tone and accent, and goes one better in refined phrasing, as at "la pauvre petite victime de Sa Divine Majesté" in Act 2. Only a singer who has taken the role on stage can provide that kind of conviction. As her light-hearted companion, Sister Constance, Brigitte Fournier is delightfully airy and eager – just right. The male characters have been cast, to say the least, from strength. Van Dam launches the opera strongly with his purposeful, fatherly Marquis and Viala quite avoids the bleating of his EMI counterpart as the Chevalier, Blanche's brother. Veteran Michel Sénéchal is ideally cast as the sympathetic Chaplain and Le Roux is suitably implacable as the accusing gaoler.

The work is given absolutely complete here (the EMI employs the four optional cuts), including the short interlude of melodrama before the finale. There is a judicious attempt at imitating stage action, and a well-balanced distribution of the characters. This highly recommendable issue has, of course, a far wider range of dynamics than its EMI predecessor. Anyone interested in the best of twentieth-century opera and – more important – wants to share in a deeply moving experience should have this set.

Poulenc Les Dialogues des Carmélites.
Denise Duval *sop* Blanche de La Force
Régine Crespin *sop* Madame Lidoine
Denise Scharley *mez* Madame de Croissy
Liliane Berton *sop* Soeur Constance
Rita Gorr *mez* Mère Marie
Xavier Depraz *bass* Marquis de La Force
Paul Finel *ten* Chevalier de La Force
Louis Rialland *ten* L'aumônier
René Bianco *bar* Le geôlier
Paris Opéra Chorus and Orchestra / Pierre Dervaux.
EMI mono ℗ ① CDS7 49331-2 (two discs: 144 minutes: AAD). Notes, text and translation included. Recorded 1958.

This classic and irreplaceable recording was made at the time of the first French performances of the work. Hailed as a rewarding addition to the slim twentieth-century list of repertory works, *Les Dialogues des Carmélites* then fell somewhat into neglect, but thanks largely to Nagano, it has regained much of its original respect. Its concise almost hypnotic mode of writing is allied to a subject of universal and compelling interest—how an enclosed group copes with matters of life and death, and of personal and group psychology which is both of its own and of every time. In the history of French opera it is a worthy successor to *Pelléas* and indeed its touching heroine Blanche shares much of the troubled, out-of-this-world, fey personality of her predecessor.

It is evident from this set that the singers were inspired by the piece to give of their considerable best. With the benefit of hindsight we can judge that this was a final flowering of the authentic school of French singing. Denise Duval is part of the long line of clear-voiced, incisive sopranos in the Heldy mould. She catches here all the conflicting facets of Blanche's personality, girlish, wilful, frightened, elated as the role requires. Crespin, even though at this early stage of her career was already not altogether happy above a high G, is a moving, authoritative Madame Lidoine. Stili better is Rita Gorr's commanding yet sympathetic Mère Marie and Denise Scharley's haunted and haunting Old Prioress, quite devastatingly desperate in her death scene. Liliane Berton is a charming Sister Constance, and the smaller roles are finely taken, not least Louis Rialland as the hapless Chaplain.

Pierre Dervaux conducts an inspired, inspiriting account of the work, attentive to both its smaller detail and to its grander, elevated passages, raising the final scene of martyrdom to a proper degree of intensity as some inner strength and group-fervour grips the nuns. As compared with the vocal score, there are a few cuts and changes in the voice parts, both sanctioned by Poulenc. The mono recording is more than adequate, but CD does reveal some uncomfortable tape edits.

Poulenc Les mamelles de Tirésias.
Denise Duval *sop* Thérèse, Fortune-teller
Marguérite Legouhy *mez* Marchande de journaux, Grosse Dame
Jean Giraudeau *ten* Husband
Emile Rousseau *bar* Policeman
Robert Jeantet *bar* Director
Julien Thirache *bar* Presto
Frédéric Leprin *ten* Lacouf
Serge Rallier *ten* Journalist
Jacques Hivert *sngr* Son
Gilbert Jullia *sngr* Monsieur Barbu
Chorus and Orchestra of the Opéra-Comique, Paris / André Cluytens.

Poulenc Le bal masqué.
Jean-Christoph Benoit *bar*
Maryse Charpentier *pf*
Paris Conservatoire Orchestra / Georges Prêtre.
EMI L'Esprit Français mono/stereo Ⓜ ① CDM5 65565-2 (70 minutes: ADD). *Les mamelles de Tirésias* recorded 1953; *Le bal maqué* recorded 1965.

If you have never hunted elephants "the Zanzibar way", now could be the time to start. Apollinaire's play, written in the 1900s, did not reach the stage until 1917. Poulenc was at the first performance – which gave the word "sur-réaliste" to the language – but he did not compose the opera until 25 years later, during the Second World War.

Les mamelles de Tirésias is Poulenc's *Così fan tutte*; the story is absurd, naïve, although the puns and rhymes of Apollinaire's poetry are a constant delight. (Mostly untranslatable, Thérèse-française-fraises-Zanzibaraise, it goes on throughout the piece.) What Poulenc has done is to express a whole range of deep emotion in the music, the homesickness of the exile, the longing for children, the mystery of masculine/feminine desires. He described the music as "producing laughter while still allowing tenderness and real lyricism". It was Leonard Bernstein who pointed out that the ensemble "Monsieur Presto à perdu son pari, puisque nous sommes à Paris" bears a striking resemblance to "Can't help lovin' dat man" from Kern's *Show Boat*. Something of the harmonic structure reappears in the finale of *Carmélites* – make of that what you will, if you care for amateur psychology.

Poulenc found his ideal interpreter in Denise Duval, who created the role of Thérèse in 1947, and went on to sing it wherever the opera was given right up until the time of its first American (concert) performance in 1960. Duval combines the "wild touch of vaudeville", as Ned Rorem put it, with her typically forward, slightly nasal, French soprano. Other survivors from the première include Serge Rallier as the Journalist, Emile Rousseau as the Policeman and Robert Jeantet as the Director. The veteran Paul Payan created the role of the Husband, but it is difficult to imagine that he was better than Jean Giraudeau, who the year before had partnered Duval in Ravel's *L'heure espagnole*.

"The work that is dearest to me" was how Poulenc described *Mamelles* at the time of this recording in 1953, and he judged Cluytens's conducting "sensational" and wrote, "it is one of the greatest joys of my life". What can one add? It is one of the greatest recordings of French opera, unchallenged and unsurpassed for 40 years. The filler, Poulenc's early cantata, *Le bal masqué*, is an ephemeral work, but it is done with style and vigour by Jean-Christoph Benoit and Prêtre. No libretto, nor even a synopsis, is included with this CD, which seems an even greater shame than usual, since the text is of such a complicated pattern. Highly recommended, nevertheless.

Sergey Prokofiev

Prokofiev The Fiery Angel.

1996

Galina Gorchakova *sop* Renata
Sergei Leiferkus *bar* Ruprecht
Vladimir Galusin *ten* Agrippa
Konstantin Pluzhnikov *ten* Mephistopheles
Sergei Alexashkin *bass* Faust
Vladimir Ognovienko *bass* Inquisitor
Evgeni Boitsov *ten* Jakob Glock
Valery Lebed *bass* Doctor
Yuri Laptev *ten* Mathias
Mikhail Kit *bar* Servant
Evgenia Perlasova *mez* Landlady
Larissa Diadkova *mez* Fortune-teller
Olga Markova-Mikhailenko *contr* Mother Superior
Yevgeny Fedotov *bass* Innkeeper
Mikhail Chernozhukov *bass* First Neighbour
Andrei Karabanov *bar* Second Neighbour
Gennadi Bezzubenkov *bass* Third Neighbour
Tatiana Kravtsova *sop* First Nun
Tatiana Filimoniva *sop* Second Nun
Chorus and Orchestra of the Kirov Opera / Valery Gergiev.
Philips Ⓟ Ⓒ 446 078-2PH2 (two discs: 119 minutes: DDD). Notes, text and translation included.
Recorded at performances in the Maryinsky Theatre, St Petersburg during September 1993.

When DG's *Fiery Angel* (conducted by Neeme Järvi) appeared everybody was loud in applauding their initiative; this is a belter of an opera and it had to wait far too long for its first CD recording. However, as regards the performance *Gramophone* was less welcoming than most critics. At the time the 1957 Charles Bruck LPs were a reminder of what was missing under Järvi; but that performance was in French and has long since been consigned to the rarity department. Soon after the DG issue came the Covent Garden production, superbly conducted by Sir Edward Downes. That was a shared enterprise with the Kirov/Maryinsky, and those who saw the London performances will know that they were only a qualified success. But now there is Gergiev and his home team in a live recording of the same production, and at last we have something close to the music's full potential revealed.

The opera itself is no blameless masterpiece – Prokofiev's indulgence in lurid sensationalism sometimes gets the better of his artistic judgement. But that sounds a pretty po-faced judgement in the face of the overwhelming power which so much of this score exudes. Or should exude. It was Järvi, in his interview with David Nice in the July 1991 issue of *Gramophone* who put his finger on the problem: "You need remarkable singers who are intelligent enough to understand what Prokofiev is asking of them, dramatically speaking, and you need a great conductor of the symphonic repertoire who can make a symphony out of the opera – but in the opera-house." The fact is that Gorchakova and Leiferkus in the Philips recording live up to that billing far more than Järvi's brave but ultimately over-faced soloists. And Gergiev, whatever his credentials in the symphonic repertoire, gets orchestral playing of far greater weight, drive, precision and character than Järvi's Gothenburgers can muster.

The comparison is of course unfair, as the Maryinsky performance comes live from what is clearly a highly-charged occasion in one of the world's great opera-houses. That brings with it the disadvantage of a constrained opera-pit acoustic, which makes some of Prokofiev's over-the-top scoring seem pretty congested. But the immediacy and clarity of the sound, plus the orchestra's rhythmic grasp, ensures that the effect is still properly blood-curdling.

If Leiferkus's distinctive rich baritone at first sounds a touch microphoney, the ear can soon adjust to that too, and Gorchakova brings intense beauty as well as intensity to Renata's hysterics, taking us inside the psychological drama in a way DG's Nadine Secunde was always struggling to achieve. The supporting roles are filled with more consistent distinction than either DG or Covent Garden could muster, and this makes a huge difference to the sustaining of dramatic tension, the crescendo which Prokofiev aimed to build through his five acts. Considering the extent of the stage goings-on there is remarkably little audience distraction on the recording. Inevitably there is some clumping around from the acrobats, and those who have not seen the staged version will not realize what an inspired touch it was on David Freeman's part to include them, as representations of Renata's delusions.

Prokofiev The Love for Three Oranges (sung in French).

1990

Gabriel Bacoiuier *bar* King of Clubs
Jean-Luc Viala *ten* Prince
Hélène Perraguin *mez* Princess Clarissa
Vincent Le Texier *bass-bar* Leandro
Georges Gautier *ten* Truffaldino
Didier Henry *bar* Pantaloon, Farfarello, Master of Ceremonies

Gregory Reinhart *bass* Tchelio
Michèle Lagrange *sop* Fata Morgana
Consuelo Caroli *mez* Linetta
Brigitte Fournier *sop* Nicoletta
Catherine Dubosc *sop* Ninetta
Jules Bastin *bass* Cook
Béatrice Uria-Monzon *mez* Smeraldina
Chorus and Orchestra of Opéra National de Lyons / Kent Nagano.
Virgin Classics Ⓟ Ⓒ VCD7 59566-2 (two discs, nas: 102 minutes: DDD). Notes, text and
translation included. Recorded 1989.

Long, long before the formulation of the concepts of the Theatre of Cruelty and the Theatre of the
Absurd, Carlo Gozzi had pointed the way in the plays he wrote around 1760 – *Turandot*, *The Stag
king*, *The Love for Three Oranges* which were designed as counterblasts to the realistic theatre of his
fellow-Venetian, Goldoni. The last-named piece was a surrealist fantasy with satirical overtones,
incorporating elements from various fairy-tales. Two and a half centuries later, Meyerhold seized on
it in a magazine he was editing, lauding its wry humour, symbolism and absurdities in a reaction
against Stanislavsky's naturalistic Moscow Arts Theatre; and a copy of this was in Prokofiev's luggage
when he left Russia for the USA in 1918. Particularly attractive to him was its scenic and textural
freedom, deploring as he did "musical dramas fixed in a statue-like rigidity and weighed down with a
thousand wearisome conventions … [such as] rhymed libretti". After translation from the original
Russian into French, his setting of *Love for Three Oranges* was produced in Chicago – after a delay
caused by the death of the opera-house director who had commissioned it, but thanks to the support
of Mary Garden – in 1921.
    It certainly broke with the conventions: musically it has no set-pieces for the singers that can be
wrenched from their context for concert-hall performance, and there is practically no development of
themes in the work – in fact, the orchestral March and Scherzo (made famous in the suite from the
opera) are the only elements that make reappearances; nevertheless the score bubbles with invention
and high spirits, and despite its apparent brittle heartlessness it has an outstanding knack of limning
a situation or mood in only a few bars. Dramatically too it is unorthodox: the course of the action is
affected by the intervention of groups of 'spectators' (variously inclined towards tragedy, comedy,
romantic pathos or just empty-headed fun), and it is thanks to this clown-like chorus that the princess
who steps from the third orange does not, like her sisters, perish of thirst in the desert, and that the
malevolent witch Fata Morgana (who, tumbling over, had at last caused the melancholy
hypochondriac prince to laugh, and as a result has cast on him a love-spell for three oranges) is
kidnapped as she is about to accomplish his ruin.
    Unlike previous recordings of the work this one, based on the stage production by Lyon Opéra (but
with a couple of cast changes), is sung in French and will thereby be comprehensible to more listeners,
who moreover will also have at their disposal an extremely good (if at times overfree) translation and
entertaining little cartoons of the characters in the story. One way or another, they are in for a
thoroughly enjoyable experience, for by one of those rare concatenations of circumstances absolutely
everything – performance, production, recording, presentation – has come out right. Kent Nagano
conducts with zest and finesse and is admirably served by his orchestra, who sound responsively on
their toes and are balanced in such a way as to produce a satisfying sonority without ever
overwhelming the singers. The cast could scarcely be better, with not a single weakness anywhere.
Invidious though it may seem to mention only a few, Jean-Luc Viala is outstanding in both character
and lyrical veins as the whining prince who is transformed into a questing hero; Georges Gautier is a
tower of strength as the unhappy Truffaldino who first is given the thankless task of making him
laugh and then has to accompany him on his adventures; Michèle Lagrange is icily imperious as the
wicked witch; Catherine Dubosc is vulnerably tender as Ninetta (surely one of the briefest parts in the
whole operatic repertory for a heroine, and undoubtedly the only heroine to be turned into a rat for
some of the time); and Jules Bastin contributes a telling vignette as the ogre's gigantic and ferocious
cook who goes weak at the knees at the sight of a piece of pretty ribbon. Preposterous? Of course,
like the oranges themselves; but great fun, and Virgin Classics have pulled it off triumphantly.

Prokofiev War and Peace.

Alexander Gergalov *bar* Prince Andrei Bolkonsky
Yelena Prokina *sop* Natasha Rostova
Vladimir Ognovienko *bass* Prince Nikolai
Svetlana Volkova *mez* Sonya
Ludmilla Kanunnikova *contr* Maria Akhrosimova
Sergei Alexashkin *bass* Count Ilya Rostov
Gegam Gregorian *ten* Count Pyotr Bezukhov
Olga Borodina *mez* Helena Bezukhova
Yuri Marusin *ten* Anatol Kuragin
Alexandr Morozov *bass* Dolokhov
Mikhail Kit *bar* Colonel Vasska Denisov

Nikolai Okhotnikov *bass* Marshal Mikhail Kutuzov
Vassili Gerelo *bar* Napoleon Bonaparte
Kirov Theatre Chorus and Orchestra / Valery Gergiev.
Philips Ⓟ Ⓓ 434 097-2PH3 (three discs: 231 minutes: DDD). Notes, text and translation
included. Recorded 1991.

Rostropovich's Erato version of *War and Peace* appeared two years before this one. The advantages
of the Philips include fitting the huge work on to three discs instead of four, without loss, and a much
better booklet. Erato had parallel translations in English, French and German, but no Russian text
or transliteration to help orientation. Philips have done Gergiev proud with the Russian text on its
own, then (in parallel) Russian transliteration, English, German and French, and separately at the
end, Italian (as well as more comprehensive introductory matter in the four Western languages).
    But there the advantages begin to run out. The Erato recording is much more vivid, and takes the
risk of including a number of of discreet battle effects (if battles can ever be discreet), as well as
presenting the work in a set of well-judged acoustical contrasts. Rostropovich conducts like a man
possessed, which may not seem very different from usual, but in this case represents a passionate
commitment to a work which the dying composer entrusted to his care. Gergiev is less invigorating,
less attentive to the multifarious musical contrasts in the work and to its calm as well as its energy. He
also has, with few exceptions, a less compelling team of singers, at any rate for the principals in what
is a notoriously huge cast-list.
    Rostropovich has Vishnevskaya as Natasha, no longer the 16-year-old innocent, understandably,
though rather harder and more forceful than is ideal; but Yelena Prokina, though tenderer and more
vulnerable, is not very secure for Gergiev. Vishnevskaya's ardent Andrei is Lajos Miller; Prokina's
rather tamer one is Alexander Gergalov. Nicola Ghiuselev for Rostropovich makes a stronger, better
focused Mikhail Kutuzov than Nikolai Okhotnikov. Napoleon is quite sensitively characterized by
Vassili Gerelo, but the slight edge of fanaticism in Eduard Tumagian's performance is closer to the
music. Rostropovich also has the advantage of Wieslaw Ochman as Pytor Bezukhov, and two 'guest'
appearances from Nicolai Gedda as Anatol and, a brief contribution, Michel Sénéchal. However,
Gergiev does have the splendid Olga Borodina as Helena Bezukhova. No one who has already
acquired the Erato set need worry, though Philips serve listeners much better with their album material.

Prokofiev War and Peace.

Lajos Miller *bar* Prince Andrei Bolkonsky
Galina Vishnevskaya *sop* Natasha Rostova
Anton Diakov *bass* Prince Nikolai
Katherine Ciesinski *mez* Sonya
Maria Paunova *mez* Maria Akhrosimova
Dimiter Petkov *bass* Count Ilya Rostov
Wieslaw Ochman *ten* Count Pytor Bezukhov
Stefania Toczyska *mez* Helena Bezukhova
Nicolai Gedda *ten* Anatol Kuragin
Vladimir de Kanel *bass-bar* Dolokhov
Mira Zakai *contr* Princess Maria Bolkonsky
Malcolm Smith *bass* Colonel Vasska Denisov
Nicola Ghiuselev *bass* Marshal Mikhail Kutuzov
Eduard Tumagian *bar* Napoleon Bonaparte
Radio France Chorus; French National Orchestra / Mstislav Rostropovich.
Erato Libretto Ⓜ 2292-45331-2 (four discs: 247 minutes: DDD). Notes, text and translation
included. Recorded 1986.

Over four hours long, 72 characters, 13 scene changes: is it any wonder that Prokofiev's *War and
Peace*, adapted from Tolstoy's famously epic novel, has had few performances and even fewer forays
into the recording studio? At the front of the booklet Rostropovich recalls how, as Prokofiev lay
dying, he reiterated one wish, that Rostropovich should make this opera known to the world. It comes
as no surprise, then, to find a deeply committed performance from both soloists (only 45 of them due
to some adroit doubling), chorus and orchestra. Prokofiev adapted the novel into seven 'peace' and
six 'war' tableaux, thus sustaining drama, through contrast, throughout its Wagnerian length.
    With few exceptions the multinational cast sing in good Russian and among them Lajos Miller is
particularly affecting as Prince Andrei, pleasingly ardent in his opening moonlit aria. The central
female role of Natasha is taken by Galina Vishnevskaya. She sang the role in the 1959 première and,
as noted above, problems are compounded by a hardness in her tone and a lack of attention to detail
in some of the quieter sections – particularly in her exchanges with Helena where the asides sound like
part of the normal conversation. Stefania Toczyska as the treacherous Helena makes a great
impression, as does Katherine Ciesinski as Natasha's confidante, Sonya. Of the men, Nicolai Gedda
as Prince Anatol sings with character and great style and Eduard Tumagian is a suitably heroic and
steadfast Napoleon. An added attraction of the recording are the sound effects, particularly in the
war scenes, convincing but never overly obtrusive.

Prokofiev War and Peace.
  Alexander Gergalov *bar* Prince Andrei Bolkonsky
  Yelena Prokina *sop* Natasha Rostova
  Vladimir Ognovienko *bass* Prince Nikolai
  Svetlana Volkova *mez* Sonya
  Ludmilla Kanunnikova *contr* Maria Akhrosimova
  Sergei Alexashkin *bass* Count Ilya Rostov
  Gegam Gregorian *ten* Count Pyotr Bezukhov
  Olga Borodina *mez* Helena Bezukhova
  Yuri Marusin *ten* Anatol Kuragin
  Alexandr Morozov *bass* Dolokhov
  Mikhail Kit *bass* Colonel Vasska Denisov
  Vassili Gerelo *bar* Napoleon Bonaparte
  Kirov Opera Chorus and Orchestra / Valery Gergiev. *Stage/Video Director:* **Graham Vick**
  Philips Ⓟ 🖭 070 427-3PH2 (two cassettes). Recorded 1991.

This is undoubtedly one of the video best-buys. Recorded at the Marinsky Theatre, Graham Vick's
wide-ranging, evocative production, caught for TV and video by Humphrey Burton, is an experience
not to be missed, a wonderful Anglo-Russian co-operative effort. The staging was supposed to come
to Covent Garden, but lack of funds prevented that happening. But this issue gives as good an idea
as possible as to what was then missed in live form. Vick's fluid, imaginative direction, in Timothy
O'Brien's simple sets, is matched by Gergiev's conducting. As we know from the CD version, he
controls the vast panoply of a score with a complete command over detail and the wider view, leaving
us in no doubt as to the inspiration of the composer's concept, 13 scenes that gives us a fair flavour
of the vast novel and its essence where emotional matters are concerned. Yelina Prokina conveys all
of Natasha's vulnerable, romantic character and her growth, by experience, to womanhood, and she
sings with her whole heart and being. Alexander Gergalov is a fine, upstanding Andrei with one of
those Russian baritones that sear the soul. Gegam Gregoriam's tortured Pierre, Vladimir
Okhotnikov's grizzled Kutuzov, Vassili Gerelo's posturing Napoleon, Olga Borodina's sexy Helena
and Yuri Marusin's cynical Kuragin are but the leading members of a close-knit ensemble
exemplifying the best aspects of Russian opera, not forgetting the vital contribution of the Kirov
chorus.

Giacomo Puccini   Italian 1858-1924

Puccini La bohème.
  Mirella Freni *sop* Mimì
  Luciano Pavarotti *ten* Rodolfo
  Elizabeth Harwood *sop* Musetta
  Rolando Panerai *bar* Marcello
  Gianni Maffeo *bar* Schaunard
  Nicolai Ghiaurov *bass* Colline
  Michel Sénéchal *bass* Benoît, Alcindoro
  Gernot Pietsch *ten* Parpignol
  Schoenberg Boys' Choir; Berlin German Opera Chorus;
  Berlin Philharmonic Orchestra / Herbert von Karajan.
  Decca Ⓟ Ⓓ 421 049-2DH2 (two discs: 110 minutes). Notes, text and translation included.
  Recorded 1972.

Although the Beecham *La bohème* on EMI remains the classic, *hors concours*, desert-island account
of this opera, a touchstone for the judgement of all others, it does not, of course, say all that can be
said about the work and thus put all other readings out of court. If only Callas had been born later
or Pavarotti earlier what a *Bohème* there might have been! Pavarotti's Rodolfo, in Karajan's reading
for Decca, is perhaps the best thing he has ever done: not only the finest recorded account of the role
since Björling's on the Beecham set, but adding the honeyed Italianate warmth that even Björling
lacked. He cannot quite match Björling's poetic refinement, no doubt, and he is less willing to sing
really quietly, but Pavarotti's honest sincerity counts for a great deal: his pride as he declares his
vocation as a poet, the desperate feigning of his "Mimì è una civetta" are points that most tenors miss
or treat as mere opportunities for a big sing. His latter-day image may sometimes tend to hide it, but
this recording is a reminder that Pavarotti is an artist of intelligence and delicacy as well as splendour
of voice. His Mimì, Freni, sings most beautifully and sensitively, but with less care than Callas for the
revelatory word or phrase inflection (for Votto on his 1956 EMI set): Freni is good but not
outstanding, in short.
  Both sets have Panerai as a strong and vividly acted Marcello; a little darker-voiced and a touch
more mannered for Karajan than for Votto. Moffo, on the Callas set, is a conventionally tarty

Musetta; Harwood, for Karajan, a much more interesting one: her tiny narration, in Act 4, of her meeting with the stricken Mimì is a gripping moment, and there is no shadow of doubt that her waltz-song in Act 2 is a passionate (and irresistible) avowal to Marcello. Between the conductors on these two sets there is no comparison: Votto is safe and efficient whenever the singers are the centre of attention, dull or even vulgar at times. Karajan, on the other hand, is a great Puccini conductor (oh yes, there is such a thing, and they are rare) who can linger over the beauties of the orchestration without ever losing his grip on the drama or relaxing his support of the singers; and of course the mono recording of the Callas/Votto set is no match, clean though it is, for the wide perspectives and the fine dynamic gradations of the Pavarotti/Karajan set.

If you can run to only one *La bohème*, we still think it should be the Beecham/EMI, despite its mono sound and the occasional fluffs and imprecisions that betray how rapidly it was made. But there are not many operas of which a better case can be made for having more than one account in one's collection. Some would plump for Serafin's Decca version, for his conducting (as detailed as Karajan and even more full-blooded), for Tebaldi (the most prima donna Mimì of them all, opulent and commanding) and for the ever elegant Bergonzi (albeit a touch strained in high passages) as Rodolfo. Davis's 1979 account on Philips has exceptional delicacy of detail and a touching Mimì in Katia Ricciarelli, but her Rodolfo, Carreras, is more conventional and Davis's account of the score gives the impression of being rather clinical and unidiomatic. Solti's highly dramatic (and excellently recorded) RCA version with Caballè and Domingo is a definite contender: both singers are in fine voice and she in particular is often subtle in her response to words and character; but is all a bit high-powered for such an intimate drama. For a modern *La bohème* to supplement the Beecham this Karajan set must go to the top of the list.

Puccini La bohème.

Renata Tebaldi *sop* Mimì
Carlo Bergonzi *ten* Rodolfo
Gianna d'Angelo *sop* Musetta
Ettore Bastianini *bar* Marcello
Renato Cesari *bar* Schaunard
Cesare Siepi *bass* Colline
Fernando Corena *bass* Benoît, Alcindoro
Piero de Palma *ten* Parpignol
Giorgio Onesti *bar* Sergeant
Chorus and Orchestra of Santa Cecilia, Rome / Tullio Serafin.
Decca Double ® ℗ ① 448 725-2DF2 (two discs: 112 minutes: ADD). Notes, text and translation included. Recorded 1959.

Quite small points can colour your reaction to a recording of *La bohème*. "Cerchi" ("look for it") says Mimì of the hastily pocketed door-key in Act 1, and in Tebaldi's authoritatively firm voice it's an order. "Cerca?" ("are you looking?"), she adds a moment or two later, and you rather feel that if Rodolfo doesn't find it soon he'll get a clout round the ear from her handbag. This Rodolfo, mark you, could melt even such a self-possessed Mimì as she is: we'll find it in the moonlight, he says, "and up here the moon is very close", with the hint of a rueful smile: even garrets have their advantages for a poet. Tebaldi can sing quietly when needed, and she can of course spin a beautiful legato line; the problem is (and for many it will be no problem at all) that the amplitude of her voice and manner is not counterbalanced by those intimate details (colouring of words, expressive subtlety of phrasing) that would have made her Mimì touching as well as finely and generously sung. Bergonzi is stylish throughout, as is Bastianini, and the rest of the cast is pretty strong, though you might find the Musetta a bit too shrill, the Benôit and Alcindoro caricatured (as usual) and the Colline is audibly corseting a vastly cavernous voice.

Tebaldi gives an undoubtedly star performance (though of Tosca, much of the time, not Mimì) but the real star of the recording is Serafin. Eighty years old when the recording was made, his ardour is as urgently youthful as his brilliance and his lightly touched detailing are so obviously the fruit of a long lifetime's loving study of the score. Serafin runs Beecham pretty close, but does not unify his cast as magically. His account was famous in its day for the spaciousness of its recording (though the voices are sometimes recessed), and it still sounds good, if rather brighter in this format than it was.

Puccini La bohème.

Victoria de los Angeles *sop* Mimì
Jussi Björling *ten* Rodolfo
Lucine Amara *sop* Musetta
Robert Merrill *bar* Marcello
John Reardon *bar* Schaunard
Giorgio Tozzi *bass* Colline
Fernando Corena *bass* Benôit, Alcindoro
William Nahr *ten* Parpignol

George de Monte *bar* Sergeant
Columbus Boychoir; RCA Victor Chorus and Orchestra / Sir Thomas Beecham.
EMI mono Ⓔ ① CDS5 56236-2 (two discs: 108 minutes: ADD). Notes, text and translation included. Recorded 1956.

The disadvantages of this famous Beecham *Bohème* are obvious when compared, for example, to Solti. It is a mono recording and is restricted in dynamic range. The sheer sense of space that is needed if the complex crowd scene of Act 2 is to emerge with the maximum impact is inevitably lacking; the climaxes here and elsewhere are somewhat constricted; no less important, it is sometimes harder to focus on the subtleties of Puccini's orchestration – Solti's orchestra on RCA and Davis's on Philips are simply both, in their very different ways, more colourful. The Beecham set was also made in a great hurry, and this shows in a number of patches of slightly insecure ensemble, even a couple of wrong entries; no such flaws mar Solti's or Davis's accounts. But there is no other important respect in which the Beecham version does not stand at least half a head (often head and shoulders) above its more recent rivals, admirable in many respects though they both are.

Katia Ricciarelli, on the Davis set, is a most touching Mimì, a little generalized in some of the fuller passages, perhaps, but beautiful at such quietly crucial moments as (in Act 4) her greeting to the Bohemians gathered at her bedside and the recollection of her first meeting with Rodolfo. Caballé, for Solti, gives one of her finest recorded performances, tenderly expressive and finely shaded, with only the occasional mannered scoop or swallowed consonant to spoil things. But neither is so predestinately right for the role as los Angeles: right both in vocal quality and in sheer involvement with every word and every musical phrase that Mimì utters. Beyond a certain point (usually a certain dynamic level) most sopranos stop being Mimì and simply produce the same sound that they would if they were singing Aida or Tosca. Los Angeles rarely does this; even under pressure (and Beecham's unhurried tempos do put her under pressure at times, as does the fact that a full-throated Italianate high C was never her strongest suit), the very difficulties themselves are used as an expressive and interpretative resource. Hers is the most moving and involving Mimì ever recorded.

And Björling's is unquestionably the most musical Rodolfo. He has the reputation of having been a bit of a dry stick, dramatically (on stage he looked like the other Bohemians' elderly, portly uncle), but on record he is the one exponent of the role to be credible both as a lover and as a poet. His voice is fine silver rather than brass, it can caress as well as weep, and his love for Mimì is more often confided than it is bellowed for all Paris to hear. Both José Carreras (for Davis) and Plácido Domingo (for Solti) are in fine voice and both are intelligent singers; of the two, Domingo is the more ardently involved (Carreras is more inclined to pour out golden tone of uniform colour) but neither is much concerned with verbal acting or with dynamic markings below *mf* or thereabouts.

This, indeed, is one of the most conspicuous differences between Beecham's account and most others: its simple belief that when Puccini wrote *pp* he meant it. Davis is most scrupulous about observing Puccini's markings in other respects (and the very fine Philips recording enables one to hear those details with great clarity), but he has not persuaded most of his singers to do likewise (his Marcello, Ingvar Wixell, sounds as though he is singing Scarpia) and for this reason and a certain tendency not to see the wood for the trees, his account lacks a degree or two both of style and of fluency. Beecham (whose spell over his entire cast – in which there is no weak link – extends as far as teaching his Schaunard, John Reardon, an irresistibly funny, cut-glass English accent for the parrot-fancying milord) makes one realize what an intimate opera this is, how much of it is quiet, how many of its exchanges are *sotto voce*, and he thus enables his singers to use the full range of their voices and to employ subtleties of colour, phrasing and diction that are simply not available to a voice at full stretch (and in the process he largely cancels out the disadvantage of his recording's restricted dynamic range).

It is the same with his handling of the orchestra: set beside Solti's exuberance and rhythmic vigour (hugely exciting in Act 2; no less responsive to the big emotional moments elsewhere), one would expect Beecham to seem understated, but again and again one turns back to his reading and discovers nothing missing – he has achieved as much or more with less. This is as complete a distillation of Puccini's drama as you are likely to hear.

Puccini La bohème.
Ileana Cotrubas *sop* Mimì
Neil Shicoff *ten* Rodolfo
Marilyn Zschau *sop* Musetta
Thomas Allen *bar* Marcello
John Rawnsley *bar* Schaunard
Gwynne Howell *bass* Colline
Brian Donlan *bar* Benoit
John Gibbs *bar* Alcindoro
Chorus and Orchestra of the Royal Opera House, Covent Garden / Lamberto Gardelli.
Stage Director: **John Copley.**
NVC Arts Ⓕ 🔲 4509-99222-3 (118 minutes). Filmed at a performance in the Royal Opera House, Covent Garden in February 1982.

La bohème is up there with the best, bringing the Bohemian world to grubby, vital life with a cast of excellent singer-actors. Cotrubas's deliberately unglamorous but winsome Mimì is more believable than most, and in freshly appealing voice. Shicoff excels himself as Rodolfo, youthfully light-voiced and elegant yet with ample power, and a credibly lightweight but likeable character. Allen's burly Marcello, golden-voiced and desperately emotional, is an excellent foil. Howell's Colline sheds his beard as promised to reveal a genial philosopher, mellow and moving, and Rawnsley injects Schaunard with as much life as the others. They have, or create, a real sense of friendly rapport. Marilyn Zschau's spitfire Musetta is not ideally steady in her waltz song, but shows something of her promise as Salome and Brünnhilde, and blends brassiness and sincerity well. Benoit and the other roles are nicely observed, as are all the details of Copley's production, translating well to video; Oman's sets again drip authenticity, to every last chunk of ceiling plaster. Gardelli contributes the kind of warm, theatrical reading you miss when faced with the latest whizz-kid. The recording is a touch grainy but you will not find a better video *Bohème* than this.

Puccini La fanciulla del West.
Carol Neblett *sop* Minnie
Plácido Domingo *ten* Dick Johnson
Sherrill Milnes *bar* Jack Rance
Francis Egerton *ten* Nick
Robert Lloyd *bass* Ashby
Jonathan Summers *bar* Sonora
John Dobson *ten* Trin
Malcolm Rivers *bar* Sid
Tom McDonnell *bar* Bello
Paul Crook *ten* Harry
Robin Leggate *ten* Joe
William Elvin *bass* Happy
Malcolm King *bass* Larkens
Paul Hudson *bass* Billy Jackrabbit
Anne Wilkens *sop* Wowkle
Gwynne Howell *bass* Jake Wallace
Eric Garrett *bass* José Castro
Handel Owen *ten* Postillion
Chorus and Orchestra of the Royal Opera House, Covent Garden / Zubin Mehta.
DG Ⓔ Ⓓ 419 640-2GH2 (two discs: 130 minutes). Notes, text and translation included. Recorded 1977.

1978

Based on the Covent Garden production of 1977, with Sherrill Milnes brought in as an extra star to make Jack Rance a noble villain, this DG set of *La fanciulla del West* remains among the most successful of Zubin Mehta's opera recordings, taking the *Gramophone* Record of the Year award in 1978. His often brisk manner gives the performance extra tautness and cohesion, never detracting from expressive warmth. In practical terms it means that the whole opera can be conveniently squeezed on to two CDs instead of three LPs, with the extra convenience that Act 1 is complete on the first disc, Acts 2 and 3 on the second with no mid-act breaks involved.

The transfer captures the fullness and boldness of the original recording, but the slight drying-out process of the digital sound makes tuttis rather more strident than before, with some hardness in the treble. That sometimes affects the recording of Domingo's tenor too. It remains a fine heroic performance, but his singing is more strenuous than we are used to now when, increasingly since his *Otello*, seems to have been such a liberating factor for him. One wishes that "Ch'ella mi creda" was more varied in dynamic, for example. Carol Neblett makes a touching Minnie, not so characterful as some but rich and true in the formidably exposed top notes. Milnes brings out the nobility of Rance without diminishing his menace, and the rest of the cast, with Covent Garden stage experience behind them, provide a formidable team, with Gwynne Howell outstanding in the haunting minstrel ballad in the opening scene. CD enhances the precision of the voice as it is first heard off-stage, highly evocative. All in all, this DG set provides an outstanding answer for anyone wanting this colourful, fascinating opera, a piece even more moving on disc, many people find, than on stage.

Puccini La fanciulla del West.
Renata Tebaldi *sop* Minnie
Mario del Monaco *ten* Dick Johnson
Cornell MacNeil *bar* Jack Rance
Piero De Palma *ten* Nick
Silvio Maionica *bass* Ashby
Giorgio Giorgetti *bar* Sonora
Enzo Guagni *ten* Trin
Virgilio Carbonari *bass* Sid

Edio Peruzzi *bar* Bello
Mario Carlin *ten* Harry
Angelo Mercuriali *ten* Joe
Michele Cazzato *bar* Happy
Giuseppe Morresi *bass* Larkens
Dario Caselli *bass* Billy Jackrabbit
Biancamaria Casoni *mez* Wowkle
Giorgio Tozzi *bass* Jake Wallace
Athos Cesarini *ten* José Castro
Santa Cecilia Academy Chorus and Orchestra, Rome / Franco Capuana.
Decca Grand Opera Ⓜ Ⓞ 421 595-2DM2 (two discs: 133 minutes: ADD). Text and translation
included. Recorded 1958.

This vintage Decca issue brings an astonishing example of early stereo engineering, now even more
sharply focused in its beauties, thanks to the transfer to CD. On two CDs instead of the original three
LPs, with a performance as beautiful as any more recent account of this opera, it makes an
outstanding issue in Decca's newly revived Grand Opera series on mid-price CD.

Capuana directs an expansive performance, but you have only to hear the haunting song of the
roving minstrel, Jake Wallace, right at the start, "Che farrano i vecchi miei", as sung here by Giorgio
Tozzi, to realize the unique atmospheric beauty of this version, with the off-stage voice as precisely
placed as those on-stage. An American critic once compared the sound of Mehta's version
unfavourably with this, and he may have been right. Forceful as the Mehta performance is, the
subtleties of the score are brought out even more by Capuana's reading, at once more spacious and
more delicate.

The Decca producer and engineers (James Walker and Roy Wallace) appreciated ahead of their time
what extra dimensions stereo could provide, and the final scene also remains a model of recording
production. After Dick Johnson has sung his aria, "Ch'ella mi creda" (del Monaco lusty but not
coarse), Minnie's arrival, Brünnhilde-like, on her horse, outdoes any stage production ever seen, and
the final farewells, in which the miners sing "Che farrano i vecchi miei" in alternate phrases with
Minnie's and Dick's love song, is timed more lovingly than ever before.

Tebaldi is in superb voice, hitting her top notes with pinging precision, del Monaco with his rich
tone was never finer, and Cornell Macneil gives Jack Rance an apt element of nobility, making him
more than a Wild West Scarpia. The two CDs are given a generous number of cueing points, 22 on
the first disc, 23 on the second disc, and like the other issues in the series a libretto with translation is
provided, but no synopsis.

Puccini La fanciulla del West.
Barbara Daniels *sop* Minnie
Plácido Domingo *ten* Dick Johnson
Sherrill Milnes *bar* Jack Rance
Anthony Laciura *ten* Nick
Julien Robbins *bass* Ashby
Kim Josephson *bar* Sonora
Charles Anthony *ten* Trin
James Courtney *bar* Sid
Richard Vernon *bass* Bello
Bernard Fitch *ten* Harry
Michael Forest *ten* Joe
Kevin Short *bar* Happy
Dwayne Croft *bass* Larkens
Hao Jiang Tian *bass* Billy Jackrabbit
Sondra Kelly *contr* Wowkle
Yanni Yannissis *bass* Jake Wallace
Vernon Hartman *bar* José Castro
Michael Best *ten* Postillion
Chorus and Orchestra of the Metropolitan Opera, New York / Leonard Slatkin.
Stage Director: **Giancarlo del Monaco.** *Video Director:* **Brian Large.**
DG Ⓟ ▣ 072 433-3GH; ◗ 072 433-1GH2 (three sides: 140 minutes). Recorded at performances
in the Metropolitan Opera House, New York during April 1992.

Do you perhaps suspect that the days are gone when Puccini could moisten the eye, evoke the furtive
tear, promote the importunate gulp? You may well think yourself proof against the assaults of this
wild-west melodrama, this absurdity of dooda-days and last-minute rescue from the gallows, but, with
the first sound of Jake Wallace's song about the old folks at home, you will probably find yourself
succumbing. The production here is thoroughly realistic, down to the snow on Minnie's window-
panes, and her supper looks almost good enough to eat. The fracas in Act 1, the shooting in Act 2,
the lynch-mob of Act 3 all look pretty well like life except, possibly, that the rope for stringing up Dick

Johnson appears to have come straight from the shop. The horses bring a further scent of the west: so many seem to pass the doors of the Polka Saloon that we must suppose the Met have a stables among their multifarious facilities. The miners are convincingly unshaven and unprepossessing, and there, while the camp-minstrel hawks his song of nostalgia, is poor seedy Larkens getting more and more homesick at the bar and by the bar. Sherrill Milnes is a superb Jack Rance, visually, and still one to be reckoned with vocally, though the voice has lost some of its resonance. Domingo, amazingly, seems to have lost nothing, save a little of the gold filling that still enriches his voice. He acts the part with touching sincerity and cuts a fine figure on entry, his hat set at a jaunty angle, his dress sporting surely more belts than are strictly necessary. The Minnie, Barbara Daniels, has a big voice and, it would seem, a big heart; not every note is as firm as one might ideally wish, but she gives a vivid performance which could well settle the form 'the girl' takes in one's mind for a long time after.

Slatkin conducts with feeling, and the orchestral playing is fine. The camera-work provides the home-viewer with many privileges, so that we needn't envy too much those fine folk we see at the start, making their way from the fountain to the opera-house, behind which the sun is already sinking into the golden west.

Puccini Gianni Schicchi.
Leo Nucci *bar* Gianni Schicchi
Mirella Freni *sop* Lauretta
Roberto Alagna *ten* Rinuccio
Ewa Podles *contr* Zita
Riccardo Cassinelli *ten* Gherardo
Barbara Frittoli *sop* Nella
Barbara Guerrini *mez* Gherardino
Giorgio Giorgetti *bar* Betto di Signa
Enrico Fissore *bar* Simone
Orazio Mori *bass* Marco
Nicoletta Curiel *mez* La Ciesca
Colin Cue *ten* Spinelloccio
Orchestra del Maggio Musicale Fiorentino / Bruno Bartoletti.
Decca Ⓟ Ⓓ 444 395-2DHO (53 minutes: DDD). Notes, text and translation included. Recorded 1991.

A likeable performance, with a likeable Schicchi at the centre of it. One does not expect Freni still to sound like a girlish *ingénue*, quiet singing is a little more of an effort for her than it once was and the tone can spread under pressure (a slightly closer than natural focus on the voices makes both of these a bit more obvious than they might be in the theatre). But her charm and her phrasing are unimpaired, and her aria is beautifully done. Alagna in 1991 sounds like a not very large-voiced lyric tenor of great intelligence and taste, with the sense not to force his voice beyond its limits. His praise of Florence and the new vigour brought to her by men like Schicchi is ardent, and he produces a lyrical, fined-down tone for the exchanges with Freni towards the end. The other singers are all reliable, though the detestable habit of giving Maestro Spinelloccio ill-fitting dentures and a penetrating whistle on every sibilant is taken to extremes. The women's trio as they disguise Schicchi is very well done by Frittoli, Podles and Curiel.

But is likeability enough for Schicchi? Nucci sings the role better than most and does not overact save in the nasal whine he adopts to impersonate Buoso Donati (but then most baritones do or overdo that). It is typical of him that "Addio Firenze" is sung very beautifully but without a hint of malice (if their ruse is found out, he is telling Buoso's heirs, they will wave the farewell of exile with a stump, their right hands having been amputated). He is, in short, not an especially characterful or dominant Schicchi; he does not command the stage from his first entrance. Still, Bartoletti knows just how to pace this not wholly jovial comedy and there is enough audible stage business to capture the sense of a real performance.

Puccini Madama Butterfly.
Mirella Freni *sop* Madama Butterfly
Luciano Pavarotti *ten* Pinkerton
Robert Kerns *bar* Sharpless
Christa Ludwig *mez* Suzuki
Michel Sénéchal *ten* Goro
Giorgio Stendoro *bar* Prince Yamadori
Elke Schary *mez* Kate Pinkerton
Mrius Rintzler *bass* The Bonze
Hans Helm *bass* Commissioner
Vienna State Opera Chorus; Vienna Philharmonic Orchestra / Herbert von Karajan.
Decca Ⓟ Ⓓ 417 577-2DH3 (three discs: 145 minutes). Notes, text and translation included. Recorded 1974.

In every way except one the transfer of Karajan's radiant Vienna recording for Decca could hardly provide a firmer recommendation. The reservation is one of price, for unlike the Maazel/Sony Classical version, and Decca's earlier transfer of Serafin's vintage recording with Tebaldi, this Karajan is on three discs, not two. Karajan's speeds are consistently expansive – some may find them too much so – but mathematically at least it would just be possible to break between discs at one of the index points in Act 2 and keep the set on two CDs. Economically the spread on to three discs is regrettable, but it does at least allow each act to be self-contained on a single disc, and for such a performance as this no extravagance is too much.

Movingly dramatic as Renata Scotto is on both the Maazel version and the Barbirolli/EMI set, Mirella Freni is even more compelling. The voice is fresher, firmer and more girlish, with more light and shade at such points as "Un bel dì", and there is an element of vulnerability that intensifies the communication. In that, one imagines Karajan played a big part, just as he must have done in presenting Luciano Pavarotti – not quite the super-star he is today but already with a will of his own in the recording studio – as a Pinkerton of exceptional subtlety, not just a roistering cad but in his way an endearing figure in the First Act. Significantly CD brings out the delicacy of the vocal balances in Act 1 with the voices deliberately distanced for much of the time, making such passages as "Vienna la sera" and "Bimba dagli occhi" the more magical in their delicacy. Karajan, both in that duet and later in the Flower duet of Act 2, draws ravishing playing from the Vienna Philharmonic strings, getting them to imitate the portamento of the singers in what is also an *echt-Viennes* manner, ravishing to the ear. For Karajan Christa Ludwig is by far the richest and most compelling of Suzukis.

Puccini Madama Butterfly.

Renata Scotto *sop* Madama Butterfly
Carlo Bergonzi *ten* Pinkerton
Rolando Panerai *bar* Sharpless
Anna di Stasio *mez* Suzuki
Piero De Palma *ten* Goro
Guiseppe Morresi *ten* Prince Yamadori
Silvana Padoan *mez* Kate Pinkerton
Paolo Montarsolo *bass* The Bonze
Mario Rinaudo *bass* Commissioner
Rome Opera House Chorus and Orchestra / Sir John Barbirolli.
EMI Ⓜ Ⓘ CMS7 69654-2 (two discs: 142 minutes: ADD). Notes, text and translation included. Recorded 1966.

This is Barbirolli's *Butterfly*; despite Scotto's expressiveness and Bergonzi's elegance it is the conductor's contribution that gives this set its durability and its hold on the affections. The Rome Opera Orchestra are not the equal of the Vienna Philharmonic for Karajan or the Philharmonia (for Maazel on CBS and Sinopoli on DG) or even the orchestra of La Scala, Milan (at least in Karajan's hands, in his earlier recording with Callas on EMI). But they are an Italian orchestra and they evidently recognized a compatriot and a seasoned fellow Puccinian in the London-born Giovanni Battista Barbirolli: he played in rehearsals at Covent Garden directed by the composer and had made his conducting début there in this opera. The rapport between conductor and orchestra and their mutual affection for Puccini are evident throughout, and they make this the most Italianate of all readings. It is hugely enjoyable, not just in the big emotional outpourings (like the Act 2 interlude, where Barbirolli's passionate gasps and groans spur the orchestra to great eloquence) but in many tiny moments where you can almost see the conductor and his players lovingly and absorbedly concentrating on subtleties of phrasing and texture.

There is a lot of good singing, too. Scotto's voice will not always take the pressure she puts on it, but her portrayal is a touching and finely detailed one, at its best in Act 2 where she has the range to respond with broken pathos to Sharpless's suggestion that Pinkerton may not come back and then to turn with real fury on the importunate marriage-broker Goro a few pages later. The ever stylish Bergonzi sings with immaculate phrasing and perfect taste, Panerai is an outstanding Sharpless (beautifully sung, the embodiment of anxious, pitying concern) and di Stasio's Suzuki is attractively light-voiced and young-sounding. The recording, however, is a bit narrow in perspective, rather close (really quiet singing and playing rarely register as such) and some of the voices are edged or slightly tarnished in loud passages; Scotto's is the most often affected, unfortunately (there is at times a touch of squalliness to her singing anyway). Although it is good to have Bergonzi's likeable Pinkerton on record he has nowhere near the vocal glamour or the accomplished acting of Karajan's Pavarotti. And for many, of course, Callas on the earlier Karajan set is simply incomparable (her "greatest achievement on records", John Steane called it).

Barbirolli's set is perhaps for those who find the meticulously refined detail of the later Karajan studied (also ravishing and stunningly recorded) and for whom the audacious liberties taken by Sinopoli are intolerable (also genuinely creative, rarely obtrusive, occasionally inspired, and his recording too is in the luxury class); those, in short, for whom Latin warmth and impulsive open-heartedness are indispensable in this opera. They will find those qualities here, with singing to match, and will not mind the occasional patch of stridency.

Puccini Madama Butterfly.

Miriam Gauci *sop* Madama Butterfly
Yordi Ramiro *ten* Pinkerton
Georg Tichy *bar* Sharpless
Nelly Boschková *mez* Suzuki
Josef Abel *ten* Goro
Robert Szücs *bar* Prince Yamadori
Alzbeta Michalková *mez* Kate Pinkerton
Jozef Spaček *bass* The Bonze
Vladimir Kubovčik *bass* Commissioner, Registrar
Slovak Philharmonic Chorus;
Bratislava Radio Symphony Orchestra, Bratislava / Alexander Rahbari.
Naxos Ⓢ Ⓓ 8 660015/6 (141 minutes: DDD). Notes and text included. Recorded 1991.

Though this would never be a first-choice *Butterfly*, it might serve quite happily as a *Butterfly* first-choice. That is, having previously known the many fine recordings that have already appeared, one would be unlikely to say "Ah, now this is the best"; but coming upon the opera fresh, never having heard it before, one could well find it a good introduction. It is consistently musical, avoids cheapness or exaggerated sentiment, and, while presenting worthily the enchanting and infinitely poignant score, it leaves plenty to be discovered with a widening knowledge of other and greater performances.

An attractive feature is the youthfulness of the Butterfly and Pinkerton. The Pinkerton, a Mexican lyric tenor, Yordi Ramiro, gives as likeable, sincere a version of the character as any, unless perhaps Nicolai Gedda in his recording with Callas . And this is not a falsification of the part, at the very heart of which is the painful truth that likeable people may do very unlikeable things. His "Dovunque al mondo" is not a coarse boast but a lyrical exposition of a view of the world which has the dignity of a simple-minded patriotism. His reception of Cio-Cio-San on arrival is affectionate and gentle, sincerely touched by her beauty and by the romance of the moment. When he comforts her after the High Priest's denunciation, he is all compassion and solicitude, and even with the "See, I have caught you" ("Io t'ho ghermita") section of the duet there is love in his voice rather than mere predatory selfishness. It is also a good voice: limited, but well defined and with a youthful freshness in its tone.

The Butterfly is also young-sounding: Miriam Gauci, born in Malta and with appearances to her credit in the States and throughout Europe, including La Scala and the Wexford Festival where she was heard in *La cena delle beffe*. She sings uncompromisingly as a light lyric soprano, with an especially lovely quality in the upper range. The lightness itself brings limitations in this colossal role, and they are compounded by the immaturity of her acting-portrayal: she does many of 'the right things' but it is rare to find in her the flash of expressiveness that illuminates a character from within. A newcomer to the opera is not likely to be troubled by this, but will on the contrary be delighted by the quality of the voice and touched by the general appeal of the character.

Alexander Rahbari conducts a performance that captures both the opera's charm and seriousness, not however, its intensity. At just the point where it should start to flame ("Il cannone del porto") it loses energy and concentration. Technically, the recording hardly excites comment one way or the other. As a performance, and particularly as an introduction, it has distinct merits: attractively priced and acquired in apt circumstances, it could earn gratitude.

Puccini Madama Butterfly.

Maria Callas *sop* Madama Butterfly
Nicolai Gedda *ten* Pinkerton
Mario Borriello *bar* Sharpless
Lucia Danieli *mez* Suzuki
Renato Ercolani *ten* Goro
Mario Carlin *ten* Prince Yamadori
Plinio Clabassi *bass* Bonze
Luisa Villa *mez* Kate Pinkerton
Enrico Campi *bass* Commissioner
Chorus and Orchestra of La Scala, Milan / Herbert von Karajan.
EMI mono Ⓜ Ⓓ CDS5 56298-2 (two discs: 139 minutes: ADD). Notes, text and translation included. Recorded 1955.

After feeling the impact of that devastating final chord on this set, you will believe devoutly that *Madama Butterfly* is the most moving of all works for the stage, that this is the best recording of it, and that it is Callas's greatest achievement on records. The morning after may bring a hesitation or two, but at present belief seems firm as Butterfly's own and a good deal more securely grounded.

Like every other artist worthy of playing the role, Callas presents the development of the woman from the child. Where she is unusual, if not unique is that she takes no exterior view of Cio-Cio-San (which then presents a pretty, childlike vulnerability), but enters the girl and finds there not the weakness of childhood but the strength. There is a natural childlike shyness ("Ieri son salita" a touchingly private confession), a natural childlike impulsiveness ("Nessuno si confessa"), as well as hurt ("mi maledice") and trust ("e felice"). But the keynote is firmness of mind: a simple factuality which sees right and wrong with the clarity of that miraculously rinsed and lightened voice. Everything here is in place. For instance, in "Un bel dì" where, in his review of the recording when it first came out, Alec Robertson found the expectancy of "Chi ssará?" too casual, Callas feels the strength of the whole utterance as residing in the calm of certainty: Butterfly is retelling what she so often has seen in her mind, and she tells it with the clarity and factual sureness of a child, exact over the details of a favourite story.

Mention of Alec Robertson is also a reminder that he was not entirely happy about Gedda as Pinkerton: "It is perfectly clear from the moment he opens his mouth that Mr Gedda would not hurt a flea, let alone a Butterfly ... This considerably alters the dramatic balance of the opera". But that was part of a common misconception which sees Pinkerton as a brash, brutish character, whereas he is what his music is: namely, in Act 1, charming, graceful, tender and fervent (that such a person can behave as he does is at the centre of the opera's tragic force). Gedda characterizes him faithfully, and sings with a sweetness that entirely explains why such a strong-minded girl as this should so trust him. Borriello, too, is a better than average Sharpless, Lucia Danieli a very adequate Suzuki, and several of the minor parts are notably well cast, including Yamadori, who should sound as though he could sing Pinkerton (his music tells us so) and who in the second Karajan recording (Decca) sounded as though he would be hard pressed to sing Goro.

It is interesting to consider this EMI set with the Decca Karajan/Freni/Pavarotti version in mind. The foreground was insistently occupied by the conductor, who too deliberately held out the score and its texture for admiring examination. However, Freni is the most involving and vocally subtle Cio-Cio-San imaginable and Pavarotti's is an incomparable Pinkerton. In this earlier EMI recording the conductor is splendid: you hardly notice him. Karajan brought to his view many details of the score which he had never previously observed but he is a relatively unassertive presence, and aurally the stage is the foreground as it is visually in the theatre. On two CDs instead of three for the Decca, the set has another advantage over its immediate rival. The change of disc in Act 2 is somewhat abrupt but greatly preferable to most arrangements that were common among the LP albums.

Puccini Manon Lescaut.
Mirella Freni *sop* Manon Lescaut
Luciano Pavarotti *ten* Des Grieux
Dwayne Croft *bar* Lescaut
Giuseppe Taddei *bar* Geronte
Ramon Vargas *ten* Edmondo
Cecilia Bartoli *mez* Singer
Federico Davià *bass* Innkeeper, Captain
Anthony Laciura *ten* Dancing master
James Courtney *bass* Sergeant
Paul Groves *ten* Lamplighter
Chorus and Orchestra of the Metropolitan Opera / James Levine.
Decca Ⓟ Ⓒ 440 200-2DHO2 (two discs: 120 minutes: DDD). Notes, text and translation included. Recorded 1992.

With Luciano Pavarotti as a powerful Des Grieux, James Levine conducts a comparably big-boned performance of *Manon Lescaut*, bringing out its red-blooded drama, while not ignoring its warmth and tender poetry. It was only five years before this that Decca issued their previous version, with Riccardo Chailly conducting Bologna forces and a cast headed by Dame Kiri Te Kanawa and José Carreras, and this one too is marked by exceptionally full, vivid sound. Decca have given Levine and his Metropolitan Opera forces the fullest, most vivid recording they have received from any company since they started to record opera in the studios of the Manhattan Center, not always an easy venue for engineers. The controversial point is the closeness of the balance of the voices, well in front of the orchestra in a way one associates with opera recordings of 35 years ago, rather than those in the digital age. Whether or not that balance has been influenced by Pavarotti, who always likes to sound as full-throated as possible, it represents an opposite view to that taken by the DG engineers when they recorded the Sinopoli version.

There, too, the title-role was taken by Mirella Freni, and though the closeness of balance on the Levine set exposes some inevitable blemishes of age in the voice, its fullness and warmth are more faithfully captured. On the DG set Manon's Act 2 aria, "In quelle trine morbide", almost sounded as if it were sung off-stage. If in that aria this time the attack is not always as clean as before, Freni's shading of tone at the end is exquisite and generally her performance is even warmer and more relaxed; she seems to respond to the thrust of Levine's view even more naturally than to the thoughtfulness and refinement of Sinopoli's. Freni's performance culminates in an account of the big Act 4 aria, "Sola, perduta, abbandonata", more involving and passionate than most other versions, with the voice showing no signs of wear, and with her sudden change of face at the words "terra di pace" ("a land of peace") bringing a magical lightening of tone. That aria makes a thrilling climax, when too often in this opera Act 4, in effect a long, static duet, can seem a let-down. In this as in so much else, Levine conveys the tensions and atmosphere of a stage performance in a way that plainly owes much to his experience at the Metropolitan. More completely than other versions, it avoids the feeling of a studio performance.

Reactions to Pavarotti as Des Grieux will differ widely. The big man launches into his little opening aria, challenging the girls to make him fall in love ("Tra voi belle") with a beefy bravado that misses some of the subtlety and point that Domingo, for example, finds in the Sinopoli recording. But then he, characteristically, points word meaning with a bright-eyed intensity that compels attention. The closeness of balance means that in volume his singing rarely drops below *mezzo forte*, and as a vocal demonstration Domingo's performance is consistently more refined, but there is little harm in having so passionate a portrait of Des Grieux as Pavarotti's. For all the closeness, he does delicately touch in such a phrase as his quotation of Manon's words in the middle of the Act 1 aria, "Donna non vidi mai" – "Manon Lescaut mi chiamo". Needless to say, the hero's big emotional climaxes in each of the first three acts come over at full force with the combination of Pavarotti and Levine.

The rest of the cast is strong too, with Dwayne Croft a magnificent Lescaut who, as well as singing with rich, firm tone, brings out the character's wry humour. The veteran, Giuseppe Taddei, is superbly cast as Geronte, very characterful and still full-throated, while Cecilia Bartoli makes the unnamed singer in the Act 2 entertainment into far more than a cipher, something which other comparably starry singers have often failed to do in rival recordings. Other small roles are also characterfully done. Many collectors, if not everyone, will count this a clear first choice among current modern versions of *Manon Lescaut*. The distanced voices in the Sinopoli versions are worrying, somewhat undermining the impact of that refreshingly strong and thoughtful reading. In quality of sound, not least in the matter of balance, the Chailly version is the best of all, and Dame Kiri sings with a purity and beauty beyond those of her rivals, even if her portrait of the heroine is not so distinctive as Freni's. The playing of the Bologna orchestra is not quite so refined as that on either the Levine or the DG sets. As for Rahbari's account, that offers, at super-budget price, very good sound and a most beautiful performance from Miriam Gauci in the title-role, in many ways fresher than any here. But for the sheer power of Puccinian drama vividly conveyed, Levine is hard to beat. One incidental advantage over the others is that Levine has the break between discs after Act 2, avoiding any break within an act.

Puccini Manon Lescaut.

Miriam Gauci *sop* Manon Lescaut
Kaludi Kaludov *ten* Des Grieux
Vicente Sardinero *bar* Lescaut
Marcel Rosca *bass* Geronte
Donald George *ten* Edmondo
Lucienne Van Deyck *contr* Singer
Henk Lauwers *bass* Innkeeper, Sergeant, Captain
Ludwig Van Gijsegem *ten* Dancing master, Lamplighter
Jack Gregoor Choir;
Belgian Radio and TV Philharmonic Chorus and Orchestra / Alexander Rahbari.
Naxos Ⓢ Ⓓ 8 660019/20 (two discs: 126 minutes: DDD). Notes and text included. Recorded 1992.

In the lovely, spring-like opening of this opera, student Edmondo offers to improvise what he calls a madrigal. Its theme is youth ("Giovinezza è il vostro nome"), and it is taken up by the "laughing young ones, full of love", "ridente, amorose adolescenti". One of the attractions of this Naxos recording is its youthfulness. Both Manon and Des Grieux, their voices a shade lighter and a degree more slender than usual, sound young, and there is a happy contrast with the brother (old, at any rate, in the ways of the world) and with the Geronte, whose voice sounds appropriate to the age which his name proclaims. So, throughout its enchanting First Act and in various of the later episodes, the opera is closer than usual to the comic genre, and of youth triumphant. When it turns to tragedy the effect is all the more grievous, and the final scene, sung by these young voices, has a heightened poignancy as it brings to such a despairing conclusion the story which had opened so gaily with the student's song of youth and hope.

Miriam Gauci has many delightful qualities, notably the gift of a pure, unthickened lyric soprano voice, and the taste to use it well. She sings with feeling though without intensity, and certainly without the deeper, tragedy-laden tones generally associated with the ill-fated heroines of this later school of Italian opera. Both vocally and dramatically she is better suited to Puccini's Manon than to his Butterfly, of which she nevertheless gave a sympathetic account (reviewed above). Kaludi Kaludov makes an admirable Des Grieux, the Italian language suiting him. The light, graceful style wanted for his first song eludes him as it does almost all (we really want to hear a Tito Schipa in it), but "Donna non vidi mai" goes well, and in all three duets with Manon he has the authentic ring in his voice and a conviction which needs no hysterical outbursts to fortify it. There is something missing both in himself and Gauci: it may be what Italians mean when they talk (approvingly) of *morbidezza*, or what to us is a kind of 'sickness' in the voice, a feeling which must colour solos such as Des Grieux's "Ah, Manon, mi tradisce il tuo folle pensiero" and "Guardate, pazzo son". Even so, this is a genuinely moving performance, and many more opulent, overtly tragic versions of the final scene can induce less emotional involvement in the listener than does this one. The remainder of the cast do well, with Vicente Sardinero as a lively, somewhat rough-voiced Lescaut, Marcel Rosca characterizing vividly as Geronte and the smaller parts all capably sung (though of course there are no star-turns, as in the Sinopoli recording which has Fassbaender as soloist in the Pastoral of Act 2, or the Callas/Serafin set which has Cossotto in the same tiny role). Rahbari's conducting has the zest and warmth of lyricism that are so essential, and he brings out more of the score's delicacy than many others do. A greater clarity of highlighted detail will be found in the Chailly/Decca (in quality of sound, not to mention balance, the best of all) and Sinopoli recordings, and they do not suffer from such backward-placing of the chorus as, in this Naxos version, makes nonsense of Edmondo, at the start, singing to and among the crowd. Still, for the super-budget price asked for this we perhaps cannot hope for everything, and for that matter it is usually no use hoping for everything in a full-price issue either.

Puccini Manon Lescaut.

Maria Callas *sop* Manon Lescaut
Giuseppe di Stefano *ten* Des Grieux
Giulio Fioravanti *bar* Lescaut
Franco Calabrese *bass* Geronte
Dino Formichini *ten* Edmondo
Fiorenza Cossotto *mez* Singer
Carlo Forti *bass* Innkeeper
Vito Tatone *ten* Dancing master
Giuseppe Morresi *bass* Sergeant
Franco Ricciardi *ten* Lamplighter
Franco Ventrigilia *bass* Captain
Chorus and Orchestra of La Scala, Milan / Tullio Serafin.
EMI Ⓟ Ⓓ CDS5 56301-2 (two discs: 120 minutes: ADD). Notes, text and translation included.
Recorded 1957.

BBC RADIO 3
90-93 FM

This performance is unique, with Act 4 for once a culmination in Callas's supreme account of the death scene. She may present a rather formidable portrait of a young girl in Act 1, but here the final act with its long duet and the big aria, "Sola, perduta, abbandonata", is far more than an epilogue to the rest, rather a culmination, with Callas at her very peak. Di Stefano, too, is on superb form and Serafin's pacing of the score is masterly. Di Stefano wipes the floor with most of his rivals past and present: in Act 4 he has a concerned tenderness for Manon that others can only sketch, his debonair charm in "Tra voi belle" is incomparable and (rarest of virtues among tenors) he never sings past the limits of his voice. Fioravanti as Lescaut and Calabrese as Geronte sing well if not very characterfully.

However, digital CD remastering in this instance loses out. A break has to be made in Act 2 – in a fairly innocuous place before the duet "Tu, tu, amore tu". The first two acts make up a total timing only a few seconds over the 75-minute limit, but evidently it was enough to prevent them going on to a single CD. That said, the CD brings the same advantages in refining the original boxy sound without glamorizing it in false stereo, plus the usual advantages of absence of background and ease of finding places. For an account of *Manon Lescaut* which comes fully to terms with the opera's huge contrasts of colour and mood you will also have to have a modern recording, for with all its improvements the sound here necessarily remains very dry and unatmospheric.

Puccini La Rondine.

Angela Gheorghiu *sop* Magda
Roberto Alagna *ten* Ruggero
Inva Mula-Tchako *sop* Lisette
William Matteuzzi *ten* Prunier
Alberto Rinaldi *bar* Rambaldo
Patricia Biccire *sop* Yvette
Patrizia Ciofi *sop* Bianca
Monica Bacelli *mez* Suzy
Riccardo Simonetti *bar* Périchaud
Toby Spence *ten* Gobin
Enrico Fissore *bar* Crébillon

1997

Puccini Le Villi – excerpts.
Prelude; L'Abbandono; La Tregenda; Ecco la casa … Torna ai felice dì.
Roberto Alagna *ten*

Puccini Morire!.
Roberto Alagna *ten*
Antonio Pappano *pf*

London Voices; London Symphony Orchestra / Antonio Pappano.
EMI Ⓟ ① CDS5 56338-2 (two discs: 131 minutes: DDD). Texts and translations included.
Recorded 1996.

It could not be more welcome when a recording transforms a work, as this one does, setting it on a new plane. *La Rondine* ("The Swallow"), Puccini's ill-timed attempt to emulate Lehár in the world of operetta, completed during the First World War, has long been counted his most serious failure, "a bird with half-broken wings" as Mosco Carner called it. The RCA recording conducted by Francesco Molinari-Pradelli with Anna Moffo characterizing splendidly in the Violetta-like role of Magda, amply demonstrated the charms of the piece, followed by Lorin Maazel's higher-powered if less idiomatic reading for Sony, with Dame Kiri Te Kanawa and Plácido Domingo giving generalized portraits of the courtesan and the student she falls in love with.

Puccini's cunning has never been in doubt either, for he and his librettists cleverly interweave elements not just of *La traviata* but of *The Merry Widow* and *Die Fledermaus*, not to mention earlier Puccini operas. His melodic style may for the most part be simpler than before, but one striking theme follows another with a profusion that any other composer might envy. What Pappano reveals far more than before is the subtlety with which Puccini interweaves his themes and motifs, with conversational passages made spontaneous-sounding in their flexibility. Above all, Pappano consistently brings out the poetry, drawing on emotions far deeper than are suggested by this operetta-like subject, thanks also to Gheorghiu's superb performance, translating her mastery as Violetta to this comparable character. Magda's first big solo, "Che il bel sogno di Doretta" (neatly forecast by the poet, Prunier, in the preceding section) finds Gheorghiu at her most ravishing, tenderly expressive in her soaring phrases, opening out only at the final climax.

Then through the following acts she makes you share the courtesan's wild dream of finding her young student, her suppressed excitement as she goes off in disguise to the student haunt of Bullier's, the dream-like meeting with Ruggero, her impulsive rejection of her protector, Rambaldo, the close of Act 2 so similar to the duetting of Rodolfo and Mimì. Most striking of all is the way she convinces you of her heartbreak, when in Act 3 she finally gives up Ruggero, not through any opposition from his family, but out of love for him, knowing the liaison would ruin him. From first to last, tenderly, often with a throb in the voice, her vocal acting convinces you that Magda's are genuine, deep emotions, painful at the end, intensified by the ravishing beauty of her voice.

As Ruggero, the hero, Alagna has a far less complex role, winningly characterizing the ardent young student, singing in his freshest voice. What will specially delight Puccinians in this set is that he is given an entrance aria about Paris, "Parigi e un citta" (first disc, track 3), which transforms his otherwise minimal contribution to Act 1. Adapting it from a song, Puccini included it in the 1920 Viennese version of the score, but never incorporated it in the original Italian version, as it certainly deserves. The partnership of Gheorghiu and Alagna highlights the way that Puccini in the melodic lines for each of his central characters makes Ruggero's more forthright, Magda's more complex. So in the Act 2 duet when the disguised Magda wonders why he should ever discover her secret ("Perche mai cercato", first disc, track 23) the style is suddenly more sophisticated with its upward *glissandos*, a point superbly reinforced by Pappano, drawing glowing sounds from the LSO. Other ravishing moments involve *pianissimo* strings, as when Magda's *Rondine* theme is recalled towards the end of Act 1, "Forse come un rondine" (first disc, track 14) and the reference back to the Doretta theme at the very end of the act (first disc, track 16). Neither previous set offers nearly as much subtlety.

Among much else, the role of the poet, Prunier, is transformed thanks to the casting of the clear-toned William Matteuzzi in what is normally a *comprimario* role. Not only is his relationship with Magda beautifully drawn, his improbable affair with the skittish maid, Lisette (clone of Adele in *Fledermaus*), is made totally convincing too, mirroring Magda's affair. Then in the Act 3 duet with Lisette his head voice for the final top D flat is a delight (second disc, track 7, 3'38"). Inva Mula-Tchako is equally well cast in the soubrette role of Lisette, bright and clear and vivacious, with Alberto Rinaldi making the sugar-daddy, Rambaldo, the dull dog Puccini intended. At least the arrival of Rambaldo at Bullier's is made more dramatic than usual. As well as bringing out the subtleties, Pappano is equally convincing in the vigorous, flamboyant music, and the big drinking ensemble which crowns the Act 2 party scene with its glorious tune has all the thrust you could want, even more than in the previous sets. The recording is warm and atmospheric, with ample clarity, fuller if not as immediate on instrumental sound as the RCA set.

The fill-ups are welcome too, particularly as neither of the rival sets has any. The excerpts from *Le Villi*, warm and dramatic, make one wish that Pappano could go on to record that first of Puccini's operas, with Alagna giving a ringing account of Roberto's aria, as he does of the song, *Morire!* – with Pappano at the piano. Originally an album-piece written for a wartime charity, Puccini used it, transposed up a semitone, with different words, as the entrance aria for Ruggero, already mentioned. The whole story is well told in Michael Kaye's invaluable annotated songbook, *The Unknown Puccini* (OUP: 1987). Altogether a set to treasure for bringing out the full genius of a tenderly moving work.

Puccini Tosca.

Montserrat Caballé *sop* Tosca
José Carreras *ten* Cavaradossi

Ingvar Wixell *bar* Scarpia
Samuel Ramey *bass* Angelotti
Piero De Palma *ten* Spoletta
Domenico Trimarchi *bar* Sacristan
William Elvin *bar* Sciarrone, Gaoler
Ann Murray *mez* Shepherd Boy
Chorus and Orchestra of the Royal Opera House, Covent Garden / Sir Colin Davis.
Philips Duo Ⓜ ① 438 359-2PM2 (two discs: 118 minutes: ADD). Recorded 1976.

Caballé's Tosca is one of the most ravishingly sung on record, with scarcely a less than beautiful note from one end of the role to the other, save where an occasional phrase lies a touch low for her. She doesn't quite have the 'prima donna' (in quotes, mind) temperament for the part (the coquettish malice of "but make her eyes black!", as Tosca forgives Cavaradossi for using a blonde stranger as model for his altarpiece of the Magdalen, is not in Caballé's armoury; either that or she knows that her voice would sound arch attempting it), but her portrayal is much more than a display of lovely sounds. She is precise with words, takes minute care over phrasing, and although some may not care for her characteristic scoops at the outset of "Vissi d'arte", she knows to a split second where dead-centre precise pitching becomes crucial. Carreras's Cavaradossi is one of his best recorded performances: the voice untarnished, the line ample, and if he's tempted at times to over-sing (he quite drowns the Sacristan's interjections in "Recondita armonia") one forgives the fault for the sake of his poetic ardour (a very good "E lucevan le stelle"). Wixell is the fly in the ointment: a capable actor and an intelligent artist, but his gritty timbre lacks centre and thus the necessary dangerous suavity.

Davis's direction is considerably flexible but dramatic and finely detailed; the secondary singers (Murray a convincingly boy-like Shepherd, Trimarchi an uncaricatured Sacristan, Ramey an aristocratic Angelotti) are all very good indeed. The recording, despite some rather unconvincing sound effects, still sounds very well, with space around the voices and a natural balance between them and the orchestra. Still a very competitive recording, in short; a pity that Philips, in their otherwise praiseworthy decision to pack two CDs into a jewel-case no thicker than those normally holding just one, should have saved space by omitting the libretto.

Puccini Tosca (sung in English).

Jane Eaglen *sop* Tosca
Dennis O'Neill *ten* Cavaradossi
Gregory Yurisich *bar* Scarpia
Peter Rose *bass* Angelotti
John Daszak *ten* Spoletta
Andrew Shore *bass* Sacristan
Christopher Booth-Jones *bass* Sciarrone
Ashley Holland *bass* Gaoler
Charbel Michael *mez* Shepherd Boy
Peter Kay Children's Choir; Geoffrey Mitchell Choir; Philharmonia Orchestra / David Parry.
Chandos Ⓟ CHAN3000 (two discs: 118 minutes: DDD). Notes and text included. Recorded 1995.

This is an issue to delight far more than devotees of opera in English, a gripping account of Puccini's red-blooded drama. Above all, it offers the first major recording to demonstrate the powers of Jane Eaglen at full stretch in one of the most formidable, vocally satisfying portrayals of the role of Tosca in years. David Parry here demonstrates his full understanding of Puccini and the bite and energy in the playing of the Philharmonia, not to mention the expressive warmth in the love music, will have you riveted as though hearing the music for the first time. The opulent Chandos sound, cleanly focused with plenty of atmosphere and presence, adds to the impact, whether in the power of the big tuttis or in the subtlety of whispered string *pianissimos*. Off-stage effects are nicely evocative, though the sequence of bell-sounds at the start of Act 3 is so clear it suggests an orchestra rather than a Roman landscape. Otherwise, the slightly forward balance of voices against orchestra is very well judged for a set in which the audibility of words is paramount.

The translation is Edmund Tracey's as used by ENO at the Coliseum and generally very good because unobtrusive, even if you get occasional awkwardnesses. Eaglen is well matched by Dennis O'Neill as Cavaradossi, aptly Italianate in every register, and betraying only a slight unevenness occasionally, not a wobble, on high notes under pressure. Gregory Yurisich makes a powerful Scarpia, younger-sounding than most, and therefore a more plausible lover. The others are well cast too, notably Peter Rose as an outstanding, fresh-voiced Angelotti.

Puccini Tosca.

Leontyne Price *sop* Tosca
Giuseppe di Stefano *ten* Cavaradossi
Giuseppe Taddei *bar* Scarpia

Carlo Cava *bass* Angelotti
Piero De Palma *ten* Spoleta
Fernando Corena *bass* Sacristan
Leonardo Monreale *bass* Sciarrone
Alfredo Mariotti *bass* Gaoler
Herbert Weiss *treb* Shepherd Boy
Vienna State Opera Chorus; Vienna Philharmonic Orchestra / Herbert von Karajan.
Decca ® ℗ 452 620-2DF2 (two discs: 114 minutes:). Text and translation included. Recorded 1962.

Karajan's classic version of *Tosca* was originally issued on the RCA label, but produced by John Culshaw of Decca at a vintage period. The first surprise is to find the sound satisfying in almost every way, with a firm sense of presence and with each voice and each section of the orchestra cleanly focused within the stereo spectrum. That is a spectacular tribute to Decca engineering of the time, and to the detailed production of Culshaw. There is some thinness at times on high violins but that is never sourly obtrusive. There are also the occasional bumps and noises which the LP process never revealed on the mastertape, which now come out on CD, but they are few enough to be undistracting.

What is less surprising is the supremacy of the Karajan version as an interpretation. He was always a master Puccinian, and this set was a prime example of that mastery. As an interpretation it is even more individual and more spontaneous-sounding than his 1985 version made for DG in Berlin. A prime instance comes at the end of Act 1, where Scarpia's *Te Deum* is taken daringly slowly, even more so than in Berlin, and conveys a quiver of menace that no other version begins to match. An extra nicety is the way that in the instrumental introduction to Cavaradossi's first aria, "Recondita armonia", he treats it as the musical equivalent of a painter mixing his colours, the very point Puccini no doubt had in mind. Karajan, though individual, and regularly challenging his singers (as he does with Taddei in the slow speed for the *Te Deum*) is most solicitous in following the voices. It is fascinating to note what expressive freedom he allows his tenor, di Stefano, and he makes Leontyne Price relax, giving a superb assumption of the role, big and rich of tone, intense of expression; the voice is the more beautiful for not being recorded too closely.

Puccini Tosca.

Maria Callas *sop* Tosca
Giuseppe di Stefano *ten* Cavaradossi
Tito Gobbi *bar* Scarpia
Franco Calabrese *bass* Angelotti
Angelo Mercuriali *ten* Spoleta
Melchiorre Luise *bass* Sacristan
Dario Caselli *bass* Sciarrone, Gaoler
Alvaro Cordova *treb* Shepherd Boy
Chorus and Orchestra of La Scala, Milan / Victor de Sabata.
EMI mono ℗ ℗ CDS5 56304-2 (two discs: 108 minutes: ADD). Notes, text and translation included. Recorded 1953.

The producer Walter Legge used to quite often question the necessity of stereo. Now more strikingly than ever in this remastering of one of the great classic performances of the gramophone, one of his own masterpieces as a creative recording producer, it is easy to see what he meant. With off-stage effects, for example – so important in Puccini – precisely placed, there is a sense of presence normally reserved for two-channel reproduction. In the long duet between Tosca and Cavaradossi in Act 3 you can even detect a difference of placing between the two singers, Callas set at a slight distance, though whether or not to offset a microphone problem with so biting a voice one can only guess. The immediacy is astonishing, and the great moment of the execution with trombones rasping and the fusillade reproduced at a true *fortissimo* has never been represented on record with greater impact.

What is especially delightful is that where on most previous CD transfers of mono originals the results have emphasized the single-channel flatness, often with sound lacking in body, this is full and weighty. A satisfyingly strong, but not boomy bass, balances the extra brightness and clarity introduced in the treble. The slightly jangling brightness on some percussion instruments gives some hint of the age of the recording, but with mono of this vintage it is amazing what bloom there is even on the violins, and when it comes to the voices, there one simply forgets the years, and drinks in the glory of one of the really great recorded opera performances as never before. Apart from Legge's skills we must not forget Christopher Parker who was responsible for the digital remastering.

The contrasts of timbre are beautifully brought out – amazingly wide with Gobbi as with Callas and with di Stefano producing his most honeyed tones. Though in the Milan acoustic there is less space than we have grown used to in the age of stereo, the separation of voices and orchestra is excellent, with the strands of the accompaniment to "Vissi d'arte", for example, finely clarified. Only in the big *Te Deum* scene at the end of Act 1 is there a hint of overloading. Wonderful as Gobbi's and di Stefano's performances are, and superbly dramatic as de Sabata's conducting is, it is the unique Callas in the title-role that provides the greatest marvel, and here more than ever one registers the facial changes implied in each phrase, with occasional hints of a chuckle (usually ironic) apparent. One only wishes that EMI had provided many more bands instead of relying on just a few index points and only bands for the separate acts. But for such a performance everything is worth it.

Puccini Tosca.
Raina Kabaivanska *sop* Tosca
Plácido Domingo *ten* Cavaradossi
Sherill Milnes *bar* Scarpia
Giancarrio Luccardi *bass* Angelotti
Mario Ferrara *ten* Spoletta
Alfredo Mariotti *bass* Sacristan
Bruno Grella *bar* Sciarrone
Domenico Medici *sngr* Gaoler
Plácido Domingo Jnr *treb* Shepherd Boy
Ambrosian Singers; New Philharmonia Orchestra / Bruno Bartoletti.
Video Director: **Gianfranco de Bosio.**
Decca Ⓟ 🔲 071 402-3DH (116 minutes). Film recorded 1976.

This film, made on location in Rome where the opera is set, is the most compelling video yet of this work (the 1992 recording for TV on site, done live, is too much of a hit-and-miss affair and not as well cast). It is intelligently directed by Gianfranco de Bosio to make the most of the evocative settings, yet manages at the same time to concentrate on the personal, specific confrontations of the principals. He achieves some really superb location photography that simply wasn't possible in the live version. Angelotti is caught running towards the church of Sant'Angelo before the music begins. Tosca is seen leaving the Palazzo Farnese at the end of Act 2 and a shepherd boy (actually Domingo's son!) is glimpsed at the start of Act 3, but by and large the dramatic verities of a performance on stage are preserved, albeit in fairly conventional form.

The singers cope convincingly with post-synchronization, and they form a cast which looks roughly the age of the characters they are portraying, unusual in this opera, and they all have voices of the right weight for their roles. Kabaivanska was reigning Tosca at the time and for many years afterwards; at the peak of her form, she catches all Tosca's sensuous, wilful, vulnerable and courageous characteristics. Her reading is exquisitely phrased, keenly sung with unforced, clear tone, bold in line and attack. Domingo, in his absolute prime in 1976, sings an impassioned Cavaradossi and shows a deal of finesse in the role's quieter moments. His great cries of "Vittoria!" are not only electrifying, they're ringingly musical as well. Milnes makes a young Scarpia, credible as a forceful dictator and feared man of action, though his scowling is a bit conventional; he should have smiled more often – the core, the obscene relish in Scarpia's music, is missing. Mariotti offers a happily unexaggerated, properly sung Sacristan. Bartoletti's conducting has a lushness to match the visual richness, unhurried but dramatic. The picture is excellent, the sound, although pre-digital, full and rich.

Puccini Il trittico.

Puccini Il tabarro[a].
Tito Gobbi *bar* Michele
Margaret Mas *sop* Giorgetta
Giacinto Prandelli *ten* Luigi
Piero De Palma *ten* Tinca
Plinio Clabassi *bar* Talpa
Miriam Pirazzini *mez* Frugola

Puccini Suor Angelica[b].
Victoria de los Angeles *sop* Suor Angelica
Fedora Barbieri *mez* Princess
Mina Doro *mez* Abbess, Mistress of the novices
Corinna Vozza *mez* Sister Monitor
Lidia Marimpietri *sop* Suor Genovieffa, Almoner First Sister
Santa Chissari *sop* Suor Osmina, Almoner Second Sister, Novice
Anna Marcangeli *sop* Suor Dolcina
Teresa Cantarini *mez* Infirmary Sister
Silvia Bertona *sop* First Lay Sister
Maria Huder *mez* Second Lay Sister

Puccini Gianni Schicchi[c].
Tito Gobbi *bar* Gianni Schicchi
Victoria de los Angeles *sop* Lauretta
Carlo del Monte *ten* Rinuccio

Anna Maria Canali *mez* Zita
Adelio Zagonara *ten* Gherardo
Lidia Marimpietri *sop* Nella
Claudio Cornoldi *ten* Gherardino
Saturno Meletti *bass* Betto di Signa
Paolo Montarsolo *bass* Simone
Fernando Valentini *bar* Marco
Giuliana Raymondi *sop* La Ciesca
Rome Opera Chorus and Orchestra / [a]**Vincenzo Bellezza,** [b]**Tullio Serafin,** [c]**Gabriele Santini.**
EMI mono/stereo Ⓜ Ⓘ CMS7 64165-2 (three discs: 161 minutes: ADD). Texts and translations
included. Recorded 1955-8.

Unless you insist on the most up-to-date recorded sound, or on buying the individual operas of
Puccini's trilogy separately, this is the classic *Trittico*, and the obvious first recommendation. Gobbi's
blackly authoritative but pitiful Michele in *Il tabarro* and his genially authoritative Schicchi (the two
outer panels of the triptych do match, in an odd sort of way) have seldom been equalled, let alone
surpassed. De los Angeles's Angelica is more purely and movingly sung than any other on record, and
her Lauretta in *Gianni Schicchi* is enchanting. Could it be said, even so, that *Il tabarro* is the weak
link in this trilogy? It is a three-hander, surely, and neither the soprano nor the tenor are quite in
Gobbi's league? Mas is a bit plummy and mezzo-ish, true, but the slight implication this gives that
Giorgetta's liaison with the young stevedore Luigi is her last chance at escape from a hateful life, and
a marriage that has soured, adds an extra twinge of pain to a plot in which all three principals are
victims. And in this context Prandelli's slightly strenuous rawness of tone characterizes Luigi
rather well.

In *Gianni Schicchi*, Carlo del Monte as Rinuccio also looks like under-casting but in fact he's one
of the few tenors who've recorded the part who sounds convincingly young, and his ardent praise of
Florence and the 'new men' who are reinvigorating the city is proudly sung. Here, too, Gobbi is
surrounded by a constellation of pungent character actors, and de los Angeles in *Suor Angelica*
is teamed with a charmingly girlish, impulsive Genovieffa and with Fedora Barbieri's rigidly
implacable Princess (is there another parallel here, with the stiff-necked Zita, 'La Vecchia', in *Gianni
Schicchi*?). With generally very stylish conducting throughout (only Bellezza in *Il tabarro* is a touch
staid, and he omits nearly all of Puccini's off-stage sound effects) only the rather elderly recordings
might be seen as a drawback. EMI boldly label the whole set 'stereo', but both *Il tabarro* and *Suor
Angelica* sound like minimally 'processed' mono: a touch congested in fuller passages, a hint of fizzy
brightness here and there, but nothing that's not abundantly worth putting up with for such
performances as these.

Puccini Turandot.
Dame Joan Sutherland *sop* Princess Turandot
Luciano Pavarotti *ten* Calaf
Monserrat Caballé *sop* Liù
Tom Krause *bar* Ping
Nicolai Ghiaurov *bass* Timur
Sir Peter Pears *ten* Emperor Altoum
Pier Francesco Poli *ten* Pang, Prince of Persia
Piero De Palma *ten* Pong
Sabin Markov *bar* Mandarin
Wandsworth School Boys' Choir; John Alldis Choir;
London Philharmonic Orchestra / Zubin Mehta.
Decca Ⓕ Ⓘ 414 274-2DH2 (two discs: 117 minutes: ADD). Recorded 1972.

When Karajan's DG Vienna recording of *Turandot* appeared on CD in 1984, many collectors
wondered how this much older Decca set would sound in the new medium. The impression then was
that this 1972 recording, even on LP, was firmer and better defined, and so it proves to be. On CD
this more than ever is confirmed as one of the very finest of the many opera recordings made in
London's Kingsway Hall, with a vivid sense of presence and reality. Even the deep tones of the bass
drum at the very start are more effectively caught here than on the digital Karajan recording, and even
the detail within the heaviest tuttis and choruses has a definition one normally associates with digital
recording. It is striking, too, how firmly placed within an identifiable acoustic each solo voice or
instrument is, and if there is a limitation of frequency range compared with the latest recordings, it is
hard to detect when the atmosphere is so realistic.

As for the performance, it can still be regarded as the most satisfying of all, with Sutherland an icy
Princess who gives signs of human vulnerability far earlier than usual, and is the more moving for
that. Caballé and Pavarotti are both on magnificent form too. Mehta equally is challenged by his
starry cast to produce an outstandingly strong and colourful reading. Two discs for the Decca set as
against three for the DG is another clear advantage. The second CD here begins with Turandot's entry
and the big aria, "In questa reggia", which is just as convenient as having one CD per act.

Puccini Turandot.

Maria Callas *sop* Princess Turandot
Eugenio Fernandi *ten* Calaf
Dame Elisabeth Schwarzkopf *sop* Liù
Mario Borriello *bar* Ping
Nicola Zaccaria *bass* Timur
Giuseppe Nessi *ten* Emperor Altoum
Renato Ercolani *ten* Pang
Piero De Palma *ten* Pong
Giulio Mauri *bass* Mandarin
Chorus and Orchestra of La Scala, Milan / Tullio Serafin.
EMI mono Ⓜ Ⓓ CDS5 56307-2 (two discs: 118 minutes: ADD). Notes, text and translation
included. Recorded 1957.

To have Callas, the most flashing-eyed of all sopranos as Turandot, is – on record at least – the
most natural piece of casting. Other sopranos may be comparably icy in their command, but
Callas with her totally distinctive tonal range was able to give the fullest possible characterization.
With her, Turandot was not just an implacable man-hater but a highly provocative female. One
quickly reads something of Callas's own underlying vulnerability into such a portrait, its tensions, the
element of brittleness. Equally, in the final arioso of Alfano's completion of Puccini's score, "Del
primo pianto", the chesty way she sings "Straniero" in the opening phrase, addressing Calaf, is
unforgettable in its continuing threat. With her the character seems so much more believably complex
than with others. It was sad that, except at the very beginning of her career, she felt unable to sing the
role in the opera-house, but this 1957 recording is far more valuable than any memory of the past,
one of the most thrillingly magnetic of all her recorded performances, the more so when Schwarzkopf
as Liù provides a comparably characterful and distinctive portrait, far more than a Puccinian 'little
woman', sweet and wilting. Even more than usual one regrets that the confrontation between princess
and slave is so brief. Though for some, Schwarzkopf's observance of markings in Liù's two arias may
seem too meticulous, the extra detail reinforces the fine-spun Straussian quality, notably in the rising
and falling octaves of "Signore ascolta".
   Next to such supreme singers it was perhaps cruel of Walter Legge to choose so relatively
uncharacterful a tenor as Eugenio Fernandi as Calaf, but at least his timbre is pleasingly distinctive.
What fully matches the singing of Callas and Schwarzkopf in its positive character is the conducting
of Serafin, sometimes surprisingly free – as in the *accelerando* at the end of Act 1, begun much earlier
than the score allows – but in its pacing invariably capturing rare colour, atmosphere and mood as
well as dramatic point. The Ping, Pang and Pong episode of Act 2 has rarely sparkled so naturally,
the work of a conductor who has known and loved the music in the theatre over a long career.
   The conducting is so vivid that the limitations of the mono sound hardly seem to matter. As the
very opening will reveal, the CD transfer makes it satisfyingly full-bodied. Like so many of Callas's
Scala sets the acoustic is on the dry side with solo voices balanced forward. The chorus are not always
well served, with sound that tends to overload at climaxes, but the propulsion of Serafin's conducting
has one readily accepting that. Though with its rich, atmospheric stereo the Mehta set remains the
best general recommendation, it is thrilling to have this historic document so vividly restored.

Gaetano Pugnani

Italian 1731-1798

Pugnani Werther.

Graziano Piazza *spkr* Werther
Luca Occelli *spkr* Narrator
Academia Montis Regalis / Luigi Mangiocavallo.
Opus 111 Ⓔ Ⓓ OPS30-197/8 (two discs: 92 minutes: DDD). 🖉 Notes, text and translation
included. Recorded 1997.

This is certainly well off the beaten track and has only recently been brought to light – a "musical
translation" of Goethe's novel *Werther*, which had been published a couple of decades previously.
(The Baker-Slonimsky Dictionary, exceptionally, is totally wrong about this work.) It consists of over
20 musical items that were so linked with the events of the story as to be self-explanatory, with the aid
only of a précis, to audiences of the time, to whom *Werther*, which had unleashed a furore of literary
discussion, was very familiar. However, the extreme brevity of some of these items, some of which end
inconclusively, and the fact that Pugnani's work was performed in 1796 in the Burgtheater in Vienna,
lend weight to the argument that it was intended as a melodrama (a genre rare in Italy though
common in Germany); and Alberto Basso has reconstituted it with an actor in the role of Werther
reading his letters (in an Italian translation), which are interspersed with, occasionally superimposed
on, the relevant music, plus a narrator to fill in a gap in the letters at the end. The music amounts to
66 minutes in all, beginning with a striking overture of tragic cast and then including not only

programmatic sections – the spring bubbling from rocks, the storm after the ball (at which a minuet and an English country dance are played) – but imaginative evocations of mood such as the hero feeling faint or his despair at the thought that Charlotte cannot be his. Conspicuous in all this is the great importance Pugnani allots to the wind, both in ensemble and when employed soloistically: a solo clarinet represents Charlotte's singing at the piano, for example, and a bassoon becomes prominent at Werther's final farewell. But the strings are also treated generously: cello and viola soloists are heard at the end of the first part of the work, and in the second, at Werther's tears, there is a substantial violin *concertante*, first *cantabile* then virtuosic. The ill-starred lovers' last meeting is vividly treated as a dramatic recitative.

Graziano Piazza is a persuasive actor with a beautiful voice; the orchestra throw themselves wholeheartedly into the music's diversity, playing expressively and with spirit; and the work is well produced. Although Pugnani was perhaps the greatest violinist of his time, his impressive dramatic sense makes one curious about his eight operas, none of which is known to us.

Henry Purcell

British 1659-1695

Purcell Dido and Aeneas.
    Catherine Bott *sop* Dido
    John Mark Ainsley *ten* Aeneas
    Emma Kirkby *sop* Belinda
    David Thomas *bass* Sorceress
    Elizabeth Priday *sop* First witch
    Sara Stowe *sop* Second witch
    Julianne Baird *sop* Second woman
    Daniel Lochmann *treb* First sailor
    Michael Chance *alto* Spirit
    Academy of Ancient Music Chorus and Orchestra / Christopher Hogwood.
    L'Oiseau-Lyre Ⓟ Ⓞ 436 992-2OHO (52 minutes: DDD). ✍ Notes and text included. Recorded 1992.

Luxury casting here. Emma Kirkby (whose Dido, for Parrott on Chandos, remains one of the finest on record) sings Belinda; David Thomas (whose Aeneas, on the same recording, was praiseworthy) sings the Sorceress; Michael Chance takes the tiny part of the Spirit, thereby putting its moment into centre stage as the gloriously conceived turning-point of the story. A few innovations, too. We have had all kinds of Sorceress on record, including the terrifying Jantina Noorman (Parrott) and the limpid tenor of Nigel Rogers (Pinnock, on Archiv; following the arguments that the Sorceress could be a man). Hogwood opts for David Thomas, who offers perhaps the most eloquent version so far. He gives full value to the words and the music. Less convincing is the use of a boy for the sailor's song; the music is indeed in treble clef in the two very late sources, and Hogwood hopefully points out that you could be a midshipman at the age of 11 but, despite direct and spirited singing, its text is so inappropriate for a boy as to make the decision seem quite wrong. Much more successful is the use of the Drottningholm wind-machines, in all their wonderful variety, to interpret the various stage-instructions and give the entire performance a real sense of verisimilitude. Here and in the unwritten dances, the solutions are thoroughly musical and thoroughly theatrical.

Catherine Bott is a fine Dido, even-voiced across the range and powerfully expressive if occasionally a touch free with the rhythms. Quite where she stands among the wonderful range of her predecessors, including Anne Sofie von Otter, Ann Murray, Emma Kirkby, Jessye Norman, Dame Janet Baker and Tatiana Troyanos, it may be too soon to say: hers is a slightly less individual reading than some, but is never for a moment outclassed. On the other hand John Mark Ainsley easily stands as the finest Aeneas since David Thomas. This is a very difficult role to handle dramatically, because its moods change so fast; and Ainsley handles all this with heartbreaking ease, allowing his tenor voice to portray the hero's confusion (most of his predecessors have been baritones or basses). This is a classic interpretation. So too is Hogwood's reading of the score, with a healthy string band (7. 7. 5. 5) that gives an unusual clarity to the contrapuntal lines and a miraculously controlled chorus, also of a healthy size. But what comes across repeatedly is Hogwood's faultless sense of the right speed and the right rhythm as well as his ability to see the moment when everything must be interrupted to give space to the drama. There are none of the extremes of tempo found on most other recordings, just absolute firmness. With that, everything falls into place and sounds right. *Dido* has done extremely well on record over the years; but collectors will find themselves returning to this one many times.

Purcell Dido and Aeneas.
    Tatiana Troyanos *sop* Dido
    Richard Stilwell *bar* Aeneas
    Felicity Palmer *sop* Belinda
    Patricia Kern *mez* Sorceress

Alfreda Hodgson *mez* First witch, Spirit
Linn Maxwell *sop* Second witch
Elizabeth Gale *sop* Second woman
Philip Langridge *ten* First sailor
English Chamber Choir and Orchestra / Raymond Leppard.
Erato Libretto Ⓜ Ⓓ 2292-45263-2 (56 minutes: ADD). Notes and text included. Recorded 1977.

This reissue came into direct competition with the Parrott full-price Chandos Chaconne reissue in 1991. These reissues perhaps offer the two extremes of *Dido* interpretation. Raymond Leppard with the English Chamber Orchestra gives a grand performance very much in the old style, one that would sound well in a large opera-house and from the very first notes declares itself to be the narrative of one of the world's most famous tragedies: the sound is opulent, all the inner details of Purcell's counterpoint are milked for their full expressive value, and the playing has all the control of shading one would expect from the English Chamber Orchestra at its best. Alongside this, Parrott can seem almost too intimate: the advantages of his lighter tone are obvious enough, and historical research decisively supports his more private approach; but Leppard surely shows that Purcell's music can well support a grander reading. Besides, Leppard gives a performance with considerable bite and verve. His only major drawback is in the chorus, which sounds leaden-footed when put alongside Parrott's bright and nimble choir (though Parrott's singers do not approach the sheer lilting happiness of the First Act chorus, "Fear no joy").

For all that it now seems dated, then, Leppard's performance has dramatic dimensions that are eminently worth retaining. These begin with the contrast between the rich-voiced Dido of Tatiana Troyanos and the clean Belinda of Felicity Palmer: the differences between their characters emerge very strongly here, whereas Emma Kirkby and Judith Nelson (Parrott) have strikingly similar voices. Troyanos and Palmer may both sound a shade miscast in terms of range, whereas Kirkby and Nelson cover their lines effortlessly; but the contrast of personality between Dido and Belinda must surely be the main dramatic force in the First Act, and Parrott misses that. Similarly the confrontation between Dido and Aeneas in the last act is more powerful in Leppard's recording. Although David Thomas is incomparably the best, most lucid and most intelligent Aeneas on disc, Parrott does not give him quite enough musical space to make the sudden changes of mind and mood comprehensible in dramatic terms; and for the same reason Kirkby cannot challenge the tragic and irascible singing of Troyanos in that scene. This is not a matter of historically appropriate colours so much as a sense of drama created by flexible tempo and declamation, matters in which Leppard's extensive experience in the theatre gave him the advantage. In other matters the two are more evenly balanced. Jantina Noorman is a distinctive and compelling Sorceress for Parrott, though not to everybody's taste, and Patricia Kern manages to generate a convincing threat by more conventional means. Both recordings come a little unstuck with the witches – those of Leppard sounding matronly and those of Parrott too absurd.

Although the Parrott recording has long been a favourite of many listeners, with Kirkby, Thomas and Nelson in the cast, Leppard's musicianship and sensitivity merit the closest attention: nobody will be disappointed with his performance.

Purcell Dido and Aeneas.
Kym Amps *sop* Dido
David van Asch *bass* Aeneas
Anna Crookes *sop* Belinda, Second witch
Sarah Connolly *mez* Sorceress
Ghislaine Morgan *sop* Second woman, First witch
Angus Davidson *alto* Spirit
The Scholars Baroque Ensemble.
Naxos Ⓢ Ⓓ 8 553108 (58 minutes: DDD). Notes and text included. Recorded 1994.

The Scholars Baroque Ensemble work all hands to the tiller, as they shun the idea of a single maestro directing the proceedings. Strong artistic leadership is something of a prerequisite in this concentrated and delicately paced opera: so often, a studio recording evokes little more than a dramatically haphazard series of tableaux. Whilst this recording cannot rival the leading versions for consistent intensity and refinement, The Scholars project a natural momentum, aided by deftly judged tempos and a refreshingly unmannered no-nonsense approach to phrasing. One-to-a-part strings leave us distinctly underwhelmed in the scrappily played Overture, and some of the most radiant dances too, but there is an immediate vocal presence with the assured and pragmatic Belinda of Anna Crookes and Kym Amps's increasingly involved Dido. Sarah Connolly's Sorceress means business and there is a real sense of the epic in her impressive voice. The chorus are exciting, robust and warm-toned and the lament-to-end-all-laments is sufficiently affecting to appeal to seasoned collectors and novices alike. David van Asch is a soft-edged Aeneas, which is certainly a most plausible characterization, though he suffers more than most from revealing close-miking.

That said, there is a compelling immediacy to the proceedings and were it not for some of the above misgivings, this would rate highly as a distinctive version on any terms – especially with some fresh and unobtrusive additions at critical moments. As it is, it is incredibly good value.

Purcell Dido and Aeneas.

Kirsten Flagstad *sop* Dido
Thomas Hemsley *bar* Aeneas
Dame Elisabeth Schwarzkopf *sop* Belinda, Second woman, Spirit
Eilidh McNab *sop* First woman
Arda Mandikian *con* Sorceress
Sheila Rex *sop* First witch
Anna Pollak *con* Second witch
David Lloyd *ten* Sailor
Mermaid Singers; Mermaid Orchestra / Geraint Jones.
EMI mono Ⓔ Ⓘ CDH7 61006-2 (59 minutes: ADD). Notes and text included. Recorded 1952.

This is a really satisfactory recording of *Dido*, if not a perfect one. Flagstad is in splendid voice and her tone, in her nobly-sung first solo, "Ah, Belinda", is perfectly controlled, her phrasing a joy; she had obviously studied the word-values with a very good coach. Not once is she tempted to call on anything like the full power of her voice, not even in the dramatic recitative in the scene where Aeneas deserts her. In the aria, "When I am laid in earth", which she had recorded before, she was good, but here she has grown more into the style and the great lament is nobly done. The orchestra, for once, falls below its high standard, the bass octaves at the start not being perfectly in tune. At all other points it produces, under the direction of Geraint Jones, musicianly playing and a lack of that lumpy rhythm that is fatal in Purcell's music. Elisabeth Schwarzkopf is a vivacious Belinda and sings her part with great assurance. One cannot think it was a good idea to cast her also for the Spirit although she does manage to make the vocal change; Arda Mandikian is a suitably spiteful Sorceress. Thomas Hemsley is a dignified and slightly diffident Aeneas, but one imagines that Dido gave him a strong inferiority complex! The chorus are lively and excellent, as are the orchestra. Jones occasionally over-refined his harpsichord part, as for example, in the Cave scene, and when the storm breaks. The recording balance is good and there is only one poor patch of orchestral tone, the accompaniment of "Oft she visits this lone mountain" which sounds confused. The Echo chorus is well engineered, and the text throughout the opera comes over very clearly.

Purcell Dioclesian, Acts 1-4.

Catherine Pierard *sop*
James Bowman *alto*
John Mark Ainsley *ten*
Mark Padmore *ten*
Michael George *bass*
Collegium Musicum 90 Chorus; Collegium Musicum 90 / Richard Hickox.
Chandos Chaconne Ⓔ Ⓘ CHAN0568 (54 minutes: DDD). Text included. Recorded 1994.

It was *Dioclesian*, the least known of the four semi-opera masterpieces of Purcell, for which the composer initially earned a reputation for writing stage music. The 'opera' was by all accounts a roaring success, though music played a less important part in the stage works of the 1690s than it did in the masque-related works of the previous decades – ironically just at the time when England could at last boast a dramatic master who could stand tall amongst the 'greats' of France and Italy. If the paucity of tableaux means a less atmospheric scenic context, such as we experience in *The Fairy Queen* or *King Arthur*, there is still much fine music which deserves to be highly regarded.

To present the complete music for *Dioclesian* in two separate releases is not quite as surprising as it might seem, given the self-contained, almost operatic nature of the mini-drama which constitutes the majority of Act 5 (the masques from Act 5 are on a separate Chandos release). That Purcell evidently found the continuity of the masque an ideal opportunity to display his considerable dramatic flair can be gauged by the trouble he took to make a typically lightweight non-plot into something substantial. The remaining music from the play, which is contained in this recording of Acts 1-4, is made up typically of an Overture, Act Tunes, First and Second Music (instrumental numbers to warn the audience that the play was about to start) and Songs. The music is not divided equally between the acts but appears where Thomas Betterton, the adaptor of Fletcher's original play, thought musical contributions could adorn the spectacle. Hence Act 1 has but a hornpipe whilst Act 2 is brimming over with fine music of all descriptions.

Hickox is evidently committed to this score: the instrumental movements are all disciplined and yet display the buoyancy and variety of expression of one who senses the freshness and special flavour of Purcell's first foray into the theatre. His soloists are authoritative Purcellians and they never disappoint; you will particularly relish the close recording in movements such as "Great Diocles" where Michael George's splendid articulation and vocal timbre reach out to the listener. So, too, Catherine Pierard in the Appendices, where she sings "Since from my dear Astrea's sight" with a touching mystery. What fine music this is. Hickox manages to sustain the tension and climate he sets from the start which is arguably what Gardiner's 1987 set on Erato never quite manages. This recording is as triumphant and beguiling an addition to the exploding Purcell catalogue as any.

Purcell The Fairy Queen.

Barbara Bonney *sop*
Elisabeth von Magnus *sop*
Sylvia McNair *sop*
Michael Chance *alto*
Laurence Dale *ten*
Anthony Michaels-Moore *bar*
Robert Holl *bass*
Arnold Schoenberg Choir; Vienna Concentus Musicus / Nikolaus Harnoncourt.
Teldec Ⓟ Ⓒ 4509-97684-2 (two discs: 119 minutes: DDD). 🖉 Notes and text included.
Recorded 1994.

If you had to live with only one version of *The Fairy Queen*, you would on balance probably be safest with Christophers, though the field is very strong and the Gallic Christie (Harmonia Mundi), meticulous Norrington (EMI), consistent Gardiner (Archiv Produktion) and now, this challenging Harnoncourt complement each other most fortuitously.

Although Harnoncourt's long flirtation with mainstream repertoire continues ever towards the *fin de siècle* with Bruckner, his work with Concentus Musicus – his trusty period-instrument colleagues of over 30 years – seems to be enjoying a second wind and here we have a personal, if idiosyncratic, account of Purcell's *The Fairy Queen*. Part of his special missionary zeal is to dissolve some of the unnecessary and delimiting distinctions between musical style and performance style: music, as he has said, is built on firmer ground than merely knowledge, taste and musical conditions. Hence, supporters will welcome his holistic ideals on interpretation. Even if Harnoncourt is blurring the boundaries of expectation for music of the period, his own contribution is such an inimitable and discernible one in baroque performance, that such generalizations hold only so much water. That said, he approaches Purcell's great 1692 'dramatick' score with fresh and open abandon; in the instrumental numbers at the start, he goes out of his way to ask new questions. Forget the easy *politesse* of the prelude. Here we have frantic hustling and bustling, percussive lower strings and rip-roaring energy. If Harnoncourt seeks to grab the attention of this magical world of Titania and Oberon (heavily watered down from Shakespeare's *A Midsummer Night's Dream*), he also renders some of the more instantly graceful airs with a contrast of exquisite refinement. The range of characterization in the instrumental music will not suit those who like a prettier, more neutral palette (he colours many wind doublings on the reprises) but others will relish, as in the Second Act Tune, the ravishing shape and care taken to find the meaning behind the notes.

There are some eccentricities which misfire, such as the Drunken Poet scene which is surprisingly wooden despite Robert Holl's notable poet. Perhaps this type of teasing is – dare one say it – too English in its ironic banter. The chorus of 'pinchers' simply don't pinch with enough conviction and Harnoncourt plays a bit safe on his sub-plot humour. Where Harnoncourt shows his true colours is in the grand and forthright Overtures to Acts 1 and 4, as well as in the choruses, whose spaciousness and expressive range, if disarmingly unintimate compared with English groups, go some way to de-parochialize Purcell and give full flight to his bold gestures. Similarly successful are the unconventionally precipitous "Come, let us leave the town" (actually it makes perfect sense) and the reflectively languid tempo of "Come all ye songsters", unnerving to start with but structurally astute given its connection to the mood of Act 1.

Where this version is strongly competitive is in the cast of singers; if there is anything the tercentenary celebrations taught us it is that Purcell's music deserves great singers. Where Ton Koopman (Erato) calls on resident soloists from his choir (with the exception of Bott, Thomas and Schopper) and is found wanting, Harnoncourt lands two world-class sopranos. The quality tells in an ambrosially starry allegory on Night and a delicious Plaint, both sung by Sylvia McNair, as well as in a focus and clarity of expression from Barbara Bonney, whose "If love's a sweet passion" makes one forget how often this is sung out of tune. There are also important contributions from Michael Chance who is rather busier with Harnoncourt than Christophers, the former opting for a countertenor more often than a high tenor.

To sum up: Harnoncourt delivers an, at times, unsettling performance but one which contains moments of unique musical insight and the singing is consistently of the highest quality (save Elisabeth von Magnus, whose enunciation is unclear and manner too earnest).

Purcell The Fairy Queen.

Gillian Fisher *sop*
Lorna Anderson *sop*
Ann Murray *mez*
Michael Chance *alto*
John Mark Ainsley *ten*
Ian Partridge *ten*
Richard Suart *bass*
Michael George *bass*

BBC RADIO 3
90-93 FM

The Sixteen Choir and Orchestra / Harry Christophers.
Collins Classics Ⓕ ① 7013-2 (two discs: 133 minutes: DDD). Text included. Recorded 1990.

Harry Christophers gives us a performance much like that of John Eliot Gardiner, though he tends to be a shade fleeter, lighter in tone and more dramatic. While few singers can compare with Gardiner's David Thomas and Judith Nelson as Purcell stylists, Christophers has Gillian Fisher, Michael Chance and John Mark Ainsley all on absolutely top form, giving classic performances every time they sing. Some of Gardiner's inner lines are a bit more clearly recorded, particularly in the chorus work. But the main reason for comparing these two recordings is that they both seem to go wrong in the same music: in the meltingly sweet love-music of Act 3 and in their jerky approach to the trochaic rhythms that are so characteristic of Purcell's music, particularly in the last scene. That is, both short-change the poetry of the work. Still, most listeners will prefer either of them to the overdriven, overcoloured and heavily Frenchified version by the normally excellent William Christie. All three recordings entirely dispense with the spoken word: the reasons are easy to understand, but it is a matter of regret that Purcell's grandest achievement remains without any of the context that generated the music.

    Where Christophers is particularly successful is in the sequence of night music in Act 2. It is magically controlled, from the breathlessly still eloquence of Fisher in "See even the Night herself", through a nicely judged "I am come" from Ann Murray, a memorable reading of "One charming night" by Chance, Michael George's all-enveloping "Hush no more" and a stunningly caught final chorus. A performance like this – as indeed of the birthday ode in Act 4, similarly set in motion by Fisher's "Now the night" – shows dimensions of Purcell's genius that are all too rarely heard on disc. Other signal achievements here are Richard Suart's performance as the drunken poet, George and Chance doing the Coridon and Mopsa duet in a gentle 'mummerset', and two arias from Ian Partridge in Act 4. Sadly, Murray sounds uncomfortable and stylistically at odds with the remainder of the cast, though many listeners may like her characterful performance of the Act 5 Plaint.

Purcell The Indian Queen.

Emma Kirkby *sop*
Catherine Bott *sop*
John Mark Ainsley *ten*
Gerald Finley *bar*
David Thomas *bass*
Tommy Williams *sngr*
Chorus and Orchestra of the Academy of Ancient Music / Christopher Hogwood.
Also includes additional Act by Daniel Purcell.
L'Oiseau-Lyre Ⓕ ① 444 339-2OHO (73 minutes: DDD). 🖉 Notes and text included. Recorded 1994.

Purcell's fourth and last full-scale semi-opera, *The Indian Queen*, is often passed over in favour of its longer and more rounded predecessors, especially *King Arthur* and *The Fairy Queen*. The reasons are plentiful: Thomas Betterton, with whom Purcell collaborated, never finished his reworking of an early Restoration tragedy and even if he had torn himself away from his business interests in 1695, Purcell would not have been alive to set the remaining music for Act 5. As it happened, Henry's brother Daniel set the masque from the final act after Betterton had hired an anonymous writer to finish his adaptation. No one can deny that neither verse nor music achieved the heights imagined in the original collaboration; given the quality of the masques in Purcell's large 'dramatick' operas (including *Dioclesian*, of course), there is an undoubted sense of anticlimax. To cap it all, the story-line – the tale of a doomed queen – hardly encouraged *réjouissance* of a conventional type, or the full range of characterful scenes upon which Purcell thrived. More fundamental, as Curtis Price points out, is that the play was not ideal for conversion into an 'opera' in the first place. Purcell must have recognized that the subject matter (delivered in antiquated heroic couplets) was to provide him with few avenues for his imagination to reign. That there is so much fine music here is proof of the composer's undaunted spirit and peerless ability.

    The difference between the Purcell Simfony's graceful and intimate performance on Linn Records, also recorded in 1994, and this new account from Christopher Hogwood is that the latter makes us realize that for all the constraints, the score is not inherently small-scale and that it warrants all the subtlety of colour that can be achieved using 12 soloists and a decent sized choir and orchestra. Needless to say, Hogwood conveys a consistent, logical and meticulous understanding of the score. The orchestral playing is crisp and transparent (as in the Symphony of Act 2), the Academy of Ancient Music's articulation allowing the integrity of the inner parts to be heard to the full without compromising blend. Amongst a distinguished line-up of singers, John Mark Ainsley gets the lion's share and is perhaps marginally more effective as the Indian Boy than as Fame, but such gloriously mellifluous and controlled singing can only enhance the reputation of this work. Emma Kirkby is in fine fettle and she executes the justly celebrated song, "I attempt from love's sickness" with her usual communicative panache. Then comes the pleasurably contrasted voice of Catherine Bott: "They tell us that your mighty powers" could not be in better hands. David Thomas as Envy, with his two followers in the Act 2 masque, highlights this brilliant scene as the work of a true connoisseur of the theatre. Mature Purcell is most strongly felt in the deftly ironic invocation by the conjurer, Ismeron, whose "Ye twice ten thousand deities" is delivered authoritatively by Gerald Finley, though the lulling to sleep, before the God of Dream's gloomy non-prediction, is strangely unconvincing. Gardiner is particularly effective here on his 1979 Erato set.

Taken as a whole, the quality of music shines very brightly in this reading. It is perhaps a touch calculated in places. The Purcell Simfony's melting chorus, "While thus we bow before your shrine" is preferable; indeed, there is a tenderness in that recording which is touching but Hogwood's version has to take its place at the top of the list. The inclusion of Daniel Purcell's Act 5 masque is interesting but not much more than that. He evidently excelled himself but he also reaffirms Henry's superiority on all levels.

Purcell King Arthur.

Véronique Gens *sop*
Claron McFadden *sop*
Sandrine Piau *sop*
Susannah Waters *sop*
Mark Padmore *ten*
Iain Paton *ten*
Jonathan Best *bass*
Petteri Salomaa *bass*
François Bazola-Minori *bass*
Les Arts Florissants Chorus and Orchestra / William Christie.
Erato Ⓟ Ⓒ 4509-98535-2 (two discs: 90 minutes: DDD).  Notes and text included. Recorded 1995.

1995

King Arthur was conceived as a libretto by John Dryden as early as 1684 but since it conveyed extreme partiality to Charles II, the King's death a year later determined its quick demise, if indeed the text ever saw the light of day. Seven years later it re-emerged when Purcell famously collaborated with Dryden in an original semi-opera, rather than merely composing music around an existing adaptation of an older play where the music rarely entered into the dramatic spirit of the whole. Dryden was doubtless forced to make several changes to his initial conception not least because courtly allegory had to fit the monarchy of the moment or else royal noses would have been put out of joint. More important, however, is the willingness of Dryden to collaborate with Purcell in an almost operatic manner.

Indeed, as far as we know, the composer did not again enjoy a librettist – let alone one of Dryden's reputation – who would state unequivocally, "I have been obliged to cramp my verses, and make them rugged to the Reader, that they may be harmonious to the Hearer". If the co-operation led to a unity of vision in terms of music's expressive role in the overall drama, Purcell was limited to a historical patriotic fantasy with little room for the magic and pathos of, say, the superior *Fairy Queen*. Yet in the context of a stage presentation, Purcell's music shines through strongly. Those who attended Graham Vick's resplendent production at Covent Garden in 1995 will know how well this drama (one which verges perilously near pantomime, as Westrup wrote) fares with the proper operatic integration of strongly propelled narrative, fantastic spectacle and musical fantasy.

We are left with just the latter in this recording made shortly after the production at the Châtelet in Paris in February 1995, though not even the dramatic powers of William Christie can restore the sense of the music's place in the overall scheme. But never mind, this is a score with some magnificent creations and Christie is evidently enchanted by it. Indeed, the difference between this and his previous Purcell recordings is that this enchantment rarely falls into the type of continental dialect (if not literally) which can distort Purcell's determinedly indigenous gait. That is not to say Purcell's music should be the preserve of the parochial few but it should surely retain something of its English simplicity and abstraction. The intricate embellishment and sophistication of Christie's *Fairy Queen*, in particular, created something of a furore amongst those who felt that its heart had been ripped out for French dramatic humours.

No danger of that here as Christie's decisions are almost universally eloquent without disorienting the subject matter. The choral singing is richly textured, sensual and long-breathed, yet always alert to a nuance which can irradiate a passage at a stroke, as Christie does in the bittersweet close of "Honour prizing" – easily the best moment in Act 1. The instrumental movements are less robust than Gardiner (on his 1983 Erato set), though finely moulded so that sinewy counterpoint and rhythmic profile are always strongly relayed. The songs, too, have been acutely prepared and are keenly characterized without resorting to excess. All the basses deliver their fine music with aplomb, the Frost Scene is as affecting as any on record: Petteri Salomaa is an outstanding Cold Genius, technically flawless in this deceptively hard song and he sports an irresistible self-pity. "Fairest isle", to mention another perennial favourite, is slow enough to be accorded just respect as a national institution but fast enough to be shaped elegantly by Véronique Gens within a recognizable dance meter. Only "How blest are shepherds" in Act 2 seems unnecessarily fussy; the solo singing is less secure here than we have become used to elsewhere.

If there is one drawback to extracting the musical numbers from the 'opera' when they have so clearly been delivered within a theatrical context, it is that the highly contextual characterizations lend themselves less well to the musical continuity of a CD. Viewed in this way, Gardiner has the edge in an account where the music largely plays itself and rolls unassumingly onward in an aura of earthy patriotism. But *King Arthur* without the play is dramatically a nonsense so why try to pretend? Christie does not but makes the strongest case for this music to date. A fine achievement.

Sergey Rachmaninov   Russian/American 1873-1943

Rachmaninov Aleko.
Sergei Leiferkus *bar* Aleko
Maria Gulegina *sop* Zemfira
Anatoly Kocherga *bass* Old Gipsy
Ilya Levinsky *ten* Young Gipsy
Anne Sofie von Otter *mez* Old Gipsy Woman.

Rachmaninov The Miserly Knight.
Anatoly Kocherga *bass* Servant
Sergei Aleksashkin *bass* Baron
Sergei Larin *ten* Albert
Ian Caley *ten* Jew
Vladimir Chernov *bar* Duke.

Rachmaninov Francesca da Rimini.
Sergei Leiferkus *bar* Lanciotto Malatesta
Maria Gulegina *sop* Francesca
Ilya Levinsky *ten* Dante
Sergei Aleksashkin *bass* Virgil
Sergei Larin *ten* Paolo
Gothenburg Opera Chorus and Orchestra / Neeme Järvi.
DG ℗ ① 453 452-2GH3 (three discs: 174 minutes: DDD). Notes, texts and translations included. Recorded 1996.

Leaving Russia at the Revolution, severed from the roots of his native language, Rachmaninov also left behind him song and opera. The three one-act operas that survive give evidence of real dramatic talent. Who else has written so accomplished a graduation exercise as *Aleko*? Tchaikovsky was dazzled, no doubt also flattered, by some suggestions of imitation. It is a number opera, based on Pushkin's dramatic poem *The Gipsies*, warning that the urban sophisticate cannot recapture pristine wildness, and has at its centre a superb soliloquy of lost love. Leiferkus takes a lyrical approach; this is a beautiful, tragic performance, ironically set against Ilya Levinsky's carelessly superficial charm as the Young Gipsy. Zemfira is sung with fierce spirit by Maria Gulegina, especially in her cruel 'Old husband' song, and at the end with a lingering caress that seems to be for neither man but for Death itself.

The other operas are different matters, both tinged with Bayreuth experiences that Rachmaninov had absorbed more thoroughly than is sometimes allowed. In her insert-note to *The Miserly Knight*, Sigrid Neef argues interestingly that he is using tempo leitmotivs to identify the different characters. This is one of the 'little tragedies' in which Pushkin presents a moral issue but does not offer a solution. Here, it is the contrast between the old knight, claiming that his devotion to gold has taken him beyond passion into a realm of serenity, and his son, who merely needs the ready. The long central soliloquy, perhaps Rachmaninov's finest piece of dramatic writing, is superbly delivered by Sergei Aleksashkin, with the wide range of his eloquence drawing sympathy to the miser. Sergei Larin portrays his son Albert as a selfish extrovert; and Ian Caley does what he can to make the Jewish moneylender more human than an unpleasant caricature.

Francesca da Rimini requires Rachmaninov to triumph over an inept libretto by Modest Tchaikovsky. This he does to a remarkable degree, using Modest's inability to produce a text for the chorus of the damned to good advantage with wordless wails, and filling out the sketchy love duet with some 50 bars of a sensuous orchestral kiss. However, he should have rejected the banal placing of the final line, about the lovers reading no more that day, in favour of its breathtaking place in Dante, when their poring over Lancelot and Guinevere reveals their own love to them. Ilya Levinsky brings a more intensely lyrical line and manner to this than in *Aleko*, and Maria Gulegina ranges from docility before Lanciotto (Leiferkus again a jealous husband) to rapture in the love duet.

Neeme Järvi leads all three operas, as the orchestra should do for much of the time, and the beautiful playing he draws from the Gothenburg orchestra helps to make these three discs a set extolling Rachmaninov's operatic talent. It is an excellent 'trilogy', excellently presented with a transliteration and good translations into English (by Joan Pemberton Smith), German and French, and helpful essays by Neef, by Harry Halbreich and by David Fanning.

Jean-Philippe Rameau French 1683-1764

Rameau Anacréon.
Véronique Gens *sop* Prêtresse
Annick Massis *sop* L'Amour
Rodrigo del Pozo *ten* Agathocle
Thierry Félix *bar* Anacréon

Rameau Le berger fidèle.
Véronique Gens *sop*
Les Musiciens du Louvre / Marc Minkowski.
Archiv Produktion Ⓔ ① 449 211-2AH (57 minutes: DDD). ✍ Texts and translations included.
Recorded 1995.

It is 15 years since William Christie recorded the later of two *actes de ballet* by Rameau centred on the ancient Greek poet, Anacreon. The piece dates from 1757 when it took its place as a freshly composed *entrée* for a revival of Rameau's opéra-ballet, *Les surprises de l'Amour*. The text, by Pierre Joseph Bernard – he'd already provided the composer with one of his strongest librettos, that for *Castor et Pollux* (1737) – is entertaining, but Rameau's music is much more so. The story, as recounted by Bernard, has little or nothing to do with Anacreon's prowess as a poet, but focuses on his amorous and bibulous reputation acquired as a result of his famous love poems. There are no historical grounds for supposing that Anacreon practised what he preached but the conjunction of convivial text and first-rate music makes for excellent entertainment.

The action centres round a *contretemps* between Bacchus and Cupid who, respectively, represent the interests of wine and women or, rather, in this instance, a particular woman, Lycoris. Eventually, Anacreon and Lycoris are reunited as, indeed, are Bacchus and Cupid: Bacchus allows us to love and Cupid allows us to drink. All very accommodating. The performance is mainly excellent, the instruments and ensemble voices of Les Musiciens du Louvre under Marc Minkowski's direction are more sharply focused than in Christie's recording on Harmonia Mundi and the music is more forcefully projected. Most of the solo contributions are convincing too, but Thierry Félix who sings the role of Anacreon is slightly disappointing. Much of the time he is quite simply out of tune. Perhaps it will bother some readers less than others but, in the company of Annick Massis, a beguiling Cupid, and Véronique Gens as a priestess of Bacchus, Félix compares unfavourably. Notwithstanding this reservation, the performance works well though Agnès Mellon's ariette, "L'Amour est le dieu de la paix" on the older recording is a hard act to follow.

Lovers of Rameau's music will want both versions. The newcomer furthermore offers an enchanting performance of Rameau's chamber cantata, *Le berger fidèle*. The soloist is Véronique Gens, who gives a touchingly poignant account of the very fine opening "Air plaintif". Thorough documentation and pleasing recorded sound.

Rameau Les Boréades.
Jennifer Smith *sop* Alphise
Anne-Marie Rodde *sop* Sémire
Edwige Bourdy *sop* Polymnie
Martine March *sop* A Nymph
Philip Langridge *ten* Abaris
John Aler *ten* Calisis
Jean-Philippe Lafont *bar* Borée
Gilles Cachemaille *bass* Borilée
François Le Roux *bar* Adamas
Stephen Varcoe *bar* Apollon
Elizabeth Priday *sop* L'Amour
Monteverdi Choir; English Baroque Soloists / John Eliot Gardiner.
Erato Ⓔ ① 4509-99763-2 (three discs: 162 minutes: DDD). ✍ Booklet included. Recorded 1982.

The "Boréades" are descendants of Boreas, god of the North Wind; by the traditions of the kingdom of Bactria the Queen is obliged to choose one of them as her consort. Alphise, however, selects Abaris, to the fury of Borée and his two sons; it is only when Apollo discloses that Abaris is his son by a nymph "jeune et charmante" of Borée's line that tranquillity is restored.

The nature of the plot tells us a good deal about the kind of work that *Les Boréades* is. There is nothing here of the tragic grandeur, indebted to ancient Greece and to Racine, of the early *tragédies-lyriques* – for example, *Hippolyte et Aricie* or *Castor et Pollux*. The nobility of those works derives from the powerful situations in which the central characters find themselves; and the music rises to those situations and articulates the characters' emotions. It may well be argued that Rameau never again reached, in his operas, the heights of those early ones. *Les Boréades* was his last, written when he was 80; he died during the rehearsals, and it was never produced. (It was almost certainly not heard, in fact, until a French Radio broadcast in 1963, then not again until John Eliot Gardiner gave a concert performance at the Queen Elizabeth Hall in 1975; and it was first staged at Aix-en-Provence in 1982 – it is those performances that form the basis of this recording.) In *Les Boréades*, the steadfast mutual love of Alphise and Abaris is the only emotion of any real consequence; everything else, like the jealousy of Calisis and Borilée, or the rage of the affronted Borée, is little more than picturesque. And this is clear in the music too. It makes no attempt to touch tragic heights. There are a few truly serious, emotionally moving scenes, including a deeply pathetic one for Abaris when he seems to have lost his beloved, and sings "Lieux désolées" – full of expressive sighs from singer and orchestra alike. And there is plenty of amorous *tendresse*. But essentially the work is a decorative one, a charming piece of decadence, one might say, in the twilight days of the *tragédie lyrique* (that is, before its new dawn with Gluck). Yet the score is as inventive and as rich as any of Rameau's, and enormously enjoyable to listen to. Dance after dance ravishes the ear – some for their scoring (listen to the piccolos and high bassoons in the Act 4 gavotte that represents a ticking clock, for example, or the oboes and bassoons in the gavottes in act 3, to cite just two of the most felicitous), some for their brilliance and ingenuity of line and rhythm (gavottes, as so often with Rameau, usually excel, but there are some rigaudons of high originality, and numerous graceful airs). The orchestral 'symphonies' or ritornellos, too, are of rare quality – some fine *entrée* pieces, a lovely entr'acte at the beginning of Act 3, and one truly exquisite, hauntingly beautiful piece in Act 4 to which Polymnie enters. The originality of line, tunefulness, grace and ingenuity of scoring is everywhere in evidence: the ear is constantly charmed, the mind constantly intrigued. If the 80-year-old composer no longer tried too hard to arouse the profounder emotions, one ought not to complain.

Les Boréades is very much John Eliot Gardiner's work: not just because it is he who has had the energy and the enterprise to revive it (in spite of extraordinary legal and copyright difficulties), but also because it seems peculiarly well suited to his style and temperament. He has a fastidious ear for orchestral detail, and makes the most of Rameau's scoring; he has a fine rhythmic sense, vital yet subtle, which serves excellently in the dances. His readiness to shape the detail and flex the pulse seem to be exactly right. He has the broad grasp, too, for the extended scenes: the great thunderstorm comes off superbly. The choral singing, as always with this group, is beyond reproach, and the orchestral playing, some imperfections in the upper woodwind apart, is excellent. Several of the soloists are those who sang at the 1975 performance, including the two who head the cast, Jennifer Smith and Philip Langridge. Smith has made this kind of role very much her own, and she brings to them real delicacy of line and clarity of tone, as well as uncommon sincerity. Hers is not a big voice, and once or twice is strained under pressure (for example in her grand rhetorical air in Act 2, but it is difficult to imagine anyone who would do the part better or more stylishly. Langridge does quite well too in Abaris's music, and copes quite happily with this high-lying role; but the tone is sometimes a little spread and wanting in focus, the interpretation careful but something short of imaginative. Anne-Marie Rodde shows charm, though not ideal linear clarity, in Sémire's music. The graceful high tenor singing of John Aler in Calisis's music is admirable, and Gilles Cachemaille makes an able if slightly lightweight Borilée. Borée himself is done with due weight and authority by Jean-Philippe Lafont. François Le Roux is barely big enough in voice for Adamas; several of the male singers give the impression of lacking weight and maturity. Among those in the smaller parts a special word of praise should go to Martine March's pleasantly crisp singing of the Nymph's music.

The recorded sound is good, with orchestral textures happily clear and choral ones reasonably so. There is one slightly too close tape-edit. There is an informative booklet with the set, but no libretto; without the help of the French text made available at the 1975 performance listeners may well become confused. It is therefore unfortunate that copyright problems have prevented Erato from remedying this deficiency in a set that otherwise offers so much delectation.

Rameau Castor et Pollux.

Howard Crook *ten* Castor
Jérôme Corréas *bass* Pollux
Agnès Mellon *sop* Télaïre
Véronique Gens *sop* Phébé
René Schirrer *bar* Mars, Jupiter
Sandrine Piau *sop* Vénus, Happy Spirit, Planet
Mark Padmore *ten* Love, High Priest
Claire Brua *sop* Minerve
Sophie Daneman *sop* Follower of Hebe, Celestial Pleasure
Adrian Brand *ten* First Athlete
Jean-Claude Sarragosse *bass* Second Athlete
Les Arts Florissants and Orchestra / William Christie.
Harmonia Mundi ℗ ① HMC90 1435/7 (three discs: 173 minutes: DDD). ✍ Notes, text and translation included. Recorded 1992.

Castor et Pollux was Rameau's second *tragédie en musique*. Its first performance took place in October 1737 but, though the cast included several of France's most celebrated singers, the opera was greeted with only moderate enthusiasm. Rameau, by then 54 years old, was none the less still a comparative newcomer to the French operatic stage, but his bold departures from the long-admired tradition established by Lully had already proved controversial. This time the theatre-going public took sides and, depending on their viewpoint, became supporters either of Lully or Rameau. For the next 15 years or so *Castor et Pollux* remained something of a *cause célèbre* and it was only with the composer's thoroughly revised version of 1754 that the opera enjoyed the popularity that it unquestionably deserved. Weighing up the pros and cons of these two versions is to some extent problematic. For the 1754 revival Rameau provided a new First Act and a reworking of the original five acts into Acts 2 to 5 with some new music, too. This tautened a drama which had never been weak but – and this point is significant to all lovers of Rameau's music – it dispensed with a very beautiful Prologue since, by the 1750s, such things were considered old-fashioned. It is this consideration above all, perhaps, that needs to be taken into account when committing *Castor et Pollux* to disc. Both versions, however, would be ideal and it would be wonderful if Erato reissued their recording of the 1754 version directed by Charles Farncombe.

William Christie and Les Arts Florissants perform Rameau's first version complete with its Prologue. The librettist, Pierre-Joseph Bernard, was one of the ablest writers with whom Rameau collaborated and his text for *Castor et Pollux* has been regarded by some as the best in the history of eighteenth-century French opera. Bernard focuses on the fraternal love of the 'heavenly twins' and specifically on the generosity with which Pollux renounces his immortality so that Castor may be restored to life. Christie's production was staged at Aix-en-Provence in the summer of 1991 but only recorded by Harmonia Mundi a year later. One feels, on listening to the Prologue, that some of the ebullient Aix spirit had evaporated in the meantime and that the production only springs to life at the outset of Act 1. Here Christie wonderfully evokes the tragic muse with a measured drum roll leading to the darkly chromatic orchestral accompaniment to the Spartans' "Que tout gémisse". This and Télaïre's profound, justifiably celebrated "Tristes apprêts, pâles flambeaux", affectingly sung by Agnès Mellon, are sensitively handled by Christie. This performance, more than that of Nikolaus Harnoncourt on Teldec, recorded ten years earlier, conveys Télaïre's inconsolable misery at Castor's death. One of the reasons for this is that of pacing – Christie allows almost a full minute and a half longer for "Tristes apprêts" to unfold; but another is one of idiom, for Christie's singers sound altogether more at home with French declamation than Harnoncourt's cast. A notable exception is Gérard Souzay's Castor which is a model of its kind. But Souzay, alas, was no longer singing at his best and his partnership with the tenor, Zeger Vandersteene, is less impressive than that of Howard Crook and Jérôme Corréas in the Harmonia Mundi set.

This may sound like a clear-cut preference for Christie's version but such is not the case. Christie's performance does seem to have the stronger solo vocal cast, and this applies to smaller roles as well as the principal ones – the sopranos Véronique Gens and Sandrine Piau are both outstanding. But Harnoncourt's cast is anything but weak and it is supported by very strong performances from the instrumentalists of the Vienna Concentus Musicus and the voices of the Stockholm Chamber Choir. And the recorded sound of Harnoncourt's version is superior to the disappointingly confined, almost boxy perspective of Christie's.

On the other hand, Christie unquestionably gives us new and subtle insights to the opera and more convincingly realizes the element of tragedy, above all in the First Act. His performing edition, by the way, is the work of the bass violist Elisabeth Matiffa who is a founder member of Les Arts Florissants. A dedicated Ramellian will need both versions, others must draw their own conclusions but can rest assured that either or both will afford deep and lasting pleasure. A very beautiful score, affectionately and perceptively interpreted by two contrasting luminaries of baroque performance.

Rameau Dardanus.

Christiane Eda-Pierre *sop* Vénus
Frederica von Stade *mez* Iphise
Georges Gautier *ten* Dardanus
Michaël Devlin *bass-bar* Anténor
Roger Soyer *bass* Teucer
José van Dam *bass-bar* Isménor
Véronique Dietschy *sop* Phrygienne
Hélène Garetti *sop* Songe
Annick Dutertre *sop* Songe
Monique Marandon *sop* Songe
Jean-Philippe Courtis *bass* Songe
Paris Opéra Chorus and Orchestra / Raymond Leppard.
Erato Ⓜ ① 4509-95312-2 (two discs: 120 minutes: ADD). Notes, text and translation included. Recorded 1980.

This great score, Rameau's third *tragédie en musique*, poses huge problems for the would-be performer since the original version of 1739 differs so much from the revised opera of 1744 that we should almost regard them as separate entities. Leppard prepared his own edition for this recording, inclining towards the 1744 version, thus omitting among other things, the Prologue and the impressive, affectingly elegiac chaconne. Leppard acknowledges the problem but does not always arrive at plausible solutions. The cast is uneven with Frederica von Stade giving us a ravishingly beautiful-sounding though unidiomatically sung Princess Iphise, on the one hand, and Michaël Devlin failing to impress as King Anténor, on the other.

José van Dam is splendid as the magician Isménor – his fine recitative at the beginning of Act 2 is admirably declaimed, but Roger Soyer as King Teucer is disappointing. The high tenor, Georges Gautier, in the title-role, has a fine voice but he can be expressively bland and occasionally insecure, as in "Ils trahiraient le secret de ma flamme" (first disc, track 18). Alas, Leppard's cuts are so severe that what we have is best consumed as a *bonne bouche*, for there is enough music in *Dardanus* to amply fill three CDs, not just two. But since, at the moment, there is no rival version of any description in the catalogue, readers are urged to acquire this one. The music is mostly vintage Rameau, let alone the purple passages such as Iphise's "O jour affreux" (Act 3), Anténor's "Monstre affreux" (Act 4) or the "Trio des Songes" (Act 4). But don't be taken in by all that you hear. There is an organ which played no part in Rameau's orchestra, for instance, and a very anachronistic, Italianate cello solo, elevated to something approaching concerto status prefacing Anténor's "Je viens vous confier le trouble de mon coeur" (Act 2).

Musically Rameau never lets us down for a moment in this work. All is wonderfully inventive and uniquely colourful – perhaps the compliment is double-edged – and the recorded sound is excellent. The booklet contains full texts in three languages. In spite of reservations, a rewarding set, but a recording of *Dardanus* which does full justice to a ravishing score is badly needed. Just listen to the opening of the prison scene (Act 4) "Lieux funestes" if you are still in doubt.

Rameau Les fêtes d'Hébé.

Sophie Daneman *sop* Hébé, Une Naïde, Eglé
Gaëlle Méchaly *sop* L'amour
Paul Agnew *ten* Momus, Le ruisseau, Lycurgue
Sarah Connolly *mez* Sapho, Iphise
Jean-Paul Fouchécourt *ten* Thélème, L'oracle, Mercure
Luc Coadou *bass* Alcée
Laurent Slaars *bar* Hymas
Matthieu Lécroart *bar* Le fleuve
Maryseult Wieczorek *mez* Une Lacédémonienne, Une bergère
Thierry Félix *bar* Tirtée, Eurilas
Les Arts Florissants / William Christie.
Erato Ⓟ Ⓒ 3984-21064-2 (two discs: 148 minutes: DDD). Notes, text and translation included. Recorded 1997.

Although dances from *Les fêtes d'Hébé*, were among the very first orchestral pieces by Rameau to appear on LP (Ducretet-Thomson) in the early-1950s, the work had to wait until 1997 to be recorded in its entirety. Though the libretto, by Antoine Gautier de Montdorge, is probably one of the weakest that Rameau ever set, and was recognized as such by Rameau's contemporaries, the piece was nevertheless an instant success and enjoyed frequent revivals during the composer's lifetime. Reasons for this paradox are not hard to find; *opéra-ballet* did not depend so much upon plot for its entertainment as upon features that were colourfully diverting and intellectually undemanding. If the costumes and sets were imaginative, the singers and dancers of high profile, and the music of a kind to capture the imagination of wealthy, pleasure-seeking Parisian society, the success of an *opéra-ballet* was virtually assured. The cast for the first performance of *Les fêtes d'Hébé*, in 1739, had its fair share of stars while subsequent revivals attracted brilliant artists and designers of a younger generation, one of whom was Boucher. His sets, we can imagine, reflected to perfection the elegant, sensuous superficiality of mid-eighteenth-century Parisian social life.

Rameau produced one of his most engaging scores for *Les fêtes d'Hébé*, consisting mainly of newly composed music, but also containing wonderfully evocative orchestral parodies of harpsichord pieces published in the 1720s. The entertainment comprises a prologue and three *entrées*, or acts which, in a manner typical of *opéra-ballet*, have self-contained rather than continuously developing plots. All is prefaced with a captivating two-movement Overture whose playful second section has much more in common with a Neapolitan *sinfonia* than a traditional opera overture in the French mould.

William Christie and Les Arts Florissants revel in Rameau's beguiling pastoral images, tender and high-spirited in turn. The dances belong to one of the composer's fruitiest vintages and Christie has capitalized upon this with a sizeable band which includes, where appropriate, a section of musettes, pipes and drums. The singers, as always with this conductor, are carefully chosen for their contrasting vocal timbres and the line-up, by and large, is strong. The leading roles in each of the opera's four sections are fairly evenly distributed between Sophie Daneman, Sarah Connolly, Jean-Paul Fouchécourt, Paul Agnew and Thierry Félix. The first three of this group are consistently engaging; their feeling for theatre, and their intuitive ability to seek out those aspects of Rameau's vocal writing which enliven it, seldom fail, and they bring considerable charm to their performances. Agnew, too, is on strong form though in the lower end of his vocal tessitura, required for the role of Momus in the Prologue, he sounds less secure than in his more accustomed *haute-contre* range. That can be heard to wonderful effect elsewhere and, above all, in a duet for a Stream and a Naïad (first *Entrée*) in which he is joined by Daneman. This beguiling little love-song is proclaimed with an innocent fervour and a tenderness which should touch the hearts of all listeners. The singing of Félix has not always been tonally well focused, though his rounded warmth and resonance are always enjoyable. Here, the weakness seems to have been addressed and the problem largely, though not entirely, overcome. *Les fêtes d'Hébé*, above all, contains a wealth of inventive, instrumentally colourful and evocative dances. Small wonder that audiences loved it so much: with music of such vital originality, how could it be otherwise? The orchestra of Les Arts Florissants have seldom been on crisper, more disciplined form than here. Strings have a warmth of tone and a unanimity which pleases throughout; and readers will not be disappointed either by the resonant and pithy contributions of pipe and drum or by the full-blooded singing of the choir.

In short Christie and his musicians have done great justice to a score of infinite and subtle allure. A ravishing entertainment, from start to finish.

Rameau Hippolyte et Aricie.

Mark Padmore *ten* Hippolyte
Anne-Maria Panzarella *sop* Aricie
Lorraine Hunt *sop* Phèdre
Laurent Naouri *bass* Thésée
Eirian James *mez* Diane
Gaëlle Mechaly *sop* L'Amour, Female Sailor
Nathan Berg *bass* Jupiter, Pluton, Neptune
Katalin Károlyi *mez* Oenone
Yann Beuron *ten* Arcas, Mercure
François Piolino *ten* Tisiphone
Christopher Josey *ten* First Fate
Matthieu Lécroart *bar* Second Fate
Bertrand Bontoux *bass* Third Fate
Mireille Delunsch *sop* High Priestess of Diana
Patricia Petibon *sop* Priestess, Shepherdess
Les Arts Florissants / William Christie.
Erato Ⓟ Ⓒ 0630-15517-2 (three discs: 182 minutes: DDD). 🎵 Notes, text and translation included. Recorded 1996.

1997

If one were pressed to nominate the greatest single acts in baroque opera, high on the list would be Act 2 of *Hippolyte et Aricie*, the first *tragédie en musique* of a 50-year-old musical theorist who had little confidence in his abilities beyond the harpsichord pieces and the few cantatas he had hitherto composed. But this act, set in the Underworld, exerts a relentless dramatic grip from its opening, with Thésée grappling with one of the Furies, to the final trio by the Fates, rejected as impracticable at the time and still astonishing today by the boldness of its enharmonic modulations. The present Thésée (who took the role of three gods on the Minkowski issue on Archiv) is a resonant, virile bass, infinitely better on his low notes than his counterpart for Minkowski, and worthy to stand comparison with Shirley-Quirk's memorable performance in Anthony Lewis's 33-year-old recording, even if slightly on the hefty side. There is an appropriately black-voiced Pluto in Nathan Berg (who also plays Jupiter and Neptune), a firm-voiced, full-blooded chorus, and an effective Mercury; but the singer of the role of Tisiphone rather overcharacterizes by adopting too nasal a tone to depict the Fury. Unlike Minkowski, who was tempted by the 1757 revision of the start of Act 2, with its re-orchestration and baritone Tisiphone, William Christie adheres throughout to Rameau's 1733 original, in so doing opening up some passages previously omitted. He uses an orchestra with more string weight than his predecessor, and they play with rather greater security both of ensemble and intonation, and with splendidly crisp rhythms.

Despite the opera's title, the main protagonists are Thésée and his queen Phèdre, whose guilty passion for his son Hippolyte precipitates the tragedy (even though there is a happy ending for the eponymous pair). In all three recordings Phèdre is strongly cast, none more so than in the present case, with Lorraine Hunt even more passionate than Dame Janet Baker was on the Decca recording, and particularly impressive in the superb aria, "Cruelle mère des amours" which begins Act 3, into which Rameau poured all his artifices of affecting suspensions and harmonies. Throughout the opera, indeed, one is also struck alike by the profusion of invention, the unobtrusive contrapuntal skill, the charm and colour of the instrumentation and the freedom allotted to the orchestra. The work's final scene, for example, set in a woodland, is filled with a truly enchanting atmosphere, ending, after the customary chaconne, with "Rossignols amoureux" (delightfully sung by Patricia Petibon). Anna-Maria Panzarella makes an appealingly youthful Aricia (to whom Rameau allocates surprisingly little on her own), and Mark Padmore is easily the best Hippolyte of the three recordings, making the most of his despairing Act 4 aria, "Ah, faut-il, en ce jour, perdre tout ce que j'aime?". Pains have been taken with the whole cast over the expressive delivery of words and their timing and over neatness of ornamentation and production values such as the proper perspective for the entry of the crowd rejoicing at Thésée's return have been well considered.

All told, this is one of William Christie's best achievements, an obvious labour of love for a masterpiece which, he confesses, has entranced him for 30 years.

Rameau Hippolyte et Aricie.

Robert Tear *ten* Hippolyte
Angela Hickey *mez* Aricie
Dame Janet Baker *mez* Phèdre
John Shirley-Quirk *bar* Thésée
Rae Woodland *sop* Diane
Roger Stalman *bass* Pluton
Patricia Blans *sop* Oenone
Christopher Keyte *bass* Neptune
Nigel Rogers *ten* Mercure
Edgar Fleet *ten* Arcas
Gerald English *ten* Tisiphone
John Whitworth *alto* First Fate
Keith Erwen *ten* Second Fate
John Noble *bar* Third Fate
Sylvia Rhys-Thomas *sop* High Priestess
Jill Gomez *sop* Priestess, Shepherdess
St Anthony Singers; English Chamber Orchestra / Sir Anthony Lewis.
Decca Serenata Ⓜ ① 444 526-2DMO2 (two discs: 146 minutes: ADD). Notes, text and
translation included. Recorded 1965.

'Twas ever thus. Rameau enthusiasts had waited 12 years for a CD version of this opera until, in 1995,
Archiv released a mainly satisfying performance under the direction of Marc Minkowski. Then came
this reissue, within the space of a few months, and Christie was to follow in 1996. But back to the
present set, which was recorded in 1965 with Dame Janet Baker as Phèdre and John Shirley-Quirk as
Thésée. The conductor, Sir Anthony Lewis, followed Rameau's first version of 1733, though unlike
Minkowski, who also broadly speaking followed this, he omitted the Prologue. Other small cuts,
mainly affecting the instrumental pieces, were also made, all this resulting in a playing time some 21
and 36 minutes shorter than Minkowski and Christie respectively.

Rameau studies and the performing style of French music have moved on apace in the last 30 years
and there are consequently features in the Decca reissue which will strike ears attuned to present-day
ideas as being a little old-fashioned. And there are problems thrown up by the musical text itself
which, though carefully revised in numerous small details, nevertheless contains orchestral textures
which have as much to do with the editor, Vincent d'Indy, as with Rameau. Such issues, however,
should not deter readers from becoming acquainted with the performance because, in Baker and
Shirley-Quirk, it boasts protagonists of extraordinary dramatic power and psychological insight.
Baker's "Cruelle mère des amours" (Act 3), her "Non, sa mort est mon seul ouvrage" (Act 4), and
Shirley-Quirk's "Ah, qu'on daigne du moins" (Act 2) and "Quels biens! Je frémis quand j'y pense"
(Act 3), are reasons enough in themselves to buy the set at once. Happily, though, there are plenty
more features of the performance which deserve unqualified recommendation: Gerald English's
Tisiphone is one of them, Thurston Dart's harpsichord continuo another.

This is, in short, a powerful realization of Rameau's first dramatic masterpiece, and at mid price too.
It cannot, indeed should not, take precedence over Christie's reading but it will be for ever treasured
by those who recognize in the contributions of Baker and Shirley-Quirk a profound and moving
account of their tragic predicament.

Rameau Les Indes galantes

Prologue:
Claron McFadden *sop* Hébé
Jérôme Corréas *bar* Bellone
Isabelle Poulenard *sop* L'Amour
Le Turc généreux:
Nicolas Rivenq *bass* Osman
Miriam Ruggeri *sop* Emilie
Howard Crook *ten* Valère
Les Incas du Pérou:
Bernard Delétré *bass* Huascar
Isabelle Poulenard *sop* Phanie
Jean-Paul Fouchécourt *ten* Carlos
Les fleurs, Fête persane:
Jean-Paul Fouchécourt *ten* Tacmas
Jérôme Corréas *bar* Ali
Sandrine Piau *sop* Zaïre
Noémi Rime *sop* Fatime
Les sauvages:
Nicolas Rivenq *bass* Adario

Howard Crook *ten* Damon
Bernard Delétré *bass* Don Alvar
Claron McFadden *sop* Zima
Les Arts Florissants / William Christie.
Harmonia Mundi Ⓟ Ⓓ HMC90 1367/9 (three discs: 203 minutes: DDD). 🗲 Notes, text and translation included.

Here we have William Christie and Les Arts Florissants in a performance of the work which revels in the affecting originality of Rameau's invention. *Opéra-ballet*, as a type of entertainment, was very well established by 1735 when Rameau and his librettist Louis Fuzelier first presented *Les Indes galantes* at the Académie Royale in Paris. At this time, more than ever before, Parisian society enjoyed dramatic entertainment in which dance and spectacle were afforded greater significance than was customary in *tragédie lyrique*. Typically, *opéra-ballet* consisted of a prologue and anything between three and five *entrées* or acts. There was no continuously developing plot but instead various sections might be linked by a general theme, often hinted at in the title. Perhaps the mid-eighteenth-century writer, Rémond de Saint-Mard, best encapsulated the essence of *opéra-ballet*: "Each act should include an intrigue, lively, lighthearted and, if you like, somewhat *galant* ... two or three scenes, and these short, will do very well. The rest of the action is in ariettes, fêtes, spectacles and altogether agreeable features."

In *Les Indes galantes* the linking theme derives from a lively taste for the exotic and the unknown cultivated at the time. Rameau's original score consisted of a prologue and two *entrées*, "Le Turc généreux" and "Les Incas du Pérou"; but shortly after the first performances composer and librettist added first "Les fleurs" and then "Les sauvages" (1736); as so often with baroque opera and oratorio a great many different versions of the work have been handed down. It was never published in its entirety and, as Sylvie Bouissou remarks in her interesting and well-informed essay, Rameau was a perfectionist and only too eager to revise the work, making the task of reassembling the score extremely difficult.

In these and other respects Christie has achieved his aims convincingly and entertainingly. His orchestra of some 46 players is almost exactly the size recorded at the Paris Opéra and his soloists comprise as strong a team of singers as you could wish for. There are 17 solo roles in all, but since no one character appears in more than one of the opera's five sections Christie is able to dispose the parts among only ten singers. In the Prologue the role of Hébé is sung by Claron McFadden, who also sings Zima in the fourth *entrée*, "Les sauvages". She has an attractive, lightly coloured voice and a fair sense of pitch, bringing a beguiling enchantment to her air, "Musettes, résonnez" (Prologue); but sometimes her vibrato is a shade uncontrolled and too generously applied. Nevertheless, she proves a worthy partner for Isabelle Poulenard who, as L'Amour, shares a duet with her at the close of the Prologue.

The first *entrée*, "Le Turc généreux", concerns the reunion of Emilie, a captive of Pasha Osman, with her lover, Valère. Miriam Ruggeri and Howard Crook – his animated "Hâtez-vous de vous embarquer" is wonderfully effective – give an ardent and stylish account of the story and the bass Nicolas Rivenq makes a sympathetic Osman; but it is the splendid tempest scene, vividly captured here, which provides the musical focal point of this section. The second *entrée*, "Les Incas du Pérou", concerns Phanie, an Inca princess, and Carlos, a Spanish officer. They love one another but Phanie, in turn is loved by Huascar, high priest of the Sun. Huascar tries to thwart them but in vain. Almost insane with jealousy he unleashes the elements and is destroyed by fire and rocks hurled from a volcano. Rameau lavishes some of his greatest dramatic skill on this *entrée* which, as well as containing one of the composer's purple passages in Huascar's air with chorus, "Clair flambeau du monde", also contains a menacing earthquake scene of considerable force, briefly foreshadowing Ismenor's incantation in the Second Act of the tragedy *Dardanus* (1739). The bass, Bernard Delétré makes an imposing, authoritative Huascar while Isabelle Poulenard strikes an innocent, appealing note as Phanie and the tenor, Jean-Paul Fouchécourt, on strong form, is a passionate suitor.

There is an intended humour in the third *entrée* "Les fleurs, Fête persane" with disguises, mistaken identities and a concluding fête celebrating a happy outcome of preceding events. Fouchécourt (Tacmas), the baritone Jérôme Corréas (Ali), and the sopranos Sandrine Piau (Zaïre) and Noémi Rime (Fatime) capture the lighthearted spirit of text and music with lively imagination and their voices blend alluringly in the beautiful quartet, "Tendre amour, que pour nous ta chaîne dure à jamais", a rarity in Rameau opera. This number, the heady chorus "Triomphez, agréable fleurs!" towards the end, and the nine dances comprising the "Ballet des fleurs" are among the loveliest pieces in this *entrée*. "Les sauvages", the fourth *entrée*, is lighthearted. Zima, a young Amerindian, is wooed by Damon, a fickle French officer and Don Alvar, a passionate Spanish one. But Zima, herself prefers Adario, an army captain of her own people. Hymen is invoked and the couple are peacefully united in a ceremony during which one of Rameau's masterpieces is heard, the "Danse du Grand Calumet de la Paix" for voices and instruments, which Rameau had first included with the title "Les sauvages" in his *Nouvelles pièces de clavecin* (*c*1728). Christie and his forces give a beautifully poised performance of this and the colourful, spaciously conceived and tautly constructed Chaconne which concludes the work.

To sum up: here is a first-rate performance of one of Rameau's most endearing stage works; Christie's control of his forces, his convincing pacing of the piece – the Prologue and first *entrée* sounded hurried and unsettled in the Aix-en-Provence production that preceded the recording – and his feeling for colour, gesture and rhythm contribute towards making this one of his finest achievements on disc. His choir are lively and well disciplined and the instrumentalists of Les Arts Florissants play with great finesse. The booklet contains full texts in French, English and German and the music is vividly recorded in a pleasing acoustic. All in all, a considerable achievement which should provide readers with enduring pleasure.

Rameau Naïs.

Linda Russell *sop* Naïs
Ian Caley *ten* Neptune
Ian Caddy *bass* Jupiter, Telenus
John Tomlinson *bass* Pluton
Richard Jackson *bass* Tiresie
Brian Parsons *ten* Asterion
Antony Ransome *bar* Palemon
Ann Mackay *sop* Flore, Second shepherdess
Jennifer Smith *sop* First shepherdess
English Bach Festival Chorus and Orchestra / Nicholas McGegan.
Erato ℗ ① 4509-98532-2 (two discs: 106 minutes: ADD). Notes, text and translation included. Recorded 1980.

Naïs was commissioned to celebrate the Treaty of Aix-la-Chapelle in 1748, and first performed the following year. Thus it was a vocal counterpart to Handel's *Music for the Royal Fireworks*, both pieces marking the conclusion of the War of the Austrian Succession. The present recording was made in 1980 following performances at London's Old Vic Theatre and at Versailles under the auspices of Lina Lalandi's enterprising English Bach Festival. Though, dramatically, *Naïs* is unremarkable, Rameau and his librettist, Louis de Cahusac, made a special point of establishing a strong relationship between dance and action. As Graham Sadler, editor of the edition and author of an informative introduction points out, Cahusac himself provided detailed choreographic outlines for the dances which feature so prominently in this piece. And Rameau responded with music which, of its kind, is much closer to the spirit of *opéra-ballet* than heroic opera, and is representative of his finest.

Nicholas McGegan has an effective understanding of French baroque style and brings out much that is graceful and enlivening in Rameau's score. Only the Prologue bears any relevance to the Treaty which occasioned the work, and this in strictly allegorical terms. Here, John Tomlinson and Ian Caddy are especially effective. In the opera itself Linda Russell is appealing in the title-role, with Ian Caley an ardent Neptune in love with her. But, as so often with Rameau's vocal music in the tenor register, the uppermost notes sometimes betray a hint of strain. For the most part, the purely instrumental numbers, whose participants seem to revel in Rameau's uniquely colourful orchestral palette, are enjoyable. Who wouldn't? From the moment that we hear the superbly inventive Overture, through to the sparkling *tambourins* which occur towards the end of Acts 1 and 3, Rameau never for a second lets us down. Only the choral singing occasionally fails to measure up to the solo and instrumental contributions. But this is, notwithstanding, a welcome and long-awaited reappearance of an exhilarating score, enhancing Erato's impressive range of Rameau's operas on CD.

Rameau Platée.

Gilles Ragon *ten* Platée
Jennifer Smith *sop* La Folie, Thalie
Guy de Mey *ten* Thespis, Mercure
Vincent le Texier *bass-bar* Jupiter, A satyr
Guillemette Laurens *mez* Junon
Bernard Delétré *bass* Cithéron, Momus
Véronique Gens *sop* L'Amour, Clarine
Michel Verschaeve *bass* Momus
Françoise Herr Vocal Ensemble; Musiciens du Louvre / Marc Minkowski.
Erato MusiFrance ℗ ① 2292-45028-2 (two discs: 135 minutes: DDD). ✍ Notes, text and translation included. Recorded 1988.

Rameau's *comédie-lyrique*, *Platée*, one of two such works from his pen, was first staged at Versailles in 1745 as part of the celebrations surrounding the marriage of the Dauphin to the Infanta Maria-Theresa of Spain. Although he wrote little in a sustained comic vein Rameau was by no means inexperienced, having earlier in his life provided incidental music for various Théâtres de la Foire in Paris. Parodies of serious plays were popular at these Fair Theatres; indeed Voltaire is known to have been offended by some of their jibes, and it may have been here that the seeds of *Platée* were sown, so to speak.

The story of Platée – a marsh nymph of unprepossessing appearance who is the butt of a cruel joke played on her by Jupiter – is perhaps a curious choice for an opera, but its mischievous, if heartless theme with its charades, disguises and comic figures, fits comfortably into Carnival tradition. That

Rameau may have had just such an idea in mind is borne out by his choice of libretto – a play by Jacques Autreau who described *Platée* in his preface as "a comedy in the manner of a divertissement suitable for the Carnival season". Having bought the play outright from Autreau, Rameau engaged the services of another librettist, Le Valois d'Orville to whom he gave detailed instructions concerning alterations, stressing that he wanted emphasis placed on the comic elements in the play.

What eventually emerged from this collaboration was a masterpiece and one that was recognized as such in Rameau's lifetime: "Connoisseurs", ran a report in the monthly periodical *Mercure de France* (March 1754), "regard *Platée* as Rameau's '*chef d'oeuvre*' ... The prologue of this work holds its earlier reputation of being the most agreeable and most light-hearted that we have. The music ... is full of pieces of song and of inspiration sufficient to render their author immortal if that is not already so by reason of his other works."

This two-disc set is the third commercial recording of *Platée* and the one that does fullest justice to Rameau's score. The oldest of them, recorded in 1956 and released by EMI Pathé Marconi on CD in the late-1980s, though not alas, in the UK, had the tenor, Michel Sénéchal, in the title-role. His performance is almost legendary, few if any singers capturing as well as he the multi-faceted character of Platée herself: vain, petulant, gullible but pathetic and deserving of our pity. Then in 1989, after a period of 33 years, came a CBS recording from Jean-Claude Malgoire with the American tenor, Bruce Brewer as Platée. This had some attractive features but also several bad ones, crucial among which was Brewer's apparent lack of sympathy for, or indeed understanding of, the character of Platée. In this, and indeed, perhaps every other respect, this recording from Erato is superior. The role of Platée, a travesti one, is sung by Gilles Ragon. His singing is lyrical, his interpretation affectionate and stylish and his awareness of Platée's foibles and her pitiable predicament acute. It may be that Sénéchal, best of all, projects the pathos in the story, if only because he responds to Rameau's music with an extraordinary sensibility; but Ragon is a worthy successor, breathing life into a role that is both technically demanding and elusive in character.

Platée is generously endowed not only with Rameau's characteristically alluring dances – only the "Marche pour la danse" (Act 3), perhaps falls short of his finest endeavours – but also with beguiling vocal airs and vigorous, indeed sometimes extraordinary choruses; among the latter is a splendid onomatopoeic colloquium of frogs (Act 1). For Platée herself, Rameau time and again provides us with music of beguiling beauty. Her first air in Act 1, "Que ce séjour est agréable!", is a halting menuet – a graceful one would have been entirely inappropriate, but the composer seldom lets us forget that Platée deserves our compassion, lavishing on her music a warmth of sentiment which she herself so anxiously seeks in her own relationships. Ragon nicely captures her wonderment and curiosity in Act 2 where Jupiter descends in a cloud, "A l'aspect de ce nuage", disguised first as a donkey – at least that is the implication from Rameau's ingenious scoring – then as an owl. And he is splendidly cantankerous in the Act 3 denouement when the practical joke becomes apparent to her.

The remainder of the cast is strong with an outstanding contribution from Jennifer Smith as the mischievous, high-spirited La Folie. Her 6/8 ariette in Act 2 is a wonderfully tricksy affair delivered with exemplary skill. At first you might think it a little overdone, but no, this is Folly in her true colours. Among other fine performances are those of Guy de Mey as Thespis (Prologue) and Mercure, Guillemette Laurens as Junon, and Véronique Gens as a fresh-sounding L'Amour, and as Clarine, one of Platée's followers.

The orchestra, too, are by and large excellent, and what occasionally is lacking in finesse is counterbalanced by robust, idiomatic playing in the dances and other instrumental movements, and by sympathetic accompaniment of the voices. The ornithological protest at Jupiter's giant owl disguise is vividly executed (Act 2), while the sour oboe C sharps in the *Passepied I* (Act 1) are colourfully evocative of the denizens of Platée's swampy domain. Effective transparency of texture frequently highlights Rameau's imaginative scoring, as for instance in the captivating *Musette* (Act 3) for piccolos, and bassoons with strings. Sometimes though, as in the *Entrée gai* (Act 3), you may feel that Marc Minkowski drives the music too hard.

Like Malgoire, Minkowski concludes the opera with the three repeated chords at the end of Platée's final defiant outburst. This extraordinary ending is in a sense entirely in keeping with the mischievous spirit of Rameau's score and it would seem that the Versailles performance in 1745 finished in this way. But the full score of that version has not survived and subsequent editions suggest that the composer intended to conclude with a return to the chorus, "Chantons Platée, egayons nous", which Platée herself interrupts. In short, this is a considerable achievement. The opera is given without any cuts and with only a handful of repeats omitted. Minkowski uses the Durand score based on the 1749 Paris version in a performing edition prepared by Graham Sadler for the English Bach Festival production in 1983. The recorded sound is lively and effective. A satisfying issue.

Maurice Ravel   French 1875-1937

Ravel L'enfant et les sortilèges.

Colette Alliot-Lugaz *sop* Child
Catherine Dubosc *sop* Sofa, Bat, Owl, Princess
Marie-Françoise Lefort *sop* Shepherdess, Fire, Nightingale

Odette Beaupré *mez* Squirrel, Dragon-fly, She-cat
Claudine Carlson *mez* Mother, Chinese cup, Shepherd
Georges Gautier *ten* Teapot, Little Old Man, Frog
Didier Henry *bar* Clock, Tom-cat
Lionel Sarrazin *bass* Armchair, Tree

Ravel Shéhérazade. Shéhérazade – fairy overture.

Catherine Dubosc *sop*
Montreal Symphony Orchestra / Charles Dutoit.
Decca Ⓟ ① 440 333-2DH (73 minutes: DDD). Notes, texts and translations included. Recorded
1992.

This fine modern Decca recording of Ravel's intoxicating opera introduces some new and very
promising singers. The sound quality is of such splendid clarity that every nuance of Ravel's witty and
highly emotional score can be heard, without any sacrifice where the voices and text are concerned.
Dutoit and the Montreal forces play with obvious care and affection. Of all operas, this is one where
orchestral texture and balance is of the utmost importance – if you don't already have *L'enfant* in your
collection, there is no need to look further.

Among the soloists Odette Beaupré is particularly impressive, a sensual and characterful Dragon-
fly and Squirrel, as well as Didier Henry as the Clock and Georges Gautier as the Teapot. Marie-
Françoise Lefort is lively as the Fire and contributes to the ensemble of the Shepherds and
Shepherdesses – perhaps the saddest, most typical Colette-Ravel moment, it seems to describe in
music all the mixed grief and joy at the loss of innocence and childhood. Catherine Dubosc is better
as the Sofa, Bat and Owl than she is in the song of the Princess – how one longs for the security of
the old-time French singers on the three classic versions (Martha Angelici for Bour, Sylvaine Gilma
for Maazel and, the best of all, Suzanne Danco for Ernest Ansermet for Decca in 1954). Colette
Alliot-Lugaz does what she can with the role of the Child – it is, of course, mostly an acting, not
singing, part but she gets the little solo about the heart of the rose, and deals with it gently.

Only the Maazel set – incredibly, 38 years old – comes anywhere near the sound quality of this
Decca recording. This opera is so utterly loveable that since there are only a few versions available, it
is suggested that Ravel enthusiasts obtain as many of them as they can afford. For others, this one
can be the standard recommendation, with either Maazel, Bour or Ansermet as a reminder of the
past glories of the French style.

One doesn't really need to hear anything else once the Child has called for his mother, but the fill-
up is generous, with a sumptuous account of the early *Shéhérazade* Overture, contrasting with the
better-known song-cycle. Dubosc performs this, making a strong impression, but of course it is a
work that has attracted every possible great singer, including Suzanne Danco herself.

Not many people under the age of umpty-five will get the puns in Colette's fake-Chinese for the
duet of the Teapot and Cup; "Sessue Hayakawa", "Mah-jong" and "Hari-kiri" come across clearly,
but can anyone identify who or what was "Keng-ca-fou"?

Ravel L'enfant et les sortilèges.

Françoise Ogéas *sop* Child
Jeanine Collard *contr* Mother, Chinese cup, Dragon-fly
Jane Berbié *sop* Sofa, She-cat, Squirrel, Shepherd
Sylvaine Gilma *sop* Fire, Princess, Nightingale
Colette Herzog *sop* Bat, Owl, Shepherdess
Heinz Rehfuss *bar* Armchair, Tree
Camille Maurane *bar* Clock, Tom-cat
Michel Sénéchal *ten* Teapot, Little Old Man, Frog
Chorus and Children's Voices of French Radio

1989

Ravel L'heure espagnole.

Jane Berbié *sop* Concepción
Michel Sénéchal *ten* Gonzalve
Jean Giraudeau *ten* Torquemada
Gabriel Bacquier *bar* Ramiro
José van Dam *bass-bar* Don Inigo Gomez
French Radio National Orchestra / Lorin Maazel.
DG The Originals Ⓜ ① 449 769-2GOR2 (two discs: 89 minutes: ADD). Notes, text and
translation included. *L'enfant et les sortilèges* recorded 1960; *L'heure espagnole* recorded 1965.

Philip Hope-Wallace, who knew a thing or two about French opera, described this *L'enfant et les
sortilèges*, when it was first issued, as "a superlative piece of recording"; and one cannot do better
than echo his words. This is, quite simply, one of the classics of the catalogue and, until Dutoit (see
above), easily the best performance available of this ever enchanting work. Everything is just right.
One couldn't ask for more vivid orchestral sound, better balance (including those double-bass

harmonics at bar 12 which are all but lost on other versions) or more marvellously clear words from everyone. Françoise Ogéas is a most convincing petulant brat finally overcome with remorse, Jeanine Collard as his mother changes her tone in a moment from gentle enquiry to disappointment to crossness to hurt reproof and as the teacup is hilariously Chinese; Camille Maurane and Michel Sénéchal are nimble-tongued as, respectively, the Clock and the Little Old Man (the latter vivaciously seconded by the children's choir), Sylvaine Gilma is brilliant in the virtuoso parts of the Fire and the Nightingale and tender as the Princess ... and so on; need one continue? Now, an open (and serious) question to connoisseurs: has there ever been a more wonderfully inventive orchestral score than this?

The return of Maazel's *L'heure espagnole* is doubly welcome in its new CD guise, since it sounds better than ever. One might be tempted to conclude that the surprising paucity of recent recordings of this delicious one-acter means that the subtlety and wit are too sophisticated for the generality of record-buyers – even of opera-fans. The music's essentially Gallic sensitivity to the words (themselves of exceptional quality), its lovingly chiselled precision and delicate ingenious scoring, rightly treasured by the discerning, sets this little masterpiece in a class apart, and that there is no modern version of *L'heure espagnole* is lamentable. The DG recording is quite satisfactory, and except for the opening pages, where the fascinating noises of the automata are much too faint, the balance is excellent, the voices not being swamped; the employment of a wide stereo image, also, makes for convincing perspectives for the entrance of Gonzalve and Don Inigo and for their lines from inside the longcase clocks. The cast in general are very willing to adopt the quasi-*parlando* style Ravel had in mind and capture the subtle inflexions of the superbly witty libretto – especially the central figures, Concepcíon and Ramiro. Sénéchal as the exasperatingly head-in-the-cloud poet, who is the only one Ravel authorized to sing lyrically, gives a particularly delicious characterization.

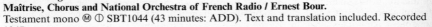

Ravel L'enfant et les sortilèges.

Nadine Sautereau *sop* Child
Denise Scharley *mez* Mother, Chinese cup, Dragon-fly
Solange Michel *mez* Sofa, Squirrel, Shepherd
Odette Turba-Rabier *sop* Fire, Nightingale
Claudine Verneuil *sop* Bat, Owl, Shepherdess
André Vessières *bass* Armchair, Tree
Yvon le Marc'Hadour *bar* Clock, Tom-cat
Joseph Peyron *ten* Teapot, Frog
Martha Angelici *sop* Princess
Marguerite Legouhy *mez* She-cat
Maurice Prigent *ten* Little Old Man
Maîtrise, Chorus and National Orchestra of French Radio / Ernest Bour.
Testament mono Ⓜ ① SBT1044 (43 minutes: ADD). Text and translation included. Recorded 1947.

1995

In some ways, *L'enfant et les sortilèges* is an ideal opera for the gramophone. One's imagination can supply things which even the most innovative stage director couldn't achieve. This performance, originally issued as a set of six 78s (and then shortly afterwards as an LP), was the first recording, made 23 years after the première. Rather than looking back to an existing tradition, it was one of the first important projects of the group of singers and musicians who for the following quarter of a century were to be an unofficial resident company in the studios of Radiodiffusion Française.

Ernest Bour was a conductor noted for his devotion to the contemporary repertory, who gave a large number of first performances on the radio in France, Germany and The Netherlands. There he led a performance of great charm – when it was first issued, Ned Rorem remembered (in *Setting the Tone*; New York: 1983), "Ernest Bour's record provoked an epidemic, we were all as bewitched as the protagonist". The 'we' was a group of young composers in New York, all of whom wished they might have composed something similar. Above all, Bour's performers are remarkable for their excellent diction and vocal acting. Inevitably, in a recording of this age, the voices are favoured so that although Ravel's wonderful characterization is clear enough in solo instrumental passages, the complexity and richness of the orchestral effects is not always caught. The remastering is first-rate, there is no crackle or hiss.

Among the singers, all great figures from the French stage and concert platform of the time, even if not all their names are familiar, Nadine Sautereau as the Child conveys the right blend of innocence and malice. She was best known as an interpreter of baroque music, but she clearly had an equal feeling for Ravel's subtle melodies and mixture of song and declamation. Denise Scharley (later the first Mme de Croissy in the French première of Poulenc's *Carmelites*) is especially effective as the Dragon-fly, with her sensual solo, "Ou es-tu?", leading to the exquisite little duet with the Nightingale. Solange Michel, a famous Carmen (her EMI version with Cluytens has been reissued on CD) sings a really heartfelt Squirrel. Perhaps the most intriguing singer is the Breton baritone, Yvon le Marc'Hadour, who makes a splendid impression as the Tom-cat.

This recording has the complete air of authenticity about it. Since all the subsequent versions (even Ansermet's) are in stereo, it is for the link with French vocal tradition that this classic performance is recommended. As such it is *hors concours*.

Ottorino Respighi Italian 1879-1936

Respighi Semirama.

Eva Marton *sop* Semirama
Veronika Kincses *sop* Susiana
Lando Bartolini *ten* Merodach
Lajos Miller *bar* Falasar
László Polgár *bass* Ormus
Tamás Clementis *bass* Satibara
Hungarian Radio and Television Chorus; Hungarian State Orchestra / Lamberto Gardelli.
Hungaroton Ⓟ Ⓓ HCD31197/8 (two discs: 143 minutes: DDD). Notes, text and translation included. Recorded 1990.

Semirama pre-dates any of Respighi's more familiar works by several years; it was his first major critical success, completed when he was 31. The morning after the first performance an Italian critic described it as "the first grand opera in the Italian repertory to be written in the Straussian style". Straussian it certainly is in its orchestral richness; it has Strauss's complexion, you might say, if not quite enough of his vigour, despite a plot of *Salome*-like gaminess (the ruthless Babylonian Queen Semirama seduces her serving-maid's lover; only in the nick of time is it revealed that he is her son). More rarely, the opera is Debussyan, even Delian in colour, and there are hints, in some of the declamatory passages, of the years Respighi had spent working and studying in Russia. More startling when one considers the date of the opera (1910) are the distinct, at times quite uncanny, apparent kinships with Puccini's *Turandot*. It would be ten years before Puccini even began to consider that subject, and he can't have heard Respighi's opera (he was in America during its run of performances and it was never revived), but taken together with the similarities of plot (oriental setting, cruel princess, tenor hero falling dismayingly for the 'wrong' soprano) it makes one wonder whether, during his long researches into Eastern music in preparation for *Turandot*, Puccini might have cast an eye over the score of *Semirama*.

One notices these things before one starts recognizing characteristic Respighian fingerprints; even at 31 his style was not yet fully formed. Its constituents are all there – sumptuous orchestral writing, grateful Italianate line (providing some of the sinew that the Straussian surface lacks), atmospheric evocation – but as yet they are not really unified. Respighi's archaizing vein, seeking roots in a pre-romantic Italian past, is as yet hardly present. For the lack of it he resorts to orientalisms learned from Rimsky-Korsakov and others, but they tap shallower dramatic soil than the conjurings of a mysterious past in his later operas. Respighi is already very skilled at seizing opportunities for flamboyant or iridescent orchestral colour: most of the solo arias have rich orchestral preludes, and there are frequent dances and processions. Indeed, much of the opera can be heard as a lavish orchestral tapestry with vocal lines embroidered upon it in relief, and the one disadvantage of Hungaroton's recording is that, by placing the soloists so far forward (and the chorus well back), it obscures some of the voluptuous richness of Respighi's orchestra.

Even so, it's in the solo numbers and duets, where orchestral opulence is given a powerful forward thrust by long-lined Italian melody, that *Semirama* really grips: the ardent duet for the serving-maid Susiana and Semirama's son Merodach at the end of Act 1, the aria and duet for Semirama and her vengeful cast-off lover Falasar in Act 2 (which builds such a head of rancorous steam that it gets away with quoting from the duet at the end of Act 1 of *Siegfried*), the long lines and high melodrama of the mother-and-son love duet in Act 3, curdled at the climax by the revelation of their relationship, the final monologue (whose fine orchestral introduction draws something like Straussian nobility from its contemplation of Semirama's shame) – all these make of the opera something more than a fascinating document of Respighi on the brink of becoming Respighi.

Marton is in as fine voice as she has ever been: excitingly full, authoritative and yet able to yield to lyricism. Kincses has a mezzoish velvetiness and hushed poignancy to modify her brightness, Bartolini is stalwart if unvaryingly loud, Miller excellently dramatic when he doesn't push his Italianate voice too hard, and Polgár is a sonorous, at times cavernous bass. Gardelli conducts with a real feeling of excited discovery, and with a fine ear for delicate texture as well as sympathy with his singers. Questions of balance aside, the recording is excellent.

Nikolay Rimsky-Korsakov Russian 1844-1908

Rimsky-Korsakov The Maid of Pskov.

Vladimir Ognovienko *bass* Ivan the Terrible
Gennadi Bezzubenkov *bass* Tokmakov
Nikolai Gassiev *ten* Matuta
Yevgeny Fedotov *bass* Vyazemsky
Yuri Laptev *ten* Bomelius
Vladimir Galusin *ten* Tucha
Georgy Zastavny *bar* Velebin

Galina Gorchakova *sop* Princess Olga
Olga Korzhenskaya *mez* Styosha
Ludmila Filatova *mez* Vlas'yevna
Evgenia Perlasova *mez* Perfil'yevna
Chorus and Orchestra of the Kirov Opera / Valery Gergiev.
Philips Ⓕ Ⓓ 446 678-2PH2 (two discs: 124 minutes: DDD). Notes, text and translation included.
Recorded 1994.

Rimsky-Korsakov's first opera is in many ways an awkward piece of work, despite his painstaking revisions (this is the third version), but it has jutting strengths that were sometimes levelled out in later operas. There is no gain in making the inescapable comparison with Mussorgsky and *Boris Godunov*: the two men shared a flat at the time, and also shared many of the ideas that went into the two operas, not least the notion of the guilty, suffering Tsar, the very Russian idea of the ruler whose actual tyranny lends him stature in the eyes of his subjects. Ivan the Terrible is sung here by Vladimir Ognovienko with less than a real sympathetic humanity, but he is not given the insight that Mussorgsky's more extended scenes allow to Boris Godunov; however, the confrontation with Olga is strikingly done. She is the Maid of Pskov, sung by Galina Gorchakova with a full, strong voice that makes much of the lyrical lines in the scenes with her lover Mikhail Tucha – a vivid characterization by Vladimir Galusin – but that scarcely seems to soften to his ardour or to defer before the Tsar's astonishment at discovering that she is in fact his illegitimate daughter. On this the plot revolves. Ravaging the countryside, Tsar Ivan turns aside from laying Pskov waste because of her, and promises to rescue her from the Boyar Nikita Matuta, whose villainy is splendidly characterized in the murky tones and sinister phrasing of Nikolai Gassiev. To no avail: the denouement comes when Tucha mounts an insurrection, in the course of which Olga is killed by a stray bullet.

There is much of interest in this score, including some very well-handled choruses and some of the brilliant orchestration that even the anxious young Rimsky-Korsakov, worried about his technique, found coming naturally to him. If Berlioz's Russian visit inspired him to a hunt and storm in the forest that could not come near its Trojan original, at least the scoring is resourceful and imaginative. Gergiev, who occasionally allows lapses in ensemble with his singers, handles this vividly, and his orchestra are responsive. They play beautifully for him, with some especially sensitive brass: Russian horns have for the most part now lost the querulous vibrato originally inherited from French example without forfeiting the silvery elegance of tone. The booklet-note, well up to Philips's high standards, includes helpful essays by Robert Layton, Detlef Gojowy and Jérémie Rousseau, plus synopses and the original Russian libretto with parallel translations into English, French and German.

Rimsky-Korsakov Sadko.

Vladimìr Galusin *ten* Sadko
Valentina Tsidipova *sop* Volkhova
Sergei Alexashkin *bass* Okean-More
Marianna Tarasova *mez* Lyubava Buslayevna
Larissa Dyadkova *contr* Nezhata
Bulat Minzhilkiev *bass* Viking merchant
Gegam Grigorian *ten* Indian merchant
Alexander Gergalov *bar* Venetian merchant
Vladimìr Ognovienko *bass* Duda
Nikolai Gassiev *ten* Sopel
Nikolai Putilin *bar* Apparition
Yevgeny Boitsov *ten* Foma Nazarich
Gennadi Bezzubenkov *bass* Luka Zinovich
Kirov Theatre Chorus and Orchestra / Valery Gergiev.
Philips Ⓕ Ⓓ 442 138-2PH3 (three discs: 173 minutes: DDD). Notes, text and translation included. Recorded at performances in the Maryinsky Theatre, St Petersburg between October 8th and 20th, 1993.

Rimsky-Korsakov's operas are not so well represented in the catalogue that one can afford to give anything but a welcome to this complete version from the Maryinsky company, for all its drawbacks. *Sadko* is a panoramic work, packed with numbers, rather less packed with event or with character, as Robert Layton points out in his helpful introductory note. It has had a good following in Russia: there was once a sumptuous production before a huge audience in the Kremlin Palace of Congresses, on a stage so vast that you did not at first notice the presence of six horses. With as much stage splendour as possible to help it along, it can make a pleasant enough evening, but much of it is static, and consists of the various characters delivering themselves of a song or a ballad or an address. These are reasonably well contrasted, partly because of Rimsky-Korsakov's skills in drawing on different Russian influences and in differentiating between a simple tonal language for the real world and a more chromatic idiom for the seductive realm of the Sea King (Okean-More) and his daughter Volkhova (points made in the essays by Detlef Gojowy and Catherine Steinegger). It needs a numerous and strong cast who can make the most of its opportunities.

Sadko himself is sung by Vladimìr Galusin pretty steadily at full volume. There is not a lot of subtlety in Sadko's nature, and he is indeed a hero: Gojowy thinks him somewhere between Peter the Great, Columbus and Siegfried, which may be stretching things a bit. The full heroic blast here is too seldom modified for the addresses to Volkhova. Galusin settles down a little as the opera proceeds, and by Act 3 is finding a somewhat more pacific manner. Valentina Tsidipova returns his advances, and makes her own, with a good feeling for line. A steady vibrato sits upon it, in a manner long familiar with Slavonic sopranos and found here also with Sadko's abandoned but eventually restored wife, Lyubava, sung by Marianna Tarasova. The Sea King is strongly sung by Sergei Alexashkin, truculent at first but warming his tone somewhat as he comes to accept Sadko. The incidental contributions vary in quality. The Varangian (or Viking) merchant is finely delivered by Bulat Minzhilkiev, and Alexander Gergalov sings the equivalent song of the Venetian merchant agreeably. But it is a pity that the best-known number from the opera, the song of the Indian merchant, should be sung as half-heartedly as it is by Gegam Grigorian. There is much more character in the ballad near the opening by the psalter-player, Nezhata. Rimsky-Korsakov took the idea of a repeated melodic phrase over a changing background from Glinka, and the Finn in *Ruslan and Lyudmila*, but it is done with all the orchestral skill the old wizard could muster, and strongly delivered by Larissa Dyadkova.

Valery Gergiev leads his forces well, and draws some vigorous, colourful singing from the choruses in their various manifestations. There is, however, a good deal of noise occasioned by the many stage comings and goings, with clumpings and hoarse whisperings as well as tunings-up and applause. The recording has difficulty in catching all the singers equally in their various peregrinations across the stage, but for the most part this is a fair representation of a score that is nothing if not colourful. There is a transliteration, with English, French and German translations. Despite the set's shortcomings, collectors of Russian opera will doubtless want to add it to their shelves, as there is unlikely to be another one for a very long time.

Rimsky-Korsakov Sadko.

Vladimir Galusin *ten* Sadko
Valentina Tsidipova *sop* Volkhova
Sergei Alexashkin *bass* Okean-More
Marianna Tarasova *mez* Lyubava Buslayevna
Larissa Dyadkova *contr* Nezhata
Bulat Minzhilkiev *bass* Viking merchant
Gegam Grigorian *ten* Indian merchant
Alexander Gergalov *bar* Venetian merchant
Vladimir Ognovienko *bass* Duda
Nikolai Gassiev *ten* Sopel
Nikolai Putilin *bar* Apparition
Yevgeny Boitsov *ten* Foma Nazarich
Gennadi Bezzunenkov *bass* Luka Zinovich
Kirov Ballet; Kirov Theatre Chorus and Orchestra / Valery Gergiev.
Stage Director: **Alexei Stepaniuk.** *Video Director:* **Brian Large.**
Philips ℗ 🎦 070 439-3PH (175 minutes). Recorded at performances in the Maryinsky Theatre, St Petersburg between October 8th and 20th, 1993. Soundtrack from the CD reviewed above.

This is a superb offering, indicative of the high standards now obtaining at the Kirov. Gergiev determined to revive the work in facsimiles of the sets of the painter, Konstantin Korovin, dating from 1920. The results, as can be judged from this video of a 1993 performance, taken live from the Maryinsky Theatre in St Petersburg, are evocative of a past age's glory as regards décor, but the direction is more ordinary: too often operatic stock gestures predominate.

That hardly matters when the performance is so musically vital and benefits from the participation of the Kirov Ballet in the big set scenes. Gergiev performs the opera uncut, thus preserving its well-constructed dimensions, and conducts it commandingly. The Kirov field a strong cast, capable of fulfilling Rimsky's appreciable demands on his singers. Galusin convincingly conveys Sadko's free spirit. His bright tenor happily blends the lyric with the heroic, even if his tone hardens under pressure. Tsidipova is an alluring Volkhova with a refulgent, big-scale soprano that she displays with artistry, most of all in her tender lullaby to the sleeping Sadko before she leaves him to turn herself into a river. As his faithful, long-suffering wife, Lyubava, Tarasova discloses a mezzo and acting ability quite out of the ordinary, her voice marrying supple warmth with Russian bite. Dyadkova, the other mezzo, makes much of the ballads of the psalter-player, Nezhata. Before Sadko sets off on his travels he is regaled by three foreign guests, three merchants, whose songs are well sung here, but not as individually as by many Russian male singers of the past. Given his reputation, Grigorian is curiously clumsy as the Indian guest. Alexashkin is an appropriately fiery Sea King, nicely warming his tone as his suspicions of Sadko are overcome.

As a whole, this is an issue to treasure. Large's video direction is as faultless as ever. The sound is a model of excellence. As no major company has staged this work in this country since the war, this issue is doubly welcome.

Rimsky-Korsakov Snow Maiden (second version).

Elena Zemenkova *sop* Snow Maiden
Alexandrina Milcheva *mez* Spring Fairy
Nikola Ghiuselev *bass* Winter
Lubomir Dyakovski *ten* Faun, Bobil
Vessela Zorova *mez* Bobilikha
Avram Andreyev *ten* Tsar Berendey
Stefka Mineva *mez* Lel
Stefka Evstatieva *sop* Kupava
Lubomir Videnov *bar* Mizgir
Bulgarian Radio Chorus and Symphony Orchestra / Stoyan Angelov.
Capriccio Ⓔ Ⓛ 10 749/51 (three discs: 209 minutes: DDD). Notes included. Recorded 1985.

Much as Rimsky-Korsakov admired his own *Snow Maiden* – almost as much as posterity has – he saw that it needed cutting, and the so-called second version is really simply his abridgement of the 1882 score with recommendations for a little further cutting if need be. It is still a long work, with nearly three-and-a-half hours of music for a touching but not very dramatic story. A good deal depends upon Rimsky-Korsakov's marvellous sense of orchestral colour, and upon his skill (as he perfectly fairly pointed out when planning a book on the opera) in drawing the various worlds of his fairy-tale with different musical devices – largely whole-tone harmony for the spirits of nature, a more straightforward idiom from Russian romantic opera for the humans who, as the plot of the tragic *Snow Maiden* reveals, cannot make real emotional contact with them, and a certain amount of Russian folk-song material to add to the colourful background.

Unfortunately, in this recording, made for Sofia National Radio in 1985, too much of the orchestral colour stays firmly in the background. It is a scintillating score, also one marked with quiet subtleties that need careful balancing between single instruments and the voice. Not only are the rich colours muted and sometimes blurred here, but it is not always possible to make out what is happening behind the voice: for instance, the distant cor anglais and flute are barely distinguishable in Lel's first song. Elena Zemenkova sings the Snow Maiden quite touchingly, phrasing sensitively though her voice is a little on the dry and edgy side, and there are nice performances of the shepherd, Lel, from Stefka Mineva, of Kupava from Stefka Evstatieva, and of Mizgir from Lubomir Videnov. However, Tsar Berendey is querulously sung by Avram Andreyev, and with too little authority. The most striking performance of the supernaturals comes, not surprisingly, from Nikola Ghiuselev as Winter. Stoyan Angelov is an attentive accompanist, but he does not take the chances which the composer gives him with some of the most captivating numbers; even the popular "Dance of the tumblers" is a trifle limp, especially for these vehement and even dangerous *skomorokhi* of Russian life and lore.

There is, culpably, no text in any language, merely a short essay, and a synopsis of some 350 words into the English version of which are inserted aria titles in German. Even a much stronger performance and recording of the work would not come near justifying this neglect of the listener's legitimate needs. This will have to satisfy us until we have a new version, or maybe EMI will consider reissuing the Fedoseyev set, with Irina Arkhipova as Spring and Lel, which was welcomed by Lionel Salter in 1977 with much enthusiasm.

Ned Rorem   American 1923

Rorem A Childhood Miracle.

Darcy Dunn *sop* Violet
Michelle Couture *sop* Peony
Madeline Tsingopoulos *contr* Mother
Peter Castaldi *bar* Father
Mary Cidoni *mez* Emma
Patrick Greene *bar* Snowman
Magic Circle Chamber Orchestra / Ray Evans Harrell.

Rorem Three Sisters Who Are Not Sisters.

Madeline Tsingopoulos *contr* Ellen
Andrea Matthews *sop* Jenny
Frederick Urrey *ten* Samuel
Carol Flamm *mez* Helen
Mark Singer *bar* Sylvester
John van Buskirk *pf*
Newport Classic Ⓔ Ⓛ NPD85594 (68 minutes: DDD). Texts included. Recorded 1994.

Ned Rorem was well qualified to take one of Gertrude Stein's plays and turn it into an opera. He chose *Three Sisters Who Are Not Sisters: a Melodrama* and set every word, unlike Virgil Thomson or

Lord Berners who both took liberties with Stein's text. Rorem, whose volumes of Diaries are consistently entertaining, had also lived in Paris for some years and knew the sophistication which lay behind Stein's apparently naïve home thoughts from abroad.

A Childhood Miracle, composed in 1952 and produced on television in 1956, is also a Stein opera, but then it was Elliott Stein who based a libretto for his young friend's uncommissioned opera – not his first – on a short story by Nathaniel Hawthorne. This is charming in a rather meandering 'Hansel and Gretel' way and the tuneful lines of the emerging song composer are grateful to sing. But 20 years later Rorem had more focus and *Three Sisters* is much less bland. The accompaniment is for piano alone, crisply written and excellently delivered by John van Buskirk. Anyone who has seen Gertrude Stein's plays on stage knows that they work, anticipating Ionesco and Beckett in a type of theatre of the absurd. This is obviously true of Rorem's half-hour, one-act piece, with its comedy crossed with horror in an invariably adept reflection of mood changes. The only time Rorem expands Stein's text is at the end, for an ensemble about death, by which time some rather silly situations involving murder have become in an odd way real. The light dismissal from Jenny is just as neatly gauged. This recording, with its well-balanced cast, ought to help to make this sparkling piece part of the repertory of every opera school.

Rorem Miss Julie.

Theodora Fried *sop* Miss Julie
Philip Torre *bar* John
Heather Sarris *mez* Christine
David Blackburn *bar* Mr Niels
Mark Mulligan *ten* Young boy
Laurelyn Watson *sop* Young girl
Judd Ernster *bass* Bass soloist
Manhattan School of Music Opera Chorus and Orchestra / David Gilbert.
Newport Classic Ⓟ Ⓓ NPD85605 (two discs: 88 minutes: DDD). Notes and text included.
Recorded at a performance in the Manhattan School of Music during December 1994.

Rorem's only full-length opera, *Miss Julie*, based on Strindberg and premièred in 1965, adds considerably to the picture of his operatic output. *Miss Julie* took a long time to settle down at the planning stage and has been much revised since then. Rorem admits that he is a song composer, never "comfortable with the opera medium, much less a buff". *Miss Julie* is an anguished story about a count's daughter who rejects her fiancé and then insists on being seduced by her father's valet during the servants' Midsummer's Eve revels. The play was attacked as immoral when it was published in 1888 and in the next year was not successful in the theatre in Denmark. Rorem delivers most of the opera in a kind of *parlando* which is too bland to reflect the growing infatuation of Act 1 but gets nearer to the nastiness and tortured remorse of Act 2, where Miss Julie and her lover plan futile expedients to escape. Nothing works and in the end Miss Julie kills herself: it all proceeds in slow motion, as in the play itself, but without access to the Strindbergian hysteria *en route*.

However, there are plenty of well-focused moments when the music is allowed to expand – the innocent duet between the boy and girl in Act 1 (track 9); Julie's aria on returning with stolen money in Act 2 (track 6); a confusion ensemble (track 7); and the drama is finally engaged when feelings turn to desperation between Miss Julie, the valet and his fiancée, the cook, Christine. Recorded live, this remains a good conservatoire production with some fine solo voices, that at last allows this corner of the American operatic repertoire to be explored.

Gioachino Rossini   Italian 1792-1868

Rossini Il barbiere di Siviglia.

Thomas Allen *bar* Figaro
Agnes Baltsa *mez* Rosina
Francisco Araiza *ten* Count Almaviva
Domenico Trimarchi *bar* Dr Bartolo
Robert Lloyd *bass* Don Basilio
Matthew Best *bass* Fiorello
Sally Burgess *mez* Berta
John Noble *bar* Official
Ambrosian Opera Chorus; Academy of St Martin in the Fields / Sir Neville Marriner.
Philips Ⓟ Ⓓ 446 448-2PH2 (two discs: 147 minutes: ADD). Notes, text and translation included.
Recorded 1982.

This was the most stylish and engaging account of *Il barbiere* to have appeared on record since the famous de los Angeles/Bruscantini set recorded by EMI with Glyndebourne forces in 1962 (reviewed below). Here, making a rare but welcome appearance in an opera recording, is the stylish Academy of St Martin in the Fields. Apart from a gabbled *Allegro vivace* midway through Dr Bartolo's aria, this is as pointed and sure-footed an account of the score as you could hope to hear, a reading which entirely belies the fact that this was Neville Marriner's operatic début on record. Played as it is here, with a fine overall line and a wealth of instrumental detail dancing attendance on the drama, the Act 1 finale is fit to be ranked with the Act 2 denouements of Mozart's *Figaro* and Verdi's *Falstaff*.

Quite how the producer, in duets, ensembles and recitatives, created so live a sense of theatre in so essentially unconvivial a place as Watford Town Hall, north west of London, must for ever remain a mystery; there is here a real and rare sense of the delighted interplay of character: a tribute, in the first place, to the degree to which Thomas Allen, Francisco Araiza, Domenico Trimarchi, Agnes Baltsa, Robert Lloyd and their fellows are inside their roles musically and dramatically. There is no vulgar horseplay in the recording; the decorum of the *ottocento* style is closely noted; but equally there is nothing slavish or literal about the way in which Rossini's, and Beaumarchais's comic felicities have been realized. The text is Zedda, more or less. Robert Lloyd takes the Calumny aria in C (D is the 'authentic' key), rightly so, for his is a magnificent bass voice. It's a grand characterization, very much in the Chaliapin style, though surer of pitch than the great man generally was. Lloyd treats the text's scabrous onomatopoeia with abundant relish whilst the orchestra seethe and fulminate below. The climax on "colpo di cannone" is a resounding one, Lloyd's voice and the splendidly placed bass drum making an unforgettable ensemble.

If that is a representative highlight, Thomas Allen's Figaro and Francisco Araiza's Count bring out the opera's virility, its peculiarly masculine strength. (Agnes Baltsa is by turns cunning, charming, and passionate; but this is a man's world, one feels, full of an ardour and energy which she complements but never initiates.) Allen has a vivid sense of character and a brilliant technique. The "Largo" is a *tour de force*, and not only in the stretto; earlier there is as much verbal pointing as you'll find in Gobbi's performance (on Galliera's famous 1957 set for EMI) or Bruscantini's (Gui), alongside an animal magnetism which will have you briefly wondering (here and in "Dunque io son" where Allen is marvellously deft) why this Rosina wasn't as taken by Figaro as the Count. Allen also has a ripe sense of comedy and a nice sense of timing; the syncopated candle-snuffing in the final vaudeville is a typical small felicity.

Araiza is similarly compelling. Technically he is first-rate. His divisions are unusually bright and clean (though rapid triplets tend to go unshaded), the top (including some flashy cadences) true. He gives us the whole role, with no cuts in the cabalettas and with the big Act 2 scene, usually omitted and invariably muffed when included, shaped in a way which is both musically vivid and dramatically right, rounding out Araiza's portrait of an aristocrat distinguished by his ability to dominate and dispel mere domestic imbroglio. Equally, Araiza can be confiding, and funny. His whining music-master (shades of Isacco in *La gazza ladra*) is a delight, right down to an unscripted attempt at a reprise of "Pace e gioia" at the end of the scene, cut off by a petulant "Basta!" from the excellent Bartolo, Domenico Trimarchi. Baltsa's Rosina lies somewhere between Victoria de los Angeles's charm (for Gui) and Maria Callas's mettlesome minx for Galliera. Baltsa, too, is infected by the set's general liveliness: witness the delighted gurgle of joy which escapes from her at the news of the Count's intentions.

Recitatives, edited down here and there, are very alert, theatrically pointed; and Nicholas Kraemer's accompaniments on a sweet-sounding fortepiano are an added pleasure. Like the engineers on the Gui set, Philips have preferred a dryish, intimate acoustic; the small-theatre atmosphere this confers is very likeable, the more so as it allows Marriner the opportunity to conduct with a tautness and vigour which a boomier, more open acoustic would disallow. Once or twice the editing appears to interrupt the dramatic flow. Would Basilio's recitative immediately after the Calumny aria really be so poised? One doubts it. Similarly, Araiza's brilliant account, with chorus, of the cabaletta to "Cessa di più resistere" sounds as if it is a product of a different session from the aria itself.

But these are minor quibbles, mere pinpricks. With excellent choral work in the all important ensembles, and with a delightful Berta from Sally Burgess, this is undoubtedly one of the very best *Barbers* the gramophone has yet given us.

Rossini Il barbiere di Siviglia.
Roberto Servile *bar* Figaro
Sonia Ganassi *mez* Rosina
Ramon Vargas *ten* Count Almaviva
Angelo Romero *bar* Dr Bartolo
Franco de Grandis *bass* Don Basilio
Kázmér Sárkány *bass* Fiorello
Ingrid Kertesi *sop* Berta
Hungarian Radio Chorus; Failoni Chamber Orchestra, Budapest / Will Humburg.
Naxos Ⓢ Ⓘ 8 660027/9 (three discs: 158 minutes: DDD). Notes and text included. Recorded 1992.

Not everyone will approve, but there are ways in which this super-budget recording of *Il barbiere di Siviglia* puts to shame just about every other version of the opera there has yet been. Those it may not please are specialist vocal collectors for whom *Il barbiere* is primarily a repository of vocal test pieces, a kind of musical Badminton. If, on the other hand, you regard *Il barbiere* (Rossini, ex-Beaumarchais) as a gloriously subversive music drama – vibrant, scurrilous, unstoppably vital – then this set is guaranteed to give a great deal of pleasure. 'Performance' is the key word here. Humburg is described in the Naxos booklet as "Conductor and Recitative Director"; and for once the recitatives really are part of the larger drama. The result is a meticulously produced, often very funny, brilliantly integrated performance that you will almost certainly find yourself listening to as a stage play – rather than an opera with eminently missable (often arbitrarily abbreviated) recitatives.

With a virtually all-Italian cast, the results are a revelation. The erotic allure of the duet "Dunque io son?" is striking, arising as it does here out of the brilliantly played teasing of Rosina by Figaro about her new admirer. Similarly, Don Basilio's Calumny aria, superbly sung by Franco de Grandis, a black-browed bass from Turin who was singing for Karajan, Muti and Abbado while still in his twenties. This takes on added character and colour from the massive sense of panic created by de Grandis and the admirable Dr Bartolo of Angelo Romero when Basilio comes in with news of Almaviva's arrival in town. The Overture is done with evident relish, the playing of the Failoni Chamber Orchestra (a group from within the Hungarian State Opera Orchestra) nothing if not articulate. Aided by a clear, forward recording, a *sine qua non* with musical comedy, the cast communicates the Rossini/Sterbini text – solo arias, ensembles, recitatives – with tremendous relish. They are never hustled by Humburg, nor are they spared: the stretta of the Act 1 finale is a model of hypertension and clarity.

It would have been nice to have an English version of the libretto, but you can't have everything at rock-bottom prices and Naxos do provide an excellent track-by-track synopsis. Super-Scrooges might complain that 158 minutes of music could have been shoe-horned on to two CDs, but three CDs is a fair deal for a complete *Il barbiere*, and the layout is first-rate.

Rossini Il barbiere di Siviglia.

Sesto Bruscantini *bar* Figaro
Victoria de los Angeles *sop* Rosina
Luigi Alva *ten* Count Almaviva
Ian Wallace *bass* Dr Bartolo
Carlo Cava *bass* Don Basilio
Duncan Robertson *ten* Fiorello
Laura Sarti *mez* Berta
Glyndebourne Festival Chorus; Royal Philharmonic Orchestra / Vittorio Gui.
EMI Rossini Edition Ⓜ Ⓘ CMS7 64162-2 (two discs: 141 minutes: ADD). Notes, text and translation included. Recorded 1962.

In a letter written in March 1882, Verdi singled out a passage in *Il barbiere di Siviglia* that was in his view a model of musical declamation: "In *Il barbiere* the phrase 'Signor giudizio per carita' is neither melody, nor harmony: it is the word declaimed, exact, true and musical ... amen". The phrase in question – an aside by Figaro to Almaviva – comes shortly after Figaro's rumbustious entrance into the Act 1 finale. On this Glyndebourne set, Sesto Bruscantini drops it in, just as it should be – singing, you might say, that is exact, true and musical ... amen.

Perhaps it is a shade misleading to refer to this classic EMI recording as a "Glyndebourne" set. It has all the ingredients of a Glyndebourne production: notably the cast, the orchestra and chorus, and that doyen of Rossini conductors, Vittorio Gui. But as far as can be ascertained, there was no actual stage production of *Il barbiere* in 1962. Nor was the recording, for all its dryness and sharp-edged immediacy, actually made in Glyndebourne. It is a well-honed, conservatively staged stereophonic studio recording made by EMI in their Abbey Road Studio No. 1 at the conclusion of the 1962 Glyndebourne season. Gui's performance is so astutely paced that whilst the music bubbles and boils every word is crystal-clear. This – to take up Verdi's point – is a wonderfully declaimed reading of the score, but also a beautifully timed one. Gui's steady tempos also allow the music to show its underlying toughness. We are reminded how radical a piece this was in 1816: a score whose initial popularity was with *aficionados* like Beethoven rather than with the public at large. Gui also secures characterful playing from the RPO, from the wind players in particular. Back in 1962, the RPO (still very much Beecham's creation) was the resident Glyndebourne orchestra.

Where Victoria de los Angeles is so memorable is in the beauty of her singing and the originality of the reading. She is much less of a virago in this role than her famous Spanish predecessor, Conchita Supervia; and less of a virago than Callas with Galliera on EMI. There has never been a Rosina who manages to be both as guileful and as charming as de los Angeles. Team her up with the incomparable Sesto Bruscantini and, in something like the nodal Act 1 duet, "Dunque io son", you have musical and dramatic perfection. Gui's Dr Bartolo, Ian Wallace, is a fine old character actor, given plenty of space by Gui, allowing his portrait of Dr Bartolo to emerge as a classic compromise between the letter and the spirit of the part. There are one or two tiny cuts in the recitatives; Almaviva's big Act 2 aria, "Cessa di più resistere" is omitted, but you probably won't miss it. Rossini was surely right to turn a blind eye to the aria's removal after the opening run in Rome.

The choice between the Gui and Galliera sets is difficult. The Galliera has, perhaps, the stronger sense of theatre about it without in any sense being crassly theatrical in the way that so many recordings of *Il barbiere* are. Gui is the more characterful conductor; but Galliera and the Philharmonia Orchestra, fluent and stylish, merely need to keep the show on the road when Callas is singing Rosina and when Gobbi is the barber. Both are classic sets. If the Galliera is *hors concours* dramatically, the Gui could none the less be said to boast the purer Rossinian pedigree.

Rossini Il barbiere di Siviglia.

John Rawnsley *bar* Figaro
Maria Ewing *sop* Rosina
Max-René Cosotti *ten* Count Almaviva
Claudio Desderi *bar* Dr Bartolo
Ferruccio Furlanetto *bass* Don Basilio
Robert Dean *bass* Fiorello
Catherine McCord *mez* Berta
Glyndebourne Festival Chorus and Orchestra / Sylvain Cambreling.
Stage Director: **John Cox.** *Video Director:* **David Heather.**
NVC Arts Ⓟ ⬛ 4509-99223-3 (155 minutes). Recorded 1981.

This Glyndebourne performance is a source of almost unalloyed delight. John Cox's stage direction is full of life, based on pertinently observed detail without ever tipping over into unwanted farce, always a danger in this overplayed piece. William Dudley's painterly décor is a feast for the eye with Seville clearly the location, romantic Spain conjured up before our eyes in foreground and background. You spy Figaro's shop in the first act, he apparently a tailor as well as a barber. In the second act you are in a canopied penthouse with a telescope for the inquisitive Dr Bartolo. Within these engrossing sets, we meet a pleasing group of principals. As Rosina, Maria Ewing gives an apposite display of charm tempered by wilfulness, an engaging, naughty smile playing around her capacious mouth, a whole heap of pouts and a general sense of fiery insubordination. She is a veritable dynamo of a Rosina, every gesture and expression acutely timed. Her tone may not be ideally full of warmth, but the touch of resin in her voice may not be inappropriate. She uses runs and embellishments to make her verbal points.

John Rawnsley's swaggering Figaro is equally alive with invention, vocal and visual. His baritone is in pristine condition, nimble in *fioriture*, firm at the top. Max-René Cosotti offers an Almaviva of lyrical delicacy in his set-pieces and witty acting in his disguises. Claudio Desderi, a younger Bartolo than usual, makes, for once, a plausible candidate for Rosina's hand and one who reveals a touch of steel behind the comic facade. "A un dottor" is delivered with keen aplomb. Ferrucio Furlanetto's Basilio is also younger than most and, vocally speaking, all the better for it. With his long, fair hair, open sandals and straw hat he looks as if he were, as one critic had it, an "eighteenth-century hippy", an eccentric reading but not implausible. Even Berta and Fiorello are for once kept from being caricatured. Cambreling's carefully considered conducting imparts an unexpected breadth to proceedings, well caught in the recording. David Heather's video direction catches the physical exuberance of this highly diverting production.

Rossini Bianca e Falliero.

Katia Ricciarelli *sop* Bianca
Marilyn Horne *mez* Falliero
Chris Merritt *ten* Contareno
Giorgio Surian *bar* Capellio
Patrizia Orciani *sop* Costanza
Ambrogio Riva *bass* Priuli
Ernesto Gavazzi *ten* Pisani
Diego d'Auria *ten* Officer, Usher
Prague Philharmonic Chorus; London Sinfonietta Opera Orchestra / Donato Renzetti.
Fonitcetra Ⓟ Ⓘ RFCD2008 (three discs: 176 minutes: DDD). Notes, text and translation included. Recorded at performances in the Rossini Conservatorio, Pesaro in August 1986.

The abiding memory of this historic revival of Rossini's *Bianca e Falliero*, semi-staged in the Auditorium Pedrotti at the 1986 Pesaro Festival, is of Marilyn Horne responding to tumultuous applause after her Act 2 *scena*, "Qual funebre apparato". Having ended this with her back to the audience, she proceeded over the next five – or was it ten? – minutes to execute a 180-degree turn back towards the footlights. To record it on film, you would have needed one of those special cameras that allows you to watch the grass grow.

This anecdote is offered, not in rebuke, but in admiration of Horne. It was, after all, a thoroughly deserved ovation. Whatever its dramatic merits (and there are several) *Bianca e Falliero* is very much a vocal showcase of an opera, a terrifyingly elaborate exploration in music of one of the world's oldest dramatic subjects, young love blighted by parental hate. To have it performed at all is a privilege; to have it performed with this degree of dash, surety and allure borders on the miraculous. None of the principals, apart perhaps from Horne, emerges wholly unscathed. Merritt begins uncomfortably, and

Ricciarelli has one or two blustery moments in the Act 2 finale (a revision of the Act 2 finale of *La donna del lago*). But much of the singing is exceptional. Ricciarelli makes a wonderfully alluring Bianca, and Chris Merritt has never sounded so well on record as he does here in his various set-piece scenes and duets.

Rossini wrote *Bianca e Falliero* for La Scala, Milan in the autumn of 1819. Working away from the San Carlo in Naples, his private artistic laboratory at the time, and with memories of his last Milanese triumph, *La gazza ladra*, still fresh in the public's mind, he clearly decided on consolidation rather than experiment. Set in seventeenth-century Venice, the story charts the machinations of a brutal father (Contareno, Merritt's role) who would rather have the brilliant young general, Falliero (Horne *en travesti*) compromised, arraigned and executed than see him marry his daughter. In the French melodrama from which Felice Romani took his libretto, Falliero comes to a grim end, much as Cavaradossi will do in *Tosca*; but Rossini and Romani, politically prudent, opted for a happier ending to the tale. The opera was a success with the Milanese and with the Italian public in the decade that followed. Soon, though, it was adapted, dismembered and forgotten. Everything apart from the glorious (and dramatically pivotal) Act 2 Quartet was banished into ill-deserved obscurity.

The problems the opera presents to our own times are obvious; yet in a performance as compelling as this, they tend to wither away. The massiveness of the piece and the close gearing of the *bel canto* style to musical and psychological ends is awe-inspiring. Amid a welter of vocal display, one is struck both by the sheer ferocity of much of the music and by its moments (rare in Rossini) of real erotic allure. The opera has its static set pieces (that big *scena* for Falliero in Act 2), but even here one senses its preoccupation with the idea of dangerous emotional excess. Musically and dramatically, it is something of a roller-coaster; the love music is often heart-easing in its beauty yet Contareno is given some of the nastiest music ever penned for the tenor voice, the writing by turns vindictive, suave and wilful.

Donato Renzetti conducts with this very much in mind. The Prague chorus are fallible but the London Sinfonietta Opera Orchestra back him to the hilt with playing of searing immediacy. The recording treats them well. Unfortunately the RAI engineers have been casual about vocal balances during the live transmission. The chorus movements don't seem to have been adequately plotted in advance. Full marks, however, to Fonitcetra for the accompanying booklet which reproduces most of the material originally issued in Pesaro's careful and scholarly programme book, plus an English translation of the Italian text.

Rossini La cambiale di matrimonio.

John del Carlo *bass* Sir Tobias Mill
Janice Hall *sop* Fanny
David Kuebler *ten* Edoardo Milfort
Alberto Rinaldi *bar* Slook
Carlos Feller *bass* Norton
Amelia Felle *sop* Clarina
Stuttgart Radio Symphony Orchestra / Gianluigi Gelmetti.
Stage Director: **Michael Hampe**. *Film Director*: **Claus Villier**.
Teldec Video Ⓕ VHS 🔲 9031-71479-3; 🌙 9031-71479-6 (two sides: 85 minutes). Filmed at performances in the Schwetzingen Festival in May 1989.

Rossini's youthful *farse* require stylish playing in a small theatre. They also need to be seen as well as heard. Which explains why these video and LaserDisc versions filmed during festival performances in the small rococo theatre in Schwetzingen are such a delight (*Il Signor Bruschino*, reviewed further on, was also filmed at the same venue). Compare this version of *La cambiale di matrimonio* with the sound-only account on the Viotti/Claves set and there is simply no contest. Yet there is still an antipathy among collectors to the idea of acquiring operas on film. It is a pity that in the age of subtitles we have only occasionally got multilingual subtitles programmed into LaserDisc's peripheral information; but Rossini's plots are not difficult to follow and Teldec's booklet annotations are excellent, with the plot outlined track by track in good clear precise form. If this is a limitation, it is a minor one.

Carlos Feller does wonders with the small part of the servant, Norton, adding a dimension to the work which you would never guess at away from the theatre. The piece is played with relish and sung, for the most part, with point and precision. The setting is London in the early nineteenth century with a grandstand view of St Paul's from the drawing-room windows. Here, though, one would query the rather dismal lighting of the backdrop. It suggests the "violet hour, the evening hour that strives homeward" of Eliot's *The Waste Land*; and the violet sky tends to clash with Clarina's lavender gown.

The orchestra is small with nimble strings and expert solo winds. The acoustic is dry, allowing Gelmetti to drive the music along at a spanking pace with plenty of zest and wry humour. With his substantial girth, handsome beard and roguish eye (he would make a marvellous Mustafà in *L'italiana in Algeri*), Gelmetti is a bit of a character in his own right. One feels he ought to be up on the stage as well. To judge by the Overture, he tends to preside rather than direct, leaving the hard-worked band to dispense the ceaseless flow of Rossini goodies.

Rossini La Cenerentola.

Teresa Berganza *mez* Angelina
Luigi Alva *ten* Don Ramiro
Renato Capecchi *bar* Dandini
Paolo Montarsolo *bar* Don Magnifico
Margherita Guglielmi *sop* Clorinda
Laura Zannini *contr* Tisbe
Ugo Trama *bass* Alidoro
Scottish Opera Chorus; London Symphony Orchestra / Claudio Abbado.
DG Ⓟ Ⓓ 423 861-2GH2 (three discs: 144 minutes: ADD). Notes, text and translation included.
Recorded 1971.

This recording of Rossini's *La Cenerentola* was Claudio Abbado's first as an opera conductor on record; the recording was also the first to use the textural research (undertaken here by Alberto Zedda) which from 1979 onwards has been incorporated into the evolving Critical Edition of all Rossini's works. Thanks to first-rate scholarship, superb recorded quality and skilled orchestral playing, the performance remains something of a triumph for Abbado and the LSO. Happily, rhythmic exactness and textural fineness have remained features of Abbado's Rossini style as the 1984 recording of *Il viaggio a Reims* triumphantly proves (reviewed further on). It is true that Vittorio Gui on the old mono Glyndebourne set conducted with more guile and affection, and with more pace and wit in the Dandini/Ramiro duet, "Zitto, zitto"; but on record, where the conductor and not the stage director is king, the kind of directness and authority which the young Abbado manifests here is most welcome.

The recording, which was made in George Watson's College in Edinburgh, derives directly from Jean Pierre Ponnelle's 1971 Edinburgh Festival production. Ponnelle reduced the events of the opera to a sequence of happenings as intricate and as finely geared as the mechanism of a Swiss watch. This is one view of *La Cenerentola*, though it denies the work much of its humanity, its capacity for pathos. these are mentioned because whilst the conductor, orchestra, and engineers all merit what in the old *Record Guide* (London: 1951) would have been the coveted two-star rating, the cast on DG's recording is perhaps less accomplished than one might have hoped. The exception is Berganza who is a sure-footed and sympathetic Cenerentola. It is the men who are occasionally disappointing. Ugo Trama makes heavy weather of the big aria Rossini wrote for Gioacchino Moncada in Rome in December 1820, and Capecchi and Montarsolo are not always so funny as one might anticipate. For example, the duet in which Dandini reveals his true identity to an astonished Don Magnifico is nowhere nearly so funny as it is with Bruscantini and Wallace on the Glyndebourne recording. Luigi Alva does very adequately as Don Ramiro but, again, memories of Gui's Juan Oncina are not entirely expunged.

Yet Abbado's mastery is such that in the big ensembles the characters are propelled brilliantly into life; the ensemble in which Magnifico claims that Cenerentola is dead is finely honed both musically and dramatically.

Rossini La Cenerentola

Marina de Gabarain *mez* Angelina
Juan Oncina *ten* Don Ramiro
Sesto Bruscantini *bar* Dandini
Ian Wallace *bass* Don Magnifico
Alda Noni *sop* Clorinda
Fernanda Cadoni *mez* Tisbe
Hervey Alan *bass* Alidoro
Glyndebourne Festival Chorus and Orchestra / Vittorio Gui.
EMI Rossini Edition mono Ⓜ Ⓓ CMS7 64183-2 (two discs: 117 minutes: ADD). Notes, text and translation included. Recorded 1953-4.

Collectors who have been more than happy over the years with Gui's stylishly conducted though strangely abbreviated 1953 Glyndebourne recording of *La Cenerentola* and, later, with Abbado's finely honed 1971 DG recording, could have quite overlooked the compelling rival set conducted by the veteran Oliviero de Fabritiis for Decca in 1963. He and his lively Florentine band catch our attention with the first note of the Overture and hold it in thrall for the next two and a half hours.

Of course, de Fabritiis's conducting won't find favour with the muesli and skimmed milk brigade who favour a more 'period' approach to Rossini, and he cannot quite get the rhythmic 'spin' on a number like "Zitto, zitto" that Gui does with Juan Oncina and Sesto Bruscantini (EMI's Dandini as well as Decca's in a part he famously made his own). With Ugo Benelli as an unwimpish, strikingly sympathetic Ramiro, the question remains: what of Simionato's Cenerentola? Hers was a Janus-like Rossini talent: an old-fashioned rather erratically schooled manner and technique that none the less thrived on the endless challenges thrown up by the tentative stirrings of revived interest in Rossini in the 1950s. Apologies for writing lengthily about the Decca *La Cenerentola*, but this is partly because its merits deserve notice; partly because it is precisely the kind of set that new converts – the hordes that are theoretically being lured to opera by Pavarotti and friends – may well buy and relish for its intoxicating mix of musical spirit, theatrical flair and technical prowess.

The Glyndebourne set ought to sound much more modest. But they knew a thing or two about making operas in mono in 1953. The recording does not quite have the almost stereophonic presence of the slightly later *Le comte Ory* (reviewed below) but in these CD transfers it emerges sounding splendidly clear and well balanced, the stage 'picture' always strikingly there. As for the performance – well, you will be lured by Gui and the matchlessly stylish Glyndebourne Festival Orchestra into two hours of more or less undiluted pleasure.

In practice, there is little to choose between the two casts. Marina de Gabarain depicts a more obviously vulnerable Cenerentola than Simionato but has similar strengths and weaknesses technically. Oncina is every bit as charming as Benelli. Bruscantini is irrefutably fine on both sets. Where Magnifico is concerned, the Glyndebourne set wins the war but loses the peace. Ian Wallace is as funny as Montarsolo (the scene with Dandini in Act 2 is done to perfection) and he is much more the Rossini stylist (Cenerentola's 'death' isn't marred by ham acting). But he loses an aria. Alidoro is also reduced to a cypher in a performing edition that cuts, sentimentalizes and partly rewrites his part. As the above timing reveals, the Glyndebourne set cuts over 20 minutes of music. True, the cuts damage Agolini more than they do Rossini. But they exist. So if you are looking for a complete *La Cenerentola* and an unimpeachably stylish one, the one to go for is still the 1971 DG set with Berganza, Alva, Capecchi and Montarsolo. It is more expensive but everything is there and beautifully in place. Abbado even manages to discipline Montarsolo into making Magnifico more man than monster. How nice to be spoilt for choice.

Rossini Le comte Ory.
John Aler *ten* Le comte Ory
Sumi Jo *sop* Comtesse Adèle
Diana Montagu *mez* Isolier
Gino Quilico *bar* Raimbaud
Gille Cachemaille *bar* La Gouverneur
Maryse Castets *sop* Alice
Raquel Pierotti *mez* Ragonde
Francis Dudziac *ten* First chevalier
Nicholas Rivenq *bar* Second chevalier
Chorus and Orchestra of Opéra National de Lyons / John Eliot Gardiner.
Philips Ⓟ Ⓒ 422 406-2PH2 (two discs: 132 minutes: DDD). Notes, text and translation included. Recorded 1988.

The last decent studio recording we had of this vintage, late-grown Rossinian *opéra-comique* was in 1957. The cover of **Gramophone** in July 1957 was apple green with EMI using a fine aerial shot of the Glyndebourne house and gardens to advertise the arrival on record of Carl Ebert's 1956 production of *Le comte Ory* beguilingly conducted by Vittorio Gui and sung in the original French by a cast that included Juan Oncina as the libidinous Comte and Sara Barabas as the Comtesse Adèle. EMI have kept the set in their catalogue in an intermittent sort of way over the years: long enough, it seems, to deter any kind of rival, so that *Le comte Ory* has become even more the connoisseur's piece and almost as rare a recorded experience as, say, Reynaldo Hahn's *Ciboulette*.

In 1988, Harmonia Mundi released on CD Le Chant du Monde's transcription of mono tapes of a live 1959 French Radio production conducted with flair and coltish abandon by the veteran Désiré-Emile Inghelbrecht. Despite cuts and acerbic studio sound; and despite, perhaps even because of, a certain nasal narrowing in the tones of Françoise Ogéas's Comtesse, it is a set that many collectors might swoon to hear, not least for Michel Sénéchal's inimitably projected Ory.

This modern *Ory*, which for better or worse is probably going to be the chosen library version for some time to come, arrives with some Gallic trappings: a French orchestra and chorus and some French singers in the *comprimario* roles. Yet, for all his Gallic airs these days, it is difficult to forget that John Eliot Gardiner is an Englishman and a Handelian at that (not necessarily a bad thing, one hears Rossini murmuring from the depths of Santa Croce) and that the present cast is headed by an American Ory, a Korean Comtesse, and a British Isolier. In the event, the principals are little affected by this. Diana Montagu's Isolier is a bright sparkling jewel of a performance that is a considerable advance on the Isolier of Glyndebourne's young Dutch mezzo, Cora Canne-Meijer. And Sumi Jo's Comtesse is a joy, too, fetching, dramatic and vocally expert. Good as Barabas was on the Glyndebourne set, she occasionally had to funk or duck some of Rossini's sudden vocal flourishes – towards the end of the opera's penultimate number, for example – and she had less in reserve dramatically. In Act 1 Sumi Jo is all aerial brilliance, singing with that polished insouciance that so captivated the late Herbert von Karajan. And yet in the Act 2 denouement, Jo brings a steely glint to her tone that leaves Ory, his fortunes sinking as fast as the vocal tessitura, in no doubt about who is the victor and who the vanquished.

John Aler, too, is an accomplished Ory, not a French Ory in the way Sénéchal naturally is, nor an Ory with the vocal allure and sly grace of Glyndebourne's Juan Oncina. The sound is darker, more back-of-the-throat, less tip-of-the-tongue, than Oncina's and there are fewer sweet elisions of rhythm and phrase than Oncina, with Gui's help, was able to give us, let alone something like the roguish lift on the final word of the response in Act 2, "C'est le répas d'innocence, mesdames!", when Ory and his roistering gang are disguised as nuns. But Aler's is a strongly projected account of the role, ably sung. Indeed, what Gardiner and his team invariably achieve is a strong sense of dramatic actuality. The Act 1 duet between Ory and Isolier, uncut and thus running to nearly twice the length of the Glyndebourne version, is a particular case in point and there are many moments, such as the Comte's re-entry near the end of Act 1 or his final submission in Act 2, where everything is immensely vivid and robust.

There is also a strong Gouverneur from Gille Cachemaille. He has the makings of a low trill, and he retains his Act 1 aria, which Ian Wallace was denied on the Glyndebourne set. This is no huge gain to one's general enjoyment of the opera; but Philips's opening up of the numerous niggling and not-so-niggling cuts is, by and large, a bonus. On the Glyndebourne recording one missed a verse in the early part of the great drinking scene, not to mention the concluding recitative and stretta of the opera's first scene, and the dramatic recitatives that lead to the Act 2 Trio, the latter a noticeably damaging cut.

Gardiner's management of the vocal ensembles, including the unaccompanied septet, is technically first-rate, with a well-balanced vocal team; and the chorus work is also strikingly robust. That said, his feel for the score – for its grace, irony, wit, and humour – seems to be distinctly limited. The little Overture which so outraged Berlioz is played by Gui as a beguiling game of musical hide-and-seek, amusingly conspiratorial. Gardiner is deadpan and rather quick, advancing purposefully to the marching 2/4 section. And as the Act gets underway it is clear that there are times when we are being offered speed or a kind of motorized energy with hardly any of the buoyancy and wit of Gui. At times the music is so forcefully directed, the seams begin to show, tub-thumping tonic and dominant cadences that a gentler interpreter would shade urbanely away. At times, the French wind playing is marvellous, full of brilliance and acerbic humour but in something like the famous song of the cellar in Act 2 it is not only Gino Quilico's rather pallid and unconfident patter that disappoints; the orchestral accompaniment itself has too little mordancy and point. Nor is Gardiner much of a colourist. In the preface to the great Act 2 Trio one longs for just one bar to be played with the ear of a real master, a Monteux, a Munch or Gui himself. But Gardiner is very much a conductor of his era and place. It is all part of the new order, borne in by the zealots of authenticity, and we must put up with it, even if in the process we are denied a good deal of the spirit of wry, smiling, sweet-sounding Francophiliac Rossini.

The set includes an excellent essay by Philip Gossett on the opera itself and its world of disguises and masquerades. The recording could have been even more tightly edited. At end-of-section rests or fermatas it is often a matter of a second or so, or less, but there is a tendency not to bother with such niceties, which is unfortunate when a longish gap highlights evidence of a separate take. Balances between voices and orchestra have generally been astutely judged but there are some variations in balance and there are times when Lawrence Collingwood's 1956 EMI mono production was at once subtler and more immediately relevant in its 'placing' of a voice. Le comte Ory is an opera where the Comte and his accomplices are much given to sly asides and subversive comments and this is something the old set often dealt with astonishingly well.

Although Gardiner is unlikely to displace the Gui in the affections of old Rossini hands, it will give considerable pleasure to anyone who has yet to discover the inexhaustible delights afforded by this delectable score.

Rossini Le comte Ory.

Juan Oncina *ten* Comte Ory
Sari Barabas *sop* Comtesse Adèle
Cora Canne-Meijer *mez* Isolier
Michel Roux *bar* Raimbaud
Ian Wallace *bass* La Gouverneur
Jeannette Sinclair *sop* Alice
Monica Sinclair *contr* Ragonde
Dermot Troy *ten* Chevalier
Glyndebourne Festival Chorus and Orchestra / Vittorio Gui.
EMI Rossini Edition mono Ⓜ ① CMS7 64180-2 (two discs: 113 minutes: ADD). Notes, text and translation included. Recorded 1956.

This production of *Le comte Ory*, finest of all French-language comic operas, was one of Glyndebourne's principal glories in the 1950s. It was seen at Glyndebourne over 30 times between 1954 and 1958; it also visited Paris (coals to Newcastle) and the Edinburgh Festival. In 1956 the stage production was rested; instead, the cast decamped to Abbey Road to make this now legendary recording.

Like Jane Austen's *Emma* it could be said to be faultless despite its faults. There are cuts. The French is not consistently good. The singing is variable, with Canne-Meijer's Isolier, Barabas's Comtesse and Wallace's Gouverneur all arguably outclassed by their opposite numbers on John Eliot Gardiner's Philips recording. Yet the Glyndebourne recording has several trump cards to play. Juan Oncina as the philandering Comte Ory has a matchless presence and charm. Like Gardiner's John Aler, he is occasionally taxed by the tessitura of the role; but his diction is superb, and, with Gui in attendance, there is a flawless ease of emission where Rossini's melodies are at their most beguiling. Where Gardiner and Aler meddle 'meaningfully' with the content of the sublime Act 2 Trio, Oncina and Gui do the supremely Rossinian thing of cultivating elegance of line and sweetness of sound above all else. Gui is also flawless in his pacing of the score, never regimenting the music as Gardiner tends to do. How well the great masters among this generation of conductors knew how to pay out the rhythms of musical comedy – one thinks of Otto Ackermann in *The Merry Widow*, of Clemens Krauss in *Die Fledermaus*, of Gui's Rossini *passim*.

This recording is one of the last masterpieces of the mono era. Don't be put off by slightly rusty sound in the Overture. As soon as the voices come into play it is clear how astutely the recording has been staged for the gramophone by Gui and the engineers. It frequently surpasses the Philips performance and recording in terms of clarity and guileful pointing of dramatic perspectives. And in Rossini's big ensembles that is a huge plus. Put on track 19 of the first disc, the Act 1 finale, and see if you don't agree. As far as many collectors are concerned, at moments like this God and Rossini are in their respective heavens and everything is right with the world. The dramas of Act 2 – Ory and his followers disguised as nuns laying siege to the women and the cellars of Castle Formoutiers – are also staged with a tremendous sense of theatrical actuality. Like champagne and the works of P. G. Wodehouse, this recording is one of life's few infallible tonics.

Rossini Le comte Ory.

Marc Laho *ten* Comte Ory
Annick Massis *sop* Comtesse Adèle
Diana Montague *mez* Isolier
Ludovic Tezier *bar* Raimbaud
Julien Robbins *bass* La Gouverneur
Stella Woodman *sop* Alice
Jane Shaulis *mez* Ragonde
Colin Judson *ten* Chevalier
Glyndebourne Festival Chorus; London Philharmonic Orchestra / Andrew Davis.
Stage Director: **Jérôme Savary.** *Video Director:* **Brian Large.**
NVC Arts Ⓟ ◫ 0630-18646-3 (140 minutes). Filmed at a performance in the Opera House, Glyndebourne in July 1997.

For Rossini in colour you cannot do better than the NVC Arts tape of the Glyndebourne production of *Le comte Ory*, not least because the settings by Ezio Toffolutti are so cheerful and so witty – in an opera with many irreligious undertones, the suggestion of Leonardo da Vinci's *The Last Supper* in the carousing scene is funny rather than sacrilegious. Marc Laho is terrific in the title-role, written for the younger Nourrit, and Diana Montague is credible in the travesti role of the Page. Director Jérôme Savary's solution to the famous trio is ingenious and the whole production, directed for video by Brian Large with English subtitles, is a romp. Andrew Davis understands the subtle change which has come over Rossini's style since the blatant hilarity of the Italian comedies; and he draws fine playing from the LPO. Not to be missed.

Rossini La donna del lago.

Katia Ricciarelli *sop* Elena
Lucia Valentini-Terrani *contr* Malcolm
Dalmacio Gonzales *ten* Uberto, Giacomo
Dano Raffanti *ten* Rodrigo di Dhu
Samuel Ramey *bass* Douglas d'Angus
Cecilia Valdenassi *sop* Albini
Oslavio di Credico *ten* Serano
Antonia d'Uva *ten* Bertram
Prague Philharmonic Chorus; Chamber Orchestra of Europe / Maurizio Pollini.
Sony Classical Ⓟ ① S2K39311 (three discs: 138 minutes: DDD). Notes, text and translation included. Recorded in conjunction with performances at the Rossini Opera Festival, Pesaro, Italy in 1983.

As the first major opera to be derived from the work of Sir Walter Scott, Rossini's *La donna del lago* (taken from Scott's *The Lady of the Lake*, 1810) was something of a trail-blazer for neo-romantics in the immediate post-Napoleonic years in Europe. In Rossini's lifetime, *La donna del lago* was also one of his most widely admired pieces. The poet Leopardi thought it "a stupendous thing" and Halévy vowed to read its First Act through once more before he died. For over 50 years it was revived, adapted, and cannibalized. Today it has a tentative hold on the repertoire as the Houston, Pesaro and Covent Garden revivals in the 1980s confirm but the work has never been officially available on record. Audiences familiar with some of Weber's music and Donizetti's, not to mention Wagner's remarkable use of the off-stage hunt at the start of Act 2 of *Tristan und Isolde*, may be less disposed than audiences of the 1820s to think the long opening scene to be in any way remarkable. But remarkable it is: musically, dramatically, and in its closeness to the letter and spirit of Scott's poem. Act 2, by contrast, has always been a problem. Chorley thought it little more than a concert in costume, and revivals and adaptations supervised or sanctioned by Rossini in later years were clearly aimed at shoring up the structure of a work which does not entirely live up to the high promise of its opening. The Pesaro production, and this recording which was made shortly afterwards in the Sala Pedrotti of the Conservatorio Rossini in Pesaro, uses H. Colin Slim's Critical Edition which gives us Rossini's original Act 2, including Serano's touching little narrative and Malcolm's second aria but omits such striking accretions as the Quartet from *Bianca e Falliero*.

The Pesaro cast is a distinguished one. It may have been tempting to cast the smallest of the principal roles, the bass Douglas, with a less remarkable singer than Samuel Ramey, but the temptation has been avoided. Marilyn Horne excepted, it would be difficult at present to find a better exponent of the travesti role of Malcolm than Lucia Valentini-Terrani; and after a slightly chilly start, Dalmacio Gonzales is an expert and affecting exponent of the role of King James V, disguised for the greater part of the drama as James Fitz-James in Scott's poem and as Uberto in Tottola's libretto. In some respects, the most demanding role is that of the fierce tribal chieftain, Roderick Dhu (Rodrigo). His cavatina is so florid that one might think it had been written for Giovanni David; in fact, it was written for Nozzari whose commanding stage presence and fierce manner were needed for the role of Rodrigo in the interests of theatrical verisimilitude. Dano Raffanti, bereft on the gramophone of any physical dimension except the vocal one, might seem lightweight; but his, too, is a creditable performance. As Elena, the lady of the lake who arrives in a skiff singing her folk-cavatina to a backdrop of loch and mountain setting, Katia Ricciarelli is not immediately successful: her diction is less than pure, her tone rather cloudy, and this doesn't quite do for the character Rossini has distilled into song from such lines in Scott as "And ne'er did Grecian chisel trace/A Nymph, a Naiad, or a Grace/Of finer form or lovelier face". But Ricciarelli settles. Her early recitatives, which should carry a Sieglinde-like charge, are rather prosaic but the voice sounds well in the duets and trios and the showpiece finale, "Tanti affetti", is sweet and true with a hint of that quality of "triumphancy" which Chorley gratefully noted in Grisi's singing when he heard her as Elena at Covent Garden in 1847.

In a work which has its own special *tinta* or colour and which (the hiatuses in Act 2 notwithstanding) is through-composed in a way remarkable for its time, the conductor's role is an important one. Maurizio Pollini, whose collaboration with the Pesaro Festival must be gratefully noted, exercises evident control over the proceedings. It's a cool, precise, at times rather quick performance, the quickness more welcome in something like the famous Chorus of Bards than it is in the hunting choruses at the start of the opera or in the Weberish chorus of Ellen's girl attendants, also in Act 1. Oddly, given the work's particular character, Pollini's direction seems to stress Rossini's roots in neo-classicism and in comic detachment. The performance registers well the drama's nodal points – the powerful C minor interlude in the fine Act 2 Trio where Rodrigo's men rise unexpectedly from the surrounding heather – but it is sometimes short on warmth and romantic sensibility.

There are occasions when the music might have benefited from a gentler pace, allowing the singers time to bring more bloom to their tone and time to point harmonic detail, such as Uberto's affecting shift to the chord of the sixth in the aside following "Deh! mi perdona, deh!". Pollini also tends to compartmentalize the opera's sustained 40-minute opening movement. The great hunting scenes don't launch and infiltrate the drama in the way they might.

And yet it is easy to criticize. Getting an overview of rarely performed works is as difficult for the conductor as it is for the musicologist; such things come only with familiarity and time. And with Rossini the scale of the whole thing is so difficult to judge. Act 1 seems to suggest a largish house and large expectations; but Rossini had some bad experiences with *La donna del lago* in big houses in Naples and Paris; so much so that when it came to his reluctantly agreeing to give an additional charity performance of *Il viaggio a Reims* in Paris in 1825, he flatly refused to allow the production to be moved from the Salle Louvois into the newer and bigger theatre, the Salle Le Peletier.

Recorded in the Sala Pedrotti of the Pesaro Conservatorio, the Sony production opts for a degree of intimacy and recorded clarity Rossini would almost certainly have approved. Whether he would have approved the parallel diminution of the work's imaginative, as opposed to merely physical, scale, is less certain. That said, the set meets its responsibilities, as the first gramophone recording of *La donna del lago*, with care and considerable distinction.

Rossini Elisabetta, regina d'Inghilterra.

Montserrat Caballé *sop* Elisabetta
José Carreras *ten* Leicester
Valerie Masterson *sop* Matilde
Rosanne Creffield *mez* Enrico
Ugo Benelli *ten* Norfolk
Neil Jenkins *ten* Guglielmo
Ambrosian Singers; London Symphony Orchestra / Gian-Franco Masini.
Philips Ⓜ Ⓛ 432 453-2PM2 (two discs: 141 minutes: ADD). Notes, text and translation included. Recorded 1975.

Rossini Otello.

José Carreras *ten* Otello
Frederica von Stade *mez* Desdemona
Gianfranco Pastine *ten* Iago
Salvatore Fisichella *ten* Rodrigo
Nucci Condo *mez* Emilia
Samuel Ramey *bass* Elmiro
Keith Lewis *ten* Lucio
Alfonso Leoz *ten* Doge, Gondoliere
Ambrosian Opera Chorus; Philharmonia Orchestra / Jesús López-Cobos.
Philips Ⓜ ① 432 456-2PM2 (two discs: 153 minutes: ADD). Notes, text and translation included.
Recorded 1978.

Rossini Mosè in Egitto.

Ruggero Raimondi *bass* Mosè
June Anderson *sop* Elcia
Zehava Gal *contr* Amaltea
Sandra Browne *mez* Amenosi
Salvatore Fisichella *ten* Aronne
Ernesto Palacio *ten* Osiride
Keith Lewis *ten* Mambre
Siegmund Nimsgern *bass-bar* Faraone
Ambrosian Opera Chorus; Philharmonia Orchestra / Claudio Scimone.
Philips Ⓜ ① 420 109-2PM2 (two discs: 146 minutes: ADD). Notes, text and translation included.
Recorded 1981.

Amid a small avalanche of new or newly reissued Rossini opera recordings, none is more important, individually or as a group, than this trio of reissues from Philips's unofficial Rossini edition. The Naples years, 1815 to 1822, are at the very centre of Rossini's creative life. It is here that genius – "I had facility and lots of instinct" – was put to school. And firmly so: the serious masterpieces of the Naples years take as their subjects the Bible and Shakespeare, Scott and Racine, Tasso and English historical romance.

Rossini made his début in Naples with *Elisabetta, regina d'Inghilterra*. It is a verse reduction of a half-remembered drama by an Italian advocate out of an English romance. It is historically dubious and dramatically ingenuous, but the central situation is interesting (whilst campaigning in Scotland, Leicester, the Queen's *inamorato*, has married a young girl, a scion of the house of Mary Queen of Scots). As a text it offered the young composer substantial spaces to fill. And being Rossini he filled them with aplomb; yet gracefully and truthfully too. The Philips recording, conducted by Masini with unhurrying grace, has a fine cast. The Matilde is Valerie Masterson, affecting and sweet-sounding. Benelli is a stylish and generally fresh-toned Norfolk; with the young Carreras trailing clouds of glory in the di Stefano style, full of fiery brilliance, well parted as Leicester.

The Elisabetta is Montserrat Caballé, no less. There are some who might want less diplomatic restraint from the jilted Queen than Caballé offers us. She talks of fierce distress but is rarely fierce; her great injunction to Matilde, "Renounce!", is eloquent rather than imperative. Stendhal described Isabella Colbran, the creator of the role, as a modern commentator might have described Callas. "When Signorina Colbran talked with Matilde it was impossible to escape the irrefutable conclusion that this woman had reigned for 20 years as a queen whose authority was absolute and supreme. It was the ingrained acceptance of manner and mannerism bred by despotic power which characterized this great artist." Caballé communicates little of this vocally. Yet she is regal, and very feminine. Rightly so, for Elisabetta's music is exquisitely rather than fiercely wrought. Elisabetta's final scene is a miracle of soft, sweet inwardness; and the glorious duet with Matilde is like an ethereal preview of "Mira, o Norma". The libretto, in fact, dictates a sweet, reasonable queen.

The *Otello* (Naples 1816) also has a strong cast, headed by Carreras's searingly noble Moor. The Desdemona is Frederica von Stade: chaste and as luminous as a sculpture in Carrara marble. The set also displays casting in depth. In Rossini's day Naples was awash with great tenors, a situation that nowadays creates prodigious difficulties. Yet both the Iago, Gianfranco Pastine, and the Rodrigo, Salvatore Fisichella, emerge with honour, barely bloodied and never for a moment bowed by Rossini's terrible arsenal of vocal effects. "They have been crucifying *Otello* into an opera", wrote Byron in 1818. Well, yes and no. By all means treat Acts 1 and 2 as flashy rodomontade, but Act 3 is glorious, inspired enough and sufficiently close to Shakespeare to have been a near fatal deterrent to what Verdi called his own "chocolate project". If you have heard it before you will thrill to it afresh – off-stage Gondolier and all – in these brilliant CD transfers.

If *Elisabetta* and *Otello* offer inspired scenes but the odd *mauvais quart-d'heure*, *Mosè in Egitto* (Naples 1819) is flawless, an exquisitely wrought small masterpiece that is still too little known. Large houses and ignorant managements have fated audiences to experience the opera in the bloated Parisian rewrite *Moïse et Pharaon* (though revivals have rarely been in French). In the original Naples version, the opera starts with the famous Scene of the Shadows – the plague of darkness that covers Egypt. It proceeds to the lovely pastoral-romantic Second Act with its terrific climax: Moses striking dead Pharoah's son. And it ends, the web of key systems miraculously intact, with the famous Prayer and crossing of the Red Sea. Moses, Michele Benedetti's part originally, draws from Raimondi the finest of all his recorded Rossini performances. June Anderson sings Elcia with stunning conviction, whilst Siegmund Nimsgern and Ernesto Palacio make a formidable father and son combination. Scimone, too, surpasses himself. A fanatical though occasionally wayward Rossinian, he has rarely directed a tauter or lyrically more beautiful performance.

Transfers to CD often find out lapses and glitches in the original productions. But these are immaculate – technically proficient, scholarly, musically memorable. There are no booklet credits, but the productions owe their existence to the unstinting work in the Rossini cause of Erik Smith, and to Philip Gossett whose influence has never been far away. There is nothing old-fashioned or fustian about these sets. All three are necessary library acquisitions for lovers of memorable opera, memorably performed.

Rossini Ermione.

Cecilia Gasdia *sop* Ermione
Margarita Zimmermann *contr* Andromaca
Ernesto Palacio *ten* Pirro
Chris Merritt *ten* Oreste
William Matteuzzi *ten* Pilade
Simone Alaimo *bass* Fenicio
Mario Bolognesi *ten* Attalo
Elisabetta Tandura *sop* Cleone, Cefisa
Prague Philharmonic Chorus; Monte Carlo Philharmonic Orchestra / Claudio Scimone.
Erato Libreto Ⓜ Ⓞ 2292-45790-2 (two discs: 123 minutes: DDD). Notes, text and translation included. Recorded 1986.

Even nowadays, with a major revival of interest in Rossini's serious operas well underway, *Ermione*, his two-set *azione tragica* taken from Racine's *Andromaque*, is a work about which even moderately well-informed opera-goers usually admit to know nothing at all. In the public imagination it sits alongside such arcana as the gelid *Zelmira* and the largely impossible *Sigismondo* as being beyond the pale. Large claims have been made for the piece (not too great a risk given Rossini's alleged remark to the Escudiers: "It is my little *Guillaume Tell* in Italian", though these claims were comparatively modest beside Professor Gossett's excited conclusion to his fine essay on the opera in the 1987 Pesaro Festival programme ("*Ermione*: Rossini's *tragédie lyrique*"). "It is a major accomplishment", he concluded "and must be reckoned one of the finest works in the history of nineteenth-century Italian opera."

For a work as neglected as this, such special pleading is entirely in order, and it should be noted that Gossett is careful to stress the historical dimension in staking out the work's claim to greatness. But whatever claims or counter-claims that have been made, there is little doubt that on the stage – the 1987 Pesaro production was the first anywhere since the 1819 Naples première – the piece makes a very real impact. This was clear in Pesaro even with Montserrat Caballé giving a brave, touching, and gracious account of a role that was written for Colbran and which cries out for a singer with Callas's ability to match *ottocento* vocalism with a lyric-tragic declamatory manner that takes its inspiration from Racine and the original Greeks. Erato's Cecilia Gasdia, has a greater feel for the drama than Caballé, but she is very much the exception here. The Erato recording, made in Monte Carlo after concert performances in Padua in June 1986, is a pre-Pesaro, non-theatrical pre-emptive strike on a piece which deserves altogether fierier advocacy.

At its première in 1819, *Ermione* clearly defied popular expectation. The off-stage cries of the grieving Trojans that interrupt the Overture's far from predictable course are not isolated strokes of dramatic *terribilità*; the score is littered with such moments. Rossini, like Beethoven and Stravinsky, is one of art's great obsessives. He was evidently drawn to the Hermione-Andromache story in part because it is a drama in which the famous Rossinian energy, driving inwards, can help define what is to some extent a tragedy of obsession. In form, *Ermione* is mature, late Neapolitan Rossini classically direct, with interest in the emotionally warring principals – Pyrrhus, Orestes and the two women who are hopelessly entangled with them – carefully marshalled and cleanly focused. Act 1, a magnificent seven-movement expository structure, runs a little over the hour; Act 2, which is largely given over to an in-depth study of Hermione's state of mind and manic behaviour, is rather shorter: just four movements making up less than an hour's music and moving with finely honed dramatic economy to a terrific conclusion that even Racine might have cared to hear.

Such a fiery, obsessive, and economically conceived music-drama needs to be conducted with a certain ferocity. In Pesaro Gustav Kuhn drove all before him to generally admirable effect; here Claudio Scimone is, for the most part, a good deal limper and more decorous. The performance briefly takes fire in the final stages but it has in general the feel of a low-powered concert-hall run-through. Margarita Zimmermann breathes some life into the grieving Andromache's music, but Ernesto Palacio is a pale-voiced Pyrrhus and fine as Chris Merritt generally is in the role of Orestes he seems better suited, and less dispensable dramatically, in the role of Pyrrhus which he sang in Pesaro.

Erato have provided a very adequate recording in their Monte Carlo venue and they provide notes and a four-language libretto in an accompanying booklet. But whoever did the editing did not know much about the structure of the piece. With Act 1 considerably longer than Act 2, it is probably necessary to spill over on to a second record. But why start the organically whole *finale primo* four minutes before the end of the first CD? Start both with "Amarti? ... Ah sì, mio ben!" and you end up with dramatic sense and two discs of about 61 minutes each.

No doubt by issuing the LPs in Europe in time for the 1987 Pesaro revival, Erato pulled off a smart marketing coup. But *Ermione* is not well served by the results. It needs more passionate advocacy than we have here if the piece is to justify to a larger public past and present claims that have been made on its behalf.

Rossini Ermione.

Anna Caterina Antonacci *sop* Ermione
Diana Montague *mez* Andromaca
Jorge Lopez-Yanez *ten* Pirro
Bruce Ford *ten* Oreste
Paul Austin Kelly *ten* Pilade
Gwynne Howell *bass* Fenicio
Paul Nilon *ten* Attalo
Julie Unwin *mez* Cleone
Lorna Windsor *sop* Cefisa
Oliver Bridge *sngr* Astianatte
Glyndebourne Chorus; London Philharmonic Orchestra / Andrew Davis.
Stage Producer: **Graham Vick.** *Video Director:* **Humphrey Burton.**
Warner Vision Ⓔ 🔳 0630 14012-3 (138 minutes). Recorded at a performance during the Glyndebourne Festival in June 1995.

To mark the start of the 1996 Glyndebourne season the Festival, in association with Warner Vision, issued videos of the first five productions presented at the Festival's new house in the Sussex Downs since May 1994, when the exciting theatre was unveiled to general praise for its looks, comfort and sound. These included this highly recommended 1995 *Ermione*, another Vick/Hudson triumph with a previously neglected work by Rossini turning out to be a tragedy of great histrionic force, at least as here staged with Hudson's lopsided theatre-within-a-theatre reflecting the incipient madness of all the characters. The work calls for no fewer than four high tenors. As the rivals for Ermione's affections, Bruce Ford (Oreste) and Jorge Lopez-Yanez (Pirro) also rival each other in vocal pyrotechnics. Anna Caterina Antonacci in the title-part, gives an exciting performance of a troubled, self-willed woman. Davis uncovers all the originality of the piece, indeed finds more in it perhaps than anyone previously thought to be there. Burton again brings the *frisson* of this vivid performance graphically into one's home. The LPO play splendidly. It is subtitled and in good stereo.

Rossini Guglielmo Tell (in Italian).

Sherrill Milnes *bar* Guglielmo Tell
Luciano Pavarotti *ten* Arnoldo
Mirella Freni *sop* Matilde
Della Jones *mez* Jemmy
Elizabeth Connell *mez* Edwige
Ferrucio Mazzoli *bass* Gessler
Nicolai Ghiaurov *bass* Gualtiero
John Tomlinson *bass* Melcthal
Cesar Antonio Suarez *ten* Un pescatore
Piero De Palma *ten* Rodolfo
Richard Van Allan *bass* Leutoldo
Ambrosian Opera Chorus; National Philharmonic Orchestra / Riccardo Chailly.
Decca Ⓟ ① 417 154-2DH4 (four discs: 235 minutes: ADD). Notes, text and translation included. Recorded 1980.

If ever there was a case for armchair opera – and on CD at that – it is Rossini's *Guglielmo Tell*. The very limitations which have made it, so far, a non-repertory work, give space for the imagination to redress the balance: the short, Rousseau-esque scenes of life by Lake Lucerne, the distant entrances and exits of shepherds and huntsmen, the leisurely but perfectly balanced side-vignettes of fisherman, hunter, child.

Thanks to the clarity and liveliness of the recording itself and, above all, the shrewd casting, this set creates a vivid *charivari* of fathers, sons, lovers and patriots, all played out against some of Rossini's most delicately painted pastoral cameos. Riccardo Chailly keeps up the undercurrent of tension between private love and public loyalty, as well as working hard the rustic jollity of the score. Tell himself could hardly have a better advocate than Sherrill Milnes, who succeeds in portraying the moral rectitude of a man who casts himself in the role of his brother's keeper, while managing to glow with true ardour and integrity in the cause for which he is fighting.

Arnoldo and Matilde, too, are cleverly cast. Pavarotti contains the coarse, direct impulsiveness of Arnoldo's shepherd stock with the tenderness of love, in his characteristic charcoal *cantabile* and, indeed, the numbness of his remorse. Even in his reflective Act 4 aria, "O muto asil", there is a rough, peasant edge gritting the vocal line which is both entirely truthful and nicely propulsive. Freni, singing opposite him as the forbidden Princess Matilde, phrases with aristocratic poise, folding into every fragment of embryonic *bel canto* the fragile ardour of a young girl's love. The vocal chemistry between them in their Act 2 declaration of love is a lively incarnation of their respective roles.

A similarly interesting patterning of vocal timbres is produced by the casting of Elizabeth Connell as Edwige, Tell's wife, and of Della Jones as Jemmy, their son. Their last act trio with Matilde is matched by the contrasting colours of the basses of Ghiaurov, Tomlinson and Van Allan: their roles may be small, but their characters are vividly stamped on what is an excellent ensemble performance.

Rossini Guillaume Tell.

Gabriel Bacquier *bar* Guillaume Tell
Nicolai Gedda *ten* Arnold
Montserrat Caballé *sop* Mathilde
Mady Mesplé *sop* Jemmy
Jocelyne Taillon *mez* Hedwige
Louis Hendrikx *bass* Gessler
Kolos Kováts *bass* Walter Furst
Gwynne Howell *bass* Melcthal
Charles Burles *ten* Fisherman
Ricardo Cassinelli *ten* Rudolph
Nicholas Christou *bar* Leuthold
Ambrosian Opera Chorus; Royal Philharmonic Orchestra / Lamberto Gardelli.
EMI Ⓜ ① CMS7 69951-2 (four discs: 238 minutes: ADD). Notes and text included. Recorded 1972.

Rossini spent several years familiarizing himself with the French language and French prosody before attempting his new grand opera for the Paris Opera and there is no doubt that *Guillaume Tell* is the genuine article, the Italian *Guglielmo Tell* a convenient artefact. As Stravinsky once observed: "Let librettos and texts be published in translation, let synopses and arguments of plots be distributed in advance ... but do not change the sound and the stress of words that have been composed to precisely certain music at precisely certain places." The rival set is powerfully cast and conducted, but it is in Italian and sounds at times like middle-period Verdi.

It is very fine but the EMI set is also strongly cast in the *comprimario* roles and has an array of principals who are sensitive to the style and dramatic manner of the French *Tell*. Bacquier's Tell, rightly, is a sympathetically paternal figure, no fervid rabble-rouser; Gedda's Arnold makes up in sensibility what it lacks in raw virility (in "Asil hereditaire" he strikes exactly the right note of heroic regret), and Caballé, the loyal and skilled Rossinian, is a fine Mathilde, the manner regal, the tone limpid, the diction idiomatic.

The contributions of Gardelli, the RPO and the Ambrosian Opera Chorus may strike you as being, in places, a shade beefy, but perhaps that is merely a consequence of the general cleanness and impact of the CD transfers of the very good 1972 recording. Unhappily, the reissue is marred by EMI's decision to supply the French text only in the accompanying booklet. How on earth they expect collectors to enjoy and understand this very long and carefully crafted opera, without a parallel text and translation, is inexplicable. It is true that the set comes now at mid price, but it is still a considerable investment for any would-be collector. The decision therefore detracts considerably from the merits of an otherwise important and successful reissue.

Rossini L'inganno felice.

Annick Massis *sop* Isabella
Raúl Giménez *ten* Bertrando
Rodney Gilfry *bar* Batone
Pietro Spagnoli *bass* Tarabotto
Lorenzo Regazzo *bar* Ormondo
Le Concert des Tuileries / Marc Minkowski.
Erato Ⓟ ① 0630-17579-2 (78 minutes: DDD). Notes, text and translation included. Recorded during performances in the Théâtre de Poissy between June 12th-17th, 1996.

Finalmente! A fine and tremendously enjoyable recording of an exquisite early Rossini one-acter that in the first flush of Rossini's national and international success in the years 1812-24 was, without question, one of his most popular operas. Within a year of its *prima* in Venice, the opera had been revived in Venice and played in Bologna, Florence (two separate productions), Trieste and Verona.

Rossini himself used it as a personal visiting card when he settled in Naples in 1815 and again when he moved to Paris in 1824. The plot resembles that of a late Shakespearian comedy. Set in a seaside mining community, it is concerned with the discovery and rehabilitation of Isabella, Duke Bertrando's wronged and, so he thinks, long-dead wife. It is a work that is comic and serious, witty and sentimental; and there, perhaps, lies the rub. Rossini, especially early Rossini, is meant to be all teeth and smiles, yet *L'inganno felice* is not quite like that. The very *mise-en-scène* is odd: 'seaside' and 'mining' being, in such a context, strangely contradictory concepts.

One-acters are difficult to programme. What do you put them with? But *L'inganno felice* has also suffered from not being known. Nowadays people want a point of reference – *in fine*, a recording – to run to; and on that front there has been very little down the years. The exception was a recording conducted by Carlo Franci, made in Naples *c*1960, a performance of great intimacy, dash and spirit recorded in a bone-dry acoustic with chamber-music forces. The tenor is rough, but Emilia Cundari is a deeply affecting Isabella, and the great conspiracy duet between the two *buffo* basses ("Va taluno mormorando") is very funny indeed, Montarsolo and Tadeo relishing every note and syllable.

The set used to be on a pair of Voce LPs but subsequently turned up on a Notes CD. (To judge from the various bits of pre-echo, copied straight off the LPs.) It is mentioned merely because it is there and it is fun, though it is clear that it is now entirely outclassed by this Erato recording.) As, indeed, is the sadly inadequate 1992 Claves CD, which is dully conducted, unimaginatively sung and recorded in an over-reverberant chapel acoustic that is quite wrong for early Rossini. The Erato set is not, however, a first choice by default. It is a splendid performance in its own right. Minkowski uses a chamber ensemble of about 30 players. It is a live performance, recorded with pleasing immediacy, that begins bullishly but settles to intimacy when the drama requires. The score is full of vocal pitfalls (another reason for companies fighting shy of it, no doubt), not least for the tenor and for the baritone Batone (Filippo Galli's role). But Giménez and Gilfry cope more than adequately, with enough in reserve to produce moments of genuine ease and beauty. Annick Massis, is a charming Isabella, good in her first aria, ravishing in her second.

The final scene of *L'inganno felice*, its finest sequence, set at night amid the mining galleys, and beautifully performed here, looks forward in some respects to the wonderful Act 2 Nocturne in *Le comte Ory*. They are, indeed, works of similar pedigree, albeit an age apart in the actual mastery of the larger operatic craft. It should be added that neither of the rival CDs is adequately annotated. The Notes CD is noteless, the Claves lacks a translation of the Italian libretto. The Erato set comes with texts in four languages, a synopsis and a scholarly essay by Damien Colas. In sum, a winner.

Rossini L'italiana in Algeri.

Marilyn Horne *mez* Isabella
Ernesto Palacio *ten* Lindoro
Domenico Trimarchi *bar* Taddeo
Samuel Ramey *bass* Mustafà
Kathleen Battle *sop* Elvira
Clara Foti *mez* Zulma
Nicola Zaccaria *bass* Haly
Prague Philharmonic Chorus; I Solisti Veneti / Claudio Scimone.
Erato Libretto Ⓜ Ⓛ 2292-45404-2 (two discs: 140 minutes: ADD). Notes and text included.
Recorded 1980.

BBC RADIO 3
90-93 FM

L'italiana in Algeri is Rossini's first fully-fledged comic masterpiece and a piece of intrinsic vitality and strength. It needs no special pleading. And yet there is little doubt that it has come fully into its own in this century – the Isabellas of Supervia and Dolukhanova notwithstanding – only since the publication in 1981 of Azio Corghi's Critical Edition which cleans up textures in an astonishing way, scouring away all the pseudo-Brahmsian clutter that the late nineteenth century has imposed on Rossini's pre-Naples orchestration.

Of the four currently available recordings of *L'italiana in Algeri* – conducted, in ascending order of seniority, by Giulini (EMI), Varviso (Decca), Scimone (Erato) and Abbado (DG) – this Scimone set is probably the all-round winner, not least for the expert and exuberant realization of the title-role by Marilyn Horne. Erato, very greyhounds in the musicological slips, recorded the Corghi edition the moment it was available, not on period instruments but with a first-rate chamber ensemble and with a cast you might reasonably expect to hear on a festival August evening in Pesaro itself. (Erato even managed to engage the young Kathleen Battle as Elvira, a clear case of apt and enterprising casting.) Unfortunately, the Erato CDs shed the alternative arias Rossini wrote between 1813 and 1815 for Venice, Milan and Naples, a marvellous complement to Corghi's notes and a first-rate chance for collectors to get a feel of how and why Rossini wrote and revised his works at this period. These appeared as fascinating addenda to the original three-LP set in 1981. In 1988 Erato decided against trying to squeeze them on to two CDs; though, tantalizingly, they are still discussed in the excellent booklet note by the editor of the Critical Edition, Azio Corghi.

In the event, this latest CD reissue is a straight re-run of the 1988 one. All that is different is the label logo. The sound is excellent and we get an act per disc, but once again the libretto is in Italian only. Why do Erato spoil so excellent a set with such cheese-paring presentation?

Rossini Maometto Secondo.

June Anderson *sop* Anna
Margarita Zimmerman *mez* Calbo
Ernesto Palacio *ten* Erisso
Samuel Ramey *bass* Maometto
Laurence Dale *ten* Condulmiero, Selimo
Ambrosian Singers; Philharmonia Orchestra / Claudio Scimone.
Philips Ⓟ Ⓓ 412 148-2PH3 (three discs: DDD). Notes, text and translation included. Recorded 1983.

Rossini's art had come a long way from his first Neapolitan opera, *Elisabetta, regina d'Inghilterra* in 1815, to *Maometto II*, his penultimate work for Naples, first seen at the San Carlo theatre on December 3rd, 1820. Beginning with the final act of *Otello* and moving through such strikingly varied experiences as *Armida*, *Mosè in Egitto*, *Ermione* and *La donna del lago*, Rossini's art had matured and deepened, his command of larger forms grown ever more complete. Like *Mosè in Egitto*, *Maometto II* was later revised for the Paris Opéra, turning up there in 1826 as *Le siège de Corinthe* after an intermediate revision prepared for the winter season of La Fenice, Venice in 1822-3. It cannot be said (as it might fairly be said of *Mosè in Egitto*) that the Neapolitan original is the finer, more integrated, more cogent piece. *Mosè in Egitto* with its effective counterpointing of the Exodus narrative with an *Aida*-like love story, is a stronger drama than that provided for Rossini by Cesare della Valle from his own verse drama, *Anna Erizo* (1820).

In *Maometto II*, Venetian forces are at bay on Euboea ("Negroponte"), about to be put to the sword by Mahomet II, the man who reversed the tide of history and terrorized the Graeco-Roman world in the middle years of the fifteenth century. The revelation that Anna, the Venetian commander's daughter, once loved a disguised and peripatetic Maometto is enough to cause well over two hours of mutual consternation. But as in *Ricciardo e Zoraide* (Naples, 1818), one feels that a less than first-rate dramatic ground-plan occasionally diffuses the interest. There is love interest – Maometto's love for Anna and her dutiful acknowledgement of the loyalty to her of the Venetian warrior, Calbo, a travesti role – but it lacks the freshness and the charge of the love of Elcia and Osiride in the original version of the *Mosè in Egitto*.

The subject of della Valle's drama came of age in the 1820s when the Greek War of Independence became for its time what Czechoslovakian and Vietnam have been for ours. With pro-Greek and anti-Turkish sentiments strongly reinforced by the romantic preoccupation with classical antiquity and by Byron's death in Greece in 1824, the 1826 revision and revival of *Maometto II* were timely. Nor did the revision bloat and diffuse the drama as was to be the case with *Moïse et Pharaon*. *Le siège de Corinthe* not only makes the drama into a tragedy which is unequivocally Greek (one of the opera's few wholly new numbers is Hiéros's blessing of the Greek banners before the final holocaust), it also tautens the musical structure in a way which gives the drama a pace and a ferocity which the much more spacious *Maometto II* rarely achieves. And yet the great majority of the music is there in *Maometto II*, and in its command of the big forms *Maometto II* makes claims on our attention which the more urgent, politically preoccupied Paris revision cannot do.

Such is Rossini's command of longer forms in *Maometto II*, the entire First Act is built out of five broad movements dominated by a *Terzettone*, a larger-than-life Trio so massive in scale that it can withstand intrusive cannon fire, popular dismay, and a melting prayer before resuming its majestic course. Indeed, it never properly ends, since by the simplest of harmonic devices Rossini builds it over into the chorus which ushers in the Islamic horde, a chorus which looks back to the utterances of the forces of darkness in Act 2 of *Armida* and forward, in its rhythms, fierce unisons, and exotic tintinnabulations to Verdi's gipsy band in *Il trovatore*. The chorus are sparingly but powerfully and evocatively used throughout *Maometto II*. The launching of Act 2, with a substantial A major chorus for Muslim women disingenuously touting the 'Gather ye rosebuds' line, is particularly remarkable for a fine-grained use of woodwind and percussion colours such as you might expect to encounter in the ballet music of Tchaikovsky or the mature Verdi. Conversely, there is a brooding quality about the score, equally typical of Rossini's later Neapolitan manner. It is not only in the opera's nocturnal opening that the brass – four horns, three trombones, two trumpets and serpentone – are atmospherically used; they feature prominently in the accompanied recitatives which Rossini scores with as much care as the ensembles themselves.

This is, of course, the first recording of *Maometto II*. In an ideal world we would have a good recording of *Le siège de Corinthe* in the catalogue, too, but Schippers on EMI and Olmi on Nuovo Era are both unsatisfactory. The former was sung in Italian and was subject to a bewildering array of cuts, and additions which ranged from Sills's own ornamentation to the otiose importation of the whole of the Act 2 Trio written for the Venetian revision of *Maometto II* in Venice in 1823. Needless to say, the Philips edition, produced by Erik Smith and conducted by Scimone, indulges no such freakish whims. Apart from what appears to be a cut in the cabaletta of the Anna/Maometto duet in Act 2, the performance is exemplary in its fidelity to the letter of the score and the style of the composer. The title-role – unusually, though *Mosè* is another exception which proves the rule – is sung by a bass. At the Naples *prima* it was Filippo Galli, the greatest Italian bass of his day; here it is Samuel Ramey. Ramey's is a magnificent performance, worthy of a role written for Galli. His tone is full and noble and he copes expertly with the complex *fioritura*. A bass like Raimondi might have made a more dangerous-sounding Maometto, but Ramey has the better technique and the sense he communicates of a love for Anna, which in the last analysis is almost paternal, is very affecting.

Equally fine is Margarita Zimmerman's Calbo. The extreme range of the part causes her few problems and she sings her big Act 2 aria less stodgily than Marilyn Horne on an important Sony Classical recital recording. Above all, Zimmerman makes us aware of Calbo's presence and personality, something not easily done when contraltos pose as warlike young men. Rossini's Erisso, Anna's father, was Nozzari, a singer of massive theatrical authority with a voice said to have been somewhat baritonal in quality. Judged by these standards, Ernesto Palacio might be thought a rather lightweight choice (initially, Laurence Dale's admirable Condulmiero makes the stronger impression) but Palacio's expertise in florid writing is needed; later on the voice is fuller and warmer than it has sometimes been on record. As Anna, June Anderson reveals a good sense of style. She was, and no doubt still is, a first-rate Elcia in *Mosè in Egitto* and is best in *Maometto II* where the writing is rapt and prayerful. In Anna's more ferocious outbursts she is, perhaps, too demure. The huge half-hour finale, designed as a series of contrasting numbers for the queenly Colbran, is only intermittently powerful in Anderson's performance. The finale exchanges with Maometto are rather palely declaimed, though Anna's dying apostrophization of her mother's ashes is touchingly done.

Scimone directs with an acute ear for Rossini's imaginative use of orchestral sonority, a fine sense of the pacing of the choruses, and a proper feel for the scale and steady reach of the drama. The recording is excellent though the battery of Muslim drums and the rent-a-crowd uproar (did Erik Smith travel to Chelsea to record this, or was it Millwall?) might have been more smoothly edited into the sound mix. But these are negligible quibbles.

Rossini L'occasione fa il ladro.

Maria Bayo *sop* Berenice
Natale De Carolis *bass-bar* Don Parmenione
Iorio Zennaro *ten* Count Alberto
Francesca Provvisionato *mez* Ernestina
Fabio Previati *bar* Martino
Fulvio Massa *ten* Don Eusebio.
English Chamber Orchestra; Turin Philharmonic Orchestra / Marcello Viotti.
Claves Ⓜ ① CD50-9208 (two discs: 85 minutes: DDD). Recorded 1992.

This performance under Marcello Viotti is spirited enough; in *L'occasione fa il ladro* (which the Buxton Festival revived, not unsuccessfully, several years ago) it is possible to think, not for the first time, that Viotti's conducting isn't sufficiently up-tempo and forward-moving. But with a charming Berenice, Maria Bayo, and Natale De Carolis successfully taking on the role of insolvent, egocentric, two-faced, wine-bibbing, womanizer, Don Parmenione, the opera comes up pretty well. What's more, this is currently the only available CD recording of the opera in the UK. (Ponnelle's uproarious Pesaro production did make its way on CD but what imported sets there were seemed to vanish as mysteriously as they appeared.) The booklet has an Italian libretto, and a plot summary in English. Unfortunately it strays over the 80-minute mark, necessitating a second CD. There is a price concession (a pair of CDs at upper mid price) but it ends up as very poor value. Had Claves provided English translations and better focused recorded sound, it would have been a winner. In the end, though, it is currently self-recommending.

Rossini La pietra del paragone.

José Carreras *ten* Giocondo
Beverly Wolff *mez* Clarice
Elaine Bonazzi *mez* Aspasia
Anne Elgar *sop* Fulvia
John Reardon *bar* Asdrubale
Andrew Foldi *bass-bar* Macrobio
Justino Diaz *bass* Pacuvio
Raymond Murcell *bar* Fabrizio
New York Clarion Concerts Chorus and Orchestra / Newell Jenkins.
Vanguard Classics Ⓜ ① 08.9031.73 (three discs: 166 minutes: ADD). Notes, text and translation included. Recorded 1971.

Here is a CD reissue of a little known LP recording (never generally obtainable in the UK) that should gladden the hearts of all Rossinians. Though it has been generally neglected by the gramophone, *La pietra del paragone* was one of Rossini's first smash-hits. It was written for La Scala, Milan in the autumn of 1812 and received 53 performances: an extraordinary run which brought Rossini instant fame and exemption from military service (a useful concession in 1812). From now on he could count himself a *maestro di cartello*, a composer whose name alone guarantees a public.

The libretto, concocted by one of La Scala's resident writers, Luigi Romanelli, is cornucopian, filling out a substantial romantic comedy with sharply etched portraits of a diverting array of social and literary gadflys. Dramatically, it suffers from some otiose manoeuvreings of plot; and Rossini added to the problems by complying with his prima donna's desire to show off her voice, and her legs, by bringing her into the denouement dressed as a Captain of the Hussars. Interestingly, the romantic lead is a bass, Count Asdrubale, a role originally written for the great Filippo Galli. It is a serious role with comic overtones; all Milan was mimicking the word "Sigillara" – the order "let the seals be affixed!" that Asdrubale repeats over and over again in the scene in which he appears in Turkish garb and affects to take over his own possessions.

The name Newell Jenkins may not be all that familiar to British audiences. His Clarion Music Society is an American initiative that was founded in the mid-1950s with the intention of reviving and promoting forgotten music from the seventeenth and eighteenth centuries. *La pietra del paragone*, recorded in New York in 1971, takes them a little way across a later frontier but the performance reflects many of those things that are commendable in the Clarion tradition – responsible scholarship, spruce and musicianly playing and conducting, and singing that is at worst adequate, at best memorable. Vanguard's Asdrubale, the distinguished baritone John Reardon, isn't a born Rossinian, but he gets by, supplementing a limited coloratura technique with a strong feel for the drama of the moment. Beverly Wolff's Clarice, sweet-toned and assured, comes into the latter category. Nor will it have escaped the notice of his many admirers that José Carreras is here, at the very start of his career, making his mark in the exquisite forest scene that begins Act 2. A strong cast of *comprimarios* includes Justino Diaz who as the poet Pacuvio has the popular nonsense aria, "Ombretta sdegnosa". Diaz is an old *Pietra* hand. He was later to sing the role of Asdrubale in the production Milan's La Piccola Scala brought to the Edinburgh Festival in 1982.

In sum, an important set that comes up especially well in the immaculately packaged and presented CD transfers. The 1992 bicentenary brought few more agreeable additions to the list of Rossini operas currently available on record.

A rival set, conducted by Claudio Desderi and taken from a live performance in 1992, is available on Nuova Era. It is a performance of great cogency, as well as fluency and flair, and is as vital and stylish as Jenkins's account. However, it is probably true to say that the Vanguard set has the stronger all-round cast. Nuova Era squeeze the opera on to two full-price CDs; Vanguard spread it over three mid-price discs. In the end, it is a close-run affair, with the beautifully produced studio set on Vanguard ahead on points if you are thinking in terms of a library acquisition and repeated hearings over the years.

Rossini Ricciardo e Zoraide.

William Matteuzzi *ten* Ricciardo
Nelly Miricioiu *sop* Zoraide
Bruce Ford *ten* Agorante
Alastair Miles *bass* Ircano
Della Jones *mez* Zomira
Paul Nilon *ten* Ernesto
Carol Smith *sop* Fatima
Alice Coote *mez* Elmira
Toby Spence *ten* Zamorre
Geoffrey Mitchell Choir; Academy of St Martin in the Fields / David Parry.
Opera Rara Ⓟ Ⓘ ORC14 (three discs: 183 minutes: DDD). Notes, text and translation included. Recorded 1995.

It was inevitable that when interest finally focused on the superb array of heavyweight operas Rossini created for Naples between 1815 and 1822, *Ricciardo e Zoraide* would be somewhat to the rear of the queue. Not because it is bereft of fine music – it has some good moments and some memorable quarters of an hour – but because the story, the essential stuff of the drama, is intrinsically less interesting than that of *Elisabetta, regina d'Inghilterra, Otello, Armida, Mosè in Egitto, Ermione* or *La donna del lago* all of which, in one way or another, draw on powerful literary sources. Nor, in what proved to be a difficult year (1818) did Rossini quite have the musical muscle to create the kind of structural epic he was later to fashion in *Maometto II*.

The tendency has been to blame the librettist for all this: Francesco Berio di Salsa, gentleman of leisure and one of Naples's leading men of letters. Having, in Lord Byron's phrase, "crucified *Otello* into an opera", he now turned his attention to two cantos from a mock-heroic epic poem by the early eighteenth-century poet and priest, Niccolò Forteguerri. The Arisoto-like ironies, such as they are, of Forteguerri's poem, *Il Ricciardetto*, appear to have passed Berio by or evaded his powers of appropriation and redeployment. Yet the libretto as such is clear enough, a workmanlike job with well-drawn dramatic sight-lines and cues aplenty for heart-stopping moments, some of which Rossini chooses to set in what was for him a new and expressively daring kind of accompanied recitative.

The drama is dominated not by Ricciardo (Giovanni David's role) or Zoraide (written for Colbran) but by Agorante, King of Nubia, Nozzarri's role. Though married to the formidable Zomira, an invention of Berio's to accommodate Rosmunda Pisaroni, a rising star in the Naples company, the king is in love with Zoraide, daughter of a stern tribal headman, and *inamorata* of the guileful paladin

Ricciardo. Agorante's character, as it is purveyed to us by the libretto and through Rossini's music, is that of a reluctant tyrant. This is immediately established in Agorante's remarkable cavatina, "Minacci pur", and proceeds to colour not only the role itself but the mood of the entire opera.

Bruce Ford, it should be said at once, sings the part magnificently. It was he who re-created it on stage in Pesaro in 1990, alongside the present Ricciardo, William Matteuzzi. Not only is Ford's singing exemplary, his pacing of the role is masterly, allowing him to dig beneath the surface of the character and reveal the 'more in sorrow than in anger' aspect of Agorante's temper. Matteuzzi is also perfectly cast in the florid, bright-toned role of Ricciardo. Matteuzzi's work on record has not always been enjoyable and there have been some stinging criticisms of his performances in the theatre, but here there is real empathy with the role, realized in page upon page of exemplary singing. He also works well with Ford. The Act 2 duet between the two men – improbably, as sexy a piece of male canoodling as you will hear in all opera – is a particular case in point.

David Parry's tempos help. Again, his work has been excoriated in print. "Overloud dynamics and unvarying timbres" was *Opera* magazine's judgement of the *Ricciardo e Zoraide* he conducted in Pesaro in 1996. There is nothing of that here. The ASMF (old Rossini hands) are exemplary and Parry's shaping of the work is both kind to the opera's prevailing *tinta* and mood and extremely solicitous of the singers' needs. Some of the tempos are daringly slow: the start of the great Act 1 Trio "Cruda sorte!", for instance. But with so much going on – powerfully fractured exclamations and a haunting off-stage chorus – the slowness seems justified.

The rest of the casting is meticulous. Nelly Miricioiu, who has a hint of Callas in her tones, makes a plausible and affecting Zoraide, Alastair Miles is superb in the Commendatore-like role of her father, Ircano, and Paul Nilon makes a strong impression in the role of Ricciardo's lieutenant, Ernesto. It was also a stroke of genius to cast Della Jones as the defiant wife, Zomira. This is a role that needs working at. The power of the character is in the ensembles and the accompanied recitatives. (A set-piece solo is late arriving, and strangely muted when it does come.) The almost exaggerated clarity of her diction ensures that everything this mistreated wife utters is etched into the listener's imagination.

And it is this sense of living engagement with the score – born of a strong belief in the virtues of the music, meticulous preparation, direct theatrical experience and solid professionalism – that makes the set the success it is. Like the various Philips productions of some of the better-known Neapolitan operas by Rossini, this is a recording that will not readily brook challenge.

The recording itself is excellent. Expertly engineered by Robert Auger, it maps Rossini's richly perspective score – the first in which he uses a complex array of separate on- and off-stage bands – with clarity and unaffected good sense. As realized here *Ricciardo e Zoraide* is a piece of which the sympathetic listener could grow very fond. Frustratingly fond. One loses count of the times when one thinks: "Now, if only that was in one of the better known operas, it would be ranked among Rossini's most memorable ideas!". Flowers, as the poet has it, born (more or less) to blush unseen and waste their sweetness on the desert air.

Rossini Semiramide.

Cheryl Studer *sop* Semiramide
Jennifer Larmore *mez* Arsace
Samuel Ramey *bass* Assur
Frank Lopardo *ten* Idreno
Julia Faulkner *sop* Azema
Jan-Hendrik Rootering *bass* Oroe
Romuald Tesarowicz *bass* Ghost of Nino
Octavio Arévalo *ten* Mitrane
Ambrosian Opera Chorus; London Symphony Orchestra / Ion Marin.
DG Ⓟ Ⓒ 437 797-2GH3 (three discs: 207 minutes: DDD). Notes, text and translation included. Recorded 1992.

Semiramide is the last opera Rossini wrote for the Italian theatre. First heard at the Teatro La Fenice, Venice in February 1823 after an unusually long period of preparation by Rossini and his librettist, Gaetano Rossi (the librettist of *Tancredi*), it is a Rolls Royce of a piece: classically proportioned, superbly engineered, unashamedly grand. What is more, there are dangerous reserves of power concealed behind the opera's outwardly sedate exterior. The exterior is the old *opera seria* style writ large; but Voltaire's plot draws on powerful dramatic archetypes. (Semiramide, Assur, and Arsace are not far removed from the likes of Gertrude, Claudius, and Hamlet.) To an extent, Rossini's music powerfully reflects this.

There has only ever been one complete (or more or less complete) recording of *Semiramide*, the one made by Decca in the winter of 1965-6 with Joan Sutherland, Marilyn Horne, Joseph Rouleau and the LSO conducted by Richard Bonynge. That set, reviewed below, remains one of Sutherland's – and Bonynge's – finest achievements on record. It has other strengths, too: a strongly characterized Assur from Rouleau and Horne's Arsace – though, as Jennifer Larmore brilliantly demonstrates on the DG set, a case was waiting to be made for an even more sharply-drawn portrait of this mettlesome royal warrior.

Texturally, *Semiramide* has never been problematic. Rossini's autograph manuscript is for the most part splendidly clear. What problems exist over individual words or notes are mainly nugatory, though it is nice to have them cleared up in the DG recording which is based on the Fondazione Rossini's 1990 Critical Edition, edited by Philip Gossett and Alberto Zedda.

If there has been a problem with *Semiramide* it is the cuts that have appeared in printed editions and found their way into accepted theatrical practice. The Decca recording is not blameless in this respect, though its only substantial omission is the first of the two (dramatically dispensable) arias for the Indian King, Idreno. Decca cast the tenor John Serge as Idreno, and though he makes a decent enough stab at Idreno's later aria, "La speranza più soave", he is completely outclassed by DG's Frank Lopardo. Sung with such elegance and searing brilliance, Idreno ceases to be a peripheral figure.

Texturally, then, the DG set is spick and span. That is not to say that it is at all points better recorded (there are times when Samuel Ramey is too far from the microphone) but the special effects – the Commendatore-like appearance of the ghost of murdered King Ninus, or the off-stage band (here authentically scored) – work much better on DG than they do on Decca where both Ninus and the band are remote to the point of being indistinct.

So how good is the DG performance? Well, it is not as well conducted as the Decca set. Bonynge on Decca not only understands the singers' every need, he also has an unerring feel for the neo-classical structuring of the piece. DG's Ion Marin is neither as ruthless nor as reckless as his astonishingly crude account of the Overture might suggest. He has fire in his belly (which seems to suit Jennifer Larmore who rides the Marin orchestra better than anyone) and he is single-minded enough to hold the big ensembles on course. But too often there is a conscripted feeling about the LSO's playing (compare this with the buoyancy and zest of their response to Bonynge) and there is no doubt that the singers are often disadvantaged by him.

The Semiramide is Cheryl Studer. By now, her versatility should come as no surprise to us. Here is a wonderful interpreter of Salome who has also proved herself to be a vocally credible Lucia di Lammermoor. Certainly, in the opening pages of Semiramide's cavatina, "Bel raggio lusinghier", one marvels at the clarity and grace of the singing as well as at the fineness of the characterization: love, terror, and bemusement all finely touched in. Only later in the cavatina, as the pace quickens at "Dolce pensiero", do doubts begin to arise. Here Marin presses on, crudely, guilelessly. There are here none of those fine elisions of tempo and tone that Bonynge achieves as part of that famously symbiotic collaboration with his wife. In the end, Studer's account of the cavatina is less radiant than Sutherland's, more mechanically driven, the ornamentation not always as unerringly right as Sutherland's seems to be.

Studer and Larmore are well contrasted vocally as queen and young soldier. They are also less inclined to dream their way through the duets. Sutherland and Horne are more sensuous; Studer and Larmore more openly intense. Studer is especially fine in the prayer at the tomb in the final scene; but then so is Sutherland. Samuel Ramey has sung the role of the murderous usurper Assur on many occasions. In the earlier part of the opera, where Rossini characterizes Assur largely through some often very florid writing in ensembles Ramey is superb. Decca's Joseph Rouleau is relatively arthritic by comparison. But things change in Act 2, first in the duet with Semiramide (shades of the Macbeths) and later in Assur's mad scene, written by Rossini for the great Fillipo Galli. Here, where the writing is less florid, the characterization more direct, Rouleau comes into his own: a wonderfully theatrical performance, coloured and declaimed in a way that Ramey's is not. At least, not here.

In fact, Ramey has already recorded Assur's Act 2 Mad Scene as part of a disc of Rossini scenes and arias he made for Teldec in 1991 with the WNO Orchestra and Chorus under Gabriele Ferro. Better conducted, with a more focused recording, it seems the more representative performance. In the central delirium, where Rossini gives Assur a series of unaccompanied outbursts – the music anticipating the king's delirium in the Banquet Scene in Verdi's *Macbeth* – Ramey is needlessly hustled by Marin. Indeed, Marin seems more interested in the prompt arrival of the next orchestral salvo than in the expressive potential of the declamation itself. As a result, half a dozen crucial shadings go by the board. Things settle down in the lyric F minor *agitato*, though you have to go to Bonynge or, best of all, to Ferro on the Teldec recital disc, to hear the sense of mental travail that is there in the syncopated accompaniment.

Rossini Semiramide.

Dame Joan Sutherland *sop* Semiramide
Marilyn Horne *mez* Arsace
Joseph Rouleau *bass* Assur
John Serge *ten* Idreno
Patricia Clark *sop* Azema
Spiro Malas *bass* Oroe
Michael Langdon *bass* Ghost of Nino
Leslie Fyson *ten* Mitrane
Ambrosian Opera Chorus; London Symphony Orchestra / Richard Bonynge.
Decca Ⓜ Ⓞ 425 481-2DM3 (three discs: 168 minutes: ADD). Notes, text and translation included. Recorded 1965-6.

It was a great joy to have this historically important, vocally superb and dramatically keen-edged recording back in the catalogues in a CD transfer that not only beautifully and vividly reproduces the clarity and sophistication of the original recording but also, if anything, adds clarity and lustre to the sound of Sutherland and Horne, very much in their Rossinian prime. Since the set first appeared in 1966, it went unchallenged for very many years, partly no doubt because of its well-nigh unassailable merit, partly because of a continuing degree of condescension to Rossini as composer of *opera seria*. Kobbe's *Complete Opera Book* still carries the dismissive opening sentence, "*Semiramide* seems to have had its day"; yet this epic reworking of the *Tancredi* model is not only one of Rossini's most carefully worked music-dramas, it is also, as his final opera in Italy (Venice, 1823), one of his richest in general scope, invention and orchestration. *Guillaume Tell* is not all that far off.

Richard Bonynge's conducting, a slightly variable phenomenon in the 1960s, is here very fine. The LSO, at the peak of their stylish 1960s form, are first-rate and Bonynge matches a fine blend of lyricism and drive with an unerring grasp of Rossini's huge music-dramatic structured designs.

Rossini Il Signor Bruschino.

Natale de Carolis *bass-bar* Bruschino padre
Fulvio Massa *ten* Bruschino figlio, Commissario
Bruno Praticò *bar* Gaudenzio
Patrizia Orciani *sop* Sofia
Lucia Canonici *ten* Florville
Pietro Spangnoli *bar* Filiberto
Katia Lytting *mez* Marianna
Turin Philharmonic Orchestra / Marcello Viotti.
Claves Ⓟ Ⓒ CD508904/5 (two discs: 84 minutes: DDD). Text included. Recorded 1988.

Rossini's vibrant one-acter, with its cruel baiting of Signor Bruschino, looks forward to aspects of Verdi's *Falstaff* even more surely than those parts of *Il barbiere* that Verdi so admired. But it is another of those operas that record companies have generally passed by. This recording is thus very welcome. It was made in Turin with a cast of mainly young Italian singers and a well-drilled chamber orchestra, all heard in a suitably intimate and keenly focused acoustic setting. The performance seemed to take a little time to settle, not to the music's general pace and zest, but to the pointing up of Rossini's sharp-eared delineation of character. Patrizia Orciani's tone sometimes hardens under pressure and Bruno Praticò occasionally coarsens Gaudenzio's outbursts in a way that an old hand like Sesto Bruscantini wouldn't quite have countenanced but, in general, it is a lively and likeable performance. Alas, the booklet contains only the Italian text. There's a plot summary in English, but that's not quite the same thing for English Rossinians who may want to follow every twist and turn of this tense little music-drama.

Rossini Il Signor Bruschino.

Alberto Rinaldi *bar* Bruschino padre
Vitto Gobbi *ten* Bruschino figlio
Alessandro Corbelli *bar* Gaudenzio
Amelia Felle *sop* Sofia
David Kuebler *ten* Florville
Carlos Feller *bass* Filiberto
Janice Hall *sop* Marianna
Stuttgart Radio Symphony Orchestra / Gianluigi Gelmetti.
Stage Director: **Michael Hampe.** *Film Director*: **Claus Villier.**
Teldec Video Ⓟ VHS ▭▭ 9031-71482-3; ◖ 9031-71482-6 (two sides: 97 minutes). Filmed at performances in the Schwetzingen Festival in May 1989.

Since its foundation in 1952, the Schwetzingen Festival has concentrated on reviving mainly eighteenth-century theatre pieces and it was not straying too far from that brief when it launched a stylishly produced cycle of the diverting one-acters Rossini wrote for Venice's Teatro San Moise between 1810 and 1813. Hampe is not as inventive a Rossini producer as the late Jean-Pierre Ponnelle who could be guaranteed to turn this Rossini piece into a riot of comic invention; but like Puccini's *Gianni Schicchi*, *Il Signor Bruschino* has sufficient comic energies of its own and Hampe's fluent, brightly-lit production serves it well. There is a handsome pair of lovers (Amelia Felle very striking in her big aria), and accomplished stage performances by Alessandro Corbelli as the prosperous Gaudenzio and Carlos Feller as Filiberto, the peasant inn-keeper who ends up turning a few dishonest lire after Bruschino's drunken son fetches up in his hostelry. Alberto Rinaldi's gout-ridden Bruschino is a bit of a dry old stick, but he is an expert in Rossinian patter and Janice Hall is a sparky Marianna. Gelmetti is a character in his own right and presides over his orchestral forces with admirable results.

There is, unfortunately, only occasional multilingual subtitles programmed into LaserDisc's peripheral information; but the booklet annotations are excellent, with the plot outlined track by track in good, clear, precise form.

Rossini Tancredi.

Ewa Podles *contr* Tancredi
Sumi Jo *sop* Amenaide
Stanford Olsen *ten* Argirio
Pietro Spagnoli *bar* Orbazzano
Anna Maria di Micco *sop* Isaura
Lucretia Lendi *mez* Roggiero
Capella Brugensis; Collegium Instrumentale Brugense / Alberto Zedda.
Naxos Ⓢ ① 8 660037/8 (two discs: 147 minutes: DDD). Notes and Italian text included.
Recorded 1994.

Tancredi is a seminal work in the Rossini canon, a work which mingles a new-found reach in the musical architecture with vocal and instrumental writing of rare wonderment and beauty. It is a difficult opera to stage (dramatically it is flawed, and its colours are as delicate at times as a butterfly's wings) yet until the appearance of this exceptionally fine recording, it has never been available on record in anything other than live theatre or concert performances. The best of them – never 'officially' available – was the one starring Marilyn Horne and the young Katia Ricciarelli, with Eve Queler conducting Philip Gossett's new Critical Edition of the score.

That is the edition which is used on this Naxos recording, albeit somewhat pragmatically, by Alberto Zedda. Zedda is an old Rossini hand and one of Gossett's fellow editors, though it is interesting to speculate how his pick-and-choose way with the *Tancredi* text is regarded in scholarly circles. Zedda encourages, most effectively, the use of a cello and double-bass as dramatic underpinning in the *secco* recitatives but the recitatives themselves are quite severely pruned. This may or may not be a concession to popular taste. What undoubtedly is a concession to popular taste is the decision in Act 2 to mix up the original Venice and Ferrara versions of 1813. What Zedda gives us is the opera's original ending, the happy ending written for Venice, as opposed to the revised 'tragic' ending written for Ferrara ("*the* fashionable ending", as Lady Bracknell might have said). However, he prefaces the original ending not with the original *Gran Scena di Tancredi* written for Venice but with the immensely popular *Rondò*, "Perché turbar la calma", which Rossini provided as part of the wholesale revision of the Act 2 finale for the Ferrara version.

Still, the proof of the pudding and all that; there is no denying that the *Rondò* is memorably sung by Ewa Podles. But, then, the singing is splendid throughout, with a cast that is unusually starry. Podles herself has sung the role of Tancredi (to acclaim) at La Scala, Milan; and the Amenaide, Sumi Jo, is too well known to need further introduction here. Jo seemed a touch cool at first, too much the pert coloratura but this is not an impression that persists. This is a performance of wonderful vocal control and flowering sensibility.

If you have heard Podles, you may be wondering how well matched she and Jo are in the opera's great nodal duets. Podles, a smoky-voiced Pole with something of Marilyn Horne's ability to turn herself into one helluva guy, likes to go her own way at times. In recitatives, rests are ignored and emphases freely redistributed. In arias, it is not unusual to find the pulse beating faster or slower as the musical temperature rises or falls. In the event, though, she and Sumi Jo work well together, and they sound marvellous. Podles also manages, chameleon-like, to adjust to the purer, more obviously stylish Rossini manner of a singer who is very unlike herself, the young American tenor, Stanford Olsen. His portrait of the conscience-stricken father, Argirio, matches singing of grace and impetus with great fineness of dramatic sensibility. As a result, something like the scene of the signing of his daughter's death-warrant emerges here as the remarkable thing it is. There could have been trouble in the duet in Act 2 between Argirio and Tancredi, where Zedda allows Podles to sing her solo lines at a slower tempo than Olsen. Ultimately, though, it all seems to work perfectly well.

Zedda is lucky to have at his disposal another of those wonderfully stylish chamber orchestras and chamber choirs that Naxos seem able to conjure at will. The aqueously lovely preface to Tancredi's first entrance is a fairly representative example of the players' ear for Rossini's delicately-limned tone-painting. And the recording itself is beautifully scaled. It is a recording, it should be added, innocent of production 'effects'; the very reverse of Naxos's radiophonically electrifying *Il barbiere di Siviglia*, which was packed to the gunnels with them. As usual with Naxos, you get a multilingual synopsis plus an original-language libretto without translation; but in the case of an opera like *Tancredi*, where it is very much a case of 'Prima la musica', this is not a great disincentive to buy. All in all, then, this is a fine set; the first-ever studio recording of *Tancredi*, and a palpable hit. It is a set that is aimed at a wide constituency of music lovers, yet it makes no compromises with the quality of the music-making.

Rossini Tancredi.

Vesselina Kasarova *mez* Tancredi
Eva Mei *sop* Amenaide
Ramón Vargas *ten* Argirio
Harry Peeters *bass* Orbazzano
Melinda Paulsen *mez* Isaura
Veronica Cangemi *sop* Roggiero

Bavarian Radio Chorus; Munich Radio Orchestra / Roberto Abbado.
RCA Victor Red Seal Ⓔ Ⓓ 09026 68349-2 (three discs: 208 minutes: DDD). Notes, text and translation included. Recorded 1995.

Naxos broke the lance with tardier rivals by releasing their super-budget-price recording of *Tancredi* that is in almost every respect superb: vividly and beautifully sung, stylishly conducted, shrewdly recorded. And then, within the year, a rival of comparable character and quality appeared. It was ever thus!

The RCA set cannot match the Naxos on price, and as a performance it equals its rival rather than surpasses it. On textural matters, though, the two sets are complementary. Only weeks after the Venetian *prima* in February 1813, Rossini reworked the end of the opera for performances in Ferrara, reproducing the so-called tragic ending of Voltaire's original drama in which Tancredi is mortally wounded in his victory over the Saracens. The fact that Tancredi dies in the Ferrara version does not render the revised opera 'tragic' in any classical sense of that term; but what it does do is provide one of the most surprising of all Rossinian closes, an end – a sad, touching, little dying fall of a *cavatina* – that must have bewildered Rossini's contemporaries.

It is an end that barely works in practice. Somehow, it is just *too* modest an end to so spacious and eloquent an opera. For the Naxos recording, which Zedda both conducts and oversees editorially, an ingenious compromise is arrived at. Zedda retains the original happy ending, but pilfers the magnificent *Rondò*, Perché turbar la calma", with which Rossini bolstered the Act 2 denouement in the Ferrara revision.

The more you hear it, the more you will think it as good a solution as any (Ewa Podles, Tancredi on the Naxos set, sings the Ferrara *Rondò* superbly). On record, though, why not offer both endings? Space is the problem. *Tancredi* sits neatly on two well-filled CDs. The only answer, if both endings are to be offered, is to go the whole hog and offer both finales and other important alternative arias which Rossini himself wrote for the piece. This is what RCA have done. The result makes the set an expensive one, three full-price CDs, but one which dedicated Rossinians will certainly want to have. In particular, it is wonderful to have Tancredi's 'other' entrance aria, the one Rossini wrote at the request of the creator of the role, Adelaide Malanotte. It is a marvellous ten-minute *Recitativo e Cavatina*, complete with a richly elaborated *concertante* violin part. Had "Di tanti palpiti" not been such a smash-hit, who knows: the alternative might have taken root of its own accord. Vesselina Kasarova sings it superbly.

Kasarova is the star of the set in other respects, too. Podles, on Naxos, is so good, it would be idle to suggest that Kasarova has it all her own way; but the Podles sound is more heavily curtained, less obviously alluring and spellbinding than Kasarova's. Since Podles does not sing the 'tragic' finale, there are no comparisons to be made there. Kasarova is very affecting, acting the thing out in a way that suggests that she is not simply the possessor of a very remarkable voice. (Not that by this juncture anyone is likely to have decided that.) And yet it does not quite come off. The conducting of Roberto Abbado may be a problem here. Much that he does is excellent, but if he has a weakness it concerns his ability to organize and sustain slow tempos. Some of Amenaide's music rather hangs fire, soloist and conductor dancing attendance a touch uncertainly on one another. Abbado's Munich players are good, but Zedda and the Collegium Instrumentale Brugense (modern instruments, old playing styles) have an added keenness of address which the more intimate, slightly more tightly focused Naxos recording nicely complements.

RCA's Amenaide, Eva Mei, is almost as persuasive as Sumi Jo on Naxos, but not quite. (It is the Podles-Kasarova situation in reverse.) Between the two tenors, Ramón Vargas (RCA) and the exciting young American Stanford Olsen (Naxos), there is little to choose. Both are first-class. RCA have the better Isaura.

Perhaps the current situation can best be summed up by saying that whenever you want to hear the opera *through* (as Dr Johnson would have put it), you should probably take the Naxos set from the shelves. You should value the RCA set too, however: for reference, for delighted dipping hither and thither, not least in the appendices, and for the remarkable Kasarova.

Rossini Il turco in Italia.
Michele Pertusi *bass* Selim
Cecilia Bartoli *mez* Fiorilla
Alessandro Corbelli *bar* Don Geronio
Ramón Vargas *ten* Don Narciso
Laura Polverelli *mez* Zaida
Francesco Piccoli *ten* Albazar
Roberto de Candia *bar* Poet
Chorus and Orchestra of La Scala, Milan / Riccardo Chailly.
Decca Ⓔ Ⓓ 458 924-2DHO2 (two discs: 142 minutes: DDD). Notes, text and translation included. Recorded 1997.

It was only natural that, with a star mezzo of Cecilia Bartoli's stature on their books, Decca should have turned to Rossini's *Il turco in Italia*, an obvious role for a singer of her temperament. Add to that a conductor of Riccardo Chailly's sympathies and the opera was asking to be recorded. Chailly, of course, has recorded the work before – for CBS back in 1981 – but in the years since, he has matured as a Rossini conductor and the Scala orchestra have this music under their collective fingers; indeed there is an energy and vitality to this playing that is wholly infectious. For Chailly's earlier recording, Montserrat Caballé was a very underpowered Fiorilla; Bartoli is full of fire and mettle (her "Sqallido veste bruna" is sensational). Michele Pertusi is a fine Selim and his performance seems to breathe stage experience – it is a characterization that is as vocally fine as it is theatrically adept. Alessandro Corbelli, reinforcing his credentials as a Rossini singer of flair and panache, is a strongly characterized Geronio.

This is a recording that smacks of the theatre, and unlike so many so-called comic operas, has lost nothing in its transfer to disc. Under Chailly's baton it fizzes and crackles like few other sets – recitatives are dispatched with the assurance of native Italian speakers and with a genuine feeling for the meaning of the text. Decca's recording is beautifully judged and the set makes a fine modern alternative to the now classic (but cut) 1954 recording under Gavazzeni with Maria Callas incomparable as Fiorilla.

Rossini Il turco in Italia.

Nicola Rossi-Lemeni *bass* Selim
Maria Callas *sop* Fiorilla
Franco Calabrese *bass* Don Geronio
Nicolai Gedda *ten* Don Narcisco
Jolanda Gardino *mez* Zaida
Piero De Palma *ten* Albazar
Mariano Stabile *bar* Poet
Chorus and Orchestra of La Scala, Milan / Gianandrea Gavazzeni.
EMI mono Ⓟ ① CDS5 56313-2 (two discs: 113 minutes: ADD). Notes, text and translation included. Recorded 1954.

It was Maria Callas who, with Franco Zeffirelli, helped restore this delectable but faintly disturbing *dramma buffo* to the stage of La Scala, Milan in the mid-1950s after an earlier run with Callas as Fiorilla in a production, partly sponsored by Luchino Visconti, at Rome's tiny Eliseo Theatre. "Our *Turco* was so refreshing, so lovely", claimed Zeffirelli. "From the beginning Maria knew it was going to be a hit." And yet he had to work hard to bring out on the stage the comédienne in Callas, that quality which was later to irradiate, on record, her Rosina and, in a more savage dimension, her Carmen.

The set contains some classic things, above all in Callas's several confrontations with her Selim, the wonderfully grave Nicola Rossi-Lemeni, and her ageing husband, Geronio, sung here with all the right hang-dog inflexions by Franco Calabrese. The hilarious duet with Geronio in Act 1 is a *locus classicus* of Callas's art, an extensive array of *bel canto* rhetoric lined up ready to be deployed with surgical precision. These fleeting appropriations of the classical tragic style are used by Rossini with an understated comic relish that Callas perfectly comprehends.

The cast Walter Legge assembled in August 1954 for the recording was more or less the cast that went into La Scala the following April. Casting the veteran Mariano Stabile as the Poet was a stroke of genius; and Legge had the additional advantage of being able to use the young Nicolai Gedda as Narciso. (Valletti sang the role in Milan.) He also, with his customary genius, managed to create a sense of genuine ensemble. Indeed, it is the special glory of this recording of *Il turco in Italia* that it allows us to hear Callas at her idiosyncratic best, not as some dominating central presence but as part of a finely-honed team. The engineers have worked miracles with the sound. Early LP pressings were dull and dry but the remasterings for CD have a presence and, almost, a brilliance that perfectly complement the exceptionally subtle and spirited performance.

Rossini Il viaggio a Reims.

Cecilia Gasdia *sop* Corinna
Katia Ricciarelli *sop* Madama Cortese
Lella Cuberli *sop* Contessa di Folleville
Lucia Valentini-Terrani *mez* Marchesa Melibea
Edoardo Gimenez *ten* Cavalier Belfiore
Francisco Araiza *ten* Conte di Libenskof
Samuel Ramey *bass* Lord Sidney
Ruggero Raimondi *bass* Don Profondo
Enzo Dara *bar* Barone di Trombonok
Giorgio Surian *bar* Don Prudenzio
Leo Nucci *bar* Don Alvaro
Prague Philharmonic Chorus; Chamber Orchestra of Europe / Claudio Abbado.
DG Ⓟ ① 415 498-2GH2 (two discs: 136 minutes: DDD). Notes, text and translation included. Recorded at performances at the Rossini Opera Festival, Pesaro, Italy in 1984.

1986

Paris always brought out the epicure in Rossini: in the 1820s and again, after years of debilitating illness, in the late 1850s and 1860s. It also stimulated him to special flights of creative fancy as we can hear in the late and still too little known *Péchés de Vieillesse*, and, most lavishly of all, in this cornucopian revel, *The Journey to Rheims*. Written as part of the festival programme surrounding the coronation of the Bourbon Charles X in 1825, *Il viaggio* has some claim to being the best of all musical parties, outgunning such later heirs presumptive as Act 2 of *Die Fledermaus* by a considerable distance.

Though the plot is slight – an array of international grandees are gathered at an inn in Plombières *en route* for the coronation in Reims – the entertainment is richly elaborated in a way which precluded easy assimilation into the standard operatic repertoire. It is for this reason that Rossini more or less simultaneously planned to dismantle one of his finest scores. Parts of *Il viaggio a Reims* turn up in more accessible form for the opera-going public in *Le comte Ory*; but some of *Il viaggio a Reims*'s finest inventions, notably the great Sextet, languished unused until, remarkably, the dismembered work was re-identified and reassembled by Philip Gossett and Janet Johnson in one of the several acts of musical restitution which placed the Fondazione Rossini in Pesaro in the forefront of contemporary musicological achievement.

The première of this lavish piece was a royal gala at the Théâtre-Italien's Salle Louvois. Its success was huge and Rossini could have filled any Parisian theatre of his choice for a substantial run had he been so minded. In the event, he played the curmudgeon, insisting the thing come off after the prescribed three performances and only agreeing to a fourth, charity performance the following September after much arm-twisting by government officials. Few composers would dream of taking a smash-hit off after four performances; but Rossini was right, of course. In the nature of things, coronations don't happen every week (and the apostrophization of Charles X is central to the design). International summitry was, and is, more in vogue; but even here we are left with the problem of the expense of mounting a work designed as a showcase for a remarkable array of top international singers. In 1825 it was Bourbon prodigality and Rossini's name which enabled *Il viaggio a Reims* to be mounted. Nowadays we need comparable, if different, names and resources – happily to hand in Pesaro where the present recording was made during the 1984 festival.

What gives *Il viaggio a Reims* a further decisive dimension is the fact that Balocchi's libretto is an elaborate appropriation of, and partial satire on, Mme de Staël's *Corinne* (1808), a remarkable travelogue-cum-autobiography-cum-romantic fantasy centred on Corinne, one of the famous improvising singers of the new romantic age. In the opera Corinna has two harp-accompanied improvisations, each stilling the entertainment, turning it in on itself at a crucial moment of transition. The first comes, dramatically, as the third movement of the great Sextet; the second comes before the apotheosis of Charles X at the end of the work. Each is a magical essay in the Ossianic style (Ellen's song in *La donna del lago* points this way) and each is magically sung on the present recording by Cecilia Gasdia.

Gasdia's presence in the performance is symptomatic of the talent, new or established, which Abbado and DG were able to attract to the enterprise. The array is stunning. As the jealous rivals for the hand of the Marchesa Melibea we have Leo Nucci as the Spanish grandee and Francisco Araiza as the impulsive Russian, Conte di Libenskof. Madama Cortese, the Sybil Fawlty of the Inn at Plombières, is sung by Katia Ricciarelli (in generally good voice here). Lucia Valentini-Terrani, on brilliant form, sings Melibea and for good measure we have two Rossini veterans, Ruggero Raimondi as Don Profondo, the fanatical lover of all things antiquarian, and Enzo Dara as the harmony-loving Barone di Trombonok who launches the great Sextet, bullishly, in C major. Most of these singers have major solo scenes, too. There is a delicious duet, unaccountably missing from *Le comte Ory*, for Libenskof and Melibea; a duet whose deft, sighing cabaletta must rank as one of the most engaging of all Rossini's inventions; and Raimondi has his witty disquisition on international types, a piece – forerunner of many numbers in Sullivan – which is heard to better effect here than in Robert's description of his voyage through the Fourmoutiers cellars in *Le comte Ory* where the prosody is less exact.

Two singers absent from the Sextet have memorable numbers of their own. The fashion-loving and flirtatious Contessa di Folleville has a splendid aria and cabaletta in which she mourns the reported loss of a favourite bonnet in a carriage accident. The Contessa is sung by Lella Cuberli, Karajan's nominated Norma, and the piece, as she sings it, is a *tour de force*. Then there is Lord Sidney, the English colonel harbouring a furtive passion for Corinna. Samuel Ramey, one of the finest Rossini singers of our day, does full justice to Sidney's big aria, omitted from *Le comte Ory*; and there is some outstanding obbligato flute-playing, too, by Wissam Boustany. Ramey also gives us a bold account of Rossini's splendid arrangement of *God Save the King* in the junketings during the final entertainment. Time and again, it comes as a revelation to hear even the *Ory* numbers in their original garb. Nothing is grander, funnier, or sonically more glorious than the *Gran Pezzo Concertato a 14 Voci* in its original form.

The Pesaro performances have been recorded with great vividness by DG. You will be bowled over by the biting immediacy of the CDs. Applause has been edited out, rightly so, but there are some reassuring bumps and creaks from the stage and murmurs of delight can clearly be heard from the audience. In every way this production seems wonderfully 'live'; there is a sense of adventure mingled with an unmistakable relish, a *joie de vivre*, about the whole thing which one might expect when fine singers get together to restore to us a masterwork by one of their greatest benefactors.

Abbado's conducting is masterly. His ear for Rossini's sonorities cannot be faulted. The wind playing is exemplary and the strings of the Chamber Orchestra of Europe wonderfully catch that peculiarly Rossinian sound, fire and ice at the same time. Rhythmically, Abbado is exceptionally brilliant; it is a very alert performance, passionate and precise in the Toscanini manner. The set is a triumph of scholarship, musicianship and managerial enterprise. It is irresistible. *Foie gras* and champagne usually come more expensive than this.

In October 1992 Abbado and the Berlin Philharmonic restaged the work in Berlin's Philharmonie, an event Sony Classical were only too keen to underwrite in exchange for another very collectable recording. 'Very collectable' with the proviso that no one who already has the DG recording need feel compelled to go out and buy the Sony. After all, the music is the same, and so are no fewer than six of the 11 principal singers. The Sony set, though, is better recorded. DG's recording is perfectly adequate but the rather hard, dry acoustic of Pesaro's Auditorium Pedrotti does jar in places, and something like Corinna's off-stage entry in the great Sextet is better managed in Berlin. Here Sylvia McNair, a lovely Corinna, is distant but focused – in a way that isn't quite the case with DG's Cecilia Gasdia. Both Samuel Ramey and Enzo Dara surpass their already superb earlier performances. In Lord Sidney's big aria, Ramey has the advantage of an exceptionally fine flute obbligato from the BPO's Andreas Blau. As for Dara, he has transformed the aria in which Baron Trombonok catalogues national foibles. What was previously more or less a straight recitation is for Sony a miracle of subversive inflexion, with Abbado and the Berlin players adding wonderful new colours that seem to lie dormant in the earlier recording. When it comes to new singers, the Sony set has its weaknesses. Not Lucio Gallo. His Don Alvaro is less cumbersome than Leo Nucci's on DG. Nor perhaps Luciana Serra as the fashion-crazed young French widow. DG's Lella Cuberli sings superbly; but, then, so does Serra in a slightly more feckless way. Madama Cortese, the Tyrolean hostess, oozes presence and style. Here the lovely and lustrous Katia Ricciarelli must be preferred on points to Sony's Cheryl Studer. With the hyperactive Russian Count Libenskof there is no contest: DG's Francisco Araiza is far more in command of the role than William Matteuzzi (Gelsomino on the earlier recording).

Incidentally, on background essays DG wins hands down – Janet Johnson, Philip Gossett, Klaus Geitel and Claudio Abbado lined up against just one essay in the Sony booklet plus a rather obsequious note by the BPO's principal oboe, Hansjörg Schellenberger. However, Sony's idea of putting explanatory footnotes to the libretto at the foot of the page rather than at the back of the booklet is another small plus in their favour.

Albert Roussel

French 1869-1937

Roussel Padmâvatî.

Marilyn Horne *mez* Padmâvatî
Nicolai Gedda *ten* Ratan-Sen
José van Dam *bass-bar* Alla-uddin
Jane Berbié *mez* Nakamti
Charles Burles *ten* Brahmmin
Marc Vento *bar* Gora
Laurence Dale *ten* Badal
Thierry Dran *ten* Old Man
Orféon Donostiarra; Toulouse Capitole Orchestra / Michel Plasson.
EMI Ⓟ Ⓒ CDS7 47891-8 (two discs: 103 minutes: DDD). Notes, text and translation included. Recorded 1982/3.

This recording of *Padmâvatî*, one of Roussel's major works and certainly the most evocative of all operas on Indian subjects, was long overdue. It was inspired by a visit Roussel made (in the chance company of Ramsay MacDonald) in 1909 to the ruins of Chitoor (in Rajputana), which had been ravaged in 1300 by the Mogul Sultan Alla-uddin. Taking slight liberties with historical detail, it tells how Ratan-Sen, prince of Chitoor, is led to believe that his long-time enemy Alla-uddin is about to make a pact with him (though in fact he has brought his army along): Alla-uddin is entertained with dances of warriors and female slaves but demands to see the uncovered face of the prince's lovely wife Padmâvatî. The sight fires him to demand her for his own, under penalty of sacking the city. Ratan-Sen tries to persuade Padmâvatî to sacrifice herself in order to save his people, but aghast at the thought of such dishonour, she stabs her beloved and commits suttee as proof of her eternal devotion.

The opera, completed in 1918 but not performed until five years later, shows Roussel shaking off early Debussyan influences and moving towards his later crisper, more pungent harmonic idiom. Richly and imaginatively scored, it employs no unorthodox instruments to create its exotic atmosphere, though Hindu melodic and rhythmic modes are used, and there is an abundance of sinuous melodic lines. A main reason for it being rarely performed is that, though lasting less than two hours (and thus needing a curtain-raiser in the theatre), it combines opera and full-scale ballet – the entertainment in Act 1 and the dread rites of Siva's daughters in Act 2. The dances, and the symbolic preludes to the two acts, are so striking that it is not inappropriate to give pride of mention here to the Toulouse orchestra, which under Michel Plasson's adroit direction brings the score vividly to life.

The chorus, which have extensive and tricky sections to negotiate, also acquit themselves well, though occasionally the sopranos are less than happy on top notes; and in some places chorus words and even tone are swamped by the orchestra. Of the principals, van Dam steals the honours as the villainous Sultan under a smiling mask; Gedda sounds harsh-voiced and rather unsympathetic (perhaps deliberately?) as the weak prince; and two small parts of a Brahmin priest and a Chitoor girl are filled with some distinction by Burles and Berbié. However, unfortunately, Horne is not the ideal choice for the title-role: Not only is she overvibrant, but her exaggerations of chest-register jar badly, and she is altogether too masterful for a portrayal of the delicate beauty who is described as "the softness of the breeze of the sea in which the earth floats ... her voice is the song of oblivion". None the less, this is a welcome, much needed issue that fills a long-standing gap in the French recorded repertoire.

Camille Saint-Saëns French 1835-1921

Saint-Saëns Samson et Dalila.
    Plácido Domingo *ten* Samson
    Waltraud Meier *mez* Dalila
    Alain Fondary *bar* Priest
    Jean-Philippe Courtis *bass* Abimelech
    Samuel Ramey *bass* Old Hebrew
    Christian Papis *ten* Messenger
    Daniel Galvez-Vallejo *ten* First Philistine
    François Harismendy *bass* Second Philistine
    Chorus and Orchestra of the Bastille Opera, Paris / Myung-Whun Chung.
EMI Ⓔ Ⓓ CDS7 54470-2 (two discs: 124 minutes: DDD). Notes, text and translation included. Recorded 1991.

B B C RADIO 3
90-93 FM

Without doubt this is the most subtly and expertly conducted performance of this work to appear on CD, excellent as others have been in this respect, and also the best played and sung. Chung's achievement is to have welded the elements of pagan ruthlessness, erotic stimulation and Wagnerian harmony that comprise Saint-Saëns's masterpiece into a convincing whole. His success is based on the essentials of a firm sense of rhythm and timing allied to a realization of the sensuousness and delicacy of the scoring. Whether in the lamenting of the Hebrews, the forceful music written for the High Priest, the heroics of Samson, the sensual outpourings of Dalila, or the empty rejoicing of the Bacchanale, he and his orchestra strike to the heart of the matter – and that orchestra play with Gallic finesse, augmented by a dedicated discipline, not always a feature of French playing. They obviously respect and admire their conductor. The choral singing, though too distantly recorded, is no less alert and refined, with a full range of dynamic contrast. Everything is as surely felt as in Sir Colin Davis's account (Philips), but it is dispensed with a surer sense of dramatic development.

The cast couldn't be bettered today, certainly superior to Davis's. Meier's Dalila is a fascinating portrayal of this equivocal anti-heroine, seductive, wheedling, exerting her female wiles with the twin objects of sexual dominance and political command. All her sense of purpose comes out in her early greeting to the High Priest, "Salut à mon père"; then she's meditative and expectant as Dalila ponders on her power at "Se pourrait-il". The set numbers are all sung with the vocal ease and long phrase of a singer at the zenith of her powers. Something of the voluptuous warmth found in Gorr's singing for Prêtre on his 1960s EMI recording is all that is missing in a performance sung in virtually faultless French. She makes more of the text than Domingo who sings in his now familiar, all-purpose style, admirable in itself, somewhat missing the particular accents brought to this music by the great French tenors of the past. They exist no more and one must salute the sterling and often eloquent tones of Domingo, now more subtly used than they were for Barenboim in 1978. You may occasionally be conscious that Domingo sounds in a different acoustic from the other singers.

Fondary is superb as the High Priest, firm and rich in tone, commanding and vengeful in delivery: the most compelling interpreter of the part on disc, *tout court*. Ramey is luxury casting as the Old Hebrew, but as this is a part once sung by Pinza, Ramey probably felt he wasn't slumming it. After an unsteady start, he sings the small but important role with breadth and dignity. As Abimelech, Courtis makes much of little. Apart from the two reservations already made, the recording is admirable, with a wide and spacious sound, and the soloists forward, but well integrated into the whole. The Bastille would seem a successful venue for opera recording. This must now be the outright recommendation for this work, one that will give constant and rewarding pleasure.

Saint-Saëns Samson et Dalila.
    Plácido Domingo *ten* Samson
    Elena Obraztsova *mez* Dalila
    Renato Bruson *bar* Priest
    Pierre Thau *bass* Abimelech
    Robert Lloyd *bass* Old Hebrew

Gérard Friedmann *ten* Messenger
Constantin Zaharia *ten* First Philistine
Michel Hubert *bass* Second Philistine
Chorus and Orchestre de Paris / Daniel Barenboim.
DG Ⓜ ① 413 297-2GX2 (two discs: 126 minutes: ADD). Notes, text and translation included.
Recorded in 1978.

This is a spacious, thoughtful, grand reading, deriving from performances in the Roman arena at
Orange in 1978. As there, Barenboim realizes the stature of this score and has the Paris forces, then
under his directorship, in idiomatic support. Excellently balanced, it gives the travails of the Israelites
and the rejoicing of the Dagon pagans just the right profile. All the supporting roles are well taken,
with special praise due to Thau's Abimelech and Lloyd's moving Old Hebrew.

Domingo as Samson, in his very best voice, is notable for his defiant heroism and dignity in his later
misery, and he sings French with a deal of feeling for the language's nuances. That can hardly be said
for Obraztsova's harshly sung Delilah. She is somewhat too much of the devil rather than the
seductress. Besides, her line in her important solos is often bumpy, the registers never integrated.
Bruson is an appropriately hectoring High Priest, but his tone isn't always keenly focused.

Apart from Chung the rival versions have much to offer. Sir Colin Davis also knows and loves the
score, and is also supported by splendid forces, but like Barenboim is inclined to take too much of the
music below the composer's metronome marks. Prêtre (EMI) is better in that respect and perhaps has,
by a small margin, the more satisfying cast, headed by Gorr's resplendent Delilah and Vickers's
impassioned Samson, not better than but different from Domingo's.

Aulis Sallinen

Finnish 1935

Sallinen The Horseman.

Matti Salminen *bass* Antti
Taru Valjakka *sop* Anna
Eero Erkkilä *ten* Merchant of Novgorod
Anita Välkki *sop* Merchant's Wife
Martti Wallén *bass* Judge
Tuula Nieminen *mez* Woman
Usko Viitanen *bar* Yeoman
Heikki Toivanen *bass* Matti Puikkanen
Savonlinna Opera Festival Chorus and Orchestra / Ulf Söderblom.
Finlandia Ⓟ ① 1576-51101-2 (two discs: 125 minutes: AAD). Notes, text and translation
included. Recorded at a performance in Savonlinna on July 17th, 1975.

The Horseman ("Ratsumies", 1972-5) was Aulis Sallinen's first opera, commissioned for a competition
organized by the Savonlinna Opera Festival to celebrate the quincentenary of Olavinlinna fortress,
within whose walls the festival plays every year (and which features in the plot). Its première – of
which this is a recording – spectacularly launched modern Finnish opera on to the mainstream
European scene, maintained shortly afterwards by his own *The Red Line* and Kokkonen's *The Last
Temptations*. Hailed in Finland as one of the great national operas, *The Horseman* propelled its
composer to international prominence. The directness of his musical language, modern in idiom but
not sufficiently extreme to alienate largely conservative opera audiences (Sallinen having abandoned
serialism in the 1960s in favour of a personal and very atmospheric style rooted in tonality), made a
terrific impact. Yet more crucially, this first effort revealed his innate and natural genius for a genre
he had previously found "strange, even alien".

The plot of *The Horseman* is highly symbolic, set in an indeterminate past when Russia held sway
over at least part of Finland (either during one of the Russian annexations in the eighteenth and
nineteenth centuries, or in a remoter time several hundred years earlier). The libretto was created by
Paavo Haavikko from his own stage play and tells the story of Antti – the horseman of the title, with
a mystical power over animals – and his wife Anna who are slaves of a merchant in the city of
Novgorod. The Merchant seduces Anna; in revenge Antti kills the Merchant, who foretells the
horseman's death. Returning to Finland, Anna tries to have herself declared a widow in order to hide
their tracks. But at an assize in Olavinlinna, the disguised Antti is accidentally embroiled in another
trial, discovered and imprisoned. Effecting their escape, Antti and Anna fall in with a band of robbers
and attempt to storm a royal estate. The horseman is killed, fulfilling the Merchant's prophecy.

This live recording is a vibrant performance, well recorded, and the odd extraneous squawk from
local Savonlinna birds or audience member does not detract from the atmosphere.

Sallinen Kullervo.

Jorma Hynninen *bar* Kullervo
Eeva-Liisa Saarinen *mez* Mother

Matti Salminen *bass* Kalervo
Jorma Silvasti *ten* Kimmo
Satu Vihavainen *sop* Sister
Anna-Lisa Jakobson *mez* Smith's wife
Pertti Mäkelä *ten* Hunter
Juha Kotilainen *bar* Unto
Paula Etelävuori *contr* Unto's wife
Matti Putkonen *bass* Tiera
Matti Heinikari *ten* First man
Esa Ruuttunen *bar* Second man
Vesa-Matti Loiri *sngr* Blind singer
Finnish National Opera Chorus and Orchestra / Ulf Söderblom.
Ondine Ⓟ Ⓒ ODE780-2 (three discs: 157 minutes: DDD). Text and translation included.
Recorded 1991.

Despite being a prolific composer of symphonies and instrumental music, Sallinen's reputation – at least in this country – rests on his operas, and in particular on his second, *The Red Line* (1976-8), which was received in some quarters with near adulation when the Finnish National Opera brought it to London in the late-1970s. Expectations were high for his next stage work, *The King Goes Forth to France* (1980-3), jointly commissioned by the Savonlinna Festival, the Royal Opera House, Covent Garden, and the BBC. Just as the starkly realistic *Red Line* was perhaps overhyped, so *The King Goes Forth To France* was roundly and unfairly dismissed as something of an aberration. To have expected Sallinen to produce another *Red Line* in the context of the satirical and surreal subject of *The King* was to miss the point completely. What is now clear from his fourth opera, *Kullervo* (1986-8), is that *The King* was an important staging-post in his development which required Sallinen to refine further both his instrumental palette and imaginative resource to a much higher level than in his earlier operas. If the music of *The Red Line* was more striking in profile, this was due in large part to the nature of the plot, but the music of *The King* served its purpose at least as well; the problems of critical perception seemed to centre on what that purpose was.

Kullervo unites the disparate strands of Sallinen's previous operas into a dramatic and musical synthesis that perhaps even surpasses his previous output. Indeed, it would be tempting to view it as his masterpiece were he not likely enough to produce another still better in the future. The dark tone of *Kullervo* recalls *The Red Line*'s grim and hostile landscape, the music depicting this bleakest of tales from the Kalevala with an awesome sense of power and foreboding. Again, the delicacy of some of the writing, particularly associated with Kullervo's mother – who shines like a beacon through the opera – is in marked contrast to the prevailing mood, providing oases of calm amidst the raging and at times feverish storm of Kullervo's life. This alone shows how well the lessons have been learned from *The King*, as does the integrated and restrained use of a synthesizer (unlike the rather awkward use of the instrument in Rautavaara's *Vincent*). Comparisons are bound to be made with Sibelius's great early symphony (which Jorma Hynninen has also recorded), and despite the wide difference in language, there are several points of concurrence between them. But Sallinen in 1986 approaching this subject was a far more mature composer than was Sibelius in 1890, and the operatic medium has suited him every bit as well as the symphony/tone-poem form fitted his predecessor. Isolating moments in such a score for particular praise is an invidious task, where the sheer variety of tone and texture is one of its strongest and most attractive features. The utterly black opening, with its low bass sonorities, and the mother's aria, "Shall I weep for you?" may indicate something of *Kullervo*'s range, as do the Blind singer's "Song of the Sister's Ravishing", where the real and legendary worlds memorably collide, and Kullervo's final immolation (nowhere near as long drawn-out as Brünnhilde's but just as effective in its own way), both extraordinary moments from a composer at the height of his powers.

Originally commissioned to open the new and still unfinished National Opera House in Helsinki, *Kullervo* was finally premièred in Los Angeles in 1992 by the Finnish National Opera. Jorma Hynninen in the title-role is on his usual exemplary form, strongly supported by all the cast and conductor Ulf Söderblom and an admirably balanced recording which allows all the detail to show.

Max von Schillings   German 1868-1933

Schillings Mona Lisa.
Beate Bilandzija *sop* Mona Lisa, Wife
Klaus Wallprecht *bass-bar* Francesco del Giocondo, Stranger
Albert Bonnema *sngr* Giovanni de Salviati, Lay brother
Marek Gasztecki *bass* Pietro Tumoni
Karsten Russ *ten* Arrigo Oldofredi
Ulrich Köberle *ten* Alessio Beneventi, Sisto
Jörg Sabrowski *sngr* Sandro da Luzzano
Bernd Gebhardt *sngr* Masolino Pedruzzi

Eva-Christine Reimer *sop* Mona Ginevra
Amy Lawrence *sop* Dianora
Gerda Kosbahn *sop* Piccarda
Kiel Opera Chorus; Kiel Philharmonic Orchestra / Klauspeter Seibel.
CPO Ⓕ Ⓓ CPO999 303-2 (two discs: 118 minutes: DDD). Notes, text and translation included.
Recorded 1994.

Mona Lisa, premièred in 1915, was Max von Schillings's fourth opera and by far his most successful:
it received nearly 2,000 performances, not only on German stages. Its predecessors were reportedly so
indebted to Wagner as to sound almost like plagiarism, but in *Mona Lisa* Schillings tempered his
Wagnerism with elements borrowed from Italian *verismo*, restrained his scoring at crucial moments to
ensure clarity of word-setting and above all found a quite un-Wagnerian plot of blatant but enjoyable
sensationalism. In this version Mona Lisa's mysterious smile is never, to his angry jealousy, directed
at her elderly husband, Francesco. He discovers its meaning – she has a lover with whom she plans to
elope – and locks him in an air-tight safe in which he keeps his collection of fabulously valuable pearls.
In a crucial scene, which must have contributed mightily to those 2,000 performances, he then tries to
seduce his own wife, her price being the key of the safe. But to prove that he loves her more than his
pearls, he throws the key into the River Arno as the lover's dying screams are heard from beyond the
locked door. In the short Second Act Mona Lisa has her revenge by tricking her husband into
entering the safe and then slamming the door on him. The action is curiously framed by a prologue
and epilogue set in the present day, two tourists sung by the same singers as Lisa and Francesco (and
in some way identifiable with them) being shown around the scene of the story by a guide.

The music matches this hokum rather well. Mona Lisa's leitmotivs (she has several) are broadly and
gratefully melodious, the duet with her lover Giovanni is deeply indebted to Wagner (including the
overheated imagery of its text) but it has effective passionate lyricism as well, and the darkness of
Francesco's miserly obsession with his pearls is well suggested, though his eloquence and later his
brutal lust are not really very strongly differentiated from the love music. No matter: it is the suspense
and the climaxes that count, and they are efficiently paced and managed. The quieter passages
between the climaxes are less striking: there are numerous scenes involving action and music off-stage,
but Schillings's operetta-ish carnival music, his counterpoint of sacred *Laude* and pagan hymn to
Venus and his penitential procession (one of the off-stage, non-singing characters is Savonarola, no
less) are rather commonplace. In one of the off-stage effects, though (a so-called Madrigal that
heightens Francesco's lust), and in a charmingly innocent folk-like theme sung by Lisa's step-daughter
before the melodramatic passions of the final scene, there's an indication of a quieter lyrical vein,
learned perhaps from Hugo Wolf, that Schillings might have tapped profitably in later operas. But he
wrote none: the rest of his life was given up to administrative work, to theatrical and marital intrigue,
to frustrated disillusionment and, briefly, to high office held under the Nazis: he died not long after
they came to power.

This is mostly a thoroughly efficient performance rather than one which can make you overlook the
opera's flaws. Wallprecht's vehement Francesco can do so: he is a pupil of Josef Metternich, and has
some of his teacher's dark authority. Bilandzija has the title-role's necessary glamour and a good deal
of its impossible range (from enigmatic serenity to spitting fury). Bonnema is ardent, but not quite
the Tauber or Patzak that Giovanni needs. Seibel paces the opera expertly and gives real heft to the
expansive lyrical pages that are the opera's principal claim on posterity. Not a major discovery, but
well worth sampling.

Franz Schmidt   Austrian 1874-1939

Schmidt Notre Dame.
Dame Gwyneth Jones *sop* Esmeralda
James King *ten* Phoebus
Horst Laubenthal *ten* Gringoire
Hartmut Welker *bar* Archdeacon
Kurt Moll *bass* Quasimodo
Hans Helm *bar* An Officer
Kaja Borris *mez* Old Falourdel
Choir of St Hedwig's Cathedral, Berlin; Berlin RIAS Chamber Choir;
Berlin Radio Symphony Orchestra / Christof Perick.
Capriccio Ⓕ Ⓓ 10 248/9 (two discs: 126 minutes: DDD). Notes, text and translation included.
Recorded 1988.

'Son of Bruckner' is Franz Schmidt's reputation, and if you can hardly imagine Bruckner writing an
opera, any apprehension you may feel at the thought of Bruckner *Sohn* writing one might be
increased by reading Gerhard Schmiedpeter's note accompanying this first ever recording of *Notre
Dame*. He describes how Schmidt wrote the orchestral music of the opera before the vocal lines (large
parts of it were in fact quarried from an abandoned Fantasy for piano and orchestra), and how one

section of the score was performed as an independent concert piece before work on the opera began. He could have gone on even further: Albert Arbeiter has shown (in *Studien zu Franz Schmidt I*: Vienna: 1976) that Schmidt sketched the opera without much reference to the libretto, merely labelling this page or that "chorus" and "dialogue" but not necessarily following even these indications when the voice parts and text were finally added. This curious method of working shows at times, not so much in awkward word-setting but in passages where the voices seem to have been skilfully inlaid into the orchestra: symphonic movements with vocal obbligatos. You might call *Notre Dame*, indeed, an 'orchestral opera': Schmidt doesn't go in for arias or duets much (moments of purely vocal lyrical effusion are usually brief), his writing for chorus is rather orator-like and formal (the Parisian mob express their feelings in fugues and Bachian *turbae*), and the presence in a shortish two-act opera of *three* orchestral entr'actes (as well as two preludes) signifies rather more than praiseworthy consideration for scene-shifters.

A 'symphonists's opera', then, an interesting but inevitably flawed demonstration of what happens when a cobbler abandons his last? Not at all; symphonic, undoubtedly, but therein lies its strength. Schmidt the symphonist knew all about writing themes that can take on new guises in development. Each of his principal characters has one: a florid gipsy melody from his own Eastern European homeland for Esmeralda (strange, then, that when she sings one of her native airs to entertain the crowd she should do so in Spanish); a proud, leaping motif for her would-be seducer, the soldier Phoebus; a solemn (indeed Brucknerian) chorale for the Archdeacon (Hugo's Frollo, though un-named in the opera), and so on. The skill with which Schmidt varies and transforms these themes, to depict the subjection and destruction of Esmeralda's joyous freedom, to show both the debonair Phoebus's love and his arrogance, to reveal the guilt beneath Frollo's reverend dignity, is remarkable, and it is one source of the opera's power. But Schmidt's feeling for the stage is strong, as well: the impressive darkness that opens Act 2 is somehow deepened by the recollections (from an ensemble of solo strings) of the fated love music from the previous act; the atmosphere of Esmeralda's trial is simply but most effectively evoked by the juxtaposition of solemn plainchant and broken lyrical phrases; Quasimodo's description of his world of air and light among the towers of Notre Dame is beautifully illustrated by lovely hovering music in the orchestra. (Quasimodo's own theme, by the way, is not transformed. He remains at the end as he began: deformed and, when threatened, terrible, but innocent; the only character in the opera whose love for Esmeralda is quite selfless and thus non-destructive.)

It would work very well on stage, so it is a slight disappointment that some of Schmidt's carefully devised spatial effects (off-stage music, mainly, and the slow procession from a distance in the trial scene) have scarcely been hinted at in this recording, and the singers have been placed in the perspective of a concert (chorus back, soloists well forward), not a stage. The part of Esmeralda was written with Maria Jeritza in mind, and then altered for Marie Gutheil-Schoder, who sang at the première. Jones has the sort of glamour and sheer heft that those names evoke and the role requires. King has the right vocal metal (now somewhat tarnished) for Phoebus, if only he would sing quietly (which he rarely does) or with genuinely ardent emotion. Welker is a sonorous and impressive Archdeacon, Laubenthal a decent Gringoire and Moll makes maximum impact in the crucial (but in this opera infrequent) scenes involving Quasimodo. The chorus are moderate, the orchestra excellent (though very slightly understaffed in the strings, by the sound of it); Perick lovingly moulds the many and subtle orchestral beauties with which this opera abounds. Despite the rather unatmospheric recording (the sound is good otherwise) the impression of a work that theatres outside Vienna have been neglecting for far too long is very strong indeed.

Othmar Schoeck
Swiss 1886-1957

Schoeck Massimilla Doni.
Edith Mathis *sop* Duchess Massimilla Doni
Hermann Winkler *ten* Duke Cattaneo
Josef Protschka *ten* Emilio Memmi
Celina Lindsley *sop* Tinti, a soprano
Harald Stamm *bass* Capraja
Roland Hermann *bar* Prince Vendramin
Deon van der Walt *ten* Genovese, a tenor
Annette Küttenbaum *mez* Maid, Shepherdess, Fruiterer
Cologne Radio Chorus and Symphony Orchestra / Gerd Albrecht.
Koch Schwann Musica Mundi Ⓟ Ⓓ 314025 (two discs: 128 minutes: DDD). Notes and text included. Recorded at a broadcast performance in January 1986.

It is time that Harry Lime's celebrated remark (through the lips of Orson Welles in *The Third Man*), that Switzerland's major achievement was the "cuckoo clock", was laid to rest. She has in Frank Martin and Othmar Schoeck produced two major composers, not to mention some of their younger contemporaries such as Conrad Beck and Willy Burkhard. The appearance of Schoeck's opera, *Massimilla Doni*, on CD was warmly welcomed. He has the distinctive quality of rendering the familiar language of Straussian opera entirely his own. The vocabulary is not dissimilar yet the world is different. You will find that the work grows stronger and its atmosphere more haunting every time you dip into it. In fact, the comparatively neo-romantic idiom of Schoeck's music is deceptive: the sound world may not seem as novel or fresh as that of his countryman, Frank Martin, who was only four years younger but who possessed an entirely different sensibility, and yet at his best Schoeck has no less depth.

Massimilla Doni is his penultimate opera, written in 1934–5, to a libretto based on Balzac by Armin Rueger with whom he had collaborated in an earlier venture. Within a few bars Schoeck has you completely under his spell. The opera differs from the better-known *Penthesilea*, as much as Richard Strauss's *Capriccio* does from *Elektra*. Indeed, since *Massimilla Doni* was first staged in Dresden in 1937, you are tempted to wonder whether it did not unconsciously inspire *Capriccio*, for there is a serene melancholy about the F major ending of the first scene that calls to mind the opening of the Strauss. This figure returns at the very end of the opera to magical effect and in fact the opera's aura of autumnal melancholy is ultimately more sympathetic than the expressionism of *Penthesilea*.

Edith Mathis gives a lovely account of the title-role, full of depth and feeling, and Celina Lindsley is an accomplished exponent of the demanding coloratura role of Tinti. Generally speaking there are no major quarrels with the performance or recording, which sound even better in this transfer than on LP. The cuts are not opened out: they are relatively trivial but they did not disfigure the 1986 Westdeutscher Rundfunk broadcast from which this performance is taken. The libretto is untranslated though there is a synopsis in French and English. Still, this is such a beautiful and rewarding opera that no one should be deterred investigating it on these grounds.

Schoeck Penthesilea.

Helga Dernesch *sop* Penthesilea
Jane Marsh *sop* Prothoe
Mechtild Gessendorf *sop* Meroe
Marjana Lipovšek *mez* High Priestess
Gabriele Sima *sop* Priestess
Theo Adam *bass-bar* Achilles
Horst Hiestermann *ten* Diomede
Peter Weber *bass* Herold
Austrian Radio Chorus and Symphony Orchestra / Gerd Albrecht.
Orfeo Ⓔ Ⓘ C364941B (80 minutes: ADD). Notes and text included. Recorded at a performance in the Felsenreitschule, Salzburg on August 17th, 1982.

Schoeck's one-act opera, *Penthesilea* is an astonishing and masterly score. It seems barely credible that a work so gripping in its dramatic intensity, and so powerful in atmosphere, should be so rarely performed and so little known. It has the listener on the edge of the seat throughout its 80 short minutes and, like any great opera, it casts a spell long after the music has ended. In the *Grove Dictionary of Opera*, Ronald Crichton wrote that "at its most intense, the language of *Penthesilea* surpasses in ferocity Strauss's *Elektra*, a work with which it invites comparison". In so far as it is a one-act work, set in the Ancient World, highly concentrated in feeling and with strongly delineated characters, it is difficult not to think of Strauss's masterpiece. Yet its sound world is quite distinctive. Vaughan Williams once spoke of originality as the power to make a C major chord sound new, citing the example of Sibelius. Though he is a lesser figure, Schoeck similarly renders the familiar language of Straussian opera entirely his own. The vocabulary is not dissimilar yet the world is different.

The action takes place during the Trojan War. Penthesilea is the queen and leader of the Amazons, female warriors who may give their love only to a man they have defeated in battle. Penthesilea believes that she has vanquished Achilles though in fact the reverse is the case. To win her love he must allow her to believe herself the victor. But when Achilles reveals the truth, she is appalled. In the subsequent combat to which he challenges her, he offers no resistance and when she realizes that he has perished by her hand, she takes her own life. Schoeck based his libretto on Kleist's tragedy of 1808, beginning at the ninth scene of the play, shortening and rearranging it but adding nothing. In conversation with Werner Vogel in 1946 Schoeck is quoted as saying that on the dramatic stage, "Kleist's language goes by too quickly and thereby has too little an effect. In the opera, words are magnified for more time is available for them. The listener has to become conscious of Kleist." The inevitable slowing-down heightens rather than hinders understanding. First given at the Staatsoper, Dresden in 1927, *Penthesilea* has rarely been heard since, even in Schoeck's native Switzerland. It was first recorded in 1973 at the Lucerne Festival with Carol Smith as Penthesilea and Roland Hermann as Achilles, and Cologne Radio forces under Zdenek Macal and issued on LP in 1975. Good though that was, this newcomer completely supersedes it.

We are immediately plunged into a vivid and completely individual world, packed with dramatic incident: off-stage war cries and exciting, dissonant trumpet calls. There is an almost symphonic handling of pace, but the sonorities are unusual: for example, there is a strong wind section, some ten clarinets at various pitches, while there are only a handful of violins; much use is made of two pianos in a way that at times almost anticipates Britten. Helga Dernesch in the title-role commands the appropriate range of emotions as Penthesilea and the remainder of the cast, including the Achilles of

Theo Adam, rise to the occasion. The important choral role and the orchestral playing under Gerd Albrecht are eminently committed and the recording is good without being state-of-the-art. There is a useful essay and libretto, though in German, not English or French. However, since the action is drawn from the *Iliad* this should hardly present problems. Schoeck was only a few years older than his better-known compatriots Frank Martin and Arthur Honegger, yet has never gained the recognition given to them. Let us hope that this recording of a marvellous opera advances his cause.

Schoeck Venus.
Frieder Lang *ten* Baron de Zarandelle
Lucia Popp *sop* Simone
James O'Neal *ten* Horace
Hedwig Fassbender *mez* Madame de Lauriens
Boje Skovhus *bar* Raimond
Zsuzsa Alföldi *sop* Lucile
Heidelberg Chamber Choir; Basle Boys' Choir;
Swiss Youth Philharmonic Orchestra / Mario Venzago.
MGB Musikszene Schweiz Ⓟ Ⓓ CD6112 (two discs: 91 minutes: DDD). Notes, text and translation included. Recorded 1991.

Venus is Schoeck's third opera and was composed in 1919-21, in the immediate wake of the First World War. Like its predecessor, *Don Ranudo*, it is based on a libretto by his school friend Armin Rüeger, and first saw the light of day in the 1922 Zurich Festival. Since then, performances have been desperately few and far between; indeed barely a handful, though the piece was revived in Zurich for Schoeck's 70th birthday in 1956. Its première abroad had to wait until 1989 at Heidelberg, and this is its first recording. Rüeger drew on two sources, the novella, *La Vénus d'Ille* of Prosper Mérimée and Eichendorff's short story, *Das Marmorbild*. The basic argument is familiar from *Ovid*, though Mérimée sets his story in the little Pyrenean hamlet of Ille-sur-Têt where he is visiting the amateur archaeologist, Peyrehorade, who has unearthed a bronze statue of Venus. The son of the house who is playing a game of pelota, a Basque ball game, immediately before his wedding finds his wedding-ring a hindrance and places it on the finger of the statue of Venus only to discover that the finger bends. During the wedding night the statue interposes itself between him and the bride, and the novella ends with his death. Rüeger moved the action to a country castle in the south of France in about 1820 but the original libretto basically follows the broad outline of the Mérimée.

There are several reasons for the opera's neglect; Ronald Crichton put his finger on the first in the *Grove Dictionary of Opera*: "the considerable demands of the tenor role may explain why *Venus* has been infrequently performed". Another would seem to be the inadequacy of the libretto. Schoeck himself seems to have changed his mind about the character of his hero during the course of 1920 and pressed ahead, leaving Rüeger to fill in the text afterwards. Large sections were added after the music was written! Thirdly, and possibly most importantly, are the factors outlined in Mario Venzago's note in the booklet which are here summarized.

The only extant score is at times difficult to decipher and is full of clef and transposition errors. Whole sections appear to have been omitted in previous performances, as there are irreconcilable differences between the piano reduction and the full score. It would seem to cry out for the ministrations of an expert scholar. Venzago is particularly scathing about the librettist and cuts about six minutes of the score on the grounds that it is "sometimes necessary to protect the composer from the poet". He goes on to say, "In good conscience we have omitted some over-ambitious or botched parts of the text, with the pertinent music, and left out the texts in the melodramatic passages where the music is particularly descriptive and has no need of textural commentaries. The present recording is therefore one of several possible performances." However, it should be said straight away that his direction of this performance radiates a total dedication.

After the glorious orchestral prelude, Lucia Popp's entry prompts one's thoughts to turn to the Strauss of *Ariadne* but as the opera unfolds the truth of Venzago's description of the opera as partly "an enormous orchestral poem (exposition, development, scherzo and recapitulation) with obbligato voices" begins to emerge. Of course this is not the only opera with a powerful symphonic dimension, and its dramatic validity is not impaired. What is really striking, however, is the sheer quality of the invention which is of a very high order. Many of the ideas – and particularly the Venus motif itself – are of great tenderness and delicacy, and exquisitely scored.

The more you hear of Schoeck's music, the more you believe him to be a master. Readers who have acquired *Penthesilea* or *Massimila Doni* or his dramatic cantata, *Vom Fischer un syner Fru*, will need no prompting to investigate this imaginative piece. Vocally the performance may not be absolutely ideal but it is worth putting up with the odd vocal infelicity for the sake of such a beautiful score, and the exacting tenor role is sung with character. The orchestral playing is shot through with great feeling and imagination. Mario Venzago takes much trouble over detail and dynamics, and obviously loves the score, and Schoeck's invention has obviously inspired sympathy and affection from the accomplished young Swiss players. The recording, too, is eminently acceptable and there is a decent perspective, and plenty of space round the sound. In any event we are not likely to get another glimpse of *Venus* for a very long time and music of such fantasy and inspiration should not be missed.

Arnold Schoenberg

Schoenberg Moses und Aron.

Franz Mazura *bass-bar* Moses
Philip Langridge *ten* Aron
Aage Haugland *bass* Priest
Barbara Bonney *sop* Young girl
Mira Zakai *contr* Invalid woman
Daniel Harper *ten* Young man, Youth
Thomas Dymit *ten* Naked youth
Herbert Wittges *bar* Ephraimite, A man
Kurt Link *bar* Another man, An elder
Glen Ellyn Children's Chorus; Chicago Symphony Chorus and Orchestra / Sir Georg Solti.
Decca Ⓕ Ⓛ 414 264-2DH2 (two discs: DDD). Notes, text and translation included. Recorded 1984.

Sir Georg Solti recorded *Moses und Aron* the best part of two decades after he conducted the opera in Peter Hall's Covent Garden production. His faith in Schoenberg's most ambitious dramatic project remained undimmed and he believed that, with increasing familiarity, the music becomes "clearer, less complicated, and more expressive and romantic". However, becoming familiar with the opera also reinforces its remarkable ambiguity and originality. *Moses und Aron* is a necessarily and challengingly diverse composition. At one extreme, the choral counterpoint with its traditional imitative techniques: at the other, the concentratedly expressionist orchestral writing. Then there is the almost blatant, post-Mahlerian vulgarity of parts of the "Dance round the Golden Calf", in complete contrast to the visionary, discomfiting density of scenes like the first, in which superimpositions of speech and song, voices and instruments, leave the listener straining to find the centre, to discover the idea behind the images in this confrontation between human and divine. Add to all this the fact that there is a text for a third act that Schoenberg never set, and we have something which, however expressive and romantic, is still very much a problem piece.

The odds are that any studio recording of *Moses* will be stronger in textural clarity and accuracy of detail than in theatrical atmosphere. Yet the latter is certainly not lacking in Solti's performance, especially in the second act. Since Act 1 is less conventionally theatrical anyway, it is not surprising that it is here that you are likely to be most aware of artists working conscientiously in a recording studio. But there are moments of excitement in Act 1, too, which seem to bear out Solti's confident claim that "the more we rehearsed and played the easier the work became". As Moses, Franz Mazura consistently stresses the character's torments of self-doubt. His approach to the relative intervals and range indicated by the *Sprechgesang* notation is very free: in particular, he shuns the lower registers which Schoenberg often indicates and which might, literally, give the character more profundity, more stature – especially at the end – and make him seem less like a close relative of Mazura's other major role in twentieth-century opera, Dr Schön in Berg's *Lulu*. Philip Langridge is an experienced Schoenbergian and, in making Aron convincingly attractive rather than merely aggressive, he provides an excellent foil to the hectoring Moses. There is not always enough sheer power, or sufficient evenness of vocal production, but he is helped by a recorded sound which seems prepared to sacrifice some clarity of orchestral detail to ensure that the principal vocal lines come through.

It is certainly good that the recording does not attempt artificially to oversimplify or stratify the work's blended textures, and it serves well the music's vertiginous exploration of the borderland between complexity and chaos, inscrutable divinity and argumentative humanity. In this precarious balance lies the impact and quality of the whole performance, with its generally good supporting cast; it also explains the abiding fascination of Schoenberg's last attempt to bring a great philosophical issue to dramatic life.

Schoenberg Moses und Aron.

Günter Reich *spkr* Moses
Louis Devos *ten* Aron
Werner Mann *bass* Priest
Eva Csapó *sop* Young girl
Elfride Obrowsky *contr* Invalid woman
Roger Lucas *ten* Young man, Naked youth
Richard Salter *bar* Another man
Ladislav Illavský *bar* Ephraimite
Vienna Boys' Choir; Austrian Radio Chorus;
Austrian Radio Symphony Orchestra / Michael Gielen.
Philips Ⓜ Ⓛ 438 667-2PM2 (two discs: 98 minutes: ADD). Notes, text and translation included. Recorded 1974.

This version of *Moses und Aron* was recorded in the same year as Pierre Boulez's account on Sony Classical (he recorded a splendid version for a second time for DG in 1995). When reviewing them,

Jeremy Noble found much to admire in both versions, concluding that whereas Boulez "rather underplays the work's rhetoric", Gielen makes the opera "more exciting". The CD transfer of Gielen's account certainly underlines the kind of raw intensity in his approach to which Boulez would never aspire, and which Schoenberg himself might have found overdone – too purely 'operatic'. The Philips sound is larger than life, the voices (especially Moses) grafted on to a close yet remarkably vivid orchestral tapestry. The Austrian Radio orchestra squeeze the last drop of expressionist exoticism out of the "Dance round the Golden Calf", and no one who likes the idea of linking Schoenberg with Puccini, and who enjoys thinking of the more sadistic aspects of *Moses und Aron* in terms of a kind of 12-note *Turandot*, will want to be without this fiery reading. The drawback is that such an emphasis on the work's pagan side inevitably reduces the impact of that tension which Schoenberg sought between sacred and profane. With Boulez you get more sense of the war between ideas and actions which lies at the heart of the drama, and even in the spacious recording the dialogues between Moses and Aron lack nothing in dramatic urgency.

Günter Reich is the Moses in both recordings, and the degree of histrionic projection in his performances reflects the different attitudes of the conductors. Both Arons – Richard Cassilly (Boulez) and Louis Devos – convey the strength as well as the seductiveness of Moses's *alter ego* with considerable success. For the rest, no performance of this opera could survive with an inadequate chorus, or with weak links in the smaller roles. Boulez's team is musically admirable, yet Gielen's chorus sound that much more at home in the pithy abstractions of Schoenberg's German text.

Two well-contrasted views of this remarkable work, then, and two sterling if not infallibly accurate performances. The difference is that the Boulez comes (at medium price) with the bonus of the Second Chamber Symphony, giving a total playing time of 121 minutes. With Solti's full-price digital recording also available, choice is even more difficult. What is clear is that Gielen remains unsurpassed in the way he links Schoenberg's score to the blood-and-thunder traditions of some very different opera composers.

Schoenberg Von Heute auf Morgen.

Richard Salter *bar* Der Mann
Christine Whittlesey *sop* Die Frau
Claudia Barainsky *sop* Die Freundin
Ryszard Karczykowski *ten* Der Sänger
Annabelle Hahn (spkr) Das Kind
Frankfurt Radio Symphony Orchestra / Michael Gielen.
CPO Ⓔ Ⓓ CPO999 532-2 (54 minutes: DDD). Notes, text and translation included. Recorded 1996.

Von Heute auf Morgen ("From Today to Tomorrow") is one of the least performed (and recorded) of Schoenberg's major compositions. With its long, unbroken span the longest of his 12-note works, by some way, when he wrote it in 1928-9 – its demands on performers are nevertheless those of technique rather than stamina. Emphatically a piece for singers with orchestral accompaniment, it should, the composer claimed, be sung with beauty of tone, without shouting or exaggeration. Yet the intensity of the expression, and the generally fast tempos, make a relaxed, conversational style difficult to achieve. The music is certainly not monotonous, any more than it is expressionistic. This is an opera with a light touch, mixing comic and serious aspects, and the music shifts constantly between recitative and aria-like writing. But it remains hard for performers whose bread and butter is earned with very different materials to achieve an idiomatic result in this story of marital misunderstanding, aggravation and – in the end – reconciliation.

By engaging reputable contemporary music specialists, CPO have gone some way to meeting this problem, and Michael Gielen conducts an account that sweeps compellingly forwards while not stinting the eloquence and lyricism. In the principal roles, Christine Whittlesey and Richard Salter undoubtedly overpoint the text in the early stages: Some of that brittle verbal clarity would willingly have been sacrificed for a more legato line. But they offer a high degree of accuracy, the moments of tenderness later on are well done and, with two strong singers in the subordinate parts, the cumulative sections of the opera are extremely convincing. The recording as such, linked to the making of a film for television, does no one any favours, and greater parity between voices and orchestra would have been welcome, but it is adequate.

Franz Schreker   Austrian 1878-1934

Schreker Die Gezeichneten.
Heinz Kruse *ten* Alviano Salvago
Elizabeth Connell *sop* Carlotta
Monte Pederson *bar* Count Vitelozzo Tamare
Alfred Muff *bass* Duke Adorno, Capitaneo di Giustizia
László Polgár *bass* Lodovico Nardi, Podesta

Christiane Berggold *mez* Martuccia
Martin Petzold *ten* Pietro
Robert Wörle *ten* Guidobald Usodimare
Endrik Wottrich *ten* Menaldo Negroni
Oliver Widmer *bar* Michelotto Cibo
Matthias Goerne *bass-bar* Gonsalvo Fieschi
Kristin Sigmundsson *bass* Julian Pinelli
Petteri Salomaa *bass* Paolo Calvi
Marita Posselt *sop* Ginevra Scotti
Reinhard Ginzel *ten* First Senator
Jörg Gottschick *bass* Second Senator
Friedrich Molsberger *bass* Third Senator
Herbert Lippert *ten* A youth
Berlin Radio Chorus; Deutsches Symphony Orchestra, Berlin / Lothar Zagrosek.
Decca Entartete Musik Ⓕ Ⓘ 444 442-2DHO3 (three discs: 171 minutes: DDD). Notes, text and
translation included. Recorded 1993-4.

Until comparatively recently all that most people knew about Franz Schreker was that he conducted
the first performance of Schoenberg's *Gurrelieder*. It is hellishly difficult, even now, but Schreker,
using an orchestra that Schoenberg feared would not be up to it and a rehearsal period that he
thought inadequate, brought off a triumph. Listening to *Die Gezeichneten* ("The Branded" or "The
Stigmatized") gives you an indication of how he managed it: his ear must have been extraordinarily
precise. *Die Gezeichneten*, hugely successful at its première in 1918 (it was soon produced at all the
major theatres in Germany and Austria) uses a large cast and a vast orchestra for a range of gorgeous
colours (Schreker's palate seems limitless) and delicate instrumental embroideries that even Strauss
hardly rivalled.

Schreker's popularity had already begun to wane some years before the Nazis pronounced him
'degenerate'. For the musical and political right wing he was tainted by his associations with
Schoenberg and with Hindemith (who he appointed to teach composition at the Berlin Hochschule
für Musik) and by the modernism of his own pupils, Alois Hába, Ernst Krenek and Berthold
Goldschmidt among them. But for the modernists these associations could not save him from seeming
a mere hangover from late romanticism, an explorer of the dead end from which modernism was
seeking to escape. And his voluptuous 'decadence' would have seemed all the more extreme as the
operas of Hindemith, Berg and Weill succeeded his on German stages. There is evidence that it
seemed so to Schreker himself, and his later operas are a fascinating dialogue with himself; one of
them is even about an opera composer who loses control of the purity of his vision as his characters
indulge in a phantasmagoria of their own.

Sexual decadence was one of the Nazis' charges against him; "his extravagant and perverted operas
have poisoned the soul of the people", was a fairly typical denunciation. The mingling in *Die
Gezeichneten* of post-*Salome* opulence (Strauss with rich admixtures of Scriabin, Szymanowski,
Korngold and Puccini is as close as you can get to describing it) with post-*Salome* gaminess of subject
matter is indeed strong stuff. Carlotta, a beautiful but gravely ill painter knows that her health would
never withstand physical love. She is loved, he believes hopelessly, by the monstrously ugly nobleman
Alviano; she is desired by the licentious Count Tamare. Drawn by the beauty of Alviano's soul she at
first declares her love for him, but then deserts him for Tamare. On learning that she gave herself to
Tamare voluntarily, knowing the fatal consequences, Alviano first kills his rival, then goes mad.

Schreker's sheer resourcefulness is breathtaking. Each character seems to have not merely an
identifying theme but a whole sound world. Scenes of extreme complexity are handled with total
assurance. The score is melodious, fabulously multi-coloured and has great cumulative power. One
reservation was hinted at by Alban Berg's reaction to the libretto: he found it superb but "a bit
kitschy". It is, and this quality is intensified in the music by a curious impassivity, as though Schreker
were observing his characters from outside. Carlotta's 'conversion' from spiritual to physical love is
not accompanied by much change in her alluringly mysterious music; her characterization is
fantastically detailed but has no depth. She, Alviano and Tamare are ideas, not people. It is an opera
in which richness of detail, complexity of texture and sheer glamour replace humanity. The end is
'effective' but not tragic.

Nevertheless, as a document of its time and as a score of unprecedented richness it abundantly
deserved a recording. Edo de Waart's performance for Marco Polo was a splendid achievement, all
the more so for being recorded live. Indeed choice between his version and the newcomer would be
tricker were it not for the fact that de Waart makes several lengthy cuts (about 20 minutes of music in
all) in the last act and his tenor is under painfully audible strain. Zagrosek's reading is superb, his cast
almost without flaw. Connell gives a splendid performance: she has all Carlotta's glamour, together
with a purity of tone and a subtle response to words and phrasing that come close to giving her a soul.
Kruse is less imaginative, one or two of Alviano's high notes give him trouble, but he sings strongly
and lyrically; Pederson makes a grippingly formidable, physical opponent. The precision and detail of
the subsidiary characters are praiseworthy throughout; even very small roles have been cast from
strength. The recording is remarkably fine, spacious and sumptuous, with not a single detail out of
focus.

Schreker Irrelohe.

Michael Pabst *ten* Count Heinrich
Luana DeVol *sop* Eva
Goran Simic *bass* Forester, Anselmus
Eva Randová *mez* Lola
Monte Pederson *bar* Peter
Heinz Zednik *ten* Christobald
Neven Belamaric *sngr* Parson, Strahlbusch
Sebastian Holecek *sngr* Miller, Ratzekahl
Helmut Wildhaber *ten* Fünkchen, A lackey
Vienna Singverein; Vienna Symphony Orchestra / Peter Gülke.
Sony Classical Ⓟ Ⓒ S2K66850 (two discs: 127 minutes: DDD). Notes, text and translation included. Recorded at a performance in the Grosser Musikvereinsaal, Vienna on March 15th, 1989.

It is good to see the upsurge of interest in Schreker's operas. There was a time when his representation in the catalogue was, to say the least, meagre but now *Der ferne Klang* (1910), *Die Gezeichneten* (1915) and *Der Schatzgräber* (1918) are all available on CD. *Irrelohe* comes immediately after *Der Schatzgräber* in the canon and was first produced in 1924 in Cologne. Immediately after the First World War Schreker was hailed by Paul Bekker as the most significant musical-dramatist after Wagner. ("The important question whether a similar type of talent would ever again resurface after Wagner ... is now answered: Franz Schreker is such a talent, the first since Wagner, that is of a similar calibre, the same phenomenon, but in a wholly different manifestation.")

His musical language is steeped in the lush and overripe orchestral textures of Strauss and Puccini, and embraces symbolism, expressionism and the Viennese *Jugendstil*. One could think of the idiom as a cross between the Strauss of *Elektra* and Korngold, albeit with a higher norm of dissonance than the latter. Schreker's star began to wane after the critical mauling *Irrelohe* received, and against a background of resentment at his success, and growing anti-Semitism (he was forced to resign as Director of the Hochschule für Musik in Berlin; subsequent Nazi persecution seems to have occasioned a stroke which led to his death in 1934). He later enjoyed the venom of that self-appointed pontiff of modernism, Theodor Wiesengrund Adorno (as did Sibelius – so he was in good company).

Irrelohe, to the composer's own libretto, is set in the eighteenth century. Count Heinrich lives as a recluse in Irrelohe castle, fearing hereditary madness should he give way to sexual passion. His love for Eva inspires the jealousy of her suitor, Peter, as well as the enmity of Christobald, whose own fiancée had been raped by Heinrich's father. Peter attempts to prevent their wedding but is killed in the ensuing struggle, and in the meantime Christobald sets fire to Irrelohe. Echoes of Valhalla's fate in *Götterdämmerung*! Eva finally sings of the redemptive power of love. (The name of the opera, incidentally, derives from a railway station: while travelling on a sleeping-car Schreker, woken up by a guard calling out the name of a station, looked out of the window and saw the name, Irrloh.)

While Schreker's mastery of dramatic and psychological effects is not in question, many critics have felt that his music is too close to the wilder shores of Hollywood for comfort (Wolfgang Molkov's note speaks of it having "quite an inventory of horror-film clichés") but we do not condemn, say, Ravel or Prokofiev, because others have pillaged and polluted their harmonic vocabulary; nor should we Schreker. While recognizably indebted, mainly to Strauss and Puccini, *Irrelohe* as drama with music holds you almost from start to finish. The characters and the vocal lines are drawn with care and the orchestral textures are sumptuous. The only reservation is that although there is a great deal of highly imaginative material and a sophisticated orchestral resource, Schreker's music is predominantly a succession of finely realized atmospheres: melodic inspiration of a strongly individual profile is less in evidence though there are inspired passages – the Prelude to Act 3 is one, though the act as a whole is the least interesting musically. Everything is dramatically effective and indeed masterly. In his thoughtful paper, "Style, Structure and Taste: Three Aspects of the Problem of Franz Schreker" (*Proceedings of the Royal Music Association*: 1982) Peter Franklin speaks of him as "a brilliant musical psychologist whose 'decadence' is a function of the range of experience on which he draws and the skill with which he manages its naturalistic representation in music".

The performance under Peter Gülke is thoroughly committed and the cast is a strong one. The recording derives from a concert performance given in the Grosser Musikvereinsaal in Vienna and although the singers are favoured there is an excellent and well-balanced orchestral detail. The break from the first CD to the second in the middle of the eighth scene of Act 2 is not well chosen but otherwise there is no cause for complaint. Those who know *Der ferne Klang* or *Der Schatzgräber* will probably need no prompting to investigate this set; for those who don't, *Irrelohe* is for the most part a gripping and imaginative score, well served by all involved in this production.

Schreker Der Schatzgräber.

Josef Protschka *ten* Elis
Gabriele Schnaut *sop* Els
Harald Stamm *bass* The King

Peter Haage *ten* The Fool
Hans Helm *bar* Bailiff
Heinz Kruse *ten* Albi
Carl Schultz *bass* Innkeeper
Peter Galliard *ten* Chancellor, Scribe
Urban Malmberg *bar* Count, Herald
Franz Ferdinand Nentwig *bass* Young nobleman
Ude Krekow *bass-bar* Schoolmaster
Dieter Weller *bass* Mayor
Hamburg State Opera Chorus and Orchestra / Gerd Albrecht.
Capriccio Ⓟ Ⓒ 60 010-2 (two discs: 140 minutes: DDD). Notes, text and translation included.
Recorded at performances in the Hamburg State Opera during May and June, 1989.

Of all Schreker's operas (in most of which he followed Wagner's example by writing his own librettos) *Der Schatzgräber* ("The treasure-seeker"), completed on the day after the 1918 armistice and first performed in Frankfurt in 1920, was the most popular, achieving over 350 performances up to the 1924/5 season. With the advent of the "new objectivity" of younger composers like Hindemith and Weill, however, Schreker's opulently-scored, late-romantic works, with their overheated erotic atmosphere, fell from favour; and to the present generation he has become an Interesting Historical Figure whose music is only latterly being rediscovered. The present issue offers the opportunity of studying his very individual style more closely. Two factors in his make-up are of significance: whereas most composers are fired to write their music by the stimulus of a plot or libretto, Schreker worked the other way round, spinning his characters and his text round basic musical ideas (a formidable essay in the booklet of the present recording says much the same thing at considerable length in impenetrably dense and pretentious polysyllabic jargon) and his plots are a strange blend of fantasy, symbolism and *verismo*, often of lurid sexual psychology. Oddly enough, Hindemith's *Mathis der Maler* treats of the same basic problem found not only in *Der Schatzgräber* but in other Schreker operas – the artist's relation to society and his commitment to his craft.

In this case the action hinges on the wandering minstrel, Elis, who owns a magic lute which (like a water-diviner's rod) vibrates in the proximity of gold or treasure, and an innkeeper's daughter, Els, a she-devil who has her suitors killed after persuading them to buy for her, from a fence, a set of jewels stolen from the queen with the magic power of ensuring their wearer eternal youth and beauty. In the course of the action these two fall passionately (and extremely suddenly) in love, Elis is accused of murdering the latest of her bridegrooms, and is saved from the gallows only on the intervention of the king, who has been told by his fool of the lute's investigative power which, he hopes, will locate the queen's prized jewels without which she is wasting away. So that her own guilt shall not be discovered, Els has the lute stolen but, in a torrid love scene, appears before Elis wearing almost nothing but the jewels, and to retain his love gives them to him on condition that he never asks their provenance. So the queen is restored and Elis fêted at court – until he is questioned as to where he found the treasure. The situation becomes tense until news arrives which identifies Els as the criminal: she is condemned to be burnt at the stake, but is saved by the king's jester, who demands her as his reward for having brought about the jewels' return. In an epilogue Elis, who had renounced her to follow his minstrel's calling, is persuaded to visit her on her deathbed, where he conjures up a rosy picture of a life beyond the grave where their love can be untrammelled and everlasting.

As with Wagner, the work's essential continuity lies in the orchestra, to which the vocal lines are more or less an obbligato; and the Hamburg orchestra here has a chance to show its admirable quality in such passages as the melancholy prelude to Act 2, the beautiful lyricism (with off-stage female voices) when Els goes out to don the jewels in Act 3 and the ecstatic impressionist writing later in that act, and in the introduction to the epilogue. The scoring, voluptuous and dramatic as it is, tends to be overlush; and there is a kind of leitmotiv treatment (as at mention of the jewels). Largely seamless as the music is, there are a number of vocal set-pieces – Elis's first ballad, his "delaying song" at the gallows (which turns into an ensemble), the rapturous love duet, Elis's narrative at court and his final vision to the dying Els – but their thematic content obstinately fails to lodge in the mind, and the only melody anyone is likely to come away with is the charming folk-like lullaby (delicately scored) which, in Act 3, Els recalls from her childhood. What is undeniable, however, is the strength of Schreker's dramatic writing, particularly in the gallows scene of Act 2 and the outburst at the festive court in Act 4.

A very positive point in this recording (put together from a run of performances in the Hamburg opera-house) is the clear enunciation of all the cast (who are occasionally overfavoured at the orchestra's expense), only the chorus remaining too far in the background. There is only one female singing role, and one might perhaps surmise that she is a wicked character from Gabriele Schnaut's heavy and wide vibrato – only in the lullaby, where she does not put pressure on the voice, is there respite from this – and from the intensity and number of screeches demanded of her. The others in the cast more than compensate for her failings: Josef Protschka is his usual sensitive and intelligent self, immediately creating sympathy for the hapless Elis, and even at the height of passion incapable of making an ugly sound; Harald Stamm's *voix noble* is well suited to the part of the frustrated king; Hans Helm produces steady and firm tone as the bailiff (a part in which Schreker seems to have lost interest halfway through); and that reliable character tenor, Peter Haage is a bright-voiced jester (perhaps a trifle high-class?). It is unlikely that *Der Schatzgräber* will ever recover its initial popularity, but to those interested in the dying days of romantic German opera it can certainly be recommended.

Franz Schubert   Austrian 1797-1828

Schubert Alfonso und Estrella.

Peter Schreier *ten* Alfonso
Edith Mathis *sop* Estrella
Dietrich Fischer-Dieskau *bar* Troila
Hermann Prey *bar* Mauregato
Theo Adam *bass-bar* Adolfo
Magdalena Falewicz *sop* Girl
Eberhard Büchner *ten* Youth
Horst Gebhardt *ten* Bodyguard leader
Berlin Radio Chorus; Berlin Staatskapelle / Otmar Suitner.
Berlin Classics Ⓟ ⓪ BC2156-2 (three discs: 163 minutes: ADD). Recorded 1978.

On the stage, *Alfonso und Estrella* makes a poor impression, for, as in other of his operas, Schubert's failure to let dramatic demands guide his invention can commit him to numbers and even long ensembles in which fine music works itself out while the plot has to wait. On disc, and especially in so splendidly sung a performance as this one, we can appreciate the beauty of the invention with less concern for a theatrical experience though even in this form, patience can be tested by the sequences of numbers (six at the start, of all places) during which nothing much happens.

For those who can rise above this problem, there is some beautiful music, given its best chance by a cast that could hardly be bettered. There is no spoken dialogue, and though the numbers are sometimes linked, they are not always exactly continuous. Occasionally, Schubert seems about to develop a theme motivically, as with "Von Fels und Wald", when a little anxiety figure trails on into the next movement. Edith Mathis sings this touchingly, and Peter Schreier's elegant tones and graceful phrasing complement her ideally. Dietrich Fischer-Dieskau does much to confer such character as is possible on Troila, and nothing in the work is more touching than the duet between Troila and Mauregato, reconciled enemies, with Fischer-Dieskau and Hermann Prey joining their voices in consummate artistry. Theo Adam has a more straightforward task with the villainous Adolfo, and does splendidly with the rather limp Vengeance aria and especially with the first big number, "Doch im Getümmel", though Otmar Suitner has to work hard to keep the repeated figuration alive. He directs a careful, well-shaped performance, even if he might have made more of Schubert's orchestration, and the chorus sound too much like the ranks of a choral society rather than peasants or soldiers.

The recording comes up well. Walther Dürr's excellent note for the original issue has been replaced by a short, helpful one by Bernd Krispin, and there is a full text with the original EMI translation.

Schubert Fierrabras.

Josef Protschka *ten* Fierrabras
Karita Mattila *sop* Emma
Robert Holl *bass* Charlemagne
Thomas Hampson *bass* Roland
Robert Gambill *ten* Eginhard
László Polgár *bass* Boland
Cheryl Studer *sop* Florinda
Brigitte Balleys *contr* Maragond
Hartmut Welker *bar* Brutamente
Arnold Schönberg Choir; Chamber Orchestra of Europe / Claudio Abbado.
DG Ⓟ ⓪ 427 341-2GH2 (two discs: 144 minutes: DDD). Notes, text and translation included.
Recorded at performances in the Theater an der Wien, Vienna in May 1988.

Schubert began at least 16 operas; he completed only half of them; only one of these was performed in his lifetime; and he seems not to have seen it. It is an extraordinary story, and a melancholy one, as he keeps up the struggle to succeed in the genre where he believed real fame for a composer must lie. There have been persistent attempts to revive them, attempts that usually founder on the realization that the greatest musical gifts cannot make a successful opera if a real dramatic instinct is lacking. Schubert never had the opportunity to see what worked or did not work in his operas on the stage; and his greatest admirers must acknowledge that such features of his style as his marvellous capacity for sustaining a simple musical figure (which can be at the centre of his songs and his symphonic movements) can rule the drama, rather than be overruled by it.

Fierrabras, his last completed opera, is not free of this fault, but the magnificence of the music has prompted attempts at resurrection. Composed in 1823, it did not get a performance until a mangled version was staged in 1897. The 1970s saw greater interest, and there followed the American première in 1980, and the British première in 1986 in Oxford, a suitable enough home for this apparently lost cause. But then along came Claudio Abbado, and his performances of the work in Vienna in May 1988 revealed the work's real power; there was a BBC broadcast, and then this set of discs made from live performances. The actual recording is not ideal, with some poor balance in ensembles, and some rather odd 'biffing' noises; but that is of no account.

The plot of *Fierrabras* is too complex for summary here, but concerns the tangled loves and loyalties of five people caught up in Charlemagne's Moorish wars. It has its awkwardnesses, for Schubert was to an extent as much at the mercy of the fashion for chivalric conventions as was Weber with *Euryanthe*, whose unsuccessful Vienna première, just as Schubert had finished his own work, probably helped to prevent a production of the latter. For all Schubert's dubious view of *Euryanthe*, the two composers can reach similar solutions, perhaps the more readily as *Fierrabras* reflects an admiration for *Der Freischütz*. There is the Singspiel basis, with use of melodrama, and a melodic manner that probably acknowledges the Viennese reputation of Cherubini as well as that of Weber. But the style is always Schubert's. The arias, including the more song-like ones, are of a different cut to his Lieder (even to the scena-like early Lieder). The choruses, among them the beautiful unaccompanied "O teures Vaterland", reflect his understanding of ensemble singing gained in youth, and are here splendidly handled especially in the scenes where they divide into opposed groups: Abbado makes of these, notably in Act 2, some of the most exciting parts of the opera. Schubert's orchestral writing, too, is marvellously effective, both in using his symphonic strengths to build up tension and in some beautiful and entirely personal strokes, such as in the Act 1 duet, "Der Abend sinkt" when Eginhard's sorrowful A minor serenade, with clarinet obbligato, is answered by Emma turning the music consolingly to the major, with the obbligato now on flute.

Robert Gambill sings the part strongly, if not as tenderly as he might; Karita Mattila is a touching Emma. Fierrabras himself, the young Moorish hero, is finely taken by Josef Protschka; the Moorish King and his principal Christian adversary, who are regrettably called Boland and Roland, are sung with suitably sustained vigour by László Polgár and Thomas Hampson. Boland's daughter, Florinda and her companion, Maragond have one of the most beautiful numbers in the score, the Act 2 duet "Weit über Glanz"; it is charmingly done by Cheryl Studer and Brigitte Balleys. Robert Holl delivers authoritatively as Charlemagne. This is not, it will be seen, a star-studded cast, but it is a well-unified one, not least by virtue of Abbado's powerful control of the work and a belief in it that is evident at every turn.

A word of praise must be found for the accompanying booklet. Elizabeth Norman McKay provides an excellent introduction for English readers; but those who have German will also gain much from Sigrid Neef's long, thorough and perceptive account of the work's genesis and nature. There is also a good Italian article by Sergio Sablich, especially concerning the stylistic tradition, but French collectors deserve better than Rémy Stricker's perfunctory essay. Full texts are provided (complete with the linking dialogue which is not recorded here) in these four languages: the English version by Lionel Salter skilfully negotiates some awkward corners on the singing translation for the Oxford production. In sum, this does splendid justice to Schubert's last opera and, for all its faults, the nearest he came to writing a masterpiece for the stage.

Schubert Die Verschworenen, oder Der häusliche Krieg.
Soile Isokoski *sop* Countess Ludmilla
Peter Lika *bass* Count Heribert von Lüdenstein
Rodrigo Orrego *ten* Astolf von Reisenberg
Andreas Fischer *ten* Garold von Nummen
Christian Dahm *bass* Friedrich von Trausdorf
Thomas Pfützner *bass* Knight
Mechthild Georg *mez* Udolin
Anke Hoffmann *sop* Isella
Lisa Larsson *sop* Helene
Susanne Behnes *sop* Luitgarde
Marion Steingötter *sop* Camilla
Iris Kupke *sop* Woman
Chorus Musicus; Das Neue Orchester / Christoph Spering.
Opus 111 Ⓔ Ⓓ OPS30-167 (64 minutes: DDD). 🎵 Notes, text and translation included.
Recorded 1996.

The Viennese dramatist, Ignaz Castelli, wrote *Die Verschworenen* ("The Conspirators") as a riposte to complaints that there were no good German librettos. "Here's one", he proclaimed in his preface. And his neatly wrought text, loosely based on Aristophanes' *Lysistrata*, prompted, early in 1823, Schubert's most dramatically viable stage-work, a one-act Singspiel which would make an entertaining double-bill in the theatre with, say, Mendelssohn's *Heimkehr aus der Fremde*. Aristophanes' story of aggrieved womenfolk withholding their favours until their husbands abandoned their warmongering is transposed here to Vienna during the Crusades and softened with a liberal injection of Biedermeier sentiment. Schubert's parodistic martial music for the macho warriors can occasionally grow wearisome, especially in the finale. Otherwise, though, he scarcely puts a foot wrong. His dramatic pacing is sure and lively, his invention witty, touching and colourful, with its intermittent echoes of Mozart (shades of the Queen of Night's final assault on Sarastro's temple, for instance, in the mock-portentous women's 'conspiracy' chorus, No. 4) and its nods to Rossini, whose music was all the rage in post-Congress Vienna.

The opera's gem is Helene's bittersweet F minor *Romanze*, with its sinuous clarinet obbligato (beautifully played here) and haunting modulation to the major in the very last bars. If this had found its way into the Peters edition of Schubert Lieder, like the *Romanze* from *Rosamunde*, it would surely be world-famous. Elsewhere, the duet for Astolf and Helene, No. 8, again with obbligato clarinet, has the mellifluous grace and innocence of some of the *Schöne Müllerin* songs; the ensemble where the page, Udolin, spills the beans on the women's conspiracy (No. 6) is a delicious piece of quicksilver comic writing; and towards the end the Countess taunts the Count by wittily parodying his self-glorying *Ariette*, No. 9, in a different key.

With his polished orchestra and fresh-toned chorus Christoph Spering gives a sympathetic, shrewdly paced account of the score, allowing the lyrical numbers plenty of breathing space and revealing a light, pointed touch in the comic ensembles. Of the singers, Peter Lika's Count has plenty of 'face', though his bass can become coarse under pressure. Rodrigo Orrego, as the knight Astolf, displays an agreeable, soft-grained tenor; and all four principal female roles are well taken, with Lisa Larsson showing a bright, pure tone and a shapely sense of phrase as Helene, and Soile Isokoski bringing real distinction to the role of the Countess, her warm, vibrant soprano, with its hint of mezzo richness and depth, more than once reminding you of Schwarzkopf. The recording is vivid and well balanced, giving ample presence to the voices while allowing Schubert's felicitous scoring its due. There is a thoughtful note by Ulrich Schreiber (perhaps over-ingenious in its exploration of the opera's implied meanings) and a reasonably idiomatic translation of the libretto, though a summary of the omitted spoken dialogue would have clarified one or two key points in the action. Warmly recommended to anyone who fancies an hour of mature Schubert at his most debonair and convivial.

Robert Schumann
German 1810-1856

Schumann Genoveva.
Ruth Ziesak *sop* Genoveva
Deon van der Walt *ten* Golo
Rodney Gilfry *bar* Hidulfus
Oliver Widmer *bar* Siegfried
Marjana Lipovšek *mez* Margaretha
Thomas Quasthoff *bar* Drago
Hiroyuki Ijichi *bass* Balthasar
Josef Krenmair *bar* Caspar
Arnold Schoenberg Choir; Chamber Orchestra of Europe / Nikolaus Harnoncourt.
Teldec Ⓟ Ⓞ 0630-13144-2 (two discs: 128 minutes: DDD). Notes, text and translation included.
Recorded during performances in the Stefaniensaal, Graz between June 27th-30th, 1996.

The medieval legend of Geneviève, wrongfully accused of adultery during her husband's absence at the Crusades, was much in the air in Schumann's day through strikingly contrasted retellings of the tale by Tieck and Hebbel – plus a tender painting of the exiled lady from Ludwig Richter. Though preparation of a composite libretto posed many problems, Schumann still hailed the subject, with its eventual triumph of good over evil, as an answer to a prayer for the German opera he had so long yearned to write. But the delayed 1850 Leipzig première proved only a *succès d'estime* as the mounting tension of the first two acts ceded to black magic in the third and an all-too-last-minute happy ending. No opera-house has since adopted it as a regular repertory work despite such gallant restagings as Liszt's at Weimar the year before Schumann's death, and Stanford's English première, with students of the Royal College of Music, in 1893. Schumann lovers can nevertheless take heart from a steadily increasing number of concert revivals, of which Harnoncourt's recording comes from live performances at the Graz Stefaniensaal in 1996.

"It's the critics themselves who deserve to be condemned for not seeing what's on offer here", so Harnoncourt writes in passionate defence of the work in the lavish accompanying booklet (with full libretto in English and French as well as German). Not for him any doubts about the scenario itself which so displeased Wagner when first shown it, nor about insufficiently contrasted musical characterization bewailed by subsequent critics, including Hanslick and Bernard Shaw. He values Schumann's freer, more interchangeable use of leitmotiv rather than as Wagnerian "luggage-labels", as the underlying source of unity in the score as a whole, to him first and foremost "a great symphony with voices". And therein lies the clue to what we hear.

The Chamber Orchestra of Europe respond wholeheartedly to his every demand – just now and again outweighing the singers in unfolding the story. It's certainly a formidable rival for Ruth Ziesak in the title-role. While luminous enough in the upper register of her two extended prayers for help, her innocently girlish, pure-toned soprano still lacks the strength and intensity of projection for moments of heightened drama such as rejection of her would-be seducer in Act 2, and joyous reunion with her husband in the last. The conductor's preference for singers with Lieder as well as operatic leanings, in deference to Schumann's abhorrence of all vocal histrionics, is particularly clear in casting of the shameful Golo himself. Deon van der Walt's liquid lyricism and musical sensitivity would melt the heart of a stone – not least in the all-revealing *sehr innig* confessions of his first-act monologue. But he conveys the pathos of unrequited love more persuasively than its sinister undertones. After the booklet's disparaging dismissal of Count Siegfried as an obtuse "petit bourgeois", it's good to encounter a younger and more impulsively romantic crusader than expected from Oliver Widmer in his carefree third-act, "Soon I'll see you again, my castle and home" (his only big chance), with feeling to match in subsequent pain and joy. Thomas Quasthoff in his turn offers a fresh-toned Drago, plausible enough as a possible lover rather than the conventional, dutiful old retainer far too wizened for the wars. And the insinuating words of the wicked Margaretha are piquantly savoured by Marjana Lipovšek without a trace of the pantomime witch so risible to Shaw at the English première.

As concessions to stage action, Harnoncourt distances the supernatural voices of Margaretha's magic mirror and the murdered Drago's ghost in Act 3 as conscientiously as he does his receding knights, or approaching squires and villagers (the admirable Schoenberg Choir) in the more ceremonial happenings of the first and last acts. But if driven to persuade any opera-house of the work's full dramatic potential, you would have to choose Kurt Masur's graphic old LP recording with Moser, Fischer-Dieskau and Schreier (never widely available in England). There is also a 1992 concert version from that excitable, even if sometimes breathlessly urgent, man of the theatre, Gerd Albrecht on Orfeo. Until the long-overdue stage revival eventually comes, many thanks to Harnoncourt for a searching, continuously evolving "symphony with voices", opening all ears anew to many purely musical subtleties and beauties.

Rodion Shchedrin
USSR 1932

Shchedrin Dead Souls.

Alexander Voroshilo *bar* Pavel Ivanovich Chichikov
Vladislav Pyavko *ten* Nozdryov
Larisa Avdeyeva *mez* Korobochka
Boris Morozov *bass* Sobakevich
Galina Borisova *mez* Plyushkin
Vitaly Vlasov *ten* Manilov
Alexei Maslennikov *ten* Selifan
Nina Larionova *mez* Lizanka Manilova
Vladimir Filippov *bass* Mizhuyev
Moscow Chamber Chorus;
Chorus and Orchestra of the Bolshoi Theatre, Moscow / Yuri Temirkanov.
Melodiya Ⓜ ① 74321 29347-2 (two discs: 130 minutes: ADD). Notes, text and translation included. Recorded 1982.

Yuri Temirkanov has described *Dead Souls* as the greatest opera of the twentieth century. Truth to tell, it is far from that. But it certainly is a fascinating, intermittently even a compelling work, and it's easy to see how it could inspire such a hyperbolic reaction.

Dead Souls was the big talking-point of the Bolshoi's 1977 season and, as with so many major events in Soviet music, the circumstances surrounding it gave the participants plenty to tell the grandchildren. According to the composer, Temirkanov travelled from Leningrad to Moscow 32 times to conduct it for no fee apart from his train fare; one of the 30 or so minor soloists, who had been the lover of Brezhnev's daughter, somehow fell foul of the authorities and disappeared off the face of the earth, so that his name had to be expunged from credits for the Melodiya LPs; almost as bizarrely, since *perestroika* Alexander Voroshilo (the phenomenal baritone in the main role of Chichikov) has given up singing and gone into business manufacturing spicy sausages.

Shchedrin worked on *Dead Souls* for ten years, apparently without heed to the practicalities of staging. The word *apparently* should be stressed, because unlike Schnittke, Gubaidulina and their associates, Shchedrin was at pains to keep his liberalism within the bounds of official acceptability. The success of his opera was not clouded by official displeasure. His score is an exercise in musical mayhem – frankly sensationalist, and from moment to moment rather enjoyable. It is always talented, often effective, yet in the long run irksome. At times its main aim seems to be to live up to the infamous *Pravda* "Muddle instead of Music" article on Shostakovich's *Lady Macbeth* ("the music quacks, grunts, growls and suffocates itself ... "); except that the pretext here is not sex and violence but a grotesquerie bordering on the Theatre of the Absurd.

The story is of Chichikov's attempts to gain social status by buying up the names of dead peasants, and of his consequential encounters with a succession of more or less barmy serf-owning gentry. As such it has been a favourite with the Russian intelligentsia, on the one hand for its observations of the eternal vanities and foibles of provincial Russians, on the other for its virtuosic use of language. Shchedrin's setting stands in a direct line from the other great Gogol operas – Shostakovich's *The Nose* and before that Mussorgsky's *The Marriage* and *Sorochintsky Fair* – without rising to their level of subtlety and control. One of his best ideas is to graft on a kind of anti-running-commentary in the shape of pseudo-folksongs, sung in ethnic open-throated manner by two female soloists supported by chamber choir who take the place of the violins in the orchestra pit. There is a certain psychedelic *frisson* when this music periodically intervenes, setting off Chichikov's various encounters with a level of far from self-explanatory allegory.

From a literary point of view, the opera was criticized after the première for having added a layer of gratuitous optimism to Gogol's tale. It's difficult to see where anyone could have heard such a thing (maybe the original staging had something to do with it). A far greater obstacle to the opera's staying power is the diminishing returns of its relentless casual extremism. That impression is heightened by a recording which was high on impact even on the 1982 Melodiya LPs, and which in its digitally remastered form is now even more overpowering. Every detail of the virtuosically intense performance comes across. Apart from the daunting vocal range negotiated with apparent ease by Voroshilo's Chichikov, you can savour Boris Morozov's Sobakevich, with a *basso profundo* sounding rather like an articulated burp, and a cameo for two horrendously bitchy 'pleasant ladies', during which the Bolshoi's principal bassoonist also does a star turn.

Temirkanov's evident belief in the opera helps to make this recording an extraordinary document. Savour it by all means, but don't expect a masterpiece.

Dmitry Shostakovich   USSR 1906-1975

Shostakovich The Gamblers (cptd K. Meyer).
Vladimir Bogachev *ten* Ikharyov
Anatoli Babikin *bass* Gavryushka
Stanislav Suleymanov *bass* Uteshityelny
Alexander Naumenko *bass* Shvokhnyev
Alexander Arkhipov *ten* Krugel
Nikolai Nizienko *bass* Alexey
Mikhail Krutikov *bass* Mikhayl Glov
Vladislav Verestnikov *bar* Alexander Glov
Alexei Maslennikov *ten* Zamukhrishkin
North-West German Philharmonic Orchestra / Mikhail Yurovsky.
Capriccio Ⓟ Ⓒ 60 062-2 (two discs: 136 minutes: DDD). Notes, text and translation included. Recorded 1993.

Despite the *Lady Macbeth* affair, which blighted his career as an opera composer, Shostakovich harboured plans for new stage works virtually to the end of his life. Some of them were probably smokescreens to keep officials at bay; some never made it beyond the drawing-board; but others, like *The Gamblers*, which occupied him in late 1941 and 1942, just after the *Leningrad* Symphony, very nearly came to fruition.

For a composer with Shostakovich's literary and human awareness of life and letters it was always going to be difficult to find a text that would pass socialist-realist muster and yet still be worth setting. Gogol's play (not the Dostoyevsky story set by Prokofiev as *The Gambler*) gives a Russian slant to the standard 'Deceiver Outwitted' comedy. Although it could be read allegorically (what story can't?) its attraction for Shostakovich was presumably just in the plot's layers of deceitfulness, plus the chance it offered him to relax from the pressures of wartime patriotism.

That of course would also be one reason why an eventual production was unlikely and why Shostakovich broke off the composition near the end of Act 1. Another was that he had chosen to work without a libretto and to set Gogol's text word by word. He had also given himself something of a problem by starting with a couple of inspired themes in the orchestral introduction (one of which he would turn to again for the second movement of his Viola Sonata). The surviving music for *The Gamblers* does suggest that he was up to the considerable challenge of pacing and variety, but the prospect of a final duration of some four-and-a-half hours finally persuaded him to abandon the project, at almost exactly the time that the Polish composer-to-be Krzysztof Meyer was born.

Meyer befriended Shostakovich in the mid-1960s, and in 1979 he produced one of the more reliable biographies of his idol (recently revised and translated into French – Paris, Fayard: 1994). In the early-1980s he was commissioned by Wuppertal Opera to produce a completion of *The Gamblers*, which he did by a mixture of very clever pastiche and allusions to the existing music of the opera as well as to half a dozen other Shostakovich works (notably *Lady Macbeth* and the Third, Fourth and Seventh Symphonies). Judicious cutting of the text kept the whole thing within bounds – two hours 16 minutes on this, the first recording of the complete work.

It is a very plausible completion. Granted it may not solve the inherent problems of the *Literaturoper* (one without a purpose-built libretto), and once in a while the musical semi-quotations do sound intrusive. The very end is rather a let-down. But on the whole the style is extremely convincing. So would you listen for pleasure? Hmm, tricky. There is a threshold between admiration and enjoyment, and maybe you have to be Russian born and bred to cross it in this instance, just as you have to be, almost certainly, with Mussorgsky's *Marriage* or Prokofiev's *The Gambler*.

Certainly there is pleasure to be had from the orchestral playing; all credit to Mikhail Yurovsky for keeping his players on the ball. Also the recording is excellently balanced and the singing never less than competent (though Vladimir Bogachev overprojects in the main role of Ikharyov, the card-sharp, and the constant dark Slavonic male timbre does get a bit oppressive). Minor drawbacks in the presentation are that the Russian text appears in a different booklet from the German and English translations and that what might have been an informative essay about the opera turns out to be little more than a long-winded waffle about the ethics and aesthetics of Meyer's completion.

Such deficiencies need not deter anyone who wants a full picture of Shostakovich's creative life; on the other hand the strengths of the work are maybe not so conspicuous as to put this near the top of the priority list for the general listener.

Shostakovich Lady Macbeth of the Mtsensk District.

Galina Vishnevskaya *sop* Katerina Lvovna Izmailova
Nicolai Gedda *ten* Sergey Dubrovin
Dimiter Petkov *bass* Boris Timofeyevich Izmailov
Werner Krenn *ten* Zinovy Borisovich Izmailov
Robert Tear *ten* Russian peasant
Taru Valjakka *sop* Aksinya
Martyn Hill *ten* Teacher
Leonard Mróz *bass* Priest
Aage Haugland *bass* Police Sergeant
Birgit Finnilä *mez* Sonyetka
Alexander Malta *bass* Old convict
Leslie Fyson *ten* Millhand, Officer
Steven Emmerson *bass* Porter
John Noble *bar* Steward
Colin Appleton *ten* Coachman, First foreman
Alan Byers *bar* Second foreman
James Lewington *ten* Third foreman
Oliver Broome *bass* Policeman
Edgar Fleet *ten* Drunken guest
David Beaven *bass* Sentry
Lynda Richardson *mez* Female convict
Ambrosian Opera Chorus; London Philharmonic Orchestra / Mstislav Rostropovich.
EMI Ⓟ Ⓒ CDS7 49955-2 (two discs: 155 minutes: ADD). Notes text and translation included. Recorded 1978.

Despite how one can fulminate against the ludicrous expurgations that transformed the 1934 *Lady Macbeth of the Mtsensk District* into the *Katerina Izmailova* of 1962, it is good to have both versions available. The latter has two substantially revised and interesting orchestral interludes and a number of considerably modified vocal lines in its favour; the former has that notoriously explicit interlude in Act 1 which Shostakovich removed in 1962 (if one were writing for a less grave publication than this one might call it the bonking interlude), and it has the libretto that he originally set. Of no great significance to non-Russian speakers, you might say, since the music is for the most part otherwise identical, but the 1962 emasculations are so extensive that they alter the very colour of the work, as though every reference to Jokanaan's head were to be removed from Salome. In this latter respect, mark you, Rostropovich himself makes one rather curious little excision in the scene after that interlude: "Now I have no husband but you" says Katerina to Sergey, to which he sniggeringly replies "All the women say that – especially the married ones". Rostropovich cuts this, and an irony is lost: in the first scene of the following act Katerina's father-in-law licks his lips over memories of his youthful whoring after other men's wives in terms very similar to Sergey's: male chauvinist piggery is the opera's leitmotiv.

Vishnevskaya's portrayal of Katerina is a bit too three-dimensional, you might think at times, especially when the recording, which favours the singers in any case, seems because of her bright and forceful tone, with its sharpish edge above the stave, to place her rather closer to you than the rest of the cast. But there is no doubt in her performance that Katerina is the opera's heroine, not just its focal character, and in any case Gedda's genially rapacious Sergey, Petkov's grippingly acted Boris, Krenn's weedy Zinovy, Mróz's sonorous Priest, even Valjakka in the tiny role of Aksinya (earthily pungent, and how right that she should laugh chubbily in her first scene!) all refuse to be upstaged. The 'minor' parts are luxuriously cast from artists who may not have had the advantage of singing their roles on stage but have clearly relished building them into vivid portraits. The close focusing on the voices and the relative distancing of the orchestra into a warmer, more ample acoustic is a bit more noticeable on CD than it was on LP; no complaints otherwise.

Bedřich Smetana

Smetana The bartered bride.

Gabriela Beňačková *sop* Mařenka
Peter Dvorský *ten* Jeník
Miroslav Kopp *ten* Vašek
Richard Novák *bass* Kecal
Jindřich Jindrák *bar* Krušina
Marie Mrázová *contr* Háta
Jaroslav Horáček *bass* Mícha
Marie Veselá *sop* Ludmila
Jana Jonášová *sop* Esmeralda
Alfréd Hampel *ten* Circus Master
Karel Hanuš *bass* Indian
Czech Philharmonic Chorus and Orchestra / Zdeněk Košler.
Supraphon Ⓟ Ⓒ 10 3511-2 (three discs: 137 minutes: ADD). Notes, text and translation included.
Recorded 1980-81.

For all its conquest of world repertories, there is something particular about a Czech performance of *The bartered bride* and this one is no exception. Not the least of it is the orchestral playing. Like any Czech conductor worth his salt, Zdeněk Košler has the rhythm and lilt of the music in his bones; but he has also thought the work out afresh, and leads the players into a performance of captivating freshness. The Overture is far from being the usual sensation-mongering scramble which we have had to endure from various Western maestros ('My violins can play faster than your violins'), but has a marvellous gaiety and lift, yet also a hint of the melancholy which runs through the work. Košler touches on this without solemnity, but it comes through time and again, especially of course with Mařenka. The Czech Philharmonic have long had one of the finest of all woodwind sections, and especially in this music they play with a sense of their instruments' folk background – there is a deliciously resiny clarinet – and with phrasing that springs from deep in Czech folk-music. The strings yield nothing to the most brilliant Western ensemble, and there is a proud timpanist.

All this sets the musical scene for some tender and touching performances. Even old Kecal comes to new life, not as the conventional Czech village bumbler, but as a human character in his own right as Richard Novák portrays him – quite put out, the old boy is, to find his plans gone astray. Miroslav Kopp makes a touching portrayal of Vašek, delivering the first stammering song with an innocence well on the right side of the ridiculous, responding to the muddled relationship with Mařenka in a state of light emotional confusion, and thoroughly enjoying his bear episode. He is clearly much better off with Jana Jonášová's bright-voiced Esmeralda, at any rate while the circus is in town.

Gabriela Beňačková begins a little heavily as Mařenka, but the warm, lyrical quality of her voice can lighten easily to encompass the character's tenderness in the first duet, "Věrné milováni", or "Faithful love", the considerable show of spirit she makes when Jeník seems to have gone off the rails, and her final rapture. Her Act 1 lament is most beautifully sung. Peter Dvorský plays lightly with the score, as he should, or the character's maintaining of the deception can come to seem merely cruel. But he delivers his love-song, "Až užiž", with great tenderness, and delivers a spirited duet with Kecal in Act 2. The chorus enjoy themselves hugely, never more so than in the Beer chorus.

Altogether a delightful, touching and warming performance: the booklet has the text in Czech, English, French and German, with an interesting essay by Hana Séquardová.

Smetana The bartered bride.

Ludmila Cervinková *sop* Mařenka
Beno Blachut *ten* Jeník
Rudolf Vonásek *ten* Vašek
Karel Kalaš *bass* Kecal
Ladislav Mráz *bar* Krušina
Věra Krilová *contr* Háta
Josef Heriban *bass* Mícha
Jarmila Palivcová *sop* Ludmila
Jarmila Pechová *sop* Esmeralda
Bohumíl Vich *ten* Circus Master
Jan Soumar *bass* Indian
Prague Radio Chorus and Symphony Orchestra / Karel Ančerl.
Multisonic mono Ⓜ Ⓒ 310185-2 (two discs: 120 minutes: AAD). Recorded 1947.

In *Opera on Record 3* (Hutchinson: 1983), Peter Tanner in his chapter on this opera commented that it was a shame Blachut never recorded the role of Jeník complete, only extracts in the 1940s. As yet another boon which arose after the opening of Eastern Europe radio archives, we can indeed hear him in the complete role, when he was in his prime, in 1947. As one would expect, he fills it not only with plangent tone but also with lyrical feeling; and his voice has just the weight the part calls for. His attention to dynamic markings and innate ability to phrase with meaning make him a near-ideal Jeník. The performance also preserves the endearing Kecal of Kalaš, one of the role's most grateful interpreters on disc, striking an apt balance between character and true singing. Without ever exaggerating expression he projects all the old rogue's mercenary instincts and love of manipulation. In addition, his tone is consistently round and firm: again, one can hardly imagine the part better done. Vonásek, another regular Czech artist of the period, finds the right sense of charm and vulnerability for Vašek, a role for which his tenor and style are ideally suited.

The drawback to the performance is the unsteady, far too mature Mařenka of Cervinková, who sounds more like Jeník's mother than his fiancée. She provides some consolation through her expressive phrasing and – of course – her command of the language, but it isn't enough to make us forget her vocal weaknesses. The smaller parts are adequately taken. Over all presides Ančerl, who offers a rousing interpretation of the wonderful music, vital in the biting rhythms that pervade the score, never exploiting the work's tendency towards the sentimental and persuading his Prague Radio forces to give of their appreciable best.

The recording is acceptable mono, but deteriorates, as the booklet tells us, in Act 3 where the original material has been damaged. While this issue is most welcome, what would be even more appreciated on CD is the classic Supraphon recording of 1952 (reissued by Rediffusion in 1977).

Smetana The Brandenburgers in Bohemia.

Karel Kalaš *bass* Volfram Olbramovič
Jiří Joran *bar* Oldřich Rokycanský
Milada Subrtová *sop* Ludiše
Ivo Zídek *ten* Junoš
Zdeněk Otava *bar* Jan Tausendmark
Antonín Votava *ten* Varneman
Bohumil Vich *ten* Jíra
Miloslava Fiedlerová *sop* Vlčenka
Věra Soukupová *mez* Děčena
Eduard Haken *bass* Old villager
Jindřich Jindrák *bar* Town crier
Prague National Theatre Chorus and Orchestra / Jan Hus Tichý.
Supraphon Ⓟ Ⓒ 11 1804-2 (two discs: 149 minutes: AAD). Notes, text and translation included. Recorded 1963.

It is not hard to point to the defects of Smetana's first opera; they cannot be denied, but especially in a vigorous, committed performance such as this, which makes emotional sense of gestures that often look rather tame on paper, they can be happily accepted. The best of the work is remarkably original: but Smetana also handles with a good deal of verve the parts that are evidently not original. He calls in help from Italian opera and the *concertato* convention for the cumulative finale to Act 1, but sets it splendidly to service; reinforcements are summoned from France for choral prayers, but the Parisian Grand Opera example is transcended in some of the finest set pieces in the work as the chorus becomes the Bohemian people and the orchestra add subtle, flexible dramatic comment.

Given the fact that the opera was the first fruit of the prize offered by Count Harrach so as to find the new Czech Provisional Theatre a repertory, it is natural for the plot to be patriotic. It deals with a thirteenth-century struggle when Bohemia was occupied by the forces of Brandenburg, and with some of the personal tragedies that ensued. These centre on the plight of Ludiše, sung with a good feeling for the lyrical line of her music by Milada Subrtová, who is abducted by a Prague burgher with the suitably mercenary name of Tausendmark. His part is uncertainly written, and Zdeněk Otava does his best to suggest villainy out of slightly indistinct material: Smetana gives him a lyrical aria without having the experience to make this enlarge his character rather than confuse it (in fairness, this was under pressure from the singer). The hero and Ludiše's lover is Junoš, sung with a fine ardour by Ivo Zídek, and the Prague 'beggar king' Jíra is nicely handled by Bohumil Vich.

The recording also has shortcomings which are worth bearing with. Made in 1963, it cannot easily accommodate the choruses which are so important, and there are places where the interaction of orchestra and voices is dramatically ineffective. Jan Hus Tichý clearly has a strong feeling for the work, as does the entire cast, but there are slips in ensemble. However, this reissue of a long-vanished set is a very welcome collectors' item, especially since performances, even in Czechoslovakia, are rare.

Smetana Dalibor.

Leo Marian Vodička *ten* Dalibor
Ivan Kusnjer *bar* Vladislav
Eva Urbanová *sop* Milada
Vratislav Kříž *bar* Budivoj
Jiří Kalendocský *bass* Beneš
Miroslav Kopp *ten* Vítek

Jiřina Marková *sop* Jitka
Bohumil Maršík *bass* Judge
Prague National Theatre Chorus and Orchestra / Zdeněk Košler.
Supraphon Ⓟ Ⓒ SU0077-2 (two discs: 155 minutes: DDD). Notes, text and translation included.
Recorded 1995.

With Jaroslav Krombholc's 1967 *Dalibor*, also on Supraphon, then the only version currently available in the domestic catalogue, a modern recording was overdue. The work has had an almost sacramental meaning for politically oppressed Czechs, with its story of a hero struggling to free himself from tyrannical imprisonment through the agency of a girl who makes her way into his cell disguised as a boy. There, the often-made comparisons with *Fidelio* cease, even though both operas have been staged at moments of national liberation. It has not been particularly popular outside its native country, and is less immediately beguiling than a number of Smetana's other operas; but it includes some of his finest music, and the atmosphere of nobility surviving in the face of tyranny is well sustained, with some splendid writing for the two main parts.

These are well taken by Leo Marian Vodička and Eva Urbanová. Vodička sings with a heroic intensity that can embrace the defiant (of his judges) and the impassioned: Dalibor's concerns seem often to centre on his dead comrade-in-arms, Zdeněk, but his almost instant love-duet with Milada, when she appears bearing a violin for his consolation, is warmly sung by them both. Urbanová's voice can have an edge, but she controls it well, phrases very sympathetically, and judges Milada's turn from avenging termagant to rescuing lover with much intelligence. The old gaoler, Beneš, is charmingly sung by Jiří Kalendocský, especially as he muses on the grimness of his trade. Ivan Kusnjer and Vratislav Kříž boom away effectively as King Vladislav and his Commandant Budivoj, and there is some nice, fresh singing from Jiřina Marková as the country girl Jitka. The orchestra play splendidly for Zdeněk Košler, who handles the score gravely but with the flexibility it needs if the action is to be clarified and the momentum sustained: there have been performances which have made a work which is actually very fluently composed sound far too static.

The booklet includes the original German text, together with the standard Czech translation which is naturally sung here. It has some odd misaccentuations, including Dalibor's very first word, "zapírat" (to deny), heftily on the second syllable in a language whose accents always fall on the first. This will hardly trouble foreign listeners; but matching the rhymes of German and Czech in the English libretto lead to misleadingly free translation, not to mention some weird locutions. Cries the infuriated Milada, "Shall I now see him? / My brother's foe? / Blood boils in me / From head to toe." The French translation sensibly avoids rhyme.

Smetana The Devil's Wall.

Václav Bednář *bass* Vok Vítkovic
Ivana Mixová *mez* Záviš Vítkovic
Ivo Zídek *ten* Jarek
Milada Subrtová *sop* Hedvika
Antonín Votava *ten* Michálek
Libuše Domanínská *sop* Katuška
Karel Berman *bass* Beneš
Ladislav Mráz *bar* Rarach
Prague National Theatre Chorus and Orchestra / Zdeněk Chalabala.
Supraphon Ⓟ Ⓒ 11 2201-2 (two discs: 136 minutes: AAD). Notes, text and translation included.
Recorded 1960.

The title refers to a group of strangely shaped rocks projecting from the Vltava, according to legend set there by the Devil so as to form a dam and flood the surrounding land. The thwarting of the diabolical plan is the climax of an opera whose plot defies summary; and its complexities are compounded by the Devil, Rarach, appearing from time to time in the guise of the hermit Beneš, a monk on the side of the angels but whose motives throughout the opera are by no means disinterested. Never mind: in among the twists and turns of this 'comic-romantic' opera there is to be found some enchanting and original music; and there is one very endearing characterization, that of Vok Vítkovic, the ageing Lord of Rosenberg, whose heart is finally warmed by Hedvika, the young daughter of the woman who once rejected him. The theme of love found late touched something in Smetana, and had done so before in *The Two Widows* and *The Kiss*: here, Vok is given some warm and affecting music, to which Václav Bednář does full justice.

Not all the music, written in Smetana's dreadful last years, is of this quality, but there is more than enough to earn this reissue of a now fairly ancient recording. The sound quality is in fact remarkably good, and accommodates most of the orchestral subtleties without trouble. These include some highly dramatic descriptions, as well as various more perfunctory ceremonial passages. Libuše Domanínská and Ivo Zídek, then in their mid thirties, have stronger music individually than as a couple, but they sing it delightfully: Jarek's first aria and Katuška's apostrophe opening Scene 2 should be enough to persuade any listener with a love for Smetana's music to persevere beyond the tedious *buffo* posturings of Michálek, with which Antonín Votava does his best. Milada Subrtová is rather less striking as

Hedvika, the girl whose heroism eventually softens Vok's heart; Ladislav Mráz and Karel Berman contend strongly as the forces of, respectively, darkness and light. Zdeněk Chalabala conducts with evident devotion to a score which this recording can persuade one is undervalued. The set includes a full text in Czech, German, French and awkward but serviceable English.

Smetana The Kiss.

Eduard Haken *bass* Paloucký
Eva Děpoltová *sop* Vendulka
Leo Marian Vodička *ten* Lukáš
Václav Zítek *bar* Tomeš
Libuše Márová *mez* Martinka
Karel Hanuš *bass* Matovš
Božena Effenberková *sop* Barče
Zdeněk Jankovský *ten* Guard
Brno Janáček Opera Chorus and Orchestra / František Vajnar.
Supraphon Ⓟ Ⓒ 11 2180-2 (two discs: 112 minutes: ADD). Notes, text and translation included.
Recorded 1980.

The Kiss turns on the slenderest of ideas, the reluctance of Vendulka to affront the memory of her betrothed Lukáš's deceased wife by accepting his kiss before their own wedding, and their eventual reconciliation. Yet although this was the first opera Smetana wrote after deafness descended on him, it proved one of his warmest and most appealing works, and the absence of much in the way of incident allows him to paint some of his most affecting portraits of simple but honest and good-hearted characters. Eva Děpoltová makes a touching Vendulka, with her initial hesitations over the kiss made part of her truthfulness of nature, and her warmth coming strongly to the fore by the close; she sings the two lullabies affectingly. Leo Marian Vodička has the ardour and impatience for Lukáš, and can command both a fine impassioned ring in the higher register and shade his tone for the melancholy reflections; he and Václav Zítek do splendidly by their duet, as the gloomy bridegroom is reassured by his friend that all need not be lost if he comes to his senses and brings himself to ask forgiveness for his rough behaviour.

There are perceptive performances of the various minor characters who surround this little village drama. Martinka, Vendulka's old aunt, sounds firm and sensible rather than merely formidable in Libuše Márová's vigorous portrayal, and there is a touching contribution from Božena Effenberková, who makes the most of one of the opera's most popular numbers, the lively little song about the skylark. Karel Hanuš adds a suitable touch of slightly eccentric comedy in the sub-plot about the smugglers. And there is Eduard Haken. He was 70 when this recording was made in 1980, but sounds in fine fettle as he presides with a good deal of grumpiness over the young lovers' betrothal and finally gives Lukáš his somewhat tetchy blessing for the sake of a quiet life. František Vajnar supervises these events with affection for a score that invites the warmest affection. The recording is vivid and well rounded, and the booklet includes text and translations into English, German and French.

Smetana Libuše.

Gabriela Beňačková *sop* Libuše
Václav Zítek *ten* Přemysl
Antonín Svorc *bass* Chrudoš
Leo Marian Vodička *ten* Stáhlav
Karel Průša *bass* Lutobor
René Tuček *bar* Radovan
Eva Děpoltová *sop* Krasava
Věra Soukupová *mez* Radmila
Prague National Theatre Chorus and Orchestra / Zdeněk Košler.
Supraphon Ⓟ Ⓒ 11 1276-2 (three discs: 166 minutes: DDD). Notes, text and translation included.
Recorded at a performance in the National Theatre, Prague on November 18th, 1983.

Libuše is, by virtue of its subject and treatment, unlikely to travel very far outside Czech lands, except through recordings; and this is one of a historic occasion. Smetana wrote the opera to celebrate the coronation of the Emperor Franz Josef as King of Bohemia, but when that event did not take place, the performance was delayed until, much more suitably, the opening of the long-awaited Czech National Theatre. The present recording was made at the reopening of that theatre in 1983.

The work is really a patriotic pageant, static and celebratory, with such plot as there is concerning the mythical founder of Prague, Libuše, and her marriage to the peasant Přemysl, founder of the first Czech dynasty. There are important parts for a large number of soloists involved in dynastic wrangling and in a not very compelling sub-plot about jealous misunderstanding: Děpoltová seizes what is almost the work's only occasion for raw human emotion when she confesses her love for Chrudoš (firmly sung by Svorc), despite having pretended to prefer his brother Stáhlav (Marian Vodička, sounding a little strained at times). Zítek makes a fine, heroic Přemysl; but the triumphant performance comes, as it must, from Beňačková. The opera concludes with a series of tableaux in which Libuše prophesies the future kings and heroes who will assure the stability and greatness of the nation. At the end of a long performance her voice is undimmed in its ringing splendour; and earlier, as near the very start, the beauty of her tone and line seeks out all the warmth, character and humanity which she proves to be latent in Smetana's spacious but seemingly plain vocal writing.

Libuše is scarcely Smetana's greatest opera, as he liked to claim, but especially in so splendid a performance from Beňačková, and under the grave but impassioned direction of Zdeněk Košler, it makes remarkably compelling gramophone listening. The live recording includes some applause, but little other audience intervention in what must have been a solemnly moving occasion in 1983. There is a good, helpful essay in the booklet and a full text and translations into English, French and German. The English version is bathetic, sometimes amusingly so, and marred by misprints: a pity.

Surprisingly, Supraphon issued a second *Libuše*, recorded in 1995 at a live performance in Prague, two years after this one. On that one, Eva Urbanová is certainly a fine Libuše, maintaining her heroic manner without hectoring and delivering her powerful melodic lines strongly; but she does not have Beňačková's golden ring of authority, and though she is well supported by the rest of the cast, and by some superb orchestral playing from the same forces listed above, under Oliver Dohnányi, there is a greater cohesion in the cast assembled by Košler. (The same text, with not very adequate translations, were used on the second set, but the misprints were cleaned up.)

Pablo Sorozábal Spanish 1897-1988

Sorozábal La tabernera del puerto.
  María Bayo *sop* Marola
  Plácido Domingo *ten* Leandro
  Juan Pons *bass* Juan de Eguía
  Enrique Baquerizo *bass* Simpson
  Rosa Maria Ysás *contr* Antigua
  Isabel Monar *mez* Abel
  Emilio Sánchez *sngr* Ripalda
  Juan Jesús Rodríguez *sngr* Verdier
  Jesús Castejón *bass-bar* Chinchorro
  Orfeón Donostiarra; Galicia Symphony Orchestra / Víctor Pablo Pérez.
  Auvidis Valois Ⓟ Ⓒ V4766 (67 minutes: DDD). Notes, text and translation included.
  Recorded 1996.

First produced in Barcelona 61 years ago, this "nautical romance", *The hostess of the harbour tavern*, was the ninth stage work of the Basque composer Sorozábal, one of the last notable writers of zarzuelas – a genre that was being overtaken by other forms, like the musical. Trained in Leipzig and Berlin, he was technically better equipped than the generality of zarzuelistas, as may be immediately heard in the orchestral prelude here (whose material is reprised at the start of Act 3): it calls for playing of superior quality, which Víctor Pablo Pérez is more fortunate in obtaining than was the case in the work's earlier Hispavox recording conducted by the composer, which included more of the dialogue. Both in harmony and orchestration Sorozábal was ahead of his fellows.

The haphazardly constructed story is uncertain whether to centre on the love of a seaman for a beautiful tavern-keeper, her subjugation by her brutal father, the jealousy of the other fishermen's wives, or a sinister plot to smuggle drugs. A lovesick youth, Abel, with an accordion on which he can play only two chords, seems surplus to requirements (and one can only applaud his eventual decision to dump it in the water), and the introduction of a group of black American sailors (who don't even sing) is a conspicuous irrelevance. It is the music which saves things. Dramatic continuity is at a low ebb in Act 1, but this contains a habanera for three men, a lively low-comedy scene, a love scene and a waltz in which Marola, the heroine, tells the women of the port that if they smelled sweeter their men would be more responsive.

The musical core of the work is Act 2, though three of the four big solos in it are dramatically superfluous set-pieces – a "bird song" for Marola, a patter-song for Juan, her father, and a warning to the black sailors by an Englishman (for some reason) that whites will maltreat them. Then comes the only well-known number, "No puede ser" (which Domingo has recorded separately no less than five times), where the hero cannot believe that his adored one could be mixed up in anything shady. Marola has a soliloquy in melodrama form (i.e. spoken over music), and the act ends with a catchy trio. Act 3 is notable for a love duet with both singers in unison, a somewhat perfunctory storm at sea, and a final confession by Juan of his wrongdoings. Pablo Pérez strikes a blow for the recrudescence of the zarzuela by gathering an admirable cast. Domingo is ardent, more forthright than the lyrical Alfredo Kraus in the earlier recording (who sounded a trifle genteel for a fisherman), and is on fine form to cope with the considerable vocal demands that are made by the role. María Bayo, once past a rather obtrusive heavy throb in her voice in Act 1, makes a sympathetic heroine, dealing lightly with her coloratura in her Act 2 aria. As the drug-running heavy father, Juan Pons, with his black-voiced bass, is ideal casting. Praise too for the other bass, Enrique Baquerizo, in the part of the Englishman.

Louis Spohr
German 1784-1859

Spohr Faust.

Boje Skovhus *bar* Faust
Franz Hawlata *bass* Mephistopheles
Hillevi Martinpelto *sop* Kunigunde
Alfred Reiter *bass* Sir Gulf, Kaylinger
Rodrigo Orrego *ten* Wohlhaldt
Ulrich Wand *ten* Wagner
Robert Swensen *ten* Count Hugo
Brigitte Wohlfarth *sop* Röschen
Christoph Späth *ten* Franz
Martina Borst *mez* Sycorax
Stuttgart Radio Chorus; Kaiserslautern Radio Orchestra / Klaus Arp.
Capriccio Ⓕ Ⓘ 60 049-2 (two discs: 114 minutes: DDD). Notes, text and translation included.
Recorded at a performance in the Festhalle, Bad Urach, Germany on October 2nd, 1993.

Hardly had there appeared a live recording of Spohr's *Faust* from the Bielefeld opera under Geoffrey Moull on CPO, hot on its heels came this one from the 1993 Bad Urach Festival, conducted by Klaus Arp. However, the versions are completely different. Spohr originally wrote the work in two acts, for Weber to conduct in Prague in 1816, the pioneering year for German romantic opera that also saw Hoffmann's *Undine*; he slightly revised it for another performance two years later, adding one or two numbers, and this is what is recorded here. In 1852 he thoroughly rewrote the work, revising it from two acts into three as a grand opera for Covent Garden, with the dialogue (not included here) abbreviated into recitative. There are a number of implications, chiefly the expansion of the character of the wicked Sir Gulf in the second version; but these will be of interest mainly to committed Spohr enthusiasts, who will want both versions whatever the shortcomings. Neither is outstandingly well sung, and the conditions of live performance involve a certain amount of audience participation and recordings that do less than full justice to orchestration which Weber, in an essay introducing his own performance, praised for its "intensely scrupulous attention to detail".

In the present performance, the principal gain is Hillevi Martinpelto's singing of Kunigunde, the seductress whose potency once caused proper-minded sopranos to recoil from taking on the part at all. She may not seem so devastating nowadays but the music has charm and allure, and her numbers especially "Ja, ich fühl' es", are elegantly shaped here and sung with a bit of smoulder. Boje Skovhus has a little difficulty with the Italianate melismata which Spohr inappropriately made part of the melodic line in this German romantic opera and some of the part lies a little low for him, but he gives a fair account of Faust's aspirations and weaknesses. His attendant, Mephistopheles, calls for a little more sheer vocal energy from Franz Hawlata, though there is a sense of the sinister and the malevolent. Robert Swensen sings the part of the young hero, Hugo, energetically, but there is a shrill, quavery performance of Röschen from Brigitte Wohlfarth. The other parts, including the important chorus, are vigorously sung with a sense of enjoyment in the whole enterprise.

The booklet includes an essay and synopsis in German, English and French, with the original text and the same English translation that was used for the previous CPO issue, complete with hilarious misprints ("how fowl a spell did blind me"). It was perhaps unwise of Susan Marie Praeder to put her name to this, as it is to all intents and purposes that by J. Wrey Mould, published in the old Boosey vocal score, and includes in this version such gems as "Be thrift in thy course, loitering sunset" and "Attempt and know the beetling Alp less steady". As the chorus rightly observe, "Pish! the thing's absurd".

Spohr Jessonda.

Julia Varady *sop* Jessonda
Renate Behle *sop* Amazili
Kurt Moll *bass* Dandau
Thomas Moser *ten* Nadori
Dietrich Fischer-Dieskau *bar* Tristan d'Acunha
Peter Haage *ten* Pedro Lopes
Hamburg State Opera Chorus; Hamburg Philharmonic Orchestra / Gerd Albrecht.
Orfeo Ⓕ Ⓘ C240912H (two discs: 127 minutes: DDD). Notes, text and translations included.
Recorded 1990.

It is not particularly surprising that *Jessonda* should have been popular in its time nor that it should have been subsequently forgotten. In a brainless and genially sanctimonious way the scenario offers agreeable situations in which love finds a way, the oriental barbarians are confounded, and everybody else ends up singing to the god of battles. Musically, it pleased both traditionalists and reformers, for while clearly a product of the schools, it also took opera a step closer to music-drama by blurring the distinction between aria and recitative. A later age lost interest partly because the innovative points had been carried, but principally because the passions were learning to speak a much more emphatic musical language and the taste for exoticism and 'local colour' would not be satisfied with such mild and decorous allusions as these.

This mildness is the first thing likely to strike the listener here. Of course Gilbert and Sullivan have come between Spohr and ourselves, so that it is hard to take a 6/8 chorus seriously, as part of a hymn of mourning for the late Rajah; similarly when 'the messenger of death' is announced and begins to a pretty *siciliana* type of melody, albeit in the minor key. The so-called War Dances might fitly take place in an eighteenth-century drawing-room. Storm, recognition, confrontation and love duet come and go in the most orderly fashion. Writers on Spohr have detected a connection with the Wagner of *Tristan und Isolde*, but it could not possibly have anything to do with the eroticism of that opera.

With one exception all the singers here do their best for the dramatic side of the entertainment. Julia Varady, in particular, brings such a fine sensitivity to the title-role that for a disconcerting moment one has to suspend disbelief and begin to wonder what it is like to be in danger of serving as a sacrifice to Brahma at the very moment when the gallant Portuguese are about to come to the rescue. They (the gallant Portuguese) are led by Tristan D'Acunha as represented by Fischer-Dieskau, inescapably Germanic in declamation but duly responsive to the rival claims of love and honour. Thomas Moser as the young Brahmin, with liberal tendencies, fortified by love for Jessonda's sister presents a sympathetic and credible character, and though the sister in question seems to be nothing more nor less than a nice girl she is so well sung by Renate Behle that one takes her on trust. The exception to this general involvement of the cast in their roles is Kurt Moll, who plays the perfidious High Priest with imperturbable sonority and (perhaps taking his cue from the score) mildness.

Albrecht conducts a workmanlike performance, and though the orchestra are a little less forward in the balance than is customary these days one is gratefully aware that the players are kept busy. Gratitude is also due for the chance to hear this opera which has retained its place in the history books, if nowhere else. At one point at least, it satisfies more than historical curiosity: that is Jessonda's prayer in Act 3, a most lovely solo and in context almost sublime when sung as beautifully as it is here by Julia Varady.

Gaspare Spontini Italian 1774-1851

Spontini La vestale.
Karen Huffstodt *sop* Julia
Anthony Michaels-Moore *bar* Licinius
J. Patrick Raftery *ten* Cinna
Denyce Graves *mez* Grande vestale
Dimitri Kavrakos *bass* Pontifex
Aldo Bramante *bass* Haruspex
Silvestro Sammaritano *bass* Consul
Chorus and Orchestra of La Scala, Milan / Riccardo Muti.
Sony Classical Ⓟ Ⓒ S3K66357 (three discs: 183 minutes: DDD). Notes, text and translation included. Recorded at performances in La Scala, Milan between December 5th and 15th, 1993.

That this work is the essential link between Gluck and Berlioz, and also pre-echoes late Rossini and Bellini, is even clearer here than on the 1991 Kuhn set on Orfeo. Muti, working with stronger forces than were available to Kuhn, emphasizes its centrality in the history of French opera and moulds the music urgently, keeping a sure grasp of the whole while observant of pertinent detail. Well aware that the piece is poised intriguingly, if precariously, between the classical and romantic worlds, he responds accordingly, aided and abetted by the chorus and orchestra of La Scala. He plays the score complete, including the ballets that close Acts 1 and 3. Thus full justice is done, in orchestral terms, to an opera that needs help if it is to work in the opera-house, because in it convention rubs shoulders with original inspiration.

Some of the singing is another matter. Muti seems somewhat injudicious in his choice of leading ladies for dramatic pieces, offering us Huffstodt's somewhat undercharacterized Julia. The American soprano certainly feels, and is able to convey, all the vestal virgin's conflicting emotions as she re-encounters her Licinius and her despair as she faces death for her illicit love, but her voice is not altogether pleasing. Its persistent tremor vitiates her good intentions, spoiling her line much of the time, and the tone itself is monotonously one-dimensional so that the many affecting phrases she sings in the last two acts suffer from weak execution. Plowright, though not ideal in the rival set, makes a grander, more positive impression and her French is much better enunciated than that of Huffstodt, who swallows her consonants.

Michaels-Moore sings much more articulate French and commands a more satisfying line than his partner. Although it is strange to hear a baritone rather than the usual tenor in the part, Michaels-Moore is quite happy in the tessitura and generally justifies the high opinion in which he is held. He begins tentatively but builds the character into something vital and positive, his tone always warm and even. Graves is an imperious if not very idiomatic Grande Vestale, Kavrakos an imposing Pontifex if you can take his quick vibrato. Raftery's move from baritone to tenor doesn't seem a happy one on this evidence: his tone as Cinna is gravelly.

Despite the reservations, the sum here is greater than the parts simply because Muti imposes a unity of purpose on the whole. He benefits from recording in the opera-house, with the extra *frisson* that brings to all the performances, making this version a more successful offering than the Kuhn set. The recording, well balanced, catches the theatre's atmosphere.

Johann Strauss II   Austrian 1825-1899

J. Strauss II Die Fledermaus.
Julia Varady *sop* Rosalinde
Lucia Popp *sop* Adele
Hermann Prey *ten* Eisenstein
René Kollo *ten* Alfred
Bernd Weikl *bar* Falke
Ivan Rebroff *bass/mez* Orlovsky
Benno Kusche *bar* Frank
Ferry Gruber *ten* Blind
Evi List *sop* Ida
Franz Muzeneder *bass* Frosch
Bavarian State Opera Chorus and Orchestra / Carlos Kleiber.
DG Ⓕ ① 415 646-2GH2 (two discs: 107 minutes: ADD). Notes, text and translation included. Recorded 1975.

B B C RADIO 3
90-93 FM

Twenty-three years after its original release there is still no recording of *Die Fledermaus* that, for many collectors, matches this one for the compelling freshness of its conductor's interpretation – the attention to every nuance of the score and the ability to bring out some new detail, all allied to extreme precision of vocal and instrumental ensemble. The ladies, too, as so often seems to be the case in recordings of *Die Fledermaus*, are quite superlatively good, with ideally characterized and projected singing. If the men are generally less outstandingly good, one can have no more than minor quibbles with the Eisenstein of Hermann Prey or the Alfred of René Kollo. But it is less easy to accept Ivan Rebroff singing the role of Orlovsky falsetto. Some collectors find that his contribution quite ruins the whole set, but most will find it tolerable enough for the glories to be found elsewhere on the recording. DG remastered the set to make it sound as though it were recorded only yesterday; but they continue to provoke puzzlement by the break between discs, which occurs during the Act 2 finale. If a split into such uneven lengths is to be made, why not have it between Acts 1 and 2? Enough of minor quibbles – this set is a 'must buy'.

J. Strauss II Die Fledermaus.
Anneliese Rothenberger *sop* Rosalinde
Renate Holm *sop* Adele
Nicolai Gedda *ten* Eisenstein
Adolf Dallapozza *ten* Alfred
Dietrich Fischer-Dieskau *bar* Falke
Brigitte Fassbaender *mez* Orlovsky
Walter Berry *bass* Frank
Jürgen Förster *ten* Blind
Senta Wengraf *sop* Ida
Otto Schenck *spkr* Frosch
Vienna Volksoper Chorus; Vienna Symphony Orchestra / Willi Boskovsky.
EMI Ⓜ ① CMS5 66223-2 (two discs: 110 minutes: ADD). Notes and text included. Recorded 1971.

Boskovsky's *Die Fledermaus* occupies a very respectable position in the ranks of recordings of this most recorded operetta. His conducting does not offer the subtle nuances of the near contemporary Kleiber version, but his cast is every bit as good and the Orlovsky of Brigitte Fassbaender – a marvellously exhilarating "Ich lade gern mir Gäste ein" – highlights the folly of DG's casting in the part. Gedda and Rothenberger, if no longer in their freshest voice, are predictably dependable in the leading roles, Renate Holm is her usual delightful self as Adele (a superb "Spiel ich die Unschuld vom Lande"), Berry is a commanding prison governor and Dallapozza an Alfred with appropriately ringing tones. The casting of Fischer-Dieskau as Falke is entirely successful. Though there is something a shade unconvincing about the production, there is much more atmosphere here than on other more modern recordings. The ballet is missing, but Fischer-Dieskau is given an interpolated number from Strauss's *Waldmeister* to help explain the background to the story.

The recorded sound is spacious and well focused, and the disc change sensible comes between acts. So, if without the character of the Kleiber or the Karajan (reviewed below), this is as thoroughly dependable and recommendable as either of them.

J. Strauss II Die Fledermaus.
Gerda Scheyrer *sop* Rosalinde
Wilma Lipp *sop* Adele
Karl Terkal *ten* Eisenstein
Anton Dermota *ten* Alfred
Eberhard Waechter *bar* Falke
Christa Ludwig *mez* Orlovsky
Walter Berry *bass* Frank
Erich Majkut *ten* Blind
Luise Martini *sop* Ida
Erich Kunz *bar* Frosch
Philharmonia Chorus and Orchestra / Otto Ackermann.
Classics for Pleasure Silver Doubles Ⓜ Ⓓ CD-CFPSD4793 (two discs: 113 minutes: ADD). Notes included. Recorded 1960.

Otto Ackermann's 1960 recording of *Die Fledermaus* is a wonderful bargain. The atmospheric stereo has remarkable depth (try the seductive opening scene). The singing is of a high degree of consistency throughout, and the vocal exchanges at the end of Act 2 are especially ingratiating. In her solos, Wilma Lipp is a delightfully pert Adele, Eberhard Waechter a rousing Falke, and Walter Berry a splendidly warm Frank. Erich Kunz predictably relishes his chance in the role of Frosch, and Christa Ludwig solves as well as anyone the problem of making a convincing young aristocrat out of the trousers role of Orlovsky. Even Gerda Scheyrer and Karl Terkal in the leading parts of Rosalinde and Eisenstein would be worthy of warm praise by any normal standard of comparison. However, admirable though they are, they lack the true star quality to be found in other sets.

Ackermann's lilting direction of the whole proceedings is underpinned by first-rate singing and playing from the Philharmonia Chorus and Orchestra. Here is a set fully worthy of the greatest of all operettas. There is no libretto but an excellent synopsis is included.

J. Strauss II Die Fledermaus (with Gala Sequence).
Hilde Gueden *sop* Rosalinde
Erika Köth *sop* Adele
Waldemar Kmentt *ten* Eisenstein
Giuseppe Zampieri *ten* Alfred
Walter Berry *bass* Falke
Regina Resnik *mez* Orlovsky
Eberhard Waechter *bar* Frank
Peter Klein *ten* Blind
Hedwig Schubert *sop* Ida
Erich Kunz *bar* Frosch
Vienna State Opera Chorus; Vienna Philharmonic Orchestra / Herbert von Karajan.
Decca Ⓕ Ⓓ 421 046-2DH2 (two discs: 143 minutes: ADD). Notes, text and translation included. Recorded 1960.

BBC RADIO 3
90-93 FM

For better and just occasionally for worse this recording represents the high watermark of the Culshaw concept of production and indeed of the Golden Age of recording in Vienna. Today it is impossible to assemble a cast almost exclusively chosen from the ensemble of a single opera-house under a conductor who has worked with them over many years. That is what happens here, and the unanimity of purpose and of idiom is all the more marked by comparison with the more polyglot casts on rival sets.

The only member of the cast who is not German speaking is, appropriately enough, Giuseppe Zambieri and he at the time was the house tenor for Italian opera in Vienna! Hilde Gueden sets some kind of ideal for Rosalinde, with a voice as frothy and creamy as a Viennese cake but without the Schwarzkopf mannerisms, though Varady for Kleiber is just as desirable. Kmentt sings, in the right register, a sappy, sensuous account of his part. Köth may be a little thin-toned for Adele, but she gives us a suitably earthy characterization and pinpoint coloratura. Berry's youthful Falke, Waechter's amusing Frank (though old Benno Kusche provides more detailed character for Kleiber), Peter Klein's amusing Blind and Erich Kunz's wholly authentic Frosch (offering a maddeningly brief snatch of "Ach! wie so herrlich") complete a near-ideal cast. Zampieri offers a bit of Lohengrin's Farewell in the Prison scene, allowing Kunz to make a joke about swans. The one piece of miscasting is Resnik as Orlovsky; she sings the couplets down a third and presents the role as an elderly *roué*, quite wrong.

The performance is firmly, sometimes too firmly, controlled by Karajan, who catches the swing of the waltz rhythms but sometimes pushes on too abruptly for the good of his singers; Kleiber is just as precise and a deal more charming. The playing of the VPO is glorious. The recording appeared in digital form in 1982, just before the introduction of CD, and was much praised for the improvement in sound. It follows the Decca practice of the time of a spacious, theatrical perspective. You have a sense of attending a live performance and the dialogue is properly integrated with the musical numbers.

J. Strauss II Die Fledermaus.

Dame Kiri Te Kanawa *sop* Rosalinde
Hildegard Heichele *sop* Adele
Hermann Prey *bar* Eisenstein
Dennis O'Neill *ten* Alfred
Benjamin Luxon *bar* Falke
Doris Soffel *mez* Orlovsky
Michael Langdon *bass* Frank
Josef Meinrad *spkr* Frosch
Chorus and Orchestra of the Royal Opera House, Covent Garden / Plácido Domingo.
Stage Director: **Leopold Lindtberg.**
NVC Arts Ⓕ 🎦 4509-99216-3 (177 minutes). Filmed at performances in the Royal Opera
House, Covent Garden in December 1983.

This Gala *Fledermaus* was a triumph: a cheerfully polyglot production far better in every way than its
desperately soggy second video incarnation, as Dame Joan Sutherland's farewell. Domingo's
conducting is a little jagged, but full of sunny energy, and if the starry cast sacrifice something of the
Sachertorte flavour to extravagant clowning, it's with a fine sense of style, enhanced by Oman's
glowingly authentic sets. Prey, Heichele and Meinrad's potty Frosch maintain the idiom, but the
Anglophones acquit themselves equally well. Luxon, although taxed by the higher lines, is ideally
debonair, and Te Kanawa gorgeously funny, reverting to Kiwi when confronted by O'Neill's Alfredo,
wielding a genuinely dangerous voice. The gala interlude remains redundant – Messrs/Mmes Hinge &
Bracket and Charles Aznavour just don't fit the milieu – but mostly harmless. Michael Langdon is a
rather elderly Frank, but only Soffel's grotesquely bald Orlovsky seems ordinary. The recording is
excellent; Act 2, previously rather recessed, sounds much improved. British critics didn't much like
this; but that archetypal Viennese, Joseph Wechsberg did.

J. Strauss Wiener Blut

Klaus Hirte *bar* Prince Ypsheim-Gindelbach
Nicolai Gedda *ten* Count Bladuin Zedlau
Anneliese Rothenberger *sop* Gabriele
Gerd W. Dieberitz *spkr* Count Bitowski
Renate Holm *sop* Franziska Cagliari
Hans Putz *spkr* Kagler
Gabriele Fuchs *sop* Pepi Pleininger
Heinz Zednik *ten* Josef
Helga Schramm *sop* Lisi vom Himmelspfortgrund
Karin Stranig *sop* Lori vom Thurybrückerl
Cologne Opera Chorus, Philharmonia Hungarica / Willi Boskovsky.
EMI Ⓕ ① CMS5 66176-2 (two discs: 97 minutes: ADD). Recorded 1976.

Perhaps it is partly because so many of the tunes are so familiar in their original orchestral forms, or
perhaps because the score sounds little more than a rather disjointed succession of bright dance tunes,
with little of the characterization or variations of mood that one might expect in a operetta, that it is
difficult to warm immediately to this work. But certainly the method in which it was created ensured
that it was lovingly sung and expertly played, with a recording that offers a good stereo spread if
rather too much reverberation. It is interesting to compare it with the Robert Stolz/Eurodisc recording
(currently out of the catalogue). Gedda and Holm easily surpass Rudolf Schock and Margit
Schramm in terms of sheer vocal beauty, but there is an earthiness in the performance of the latter
pair that is perhaps more appropriate for their roles. In the orchestral and choral contributions too,
one feels that the German (or German-based) forces are not quite so much at home in this very
Viennese work as Stolz's Vienna forces.

  But these will be considered small points in consideration of the performance as a whole, and on
one point there is a distinct advantage with this recording. EMI used to be criticized for including
dialogue at the expense of some of the musical numbers, but here every number is included (though
there has been some rewriting of the orchestral introduction), and in this respect it puts itself ahead
of the Stolz version and a long way ahead of the old Columbia mono issue with Schwarzkopf.

Richard Strauss   German 1864-1949

R. Strauss Die aegyptische Helena.

Dame Gwyneth Jones *sop* Helena
Matti Kastu *ten* Menelaus
Dinah Bryant *sop* Hermione, First Elf

Barbara Hendricks *sop* Aithra
Willard White *bass* Altair
Curtis Rayam *ten* Da-ud
Betty Lane *sop* First servant
Glenda Kirkland *mez* Second servant
Patti Dell *sop* Second elf
Maria Cimarelli *contr* Third elf
Katherine Grimshaw *contr* Fourth elf
Birgit Finnila Finnilä *contr* The Omniscient Mussel
Kenneth Jewell Chorale; Detroit Symphony Orchestra / Antal Dorati.
Decca Grand Opera Ⓜ Ⓓ 430 381-2DM2 (two discs: 128 minutes: ADD). Notes, text and
translation included. Recorded 1979.

Die aegyptische Helena is a problem-piece, that cannot be denied. Strauss hoped for a light-hearted,
satirical treatment of Helen of Troy but Hofmannsthal changed course midway and ended by
complicating the plot with desert sheikhs and his fatal penchant for symbolism, this time about death
and marriage. Yet Strauss summoned enthusiasm for what must have been one of his most difficult
tasks and in the end declared that it had turned out "very beautiful, brilliant yet simple", though the
last adjective is perhaps optimistic!

The opera, first performed in 1928, was not a success on stage until this Munich production showed
that it could work, and it predictably called forth the stock abuse of post-*Ariadne* Strauss: "dated",
"the mixture as before", "composing from memory", and so on. Undeniably, the music is not out of
his top drawer, not all of it anyway, but there is much that is powerful and inspired, while the scoring
throughout is masterly and often of striking beauty.

It has been called Strauss's *bel canto* opera, and this seems to be an apt description. It was composed
just after he had been working with the great Vienna State Opera singers of the 1920s and the two
principal roles of Helena and Menelaus require a dramatic soprano and Heldentenor of the finest
quality. Strauss has composed exultant arias for them, of which Helena's "Zweite Brautnacht" is the
best known, but it is not alone. There is also a delightful lyric soprano role, that of Aithra, the
sorceress – her scene at the start of the opera is a sign of how successful the work could have been if
Hofmannsthal had continued in this vein.

The recording is a transfer of the LP set issued in 1979. Dorati drives the music hard but was
obviously an enthusiast for the work and it shows. As Helena, Gwyneth Jones has moments when the
radiance the part ideally needs can be glimpsed, but her familiar vocal flaws are also fully deployed.
Nevertheless, she has often sung the role on stage, for which she deserves high praise, and brings real
dramatic flair to it. Unfortunately Matti Kastu as Menelaus has all the vocal allure of a rusty fretsaw:
no wonder people say Strauss hated the tenor voice (he didn't) when his music for it is sung like this.
As Aithra, Barbara Hendricks is delightful and Willard White and Curtis Rayam, as the desert
warriors, restore the male balance. As this is its only representation in the catalogue, until something
better comes along, Straussians must make do with this not altogether unsatisfactory performance.

R. Strauss Arabella.

Julia Varady *sop* Arabella
Helen Donath *sop* Zdenka
Dietrich Fischer-Dieskau *bar* Mandryka
Walter Berry *bass* Waldner
Helga Schmidt *mez* Adelaide
Elfriede Höbarth *sop* Fiakermilli
Adolf Dallapozza *ten* Matteo
Hermann Winkler *ten* Elemer
Klaus-Jürgen Küper *bar* Dominik
Hermann Becht *bar* Lamoral
Doris Soffel *mez* Fortune-teller
Arno Lemberg *spkr* Welko
Bavarian State Opera Chorus; Bavarian State Orchestra / Wolfgang Sawallisch.
Orfeo Ⓟ Ⓓ C169882H (two discs: 144 minutes: ADD). Notes, text and translation included.
Recorded 1981.

Complete except for a brief cut in Matteo's part in Act 3, Sawallisch's Orfeo recording of *Arabella* has
been easily fitted on to two CDs. Sawallisch is the most experienced conductor of Strauss's operas
alive today and at his best in this one, his tempos just right, his appreciation of its flavour (sometimes
sentimental, at others gently ironic and detached) unequalled. Helen Donath's delightful Zdenka is a
perfect foil for Varady's Arabella. Varady's singing of the title-role is characterful and intelligent. One
should be left with ambivalent feelings about this heroine; is she lovable or a chilling opportunist? Or
both? And while Fischer-Dieskau's singing of Mandryka has not the total security of his earlier
Keilberth performance recorded live by DG at Munich in 1963, he remains the best Mandryka heard
since the war.

R. Strauss Arabella.

Lisa della Casa *sop* Arabella
Hilde Gueden *sop* Zdenka
George London *bass-bar* Mandryka
Otto Edelmann *bass* Waldner
Ira Malaniuk *mez* Adelaide
Mimi Coertse *sop* Fiakermilli
Anton Dermota *ten* Matteo
Waldemar Kmentt *ten* Elemer
Eberhard Waechter *bar* Dominik
Harald Pröglhöf *bass* Lamoral
Judith Hellwig *sop* Fortune-teller
Wilhelm Lenninger *ten* Welko
Vienna State Opera Chorus; Vienna Philharmonic Orchestra / Sir Georg Solti.
Decca Grand Opera Ⓜ ① 430 387-2DM2 (two discs: 144 minutes: ADD). Notes, text and
translation included. Recorded 1957.

This performance, made in Vienna, is particularly valuable because it preserves Lisa della Casa's
cherished performance of the title-role, the best of her Strauss characterizations. She is a believable
Arabella, loving and lovable but with that touch of cold calculation that is inseparable from the role.
Even so, to hear her Arabella at its best, one must go to the Keilberth performance referred to above.
Keilberth's tempos are slower, more indulgent and less apparently fearful of the romance in the score
than Solti's.

For some, Solti could be seen as the drawback of this performance. He was frequently quoted as
saying that the libretto of *Arabella* is superior to the music and he conducts the opera as if trying to
prove his point. This is Solti in unrelenting mood, not so much rushing the Act 2 love-duet as
understating all its tenderness. According to John Culshaw's memoirs, Solti and the Vienna
Philharmonic were at odds throughout the recording and there was bad blood between della Casa and
Hilde Gueden. Even so, all these artists were sufficiently professional not to let their peccadillos show
in their work; indeed, they might have brought a bit of extra spice into the proceedings. Alas, not so.

The Decca recording is good and wears its years well. Gueden is an attractive Zdenka, though a bit
characterless, and George London's Mandryka is a reliable performance. Both Otto Edelmann as
Waldner and Anton Dermota as Matteo uphold Viennese tradition in these roles, as does the late
Eberhard Waechter as Dominik. Recommended mainly, though, for della Casa, whose "Aber der
Richtige" evidently cast a momentary spell over Solti. The recording is of the three-act version, not
the 1939 Munich running-together of Acts 2 and 3. However, if money is no object the best choice of
all is undoubtedly the Sawallisch with Varady an apt successor to della Casa.

R. Strauss Arabella.

Dame Kiri Te Kanawa *sop* Arabella
Marie McLaughlin *sop* Zdenka
Wolfgang Brendel *bar* Mandryka
Sir Donald McIntyre *bass-bar* Waldner
Helga Dernesch *mez* Adelaide
Natalie Dessay *sop* Fiakermilli
David Kuebler *ten* Matteo
Charles Workman *ten* Elemer
Kim Josephson *bar* Dominik
Julien Robbins *bass* Lamoral
Jane Shaulis *mez* Fortune-teller
Roger Crouthamel *bar* Welko
Chorus and Orchestra of the Metropolitan Opera, New York / Christian Thielemann.
Stage Producer: Otto Schenk. *Video Director:* Brian Large.
DG Ⓕ 🔲 072 449-3GH (166 minutes). Synopsis included. Recorded at performances in the
Metropolitan Opera House, New York during November 1994.

Based on a revival at the Metropolitan in late 1994 this performance preserves for posterity Dame Kiri
in one of her most alluring portrayals. Her reading has deepened significantly over the years and she
now conveys from the inside all of Arabella's conflicting emotions and her strong-willed nature, while
her voice has lost only a little of its sheen. She is surrounded by the Schenk staging, then already ten
years old. It is traditional in the best sense, with innumerable touches that bespeak knowledge of
Viennese etiquette, and he persuades his singers to act with real conviction. Thielemann's flowingly
unobtrusive interpretation is one of the performance's greatest assets, confirming his reputation in
German repertory, although the orchestra could with advantage have been given greater prominence.

Others in the cast besides its heroine look mature for their roles, something inevitably emphasized
by close-ups. Brendel as Mandryka is quite a few years older than the 35 stipulated in the libretto so

inevitably this looks like a middle-aged romance, but, like his partner, he acts and sings his part with experienced aplomb although in the cruelly high-lying passages he can't wholly hide a sense of strain. McLaughlin, poorly made-up and coiffured, is also hard to believe as the youthful boy/girl Zdenka/Zdenko and the role lies uncomfortably for her at this stage of her career. Kuebler is hardly the ardent, reckless spirit Matteo should be.

There need be no reservations about McIntyre's minutely observed, warmly sung Waldner or Dernesch's fruity Adelaide. Dessay makes a perky Fiakermilli, and the smaller roles are more than adequately taken. Brian Large does his usual excellent job as video director. It is a great pity that no subtitles are provided. This issue has two significant rivals.

The Solti/Decca film from 1977 is also directed by Schenk, again with a fine eye for relevant detail. Janowitz is an appealing Arabella but has trouble with post-synchronization. Weikl is ideally cast as Mandryka, far superior to Brendel, and Sonia Ghazarian is a wholly credible Zdenka. Solti and the Vienna Philharmonic are in their element in this score, delivering it with the right *Schwung*. Picture and sound are faultless. An NVC Arts video enshrines a 1984 Glyndebourne performance, sensitively conducted by Haitink (though the LPO don't play quite as well as the Met's orchestra) and produced, with several amusing touches, by John Cox in Julia Trevelyan Oman's subtly observed décor. There, Ashley Putnam is perhaps the most convincing of all three Arabellas, and the remainder of the cast, an indifferent Zdenka apart, integrated into a strong ensemble. The picture is excellent, but the sound is a shade dated. Choice among these sets, none wholly recommendable but each offering individual delights, will probably depend on your preference of singer in the title-role and/or conductor, and each is visually faithful to the work.

R. Strauss Ariadne auf Naxos.

Jessye Norman *sop* Ariadne
Julia Varady *sop* Composer
Edita Gruberová *sop* Zerbinetta
Paul Frey *ten* Bacchus
Dietrich Fischer-Dieskau *bar* Music master
Olaf Bär *bar* Harlequin
Gerd Wolf *bass* Truffaldino
Martin Finke *ten* Scaramuccio, Dancing master
Eva Lind *sop* Naïad
Marianne Rørholm *contr* Dryad
Julie Kaufmann *sop* Echo
Rudolf Asmus *spkr* Major-domo
Leipzig Gewandhaus Orchestra / Kurt Masur.
Philips Ⓟ Ⓒ 422 084-2PH2 (two discs: 118 minutes: DDD). Notes, text and translation included. Recorded 1988.

B B C RADIO 3
90-93 FM

If you are one of those listeners who found Levine's tempos in his 1987 DG *Ariadne* too mercurial and wayward, you will probably prefer Kurt Masur's approach on this Philips recording. He keeps nearer to the score's indications, though occasionally he is rather staid, but he is always deeply musical. Although Levine's interpretation seems to match the quixotic spirit of the opera, there have to be others reasons why, if given a choice, you should opt for Masur's as the best of present-day recordings of this difficult and ever-fascinating piece. The principal reasons are the singing and the actual recording, which has a bloom to it that, again, suits the music. It is very well balanced and, although made in the studio, it does give an impression of the theatre.

First, the Prologue. Neither DG nor Philips can match the sparkle of the Karajan EMI issue from 1954 (reviewed below), transferred to CD so successfully, which has the incomparable advantage of Irmgard Seefried's Composer. But Julia Varady is very good indeed, singing with fire and, where required, tenderness (a lovely "Du Venus sohn"), her tone always steady and rich. She has no trouble with the high-lying parts of the role, whereas Baltsa on DG does (and is, arguably, miscast anyway). A splendid performance. Fischer-Dieskau is in good gruff voice as the Music master, avoiding that hectoring tone which often afflicted him latterly, and his exchanges with the Major-domo – a low-key performance by Rudolf Asmus, condescending and nicely understated – are properly entertaining (but how disconcerting to hear him twice sing "Ari-hadne"!).

Edita Gruberová is the Zerbinetta, a role for which she has rightly enjoyed world-wide acclaim as has Kathleen Battle, who sings it for DG. Like Battle in her recording, Gruberová is not quite at her most brilliant and incisive, 98 per cent, say. She does not conceal some breath-control problems in her big aria, but one feels churlish to criticize such a brilliant achievement with its crystalline trills. Battle is more coquettish, but Gruberová's stronger and fuller tone is more Straussian. The males in her troupe are well cast, headed by Olaf Bär as an outstanding Harlequin, easily the best on record.

But where the recording scores most convincingly over any recent rivals is in the casting of Ariadne and Bacchus. Jessye Norman brings to the title-role opulence of tone, nobility of phrasing and Straussian richness, none of which Tomowa-Sintow (DG) commands in equal degree. She is not a Straussian soprano in the Viennese or Munich mould – some charm lacking, some may feel. But charm is not a prerequisite for Ariadne and Norman gives us the classical dignity and tragedy of the role in generous measure. Both "Ein Schönes war" and "Es gibt ein Reich" are marvellously sung. Her trio of nymphs are excellent, with Julie Kaufmann particularly impressive as Echo.

And we all know how *Ariadne* can be wrecked by the tenor who sings Bacchus, to the extent that one sometimes wonders if it is Strauss's fault and the role is really impossible to perform satisfactorily except by the likes of Roswaenge and Lorenz in the past. The Canadian Heldentenor Paul Frey, who has had successes in Wagner and Strauss at Bayreuth and Munich respectively, here makes one ashamed of these doubts and misgivings by really singing the role, riding the climaxes effortlessly and tunefully and, with Norman, making the final duet the ecstatic experience Strauss had in mind but which so rarely materializes. The playing of the instrumentalists from the Leipzig Gewandhaus Orchestra is exemplary, with some exquisite work by the solo cello and horn and a particularly nimble pianist. The recording captures much detail without exaggerating it and has exceptional clarity. There's no doubt that this is an *Ariadne* with outstanding virtues.

R. Strauss Ariadne auf Naxos.

Gundula Janowitz *sop* Ariadne
Teresa Zylis-Gara *sop* Composer
Sylvia Geszty *sop* Zerbinetta
James King *ten* Bacchus
Theo Adam *bass-bar* Music master
Hermann Prey *bar* Harlequin
Siegfried Vogel *bass* Truffaldino
Hans Joachim Rotzsch *ten* Brighella
Peter Schreier *ten* Scaramuccio, Dancing master
Erika Wüstmann *sop* Naïad
Annelies Burmeister *mez* Dryad
Adele Stolte *sop* Echo
Erich-Alexander Winds *spkr* Major-domo
Staatskapelle Dresden / Rudolf Kempe.
EMI Opera ⓜ ① CMS7 64159-2 (two discs: 118 minutes: ADD). Notes, text and translation included. Recorded 1968.

This admirable and enjoyable set of what some consider Strauss's most satisfying opera all-round was out of circulation for far too long. Beyond any other conductor who has tackled the work on disc except Böhm (available variously on DG, Preiser and Schwann), Kempe understands both the lyrical and humorous aspects of the opera and hones them into a coherent whole. You can hear his attention to detail in his handling of the delicate accompaniment to the Dancing master's little homily in the Prologue and in the recitative-like introduction to Zerbinetta's aria. His strict control of minutiae is underpinned by his unerring sense of rhythm and tempo, and in the final scene an ability to tighten the tension. Only Böhm can here surpass Kempe by virtue of an even greater sense of dramatic movement and an overview of the score, characteristics notably lacking in both the Solti (Decca) and Levine (DG) sets, though present to an extent in the Masur (Philips) and Karajan (EMI). Kempe is inestimably helped by the *echt*-Strauss orchestra, the Dresden Staatskapelle.

Very rarely has any soprano sung Ariadne with such complete control of tone and technique as that shown by Janowitz. Her aristocratic phrasing, with an ideal movement between notes and a judicious use of portamento, is exemplary. Hers is the ideal kind of voice for the part, warm, lyrical and slightly vibrant, avoiding the heaviness of Price (Solti), who recorded the role too late in her career, and Norman on the Masur. Schwarzkopf (Karajan) brings more light and shade than Janowitz to the role and she is a shade more inside the role thanks to those subtle nuances for which she is famous. Not to mention the radiant Reining on the 1944 Vienna performance (Preiser and Schwann). Zylis-Gara's Composer is a kind of mirror-image of Janowitz's Ariadne. Apparently a shade cool, the inner fires surely burn intensely underneath the surface. Happily a soprano in the part rather than the mezzo preferred today – but not by Strauss – she marries creamy tone with a near-perfect technique, and is wonderfully radiant in the Composer's glorious outburst near the end of the Prologue. She is different from, but not superior to Seefried's marvellously impulsive assumption on the older EMI version. Zylis-Gara is especially affecting in her romantic colloquy with Zerbinetta, here sung by Geszty with tremendous brio, character and fluency. As in the theatre, her assumption is breathtakingly accurate and vivid, superior even to Gruberová's (Solti and Masur), complementary to the softer-grained more musing Streich (Karajan).

Adam is a nicely concerned Music master, Prey an attractive though slightly too heavy Harlequin – as he is *chez* Karajan and Levine. Schreier doubles ebulliently as the Dancing master and Scaramuccio, and the smaller roles are all filled by Dresden regulars of the 1960s. Reservations concern only the Bacchus of James King, efficiently and accurately sung but dry in tone and hardly ardent enough until the concluding moments. Schock (Karajan) is more beguiling in tone, more fervent in style. The recording, made in Dresden's Lukaskirche, tends to be a shade too reverberant, but the balance is natural and excellent between voices and instruments, with both well forward. This is an unhesitating recommendation of a stereo version at medium price. The Karajan, in mono, remains a strong contender, with different and complementary attributes.

R. Strauss Ariadne auf Naxos.

Dame Elisabeth Schwarzkopf *sop* Ariadne
Irmgard Seefried *sop* Composer
Rita Streich *sop* Zerbinetta
Rudolf Schock *ten* Bacchus
Karl Dönch *bar* Music master
Hermann Prey *bar* Harlequin
Fritz Ollendorff *bass* Truffaldino
Helmut Krebs *ten* Brighella
Gerhard Unger *ten* Scaramuccio
Lisa Otto *sop* Naïad
Grace Hoffmann *contr* Dryad
Anny Felbermayer *sop* Echo
Hugues Cuénod *ten* Dancing master
Alfred Neugebauer *spkr* Major-domo
Philharmonia Orchestra / Herbert von Karajan.
EMI mono Ⓜ ① CDS5 55176-2 (two discs: 128 minutes: ADD). Notes and text included.
Recorded 1954.

B B C RADIO 3
90-93 FM

This classic performance is 44 years old but wears its years lightly and although it is in mono it is such a superb recording that one scarcely notices nor minds. It is a joy to have it on CD, first and foremost because of Irmgard Seefried's unsurpassed singing of the Composer. No one else on record (and one suspects on the stage, too, at any rate since Lehmann) has conveyed with such ardour, charm and youthful impetuosity the changeable moods of this brilliantly-drawn character. Her lack of strain in the part's highest reaches gives the music a special radiance. Her "Du Venus sohn" is something to treasure.

Then there is Rita Streich's Zerbinetta, unchallenged until Gruberová came along and some would still award her the palm. All the coloratura fireworks are there, but sung with such feeling and meaning that they take on an extra dimension, which is surely what the composer intended. And here are the young Hermann Prey as Harlequin, and the ageless Hugues Cuénod as a Dancing master of such rapier wit that one could wish the part thrice as long. With Walter Legge's Philharmonia playing like angels, Karajan was enabled to put one of his most stylish performances on record, the tempos exemplary, the love duet passionate (and tender) and convincing, the wit sparkling and exquisitely pointed. Elisabeth Schwarzkopf as Ariadne sings very beautifully, not without strain at times and not without mannerisms, but with marvellous tone colour. Her haughty caricature of the Prima Donna in the Prologue is a gem. Rudolf Schock's Bacchus is invariably musical, a singer not a shouter. The decision to record the spoken utterances of the Major-domo in the Prologue in a different acoustic was always disconcerting but, again, not a disaster. One can't escape the conclusion that this Karajan set belongs to a world of Straussian interpretation that has long since receded.

R. Strauss Ariadne auf Naxos.

Gundula Janowitz *sop* Ariadne
Trudeliese Schmidt *mez* Composer
Edita Gruberová *sop* Zerbinetta
René Kollo *ten* Bacchus
Walter Berry *bar* Music master
Barry McDaniel *bar* Harlequin
Manfred Jungwirth *bass* Truffaldino
Heinz Zednik *ten* Brighella, Dancing master
Kurt Equiluz *ten* Scaramuccio
Hilda de Groote *sop* Naïad
Axelle Gall *sop* Dryad
Olivera Miljakovic *sop* Echo
Erich Kunz *spkr* Major-domo
Vienna Philharmonic Orchestra / Karl Böhm.
Stage Director: **Filippo Sanjust.** *Video Director:* **John Vernon.**
DG Ⓔ ⚏ 072 442-3GH (128 minutes). Recorded 1978.

This is a worthy visual supplement to the audio-only *Ariadnes* conducted by Böhm. Obviously the work was always a great favourite with the conductor and in his eighties he shows little or no decline in his direction of it. This being a film version, without an audience present, one misses that *frisson* of spontaneity found on his live sets. A cinematic adaptation of a production, by Sanjust, for the Vienna State Opera, the view of the work is fairly traditional, attractive in décor, full of pertinent detail and, where the *commedia dell'arte* figures are concerned, balletic movement. Above all the video director, the experienced John Vernon, persuaded all his principals to act with great conviction so that the very many close-ups reveal few specifically operatic gestures and plenty of genuine feeling.

Of course Gruberová, the Zerbinetta of her generation, vocally stronger than the mercurial Kathleen Battle on Levine's DG video production, is completely natural in front of the cameras, presenting her appealingly seductive portrait by means of facial and bodily expression .She sings the role with her accustomed confidence, indeed insouciance, troubled not at all by the demands of her long aria. She moves into a serious vein when this flighty Zerbinetta finds herself falling seriously in love with Trudeliese Schmidt's personable Composer in the Prologue. Comparison with Seefried for Karajan (reviewed above) in that role proves Strauss right when he cast the part for a soprano. Schmidt and Troyanos (Levine), though both look suitably boyish and sing strongly, show strain at the top. In this Prologue Vienna scores with Berry's classic Music master and Kunz's unerringly accented and wonderfully sardonic Major-domo.

Janowitz is quite in the vocal class of her famous predecessors, leaning more towards della Casa than Reining or Schwarzkopf, and slimmer of voice and figure than the refulgent Norman (Levine). She is on ecstatic form when Bacchus arrives on the scene and particularly moving at "Gibt es ein Vorüber?" in the final duet. Although her acting is sometimes awkward, she makes a conscious effort to convey Ariadne's infatuation with Bacchus. Kollo looks the handsome god to the life, but his tone is sometimes strained and he doesn't have the warmth of Lorenz or Schock on the Böhm CD versions. He is, however, more subtle than James King (Levine), indeed wholly obedient to the score's markings. The *commedia dell'arte* figures are fleetly led by Zednik (doubling as a nicely adaptable Dancing master) and McDaniel. The video picture is reasonably good, the sound excellent. This version is preferable to the Levine, not least because of Böhm's slimmer, more diaphanous account of the miraculous score.

R. Strauss Ariadne auf Naxos (1912 version).
Dame Margaret Price *sop* Ariadne
Veronica Cangemi *sop* Singer
Sumi Jo *sop* Zerbinetta
Gösta Winbergh *ten* Bacchus
Thomas Mohr *bar* Harlequin
Alfred Kuhn *bass* Truffaldina
Markus Schäfer *ten* Brighella
Steven Cole *ten* Scaramuccio
Doris Lamprecht *mez* Shepherd, Dryad
Brigitte Fournier *sop* Naïad, Shepherdess
Virginie Pochon *sop* Echo
Ernst Theo Richter *spkr* Monsieur Jourdain
Orchestra of Opéra National de Lyons / Kent Nagano.
Virgin Classics Ⓕ Ⓞ VCD5 45111-2 (two discs: 136 minutes: DDD). Notes, text and translation included. Recorded 1990s.

There are still important first recordings to be made and this is one of them. The 1912 *Ariadne auf Naxos* is a work in its own right, different from its popular successor both in content and in tone, and it is high time we had the chance to hear the artistic collaboration that Strauss and Hofmannsthal originally intended. No matter that it failed to hold the stage: other mixed theatre works, like Purcell's *Fairy Queen* and *King Arthur*, have struggled to win popular favour, but that is no reason not to give them a try from time to time. Full marks to Virgin for rescuing this long-abandoned *Ariadne*.

What exactly do we get here? The point of the original was that Hofmannsthal wanted to adapt a Molière comedy for the Berlin stage and so the first half of the entertainment was not the operatic Prologue we hear today, but a reduced version of the play, *Le bourgeois gentilhomme*, accompanied by incidental music by Strauss. There are just 11 numbers, totalling about half-an-hour and comprising a different selection from either the enlarged 1917 score that Strauss put together later or the 1920 Suite. The Overture and Dinner sequence, serving up *Rheingold* salmon and roast lamb courtesy of *Don Quixote*, are familiar, but there are also a couple of attractive vocal numbers.

The style is trim classical pastiche. Nagano has trained his small band of musicians from the Orchestra of Opéra National de Lyons to play with a light touch. In fact, this performance is rather more graceful than Strauss's own earlier recording of the Suite (available on Pearl). Nagano's Minuet dances with a spring in its step and his Fencing master parries with rapier-like precision. Veronica Cangemi sings nicely in the brief arietta "Du, Venus' Sohn", which Strauss was later to expand into the Composer's music, and Doris Lamprecht and Brigitte Fournier duet fluently as the Shepherd and Shepherdess. The big problem is what to do with the play. Virgin have elected not to record Hofmannsthal's cut version of the text, which may seem to negate the purpose of this first recording, but one cannot help feeling it was the right decision. Like the restless audience at the Stuttgart première, most of us do not want to sit through two hours of Molière in German, and the provision of short snatches of spoken narration seems as good a compromise as any. In any case, a dab hand at the CD programming button can easily cut out the speech altogether.

And so to the opera. There are differences here too, because Strauss evidently felt the evening lasted too long as it stood and made a few deft cuts before *Ariadne* returned to the stage in 1916. The big loser was Zerbinetta, who in the original version has a longer – and much more difficult – aria and an extra solo scene before Ariadne and Bacchus get down to the serious business of their duet. A number of adventurous sopranos have recorded the earlier "Grossmächtige Prinzessin" (up a tone with higher-than-the-Queen-of-Night F sharps) but there cannot be many who sound happier with it than Sumi Jo. Her singing is almost always sweet-toned and playful, as though tightrope-walking in the leger lines is the most natural thing in the world. She leads an amiable *commedia dell'arte* quartet, with Thomas Mohr an able Harlequin, and there is a first-rate trio of nymphs from Lamprecht, Fournier and Pochon.

This set also marks the belated first recording in a Strauss opera by Dame Margaret Price. (Oh, the missed opportunities! Where are her Chrysothemis, her Marschallin, her Countess in *Capriccio*?). If only the recording team could have set sail for her "wüste Insel" ten years earlier. The aristocratic Straussian line and her excellent German mean there is still much to enjoy here, but it would be less than truthful if one did not report passages when the intonation is touch-and-go or her nervousness at facing Ariadne's noble high B flats. Her best singing comes in the final duet, where she is paired with the ideally weighted tenor of Gösta Winbergh, a Bacchus who for once makes his horribly difficult music sound beautiful. Nagano supports them with a fine blend of classical poise and theatrical sweep. Maybe there is not the depth that Karajan found, but the orchestral playing in this performance is as clear as a crystal glass and that is in keeping with the lighter, glinting comedy of the 1912 *Ariadne*.

The last word in this version goes to the *commedia dell'arte* characters, who creep back on stage to reprise Zerbinetta's sparkling aria, and then Molière's host, Monsieur Jourdain, who wakes up to find that the rest of the guests have slipped away – a delightfully ironic ending, so much better than the overblown conclusion we usually hear. For Strauss enthusiasts this excellent set is self-recommending. For those wanting to broaden their operatic outlook, it offers much to discover and delight.

R. Strauss Capriccio.

Dame Elisabeth Schwarzkopf *sop* Countess
Eberhard Waechter *bar* Count
Nicolai Gedda *ten* Flamand
Dietrich Fischer-Dieskau *bar* Olivier
Hans Hotter *bass-bar* La Roche
Christa Ludwig *mez* Clairon
Ruldof Christ *ten* Taupe
Anna Moffo *sop* Italian soprano
Dermot Troy *ten* Italian tenor
Karl Schmitt-Walter *bar* Major-domo
Philharmonia Orchestra / Wolfgang Sawallisch.
EMI mono Ⓟ Ⓤ CDS7 49014-8 (two discs: 135 minutes: ADD). Notes, text and translation included. Recorded 1957-8.

If you could take only a single studio-made (as distinct from live) recording to your desert island, it might well be this one. Not only is the work a source of constant and none-too-demanding delight but its performance and recording, especially in this CD reincarnation, are well-nigh faultless. Indeed, it is one of the most welcome happenings of the CD revolution that so many half-forgotten sets such as this one have earned a new life, and in this case the resuscitation could hardly be more welcome.

Walter Legge assembled for the recording in 1957 what was almost his house cast, each singer virtually ideal for his or her part. Some might say that no role she recorded suited Schwarzkopf's particular talents more snugly than Countess Madeleine. Her ability to mould words and music into one can be heard here to absolute advantage. Then the charming, flirtatious, sophisticated, slightly artificial character, with the surface attraction hiding deeper feelings revealed in the closing scene (quite beautifully sung), suit her to the life. She, like her colleagues, is superbly adept at the quick repartee so important an element in this work.

As her brother, the light-hearted, libidinous Count, the young Eberhard Waechter is in his element. So are the equally young Nicolai Gedda as the composer, Flamand, the Sonnet so gently yet ardently delivered, and Fischer-Dieskau as the more fiery poet, Olivier. Christa Ludwig is nicely intimate, conversational and cynical as the actress Clairon, handling her affairs, waning with Olivier, waxing with the Count, expertly. Above all towers the dominating presence of Hotter as the theatre director, La Roche, impassioned in his defence of the theatre's conventions, dismissive of new and untried methods, yet himself not above a trivial flirtation – and how delicately Hotter manages his remarks about his latest protégée as she dances for the assembled company.

Even with so many distinguished singers gathered together, it is the closeness of the ensemble, the sense of a real as distinct from a manufactured performance that is so strongly conveyed. And Legge did not neglect the smaller roles: Rudolf Christ makes an endearingly eccentric Monsieur Taupe, the veteran Schmitt-Walter a concerned Major-domo. Anna Moffo and Dermot Troy sing the music of the Italian soprano and tenor with almost too much sensitivity. Crowning the performance is the musical direction of Wolfgang Sawallisch, always keeping the score on the move, yet fully aware of its sensuous and witty qualities: Krauss's amusing libretto has much to do with the work's fascination. Both the extended Prelude and the interludes are gloriously played by the vintage Philharmonia

Orchestra, who are throughout alert to the old wizard's deft scoring, as refined here as in any of his earlier operas. The recording might possibly have given a little more prominence to the instruments; in every other respect, although it is in mono, it hardly shows its age. It will be a source of enduring pleasure to those familiar or unfamiliar with Strauss's inspired swan-song.

R. Strauss Capriccio.

Gundula Janowitz *sop* Countess
Dietrich Fischer-Dieskau *bar* Count
Peter Schreier *ten* Flamand
Hermann Prey *bar* Olivier
Karl Ridderbusch *bass* La Roche
Tatiana Troyanos *mez* Clairon
David Thaw *ten* Taupe
Arleen Auger *sop* Italian soprano
Anton de Ridder *ten* Italian tenor
Karl Christian Kohn *bass* Major-domo
Bavarian Radio Symphony Orchestra / Karl Böhm.
DG Strauss Opera Edition Ⓜ ① 445 347-2GX2 (two discs: 142 minutes: ADD). Notes, text and translation included. Recorded 1971.

"Böhmerl" was Strauss's endearing diminutive for the conductor who did most to propagate the composer's music during his lifetime and thereafter. If Böhm wasn't conducting the première of a work in Dresden he was giving the first performance in some other centre. The 1971 *Capriccio*, a famous performance, hardly needs new commendation. It stands on a par with the Sawallisch, but is better recorded. It captures the glorious Janowitz voice in its prime. Her lovely Countess Madeleine is supported by portrayals of a comparative stature, all woven together by Böhm in to a skein of harmonious sound, finely recorded. Listening to this work, one hears the interesting correlation and development of Strauss's conversational style from *Rosenkavalier*, through *Ariadne* and *Die schweigsame Frau* to its distillation in *Capriccio*, and wonders anew at his prolific invention.
　　Strauss loved his creations and Böhm was instrumental in conveying his mentor's wishes.

R. Strauss Capriccio.

Dame Kiri Te Kanawa *sop* Countess
Håkan Hagegård *bar* Count
David Kuebler *ten* Flamand
Simon Keenlyside *bass* Olivier
Victor Braun *bar* La Roche
Tatiana Troyanos *mez* Clairon
Michel Sénéchal *ten* Taupe
Dale Travis *bar* Major-domo
San Francisco Opera Orchestra / Donald Runnicles.
Stage Director: **Stephen Lawless.** *Video Director:* **Peter Maniura.**
Decca 🔳 071 426-3DH (138 minutes). Recorded 1993.

In between close-ups and group shots, the camera shows the vast stage of the San Francisco Opera, its height dwarfing that of any Parisian garden-salon, so that we reflect on the benefits of video. Here the conversation piece can be followed from a position almost as privileged as that of the Major-domo and his staff, silent presences throughout the discussions. Stephen Lawless's production ensures that it is a pleasure too, and Peter Maniura's direction of the filming eliminates any problem about looking in the right place. There is just one exception to that, for we don't do well to be looking at the orchestra and Donald Runnicles during the string sextet at the start.
　　Visually and vocally, two characters are almost equally at the centre of this performance. The Countess has her central position mapped out for her, but the relative importance of the men is to some extent the debating point of the whole opera. Here the place goes to La Roche. Wryly and ruefully, the man of the theatre speculates that in the projected opera with themselves as subject he will be cast as the bass-*buffo*. Victor Braun does a delicious five-second 'ham' act of the arthritic caricature he expects, but he himself has made far too strong, real and likeable a character for that kind of Dr Bartolo-routine to be thinkable. In this performance, only the first sight of him, asleep with mouth agape during the chamber music, suggests anything of the cousin-to-Baron Ochs figure either; after that, he is a man of resource and some charm, and his honest preference for arias over recitative and an orchestra that does not drown the singers will win him more friends than his creators may have intended. Braun, 58 when this was recorded, has preserved his fine voice well, and his Herculean solo is well and truly sung. This is an opera without a hero, but if one had to be cast from its ranks, on this showing it should be La Roche.
　　All do well. Simon Keenlyside is in resonant voice and has impeccable stage manners. Michel Sénéchal comes in blinking from the dark as Mr Mole the prompter. Tatiana Troyanos, within months

of her lamentable death, is a gallant Clairon. Then there is Dame Kiri: her tone not quite so pure and radiant as of yore, yet steady and often beautiful, her presence that of a gracious aristocrat, a woman of charm, feeling and intelligence. The ending of the opera is commonly held to be enigmatic. The smile which the Countess flashed at the Major-domo (who looked as though but for his wig he would have scratched his head) suggested an improbable solution.

R. Strauss Daphne.

Lucia Popp *sop* Daphne
Reiner Goldberg *ten* Apollo
Ortrun Wenkel *contr* Gaea
Kurt Moll *bass* Peneios
Peter Schreier *ten* Leukippos
Ludwig Baumann *bar* First shepherd
Alexander Senger *ten* Second shepherd
Wolfgang Vater *bass* Third shepherd
Matthias Hölle *bass* Fourth shepherd
Dorothea Wirtz *sop* First servant
Uta-Maria Flake *sop* Second servant
Bavarian Radio Chorus and Symphony Orchestra / Bernard Haitink.
EMI Ⓟ Ⓒ CDS7 49309-2 (two discs: 104 minutes: DDD). Notes and text included. Recorded 1982.

Strauss's pastoral opera, although an awkward work to stage because of its static plot and unsatisfactory length, is almost ideal material for records, where one can bask in its early flowering of the composer's late, ethereal manner, which culminated in the *Vier letzte Lieder*. William Mann, in his book on the operas (Cassell: 1964), commented that "for much of the time we may think to hear Strauss playing amiably with the utmost expertise on pentatonic and diatonic ideas that do not leave much impression on the mind after a performance", but he admitted to a more favourable view of the piece on the strength of the reissued 1964 live Vienna recording conducted by Karl Böhm (reviewed below).

Interest was once again rekindled by this enjoyable though not flawless set. Certainly Mann's earlier strictures on the work's musical development are to an extent confirmed, and the pace dictated by Gregor's indifferent libretto is erratic, but there is so much beautiful music in Daphne's own part, above all in her long duet with Apollo (on a par with the Ariadne/Bacchus encounter for erotic suggestion) as to make it a worthwhile acquisition for any collection. Haitink does everything in his appreciable power to convince us of the diaphanous quality of the scoring, sustains the long paragraphs of what is, in effect, a long symphonic poem with an unfailing grip on structure, and supports his singers splendidly. Böhm's version must be taken into account as he conducted the opera's première, and Haitink cannot quite equal the peculiar quality of incandescence that Böhm could bring to Strauss. Moving that little bit more quickly, Böhm is often the more gripping interpreter. But this modern version, studio-made in finely balanced and spacious sound, has none of the mistakes found in the older (live) set.

Lucia Popp, predictably, makes a lovely Daphne, progressing from the cool creature of her opening scene, a solo keenly articulated, to the self-awareness made available by Apollo's intervention, and then to the final, serene resignation as she becomes a laurel tree. Gueden, for Böhm, provided smoother vocalization but an altogether blander interpretation. A slight edge sometimes invades Popp's tone under the considerable pressure Strauss demands of his soprano, but the total accomplishment of the portrayal puts that reservation into perspective. Leukippos, the human lover of Daphne destroyed by the god Apollo, has been lucky in his recorded interpreters. Wunderlich (Böhm) was possibly more lyrically youthful than Schreier, but Schreier makes more of the text, and sings with his accustomed feeling for a phrase: his short and sweet death scene is most touching.

Apollo is a beast of a part; it calls for the combination of a Tauber and a Vickers (neither sang it). Goldberg finds it hard going, his tone often uningratiating, but he has his moments and is seldom less than adequate. King, for Böhm, was more refulgent but less accurate. The minor characters, reduced to the fringe by Gregor at Strauss's insistence, have to make their mark quickly. Moll succeeds in this more easily than Wenkel, who finds the low tessitura of Gaea not unnaturally uninviting.

The Bavarian orchestra revel in their opportunities, with some particularly sensitive solos from the wind section. Once or twice you may feel that players and chorus are a little too backward in relation to the soloists, especially where Goldberg was concerned. As a whole, the set provides a welcome opportunity to get to know a slightly off-centre work in a strong performance.

R. Strauss Daphne.

Hilde Gueden *sop* Daphne
James King *ten* Apollo
Vera Little *contr* Gaea
Paul Schöffler *bass* Peneios

Fritz Wunderlich *ten* Leukippos
Hans Braun *bar* First shepherd
Kurt Equiluz *ten* Second shepherd
Harald Pröglhöf *bass* Third shepherd
Ludwig Welter *bass* Fourth shepherd
Rita Streich *sop* First servant
Erika Mechera *sop* Second servant
Vienna State Opera Chorus; Vienna Symphony Orchestra / Karl Böhm.
DG Strauss Opera Edition Ⓜ Ⓞ 445 322-2GX2 (two discs: 95 minutes: ADD). Notes, text and translation included. Recorded at a performance in the Theater an der Wien, Vienna during the 1964 Wiener Festwochen.

Böhm's *Daphne* recording is another Strauss classic and here, in the opera dedicated to him and of which he conducted the first performance in 1938, he is peerless. The Haitink, in many opinions, came nowhere near it, even though Böhm makes some irritating cuts. Yes, there are the inaccuracies inseparable from live recording, balance is not as it would be (or should be) in the studio, and there are stage noises but what a performance; that's what counts, and it sounds much better on CD than on the LPs many of us have treasured for years.

This is Strauss's most lyrical opera and occupies a special place in the affections of his admirers. Böhm's unfolding of the marvellous orchestral score, from that first oboe melody to its final metamorphosis, is the work of a master-interpreter – one has only to hear his majestic phrasing of the cellos' Peneios melody to recognize that. Hilde Gueden's Daphne is a lovely performance, sung with an engaging innocence, as befits this mysterious heroine, but also with the soaring richness that the part requires in its most dramatic passages, such as the duet with Apollo, sung by James King with power and conviction. He has never possessed a voice notable for its tonal beauty, but he is really rather impressive here. For tonal beauty, however, there is Wunderlich as Leukippos, making something exceptionally expressive out of every phrase. Schöffler's Peneois must have been better a few years earlier, but it has a noble dignity one would be hard-pressed to equal today, and Vera Little copes well with all but the lowest notes of the Erda-like part of Gaea.

R. Strauss Elektra.
Birgit Nilsson *sop* Elektra
Regina Resnik *mez* Clytemnestra
Maria Collier *sop* Chrysothemis
Tom Krause *bar* Orestes
Gerhard Stolze *ten* Aegisthus
Vienna Philharmonic Orchestra / Sir Georg Solti.
Decca Ⓕ Ⓞ 417 345-2DH2 (two discs: 108 minutes: ADD). Notes, text and translation included. Recorded 1966-7.

What is undoubtedly one of the greatest performances ever on record sounds even more terrifyingly realistic on this magnificent transfer to CD. There are many who believe that Elektra was Nilsson's most exciting accomplishment for the gramophone, surpassing even her Brünnhilde. Her unflinching attack, magnificent high Bs and Cs, her subtle shadings (listen to the caressing of the line at "Von jetzt an will ich deine Schwester sein"), her depth of feeling, as in the great lamenting passage, "Kannst du nicht die Botschaft austrompeten dort ... " when Elektra believes Orestes dead; these, coupled with her absolute steadiness of tone, are something we are lucky to hear once in a lifetime. Now that the assumption has become something of a historical document its achievement seems that much more amazing.

Then this is possibly Solti's most notable operatic recording. The nervous tension of this work finds a keen empathy in his gripping, taut and highly detailed conducting, to which the VPO responded with their finest playing, and every strand of the score, given – for once – complete, is caught by John Culshaw's recording. There are aspects of the SonicStage approach that seem even more aggravating than they did on LP. The stage noises, though too loud, are understandable, and with movement of the singers in different acoustics is often convincing, but Clytemnestra's electronically enhanced cackles and Chrysothemis's unnatural wailing simply exaggerate what Strauss has already made plain in the score. Both those roles are aptly taken. Regina Resnik is the raddled old Queen to the life, and generates the feel of a theatrical encounter in her long duologue with Elektra. Marie Collier, though inclined to yowl, conveys all Chrysothemis's neurosis and frustration and her voice can soar almost as easily as Nilsson's. Tom Krause's Orestes is the epitome of youthful nobility and firm resolution. The insert-booklet has an enlightening essay on the work by Michael Kennedy, who nicely contrasts and compares it with *Salome*.

R. Strauss Elektra.
Inge Borkh *sop* Elektra
Jean Madeira *mez* Clytemnestra

Marianne Schech *sop* Chrysothemis
Dietrich Fischer-Dieskau *bar* Orestes
Fritz Uhl *ten* Aegisthus
Dresden State Opera Chorus; Staatskapelle Dresden / Karl Böhm.
DG Strauss Opera Edition Ⓜ ① 445 329-2GX2 (two discs: 100 minutes: ADD). Notes, text and
translation included. Recorded 1960.

Böhm, writing of his first meeting with Strauss at Munich in 1924, tells of the composer, when
rehearsing the Maids' Scene in *Elektra*, asking the orchestra to play softly as "the composition itself
is already so loud", and goes on to discuss the difficulty of securing a just balance in the opera-house
between singers and orchestra in the final duet; a difficulty, Böhm says, eliminated in the studio by
the use of microphones for each group so that the singers can be subject to the most brilliant
orchestral tone and yet remain audible. In this recording we hear the orchestra only at their fullest,
and most powerful, in the sections in which they alone play, such as those before and after the
Clytemnestra-Elektra scene, or in the final duet.

The voices of the singers are, in consequence, greatly exposed, and we can hear the words, vocal
nuances, and the stresses and strains of some of the very trying and testing passages, with absolute
clarity. Let it be said at once that two of the three principals affected by this process come through
their ordeal with flying colours. These are Inge Borkh and Jean Madeira. Marianne Schech is not so
successful. It is a joy to hear Borkh's high notes, loud or soft, taken so securely and so dead-centre.
She makes such things as the end of the Agamemnon monologue, the trying passages at the end of
her scene with Clytemnestra, and her part in the final duet, absolutely thrilling: and her singing of the
exquisite lyrical music of the Recognition scene, if perhaps a little lacking in tenderness, is most
beautiful. Her first words, "Allein! weh, ganz allein" ("Alone! woe! quite alone!") are full of deep
pathos" and she ranges from this emotion to biting contempt and hatred for her mother and lust for
vengeance on that lady and her paramour, and triumphant joy when that vengeance is accomplished
by Orestes.

Marianne Schech is not a singer of this order. She is apt to slide up to her high notes – which are
sometimes shrill – but she throws herself with abandon into Chrysothemis's monologue of longing
for husband and children and home, in a world far from the evil atmosphere of the Palace and its
inmates. She sings always with conviction and it is given to her to end the ecstatic final duet with
Elektra, before the latter's dance of death, on a phrase with a high B natural, and to give the great cry
of "Orestes" just before the curtain falls. She achieves both these climaxes splendidly. Jane Madeira's
dark, rich-toned voice is a natural for the part of Clytemnestra. Her long monologue and her duet
with Elektra are one of the marvels of *Elektra* (and of musical psychology): in these Madeira gives
us splendid singing and a vividly drawn portrait of the bloated, diseased, and dream-haunted woman.
It goes without saying that Fischer-Dieskau makes a living person of Orestes – a character often made
to appear a lay figure. His feeling for words, the emotion – for example – with which he sings "Orest
gestorben bin" ("Orestes is dead indeed"), his growing excitement when Elektra tells him she is not a
servant but of royal blood – these are a few pointers to a noble presentation of the part. Fritz Uhl
gives an excellent portrayal of the ill-fated Aegisthus, at first jaunty, then nervous and fearful, and at
length terrified. He really sings his notes. The small parts are all well taken.

And so to the conductor and the orchestra. Böhm seems to find the right tempos, the right tensions
and relaxations, in his interpretation of the complicated score with its graded series of great
crescendos from the Agamemnon monologue to the final pages. It is an overall conception that
commands the greatest admiration, the interpretation of a musician who had conducted a large
number of Strauss's operas in the presence of the composer. The lovely tone of the strings in the
haunting "Children of Agamemnon" theme, the baleful braying of the horns as Clytemnestra appears
at the window of the Palace, the sinister fluttering of the flutes in her monologue, the terrifying music
for the whole orchestra as she returns to the Palace, the glorious playing in the Recognition Scene and
in Elektra's dance – these are a few of the outstanding things in their performance of Strauss's
amazingly imaginative and colourful orchestration. The recording is good and spacious.

R. Strauss Elektra.

Leonie Rysanek *sop* Elektra
Astrid Varnay *sop/mez* Clytemnestra
Catarina Ligendza *sop* Chrysothemis
Dietrich Fischer-Dieskau *bar* Orestes
Hans Beirer *ten* Aegistheus
Vienna State Opera Chorus; Vienna Philharmonic Orchestra / Karl Böhm.
Stage/Video Director: **Götz Friedrich.**
Decca ⊟ 071 400-3DH; ✆ 071 400-1DH2 (two discs: 117 minutes). Recorded 1982.

Götz Friedrich's film is set in some dark, dank, doom-laden courtyard (actually a disused factory),
with the House of Atreus a grim-looking range of sinister, grey shutters. He opts for an almost silent-
film style of acting reminiscent of the films of Fritz Lang, highly stylized and enhanced by a deal of
close camerawork, characters confronting each other literally face to face, most notably in the

Elektra/Clytemnestra scene. The appearance of Agamemnon's ghost, the pawing of Chrysothemis by Elektra, the horribly vivid murder of Aegistheus and much else makes manifest what Hofmannsthal intended us to imagine in our mind's eye. This is the work of an imaginative man of the theatre with his own vital vision of the work, replete with an extravagantly fantastic retinue for Clytemnestra.

The cast is authoritative and experienced enough to carry out Friedrich's intentions with complete conviction and they effortlessly manage lip-synch. Rysanek's unforgettable Elektra, distraught, deranged, eventually maniacal, crowned her career as a Strauss soprano with this interpretation and vocally she encompasses every facet of the demanding role. The recognition scene, with Fischer-Dieskau's nobly sung and acted, solemn and still Orestes, is a heart-stopping experience. As Chrysothemis Ligendza, robed in white against Elektra's black, is keen-edged, clear in contrast to Rysanek's warmer, more occluded tone. Encouraged by the staging, Varnay exults in Clytemnestra's superstitions, fears and decadence, mightily convincing if a bit over the top. Beirer is a fittingly eupeptic, feeble Aegistheus. Greindl makes a farewell appearance in the small role of the Tutor.

In their last co-operation with their revered conductor, the Vienna Philharmonic play refulgently for Böhm and his reading is, as expected, elemental, taut and emotionally overwhelming, a fit *adieu* to a composer he served so faithfully over such a long period.

R. Strauss Die Frau ohne Schatten.

Julia Varady *sop* Empress
Plácido Domingo *ten* Emperor
Hildegard Behrens *sop* Dyer's wife
José van Dam *bar* Barak the Dyer
Reinhild Runkel *contr* Nurse
Albert Dohmen *bar* Spirit-messenger
Sumi Jo *sop* Voice of the Falcon
Robert Gambill *ten* Apparition of a young yan
Elzbieta Ardam *mez* Voice from above
Eva Lind *sop* Guardian of the temple
Gottfried Hornik *bar* One-eyed brother
Hans Franzen *bass* One-armed brother
Wilfried Gahmlich *ten* Hunchback brother
Vienna Boys' Choir; Vienna State Opera Chorus; Vienna Philharmonic Orchestra / Sir Georg Solti.
Decca Ⓟ Ⓒ 436 243-2DHO3 (three discs: 195 minutes: DDD). Notes, text and translation included. Recorded 1989/91.

1992

This qualifies as being one of the most excitingly recorded operas of any. The range of sound is extraordinary yet it is never gained at the expense of detail. Warmth and range are self-evident; at the same time the most intricate passage can be clearly heard. The Decca producers and engineers who set standards 25 and more years ago with Solti's sets of *Salome*, *Elektra* and *Der Rosenkavalier* here scored another triumph. The EMI/Sawallisch version has nothing like the same immediacy.

Such a glorious sound picture is all of a piece with Solti's interpretation. As one might have surmised from the aforementioned sets he brings out all the histrionic power of the score, all its elemental force and passion. As ever, this sometimes means living from bar to bar on a consistent high, with little room left for relaxation, but it does give this many-sided score a dramatic tautness – as was the case when he first conducted at Covent Garden in a famous staging back in the 1960s. As he tells us in a note in the booklet, the work has "always been one of the greatest loves of my operatic life" and he conducts it *con amore* as at the great D major theme in Act 1, or in the heartfelt duet for Barak and his wife in Act 3. He also concentrates, as much as any version, on the fantastic/allegorical side of the work: every fish, unborn child and visionary youth comes vividly before us.

If you think you might tire of Solti's frontal attack you may prefer the slightly more lyrical, even-tempered readings of Sawallisch and Böhm. The blatancy of the G major/C major rejoicing at the work's close, when done with so much extroversion, becomes a shade trying. On the other hand, there are one or two moments where Solti's performance hangs fire – at fig. 69 in Act 1 for instance, surely taken too stiffly, and in some of the Emperor's music where the conductor goes carefully, perhaps in deference to the relative unfamiliarity of his tenor with this music. In his note Solti makes the point that the musical problems "are enormous, the greatest being the problem of balance". Of course on disc the need to keep the text clear, while not holding back the glories of the orchestration, can be overcome so that here the sometimes conflicting demands of words and music to which Solti refers are reconciled.

In his achievement, Solti has the inestimable co-operation of the Vienna Philharmonic, as did Böhm (on Decca), and there can be no doubt that they live the work and play it with greater authority than their Bavarian Radio colleagues (Sawallisch). While the sound for Böhm is still incredible considering its age (1955), Solti's recording inevitably has a broader spectrum.

As ever, when one turns to the singers, an ideal would be a composite of the best elements in each cast. The soprano roles in this version are both superbly taken. As the Dyer's wife, Behrens is far and away superior to Sawallisch's Vinzing and Böhm's Goltz (Decca), rivalling the classic interpretation of Nilsson (Böhm/DG, reviewed below). It may be that both dramatic sopranos were vocally a shade past their best when they turned to this role, but both show an instinctive understanding of its needs. Behrens tugs at the heart in every one of her solos – notably in her frustrated outburst in Act 2, culminating in the heartbreak of the line, "Barak, ich habe es nicht getan". But she caps this with her deeply eloquent singing in the long solo at the start of Act 3, the very centre of the part. Praise cannot be higher for Varady than to say that she challenges Rysanek's hegemony in the role of the Empress (both of the Böhm sets). Varady's highly charged, vibrating tone invests the part with just the right sense of growing knowledge of the self, and time after time her singing, on a technical level, is rewarding in its sensitivity and accuracy. Rysanek perceives the part in a more inward manner; Varady is the more intense. Both have a better understanding of the part's needs than Studer (Sawallisch).

José van Dam sings Barak with the strength of tone and line, the sincerity of purpose one would expect, but – perhaps because he hadn't much experience of it on stage – he doesn't catch at the heart as do Berry (Böhm/DG), even more Schöffler (Böhm/Decca). Many will buy the set for Domingo's Emperor (the wrong reason) and not be disappointed by his stalwart, straightforward, blessedly steady singing. But Kollo (Sawallisch), once you make allowance for the beat in his tone, sings the role with more idiomatic diction and more involvement; so does the admirable King (Böhm/DG). Hopf's voice for Böhm/Decca is best fitted for the part, but he doesn't show much imagination. The Nurse, being a gift of a part, is well sung by all the mezzos. Runkel certainly conveys malign force. The minor roles are all carefully cast by Decca. Dohmen confirms his talent as the Spirit-messenger and Sumi Jo as the Falcon's voice is luxury casting indeed.

This version must be first choice now, not only as a splendid achievement all round; however, those for whom economy is a necessity need hardly consider that they are being fobbed off with second best if they buy either of the older Böhm sets.

R. Strauss Die Frau ohne Schatten.

Leonie Rysanek *sop* Empress
James King *ten* Emperor
Birgit Nilsson *sop* Dyer's wife
Walter Berry *bass* Barak the Dyer
Ruth Hesse *mez* Nurse
Peter Wimberger *bass-bar* Spirit-messenger
Lotte Rysanek *sop* Voice of the falcon, Guardian of the temple
Ewald Aichberger *ten* Apparition of a young man
Gertrude Jahn *mez* Voice from above
Hans Helm *bar* One-eyed brother
Lorenzo Alvary *bass* One-armed brother
Murray Dickie *ten* Hunchback brother
Vienna State Opera Chorus and Orchestra / Karl Böhm.
DG Strauss Opera Edition Ⓜ ① 445 325-2GX3 (three discs: 175 minutes: ADD). Notes, text and translation included. Recorded at performances in the Vienna State Opera on October 23rd and 27th, 1977.

There were rumours for a long time that a 'live performance' version of *Die Frau ohne Schatten* had been recorded at performances in Vienna under the direction of Karl Böhm, and this is the proof that they were true – so is preserved what was the classic cast for the work during the 1960s and 1970s. Böhm himself had always been closely connected with the opera and his 1955 Decca recording has always survived in the catalogue. Böhm makes the standard theatre cuts, rather more damaging than those in that Decca version, but not so many as those on DG conducted by Keilberth, recorded live at Munich in 1963.

Böhm's direction on the Decca set was described as possessing "a fantastic, absolutely appropriate dynamism", and he never lost that even in his later years, as you can judge here. Of course, in every way the sound is superior to that on the older set, and throughout, the Vienna strings play with an unmatchable Straussian glow, while the rest of the orchestra cope unflinchingly with this unbelievably complex score.

Opinions of the work itself will always differ. The banal and bombastic seem often to rub shoulders with passages where Strauss is at his most sublime; Strauss too often seems defeated by the confused symbolism of the libretto and what Norman Del Mar calls its "impenetrable intricacies". At the same time, much of the Third Act lives at an elevated level hardly found in earlier or later works. It is Böhm's skill to make us forget, much of the time, the obfuscation and enjoy the beauties and fantasies. If the cast occasionally sounds a little elderly, its unrivalled understanding of its collective task wins through by the end. Nilsson's Dyer's wife is least worried by the passing years, and here she gives a performance of a role that demands a rich lower register as well as a gleaming top to set beside her Elektra and Salome, indeed at certain points surpass them in sheer involvement and moving utterance. Anyone who may have thought her a cold singer needs to hear her remorse when she realizes the anguish she has caused her husband, Barak, sung here – as it was at Covent Garden – with sympathetic warmth and generous breadth by Walter Berry. He is not always quite secure in line or pitch, but who cares when he is so obviously singing from deep within himself. At the time of this recording Leonie Rysanek had remained unrivalled as the Empress for some 35 years. Here, after an initial huskiness, she gives an interpretation of more depth and understanding than she did on the 1955 set, and soars to the heights with almost equal ease. Her two long solos explore to the full the character's agony of soul and growing self-realization. As her Emperor, James King copes well with the role's awkward tessitura, but his tone is often on the dry side.

Ruth Hesse makes the Nurse into a ruthless schemer, as she did on stage at Covent Garden, and the microphone often catches an edge on her tone. Smaller roles are taken with understanding by members of the Vienna ensemble. The recording faithfully captures the excellent acoustics of the Vienna State Opera.

Although out-and-out Straussians will have to have the complete version, few other sets are likely to surpass the conductor, orchestra and cast assembled here, all of whom had benefited by career-long experience of the work, and convey with entire conviction the moral dilemmas and psychological confusions of Hofmannsthal's involved scenario. Strauss is well served by them. The work itself, being so difficult to stage, benefits a lot from being heard in the home where one can imagine for oneself the fantastical milieus and supernatural interventions predicated by the authors.

R. Strauss Die Frau ohne Schatten.

Cheryl Studer *sop* Empress
Thomas Moser *ten* Emperor
Eva Marton *sop* Dyer's wife
Robert Hale *bass* Barak the Dyer
Marjana Lipovšek *contr* Nurse
Bryn Terfel *bass-bar* Spirit-messenger
Andrea Rost *sop* Voice of the falcon
Herbert Lippert *ten* Apparition of a young man
Elizabeth Norberg-Schulz *sop* Guardian of the temple
Elzbieta Ardam *mez* Voice from above
Manfred Hemm *bar* One-eyed brother
Hans Franzen *bass* One-armed brother
Wilfried Gahmlich *ten* Hunchback brother
Salzburg Children's Choir; Vienna State Opera Chorus; Vienna Philharmonic Orchestra / Sir Georg Solti. *Stage Director:* **Götz Friedrich.** *Video Director:* **Brian Large.**
Decca Ⓟ 🔲 071 425-3DH2 (204 minutes). Recorded at performances during the Salzburg Festival in 1992.

This performance is taken from the Salzburg Festival of 1992 and has nothing to do with the CD-only recording – indeed this video's Empress, Cheryl Studer, appears on the EMI set, conducted by Sawallisch. And Studer's performance would be the most compelling reason for investing in this video version: she gives her taxing role a vocal interpretation that is technically and expressively accomplished and she is totally committed dramatically, if not quite so vulnerable and affecting as Varady on the Decca CD set. Her tone cuts strongly and vibrantly through the complex orchestration and Solti's somewhat blatant projection of it.

Marton achieves the same effect but in her case the tone sounds worn and ugly (no other words will do) and often painful to the ear; nor can it be said that her acting, submitted to close-up, is convincing. Hale makes a suitably moving figure of Barak, but his voice isn't as steady as it once was and he sometimes fights a losing battle with the pit. As the Emperor, Moser finds the right heroic timbre, but his tone lacks sap. While Lipovšek has the measure of the Nurse's music, the butch interpretation imposed on her by Friedrich, suggesting a lesbian attachment to the Empress, is uncomfortable. Bryn Terfel makes a strong showing as the Spirit-messenger.

Some day a designer and director will find an inspiring solution to the almost insoluble problems set by the creators. Here the basically plain, unimaginative sets fail to match the metaphysical aspects of the libretto and not all the more outrageous elements are confronted. Nor does Friedrich seem to be giving much detailed guidance to his singers as regards interpretation: perhaps such starry singers were not always easy to direct. The Baraks should surely not be present at the Emperor's trial. For all these strictures, the production has its moments of wonder and of emotional force, thanks mainly to Strauss.

The natural flow of the work often eludes Solti. There is excitement enough but it is too often of the moment. The Vienna Philharmonic play magnificently and the richness of their contribution comes across on video. Brian Large's video direction is exemplary in deciphering the action for newcomers to the work, who also have subtitles to aid them.

R. Strauss Friedenstag.

Roger Roloff *bass-bar* Commandant
Alessandra Marc *sop* Maria
William Wildermann *bass* Sergeant
George Shirley *ten* Rifleman
Max Wittges *bass-bar* Corporal

Peter van Derick *bar* Musketeer
Paul Schmidt *bass* Bugler
Ruben Broitman *ten* A Piedmontese
Stephen Lusmann *bar* Officer, Front-line Officer
Terry Cook *bass* Holsteiner
Richard Cassilly *ten* Burgomaster
James Wood *bas* Prelate
Karen Williams *sop* Woman of the People
New York City Gay Men's Chorus; Collegiate Chorale and Orchestra / Robert Bass.
Koch International Classics Ⓟ Ⓒ 37111-2 (80 minutes: DDD). Notes, text and translation
included. Recorded at a performance in Carnegie Hall, New York on November 19th, 1989.

With the possible exception of *Guntram* (his first opera), the one-act *Friedenstag* is the least known of
Strauss's operas and in many respects the least characteristic. The music is so different from most of
what Strauss was writing at the time. Instead of harking back to romanticism, as in *Arabella* and
Daphne, he composes here in a tougher style more in keeping with his own time, bringing into play
Hindemithian, even Bergian ideas. The final paean to peace recalls the Mahler of the symphonies'
choral sections. The piece is more dramatic oratorio than opera. It was to have been his second
collaboration with Stefan Zweig as librettist, but after the Nazis came to power there was no further
chance of working with a Jewish writer so the text was written by Joseph Gregor, much to Strauss's
irritation, although Zweig acted as adviser and indeed revised some of the scenes.

    Friedenstag was first performed in Munich in 1938 and a few months later in Dresden in a double
bill with *Daphne*. Considering that its theme is anti-war – it is set in a besieged city on the last day of
the Thirty Years' War in 1648 – it is extraordinary that the Nazis permitted it to have over 100
performances in two years, especially as Strauss was already out of favour. Perhaps they were
bamboozled by the final chorus, which might have suited them and has a Shostakovich-like
ambivalence. It is an austere score, strongly diatonic, its sombreness relieved only by the Piedmontese
youth's Italian aria and the long soprano aria for the Commandant's wife, Maria. It was made at a
public concert performance in Carnegie Hall, finely conducted by Robert Bass and with splendid
singing of the roles of the Commandant and his wife by Roger Roloff and Alessandra Marc, with
some excellent smaller cameos by William Wildermann, George Shirley and Richard Cassilly. The
recording is pretty well balanced and has real 'presence'.

    It is recommended to all Straussians but be warned not to rush back to the shop after purchasing
it, thinking that a disc is missing. The case is designed for two discs, but all 80 minutes are
accommodated on one. Also, although there are 21 index points, there is no indication in the booklet
of where each of them begins, though a loose 'insert' has been provided.

R. Strauss Friedenstag.
Hans Hotter *bass-bar* Commandant
Viorica Ursuleac *sop* Maria
Herbert Alsen *bass* Sergeant
Josef Witt *ten* Rifleman
Hermann Wiedemann *bass* Corporal
Carl Bissuti *bass* Musketeer
Nikolaus Zec *bass* Bugler
Anton Dermota *ten* A Piedmontese
Hermann Gallos *ten* Officer
Georg Monthy *bass* Front-line Officer
Karl Kamann *bass* Holsteiner
Willy Franter *ten* Burgomaster
Viktor Madin *bar* Prelate
Mela Bugarinovic *mez* Woman of the People

R. Strauss Arabella – excerpts.
Margit Bokor *sop*
Adele Kern *sop*
Viorica Ursuleac *sop*
Gertrud Rünger *mez*
Alfred Jerger *bass-bar*
Richard Mayr *bass*
Vienna State Opera Chorus and Orchestra / Clemens Krauss.

R. Strauss Ariadne auf Naxos – excerpts.
Adele Kern *sop*
Dora Komarek *sop*
Anny Konetzni *sop*
Elisabeth Rutgers *sop*

Else Schulz *sop*
Elena Nikolaidi *mez*
Friedrich Jelinek *ten*
Alexander Pichler *ten*
Richard Sallaba *ten*
Set Svanholm *ten*
William Wernigk *ten*
Hermann Baier *bar*
Alfred Poell *bar*
Alfred Jerger *bass-bar*
Alfred Vogel *bass*
Alfred Muzzarelli *spkr*
Vienna State Opera Orchestra / Rudolf Moralt.
Koch Schwann mono Ⓜ Ⓒ 314652 (two discs: 143 minutes: ADD). *Friedenstag* recorded from a
broadcast performance from the Vienna State Opera on June 10th, 1939; *Arabella* from a
performance on October 29th, 1933; *Ariadne auf Naxos* from a performance on October 16th,
1941.

This issue alone would be justification enough for the whole Vienna State Opera archive project,
simply because it offers us a complete performance of *Friedenstag* given by its creators in 1939,
shortly after its première. Here Krauss, his wife, Viorica Ursuleac and Hotter prove incontrovertibly
that the work has a strength and validity not often accorded it by even the most dedicated of
Straussians. Krauss brings immense conviction and energy to it – *he* obviously believed in the work.
Then Ursuleac gives the performance of her life as Maria. She is fearless and tireless in tackling the
high As, B flats and Bs in which the role abounds, singing with vibrant tone and in a possessed manner
fitting an overwrought woman starved of the love of her husband who has poured all his energies into
war. Finally, she provides the necessary ecstasy when she wins him back and sees the war come to an
end. As ever, Strauss glories in his writing for a *lirico-spinto*, and Ursuleac glories with him.

The 30-year-old Hotter, in towering voice, gives to the Commandant's part the right sense of a man
dedicated to his role of defending his Kaiser's cause and honour at whatever cost to his men or to his
personal life. A team of Viennese stalwarts of the day fills the smaller roles satisfactorily, with the
young Dermota notable as the Piedmontese youth musing on his beloved Italy and its girls: it's
another role nicely etched in by the composer. The recorded sound, taken in this case off a broadcast,
is good by the standard of the day, but by no means anything special. However, the voices don't
distort and much of the orchestral detail can be gleaned.

Friedenstag is flanked by excerpts from two other works. Those from a 1933 *Arabella*, also a
Viennese 'first', featuring the original singers of the two main roles, are not so desirable since Ursuleac
and Jerger recorded the most important passages commercially (on Decca-Polydor, also in 1933).
Nevertheless, it is good to hear Krauss conducting with such élan.

The excerpts from the 1941 *Ariadne*, with the reliable Moralt in the pit, are interesting mainly for
the opportunity to hear artists in unaccustomed roles, of which they left no recorded evidence, the
one exception being Kern, who made Zerbinetta's aria in the 1930s – she remains a delightful
interpreter of the part. Anny Konetzni, more renowned as a Brünnhilde and Isolde, lightens her tone
successfully to present a sympathetic, lovingly sung heroine. Svanholm's somewhat intractable tenor
makes a strong effect as an ardent Bacchus. Else Schulz seems miscast as the Composer, and erratic
in her execution.

R. Strauss Intermezzo.
Lucia Popp *sop* Christine Storch
Philipp Brammer *spkr* Little Franz
Dietrich Fischer-Dieskau *bar* Robert Storch
Gabriele Fuchs *sop* Anna
Adolf Dallapozza *ten* Baron Lummer
Klaus Hirte *bar* Notary
Gudrun Greindl-Rosner *sop* Notary's wife
Raimund Grumbach *bar* Businessman
Martin Finke *ten* Conductor
Jörn W. Wilsing *bar* Lawyer
Kurt Moll *bass* Singer
Elisabeth Woska *spkr* Cook
Erika Rüggeberg *spkr* Marie, Therese
Karin Hautermann *spkr* Resi
Bavarian Radio Symphony Orchestra / Wolfgang Sawallisch.
EMI Ⓟ Ⓒ CDS7 49337-2 (two discs: 133 minutes: ADD). Notes included. Recorded 1980.

Sheer joy, this transfer, still the only CD recording easily available of what is increasingly coming to
be regarded as one of Strauss's finest operas. This account of a crisis in his marriage, all caused by a

girl mistaking his name for someone else's, drew a brilliant score from Strauss. He set his own sparkling libretto to music in which wit, sentiment and satire sit easily together. The conversational recitative is a masterly example of continuous melody, matched by orchestral virtuosity in evolving melody from fragmentary phrases. The role of Christine is a gift to a lyric soprano and is marvellously characterized by Lucia Popp, neither too shrewish nor too soft-grained, conveying her irresistible attraction for her husband, Robert Storch (alias Strauss). The latter role is forcefully sung by Fischer-Dieskau and there are excellent portrayals by the rest of the cast, especially from Adolf Dallapozza as Baron Lummer. But the prime pleasure in this technically brilliant recording – every word and note crystal-clear – is Sawallisch's comprehensive command of the opera and the flawless orchestral performance by the Bavarian Radio Symphony Orchestra. The interludes, miniature tone-poems in themselves, are sumptuously played. But why no English translation in the booklet, as there was with the LP set? This, of all operas, needs one.

R. Strauss Der Rosenkavalier.

Dame Elisabeth Schwarzkopf *sop* Die Feldmarschallin, First orphan
Christa Ludwig *mez* Octavian, Second orphan
Otto Edelmann *bass* Baron Ochs
Teresa Stich-Randall *sop* Sophie
Eberhard Waechter *bar* Faninal
Nicolai Gedda *ten* Italian tenor
Kerstin Meyer *contr* Annina, Third orphan
Paul Kuen *ten* Valzacchi
Anny Felbermayer *sop* Milliner
Harald Pröghlöf *bar* Notary
Franz Bierbach *bass* Police Commissioner
Erich Majkut *ten* Feldmarschallin's Major-domo
Gerhard Unger *ten* Faninal's Major-domo, Animal seller
Karl Friedrich *ten* Landlord
Ljuba Welitsch *sop* Leitmetzerin
Loughton High School for Girls and Bancroft's School Choirs;
Philharmonia Chorus and Orchestra / Herbert von Karajan.
EMI ℗ ① CDS5 56242-2 (three discs: 191 minutes: ADD). Notes, text and translation included. Recorded 1956.

1988

This really does triumph over just about every other stereo reading of *Rosenkavalier* – even the outstanding 1969 Solti/Decca set – and the triumph is, almost entirely, Schwarzkopf's own. She stands at the centre of it as a Marschallin who incarnates that sense of "the holiest exuberance of life" about which Stefan Zweig wrote of the pre-war years, and which is, in turn, incarnated uniquely in this opera. There is never any sense of mere manner: rather her volatility, dignity, and her ability to catch the evanescent life-breath of each word and phrase as it is spun into line sets the pace and spirit of the performance as a whole. When she and the orchestra are alone together for the first time, in "Da geht er hin", there is a tension to be found nowhere else.

Karajan, without the opulent acoustic or playing of the Vienna Philharmonic for DG 25 years later, captures the essential fragility and ambiguity as well as the hedonism of the score, springing into dance under the feet of the dialogue, catching the transparent, Mozartian element of its writing as he has never done since. For his later *Der Rosenkavalier*, he adopts textures and tempos which, to extend a metaphor, certainly don't permit the performance to pass the diabetic test. If it's Sachertorte you want, then the 1982-4 recording is for you, though you must also be prepared for the comparatively lack-lustre singing of Anna Tomowa-Sintow, a sepulchral Ochs in Kurt Moll, and an uneasy Sophie in Janet Perry.

Agnes Baltsa's Octavian is the strong point on this later recording: strong in interest anyway. But to hear Christa Ludwig in 1956 is to see light streaming in through a window; and to listen to Otto Edelmann's Ochs is, to know a truly Austrian gentleman singer who, as Strauss specified, is only "a bounder inwardly". Teresa Stich-Randall's Sophie is very much a young woman in the world, yet not of it: Karajan's handling of Act 2 is a masterpiece of timing and sense of moment.

Solti's performance (Decca) is also very difficult to live without. The dramatic presence, the orchestral playing, the singing of Yvonne Minton's Octavian and Helen Donath's Sophie are unsurpassed, and the casting of the minor parts (Anton Dermota as Landlord, Kurt Equiluz as Major-domo, Arleen Auger as one of the three orphans) is as irresistible as the production quality as a whole.

R. Strauss Der Rosenkavalier.
Maria Reining *sop* Die Feldmarschallin
Sena Jurinac *sop* Octavian
Ludwig Weber *bass* Baron Ochs
Hilde Gueden *sop* Sophie

Alfred Poell *bar* Faninal
Anton Dermota *ten* Italian tenor
Hilde Rössl-Majdan *mez* Annina
Peter Klein *ten* Valzacchi
Berta Seidl *sop* Milliner
Franz Bierbach *bass* Notary
Walter Berry *bass* Police Commissioner
Harald Pröglhöf *bass* Feldmarschallin's Major-domo
August Jaresch *ten* Faninal's Major-domo
Erich Majkut *ten* Animal Seller, Landlord
Judith Hellweig *sop* Leitmetzerin
Vienna State Opera Chorus; Vienna Philharmonic Orchestra / Erich Kleiber.
Decca Historic mono Ⓜ ① 425 950-2DM3 (three discs: 197 minutes: ADD). Notes, text and
translation included. Recorded 1954.

Another classic performance. It is heartily welcome, especially as Decca have done wonders in
cleaning the sound, the set seeming warmer and more spacious than in any of its LP guises. The
bloom on the playing of the Vienna Philharmonic is grateful to the ear and the voices stand ideally
in relation to the instruments. That is doubly heartening given the fact that for many Kleiber's
interpretation still stands above that of any of his successors, except perhaps his son Carlos's similar
reading. Kleiber senior's innate and deep understanding of the score and his instinctive feeling for this
area of the Viennese idiom remains unsurpassed; so does his convincing treatment of the score's
weaker pages (it is here given complete). Above all, Kleiber never makes the mistake, as many believe
Karajan did, of lingering too long over the work's purple passage, nor does he overheat its more active
ones as Solti was inclined to do: the key to his reading is a combination of lightness, line and
incandescence – try the opening of Act 2. Kleiber is the *fons et origo* in interpreting this work: once
you have his reading under your skin you can proceed to more self-indulgent and/or brilliant
performances.

The vocal glory of the set remains Sena Jurinac's Octavian. Here in more refulgent voice, perhaps,
than anywhere else on disc, she gives the performance of one's dreams. How gleaming yet how warm
is her voice, how naturally impetuous and intense her colloquies with her elders. Jurinac carefully
denotes Octavian's growing fascination with Sophie. Then, as the maudlin Mariandl of Act 3, she
changes her tone subtly, never exaggerating. Finally, her voice soars gloriously in the trio and duet
that crown the work. It is a definitive interpretation, and will surely remain so.

Maria Reining's Marschallin has been badly underrated. Her approach is natural, stylish and very
moving in its simplicity – and its obedience to the score. Not a trace of self-consciousness or arch
phrasing spoils the patent honesty of her portrayal. The voice itself sounds a little tremulous at the
start, and it never quite gains the warmth other Marschallins achieve, but the unmannered yet
absolutely idiomatic enunciation of the text is compensation enough, and her partnership with
Jurinac's Octavian is often memorable. As a whole this set, above all, recalls the kind of rapport
between the artists you would have heard at the time in Vienna: as the booklet writers say, those who
took part in this recording emphasize "the homogeneity of the ensemble". Gueden was part of that
ensemble: her singing may be a shade sophisticated for the part (and she shouldn't show dislike for
Ochs before she has met him), but the accuracy and firm focus of her singing count for much. In any
case, she is preferable to other Sophies on disc, except for Bernstein's Lucia Popp on Sony Classical.

Ludwig Weber's Ochs is a ripe, assured assumption, sung with total command of the text and in an
authentic Viennese accent. There is no better, not even Mayr on the 1933 Hager/HMV set (now
transferred to Pearl). For such a large bass, Weber is amazingly nimble of tongue in the restored
passages in Act 1. Among the smaller parts, one notes Dermota's lyrical Italian Tenor, Alfred Poell's
fussily excited Faninal, Peter Klein's properly nasty Valzacchi and Walter Berry's imposing Police
Commissioner (his role includes the opening of passages usually omitted). All are versed in that
essential, command of Strauss's *parlando* style, so that Hofmannsthal's racy, keenly fashioned libretto
is given wit and point.

Although admiration for the Solti and the first Karajan sets remains undiminished – and, of course,
they benefit from stereo placing as compared with the mono here – the Kleiber is the performance
many seasoned collectors would choose to take to their desert island.

R. Strauss Der Rosenkavalier.

Dame Gwyneth Jones *sop* Die Feldmarschallin
Brigitte Fassbaender *mez* Octavian
Manfred Jungwirth *bass* Baron Ochs
Lucia Popp *sop* Sophie
Benno Kusche *bar* Faninal
Francisco Araiza *ten* Italian Tenor
Gudrun Wewezow *mez* Annina
David Thaw *ten* Valzacchi
Susanne Sonnenschein *sop* Milliner

Hans Wilbrink *bar* Notary
Albrecht Peter *bar* Police Commissioner
Georg Paskuda *ten* Feldmarschallin's Major-domo
Friedrich Lenz *ten* Faninal's Major-domo
Norbert Orth *ten* Landlord
Anneliese Waas *sop* Leitmetzerin
Bavarian State Opera Chorus and Orchestra / Carlos Kleiber.
Stage Director: **Otto Schenk.** *ideo Director:* **Horant H. Hohlfeld.**
DG ⬚⬚ 072 405-3GH; ☙ 072 405-1GH2 (182 minutes). Recorded 1979.

The famous Otto Schenk representation of Strauss's best-loved score at the Bavarian State Opera, memorably conducted by Carlos Kleiber, is here enshrined on video. It remains a benchmark by which other performances can be judged. Schenk's orthodox, highly detailed and perceptive staging within Jürgen Rose's handsome sets eschewed fashionable modernities and so has stood the test of time. Kleiber's interpretation, unsurpassed since his father Erich conducted the work, has that combination of warmth, lightness and élan the score calls for, allied to controlled but never effusive sentiment. The orchestra play for him with a confidence gained from long experience of Kleiber's impulsive ways. Shots of him in the pit during the preludes to Acts 1 and 3 show how incisive his beat can be and how much he actually enjoys conducting the piece.

The instinctive, natural way the principals react to each other is further evidence of the rapport achieved in this production, especially in the intimacies of the dialogues between the Marschallin and Octavian, the Octavian and Sophie, then the interplay among the three in the closing scenes, that lie at the heart of the piece. In the name part Fassbaender acts the ardent, impetuous youth to the life, sensual with the Marschallin in Act 1, lovestruck with Sophie in Act 2, and highly amusing in the Mariandl disguise. Although by the time this video was made, Popp was looking a shade mature for Sophie, she conveys by turn, charm, mettle, indignation (at Ochs's boorish behaviour) and confusion at her final predicament, singing with the right blend of sensuousness and purity. Jones's Marschallin looks appealing, even girlishly flirtatious, in Act 1, then switches to dignified authority in Act 3, suggesting all the heartbreak of the close. Jungwirth is a ripe, experienced Ochs, occasionally too boorish in behaviour and a shade approximate with his note values. Kusche is a too elderly but rightly tetchy Faninal, Araiza a mellifluous Italian Tenor. Smaller roles are filled with long-serving artists of the house. The sound is excellent, especially on LaserDisc.

R. Strauss Salome.
Cheryl Studer *sop* Salome
Horst Hiestermann *ten* Herod
Leonie Rysanek *sop* Herodias
Bryn Terfel *bar* Jokanaan
Clemens Bieber *ten* Narraboth
Marianne Rorhølm *contr* Page
Friedrich Molsberger *bass* First Nazarene
Ralf Lukas *bass* Second Nazarene
William Murray *bass* First soldier
Bengt Rundgren *bass* Second soldier
Klaus Lang *bar* Cappadocian
Orchestra of the Deutsche Oper, Berlin / Giuseppe Sinopoli.
DG Ⓔ Ⓛ 431 810-2GH2 (two discs: 102 minutes: DDD). Text and translation included. Recorded 1990.

This is a magnificent achievement on all sides, but chief praise must go to Cheryl Studer for giving such an all-consuming account of the title-role, one to set beside those of Nilsson (for Solti, reviewed below) and Behrens (Karajan on his 1977 EMI set) on disc, and to be spoken of in the same breath as the legendary Ljuba Welitsch, whom Studer most recalls. Studer has every qualification for the part. The voice, fresh, vibrant and sensuous in tone, carries total conviction as she presents Salome's growing fascination, infatuation and eventual obsession with the body of Jokanaan, ending in the arresting necrophilia of the famous final scene. Studer expresses Salome's wheedling, spoilt nature, strong will, and eventual ecstasy in tones apt for every aspect of the strenuous role.

What strikes you more than anything is her wonderful control of sweet *pianissimos*, as at "Lass mich ihn beru'hren dein Leib" ("Let me touch your body") in her attempted seduction of Jokanaan. Throughout, her voice is at once flexible and powerful enough to fulfil every demand of the composer without exaggeration or false gesture: Strauss would surely have been delighted with her assumption, which culminates in the growing intensity and voluptuousness of the final scene, carried through with not a trace of strain. She seems to have the power of Nilsson, the understanding of Behrens and the subtlety of Caballé (for Leinsdorf on his 1968 RCA set).

She is supported up to the hilt by Sinopoli's incandescent conducting. In another score his forceful, overwhelming direction might seem a mite exaggerated but *Salome*, for better or worse, can take such treatment as Solti has already shown. Sinopoli certainly matches him in decibels but also in expounding Strauss's inspired scoring, although the spacious DG recording seems rather more intent on emphasizing the general picture rather than focusing on detail. Nor can Sinopoli here be accused of going slow. Indeed, his reading is if anything on the swift side, his speeds similar to those of Leinsdorf, never one to linger. Sinopoli appears to have honed his own Berlin orchestra into an instrument that willingly does his bidding. Though his reading certainly isn't as finely honed as Karajan's it is happily more subjective, more immediate in impact.

Sinopoli seems to have inspired his entire cast to great things. Bryn Terfel's Jokanaan was his notable début in a substantial role on disc. His voice sounds too distant when he is heard from his dungeon, a misjudgement on the producer's part, but once above ground he delivers Jokanaan's imprecations with splendid conviction and unflagging tone. His voice sounds uncannily like Thomas Allen's writ large, particularly so at Jokanaan's prophesy of Christ's coming. He is no more nor less commanding in the role than Solti's Krauss or Karajan's van Dam. Leonie Rysanek, a former Salome herself, is a predictably colourful and wilful Herodias. Hiestermann's Herod is properly neurotic and crazed, though his keen-edged tenor occasionally becomes unsteady when he puts too much pressure on it. Clemens Bieber provides a pleasingly lyrical Narraboth. Marianne Rørholm makes her mark as the Page. The other small roles are filled by stalwarts of the Deutsche Oper, some of them not as ingratiating as those on the rival versions.

Nobody is going to dispense lightly with their Solti or Karajan versions, both valid and well-tried views of the work, but the Sinopoli is fully worthy of standing beside them. For a newcomer to the work Studer's superb portrayal tips the balance in favour of this set. She has all her rivals' accomplishments and something more.

R. Strauss Salome.
Christel Goltz *sop* Salome
Helmut Melchert *ten* Herod
Siw Ericsdotter *sop* Herodias
Ernst Gutstein *bar* Jokanaan
Heinz Hoppe *ten* Narraboth
Eva Fleischer *contr* Page
Theo Adam *bass-bar* First Nazarene
Johannes Kemter *ten* Second Nazarene
Rainer Lüdeke, Helmut Eyle *basses* First and Second soldiers
Fred Teschler *bass* Cappadocian
Friederike Apelt *sop* Slave
Staatskapelle Dresden / Otmar Suitner.
Berlin Classics Ⓜ ① 0091 012BC (two discs: 94 minutes: ADD). Text and translation included. Recorded 1963.

Text and musical gesture shine as bright as the moon over Judaea in this remarkably fresh-sounding *Salome*. Suitner was lucky to have such vivid recording at his service: astonishing for 1963, less manipulated than the Culshaw-produced Decca 'soundstage' for Solti and hardly prone to the distortions that afflict Karajan's otherwise overwhelming Salzburg spectacular. But in any case the conductor looks well enough to the balances – diaphanous when they need to be, though not perhaps sensual, the brass packing quite a punch when finally they're unleashed in the interlude of Jokanaan's return to the cistern. Suitner is easily in command of 'difficult' passages such as the Jews' quarrel, and he follows the dramaturgy so keenly that one never feels any jolt between extreme breadth and whirlwind fury (very well articulated, too, especially towards the end of the dance).

Goltz, in the last of her four studio recordings, plays her part in this quick-change artistry: her proud announcement "I am Salome, daughter of Herodias, princess of Judaea" so commands our attention that the sudden blast of Jokanaan's wrath comes as a complete surprise, as does the uproar after the innocuous demand for the prophet's head. It's not hard to realize why she was regarded as the complete Salome of her time: reasons enough are the seductive giggle in the voice when asking Narraboth a special favour, the compound of irony, disgust (chest-voice colour on "Scharlachnatter") and searing nostalgia ("du hättest mich geliebt") in a near-ideal final scene. 'Near-ideal' because while the energetic technique is used to project the meaning of the words as well as sheer vocal power in the upper register, Goltz was after all in her early fifties and there are times when she doesn't quite reach her desired goal. Still, she remains as interesting a Salome as Behrens for Karajan).

Ernst Gutstein finds much natural beauty of line in Jokanaan's prophecies: never hectoring, though with a hint of tearfulness that verges on the sentimental in the 'Sea of Galilee' solo (and sentimentality sits especially uneasily alongside the rant). Melchert is the perfect Herod, a lyric-heroic tenor who makes the drinking-song and the desperate promises sound rather beautiful, but who is allowed to depart from the notes when neuroses need to come to the fore; Ericsdotter, his (soprano) spouse, plays safer but puts across the gloating well enough. All the minor roles are taken with exemplary diction if not always the greatest ease of phrasing or pitching. The interesting documentation, going perhaps a little too far in giving us the career-histories of each soldier and Nazarene, overstates the case when it suggests the recording may be remembered as "the last monument to genuine musical teamwork", but it certainly has a point.

R. Strauss Salome

Birgit Nilsson *sop* Salome
Gerhard Stolze *ten* Herod
Grace Hoffman *mez* Herodias
Eberhard Waechter *bar* Jokanaan
Waldemar Kmentt *ten* Narraboth
Josephine Veasey *mez* Page
Tom Krause *bar* First Nazarene
Nigel Douglas *ten* Second Nazarene
Zenon Koznowski *bass* First soldier
Heinz Holecek *bass* Second soldier
Theodore Kirschbichler *bass* Cappadocian
Liselotte Maikl *sop* Slave
Vienna Philharmonic Orchestra / Sir Georg Solti.
Decca Ⓟ Ⓓ 414 414-2DH2 (two discs: 90 minutes: ADD). Notes, text and translation included. Recorded 1961.

Salome was one of Decca's notable 'Sonic-stage' successes, now all of 37 years ago. It still beats most of its operatic competitors in terms of sound alone. There is a real sense here of a theatrical performance, as directed by John Culshaw, with an imaginative use of movement that is all the more obvious in its CD recension. The transfer also improves on the already very clear recording of the orchestra, so that all the detail of the extraordinary scoring, so often obscured in the opera-house, can be easily heard. It must be added that it also makes more plain the Solti stomp on the platform at climactic moments.

Of course, the vivid, nervous energy of Strauss has always been Solti's territory and this is an overwhelming account of Strauss's sensual piece, sometimes a little too hard-hitting for its or our good: there are places where the tension might be relaxed just a shade. But throughout, the VPO answer Solti's extreme demands with their most aristocratic playing, which is even more exciting in the remastering. With only a single break, the sense of mounting fever is all the more felt.

Nilsson's account of the title-role remains another towering monument to her tireless singing. Here, more even than as Brünnhilde, one notices just how she could fine away her tone to a sweet and fully supported *pianissimo*, and her whole interpretation wants nothing of the erotic suggestiveness of sopranos more familiar with the role on stage. Stolze's Herod is properly wheedling, worried and, in the final resort, crazed, but there are times, particularly towards the end of his contribution, when exaggeration takes over from characterization in a kind of braying *Sprechgesang*. Others, most notably Patzak on Decca's earlier mono recording under Clemens Krauss, showed how effects can be created without distortion of the vocal line. Waechter is an aggressive rather than a visionary Jokanaan; I prefer a nobler tone in this role. Grace Hoffman is a suitably gloating Herodias. Much better than any of these, Nilsson apart, is Kmentt's wonderfully ardent Narraboth.

None of the rivals since 1962 has managed a true challenge.

R. Strauss Salome.

Catherine Malfitano *sop* Salome
Horst Hiestermann *ten* Herod
Leonie Rysanek *sop* Herodias
Simon Estes *bass* Jokanaan
Clemens Bieber *ten* Narraboth
Camille Capasso *treb* Page
Friedrich Molsberger *bass* First Nazarene
Ralf Lukas *bass* Second Nazarene
William Murray *bass* First soldier
Bengt Rundgren *bass* Second soldier
Klaus Lang *bar* Cappadocian
Aimée Elizabeth Willis *sop* Slave
Berlin Deutsche Oper Orchestra / Giuseppe Sinopoli.
Stage Director: **Petr Weigl**. *Film Director*: **Brian Large**.
Teldec Ⓟ VHS ▭ 9031-73827-3; ◖ 9031-73827-6 (two sides: 109 minutes).

This all-in, all-revealing performance is not for the fainthearted. In keeping with the times, Malfitano presents Salome blatantly as a repressed and selfish teenager whose erotic desires are awakened by the sight of Jokanaan and who then becomes totally obsessed by his physical presence. Casting off all pretension of modesty, this Salome writhes orgasmically on stage after he has refused her, then dances down to complete nudity before Herod in order to get what she wants – the head of her idol, which she then proceeds to kiss lasciviously. In all this Malfitano rivals if not surpasses Maria Ewing at Covent Garden in a production (Petr Weigl), conducted by Downes, for the Deutsche Oper, Berlin, that centres entirely on the girl's sexual awakening and leads to the unhinging of her mind.

Malfitano carries out this reading with astounding, almost repulsive conviction, a performance of acrobatic dexterity and single-minded devotion, not the least notable for her use of her expressive eyes. That her vocal performance is as convincing makes the whole thing all the more magnetic. Her singing is consistently steady, controlled and flexible. Although her voice is not large she finds no difficulty in riding the orchestra by dint of firmly focused tone, and she misses few of the dynamic contrasts Strauss demands. Indeed one imagines Strauss would have been well pleased with her entire interpretation. All this is achieved not in the somewhat unreal atmosphere of a film or recording studio but a live performance in Berlin, so that we see from her perspiration what the effort of her athletic dance has cost Malfitano. We also see the beads of sweat on the forehead of Hiestermann whose Herod is a nice study in neurotic, superstitious desperation. While one noticed some unsteadiness in his CD recording for DG under Sinopoli, it can here be considered as part of his whole and convincing portrait. Similarly Rysanek's Herodias is all the more effective for being viewed as well as heard. This indestructible singing actress, active now on stage for nearly half a century, turns in a magnificent portrait of raddled, epicene decline. Estes gives his best performance since his Dutchman. A towering, though somewhat too eupeptic figure, he declaims the prophet's words with strength and eloquence. Bieber's lyrical Narraboth completes a splendid team of principals.

As in his CD version, Sinopoli conducts with understanding of every aspect of the highly coloured score without any resort to exaggeration. The balance with the singers is very much what you would encounter in the theatre. In sum the sound is truthful and spacious. Visually Brian Large's experienced hand makes sure the cameras are in the right place at the right time, but he is a little hampered by the predominantly dark nature of the original staging, which doesn't leave much lee-way for contrasts. Weigl's staging is economic with a nice sense of making the most of key events. He is particularly successful in showing how Salome gradually comes into physical contact with Jokanaan's body. Svoboda's set, inevitably with this designer dominated by staircases, appears cleverly to marry the real with the abstract, but as suggested the lighting leaves much in the shade. The Berlin audience's enthusiasm at the end knows no bounds. There are no subtitles.

R. Strauss Salomé.

Karen Huffstodt *sop* Salomé
Hélène Jossoud *mez* Hérodias
Jean Dupouy *ten* Hérode
José van Dam *bar* Iokanaan
Jean-Luc Viala *ten* Narraboth
Hélène Perraguin *mez* Page
Jules Bastin *bass* First Nazarene
Alain Gabriel *bar* Second Nazarene
Vincent Le Texier *bass-bar* First soldier
Fernand Dumont *bass* Second soldier
Orchestra of Opéra National de Lyons / Kent Nagano.
Virgin Classics Ⓟ Ⓒ VCD7 59054-2 (two discs: 105 minutes: DDD). Notes, text and translation included. Recorded 1991.

Oscar Wilde wrote his *Salomé* in French, in a bid to interest Sarah Bernhardt in playing the title-role in a London production. This never took place, although Bernhardt was said to be enthusiastic (the dance, in those days, would not have posed her any problems as she still had both legs). When the play was eventually put on in Paris the programme cover was designed by Toulouse-Lautrec. Shortly after the first performance of his opera (in a German translation of the Wilde), Strauss decided to adapt the score to fit Wilde's French text (or as much of it as he had used), and to do this he made numerous tiny adjustments to fit the new vocal stresses. This version was performed, and also translated into Italian. When Mary Garden sang the role for the first time in New York in 1909, she remembered in her autobiography, "We gave the opera in the French of Oscar Wilde, word for word. I would like to see it done that way always ... I could think and feel it only in French".

Garden's performances were probably the last of that French version in Strauss's lifetime, since for a new production in Paris, also in 1909, a translation back into French of the German was made to accommodate the singers, and that has been the version performed there until the Lyon Opéra, sponsored by Rhône-Poulenc, resurrected the Strauss-Wilde version; this enterprising recording is based on those performances. The changes Strauss made in adapting his original score to suite Wilde's French text are mostly to do with the stress on certain syllables, but sometimes result in a complete reversal of a phrase, ending on a different note; for instance Hérodias, refuting the Tetrarch's claim that the moon looks different, ends a whole octave higher in the French score.

The greatest change noticeable is of course the lightening of the general feel, when everyone is singing with those difficult nasal French sounds, as opposed to the gutsier German. The booklet accompanying the discs contains some fascinating material, including part of the Strauss/Romain Rolland correspondence, particularly relevant to this project. The orchestration used is that of the 1905 première rather than the version for smaller forces that Strauss made for Elisabeth Schumann when he was trying to persuade her to undertake the part. In the title-role the American soprano, Karen Huffstodt, does not immediately sound a natural for the part dynamically. Her voice has a quavery, plaintive quality that is reminiscent of Beverly Sills, but once past the dance she manages to produce some impressive, full tone. While her singing is hardly a competition for the heavyweights like Nilsson or Jones, and she hasn't the sheer beauty of tone that Welitsch or Caballé brought to the part, her little laugh when she asks for the head and the sense of theatricality that she brings throughout add to the enjoyment of the enjoyment of the performance. José van Dam is a resonant Iokanaan, and like the rest of the cast he sings the French text with enough conviction to make you begin to accept the opera in this unfamiliar language.

Jean-Luc Viala is a very good Narraboth; his scene with Salomé near the beginning suddenly sounds uncannily like a passage from *Pelléas* and of course all the comparisons are apt, since Strauss studied the Debussy score while working on the French *Salomé* and Mary Garden herself had been the first Mélisande. Jean Dupouy and Hélène Jossoud as the unhappy regal couple are both positive assumptions. The Lyon Opéra Orchestra under Kent Nagano play the piece with a good deal of elegance and delicacy, though it is difficult to be altogether certain that those qualities are the ones that should first come to mind when approaching this opera. Since it is still the only recording of this version, a specialist item, it wouldn't be a first recommendation, but it is well worth investigating and adds considerably to our knowledge of the opera.

R. Strauss Die schweigsame Frau.

Theo Adam *bass-bar* Sir Morosus
Annelies Burmeister *mez* Housekeeper
Wolfgang Schöne *bass* Barber
Eberhard Büchner *ten* Henry Morosus
Jeannette Scovotti *sop* Aminta
Carola Nossek *sop* Isotta
Trudeliese Schmidt *mez* Carlotta
Klaus Hirte *ten* Morbio
Werner Haseleu *bar* Vanuzzi
Helmut Berger-Tuna *bass* Farfallo
Johannes Kemter *spkr* Parrot
Dresden State Opera Chorus; Staatskapelle Dresden / Marek Janowski.
EMI Ⓜ Ⓓ CMS5 66033-2 (three discs: 174 minutes: ADD). Notes, text and translation included. Recorded 1976-7.

Brilliant, elaborate ensembles contrasted with warm, affectionate passages (especially the Act 2 duet for old Morosus and Aminta) in Strauss's most grateful vein do not quite release this translation into opera of Ben Jonson's typically cruel comedy (somewhat akin in plot to *Don Pasquale*) from the charge of wordiness (Stefan Zweig's libretto) and note-spinning. Its lengthy tomfoolery can seem a trifle laboured, its dramaturgy weak, reasons enough why it resists attempts to become part of the regular repertory – and why Böhm judiciously cut it for the 1959 Salzburg revival recorded live.

This performance, following a revival at Dresden, where the piece had its 1935 première, bowls along with undeniable conviction under Janowski's punctilious and lively baton, all the orchestral parodies and touches of onomatopoeia promptly dealt with by the excellent band, so that the score's *longueurs* can almost be overlooked. His cast has many strengths. Although Adam's voice is a trifle light for Morosus, he proves to be right inside the character of the retired admiral, who can't stand noise around him, delivering the long part tirelessly and intelligently, a vividly sympathetic portrait. Schöne is rightly the linchpin of the action as the Barber, his warm baritone deployed to good effect in his lengthy passages of *parlando*. Henry, Morosus's nephew who has joined a travelling troupe and is thus disinherited by his old uncle, is taken lightly and neatly by Büchner. As his beloved Aminta, a Zerbinetta-like role, Scovotti has all the notes, but misses some of the warmth called for. The character parts are all filled reliably so that, as a whole, the opera is made to 'work'. This version is, of course, better recorded than the Salzburg set, but that has the unbeatable quartet of Hotter, Gueden, Wunderlich and Prey in the central roles, plus Böhm in the pit, and fits the attenuated version on to two mid-price discs (in mono) against this set's three. The choice is difficult, but unless you must have the work in its entirety and in stereo the Böhm will probably suffice.

R. Strauss Die schweigsame Frau.

Hans Hotter *bass-bar* Sir Morosus
Georgine von Milinkovic *mez* Housekeeper
Hermann Prey *bar* Barber
Fritz Wunderlich *ten* Henry Morosus
Hilde Gueden *sop* Aminta
Pierrette Alarie *sop* Isotta
Hetty Plümacher *contr* Carlotta
Josef Knapp *bar* Morbio
Karl Dönch *bar* Vanuzzi
Alois Pernerstorfer *bass-bar* Farfallo

Vienna State Opera Chorus; Vienna Philharmonic Orchestra / Karl Böhm.
DG Strauss Opera Edition mono Ⓜ ① 445 335-2GX2 (two discs: 146 minutes: ADD). Recorded at a performance in the Festspielhaus, Salzburg on August 6th, 1959.

To mark the centenary of Böhm's birth, DG issued a magnificent box of nine Strauss operas which included this invaluable live performance from the Salzburg Festival, never available before except on a dim 'private' issue. Hans Hotter is one of the stars of *Schweigsame Frau* of which Böhm gave the première in 1936 under inauspicious circumstances (here he conducts it lightly, engagingly). Hotter as Sir Morosus shows his amazing versatility (at this time he was also tackling Gurnemanz) and his ability to cope with the detail of Zweig's brilliant libretto, the wittiest and most amusing Strauss ever set. Hotter finds a calm, warm legato for the quiet solos that end Acts 2 and 3 and for the plaintive love duet with Aminta, so soon to make Morosus's life an obstreperous hell on earth, and the power for his outbursts of incontinent outrage. As Sir Henry, Morosus's equivocal nephew, Fritz Wunderlich discloses, for the first time at Salzburg, his sappy tone and immaculate style. His Aminta is the delightful Hilde Gueden, who sings the Norina-like part with charm and brilliance. Altogether we learn here why Strauss had such a deep affection for this piece.

Igor Stravinsky
USSR/French/American 1882-1971

Stravinsky Oedipus Rex.
Thomas Moser *ten* Oedipus
Jessye Norman *sop* Jocasta
Siegmund Nimsgern *bass-bar* Créon, Messenger
Roland Bracht *bass* Tirésias
Alexandru Ionita *ten* Shepherd
Michel Piccoli *spkr* Narrator
Bavarian Radio Male Chorus; Bavarian Radio Symphony Orchestra / Sir Colin Davis.
Orfeo Ⓟ ① C071831A (DDD). Text and translation included. Recorded at performances in the Herkulessaal, Munich on January 27th and 28th and June 27th, 1983.

BBC RADIO 3
90-93 FM

Stravinsky's *Oedipus Rex* was written for the twentieth anniversary of the Diaghilev company, but his only recorded comment on the work was an uncomplimentary "C'est ennuyeux". On this recording, the virtues of a fine Stravinskian are apparent. The pace is unerringly right, the rhythms never monotonously mechanical, the score's phrasing and accents scrupulously realized. The singers are, on balance, the best possible team available at the time, with Thomas Moser anguished and expressive in ways which occasionally recall the Pears of the 1951 Stravinsky/CBS recording (released in the UK in 1955). That version remains a classic (it is not represented in the current catalogue). Moser lacks the sheer individuality of Pears, but even his more conventional forcefulness at moments of tension is always well controlled. Jocastas notoriously tend to unsteadiness, but Jessye Norman is never tempted to push urgency of attack to the point where the actual sound becomes rough or distorted. The role – and the recording – brings out the distinctive colour of her voice, and although she may not be ideally suited to the more mannered aspects of the part she gives a memorable performance. So too does Siegmund Nimsgern, a commanding Créon and Messenger. For the rest, Roland Bracht is not quite bass enough for Tirésias, while Alexandru Ionita allows some intrusive aspiration to mar the Shepherd's song. Michel Piccoli is a powerful narrator – using Cocteau's original French – even if he does overdo the rhetorical pauses.
The performance achieves a good balance between neo-classical stylization and vivid dramatic force: only at one crucial point, Oedipus's terrible confession "Lux facta est", does it seem too restrained, too *sotto voce*, to carry complete dramatic conviction? A rather low-level transfer means that careful attention to the volume control is required, and this can affect the audibility of orchestral detail in what is, essentially, a well-balanced recording. But Sir Colin's rapport with his Munich forces is complete.

Stravinsky Oedipus Rex
Ivo Zídek *ten* Oedipus
Věra Soukupová *mez* Jocasta
Karel Berman *bass* Créon
Eduard Haken *bass* Tirésias
Antonín Zlesak *ten* Shepherd
Zdeněk Kroupa *bar* Messenger
Jean Desailly *spkr* Narrator

Stravinsky Symphony of Psalms.
Czech Philharmonic Chorus and Orchestra / Karel Ančerl.
Supraphon Historical Ⓟ ① 11 1947-2 (73 minutes: AAD). Recorded 1964.

After Václav Talich and Rafael Kubelík, Karel Ančerl (1908-73) was probably the finest of those Czech conductors who were still active post-war. His overall style combined feeling without fussiness, rhythmic precision and crisp instrumental articulation (most notably from the incisive Czech Philharmonic woodwinds). However, his significant Supraphon legacy made it on to CD only in fits and starts: after some encouraging representation at mid price and below, Ančerl then somewhat bizarrely moved to full price. So much for economy! This irritating caveat merely scuffs what is basically a shining recommendation. *Oedipus Rex* is among the best ever recorded, with Věra Soukupová a superb Jocasta (sample her solo at the beginning of Act 2) and Ivo Zídek a tortured (and occasionally unsteady) Oedipus; Karel Berman's Créon is also memorable, and the Czech Philharmonic Chorus support the action with admirable zeal. The *Symphony of Psalms* is a better recording – fuller in texture, primarily – and, like *Oedipus*, has the benefit of a controlled and moving finale, furthermore, the music's native austerity is effectively offset by the breezy, open-air quality of those Czech winds.

Stravinsky The Rake's Progress.

Jerry Hadley *ten* Tom Rakewell
Dawn Upshaw *sop* Anne Trulove
Samuel Ramey *bass* Nick Shadow
Grace Bumbry *mez* Baba the Turk
Steven Cole *ten* Auctioneer
Anne Collins *contr* Mother Goose
Robert Lloyd *bass* Trulove
Roderick Earle *bass* Keeper of the Mad House
Chorus and Orchestra of Opéra National de Lyons / Kent Nagano.
Erato Ⓕ Ⓓ 0630-12715-2 (two discs: 138 minutes: DDD). Recorded 1995.

Any number of the world's opera-houses would have given their eye teeth for the privilege of presenting the première of Stravinsky's only true opera, but he, intensely money-conscious though he was (and he had worked on the piece for three years without a commission fee), insisted on La Fenice in Venice. Because he was fond of the city, of course, but also because *The Rake's Progress* is a chamber opera. And this is a chamber performance of it, with a fairly small orchestra, much singing of almost *parlando* quality and crystal-clear words. It is also intimate, with a strong sense of the stage, of characters reacting to each other. Together with Nagano's on the whole brisk tempos, and no time wasted on pauses between numbers that should follow each other without a break, it gives the impression of a real performance, and a gripping one.

Upshaw's is not the purest soprano voice to have attempted the role of Anne, and there have been more spectacular high Cs than hers, but she is movingly vulnerable, totally believable. So is Hadley, acting at times almost too vividly for the music's line: as he occasionally demonstrates, he has a wonderfully beautiful head voice; one wishes he had used it more often. He is not, therefore, quite the touchingly likeable "shuttle-headed lad" that Alexander Young portrayed so unforgettably in the composer's own second recording, but no other Tom Rakewell surpasses him. Ramey's is a bigger voice than most of the others here, and in the past his firm, superbly produced sound has sometimes sounded a bit unvaried: not here. He has recorded the role twice before (for Chailly on Decca, and on a video of the Glyndebourne production conducted by Haitink, on Carlton Classics), but never with such a light touch, and all the more dangerous for it. Collins and Lloyd are both first-class as Mother Goose and Truelove, Cole an unusually light-voiced, confidingly conspiratorial Sellem. Bumbry is the disappointment of the cast, overloud and baritonal almost throughout, but the French chorus sing nimbly and in admirable English.

Stravinsky's own recording, particularly on account of Young, also for the composer's infectious enthusiasm and sheer rhythmic zest, is unbeatable, but of modern recordings of *The Rake's Progress* this is by some way the most enjoyable.

Stravinsky The Rake's Progress.

Alexander Young *ten* Tom Rakewell
Judith Raskin *sop* Anne Trulove
John Reardon *bass* Nick Shadow
Regina Sarfaty *mez* Baba the Turk
Kevin Miller *ten* Auctioneer
Jean Manning *mez* Mother Goose
Don Garrard *bass* Trulove
Peter Tracey *bar* Keeper of the Mad House
Sadler's Wells Opera Chorus; Royal Philharmonic Orchestra / Igor Stravinsky.
Sony Classical Ⓜ Ⓓ SM2K46299 (two discs: 140 minutes: ADD). Recorded 1964.

No composer has ever forged a closer relationship with the recording process than Stravinsky. He made his first records in 1928, and quickly saw the gramophone as an important medium; one which enabled him to take a written score a stage further in the creative process and realize it in the form of preserved sound. Stravinsky's early records for Columbia suggest that he had not quite mastered the art of conducting, but by the mid-1930s he was perfectly competent, and until 1967 performed regularly in the concert-hall and in the studios.

By 1959 Stravinsky's discography was quite large and he had already recorded some of his works on two occasions, when American CBS decided that they should use the then fairly new stereo medium to commit to disc as many of his readings as possible. This decision was taken just in time, since the elderly Stravinsky was able to conduct for just another seven years, during which period he directed new recordings of nearly all his output. Sometimes, particularly near the end of this phase, ill health intervened, and he was only able to supervise a recording, which was then directed by his assistant Robert Craft.

Practically all the late recordings are contained in Sony's marvellous enterprise, the Stravinsky Edition, of which *The Rake's Progress* is but a small part. Both Judith Raskin as Anne and Alexander Young as Tom are superb, but all the soloists are more than adequate and Stravinsky paces the opera with much dramatic flair. He is a highly communicative, convincing advocate. He remains one of the most extraordinary figures of our or any time, and his own reading will remain (or should remain) a touchstone for later interpreters. The transfer to CD was most expertly carried out under the guidance of producer John McClure himself.

Pyotr Il'yich Tchaikovsky USSR 1840-1893

Tchaikovsky Eugene Onegin.
Dmitri Hvorostovsky *bar* Eugene Onegin
Nuccia Focile *sop* Tatyana
Neil Shicoff *ten* Lensky
Olga Borodina *mez* Olga
Alexander Anisimov *bass* Prince Gremin
Sarah Walker *mez* Larina
Irina Arkhipova *mez* Filipyevna
Francis Egerton *ten* Triquet
Hervé Hennequin *bass-bar* Captain
Sergei Zadvorny *bass* Zaretsky
St Petersburg Chamber Choir; Orchestre de Paris / Semyon Bychkov.
Philips Ⓟ Ⓒ 438 235-2PH2 (two discs: 141 minutes: DDD). Notes, text and translation included.
Recorded 1990.

This is a magnificent achievement on all sides. In a recording that is wider in range, more immediate than almost any other on record, the work comes to arresting life under Bychkov's vital direction. Too often, on disc and in the theatre, the score has been treated self-indulgently and on too large a scale. Bychkov makes neither mistake, emphasizing the unity of its various scenes, never lingering at slower tempos than Tchaikovsky predicates, yet never moving too fast for his singers. Entirely at the service of Tchaikovsky's marvellous invention, he illuminates every detail of the composer's wondrous scoring with pointed delicacy and draws playing of the utmost acuity and beauty from his own Paris orchestra, enhanced by the clear, open recording. It is difficult to imagine a more captivating and idiomatic account of the piece, even if Tchakarov on Sony Classical runs it close in some respects, and excellent as are Tchakarov's chorus, the St Petersburg Choir are even better, superbly disciplined, alert with their words.

Focile and Hvorostovsky prove almost ideal interpreters of the central roles. Focile offers keen-edged yet warm tone and total immersion in Tatyana's character. Aware throughout of the part's dynamic demands, she phrases with complete confidence, eagerly catching the girl's dreamy vulnerability and heightened imagination in the Letter scene, which has that sense of awakened love so essential to it. Then she exhibits Tatyana's new-found dignity on Gremin's arm and finally her desperation when Onegin reappears to rekindle her romantic feelings. Her voice may not have the richer overtones of Tomowa-Sintow (Tchakarov), but she is more capable of indicating Tatyana's palpitating youthfulness, missing only something of the sheerly Russian quality in the young Galina Vishnevskaya's classic reading conducted by Boris Khaikin (reviewed below).

Hvorostovsky is wholly in his element. His singing has at once the warmth, elegance and refinement Tchaikovsky demands from his anti-hero. He suggests all Onegin's initial disdain, phrasing his address to the distraught and humiliated Tatyana – Focile so touching here – with distinction, and brings to it just the correct *bon ton*, a kind of detached humanity. He fires to anger with a touch of the heroic in his tone when challenged by Lensky, becomes transformed and single-minded when he catches sight of the 'new' Tatyana at the St Petersburg Ball. Together he, Focile and Bychkov make the finale the tragic climax it should be: indeed this passage is almost unbearably moving in this reading.

Shicoff has refined and expanded his Lensky since he recorded it for Levine on DG. His somewhat lachrymose delivery suits the character of the lovelorn poet, and he gives his big aria a sensitive, Russian profile, full of much subtlety of accent, the voice sounding in excellent shape, but there is a shade too much self-regard when he opens the ensemble at Larin's party with "Yes, in your house". Anisimov is a model Gremin, singing his aria with generous tone and phrasing while not making a meal of it. Olga Borodina is a perfect Olga, spirited, a touch sensual, wholly idiomatic with the text – as, of course, is the revered veteran Russian mezzo, Arkhipova, as Filipyevna, an inspired piece of casting. Sarah Walker is a sympathetic Larina. Egerton is a lovable Triquet, but whereas Gergiev, in the theatre, dragged out his couplets inordinately, Bychkov once more strikes precisely the right tempo.

Levine's superficial reading and his less idiomatic cast are totally eclipsed. Not so Tchakarov's version, which has Tomowa-Sintow as a particularly appealing Tatyana, but the ageing Mazurok and Gedda are no match for their successors on this newer recording. The Khaikin will always hold a very special place in the discography of the opera, but as a recording it is naturally outclassed by the Philips, which must be the outright recommendation.

Tchaikovsky Eugene Onegin (sung in English).

Thomas Hampson *bar* Eugene Onegin
Dame Kiri Te Kanawa *sop* Tatyana
Neil Rosenshein *ten* Lensky
Patricia Bardon *mez* Olga
John Connell *bass* Prince Gremin
Linda Finnie *mez* Larina
Elizabeth Bainbridge *mez* Filipyevna
Nicolai Gedda *ten* Triquet
Richard Van Allan *bass* Captain, Zaretsky
Welsh National Opera Chorus and Orchestra / Sir Charles Mackerras.
EMI Ⓕ Ⓘ CDS5 55004-2 (two discs: 142 minutes: DDD). Notes and text included. Recorded 1992.

How sensible to record an English-speaking cast singing in the vernacular (thanks to Peter Moores's advocacy) rather than in Russian learnt by rote. As every single member makes the most of David Lloyd-Jones's familiar translation (slightly amended here), they communicate the meaning of the piece immediately to their unseen audience, at least those in the English-speaking world for whom the set is surely intended.

Its rightful hero is Thomas Hampson. Blessed with a baritone of ideal weight for Onegin, he sings the role with the sense of *bon ton* it requires. Tchaikovsky's grateful lines are firmly held, even caressed and filled with warm yet flexible and nicely coloured tone. When finally roused to genuine passion in Act 3, Hampson's Onegin adds an emotional thrust just right for the possessed man, even if, in that respect he isn't quite as seized by infatuation as Thomas Allen for Levine or Hvorostovsky for Bychkov.

He may be hindered there, in the final scene, by Dame Kiri's seeming unwillingness to go the whole way in emotional commitment. Hers is a curious performance that might with advantage have been caught ten years ago when she was singing the part at Covent Garden. Here she gives a carefully studied and crafted performance, often phrased with subtlety and enunciated with a feeling for the words (indeed, hers are as clear as everyone else's), but there is a kind of *faux naïf* approach, a touch of archness to her portrayal as if she were deliberately trying to sound the young, ingenuous girl, particularly in the early scenes. The Letter scene seems to be put together piecemeal, wanting that passionate, impulsive sincerity of expression Focile (for Bychkov), even more the young Vishnevskaya (for Khaikin), brought to it. However, despite a few worn patches in the lower part of the voice, there is much lovely singing here *qua* singing even when the soul of the part sometimes goes missing.

Neil Rosenshein once sang an almost ideal Lensky at Covent Garden (in 1986). Time passes and his tenor is no longer as fresh-sounding or easily produced, at least at the top, as it then was. Against that must be set as full an understanding of the part – he is the lovelorn poet to the life – as you'll find on disc, except from Lemeshev on the old Russian versions (Nebolsin on Dante and Khaikin), and many turns of phrase that are heart-stopping so that one can overlook the few grating notes.

For the rest there is nothing but praise. The young mezzo, Patricia Bardon, is a lively, rich-toned and eager Olga, one who very much relishes singing in her native tongue. So does Elizabeth Bainbridge: here at the very end of her career (she was about to retire) we have a fit memento of her art in a role, Filipyevna, that she often sang with distinction at Covent Garden. She is in excellent voice and characterizes the part with unforced dignity. John Connell is a model Gremin, singing his aria with just the grave, gentle ardour it calls for and placing the words ideally on his ingratiating tone without making a meal of them. Linda Finnie is equally praiseworthy as Larina. Gedda, once a fine Lensky, lavishes his skills and his still-strong voice on Triquet's couplets, shading the second to a *piano* where the first is sung *forte*.

It is good to have Mackerras's sane, secure and vital reading of the score enshrined on disc. He and his Welsh forces play alternately with vigour and sensitivity. The WNO Chorus are predictably excellent. Each scene is well timed and shaped in itself, but one sometimes feels a sense that the score had been put together in sections not quite conceived as a whole and that, when accompanying his diva, Sir Charles was being more cautious than elsewhere, to the detriment of the drama.

In spite of these few strictures, this well-recorded and prepared version, nicely produced by John Fraser, is hugely enjoyable. It doesn't replace as first choice either the Bychkov, which is just that much better played and more passionately conducted, or the Khaikin, the most authentic performance of all apart from the even older Nebolsin, but after hearing this set you may find that you would not willingly be without the various constituents that are praised above, and there will be many, in any case, who will prefer the directness of hearing the piece sung in their own language: they will not be disappointed.

Tchaikovsky Eugene Onegin.
  Evgeny Belov *bar* Eugene Onegin
  Galina Vishnevskaya *sop* Tatyana
  Sergei Lemeshev *ten* Lensky
  Larissa Adeyeva *mez* Olga
  Ivan Petrov *bass* Prince Gremin
  Valentina Petrova *sop* Larina
  Evgenya Verbitskaya *mez* Filipyevna
  Andrei Sokolov *ten* Triquet
  Georgi Pankov *bass* Captain
  Igor Mikhailov *bass* Zaretsky
  Bolshoi Theatre Chorus and Orchestra / Boris Khaikin.
  Melodiya mono Ⓜ ① 74321 17090-2 (two discs: 140 minutes: ADD). Recorded 1955. Booklet included.

B B C RADIO 3
90-93 FM

This classic version, generally accepted as the most convincing and knowledgeable performance the work has ever received, was available on Legato for a while, but the reissue here, presumably from the original Melodiya tapes, is greatly preferable. The set wears its years lightly: indeed, the recording of the voices and even the orchestra, albeit in mono, has a great deal to teach producers today in terms of a natural sound. The reading's virtues have already been praised, above all Khaikin's unforced, unexaggerated, wholly integrated direction, with players and singers who know the score from the inside, giving an entirely idiomatic reading (if you can forgive the watery horns). From the very first scene you feel the impetus of the performance and are drawn into its truly Russian ambience. Khaikin brings into perfect balance the dramatic and yearning aspects of the score in a lyrical, delicate reading. With his incisive but sympathetic beat, he clearly characterizes those many passages of intimate feeling without which any account of the piece crucially fails.

  The young Vishnevskaya is a near-ideal Tatyana, having exactly the right voice for the part and totally convincing us that she is Tatyana. She is incomparable. What a genuine, unsophisticated outpouring of passion the Letter scene becomes as she interprets it, and how superbly she sings it! Adyeva makes much of little as Olga. Few tenors before or since Lemeshev have offered precisely the right tone and character for Lensky – except his younger self on the 1936 set on Dante. From his first entry we hear a plaintive timbre and easy way with the language that proclaim a true poet. Belov's Onegin, though not quite in that class, is a resolute member of a real ensemble and rises to the challenge of the final scenes. Petrov offers Gremin's aria in its most loving form. Verbitskaya is an appreciable nurse, steadier than most.

  All that disappoints is the presentation: many spelling mistakes (e.g. Pretrov for Petrov), no libretto, and – worst of all – no indication of the historic significance of the performance in the accompanying booklet. Yet you are urged to acquire this interpretation: an Onegin of national character and great eloquence, before international artists got to it, generalizing and overplaying the emotional content.

Tchaikovsky Eugene Onegin.
  Wojciech Drabowicz *ten* Eugene Onegin
  Yelena Prokina *sop* Tatyana
  Martin Thompson *ten* Lensky
  Louise Winter *mez* Olga
  Frode Olsen *bass* Prince Gremin
  Yvonne Minton *mez* Larina
  Ludmilla Filatova *mez* Filipyevna
  John Fryatt *ten* Triquet
  Christopher Thornton-Holmes *bar* Zaretsky
  Howard Quilla Croft *bass* Captain
  Glyndebourne Chorus; London Philharmonic Orchestra / Andrew Davis.
  Stage Producer: **Graham Vick.** *Video Director:* **Humphrey Burton.**
  Warner Vision Ⓕ 🔲 0630 14014-3 (156 minutes). Recorded at a performance during the Glyndebourne Festival in June 1994.

The undoubted triumph of the 1994 Glyndebourne Festival was Graham Vick's *Onegin*, and most of its portrait of personal trauma in a spare, pointed Russian setting (Richard Hudson's work) is happily transferred on to video through Humphrey Burton's sympathetic direction. Yelena Prokina's vulnerable Tatyana is sung in tones that only a Russian soprano can provide. The remainder of the cast, apart from Filatova's authentic Nurse, is not so special, but here it is the ensemble, the taut choral work and the general air of a concept properly worked out and rehearsed that counts for so much. The LPO play splendidly and Andrew Davis catches all the yearning and dark-hued colour of the score in a well-paced interpretation. It is subtitled and the recording is excellent.

Tchaikovsky Mazeppa.

Sergei Leiferkus *bar* Mazeppa
Galina Gorchakova *sop* Mariya
Anatoly Kotscherga *bass* Kochubey
Larissa Dyadkova *mez* Liubov
Sergei Larin *ten* Andrei
Monte Pederson *bar* Orlik
Richard Margison *ten* Iskra
Heinz Zednik *ten* Drunken Cossack
Stockholm Royal Opera Chorus; Gothenburg Symphony Orchestra / Neeme Järvi.
DG Ⓟ Ⓒ 439 906-2GH3 (three discs: 166 minutes: DDD). Notes, text and translation included. Recorded 1993.

Call it cynicism or simply a composer's desire to reach a wider public at a time before film scores brought in the money, but Tchaikovsky's new-found concept of opera as a popular art-form in the 1880s was hardly likely to yield any consistent masterpieces. Ironically, it was the earlier *Eugene Onegin* that now took on a new lease of life and turned Tchaikovsky into Russia's best-loved composer, not the more calculated recipes for success of *The Maid of Orléans*, *Mazeppa* or *Charodeyka* ("The Enchantress"). *Onegin* works for us today because it is sincerely felt from start to finish; but the fascination of those lesser-known operas lies in the way they move in and out of scenes and predicaments which clearly touched the composer. Of the three, *Mazeppa* has the greatest share of first-rate music, extending our appreciation of Tchaikovsky's bleaker side as he attempts to reflect the cruelty inflicted by the anti-hero (no noble Ukrainian freedom-fighter either here or in the Pushkin poem on which the opera is based), though the centres of gravity on this recording do not always fall where received critical wisdom has suggested they should.

Tchaikovsky has supposedly invested most in the portrayal of the unhappy heroine Mariya; but the celebrated 'quiet curtain' to the last act where, driven gently mad by her elderly lover's execution of her disaffected father, she cradles the body of her childhood sweetheart in her arms, registers its restraint without proving deeply moving. There is a matter-of-factness about Galina Gorchakova's delivery which holds us at arm's length, begging admiration for the unique brilliance of her upper register without beginning to touch the core either of the necessary intimacy here nor the bigger emotions of previous scenes. Her response to Mazeppa's patriotic scheme in Act 2 (second disc, track 4, index point 8) gives us a fairer picture of the Gorchakova phenomenon than ill-focused earlier stages of this semi-interpretation: shining strength above the stave goes some way towards redeeming the placidity of the whole. It takes Larissa Dyadkova's far more committed cut and thrust in the electrifying scene between Mariya and her mother to spur Gorchakova to a more consistent sense of occasion (though one wonders, incidentally, if the final clash here of the soprano's top B with the mezzo's A can ever sound quite right).

Anatoly Kotscherga as Kochubey would clearly like to deliver more than his limited vocal resources permit him as the outraged father seethes in Act 1 – Chaliapinesque ranting might just have carried the ensemble scenes of the act, much the weakest of the three – but he rises to his supreme challenge as Tchaikovsky plumbs the depths for Kochubey's prison monologue: here, indeed, are the range of tone colour and introspection missing from Gorchakova's mad scenes. Leiferkus has less to deal with as the headstrong tyrant (though more, certainly, than Sergei Larin, who does his best with the lachrymose heroics of the token tenor); even so, he strikes firmly at the heart of darkness, and there could be no more free- and easy-sounding delivery of the wonderful aria that Tchaikovsky gave his baritone at a late stage in the compositional process. In the cases of both the victim's darkest hour and this, the conqueror's most sensitive one, Järvi reinforces the orchestra's role as an equal partner in characterization – driving home the lower-instrument gloom and terror of Kochubey's circumstances, underlining the light and lovely, woodwind-dominated scoring of "O, Mariya!" as Mazeppa muses, Gremin-like, on the sincerity of his late-flowering love.

Järvi's swift, fluent way with the outward drama of the piece is strikingly established in the Introduction, where the Gothenburg Symphony Orchestra are lucky to be able to establish their greatest asset in the first, brusque announcement of Mazeppa's theme: powerful cellos and basses register richly in this spacious Gothenburg Concert Hall recording. He takes the orchestral set-pieces, the gopak and the "Battle of Poltava" sequence at heady speeds, though the fire dims a little for the big execution-finale of Act 2, where neither the brass nor the chorus (from Stockholm's Royal Opera) are as ruthless as their Russian counterparts would surely be. A short Third Act means that there is (unused) space on the third disc for the conventional finale that Tchaikovsky originally wrote (it is included as a supplement to the full score); our respect for his last-minute decision to keep it simple would surely be all the greater had we been allowed to hear that alternative. Slight disappointment with the much-vaunted Gorchakova apart, then, this is a faithful testament to *Mazeppa*'s intermittent power to move and appal.

Tchaikovsky The Queen of Spades.

Gegam Grigorian *ten* Herman
Maria Gulegina *sop* Lisa
Irina Arkhipova *mez* Countess
Nikolai Putilin *bar* Count Tomsky
Vladimir Chernov *bar* Prince Yeletsky
Olga Borodina *mez* Pauline
Vladimir Solodovnikov *ten* Chekalinsky
Sergei Alexashkin *bass* Surin
Evgeni Boitsov *ten* Chaplitsky
Nikolai Gassiev *ten* Major-domo
Gennadi Bezzubenkov *bass* Narumov
Ludmila Filatova *mez* Governess
Tatiana Filimonova *sop* Masha
Kirov Theatre Chorus and Orchestra / Valery Gergiev.
Philips Ⓕ Ⓓ 438 141-2PH3 (three discs: 166 minutes: DDD). Notes, text and translation included. Recorded 1992.

There are major problems with all the current sets of Tchaikovsky's most melodramatic opera. If melodrama were all, the mid-1970s Bolshoi version with Ermler on Melodiya would be the one to have, but the cavernous recording, raw orchestral playing and, especially, the continuously loud singing are hard to live with. Tchakarov and his largely Bulgarian forces (Sony Classical) reveal far more subtlety, but at the expense of dramatic immediacy and with a dry, uninvolving recording quality. Ozawa's set (RCA) is blessed with a distinguished Tomsky from Sergei Leiferkus, who however, also shows up the inadequacy, in some cases almost amateurishness, of the rest of the cast.

Somewhere in between the extremes of visceral impact and the arm's-length approach comes this Kirov version, and in many ways the medium it strikes is a happy one. Valery Gergiev is, of course, one of the outstanding Tchaikovskians of the day. Here again he persuades a thoroughly Western-sounding Kirov Theatre Orchestra to what is surely the most refined account of the score yet recorded, and one that is never lacking energy or full-blooded attack. His is not so much a compromise approach as one which stresses fatalism and underlying sadness. The recording was made in the Kirov Theatre itself, and there is admittedly some constriction to the orchestral sound picture. But for many the atmosphere of a real stage-venue will be a plus, and the all-important balance between voices and orchestra is just right.

If the spine still fails to tingle as one feels it should that is mainly a reflection of the respectable but unexciting singing. The bass and baritone soloists are rather samey in timbre, none of them having the distinction of a Leiferkus; Gegam Grigorian brings an impressive all-purpose ardour to Herman, but he is still hammy in his *primo tenore* mannerisms – typical that he disregards the score and joins Lisa on an audience-massaging top B at the end of Act 1. Of the women Arkhipova is well cast as the decaying Countess, but Maria Gulegina, for all that she commands some microphone-splitting top notes, is too uniformly tremulous and matronly in tone for Lisa while Olga Borodina is a pleasant but rather unvaried Pauline.

As suggested, it would be folly to expect greater thrills from any of the rival sets, and in many ways Gergiev's conducting elevates this one above them all. However, the old Melik-Pashayev/Melodiya set (released on LP in 1961) must be the classic recorded version – above all, but not exclusively, for the plangent Herman of Georgi Nelepp. When the ex-Soviet archives are still being so greedily plundered, is it not possible for someone to put this genuine treasure somewhere near the top of the list?

Tchaikovsky The Queen of Spades.

Gegam Grigorian *ten* Herman
Maria Gulegina *sop* Lisa
Ludmila Filatova *mez* Countess
Sergei Leiferkus *bar* Count Tomsky
Alexander Gergalov *bar* Prince Yeletsky
Olga Borodina *mez* Pauline
Vladimir Solodovnikov *ten* Chekalinsky
Sergei Alexashkin *bass* Surin
Evgeni Boitsov *ten* Chaplitsky
Nikolai Gassiev *ten* Major-domo
Gennadi Bezzubenkov *bass* Narumov
Evgenia Perlasova *mez* Governess
Tatiana Filimonova *sop* Masha

Kirov Theatre Chorus and Orchestra / Valery Gergiev.
Stage Director: **Yuri Temirkanov.** *Video Director:* **Brian Large.**
Philips Ⓕ 🎥 070 434-3PH (179 minutes). Recorded 1992.

At first sight this looks like the video equivalent of the above account of the opera. In fact, not only are the performances different, but there are two important changes in the cast. This video recording was made in April 1992, to be followed a month later by the CD version, made on the same stage but without an audience present. Gergiev repeats a reading that is possibly even more enjoyable, one that is at once refined, energetic, fashioned as a total concept, an important attribute in this superb score that can nevertheless tend to sprawl without a tight hand at the helm; and the playing is at once idiomatic and technically admirable. It underpins a production, one oddly enough by Temirkanov, Gergiev's predecessor as Music Director of the Kirov, that is by and large conventional – set in its correct surroundings, dressed in period and conforming to the generalized tradition of acting familiar in many Russian stagings.

There are exceptions, such as the old Countess rising from her chair at Herman's stealthy approach, not merely sitting transfixed and terrified. That is a role differently cast than on the CD set. Filatova is demonstrably a younger singer than Arkhipova and the make-up cannot hide that fact, especially when the cameras are close up, but her acting in her big scene is so moving and convincing, her singing so affecting, that she overcomes the disadvantage, and – surprisingly – makes rather more of her words, by subtle inflexion, than her more famous and experienced colleague.

Leiferkus returns to the role of Tomsky, which he sang so superbly on the Ozawa CD set (RCA), magnificent in his airy definition of this equivocal character, deserting his supposed friend Herman at the end to second Yeletsky in a proposed duel. He sings both his solos with immense panache. Gergalov does not sing Yeletsky's sad, grateful aria with quite Chernov's breadth and warmth, but his shading of line and soft-grained tone are a pleasure to hear: Russia seems to have an inexhaustible supply of exceptional baritones, and sopranos, of whom Gulegina is just one. She sings with such vibrancy and intensity that one forgives a reluctance to moderate to a *piano*. Her acting suggests all Lisa's unjustified faith in Herman's intentions and the desperation at each disillusionment. Grigorian begins by seeming little more than a conventional tenor, but as the role develops he begins to catch the man's unhinged state of mind in his voice, eyes and body movement; and his utterly secure singing is something seldom heard before in any version. It is just the peculiarly Russian timbre of Nelepp on Melodiya, and other tenors further back in the recording of Russian opera, that is missing. With her comely presence before us Borodina is something like an ideal Pauline.

Brian Large is, as ever, exemplary in his video direction. The sound is somewhat limited in range and rather under-recorded, but not so much as to prevent a recommendation *tout court*.

Georg Telemann   German 1681-1767

Telemann Don Quichotte auf der Hochzeit des Comacho.

Raimund Nolte *bass* Don Quichotte
Michael Schopper *bass* Sancho Panza
Silke Stapf *sop* Pedrillo
Mechthild Bach *sop* Grisostomo
Heike Hallaschka *sop* Quiteria
Annette Köhler *mez* Comacho
Karl-Heinz Brandt *ten* Basilio
Bremen Vocal Ensemble for Ancient Music; La Stagione / Michael Schneider.
CPO Ⓕ ① CPO999 210-2 (59 minutes: DDD). 📖 Notes, text and translation included.
Recorded at a performance in Kirche Unser Lieben Frauen, Bremen, Germany on March 14th, 1993.

Telemann's delightful serenata, *Don Quichotte auf der Hochzeit des Comacho* ("Don Quixote at Comacho's Wedding"), dates from the end of his life. He wrote it in 1761, at the age of 80, choosing for a libretto a text by a young Hamburg poet, Daniel Schiebeler. Schiebeler was only 20 years old at the time but Telemann, forward-looking as ever, was evidently attracted by a text, or "song-poem" as Schiebeler himself called it, whose type was to become very popular, in which the daydreams and fantasies of incredible fiction were treated dramatically.

Other than in its choice of subject, Telemann's serenata has nothing to do with his very much better known depictive orchestral suite, *Don Quichotte*, probably written well before the vocal work. However, since the serenata has no introductory overture or sinfonia, the suite does offer itself as a pleasing companion piece, complementary in spirit and in subject matter and it would have been good to have had it here. Never mind, the serenata itself (in five scenes) is given complete.

Schiebeler took an episode from Part 2 of Cervantes's celebrated burlesque novel, in which the Knight of the Lions and his squire, Sancho Panza, encounter some rather strange wedding celebrations as they roam the world in search of adventure. The bride, Quiteria is to marry Comacho, a rich sheep farmer. But *she* loves Basilio who is, however, poor and therefore disqualified from marrying his childhood sweetheart. Just as the marriage is about to take place Basilio is led in with a dagger in his breast. He implores Quiteria to grant him one last wish – to give a dying man her hand in marriage, since that would strengthen his heart and give him breath for confession. Quiteria agrees to this, gives Basilio her hand and the priest blesses them, whereupon Basilio leaps to his feet pulling the dagger deftly from his breast. It was all a trick, he exclaims, jubilantly. Comocho is furious and demands instant justice but Don Quixote intervenes: "Quiteria was Basilio's, and Basilio Quiteria's, by Heaven's just and favourable decree". Drinking, dancing and merrymaking follow as Quixote and a reluctant Sancho leave the feast for the open road once more.

The story afforded Telemann numerous opportunities for little humorous touches and the score, if not a masterpiece, is never dull or long-winded, drawing on widely flung stylistic terms of reference ranging from *opera seria* to folk-song (tracks 9 and 17). Most sharply and wittily characterized is the role of Sancho, a character in whom Telemann, like us, clearly delighted. Athletic leaps accompany his recollection of an earlier unpleasant escapade when playful rogues tossed him in a blanket. Michael Schopper revels in the part, giving a larger-than-life picture of this lovable squire. Quixote is another bass role, here sung by Raimund Nolte. His, too, is a splendidly robust performance, as we can hear, for instance, in his vigorous chiding of the timorous tendencies in Sancho's nature (tracks 5 and 6). The remaining roles are smaller, but uniformly well sung and the choruses, often adorned with rhythmic and instrumental ideas which evoke splashes of local colour, are first-rate. The distant popping of a cork from a wine bottle, at the end of track 18, though contextually apposite is not, however, in Telemann's score.

In summary, here is a work which should have a wide appeal for its musical diversity, skilful characterization and captivating melodies. In works such as this, the tension between established and newly emerging ideas, musical and dramatic, is to the fore, underlining both Telemann's almost ceaseless interest in experimentation, and a seemingly ever-youthful curiosity which belies his advanced years. The sound is excellent and the booklet contains full German texts with translations; the enthusiastic and informative introductory note is by Bernd Baselt, whose edition of the work was presumably used for the performance. The soloists, choir and Schneider's instrumental group, La Stagione, turn in an effectively paced and warm-blooded performance with a keen sense of the humour inherent in both text and music. An enterprising release from a small company that have been exploring some fascinating by-ways of German seventeenth- and eighteenth-century repertory.

Telemann Orpheus.

Roman Trekel *bar* Orpheus
Ruth Ziesak *sop* Eurydice
Dorothea Röschmann *sop* Orasia
Werner Güra *ten* Eurimedes
Maria Cristina Kiehr *sop* Ismene
Hanno Müller-Brachmann *bar* Pluto
Isabelle Poulenard *sop* Cephisa, Priestess
Axel Köhler *alto* Ascalax
RIAS Chamber Choir, Berlin; Academy for Ancient Music, Berlin / René Jacobs.
Harmonia Mundi ℗ ① HMC90 1618/9 (two discs: 159 minutes: DDD). ✍ Notes, text and translation included. Recorded 1996.

Some readers may already have heard this performance of Telemann's three-act opera, *Orpheus, oder die wunderbare Beständigkeit der Liebe* ("Orpheus, or the marvellous constancy of Love") from broadcasts on BBC Radio 3, German networks and, perhaps, others too. Its release on Harmonia Mundi, though, is the first on disc of an opera that was recognized as being the product of Telemann's pen only some 20 years ago. The first performance of *Orpheus* took place in Hamburg, at the famous Gänsemarkt Opera, of which Telemann himself was Music Director, in 1726. Two years later it was revived in Karlsruhe and, in 1736 was given, once again, in Hamburg, this time with adjustments, and a new title in which the constant love of Orpheus was supplanted by "Vengeful love, for Orasia, the widowed Queen of Thrace". The original libretto was by a Frenchman, Michel du Boullay, who had collaborated with Louis Lully, son of the redoubtable Jean-Baptiste, in an opera, *Orphée*, given in Paris in 1690. Telemann himself seems to have adapted the text to suit Hamburg taste – there is, for instance, a tragicomic element in the characters of Cephisa and Eurimedes, apparent above all in the First Act; but though the libretto has survived virtually complete, a small part of the score is lost. For the edition used here, Peter Huth – who has also contributed a useful essay – Jakob Peters-Messer and the director of the performance, René Jacobs, have filled the lacunae with music from other Telemann sources. Among the most important of these are the operas, *Emma und Eginhard* (1728) and *Flavius Bertaridus* (1729), from each of which a single aria has been borrowed. Other, smaller interpolations and editorial decisions are acknowledged in Huth's essay; but his declaration that the Overture, missing from Telemann's score, has been replaced by one belonging to "the orchestral Suite in F major" is unhelpful and furthermore betrays a startling disregard for the composer's well-attested fecundity in this sphere of composition. There are at least 18 orchestral suites in this key, of which the present one answers to the catalogue number TWV55:F14.

Telemann's *Orpheus* has an additional dimension to the standard version of the legend in the person of Orasia, widowed Queen of Thrace. She occupies a key position in the drama, first as murderess of

Eurydice of whose love for Orpheus she is jealous, then of Orpheus himself, since he, understandably, rejects her advances. The plot develops effectively, contributing greatly to the dramatic coherence and overall satisfaction provided by text and music alike. Indeed, it is a work that, in certain respects, reveals Telemann's theatrical talents more tautly than the piece by which he is best known, *Der geduldige Socrates* (1721); for though it differs from *Orpheus* in being an entirely comic opera, the plot is slender for a work of almost unwieldy dimensions.

In common with a great many operas for the Hamburg stage, *Orpheus* contains arias sung in languages other than the German vernacular. Italian was the usual alternative, but here there are airs in French, too, and Telemann, on these occasions, lends emphasis to the 'mixed style' aesthetic, in which he was an ardent believer, by retaining the distinctive stylistic character of each country. Thus the Italian arias tend to be virtuosic da capo pieces, while the French ones offer compelling evidence of the composer's assimilation of the *air de cour* (disc 1, tracks 20 and 32; disc 2, track 40). But it is the German arias that are often both the most interesting and the most varied, since it is the Lied and the arioso, as developed in the Passion-Oratorio settings, that provide those additional ingredients which vitalize, refresh and give distinction to his music.

Jacobs has assembled a first-rate cast for this opera, which he has previously directed in stage productions at Innsbruck and Berlin. Dorothea Röschmann projects a passionate and temperamental Orasia for whom Telemann has provided several strongly characterized arias. One of them, "Vieni, o sdegno, e fuggi, Amor!", is worthy of comparison with Handel for the forcefulness of its declamation, the boldness of its contours and the lively nature of its accompaniment. Another, "Furcht und Hoffnung", one of the best sustained arias in the work, demonstrates Telemann's skill in projecting the conflicting emotions of the text – fear and hope, love and hate. Orpheus is sung by Roman Trekel, Eurydice by Ruth Ziesak. Telemann adorns both roles with an affecting blend of lyricism and pathos. Eurydice's part in the drama is, perforce, relatively small – she is dead well before the end of Act 1 and has little to sing during her all too brief journey from the Underworld. But her music is often alluring and nowhere more so, perhaps, than when she welcomes the Shades, who gather to prevent an opportunity for the lovers to look upon one another during the rescue scene. There are some forward-looking harmonies here which foreshadow later developments in opera. Orpheus's music is, appropriately, captivating more often than not; and it is strikingly varied in character, ranging from the light-hearted, enchanting "Vezzosi lumi", to his deeply felt "Fliesst ihr Zeugen meiner Schmerzen", which is followed by a sharply poignant, despairing arioso with solo oboe and string pizzicato. Such music as this is hardly distinguishable from the sort of Passion music that Telemann was setting for the annual Lenten performances for which he was responsible throughout his Hamburg years.

This is an important and hugely enjoyable release which enriches our hitherto somewhat limited view of Telemann the opera composer and, indeed, enhances for us his reputation in this sphere. Jacobs and his musicians deserve congratulations, and so do Harmonia Mundi for their first-rate recording in which almost two hours and 40 minutes of music have been accommodated on two discs. No opera lover should miss this.

Ambroise Thomas
French 1811-1896

Thomas Hamlet.
Thomas Hampson *bass* Hamlet
June Anderson *sop* Ophélie
Gregory Kunde *ten* Laërte
Denyce Graves *mez* Gertrude
Samuel Ramey *bass* Claudius
Jean-Philippe Courtis *bass* Ghost
Gérard Garino *ten* Marcellus
Michel Trempont *ten* Polonius
François Le Roux *bar* Horatio
Thierry Félix *bar* First gravedigger
Jean-Pierre Furlan *ten* Second gravedigger
Ambrosian Opera Chorus; London Philharmonic Orchestra / Antonio de Almeida.
EMI Ⓟ Ⓓ CDS7 54820-2 (three discs: 198 minutes: DDD). Notes, text and translation included. Recorded 1993.

Variously described as a "powerful, dark-hued masterpiece" and as, dramatically, a travesty with some musical high spots amid a sea of commonplace sentimentalities, Thomas's *Hamlet* seems to demand being looked at afresh. Forget Shakespeare if you can (although much of his text is employed) for, after all, he was already making his own version of an old story, and do not repine at the absence of Rosencrantz, Guildenstern or Fortinbras, nor that Polonius's part is reduced to a mere eight bars; and though the contrived happy ending, with Hamlet being proclaimed king, takes some swallowing, responsibility for this lies not with Thomas but with the French audiences of the 1860s, whose bourgeois tastes, unable to take stronger meat, had already forced his librettists, Carré and Barbier (in

Gounod's *Faust* and Thomas's *Mignon*) to emasculate Goethe. For the Covent Garden production of *Hamlet* a year after the Paris première, the ending was changed as a sop to British sensibilities, and Hamlet kills himself. Richard Bonynge, in his version on Decca, tries to effect a *rapprochement* with Shakespeare and has Hamlet fatally wounded at the very start of the duel. The present recording goes back to Thomas's original but also includes the Covent Garden ending in an appendix, to which is also banished the musically shallow and banal ballet (dramatically irrelevant) on which Parisian audiences insisted. An extra point of interest in this set is the inclusion (also in an appendix) of a duet between Claudius and Gertrude which had only recently been discovered in the Bibliothèque National and which has not previously been recorded. In any case, this recording – over three hours of it – is more complete than the Decca issue, in which there were a number of small cuts.

So, viewing the work objectively, what impression does it make? There are indeed undistinguished sections, where Thomas lapses into the conventional and pretty-pretty – and lead-ins to arias are too often like ballet-dancers' "take up position" (though the introduction to "To be or not to be" is almost Verdian) – but against this must be set the tense scene of the ghost's appearance, Hamlet's highly dramatic confrontation of Gertrude (with a further manifestation by the ghost), and such arias as Claudius's prayer for forgiveness and Hamlet's "Comme une pâle fleur". Thomas's orchestration is colourful and full of felicities (and not merely because of his employment of a saxophone), with highly effective use of the trombones, and the Intermezzo to Act 4, a clarinet solo, is singularly lovely. This good impression owes much to the excellent performance here. Almeida secures the utmost in commitment from the LPO – the initial coronation march has tremendous impact – (though occasionally, as in Act 1, the orchestra are allowed to outbalance the singers) and the splendidly firm-voiced and tonally sensitive Ambrosian Singers; and the casting is admirable, with not a single weakness. The principals sound younger, and therefore more plausible, than in the Bonynge set. Anderson, with her seductive voice and sparkling technique, presents a more touching and vulnerable Ophelia, and manages even to make the protracted mad scene that occupies all of Act 3 something more than the mere display-piece for prima donnas and canary-fanciers it was long considered to be. (Her Ballad here, which is movingly taken up by the wordless chorus, bears a close resemblance to the first movement of Grieg's Op. 63, and proves to have been suggested to Thomas by his Scandinavian first Ophelia, Christine Nilsson.) Hampson's Hamlet is full of subtle shadings of tone and colour, and the recitatives (his as well as the others') are invested with life and character in a way that leaves the Bonynge set standing. Ramey brings weight (if perhaps not ideal steadiness) to his portrayal of Claudius, Denyce Graves has a secure facility as Gertrude, and in the minor parts, all of which are well taken, one distinct advantage over the earlier set is the fine First gravedigger of Thierry Félix instead of his dreadfully wobbly predecessor. The overall standard of the French is notably superior. The one criticism is that, as compared with John Tomlinson's awe-inspiring ghost, set in a hollow acoustic, Courtis here is given insufficient presence, so that his all-important narration fails to make its proper effect. In sum, however, this is recommended to listeners to give Thomas another chance and not just to dismiss him as an operatic lightweight.

Virgil Thomson
American 1896-1989

Thomson Lord Byron.
Matthew Lord *ten* Lord Byron
Richard Zeller *bar* Thomas Moore
D'Anna Fortunato *contr* Lady Byron
Richard Johnson *bass* John Hobhouse
Jeanne Ommerlé *sop* Mrs Leigh
Gregory Mercer *ten* John Murray
Adrienne Csengery *sop* Contessa Guiccioli
Thomas Woodman *bar* Count Gamba
Stephen Owen *bass* John Ireland
Louisa Jonason *sop* Lady Melbourne
Debra Vanderlinde *sop* Lady Charlotte
Marion Dry *mez* Lady Jane
Monadnock Festival Chorus and Orchestra / James Bolle.
Koch International Classics Ⓟ Ⓒ 37124-2 (two discs: 118 minutes: DDD). Text included.
Recorded at performances in Wilton, New Hampshire on August 31st and September 2nd, 1991.

One wonders how far the awkwardness of this often striking but flawed opera was due to the Metropolitan Opera coming up with a commission well after Thomson had planned it, and then, according to his librettist, demanding substantial changes to make it suitable for their new Lincoln Center auditorium? In the event they never performed *Lord Byron*, and after its première at the Juilliard School the composer subjected it to severe cuts (restored in this recording). Whatever the reason, the opera is oddly proportioned (a very short First Act: the Met had demanded two intervals in what had palpably been a one- or two-act structure), oscillates curiously between chamber and 'grand' opera and takes rather a long time to get off the ground. The stark and gritty choral scenes at the beginning and end may have been late responses to the Met's demand for bigger music to fill their vast stage; they certainly delay the arrival of anything that the admirer of *Four Saints in Three Acts* or *The Mother of us all* would recognize as characteristic Thomson.

The opera takes place after Byron's death; the intention was that it should be set in Poets' Corner in Westminster Abbey, as his friends, his widow and his half-sister Augusta Leigh attempt to persuade the authorities to allow his burial there. Byron himself arrives (and so does the real Virgil Thomson, to the sound of castanets) as an ironic observer of the unveiling of his own statue, and a series of 'memory scenes' or flashbacks recall his first meeting with his wife, the scandal surrounding his relationship with Augusta, his wedding and his exile after Lady Byron discovers him and Augusta embracing. Back in the Abbey, Byron's publisher burns unread the poet's presumably scandalous memoirs, the Dean decrees that a man whose life is not fit to print cannot be buried in such holy ground and the statue is removed. As night falls, however, the shades of the Abbey's other poets welcome Byron to their number in an almost martially jubilant finale.

Thomson's lyricism, his affinities with demotic music and his humour are most apparent in the 'memory scenes'. The third of them, set on the night before Byron's wedding, is especially ingenious: on a split stage Byron's fiancée, Annabella, with Augusta and Lady Melbourne, surveys her trousseau and hopes for the best, while Byron and his friends, drunk at a bachelor party, stage a mock-marriage. The music ironically interweaves *Auld lang syne*, *O, du lieber Augustin* (already associated in the previous scene with Byron's 'degeneracy') and an owlish canon, very close to *Ding dong bell, pussy's in the well*. Eventually, the two scenes combine in a complex and lively ensemble, crowned with a derisive transformation of *Auld lang syne* into a waltz.

The first 'memory scene' has a vintage Thomson aria (Byron's own "Alas! The love of woman", accompanied by a languishing chorus of adoring young ladies), the second a burlesque Italian mad scene for Lady Caroline Lamb and a gently expressive duet for Byron and Augusta, while the fourth riskily but effectively presents their relationship as an infantile one, the passion beneath their baby-talk only gradually recognized by Lady Byron; this, with Byron's arias, is one of the lyrical high points of the score. The outer scenes, despite incidental felicities – Thomas Moore's presence is an excuse for both real and pastiche 'Irish Melodies', Augusta's aria to the statue, "He will be remembered for his beauty" is touching, so is Shelley's ode of welcome – seem to come from another opera, and a much less interesting one.

Some allowances have to be made for the performance. The principals are mostly at least adequate, though Lord's vociferous manner and his raw vowels come nowhere near an evocation of Byron. Some of the secondary singers are decidedly rough, and the sound has most of the vices of live recording (mysterious pauses and stage noises, patches of unfocused ensemble) and few of its virtues. The orchestra sound a bit under strength. Cueing bands have apparently been flung in at random (they vary in duration from 17 seconds to a quarter of an hour, and do not always correspond with the key points in the accompanying booklet). Thomson enthusiasts will need no urging to acquire this set despite its disadvantages; enquiring newcomers to his music, however, would do better to begin with the orchestral pieces, the 'portraits' and songs or the other two operas, of which only *The Mother of us all* is currently in the catalogue.

Thomson The Mother of us all.
Mignon Dunn *mez* Susan B. Anthony
James Atherton *ten* Jo the Loiterer
Philip Booth *bass* Daniel Webster
Batyah Godfrey *contr* Anne
William Lewis *ten* John Adams
Linn Maxwell *mez* Indiana Elliot
Helen Vanni *mez* Constance Fletcher
Douglas Perry *ten* Thaddeus Stevens
Ashley Putnam *sop* Angel More
Joseph McKee *bass* Chris the Citizen
Gene Ives *bar* Virgil Thomas
Santa Fé Opera Chorus and Orchestra / Raymond Leppard.
New World ℗ ① NW288/9-2 (two discs: 107 minutes: ADD). Text included. Recorded 1976.

Thomson's second opera was originally released on New World in the USA in 1977, although the orchestral suite had been recorded three times before that. *The Mother of us all* is more immediately successful on record than *Four Saints in Three Acts*, which was issued complete by Nonesuch in 1982 (not generally available in the UK) after being recorded only in abridged form for over 40 years. *Four Saints* is more repetitive and abstract, whereas *The Mother of us all* has a fashionable cause and, near enough, a plot. In fact this opera, so characteristic of both Thomson and his librettist, Gertrude Stein, is more likely than anything else to augment Thomson's audience outside the USA.

The opera's cause is women's suffrage and its heroine the historic pioneer, Susan B. Anthony (1820-1906), who lived long enough to see some American states grant women the vote. She is the factual part of the libretto, but the opera is also rich in fantasy. Even the composer, his librettist and her literary executor are included as characters and people from different periods who never actually met encounter each other on stage. This is all fairly normal within the studied abnormality of Gertrude Stein whose writing profoundly affected Thomson, so that his music is in many ways a precise counterpart of her literary innovations.

This set has transferred well to CD. The cast was based on the Santa Fé Opera production of 1976 conducted by Raymond Leppard, who came fresh from his exploits in Monteverdi and Cavalli. That experience cannot have been wasted on the Thomson opera, equally concerned with delivering text audibly, pacing varied textures and balancing the changes from arioso to recitative. What has altered since then is that opera audiences in many parts of the world have succumbed to non-narrative opera, whether Philip Glass, Harrison Birtwistle or John Adams. Thomson, with *Four Saints* in 1934, and *The Mother* in 1947, is the ancestor of the American part of this process and by comparison with Glass's seems generously inventive. Alongside the serious topic of women's lib in days when such ideas were embryonic at best, there are witty asides arising from both text and context. In waltz time the character John Adams (what prophetic anticipation!) explains: "I never marry. I have been twice divorced but I have never married".

Major roles are sung by Mignon Dunn, Philip Booth (magisterial but straining a bit at the top as Daniel Webster), and James Atherton (who is engaging) in a well-balanced team with no weak links. There are times when ensemble is not as clean as it should be but the overall impact of the performance is utterly authentic and convincing. Apart from "London Bridge is falling down", all the tunes are supposed to be original, but they are so close to various diatonic types, ranging from hymns to Viennese waltzes, that they soon become really catchy. The whole of the First Act sparkles with invention and it is only towards the end of the Second Act that Thomson's technique seems to freewheel into final sad reminiscences with the Wedding Hymn possibly overdone.

The original New World LPs were issued in a double sleeve, as usual replete with documentation. It has not been possible to get all this on to a CD booklet but you are invited to apply for it. (Neither, apparently, was it possible to bring artists' biographies up to date.) This detail could only enhance a most enjoyable and unusual operatic release.

Sir Michael Tippett
British 1905-1998

Tippett King Priam.
  Norman Bailey *bar* Priam
  Heather Harper *sop* Hecuba
  Thomas Allen *bar* Hector
  Felicity Palmer *sop* Andromache
  Philip Langridge *ten* Paris
  Yvonne Minton *mez* Helen
  Robert Tear *ten* Achilles
  Stephen Roberts *bar* Patroclus
  Ann Murray *mez* Nurse
  David Wilson-Johnson *bar* Old man
  Peter Hall *ten* Young guard
  Kenneth Bowen *ten* Hermes
  Julian Saipe *treb* Young Paris
  Linda Hirst *sop* Servant
  London Sinfonietta Chorus; London Sinfonietta / David Atherton.
  Chandos Ⓟ Ⓓ CHAN9406/7 (two discs: 127 minutes: ADD). Notes and text included. Recorded 1980.

1981

King Priam was a great shock when it was first performed in 1962. In place of the ecstatic lyrical warmth of Tippett's previous opera, *The Midsummer Marriage*, a plot drawn from the Trojan War drew from him a new and bracing style, hard-edged, disjunct and often barbaric in colour. His vocal writing also became very much more taxing. All the principal roles demand unsparing vocal intensity, precision in pitching the often very awkward intervals and, often enough, athletic flexibility. In its own way it is as difficult to cast as *Il trovatore*, and the fearlessness of, in particular, Harper, Minton, Palmer, Langridge and Tear is quite remarkable. But a lot more is required of the singers than merely standing up with fortitude to the demands made of them. In that way, too, this is an exceptionally fine performance. One only has to compare the ardour of Langridge's Paris with the range from languor to ferocity of Tear's Achilles to realize that Tippett is very far from writing all-purpose angular modernisms for both his principal tenors. Hecuba, Andromache and Helen are equally sharply characterized by the composer, and as vividly realized by these singers.

Alongside the shock at this opera's new sound world went a deeper shock at how poignantly moving it could be. The title-role is less spectacularly difficult than some of the others, but Priam is given many of the opera's most telling pages, from 'his' motif of sonorous chordal strings (an archetypal Tippett sound) to the bare but profoundly affecting scene in which he begs Achilles for the body of his son. Bailey has just the right blend of proud dignity and vulnerability for the role, and his projection of the text is immaculate. Atherton is at his best, not just steering the cast and the orchestra past the score's many pitfalls but searching out all the wonderfully sensuous sounds that it contains. He knows just what Tippett means by marking Paris's love music 'winged' (*alato*, though the composer misspells it), and that is exactly how it sounds.

The performance and the clean, transparent recording are in short fully worthy of this wonderful opera. Nevertheless one hopes that it will have a rival one day. A more robust tenor than the very musicianly Kenneth Bowen would make a more magical figure of Hermes. Much more important, Tippett's virtuoso violin lines were for a long time thought unplayable by a full violin section, and they are here given, as in stage performances until recently, to a soloist. Now that we know how magnificent they sound on a dozen or more violins it's hard not to feel cheated, brilliantly though Nona Liddell (uncredited) plays them. But let us not be ungrateful for what is a remarkably fine set.

Tippett The Knot Garden.
Raimund Herincx *bass* Faber
Yvonne Minton *mez* Thea
Jill Gomez *sop* Flora
Dame Josephine Barstow *sop* Denise
Thomas Carey *bar* Mel
Robert Tear *ten* Dov
Thomas Hemsley *bar* Mangus
Orchestra of the Royal Opera House, Covent Garden / Sir Colin Davis.

Tippett A Child of Our Time.
Jessye Norman *sop*
Dame Janet Baker *mez*
Richard Cassilly *ten*
John Shirley-Quirk *bar*
BBC Singers; BBC Choral Society; BBC Symphony Orchestra / Sir Colin Davis.
Philips Ⓟ ① 446 331-2PH2 (two discs: 145 minutes: ADD). *The Knot Garden* recorded 1973;
A Child of Our Time recorded 1975.

Even some of the more enthusiastic reviews after the first performance of *The Knot Garden* were rather perplexed by its structure: it is a short opera, but its three acts are divided into 23 scenes, often brief and abruptly juxtaposed. However, the form of the piece will strike you as admirably clear, musically strong and ideally appropriate to the subject. *The Knot Garden* is not so much a narrative as an examination of a set of relationships; the structure is a device to bring about confrontations. Thus, the First Act introduces six of the seven characters, briefly demonstrates their problems and then introduces a catalyst in the person of Denise, the freedom-fighter disfigured by torture. She sings an updated version of an ancient operatic form – the virtuoso display aria, here brilliantly put to new purposes – which in turn prompts an ensemble-finale in the again updated form of a blues with a fast boogie-woogie middle section.

The Second Act, apparently still more labyrinthine (its subtitle is "Labyrinth"), contains the opera's most violent cross-cuttings – the technique is cinematic – but it has two scenes of stillness, both of them very beautiful (fantasias respectively on *We shall overcome* and Schubert's *Die liebe Farbe*) which together allow a vision of healed relationships, crystallizing (Mozartian or even Verdian practice again) in a concluding aria of belief in love and beauty. It is full, that aria, of Tippett's (some would say) notorious colloquialisms. In this opera they go along with musical colloquialisms (the blues, the electric guitar) to convey a tough but vulnerable urban poetry that it would have been hard to evoke without their use. At times the same seems to be true of Tippett's words: you may wince a bit at "Play it cool" and "A man is for real", but you also wonder whether they are not the equivalent of his unerringly-used electric guitar; that 'aria' would be diminished without its cries of "Oh boy!".

The Knot Garden is a classic of its period, and a central work in its composer's output, As an opera about relationships it needs particularly sensitive handling by the singers, and the cast (that of the first performance) is outstanding. Tear gives his character ("a homosexual in pink socks!", sneered one reviewer) real charm and pathos as well as singing his uncommonly difficult lines with great flair. Barstow is even finer: an electric presence with a visionary intensity to her aria of remembered anguish. Minton and Herincx are both excellent, Gomez touchingly vulnerable, while Hemsley's immaculate diction and gentlemanly tones are perfect for Mangus, the psychiatrist Prospero.

Davis is as eloquently urgent in the opera as in the oratorio, *A Child of Our Time*, which, in a generally fine, rather opera-scaled reading, makes an ideal coupling: two complementary aspects of Tippett the maker of healing images. In the opera the voices sound a little further forward than on the LPs, the sound a bit harder-edged; the oratorio, appropriately, is placed in a warmer acoustic.

Tippett The Midsummer Marriage.
Alberto Remedios *ten* Mark
Joan Carlyle *sop* Jenifer
Raimund Herincx *bass* King Fisher

Elizabeth Harwood *sop* Bella
Stuart Burrows *ten* Jack
Helen Watts *contr* Sosostris
Stafford Dean *bass* He-Ancient
Elizabeth Bainbridge *mez* She-Ancient
David Whelan *bar* Half-Tipsy man
Andrew Daniels *ten* Dancing man
Chorus and Orchestra of the Royal Opera House, Covent Garden / Sir Colin Davis.
Lyrita Ⓟ Ⓒ SRCD2217 (two discs: 154 minutes: ADD). Notes and text included. Recorded 1970.

It is as though Turner's *The Fighting Temeraire* were not on show because no one could be bothered to clean it, or as though Wordsworth's *The Prelude* had been allowed to go out of print. How did it take so long for this great and magical opera to appear on CD? So many of the expressions of our age have frowned in their contemplation of it, or have turned away to cultivate arcane, private gardens. But here was Tippett in 1955 expressing joy, boundless optimism and faith in beauty and humanity; doing so, moreover, with such richness of imagery that even those who loved it at first hearing were a bit taken aback by its overwhelming abundance.

As so often with his pieces, it took a while to sink in, and for players and singers to get their fingers and their vocal chords around those springing rhythms and sinewy lines. The moment at which that happened was the moment of this recording and the performances that preceded it. Remedios and Carlyle are not simply managing those exuberant hocketings above the stave in their final duet; you would swear that they were enjoying them, and as they do so the image of love as a consuming flame is vividly projected. Burrows and the adorable Harwood are audibly moved by how much tenderness and innocence there is in their music, and they make a real and most touching couple. Herincx is wonderfully suave and bossy as King Fisher; Watts not only survives her forays into the bass-baritone register but makes an awesomely Sibylline figure of Sosostris. And Davis, raptly in love with this score and communicating that to his singers and players so effectively that one is never aware of them gritting their teeth and counting beats as though their lives depended on it, reveals again and again the opera's magical sonorities. It is a superb performance: after it one can hardly read those early reviews ("incomprehensible libretto", "too much counterpoint", "half an hour too long") without laughing. The recording, too, communicates a real sense of live performance. A masterpiece, in short, and one that can be listened to again and again without exhausting its exuberant generosity.

Eduard Tubin
Estonian 1905-1982

Tubin Barbara von Tisenhusen.
Helvi Raamat *sop* Barbara von Tisenhusen
Tarmo Sild *bar* Matthias Jeremias Friesner
Mare Jõgeva *mez* Anna von Tödwen
Uno Kreen *bass* Johann von Tödwen
Ivo Kuusk *ten* Franz Bonnius
Väino Puura *bar* Jürgen
Ants Kollo *ten* Reinhold
Hans Miilberg *bass* Bartholomeus
Mati Palm *bass* Reinhold von Tisenhusen
Estonian Opera Chorus and Orchestra / Peeter Lilje.
Ondine Ⓟ Ⓒ ODE776-2 (two discs: 95 minutes: DDD). Notes, text and translation included. Recorded 1991.

Eduard Tubin first tried his hand at opera in 1941 with *Puhajarv* ("Holy Lake"), and a little later, *Libahunt* ("Werewolf") though he finished neither. Then in 1944, when the Red Army was at the gates of Tallinn, he fled to Sweden where he lived for the remainder of his life. But in the mid-1960s, relations with Soviet Estonia began to thaw, and performances of his music were once again permitted. Tubin was invited to Tallinn in 1966, when the Estonian Opera put on his ballet, *Kratt* and its success prompted a commission from the Opera: *Barbara von Tisenhusen* was the result.

It has much in common with his second opera, *The Parson of Reigi*. They are both relatively short: in the present opera there are three acts of about half-an-hour apiece, and it, too, turns for its inspiration to the Finnish-born Aino Kallas (1878-1956). Moreover, the plot is not dissimilar both in its simplicity and substance It concerns illicit love, the attraction of a noblewoman (Barbara von Tisenhusen) for a commoner (Franz Bonnius), their subsequent elopement, their attempted escape to Lithuania and the disastrous consequences that ensue. Like Catharina in *The Parson of Reigi*, she is condemned to death, though in this instance her lover escapes her fate and is drowned in an ice-covered lake. There is one important difference in that the musical organization is more symphonic.

The thematic substance is largely drawn from a chaconne-like motif heard as the curtain rises. It changes so subtly and unobtrusively in dramatic character in each scene that one wonders whether most opera-goers would notice it. As with all composers of quality, Tubin's is the art that conceals art. *Barbara von Tisenhusen* has no want of variety of pace and texture, and is probably more effective as theatre than its successor. The fourth scene, in which the Tisenhusen brothers arrange for a bear to be savaged by a pack of dogs for their amusement, which Harri Kiirsk calls "the cruel scherzo of the opera", comes close to the dark world of the Eighth Symphony on which he worked at about the same time. Again characterization is far more vivid than one might expect for a composer whose thought processes are predominantly symphonic in temperament and character but then you must not forget that Tubin had stage experience when he worked at the Vanemuine Theatre in Tallinn before the Second World War. The opening of the Third Act is very characteristic and an ideal passage to sample for it conveys much of the excitement, atmosphere and dramatic skill that the score exhibits.

The singers are excellent without being of 'star quality' and the orchestral playing under Peeter Lilje is committed and serviceable. The sound is rather like that of any broadcast opera relay rather than a commercial studio recording, and needs more space in which to expand. When *Barbara von Tisenhusen* was first staged it played to full houses for 50 performances – this is not surprising for it is a work of dramatic and musical coherence that deserves a strong recommendation.

Mark-Anthony Turnage
British 1960-

Turnage Greek.
Quentin Hayes *bass* Eddy
Richard Suart *bass* Dad, Café manager, Chief of Police
Fiona Kimm *mez* Wife, Doreen, First maitress, Second mphinx
Helen Charnock *sop* Mum, Second waitress, First sphinx
Greek Ensemble / Richard Bernas.
Argo Ⓔ Ⓓ 440 368-2ZHO (78 minutes: DDD). Notes and text included. Recorded 1992.

Mark-Anthony Turnage's *Greek* (to a libretto by Steven Berkoff from his own *Oedipus-in-the-East-End* play) won two awards and a standing ovation at its première in Munich in 1988, capacity audiences at the Edinburgh Festival that year and both enthusiastic acclaim and public response when it later appeared at the English National Opera, on BBC television and in subsequent productions in Europe and Australia. Deprived of Jonathan Moore's staging there might have been a risk of its impact being lessened in the colder, sound-only medium of CD, but the by now seasoned cast and Richard Bernas's pungent, saxophone- and percussion-dominated band ensure that it is not.

But *Greek* has certainly changed, and this is not a reference to the excision of a few four-letter words from the libretto. The libretto's Cockney has become something of a problem, which it was not on stage. It's partly that twisted vowels and glottal stops don't sit comfortably on classically trained voices (the cast do wonders, but can't avoid reverting to Home Counties English whenever an awkward note needs genuinely to be sung). It's also hard to know how singers who've been trying very hard at their "gorblimeys" and their "'ere we gos" should enunciate Berkoff's perplexing side-lurches into "Confess, my dear, the quandary that doth crease your brow" and the like. If it comes to that, Eddie/Oedipus tells us that he was "spawned in a Tufnell Park that's no more than a stone's throw from the Angel, a monkey's fart from Tottenham or a bolt of phlegm from Stamford Hill. It's a cesspit, right … ". Is it mere pedantry in a former resident of that cesspit to remark that the Angel, two miles off, Tottenham and Stamford Hill, five and four miles respectively, would tax most stone-throwers, monkeys or bronchitics, and that none of these agreeable places is in the East End? Probably, and yet a lack of focus, a sense of opera singers pretending to be not quite accurately observed 'Cockneys', does undermine the opera's otherwise luridly alluring vision of racism, police violence, strikes and inner city decay as Thatcher's Britain equivalent of the Theban plagues. For all its demotic language and brilliant devices (a chorus of shouting policemen accompanied by stamping feet, a vividly gruesome duet of exclamatory verbal violence, the Sphinx portrayed by two singers as a multiple image of destruction: the eternal feminine/feminist and the old slag) this is an apocalyptic vision seen from the comfortable vantage point of a decent restaurant well up West.

But that skewed focus doesn't diminish the directness and ingenuity of Turnage's idiom, which for all its echoes of Weill and rock, its obvious roots in Stravinsky, centres on a moody, often beautiful lyricism (the Wife's 'love aria' in Act 2), which is indeed genuinely urban, his instinct for the *musical* demotic is very shrewd. The opera's sonorities are precise and memorable, it has in the crucial scenes a gravity that can rise (the stricken duet and quartet after Eddy's incest and patricide are revealed) to eloquence, even nobility. The performance, those heroic efforts to reconcile Cockney and quasi-*bel canto* aside, could hardly be bettered; the recording pitches the opera at you hot and strong.

Viktor Ullmann
Austrian/Hungarian 1898-1944

Ullmann Der Kaiser von Atlantis, oder Die Tod-Verweigerung.
Michael Kraus *bar* Kaiser Overall
Franz Mazura *bar* Loudspeaker

Martin Petzold *ten* Soldier
Christiane Oelze *sop* Bubikopf
Walter Berry *bass* Death
Herbert Lippert *ten* Harlequin
Iris Vermillion *mez* Drummer-girl
Leipzig Gewandhaus Orchestra / Lothar Zagrosek.

Ullmann Hölderlin-Lieder – Abendphantasie; Der Frühling; Wo bist du?.

Iris Vermillion *mez*
Jonathan Alder *pf*
Decca Entartete Musik Ⓕ ① 440 854-2DH (68 minutes: DDD). Notes, texts and translations included. Recorded 1993.

The subtitle of Viktor Ullmann's opera means "The denial of death". Death is portrayed as an old soldier, proud of the dignity of his calling. In his opening aria he reminiscences about the way war was in his young days, "when people wore the most magnificent clothes to do me honour". But now the Emperor Overall (an obvious Hitler-caricature, his first announcement greeted by a derisive parody of the German National Anthem) decrees total war and conscripts Death to his cause without so much as a by-your-leave. Death is outraged, and resigns his office; soon even the mortally wounded, the terminally ill are denied his solace. Eventually Death appears to the distraught Emperor and demands his life as the price of taking up his work again.

All this was written and prepared for performance (not actually performed: the SS saw to that) in that hideously fascinating place, the 'model ghetto' of Terezin or Theresienstadt, ostensibly a benign application of 'the final solution', in fact a transit camp for Auschwitz. It would deserve a recording as a memorial to that place and to the 'will to live' that, according to Ullmann himself, drove the score or so composers and the hundreds of other artists and performers who passed through it on the way to their deaths. It would deserve a recording even if it were not especially good. It is in fact moving and at times inspired, owing some of its musical quality as well as its terrible dramatic ironies to the place where it was written. Terezin must have contained a higher proportion of cultivated and musically literate people than almost any community of its size at that time. Ullmann, whose career had been slow in developing before the war, was confronted with an ideal audience, able to pick up without prompting the fact that the opera's leitmotiv is the 'theme of death' from Suk's *Asrael* Symphony, fully able to appreciate the resonance of building the work's finale on Luther's *Ein feste Burg* (used, most memorably, in monuments to Protestant Germany by composers banned by the Third Reich, Meyerbeer and Mendelssohn), and to understand why Harlequin, in the opera's opening number, should quote Mahler as an image of irrecoverable innocence.

Even more than that, though, it took a musical dramatist of exceptional quality to turn the Emperor-image in the opening scenes of Hitler-as-Behemoth, at the end into Death's most lyrical eulogist. There are two versions of this scene (both are recorded here), one mysterious and elegiac, the other still more Mahlerian but also a warning against future dictators, and this perhaps sets the poignantly beautiful final chorale fantasy best in context.

Walter Berry's voice was by the time of this recording a little worn, but its warm geniality and the associations it conjures up are characteristic of the shrewdness with which the casting has been done: for 'casting' read 'dramatization'. The scratch ghetto orchestra (11 players) for which Ullmann wrote, points up the overtones of Weill and Krenek and Zemlinsky, but also his own evocative use of limited resources. The expressively lyrical, tonally ambiguous Hölderlin songs, richly sung, were written in the same year as the opera. Together they suggest that, a few months before Ullmann's death, Terezin had matured him into a composer of rare subtlety as well as poignant directness.

Ullmann Der Sturz des Antichrist.

Ulrich Neuweiler *ten* Regent, Demon of the Regent
Richard Decker *ten* Priest, Imperfect Angel of the Priest
William Oberholtzer *bar* Technician, Spectre of the Technician
Louis Gentile *ten* Artist
Monte Jaffe *bass* Warden
Lassi Partanen *ten* Crier
Bielefeld Opera Chorus; Bielefeld Philharmonic Orchestra / Rainer Koch.
CPO Ⓕ ① CPO999 321-2 (two discs: 106 minutes: DDD). Notes, text and translation included. Recorded at performances in the Oetkerhalle, Bielefeld on February 15th and 16th, 1995.

Even in the desperate conditions of Theresienstadt, Ullmann followed a more recognizably German compositional path than his fellow internees. Schoenberg was his teacher but he was never a slavish Schoenbergian and the stylistic variety of his work is one of its more notable features (or weaknesses; it depends on your point of view). Following several successful stagings of *Der Kaiser von Atlantis*, his first opera, *Der Sturz des Antichrist* was given a belated première in Bielefeld in 1995. This recording was made in conjunction with that production and is a welcome, if not ideally polished, representation of Ullmann's prophetic music drama – an allegorical depiction of the rise of a dictator, the destruction he causes and his ultimate defeat. Having mounted revivals of operas by Schreker, Brand and Korngold in the last ten years or so, the Bielefeld company was perhaps uniquely well placed to tackle Ullmann's *magnum opus*.

Der Sturz des Antichrist is an ambitious work in all respects – philosophical, dramatic, vocal and technical. It is based on (and remains slavishly faithful to) a dramatic sketch by Albert Steffen, a fellow disciple of the philosopher and teacher, Rudolf Steiner. The opera's Hitler figure is the Regent, who commands technician, priest and poet to submit to his will, symbolic figures representing science, religion and the artist as state propagandist. The poet (Ullmann?) resists and is thrown into prison whereupon his gaoler helps him to unlock his spiritual resources (the scene contains the opera's most nearly sublime music which CPO quite unnecessarily split between discs). In the final act, the poet denounces the Regent as the Antichrist, and the dictator overreaches himself, inviting destruction as he takes to the skies in a Tippettian aircraft or spaceship.

It is difficult to judge the quality of such an extraordinary piece from a first recording. The recorded balance ensures that the music remains subservient to the words, and such would appear to be the composer's intention. The work is a metaphysical fantasy squarely in the Wagnerian tradition – which here means few opportunities for dramatic action, scant melodic interest (despite the broadly tonal idiom) and yet plenty of recognizable leitmotivs. While there is a hint of Korngold and even Scriabin in the work's riper moments, Schoenberg and Debussy are more perceptible influences than the Weill or Hindemith one might have expected. So too is Mahler. The main leitmotiv is cribbed from "Ich ging mit Lust" (a *Wunderhorn* setting from the *Lieder und Gesänge aus der Jugendzeit*), although there might be no significance in this beyond Ullmann's inability to write his own tunes. Whole-tone and augmented harmonies are identified with the perverted value system of the villainous Regent and the work as a whole is claimed to be tightly structured.

Whatever else it may be, *Der Sturz des Antichrist* is a sombre affair – the effect of an all-male cast and a brooding orchestral palette featuring contrabassoon, two bass clarinets and even basset horns. The wordless female chorus are used sparingly in the last act. The one outstanding performance is Monte Jaffe's as the Warden, but then he does have the best music to sing. It is tempting to give this set an uncritical welcome in the light of the composer's fate but it is also true to say that many readers may find it hard going.

Ralph Vaughan Williams
British 1872-1958

Vaughan Williams Hugh the Drover.
Bonaventura Bottone *ten* Hugh
Rebecca Evans *sop* Mary
Richard Van Allan *bass* Constable
Alan Opie *bar* John the Butcher
Sarah Walker *mez* Aunt Jane
Neil Jenkins *ten* Turnkey
Robert Poulton *bar* Sergeant
Karl Morgan Daymond *bar* Showman
Harry Nicoll *ten* Cheap-Jack
Adrian Hutton *bass* Shellfish seller
Julia Gooding *sop* Primrose seller
Wynford Evans *ten* Ballad seller
Jenny Saunders *sop* Susan
Alice Coote *mez* Nancy
Lynton Atkinson *ten* William
Paul Robinson *bar* Robert
John Pearce *ten* Fool
Paul Im Thurn *bar* Innkeeper
New London Children's Choir; Corydon Singers; Corydon Orchestra / Matthew Best.
Hyperion Ⓟ Ⓞ CDA66901/2 (two discs: 102 minutes: DDD). Notes and text included. Recorded 1994.

Vaughan Williams Hugh the Drover.
Robert Tear *ten* Hugh
Sheila Armstrong *sop* Mary
Robert Lloyd *bass* Constable
Michael Rippon *bass* John the Butcher
Helen Watts *contr* Aunt Jane
John Fryatt *ten* Turnkey
Henry Newman *bass* Sergeant
Terence Sharpe *bar* Showman
Leslie Fyson *ten* Cheap-Jack
Oliver Broome *bass* Shellfish seller

Sally Burgess *mez* Primrose seller
David Johnston *ten* Ballad seller
Linda Richardson *mez* Susan
Shirley Minty *mez* Nancy
Neil Jenkins *ten* William
Bruce Ogston *bar* Robert
Steve Davies *bass* Fool
David Read *bass* Innkeeper
**St Paul's Cathedral Choir; Ambrosian Opera Chorus;
Royal Philharmonic Orchestra / Sir Charles Groves.**
EMI British Composers Ⓜ Ⓞ CMS5 65224-2 (two discs: 106 minutes: ADD). Notes and text
included. Recorded 1978.

In the publicity surrounding the revival at the 1994 Proms performance of Ethel Smyth's *The Wreckers*, it was as though everything between that work (1906) and *Peter Grimes* (1945) in British opera had been conveniently forgotten. The Hyperion set of *Hugh the Drover* (written in 1910) puts that to rights and proves, conclusively that, whereas Smyth was fashioning herself, albeit with craft, on continental models, Vaughan Williams was striking out on his own, in a specifically English way, and his work has a dramatic tautness Smyth's woefully lacks. But enough of odious comparison. Let us once more enjoy on its own the forthright, lyrical energy and subtlety of *Hugh*, admirably adumbrated in the modern version conducted enthusiastically by Best, supported by his Corydon forces. They almost make the work sound like the first British musical – if that's not a heresy!

They make sure we enjoy Vaughan Williams's innate gift as an orchestrator, the vigour of his writing for the chorus, and the richness of invention all round. In its revised form at any rate, the piece has very few *longueurs* and many moments of great beauty, particularly in the scenes for Mary and Hugh. Which British composer has written better love duets? None, probably, and the influence of Puccini sometimes seems hard to gainsay. Some of the hearty ingenuousness of the libretto and setting might be difficult to take on stage today, but some enterprising company – perhaps Opera North – should have a go, because in most respects the work is eminently stageworthy.

A post-war Sadler's Wells revival had the sturdy and forthright James Johnston as hero. Bonaventura Bottone's more sophisticated and eloquently accented performance misses some of the Drover's verve, but his singing is at all times finely shaped and accented, and his tone is equal to the appreciable demands placed on it. What we miss in his and Tear's larger-scale but too sophisticated reading on EMI is Johnston's vigour, even more that of the creator, the young and ebullient Tudor Davies, who can be heard on a contemporary recording of extracts made by HMV in 1924, the year of the première (reissued on Pearl); his verve and his heroic tang make him a hard act to follow.

Rebecca Evans, on the other hand, need fear no comparison with any predecessor. It is she alone who conveys the youthful vulnerability of Mary, and does so in the most sweet and tender way, both in solo and duet, while having the necessary mettle in her voice when Mary turns courageous in Act 2. The voice soars easily, the tone remains ever fresh and attractive. Sheila Armstrong (EMI) has a fuller, maturer tone suggesting a more introverted Mary than Evans attempts. Alan Opie is ideally biting and virile as John the Butcher, projecting the man's undoubted hubris in his vital treatment of the text, and he is steadier in voice than EMI's Michael Rippon. As the Constable, Mary's tetchy father, Van Allan – perhaps appropriately – sounds more elderly than EMI's Robert Lloyd: both make the role as important as their few appearances allow. Sarah Walker's Aunt Jane is as thoughtfully sung as one would expect from this experienced artist, but in her solo near the end of Act 1 she yields points to the extra feeling the more even-voiced Helen Watts (EMI) finds in the part. Smaller roles are well taken in both sets.

A major difference between the two readings comes in the conductor's approach, a lesser one in the recorded quality. In almost all cases Best takes faster speeds, chooses lighter textures than Groves (Best is closer to Sargent on the old HMV 78s). As a whole, Groves's interpretation runs deeper, as one might expect from the older man. The recording of the Hyperion often places the singers further back than the EMI set, and you may need a high volume setting to get the best out of it overall. The EMI set is certainly not outclassed in that respect and benefits from the Ambrosian Chorus on tiptop form. Both versions are most enjoyable, each worthy of the work. Choice will lie with a preference for an individual singer or for character of interpretation. Those who are really interested in the work may want to have both sets and as an extra, the abridged Pearl CD for passages the composer omitted in his revision and for Davies's unsurpassed Hugh.

Vaughan Williams The Pilgrim's Progress
John Noble *bar* The Pilgrim
Raimund Herincx *bar* John Bunyan, Lord Hate-Good
John Carol Case *bar* Evangelist
Wynford Evans *ten* Pliable, Second shepherd
Christopher Keyte *bass* Obstinate, Judas Iscariot, Pontius Pilate
Geoffrey Shaw *bar* Mistrust, Demas
Bernard Dickerson *ten* Timorous, Usher

Sheila Armstrong *sop* First Shining One, Voice of the Bird
Marie Hayward Segal *sop* Second Shining One, Madam Wanton
Gloria Jennings *contr* Third Shining One, Madam By-Ends
Ian Partridge *ten* Interpreter, Superstition
John Shirley-Quirk *bar* Watchful, the Porter
Terence Sharpe *bar* A Herald, First shepherd
Robert Lloyd *bass* Apollyon, Third shepherd
Norma Burrowes *sop* Branch Bearer
Alfreda Hodgson *contr* Cup Bearer, Pickthank
Joseph Ward *ten* Lord Lechery
Richard Angas *bass* Simon Magus, Envy
John Elwes *ten* Worldly Glory, Celestial messenger
Delia Wallis *mez* Madam Bubble
Wendy Eathorne *sop* A woodcutter's boy
Gerald English *ten* Mister By-Ends
Doreen Price *sop* Voice from Heaven
Jean Temperley *mez* Voice from Heaven
Kenneth Woolam *ten* Voice from Heaven
London Philharmonic Choir and Orchestra / Sir Adrian Boult.
EMI Ⓜ ① CMS7 64212-2 (two discs: 153 minutes: ADD). Notes and text included. Recorded 1972.

When this glowing performance of one of Vaughan Williams's most raptly beautiful works first appeared as a centenary offering to the composer, hope was expressed that the record would lead to more stage performances on both sides of the Atlantic. That hope, alas, has not been fulfilled, but hearing the opera again convinces you afresh that far from being loose-limbed, it is unusually concentrated musically. That Vaughan Williams drew from a whole series of Bunyan inspirations over 30 years has made for meatiness of material and little or no inconsistency of style. "They won't like it", predicted the composer after the first performance at Covent Garden. "They don't want an opera with no heroine and no love duets – and I don't care. It's what I meant, and there it is." Though he described the work as a "morality", he was aggressively concerned that it should be treated as an opera, not as an oratorio. One can see what he meant. He wanted the work's strength and cohesion brought out, not just its piety; but in truth precious little is lost from not having it staged, and CD format might well be counted as ideal, allowing the listener to picture his own staging.

This stands as one of Sir Adrian's very finest of his many records of Vaughan Williams's music, beautifully paced and textured with the fascinating references to the symphonies – not just No. 5 which took material from the previously written Act 1 but (at least by implication) Nos. 3, 4 and 7 as well, not to mention the *Serenade to Music*. In every way, Vaughan Williams's Bunyan inspirations permeated his music, and this opera stands as their centre-point.

John Noble, who as a very young singer scored a great success in the 1954 Cambridge production, may not have the richest or most characterful baritone, but his dedication and understanding make for compelling results. Outstanding among the others are Sheila Armstrong, Ian Partridge, Norma Burrowes and John Shirley-Quirk. The chorus – subject of rather tough treatment from Boult as the old rehearsal excerpts suggested – sing with fervour, and the sound remains first-rate.

Giuseppe Verdi   Italian 1813-1901

Verdi Aida.
    Montserrat Caballé *sop* Aida
    Plácido Domingo *ten* Radames
    Fiorenza Cossotto *mez* Amneris
    Piero Cappuccilli *bar* Amonasro
    Nicolai Ghiaurov *bass* Ramphis
    Luigi Roni *bass* King of Egypt
    Esther Casas *sop* Priestess
    Nicola Martinucci *ten* Messenger
    Chorus of the Royal Opera House, Covent Garden; New Philharmonia Orchestra;
    Trumpeters of the Royal Military School of Music, Kneller Hall / Riccardo Muti.
    EMI Ⓕ ① CDS5 56246-2 (three discs: 148 minutes: ADD). Notes, text and translation included.
    Recorded 1974.

BBC RADIO 3
90-93 FM

The rivalry between Muti and Claudio Abbado (for DG), so close on LP, transferred to CD. The virtues of the Muti are unchanged. Caballé gives what is generally considered her most successful Verdi performance on record, full of those vocal subtleties and beauties that inform her best singing, at its finest perhaps in the lovely floated passage at the close of "O patria mia", but no less effective when it comes to the power needed to fill Verdi's phrases generously. Moreover, the characterization, perhaps inspired by Muti, fulfils almost every aspect of the role's demands. In contrast to Caballé's delicacy and plangency, there is Cossotto's imperious, fiercely sung Amneris, just as electrifying when she is at the end of her tether in Act 4 as when she is baiting Aida in Act 2. Domingo, though not so vital as for Abbado, sings an upright, musical Radames, Cappuccilli is a forthright, unsubtle Amonasro, Ghiaurov a properly merciless Ramphis. Interesting to note Martinucci, later to become a Radames, in the tiny role of the Messenger.

Muti gives an impassioned, subjective account of the score, in many cases slower than Abbado's, but his pace in the final duet still strikes one as on the quick side and, in contrast to his Italian colleague, he does sometimes indulge in sudden accelerandos and crescendos that are unwarranted by the score. The balance between the sets is still a fine one. Ricciarelli (Abbado), though not vocally anywhere near so reliable as Caballé, is still an Aida to be reckoned with because she understands the emotions of the part so well. Abbado's great weakness is his insensitive Amneris: Obraztsova's raw, poorly articulated performance is no match for Cossotto's. Nucci, though well enough in the picture, is not so imposing as Cappuccilli. Ghiaurov is a little rusty as compared with his younger self. But Domingo there offers the most heroic Radames on any available set, and one fashioned in long breaths and refined phrasing. Abbado himself is inclined to take a more measured view of the score than Muti; his tempos seem "correctly regulated one with the other", and he is just as able as Muti to create the right atmosphere for a scene, by his attention to Verdi's illustrative detail.

With Muti digitally remastered, the differences in recorded quality are even more marked. The EMI sound is bigger in scale, more reverberant and spacious, but in the indoor scenes, as it were, the Abbado often seems the more natural. Both choruses and orchestras are well caught, and distinguish themselves with splendidly vital contributions. By a hair's breadth Muti is preferable, mainly because an *Aida* with an inadequate Anmeris is an *Aida* seriously faulted; in other respects honours remain equal.

Verdi Aida.

Mirella Freni *sop* Aida
José Carreras *ten* Radames
Agnes Baltsa *mez* Amneris
Piero Cappuccilli *bar* Amonasro
Ruggero Raimondi *bass* Ramphis
José van Dam *bass-bar* King of Egypt
Katia Ricciarelli *sop* Priestess
Vienna State Opera Chorus; Vienna Philharmonic Orchestra / Herbert von Karajan.
EMI Ⓜ ① CMS7 69300-2 (three discs: 155 minutes: ADD). Notes, text and translation included.
Recorded 1979.

Why bother about millionaire schemes for *Aida* and the elephants at Giza when the imagination, with this performance to work on, can conjure up greater worlds by far? The remastering of this outstanding recording recharges it with extraordinary physical immediacy. Even at *fortissimo* climaxes, there is an absence of distortion: the recording balance itself scatters and spreads the distribution of resources, particularly in ensemble and chorus, for maximum mobility and energy. The Vienna Philharmonic, of course, help matters, and so does the Musikvereinsaal where it was recorded. Where else (and, indeed, under who else's baton?) would the opening violin playing sound so incorporeal? And where else would the opening of Act 3 so palpably re-create the cricket-whirring nights by the Nile?

The performance is, of course, far more than the sum of its excellent parts. Again, the remastering emphasizes Karajan's skill in dramatic pacing and his alertness in Verdi's musical *coups de théâtre*. So often he whips up the muttered thoughts and asides into the central impetus of the drama, hastening this opera's particular nervous chain reactions and responses, and bringing the orchestral subtext up and over the voices in moments of remarkable tension. For his soloists, there is time and space enough, and they are a formidable band. Mirella Freni's fragile, volatile recitatives, with their mercurial expressive range, are the barometer of her entire performance, just as her "O patria mia, mai più ti rivedrò!" is some indication of the expressive distance she can cover in a single line. José Carreras was on top form when this recording was made, with muscle as well as a sensibility propelling Radames's vigorous appetite for both love and war. There have seldom been such complementary timbres and colours of Verdi's two basses as in this King of Egypt and this Ramphis: José van Dam lyrical, elegant, compact; Ruggero Raimondi sensuous in his very austerity.

Agnes Baltsa brings sympathy to the role of Amneris through the vulnerability and generosity which surfaces out of her potent *cantabile*, and Piero Cappuccilli is a noble, sombre Amonasro who benefits a great deal from the yearning sense of time and space afforded to him by Karajan.

Verdi Aida.

Maria Callas *sop* Aida
Richard Tucker *ten* Radames
Fedora Barbieri *mez* Amneris
Tito Gobbi *bar* Amonasro

Giuseppe Modesti *bass* Ramphis
Nicola Zaccaria *bass* King of Egypt
Elvira Galassi *sop* Priestess
Franco Ricciardi *ten* Messenger
Chorus and Orchestra of La Scala, Milan / Tullio Serafin.
EMI Callas Edition mono Ⓜ ① CDS5 56316-2 (two discs: 144 minutes: ADD). Notes, text and translation included. Recorded 1955.

If you want *Aida* as music-theatre, this is undoubtedly the set to have. On none of the rival sets will you hear the words treated with so much attention as the music. On none of them will you hear a complete cast that so conveys to you the inner feelings of the characters with such utter conviction. Chief among these, of course, is Maria Callas. She starts a little tentatively, but by the time she has reached "Ritorna vincitor", you are at once aware that she has totally immersed herself in the slave-girl's feelings, aware of herself as the daughter of a king, and torn between her duty to her homeland and her love for Radames. The hate she registers in spitting out the words "dell'Egiziecoorte", the sudden change of tonal colour at "Sventurata! che dissi!", the observance of the *triste* marking at "I sacri numi", finally the withdrawn quality at "numi pietà" illumine text and music and give them a dramatic relevance found in the performances of no other *Aida* on a disc or indeed elsewhere. That is what Callas is about and to appreciate it, you have to follow the score, or at least the text scrupulously. Listening with only half your attention you will find faults in the vocal production, even in the calibre of the voice compared with some other sopranos.

The instances of verbal and musical imagination could be multiplied here, but that might spoil your own discovery of them yourself, whether you are hearing the assumption for the first or umpteenth time. Your attention is drawn only to the wonderful recollection of the beauties of her homeland, "O freschi valle" in the Third Act aria, making you forgive a few ugly sounds at the piece's close. Once it is over, this Aida is joined by that *nonpareil* of an Amonasro, Tito Gobbi. They never encountered each other on stage in these roles, but that did not prevent a theatrical electricity informing their confrontation here. Gobbi is as frightening as the angry general as he is consolatory and plangent when he has Aida at his feet. His catches the pride, the regality and the paternal feelings, all within the short space of time allotted Amonasro.

But the performance that will really 'get' you is Barbieri's Amneris, simply because he portrays what a genuine Italian mezzo can sound like in this part. True, there is Cossotto on the Muti set, but Barbieri is subtler and, like Callas and Gobbi, marvellous at conveying feelings – in her case unrequited love and fierce jealousy – through the text. That makes her duet in Act 2 with Callas and her great scena in Act 4 quite riveting; how you sympathize with this rejected yet proud woman. On the other hand, Tucker's Radames is slightly less impressive than in the past, not quite Italianate enough in diction and a little superficial when set beside Domingo on both the Muti and Abbado sets. Still, his is a genuinely heroic tenor, and in both his duets with Callas he is roused to impassioned utterance seconded by some often distinctive phrasing. It is good to hear Italian sounds from the two excellent basses.

Serafin's reading is in the central Italian tradition of over 30 years ago; that is to say it is unobtrusively right in matters of tempo, emphasis and phrasing while occasionally passing indifferent ensemble in the choral and orchestral contribution. Muti is both more exact and more exciting, but at times more superficial, Abbado a little cool. Of course, the recorded sound cannot compete with its more modern rivals and even for its day it was hardly a model of clarity. On the other hand, nowhere else will you find the characters or their relationships so sharply defined. As John Steane commented in *Opera on Record* (Hutchinson: 1979): "If reduced to just one recording of *Aida* many of us would, I fancy, be found clinging to this one." That is even more likely since it turned up in the new, clearer format.

Verdi Aida.
Maria Chiara *sop* Aida
Nicola Martinucci *ten* Radames
Fiorenza Cossotto *mez* Amneris
Giuseppe Scandola *bar* Amonasro
Carlo Zardo *bass* Ramphis
Alfredo Zanazzo *bass* King of Egypt
Maria Gabriella Onesti *sop* Priestess
Giampaolo Corradi *ten* Messenger
Verona Arena Corps de Ballet; Verona Arena Chorus and Orchestra / Anton Guadagno.
Stage Director: **Giancarlo Sbragia.** *Video Director:* **Brian Large.**
NVC Arts Ⓕ 〔▭▭〕 0630-19389-3 (160 minutes). Recorded 1981.

It is fruitless, these days, to try to find an ideal account of this demanding opera, but this performance in the Verona Arena, which has a long tradition of staging the work, fulfils most of Verdi's requirements. The all-Italian cast brings an authentic sound to declamation of the text, an important essential. As Aida, Chiara looks the part, acts with dignity and sings with sovereign phrasing and fine-limned tone: her *piano* effects are often quite ravishing. No wonder she has the large audience in the palm of her hands. Cossotto, for years the reigning Amneris in the Arena, projects a grand, imperious reading, boldly voiced though a shade reluctant in the matter of singing quietly. She rightly brings down the house at the end of the Judgement scene. Martinucci, macho in looks, sings Radames with inspiriting élan, and duets impressively with both Aida and Amneris. Scandola, a great bear of an Amonasro, offers a baritone of truly Verdian weight. The basses singing Ramphis and the King might well have exchanged roles as the singer of the latter, lesser part has the stronger voice. The Verona Arena forces respond eagerly to Guadagno's unaffected, lively beat, another of the performance's telling assets.

The production was new in the previous season at Verona. Vittorio Rossi, designing his third *Aida* for the huge Arena, creates memorable stage pictures, including a *coup de théâtre* for the triumphal scene that provokes spontaneous applause. The director, Giancarlo Sbragia, handles his large forces skilfully, the choreography is stylish and in character, and Brian Large does his appreciable best to catch as much as possible with his astute video direction. The sound is average and subtitles are provided.

Verdi Aroldo.

Montserrat Caballé *sop* Mina
Gianfranco Cecchele *ten* Aroldo
Louis Lebherz *bass* Brian
Juan Pons *bar* Egberto
Vincenzo Manno *ten* Godvino
Paul Rogers *ten* Enrico
Marianna Busching *mez* Elena
New York Oratorio Society; Westchester Choral Society; New York Opera Orchestra / Eve Queler.
Sony Classical Ⓟ Ⓘ M2K79328 (two discs: 125 minutes: ADD). Notes, text and translation included. Recorded at a performance in Carnegie Hall, New York on April 8th, 1979.

This set was made at a concert performance in 1979, and received reasonably enthusiastic critical approval the following year. The revised version of *Stiffelio*, it hasn't quite the conviction of the earlier piece because the story has become more implausible in the transformation, but it is still worth hearing. The key role is that of the unfaithful, remorseful Mina; it is sung here with great feeling and technical assurance by Caballé, encapsulated by the "Salvemi tu, gran Dio" prayer in Act 1 and the scene at the start of Act 2. None of the other singers is on that level of achievement. Cecchele gives a standard tenor performance, replete with lachrymose touches, as Aroldo and Juan Pons is powerful as old Egberto. Queler knows how to light an early Verdi score but does sometimes sit on the rhythms. The voices have plenty of space round them and are well balanced with the orchestra. There is a certain amount of audience participation.

Verdi Attila.

Samuel Ramey *bass* Attila
Cheryl Studer *sop* Odabella
Giorgio Zancanaro *bar* Ezio
Neil Shicoff *ten* Foresto
Ernesto Gavazzi *ten* Uldino
Giorgio Surian *bass* Leone
Chorus and Orchestra of La Scala, Milan / Riccardo Muti.
EMI Ⓟ Ⓘ CDS7 49952-2 (two discs: 109 minutes: DDD). Notes, text and translation included. Recorded 1989.

Lamberto Gardelli's two readings of *Attila*, for Hungaroton and Philips respectively, have such strongly contrasted basses in the title-role that they seem to state two different views of the opera, consistent though Gardelli's own way with it has remained. Philips's *Attila* (reviewed below) is the young Ruggero Raimondi, a nobly Italianate *basso cantante*, with at that stage of his career not quite the authority or the weight of tone that the role ideally demands, but a fine control of its great arches of melody. Evgeni Nesterenko, for Hungaroton, brings Slavonic blackness and vehemence to the part: he is the scourge of God to the life and hugely impressive, but his profoundly un-Italian voice leaves you with the slight feeling that for him Attila is spelled 'Genghis'; Verdi's *Attila* is at least an honorary Italian, and much the most sympathetic character in the opera.

Ramey is in many respects the ideal third alternative: weightier and darker than Raimondi, the incisiveness of his diction not impeding a fine sense of line. His is truly an Attila-size voice, used with impressively commanding authority, but it is a pity that he so seldom sings quietly. Finely controlled *mezza voce*, allowing great beauty of tone as well as an impressive opening out to grander or denunciatory passages, is one of Raimondi's great virtues, and Ramey cannot quite match him in it.

The recording is partly responsible for this impression. The orchestra has bloom to it and space around it but the singers seem to be more closely microphoned and in a different and much crueller acoustic. They are not as absurdly close as in some opera recordings, but the perspective strips their voices raw. Shicoff's is a useful rather than a robust tenor, but he has a beautiful half-voice and a good sense of Verdian style: he was a sensible choice for Foresto. But a sense of strain, a certain nasality, the rather terrier-like doggedness of a voice being stretched a little too far, these are all emphasized by the recording; in a word, he sounds puny. Zancanaro's voice is forwardly placed and vehement anyway, and this too is exaggerated into a rather gritty barking. Even Studer, better equipped for the role of Odabella than any other soprano who has recorded it (save for the incisive low notes which, like most exponents of the part, she lacks), sounds bright and oddly substanceless in her fiercely demanding entrance music, and a single awkwardly approached high note in Act 3 is mercilessly exposed. But she phrases beautifully, has a floatingly free upper register and the clarity to dominate an ensemble. Since the sopranos on the other two sets are inadequate (Sylvia Sass, her voice worn, pinched and insecure, for Hungaroton; Philips has the fundamentally miscast Cristina Deutekom, uncomfortably shrill and with no lower register at all) the EMI would seem to have moved into first place, despite reservations, on Studer's account and on Ramey's.

The Philips version, however, has Carlo Bergonzi bringing a real sense of character as well as impeccably stylish vocalism to the role of Foresto (Hungaroton's tenor, János B. Nagy, is no more than serviceable) and Sherrill Milnes doing much the same for Ezio (he has a finer, indeed a more Italianate sense of line than Zancanaro; the Hungaroton baritone, again, is adequate but no more). Many collectors find Gardelli both a more subtle and a more characterful Verdian than Muti, and his account of this strange, flawed but disquieting opera is a good riposte to those who might smile at the application of the adjective 'subtle' to it. Finally and crucially, the Philips is much more sympathetically recorded than the EMI, the voices more naturally integrated with the orchestra and in a kinder perspective.

Verdi Attila.

Ruggero Raimondi *bass* Attila
Cristina Deutekom *sop* Odabella
Sherrill Milnes *bar* Ezio
Carlo Bergonzi *ten* Foresto
Ricardo Cassinelli *ten* Uldino
Jules Bastin *bass* Leone
Finchley Childrens Music Group; Ambrosian Singers;
Royal Philharmonic Orchestra / Lamberto Gardelli.
Philips Ⓜ Ⓒ 426 115-2PM2 (two discs: 106 minutes: ADD). Notes, text and translation included. Recorded 1972.

One of the earliest of Philips's Verdi 'collection', this set was welcomed in its CD format as it represented the very best aspects of the series. Gardelli has an innate feeling for the merits of early Verdi, never presses the music too hard, and makes the very most of this score's many vivid and exciting passages. Though not all sing with the fine combination of fervour and style shown by Bergonzi as the knight, Foresto, none is less than satisfying. Raimondi wants some of the weight and vigour needed for the rough, vicious Attila, but he characterizes the tyrant well enough. Milnes is a rugged, lively Ezio, but his tone is sometimes less than ideally focused. Deutekom's range of expression as Odabella is limited, but she is splendid in her big scene in the Prologue and finds the gentle manner for her First Act cavatina. The Ambrosians and the RPO are well in the picture. The recording, nicely balanced and with a few 'distancings' where needed, has stood the test of time.

Verdi Un ballo in maschera.

Katia Ricciarelli *sop* Amelia
Plácido Domingo *ten* Riccardo
Renato Bruson *bar* Renato
Edita Gruberová *sop* Oscar
Elena Obraztsova *mez* Ulrica
Ruggero Raimondi *bass* Sam
Giovanni Foiani *bass* Tom
Luigi De Corato *bar* Silvano
Antonio Savastano *bar* Judge
Gianfranco Manganotti *ten* Servant
Chorus and Orchestra of La Scala, Milan / Claudio Abbado.
DG Ⓜ Ⓒ 453 148-2GTA2 (two discs: 127 minutes: ADD). Notes included. Recorded 1981.

Well sung as the Solti/Decca set may be (recorded a year after this one), this recording is a far more satisfying and unified performance of *Un ballo in maschera*, largely because Abbado and his La Scala forces give us much more of a sense of a theatrical experience and because Abbado's conducting is so much more stable and of a piece. Listening to Abbado's direction, you will be struck by his attention to detail and his sensible tempos. Though not quite so exciting as Muti's on EMI, it seems to make better sense as a whole. Margaret Price sings far the more secure Amelia for Solti, but she doesn't always get inside the part as does the vocally more variable Ricciarelli, who gives us the very epitome of the girl torn between love and duty. Domingo doesn't have, never has had, the 'ping' of Pavarotti, but his Riccardo is as involved and as involving a performance as that of his Amelia; together with Abbado, they give an eloquent account of the love duet. Bruson, in better voice than for Solti, is hardly less expressive. Solti scores with the better Oscar and Ulrica. The sound could be a little more open and clear but at least it isn't so blatant as the Solti.

Verdi Un ballo in maschera.
Martina Arroyo *sop* Amelia
Plácido Domingo *ten* Riccardo
Piero Cappuccilli *bar* Renato
Reri Grist *sop* Oscar
Fiorenza Cossotto *mez* Ulrica
Gwynne Howell *bass* Sam
Richard Van Allan *bass* Tom
Giorgio Giorgetti *bar* Silvano
Kenneth Collins *ten* Judge
Haberdashers' Aske's School Girls' Choir; Medici Quartet;
Chorus of the Royal Opera House, Covent Garden; New Philharmonia Orchestra / Riccardo Muti.
EMI Ⓜ ① CMS5 66510-2 (two discs: 127 minutes: ADD). Notes, text and translation included. Recorded 1975.

Any recording of this opera runs the risk of being compared to the Metropolitan Opera historic broadcast of 1940, a legendary performance (now available on Myto) in reasonably good sound, with Milanov, Björling and Sved in the leading roles and conducted by the greatly underrated, Toscanini-like Ettore Panizza. Both cast and conducting have always made this performance a once-in-a-lifetime experience. By its side other sets, for all their incidental merits, can sound somewhat low in voltage.

However, Muti's *Ballo*, above all else, glories in the conductor as an exuberant man of the theatre. The impetus with which he whips up the constituent parts of an ensemble into the vortex, and the juxtaposition of blasting tutti with slim, sweetly phrased woodwind detail, so typical of this opera, hits the ear thrillingly. So does the equally characteristic tugging undercurrent of the ballo against the intrigue of the maschera, activated by Muti with such acute perception and élan.

He provides pliant, springing support for all his singers too: Domingo, a warm, generous Riccardo, is every bit as happy with Muti as with Abbado on his DG set. The same cannot be said of Martina Arroyo, the weak link on this recording. Dramatically forceful, but curiously cool and detached from the expressive nuancing of her part, she has little of the vulnerability of a Ricciarelli (Abbado), or the individuality of a Price (for Solti on his 1982 Decca set). But, although this mid-price recording may not offer the most consistently luxurious vocal banquet, none the less, with Cossotto's stentorian Ulrica and Cappuccilli's staunch, resilient Renato, its strong sense of theatrical presence and its dramatic integrity will make it the chosen version for many new collectors.

Verdi Un ballo in maschera.
Maria Callas *sop* Amelia
Giuseppe di Stefano *ten* Riccardo
Tito Gobbi *bar* Renato
Eugenia Ratti *sop* Oscar
Fedora Barbieri *mez* Ulrica
Silvio Maionica *bass* Sam
Nicola Zaccaria *bass* Tom
Ezio Giordano *bass* Silvano
Renato Ercolani *bar* Judge, Servant
Chorus and Orchestra of La Scala, Milan / Antonino Votto.
EMI mono Ⓜ ① CDS5 56320-2 (two discs: 130 minutes: ADD). Notes, text and translation included. Recorded 1956.

This reissue of *Ballo* was a welcome reminder of the special qualities of its principals. Votto was underrated as a Verdi conductor: his direction has a truly Verdian élan. This is one of Callas's most compelling assumptions. Certain phrases, such as when she sings "Son di lui" – "I am his", meaning her husband, to Riccardo – remain uniquely accented and convincing. Her Amelia does have more character, presence and sheer *spinto* quality than that of either soprano on the Solti and Abbado sets (Price and Ricciarelli respectively). Gobbi is a very different Renato than Bruson, who appears for both Solti (Decca) and Abbado (DG); more incisive, more threatening, but by the same token, rather less smooth in his vocalization; for an ideal "Eri tu", you would want to go far further back in recorded history, to Amato and de Luca. Where Riccardo is concerned, di Stefano is closer to

Pavarotti (Solti) than to Domingo (Abbado) in giving face to the role. He hasn't so secure a top register as either of his rivals, but in the ballata and the love duet he does surpass them both in the involvement and daring of his performance; indeed all these three principals are superior to their successors in creating the tension of a live performance as against a studio one. In that respect this is the recording collectors have always turned to most often, even though Abbado is the more finished and better-produced set. It should be added that Barbieri makes a vivid and resourceful Ulrica and Ratti a smiling, pert, if sometimes shrill Oscar.

The recording is more than respectable in terms of sound. Callas enthusiasts will want this version in any case. Others may find the choice more difficult depending on whether they value the character of individual performances over all-round finish.

Verdi La battaglia di Legnano.
  Katia Ricciarelli *sop* Lida
  José Carreras *ten* Arrigo
  Matteo Manuguerra *bar* Rolando
  Nikola Ghiuselev *bass* Barbarossa
  Hannes Lichtenberger *bass* First Consul
  Dimitri Kavrakos *bass* Second Consul
  Jonathan Summers *bar* Marcovaldo
  Franz Handlos *bass* Podestà
  Ann Murray *mez* Imelda
  Mieczyslaw Antoniak *ten* Herald
  Austrian Radio Chorus and Symphony Orchestra / Lamberto Gardelli.
  Philips Ⓜ Ⓓ 422 435-2PM2 (two discs: 108 minutes: ADD). Notes, text and translation included.
  Recorded 1977.

Written for a première in Rome at a time when the city was seething with nationalist and republican passions, an opera which celebrates the Italian victory against Barbarossa, and in which the hero leaps from a window crying "Viva Italia", had a better than average chance of success. The excitement was in fact such that the final act (admittedly only 15 minutes long) was encored in its entirety, and at one performance a soldier in the audience followed the hero's example and jumped from the gallery into the orchestra pit. Subsequently the opera's initial *succès fou* caused it to be associated with the mood of the moment and neglected even as an example of 'early Verdi'. By January 1849 Verdi had already seen 12 of his operas produced (13 with the French revision of *I lombardi*) and had been a full decade in the business. *Rigoletto* was only two years away.

La battaglia has many fine qualities, but curiously for an opera making such a popular appeal in its time, there is no broad, immediately memorable melody to compare with the Hebrews' chorus in *Nabucco* or the big tunes of *Ernani*. A good deal of chorus work is involved (including two consecutive scenes for men's voices only), and a full allowance of arias, duets and ensembles. But only at the very end does the Grand Tune appear, and almost immediately it finishes: perhaps that is the way to make sure of an encore. Musically, the impressive feature of the score is its orchestration; dramatically, interest focuses on the predicament of the afflicted heroine and the relationship between tenor and baritone; artistically, popular nationalism is not the matter closest to its heart.

As the three interesting human beings concerned, Ricciarelli, Carreras and Manuguerra are remarkably good at creating genuine characters. The first two are also at the top of their form as singers; indeed, Ricciarelli is almost unrecognizable in most of the First Act. Manuguerra, though often impressive, was just past his best (he had made his début 16 years previously and was here over 50). In minor roles, the sort of part where one turns to the cast-list afterwards to ascertain identities, Dimitri Kavrakos distinguishes himself and Ann Murray does not. Gardelli conducts a splendid performance and the work of the Austrian orchestra and chorus is fine – how good, moreover, that the then hated enemy should be the country to provide them.

Verdi Il corsaro.
  Jessye Norman *sop* Medora
  Monserrat Caballé *sop* Gulnara
  José Carreras *ten* Corrado
  Gian-Piero Mastromei *bar* Seid
  Clifford Grant *bass* Giovanni
  John Noble *bar* Selimo
  Alexander Oliver *ten* Eunuch
  Ambrosian Singers; New Philharmonia Orchestra / Lamberto Gardelli.
  Philips Ⓜ Ⓓ 426 118-2PM2 (two discs: 94 minutes: ADD). Notes, text and translation included.
  Recorded 1975.

This work, based on Byron's poem, *The Corsair*, is one of the most economic and inspired of Verdi's early scores. Piave's libretto is serviceable. It's filled with poetic conceits not found in all the works of the 'galley' years, and also prophetic of many glories to come. Its success owes much to the quality of the performance here. Gardelli once again shows how well attuned he is to both the vigour and unguarded lyricism of this period in Verdi's career. Around him is assembled a near-ideal cast for this particular opera. In the first place it is a treat, hardly to be repeated, of having Caballé and Norman in the same recording. The latter sings Medora's beautiful cavatina with just the right sweet vulnerability. Caballé, at the peak of her career in the mid-1970s, sings with a nice combination of strength and sensitivity, and in the faster music her scales and coloratura have that gentle lightness that has always been a feature of her best performances. Then Carreras is perfect casting as the buccaneer of the title. He has the most original scene in the score, in prison in Act 3, and sings it with just the right plaintive sound. When Gulnara joins Corrado, his lyrical passion matches Caballé's. All three are superb in the marvellous finale to the whole work, offering a classic of Verdi singing. Mastromei may not be quite in his colleagues' class – in any case his music is less interesting – but he characterizes the villain well enough.

The New Philharmonia play with assurance for Gardelli. The recording is well up to the high Philips standard and these CDs are really essential for anyone wanting early Verdi at his most convincing.

Verdi Don Carlo.
Plácido Domingo *ten* Don Carlo
Montserrat Caballé *sop* Elisabetta
Shirley Verrett *mez* Eboli
Sherrill Milnes *bar* Rodrigo
Ruggero Raimondi *bass* Philip II
Giovani Foiani *bass* Grand Inquisitor
Delia Wallis *mez* Tebaldo
Ryland Davies *ten* Conte di Lerma
Simon Estes *bass* Monk
John Noble *bar* Herald
Ambrosian Opera Chorus;
Orchestra of the Royal Opera House, Covent Garden / Carlo Maria Giulini.
EMI Ⓟ Ⓒ CDS7 47701-8 (three discs: 208 minutes: ADD). Recorded 1970.

BBC RADIO 3
90-93 FM

It is almost 40 years since Giulini's epoch-making and revealing revival of *Don Carlos* at Covent Garden; it is 28 years since this recording of virtually what was heard at Covent Garden appeared (the 1886 version of the score) using Royal Opera forces – the work had been regularly revived there in the years between. Its reissue on CD was more than welcome and really didn't come into rivalry with the Abbado set on DG because that uses the original version (with appendices) and is sung in French rather than the much more familiar Italian translation encountered on EMI.

Its overriding advantage lies in Giulini's commanding and searching direction, encountering the work as the huge canvas it is and holding together its disparate elements with an unerring control. Not all the the members of the cast are ideal. Raimondi is too light and too characterless for Philip, Milnes hardly the equal of Gobbi on the Santini set. On the other hand, Elisabetta's music can scarcely ever have been sung more beautifully than by Caballé, in her absolute prime in 1970 – as was Verrett, a properly nervous and eager Eboli. Domingo was at the start of his career, and did not have quite the personality and commitment he later showed for Abbado, but his actual singing has a security seldom matched elsewhere in this role, at once heroic, ardent and impulsive. Two caveats, however: the bells which should accompany the opening of the *auto da fé* scene have been left off this CD transfer and the disc layout details in the booklet are hopelessly confused.

The 1992 Levine set on Sony comes tantalizingly close to being given preference over Giulini. It isn't so lovingly conducted, but the immediacy of the recording, excellent apart from one big proviso, and the general dedication of the whole unified cast creates a compelling experience. He realizes the nobility and inner intensity of Verdi's broad concept. The main criticism is the familiar one with this conductor: he overemphasizes the double-*forte* effects in a vulgar way; do the beginning of the Inquisition scene and the death of Posa really need to sound so blatant? It quickly leads to ear fatigue. You need only listen to the sensitively balanced Giulini version to hear a fairer balance, although Giulini's set has nothing like the range of dynamics or clarity of the newer one. Although that fault may not be serious enough to worry too many collectors, since the moments of overkill in this score are few and far between, more worrying is the frequent change of levels, possibly signifying different sessions. However, Levine's singers would be hard to surpass today and make a substantial case for preferring his to any of the other five-act versions. They include Sylvester, Millo, Zajick, Chernov and Furlanetto.

Verdi Don Carlo.
Mario Filippeschi *ten* Don Carlo
Antonietta Stella *sop* Elisabetta
Elena Nicolai *mez* Eboli
Tito Gobbi *bar* Rodrigo

Boris Christoff *bass* Philip II
Giulio Neri *bass* Grand Inquisitor
Loretta di Lelio *sop* Tebaldo
Paolo Caroli *ten* Conte di Lerma, Herald
Plinio Clabassi *bass* Monk
Orietta Moscucci *sop* Voice from Heaven
Rome Opera Chorus and Orchestra / Gabriele Santini.
EMI Opera mono Ⓜ ① CMS7 64642-2 (three discs: 169 minutes: ADD). Notes, text and translation included. Recorded 1954.

This EMI reissue opts for the four-act version of 1884 and that is substantially truncated in a manner not tolerated today – rightly so. But it is an essential supplement to any other version because of the incomparable performances of the lower voices. No decent collection should really be without Gobbi's eloquent Rodrigo (bringing to the role a plangent timbre that makes the death scene more moving than any other portrayal) and Christoff's deeply expressive, subtly shaded king. Their encounter at the close of Act 1 is one of the classics of recorded history, not be missed. Their attention to phrasing and word-painting and the individual character of each voice are in a class of their own, superior to any other on disc. To hear Christoff utter such lines as "sgraziato genitor! sposo più triste ancor!" is to be reminded of a school of acting with the voice and through the words that seems dormant today. The confrontation between Christoff's Philip and Neri's towering Grand Inquisitor is almost in the same category. After hearing these interpretations, you may well be content with just this old mono set, simply for these precious insights.

The other singers are much more ordinary. Filippeschi is steely, somewhat untutored as Carlo, likewise Nicolai as Eboli. Stella defines many phrases unerringly, but isn't technically in the class of her rivals. Santini is a capable, routine conductor, no more, though one sometimes admires his self-effacement compared with the interventionist approach of other conductors.

Verdi Don Carlo.

Luciano Pavarotti *ten* Don Carlo
Daniella Dessì *sop* Elisabetta
Luciana d'Intino *mez* Eboli
Paolo Coni *bar* Rodrigo
Samuel Ramey *bass* Philip II
Alexander Anisimov *bass* Grand Inquisitor
Marilena Laurenza *sop* Tebaldo
Orfeo Zanetti *ten* Conte di Lerma
Andrea Silvestrelli *bass* Monk
Mario Bolognesi *ten* Herald
Nuccia Focile *sop* Voice from Heaven
Chorus and Orchestra of La Scala, Milan / Riccardo Muti.
Stage/Video Director: **Franco Zeffirelli.**
EMI Ⓟ 🔲 MVB4 91134-3; 🌑 LDD4 91134-1 (two discs: 196 minutes). Recorded 1992.

If you want a video of the four-act Italian version of Verdi's masterpiece, this staging at La Scala by Zeffirelli will fill the bill, not least because energy, rhythmic vitality and quick emotions inform Muti's reading, enhanced by his understanding of the work's *tinta*. He keeps his players on a tight but never stifling rein. He also has the advantage of four Italian principals (out of six), headed by the golden-voiced Pavarotti, singing with his customary ardour, words ideally on the voice, and with his line liquid and flowing. His girth makes him an unconvincing Carlo, who ought to be lean and nervous, but he acts with his usual sincerity.

In contrast to her lover, Dessì's Elisabetta looks the very image of the wronged, sympathetic Queen, but she sings with less than ideal steadiness. The timbre and style are right, but her technique is consistently under siege, a case of the spirit being willing, the flesh weak. Coni makes an upright, affecting Rodrigo but under pressure his tone tends to lose focus; like Dessì, he is a shade overparted. Not so D'Intino who sings most of Eboli's part with fearless brio, and acts it with a deal of credibility. Ramey's well-focused bass is appropriate to Muti's sharply etched reading, but he doesn't probe the depths of Philip II's misery, a man of action rather than anguish. Anisimov is a rather ordinary Inquisitor. Zeffirelli's production evokes the atmosphere of political threat and religious bigotry with dark-hued sets (hard to light for video) and shafts of ceremonial panoply. The sound is admirable and subtitles are provided.

Verdi Don Carlos.

Roberto Alagna *ten* Don Carlos
Karita Mattila *sop* Elisabeth
Waltraud Meier *mez* Eboli
Thomas Hampson *bar* Rodrigue

José van Dam *bass-bar* Philippe II
Eric Halfvarson *bass* Grand Inquisitor
Csaba Airizer *bass* Monk
Anat Efraty *sop* Thibault
Scot Weir *ten* Comte de Lerme, Herald
Donna Brown *sop* Voice from Heaven
Chorus of the Théâtre du Châtelet; Orchestre de Paris / Antonio Pappano.
EMI Ⓟ Ⓒ CDS5 56152-2 (three discs: 206 minutes: DDD). Notes, text and translation included.
Recorded at performances in the Théâtre du Châtelet, Paris on March 10th, 13th and 16th, 1996.

This recording of the French version was made by EMI at the Théâtre du Châtelet during
performances in 1996 of a production by Luc Bondy. The staging later moved to Covent Garden with
Haitink in the pit and with one major change of cast (Martine Dupuy for Meier). Then Haitink
recorded the opera for Philips using the five-act Italian edition (1884 plus the Fontainebleau scene at
the start) and a wholly different, Russian-orientated cast. After the sessions, he brought the work to
the Proms (with Valayre replacing Gorchakova as Elisabeth): it was an exhilarating performance,
more exciting than Haitink's direction of the French recension at the Royal Opera. However, for
anyone wanting the original French, which is, after all, the text Verdi adhered to throughout myriad
versions, the only CD rival to this set is the Abbado version on DG.

Text-wise, Pappano excludes the opening scene for the chorus at Fontainebleau, cut by the
composer before the first night; he includes the important dress-changing scene at the start of Act 3
(which explains Carlos's ardour towards the 'wrong' woman), a snippet of the Elisabeth-Eboli duet in
Act 4, and the whole of the Carlos/Philippe duet after Posa's death (the theme of which was reused
in the Requiem). Pappano also chooses some of the alternative settings, notably in the Posa-Philippe
duet in Act 2 and the farewell encounter of Elisabeth and Carlos in Act 5, amendments that Verdi
made for the neglected 1872 Naples revision. Neither seems to be an improvement: you can judge for
yourself by listening to the Abbado version on DG which remains faithful to what we usually hear –
and what Verdi finally decided on his last revision. Indeed on the Abbado we hear the 'orthodox'
version throughout the main recording: alternatives are consigned to appendices which you can then
programme in at your own discretion.

On practically all counts Pappano stands comparison with his senior Italian colleague. His is a
subtly shaped, superbly paced and vital interpretation from start to finish. He is as able to encompass
the delicacies of the Veil Song and the succeeding exchanges as he is to purvey the grand, tragic
passion of Elisabeth and Carlos in Act 2, the intricacies and changes of feeling in the colloquy
between Rodrigue and Philippe, the terrible menace of the Grand Inquisitor. The Orchestre de Paris
support him with playing of dedication and sensitivity. Giulini's noble conducting of the Italian
version comes to mind when listening to Pappano and his players. Praise cannot be higher.

By and large he has singers who can sustain his vision. Mattila, who sometimes sounded out of sorts
at Covent Garden, here sings a lovely Elisabeth. Her soft-grained yet strong tone and exquisite
phrasing in all her solos and duets is balm to the ear, crowned by her deeply appealing account of
Elisabeth's Act 5 *Scène*, most touching in the recollection of Fontainebleau happiness. One or two
moments of questionable intonation in the farewell to the Countess of Aremberg can be excused in a
live performance. Ricciarelli (Abbado) is also affecting but not so secure and at times too moony. By
Mattila's side Alagna offers an equally involving Carlos. Without quite the fullness of voice or sheer
vocal opulence offered by Domingo (Abbado), Alagna presents a more vulnerable picture of the
unbalanced infante with the *larmes dans la voix* so essential to the part heard at "Au couvent de Saint-
Just" at his entry in the first cloister scene, again at "parlez, parlez" when intoxicated by Elisabeth's
voice in their private colloquy in Act 2. His is a fully rounded portrayal that will please his many
admirers, the difficult tessitura seldom troubling him and his French, of course, is impeccable.

As Rodrigue, Marquis de Posa, Hampson also has idiomatic French. His mellifluous baritone well
suits this French version and he provides many moments of vocal beauty, not least his solo addressed
to Elisabeth in Act 2. His elegiac account of Rodrigue's famous aria in the Prison scene is, sensibly,
taken faster by Pappano than by Haitink, never allowing it to drop into sentimentality. Arguably, the
death needs a more imposing voice but the added decibels can easily be borne to appreciate
Hampson's intelligence. By his side, Nucci (Abbado) sounds cool and uninteresting.

Meier's Eboli is more uneven. Few singers can encompass both the Veil Song and "O don fatale".
Meier is awkward and blowzy in the first but, with her dramatic presence to the fore, sings her
challenging aria of remorse with tremendous panache and intensity. Van Dam nicely balances the
exterior authority and interior agony of Philippe, everywhere in command of line, language, phrase,
much more incisive than Abbado's woolly Raimondi. His encounter with Halfvarson's frighteningly
dour Inquisitor is rightly at the very heart of the drama (Pappano is superb here): church and state
are admirably represented, neither winning the battle of wills. There's a good, strong Monk, and sure
support in even the smallest roles. The smooth sextet of Flemish deputies in the *auto da fé* scene is a
great improvement on the usual unsteady drone of played-out basses.

The recording catches the *frisson* of the theatrical experience. One can easily bear a few moments
of stage noise and properly enthusiastic applause in the cause of capturing the atmosphere and
immediacy of an evening in the opera-house that cannot be simulated in the studio, as for example
the desperate passion van Dam puts into his part. The positioning of the singers on stage never causes

problems, everything is clear and in its place, and the balance with the pit sounds natural. This must take preference over the Abbado version (which takes four CDs against EMI's three) except for those who want more of the alternative music. The Abbado has certainly been underrated in some quarters – it is a formidable achievement as a whole and a trail-blazer – but this one catches more truly the surge and swell of emotional and dramatic tensions so vital in the work's interpretation. It is a landmark in the *Don Carlos* discography.

Verdi Don Carlos.

Roberto Alagna *ten* Don Carlos
Karita Mattila *sop* Elisabeth
Waltraud Meier *mez* Eboli
Thomas Hampson *bar* Rodrigue
José van Dam *bass-bar* Philippe II
Eric Halfvarson *bass* Grand Inquisitor
Csaba Airizer *bass* Monk
Anat Efraty *sop* Thibault
Scot Weir *bar* Comte de Lerme, Herald
Donna Brown *sop* Voice from Heaven
Choeur du Théâtre du Châtelet; Orchestre de Paris / Antonio Pappano.
Stage Director: **Luc Bondy.** *Video Director:* **Yves André Hubert.**
NVC Arts Ⓟ 🅭🅭 0630 16318-3 (two cassettes: 211 minutes). Notes included. Recorded at performances in the Théâtre du Châtelet, Paris on March 10th, 13th and 16th, 1996.

Luc Bondy's staging of this five-act French version of Verdi's masterpiece (reviewed above on CD) received mixed reviews when it was seen at both the Châtelet in Paris (from which this video derives) and Covent Garden. In London it was certainly a shock to those of us brought up on Visconti's marvellously evocative production of 1958, preserved – though not quite in pristine form – on the 1985 Haitink/Castle video. While the simple décor of Gilles Aillaud has something to be said for it – a small amount of scenery and props manages economically to suggest the various milieux and keep the action flowing – Bondy's direction of the principals leaves much to be desired in the opening acts, and the exterior scenes are tame indeed, especially when compared with the Visconti inscenation or even that of Zeffirelli in the 1992 La Scala production (Muti).

Suddenly in Act 4, the work's greatest, everything falls into place. The spare walls of the King's study, the atmospheric lighting and José van Dam's searing portrait here of the King's misery are riveting (though you may not be convinced that the Queen's presence on stage at this moment of the King's loneliness is a good idea), the scene with the Grand Inquisitor even more so with Halfvarson's gnarled, toad-like old cleric lumbering menacingly about the stage, a superb antagonist for this Philippe. The rest of the act is hardly less compelling.

Although the cast is clothed in handsome period dress, with one exception they appear to be bereft of wigs which leaves them looking curiously modern. The exception is the now infamous wig for Thomas Hampson, which makes him look like a cross between Charles II and Tiny Tim. His acting is often plausible, occasionally a shade exaggerated. Van Dam is in all respects a magnificent Philippe II, his pain exhibited in his taut, strained body language as much as in his superbly articulated singing. Meier acts Eboli, a scheming, seductive presence, more successfully than she sings the role. Mattila is a lovely Elisabeth in both aspects of her portrayal, conveying the unhappy Queen's agony at being torn between loyalty to the King and love of his son. Alagna is the fierily impetuous Carlos to the life and vocally absolutely right for the part, particularly when supported by his lithe, personable presence. Pappano's pacing of the long work, his conducting keenly focused from start to finish, is admirable. The video direction is a shade wayward, not always sensitive in choosing between close-ups and the longer view.

The performance, lasting 211 minutes, is spread over two videos, an odd fact. As this was also an HDV issue, the top and bottom of the pictures on VHS are black. The picture and sound quality are excellent; subtitles are provided. As a whole, this performance at the very least allows us to see and hear what is basically Verdi's original concept of a French opera as he intended it to be, give or take a few strange decisions on variant readings. The other versions, all in Italian, are not strictly comparable. Karajan (Sony Classical) has some fine singing but is feebly staged and rudely foreshortened. The Haitink suffers from his ponderous conducting and indifferent sound but has an interesting cast (Cotrubas, Baglioni, Lima, Zancanaro, Lloyd), but for an Italian version go for Muti with Dessì, Intino, Pavarotti, Coni and Ramey all very much inside their parts and Muti rousing them to great things within Zeffirelli's grand staging.

Verdi I due Foscari.

Piero Cappuccilli *bar* Francesco Foscari
José Carreras *ten* Jacopo Foscari
Katia Ricciarelli *sop* Lucrezia
Samuel Ramey *bass* Jacopo Loredano

Vincenzo Bello *ten* Barbarigo
Elizabeth Connell *sop* Pisana
Mieczyslaw Antoniak *ten* Officer
Franz Handlos *bass* Doge's servant
Austrian Radio Chorus and Symphony Orchestra / Lamberto Gardelli.
Philips Ⓜ ① 422 426-2PM2 (two discs: 104 minutes: ADD). Notes, text and translation included.
Recorded 1976.

It is invaluable to have this piece complete rather than cut as on the flawed Giulini 1951 version on Fonit Cetra. It isn't a long opera, and it deserves to be heard as an entity. Gardelli's unfussy, direct, supportive conducting can hardly be praised enough. When ideal Verdi interpreters are so few and far between how admirable it is to hear Gardelli provide the right tempos, dynamics and rhythmic emphasis every time. Carreras may lack some of the delicacies his role of the condemned Jacopo calls for and which Bergonzi provided for Giulini, but he is here in pristine voice, singing his great prison scene with the utmost sincerity, adumbrating the character's desperation. Cappuccilli is absolutely in his element as the gloomy old Doge and father, a portrait to set alongside his superb Boccanegra. The breath control and *cantabile* he displays in his first aria, "O vecchio cor", is a classic of Verdi singing, and he is just as sensitive in his final scene of resignation and in his duet with Lucrezia. Ricciarelli sings this difficult role with lustrous tone and unflinching attack: she has done nothing better on record. She floats a glorious A over the chorus in her first aria and finds no difficulty in the divisions, where she (and Verdi) condemn injustice. The very young Samuel Ramey makes much of little as the intriguing, vicious Loredano.

The recording, made in Vienna, is up to the high standards of the Philips Verdi series, and the radio forces there contribute effectively to the set's undoubted success.

Verdi Ernani.

Plácido Domingo *ten* Ernani
Mirella Freni *sop* Elvira
Renato Bruson *bar* Don Carlos
Nicolai Ghiaurov *bass* Don Ruy Gomez de Silva
Jolanda Michieli *sop* Giovanna
Gianfranco Manganotti *ten* Don Riccardo
Alfredo Giacomotti *bass* Iago
Chorus and Orchestra of La Scala, Milan / Riccardo Muti.
EMI Ⓟ ① CDS7 47083-8 (three discs: 128 minutes: DDD). Notes, text and translation included.
Recorded at performances in La Scala, Milan during December 1982.

Gnarled and cynical old opera-goers were known to wobble like jellies after the BBC showed a video of the La Scala *Ernani* in 1983. "Best Verdi singing for 20 years" was among the comments to be heard. Praise all round from critics, professional and amateur alike. No doubt there was electricity on the Scala stage that evening; no doubt that the four principals gave their all in a thrilling realization – under Muti – of this, the best of Verdi's 'galley' dramas, catching what Shaw called the "fierce noonday sun" of this thrusting score.

Most honour was given to Bruson's Don Carlo, an assumption that was as gripping dramatically – that tortured look of his, encapsulating Carlo's emotional turmoil – as it was vocally; now with only the ear to be satisfied, it seems no less arresting a performance. In his portrayal more than anywhere, the musical tension, captured at a live performance, becomes manifest. From the *sotto voce* of "Vedi come il buon vegliardo" through the Battistini-like velvet *mezza voce* of "Vieni meco" to the tragic accents of "Oh! de' verdi'anni miei" and the awe of "O sommo Carlo", Bruson offers a great piece of Verdi singing, only a slight woolliness in the tone at "Lo vedremo" to mar it. That might have been improved on in the studio, but how much else might have been less vivid?

Domingo's Ernani is hardly less impressive. Combining the correct style of Bergonzi (Schippers/RCA) and the insolent pride exhibited by Lamberti (Gardelli), he – as much as anyone – benefits from being caught live on stage. His opening aria and cabaletta are full of delicate touches and obedience to the dynamic marks (as, of course, is all Bruson's performance). In the last act, his recitative, "Tutto ora tace d'intorno" has a Martinelli-like pathos, and his contributions to the final trio an overwhelming eloquence. He has done nothing better for the gramophone than this final act. Here, too, Freni achieves most, the etching in of "Il riso del tuo volto fa ch'io veda", a brief utterance of happiness, most affecting, and her desperate, unavailing appeals to Silva for mercy sung with brio. In her opening aria and cabaletta, the famous "Ernani, Ernani", too many breaks in register are evident, too much is asked of a voice not really meant by nature for this kind of heavy duty. Here she yields in sheer opulence of tone to Leontyne Price (Schippers), and the grace and magnetism in Sass's assumption, but somehow in the studio neither of these excellent sopranos quite matches the sorrow and heartbreak of Elvira's predicament that Freni manages in the theatre.

Ghiaurov, rusty as his voice had become, created a great impression of dignity and implacable strength on television as Silva, and many of those qualities are carried over into his singing. "Infelice" is delivered with mature nobility, "Ah, io l'amo" is intensely moving. Compare him with Flagello

(Schippers) or Kováts (Gardelli) in the latter solo, and you will again find Ghiaurov authoritative and moving, where the others are blank and/or untidy. Ghiaurov is denied Silva's probably spurious cabaletta. Otherwise the work is given complete. Muti conducts the score in exemplary manner. He has learnt when to allow his singers licence to phrase with meaning – many touches of rubato are gratefully received and used by Domingo and Bruson – when to press on. Sometimes the *strettos* are over-energized in a way Gardelli wouldn't contemplate, but as a rule Muti judges the moments when the tension should be increased to a nicety, as in the sudden surge of emotion in "Fino al sospiro estremo", the unison passage of ecstasy for Elvira and Ernani in the Fourth Act – "crescendo e stringendo" is Verdi's marking and that is what we get.

The La Scala chorus give us the genuine sound of Italian voices in full flight, sounding much more inside their various assumptions than their rivals. Ensemble isn't perfect at every point, but never far enough astray to be worrying on repeated hearings. Italian audiences are not renowned for their silences. Their movements are occasionally in evidence as are the on-stage effects, but the atmosphere of being in an opera-house and taking part, as it were, in a real occasion has all the advantages over the aseptic feeling of a studio. Nor is there anything to complain about in voice-orchestra balance.

Verdi Ernani.
Carlo Bergonzi *ten* Ernani
Leontyne Price *sop* Elvira
Mario Sereni *bar* Don Carlos
Ezio Flagello *bass* Don Ruy Gomez de Silva
Júlia Hamari *contr* Giovanna
Fernando Iacopucci *ten* Don Riccardo
Hartje Mueller *bass* Iago
RCA Italiana Opera Chorus and Orchestra / Thomas Schippers.
RCA Victor Ⓜ Ⓓ GD86503 (two discs: 130 minutes: ADD). Text and translation included.
Recorded 1967.

An initial attraction of this issue over Muti's must be that it is on two discs instead of three. It's a studio recording very much of its period, favouring the soloists rather than the orchestra, with the producer moving the characters about in a stereophonic display of doubtful merit. The live EMI recording means that 100 or so human feet are added to the scoring; on the other hand, there is an undeniable sense of occasion and the sound is altogether more opulent. Muti conducts with more intensity than Schippers, and the choruses and concerted work have more life and urgency. The honours are probably about equal among the two sets of soloists. Ezio Flagello is a sonorous, conventional Silva; Ghiaurov (for Muti) sings with finer care of the melodic line and bears himself with greater dignity. Mario Sereni lacks Bruson's shining tone and grandeur, but despite some rough moments in "O de' verd'anni miei" sings the lyrical music well.

Leontyne Price has moments when she sounds like the greatest Verdi soprano of the age (the phrases where, forlornly, she asks Ernani for a smile, "il riso del tuo volto", provide an example) and she is more than Mirella Freni's equal. And Bergonzi is decidedly Domingo's superior here. His singing is the principal recommendation of the set, not that he is particularly subtle or intense, but that he never wrenches out of shape the melodic line for which his finely produced voice is an ideal instrument. The Muti recording gives very limited satisfaction in the arias, which are such an important part of the opera; the RCA issue (texturally complete), while not rising to the standard of the famous old recordings of individual items, presents an attractive alternative.

Verdi Falstaff.
Tito Gobbi *bar* Falstaff
Rolando Panerai *bar* Ford
Luigi Alva *ten* Fenton
Dame Elisabeth Schwarzkopf *sop* Alice Ford
Anna Moffo *sop* Nannetta
Fedora Barbieri *mez* Mistress Quickly
Renato Ercolani *ten* Bardolfo
Nicola Zaccaria *bass* Pistola
Tomaso Spataro *ten* Dr Caius
Nan Merriman *mez* Meg Page
Philharmonia Chorus and Orchestra / Herbert von Karajan.
EMI Ⓟ Ⓓ CDS7 49668-2 (two discs: 120 minutes: ADD). Notes, text and translation included.
Recorded 1956.

BBC RADIO 3
90-93 FM

For once the record company's words could be taken at face value: this *Falstaff* is, indeed, an "outstanding musical document" and one which, since its transfer to CD, still stands (with Toscanini) peerless in the catalogue. At its centre stands Tito Gobbi, and his is a presence large enough to encompass both the lord and the jester, the sensuous and the sensual, and the deep seriousness as well as the deep absurdity of his vision. Few Falstaffs have such a measure of the simplicity of his first monosyllables in the bustle around him; few find the poise as well as the confusion within his music. Gobbi offers everything which Giuseppe Taddei, in the later Karajan recording (for Philips), denies us. By playing tiringly relentless verbal and vocal games, Taddei robs the role of its ambiguities: a comparison of their "Honour" monologues is deeply revealing.

Renato Bruson's hugely human Falstaff, solemn, vulnerable, yet properly volatile, will continue to make Giulini's 1982 DG recording irresistibly tempting. Neither Giulini, though, nor Karajan in 1980, had the benefit of Walter Legge's artistic directorship, and in the casting kaleidoscope this makes all the difference. This recording is incomparable in its quartet of merry wives. Schwarzkopf's Alice radiates both the "gioia nell'aria" and the "gioia nel'cor" of Verdi's writing, Fedora Barbieri's redoubtable Mistress Quickly, with her stentorian cries of "Povera donna!", puts both Christa Ludwig and Valentini-Terrani (for Giulini) in the shade; Anna Moffo's Nannetta, perfectly matched in timbre and agility with Luigi Alva's Fenton, is a constant delight. It is, above all, their corporate presence which works at such a distinctively higher level. They enable us to feel the dappled sunlight of the score; in the later Karajan all we see is music-stands.

Rolando Panerai rules as Ford in both the Karajan recordings and, indeed, takes over as the most resonant presence in the later one. His "E sogno? o realtà?" is a high point of both performances, scoring over Leo Nucci for Giulini at every turn. This 1956 recording has been discreetly and skilfully doctored, but a little background hiss does remain: no one could deny that the Vienna Philharmonic in 1980 have more acoustic space than the Philharmonia to stretch their muscles and luxuriate in Verdi's late summer sun. But one doesn't actually end up hearing more. Whereas Karajan's baton has slackened somewhat in 1980, with not a few moments of sluggish pacing, this first great recording is a-flutter with pungent solo detail, realizing, with Nannetta, that the world is "tutto deliro, sospiro e riso". Giulini relishes the score no less affectionately, offering at times a still more supple approach to the vocal writing. But the heavier, closer presence of the orchestra on DG's recording sometimes misses the essential elusive quality of the score. Only in this early release do the episodes of the opera, its exits and entrances, its subjects and counter-subjects, pass with the unique sensibility of Verdi's final great exuberant fugue of life.

Verdi Falstaff.

Sir Geraint Evans *bar* Falstaff
Robert Merrill *bar* Ford
Alfredo Kraus *ten* Fenton
Ilva Ligabue *sop* Alice Ford
Mirella Freni *sop* Nannetta
Giulietta Simionato *mez* Mistress Quickly
Piero de Palma *ten* Bardolfo
Giovanni Foiani *bass* Pistola
John Lanigan *ten* Dr Caius
Rosalind Elias *mez* Meg Page
RCA Italiana Opera Chorus and Orchestra / Sir Georg Solti.
Decca Grand Opera Ⓜ ① 417 168-2DM2 (two discs: 115 minutes: ADD). Notes, text and translation included. Recorded 1963.

The fact that this issue is at mid price may influence you in its favour. You'll be presented with a thoroughly lively and enjoyable reading, but one without the special warmth of the Giulini, slightly spoilt by the heavy recording of the orchestra, or the grace and vitality of the Karajan, still the top recommendation or, indeed, the classic Toscanini. In the context of the these versions, Solti's combination of exuberance and precision is certainly to be admired, but the explosive outbursts of the brass, more evident on CD than LP, are foreign to the spirit of this light-fingered score, and become more troublesome on repetition. Solti certainly brings out the refinement of the writing but is less aristocratic and subtle than either Karajan or Giulini, who are both more affectionate in their approach.

By the time of this recording Sir Geraint Evans was already an experienced Falstaff, and he knows how to savour a phrase as well as Gobbi on the Karajan set, but he is also inclined to exaggerate expression sometimes at the expense of the music, a fault both Gobbi and Bruson (for Giulini) avoid. Both his rivals suggest more of the character's inner warmth and vulnerability, but Evans is always a living and lovable personality. All three baritones give appreciable performances, but Gobbi is just the most interesting by dint of the way in which he encompasses both the absurdity and the seriousness of the role through his command of vocal colour. Robert Merrill is an authoritative but not particularly individual Ford, wanting the incisiveness of Panerai (Karajan). On the other hand Solti's Alice is much more idiomatically sung by Ligabue, the best portrayal on any set, even better than Schwarzkopf. Simionato is a straighter Quickly than either the ebullient Barbieri (Karajan) or Valentini Terrani (Giulini). Alva (Karajan) is the most appealing Fenton but Kraus's elegant singing runs him close. Moffo (Karajan) is a more charming Nannetta than Freni, who has the warmer voice. Solti's version sports a splendid Bardolph and Pistol, but so does Karajan.

Verdi Falstaff.

Giuseppe Valdengo *bar* Falstaff
Frank Guarrera *bar* Ford
Antonio Madasi *ten* Fenton
Herva Nelli *sop* Alice Ford
Teresa Stich-Randall *sop* Nannetta
Cloe Elmo *contr* Mistress Quickly
John Carmen Rossi *ten* Bardolfo
Norman Scott *bass* Pistola
Gabor Carelli *ten* Dr Caius
Nan Merriman *mez* Meg Page
Robert Shaw Chorale; NBC Symphony Orchestra / Arturo Toscanini.

RCA Gold Seal mono Ⓜ Ⓘ GD60251 (two discs: 117 minutes: ADD). Notes, text and translation included. Recorded at NBC broadcasts on April 1st and 8th, 1950.

This *Falstaff* remains, as it always has been, one of the half a dozen greatest opera sets ever recorded. It is a miracle in every respect. How Toscanini loved Verdi and how he strained every sinew to fulfil this amazing score's variety in line, feeling and colour. Whether it is the clarity and discipline of the ensembles, the extraordinary care taken over orchestral detail (most arresting in the whole of the final act's first scene) or the alert control of dynamics, Toscanini is supreme, yet nothing is done for effect's sake; everything seems natural, inevitable, unforced, as though the score was being crated anew before us with chamber-music finesse – and the atmosphere of a live performance adds to the feeling of immediacy. Nobody dares, or seems to want to interrupt the magic being laid before them. Toscanini in his old age is matching the subtlety and vitality of the composer's own Indian summer – or one might say spring, so delicate and effervescent does the scoring sound.

The other overriding impression of Toscanini's reading is the perfect relationship of tempos, not always precisely Verdi's, and the way he accommodates his singers, quite putting to flight any idea of him as a strict taskmaster. If, vocally, the main glory is the wonderful sense of ensemble gained through hours of hard rehearsals, individual contributions are almost all rewarding. Indeed, Valdengo's Falstaff, under Toscanini's tutelage, has not been surpassed on disc even by Gobbi. Flexibility, charm, exactness, refinement inform his beautifully and wisely sung portrayal (extraordinary for a singer in his mid thirties) – listen to the whole of the monologue at the start of Act 3 and you'll hear what a great singer working with a great conductor can make of a great role – mainly by observing what the composer has written. He is no less pointed and subtle in his encounter with Frank Guarrera's imposing Ford, and Guarrera himself, again with Toscanini's help, reminds us how much the writing in the Jealousy aria relates to Otello's music. Another great joy of the set is the women's ensemble, their contribution the very epitome of smiling chatter. The Alice, Meg and Nanetta (Stich-Randall – none better), all sound, as they were, fresh and youthful. Herva Nelli is a lively and delightful Alice and Cloe Elmo's Quickly is as rich and ripe of voice and diction as any on disc, though a trifle coarse at times. The Fenton is sweet and Italianate in tone, but not as stylish as others. The smaller roles are all very much part of the team.

This set is a repository of the very best in Verdi conducting, worthy of study by aspiring (or established) conductors. More important than that, it should be a source of revelation to a new generation of collectors who may have a dim and/or wrong-headed view of what Toscanini was about. The remastering gives it clearer, more immediate sound than ever heard before from the originals.

Verdi La forza del destino.

Rosalind Plowright *sop* Leonora
José Carreras *ten* Don Alvaro
Renato Bruson *bar* Don Carlo
Paata Burchuladze *bass* Padre Guardiano
Agnes Baltsa *mez* Preziosilla
Juan Pons *bar* Fra Melitone
John Tomlinson *bass* Marchese
Mark Curtis *ten* Trabuco
Jean Rigby *mez* Curra
Richard Van Allan *bass* Mayor
Ambrosian Opera Chorus; Philharmonia Orchestra / Giuseppe Sinopoli.

1987

DG Ⓔ Ⓘ 419 203-2GH3 (three discs: 178 minutes: DDD). Notes, text and translation included. Recorded 1985.

It was ever thus: the more or less simultaneous release of two recordings of distinction in a then limited field (the other was Muti on EMI). In practice, they vie tantalizingly with one another; if we could selectively combine the two casts then we would indeed have untrammelled pleasure. The glorious centrepiece of EMI's La Scala, Milan recording is Domingo's Don Alvaro, powerfully complemented by Zancanaro's Don Carlo. If DG's set has a weakness it is in the great central movement of Act 3 ("Solenne in quest'ora", "Urna fatale", and so on) where Carreras sings with ardour but suddenly diminished control and where Bruson rather sadly begins to show his years. That said, their great Act 4 confrontation goes well, despite the usual impossibly gabbled end, and there are few quarrels with Carreras's singing earlier in the opera. As a performance it lacks the penetrating interpretative distinction of Domingo's. His Don Alvaro is an aristocratic warrior capable of high passion and chilling irony; Carreras's Don Alvaro is a personable hot-head. Sounding remarkably like Giuseppe di Stefano in his prime, Carreras's singing stimulates a physical sensation not dissimilar to a warming double brandy tossed gratefully back with promise of more to come.

But *La forza del destino* is more, far more, than a single big duet; elsewhere DG's set nudges, elbows, and frequently knocks the EMI set into second place. For one thing, there are no weaknesses in DG's casting of the mass of tiny but dramatically crucial *comprimario* roles, from perfectly shaped vignettes (Mark Curtis's Trabuco, Jean Rigby's Curra, John Tomlinson's Marchese, and the Mayor of Richard Van Allan, no less) to full-drawn small portraits: a glorious Melitone from Juan Pons (outpointing EMI's veteran Sesto Bruscantini at every juncture) and quite the best Preziosilla we have had on record, from Agnes Baltsa. The freedom and verve of Baltsa's singing in the Act 1 Inn scene and the brilliance of Verdi's orchestral commentary as revealed to us by Sinopoli and the Philharmonia Orchestra (who play supremely well throughout the set) are a joy from start to finish. Add Burchuladze's immensely imposing portrayal of Padre Guardiano (richer voiced than Plishka and occasionally nimbler, too) and the stage is well set for the opera in general and Leonora in particular to make their mark.

Which is precisely what Rosalind Plowright proceeds to do. Yes, she has studied Callas (for Serafin on EMI), and even occasionally risks sounding like her; but the vigour of Plowright's portrayal seems to come from within, not from the conscientious application of second-hand interpretative points. Exposed above the stave, Plowright's voice may not have the poise of a Tebaldi or a Milanov, but poise is not a characteristic one necessarily looks for in a great Leonora. After Freni's conscientious professionalism on EMI it is a great joy to hear a singer to whom every jot and title of recitative, every lyric phrase, every new situation unmistakably matters. What flaws there are – the distant balance in "Pace, pace" and Plowright's blank diction on the initial word, or the awkward jab of sound at the top of the solo cello's second ascent in "Me, pellegrina" – are containable in the context of a performance by Plowright whose ardour and sincerity cast over the whole enterprise a special radiance and point.

Of the two conductors, Muti is the more consistent, Sinopoli the more interesting, with both playing long stretches of the score in ways that are undeniably exciting. Sinopoli's conducting is immensely careful. There are passages when he is teasingly slow and one or two reckless sallies in some of Verdi's cheaper music, but it is in general an eminently responsible, dramatically intelligent reading, based on a conception of Verdi's sound world that emphasizes the music's urgency and simplicity, its concern with the earthy, the primal, the *naïf*. Brass tone is cool and concentrated, but blazing fiercely at nodal points; strings are often encouraged to play with a refreshing absence of vibrato. These are radical, innovatory points considerably removed from the run-of-the-mill Verdi conducting we often get on record and in the theatre. The choral work is also first-rate.

Where Sinopoli is decisively superior to Muti is in the crucial closing trio. Here is the stuff of which great music drama is made, wonderfully enacted by Burchuladze, Plowright and Carreras, with subtle changes of pace and perspective from Sinopoli and glorious string playing in the opera's closing pages. Both recordings have a wide dynamic range. DG's sound is generally more immediate though with a greater range of quasi-theatrical perspectives. They don't all work – as already indicated, Leonora seems to stay in the grotto for "Pace, pace" – but there is evidence that the production team have taken a lot of care with the recording. The difficulties the team encountered with illness and rescheduling during the sessions don't show up in the finished product.

With the Callas/Serafin set on EMI, we are spoilt for choice. Go for Muti on EMI if you see *La forza del destino* as ritual drama in a man's world; but if it is all-round accomplishment that you seek then Sinopoli has it, if not by a furlong, then at least by a couple of lengths.

Verdi La forza del destino.

Martina Arroyo *sop* Leonora
Carlo Bergonzi *ten* Don Alvaro
Piero Cappuccilli *bar* Don Carlo
Ruggero Raimondo *bass* Padre Guardiano
Biancamaria Casoni *mez* Preziosilla
Sir Geraint Evans *bar* Fra Melitone
Antonio Zerbini *bass* Marchese
Florindo Andreolli *ten* Trabuco
Mila Cova *mez* Curra
Virgilio Carbonari *ten* Mayor
Derek Hammond-Stroud *bar* Surgeon
Ambrosian Opera Chorus; Royal Philharmonic Orchestra / Lamberto Gardelli.
EMI Opera Ⓜ Ⓘ CMS7 64646-2 (three discs: 168 minutes: ADD). Notes, text and translation included. Recorded 1969.

Listening to Verdi's four great mid-period operas – *Boccanegra* (revised version), *Ballo*, *La forza del destino* and *Don Carlos* – is enough to persuade one that they are, by virtue of their marvellous melding of private emotions within a huge public panorama, their bold ambitions fully realized, the greatest works in the whole *oeuvre*. And *Forza*, though sometimes criticized for being sprawling, is not the least of the four. It is a 'chase' opera in which Carlo pursues Alvaro and Leonora through two countries, through cloister and convent, through scenes popular and martial, all treated on the most expansive scale. It is dominated by its series of magnificent duets that are composed so that the music marches with the development of situation and character. All the work's qualities are made manifest in this magnificent performance that was unavailable for far too long.

Much of its success is owed to Gardelli, a Verdian in a class above his contemporaries in this field. He is not one of those conductors who ruin Verdi's music by applying a metronomic drive; the singers, and the phrases, breathe and live under this baton. There is a Serafin-like suppleness to his reading; he neither drives the music nor allows it to flag. Under these conditions his singers blossom. In the best of her too few recordings, made when she was at the peak of her powers, Arroyo sings a lovely Leonora, feminine, concerned, eventually harrowed by her experiences. Phrases soar naturally; dynamic markings are observed; the personality appeals. She can sing a broad phrase, strike a high note *pianissimo*. Callas brought more character to the music; but no one else, not even Leontyne Price (Levine), sings it better.

The male antagonists are in a similar class. One could argue quite cogently and at length, on the strengths of this performance, that Bergonzi is the greatest Verdi tenor of the century (there is, of course, much more evidence to support that case) and certainly superior to Domingo and Pavarotti. The way he sings Alvaro's music with a passion always tempered by the needs for a firm line, long phrase, and dynamic control is a model of such things, even if he misses the sheer volume of a *tenore di forza*, such as Pertile or Giacomini. Cappuccilli, whose voice has just the right weight for Don Carlos and, like Bergonzi, was at the height of his powers in 1969, is another exemplary Verdian. Although neither he, nor any other baritone, sings the student song as Verdi intends it to be sung, he is subtle in his big aria and superb in the three duets with Bergonzi's Alvaro. As an example of the set's quality, try, if you can, their second encounter on the battlefield in which Carlos first forces Alvaro into a duel. Bergonzi's moving pleas for peace between them (second disc, track 12, 2'30") is as eloquent as one of Cappuccilli's fierce replies, "Stolto, stolto", is vicious (20'27"), and Gardelli marvellously realizes the disturbing accompaniment to this second section.

Casoni is a colourful, characterful Preziosilla but lacks a trill (Stignani on the wholly forgotten Cetra wartime version is the benchmark here). As the Father Superior, Raimondi is firm but a shade too lugubrious. Evans is a worthy but not very witty Melitone. Andreolli is a trim Trabuco. The RPO of the day was still substantially Beecham's band and play with the flair and individuality that implies – listen to what must be Jack Brymer's clarinet in the introduction to Alvaro's Act 3 aria, a fit prologue to a superb piece of singing from Bergonzi. They and Gardelli ensure that the genre scenes don't hang fire. The recording, through subtle movements of the singers, convincingly suggests a stage performance. At mid price, there is little even in newer sets to shake one's confidence in the desirability of this version.

Verdi La forza del destino.
Maria Callas *sop* Leonora
Richard Tucker *ten* Don Alvaro
Carlo Tagliabue *bar* Don Carlo
Nicola Rossi-Lemeni *bass* Padre Guardiano
Elena Nicolai *mez* Preziosilla
Renato Capecchi *bass* Fra Melitone
Plinio Clabassi *bass* Marchese
Gino del Signore *ten* Trabuco
Rina Cavallari *sop* Curra
Dario Caselli *bass* Mayor
Chorus and Orchestra of La Scala, Milan / Tullio Serafin.
EMI mono Ⓜ ① CDS5 56323-2 (three discs: 164 minutes: ADD). Notes, text and translation included. Recorded 1955.

The two EMI recordings of *La forza del destino* are rendered unignorable, their shortcomings pushed into the shadows, by two transforming performances: Callas's Leonora here and Domingo's Don Alvaro on the Muti. Both sets are complete and strongly cast down to the smallest *comprimario* roles. Leonora was a role to which Callas was particularly well attuned. Leonora's ardour, sincerity, and desperate vulnerability are etched by this great artist into her every utterance. *Forza* begins with a subdued conversation and ends with the great trio and Callas is unforgettable in both; whenever she is before the microphone – throughout Act 1, in the great scene with the Padre Guardiano and in Act 4 – we are aware of the greatness of *La forza del destino* as music-drama. There are some flaws in execution but fewer than might be expected given the rough patch Callas (generally in fine fettle around this period) had gone through in the spring of 1954. Walter Legge, whose advice Callas respected and whose authority she acknowledged, told her that unless the wobble was sorted out EMI and Angel would have to issue sea-sickness pills with the records. In the event, they weren't necessary. Callas is also helped by the digital remastering, and by CD; her voice never really sat comfortably in 1950s vinyl which bucked and jabbered at her emissions as surely as any dyed-in-the-wool canary-fancier. The sound is clear and true. The Legge/Beckett mono recording is generally excellent. The strings perhaps lack weight but one quickly forgets this as one listens to the unruffled good sense of Serafin's direction. It is a pity about the cuts (notably the foreshortening of the Padre Guardiano/Melitone exchanges in Act 4) and about Tagliabue's leathery Don Carlo, since the rest of the cast is admirable. Richard Tucker is glorious, some lachrymose moments notwithstanding. Even if you opt for a rival version of the opera, because of Callas this set is unmissable.

Another obvious rival is Schippers on his 1965 RCA recording. At mid price, this is also a set by which you could get to know *Forza*, the more so as it is complete. No recording of *Forza* can be definitive, or even self-evidently a better buy than any of its rivals. One is, alas, bound to choose here and there for this and that. In the case of Schippers it must be, at this distance of time, for the youthfully radiant portrayal by Leontyne Price who was always a fine Leonora. Merrill also sings well on this RCA version, a top-class 'house' performance, and the set – which still sounds very clean and fresh and which is cleanly, freshly conducted by Schippers – has the advantage of general all-round strengths, or rather a lack of noticeable weaknesses, unless it is the rather humourless Melitone of Flagello. However, Serafin's is a more characterful performance, notwithstanding its weak Don Carlo and the cuts.

Verdi La forza del destino.
Leontyne Price *sop* Leonora
Giuseppe Giacomini *ten* Don Alvaro
Leo Nucci *bar* Don Carlo
Bonaldo Giaiotti *bass* Padre Guardiano
Isola Jones *mez* Preziosilla
Enrico Fissore *bar* Melitone
Richard Vernon *bass* Marchese
Anthony Laciura *ten* Trabuco
Diane Kesling *mez* Curra
James Courtney *bar* Mayor
John Darrenkemp *ten* Surgeon
Chorus and Orchestra of the Metropolitan Opera, New York / James Levine.
Stage Director: **John Dexter.** *Video Director:* **Kirk Browning.**
DG Ⓕ ⚏⚏ 072 427-3GH (180 minutes). Recorded 1984.

This stand-and-deliver performance is a great relief from the producers' concepts and gimmicks we have endured in such a piece as *Forza* for far too long, particularly with the calibre of the cast as seen and heard here. Initially, it looked as if it might be disappointing. In the first scene, Price seemed all of her 57 years (the performance was taken from a Metropolitan evening) and Giacomini looked inexpressive and sounded a trifle hesitant. Happily this wasn't a harbinger of the rest. Price could still give her younger contemporaries a lesson or two in shaping and projecting a Verdi phrase – they should listen to her "Pace, pace" – and much of what she does here has a majestic confidence of tone, a sweep of line such as we haven't heard since she was in her prime. To add to that her dignified acting, so much more moving than the exaggerated histrionics sometimes encountered in this role, was in every respect arresting: the voice tells us what Leonora felt, what she wanted to express of her troubled existence.

Giacomini is superb. One or two clumsy phrases around the *passagio* apart, he sings Alvaro's extremely taxing music with the breadth of phrase, the security of tone, the confidence in attack that only a true *tenore di forza*, which he is, can provide, calling to mind Francesco Merli, on pre-war records, of Alvaro's part. But not everything in his reading is mere *spinto* strength: in the duets that lie at the centre of his role, he evinces the tenderness and vulnerability that makes Alvaro such a complex character, and conveys as much in both his quieter singing and in his sensitive acting. And it has to be said it is a relief to hear a tenor other than Domingo, for all his gifts, in this kind of music. Variety is the spice in singing as much as in life.

Beside him Nucci sounds relatively coarse, belting out his music with an eye for the gallery, very seldom moderating his forceful tone. Allowing for that, his Carlo is enjoyable and truly Italianate in manner – likewise a Guardiano (the reliable if somewhat rusty Giaiotti) and a Melitone (the compact and amusing Fissore) in similar mould. Isola Jones sounds as if she is doing herself no favours by essaying such a beefy part as Preziosilla without the means to encompass it. Still, she makes her mark, looking every inch the camp-follower.

Levine has always favoured this score – remember the classic RCA set from 1987 with the much younger Price – and he manages to hold together its sprawling structure through sensibly related speeds, never allowing the continuity to break, in spite of the insistent applause that greets every number. He plays the score complete and makes the most of all of it, supported by some finely shaped playing. The revival of John Dexter's sensible, unforced staging, well lit, is unobtrusive, but the video director relies rather too much on very close close-ups, which are sometimes unkind to singers attempting to reach the furthermost parts of a large house. The picture and sound are of the exemplary quality we expect from DG in this field, but there are no subtitles. This is a performance not to be missed by enthusiastic Verdians, or those who appreciate generous-hearted singing in a real performance rather than a manufactured one.

Verdi Un giorno di regno.

Ingvar Wixell *bar* Cavaliere di Belfiore
Fiorenza Cossotto *mez* Marchesa del Poggio
Jessye Norman *sop* Giulietta
José Carreras *ten* Edoardo di Sanval
Wladimiro Ganzarolli *bar* Baron Kelbar
Vincenzo Sardinero *bar* Gasparo Antonio della Rocca
William Elvin *bar* Delmonte, A servant
Ricardo Cassinelli *ten* Count Ivrea
Ambrosian Singers; Royal Philharmonic Orchestra / Lamberto Gardelli.
Philips Ⓜ ⓪ 422 429-2PM2 (two discs: 119 minutes: ADD). Notes, text and translation included.
Recorded 1973.

When this set first appeared in 1974, Richard Osborne graphically stated: "In *Un giorno* Verdi can be seen teeing up the *opera buffa* style and driving lustily over the fairway. It's an unfamiliar and exhilarating sight, and the fact that three years later in *Don Pasquale* Donizetti drove even further and with a still sweeter swing, doesn't detract a jot from either quality." This was one of the first fruits of Philips's intention to record all Verdi's early operas, and it remains one of the most rewarding results of that policy. The true and forward recording sounds even fresher and more attractive on CD, and the hand-picked cast obviously enjoy themselves in a theatre-like performance. Gardelli was the house conductor for the Verdi project, an apt choice as can be once more confirmed by listening to his expert management of the many fizzing ensembles and his innate sense of what a Verdi *melodia* requires.

Ingvar Wixell fills the major role of Belfiore, the false King Stanislaus of the original libretto, with relish and panache, though not quite enough Italianate brio. The two *buffo* bass parts are in fact sung by baritones, but Ganzarolli and Sardinero make one forget that they haven't quite the requisite bottom to their voices by dint of their lively characterization. Although the Marchesa is supposedly the soprano role, the mezzo Giulietta has the higher-lying line and the Marchesa was sung originally by a mezzo, so the casting here is apt enough. As ever, Cossotto provides strong tone and clean attack. The young Jessye Norman sings with just the warmth her part needs. It is also a pleasure to hear the youthful Carreras providing the plaintive voice the romantic lead calls for. Altogether, this set is a delight to the ear and should be in every Verdian's library.

Verdi Giovanna d'Arco.

Montserrat Caballé *sop* Giovanna
Plácido Domingo *ten* Carlo VII
Sherrill Milnes *bar* Giacomo
Keith Erwen *ten* Delil
Robert Lloyd *bass* Talbot
Ambrosian Opera Chorus; London Symphony Orchestra / James Levine.
EMI Ⓜ ⓪ CMS7 63226-2 (two discs: 121 minutes: ADD). Notes, text and translation included.
Recorded 1972.

The most brassy of Verdi's scores, *Giovanna d'Arco* has a brashness which James Levine's conducting brings into a glaring light. The punchy style is established immediately in the Overture. Then the French curse the English to a thumping accompaniment in the first scene, Joan's fighting spirit emerges in the second but not half so assertively as does that of the orchestra, and when shortly afterwards she falls asleep the banality of the accompanying figure stands no chance of escaping attention as it is thrust characteristically into the foreground. When she wakes up it is to lead into one of those cabaletta tunes that can be a delight if the conductor encourages the natural spring in their rhythm and avoids the vulgarity of overemphasis; unhappily, Levine seems to take the opposite view.

The ruling trio of the time, Caballé, Domingo and Milnes, are on excellent form. Caballé does her best to make a credible character out of the opera's conventionalized treatment of this supremely unconventional woman. She sings beautifully throughout, and at certain moments (the ending of the 'forest' aria, for instance, and her solo in the ensemble of Act 2) is sublime. Domingo, the voice at its loveliest and with the strong heroic steel already showing through, brings conviction if not subtlety to his unconvincing role. Milnes as the father who conscientiously denounces Joan and discovers his mistake too late has plenty of authority and, at *forte*, there is an exciting ring in his voice. Good work by the Ambrosian chorus and the LSO is a further asset. But it is an opera with many weaknesses, Verdi's best self having scope only in the first part of the father-and-daughter duet in Act 3, and it needs to be conducted with slightly more refined taste than is shown here. There is, however, no current CD competition.

Verdi Giovanna d'Arco.

Susan Dunn *sop* Giovanna
Vincenzo La Scola *ten* Carlo VII
Renato Bruson *bar* Giacomo
Pierre Lefebvre *ten* Delil
Pietro Spagnoli *bass* Talbot
Chorus and Orchestra of the Teatro Comunale, Bologna / Riccardo Chailly.
Stage Director: **Werner Herzog.** *Film Director:* **Keith Cheetham.**
Teldec Video Ⓟ ⊡ 9031 71478-3; ◑ 9031 71478-6 (three sides: 127 minutes). Recorded 1989.

Here's an issue to delight all those who enjoy Verdian singing of the highest quality. Musically speaking, this set need hardly fear comparison with the CD version reviewed above. Susan Dunn shows that she is a Verdi interpreter, vocally speaking, of class. She projects both her Act 1 and Act 2 arias and her contributions to the ensembles, with lovely tone, finely honed to the needs of the moment, and phrasing that puts her in the Caballé class.

In the first of the great father-daughter duets in Verdi, in the final act when Giacomo realizes Giovanna is indeed pure and not sullied as he had imagined, Dunn is aptly partnered by Bruson, here at the peak of his powers. Together they give as rewarding and moving an example of Verdi singing as any you will hear for many a day. Listen to how Dunn phrases so eloquently and classically "Amai, ma un solo istante" and then how Bruson answers with his forgiving sad phrase, "Ella innocente e paura!" – enough to move the proverbial stone to tears. When you listen to Bruson here and in his Act 1 aria and cabaletta, indeed throughout, you hear a perfection of moulding line, tone and text into an integrated whole that is the very essence of great singing. Add to that the emotional content of Bruson's performance, and his imposing presence, and you have an interpretation to treasure. As regards Dunn and Bruson, this will one day be a historic document of what the late twentieth century could offer in vocal aristocracy. Bruson far outsings Milnes, admirable as he is for Levine.

La Scola isn't in the same class as his partners and no match for the young Domingo. His tenor is more reliable than pleasing, the tone being somewhat tight and restricted, but time and again he surpasses the form expected of him with a long-breathed phrase and a touch of Italianate brio. In any case, King Charles is a cardboard figure set beside those of Giovanna and Giacomo. All three principals shine in the last-act finale, a trio foretelling the very best of Verdi to come. All three, and the good artists in the *comprimario* roles, are convincingly led by Chailly who manages to keep a balance between raw energy and lyrical poetry – both sides of Verdi's musical character are truly adumbrated in this score. His Bologna orchestra play splendidly for him, but his chorus is a trial. Its members wobble and sing out of tune, particularly annoying when they are supposed to be portraying Angels: the contrasted writing for Angels and Demons is one of the most inspired features of this score.

The production is by film director, Werner Herzog, in association with his designer, Henning von Gierke. It worked rather better in the theatre than it does on video, where the rather grand décor hardly has the space to make its mark, and there is no evidence of the Angels and Demons being represented properly. There is intelligent use of emblems such as brightly coloured sheets, crosses, rocks and chains. The staging is strangely static and dull, coming from a film director. Herzog and his colleague appear to have left the principals to their own devices – not surprisingly, the experienced Bruson fares better than his inexperienced colleagues. Dunn does little except look elated or frightened in a conventional way – even so, her very simplicity is in its way touching. La Scola merely stands and sings in a typically Italian-tenor manner. Nor do they react very convincingly to each other. Still, little stands in the way of enjoyment of the excellent singing. The sound is a true representation of what you might have heard in the opera-house, somewhat more confined but more realistic than what is customarily caught in the studio. The piece itself may suffer from Solera's cackhanded libretto, wholly unhistorical, but Verdi's music – and here its refined execution – makes something memorable out of the improbably story.

Verdi I Lombardi alla prima crociata.

June Anderson *sop* Giselda
Luciano Pavarotti *ten* Oronte
Samuel Ramey *bass* Pagano
Richard Leech *ten* Arvino
Ildebrando d'Arcangelo *bass* Pirro
Yanni Yannissis *bass* Acciano
Jane Shaulis *mez* Sofia
Anthony Dean Griffey *ten* Prior
Patricia Racette *mez* Viclinda
Chorus and Orchestra of the Metropolitan Opera, New York / James Levine.
Decca Ⓟ ① 455 287-2DHO2 (two discs: 129 minutes: DDD). Notes, text and translation included. Recorded 1996.

At this stage of his career it is good to hear Pavarotti in a new role on disc, even if Oronte is not one of Verdi's biggest challenges for a tenor. Having failed to appear in the First Act, the Turkish tyrant's son soon gets killed off and goes to heaven – a noble demise, although the average operatic tenor would far rather be on stage hogging the limelight to the end. The sum total of Oronte's role is his lovely entrance aria, a duet with the soprano, and the opportunity to lead off the big trio, as Verdi was to have his tenor do in the *Rigoletto* quartet.

Pavarotti appeared in the Metropolitan Opera production of *I Lombardi* in 1993 and this recording is the delayed result, following after a gap of three years. Little, if anything, seems to have been lost in the interim. He is in good voice and sings Oronte's aria with a fine sense of legato, binding the decorative turns of the cabaletta beautifully into the vocal line and throwing in a respectable top C to show us he still can. In the opening to the trio, "Qual voluttà trascorrere", Pavarotti imparts a vivid sense of the situation: this Oronte really sounds as if he has been wounded, turning Verdi's broken vocal line into the mortal gasps for breath the composer clearly envisaged, while still delivering singing of the highest quality. There are few operatic voices around that are ageing so gracefully.

I Lombardi is a viscerally exciting opera and contains far more of interest than just that trio, made famous on disc by Caruso, Alda and Journet, and later Gigli, Rethberg and Pinza. The first complete recording, conducted by Lamberto Gardelli (reviewed below), set a good benchmark in 1971, but that need not deter us from welcoming this lively newcomer. Levine's home company is in excellent shape. The Metropolitan Opera Orchestra play with splendid precision, every string *tremolo* seething with intensity, and Raymond Gniewek makes a nice job of the miniature violin concerto that opens the Third Act finale. As Turks and Crusaders, women of the harem and virgins, the Met Chorus have a high old time on both sides of *I Lombardi*'s war-zone. Levine himself has improved beyond recognition as a Verdian since his youthful, slightly vulgar, set of *Giovanna d'Arco* for EMI (reviewed above). This studio recording is well paced, has a good sense of theatre, and does not overplay its hand in the old Levine manner. Everything is swift and crisp on the surface, though the Philips set sometimes has a deeper sense of Italianate *rubato* that probes to the emotions below. Typically, it is Gardelli rather than the correct Levine, who makes an unwritten, millisecond's holding-back in the great trio, so as to clinch the final climax.

The best role goes to the soprano, Giselda, specially tailored for the delicate skills of Erminia Frezzolini. Among the current crop of Verdi sopranos, June Anderson is probably as plausible a modern Frezzolini as any. Although her opening prayer is less than heavenly, because of a sinful lapse in approaching notes from below, she soon makes due atonement. There is some lovely, pure-toned singing in Giselda's big scene at the end of the Second Act and her coloratura is shining bright, both in this cabaletta and later in "In fondo all'alma". Cristina Deutekom on the Philips set has more guts and spontaneity, but Anderson is the one with the quality voice (Deutekom's fast vibrato and tendency to yodel at speed have always been an acquired taste). Samuel Ramey makes a relatively lightweight Pagano, who alone decorates his second verses. His counterpart on Philips, Ruggero Raimondi, who is stronger and tougher, offers a no less valid view of Pagano's character. In the second tenor role Richard Leech holds his own, though his voice does not take well to the microphone. Ildebrando d'Arcangelo proudly represents the younger generation of Italian singers in the small role of Pirro and Patricia Racette sings brightly as Viclinda. Jane Shaulis's tired mezzo makes Sofia sound more like Oronte's granny than his mother. On balance, with Pavarotti having the edge over Domingo's warmly-sung, but less interesting Oronte, Decca have probably assembled the better cast.

It is difficult to declare a straight victor between these two competing sets. Gardelli's crusading first recording has a rough Italianate vigour that lovers of early Verdi will enjoy, but Levine and his forces fight back with pace and brilliance, and a bright, modern recording with the voices well forward. This young Turk of a set is more than able to hold its ground.

Verdi I Lombardi alla prima crociata.
   Cristina Deutekom *sop* Giselda
   Plácido Domingo *ten* Oronte
   Ruggero Raimondi *bass* Pagano
   Jerome Lo Monaco *ten* Arvino
   Stafford Dean *bass* Pirro
   Clifford Grant *bass* Acciano
   Montserrat Aparici *sop* Sofia
   Keith Erwen *ten* Prior
   Desdemona Malvisi *sop* Viclinda
   Ambrosian Singers; Royal Philharmonic Orchestra / Lamberto Gardelli.
   Philips Ⓜ ① 422 420-2PM2 (two discs: 135 minutes: ADD). Notes, text and translation included. Recorded 1971.

"Full of life, musical colour and emotion, yet incapable of a satisfactory production except perhaps in symbolical terms, *I lombardi* surely emerges as an ideal opera for the gramophone record, for the theatre of the mind." Thus spake the producer in his note for the booklet accompanying the original LP issue. He was right, no doubt, in so far as there do seem to be formidable difficulties in the way of successful stage production. The First Act promises well and turns out to be much the best. After that, apart from the famous trio, nothing quite rises to the point of inspiration, and a good deal of it sinks into banality. The character of the villain-turned-hermit appears to have interested Verdi less than his central position in the libretto would signify, and there are none of those duets which so frequently quicken his creative abilities, because of the moving nature of the human relationship involved. One imagines, too, that in practical terms a factor working against regular performance in the past has been the restrictions of the principal tenor role. Not only is Oronte absent from the First Act but he is dead by the last scene (though briefly singing in spirit from off-stage). Moreover, to add insult to injury, the second tenor has the effrontery to survive him and take part in a further trio on his own account.

The young Domingo, singing with a rich, throaty lustre, makes a good job of what he has to do (and no exhibitionism or excitement – through additional high notes in "La mia letizia"). The second tenor, Jerome Lo Monaco, presents a suitable contrast, with his lighter, reedier tone. The soprano part is difficult to cast, for it wants dramatic weight as well as the agility of a virtuoso and an extensive upper range: Cristina Deutekom copes well with the tessitura but her somewhat tremulous tone gives limited pleasure. Raimondi, on the other hand, is heard in one of his finest performances on record, the opulent resonance being spread evenly throughout the whole voice and his characterization showing imaginative involvement. The chorus work is strong, and Gardelli leads the orchestra in a well-played, finely recorded account of the score.

Verdi Luisa Miller.
Montserrat Caballé *sop* Luisa
Luciano Pavarotti *ten* Rodolfo
Sherrill Milnes *bar* Miller
Bonaldo Giaiotti *bass* Count Walter
Anna Reynolds *mez* Federica
Richard van Allen *bass* Wurm
Annette Céline *mez* Laura
Fernando Pavarotti *ten* Peasant
London Opera Chorus; National Philharmonic Orchestra / Peter Maag.
Decca Ⓟ Ⓒ 417 420-2DH2 (two discs: 144 minutes: ADD). Notes, text and translation included. Recorded 1975.

Verdi Luisa Miller.
Anna Moffo *sop* Luisa
Carlo Bergonzi *ten* Rodolfo
Cornell MacNeil *bar* Miller
Giorgio Tozzi *bass* Count Walter
Shirley Verrett *mez* Federica
Ezio Flagello *bass* Wurm
Gabriella Carturan *mez* Laura
Piero De Palma *ten* Peasant
RCA Italiana Opera Chorus and Orchestra / Fausto Cleva.
RCA Ⓜ Ⓒ GD86646 (two discs: 132 minutes: ADD). Notes, text and translation included. Recorded 1964.

The vote goes to the Decca recording under Peter Maag, though that is not to present it with a complete bill of health or to put Cleva's or Lorin Maazel's DG sets into permanent quarantine. In fact, if we were simply to go through the casts, honours would be fairly evenly spread. Maazel has the most touching, aptly-cast heroine in Ricciarelli, yet Caballé, though at first sounding too mature, has the more lovely voice, while Moffo is firmer in tone than Ricciarelli and more assured in certain technical matters than Caballé. Maag has the most fully human of the Millers in Sherrill Milnes, though both Bruson (with Maazel) and MacNeil have a deeper lustre in their voices. Cleva has the most stylish of the three distinguished Rodolfos in Bergonzi, but both Pavarotti and Domingo are on top form, fully committed in feeling as in vocal resource. If we look further down the lists we see Cleva strengthen his performance with Verrett, who makes the somewhat colourless character of Federica memorable in the right way (Obraztsova, with Maazel, in the wrong way, and Anna Reynolds not at all). Of the villains, Ganzarolli (Maazel) is the nastiest but partly because his singing is the least enjoyable, Van Allen introduces an appropriate snarl into his Italian pronunciation, and in the Cleva recording there is a sonorous repertory double-act by Tozi and Flagello who might have wandered in from almost any other opera.

The deciding factor is not solely the conducting but a feeling for the work which may originate in the conductor and has spread to all concerned. They all give the impression of being in love with this opera. From the start, where Cleva and Maazel, in their different ways, appear as good workmen doing a businesslike job, Maag has gone to the heart of the score, finding its seriousness as well as its fire. Sometimes an *allegro moderato* comes out more like an *andantino*, but the slower speeds are usually well placed so that pace and tension are not lost. The last act is especially fine, containing what should be regarded as among the gramophone classics – the two duets of Luisa, first with her father, then with Rodolfo. Ray Minshull's production for Decca is unobtrusively effective in creation of atmosphere, to which the London Underground makes an ominous contribution from time to time.

Verdi Macbeth.
Piero Cappuccilli *bar* Macbeth
Shirley Verrett *mez* Lady Macbeth
Nicolai Ghiaurov *bass* Banquo
Plácido Domingo *ten* Macduff
Antonio Savastano *ten* Malcolm
Carlo Zardo *bass* Doctor
Giovanni Foiani *bass* Servant
Sergio Fontana *bass* Herald
Alfredo Mariotti *bass* Assassin
Stefania Malagù *mez* Lady-in-waiting
Chorus and Orchestra of La Scala, Milan / Claudio Abbado.
DG The Originals Ⓜ Ⓓ 449 732-2GOR2 (two discs: 154 minutes: ADD). Notes, text and translation included. Recorded 1976.

When the Muti/EMI version appeared on two CDs at mid price, it was suggested that, to be competitive, this Abbado set would have to follow suit. And eventually it did so, as part of the Originals series. On comparing the two sets, made at roughly the same time, one is struck by one startling contrast in approach. On the Muti recording we are presented with a sound picture suggesting a theatrical ambience and a performance to accompany it that depends on grand, opera-house gestures. By contrast DG and Abbado opt for a more confined acoustic and a much more intimate performance. In their crucial Act 1 duet, Cappuccilli and Verrett seem to be communing with themselves and with us in the privacy of our home; Milnes and Cossotto on EMI are more extrovert, directing their interpretations to the mid-stalls. As between these principals, Cappuccilli has a better focused tone than Milnes and the Italian baritone gives us a more haunted, subtle portrayal of the Thane. Verrett matches him in nuance, but vocally she is no match for Cossotto's Italianate tone and brio for Muti. As for the rest, Ghiaurov is to be preferred, as Banquo, to Raimondi (EMI); honours are equal between the two starry Macduffs.

Abbado just has the edge over Muti because of the slight superiority of his La Scala forces over their British counterparts, while the DG recording offers us marginally more detail. Don't entirely rule out of the equation the 1959 Leinsdorf/RCA set where Rysanek's superior singing and acting and Warren's compelling Macbeth remain in the frame; so even more do Nilsson and Taddei (best of all Macbeths) on the 1964 Schippers/Decca set, an arresting performance despite minor excisions. But a newcomer won't find much fault with this Abbado set, scrupulously prepared, executed and recorded.

Verdi Macbeth.
Sherrill Milnes *bar* Macbeth
Fiorenza Cossotto *mez* Lady Macbeth
Ruggero Raimondi *bass* Banquo
José Carreras *ten* Macduff
Giuliano Bernardi *ten* Malcolm
Carlo del Bosco *bass* Doctor
Leslie Fyson *bar* Servant
Neilson Taylor *bar* Herald
John Noble *bass* Assassin
Maria Borgato *mez* Lady-in-waiting
Ambrosian Opera Chorus; New Philharmonic Orchestra / Riccardo Muti.
EMI Ⓜ Ⓓ CMS7 64339-2 (two discs: 151 minutes: ADD). Recorded 1976.

Since it was first reissued on CD at full price in 1986, this set has shed a disc and is here available at mid price, but at the severe cost of leaving out the Appendix that included numbers from the first version excluded by Verdi on revision. That's a thousand pities because it thus takes away, at a stroke, one of this version's main advantages over its close rivals. Nevertheless, what remains is a vivid, exciting traversal of this ever-original score, though not one that can always be easily placed above its rivals. The conducting of the youthful Muti is tauter and more histrionic (sometimes to the point of being vulgar) even than Abbado's, which has always been its main rival with Abbado tending to probe deeper into the soul of the Macbeths. At no point does Muti allow tension to slacken nor does he indulge in the frequent eccentricities of Sinopoli (Philips). There is no weakness among the set's principals. Cossotto remains just about the most idiomatic of Ladies on disc and, apart from one or two moments of strain at the top, encompasses the role with full tone and biting diction – in both respects superior to Verrett (DG). Nilsson (Schippers/Decca) is the type of soprano Verdi intended for the role, but she is not as convincing as Cossotto as the maladjusted 'heroine'.

As Macbeth all four baritones are, in their varied ways, interesting, but Milnes's interpretation is more externalized than that of Cappuccilli (Abbado) or the alert and intelligent Taddei (Schippers), an ideal interpreter. Carreras is the most eloquent of the Macduffs ("Ah, la paterna mana" a model of the genre). There's not much to choose among the three excellent basses who sing Banquo, nor among the excellent orchestras. The EMI recording is at times too reverberant, the Abbado a shade too close and overbearing. At mid price the Muti represents very good value and the performance is in any case close to being the most persuasive. It is marginally to be preferred to the (spaciously recorded) mid-price Decca since Schippers sanctioned disfiguring cuts. However, Taddei is such a superb Macbeth that many collectors would be loath to be without that version.

Verdi Macbeth.

Enzo Mascherini *bar* Macbeth
Maria Callas *sop* Lady Macbeth
Italo Tajo *bass* Banquo
Gino Penno *ten* Macduff
Luciano della Pergola *ten* Malcolm
Dario Caselli *bass* Doctor
Attilio Barbesi *bass* Servant
Ivo Vincò *bass* Herald
Mario Tommasini *bass* Assassin
Angela Vercelli *mez* Lady-in-waiting
Chorus and Orchestra of La Scala, Milan / Victor de Sabata.
EMI mono Ⓜ Ⓒ CMS7 64944-2 (two discs: 139 minutes: ADD). Notes, text and translation included. Recorded at a performance in La Scala, Milan on December 7th, 1952.

Lady Macbeth, or "Lady" as Verdi so endearingly called her, was a role Callas was born to play. Indeed, there are those who believe that this performance, recorded live on the opening night of the 1952-3 La Scala season, is one of the great representative performances of her career. That is not a judgement to unreservedly go along with. A great representative performance requires a coming together of all the elements: not only within the reading itself but of the various contingent details. And on both counts this – in many ways revelatory – La Scala recording is seriously flawed.

The recording itself is a problem, though not in the end an insurmountable one. As always, the ear adjusts. Once past the opening scenes, it is possible increasingly to discount vagaries of vocal and instrumental balance. The ear adjusts even to the troublesome shadows thrown over the performance by an unusual amount of pre- and post-echo. If there is real frustration it comes in a short section of the Sleepwalking scene when the sound is fogged by what seems like indifferent radio reception. On the other hand, there is none of the overloading or distortion in high frequencies that we have in the Mad scene in Callas's famous live 1955 EMI Berlin recording of *Lucia* (see the review under Donizetti).

It has often been said that a Callas/Gobbi studio version of *Macbeth* was one of the century's great unmade recordings. Though Gobbi had recorded Macbeth's Act 4 lament, "Pietà, rispetto, amore" for HMV in 1950, it was several more years before he completed his study of a role he felt distinctly challenged by. ("Highly dramatic declamation, tessitura of an almost giddy height" as he put it in his autobiography, *My Life* – Macdonald and Jane: 1979.) La Scala's Macbeth, Enzo Mascherini, is barely adequate. (Lady Macbeth's "Leave all the rest to me" seems at the time like a production note, an injunction from Callas herself as well as from the character she is playing.) That said, the portrait gathers power as the drama unfolds. The Banquo, Italo Tajo, also makes steady progress after a desperately uncertain start.

The other key collaborator in the La Scala production is the conductor, Victor de Sabata. Much of his conducting is superb. In particular, there is the way scenes build, taking on weight and fire at nodal points. He makes cuts in the score but they are usually strategic cuts. (The pacing of the Banquet scene is effectively tightened by a one-verse-only start to Lady Macbeth's drinking song.) It is also marvellous to have the Act 3 ballet music, to which Verdi attached considerable importance, included in so purposeful a reading.

There are, however, miscalculations. There is a curiously muzzy, unfocused feel about the crucial hushed colloquy after the murder. Worse, there is the very rapid speed adopted by de Sabata and Callas in the Sleepwalking scene. True, the tempo is only marginally quicker than the printed metronome mark, but the metronome mark itself is clearly too fast. The result is a mere sketch, a fleeting impression of the scene. This in turn means there is no real moment of catharsis in the opera's (otherwise perilously banal) denouement. Callas's later studio recording of the Sleepwalking scene, conducted by Rescigno and produced by Walter Legge (also on EMI), is much to be preferred. (As Callas later acknowledged, Legge's insistence on a completely new take after an apparently perfect first-time effort turned a technically secure performance into a genuinely penetrating one, psychologically.)

This unforgettable account of that scene is the recital disc's one claim to indispensability. In the two other scenes the 1952 live performance is much to be preferred. In the first place, there is the commanding sweep of the whole – Callas's Lady Macbeth determining everything from her first moments, where majesty and brooding power are attended by a viper's power to strike and wound, through to the traumas of the Banquet scene where Lady Macbeth is both the dauntless hostess and urgently confiding psychotherapist. And then there are the telling details. Above all, they come in Act 2 in a supreme account of "La luce langue" which far outshines what Callas was later to give us, out of context, on the Rescigno disc. The text of "La luce langue" is more or less Verdi's own, closely based on words Macbeth utters in the original play ("Light thickens; and the crow / Makes wing to th' rooky wood"). The music is also new; it dates from the 1865 revision. Here, indeed, we have Callas at her greatest. "An eagle among chickens" is how Julian Budden describes the revised scene, sitting, as it does, in the midst of the 1847 original. On this recording Callas, too, is an eagle among chickens.

Verdi Macbeth.

Leo Nucci *bar* Macbeth
Shirley Verrett *mez* Lady Macbeth
Samuel Ramey *bass* Banquo
Veriano Luchetti *ten* Macduff
Antonio Barasorda *ten* Malcolm
Serio Fontana *bass* Doctor
Gianfranco Casarini *bass* Servant
Giuseppe Morresi *bass* Herald
Gastone Sarti *bar* Assassin
Anna Caterina Antonacci *sop* Lady-in-waiting
Chorus and Orchestra of the Teatro Comunale, Bologna / Riccardo Chailly.
Film Director: **Claude D'Anna.**
Decca Ⓕ 🔲 071 422-3DH (140 minutes). Recorded 1986.

Claude D'Anna, who directed this film, certainly has a lively, imaginative mind – the idea of having Macduff and the exiles perform their scene at the funeral of Macbeth's family is truly inspired – but too often the results come perilously close to Monty Python antics, as in the treatment of the witches and Macbeth's banquet. At any moment you expect a bearded Palin or Jones to pop up on the screen. Even more troubling is to have singers' voices dubbed onto actors' miming. When most of us have such a clear idea of what Ramey looks like, it is disorientating to see another face when listening to the familiar tones, although it has to be said that great care has been taken, with a single exception, over lip synchronization. That exception is Verrett, who cannot have taken kindly to the process. Nor does she often suggest Lady Macbeth's fanaticism caused by her distracted mind. Nucci is by far the most convincing performer on all counts, even if he is inclined to force his voice in attempting dramatic effects.

In spite of these reservations, the performance generates a degree of tension, by virtue of the dark-hued unity D'Anna and Chailly impose on the piece, very much in sympathy with the *tinta* of the music ... and what music: any chance to renew acquaintance with this extraordinary score is to be welcomed. So much in advance of its time, so subtly tailored to the feeling of the play it remains, for all its many rivals, underrated in the canon, and Chailly is expert at exploring its originality. The picture and sound are as expertly managed as always with Decca, and even the slight reverberation (the recording was made in a Bologna church) seems appropriate in this context.

Verdi I masnadieri.

Montserrat Caballé *sop* Amalia
Carlo Bergonzi *ten* Carlo
Piero Cappuccilli *bar* Francesco
Ruggero Raimondi *bass* Massimiliano
John Sandor *ten* Arminio
Maurizio Mazzieri *bass* Moser
William Elvin *bar* Rolla
Ambrosian Singers; New Philharmonia Orchestra / Lamberto Gardelli.
Philips Ⓜ ① 422 423-2PM2 (two discs: 127 minutes: ADD). Notes, text and translation included. Recorded 1974.

Musically this is surely among the best of those operas mostly conducted by Gardelli, which were discoveries for many of us when they first appeared on LP. Dramatically it is harder to accept, and only by the most lax of aesthetic codes could it be called an artistic success: its material includes some extreme states of mind for which Verdi's music was not at that time ready. Still, if we are willing to take seriously those parts of the opera in which the music does give reality to the drama and for the rest have it with a pinch of salt and enjoy the tunes, then *I masnadieri* becomes a valued addition to the Verdi repertory. Rather as with *La battaglia di Legnano* (reviewed above) there is some discrepancy between the rumbustious plot and the mainspring of emotion. Here the drama is crammed full of action, and the ostensible subject is the band of brigands, or thugs, with whom the hero becomes involved; yet what touches the heart of the composer (to judge from his music) is the unhappiness of separation and the plight of a cruelly treated old man. So if we take the mood from the Overture, it is defined in the sad cello solo and then the yearning phrases for the violins. Similarly, the eloquently sighing prelude to Act 2 helps to guide a listener towards the quieter, more personal part as what really matters, with the brigands' choruses and some of the more melodramatic developments of the plot being of relatively nominal interest only.

Not long after this first recording, there appeared another, on Decca, under Richard Bonynge whose somewhat more imaginative handling of the score showed that there was more to it than even this fine performance under Gardelli had suggested. However, as far as the singing is concerned this Philips version is generally preferable. Bergonzi's clean-cut line is always a pleasure, and Caballé brings warmth, accomplishment and conviction to the difficult role first sung by Jenny Lind. Cappuccilli has some fine and some uneven tones, but it would need an Amato, Gobbi or Tibbett to bring the character to effective life. Particularly impressive is Raimondi, then with more of the deep bass in his voice than later in his career; it can be no easy task to sing magnificently while playing an old man who is being starved to death, and he succeeds remarkably well. His utterances from underground set a problem for the producer and staff; not quite happily solved perhaps, but generally the recorded sound is fine, as is the playing of the Philharmonia Orchestra. The Ambrosians sing the music of the Masnadieri with relish, telling in waltz time of their pleasure in the cries of mothers and orphans, and in the most genial of tunes attesting, in the English translation, that "Plunder, rape, arson, killing, for us are pastimes, sheer amusements".

Verdi Nabucco.
Tito Gobbi *bar* Nabucco
Bruno Prevedi *ten* Ismaele
Carlo Cava *bass* Zaccaria
Elena Souliotis *sop* Abigaille
Dora Carral *sop* Fenena
Anna d'Auria *sop* Anna
Giovanni Foiani *bass* High Priest of Baal
Walter Kräutler *ten* Abdallo
Vienna State Opera Chorus; Vienna Opera Orchestra / Lamberto Gardelli.
Decca Ⓟ Ⓛ 417 407-2DH2 (two discs: 121 minutes: ADD). Notes, text and translation included. Recorded 1965.

Thirty-three years have hardly lessened the excitement of listening to this vigorous, closely-knit performance. One realizes why we were all amazed by Souliotis's account of the role of Abigaille. Her singing seizes you by the throat through its raw depiction of malice and through its youthful, uninhibited power. With the benefit of hindsight one can hear how a voice treated so carelessly and unstintingly could not last long, and so it was to be; but we should be glad for the brightness of the meteor while it flashed all too briefly through the operatic firmament. As an interpretation, her Abigaille seems a little coarse set beside the refinements shown by Scotto for Muti on EMI, a set that must surely appear on CD. However, Suliotis can manage by nature what Scotto has to conjure up by art, and she is certainly a subtler artist than Dimitrova on the wayward Sinopoli/DG version.

Gobbi, here nearing the end of his illustrious career, remains the most convincing interpreter on record of the crazed king. The voice may have become a shade hard and uningratiating, but his use of Italian and his colouring of his tone, finally his pathos, are certainly not rivalled by Cappuccilli (Sinopoli). Carlo Cava exudes implacable fury as old Zaccaria, but he is inclined to go through his tone at *forte*. Prevedi is more than adequate as Ismaele, Carral less than adequate as Fenena (here DG score with Valentini Terrani).

One of the main assets of the Decca remains Gardelli's prompt, unfussy, yet thrillingly delivered interpretation, clearly conveyed to his excellent Viennese forces. It is much more steadily and convincingly paced than Sinopoli's reading. The recording is forward and has plenty of presence, but now sounds a little boxy beside the greater spaciousness of the DG. But the panache of the Decca enterprise silences criticism (except when the minute cuts in Nabucco's part are conceived). It is a pleasure to hear the bold inspiration of Verdi's first triumph conveyed with such conviction. Listen to the First Act finale and you will be won over to the set as an entity.

Verdi Nabucco.
Renato Bruson *bar* Nabucco
Ottavio Garaventa *ten* Ismaele
Dimiter Petkov *bass* Zaccaria
Ghena Dimitrova *sop* Abigaille
Bruna Baglioni *mez* Fenena
Giovanni di Rocco *sop* Anna
Francesco Ellero d'Artegna *bass* High Priest of Baal
Aronne Ceroni *ten* Abdallo

Chorus and Orchestra of Verona Arena / Maurizio Arena.
Stage/Video Director: **Renato Giaccheri.**
NVC Arts ⬜⬜ 0630-19390-3 (140 minutes). Recorded 1981.

This is an archetypal opera for the Arena at Verona, and its vast stage is here used cleverly to suggest, in monolithic structures, the biblical setting. The costumes are of a magnificence to match, larger than life but so is the whole effort. Bruson is ideal casting in the title-part. His keenly focused baritone and his gift for projecting an unstable yet formidable character such as Nabucco are a match for Verdi's concept. He admirably suggests the different facets of this complex character: his violence, sense of terror, eventually love, and offers an unforgettable account of his "Dio de Giuda" solo. Dimitrova, as the evil Abigaille, one of her best roles, matches him decibel for decibel, gesture for gesture, *bel canto* nicely allied to raw power, Petkov is a disappointing Zaccaria, and smaller roles are cast no more than adequately. Arena leads a well-co-ordinated account of the score and gives his singers secure support. The chorus, important here, sing magnificently. The picture and sound are acceptable and there are subtitles.

Verdi Oberto, Conte di San Bonifaco.

Samuel Ramey *bass* Oberto
Maria Gulegina *sop* Leonora
Stuart Neill *ten* Riccardo
Violeta Urmana *mez* Cuniza
Sara Fulgoni *mez* Imelda
London Voices; Academy of St Martin in the Fields / Sir Neville Marriner.
Philips Ⓟ Ⓓ 454 472-2PH2 (two discs: 149 minutes: DDD). Notes, text and translation included. Recorded 1996.

An exciting cast, suitably vigorous conducting and a lifelike recording make this a spectacular addition to Philips's repertory of Young Verdi, as the company now call the series. The composer's compositional technique may have been in a fairly undeveloped state in 1839 but when a performance of his first opera is as convincing as this, one hears more than a few pre-echoes of glories in the making. In its best moments the inspiration is already presaging a talent, a genius for original thought and construction beyond those of Bellini and Donizetti, while encompassing the best of what they had to offer. By adding as appendices three numbers Verdi wrote for later revivals and never recorded before, Philips put us further in their debt.

Gulegina is thought to be the best *spinto* of the day, and she confirms that opinion here in singing that suggests the dramatic conviction of Vishnevskaya in her prime. Like her great predecessor she shirks nothing in projecting the emotions of the character she is portraying. Her tone is big and vibrant, her feeling for the shape of Verdian phrase, as at "Misero padre mio!" in the work's finale, instinctive. Only the colouring and shading of tone and words is rudimentary, a common fault today. The same failing slightly, but only slightly, detracts from the arresting impression made by the Lithuanian mezzo, Violeta Urmana, in the part of Cuniza. The operatic world seems to be bursting with exciting mezzos these days. Following on Bartoli, Larmore, Kasarova and Sara Mingardo (a Handelian second to none), Urmana can meet that challenge, her sappy, forthright tone gratefully recalling that of Cossotto. She comes into her own in the additional aria Verdi wrote for Milan, but in her less prominent contributions to the work proper she already makes a deep impression through her confident and spirited delivery.

Ramey is well suited to the title part, portraying the grieving, vengeful father to the life, imperiously declaiming recitative, singing *cantabile* passages in rich, finely shaped phraseology. The American tenor, Stuart Neill, rather in the school of Chris Merritt with the advantages and disadvantages that suggests, sings rousingly but often too loudly as the villain, Riccardo. He imitates the Italian tenor style successfully but when you go back to the real thing, in Bergonzi's portrayal on the 1983 Gardelli/Orfeo set, you hear what's missing in Neill's otherwise estimable contribution. Marriner conducts a direct, forward-moving interpretation that matches the raw energy in the score. His old orchestra offer playing of admirable thrust and delicacy as required. The London Voices sound properly Italianate. In his otherwise informative notes, Roger Parker is obviously unaware that there are three rather than two additional pieces in the Appendix. As it happens, the one he omits to mention, a duet found at the end of the Autograph, "Nel cangiar di sorte infida", is the most interesting, recalling the Bellini of "Mira, o Norma". It is gratifyingly voiced by Gulegina and Urmana whose voices smoothly intertwine. Cuniza's aria, written for Milan in 1840, is brought vividly to life by Urmana though it is a dullish piece. By contrast the Act 1 duet for Riccardo and Cuniza composed for the same performance shows Verdi already extending his melodic and harmonic skills. Urmana and Neill sing it with feeling.

The recording deserves and shall have a paragraph to itself. When you began listening you will hear the ideal balance and natural sound so often missing in so many opera sets. It makes you wonder if Erik Smith had been recalled to the Philips colours. Indeed he had and with the expected results. Nothing here of added resonance or distanced soloists, just a sense that one is in a good seat in the stalls and with enough attempt at moving the singers to simulate a live performance.

Verdi Otello.

Plácido Domingo *ten* Otello
Cheryl Studer *sop* Desdemona
Sergei Leiferkus *bar* Iago
Ramon Vargan *ten* Cassio
Michael Schade *ten* Roderigo
Denyce Graves *mez* Emilia
Ildebrando d'Arcangelo *bass* Lodovico
Giacomo Prestia *bass-bar* Montano
Philippe Duminy *bass* Herald
Hauts-de-Seine Maîtrise;
Chorus and Orchestra of the Opera-Bastille, Paris / Myung-Whun Chung.
DG Ⓔ Ⓓ 439 805-2GH2 (two discs: 132 minutes: DDD). Notes, text and translation included.
Recorded 1993.

Just as *Othello* is a difficult play to bring off in the theatre, so *Otello* is a difficult opera to bring off out of it. For some years Domingo has been, on stage, the greatest Otello of our age. On record, though, he has had less success. The 1978 RCA set, conducted by Levine, was frankly a trial run. After this he was caught in the toils of a Zeffirelli film, strangely conducted by Maazel, the oddly muted soundtrack of which was issued by EMI. Both sets are still in the catalogue though neither is recommendable, not least because neither of the Iagos – Sherrill Milnes for Levine or Justino Diaz for Maazel – is up to much technically or theatrically. Leiferkus is both.

Leiferkus and Domingo have worked closely together in the theatre; and it shows in scene after scene – nowhere more so than in the crucial sequence in Act 2 where Otello so rapidly ingests Iago's lethal poison. By bringing into the recording studio the feel and experience of a stage performance – meticulous study subtly modified by the improvised charge of the moment – both singers help defy the jinx that so often afflicts *Otello* on record. Leiferkus is not a great colourist. If there is a point at which he seems to fall short of the letter of Verdi's score (or, rather, Giulio Ricordi's Production Book) it is when he fails to make sufficient distinction between Iago's voice and the imagined voice of Cassio in the dream narrative, "Era la notte". Toscanini's Iago, Giuseppe Valdengo, whom Leiferkus to some extent resembles, is rather more effective here. Yet listen to Leiferkus's phrasing of Cassio's first murmurings and you will hear how effortlessly he meets Verdi's technically demanding insistence on the elision of two sentences, "cauti vegliamo" hypnotically grafted on to the word "l'estasi": natural caution subverted by passion.

The skill of Leiferkus's performance is rooted in voice and technique: clear diction, a disciplined rhythmic sense and a mastery of all ornament down to the most mordant of mordents. Above all, he is always there (usually stage right in this recording), steely-voiced, rabbiting obsessively on. We even hear his crucial interventions in the great Act 3 *concertato*. This is something of a miracle, given the fact that Iago's plotting goes by the board in just about every recording except the RCA/Toscanini and the superbly 'staged' 1961 Decca production, masterminded by Culshaw and Karajan. (Or, perhaps more correctly, by Culshaw; in his 1973 EMI remake Karajan cuts the section in question!)

Otello is a role a tenor must live with for years, hoping the voice will retain its flexibility and sheen whilst at the same time acquiring fresh colours with which to meet new demands, new insights. This is Domingo's great achievement. He is in superb voice on this recording; the sound seems golden as never before. Yet at the same time, it is a voice that is being more astutely deployed. To take that cruellest of all challenges to a studio-bound Otello, the great Act 3 soliloquy "Dio! mi potevi", Domingo's performance is here simpler, more inward, more intense. It isn't, as he told one of DG's attendant journalists, his slowest performance to date. The Maazel is slower than this, a kind of ritual embalming. Rather, it is as though Domingo has rethought the role for the microphone, much as a great actor might adapt his Othello for the radio, or a singer might shift from the broad brush-strokes of theatre performance to the keener disciplines of Lieder-singing. It helps, perhaps, that Domingo's voice has darkened, winning back some of its russet baritonal colourings. But in the end the genius of the performance lies in its ability to distil. Nowhere is this more evident than in the death scene itself. On the Maazel recording the final "morta!" is turned into a fermata, an egregiously self-contained dying fall. Here it is more or less in time, very simple, unerringly 'placed', no longer 'acted'. And ten times more effective.

Of course, Domingo is never quite as trumpet-toned as Martinelli. Nor does he attempt to portray Otello as a stricken visionary after the manner of Jon Vickers with Serafin in 1960 or more symbiotically, with Karajan in 1973. In the later of those recordings, at the moment where Otello twice intones the name of the dead Desdemona, Vickers's voice takes on a quality such as we haven't heard before – the voice of a man who is, almost literally, beside himself with grief. The problem is that away from these sublime manifestations of Vickers's art this Berlin-made EMI set too often slumps back into the worst kind of German bombast. Chung's conducting, by contrast, is almost disarmingly vital. Verdi's scoring is more Gallic than Germanic (though less so than the scoring of *Falstaff*). The score sounds very brilliant in the hands of the excellent Opera-Bastille orchestra, and, in Act 4, very beautiful. That said, Chung's conducting has its limitations. He seems especially wary of those emotional depths – expanses, what you will – that sit in the score's main shipping-lane like

Scylla and Charybdis, wrecking those who try to sail briskly by, dragging under those who are tempted to linger too long. No one steers a better course than Serafin on RCA (Toscanini, too, who gets better orchestral playing than Serafin). Verdi's score is littered with restraining marks. Iago's "Credo" is marked *Allegro sostenuto*; yet Chung goes quickly, staying in tempo at the fanfares of fig. E, and hustling Leiferkus. Otello's "Ora e per sempre" is marked *assai ritenuto* and *larga la frase*; Chung isn't unduly quick, but the rhythmic infrastructure is muddled and unclear. The oath-swearing "Si, pel ciel" has a splendid swing to it, but the marking is *molto sostenuto*. And so on. And yet, Chung's freshness is all gain. He is a master of the big ensemble, and the line of an act. Tension rarely slackens. Where it does the mixing and matching of takes is probably to blame.

If there are reservations creeping in about some of the conducting, the reverse is the case with Cheryl Studer's Desdemona. Her very ubiquity sows doubt in the critic's mind and it is tempting to look for faults: a less than perfectly sounded top A flat near the start of the love duet, and a distinctly uncertain one at the end of the "Ave Maria". (And for real nigglers, a break in the line in the love duet at "sofferti e le catene" – "not the kind of thing you'd catch Margaret Price doing, dear".) And yet Studer's is a carefully drawn portrait of a chaste and sober-suited lady. Perhaps Verdi had a sweeter-voiced singer in mind for this paragon of "goodness, resignation, and self-sacrifice" (Verdi's words, not Shakespeare's). Studer's oboe tones keep us at a certain distance. There is little of Rysanek's warmth and vulnerability (Serafin) and yet you will look in vain for a better Desdemona. What's more, Studer is a singer who can single-mindedly focus the drama afresh, as she does in Act 3.

DG's recording is clear and unfussy and satisfyingly varied; Studer, in particular, is much helped by the beautifully open acoustic the engineers provide for the closing act. It is not a SonicStage production after the manner of the Culshaw/Karajan with its grandstand view of the orchestra and the characters playing out the drama, as they do in Shakespeare, under Heaven's vault. But, then, no recording matches that. Despite some occasionally less than enthralling singing of the *comprimario* roles, this is undoubtedly the best *Otello* the gramophone has given us since 1960. It also happens to be the first time on record that a great Otello at the height of his powers has been successfully caught in the context of a recording that can itself be generally considered worthy of the event, musically and technically.

Verdi Otello.
Jon Vickers *ten* Otello
Leonie Rysanek *sop* Desdemona
Tito Gobbi *bar* Iago
Florindo Andreolli *ten* Cassio
Mario Carlin *ten* Roderigo
Miriam Pirazzini *mez* Emilia
Ferrucio Mazzoli *bass* Lodovico
Franco Calabrese *bass.* Montano
Robert Kerns *bar* Herald
Rome Opera Chorus and Orchestra / Tullio Serafin.
RCA ⓜ ① GD81969 (two discs: 144 minutes: ADD). Text and translation included. Recorded 1960.

BBC RADIO 3
90-93 FM

This set has always been somewhat underrated. Since RCA have remastered it to such excellent effect on CD, a reassessment in its favour seems the more imperative. In terms of sound alone it stands up very well to its more modern rivals; indeed it is certainly preferable to the 1978 RCA set under Levine or to the 1985 EMI under Maazel. It has more sense of a real performance to it with an ideal balance between voices and orchestra. But then Richard Mohr was a very experienced producer, who even moved his singers about in an appropriate way to describe the action. Without the nasty side breaks on LP, we can appreciate even better the consistency of the recording and, of course, of Serafin's unfussy conducting, not as immediately exciting as Maazel's could be, but yielding up its benefits over the long span. It is true that the Rome Opera Orchestra and Chorus do not always sound totally unanimous but you do feel they have the music in their bones.

Vickers may not be quite such an anguished, totally involved Moor as he was later to become in Karajan's second version (EMI), but here he is in securer voice and his singing as such comes close to some kind of Otello ideal, more metallic and heroic than Domingo's (for Levine, Maazel and Chung) though not necessarily more sensitive than that of the younger tenor. Gobbi's Iago remains irreplaceable – except possibly by Valdengo's on the Toscanini. His imagining of the part in purely vocal terms is something of a classic, varied in diction and tone, alert in mind so that a presence comes before us at home: listen to him in the recitative after the *Credo* – "aiuto Satana" indeed. The whole scene following with Vickers is an object-lesson in vocal acting. Rysanek isn't everyone's first choice as Desdemona; she isn't completely happy in her Italian phraseology or ideally steady. In compensation she sings with a gentleness and tender pathos that many Italian sopranos cannot match – listen to "dammi la dolce e lieta parola" in the Second Act *concertato*.

So this version is certainly competitive, particularly at mid price. An outright choice is clearly impossible, with so many mid-price rivals, but collectors will certainly want this one, particularly for Gobbi's Iago and for the earlier of Vickers's tragic portrayals of the tormented Moor.

Verdi Otello.

Ramon Vinay *ten* Otello
Herva Nelli *sop* Desdemona
Giuseppe Valdengo *bar* Iago
Virginio Assandri *ten* Cassio
Leslie Chabay *ten* Roderigo
Nan Merriman *mez* Emilia
Nicola Moscona *bass* Lodovico
Arthur Newman *bass* Montano
NBC Chorus and Symphony Orchestra / Arturo Toscanini.
RCA Victor Gold Seal mono Ⓜ ① GD60302 (two discs: 125 minutes: ADD). Recorded from
broadcast performances on December 6th and 13th, 1947.

One of the century's legendary achievements on record confirms its reputation on this well-managed
reissue. Here Toscanini's blazing intensity, his full comprehension of every facet of the score are
evident throughout. In the very first scene the crackling of the fire in "Fuoco di gioia", the bubbling
strings as illustration of Cassio getting drunk, the complete fidelity to the score of Valdengo's Iago,
tell of long preparation and immediately excite the ear. They are but harbingers of the legendary
maestro's total command and of his wholehearted empathy with the opera's faultless structure and
deep-felt emotions, all achieved within correct tempos and with an overview of the acts, each of which
courses tautly to its inevitable conclusion. Just one little detail – the stab of pain in the orchestra at
Otello's first thought of jealousy, before "Perchè fai tale inchiesti" – shows just how intimately
Toscanini knows his music; that and so much else left uncovered by other conductors sets him far
above all, except his disciple Panizza on the equally satisfying Metropolitan performance on Music
& Arts.

The attack and dedication of chorus and orchestra are apparent throughout; so is the discipline and
textural clarity on all sides. Nothing escapes Toscanini, yet at the same time nothing obtrudes in a
manner that calls attention to itself – unless it be the conductor's groans and encouragement now
more audible in the digital transfer. The sound remains dry but somehow this very close, confined
quality accords with the work's own claustrophobic quality – if only Otello had gone out into the
open air and thought about the reality of the evidence before him, he might not have been so easily
caught up in Iago's web of deceit. Valdengo's Iago continues to put all but Gobbi's for Serafin and
Tibbett's for Panizza, in the shade. His light, almost elegant and seemingly cheerful tone, his mordant,
sinister delivery of the *Credo*, his insinuating and perfectly accurate delivery of the imagined Dream
all tell of his willingness to follow Toscanini's guidance, for he never sang so well for anyone else. This
is a faultless performance. So, in terms of interpretation, is Vinay's Otello – the tormented, fearsomely
commanding Moor to the life. It's only when you compare his too baritonal tone with Martinelli's
(Panizza) or Pavarotti's incisive, Italianate delivery (Solti) or Domingo's absolute security (Levine)
that Vinay's thicker tone and the throb in it seem a shade below an ideal; but no one conveys better
the sense of Otello's world falling about him. Nelli always turns out to be more satisfying than one
expects, because her sincerity of purpose, her accuracy and her true tone compensate for a slightly
pallid reading of Desdemona's thoughts and feelings. Certainly she makes more of the text than
Dame Kiri Te Kanawa (Solti/Decca) and often sings with a finer line, while missing Rethberg's
warmth on the Panizza version – and indeed the sense of suffering heard from Scotto (Chung and
Levine). The smaller roles are all worthily taken.

Any incidental drawback should not prevent anyone hearing this overwhelming interpretation.
Once the vivid storm is launched it is impossible to leave the performance until the tragic, stricken
figure of Otello falls lifeless by his wronged wife's side: Toscanini identifies so sympathetically with
the human condition, as did Verdi himself – and it is from Verdi, at whose feet he sat, that Toscanini
learnt his trade.

Verdi Otello.

Mario del Monaco *ten* Otello
Rosanna Carteri *sop* Desdemona
Renato Capecchi *bar* Iago
Gino Mattera *ten* Cassio
Athos Cesarini *ten* Roderigo
Luisella Ciaffi *mez* Emilia
Plinio Clabassi *bass* Lodovico
Nestore Catalani *bass* Montano
Bruno Cioni *bass* Herald
Chorus and Orchestra of RAI, Milan / Tullio Serafin. *Director:* **Franco Enriquez.**
Bel Canto Society Ⓕ ⚏ BCS0004 (134 minutes). Filmed in 1958.

As with other Bel Canto Society issues, the films made in the studio for television have to be
distinguished from those made, sometimes on location, for the cinema. *Otello*, directed by Franco

Enriquez (who later gained fame at Glyndebourne), was in the former category and ranks among the most successful video representations of this work. It has an exemplary cast, with the grossly underrated Rosanna Carteri as the heroine. Enriquez uses subtle lighting to make the most of black and white and to portray the dark doings of the plot. His close-up technique never worries Carteri who sings a glorious, full-throated, tender Desdemona. Her portrayal breathes heartbreaking sincerity and is sung with the natural, easy, warm Italian tone now in such scarce supply. You really can't fault her singing and her portrayal is deeply moving on every level. As her Otello, del Monaco is more sensitive than on either of his audio-only recordings and suggests, vocally and dramatically, all the Moor's outer power and inner agony, using his piercing eyes to unerring effect. One is also reminded that he was the best-equipped tenor ever to essay the part. Capecchi, more familiar in *buffo* roles and in Mozart, proves a wholly plausible Iago, bluff, charming, insinuating. Studio confines sometimes inhibit the truth of the outside scenes, but rather this than Zeffirelli's overdone film.

Verdi Rigoletto.

Robert Merrill *bar* Rigoletto
Anna Moffo *sop* Gilda
Alfredo Kraus *ten* Duke
Ezio Flagello *bass* Sparafucile
Rosalind Elias *mez* Maddalena
David Ward *bass* Monterone
Anna di Stasio *mez* Giovanna
Piero De Palma *ten* Borsa
Robert Kerns *bar* Marullo
Corinna Vozza *mez* Countess Ceprano
Marino Rinaudo *bass* Count Ceprano
Tina Toscano *sop* Page
RCA Italiana Chorus and Orchestra / Sir Georg Solti.
RCA Victor Ⓜ Ⓒ GD86506 (two discs: 113 minutes: ADD). Text and translation included. Recorded 1963.

This has always been a competitive set, and it remains so at mid price. Solti may drive hard at times but there's no doubting the vivid, histrionic quality of his conducting. Alfredo Kraus is a fine, fiery Duke, in every way distinguished; he is certainly preferable to his older self elsewhere. Merrill isn't such a compelling artist but he is a strong, honest interpreter of the role, who never does much wrong without quite impressing himself on the mind's eye and ear as does Gobbi for Serafin (on EMI, reviewed below). Moffo is quite a touching Gilda, but not so individual, to say the least, as Callas (Serafin) or indeed Cotrubas (Giulini on DG), and vocally Sutherland's inferior (Bonynge on Decca), but in some ways her simple reading of the role is preferable to any of these. Support is variable. This set is not only complete but also gives the score exactly as Verdi wrote it, which allows us to hear Verdi's cadenzas rather than nineteenth-century amendments. The recording is rather boomy and blatant. In absolute terms this couldn't be recommended above the full-price Serafin, Giulini or indeed Sinopoli (Philips) versions, but it has much to offer.

Verdi Rigoletto.

Eduard Tumagian *bar* Rigoletto
Alida Ferrarini *sop* Gilda
Yordi Ramiro *ten* Duke
Josef Spaček *bass* Sparafucile
Jitka Saparová *mez* Maddalena
Ladislav Neshyba *bass* Monterone
Alžbeta Michalková *mez* Giovanna
Josef Abel *ten* Borsa
Peter Subert *bar* Marullo
Ivica Neshybová *mez* Countess Ceprano
Robert Szücs *bass* Count Ceprano
Slovak Philharmonic Chorus; Bratislava Radio Symphony Orchestra / Alexander Rahbari.
Naxos Ⓢ Ⓒ 8 660013/4 (two discs: 115 minutes: DDD). Notes and text included. Recorded 1991.

This recording of *Rigoletto* is astonishing value for less than £12. There are no big names in the cast – though the Rigoletto, the Hungarian baritone Eduard Tumagian, has sung leading roles with Muti in Milan – but the absence of big names doesn't stop this being a lucidly thought-through performance, dramatically sensitive, and more than acceptable musically. There used to be a time when it was Cetra who provided the bargains. Indeed, their *Rigoletto* with Taddei, Pagliughi, Ferruccio Tagliavini and Angelo Questa conducting the Turin Radio Orchestra, was a classic in its day. This set isn't quite in that class, and it probably won't be preferred by experienced collectors to the famous Serafin set (full price, despite the ageing 1955 mono recording). Yet the Naxos set is no hole-in-the-corner affair. In the first place, it is extremely well conducted. Persian by birth and Viennese by training, Alexander Rahbari won various conducting prizes in the 1970s and later became one of Karajan's assistants in Salzburg. Under Rahbari the orchestral playing is a cut above what one normally hears from an opera-house pit. The playing is sweet-toned, the rhythms exact and well sprung, the pacing shrewd. Ideally, there would be a slightly more forward placement of the orchestra; you need to play the discs at quite a high level to get a real taste of what is going on.

The weakest of the principals is the Duke. The Mexican tenor, Yordi Ramiro, has to work at the voice to make it at all agreeable or debonair, and the effort shows. Distance lends enchantment to the view in "La donna è mobile", where Ramiro is placed to the right and rather far upstage. On the other hand, he leads the Quartet decisively and with a good deal of eloquence. The Gilda of Alida Ferrarini is occasionally sharp-toned, the sound slightly blanched or pinched, but this is not a criticism that can be consistently levelled. She is often every inch the affecting *ingénue*, and there is quite a good coloratura technique, the trills precise, the vocal lines sympathetically traced. It is typical of the set as a whole that the death scene is affectingly done, neither sour-toned nor crudely histrionic. Tumagian's Rigoletto is more or less unfailingly reliable. The voice is mellow and well focused, yet one senses quickly a growing bitterness in the court scene. He lacks the grand commanding line of the greatest Rigolettos on the final page of "Cortigiani", but "Pari siamo" is sensitively handled. A broader pace at the critical "Il retaggio d'ogni uom m'è tolto, il pianto" would have given the reading even more depth, edging a good performance towards a great one.

There are no real weaknesses in the *comprimario* roles. You expect fine basses from Eastern Europe and there are sterling portrayals of both Monterone and Sparafucile. In the first scene the Borsa sounds as though he has been recorded in a private cubicle, but that is an engineering problem, not a singing one. And though the Maddalena is rather foreign-sounding, she is none the worse for that. Despite what seems to be inexpert mixing in the opening scene, the recording is clear and easy on the ear. If anything it understates things, which is preferable to some of the overmiking that goes on these days. Off-stage contributions are atmospherically handled; only the Page seems unaccountably distant. The booklet doesn't run to an English libretto, but the Italian is included and there is a very serviceable track-by-track synopsis for anyone who doesn't know the story. More importantly, the score is played complete. The only cut, a handful of bars, is the two-voice cadenza at the end of the duet for Gilda and the Duke.

This is not a set, then, that will please operatic name-droppers, but it offers first-rate value for money. Indeed, it is a more cogent *Rigoletto* than several more expensive and more starrily cast versions currently on offer. As a recording, it has the edge technically on older bargain rivals such as the hyper-tense Perlea (on RCA) with Merrill, Peters and Björling or the rather dowdy Molinari-Pradelli on Classics for Pleasure.

Verdi Rigoletto.
   Tito Gobbi *bar* Rigoletto
   Maria Callas *sop* Gilda
   Giuseppe di Stefano *ten* Duke
   Nicola Zaccaria *bass* Sparafucile
   Adriana Lazzarini *mez* Maddalena
   Plinio Clabassi *bass* Monterone
   Giuse Gerbino *mez* Giovanna
   Renato Ercolani *ten* Borsa
   William Dickie *bar* Marullo
   Elvira Galassi *sop* Countess Ceprano
   Carlo Forti *bar* Count Ceprano
   Chorus and Orchestra of La Scala, Milan / Tullio Serafin.
   EMI mono Ⓟ Ⓒ CDS5 56327-2 (two discs: 118 minutes: ADD). Notes, text and translation
   included. Recorded 1955.

That one recording should continue to hold sway over many other attractive comers after 33 years is simply a tribute to Callas, Gobbi, Serafin and Walter Legge. Whatever the merits of its successors, and they are many, no *Rigoletto* has surpassed Gobbi in tonal variety, line, projection of character and understanding of what Rigoletto is about; no Gilda has come anywhere near Callas in meaningful phrasing – listen to the comparative versions of "Caro nome" or "Tutte le feste" on any and each of the sets if you are disbelieving – nor achieved such a careful differentiation of timbre before and after her seduction; no conductor, not even Giulini on DG, though he comes near it, matches Serafin in judging tempo and instrumental detail on a nicety; nor benefited from a chorus and orchestra bred in the tradition of La Scala; no producer has equalled Legge in recording voices rather than the space round them (why won't producers today listen to how truthfully their predecessors caught the actual sound of a voice?). And di Stefano? Well, he may not be so stylish a Duke as Domingo and some others, but the 'face' he gives his singing, and the sheer physical presence he conveys, not to forget his forward diction, are also unique in this opera.

Nothing in this world is perfect, and so there are some small drawbacks here. Serafin sadly makes small cuts in the first Gilda/Rigoletto duet and omits entirely the Duke's cabaletta as used to be practice in the theatre. Gobbi could be said not to have quite the weight of voice ideally called for by a Verdi baritone role; in that he yields to Bruson, who is also an appreciable interpreter of the part (Sinopoli/Philips). Finally, the recording, although immeasurably improved from previous issues of the set, still has one or two places of distortion obviously present on the original tape. In every other way, this remains the classic performance of the opera on record, and one that should be on every Verdi collector's itself.

Verdi Rigoletto.

Ingvar Wixell *bar* Rigoletto, Monterone
Edita Gruberová *sop* Gilda
Luciano Pavarotti *ten* Duke
Ferruccio Furlanetto *bass* Sparafucile
Victoria Vergara *mez* Maddalena
Fedora Barbieri *mez* Giovanna
Remy Corazza *ten* Borsa
Bernd Weikl *bar* Marullo
Kathleen Kuhlmann *mez* Countess Ceprano
Roland Bracht *bass* Count Ceprano
Vienna State Opera Chorus; Vienna Philharmonic Orchestra / Riccardo Chailly.
Stage/Video Director: **Jean-Pierre Ponnelle.**
Decca 📀 071 401-3DH; 💿 071 401-1DH2 (two discs: 116 minutes). Recorded 1983.

Ponnelle's film, made on location in Mantua, is a most imaginative concept, full of atmosphere and colour. We see a really nasty, licentious court and an orgy in the first scene that is frankly lewd while the relationship between Gilda and Rigoletto is near being incestuous. Altogether the visual aspect, both as regards scenery and camerawork, has a startling immediacy that makes one think anew about the characters' relationships and Verdi's reactions to them.

In Wixell's Rigoletto, which he arrestingly doubles with that other wronged father, Monterone, the performance has a dominating, intense protagonist, an interpretation that goes well beyond the customary traditions of acting this part. Although Wixell's baritone may not be exactly Italianate, he uses his voice to stunning effect. Pavarotti consoles us for his conventionally acted Duke by the generosity and brio of his singing. With her pre-Raphaelite curls and pure tone, Gruberová is a touching Gilda, but not quite the protected virgin of Verdi's imagining: something of artifice spoils her acting, though she goes to her death with real feeling. You also sense her agony in the great quartet as she sees the Duke, whom she still loves, wooing Maddalena (the excellent Vergara), and here Ponnelle shows his skills as Gilda and Rigoletto look through a window at the flirtatious couple. Veteran Fedora Barbieri makes something of Giovanni with her venal eyes as she colludes with the Duke entering the Rigoletto establishment. Chailly conducts a strong-limned, unfussy performance of the score (every bar included). Picture and sound are first-rate, so is lip-synch, but there are no subtitles.

Verdi Simon Boccanegra.

Piero Cappuccilli *bar* Simon Boccanegra
Mirella Freni *sop* Amelia
José Carreras *ten* Gabriele
Nicolai Ghiaurov *bass* Fiesco
José van Dam *bass-bar* Paolo
Giovanni Foiani *bass* Pietro
Antonio Savastano *ten* Captain
Maria Fausta Gallamini *sop* Maid
Chorus and Orchestra of La Scala, Milan / Claudio Abbado.
DG The Originals Ⓜ ① 449 752-2GOR2 (two discs: 136 minutes: ADD). Notes, text and translation included. Recorded 1977.

BBC RADIO 3
90-93 FM

In its latest guise, remastered, at mid price, the Abbado has become a gramophone classic, a performance in the studio after a series of performances at La Scala in the Strehler staging, which none of us lucky enough to have caught it on the company's cherished visit to Covent Garden in 1976 is ever likely to forget. The close, slightly claustrophobic recording exactly mirrors the mood of nefarious activities and intrigues following Boccanegra's rise to be Doge of Genoa, he and his lovely daughter victims of the dark deeds round them. In his plebeian being, clement exercise of authority and warm, fatherly love, Simon Boccanegra is made for Cappuccilli who, under Abbado's tutelage, sings it not only *con amore* but with exemplary, delicately tinted tone and unbelievably long-breathed phrasing. As his daughter Amelia, Freni was just entering her quasi-*spinto* phase, and expands her lyric voice easily into the greater demands of this more dramatic role. Similarly heavier duties had not yet tarnished the youthful ardour and sap in the tone of the 30-year-old Carreras. As implacable Fiesco, Ghiaurov exudes vengeful command and van Dam evil machinations as the villain Paolo.

Over all presides Abbado in what remains one of his greatest recordings, alert to every facet of the wondrous score, timing every scene, in an opera tricky to pace, to near-perfection, and in sum bringing theatrical drama into the home. You may prefer this or that aspect of the other sets, but this one should be an essential adornment to any reputable collection of Verdi.

Verdi Simon Boccanegra.
   Tito Gobbi *bar* Simon Boccanegra
   Victoria de los Angeles *sop* Amelia
   Giuseppe Campora *ten* Gabriele
   Boris Christoff *bass* Fiesco
   Walter Monachesi *bar* Paolo
   Paolo Dari *bar* Pietro
   Paolo Caroli *bar* Captain
   Silvia Bertona *mez* Maid
   Chorus and Orchestra of the Rome Opera House / Gabriele Santini.
   EMI mono Ⓜ ① CMS7 63513-2 (two discs: 119 minutes: ADD). Notes, text and translations
   included. Recorded 1957.

BBC RADIO 3
90-93 FM

Simon Boccanegra has had a strange history. Neglected for some 70 years, it was awoken from its long sleep by the kindly kisses of the conductors, Serafin and Gui in the 1930s at, successively, the Metropolitan, La Scala and the Maggio Musicale in Florence. It gained ground in the UK through the famous Sadler's Wells staging in 1948, since when it has been in the regular repertory of most major houses. On disc it has enjoyed a similar second coming.
   Although the sound of Santini's version, even in its refurbished state, is indifferent, as it was even for the standards of its day, it simply cannot be overlooked because it preserves two interpretations that are now of historic importance – Gobbi's Boccanegra and Christoff's Fiesco, the brothers-in-law (in real life) rivalling each other in projecting dramatic conviction. Even with Cappuccilli's superb reading in mind (he recorded Boccanegra both for Gavazzeni and Abbado – on RCA and DG, respectively), Gobbi's still remains definitive. Through his sensitive diction and fine gradations of tone he portrays unforgettably the Doge's changes of character, so unerringly delineated by Verdi himself, from unruly pirate to commanding Doge to loving father and, after the poisoning, to tragic hero. The weary acceptance and sad accents of the final scene match those of Cappuccilli in his equally moving interpretations, especially that on the Abbado set. Gobbi at the time was at the height of his vocal powers so that the often high tessitura bothers him little, though it is certainly true that Cappuccilli has still greater resources to call on.
   Christoff may not have quite the vocal amplitude of Ghiaurov (Abbado), but his reading has more vocal character. His pungent, crisply articulated singing is ideally suited to the proud, implacable, patrician Fiesco. His singing shades into deeply felt remorse in the final, conciliatory meeting with Boccanegra. If you want to judge the calibre of both portrayals you need look no further than the close of the Prologue and listen to Christoff's relishing of Boccanegra's discomfiture at "L'ora suonò del tuo castigo" ("the hour of your punishment is at hand") as Boccanegra discovers his beloved Maria is dead, followed by Gobbi's cry "Sì; spaventoso, atroce sogno il mio!" ("Yes, a terrible and fearful dream is mine"), so eloquently accented.
   Los Angeles is an Amelia very much in the mould of Ricciarelli (Gavazzeni), vulnerable in character, gentle and elegiac in voice with just a suggestion of strain in the highest register. Los Angeles's tone is actually clearer, more girlish than that of either of her rivals, and she is more adept than either of them at suggesting passion for Gabriele and a daughter's love for her father through her sensitive painting of words. She is quite exquisite in the downward runs in the final ensemble. Campora makes a likeable, fiery Gabriele, more in the mould of Carrreras (Abbado) than Domingo (Gavazzeni). Monachesi is an imposing Paolo.
   Neither Santini's conducting nor the playing of the Rome Opera Orchestra matches that of their La Scala counterparts. Abbado's realization of this work is unlikely to be surpassed, though Gavazzeni's reading has much to commend it. The voices in this mono recording are more fairly caught than the chorus and orchestra, but there is a persistent though hardly disturbing tape hiss. EMI are to be castigated for not giving us any details about the performers or recording: surely in reissuing a 41-year-old set that has such historic importance they should blow their own trumpet a little. It is a pity, too, that they did not retain the picture of Gobbi in the title-role as on the cover of the LP reissue (in 1977) rather than the portrait of him here in real life. That said, this is a set those interested in great recordings of Verdi operas must get (even if they may regret the needless cuts), whether or not they have recommendable stereo sets in their collection.

Verdi Simon Boccanegra.
   Alexander Agache *bar* Simon Boccanegra
   Dame Kiri Te Kanawa *sop* Amelia
   Michael Sylvester *ten* Gabriele
   Roberto Scandiuzzi *bass* Fiesco

BBC RADIO 3
90-93 FM

Alan Opie *bar* Paolo
Mark Beesley *bar* Pietro
Rodney Gibson *ten* Captain
Elizabeth Sikora *sop* Maid
Chorus and Orchestra of the Royal Opera House, Covent Garden / Sir Georg Solti.
Stage Director: **Elijah Moshinsky.** *Film Director:* **Brian Large.**
Decca Ⓟ ⬛⬛ 071 423-3DH (137 minutes). Recorded 1991.

This is an exemplary issue in almost every way. Brian Large's video direction of Elijah Moshinsky's excellent staging for Covent Garden catches the dour, dark mood of the work to perfection within Michael Yeargan's evocative sets and Peter J. Hall's refined lighting. This sensible backcloth allows Verdi's taut drama to unfold unerringly under Moshinsky's eager eye. The personal trauma within the public feuds are all admirably delineated and faithfully executed by a uniformly committed cast.

Indeed the singers here are a much more successful ensemble than the team on Solti's disappointing 1989 CD version. Only Dame Kiri is common to both: here in the context of a performance in the theatre she is much more involved and involving. Amelia has always been the best of her Verdian roles, and once again she suggests all the girl's innocent radiance both in her acting and her singing, which – on this occasion – was full-blooded, even and thoughtfully phrased. As Boccanegra Agache is a notable improvement on Nucci in the CD-only version. His voice is larger, has more resonance and moves easily through every aspect of the taxing role. Agache acts the role magnificently, challenging memories of Gobbi and Cappuccilli as the protagonist. His expressive eyes tell us of the Doge's hopes, fears and fatherly love, and in the Council Chamber he shows a dignity and power that dominate disputants and the stage. He dies with tender sadness in his tones.

As Boccanegra's antagonist, the formidable Fiesco, Scandiuzzi, singing with Pasero-like authority, shows he is the most notable *basso cantante* to emerge from Italy in a generation but in spite of make-up he looks far too young for the role in general (it is a pity that none of the characters seem to have aged one jot between the Prologue and Act 1, although 25 years have intervened). Scandiuzzi sings his aria in the Prologue with long breath and vibrant tone, then makes his confrontations with Simone the superb moments of music-drama they should be. As the evil Paolo, Alan Opie confirms all his gifts as a physical and vocal actor. Michael Sylvester has just the *squillo* characteristics the part of the fiery Gabriele needs and also a welcome feeling for Verdian line.

The only reservations concern Solti's conducting. He directs a well-prepared, carefully phrased and supportive performance but one that is often stiff-limbed and wanting in dramatic propulsion. A few bars of the Abbado recording demonstrates what is missing here. But he is always supportive of his singers and draws subtle phrasing from the orchestra. The sound and picture are of the high standard we expect from Decca and the balance between stage and pit is just right. So you can sit back and enjoy a riveting performance of a marvellous piece.

Verdi Stiffelio.

José Carreras *ten* Stiffelio
Sylvia Sass *sop* Lina
Matteo Manuguerra *bar* Stankar
Wladimiro Ganzarolli *bass* Jorg
Ezio di Cesare *ten* Raffaele
Maria Venuti *mez* Dorotea
Thomas Moser *ten* Federico
Austrian Radio Chorus and Symphony Orchestra / Lamberto Gardelli.
Philips Ⓜ Ⓘ 422 432-2PM2 (two discs: 109 minutes: ADD). Notes, text and translation included. Recorded 1979.

It is generally agreed now that *Stiffelio* is more successful than its revised successor, *Aroldo*. Its rediscovery in the late-1960s has enabled this reassessment, fully discussed in Julian Budden's introduction to the set. The drama has greater unity. Stiffelio himself is almost a dry run for Otello, a man of generous instincts who is forced into a ruinous situation. As a whole the score is, as Budden suggests, the most unjustly neglected of Verdi's operas. Had it not been suppressed by the censors, and then unsatisfactorily revised, it would surely have a regular part in the repertory, as the story and its handling are far superior to what preceded them in the Verdi canon.

The title-role is a gift for an accomplished tenor: Carreras catches the moral fervour and uncertainties of the part with his open-hearted, spontaneous performance, another in a gallery that, in perspective, places him in a high place among Verdi tenors on record. As Lina, who is torn between steadfastness and vulnerability, Sylvia Sass also offers a rewarding performance, alternating delicacy with fiery strength, though technically she isn't always as secure as one might ideally wish. Manuguerra is appropriately venomous as Stankar but his voice hasn't any particular distinction, tending to sound nasal, nor has his reading much individuality, but he is never less than adequate.

Gardelli here adds another vital performance to his long series of Verdi readings, even if he isn't quite as alert as in his London-made sets, possibly because the recording has somewhat less clarity and the Austrian Radio orchestra are not that acute. But any reservations pale before the importance of the work in hand to all Verdians, and enough is achieved to prove its worth. Besides, it is an essential purchase for Carreras enthusiasts.

Verdi Stiffelio.

Plácido Domingo *ten* Stiffelio
Sharon Sweet *sop* Lina
Vladimir Chernov *bar* Stankar
Paul Plishka *bass* Jorg
Peter Riberi *ten* Raffaele
Margaret Lattimore *sop* Dorotea
Charles Anthony *ten* Federico
Chorus and Orchestra of the Metropolitan Opera, New York / James Levine.
Stage Producer: **Giancarlo del Monaco.** *Video Director:* **Brian Large.**
DG Ⓕ ⚏ 073 116-3GH (115 minutes). Synopsis included. Recorded at performances in the Metropolitan Opera House, New York during November 1993.

Although the compelling performance conducted by Sir Edward Downes emanating from Covent Garden was highly recommended (it is currently out of the catalogue), this staging from the Met is just as vital and in some respects preferable. Both readings surely confirm that this long-neglected work deserves a place in the regular repertory not only for its musical distinction but also for the dramatic conviction of its tale about guilt, adultery and forgiveness within a strict, small sect.

Del Monaco sets it in a dark, almost Gothic Victorian milieu, lavishly designed by Michael Scott (the church in the finale must have cost a bomb, generous indeed given the shortness of the scene). Levine conducts a gripping performance – he always shows a close affinity with early and middle Verdi – and brings out the originality of this tautly composed score. The title-role of the priest torn between revenge, remorse and forgiveness, a kind of proto-Otello, is ideal for Domingo. He conveys every change of mood in the role through his wholly convincing acting, an improvement, vocally and dramatically, on Carreras on the rival set, and he finds the declamatory, heroic cut of the vocal writing much to his liking. Chernov is superb as the vengeful father of Lina (Stiffelio's guilty wife). Stiff and upright in a military uniform, his eyes and body language speak of internal anger, and he dispatches his Act 2 aria and cabaletta with a force that suggests he's right at the top of the current Verdi baritone ranking. Plishka is in his element as the single-minded minister seeking peace in the community.

Doubts concern only Sweet's Lina. She provides some moments of deeply felt singing, but her acting is skin-deep as compared with Catherine Malfitano's projection of inner anguish in the Covent Garden performance, and Sweet's voice, for all its strength, is often an unwieldy instrument to bring to bear on a fine Verdian line. That said, this interpretation as a whole is worthy to set beside its rival. One thing is sure: it is a very desirable purchase.

Verdi La traviata.

Ileana Cotrubas *sop* Violetta
Plácido Domingo *ten* Alfredo
Sherrill Milnes *bar* Germont
Stefania Malagù *mez* Flora
Helena Jungwirth *sop* Annina
Walter Gullino *ten* Gastone
Bruno Grella *bar* Baron
Alfredo Giacomotti *bass* Marquis
Giovanni Foiani *bass* Doctor
Walter Gullino *ten* Giuseppe
Bavarian State Opera Chorus and Orchestra / Carlos Kleiber.
DG Ⓕ ① 415 132-2GH2 (two discs: 106 minutes: ADD). Notes, text and translation included. Recorded 1977.

This performance is so compelling dramatically, and as a recording much more natural than most of its rivals, that it could well be a newcomer's first choice. The interpretation of Violetta by Ileana Cotrubas, superbly partnered by Kleiber's conducting, makes it an imperative. Cotrubas's peculiarly plaintive, vibrating timbre and highly individual nuances seem to be perfectly fitted to the part. To those she adds more of a sense of involvement and spontaneity than any other on disc. In Act 2, if she does not have you close to tears, you must have a hard heart indeed. At "Più non esiste", this Violetta leaves no doubt that all previous experience has been erased from her mind in Alfredo's arms. Then, the very precise articulation and observance of note values, so typical of the set as a whole, at "non sapete" emphasizes the sudden realization that all she now lives for is to be taken from her, just as at "Così alla misera" she feels the blow has fallen as she communes to herself, the tears held back on the accentuated word "implacabil". At "Amavi, Alfredo" the whole bottled-up sense of mortality and lost happiness breaks forth uncontrollably. This is interpretation on the highest plain.

That first scene of Act 2 is the clue to any great reading of the role of Violetta. It is not undermined by the rest of Cotrubas's performance. "Sempre libera", at Kleiber's fast pace, is nervously exciting as it should be, with firm attack from the singer. The exchanges with Annina and the Doctor in Act 3 could not be more touching, the dots over the semiquavers at "ogni speranza è morta!" properly observed and proving the dramatic effect Verdi intended for them. Kleiber gives the score a Toscanini-like sense of dramatic purpose and impending doom without being quite as strict with his singers as Serafin (reviewed below), who is content to be an accompanist. You can hear that in the final *allegro* section of the Violetta/Germont duet, with note values, double dots and the like, firmly observed, or in the succeeding scene where the accompaniment to Violetta's letter writing has a precision not to be found with Serafin.

Much earlier in the score Kleiber and his excellent Munich players give the dance music *chez* Violetta a chilling emptiness whereas Serafin in Rome sounds ordinary. The Munich opera's chorus is also superior to its Roman counterpart. Indeed throughout this first scene the differences between the performances are very marked, Kleiber emphasizing the hectic bustle of the party, seconding the nervous, consumptive aspect of Cotrubas's Violetta, whereas los Angeles's Violetta (Serafin) keeps a very tame house. Again at Flora's gathering, the dances have been rethought by Kleiber to arresting effect. Domingo gives Alfredo one of his most winning performances, singing with sensitivity and grace – note the real *pianissimo* at the end of the first-act duet with Violetta – and altogether following her and their conductor away from routine. His outburst at Flora's party has an Otello-like sense of wrong and jealousy. Still, Del Monte (Serafin) is just that much lighter and more individual in accent. Milnes quite surpasses his Germont, good as that was, for Prêtre (on his 1967 RCA set), seemingly inspired by Kleiber. The line and tone are more firmly controlled than other interpretations and, with Cotrubas, he sings "Dite alla giovine" in a most intimate and tender *mezza voce*. His "Di Provenza" has more light and shade than Sereni's (Serafin).

Kleiber's volatile, incisive direction, sometimes in questionable tempos, has worn perhaps a little less well than the rest. But then you hear Cotrubas's heart-rending "Amami, Alfredo" and inevitably lean towards this set. You won't be disappointed, and will certainly enjoy the theatrical-like sound and you will be unable to avoid getting caught up in the drama.

Verdi La traviata.
   Maria Callas *sop* Violetta
   Giuseppe di Stefano *ten* Alfredo
   Ettore Bastianini *bar* Germont
   Silvana Zanolli *sop* Flora
   Luisa Mandelli *sop* Annina
   Giuseppe Zampieri *ten* Gastone
   Arturo la Porta *bass* Baron
   Antonio Zerbini *bass* Marquis
   Silvio Maionica *bass* Doctor
   Franco Ricciardi *ten* Giuseppe
   Chorus and Orchestra of La Scala, Milan / Carlo Maria Giulini.
   EMI mono Ⓜ Ⓓ CMS7 63628-2 (two discs: 124 minutes: ADD). Notes, text and translation included. Recorded at a performance in La Scala, Milan on May 28th, 1955.

Possibly the most famous production of *La traviata* since its première, this of Visconti's at La Scala in 1955 proved almost as controversial as its ill-fated original. In dispute were the producer's updating of setting and costumes to the 1880s, the prominence of his name on the hoardings, the conductor's speeds, the soprano's voice and the tenor's general exasperation. For Callas it was the culmination of all artistic endeavour, to work on the great role in the great house and in such enriching detail with the aristocracy of Italy's theatrical and musical world as represented by Visconti and Giulini. This was the year of fulfilment. Her voice and art enjoyed a brief period of equilibrium, and there still tingled a sense of discovery, of widening prospects and changing perspectives. Her recordings that year included the *Madama Butterfly* (on EMI, reviewed under Puccini) which stands supreme among her achievements in the studios, and then two other masterpieces, recorded live that same year: the Berlin *Lucia di Lammermoor* (reviewed under Donizetti) and this *La traviata*. It survives the controversies of its day with remarkable serenity, to re-emerge quite simply as a performance of rare depth and beauty. This is in spite of faults both technical and artistic. As recorded sound, it improves on the unauthorized issues through which the performance has previously been most widely known to collectors, though it compares unfavourably with the EMI Lisbon/Ghione version of 1958. The Scala orchestra is recorded at closer range, with greater volume but less clarity of texture, and the whole effect is more confined, more liable to the distortion which in the second party-scene (Act 2 scene 2) remains endemic.

Among the principals, Bastianini as Germont *père* seems totally unresponsive. Di Stefano, by contrast, presents a vividly living character: aspects of his singing will come in for criticism no doubt, but he involves himself, whereas Bastianini stands apart. The baritone's is, of course, a splendid voice produced in the fine Italian tradition, but his manner is wooden, his style unpolished. Mario Sereni, Callas's Germont in Lisbon, sings with far greater warmth and sensitivity, his rounder tone suiting the music as in an earlier age de Luca's did compared with the more dramatic voices of Ruffo or Amato. It is still mildly astonishing that Bastianini could have been on stage with Callas for these 20 minutes without something touching his art into a different kind of life, and, almost equally, that Callas could have played her own part so movingly with so little coming back from her colleague. Yet she does. Nothing could carry more sure and touching conviction than her "Oh come dolce mi suona il vostro accento", and rarely can the remark have had less to prompt it. There are marvels in this scene. "Non sapete" struggles against fate like a caged bird. The desolate acknowledgement, "Ever", just escapes from the lips, and the despairing "Morrò" has an annihilating force that should have sunk father Germont and his middle-class morality into the ground. The final act is greatness itself, and indeed no part, and hardly any phrase, of Callas's performance throughout the opera fails to provoke and deserve special comment.

At one point the Milan audience makes its own comment in the way it knows best, by applauding while the music and action still continue. This is after the outburst of "Amami, Alfredo" sung with such blazing sincerity that Alfredo's reaction to the letter five minutes later seems not merely unperceptive but moronic. Callas's intensity here has powerful support from Giulini, who builds the orchestral crescendos with overwhelming passion. Here and elsewhere we recognize that a great conductor is at work. Yet there are times when the less demonstrative but more quietly sympathetic touch of Franco Ghione in the Lisbon performance is preferable. Ghione is a good accompanist: hear, for instance, how responsively he accompanies Alfredo Kraus in the Brindisi, and, by contrast, how monotonously Giulini lets the one-two-three call the tune. Giulini's liking for slow speeds could be debilitating even in those days, and we find, for instance, "Un dì felice" moving sluggishly, an effect not risked by Ghione whose tempo is far more natural. So at least one element in the performance remains controversial. And in a straight comparison, the Lisbon recording has much in its favour – even the deterioration in Callas's voice is to some extent offset by a development in characterization. Even so, somewhere at the heart of this one, from La Scala, there glows a warmer, fuller life of voice and spirit.

Verdi La traviata.
Victoria de los Angeles *sop* Violetta
Carlo del Monte *ten* Alfredo
Mario Sereni *bar* Germont
Santa Chissari *sop* Flora
Silvia Bertona *sop* Annina
Sergio Tedesco *bar* Gastone
Vico Polotto *bar* Baron
Silvia Maionica *bass* Marquis
Bonaldo Giaiotti *bass* Doctor
Renato Ercolani *ten* Giuseppe
Rome Opera Chorus and Orchestra / Tullio Serafin.
Classics for Pleasure ® ① CD-CFPD4450 (two discs: 119 minutes: ADD). Notes, text and translation included. Recorded 1959.

"Anyone who is supposed to 'know about records' finds himself asked one question more often, perhaps, than any other: 'Which *Traviata* should I buy?'." The sentence comes from Desmond Shawe-Taylor in the 1961 issue of **Gramophone**. He answered that Serafin's set, then new, was probably the one, though by a narrower margin than he had at first supposed. The years have flown (nearly 40 of them), bringing many more *Traviatas*, but the question still remains, and one can only say that it is hard to foresee a time when the los Angeles recording will be out of the running.

Serafin's slow speeds trouble less than they did when the set was new (except in "Addio del passato" which would certainly be intolerable if the second verse had been included). The recording itself has worn well, with imaginative but unobtrusive production by Victor Olof. Moreover, the virtues of Serafin's conducting emerge more clearly after our subjection in the intervening years to conductors who see it as 'their' *Traviata*: Serafin is modest but not self-effacing, and one is aware of sensitive guidance right from the opening bars of the Prelude. He is the soul of discretion, his caring hand and steady tempos always supporting his singers sympathetically. "Alfredo, Alfredo" in the Act 2 scene 2 *concertato* is a fair example of what is so right about the set: clear diction, perfect legato, ideal pacing.

Most depends on the singing of the three major roles. Here, the Alfredo has plenty of character, a good voice and some sense of style. The father has sufficient gravity and sympathy, and though his voice is 'standard' rather than particularly individual he is in a good tradition of Italian baritones. Victoria de los Angeles has so many moments of adorable vivacity and pathos that her Violetta is quite unforgettable. She copes well with the high tessitura of Act 1, and in Act 2 the great duet finds her at her very best. To take a single example, the lamenting phrases starting "Cosi alla misera" have a heart-rending poignancy. The discs are worth buying for such things alone.

Serafin makes the old theatrical cuts, which to many are now quite unacceptable but then so does Callas in the set which, without a doubt, many collectors would take to their desert island, and Kleiber with Cotrubas also makes many of the excisions. And the truth about Violetta lies with los Angeles, Callas and Cotrubas and their various tenors and conductors.

Verdi La traviata (sung in English).

Valerie Masterson *sop* Violetta
John Brecknock *ten* Alfredo
Christian du Plessis *bar* Germont
Della Jones *mez* Flora
Shelagh Squires *mez* Annina
Geoffrey Pogson *ten* Gaston
John Gibbs *bar* Baron
Denis Dowling *bar* Marquis
Roderick Earle *bass* Doctor
Edward Byles *ten* Giuseppe
Chorus and Orchestra of English National Opera / Sir Charles Mackerras.
Classics for Pleasure Silver Doubles ⑤ ① CD-CFPSD4799 (two discs: 119 minutes: ADD).
Recorded 1980.

"That's how to take it – splendid!" declares the chorus *en masse* with delightfully old-fashioned stiff upper lip. This recording dates from 1980, after the end of Sir Charles Mackerras's reign at the London Coliseum, but still in time to capture the traditional values over which he presided at English National Opera. Above all, the set is a perfect example of what recording opera in English should be about. Edmund Tracey's translation is remarkably close to the Italian, always using words with the same linguistic origin where possible, and the singers take the text to heart. There is no libretto in the booklet and none is needed. John Brecknock, in particular, used to be renowned for the clarity of his words in the theatre, one of the traditions now in danger of being lost for good. His Alfredo sounds a young man of good bearing, singing with an attractive English ardour even if he was slightly past his best by this time. Christian du Plessis makes a Giorgio Germont with enough voice, but limited imagination. Both artists get a single verse of their cabalettas, Brecknock ending his with a dutiful top C. Among the supporting cast Della Jones's spitfire Flora briefly snatches the spotlight, as she makes her consonants crackle with energy. All of them worked regularly with Mackerras at ENO and sing with a care for the details of the score that must emanate from him. There is not, however, much passion about the performance. At the height of the drama one wishes they would let themselves go.

So far the set's virtues may be ephemeral, but Valerie Masterson's delectable Violetta deserves her chance with posterity. There is a moment towards the end of "Un dì felice" where Mackerras gives her a little extra time and she floats the high A with an intuitive freedom that seems to cradle the very spirit of the opera in the palm of her hand. As much as any international singer, Masterson knows where to find Violetta's heart in the music. She is not in equally good voice throughout (the recording was made over a period of three months) but at its best her soprano has a delicate, bone-china fragility that very nearly embodies the role. It is difficult to imagine anyone who wants *La traviata* in English being disappointed.

Verdi La traviata.

Tiziana Fabbricini *sop* Violetta
Roberto Alagna *ten* Alfredo
Paolo Coni *bar* Germont
Nicoletta Curiel *mez* Flora
Antonella Trevisan *mez* Annina
Enrico Cossutta *ten* Gaston
Orazio Mori *bass* Baron
Enzo Capuano *bass* Marquis
Rancesco Musinu *bass* Doctor
Ernesto Gavazzi *ten* Giuseppe
Ernesto Panariello *bass* Messenger
Chorus and Orchestra of La Scala, Milan / Riccardo Muti.
Stage and Video Director: **Liliana Cavani.**
Sony Classical Ⓕ 📼 SHV48353 (136 minutes). Also available on Ⓕ ① S2K52486 (136 minutes: DDD). Recorded at performances at La Scala, Milan in March and April 1992.

An exciting and eloquent reading on all sides, this version must be rated with the established front runners. It is not for the faint-hearted, or for those who like their Violettas to have full, equally, produced voices. Fabbriccini is evidently not an Act 1 Violetta. She has problems with the Brindisi and to an extent with "Un dì felice". One is just about to write her off as technically too flawed, when in "Ah, fors'é lui" she suddenly alerts the mind and senses to her quality with her inflexions of the single word "palpito", and in the second verse (we have here an utterly complete and accurate *La traviata*) she again and again phrases with distinction or colours words significantly – listen to the infinite tenderness of "O amore". So after all, this is a Violetta, even without assured coloratura and with problems at the *passagio*, who is going to hold our attention and move us.

Once confronted by father Germont in the Second Act she makes us aware that we are in the presence of a notable and individual artist, with a tear in the voice and what the Italians term *morbidezza*. The urgency of "più non esiste" as if this Violetta is aware that a blow is about to hit her, the weight of sorrow on "L'uomo giovane", these and so much else bespeak not only complete identification with Violetta's predicament but also vocal acumen of an exceptional kind, often based on the seemingly lost art of portamento. Maybe the power and security are not there for "Amami, Alfredo", yet the passion is very much present, as is the Italianate rightness of sound and accent. She is partnered in the earlier part of the scene by the sensitive, sympathetic Germont of Coni, very much in the Bruson mould: an excellent model, revealing his merits of alert diction and sure tone at "Pura siccome un angelo" and singing throughout with firm and intelligent phrasing, sustaining "Di Provenza" even at Muti's slow tempo and showing concern for different dynamics, making its oft-omitted cabaletta sound interesting by virtue of his light, easy touch.

Fabbriccini is no less arresting in the second part of this act. Enormously helped by Muti, as she is throughout, she catches the nervous anxiety of Violetta, culminating in the sad, sustained appeal at "Alfredo, Alfredo". The final tragedy is still better, very much modelled on Callas. The voice, more settled now than anywhere in the performance, manages "Addio del passato", both verses, with long-breathed phrasing and pathetic accents, the result of a true understanding of Verdian style yet never self-conscious in its effect – this is undoubtedly great singing and interpretation The death is deeply moving. Alagna, in the role that brought him to wide attention, is just the Alfredo for this Violetta; youthfully ardent, with keen-edged tone, finely attuned to the legato essential in Verdi, neat in his phrasing, not always individual in utterance, at his appreciable best in "Parigi, o cara".

The recording is taken from four performances given at La Scala. It is a theatrical view full of electricity, vitally executed by the forces of La Scala, as vital as any in the recorded history of the work – and all the more welcome for that and the unanimity of approach felt on all sides, not achievable, or rarely so, under studio conditions. We are really present on a great night at La Scala. Liliana Cavani's honest, unaffected traditional staging underlines and supports the readings of the principals, particularly that of Fabbriccini.

The comparison with Callas cannot now be avoided. Taking Fabbriccini's portrayal all-round, dramatic and vocal – she is the most moving, most searing Violetta since that of her legendary predecessor. While obviously modelling her singing and acting on that of her forbear at La Scala, she is yet no carbon copy – the personality is different in that Fabbriccini seems the more lost, the more vulnerable when assaulted by the Germonts in Act 2 – her look at Flora's party when Alfredo denounces her says everything, and her final act is filled with poignancy. Alagna looks handsome but is a shade sparing in facial expression. Coni contrives to add years to his real age and is at once implacable and dignified.

Cavani's own video production manages to convey the aptness of Dante Ferretti's decor and at the same time gives us an intimate view of the drama. In sound terms, even more than on the CDs, the chorus and orchestra are rather too loud in relation to the soloists. No subtitles are provided by Sony, and the top and bottom of the screen are blank presumably because the production is expressly designed for the different demands of High Definition video. This production excels by virtue of the cast and conductor being authentically Italian. Not to be missed.

Verdi Il trovatore.
Maria Callas *sop* Leonora
Giuseppe di Stefano *ten* Manrico
Rolando Panerai *bar* Count di Luna
Fedora Barbieri *mez* Azucena
Nicola Zaccaria *bass* Ferrando
Luisa Villa *mez* Ines
Renato Ercolani *ten* Ruiz, Messenger
Giulio Mauri *bass* Old Gipsy
Chorus and Orchestra of La Scala, Milan / Herbert von Karajan.
EMI Ⓟ Ⓒ CDS5 56333-2 (two discs: 129 minutes: ADD). Notes, text and translation included. Recorded 1956.

Callas and Karajan took the world by the ears in the 1950s with this *Il trovatore*. Leonora was one of Callas's finest stage roles and this recording is wonderfully intense, with a dark concentrated loveliness of sound in the principal arias that puts one in mind of Muzio or Ponselle at their best. Walter Legge always managed to team Callas with the right conductor for the work in question. Often it was Serafin, but Karajan in *Il trovatore* is as compelling a prospect as de Sabata in *Tosca* (see the review under Puccini). This opera, like Beethoven's Seventh Symphony and Stravinsky's *The Rite of Spring*, is one of music's great essays in sustained rhythmic intensity; dramatically it deals powerfully in human archetypes. All this is realized by the young Karajan with that almost insolent mastery of score and orchestra that made him such a phenomenon at this period of his career.

There are some cuts, but, equally, some welcome inclusions (such as the second verse of "Di quella pira", sung by di Stefano with his own unique kind of *slancio*). Although the EMI sound is very good, one or two climaxes suggest that in the heat of the moment, the engineer, Robert Beckett, let the needle run into the red and you might care to play the set in mono to restore that peculiar clarity and homogeneity of sound which are the mark of Legge's finest productions of the mono era. But whatever you do don't miss this set.

Verdi Il trovatore.

Leontyne Price *sop* Leonora
Plácido Domingo *ten* Manrico
Sherrill Milnes *bar* Count di Luna
Fiorenza Cossotto *mez* Azucena
Bonaldo Giaiotti *bass* Ferrando
Elizabeth Bainbridge *mez* Ines
Ryland Davies *ten* Ruiz
Stanley Riley *bass* Old Gipsy
Neilson Taylor *bar* Messenger
Ambrosian Opera Chorus; New Philharmonia Orchestra / Zubin Mehta.
RCA Red Seal Ⓜ ① 74321 39504-2 (two discs: 137 minutes: ADD). Notes, text and translation included. Recorded 1969.

BBC RADIO 3
90-93 FM

While you cannot compare this set with the above Karajan (or Giulini on his full-price DG set, which is probably the best all-round performance, with Rosalind Plowright and Fassbaender providing riches for many repeated listenings), as a total and totally compelling performance, there are details here which fully justify its existence and will be enough to tempt any collector's palette. Giulini's version is complete, with the older Domingo's Manrico and the remarkable Azucena of Brigitte Fassbaender. However, the Leonora of Leontyne Price is the high point of the Mehta recording: her velvety, sensuous articulation of what is certainly an "immenso, eterno amor" is entirely distinctive and dramatically astute. The New Philharmonia are a no less ardent protagonist. Mehta's pacing may be uneven, his accompanying breathless, but he draws robust playing in bold primary colours to which the recording gives vivid presence. The acoustic serves Manrico less well: he seems to be singing in the bath when we first overhear him. This, though, is a younger, simpler Domingo than the one we encounter with Giulini, and there are passages of wonderfully sustained intensity. Cossotto's Azucena is disappointing. All the vocal tricks and techniques are there, but it is very much a concert performance in which she, and therefore we, are never entirely engaged.

Verdi Il trovatore.

Antonietta Stella *sop* Leonora
Carlo Bergonzi *ten* Manrico
Ettore Bastianini *bar* Count di Luna
Fiorenza Cossotto *mez* Azucena
Ivo Vincò *bass* Ferrando
Armanda Bonato *mez* Ines
Franco Ricciardi *ten* Ruiz
Giuseppe Morresi *bass* Old Gipsy
Angelo Mercuriali *ten* Messenger
Chorus and Orchestra of La Scala, Milan / Tullio Serafin.
DG Double ⑧ ① 445 451-2GX2 (two discs: 126 minutes: ADD). Recorded 1962.

This set has been grossly underrated in the work's not altogether overpopulated discography. In the first place it is blessed with Serafin's lithe, clear, unforced conducting based on strongly articulated rhythms, but there is nothing of the modern fault of the orchestra dominating the sound and therefore drawing attention to itself. Secondly, Serafin's presence obviously had a good influence on the singers in the matter of obedience to what Verdi wrote. And here we have an Italian conductor in charge of a cast all of whose members are Italian.

Bergonzi, it hardly needs restating, is a paragon of a Verdi tenor. In his only interpretation of Manrico on disc he offers finely schooled tone matched to an immaculate line and a fair rapport with the character. Bastianini is far more disciplined here than in Karajan's contemporaneous, live version from the Salzburg Festival on DG, where his phrasing is often sloppy. Even if one would still like some more light and shade in his singing, his brazen, vibrant voice is ideal at conveying the malevolence appropriate to Luna. Cossotto, in the first of her recorded Azucenas, sings with a firmly etched line and the drive that always characterized her Verdi. Stella isn't quite in the same class as her colleagues. She has the right voice for Leonora but it doesn't always quite obey her will. Still, her arias are shaped intelligently and honestly, and at least her voice has a true *spinto* tone to it. Vincò is an admirably positive Ferrando.

A reasonably full version of the score is given; a few second verses of cabalettas are missing. With sound that is often an improvement on what we hear today, this is a bargain not to be missed, even if the supporting material is inadequate. You will derive more pleasure from it than from all but two or three of the full-price sets.

Verdi Il trovatore.

Rosalind Plowright *sop* Leonora
Franco Bonisolli *ten* Manrico
Giorgio Zancanaro *bar* Count di Luna
Fiorenza Cossotto *mez* Azucena
Paolo Washington *bass* Ferrando
Giuliana Matteini *mez* Ines
Giampaolo Corradi *ten* Ruiz
Bruno Grella *bar* Gipsy
Bruno Balbo *ten* Messenger
Chorus and Orchestra of Verona Arena / Reynald Giovaninetti.
Stage Director: **Giuseppe Patroni Griffi.** *Video Director:* **Brian Large.**
NVC Arts Ⓕ ▨ 4509-99215-3 (144 minutes). Recorded 1985.

This performance in the Verona Arena has just the kind of vocal and dramatic élan the work demands. The sculptor, Mario Ceroli, known for his work in unpainted wood, has here designed grand-scale artefacts and emblems hurriedly moved around the huge venue to make contrasting backgrounds to a vital, inspiriting performance. Giuseppe Patroni Griffi's direction of his principals is less convincing and he has his chorus running from side to side for no apparent reason, but the sum is greater than the parts and anyway, it hardly matters when they sing so convincingly.

Plowright was then at the peak of her powers. Her warm soprano apparently carried easily into the Arena's wide spaces and she offers a generous-voiced, ably acted performance as Leonora, one or two stressed high notes apart. She is particularly exciting in the closing scene, when she throws caution to the winds. Bonisolli, with his macho voice and presence, viscerally excites his audience throughout and even indulges them with an encore of "Di quella pira", his high Cs more secure the second time round. His sense of Verdian style is variable, but he often evinces more stylistic intelligence than he was given credit for. His acting is something else. Cossotto knows from long experience how to project her voice into the Arena. If her voice isn't as secure as it once was, it still rings with authentic fire and passion. But the vocal star of the performance is Zancanaro who rightly stops the show with his account of "Il balen", sung with impeccable style in that vibrant voice of his, and he continues in the same vein throughout, a Verdian baritone of compelling authority tempered by elegance of phrase.

Reynald Giovaninetti keeps his four thoroughbreds just about about in harness. It's all good, clean fun and in many ways thrilling, in excellent vision and sound. Subtitles are provided.

Verdi I vespri Siciliani.

Cheryl Studer *sop* Elena
Chris Merritt *ten* Arrigo
Giorgio Zancanaro *bar* Montforte
Ferruccio Furlanetto *bass* Procida
Gloria Banditelli *contr* Ninetta
Enzo Capuano *bass* De Béthune
Francesco Musinu *bass* Vaudemont
Ernesto Gavazzi *ten* Danieli
Paolo Barbacini *ten* Tebaldo
Marco Chingari *bass* Roberto
Ferrero Poggi *ten* Manfredo
Chorus and Orchestra of La Scala, Milan / Riccardo Muti.
EMI Ⓕ Ⓞ CDS7 54043-2 (three discs: 199 minutes: DDD). Notes, text and translation included.
Recorded at performances in La Scala, Milan during December 1989 and January 1990.

This was considered to be the most exciting set of a Verdi opera for a very long time when it appeared in 1991. It is justification, if that were needed, for EMI's policy – and Muti's desire – to record live at La Scala (and it follows up the success of the earlier Scala/Muti *Ernani* – reviewed above). The production from which the discs derive was not well received either scenically or musically when it was first given, and the broadcast relay of the first night wasn't encouraging. It's apparent that things improved enormously as the run continued so what we have here is a thrilling record of Italy's leading house at its best – and that's something impossible to simulate in the studio.

Vespri is one of the most difficult of Verdi's operas to bring off. Scribe's libretto, true to Parisian taste nurtured on Auber and Meyerbeer, is a somewhat superficial, broken-backed affair (though Verdi accepted it with alterations); Verdi's attempt to fulfil Parisian tastes, long ballet and all, isn't at all times convincing, yet for the most part the composer rose above the demands for show and grandeur to disclose the real feelings of his characters, none of whom is a particularly lovable creature (in that they resemble those in *Attila*, the last of Muti's EMI Verdi sets, also reviewed above). The opera is a structure involving large ensembles, elaborate spectacle, intricate and novel orchestral effects, a big ballet, and virtuoso singers pushed to the limits of their technique. Muti realizes all these assets with unperturbed ease and easily overcomes any drawbacks, real or imagined. He rouses his forces, solo and concerted, with all his old gifts for energizing rhythms and shaping a Verdian line. He yields where wanted to the needs of his singers, presses on when the drama or a dull page demands it, and draws the best out of what is generally considered Verdi's most telling ballet music. He is less impulsive, more ready to take his time than Levine on his 1973 RCA recording. La Scala's Orchestra and Chorus play and sing with the flair of authenticity – as indeed they should.

The set is graced by some superb singing – at least in the two most important and interesting roles, those of Elena and Monforte. Cheryl Studer confirms her ebullient form in *Attila* as a *lirico-spinto* with full control of coloratura, thus placing her in the royal line of Ponselle, Callas, Sutherland and Caballé (the last two of whom encouraged Studer to undertake this kind of repertory). In her first appearance, as she instils the Sicilians with courage, "Coraggio, su coraggio" (disc 1, track 4), she immediately shows her mettle with confident, inspiriting attack, the tone vibrant, the diction fiery. In Act 2, in the duet with Arrigo at "Pressa alla tomba" (track 11), she discloses with the deepest eloquence her feeling for her lover, most tellingly at the phrase "Tu, dall'eccelse". In the later duet with Arrigo in Act 4, her long solo, "Arrigo! ah, parli ad un core" (disc 3, track 3), a passage made famous by Callas, she floats her tone most appealingly, the accents delicate, affecting. In the *Bolero* (track 9) she rivals any of her predecessors in delicacy, a real smile in the voice, the phrasing long-breathed, the coloratura, not quite perfect, but near it. Taken with her soaring contributions to the ensembles, this is great singing by any standards, past or present. Her characterization catches Elena's combination of fire and softness. In sum she finds what Berlioz termed the "penetrating intensity of melodic expression" that characterizes her writing.

To find Zancanaro on equally impressive form is an added blessing. Monforte is the work's most interesting character, the French governor of Sicily, father of the Sicilian Arrigo, who is his sworn enemy. In his great scene at the start of Act 3 (disc 2, track 1), Zancanaro finds deeper strains of feeling than heard from him in any other role, and then sings the subtly written aria, "In braccio alle dovizie", with a refinement of line and variety of dynamics that enhance the strength of voice and clarity of diction we have always admired in his singing. Here, authority and vocal presence are tempered by grace and emotional involvement. He is just as eloquent in the ensuing duet with Arrigo, taken here by Chris Merritt, another singer inspired by the occasion or the work to surpass himself. Although not entirely convincing as a Verdian tenor – his voice seems a shade thin, his technique too uncertain for that – he delivers all his music with such conviction and such a belief in himself that criticism is almost silenced. His solo in Act 4, "Giorno di pianto" (disc 3, track 1), is well managed as is his duet in the same act with Elena; even better is the very French "La brezza aleggia intorno" (track 10) in Act 5, delicately sung (high D and all) and delicately answered and joined by Studer.

Which leaves, of the principals, Furlanetto. So accomplished and heard to such advantage in Mozart and Rossini, he here sounds overparted. "O tu Palermo" lacks the weight and authority of a Pinza, Pasero or Christoff – or even Raimondi on RCA – but he improves immeasurably after that, pronouncing his anathemas on the French and stirring his supporters with a verve that compensates for any failings in vocal power. Small roles are taken with accomplishment.

The recording is a considerable improvement on previous sets recorded at La Scala. Those who want their orchestras to be big and resonant may be disappointed by the confined sound heard here, a bit like listening to Toscanini's old sets. The voices are, on the whole, caught well in a true theatre perspective, with the movement seeming quite logical and not disorientating. A few coughs and some applause will only worry those who must have complete silence – or the often aseptic acoustics of the studio. There's no applause after Monforte's aria, which suggests it may have been recorded later, especially as the acoustic seems slightly different here.

The older RCA set has much to commend it, most of all Domingo's full-flooded Arrigo, though he gives points to Merritt in the *mélodie* in Act 5 already referred to. The newer one is, on balance, more convincingly cast and conducted. It won't please those who are longing to hear the piece in the original, but Verdi did approve of the Italian version and certainly would have approved of its vital execution here. Noel Goodwin contributes a well-researched note to the accompanying booklet, which has some rather dimly reproduced pictures of the staging.

Antonio Vivaldi
Italian 1678-1741

Vivaldi Ottone in Villa.
Monica Groop *mez* Ottone
Nancy Argenta *sop* Caio Silio
Susan Gritton *sop* Cleonilla
Sophie Daneman *sop* Tullia
Mark Padmore *ten* Decio
Collegium Musicum 90 / Richard Hickox.
Chandos Chaconne Ⓕ Ⓛ CHAN0614 (two discs: 145 minutes: DDD). 🗲 Notes, text and translation included. Recorded 1997.

Vivaldi claimed to have written over 90 stage works, but he may have been exaggerating. What is undeniable is that, much as we may marvel at the profusion of his concertos, which certainly brought him fame, he was most successful in his day as an opera composer. This, his very first opera, premièred in Vicenza in 1713, was an instant hit, and Vivaldi himself thought well enough of it to employ the music of one aria no fewer than five more times. The work was produced very simply, without special scenery or effects, and with modest forces – only five singers (one a castrato) and a small orchestra of strings, a pair of very economically used oboes doubling recorders, and continuo. The story – nothing to do with Handel's *Ottone*, produced ten years later – is a relatively uncomplicated one by the standards of baroque opera, of amatory pretences and misunderstandings: it has been admirably summarized by Eric Cross (who has edited the work) as a "light-weight, amoral entertainment in which the flirtatious Cleonilla consistently has the upper hand, and gullible Emperor Ottone (a far from heroic figure) never discovers the truth about the way he has been deceived".

The score proceeds in a succession of *secco* recitatives (with just a very occasional *accompagnato*) and *da capo* arias – which the present cast ornament very stylishly. There are no duets or ensembles except for a perfunctory final chorus in which the characters merely sing in unison; but there is an abundance of tuneful arias, and when Vivaldi can be bothered to write proper accompaniments to them – he often merely has violins doubling the voice, plus a bass-line (surely the harpsichord was intended to fill in the harmonic hiatus?) – he can provide interesting imitative counterpoint. Several arias employ only the upper strings without cello and bass except in ritornellos. It was not to be expected that Vivaldi's first venture into opera would break new ground, but some features do grab our attention. He has a penchant for changing tempo within an aria to denote a change of mood, notably, for example, in the ornate bravura aria that ends Act 1, where furious violin semiquavers underlining Caio's jealousy give way to a slow, grieving section, Cleonilla's heartless "Tu vedrai" shortly after, and even more in the closing aria of Act 2, where the unhappiness of Tullia (disguised as Cleonilla's page) finds outlet in an alternation of pathetic expressive harmonies and spirited agitation. There is an echo aria (the word-endings conveying a different meaning) with trilling recorders (their only appearances in the work); a quite lovely tender aria for Caio, "Leggi almeno"; an unexpected French-style aria in crisp dotted rhythm; and in Act 3, one aria with a big violin cadenza in the final ritornello (presumably for Vivaldi himself to play). This is brilliantly flaunted by Simon Standage, who also features with another (unnamed) violinist in florid duetting at the start of the sprightly overture, whose spring-heeled vivacity sets the tone for the orchestral approach throughout the work.

The small Vicenza theatre could not afford star singers, so only limited opportunities were provided for vocal virtuosity; but the present cast makes the most of its opportunities, both in display and in meditative mood. It is not always easy to tell the three sopranos apart, but Susan Gritton well suggests the scheming minx, Cleonilla; Nancy Argenta with her bright voice has the castrato role that includes the fine arias mentioned, and displays a *messa di voce* in the echo aria; and Sophie Daneman, in a breeches role, produces a wide range of colour. Monica Groop slightly undercharacterizes Ottone (who is indeed a bit of a drip) except when roused to dismiss Rome's anxiety at his dalliance. It is quite a relief to hear one male voice, and Mark Padmore is excellent, especially in his elaborate "Che giova il trono al Re". Richard Hickox keeps a firm rhythmic hand on everything and delivers quite the best and neatest Vivaldi operatic recording yet.

Vivaldi Tito Manlio.

Giancarlo Luccardi *bass* Tito Manlio
Norma Lerer *mez* Decio
Margaret Marshall *sop* Lucio
Júlia Hamari *mez* Servilia
Rose Wagemann *mez* Manlio
Birgit Finnilä *mez* Vitellia
Domenico Trimarchi *bar* Lindo
Claes Hakon Ahnsjö *ten* Geminio
Berlin Radio Chorus; Berlin Chamber Orchestra / Vittorio Negri.
Philips Ⓜ ① 446 332-2PM4 (four discs: 238 minutes: ADD). Notes, text and translation included. Recorded 1977.

In 1718 Vivaldi entered the employment of Prince Philip of Hesse-Darmstadt who had been appointed governor of Mantua, then part of the Austrian Empire. His responsibilities seem to have been varied but probably the most important of them was to provide operas for his employer's court. One of these was *Tito Manlio*, which was produced for the Mantuan Carnival season in 1719; and, if we are to believe a note by Vivaldi himself at the head of the score, written in the space of five days.

On its first appearance in 1978 the late Roger Fiske, while acknowledging that Vivaldi was no Handel, nevertheless gave *Tito Manlio* an enthusiastic, if qualified welcome. Listening to it freshly and effectively transferred on to CD one has to agree that the work deserves at least that, and it certainly ranks among the most successful of all Vivaldi operas so far commercially recorded. The libretto, by Matteo Noris, whom Vivaldi set on more than one occasion, centres round a dispute between the Romans and the Latins which has arisen because the Roman Senate, headed by Titus Manlius, has denied the Latins a consul of Latin birth. The Latins declare war on Rome but, since until now the opposing camps have been on friendly terms, Titus forbids his son Manlius to engage the enemy in single combat. Manlius disobeys him and is sentenced to death by his father. These events, together with drama provided by lovers separated by war, sustain the opera successfully by and large, through three substantial acts. All this takes place in about 340 BC, by the way.

Readers familiar with Vivaldi's oratorio, *Juditha Triumphans*, will know how resourceful the composer could be in achieving variety within a long sequence of arias. In *Tito Manlio* his melodic invention is often as alluring and, if the libretto is no masterpiece, at least it provides a wealth of opportunities for evocative image painting. Latin knight Lucius's "Alla caccia d'un ben adorato" (first disc, track 12), with its colourful writing for hunting horn, is a splendid piece which Vivaldi devotees may recognize from its inclusion in the *Serenata a Tre* (RV690), probably composed at about the same time. No less effective is Lucius's "Parla a me speranza amica" (first disc, track 20), but simple sentiments often call for simple means with Vivaldi and there is a delightful ingenuousness here. Of an entirely different character again is Lucius's Act 3 "Non basta al labbro" (fourth disc, track 4) in which Vivaldi affectingly expresses a dichotomy between head and heart. The role is stylishly sung by Margaret Marshall. Titus's daughter Vitellia, sung by Birgit Finnilä, is also allotted some engaging music. Her Act 1 "Di verde ulivo" (first disc, track 22) is a virtuoso partnership between voice and cello in which Vivaldi skilfully portrays her agitated state of mind.

Then there is Titus's music, sung by Giancarlo Luccardi; he had a reputation as a stern consul and Vivaldi underlines this side of his character with some robust arias. The Act 1 "Orribile lo scempio" (first disc, track 18) is especially enjoyable, with its busy string accompaniment, sung with great authority by Luccardi. Manlius, Titus's son, sung by Rose Wagemann, also has some strong arias – not surprisingly since his predicament seems hopeless on all fronts, so much so, in fact, that even the customary "lieto fine" begins to look in jeopardy. After listening to the death sentence pronounced upon him at the end of Act 2, he reflects upon his desperate situation in an impassioned "Vedrà Roma e vedrà il Campidoglio" (second disc, track 2).

In short, this is an opera which both in content and performance, albeit dated in some respects, goes some way towards rehabilitating Vivaldi in the minds of readers who, over the years, have encountered more than their fair share of indifferent recordings. The cast, as implied, is mainly a strong one with the Berlin Chamber Orchestra of modern instruments providing solid support. If the Overture to the work has survived it can no longer be identified. Negri, instead, has chosen three movements from three different concertos (RV562, RV579 and RV141). The solution is both apt in context and extremely effective. A welcome and stimulating reissue.

Amadeo Vives
Spanish 1871-1932

Vives Bohemios.
María Bayo *sop* Cossette
Luis Lima *ten* Roberto
Santiago S. Jerico *bar* Victor
Carlos Alvarez *bass* Bohemio
Rosa Maria Ysás *contr* Pelagia
María José Martos *sop* Juana
Isabel Monar *mez* Cecilia
Alfonso Echeverria *bass* Girard
Emilio Sánchez *bar* Marcello
**La Laguna University Polyphonic Chorus and Choir; "Reyes Bartlet" Choir;
Puerto de la Cruz Choir; Tenerife Symphony Orchestra / Antoni Ros Marbà.**
Auvidis Valois Ⓟ Ⓒ V4711 (43 minutes: DDD). Notes, text and translation included. Recorded 1993.

When Puccini wrote *La bohème* he had the advantage of two excellent librettists with whom he had already worked on *Manon Lescaut*; Leoncavallo in his *Bohème* was as skilful in his book as in his score; but Vives, who likewise drew on Mürger's *Vie de bohème* for the background of his one-act zarzuela, had to collaborate for the first time with a pair of hacks, of whose librettos it was often said that "there was a difference of opinion: some booed Perrín, others booed Palacio". What they offered Vives (who already had a large number of zarzuelas, and even some operas, behind him) was a naïve little story: the fumblings of a struggling composer, Roberto, are overheard by a young singer, Cossette, who falls in love with him from afar and, without his knowledge, takes his score to her audition at the Opéra-Comique, where, as in some conventional Hollywood B-movie, the genius of both is recognized and they fall into each other's arms.

This novelettish nonsense is saved by Vives's attractive and well-written score (he was a much more cultivated musician than many zarzuela composers), although apart from the two principal characters the others' singing parts are very minor indeed (but they say quite a lot in the connecting dialogue, which is not recorded here; the chorus in the second scene (outside a dance-hall), however, are given plenty to do, if only in providing local colour. The orchestration is delicate and neat – the intermezzo before Scene 3, with its pizzicato theme, is a highlight not only of this work but of the zarzuela repertoire – and Ros Marbà, commendably taking his time over the music, brings out its character admirably: he is fortunate in having a good orchestra and chorus. María Bayo is delightfully pure-voiced and agile in her coloratura, and Luis Lima sounds young and romantic. Together they have one of the score's best numbers, the final duo; but the elegant waltz at the start of the second scene is also of great appeal. The booklet usefully indicates the action in the intervening dialogue sections; but Auvidis's usual translator makes, as ever, numerous elementary mistakes and makes Auber a librettist instead of a composer.

Vives Doña Francisquita.
   María Bayo *sop* Doña Francisquita
   Raquel Pierotti *sop* Aurora la Beltrana
   Alfredo Kraus *ten* Fernando
   Santiago S. Jerico *ten* Cardona
   Alfonso Echeverria *bass* Don Matías
   Rosa Maria Ysás *contr* Doña Francisca
   Ismael Pons *bar* Lorenzo
   La Laguna University Polyphonic Chorus; Tenerife Symphony Orchestra / Antoni Ros Marbà.
   Auvidis Valois Ⓟ Ⓒ V4710 (two discs: 100 minutes: DDD). Notes, text and translation included.
   Recorded 1993.

One of the most cultured and technically accomplished writers for the Spanish musical theatre, Vives composed over 100 zarzuelas and operettas, but held something of a record with his 1923 masterpiece *Doña Francisquita*, which clocked up 5,000 performances in 20 years. Based on a comedy by the seventeenth-century Lope de Vega, the plot is a complicated amorous intrigue: a young student infatuated with an actress is loved by a girl who, in her determination to win him, pretends to accept the hand of his father, whose advances are mistakenly thought by her mother to be directed to *her*: throw in carnival scenes and the young man's companion who – for somewhat obscure reasons – disguises himself as a woman, and the action becomes elusive to follow. All the more since what we hear are isolated scenes without any of the dialogue (a good half of the libretto): especially in Act 3, this leaves huge gaps in the continuity that are papered over only by brief summaries in the booklet.

This throws all the emphasis, therefore, on the music, which for all its popular appeal, with a fandango, mazurka, bolero and bands of folk instruments (in the best zarzuela tradition) is of a distinction seldom found in this repertoire: alike in construction (the conspicuous weakness in so much Spanish music), in harmony and in orchestration (endlessly inventive here) *Doña Francisquita* is in an altogether superior class. Highlights of the score, apart from the dance movements, are a charming 'nightingale' song in Act 1, Fernando's big solo and a lively quintet in Act 2, and a dramatically superfluous but musically endearing romantic interlude at the start of Act 3, in which the orchestra and chorus have a chance to show their sensitivity.

Rather wryly, it has to be admitted that the chief virtues of this issue are indeed the orchestral playing and the excellent singing of the chorus (though the male section sounds rather large for the stage situation). Alfredo Kraus is a much respected artist but does not sound like a young student (particularly beside the very light tenor of Santiago Jerico as his companion) and is too beefy by half – as was Pedro Lavirgen in another recording under Sorozábal on Hispavox: the role is a romantic one, not heroic. María Bayo, also a much admired singer, is heard to less advantage than had been hoped: the recording seems to catch an edge to her voice, in places giving it a shrillness that accords ill with the heroine whom she is portraying: Teresa Tourné, in the earlier recording, is more appealing. The most successful artist here is Raquel Pierotti, who brings real character to her part as the haughty actress who at first disdains the hero's adoration. The production takes insufficient care over perspectives in Act 1 – asides are blurted out in full voice – but noticeably improves thereafter.

Richard Wagner   German 1813-1883

Wagner Der fliegende Holländer.
   Theo Adam *bar* Holländer
   Anja Silja *sop* Senta
   Martti Talvela *bass* Daland
   Ernst Kozub *ten* Erik
   Annelies Burmeister *mez* Mary
   Gerhard Unger *ten* Steuermann
   BBC Chorus; New Philharmonia Orchestra / Otto Klemperer.
   EMI Ⓟ Ⓒ CDS5 55179-2 (three discs: 152 minutes: ADD). Notes, text and translation included.
   Recorded 1968.

Klemperer's magisterial interpretation of this work was unavailable in any form for far too long so that its reissue was most welcome. It has a deal in common with the 1981-3 Karajan/EMI set in treating the work symphonically. This is something of a contrast with the 1985 Bayreuth/Philips version under Woldemar Nelsson which employs faster speeds and a more dynamic view of the score like the famous 1955 Keilberth set from Bayreuth (reviewed below). As ever, Klemperer by and large justifies some moderate tempos by the way in which he sustains line and emphasizes detail. Only once or twice – in the Spinning and Sailors choruses – do you sense a lack of propulsion. Otherwise there is throughout a blazing intensity to the reading that brooks no denial. The storm and sea music in the Overture and thereafter is given stunning power, and the Dutchman's torture and passion is evoked in the orchestra – the accompaniment to his long monologue has both inner depth and finely realized detail. Indeed, the playing of the New Philharmonia, forwardly recorded in Studio No. 1 at Abbey Road, is a bonus throughout. Klemperer catches as convincingly as anyone the elemental feeling of the work – the sense of the sea, basic passions and the interplay of character unerringly adumbrated.

Theo Adam's Dutchman was rather severely treated when the set first appeared, but there have been few baritones before or since who have sustained the line of the role so well and so intelligently reached the heart of the matter where the text is concerned. José van Dam on the Karajan set sings more beautifully but doesn't convey so much of the role's anguish. Estes for Nelsson is stolid by comparison. As at the concert performance that was given concurrently with this recording, Adam seemed inspired by Klemperer to give of his considerable best, and the results are profoundly moving. Silja's bright, sometimes piercing timbre isn't to everyone's taste, but she is certainly easier to listen to than either Karajan's or Nelsson's Senta, and sings with just as much if not more conviction as Balslev (Nelsson). Hers is a most moving portrayal of trust and loyalty and love unto death, the interpretation of an outstanding singing-actress.

Martti Talvela was in his absolute prime in 1968. Singing magnificently and suggesting a formidable presence, he is a bluff, burly Daland. Ernst Kozub was then the white hope for a new Heldentenor, but died too young to fulfil his potential. His Erik has its clumsy moments but one admires the shining tone, and Kozub evinces sympathy for the character in Erik's Third Act cavatina. Gerhard Unger offers an ardent, cleanly articulated Sailor. Annelies Burmeister is a ripe Mary. The BBC Chorus are not the equal of their Bayreuth counterparts on either the Keilberth or Nelsson sets, but are none the less very much in the picture. The set was carefully produced in the placing of voices against the instruments and the provision of stage effects (breaking waves, spinning wheels, howling winds and so on) without these becoming unduly intrusive. The overall sound is a shade on the dry side, but better that than the excessive reverberation on so many opera sets today. This has got to be the prime recommended version of the work.

Wagner Der fliegende Holländer.
George London bass-bar Holländer
Leonie Rysanek sop Senta
Giorgio Tozzi bass Daland
Karl Liebl ten Erik
Rosalind Elias mez Mary
Richard Lewis ten Steuermann
Chorus and Orchestra of the Royal Opera House, Covent Garden / Antál Dorati.
Decca Grand Opera ⓜ ① 417 319-2DM2 (two discs: 145 minutes: ADD). Notes, text and translation included. Recorded 1960.

There are several reasons why Dorati's account deserves a hearing, and a place on shelves with space and time for more than one *Dutchman*. George London is commanding in the title-role, his tone grainy but never dry, his phrasing eloquent, his characterization complete. Despite the recording's modish, early-1960s tendency to place him in the middle distance, London is still able to convey all the necessary weight and passion, save possibly in the later stages of the great Act 2 duet, where Dorati pushes the music forward too impatiently. London's partner here, Leonie Rysanek, might have welcomed this briskness as insurance against uncomfortably lengthy high notes. On the whole, however, her performance has worn better than some early reviewers of the set might have expected. The extraordinary intensity of Rysanek's smoky, full-bodied tone may make her an improbably mature-sounding Senta, but, like London, she is a strong asset in a performance which is distinctly studio-bound at times – most obviously in the lacklustre conclusion to Act 1.

The remaining solo singers are generally excellent, too. Karl Liebl's Erik has an intimate tenderness but he also conveys Erik's despair without excessive melodrama. Giorgio Tozzi is not the most sonorous or sinister Daland ever heard on disc, but he provides a good foil to the charismatic London. Antál Dorati is to be commended for using the original one-act version of the score (with Wagner's revised endings for the Overture and the final scene); but his decisions about when to broaden out and when to push on suggest that he was a less than natural Wagnerian: and the sound, recessing the solo singers while still losing orchestral detail, show its age. These are not trivial flaws: yet the finely characterized singing of London and Rysanek remains memorable.

Wagner Der fliegende Holländer.
Alfred Muff bass-bar Holländer
Ingrid Haubold sop Senta

Erich Knodt *bass* Daland
Peter Seiffert *ten* Erik
Marga Schiml *mez* Mary
Jörg Hering *ten* Steuermann
Budapest Radio Chorus; Austrian Radio Symphony Orchestra / Pinchas Steinberg.
Naxos Ⓢ Ⓓ 8 660025/6 (two discs: 139 minutes: DDD). Recorded 1992.

Well, here's a surprise: this super-bargain version entered the lists and – to mix a metaphor – virtually jumped to the top of the pile at a single leap. As a direct, no-nonsense version well sung all round, no weakness in the cast and many strengths, it immediately has an advantage over its rivals. Add to that an interpretation that rivals Böhm's mid-price 1971 DG version in theatrical excitement and urgency of delivery and you'll appreciate why it is so enjoyable. Steinberg doesn't attempt a 'deep' interpretation, conducting the work as a straightforward opera, not a music-drama viewed from the other end of Wagner's achievement, and there's much to be said for this approach. He draws from his Austrian Radio forces playing and singing that has an inspiriting verve to it. The orchestra seem to be full of players of individual distinction, particularly where the winds are concerned and the choir, as sailors and townspeople, deliver their words and notes with tone and a unanimity that rivals that of their famous Leipzig counterparts. So all the big scenes, especially those at the start of the second and third 'acts' (actually we have here the single-act version), are conducted with rhythmic élan and tight control by Steinberg. This is tremendous stuff.

Ingrid Haubold is a discovery. Here is a lyric-dramatic soprano who has just the steadiness and strength to encompass Senta's music and, as important, the histrionic power to convey most of the girl's obsession. As with the rest of the performance there is a refreshing directness to her reading, quite free of artifice or prima-donna pretensions, and she rises with only an occasional sense of not entirely inappropriate strain to the climaxes of the love duet and to the final moments of the opera as a whole. Her voice has a certain raw edge to it that may put off some but seems apt in this part. Her Dutchman is better known: Alfred Muff has been singing this part and others of the same dimension for some years in Germany. He may miss some of the inner tension and torment of the role, but he sings with a welcome sense of line and in a tone that is consistently firm and pleasing from start to finish – and of how many Höllanders can that be said?

Then there are two matchless tenors as Erik and the Steuermann. On few other versions, or indeed performances on stage, has there been an Erik to equal Seiffert, a tenor ever growing in stature, in voice and technical ability. For once Erik's music is not only a pleasure to hear but also sounds as Wagner surely imagined it, lyrically impassioned. Jörg Hering is a tenor in the Ainsley and Heilmann class: he sings the youth's recollection of home and love with the utmost eloquence of tone and phrase. Knodt is a perfectly adequate Daland, but his somewhat woolly tone isn't ideal for the old sailor. The well-known Schiml is an excellent Mary with none of the wobble heard when the part is taken by superannuated mezzos.

The recording is at once spacious and immediate although the singers, especially Senta, are placed a shade backwards. This performance hasn't the epic dimension of the Klemperer, nor a Senta, in spite of all her qualities, in the Silja class, but it is highly competitive and at the price, should be snapped up by all aspiring Wagnerians.

Wagner Der fliegende Holländer.
Hermann Uhde *bar* Holländer
Astrid Varnay *sop* Senta
Ludwig Weber *bass* Daland
Rudolf Lustig *ten* Erik
Elisabeth Schärtel *mez* Mary
Josef Traxel *ten* Steuermann
Chorus and Orchestra of the Bayreuth Festival / Joseph Keilberth.
Teldec mono Ⓜ Ⓓ 4509-97491-2 (two discs: 139 minutes: ADD). Recorded at performances in the Festspielhaus, Bayreuth during August 1955.

It is the regret of many older Wagnerians to have missed visiting Bayreuth to catch this *Holländer* of 1955. In its first post-war staging at the festival, Wolfgang Wagner appears to have done his best work ever and in an interview for this set's booklet he describes his intentions and their execution. Knappertsbusch conducted the first night, and that performance can be heard on a Music & Arts issue. Decca, then allied to Telefunken, recorded later performances conducted by Keilberth, a version appearing, belatedly, on CD for the first time.

You will miss one of the greatest pieces of dramatic singing ever committed to disc if you overlook Uhde's superb reading of the title-part. His pained tone transferred into a haunting realization of the text is ideal in the role and sears one's soul from start to finish. Listen, in his Monologue to "Nirgends ein Grab!" or "Vergeb'ne Hoffnung!" or again to "Ihr Welten, endet euren Lauf!" and you will hear the man's anguish ideally conveyed. Then in the opening of the duet with Senta (second disc, beginning of track 5) Uhde commands the line and the intimate tone to suggest the Dutchman's dreamlike wonder as he contemplates this woman who has appeared from nowhere, apparently to ease his torment. As that woman, Varnay is almost as good. It is true that by then she had become the leading Brünnhilde and Elektra of her day so that the voice is a shade unwieldy for the part, but one soon forgets that, and an occasional sourness at the top, for her understanding shown in the Ballad but even more in her opening phrase in the duet, beginning "Versank ich jetzt". Windgassen on the first night (Knappertsbusch) is the more interesting and involved Erik, but Lustig has the stronger voice and sings with welcome conviction. Weber's Daland is common to both performances and entirely admirable, a real character in terms of sound alone. Traxel is star casting for the Steuermann, singing his elegiac song with inner rapture.

Keilberth's conducting has been unjustly denigrated. He can stand comparison with most of those who have been in charge of the work on disc, but Knappertsbusch conducts a more deliberate and intense interpretation. On both occasions the chorus and orchestra excel themselves. There may be moments of hesitant ensemble but these are as nothing when the immediacy of a live occasion is taken into account, with very few intrusions from stage or audience.

The sound emphasizes some grittiness in the strings, not present on LP or on the Music & Arts issue. These drawbacks are small in the face of the performance's visceral excitement. Of course you can also hear that in the 1980s Bayreuth account on the Nelsson/Philips set, but that isn't as vividly sung. Between Keilberth and Knappertsbusch, it is hard to choose but whatever you do, when buying a set of this work, hear one or the other before making your decision.

Wagner Der fliegende Holländer.

Robert Hale *bass* Holländer
Julia Varady *sop* Senta
Jaakko Ryhänen *bass* Daland
Peter Seiffert *ten* Erik
Anny Schlemm *mez* Mary
Ulrich Ress *ten* Steuermann
Bavarian State Opera Chorus and Orchestra / Wolfgang Sawallisch.
Stage Director: **Henning von Gierke.** *Video Director:* **Eckhart Schmidt.**
EMI Ⓟ 📷 MVD99 1311-3 (105 minutes). Recorded 1991.

It is ironic that, when this was released in 1993, it was probably the best conducted and sung performance of the work then available on any format, while its visual side leaves something to be desired. Sawallisch's command of this score is probably unrivalled among today's conductors. As with his video *Ring* you feel from first to last that you are in the hands of an experienced interpreter who knows the score inside out and has conveyed his knowledge convincingly to his dedicated players. No tempo seems wrong-headed, each is unerringly related to the next, the whole is a unified concept. Lest that suggests an element of dullness, be assured that in the tautest of readings the surge and sway of the sea and of tormented emotions are as vividly portrayed here as in any other recording.

Hale complements his admired Wotan, for Sawallisch's video *Ring* (reviewed below), with an intensely sung Dutchman, firm in line and tone, superbly articulated, very much in the vein of Uhde's memorable reading for Decca (now on Teldec, see above), more baritone than bass in weight. Beside him is the equally intense, single-minded Senta of Varady. Like her Dutchman, she is blessedly free from wobble, exemplary in style and phrasing, moving in looks and tone. A performance already admired at Covent Garden, it is here rightly preserved for posterity. It is amazing with this singer that so small a frame can produce such a solid tone. Focus and projection are the names of the game.

To add to one's pleasure Seiffert is a superior Erik, one who encompasses the awkward, high-lying tessitura, and its need for fluid singing with apparent ease – and with the heroic tone appropriate to the writing. Ryhänen, the Daland, is another of those massively built Finnish basses with voices to match, but he needs help with his acting and characterization, evidently not provided by the young producer, Henning von Gierke. Likewise, Ulrich Ress, who on the evidence of his Steuermann is another promising Heldentenor in the making.

Gierke's own sets (he had till this been known as a designer, notably of Bayreuth's *Lohengrin*) are a pleasing enough frame for the work, but for the most part lack the sense of the visionary and the mysterious demanded by the piece. Within them he does little more than place the singers strategically and let them make the most of their opportunities, which the two principals gratefully accept, but most of the problems of the work, such as the arrival of the Dutchman's ship, the first appearance of the Dutchman before Senta, the ghost-sailors' Act 3 interventions, the closing apotheosis, are muffed. Within the customary conventions – the Savonlinna outdoor performance by Segerstam on Teldec is visually more exciting; Kupfer's Bayreuth production by Nelsson on Philips is a personal and controversial creation that always holds the attention – neither performance is sung with such consistent security as this one which is, on that account, a riveting experience.

Wagner Lohengrin.

Jess Thomas *ten* Lohengrin
Elisabeth Grümmer *sop* Elsa of Brabant
Christa Ludwig *mez* Ortrud

Dietrich Fischer-Dieskau *bar* Telramund
Gottlob Frick *bass* King Henry
Otto Wiener *bass* Herald
Vienna State Opera Chorus; Vienna Philharmonic Orchestra / Rudolf Kempe.
EMI Ⓟ Ⓘ CDS7 49017-8 (three discs: 219 minutes: ADD). Notes, text and translation included.
Recorded 1962-3.

You needn't do more than compare the Act 1 Prelude on these performances to hear the superior sound quality of Sir Georg Solti's 1985/6 Decca recording. Even after digital remastering Rudolf Kempe's account on EMI has less presence, a narrower perspective. There's a difference in interpretation, too. Solti phrases spaciously, but with no sense of sluggishness: Kempe is less expansive, with a hint of urgency verging on restlessness. However, Kempe doesn't invariably drive the music more forcefully than Solti – his Act 3 Prelude is relatively sedate: and Kempe sustains the theatrical dynamism of the work in the recording studio no less successfully than his rival. When it comes to singers, Kempe's pair of plotters (Ludwig and Fischer-Dieskau) are superior to Solti's, both musically and dramatically (Plácido Domingo and Jessye Norman). There is also much to admire in Elisabeth Grümmer's vulnerable Elsa and Jess Thomas's plangent but never merely lachrymose Lohengrin. Thomas has the full dramatic range for the part, but in Act 3 the voice sounds less fresh and full than it might. Domingo, for Solti, conveys more passion with less effort, inspired by Jessye Norman's powerful yet never overbearing Elsa. Solti's performance as a whole reaches a significantly higher peak in Act 3 than Kempe's. It should nevertheless be stressed that Kempe's performance has no real weaknesses. Moreover, it has been issued on three well-filled CDs, as opposed to Solti's four. This means that side-breaks come in irritating places but, given the saving, it may prove a minor irritation.

Wagner Lohengrin.
James King *ten* Lohengrin
Gundula Janowitz *sop* Elsa of Brabant
Dame Gwyneth Jones *sop* Ortrud
Thomas Stewart *bar* Telramund
Karl Ridderbusch *bass* King Henry
Gerd Nienstedt *bass* Herald
Bavarian Radio Chorus and Symphony Orchestra / Rafael Kubelík.
DG Ⓜ Ⓘ 449 591-2GX3 (three discs: 222 minutes: ADD). Notes, text and translation included.
Recorded 1971.

Lohengrin has fared reasonably well on disc, with many excellent performances from which to choose. The attributes of Kubelík's version have been underestimated. It will hold your interest from first to last, not least thanks to Kubelík's masterly overview. Not only does he successfully hold together all the disparate strands of the sprawling work, he also imparts to them a sense of inner excitement through his close attention to the small notes and phrases that so often delineate character in this score and through his vital control of the large ensembles. He is helped inestimably by the Bavarian Radio forces – gloriously singing strings, characterful winds, trenchant, involving chorus – of which he was, in 1971, a beloved chief. There's never a dull moment in this vivid, theatrical *Lohengrin*. The recording, produced by Hans Hirsch, imparts a suitably spacious atmosphere to the piece but also places the principals up front where they should be except when distancing is required – as at Lohengrin's first appearance and at the moment when Elsa appears on the balcony to address the night breezes.

Janowitz's Elsa is one of the set's major assets. Pure in tone, imaginative in phrasing, she catches the ear from her first entry, very much suggesting Elsa's vulnerability, then implies all her blind faith and belief in her saviour – listen to the single phrase "Verzeih euch mir!" when she is telling evil Ortrud of her love for the unnamed knight – though her part in the big Act 2 ensembles sometimes puts a strain on her lovely tone. Later she eloquently conveys her deep feelings in the love duet, followed by her voicing of all the doubts that beset confused Elsa. Silja (for Sawallisch on his 1962 Philips set) offers a more 'modern', intense reading, Grümmer (Kempe) a more radiant and verbally meaningful one, Studer (for Abbado on his 1991 DG set) a more obviously Wagnerian timbre, but Janowitz can well stand up to all that formidable competition.

King's Lohengrin is more ordinary; today we would be grateful for such solid, musical and well-judged singing, but one wants the ear to be cajoled a little more, and that's what Schock (for Schüchter on his 1953 EMI set) manages to do, not to mention the irreplaceable Franz Völker further back in the work's recorded history. However, few if any Lohengrins can sing the passage starting "Höchstes Vertraun" (third disc, track 5) with anything like King's true tone and powerful conviction. Though not as detailed or subtle in his colouring of the text as Fischer-Dieskau (Kempe) or quite as anguished as Uhde for Keilberth, Thomas Stewart sings a sturdy Telramund, managing the high tessitura with consummate ease. He is horribly plausible in his complaints against Elsa. This portrayal discloses him as a grossly undervalued singer, possibly because he lay under the long shadow of Hotter in the late-1960s and early-1970s.

Dame Gwyneth Jones's voice spreads, turning a vibrato that might flatteringly be called opulent into something far more objectionable. However, her portrayal, taken all-round, is reasonably convincing. Though not in the class of Klose (Schüchter), Varnay (Keilberth) or Meier (Abbado), it registers high on the scale of vicious malevolence in the part. The difficulty, as it always has been with this intelligent artist, is that the subtlety evinced in quiet passages is vitiated when the tone comes under pressure – but some Ortruds today are far more guilty in that respect than Jones. As King Henry, Ridderbusch offers a judicious blend of sympathy and authority dispensed in fluent, warm tone. Nienstedt makes the Herald's pronouncements moments to savour. The chorus are, as already suggested, nothing short of superb. So, although Kempe remains the prime recommendation for *Lohengrin*, this one makes an almost irresistible bid for recommendation, not least because of the wholly resplendent recording.

Wagner Lohengrin.

Wolfgang Windgassen *ten* Lohengrin
Eleanor Steber *sop* Elsa of Brabant
Astrid Varnay *sop* Ortrud
Hermann Uhde *bar* Telramund
Josef Greindl *bass* King Henry
Hans Braun *bar* Herald
Bayreuth Festival Chorus and Orchestra / Joseph Keilberth.
Teldec Historic Series mono Ⓜ ① 4509-93674-2 (four discs: 220 minutes: ADD). Notes, text and translation included. Recorded at performances in the Festspielhaus, Bayreuth in July 1953.

The return of this renowned performance to the catalogue is very welcome. For years, until the appearance of Kempe's stereo set, it stood sturdy duty for the work in the LP catalogue, one of the early post-war Bayreuth sets demonstrating the dedication of the new regime there. Three of the interpretations have not been surpassed on more recent recordings – those of Varnay, Uhde and Steber. Magnificent as are Ludwig, Fischer-Dieskau and Grümmer for Kempe, their predecessors just surpass them by virtue of being recorded in a live context. Varnay, with a voice ideally suited to Ortrud, commands the role with her dramatic soprano and gift in portraying all the character's venom and hatred. She also towers over Uhde's cringing, neurotic Telramund, an interpretation never likely to be bettered for its intelligent projection of the text and insight into the character's psychological make-up. The pair's scene together at the beginning of Act 2 evinces a hair-raising response from the listener.

Steber, still an underrated singer, makes Elsa at once pure and characterful, thinking herself into the girl's predicament and her response to it, singing her solos and contribution to the love duet with real feeling. She matches her American successor, Cheryl Studer, on the 1990 Schneider/Philips Bayreuth version, in vocal warmth and varied dynamics. Her partner is the equally sensitive Windgassen as Lohengrin, but in his case the means are not always responsive to the singer's wishes and on occasion he is not accurate rhythmically in Act 1. He finds his best voice for the all-important Act 3, the Narration being particularly eloquent. In any case, few other tenors, apart from perhaps Jess Thomas for Kempe and Domingo for Solti, surpass him in the role if we except that *nonpareil* Völker in the wartime Heger 1942 version of the opera (Preiser), where he has Maria Müller as an equally peerless Elsa. Greindl's King is impressive in utterance but inclined to unsteadiness.

Keilberth's reading is forthright, sensible and well co-ordinated, lacking only the visionary quality that Kempe finds in the score. The recording sounds well in its digitally remastered form.

Wagner Lohengrin.

Peter Hofmann *ten* Lohengrin
Karan Armstrong *sop* Elsa of Brabant
Elizabeth Connell *sop* Ortrud
Leif Roar *bass* Telramund
Siegfried Vogel *bass* King Henry
Bernd Weikl *bar* Herald
Bayreuth Festival Chorus and Orchestra / Woldemar Nelsson.
Stage Director: **Götz Friedrich.** *Video Director:* **Brian Large.**
Philips Video Classics Ⓟ ⬛⬛ 070 411-3PH2; ⬤ 070 411-1PH2 (two discs: 199 minutes).
LaserDisc has optional teletext subtitles in English. Recorded 1982.

This Bayreuth performance is just to be preferred to its 1987 successor, but by discarding the latter, also on Philips, you lose Cheryl Studer's lovely Elsa and some striking stage pictures. On the whole Götz Friedrich's staging offers a more penetrating experience that that of film director, Werner Herzog, in the later version. Günther Uecker's sets offer a pattern of black squares pierced with silver studs as a background to most scenes. The swan is a swirling projection on the scrim. The love couch in Act 3 is quite an evocative prop. Within this economic setting Friedrich moves his principals with the kind of conviction typical of his best work: the first contact of Elsa with Lohengrin and the tender concern of Elsa for Ortrud after the former's dream are just two examples of Friedrich's skills. He is also masterly in his control of the seemingly interminable assemblies in Act 2. Karan Armstrong's psychologically interesting Elsa is somewhat lamed by laboured singing. Hofmann looks like everyone's ideal Lohengrin, proud and ardent, and he climaxes a well-sung performance with a fine narration. Disharmony and evil are forcefully represented by Connell's viciously malevolent Ortrud, potently activating the weak soul of Telramund, a part forcefully delivered by Roar. Vogel is a dull King, Weikl a quite out-of-the-ordinary Herald. The sound recording ideally captures the Bayreuth acoustic, allowing us to hear Nelsson's firm command of the work's sprawling structure and his sensitivity to its lyrical aspects.

Wagner Die Meistersinger von Nürnberg.

Thomas Stewart *bar* Hans Sachs
Sándor Kónya *ten* Walther
Gundula Janowitz *sop* Eva
Franz Crass *bass* Pogner
Thomas Hemsley *bar* Beckmesser
Gerhard Unger *ten* David
Brigitte Fassbaender *mez* Magdalene
Kieth Engen *bass* Kothner
Horst Wilhelm *ten* Vogelgesang
Richard Kogel *bass* Nachtigall
Manfred Schmidt *ten* Zorn
Friedrich Lenz *ten* Eisslinger
Peter Baille *ten* Moser
Anton Diakov *bass* Ortel
Karl Christian Kohn *bass* Schwartz
Dieter Slembeck *bass* Foltz
Raimund Grumbach *bass* Nightwatchman
Bavarian Radio Chorus and Symphony Orchestra / Rafael Kubelík.
Calig Ⓟ Ⓒ CAL50971/4 (four discs: 272 minutes: ADD). Recorded 1967.

There could be no more fitting memorial to Kubelík than the appearance of this, probably the most all-round satisfying *Meistersinger* in the era of stereo LP. It has circulated on an 'unofficial' label for a while now, but this is the first time it has become generally available. The reasons why it was originally held back from release are mysterious. It was recorded in 1967 by Bavarian Radio to mark the work's centenary the following year (it was broadcast appropriately enough on Midsummer's Day), apparently in co-operation with DG, but allegedly a dispute over an important piece of casting prevented it being issued at the time it was made. The loss for Wagner lovers all these years has been a severe one.

Kubelík conducts an unforced, loving interpretation, showing a gratifying grasp of overall structure, matching Kempe (EMI) in those respects. At the time it was broadcast, the German critic Karl Schumann rightly commented on Kubelík's "irresistible combination of intellect and passion". As a whole the reading has an unobtrusive cohesion achieved within flexible tempos and dynamics. Everything proceeds at an even, well-judged pace with just the right surge of emotion at the climaxes. All this is conveyed unerringly to his own Bavarian Radio Symphony forces with whom he made so many successful recordings. This one was committed to disc in Munich's Herkulessaal, the venue for the most recent EMI recording (Sawallisch in 1993). Even more than there, this one catches the excellent acoustic of the hall, which contributes to the spacious, natural results, the soloists well forward, making it as resplendent as any recorded version of this opera.

Fortunately there is a cast at hand willing and able to respond to Kubelík's mastery. Stewart's Sachs is certainly his most successful performance on disc. He offers a finely moulded, deeply considered reading that relies on honest, evenly produced, mostly warm tone to create a darkish, philosophical poet-cobbler, one on a par with Adam's reading for Karajan's second version in 1970 at Dresden (EMI) but more steadily sung, and bettered only by Paul Schoeffler on older, mono versions conducted by Knappertsbusch (Decca, 1950/51), Abendroth (Preiser, 1943) and Böhm (Preiser, 1944) – and then only because the senior baritone has bass resonances not available to Stewart. Kónya is simply the most winning Walther on any set, superseding Sawallisch's excellent Heppner by virtue of a greater ardour in his delivery and Kempe's admirable Schock because he has the more pleasing voice. Kónya pours out consistently warm, clear tone, his tenor hovering ideally between the lyric and the heroic. In this highly demanding role he never comes under strain and manages also to be poetic. What more can one ask? Nor are there many better Evas than the young Janowitz, certainly none with a lovelier voice. Scheppan on the 1943 Bayreuth version (Abendroth), Schwarzkopf for Karajan (EMI, 1951) and Grümmer for Kempe may achieve a greater intensity of phrase (as at the start of the Quintet) but Janowitz is very nearly their equal.

Franz Crass, a less pompous Pogner than some, sings his part effortlessly, with noble feeling. Hemsley, though singing his first Beckmesser, evinces a close affinity with the Town Clerk's mean-mindedness, and his German is faultless. As in his two previous assumptions of the role (the first

Karajan and Kempe), Unger is a paragon among Davids, so eager in his responses and finding just the right timbre for the role. His Magdalene, again perfect casting, is the young Fassbaender. With a characterful Kothner in Engen, the requirements for a near-ideal *Meistersinger* ensemble are in place. As the recording doesn't betray its age this would undoubtedly be the first choice among stereo versions, superseding even the second Karajan because Kubelík's cast is superior.

Wagner Die Meistersinger von Nürnberg.

Ferdinand Frantz *bass-bar* Hans Sachs
Rudolf Schock *ten* Walther
Elisabeth Grümmer *sop* Eva
Gottlob Frick *bass* Pogner
Benno Kusche *bar* Beckmesser
Gerhard Unger *ten* David
Marga Höffgen *contr* Magdalene
Gustav Neidlinger *bass-bar* Kothner
Horst Wilhelm *ten* Vogelgesang
Walter Stoll *bass* Nachtigall
Manfred Schmidt *ten* Zorn
Leopold Clam *ten* Eisslinger
Herbert Kraus *ten* Moser
Robert Koffmane *bar* Ortel
Anton Metternich *bass* Schwarz
Hanns Pick *bass* Foltz
Hermann Prey *bar* Nightwatchman
**St Hedwig's Cathedral Choir, Berlin; Chorus of the Deutsche Oper, Berlin;
Berlin State Opera Chorus; Berlin Philharmonic Orchestra / Rudolf Kempe.**
EMI mono Ⓜ Ⓘ CMS7 64154-2 (four discs: 260 minutes: ADD). Notes, text and translation included. Recorded 1956.

This famous set, its reissue long awaited, finally made its re-entry into the catalogue. If one had to express some disappointment, that is because it had been preceded on to CD by two other recommendable sets from the same company (EMI – from Dresden, 1970 and Bayreuth, 1951), both conducted, in different circumstances, by Karajan. It should be said at once that Kempe's interpretation remains his version's main glory, a wonderfully consistent, life-enhancing view of the piece, unexaggerated in tempo, all of a piece structurally – just as it used to be at Covent Garden. No other conductor on disc, not even Kuijken or Karajan, surpasses Kempe in the long view, in generosity of phrasing, subtlety or rubato, or in a sharp eye for instrumental detail. In particular, the whole of Act 3, from Eva's entrance, after all the heart of the work, sweeps forward with an inevitability of pulse and a depth of feeling that warm the heart.

It is a thousand pities then that the recording wasn't made in stereo (which should have been possible in 1956) and that the mono sound isn't up to the high standards of the day. The orchestral contribution now seems constricted – even by comparison with the Karajan/Legge recording at Bayreuth from 1951. The other major regret is that the role of Sachs wasn't assigned to Hotter, then at the height of his powers and a noble interpreter, but to the reliable, articulate but sometimes gravelly and prosaic Ferdinand Frantz. He is surpassed in almost every respect by Edelmann (first Karajan). Nor is the rest of Kempe's cast quite as convincing as one had remembered especially in relation to that Bayreuth set. Grümmer remains a sincere, outgoing Eva of a kind hard or impossible to emulate today, product of a lost tradition perhaps, but even she cannot quite match the absolutely inspired Schwarzkopf of 1951, singing on stage with a fervour and spontaneity that she didn't always match in the studio. This, like other other judgements, has been made by fresh and detailed comparisons. Listen to "O Sachs, mein Freund" or the opening of the Quintet in both versions: it is simply a case of the excellent being trumped by the superb and from here to the end of the work, Karajan conducts like a man possessed.

Similarly although Schock is an ardent and idiomatic Walther, he hasn't the Heldentenor strength and stamina of Hopf (first Karajan) whose only rival in the role on disc is the golden-voiced but unauthentic Domingo, on the unevenly cast Jochum 1976 DG set. Try the opening of the Prize Song – Schock is quite poetic but Hopf manages a smile in his tone and a smooth line, indeed sings the whole piece, and most of the rest of his part, with an ardour and breadth that, for once in a way, responds fittingly to Wagner's inordinately taxing challenge to his tenor. But Schock is still preferable to any Walther you're likely to hear in the opera-house today. Kunz (first Karajan) and Kusche both take a broadish view of Beckmesser's role, declaiming with bite and bile. Kunz's reading is the better sung. As David, Unger is common to both Kempe and the first Karajan, and has few equals in the part, a reading full of youthful bounce and good humour. For some 20 years, he had few rivals in the role. Frick is a wise, clear and sonorous Pogner, though Ridderbusch finds more poetry in the role and sings it with a firmer legato on the second Karajan.

Mention of that set, yet another EMI classic, reminds us that stereo inevitably adds a breadth and depth to the sound picture, an important advantage in this work, especially when the recording, made in Dresden, is so beautifully and naturally balanced, enhancing the superb playing and singing of the Dresden forces. None of its successors has rivalled it in that respect, but Kempe's mono version has the benefit of the same orchestra on just as gratifying a form and a choir from Berlin renowned in its day as one of the best in Germany, West or East. In most respects Karajan's second recording is not as convincingly sung as his first or Kempe's. One would hate to be without Kempe, or indeed the second Karajan, but the first Karajan is an imperative, a truly inspired rendering, replete from start to finish with that special sense of Bayreuth dedication – and in very reasonable sound.

Wagner Die Meistersinger von Nürnberg.

Otto Edelmann *bass* Hans Sachs
Hans Hopf *ten* Walther
Dame Elisabeth Schwarzkopf *sop* Eva
Friedrich Dalberg *bass* Pogner
Erich Kunz *bar* Beckmesser
Gerhard Unger *ten* David
Ira Malaniuk *contr* Magdalene
Heinrich Pflanzl *bass* Kothner
Erich Majkut *ten* Vogelgesang
Hans Berg *bass* Nachtigall
Josef Janko *ten* Zorn
Krl Mikorey *ten* Eisslinger
Gerhard Stolze *ten* Moser
Heinz Tandler *bass* Ortel
Heinz Borst *bass* Schwarz
Arnold van Mill *bass* Foltz
Werner Faulhaber *bass* Nightwatchman
Bayreuth Festival Chorus and Orchestra / Herbert von Karajan.
EMI Références mono Ⓜ Ⓞ CHS7 63500-2 (four discs: 267 minutes: ADD). Notes and text included. Recorded at performances in the Festspielhaus, Bayreuth in August 1951.

Karajan's Dresden/EMI *Die Meistersinger* is generally acknowledged, with Kubelík's, to be the most gratifying performances of this opera in stereo. The only rivals in mono are Kempe's reading and Karajan's other recording reissued here and recorded at the Bayreuth Festival in 1951, the only work during the first post-war season to escape Wieland Wagner's new and ascetic look (it was staged by the Munich conservative, Rudolf Hartmann, in traditional but apparently far from dull fashion). Because this is a live performance Karajan's conducting has always impressed as being even more vivid and penetrating than in his more considered Dresden version, an impression enhanced by the fact that he was 20 years younger. In his well-researched note to this CD reissue, Richard Osborne very properly writes that "the miracle of Karajan's conducting is that it marries fervour with lucidity in particular measure". That can be heard most tellingly in the work's most inspired section – the first four scenes of Act 3. The instrumental detail that characterizes and describes Beckmesser's movements as he steals into Sachs's study is delineated with a refined clarity that ideally brings out its humour. Then in the following scene Karajan is inspired to heights of intensity and concentration as Sachs and Eva play out their emotional entanglement culminating in "O Sachs, mein Freund" and the Quintet.

It is here, too, that Schwarzkopf's Eva and Edelmann's Sachs add a further touch of eloquence to their already finely wrought performances. The underrated Edelmann gives the best sung Sachs in any complete recording. He has the prime virtues of perfect firmness, a true legato and a strong, full-bodied, unforced, totally likeable tone. You may not find the individuality of phrase here that other, older interpreters give us, but in his varied responses to the masters, Eva, Walther and Beckmesser, he is unfailingly true to Sachs as the poet-cobbler, and his voice proves virtually tireless. One might argue as to whether the youthful Schwarzkopf is quite as lovable and outgoing an Eva as Grümmer for Kempe, but in respect of radiant tone, musical phrasing, wit allied to beauty, she hasn't a peer. Nor has Gerhard Unger as David, who sings his role with the fresh tone and eager responses it calls for.

With the rest of the singers, a few – but not many – reservations have to be made. Hopf, the Walther, can be ungainly and at times his tone becomes a trifle gluey, but he has all the notes, his tone is unconstricted and full at the top and he attempts many touches of piano singing – and you can't say that of many of his successors, Domingo (Jochum/DG) apart. Dalberg can be excused some unsteadiness for the sake of his warm, sympathetic portrait of Pogner. Kunz, though somewhat free with Beckmesser's music, creates a vivid, unexaggerated portrait of the dried-up town clerk. Malaniuk is a lively Magdalene. Werner Faulhaber, a promising baritone who had his life cruelly ended by a mountaineering accident two years after this recording was made, is a warm, reflective Nightwatchman.

This set won't be for those who mind occasional coughs – they're most troublesome in the Third Act Prelude, just when you want silence to admire Karajan's deeply moving interpretation – or who must have stereo and perfect voice/orchestra balance. They are directed to Kubelík or the second Karajan, but for anyone who appreciates a true-to-life, responsive and exceptionally intense experience this is a version to cherish. Only two things are worrying – and they have nothing to do with the set's age or provenance: EMI, being parsimonious, provide only the German text, and the changeover from the third to fourth CD is most inartistically made, just before the words, "Die selige Morgentraum-Deutweise".

Wagner Die Meistersinger von Nürnberg.

Sir Donald McIntyre *bass-bar* Hans Sachs
Paul Frey *ten* Walther
Helena Doese *sop* Eva
Donald Shanks *bass* Pogner
John Pringle *bar* Beckmesser
Christopher Doig *ten* David
Rosemary Gunn *mez* Magdalene
Robert Allman *bass* Kothner
Gerald Sword *ten* Vogelgesang
Neville Wilkie *bass* Nachtigall
Lawrence Allen *ten* Zorn
John Miley *ten* Eisslinger
Christopher Dawes *ten* Moser
Stephen Bennett *bass* Ortel
Arend Baumann *bass* Schwarz
David Hibbard *bass* Foltz
Australian Opera Chorus; Elizabethan Philharmonic Orchestra / Sir Charles Mackerras.
Stage Director: **Michael Hampe.** *Video Directors:* **Peter Butler, Virginia Lumsden.**
PolyGram RM Great Opera Collection Ⓔ 〰 079 229-3 (two cassettes: 277 minutes). Recorded at a performance in the Opera House, Sydney on October 14th, 1988.

Two expatriate Antipodean knights ensure that this performance is an outright triumph. Sir Charles in the pit catches the full range of Wagner's masterpiece, its drive, humanity and inner spirit. With an orchestra not perhaps quite of the highest class and a shade small for their task, he none the less ensures that every strand of the musical argument, and every side of the many-faceted score is exposed in a mature, warm interpretation.

On stage Sir Donald crowns his distinguished career as a Wagnerian bass-baritone with a rounded, wholly convincing portrayal of Sachs. A grizzled, bearded figure, he truly dominates the stage as he encompasses Sachs as shoemaker, thwarted lover and poet, all aspects coming together as he throws objects around his workshop when he realizes his scheme to bring Eva and Walther together has succeeded all too well and this Sachs expresses his pent-up feelings with physical action. That makes his falling into Eva's arms at "O Sachs, mein Freund", just after, that much more moving. At the beginning of this, the opera's crucial scene, the first of Act 3, McIntyre's still presence as he muses philosophically on the previous night's unruly events is just as arresting, and in the scenes with Beckmesser he also catches the witty side of Sachs's character. If in the monologues we do notice that his rich bass-baritone has dried out somewhat and the line is now hard for him to sustain, we are compensated for that by the meaningful way he 'speaks' the text. There's no better modern Sachs on CD or video.

By his side John Pringle's Beckmesser is just as impressive, a black streak of misery, tautly vindictive, literally pointing his finger at everything that displeases his mean mind. It's a properly prickly characterization that never dips over, dramatically or vocally, into caricature. Like McIntyre, he makes all he can of the text. Veterans Robert Allman and Donald Shanks bring all their experience to bear on Kothner and Pogner respectively. Allman's pompous pleasure in reading out the tablature is particularly striking. Helena Doese may look a shade mature for the youthful Eva but few younger sopranos can fill the role with such lustrous tone or match it so confidently to the text. There's a lively local Magdalene. Unfortunately the performance is not so well served in the tenor department. Frey is barely adequate vocally as Walther and a cipher in his portrayal of the proud Junker. Doig's tenor and appearance are a shade heavy for David, though he recites the modes charmingly enough.

Hampe's staging, much admired in Sydney, renews the traditional without ever offending against Wagnerian proprieties. His *Personenregie* evinces his long experience in directing opera. You catch all the exchange of grudges among the fussy masters, all the shades of feeling among the principals, and the choral scenes are expertly managed. John Gunter's sets and Reinhard Heinrich's costumes, mostly in brown and beige, are wonderfully evocative of the opera's period, and the designs make the best possible use of the small stage, itself an advantage when it comes to video as we can see much of it for most of the time in the sympathetic direction for video of Peter Butler and Virginia Lumsden.

The sound picture is exemplary, though some might like the orchestra a little more forward. The absence of subtitles is a serious drawback. Barry Millington's notes repeat gratuitously his hang-up over Wagner's portrayal of Beckmesser as a Jew, which is quite irrelevant to this production where there's no suggestion of that misconceived premise. As a whole this staging is preferable to the Bayreuth one by Wolfgang Wagner on Philips. Although that is strongly cast it is not as perceptively directed on stage as this one, which should be seen and heard by all lovers of this ever-fresh work.

Wagner Parsifal.

Peter Hofmann *ten* Parsifal
José van Dam *bass-bar* Amfortas
Kurt Moll *bass* Gurnemanz
Dunja Vejzovic *mez* Kundry
Siegmund Nimsgern *bass* Klingsor
Victor von Halem *bass* Titurel
Claes Hakon Ahnsjö *ten* First knight
Kurt Rydl *bass* Second knight
Marjon Lambriks *mez* First squire
Anne Gjevang *mez* Second squire
Heiner Hopfner *ten* Third squire
Georg Tichy *bass* Fourth squire
Barbara Hendricks *sop* First flower maiden
Janet Perry *sop* Second flower maiden
Inga Nielsen *sop* Third flower maiden
Audrey Michael *mez* Fourth flower maiden
Doris Soffel *contr* Fifth flower maiden
Rohângiz Yachmi Caucig *contr* Sixth flower maiden
Hanna Schwarz *mez* Voice from above
Berlin Deutsch Opera Chorus; Berlin Philharmonic Orchestra / Herbert von Karajan.
DG Ⓔ Ⓛ 413 347-2GH4 (four discs: 256 minutes: ADD). Notes, text and translation included.
Recorded 1979-80.

1981

Karajan's *Parsifal* seems to grow in stature as an interpretation on each rehearing; on its CD transfer it appears to have acquired a new depth, in terms of sound, because of the greater range of the recording and the greater presence of both singers and orchestra. As in practically all cases, CD offers a more immediate experience. Karajan's reading, a trifle stodgy in Act 1, grows in intensity and feeling with the work itself, reaching an almost terrifying force in the Prelude to Act 3 which is sustained to the end of the opera. Moll's Gurnemanz is a deeply expressive, softly-moulded performance of notable beauty. Vejzovic, carefully nurtured by Karajan, gives the performance of her life as Kundry. Hoffmann's tone isn't all times so steady as a Parsifal's should be, but he depicts the character's anguish and eventual serenity in his sincere, inward interpretation. Van Dam is a trifle too placid as Amfortas but his singing has admirable power and steadiness. Nimsgern is the epitome of malice as Klingsor. The choral singing hasn't quite the confidence of the superb orchestral playing which has both qualities of Keats's imagining of beauty and truth in abundance.

Wagner Parsifal.

Warren Ellsworth *ten* Parsifal
Phillip Joll *bass-bar* Amfortas
Sir Donald McIntyre *bass-bar* Gurnemanz
Waltraud Meier *mez* Kundry
Nicholas Folwell *bar* Klingsor
David Gwynne *bass* Titurel
Timothy German *ten* First knight
William Mackie *bass* Second knight
Mary Davies *sop* First squire
Margaret Morgan *sop* Second squire
John Harris *ten* Third squire
Neville Ackerman *ten* Fourth squire
Elisabeth Ritchie *sop* First flower maiden
Christine Teare *sop* Second flower maiden
Rita Cullis *sop* Third flower maiden
Elizabeth Collier *sop* Fourth flower maiden
Kathryn Harries *sop* Fifth flower maiden
Catriona Bell *mez* Sixth flower maiden
Welsh National Opera Chorus and Orchestra / Sir Reginald Goodall.
EMI Ⓜ Ⓛ CMS5 65665-2 (four discs: 295 minutes: DDD). Notes, text and translation included.
Recorded 1984.

The more one hears this work, the more one wonders at Wagner's glorious command of his motifs, counterpoint and harmony. No conductor today has a greater understanding of this complex structure and, as he himself would have it, its *Klang*, than Goodall. So, on that ground alone, this is an important and deeply satisfying performance. But, it hardly needs saying that the opera has always brought the very best out of its interpreters. The two early Knappertsbusch versions on Decca and Philips, and the Karajan on DG, reviewed above, must rate in any canon of great recordings of the past. The Jordan (Erato) has much to offer and the Solti (Decca), though some way behind as a spiritual experience, is admirable purely as a recording. It is perhaps, progressing from purely musical to metaphysical considerations, the spiritual element in Goodall's reading that so impresses. In his eighties, Goodall seems to have peered even further into the work's meaning than in the past, and in page after page of the outer acts he conveys its mystical calibre in a way Knappertsbusch and to a slightly lesser extent Karajan have done in their recordings. The rich sonority Goodall demands can already be heard in the Prelude, and through the rich texture the trumpet line pierces like a spear. The First Act transformation music is similarly broad and timeless in its feeling. In the first Grail scene, the Eucharist motif is as luminous as it should be; even the slightly less inspired Communion-serving theme here has its due gravity.

In the Prelude to Act 3, the sense of Parsifal's effortful wandering is unerringly felt at Goodall's deliberate pace. The baptismal, 'coronation' and Good Friday music are ideally long in phrasing yet never over-emphasized, and the whole work moves to an inevitable, and incandescent climax in the second transformation and Parsifal's redeeming close. Against that must be set an unduly laboured account of the Flower maidens' music, following on a call to arms from Klingsor, that is stickily conducted. These kind of energetic passages have never been Goodall's strength, and he takes time to recover. "Ich sah das Kind" is too slow and sleepy, but from Amfortas's moment of truth Goodall builds the tension of the act's battle of wills between Kundry and the hero. What you miss throughout are the incisive accents and command of ensemble exhibited by Knappertsbusch and Karajan.

Of course, Goodall is renowned both as an orchestral and vocal coach. Here he persuades the WNO orchestra to play to the considerable limit of their capabilities. Though it is not quite in the BPO or Bayreuth class, the execution is quite dedicated enough to carry out their conductor's exigent demands. All of the cast have benefited enormously from the long preparation Goodall expects – most of all Donald McIntyre. At Cardiff, when a Goodall disciple convincingly took over from the master, his performance as Gurnemanz was appreciable, but it has now gained immeasurably in stature to be among the most compelling on record. In both the First Act and Third Act narrations, Goodall's long line supports McIntyre's vivid story-telling. His description of the dying swan's wounds is as moving as his recollection of Titurel's death, and the blessing of Parsifal in Act 3 has impressive authority. Throughout, line and words are kept in rewarding balance. Perhaps he lacks the sheer weight of tone that Weber (Knappertsbusch on Decca) and Moll (Karajan) exhibit, and just a little of the inner feeling of Hotter (Knappertsbusch on Philips) but his interpretation can certainly hold its own with all three, and it is more deeply considered than Robert Lloyd's for Jordan.

Another special performance comes from Warren Ellsworth, the young American tenor. Deeply committed, almost to a fault, he lives every moment of the role as he did on stage, and he develops the character from uncomprehending stripling to saint-like redeemer by vocal means alone. And his voice is undoubtedly a true Heldentenor, perhaps best described as having the timbre of James King and the dramatic projection of Max Lorenz with some of the latter's propensity to take liberties over note values. He is securer at full voice than at *mezza voce* – which means that the quiet close to the end of Act 2 is a bit of a trial. His repelling of Kundry earlier in the act has a Vickers-like force. All in all, an exciting début – a more vital Parsifal than any of his rivals.

Waltraud Meier didn't sing Kundry at Cardiff but had been imported for this recording. Hers is an exciting, not ideally smooth voice, rather happier in the dramatic encounter with Parsifal than in the earlier seductions. The modern trend for casting mezzos in this part which often lies very high, is questionable, and Meier cannot hide signs of strain. Though she is already well within the part, she makes less of the text than her foreign colleagues, possibly because she hasn't worked so long with Goodall. The one real disappointment of the set is Phillip Joll's wobbly, drily sung and over-emoting Amfortas. This simply will not do on record. Nicholas Folwell makes a suitably biting Klingsor, though not one to match Uhde (Knappertsbusch/Decca) or Nimsgern (Karajan). Flower maidens are no more than adequate, the choral singing superb.

Wagnerians will want to have this for the truthfulness and elevation of Goodall's reading, particularly in Act 3, which has breadth and authority. The recording is unobtrusively balanced and forward, with some indication of stage movement. You may be less happy about the fades in and out on some sides, or with the overlapping of some bars on others, but that is a small drawback to a major achievement.

Wagner Parsifal.

Jess Thomas *ten* Parsifal
George London *bass-bar* Amfortas
Hans Hotter *bass-bar* Gurnemanz
Irene Dalis *mez* Kundry
Gustav Neidlinger *bass* Klingsor
Martti Talvela *bass* Titurel
Niels Møller *ten* First knight
Gerd Nienstedt *bass* Second knight
Sona Cervená *mez* First squire
Ursula Boese *contr* Second squire
Gerhard Stolze *ten* Third squire

Georg Paskuda *ten* Fourth squire
Gundula Janowitz *sop* First flower maiden
Anja Silja *sop* Second flower maiden
Else-Margrete Gardelli *sop* Third flower maiden
Dorothea Siebert *sop* Fourth flower maiden
Rita Bartos *sop* Fifth flower maiden
Sona Cervená *mez* Sixth flower maiden
Bayreuth Festival Chorus and Orchestra / Hans Knappertsbusch.
Philips Ⓕ ① 416 390-2PH4 (four discs: 250 minutes: ADD). Notes, text and translation included.
Recorded at a performance during the 1962 Bayreuth Festival.

Transfer to CD left many collectors in no doubt that this is the most moving and satisfying account of *Parsifal* ever recorded, and one that for various reasons will not easily be surpassed. Nobody today, not even Goodall, can match Knappertsbusch's combination of line and emotional power. Nobody else manages to sustain the breadth and gravity of Act 1 so effortlessly as "Kna" – not even his own 1951 Decca mono LP Doppelgänger; nobody quite equals his sense of searing remorse in the latter part of Act 2; none manages the architectural grandeur and solemnity of Act 3. The weight of the interpretation isn't compromised by slow tempos as it sometimes can be in the 1951 performance. All this makes the conductor quite incomparable in this work. An essay by Deryck Cooke extolling Knappertsbusch's reading happily accompanies this issue. On it can be heard, at its most compelling, the magnificence of the Bayreuth chorus and orchestra, and the marvellous blend achieved between stage and pit that is Bayreuth's unique secret.

Another reason this version will be so hard to rival is the Wagnerian heights of achievement in the singing. As Robin Holloway commented in *Opera on record* (Hutchinson: 1979), "Hotter is all-surpassing and makes every other Gurnemanz seem generalized". Whether being sad, admonitory, spiritual or celebratory, this Gurnemanz commands the stage by virtue of warm, grand tone and verbal detailing. George London's Amfortas, also heard on the 1951 set, is as urgent and tormented as Amfortas should be, quite frightening in his anguished declamation. Neidlinger isn't a match for Uhde as Klingsor (1951), but his biting interpretation falls little short of Uhde's ideal.

Jess Thomas, a little too non-committal in Act 1 (though this standing-apart isn't wholly inappropriate), comes into his own in Act 2, playful with the Flowers, forcefully dismissive and pained with Kundry. Inspired by Hotter, he rises to heights of feeling in the Good Friday music. Only the touch of mysticism in the finale is missing. Dalis has always been accused of aping Mödl, but that is hardly worrying as her performance has presence and is articulated intelligently. The sensuousness of "Ich sah das Kind" is missing, however. Talvela is a sonorous, too youthful-sounding Titurel.

No other recording can quite catch the very special Bayreuth aura, or indeed Knappertsbusch's total concept, and the vocal calibre of his cast, all so vitally heard here.

Wagner Parsifal.

Siegfried Jerusalem *ten* Parsifal
Bernd Weikl *bar* Amfortas
Kurt Moll *bass* Gurnemanz
Waltraud Meier *mez* Kundry
Franz Mazura *bar* Klingsor
Jan-Hendrik Rootering *bass* Titurel
Paul Groves *ten* First knight
Jeffrey Wells *bass-bar* Second knight
Heidi Grant Murphy *mez* First squire, First flower maiden
Jane Bunnell *mez* Second squire, Third flower maiden
John Horton Murray *bar* Third squire
Bernard Fitch *ten* Fourth squire
Kaaren Erickson *sop* Second flower maiden
Korliss Uecker *sop* Fourth flower maiden
Gwynne Geyer *sop* Fifth flower maiden
Wendy White *mez* Sixth Flower Maiden
Gwenneth Bean *contr* Voice from above
Chorus and Orchestra of the Metropolitan Opera, New York / James Levine.
Stage Director: **Otto Schenk.** *Video Director:* **Brian Large.**
DG Ⓕ ⬛⬛ 072 435-3GH2 (four cassettes: 266 minutes). Recorded 1992.

This isn't half as tedious a performance as its CD counterpart, partly because the context of a live performance prevents Levine from slowing down so excessively and confines his orchestra to the pit, thereby avoiding the false balance on CD, but mainly because of Meier's electrifying Kundry. Impressive as is Norman on the sound-only version and Meier herself on the Barenboim set (Teldec) she here surpasses both those portrayals by virtue of creating a wholly convincing temptress in Act 2 and tortured soul in Acts 1 and 3. As in her portrayal of the role at Bayreuth, she simply is Kundry, having thought herself voice, body and soul into the part, a wholly remarkable achievement which is the stuff of legends, on a par with, say, Callas's Tosca or Sutherland's Lucia. Nothing in the performance could hope to match that assumption, but all the parts, save the tired-sounding Klingsor, are more effectively cast than on the CD set, with Moll that much more eloquent live than he was in the studio. Jerusalem, although his voice has lost some of the bloom and ease it had when he recorded the part for Barenboim, is still a more than welcome Parsifal, enacting the petulant youth as well as he does the experienced Knight. Weikl's Amfortas is well routined though not exceptional in accents or tone. Levine is, as already suggested, a shade more lively here than on CD and cannot allow his orchestra to revel in their own virtuosity.

When it was new in 1991, Schenk's staging was accepted as a sensible if conventional piece of work. Within Schneider-Siemssen's dated-looking sets, it is almost pre-Wieland in its realism, but with topless maidens and a good deal of sexual imagery and erotic play allowed in Act 2. Brian Large has filmed it all with his customary acuity. He was also responsible for the previous, Bayreuth 1983, video of another conventional staging, Wolfgang Wagner's, conducted by Stein on Philips. That has a younger, more personable Jerusalem as Parsifal and a steadier Weikl as Amfortas. Randová is a strong but monochrome Kundry, less articulate and seductive than Meier. Sotin is as reliable a Gurnemanz as Moll. Because of Meier, though, this more recent set is preferable.

Wagner Rienzi.

René Kollo *ten* Rienzi
Cheryl Studer *sop* Irene
Jan-Hendrik Rootering *bass* Steffano Colonna
John Janssen *bar* Adriano Colonna
Bodo Brinkmann *bar* Paolo Orsini
Karl Helm *bass* Raimondo
Norbert Orth *ten* Baroncelli
Kieth Engen *bass* Cecco del Vecchio
Carmen Anhorn *sop* Messenger of Peace
Bavarian State Opera Chorus and Orchestra / Wolfgang Sawallisch.
Orfeo d'Or Ⓔ Ⓒ C346953D (three discs: 195 minutes: ADD). Notes included. Recorded at a performance in the Nationaltheater, Munich on July 6th, 1983.

In 1983 Sawallisch had just taken over as Intendant at the Bavarian State Opera and managed to present all 13 of Wagner's stage works to mark the centenary of the composer's death. So this performance was quite an occasion, made more so by Sawallisch's obvious dedication to his manifold tasks, not least this arduous one. That said, the evening seemed interminable. The staging was feeble, and four hours of indifferent, immature, Meyerbeerian Wagner on a hot night gave little pleasure.

At the time a record of the occasion was promised but it took more than 12 years to appear. *Rienzi* is remarkable only in that within a few years Wagner could be transformed from the garrulous writer of this score, which would surely never be performed were it not by Wagner, into the taut and inspired composer of *Der fliegende Holländer*, even though some of the less attractive features of *Tannhäuser* are already discernible. Sawallisch's conducting, confident, long-breathed and thus managing to make us forget many of the score's banalities, and the playing of his orchestra are good reasons for hearing the set, and a further one is the fledgling Studer, who on stage made a distinct impression as the put-upon Irene and does so again in purely vocal terms. Kollo is a more appealing Rienzi here than for Hollreiser and encompasses his long part in the proceedings with decent tone and amazing stamina. But the performance is lamed by Sawallisch's casting of Adriano with a high baritone rather than a mezzo. Janssen, singing the part down an octave, often sounds pressed by its tessitura. The remainder of the cast is drawn from Munich regulars of varying ability.

Sawallisch is said to have restored cuts but he conducts 30 or so minutes less than Hollreiser of what was originally a six-hour score. For those who want more of the music, Hollreiser remains the choice. In any case, he yields nothing to Sawallisch in his interpretation and his orchestra are also excellent. EMI also offer the advantage of a libretto and translation, Orfeo only a synopsis, a serious drawback.

Wagner Rienzi.

René Kollo *ten* Rienzi
Siv Wennberg *sop* Irene
Nikolaus Hillebrand *bass* Steffano Colonna
Janis Martin *sop* Adriano Colonna
Theo Adam *bass* Paolo Orsini
Siegfried Vogel *bass* Raimondo
Peter Schreier *ten* Baroncelli
Gunther Leib *bass* Cecco del Vecchio
Ingeborg Springer *sop* Messenger of Peace
Leipzig Radio Chorus; Dresden State Opera Chorus; Staatskapelle Dresden / Heinrich Hollreiser.
EMI Ⓜ Ⓒ CMS7 63980-2 (three discs: 225 minutes: ADD). Notes, text and translation included. Recorded 1974-6.

"First recording" proclaimed the five-LP box in 1976. In these circumstances, three very well-filled CDs at medium price of a performance that has undeniable virtues were to be welcomed for restoring a milestone in the history of opera to circulation. Listeners persuaded that Wagner only really found himself with *Der fliegende Holländer* may well be surprised to hear how much of that work – and of *Tannhäuser* and *Lohengrin* – is prefigured in *Rienzi*. It is nevertheless more grand opera than romantic opera, not least because the hero (the tragic Roman tribune of Bulwer Lytton's novel) is so completely a political animal; his bride, he declares to his sister in Act 5, is Rome. As for the 'grandness', this is all too evident in the extensive marches, choruses and ballet music, as well as in the predominantly forceful rhetoric of the solo vocal writing. Even in his greatest works, Wagner was not exactly addicted to understatement. In *Rienzi* (especially Act 3) the sustained tone of hectic aggressiveness threatens to become monotonous, and it would certainly be hard to take in a performance with less sense of theatrical impetus than this one.

The principal credit for the recording's success – all the more remarkable since it was made in two quite separate periods in 1974 and 1976 – is due to the conductor, Heinrich Hollreiser. He prevents the more routine material from sounding merely mechanical, and ensures that the whole work has a sweep and a conviction that persuades you that there is no reason for its continued exclusion from the Bayreuth canon: indeed, Bayreuth might be the ideal theatre for its large-scale spectacle. Hollreiser's cast is uneven: distinguished singers like Theo Adam and Peter Schreier have little to do, whereas the main parts would tax the greatest artists in best voice. The chief disappointment is Siv Wennberg, who had promised well in Wagner in the theatre but who was clearly under strain when this recording was made. René Kollo often sounds as though he is singing through gritted teeth, but the character's impulsiveness is here, and this quality is probably more crucial than any heroic nobility or religious sensibility. Janis Martin also conveys youthful impetuosity, and she, at least, is able to discover a gentler vein now and again.

There are some minor problems with the booklet – an incorrect cue for track 13 on the first disc, a missing line of text near the start of the third: but at least the libretto is included. The recording is no more than adequate by today's standards. Fortunately, the conductor's evident (and justified) belief in the significance of the enterprise remains as persuasive as ever.

Wagner Der Ring des Nibelungen.

Das Rheingold.
George London *bass-bar* Wotan
Kirsten Flagstad *sop* Fricka
Set Svanholm *ten* Loge
Paul Kuen *ten* Mime
Gustav Neidlinger *bass* Alberich
Claire Watson *sop* Freia
Waldemar Kmentt *ten* Froh
Eberhard Waechter *bar* Donner
Jean Madeira *contr* Erda
Walter Kreppel *bass* Fasolt
Kurt Böhme *bass* Fafner
Oda Balsborg *sop* Woglinde
Hetty Plümacher *sop* Wellgunde
Ira Malaniuk *mez* Flosshilde

Die Walküre.
James King *ten* Siegmund
Régine Crespin *sop* Sieglinde
Birgit Nilsson *sop* Brünnhilde
Hans Hotter *bass-bar* Wotan
Christa Ludwig *mez* Fricka
Gottlob Frick *bass* Hunding
Vera Schlosser *sop* Gerhilde
Berit Lindholm *sop* Helmwige
Helga Dernesch *sop* Ortlinde
Brigitte Fassbaender *mez* Waltraute
Claudia Hellmann *sop* Rossweisse
Vera Little *contr* Siegrune
Marilyn Tyler *sop* Grimgerde
Helen Watts *contr* Schwertleite

Siegfried.
Wolfgang Windgassen *ten* Siegfried
Hans Hotter *bass-bar* Wanderer
Birgit Nilsson *sop* Brünnhilde

Gerhard Stolze *ten* Mime
Gustav Neidlinger *bass* Alberich
Marga Höffgen *contr* Erda
Kurt Böhme *bass* Fafner
Dame Joan Sutherland *sop* Woodbird

Götterdämmerung.

Birgit Nilsson *sop* Brünnhilde
Wolfgang Windgassen *ten* Siegfried
Gottlob Frick *bass* Hagen
Gustav Neidlinger *bass* Alberich
Dietrich Fischer-Dieskau *bar* Gunther
Claire Watson *sop* Gutrune
Christa Ludwig *mez* Waltraute
Dame Gwyneth Jones *sop* Wellgunde
Lucia Popp *sop* Woglinde
Maureen Guy *mez* Flosshilde
Helen Watts *contr* First Norn
Grace Hoffman *mez* Second Norn
Anita Välkki *sop* Third Norn
Vienna State Opera Chorus; Vienna Philharmonic Orchestra / Sir Georg Solti.
Decca Ⓑ Ⓓ 455 555-2DMO14 (14 discs: 876 minutes: ADD). Notes, texts and translations
included. Recorded 1958-65. *Also available separately.*

Classics of the gramophone have to move with the times, and in its latest manifestation, 40 years from
the first LP issue of *Das Rheingold*, the Solti/Decca *Ring*, first issued on CD in 1985, is now available
at bargain price. As perspectives on the Solti/Culshaw enterprise lengthen, and critical reactions are
kept alert by the regular appearance of new, or newly issued, and very different recordings, it may
seem increasingly ironic that of all conductors the ultra-theatrical Solti should have been denied a live
performance. There are indeed episodes in this recording that convey more of the mechanics of the
studio than of the electricity of the opera-house – the opening of *Die Walküre*, Act 2, and the closing
scenes of *Siegfried* and *Götterdämmerung*, for example. Yet, in general, dramatic impetus and
atmosphere are strongly established and well sustained, sometimes more powerfully than is usually
managed in the theatre. As just one example one would instance the superb control with which the
intensity of Donner's summoning up of the thunder in *Das Rheingold* is maintained across Froh's
greeting to the rainbow bridge (which often falls flat in the theatre) into Wotan's own great salutation.
At the majestic climax of this scene the power of feeling conveyed by George London's fine
performance counts for more than any 'artificiality' in the way the voice is balanced against the
orchestra. Equally memorable in a totally different context is Solti's management of the long
transition in *Götterdämmerung* between Hagen's Watch and the appearance of Waltraute. Nothing
could be less mannered or unnatural than Solti's grasp of perspective and feeling for the life of each
phrase in this music.
    Even so, we are not proposing to offer a full-blown revisionist interpretation of Solti's *Ring*, arguing
that he always prefers deliberation to impetuosity and that the recording itself has the ideal natural
balance. On CD the clarity of instrumental detail is consistently remarkable, and while not all the
singers sound as if they are constantly in danger of being overwhelmed (Hagen's Watch is a good
example of an appropriately forward vocal balance) there are some vital episodes especially those
involving Wolfgang Windgassen and Birgit Nilsson. Awareness of what these artists achieved in other
recordings strengthens the suspicion that they may have been giving more than we actually get in this
case. Windgassen in particular is not allowed to dominate the sound picture in the way his part
demands, and Nilsson can seem all-too relaxed within the comforting cocoon of the orchestral
texture. Factors like these, coupled with those distinctive Soltian confrontations between the hard-
driven and the hammily protracted, have prevented the Decca cycle from decisively seeing off all its
various rivals over the years.
    It is nevertheless still open to question whether any studio recording of *The Ring* could reasonably
be expected to be more atmospheric, exciting or better performed than this one. The Vienna
Philharmonic are not merely prominent, but excellent, and such interpretations as Svanholm's Loge,
Neidlinger's Alberich and Frick's Hagen remain immensely impressive. Above all, there is Hans
Hotter, whose incomparably authoritative, unfailingly alert and responsive Wotan stands up well
when compared to his earlier Bayreuth accounts. Nowhere is he more commanding than in *Siegfried*,
Act 1, where one even welcomes Stolze's mannerisms as Mime for the sparks they strike off the great
bass-baritone. Earlier in this act the interplay of equally balanced instruments and voices in relatively
intimate conversational phrases displays the Culshaw concept at its most convincing. The care taken
over the SonicStage production was graphically chronicled by Culshaw in *Ring Resounding* (Secker
& Warburg: 1967). He would have been astonished to hear what his successors have achieved in
renewing his production through digital remastering. One now realizes how much of the original
sound was lost on the old pressings. What we now have is exactly what was achieved and recorded in
the Sofiensaal in Vienna in those pioneering days back in 1958. Which brings us to comparisons with

the 1980 Janowski/RCA version (reviewed below). The approaches of the two recordings are so different that they almost seem like different experiences. Whereas Culshaw was intent on creating a theatre on record with all the well-known stage effects, the rival version eschews all such manifestations. In general, Janowski presents a much more intimate view of the work, more contained than Solti's.

So there can be no doubt that, despite the occasional thumps from Solti, despite somewhat skimpy presentation (the *Götterdämmerung* tracks are not timed), and however many other *Rings* you may have, your collection will be the poorer without this one.

Wagner Der Ring des Nibelungen.

Das Rheingold.

Theo Adam *bass-bar* Wotan
Yvonne Minton *mez* Fricka
Peter Schreier *ten* Loge
Christian Vogel *ten* Mime
Siegmund Nimsgern *bass-bar* Alberich
Marita Napier *sop* Freia
Eberhard Büchner *ten* Froh
Karl-Heinz Stryczek *bass* Donner
Ortrun Wenkel *contr* Erda
Roland Bracht *bass* Fasolt
Matti Salminen *bass* Fafner
Lucia Popp *sop* Woglinde
Uta Priew *mez* Wellgunde
Hanna Schwarz *contr* Flosshilde

Die Walküre.

Siegfried Jerusalem *ten* Siegmund
Jessye Norman *sop* Sieglinde
Jeannine Altmeyer *sop* Brünnhilde
Theo Adam *bass-bar* Wotan
Yvonne Minton *mez* Fricka
Kurt Moll *bass* Hunding
Eva-Maria Bundschuh *sop* Gerhilde
Ruth Falcon *sop* Helmwige
Cheryl Studer *sop* Ortlinde
Ortrun Wenkel *contr* Waltraute
Uta Priew *mez* Rossweisse
Christel Borchers *mez* Siegrune
Kathleen Kuhlmann *contr* Grimgerde
Anne Gjevang *contr* Schwertleite

Siegfried.

René Kollo *ten* Siegfried
Theo Adam *bass-bar* Wanderer
Jeannine Altmeyer *sop* Brünnhilde
Peter Schreier *ten* Mime
Siegmund Nimsgern *bass-bar* Alberich
Ortrun Wenkel *contr* Erda
Matti Salminen *bass* Fafner
Norma Sharp *sop* Woodbird

Götterdämmerung.

Jeannine Altmeyer *sop* Brünnhilde
René Kollo *ten* Siegfried
Matti Salminen *bass* Hagen
Siegmund Nimsgern *bass-bar* Alberich
Hans Günter Nöcker *bar* Gunther
Norma Sharp *sop* Gutrune
Ortrun Wenkel *contr* Waltraute
Uta Priew *mez* Wellgunde
Lucia Popp *sop* Woglinde
Hanna Schwarz *contr* Flosshilde
Anne Gjevang *contr* First Norn
Daphne Evangelotos *mez* Second Norn
Ruth Falcon *sop* Third Norn

**Mens' Voices of the Leipzig State Opera; Dresden State Opera Chorus;
Staatskapelle Dresden / Marek Janowski.**
RCA Victor Red Seal ® ℗ 74321 45417-2 (14 discs: 839 minutes: DDD). Notes, texts and
translations included. Recorded 1980.

Here's another true and desirable bargain. This, the first digitally recorded cycle to appear on CD, has
always had a great deal to commend it even at full price. Now at the budget level, it becomes even
more attractive. One of its most telling assets is the actual recording, still the most natural, clear and
most sensitively balanced available. Then it has the Dresden Staatskapelle playing with the utmost
beauty from start to finish – try the start of Act 3 of *Götterdämmerung* – and with lean power when
that's called for. There's no feeling, as with some of its predecessors or successors, that the orchestral
sound is being artificially boosted: voices and players are in an ideal relationship. Which is not to say
that such purple passages as the Magic Fire Music, Ride of the Valkyries, Rhine Journey and Funeral
March want anything in visceral excitement.

Janowski conducts a direct, dramatic interpretation, concerned throughout with forward
movement. His clear-sighted conducting, based on textural clarity, conveys theatrical excitement from
start to finish without fuss or attempts at portentous readings. Janowski sees the cycle more as the
culmination of what has gone before in the nineteenth century rather than as a new art. All this makes
it an ideal introduction to the *Ring* for any young collector, who can later go on to more
philosophically inclined interpretations. Even Wagnerians who are not quite so young will themselves
again be enthralled by these recordings.

The casts are by and large excellent. *Das Rheingold* is dominated by three central performances –
Nimsgern's vibrant, articulate Alberich, Schreier's wonderfully vital, strikingly intelligent and
articulate Loge and Adam's experienced Wotan. But Fricka, Giants and Rhinemaidens are all well
cast, and the whole performance grips one's attention from start to finish as the kaleidoscopic drama
unfolds. *Die Walküre* introduces us to Norman's involving if not wholly idiomatic Sieglinde and, even
better, the youthful Jerusalem's near-ideal Siegmund, forthright and sincere, not forgetting Moll's
granite Hunding. Adam is so authoritative, so keen with the text, so inside his part that an occasional
unsteadiness can be overlooked. With Altmeyer's Brünnhilde we come to the one drawback of the set.
Though in this and the succeeding operas, we are thankful for such clear, clean and youthful tone, her
reading is unformed and one-dimensional, lacking the essential insights of a Varnay or Behrens. The
other Valkyries need to be mentioned because they include singers such as Studer, soon to go on to
greater things; as such they stand out among recorded broods.

In the title-role in *Siegfried* Kollo gives one of his most attractive portrayals on disc, full of
thoughtful diction poised on clear-cut tone. Schreier misses nothing in his interpretation of the
dissembling, wily Mime, Adam is at his very best as the wise, old Wanderer, and the smaller parts are
well catered for. In *Götterdämmerung*, Salminen is a commanding, often subtle Hagen, though
inclined to bark in his call, Nöcker a splendid Gunther. Kollo is here harder pressed than in the
previous work, and inclined to force, but as ever his musical singing compensates for the faults.
Altmeyer fails to dominate as she should, but is never less than adequate, sometimes more than that.
Again the smaller parts, especially Rhinemaidens, led by Popp, are well taken.

We wouldn't hesitate to recommend this *Ring* to anyone wanting a reasonably priced introduction
to the cycle. Even at a higher level, it has much going for it in comparison with supposedly more
prestigious recordings.

Wagner Der Ring Des Nibelungen.

Das Rheingold.

Theo Adam *bass-bar* Wotan
Annelies Burmeister *mez* Fricka
Wolfgang Windgassen *ten* Loge
Erwin Wohlfahrt *ten* Mime
Gustav Neidlinger *bass* Alberich
Anja Silja *sop* Freia
Hermin Esser *ten* Froh
Gerd Nienstedt *bass* Donner
Vera Soukupová *mez* Erda
Martti Talvela *bass* Fasolt
Kurt Böhme *bass* Fafner
Dorothea Siebert *sop* Woglinde
Helga Dernesch *sop* Wellgunde
Ruth Hesse *mez* Flosshilde
Bayreuth Festival Chorus and Orchestra / Karl Böhm.
Philips Ⓟ ℗ 412 475-2PH2 (two discs: 137 minutes: ADD). Notes, text and translation included.
Recorded at a performance at the Bayreuth Festival in 1967.
Der Ring Des Nibelungen (complete) available on Philips ® ℗ 446 057-2PB14 (14 discs:
819 minutes: ADD). Synopsis included.

Die Walküre.

James King *ten* Siegmund
Leonie Rysanek *sop* Sieglinde
Birgit Nilsson *sop* Brünnhilde
Theo Adam *bass* Wotan
Annelies Burmeister *mez* Fricka, Siegrune
Gerd Nienstedt *bass* Hunding
Danica Mastilovic *sop* Gerthilde
Liane Synek *sop* Helmwige
Helga Dernesch *sop* Ortlinde
Gertraud Hopf *mez* Waltraute
Sona Cervená *mez* Rossweisse
Elisabeth Schärtel *contr* Grimgarde
Sieglinde Wagner *contr* Schwertleite
Bayreuth Festival Chorus and Orchestra / Karl Böhm.
Philips Ⓕ ① 412 478-2PH4 (four discs: 210 minutes: ADD).Notes, text and translation included.
Recorded at a performance at the 1967 Bayreuth Festival.

Siegfried.

Wolfgang Windgassen *ten* Siegfried
Theo Adam *bass* Wanderer
Birgit Nilsson *sop* Brünnhilde
Erwin Wohlfahrt *ten* Mime
Gustav Neidlinger *bass* Alberich
Vera Soukupová *mez* Erda
Kurt Böhme *bass* Fafner
Erika Köth *sop* Woodbird
Bayreuth Festival Orchestra / Karl Böhm.
Philips Ⓕ ① 412 483-2PH4 (four discs: 223 minutes: ADD). Notes, text and translation included.
Recorded at performances at the Bayreuth Festival during 1967.

Götterdämmerung.

Birgit Nilsson *sop* Brünnhilde
Wolfgang Windgassen *ten* Siegfried
Josef Greindl *bass* Hagen
Gustav Neidlinger *bass-bar* Alberich
Thomas Stewart *bar* Gunther
Ludmila Dvořaková *sop* Gutrune
Martha Mödl *mez* Waltraute
Helga Dernesch *sop* Wellgunde
Dorothea Siebert *sop* Woglinde
Sieglinde Wagner *contr* Flosshilde
Marga Höffgen *contr* First Norn
Annelies Burmeister *mez* Second Norn
Anja Silja *sop* Third Norn
Bayreuth Festival Chorus and Orchestra / Karl Böhm.
Philips Ⓕ ① 412 488-2PH4 (four discs: 249 minutes: ADD). Notes, text and translation included.
Recorded at a performance at the Bayreuth Festival in 1967.

Charting a path through the maze of *Ring* recordings becomes ever more complex as the sets pile up on the shelves. Philips have neatly recycled Böhm's classic Bayreuth set as a budget box (no libretto) comprising 14 discs. Parts 1-4 are, of course, still available separately. Now that we have so many complete *Ring* cycles available on CD, it is impossible to make an absolute decision on which is best. Discussion about the front runners is therefore in order. Those who have opted for Janowski (RCA) need not, by any means, feel that they were short-changed; in some vocal matters, it is deficient, but the interpretation remains remarkably consistent and consistently cast, which cannot be said of either Karajan (DG, 1967/8) or Solti (Decca).

For all his avowed aim at a chamber-music texture, Karajan never skimps climaxes: quite the contrary, as you can easily test in the Valkyrie ride, the close of *Das Rheingold*, or the awakening of Brünnhilde. Solti's whole interpretation tends to be more histrionic and energetic, Karajan's the more reflective; it is also more refined and, at times, more ecstatic than Solti's, and that is only emphasized on CD, where one is time and again ravished by sound alone. But, if we take as an example the conversation between Brünnhilde and Wotan in Act 3 of *Die Walküre*, both conductors, and the singers, sound less involved and so less communicative than their Böhm counterparts, and it is the acoustic on the Böhm set that both gains most by the digital reprocessing and by its natural, theatre balance. Of course, Brünnhilde and Wotan are two of the most important characters in *The Ring*. As Crespin points out in her autobiography (available only in France), when she was approached by Michel Glotz (DG's producer) she thought Sieglinde was to be her role, as it is for Solti. She enjoyed working with Karajan on Brünnhilde, in recording and the theatre, but knew all too well that this was a once-only performance. In the dialogue just mentioned she is at her most persuasive, a young warrior-maid as Karajan intended, and certain phrases have never been so touchingly inflected; the soft entreaty to her father is gentler than any in memory. She cannot match Nilsson's heroic utterance and, for Böhm, her radiant and detailed interpretation. Nor is Dernesch, in the last two operas, Nilsson's peer. This is, again, a youthful goddess, but fallible vocally at times, where Nilsson is infallible; but there is much womanly inflection to admire in Dernesch's often noble portrayal.

Fischer-Dieskau's highly intelligent *Das Rheingold* Wotan (Karajan) is occasionally barked when Wagner forces him beyond his natural capabilities. Otherwise his account of the part is as musical and intelligent as one would expect it to be. Altogether, Karajan's *Das Rheingold* is a delight. A superb trio of Rhinemaidens starts it glowingly (Anna Reynolds the best Flosshilde ever heard). Kelemen is almost Neidlinger's equal as Alberich (Solti). Stolze's Loge is a noteworthy creation, but its verbal mannerisms are even more apparent on CD. Talvela is the best of all Fasolts, so warm of expression, so commanding of voice. He changes to menace as Hunding in *Die Walküre*. Veasey, in both works, is a nagging, fluent Fricka, few better. Janowitz's Sieglinde is lovely to hear, but cool, no match for Vickers's intense but overarticulated Siegmund: Act 1 never sounds the overwhelming, urgent matter it is with Böhm and on Furtwängler's set (Music & Arts, 1950). Act 2 brings us Thomas Stewart's fatherly, firmly-sung Wotan (but his Wanderer, less secure, is no match for Decca's Hotter in authority). Adam (Böhm), with a deeper understanding of the text, exerts greater authority.

On the whole, Karajan's *Die Walküre*·is still 'undercooked', for all its aural splendour on CD. His *Siegfried* is more powerfully imagined but its casting is faulty. Thomas, for all his occasional moments of youthful exuberance not found in Windgassen's mature reading (Solti and Böhm), hasn't the experience to convey a rounded characterization. Dominguez, whose voice is recessed deliberately, sounds suitably other-wordly. With *Götterdämmerung*, Karajan's *Ring* reaches the stature one looks for – but so do his rivals. The recording is again electrifying, with much sense of the theatre. Though vocally still not a match for Nilsson, Dernesch makes a noble, appealing Brünnhilde, a reminder of what should have been a great career as a Hochdramatische. Her "Welchen Unholds List" in Act 2 shows her and Karajan's interior way with the music. Brilioth gains in assurance and communication as the work progresses; again great promise remained unfulfilled. But both artists have suitable memorials here. Riddderbusch is much softer grained as Hagen than Frick (Solti), a world-weary, subtle half-dwarf, rather than Frick's more melodramatic, black reading. Greindl (Böhm) is preferable to either. Claire Watson (Solti) is a more pointed, sensuous Gutrune than Janowitz, Fischer-Dieskau (Solti) a more nervous Gunther than the more conventionally vacillating Stewart. Ludwig's highly-charged Waltraute fits in with both the Karajan and Solti interpretations. Good Norns on both sets, better Rhinemaindens with Karajan.

Throughout all the Karajan sets, one is consistently aware of the lyrical beauty of the whole work, just how much unsurpassed orchestration, and subtle transformations there are in the score. It is a version that needs to be heard for almost the ultimate in orchestral playing. Yet Karajan remains always thoughtful to his singers, as did the DG engineers; the balance between voices and orchestra is unfailingly right throughout, as it is not on the Decca, so you could say that this is the most truthful of all *The Ring* sets.

But then listen to Böhm to remind you that it is impossible in the studio, even the acoustically splendid church in which Karajan recorded his *Ring*, wholly to conjure up a theatre ambience, so arrestingly caught in this *Rheingold* as in the other instalments of the Böhm *Ring*. Special recording devices do not necessarily ensure the greatest drama in a recorded performance, and the naturalness of the Bayreuth sound once again impresses; so does the immediacy of the performance. In *Rheingold* one has to admit that Böhm sometimes presses forward too hard, particularly so in the opening scene, and later when Fasolt is speaking of the golden apples, but by and large his incandescent approach fires the stage of great things. Neidlinger, who appears with Solti, and Talvela, Karajan's Fasolt, are even more vital here, both giving readings unsurpassed on record: Neidlinger's curse is chilling. Windgassen's Loge seems to be full of interpretative insight without Stolze's exaggerations, and his few alterations to the text matter little. Adam, once over some initial wobbling, is as authoritative as ever; his tone is more grainy but also more even than Fischer-Dieskau's. Burmeister is more than adequate as Fricka. The lesser gods are excellent, Silja's Freia more urgent in her appeals to her brothers than those on any other version. Where Karajan has the best Flosshilde, Böhm benefits from the warmest Wellgunde in the young Dernesch. Wohlfahrt, as for Karajan, is a subtle Mime, and in Böhm's cycle, he is heard again in *Siegfried*.

The Nibelungs' hammerings (Böhm) aren't so overwhelming as on either the Decca or DG sets, and the same applies to other effects. Occasional changes in perspective and stage noises only add to the illusion of attending the theatre at Bayreuth. The experience is perhaps not so all-enveloping as with the Karajan, but it is certainly as engrossing as any other. It won't have escaped the notice of the economy-minded that Philips have managed to transfer the recording on to two CDs. Those who have been gradually collecting the Böhm *Ring* needn't hesitate. Newcomers need not feel it is inferior to Solti and Karajan, and as part of a consistent performance of the cycle, the casts remain uniform.

Böhm's swift-footed, openly histrionic *Walküre* will obviously not please those who prefer a more reflective, metaphysical reading, but – like other Wagner music-dramas – this is a work for the stage and about people and events, and Böhm makes you believe that this is a here-and-now story set to magnificent music: he lives every moment of both without letting you forget the longer view, or being unaware of the need to allow the music to soar and surge at climaxes. Here we have the real passion of the illicit lovers in Act 1, the fury and anguish of a father-god and the impetuous, womanly feelings of his daughter-goddess in the succeeding acts. That sense of immediacy is greatly enhanced by virtue of the live recording at Bayreuth. Neither Solti's or Janowski's sets, in the nature of things, has that sense of something coming at you from a real theatrical event in honest, totally unvarnished sound. To add to its benefits we have a Bayreuth orchestra of vintage quality, or perhaps one trained to a pitch of excellence by Böhm, who would never let any kind of *Schlamperei* past his acute ears.

The cast, though far from perfect, is at least the equal of any that could be assembled today, and in one respect decidedly superior. This is, of course, Nilsson's Brünnhilde caught at the peak of that soprano's powers and throughout more involved, quite naturally, than in the Decca studio recording. Theo Adam, in fresher voice than for Janowski, is a straightforward, articulate Wotan, who fits in very well with Böhm's reading, while not having Hotter's (for Solti) interior, spiritual dimension to his singing. Rysanek sings unevenly as Sieglinde, but as ever offers a moving portrayal of Sieglinde's plight and an ecstatic adumbration of her passion, which is vividly responded to by James King's Siegmund. Indeed, in the light of what we hear today, King's attributes may have been undervalued when he was in his prime. Gerd Nienstedt is a vigorous, properly nasty Hunting.

The Böhm *Siegfried* convinces you that this is the most truthful and natural-sounding, not to say the most exciting available. You are struck by the excellence of the theatrical balance, its immediacy, its absence of electronic device. Each singer seems to give that extra bit of dramatic conviction while performing on stage, and marvelled at the standard of Wagnerian singing to be heard in the performance as throughout the cycle. Windgassen is an untiring Siegfried, also in Acts 2 and 3 a most poetic one. His sterling qualities need rehearsing once more in view of the limitations of his successors, and in the final duet he remains a match for Nilsson's resplendent Brünnhilde, a priceless asset here, as on the Solti/Decca version, but just that much more involving at Bayreuth.

Theo Adam is perhaps in his most stirring, articulate and broad-phrasing form as the Wanderer, worldly-wise with Mime, authoritative with Alberich, urgent with Erda, sympathetic with Siegfried in four of the duologues that are the essence of *Siegfried*. Neidlinger remains unsurpassed as Alberich and Wohlfahrt is among the most accurate of Mimes, but he does occasionally indulge in Stolze-like cackling. Köth isn't the most airy of Woodbirds, but at the other end of the scale, Böhme is an imposing Fafner.

Over all presides Böhm, ever alive to the vivid, illustrative side of Wagner's writing as he is to its incandescence. Where he can fail is in moment of moving reposes as after the splitting of Wotan's spear; these call for the more metaphysical approach of a Furtwängler. But in this, nor any other respect, is Böhm in any way inferior to his rivals. The recording balance is superior on Karajan's DG; orchestral detail is clearer on Solti's Decca. But for a real experience of *Siegfried* as music drama (listen to the Siegfried/Fafner encounter), Böhm is the man, Bayreuth the place. The immediacy of it is still astounding.

The Böhm and Solti performances of *Götterdämmerung* have always been fitting climaxes to their respective *Ring* cycles, and at the same time they are wholly typical of the characteristics of conductors and recordings. The effect of either, taken on its own, is as overwhelming as any performance of *Götterdämmerung* should be. Whether you prefer one to the other depends not so much on the calibre of the interpretation, which is mighty in each case, but on what you want to hear in your home. While the reading of each is not so dissimilar, stemming from the innate dramatic response of both Solti and Böhm, the results are quite contrasted, mainly because of the differences in recording venues and techniques.

The Decca remains a startling experience in the home, a revelation in sound quality enhanced by CD. It also remains a performance dominated by conductor and orchestra. You will never hear so much detail of the orchestral score in the opera-house, and you certainly hear less on the Philips. At times, such as in Waltraute's warning and the consequent disaster for Brünnhilde, then again in the closing scenes of the whole work, you feel as if you were in the theatre, so involving are the performers; at other times, particularly in direct comparison with the Bayreuth set, you become aware this is a studio performance; the ambience is that of the studio, and the total silence of the background on CD only brings home the point. The very immediacy of the recording also calls attention to the aggressive energy of Solti's conducting, as in the great Second Act confrontation or the Funeral March. If you are in the mood for it, and the neighbours are out of earshot, it is thrilling on its own terms.

By direct comparison, the Philips, its sound quality enormously improved on CD, suggests the natural and excellent acoustic of the Bayreuth theatre; as with the Böhm *Die Walküre*, you imagine yourself in a Bayreuth stall on what must have been a memorable evening in 1967, and even by the side of the Decca, you will be surprised how much of the orchestral tissue can be heard. By the same token, you can also catch the occasional cough, prompter's whisper, and stage movement and that may deter some from appreciation of the Böhm set. However, most collectors prefer this evidence of human activity to the sometimes artificially contrived or electronic effects on the Decca – the added thunder at Waltraute's appearance, the baritonal resonance given to Siegfried's voice when disguised as Gunther by the Tarnhelm, the odd back-stage focusing of Alberich, the sword play of Hagen and Gunther in their fight, realistically as some of these are achieved.

Where the casts are concerned, honours are about even. Both performances are dominated by Nilsson's Brünnhilde. Magnificent as she is for Solti, her Bayreuth interpretation is just that much more taut and consistent, though allowance has to be made for one or two word fluffs. Indeed, with Böhm at his most incandescent, the Immolation must rank as one of the noblest accounts of this music ever recorded. Whichever performance you choose, you will hear a Brünnhilde unlikely to be equalled, vocally quite tireless even on stage and full of interpretative insights that she was not often given credit for during her distinguished career. With Windgassen, the balance favours his Decca performance, where he is in marginally fresher voice, but in both cases his reliability and musicianship are abiding assets, and his death scene is movingly tender in both versions.

Frick and Greindl were great Hagens. Greindl's is not quite so securely vocalized as his rival's, but Greindl manages to be the more implacable and nasty, his verbal declamation quite frightening, as he could be in the role on stage; here is a case where actuality does tell. His Watch and call to the vassals are performances to savour again and again. Like Greindl, Mödl's Waltraute is intent on giving every consonant its due; her performance is very much sung off the words. But she is unsteady and sometimes takes awkward breaths. With a voice in better condition, Ludwig is hardly less vital or concerned in her declamation. Fischer-Dieskau sounds almost too noble for poor, ineffectual Gunther; Stewart, by contrast, has a rough-hewn voice that suits this music. The Norns' scene sounds rather static on Decca; both Silja and Burmeister are superior to their Decca colleagues in conveying the Norns' anxious state of mind. Both sets have delightful Rhinemaidens. Neither Gutrune is ideal, but Watson is steadier, more blonde in tone than Dvořáková.

So Böhm seems to be at the top of the list for either the complete cycle (now at a most enticing bargain price for the complete set, or individual bricks), although the Janowski is a reasonable middle-of-the-road, studio-made (there are no stage noises) alternative. If you are wanting to build up a *Ring* by individual sets from various sources, Solti's 1959 *Das Rheingold* (still an amazing experience), the 1954 Furtwängler/VPO *Die Walküre*, the Barenboim Teldec *Siegfried* (with Jerusalem) as the best singer in the title-role, and many visceral excitements from the orchestra) and the Levine *Götterdämmerung*, a grand, well-considered interpretation, with Behrens's deeply eloquent Brünnhilde, Goldberg's serviceable Siegfried, Salminen's menacing, massive Hagen and Schwarz's unsurpassed Waltraute, are all in the frame. However, in the end you will derive most satisfaction from Böhm.

Wagner Der Ring des Nibelungen.

Das Rheingold.
Sir Donald McIntyre *bar* Wotan
Hanna Schwarz *mez* Fricka
Heinz Zednik *ten* Loge
Helmut Pampuch *ten* Mime
Hermann Becht *bass-bar* Alberich
Carmen Reppel *mez* Freia
Siegfried Jerusalem *ten* Froh
Martin Egel *bar* Donner
Ortrun Wenkel *mez* Erda
Matti Salminen *bass* Fasolt
Fritz Hübner *bass* Fafner
Norma Sharp *sop* Woglinde
Ilse Gramatzki *sop* Wellgunde
Marga Schiml *contr* Flosshilde
Bayreuth Festival Orchestra / Pierre Boulez.
Stage Director: **Patrice Chéreau.** *Television Director:* **Brian Large.**
Philips Ⓟ **⚟** 070 401-3PH (163 minutes). Recorded during the 1980 Bayreuth Festival.

B B C RADIO 3
90-93 FM

Die Walküre.
Peter Hofmann *ten* Siegmund
Jeannine Altmeyer *sop* Sieglinde
Dame Gwyneth Jones *sop* Brünnhilde
Sir Donald McIntyre *bar* Wotan
Hanna Schwarz *mez* Fricka
Matti Salminen *bass* Hunding
Carmen Reppel *mez* Gerhilde
Katie Clarke *mez* Helmwige
Karen Middleton *sop* Ortlinde
Gabriele Schnaut *mez* Waltraute
Elisabeth Glauser *mez* Rossweisse
Marga Schiml *mez* Siegrune
Ilse Gramatzki *mez* Grimgerde
Gwendolyn Killibrew *mez* Schwertleite
Bayreuth Festival Orchestra / Pierre Boulez.
Stage Director: **Patrice Chéreau.** *Television Director:* **Brian Large.**
Philips Ⓟ **⚟** 070 402-3PH2 (two cassettes: 216 minutes). Recorded 1980.

Siegfried.

Manfred Jung *ten* Siegfried
Sir Donald McIntyre *bar* Wanderer
Dame Gwyneth Jones *sop* Brünnhilde
Heinz Zednik *ten* Mime
Hermann Becht *bass-bar* Alberich
Ortrun Wenkel *mez* Erda
Fritz Hübner *bass* Fafner
Norma Sharp *sop* Woodbird
Bayreuth Festival Orchestra / Pierre Boulez.
Stage Director: **Patrice Chéreau.** *Television Director:* **Brian Large.**
Philips Ⓕ 🄳🄳 070 403-3PH2 (two cassettes: 225 minutes). Recorded 1980.

Götterdämmerung.

Dame Gwyneth Jones *sop* Brünnhilde
Manfred Jung *ten* Siegfried
Fritz Hübner *bass* Hagen
Hermann Becht *bass-bar* Alberich
Franz Mazura *bass* Gunther
Jeannine Altmeyer *sop* Gutrune
Gwendolyn Killibrew *mez* Waltraute
Norma Sharp *sop* Woglinde
Ilse Gramatzki *mez* Wellgunde
Marga Schiml *mez* Flosshilde
Ortun Wenkel *mez* First Norn
Gabriele Schnaut *mez* Second Norn
Katie Clarke *mez* Third Norn
Bayreuth Festival Chorus and Orchestra / Pierre Boulez.
Stage Director: **Patrice Chéreau.** *Television Director:* **Brian Large.**
Philips Ⓕ 🄳🄳 070 404-3PH2 (two cassettes: 250 minutes). Recorded 1980.

Wagner Der Ring des Nibelungen.

Das Rheingold.

Robert Hale *bass-bar* Wotan
Marjana Lipovšek *mez* Fricka
Robert Tear *ten* Loge
Helmut Pampuch *ten* Mime
Ekkehard Wlaschiha *bass-bar* Alberich
Nancy Gustafson *mez* Freia
Josef Hopferweiser *ten* Froh
Florian Cerny *bar* Donner
Hanna Schwarz *mez* Erda
Jan-Hendrik Rootering *bass* Fasolt
Kurt Moll *bass* Fafner
Julie Kaufmann *sop* Woglinde
Angela Maria Blasi *sop* Wellgunde
Birgit Calm *contr* Flosshilde
Bavarian State Opera Orchestra / Wolfgang Sawallisch.
Stage Director: **Nikolaus Lehnhoff.** *Television Direction:* **NHK Enterprises.**
EMI Ⓕ 🄳🄳 MVB9 91276-3 (two cassettes: 151 minutes). Recorded 1989.

1993

Die Walküre.

Robert Schunk *ten* Siegmund
Julia Varady *sop* Sieglinde
Hildegard Behrens *sop* Brünnhilde
Robert Hale *bass-bar* Wotan
Marjana Lipovšek *mez* Fricka
Kurt Moll *bass* Hunding
Andrea Trauboth *mez* Gerhilde
Nancy Gustafson *mez* Helmwige
Marianna Siebel *sop* Ortlinde
Cornelia Wulkopf *mez* Waltraute
Gudrun Wewezow *mez* Rossweisse
Christel Borchers *mez* Siegrune
Birgit Calm *mez* Grimgerde
Anna Pellekoorne *mez* Schwertleite

1993

Bavarian State Opera Orchestra / Wolfgang Sawallisch.
Stage Director: **Nikolaus Lehnhoff.** *Television Direction:* **NHK Enterprises.**
EMI Ⓕ **ᴄᴄ** MVB9 91279-3 (two cassettes: 225 minutes). Recorded 1989.

Siegfried.

René Kollo *ten* Siegfried
Robert Hale *bass-bar* Wanderer
Hildegard Behrens *sop* Brünnhilde
Helmut Pampuch *ten* Mime
Ekkehard Wlaschiha *bass-bar* Alberich
Hanna Schwarz *bass* Fafner
Julie Kaufmann *sop* Woodbird
Bavarian State Opera Orchestra / Wolfgang Sawallisch.
Stage Director. **Nikolaus Lehnhoff.** *Television Direction:* **NHK Enterprises.**
EMI Ⓕ **ᴄᴄ** MVD9 91283-3 (two cassettes: 235 minutes). Recorded 1989.

1993

Götterdämmerung.

Hildegard Behrens *sop* Brünnhilde
René Kollo *ten* Siegfried
Matti Salminen *bass* Hagen
Ekkehard Wlaschiha *bass-bar* Alberich
Hans Günter Nöcker *bass* Gunther
Lisbeth Balslev *sop* Gutrune
Waltraud Meier *mez* Waltraute
Julie Kaufmann *sop* Woglinde
Angela Maria Blasi *mez* Flosshilde
Marjana Lipovšek *mez* First Norn
Ingrid Karrasch *mez* Second Norn
Penelope Thorn *mez* Third Norn
Bavarian State Opera Chorus and Orchestra / Wolfgang Sawallisch.
Stage Director: **Nikolaus Lehnhoff.** *Television Direction:* **NHK Enterprises.**
EMI Ⓕ **ᴄᴄ** MVD9 91287-3 (two cassettes: 257 minutes). Recorded 1989.
The complete *Ring* is available as **ᴄᴄ** MVX9 91275-3 (eight cassettes).

1993

The scene between Brünnhilde and Waltraute on the EMI/Munich set says everything that needs to be said about how the cycle should be performed. Here Behrens and Meier, in total control of their voices and their bodies, create music drama under a director, Nikolaus Lehnhoff, who has encouraged them to look at and touch each other in a manner wholly apt to conveying Brünnhilde's complacent belief in the power of love, Waltraute's urgent concern and pleading (unsuccessful) to relinquish the ring for the good of everyone. Had Waltraute succeeded the whole story would have stopped there. If everything in the EMI performance were as arresting and vivid as this there would be no contest, but – of course – no interpretation of the *Ring* can ever tell the whole story, but only alight on a few facts.

These performances, the Bayreuth (with the famous Chéreau staging in its final, 1980 form), are specific in their aims of creating concepts that haven't and won't please traditionalists, but constantly provoke thought even when in the case of the Munich *Rheingold* they seem completely wrong-headed. They are in the end more satisfying and more likely to bear repetition than Schenk's production for the Metropolitan (Levine on DG), which largely follows Wagner's explicit stage directions, sets the work in myth-land and seldom requires its performers to touch, let alone feel each other. Nor does it challenge the viewer. We can now see that Chéreau set a new tradition in that area, for many close-contact moments in his staging are repeated in Lehnhoff's, particularly as regards the pairs of lovers. We are left in no doubt that they are infatuated with each other and will couple just before, or when the curtain comes down (Kupfer took things even further in the 1992 Bayreuth staging). Similarly both jump decades in the matter of setting and clothes. And Chéreau above anyone doesn't shirk the cruelty inherent in the cycle.

In this, as in much else, Chéreau is the more consistent and convincing: his view of the participants as roughly the children of the industrial revolution is carried out with thorough conviction helped by the genius of his designer, Richard Peduzi. Although the Lehnhoff staging has its moments – as in the finely proportioned, geometric set (Erich Wonder) for *Walküre* Act 2 and when the back of the stage opens up in *Siegfried* to reveal the Rhineland, it is Chéreau who manages not to throw out entirely the feeling of colour, nature (his *Siegfried* Act 2 forest is a mysterious yet beautiful place) and place, even offering a plausible Gibichung Hall, while at the same time emphasizing the work's relevance for our time. Of course, for DG Schenk's staging places scenes where the author predicates, but without enough imagination. However, he does score with a dragon that really looks dangerous, actually claws Siegfried and thrusts him down a slope before the hero finally lands his death blow.

As far as the filming is concerned, all three versions are well managed – that at Bayreuth and the Metropolitan by Brian Large, that at Munich by a Japanese director (the whole project was undertaken in co-operation with NHK). The cameras nearly always manage to be on the right person at the right time yet to convey the impression of a complete scene, but Bayreuth again scores by virtue of being so strongly lit in the first place: the others take place in too much gloom. It has been said that the Chéreau was made with the television in mind: however that may be, it works superbly on the home screen, now enhanced by superb sound. In that respect, the Bayreuth and Munich (National Theatre) sets faithfully reproduce what you would hear in either opera-house (both possessing near-ideal acoustics) with a fair balance between stage and pit, the Bayreuth having marginally more reverberation.

The Met is quite different, with the orchestra more forward than you would hear in the house and offering – as it does on CD – a fatter sound than do the European orchestras. Direct comparison here indicates that Levine favours saturation at the expense of the translucency and beauty heard on the other two sets. A certain emphasis on the conductor is made manifest when Levine is seen conducting at the start of each act, while Sawallisch and Boulez remain discreetly hidden throughout. Similarly there are curtain calls after every act on DG, which are unnecessary and break the spell. Obviously the DG set was recorded at live performances, a few coughs audible; the same is true of the Munich version. The Bayreuth loses out in its appallingly insensitive side-breaks – the one just after Brünnhilde has delivered the line "War es so schmählich" is particularly galling. The Munich version has artistic fades in and out. The Met changes are all discreet.

Two of the conductors' interpretations are familiar from their CD recordings, the Boulez identical with his sound-only version, which has been issued on CD as part of Philips's Bayreuth Series. Levine is less convincing than in the studio, his tendency to 'sit' on passages more irritating here and the relationship of tempos not wholly convincing, even if the reading as a whole is well considered, weighty and, of course, superbly played. The merits of Boulez's interpretation are obvious. After four years playing with an initially recalcitrant orchestra, he had by 1980 gained their total loyalty born out of conviction in his attempt to cleanse the scores of traditional accretions. With the pictures before you his fast direction and absolute insistence on playing the written note is convincing in a curiously exhilarating way. There are times, as at Wotan's farewell, when one would like more relaxation, nor does he attempt to measure up to the metaphysical element in the vast work, but by dint of relating his direction closely to what is going on above, a thrilling unity and unanimity is achieved.

The same could be said in a slightly different sense of Sawallisch's reading. He conducted several cycles before this recording was made, with most of the same singers. His is a more lyrical interpretation than either of the others, with a very definite emphasis on legato, on finely honed speeds, and an indefinable but irresistible sense of forward movement. In this his reading often resembles that of Böhm. The playing of the orchestra of the Bavarian State Opera is on a par with that at Bayreuth and the Metropolitan.

It is a case of swings and roundabouts where the casts are concerned. Levine and Sawallisch share their Brünnhilde. The steady beat that sometimes afflicts Behrens's voice disturbs many and by the time she made both these cycles, the lower part of her range was proving recalcitrant, but on both sets she creates an utterly convincing character, from challenging Valkyrie, sympathetic love-mate to dramatic heroine, conveying the minutiae of Brünnhilde's emotions through her feeling for words, deeply expressive eyes and supple movements. Vocally she rises magnificently to the part's great moments never more than in the sad, inner monologue before the trio at the end of Act 3 of the final opera. Her radiance at her awakening, her absolute joy at "O heiligste Wunder", and the whole delivery of the Immolation will surely stand time's test. Dame Gwyneth is as sympathetic though a very different actress, more overtly feminine and vulnerable, even more shattered by Siegfried's betrayal. Vocally she is very variable, scooping and wobbling in Act 3 of *Siegfried*, but magnificent for most of *Götterdämmerung*. Some will find her less appealing than the softer grained Behrens; others will disagree.

None of the Siegfrieds is satisfying in every way. Kollo has the deepest understanding of the role but is often strained in tone and a shade podgy in appearance. Jung, surely inspired by his producer, alternates between being a chunky bully and a chubby charmer. His delivery tends to be jerky and overemphatic but all the notes are hit in the middle and securely, and he is responsive to all the drama's needs. Jerusalem, though vocally the most lyrical, proves unexpectedly disappointing. He is certainly the most personable of the three, but the camera exposes him as a poor actor, inclined to be a bit of a booby.

Hale is the most underrated Wotan of the day. He pours his whole soul and body into the role, compensating by his intensity for a bass-baritone less powerful than those of his rivals. His tone is consistently pleasing and he fills phrase after phrase with a deep undertow of meaning. His world-weary Wanderer follows on his vigorous Wotan in *Rheingold*, his anguished God in *Walküre* – his "O heilige Schmach" here and the ensuing monologue rank with those of Hotter, than which there can be no higher praise. McIntyre, given a fundamentally unsympathetic interpretation of the role by Chéreau, executes it with absolute command throughout. Morris, as ever, sings with strength and authority but conveys little of the role's heart.

Altmeyer and Hofmann are a properly and believably ecstatic Volsung pair, which is more than can be said for the unconvincing Norman and Lakes. Varady and Schunk have their moments but are a shade overparted (Moll commands EMI's *Walküre* Act 1 with his overbearing, magnificent Hunding). Space forbids comments on all the participants, many of them well-known quantities, such as Tear's cynical, foppish Loge (a role Jerusalem sings but hardly acts for Levine), and Zednik's comic-tragic Mime, younger and more athletic for Chéreau than for Schenk. Salminen tailors his vast and louring presence as Hagen to suit the needs of two very different stagings, but all the basses are splendid throughout the three cycles. Lipovšek and Schwarz vie for honours as Fricka: the former is the more commanding, the latter the more wifely (another Chéreau coup is her attempt to re-seduce Wotan). Schwarz is just as compelling as Sawallisch's Erda, but her two rivals are both more than adequate. Meier towers above her rivals as Waltraute. All three Gunthers are on the mature side: surely he should be a younger man.

All these performances are enjoyable as complete, integrated stage productions, evincing a logic and consistency not available to the studio-made CD sets, and comparing more readily with the great live sets on CD from the 1950s and 1960s. The DG (no subtitles are provided) is not such a vital and engrossing experience as either of the other two, between which it is hard to choose – both are absorbing and satisfying experiences in their own right. Forced to choose, one might opt for Sawallisch/Lehnhoff (complete with Teletext subtitles) in spite of its quirky *Rheingold* simply because its individual interpretations, and especially Hale's Wotan, are marginally preferable to those on the Boulez/Chéreau (no subtitles) but that would deprive an intending buyer of Chéreau's many *aperçus* so the decision is difficult. With such an outlay involved it might be wise to try to sample both.

Wagner Tannhäuser (Paris version).

Plácido Domingo *ten* Tannhäuser
Cheryl Studer *sop* Elisabeth
Andreas Schmidt *bar* Wolfram
Agnes Baltsa *mez* Venus
Matti Salminen *bass* Hermann
William Pell *ten* Walther
Kurt Rydl *bass* Biterolf
Clemens Biber *ten* Heinrich
Oskar Hillebrandt *bass* Reinmar
Barbara Bonney *sop* Shepherd Boy
Chorus of the Royal Opera House, Covent Garden; Philharmonia Orchestra / Giuseppe Sinopoli.
DG Ⓟ Ⓓ 427 625-2GH3 (three discs: 176 minutes: DDD). Notes, text and translation included.
Recorded 1988.

This is Plácido Domingo's *Tannhäuser*. Domingo's third attack on a Wagnerian role (the others being Walther and Lohengrin) is a success in almost every respect. He evokes the erotic passion of the Venusberg scene and brings to it just the right touch of nervous energy. This is boldly contrasted with the desperation and bitterness of the Rome Narration after the hero's fruitless visit to the Pope seeking forgiveness: Domingo's description of how Tannhäuser avoided every earthly delight on his pilgrimage is delivered with total conviction. In between he berates the slightly prissy attitude of his fellow knights on the Wartburg with the dangerous conceit of someone who knows a secret delight that they will never enjoy in their measured complacency.

His tenor must be the steadiest and most resplendent ever to have tackled the part. He has his disadvantages. Domingo's German is far from idiomatic with several vowel sounds distorted, which sometimes detracts from the strength of his declamation. Then, occasionally, his voice seems in a different acoustic from the orchestra and his vocal partners – listen to the encounter with Venus – but this hardly diminishes an appreciable achievement, another jewel in a many-sided recording crown. Domingo and Baltsa, as Venus, bring a remarkable intensity to their scene together, suggesting a forerunner of the Kundry/Parisfal encounter. Baltsa also has some difficulties with her German, and her voice doesn't always sound as seductive as it ought, but she has the range and attack, particularly in the upper register, for an awkwardly-lying part. Here comparisons have to be made with Christa Ludwig in one of her most successful assumptions, heard on the Solti version (Decca). Ludwig is not only more familiar with her role but also has the more voluptuous voice. She is aided by her creative use of the text – something that for all her vocal acumen, isn't available to Baltsa. And Ludwig is superbly seconded by Solti.

And this brings us to Sinopoli. It is obviously his concern throughout to bring out every last ounce of the drama in the piece, both in terms of orchestral detail, which receives very special attention from the Overture, given a big, full-blooded reading, onwards, but as in his direction of the work over the past few years at Bayreuth, Sinopoli is aware in this opera of the longer line, often sustained by the upper strings. The Philharmonia's violins respond with their most eloquent playing. The kind of *frisson* Sinopoli offers is evident in the anticipatory excitement at the start of Act 2 and the iron control he maintains in the big ensemble later in the same act. Nor does he overlook the elevated side of the score. All Elisabeth's music is delivered with the right sense of serenity tinged with sorrow. But he can sometimes relapse into his self-indulgent vein: the middle section of Elisabeth's solo in her duet with Tannhäuser is unendurably slow; so is her colloquy with the Landgrave. At the end one isn't surprised to find that he takes quite a few minutes longer over each act than Solti, himself not exactly a speed merchant in this piece.

Cheryl Studer's secure, beautiful voice has no difficulty coping with Sinopoli's deliberate tempos. She has taken this part to universal acclaim at Bayreuth, and repeats it here with total conviction, both vocal and interpretative, phrasing with consistent intelligence. Andreas Schmidt is a mellifluous, concerned Wolfram, his voice a trifle light for the part. He often recalls Fischer-Dieskau, but his approach is rather more intent on firm line. Salminen is a rugged, characterful Landgrave, not quite as smooth but more interesting than Sotin (Solti). Barbara Bonney is an ideally fresh Shepherd Boy. The Covent Garden Chorus have obviously benefited by being trained specifically for this work by Bayreuth's Norbert Balatsch. As knights, ladies and pilgrims they sing with consistent beauty of sound, and have been sensibly balanced with the orchestra. They need not fear comparison with Decca's Vienna choir, also Balatsch trained.

As Sinopoli has chosen to conduct the Paris version, the Solti set is its main rival. It has always been one of Solti's most recommendable opera recordings, and in its CD format it remains a formidable achievement. Its cast has no weaknesses and many strengths. Solti is no less vital than Sinopoli in conveying the rich sonority, the elemental passions, and the sublime clarity experienced in the best parts of this uneven work. The Vienna Philharmonic play superbly for Solti, but as implied the Philharmonia on this form are just as impressive. Decca attempt much more 'production' than DG. If that appeals to you and you are satisfied with Kollo's thoughtful, deeply felt but sometimes uningratiating Tannhäuser then you may prefer the older version. You will also enjoy Ludwig's unrivalled Venus and the sympathetic Elisabeth of Dernesch. But Domingo and Studer just incline one towards Sinopoli.

Wagner Tannhäuser (Dresden version).
Hans Hopf *ten* Tannhäuser
Elisabeth Grümmer *sop* Elisabeth
Dietrich Fischer-Dieskau *bar* Wolfram
Marianne Schech *sop* Venus
Gottlob Frick *bass* Hermann
Fritz Wunderlich *ten* Walther
Rudolf Gonszar *bass* Biterolf
Gerhard Unger *ten* Heinrich
Reiner Süss *bar* Reinmar
Lisa Otto *sop* Shepherd Boy
Chorus and Orchestra of the Berlin State Opera / Franz Konwitschny.
EMI Studio Ⓜ Ⓓ CMS7 63214-2 (three discs: 183 minutes: ADD). Notes and text included. Recorded 1961.

Listen to how Konwitschny conducts the Overture, the large ensemble in Act 2, and indeed much of the solo work and be reminded of the lost art of pacing and shaping a Wagnerian paragraph. Above all he evinces the secret of steady, forward movement in Wagner; he unerringly feels the pulse of this score. He's helped by having an orchestra fully versed in this opera's tradition and by having perhaps the best chorus, Bayreuth's excepted (on the Sawallisch set for Philips), ever to have recorded the piece. Add to that an ideal balance on the engineers' part between all these elements and you have a formidable argument in this version's favour. Indeed some slight tape noise apart, you would hardly guess that this set was recorded some 37 years ago – or perhaps, given the unsatisfactory nature of so many recent sets, from the point of view of recording, you might indeed well guess that this wasn't a recent attempt. The sound on the Solti/Decca is the only one to have the presence and clear balance found on this EMI version, though the Bayreuth set captures the unique acoustics of that theatre.

Where the soloists are concerned, in all but one crucial respect, those on this reissue are second to none. Indeed, as is the case with the Berlin orchestra, Grümmer as Elisabeth, Frick as the Landgrave (for once no bore) and Fischer-Dieskau as Wolfram, display quite unreservedly the advantage of long acquaintance with a particular idiom. If you are doubtful, try the exchange in Act 2 between Elisabeth and the Landgrave (disc 2, track 4), where Grümmer and Frick provide a marriage between line and expression that's little short of ideal. The same is true of all Fischer-Dieskau's confidently and sensitively managed solos. It's true that Grümmer's tone has some threads in it during "Dich, teure Halle" but thereafter her sincerity, as when she puts herself on the line in Act 2 and in the Prayer in Act 3, is unrivalled, as is her unerring instinct for the shape of a phrase. Wunderlich and Unger both contribute positively to the ensemble in the Hall of Song.

The exception referred to above is Hopf's clumsy account of Tannhäuser's music. He has little problem with the role's cruel tessitura, indeed often makes a pleasanter sound than Kollo (Solti) or Windgassen (Sawallisch), but his aspirating of runs and turns, and his generally heavy-handed delivery, are at times hard to take, especially in the earlier acts. He makes some amends by his intense utterance in the Rome Narration, and throughout he always attempts to find his way to the heart of the role, even when fluent execution fails him. Schech isn't the most glamorous of Venuses; no match for Solti's Ludwig, or indeed for Haitink's Meier (EMI), but her contribution is never less then secure. All in all, if it's the Dresden version you are looking for, you could do worse than choose this mid-price reissue in front of the more recent and less convincing Haitink version, though the Philips reissue of the Sawallisch/Bayreuth version is well worth listening to – that offers a Wagner-approved conflation of the Dresden and Paris versions and is a truthful record of a dedicated evening at Bayreuth in 1962, much enhanced by Sawallisch's conducting, which has many of Konwitschny's qualities, if not quite the older conductor's overview of the piece. His cast, including Silja, Windgassen and Waechter, are also singers in the class of those on the Konwitschny. For the Paris version choose Sinopoli or Solti, the former just ahead because of Domingo's splendid Tannhäuser.

Wagner Tannhäuser.

Spas Wenkoff *ten* Tannhäuser
Dame Gwyneth Jones *sop* Elisabeth, Venus
Bernd Weikl *bar* Wolfram
Hans Sotin *bass* Hermann
Robert Schunk *ten* Walther
Franz Mazura *bar* Biterolf
John Pickering *ten* Heinrich
Heinz Feldhoff *bass* Reinmar
Klaus Brettschneider *treb* Shepherd Boy
Bayreuth Festival Chorus and Orchestra / Sir Colin Davis.
Stage Director: **Götz Friedrich.** *Video Director:* **Brian Large.**
Philips ⟨CD⟩ 070 412-3PH2; 🔅 070 412-1PH2 (two discs: 190 minutes). Recorded 1978.

Friedrich's 1978 staging at Bayreuth was a memorable experience and its preservation on video is therefore very welcome. He presents the eponymous anti-hero as fighting against one of the most self-satisfied, obviously uniform and uniformed societies that can be imagined so that the long Act 2 set pieces simply emphasize his isolation, their smugness. Venusberg, finely choreographed by John Neumeier, is an overtly erotic place, super-sensual, justifying choice of the Paris version at this point: later the performance reverts to the Dresden original. Alone of the conformists, Elisabeth perceives the knight's torment and suffers with him. Movement of the principals and chorus is at one with Friedrich's concept. Wagner would surely have applauded this true example of music-drama. Davis reveals both the work's internal and external elements, evincing a keen ear for sonority and balance between voices and instruments and within the orchestra itself, while realizing an overview of the score.

Jones's doubling of Venus and Elisabeth is a convincing *tour de force*, one of her best achievements, her seductive, quivering sex-goddess succeeded by her ingenuous, faithful Elisabeth, whose suffering is graphically conveyed in Act 3, particularly as she drags herself off-stage, a broken, dying figure. Jones is on untiring form, though you have to cope with the familiar beat in her tone. Wenkoff is an intense, involved Tannhäuser, with the wherewithal, vocally, to do justice to the role by virtue of firm tone, stylish phrasing and deep feeling, carrying out Friedrich's vision of the role. Weikl sings Wolfram in a warm, easy manner and acts with due concern. Sotin's experienced, upright Landgrave and excellent knights complete a near-faultless cast. The recording is reasonably clear. LaserDisc has optional teletext subtitles in English.

Wagner Tristan und Isolde.

Siegfried Jerusalem *ten* Tristan
Waltraud Meier *mez* Isolde
Marjana Lipovšek *mez* Brangäne
Matti Salminen *bass* King Marke
Falk Struckmann *bar* Kurwenal
Johan Botha *ten* Melot
Peter Maus *ten* Shepherd
Roman Trekel *bar* Helmsman
Uwe Heilmann *ten* Sailor
Berlin State Opera Chorus; Berlin Philharmonic Orchestra / Daniel Barenboim.
Teldec ⓟ ① 4509-94568-2 (four discs: 235 minutes: DDD). Notes, text and translation included. Recorded 1994.

Over several seasons of conducting the work at Bayreuth, Barenboim has by now thoroughly mastered the pacing and shaping of the score as a unified entity. Even more important he has peered into the depths of both its construction and meaning, emerging with answers that satisfy on almost all counts, most tellingly so in the melancholic adumbration of Isolde's thoughts during her narration, in the sadly eloquent counterpoint of bass clarinet, lower strings and cor anglais underpinning King Marke's lament, and in the searingly tense support to Tristan's second hallucination.

These are but the most salient moments in a reading that thoughtfully and unerringly reveals the inner parts of this astounding score. The obverse of this caring manner is a certain want of spontaneity, and a tendency to become a shade self-regarding. You occasionally miss the overwhelming force of Furtwängler's metaphysical account or the immediacy and excitement of Böhm's famous, live Bayreuth reading but the very mention of those conductors suggests that Barenboim can live in their world and survive the comparisons with his own perfectly valid interpretation. Besides, he has the most gloriously spacious yet well-focused recording so far of this opera and an orchestra not only familiar with his ways but ready to execute them in a disciplined and sensitive manner. The recording also takes account of spatial questions, in particular the placing of the horns off-stage at the start of Act 2 and the approach of the subsidiary characters after Tristan's death in Act 3.

Salminen delivers a classic account of Marke's anguished reproaches to Tristan, his singing at once sonorous, dignified and reaching to the heart, a reading on a par with that of his fellow-countryman, Talvela for Böhm. Barenboim's Berlin bass-baritone, Struckmann is splendid: his Kurwenal ranks among the best even though a few notes at the top stretch him. Heilmann's fresh, vibrant Sailor is a pleasure to hear; even more so Peter Maus's refined tone and diction as the Shepherd.

So, you'll be asking, why leave the lovers and Brangäne so long in the wings? The answer is that with them reservations set in. In view of her acting ability Meier must undoubtedly be an arresting Isolde in the theatre. Some of her vividness as a stage performer spills over into her vitally wrought, verbally alert reading, which catches much of the venom of Act 1, the visceral excitement of Act 2, the lambent utterance of the Liebestod. Nothing she does is unmusical; everything is keenly intelligent. Yet many may find her tone too narrow for the role and lacking in variety. Until Act 3 you miss the touch of *Schmerz* that has to be there in the voice of an ideal Isolde. Maybe this is a very *modern* interpretation of a role that needs a more timeless approach. That is even truer of Lipovšek's Brangäne. She tends to slide and swim in an ungainly fashion, sounding at times definitely overparted. Listening to Ludwig (Böhm) only serves to emphasize Lipovšek's deficiencies. Then it is often hard to tell Isolde and Brangäne apart, so alike can be their timbre.

As with his partner, Jerusalem sings his role with immaculate musicality; indeed he may be the most accurate Tristan on disc where note values are concerned, one also consistently attentive to dynamics and long-breathed phrasing. On the other hand, although he puts a deal of feeling into his interpretation, he hasn't quite the intensity of utterance of either Windgassen (Böhm), or, even more, Suthaus (Furtwängler). His actual timbre is dry and occasionally rasping: in vocal terms alone Suthaus is in a class of his own. Yet, even with the reservations about the Isolde and Tristan, this is a version that will undoubtedly hold a high place in any survey of this work, for which one performance can never hope to tell the whole story.

Wagner Tristan und Isolde.
Wolfgang Windgassen *ten* Tristan
Birgit Nilsson *sop* Isolde
Christa Ludwig *mez* Brangäne
Martti Talvela *bass* King Marke
Eberhard Waechter *bar* Kurwenal
Claude Heater *ten* Melot
Erwin Wohlfahrt *ten* Shepherd
Gerd Nienstedt *bass* Helmsman
Peter Schreier *ten* Sailor
Bayreuth Festival Chorus and Orchestra / Karl Böhm.
Philips Ⓜ ① 434 425-2PH3 (three discs: 219 minutes: ADD). Recorded at performances at the Bayreuth Festival in 1966.

BBC RADIO 3
90-93 FM

Glowing reports have been written about this set on more than one occasion. On reissue, it seems no less recommendable. The Bayreuth acoustic imparts a warmth and atmosphere that no studio or hall can imitate, and it was caught so accurately back in 1966 by the DG engineers that it stands up well to recent competition. By and large, it surpasses its rivals in terms of performance. The dramatic truth of Böhm's direct, surging interpretation is as overwhelming as it was in the theatre. So is Nilsson's Isolde, which for Wagnerian strength hasn't been anywhere near matched since on record. She is quite superb in the biting anger and frustration of Act 1, hardly less impressive as the 'melted' Isolde. As always, one begins by worrying about the dryness of Windgassen's tone and ends by admiring his stamina and understanding, particularly in Act 3. Ludwig remains a *nonpareil* of a Brangäne, Waechter a fiery Kurwenal. Talvela's Marke, younger than most, is as tenderly vulnerable as any on record. The young Schreier launches the vocal part of the work after Böhm's searing Prelude, with a lyrically fresh account of the Sailor's song. This issue is more deserving than most for a place on the Wagner shelf.

Wagner Tristan und Isolde.
Ludwig Suthaus *ten* Tristan
Kirsten Flagstad *sop* Isolde
Blanche Thebom *mez* Brangäne
Josef Greindl *bass* King Marke
Dietrich Fischer-Dieskau *bar* Kurwenal
Edgar Evans *ten* Melot
Rudolf Schock *ten* Shepherd, Sailor
Rhoderick Davies *ten* Helmsman

BBC RADIO 3
90-93 FM

Chorus of the Royal Opera House, Covent Garden; Philharmonia Orchestra / Wilhelm Furtwängler.
EMI mono Ⓟ Ⓛ CDS5 56254-2 (four discs: 236 minutes: ADD). Notes, text and translation included. Recorded 1952.

Those of us who had worn out our original HMV pressings of the famous Furtwängler recording of *Tristan und Isolde* were grateful to EMI for taking the cue offered by the Furtwängler centenary to reissue this recording on CD. We should now be doubly grateful. It was remastered again in 1997, achieving a marked improvement over its 1985 transfer. At best, the sound is remarkable. At the start of Act 2, for instance, there is an exceptional depth of perspective to the mono sound. Elsewhere, in the big climaxes, the sound does become congested; though it never breaks up or distorts, there is some perceptible hardening of the musical arteries. The digital remastering also makes studio noises more audible: for instance, the brief rumpus at the end of Tristan's first phrase in "O sink hernieder". The performance, as is well known by now, is memorable for the reach, beauty and re-creative power of Furtwängler's conducting and Flagstad's authoritative, beautifully pointed account of Isolde's role.

    Though they lacked opera-house experience, the Philharmonia Orchestra, in 1952, were probably the world's finest orchestra. It is difficult to accept the view, sometimes stated, that Flagstad was unsuited at this time to the role of Isolde. Like Gielgud's *Hamlet*, which was put on LP at much the same time, it would have been better caught younger; but that said, there were no contemporary Isoldes to better Flagstad's any more than there was a contemporary Hamlet to outshine Gielgud's. The young Dietrich Fischer-Dieskau is a superb Kurwenal; there could be tiny reservations about other members of the cast: the hugely impressive but perhaps rather too formal Tristan of Ludwig Suthaus, Josef Greindl's King Marke, and so on. However, the fact remains that this is a unique listening experience.

Wagner Tristan und Isolde.
René Kollo *ten* Tristan
Johanna Meier *sop* Isolde
Hanna Schwarz *mez* Brangäne
Matti Salminen *bass* King Marke
Hermann Becht *bar* Kurwenal
Robert Schunk *ten* Melot, Sailor
Helmut Pampuch *ten* Shepherd
Martin Egel *bass* Helmsman
Bayreuth Festival Chorus and Orchestra / Daniel Barenboim.
Stage Director: **Jean-Pierre Ponnelle.** *Video Director:* **Brian Large.**
Philips 🔲 070 409-3PH2; 🔲 070 409-1PH3 (three discs: 245 minutes). Recorded 1982.

This video derives from the 1982 revival of Jean-Pierre Ponnelle's 1981 production at Bayreuth. Each act, in his own scenery, is dominated by a single symbol: the huge prow of a ship in Act 1; a vast, gnarled oak in Act 2; the splintered shell of a tree set on a bleak promontory in Act 3. To this impressive array of sets is added an inspired use of colour and light, most telling in the love duet where Ponnelle conjures up a woodland scene of magical delight, then plunging the loving pair into utter darkness for their moment of supreme bliss. When King Marke breaks in on them, we see the drab light of dawn manifestly destroying the lovers' illusions.

    A few stage props contribute to the consistency of Ponnelle's concept, Isolde is first seen in the Prelude enveloped in a massive silver cloak, presumably hiding her true soul. The potential lovers drink their draught from a copper dish. They swear love in death beside a pool from which they drink as they begin their rapturous duet. Controversy arises only in the final scenes, in which Tristan – rather than dying at the point Wagner intended – imagines the final events in a dying delirium. Isolde appear to him as an angelic saviour, all in white, the others remaining shadowy figures on a backcloth. Ponnelle directs his principals to good purpose, emphasizing physical contact. Meier's Isolde is a slim, affecting figure, well matched to Kollo's dark-hued, intense Tristan, wild and searing in his last-act hallucinations. Meier's voice is compact and appealing, though short on sheer power. Kollo's voice was never the most tractable of instruments, but as ever he uses it intelligently. Schwarz's warm, concerned Brangäne and Salminen's dignified, moving Marke are notable assets, Becht's rough-hewn Kurwenal a single drawback. Barenboim doesn't always knit episodes into a convincing whole, but in this, his first attempt at the score, he is sympathetic, and draws some wonderful playing from his orchestra. Picture and sound, as ever in this venue, are of high quality as is Large's direction.

Vincent Wallace   Irish 1812-1865

Wallace Maritana.
Majella Cullagh *sop* Maritana
Lynda Lee *mez* Lazarello
Paul Charles Clarke *ten* Don Caesar

Ian Caddy *bass* Don José
Damien Smith *bar* Captain
Quentin Hayes *bass* King of Spain
RTE Philharmonic Choir and Concert Orchestra / Prionnsías O'Duinn.
Marco Polo Ⓟ Ⓒ 8 223406/7 (two discs: 198 minutes: DDD). Notes and text included. Recorded 1997.

All the histories and encyclopaedias tell us that there were no 'successful' operas composed in Britain between Purcell's *Dido and Aeneas* and Britten's *Peter Grimes*. We have become so used to hearing this that it gets repeated without question. But London, Dublin and later Manchester all knew a vigorous operatic life in the eighteenth and nineteenth centuries. As John Allen points out in his excellent introduction to this recording of William Vincent Wallace's *Maritana*, there existed a "now largely forgotten school of Romantic English opera".

Wallace was born in the Pyrénées in 1812, of Irish parents. His career took him from Dublin, where he was a violinist in the Theatre Royal Orchestra, to Australia, New Zealand and South America. He conducted an opera season in Mexico. Coming to London in 1845, he composed *Maritana* for Drury Lane, where it was an immediate success, following Balfe's *The Bohemian Girl* (1843). It was some 17 years before they were succeeded by Benedict's *The Lily of Killarney*, the three operas eventually being nicknamed "the Celtic *Ring*". Wallace's music is clearly influenced by the operas of Rossini and Donizetti. One wonders whether people would find it so ridiculous were it translated into Italian. The plot is based on D'Ennery's and Dumanoir's play *Don César de Bazan*, which itself derives from Victor Hugo's *Ruy Blas*, or at least characters in it. The same play was later used for Massenet's *Don César de Bazan*, and the broad outline – condemned man marries a girl he has never met on the eve of his execution – was parodied by Gilbert in *The Yeomen of the Guard*.

In a way, *Maritana* is one of the first musicals. Although Wallace takes the style of Donizetti as his starting-point, he departs from it sharply at key moments to insert popular ballads. "In happy moments", "'Tis the harp in the air", "Let me like a soldier fall" and above all "Scenes that are brightest" were relentlessly plugged up and down the land in hundreds of arrangements.

Prionnsías O'Duinn leads a vigorous performance, suggesting a bit more than a concert reading, even if the disparity of styles, half-Italian, half-Victorian drawing-room, doesn't quite come off all the time. However, it is good to be given the opportunity to hear a modern performance of this very important work. It's part of the missing link in our knowledge of British music theatre. Majella Cullagh in the title-role, Lynda Lee as the put-upon apprentice lad Lazarello, Paul Charles Clarke as Don Caesar and Ian Caddy as the evil Don José all sing with total dedication and conviction. It isn't at all difficult to understand *Maritana*'s popularity, nor with the ensuing snobbery of the twentieth century, why it fell out of favour.

Sir William Walton   British 1902-1983

Walton The Bear.
Della Jones *mez* Madame Popova
Alan Opie *bar* Smirnov
John Shirley-Quirk *bar* Luka
Northern Sinfonia / Richard Hickox.
Chandos Ⓟ Ⓒ CHAN9245 (53 minutes: DDD). Text included. Recorded 1993.

If Walton's sense of humour was firmly established from the start in *Façade*, his one-acter, *The Bear*, among his later works, brings out very clearly how strong that quality remained throughout his life. It was commissioned for Benjamin Britten's Aldeburgh Festival, in a sense a peace-offering on both sides between rivals. It was Sir Peter Pears who suggested the subject, and happily Walton found an ideal collaborator in Paul Dehn, who provided wittily rhymed verses for some of the set-numbers at melodramatic high-points. Otherwise Walton and Dehn together deftly slimmed down the Chekhov text. The composition was held up by the serious cancer operation which Walton underwent in 1966, but he completed the score in time for the piece to be given its première at the 20th Aldeburgh Festival in June 1967. It was recorded for EMI soon after with the original cast – Monica Sinclair, John Shaw and Norman Lumsden with James Lockhart conducting the English Chamber Orchestra – but sadly that fine recording has long been unavailable .

Happily this version in the Chandos Walton series is even finer, and hopefully it will encourage more performances of one of the wittiest operas in the repertory, and one which requires minimal forces. Walton used to complain how hard it was to use the Britten chamber layout with only single woodwind, but amazingly his textures have a Waltonian lushness rather than a Britten-like spareness. Walton times the melodramatic moments marvellously – notably the climactic duel between the mourning widow and her husband's creditor (the bear of the title) and Hickox here, more flexible than Lockhart was, brings that out most effectively. Walton also deftly heightens the farcical element in the Chekhov by introducing dozens of parodies and tongue-in-cheek musical references, starting cheekily with echoes of Britten's own *Midsummer Night's Dream*. There are so many such references and echoes that Christopher Palmer in his excellent note refuses to specify them, challenging listeners to draw up their own lists, which, as he says, are all bound to be different.

Hickox brings out the richness of the piece as well as its wit, helped by the opulent Chandos recording which still allows words to be heard clearly. The casting of the three characters is as near ideal as could be. Della Jones is even more commanding as the affronted widow than Monica Sinclair was before, with words much clearer, consistently relishing the melodrama like a young Edith Evans. Alan Opie far outshines his predecessor, John Shaw, as Smirnov, 'the bear'. His singing is clean-cut and incisive, powerfully bringing out the irate creditor's changing emotions, while John Shirley-Quirk, not quite so firm as he once was but still rich and resonant, is very well cast as the old retainer, Luka. With the duel scene leading delectably to an amorous *coup de foudre* – *The Bear* in many ways comes off even better on disc than on stage.

Walton Troilus and Cressida.

Judith Howarth *sop* Cressida
Arthur Davies *ten* Troilus
Clive Bayley *bass* Calkas
Nigel Robson *ten* Pandarus
Alan Opie *bar* Diomede
James Thornton *bar* Antenor
David Owen-Lewis *bass* Horaste
Yvonne Howard *mez* Evadne
Peter Bodenham *ten* Priest
Keith Mills *ten* Soldier
Bruce Budd *bass* First Watchman
Stephen Dowson *bass* Second Watchman
Brian Cookson *ten* Third Watchman
Chorus of Opera North; English Northern Philharmonia / Richard Hickox.
Chandos Ⓟ Ⓓ CHAN9370/1 (two discs: 133 minutes: DDD). Notes and text included. Recorded 1995.

1995

Troilus and Cressida here receives a recording which lives up to all possible hopes and more. It is powerfully presented as an opera for the central repertory, traditional in its red-blooded treatment of a big classical subject, with the composer revelling in big, tonal melodies presented with many *frisson*-making modulations. Few if any operas since Puccini have such a rich store of instantly memorable tunes as *Troilus and Cressida*.

So what went wrong? Walton wrote the piece in the wake of the first great – and well-deserved – operatic success of his rival, Benjamin Britten. What more natural than for Walton, by this time no longer an *enfant terrible* of British music but an Establishment figure, to turn his back on operas devoted like Britten's to off-beat subjects, and to go back to an older operatic tradition using a classical love story, based on Chaucer (not Shakespeare). Though he was much praised for this by early critics in 1954, he was quickly attacked for being old-fashioned. Even when in the tautened version of the score he offered for the 1976 Covent Garden revival – with the role of the heroine adapted for the mezzo voice of Dame Janet Baker – the piece was described by one critic as a dodo. Yet as Richard Hickox suggests, fashion matters little, and the success of the Opera North production in 1995 suggested that at last the time had come for a big, warmly romantic, sharply dramatic work to be appreciated on its own terms.

This recording was made under studio conditions during the run of the opera in Leeds. The discs amply confirm what the live performances suggested, that Walton's tautening of the score, coupled with a restoration of the original soprano register for Cressida, has provided the answer. Hickox, who first fell in love with the piece at the time of the 1976 Covent Garden revival, conducts a performance that is magnetic from beginning to end. If the First Act, setting out a complex plot, has always been the principal problem, both for Walton and his librettist, Christopher Hassall, during the composition and latterly in staging the opera, this recorded performance, with natural tensions reflecting stage experience, gives the crispest exposition. Each development is unerringly heightened by Walton's music, whether in choral writing as electric, often violent, as that in *Belshazzar's Feast*, or in an atmospheric scene-painting, or in the melodic warmth of the heartfelt music illustrating the love of Troilus and Cressida.

Walton wrote the opera soon after his marriage to his young wife, Susana, during their early years in Ischia. The score bears a dedication to her, and plainly the opera reflects Walton's new happiness, which he cherished the more in reaction to the painful death of his previous partner, Alice, Lady Wimborne. Until near the end of his life Walton was very cagey indeed about revealing his private life, but more clearly than ever with this recording we can see this, his only full-length opera, as a watershed work in his career, at once the last of the electrically intense, passionately romantic works which marked the first half of his career, and the first of the refined, more reflective works of the post-war period.

The scene is atmospherically set in Act 1 by the chorus, initially off-stage, but then ever more *Belshazzar*-like, with the incisive Opera North chorus snapping out thrilling cries of "We are accurs'd!". Hassall's libretto is unashamedly archaic in its use of 'opera-speak' like that, with "thee"s and "thou"s and the occasional "perchance". Though the text may put some off, it is plainly apt for a traditional 'well-made opera' on a classical subject. The first soloist one hears is the High Priest, Calkas, Cressida's father, about to defect to the Greeks, and the role is superbly taken by the firm, dark-toned Clive Bayley. Some have regretted Walton's decision to cut Calkas's big monologue in Act 1, one of the most substantial passages omitted, but here thanks to Bayley the character is very clearly established without it.

Troilus's entry and his declaration of love for Cressida bring Waltonian sensuousness and the first statements of the soaring Cressida theme. Arthur Davies is not afraid of using his head voice for *pianissimos*, so contrasting the more dramatically with the big outbursts and his ringing top notes. Judith Howarth's Cressida is much more girlish than Dame Janet Baker in the Covent Garden set. She brings out the vulnerability of the character along with sweetness and warmth. After Calkas has defected to the Greeks, her cry of "He has deserted us and Troy!" conveys genuine fear, with her will undermined.

It is surprising that in lowering the tessitura of the role for Dame Janet, Walton did not have to transpose much more of the role. Cressida's final agonized solo in Act 3 before her suicide remains substantially at the same pitch, but the final high outburst then makes all the difference, a thrilling climax with Howarth delivering a shining top B. Cressida's solos in the Act 2 love scene – starting with "At the haunted end of the day" – are largely a minor third higher in the soprano version, adding tenderness and again vulnerability. The climax of the duet has been restored as in the original, with the "Aphrodite" phrases expanded. The only tiny cut noted here beyond the Covent Garden text comes in Act 1 in Cressida's final exchanges with Calkas before he defects, where the off-stage chorus on Walton's suggestion has been eliminated. All told, though some fine music has been cut, the tautened version is far more effective both musically and dramatically, with no *longueurs* at all. It all leads to the big set-piece sextet at the climax of Act 3, before Cressida's last solo, an old-style culmination that works in a way you can compare with the *Meistersinger* Quintet or the *Rosenkavalier* Trio.

Rather like Gerald English – Pandarus in the Covent Garden recording – Nigel Robson does not try to echo the original tenor, Sir Peter Pears, for whom the role was written. With the campness muted, the character becomes an urbane know-all, manipulating everyone. The musical characterization, as well as Hassall's text, are aptly pointed here, and the sly echoes of Britten's writing for Pears – as in the melismatic triplets for the witty passage as he leaves the lovers, "He seems to have reached the kneeling stage" – remain as effective as ever. The role of Diomede, Cressida's Greek suitor, can seem one-dimensional, but Alan Opie in one of his finest performances on record sharpens the focus, making him a genuine threat, with the element of nobility fully allowed. As Antenor, James Thornton sings strongly, but is less steady than the others, while Yvonne Howard is superb in the mezzo role of Evadne, Cressida's treacherous servant and confidante. With such firm, rich tone the only danger is that the voice can be confused with that of Cressida, even though the dangers were obviously greater when Cressida too was a mezzo. Not just the chorus but the orchestra of Opera North, the English Northern Philharmonia, respond with fervour. Naturally and idiomatically they observe the Waltonian rubato and the lifting of jazzily syncopated rhythms which Hickox as a dedicated Waltonian instils, echoing the composer's own example.

As for the recorded sound, it brings a complete contrast with the dry Covent Garden acoustic on the old EMI set. The bloom of the Leeds Town Hall acoustic allows the fullest detail from the orchestra, enhancing the Mediterranean warmth of the score, helped by the wide dynamic range. The many atmospheric effects, often off-stage, are clearly and precisely focused, and the placing of voices on the stereo stage is unusually precise too. The complete Walton Chandos Edition could not have been rounded off with a more fulfilling set.

Robert Ward
American 1917

Ward The Crucible.
Joyce Ebert *mez* Betty Parris
Norman Kelly *ten* Rev. Samuel Parris
Gloria Wynder *contr* Tituba
Patricia Brooks *sop* Abigail Williams
Naomi Farr *sop* Ann Putnam, Sarah Good
Paul Ukena *bar* Thomas Putnam
Eunice Alberts *contr* Rebecca Nurse
Spiro Malas *bass* Francis Nurse
Maurice Stern *ten* Giles Corey
Chester Ludgin *bar* John Proctor
John Macurdy *bass* Rev. John Hale
Frances Bible *mez* Elizabeth Proctor
Nancy Foster *sop* Mary Warren
Richard Krause *ten* Ezekiel Cheever

Jack DeLon *ten* Judge Janforth
Lorna Ceniceros *sop* Ruth Putnam
Helen Guile *contr* Susanna Walcott
Marija Kova *sop* Martha Sheldon
Elizabeth Schwering *contr* Mercy Lewis
Beverly Evans *sop* Bridget Booth
New York City Opera Orchestra / Emerson Buckley.
Albany Troy Ⓟ Ⓓ TROY025/6-2 (two discs: 110 minutes: ADD). Notes and text included.
Recorded 1989.

Robert Ward's *The Crucible* was warmly received on its first production in New York in 1961, and it has since been very widely performed, not only in the United States. For obvious reasons: its plot, after Henry Miller's play about the Salem witch trials, is a strong one (with powerful resonances in 1961: Senator McCarthy was a very recent memory) and Ward's music is swift-moving and gratefully lyrical. His language owes a lot to the American vernacular of his teachers Howard Hanson and Aaron Copland; no folk-songs or hymn-tunes are actually quoted, but there are plentiful suggestions of them to give a strong sense of place, and something also to an operatic vernacular rooted in Puccini (via the example of Menotti, perhaps, several of whose most popular works had already appeared). There is a certain cragginess, too, drawn partly from very careful word-setting of Miller's archaizing text and very apt for evoking the starched rigour of a closed and in-turned community, that seems to be Ward's own.

His stage craft is his own, too, and each act builds to its curtain with real power and urgency. For such a concise opera – four acts playing for well under two hours – it has a large cast, none of whom, by the nature of the drama (it is a study of the stresses within a community) can be presented from the outset as 'principals'. Within that context the way that the rough-tongued, insecure John Proctor and his wife Elizabeth (driven into apathy and shrewishness by his adultery and her own lack of faith in herself) not only grow but grow towards each other as events tear them apart is impressive; several of the 'secondary' characters, too, are deftly given a third dimension. It is a highly skilful piece of popular music theatre, in short, and would work stunningly on stage.

Its drawbacks, noticeable in the pitiless concentration on the essentials of a recording, would also be put into fairer perspective in the theatre, where the opera belongs. The word-setting, splendidly judged for communicating the text (you will not need the printed libretto provided) is sometimes awkwardly jogging, sequential or repetitive. More seriously, the sort of hypnotic terror that the scenes of mass hysteria demand is not within Ward's range; indeed at such points his stage directions – "singing wildly", "with terrible intensity" – are not matched by his music, nor is the final scene (Elizabeth could save John from death by colluding with him in a lie, but will not: "He has found his name and goodness now. God forbid I take it from him") the wrenchingly moving conclusion that it tries so hard to be. But if *The Crucible* fails it does so honorably – the decency and plainness of its language are strengths as well as weaknesses when evoking such a community – and it deserved a recording.

This one, although the fact is nowhere acknowledged, was made not long after the first performance, by the company that created it; under Emerson Buckley's direction there is a crackling sense of pace and of stage-seasoned ensemble. The singers are all very competent, with Bible and Ludgin making the most of the touching eloquence of John's and Elizabeth's scenes together. The orchestra are placed well behind the voices and there is a touch of distortion at times, but the set sounds not too badly for its age.

Carl Weber   German 1786-1826

Weber Der Freischütz.
  Gundula Janowitz *sop* Agathe
  Peter Schreier *ten* Max
  Edith Mathis *sop* Aennchen
  Theo Adam *bass* Caspar
  Bernd Weikl *bar* Ottakar
  Franz Crass *bass* Hermit
  Siegfried Vogel *bass* Kuno
  Gerhard Paul *spkr* Samiel
  Günther Leib *bar* Kilian
  Leipzig Radio Chorus; Staatskapelle, Dresden / Carlos Kleiber.
DG Ⓟ Ⓓ 415 432-2GH2 (two discs: 130 minutes: ADD). Notes, text and translation included.
Recorded 1973.

BBC RADIO 3
90-93 FM

Carlos Kleiber's fine set of *Der Freischütz* earns reissue on CD for a number of reasons. One is the excellence of the actual recorded sound with a score that profits greatly from such attention. Weber's famous attention to details of orchestration is lovingly explored by a conductor who has taken the trouble to go back to the score in manuscript and observe that there are differences between that and most of the published versions (this recording was made before Joachim Freyer's invaluable edition for Peters in 1976). So not only do we hear the eerie sound of low flute thirds and the subtle contrast of unmuted viola with four-part muted violins in Agathe's "Leise, leise", among much else, with a new freshness and point, but all the diabolical effects in the Wolf's Glen come up with a greater sense of depth, down to the grisliest detail. The beginning of the Overture, and the opening of the Wolf's Glen scene, steal upon us out of a primeval silence, as they should.

All this would be of little point were the performance itself not of such interest. There is a good deal to argue about but this is because the performance is so interesting. Whatever one may feel about some of Kleiber's tempos, and one may feel some of them to be unwise in both directions, they spring beyond doubt from a careful, thoughtful and musical mind. The singing cast is excellent, with Gundula Janowitz an outstanding Agathe to a somewhat reflective Max from Peter Schreier, at his best when the hero is brought low by the devilish machinations; Edith Mathis is a pretty Aennchen, Theo Adam a fine, murky Caspar. The dialogue, spoken by actors, is slightly abbreviated and in one or two respects amended.

Kubelik's performance is the more subtle and commanding, and also the more colourful. It is more traditional than Kleiber's, without any loss of freshness; Kleiber produces much new insight, however, often penetratingly. The magical old score can take both approaches.

Weber Der Freischütz.

Hildegard Behrens *sop* Agathe
René Kollo *ten* Max
Helen Donath *sop* Aennchen
Peter Meven *bass* Caspar
Wolfgang Brendel *bar* Ottakar
Kurt Moll *bass* Hermit
Raimund Grumbach *bass* Kuno
Rolf Boysen *spkr* Samiel
Hermann Sapell *bar* Kilian
Bavarian Radio Chorus and Symphony Orchestra / Rafael Kubelík.
Decca Ⓜ ① 443 672-2DMO2 (two discs: 134 minutes: ADD). Notes, text and translation included. Recorded 1979.

Versions of *Der Freischütz* now abound, but this reissue was most welcome. Its strengths are many, not least among them being Kubelík's perceptive, well-judged handling of the score. His tempos are just, his sense of orchestral excitement high (the Wolf's Glen casts its usual spell), his understanding of Weber's subtle sense of instrumental balance and colour acute; and over it all there is a freshness and bloom that make the incursion of darkness the more terrifying. Kollo sings Max with a fine ardour, tinged with anxiety, to Behrens's Agathe, a tender performance and one with a livelier cut than some; she contrasts well with Donath's warm-hearted Aennchen. Peter Meven's Caspar is splendid, singing his drinking song with a sinister compulsion and brooding darkly over events in the Wolf's Glen. There is a certain amount of incidental din here, as the producers enjoy themselves with stage effects and make Samiel's voice loom from everywhere.

The booklet, with German text and English translation, is rather shoddily reproduced, and has regrettably lost Rodney Milnes's original essay, retaining his synopsis, translated into French, German, Italian and Spanish. Davis's 1990 Philips set is probably also a good bet for the opera, despite a less than ideal Agathe in Karita Mattila, with Carlos Kleiber's sometimes eccentric version always commanding attention; Kubelík's return provides a very good alternative which many may put at the top of their preferences.

Weber Der Freischütz.

Elisabeth Grümmer *sop* Agathe
Rudolf Schock *ten* Max
Lisa Otto *sop* Aennchen
Karl Christian Kohn *bass* Caspar
Hermann Prey *bar* Ottakar
Gottlob Frick *bass* Hermit
Ernst Wiemann *bass* Kuno
Fritz Hoppe *spkr* Samiel
Wilhelm Walter Dicks *bar* Kilian
Chorus of the Deutsche Oper, Berlin; Berlin Philharmonic Orchestra / Joseph Keilberth.
EMI Ⓜ ① CMS7 69342-2 (two discs: 134 minutes: ADD). Notes and text included. Recorded 1958.

Keilberth's *Freischütz* was a classic in its day, and long held the field. Its memorable performances include Rudolf Schock's elegant if slightly aloof Max to one of the most famous Agathes of the century, Elisabeth Grümmer, then still at the peak of her career, and singing here strongly and affectingly. Young Hermann Prey, then just turned 30, contributes a splendid Ottakar, and the ever-reliable Gottlob Frick is for once cast not in the role of black villain but as a Hermit, here both sonorous and consoling. Lisa Otto nips about nimbly as Aennchen, and Karl Christian Kohn is a Caspar of rather less distinction. It is for the memory of these well-loved performances that the set earns its reissue, and no less for Keilberth's loyal and loving direction of the score. It was good to find how well all the spookery in the Wolf's Glen comes up in a recording that is now 40 years old; but inevitably there is more immediacy in the Kleiber set. However, Kleiber takes some original views of tempos and other matters; Keilberth's was a straight, traditional, expert *Freischütz* of the kind that remains in the mainstream of German operatic repertories.

An abbreviated version of the dialogue is included, but banded off so that you can skip if you like. The booklet contains an anonymous German article, translated into French, and an English article by Peter Branscombe. The German text is included, but no translation.

Weber Oberon.

Deon van der Walt *ten* Oberon
Inga Nielsen *sop* Rezia
Peter Seiffert *ten* Hüon
Bo Skovhus *bar* Scherasmin
Vesselina Kasarova *mez* Fatime
Melinda Paulsen *mez* Puck
Heidi Person *sop* First mermaid
Hermine May *sop* Second mermaid
Berlin Radio Chorus; Deutsches Symphony Orchestra, Berlin / Marek Janowski.
RCA Victor Red Seal Ⓟ Ⓓ 09026 68505-2 (two discs: 121 minutes: DDD). Notes, text and translation included. Recorded 1996.

Oberon has always been a problem opera, ever since Weber conducted it at Covent Garden in 1826. Compelled to fit his exquisite numbers into a ramshackle entertainment in which décor and stage machinery counted for more than music, he planned to rewrite it as a German opera on the return home which, tragically, he never made. There have been various stage versions, the best of them by Mahler, but the problems do not end with recording. A set made under Hans Müller-Kray for Period Thrift in the 1950s cut the dialogue completely. Kubelík's set has some dialogue with the addition of an extra fairy, Droll. The present set has the singers speaking a shortened version of the dialogue, with an English translation in the booklet that does not reproduce Planché's dire original. This is probably the best solution, and provides a dramatic convention for the passage of the plot. Incidentally, every note of the score is included apart from the aria Weber was forced to substitute for his superior original by John Braham, who sang Hüon.

Janowski has a light hand, listening (as do the record producers) to all Weber's delicate combinations of instruments, judging tempos nicely (apart from some rather speedy Mermaids), generating a fine fury in what is the best storm in German opera before *The Flying Dutchman*. There are plenty of other Wagner adumbrations in the score. Some of them come in the opera's most famous aria, "Ocean! thou mighty monster", delivered with full Wagnerian relish by Birgit Nilsson for Kubelík. Inga Nielsen is less grand, but subtler: she describes the shifting moods of the sea with a beautiful ear for Weber's detail, and can rise with a full tone to the occasion of the sun bursting forth, as well as spinning a long line in the beautiful Cavatina, "Mourn thou, poor heart". Peter Seiffert is lighter, less lyrical than Plácido Domingo for Kubelík, but he can produce a heroic ring and he is undaunted by some taxing vocal lines. His Preghiera, "Ruler of this awful hour", is beautifully done, and he gets nimbly round the tricky Rondo, "I revel in hope and joy". For Kubelík, Hermann Prey was an engaging Scherasmin; Bo Skovhus does not have the same lightness of touch, but Vesselina Kasarova manages more liveliness with her fairly strong tone than does Júlia Hamari for Kubelík. Melinda Paulsen does well with Puck.

In sum, this set is a very enjoyable, idiomatic performance, with delightful and perceptive ideas, at every turn, even if it would be difficult to give it preference over Kubelík's powerful soloists.

Weber Oberon.

Donald Grobe *ten* Oberon
Birgit Nilsson *sop* Rezia
Plácido Domingo *ten* Hüon
Hermann Prey *bar* Scherasmin
Júlia Hamari *contr* Fatime
Marga Schiml *sop* Puck
Arleen Auger *sop* Mermaid
Bavarian Radio Chorus and Symphony Orchestra / Rafael Kubelík.
DG Ⓜ Ⓓ 419 038-2GX2 (two discs: 139 minutes: ADD). Notes and translation included. Recorded 1970.

It is a pity that the version used here has to be in the German translation, not much better in its way than Planché's sorry original; but an attempt to confer an illusion of dramatic continuity is made by using a linking narrative intended by Oscar Fritz Schuh and Friedrich Schreyvogel for a Vienna production that never materialized. It includes a figure called Droll: those who have no wish to sit through his confidings can of course skip more easily now than with the original LP.

Kubelík handles the score beautifully. He responds more readily to the atmosphere of magic and mystery than to the wit and the colour: thus, the ravishing Mermaids' Song is soft and lulling, but lacks some sparkle in the succeeding music. It can also lead him to underplay the Wagnerian tensions underlying Oberon's first aria, "Fatal vow!", though he is superb with that other great Wagnerian moment, the sun breaking through the clouds in "Ocean! thou mighty monster". There is, of course, no lack of Wagnerian response here from Birgit Nilsson; more surprisingly, perhaps, she can also refine and lighten her tone to encompass the more soubrette-like music which Weber, with less than his best judgement, also wrote for Reiza. Plácido Domingo responds no less happily to the Italianate elements in the writing for Hüon, both to the heroics and to the caressing manner for the Preghiera. Hermann Prey is a delightful Scherasmin and Júlia Hamari a pleasant if none too sprightly Fatime. Oberon himself is Donald Grobe, world-weary and burdened in the first aria; and there is a pretty piece of singing from Arleen Auger as the Mermaid.

Pleasure at the work's return is only tempered by the fact that the booklet has fallen victim to the problems of the small CD format. It is a serious misjudgement on DG's part for Franz Willnauer's sensible essays in three languages, accompanying the English, French and German libretto, now to be replaced by just a translation of his brief synopsis in Italian. Not good enough.

Weber Peter Schmoll und seine Nachbarn.
Rupert Busching *bar* Peter Schmoll
Johannes Schmidt *bass* Martin Schmoll
Anneli Pfeffer *sop* Minette
Sibrand Basa *ten* Karl Pikner
Hans-Joachim Porcher *bass* Hans Bast
Hans-Jürgen Schöpflin *ten* Niklas
Hagen Philharmonic Orchestra / Gerhard Markson.
Marco Polo Ⓟ Ⓒ ⑧ 8 223592/3 (two discs: 92 minutes: DDD). Notes and text included. Recorded 1993.

Peter Schmoll was Weber's second opera, and the first to survive, written in 1802 when he was all of 15. It is a *Singspiel*, a sentimental comedy set on the German side of the frontier across which a group of *émigrés* have fled the Revolution, and deriving from a once popular novel by C. G. Cramer. Unfortunately the adaptation was clumsily made, keeping nervously close to a contrived and confused plot. More unfortunately, the dialogue is lost, so that the course of the plot can only be understood by reference to the novel. Most unfortunately of all, the loss of the dialogue has encouraged several versions, of which the one to have some modern currency is by Willy Werner Göttig: it was published by Peters in 1963, performed in Germany and England (at Hintlesham in 1968), and is used here.

We must be grateful for small mercies, and this recording counts as just that. The Göttig version produces a completely new but unimproved plot that often goes directly against the music, gives arias to the wrong characters even when this involves a change of vocal register, and alters the order of the numbers to make rubbish of rather a good dramatic musical sequence and a very careful tonal scheme anticipating the scrupulousness of Weber's mature operas. Thus a fine storm aria, with booming trombones and flashing piccolos, is rendered meaningless in a completely new context. The character of Hans Bast, Schmoll's steward, is emasculated by the removal of two of his solos; and the only female character, Minette, is put into a new light that does not show up her features to advantage.

At least there does survive the orchestration, which even at his tender age was already one of Weber's claims to fame. There are some bold and imaginative instrumental effects, not only the piccolo and trombone writing for the storm but a mature and sympathetic use of the horn and the clarinet; and in one number Weber demanded (too impracticably for modern performance) a curious combination of recorders and basset-horns. The general manner of the music is, as one would expect, the *Singspiel* of the day, close in spirit to Dittersdorf or Wenzel Müller or Conradin Kreutzer. Melodically, the manner ranges from plain jollity to some very eloquent, rather French-influenced writing (there is a beautiful love duet). Sometimes there are remarkable touches that turn a plain phrase into something memorable; sometimes a phrase remains plain. Similarly, the harmony is often simple, even a little clumsy; then Weber will look right forward to his mature chromatic manner with a strange, effective progression.

The singers deal directly and quite effectively with music that does not give them very much occasion for characterization, especially in Göttig's rewriting; and Gerhard Markson has a good feel for the colour and charm of this very agreeable little opera. There is an essay and synopsis in German and English, with Göttig's text in German only. Whatever the necessary reservations, this version of *Peter Schmoll* should be snapped up by any collector interested in Weber and his period, pending a recording of the correct musical and verbal text, in the correct order: there is, after all, no need on a recording for spoken linking dialogue.

Weber Silvana.

Katja Isken *spkr* Silvana
Alexander Spemann *ten* Rudolph von Helfenstein
Andreas Haller *bass-bar* Krips
Stefan Adam *bar* Adelhart
Angelina Ruzzafante *sop* Mechthilde
Volker Thies *ten* Albert von Cleeburg
Sergio Gómez *bass* Kurt
Horst Fiehl *bar* Fust von Grimmbach
Anneli Pfeffer *sop* Klärchen
Jürgen Dittebrand *spkr* Ulrich
Peer-Martin Sturm *ten* Herald
Hagen Opera Chorus; Hagen Philharmonic Orchestra / Gerhard Markson.
Marco Polo Ⓟ Ⓒ 8 223844/5 (two discs: 124 minutes: DDD). Notes, text and translation included. Recorded 1996.

Silvana is well worth rehabilitation. Weber wrote it (or rather, rewrote it from a lost juvenile effort) during his Stuttgart years in 1808-10 as a young man more attracted to the delights of wine and women than those of song. It was the kindly Franz Danzi who made him pull himself together, and consequently helped to rekindle his sense of vocation. The complicated tale concerns a forest waif, bereft of her voice, wooed and won by a knight, Rudolph, who no more wants to marry Mechthilde, daughter of the dynastically ambitious Adelhart, than Mechthilde, in love with Albert, wants to marry him. All is straightened out in the end when 'Silvana', the sylvan child, turns out to be Adelhart's long-lost daughter Ottilie, and reassumes her voice. She can now marry Rudolph; Mechthilde can marry Albert.

There are many signs of what was to come in Weber's career. The knightly world anticipates *Euryanthe*, the forest world *Der Freischütz*. The invention cannot, of course, match the best of either work, but there is much to lift it above the conventions which are its starting-point. Not many *Singspiel* composers had such an instinct for finales propelled by dramatic necessity (something Schubert never learnt), and none had such an ear for the sounds of the forest. Already, in his early twenties, Weber had an extraordinary feeling for instrumental colour as part of the dramatic expression, one considerably greater than his skill with the human voice. So the idea of a dumb heroine suited him well. It is a pity that the text and translation with these records do not include more of the score's stage directions for Silvana, to whose movement, gesture and mime Weber responds with enchanting detail. She is largely associated with an oboe for her lively, engaging side, and for her amorous warmth with a cello that can lead her into kinship with Wagner's Sieglinde. Weber gives a pioneering portrayal of character through instruments alone. We know Silvana as closely as anyone in the opera. Rudolph, gracefully sung by Alexander Spemann, is clearly denied a love duet with her, but Weber turns matters to advantage by creating a Silvana-oboe obbligato for his ardent lines.

The other characters are more conventional. Rudolph's squire Krips, in the person of the lively Andreas Haller, bumbles away in the tones of any Hiller or Reichardt buffoon, though he has a better tune (it quickly went into the taverns) and he is more wittily orchestrated. Adelhart rages on in the Vengeance Aria convention of the day, and is (like others of his ilk) too often shaken with unsuitable fits of coloratura; Stefan Adam does well with him. Weber cannot manage much with Mechthilde, torn between duty to her father and love for the mysterious Albert, who is mild to the point of nonentity; but Angelina Ruzzafante takes the opportunity of making her vigorous melodic line, coloratura and all, reflect a character of considerable spirit.

Gerhard Markson (who has also recorded Weber's even more youthful *Peter Schmoll*, reviewed above) directs a well-turned performance that began life on the stage in Hagen in February 1995. He might have stirred the chorus into livelier action, especially with a huntsmen's chorus that is some way short of those in *Freischütz* or *Euryanthe* but that has cheerful lines and whooping horns. He does excellently with a storm that will later blow up again in the Wolf's Glen, and with the many instrumental felicities that belong to Weber alone. There is much to enjoy here.

Kurt Weill
German/American 1900-1950

Weill Aufstieg und Fall der Stadt Mahagonny.

Wolfgang Neumann *ten* Jimmy Mahoney
Anja Silja *sop* Jenny
Anny Schlemm *mez* Widow Begbick
Klaus Hirte *bass* Trinity Moses
Paul Wolfrum *bar* Pennybank Bill
Frederic Mayer *ten* Jake, Toby
Hans Franzen *bass* Alska-Wolf-Joe
Thomas Lehrberger *ten* Fatty the Book-keeper

Cologne State High School for Music; Pro Musica Vocal Ensemble;
Cologne Radio Symphony Orchestra / Jan Latham-König.
Capriccio Ⓕ ① 10 160/1 (two discs: 141 minutes: DDD). Notes, text and translation included.
Recorded 1985.

Weill Aufstieg und Fall der Stadt Mahagonny.
Heinz Sauerbaum *ten* Jimmy Mahoney
Lotte Lenya *sngr* Jenny
Gisele Litz *mez* Widow Begbick
Horst Günter *bar* Trinity Moses
Georg Mund *bar* Pennybank Bill
Fritz Göllnitz *ten* Jake, Toby
Sigmund Roth *bass* Alska-Wolf-Joe
Peter Markwort *ten* Fatty the Book-keeper
North West German Radio Chorus and Orchestra / Wilhelm Brückner-Rüggeberg.
Sony Classical mono Ⓕ ① M2K77341 (two discs: 136 minutes: ADD). Notes, text and
translation included. Recorded 1958.

Older readers may remember the sense of anticipation created by Andrew Porter's original review
back in 1960 of the Sony recording of *Aufstieg und Fall der Stadt Mahagonny* conducted by Brückner-
Rüggeberg and may have gone on to fall under the spell of this opera. On the one hand it has melodies
no less haunting than those in *Die Dreigroschenoper*, while on the other it has compelling operatic
structures flavoured with crafty, pungent, eerie harmonies. Of one aspect without the other one might
easily tire, but with the two juxtaposed one has something uniquely fascinating.

That recording reappeared, cleanly remastered on two CDs, at the same time as a modern version
from Capriccio. If no new recording can quite recapture the thrill of that original discovery, this one
comes remarkably close to doing so. For one thing there is the digital stereo sound (the Sony is in
mono). The difference in bringing out the full flavour of Weill's harmonies and orchestral detail is
almost the difference between monochrome and colour. But it is not merely in sound quality that
there is the impression of an extra dimension. Sony's major attraction was Lotte Lenya and yet at the
same time she is its greatest drawback, since she is totally unable to encompass Weill's original
soprano line in the part of Jenny. On Capriccio the part is sung, and superbly too, by Anja Silja – a
performance both dramatically and lyrically outstanding. If Silja does not always achieve complete
vocal purity in "Denn wie man sich bettet", her Havana Song, with its twangy Hawaiian guitars, is
captivating. Her Alabama Song, especially, creates a quite different effect, with her voice haloed by
those of her friends, as it is not in the older recording.

Other parts are strongly taken, too – most notably Anny Schlemm, with her fruity mezzo perfectly
suited to the part of the Widow Begbick, and Hans Franzen, with a rich bass in the part of Alaska-
Wolf-Joe. The choral and orchestral contributions are superb, and the cumulative sonic effect is at
times overwhelming. Even so, the newer recording is not all gain. The major disappointment is
Wolfgang Neumann in the leading role of Jimmy Mahoney. His is a pinched, strained, unattractive
voice. Then again, one of the potential major advantages of a soprano Jenny is lost by the omission
of the Cranes duet, one of the highlights of the score. Dramatically this is fair enough, since Weill
added it merely to tone down the sexuality of the Act 2 brothel scene, where it sits uneasily. But to
have it neither there (as in the Sony recording) nor in Act 3, where David Drew has stated Weill later
wished to put it, is a pity. Also, compelling though Latham-König's conducting mostly is, you do miss
the bounce and onward movement of Brückner-Rüggeberg's interpretation. Latham-König's tempos
are consistently slower than Brückner-Rüggeberg's and the Alabama Song, particularly, loses some of
its haunting fluency when pounded out insistently, as it is here. However, even though retaining
affection for the older recording, the Capriccio set has to be the preferred choice. Either way, though,
nobody who does not already know this haunting score should miss this opportunity to do so.

Weill Die Dreigroschenoper.
René Kollo Macheath
Ute Lemper Polly Peachum
Milva Jenny Smith
Mario Adorf Peachum
Helga Dernesch Frau Peachum
Wolfgang Reichmann Brown
Susanne Tremper Lucy Brown
Rolf Boysen Street Singer
Berlin RIAS Chamber Choir and Sinfonietta / John Mauceri.
Decca Ⓕ ① 430 075-2DH (74 minutes: DDD). Recorded 1988.

For 40 years the Sony *Dreigroschenoper* under Wilhelm Brückner-Rüggeberg, with Lotte Lenya in the
role of Jenny, has towered head and shoulders above any rival. That supremacy faces its sternest
challenge in this release which boasts such assets as John Mauceri's authoritative conducting and a

leading role for the exciting musical theatre singer, Ute Lemper. Mauceri's presence makes itself felt immediately in the clarity of instrumental detail and the bounciness of the dance rhythms. Lemper, too, is soon well in evidence in a splendidly shaped "Barbara-Song". There is also a superbly rounded Mrs Peachum in Helga Dernesch, whose "Ballad of Sexual Dependency" is a *tour de force* – albeit sadly shorn of its third verse. It is followed by an absolutely irresistible "Zuhälter-Ballade", in which the innocently spun out melody serves to accompany some wickedly expressive handling of the text by René Kollo as Macheath, and by the husky Milva (another impressive singing actress) as the whore, Jenny. Kollo is no less impressive in his handling of Macheath's Epitaph, again tellingly accompanied by Mauceri.

Yet the challenges that a new *Dreigroschenoper* has to face are indeed formidable ones. Much has been said of the distorted ideas we have of Weill's music due to its subjection over the years to firstly, Brecht's alienation style (encouraging the familiar 'snarl-and-shout' type of delivery) and, secondly, the lowering of vocal line to suit Lotte Lenya's changing vocal powers. The response of this recording is somewhat ambivalent. On the one hand, Mauceri has gone back to Weill's original manuscript material, has reconsidered tempos, and has ensured, for instance, that Macheath's music is properly sung by an operatic tenor. On the other hand, Jenny's music is sung by a performer for whom – as for Lenya – downward transpositions have to be made.

Perhaps this reaction is equally ambivalent. On the one hand, you wonder whether Kollo, with his light tenor, sounds at all like a gangster, and whether Mauceri's recording quite catches the seediness associated with the work. On the other, you wonder whether in the interest of hearing the music sung at closer to the original pitch, Ute Lemper might more appropriately have been cast as Jenny. It should be added that this is in no way to decry the splendid Milva. It does, though, seem to highlight a lack of assurance about the casting that the problem of which of them should sing "Pirate Jenny" is resolved by giving it to both. Polly sings it in Act 1, Jenny in Act 2 – a most curious arrangement.

Ultimately the old recording retains a special magic of its own that makes it foolish to pretend to its devotees that the Mauceri recording should replace it. On the other hand, there can scarcely be any doubt that it is to this newer version that the uncommitted should be directed. For all the remarkably good quality of the Sony recording, the clearer Decca digital sound is obviously superior. Likewise, the singing on the newer version is undeniably of a higher standard, whilst no less appropriate in terms of Weill's requirement for singing actors. In orchestral playing, too, there is a clear advantage, no less than in John Mauceri's imaginative conducting. In the "Zuhälter-Ballade", above all, these characteristics come together to give this recording a quite haunting quality.

Weill Die Dreigroschenoper.
   Erich Schellow Macheath
   Johanna von Kóczián Polly Peachum
   Lotte Lenya Jenny Smith
   Willy Trenk-Trebitsch Peachum
   Trude Hesterburg Frau Peachum
   Wolfgang Grunert Brown
   Inge Wolffberg Lucy Brown
   Wolfgang Neuss Street Singer
   Günther-Arndt Choir;
   members of the Dance Orchestras of Radio Free Berlin / Wilhelm Brückner-Rüggeberg.
   Sony Classical Ⓟ Ⓓ MK42637 (68 minutes: ADD). Notes, text and translation included.
   Recorded 1958.

This is, of course, the classic recording of *Die Dreigroschenoper*, featuring the composer's widow, Lotte Lenya, in the role of Jenny that she created back in 1928. Though 30 years on Lenya's voice had lost its youthful characteristics, no other recording of the work has approached this for bringing out, on the one hand, the pungency of its satire and, on the other, the catchiness of the dance-band rhythm. Probably none ever will. It is also the absolutely complete version, since it includes not only Mrs Peachum's "Ballad of Sexual Dependency" but even Lucy's rarely heard "Jealousy Song". The sound is very good early stereo.

Weill Lady in the Dark.
   Risë Stevens *mez* Liza Elliott
   Adolph Green *sngr* Beekman, Ringmaster
   John Reardon *bar* Randy Curtis
   Stephanie Augustine *sngr* Sutton
   Kenneth Bridges *sngr* Charley Johnson
   Roger White *sngr* Kendall Nesbitt
   chorus; orchestra / Lehman Engel.

Weill Lady in the Dark – excerpts.
   Danny Kaye *sngr*

chorus; orchestra / Maurice Abravanel.
Sony Classical Masterworks Heritage mono/stereo Ⓜ ① MHK62869 (64 minutes: ADD).
Lady in the Dark recorded 1963; excerpts recorded1941.

No qualms at all about this sumptuous reissue of the 1963 studio recording of *Lady in the Dark*. Presented with evocative photographs of the recording sessions, this is an almost complete recording of the musical numbers from this fascinating, curious work. Risë Stevens makes no attempt to imitate Gertrude Lawrence, and her rich operatic mezzo sounds suitably tough – after all she is meant to be the Editor-in-Chief of a glossy magazine, a woman succeeding in a predominantly male world. Ira Gershwin's lyrics are delivered with superb clarity by the unnamed chorus, and John Reardon is fine in the Victor Mature role of Randy Curtis, who sings "This is news". In the Danny Kaye part, Adolph Green provides an alternative interpretation of "Tchaikovsky". As a fill-up, Sony provide Danny Kaye's cover versions of six of the numbers from the show – he failed to upstage Gertrude Lawrence in the production, so he had another go in the recording studio. He takes liberties with the words and music, but it has to be said that his version of "The Princess of Pure Delight" is second to none. Lehman Engel, who had known Weill since 1936 when he helped with the auditions for *Johnny Johnson*, leads a performance that seems ideal.

Weill Lost in the Stars.

Gregory Hopkins *ten* Leader
Arthur Woodley *bass-bar* Stephen Kumalo
Reginald Pindell *bar* Absalom, John, Man, Villager
Cynthia Clarey *sop* Irina
Carol Woods *sngr* Linda
Jamal Howard *treb* Alex
Richard Vogt *spkr* Stationmaster, Judge
New York Concert Chorale; St Luke's Orchestra / Julius Rudel.
MusicMasters Ⓟ ① 67100-2 (72 minutes: DDD). Recorded 1992.

Julius Rudel conducted a production of *Lost in the Stars* for the New York City Opera in 1959, part of the breakthrough seasons featuring American operas that helped to alter the musical establishment's perception of American opera in general and Weill's contribution to it in particular. *Lost in the Stars* is subtitled "A Musical Tragedy" and was adapted by Maxwell Anderson from Alan Paton's novel, *Cry the Beloved Country*. Weill and Anderson's use of a chorus to comment on the action and advance the story makes the play difficult to stage, and Andersen's sentimentalization of the Paton original has made it one of the most dated of Weill's works. However, these very limitations have enhanced its potential on the concert platform. A sequence devised by David Drew, augmenting the oratorio-like choruses with a speaker reading passages from the novel, has been heard at Carnegie Hall, the Almeida Festival and at the 1993 Proms.

Rudel comments in the booklet that he found the recording sessions "somewhat akin to a religious experience" and this certainly communicates itself, especially in the choral sequence, "Cry the beloved country" which frames the death-cell confrontation between father and son. Without much recorded dialogue, the condescending sugariness of the Anderson contribution is reduced and Weill's experimentation with the choruses as well as his usual high quota of great melodies make this one of the finest modern recordings of his work.

Several of the numbers were lifted from an earlier project, *Ulysses Africanus*, which Weill and Anderson had planned as a vehicle for Paul Robeson: the title-song and "Trouble man" (both of which were recorded by Lotte Lenya with Weill at the piano in 1943 (reissued on Capriccio). There is another curious example of Weill's plundering of his own work, the melody of his setting of Brecht's *Nana's Lied* from 1939, is used here as a solo for Stephen Kumolo, "The little grey house". In the main role of the black preacher, Kumolo – created on Broadway in 1949 by Todd Duncan, the first Porgy – Arthur Woodley sings with fervour and fine diction. Cynthia Clarey as his son's lover, Irina, gets "Trouble man" and "Stay well", while Carol Woods launches "Who'll buy?", the most raucous saloon ballad of Weill's American career. (There is an amazing photograph in the booklet of José Quintero rehearsing the 1959 NYCO cast with "Shirley Carter" as Irina – better known as Shirley Verrett.) The Orchestra of St Luke's manage an accurate 1940s sound; a real achievement. This is a major addition to the catalogue and essential to any collection of Weill's work – or of twentieth-century opera.

Weill Die sieben Todsünden.

Weill Symphony No. 2.

Teresa Stratas, Nora Kimball *sops*
Frank Kelley, Howard Haskin *tens*
Herbert Perry, Peter Rose *basses*
Chorus and Orchestra of Opéra National de Lyons / Kent Nagano.
Erato Ⓟ ① 0630-17068-2 (65 minutes: DDD). Text and translation included. Recorded 1996.

This is the first recording of *Die sieben Todsünden*, Weill's last major collaboration with Brecht, to couple this *ballet-chanté* with the Second Symphony. It is the most appropriate pairing, for both works were finished in France in 1933, in the months after Weill had left Germany after the Nazis came to power. There are many cross-references in the two pieces, rhythmically and even melodically (although the Symphony has more direct quotes from *Der Silbersee*, the last piece Weill composed in Germany).

Teresa Stratas has long been admired for her performances of Weill's songs. This performance of *Sins* was recorded at the same time that Stratas performed it for Peter Sellars's film of the work (Decca). That interpretation largely removes the dance element, and replaces it with a typically provocative modern scenario, intercut with documentary footage of urban decay. There is a certain amount of stage noise in this recording, especially in "Lust" – the heart of the work. Stratas's singing isn't pretty, but then it's not meant to be; she uses all her declamatory powers, and projects text and music in such a dramatic and heartfelt way that it puts this version immediately in the front rank.

Nagano's conducting begins with a very slow introduction, which may sound off-putting to those familiar with the much sprightlier Rattle (EMI) or Masur (Teldec) versions, the obvious comparisons with this, both with soprano soloists. (The versions by Lenya, the creator, Gisela May, Ute Lemper and Julia Migenes all use the transposed version made in the 1950s, and although they sing in the original keys, both Fassbaender and von Otter as mezzos give Anna I a darker, even more world-weary sound.) As the performance progresses though, Nagano's control of the drama seems just right – this isn't a concert reading, but a full-scale theatrical event.

The recorded sound of the symphony is noticeably better than that of *Sins*. As Weill's only major orchestral work, it has never really caught on, which seems very strange; the orchestral writing is as sophisticated as anything in his operas, the mood though pessimistic is beautifully conveyed by the haunting opening solo. The symphony shows where Weill might have been heading, had his career not been diverted by history. With *Die Burgschaft* and *Der Silbersee* one can hear how he had already advanced away from the jazz-influenced late-1920s period that culminated in the completion of the opera *Mahagonny*, and was moving towards something more severe and controlled.

With so many versions of *Die sieben Todsünden*, preferences for voice and coupling are important. Fassbaender and von Otter both have a selection of Weill songs and arias, Réaux with Masur has the *Lulu* suite, Ross with Rattle, Stravinsky's *Pulcinella*. For first-time Weill buyers, this version is recommended over all the others; Stratas is terrific and the coupling is perfect.

Weill Der Silbersee.

Wolfgang Schmidt *ten* Severin
Hildegard Heichele *sop* Fennimore
Hans Korte *bar* Olim
Eva Tamassy *mez* Frau von Luber
Udo Holdorf *ten* Baron Laur
Frederic Mayer *ten* Lottery Agent
Cologne Pro Musica; Cologne Radio Symphony Orchestra / Jan Latham-König.
Capriccio Ⓔ ① 60 011-2 (two discs: 107 minutes: DDD). Notes, text and translation included. Recorded 1981.

There can be few works of art more intimately and poignantly bound up with twentieth-century political events than *Der Silbersee*. True, scores that comment on tyranny, outrage or holocaust roll from composers' pens with steady regularity, but they usually make their point by reflecting on past events. In *Der Silbersee* we hear the angry voice of protest on the eve of tragic events. The opera was premièred, simultaneously in Leipzig, Magdeburg and Erfurt, on February 18th, 1933, a matter of days before the Reichstag fire and the Nazi seizure of power. A month later, Weill was in exile in Paris, the subject of anti-Semitic abuse. Georg Kaiser, his librettist, fell into disgrace, was forbidden to write, and eventually emigrated.

It is not a work that minces its words. Expressed as a barely-concealed allegory – a 'winter's tale' is how the authors describe it, in both the literal and metaphorical sense – the scene is unmistakably contemporary Germany, bleakly portrayed as a country torn apart by inequality, unemployment, poverty and famine. The two protagonists, Severin and Olim, stand respectively for the hopeless unemployed and the ruling Socialist party, whose antagonism eventually gives way to unity after both have been ousted by an upstart rival (personified in the sinister Frau von Luber). Seeking oblivion in the waters of the Silver Lake, they discover that the surface has miraculously frozen over, leading them on a path to an unknown future. It is a depressing image, but not a pessimistic one; the year, after all, was 1933, not 1939.

Although technically a Singspiel, truly in the tradition of *Die Zauberflöte* and *Der Freischütz*, the proportion of music to original dialogue is relatively low. In this concert version, Kaiser's text has been pruned back hard, yet the opera still packs its punches, and not a note of Weill's score has been denied us. The result is very good indeed. From the first bar of the overture the vitality of Jan Latham-König's direction is evident, and rarely does he allow the pace to slacken. For a cast we have singers, not actors: Weill's musical demands are heavy, and the problem of finding principals who can both sing and act are at least partly relieved by the compression of the dialogue. In the event, even the spoken portions of the work have been directed with a firm hand, and connections between speech and music are mostly well achieved. Hildegard Heichele is impressive in the heroine role of Fennimore – the only character who breathes hope into the story – and she sings the famous Ballad of Caesar's Death, the most politically sensitive number in the opera, with fiery passion and real courage. Everyone around her assists in keeping the atmosphere electric, from Hans Korte as the confused, institutionalized Olim, Wolfgang Schmidt as an angry Severin and Eva Tamassy as the dastardly Frau von Luber, right down to Frederic Mayer as the brash Lottery Agent, who deserves special mention for his splendidly avaricious Act 1 aria – "interest, and compound interest!"

As always in this Capriccio series of Weill reconstructions, the documentation is superb, progressing from a historically sensitive introductory essay by Josef Heinzelmann and extracts from letters to or by Weill via a selection of photographs to an excellent English translation of the libretto by Lionel Salter. The recording is deliberately coarse in texture and entirely appropriate. This is a thrilling release, beautiful as well as moving in its black humour; definitely not to be missed.

Weill Street Scene.

Kristine Ciesinski *sop* Anna Maurrant
Richard Van Allan *bass* Frank Maurrant
Janis Kelly *sop* Rose Maurrant
Bonaventura Bottone *ten* Sam Kaplan
Terry Jenkins *ten* Abraham Kaplan
Meriel Dickinson *mez* Emma Jones
Angela Hickey *mez* Olga Olsen
Claire Daniels *sop* Jennie Hildebrand
Fiametta Doria *sop* First nursemaid
Judith Douglas *mez* Second nursemaid
English National Opera Chorus and Orchestra / Carl Davis.
TER Classics Ⓟ Ⓘ CDTER21185 (two discs: 146 minutes: DDD). Recorded 1989.

When, in 1989, Scottish Opera and English National Opera shared a production of Kurt Weill's *Street Scene*, two separate complete recordings came out of it. This was despite the fact that several singers were common to Glasgow and London. Where John Mauceri for Decca used the conductor, orchestra and chorus of the Scottish production, they imported internationally known singers for the leading roles. TER, by contrast, recorded the ENO production as it stood – apart from a couple of relatively minor substitutions. Only Meriel Dickinson, in the role of the bitchy Mrs Jones, appears in both recordings.

Listening to it, the main result is to heighten admiration for a work that integrates such marvellous melodies into a score of genuine passion, and such wit and humour into a tragic story with a deep-hitting social message. As for a choice between the two recordings, there is really no overall preference. Both are of a very high standard, and both have relative advantages. One can only guide readers towards the one that will suit them better. First, there is about the TER a definitely greater feeling of continuity and uniformity – a feeling that the performers are inside their roles – than there is with Decca. This must owe something to the fact that the TER recording was made during the London run, whereas the Decca was made at sessions seven months apart with singers who presumably flew in and then departed. Maybe, also, it owes something to the type of singer that Decca imported. The major disappointment with that recording (but it may be a disappointment that will not be shared by everyone) came from the contribution of Josephine Barstow. Her very deliberately produced, operatic-style delivery seems unsuitable for this Broadway opera. Kristine Ciesinski may sound too young for Anna Maurrant, but her more natural style of delivery seems to be far more suitable for this work.

To a much lesser extent the same stricture applies to the contribution of Angelina Réaux as young Rose Maurrant on the Decca, though on any grounds the contribution of Janis Kelly to the TER recording is outstanding. Her beautifully clear but natural enunciation, her sense of emotional involvement, make "What good would the moon be?" a performance of real beauty. Yet perhaps the most striking 'plus' about this TER version is the performance of Richard Van Allan as the murderous Frank Maurrant. His "Let things be like they always was" shows far more expression than Samuel Ramey does for Decca and creates a far more sinister effect, a far greater sense of foreboding that is carried through the whole work. On the other hand, Bonaventura Bottone cannot really match the winning tones of Jerry Hadley in the role of Sam Kaplan.

Carl Davis's conducting makes its contribution to the effect of Frank Maurrant's number with its slightly slower tempo. Elsewhere, though, the balance seems to be strongly in favour of John Mauceri for Decca. Time and again Mauceri gives the music an element of life that is missing with Davis. Note at the very start, for instance, the way that Mauceri builds up the atmosphere. Note likewise, in "Wouldn't you like to be on Broadway?", how much more successfully Mauceri captures the change of mood as Harry Easter's attempt to seduce Rose is interrupted by the arrival of Mrs Jones. Whereas "Moon-faced, starry-eyed" (with Catherine Zeta Jones of ITV's *The Darling Buds of May*, incidentally) is really a piece of sweet dance music under Carl Davis, under John Mauceri it really swings.

So there it is. Both recordings reach a very high standard, both in terms of performance and also in the first-class, atmospheric sound quality. Those who want star names and more inspiring conducting should go for the Decca; but the TER is the one that is the more consistently enjoyably sung.

Weill Der Zar lässt sich photographieren.

Barry McDaniel *bass* Tsar
Carla Pohl *sop* Angèle
Thomas Lehrberger *ten* Assistant
Ulla Tocha *mez* Boy
Marita Napier *sop* False Angèle
Heinz Kruse *ten* False Assistant
Hilke Helling *contr* False Boy
Mario Brell *ten* Leader
Hans Franzen *bass* Tsar's equerry
Cologne Radio Chorus and Symphony Orchestra / Jan Latham-König.
Capriccio Ⓕ Ⓓ 10 147 (47 minutes: DDD). Notes, text and translation included. Recorded 1984.

Here is a marvellous little opera, superbly researched, most winningly performed and handsomely produced in a 1984 studio recording by West German Radio. In its day – the first performance was in 1928 – *Der Zar* was supremely popular on the German stage; only *Der Rosenkavalier* was produced more often. It fell from grace with the Nazis, and has only intermittently been revived since, an oversight bordering on iniquity which this recording will hopefully help to remedy.

With an act of terrorism at the heart of the story-line, a certain Zeitgeist hovers in the plot. But Georg Kaiser's libretto borders more obviously on farce than political comment, and it's the sheer fun of the show, combined with its aura of period chic, that gives the work its continued appeal. The plot is deliciously absurd. Photographer Angèle and her staff are hijacked in their Parisian studio by a team of would-be assassins, who disguise themselves and lure the Tsar to a portrait session. Under its black cloth, the camera now conceals a gun. Left alone to shoot (as it were) her customer, the imposter Angèle finds herself being seduced by the Tsar, who on several occasions manages to swap roles and take control of the camera. As the pace quickens, the police move in. The criminals hastily abort their scheme and escape, leaving the Tsar faced with a new, plainer but authentic Angèle. As her (disarmed) camera successfully performs its task, the curtain falls.

Weill's music is wickedly apt. Never does the score allow any moment of wit or irony in the story to go unmarked, and it brilliantly underlines the characterization. Decadent music, part dance, part pure romance, accompanies the Tsar's entry and lingers around his every word. As the two protagonists tussle over possession of the camera, so the heartbeat of the music increases, always to be teasingly interrupted. At the moment of highest drama, Weill plays his trump card: the orchestra fall silent, and instead a gramophone record plays the sultry "Tango Angèle", recorded under Weill's supervision in 1927; the imposter, Angèle, drawing the Tsar to the couch, piles him with cushions and makes her getaway. Throughout all this, a male chorus in evening dress make intermittent comments on the action in the detached manner of a Greek chorus.

Everything about the performance, under Jan Latham-König's well-paced direction, does the work justice, and the casting is apt throughout. There is an uneasiness of balance in the section of melodrama, where the spoken dialogue is too obviously suggestive of the studio rather than the stage; but otherwise the recording is attractive. We are given the complete text, together with Lionel Salter's lively English singing translation. Helpful documentation, including some splendid photographs, further add to the pleasure.

Judith Weir
Scottish 1954-

Weir Blond Eckbert.

Nicholas Folwell *bar* Blond Eckbert
Nerys Jones *sop* A Bird
Anne-Marie Owens *mez* Berthe
Christopher Ventris *ten* Walther, Hugh, An Old Woman
English National Opera Chorus and Orchestra / Sîan Edwards.
Collins Classics Ⓕ Ⓓ 1461-2 (65 minutes: DDD). Recorded at a performance in the Coliseum, London on May 14th, 1994.

Few recent operas so richly repay repeated hearing as Judith Weir's *Blond Eckbert*. Not that it's a 'difficult' score, giving up its secrets only after prolonged grappling; in fact its lucid textures and tensely lyrical lines are immediately appealing, drawing you effortlessly into the work's alluring mystery. It is based (libretto by the composer herself) on a short story by Ludwig Tieck, at once a strange folk tale from the forests of German romanticism and an absorbing detective story. At its centre are two secrets, ticking away like time bombs, one of them exploding bafflingly at the end of the First Act, the other shatteringly in the opera's final scene. The two explosions are timed, placed and led up to with masterly precision. One pleasure of rehearing this opera is to observe how single lines, seemingly very simple on first hearing, have contributed to this cumulative effect. Berthe's 'ballad' in the First Act, for example (at her husband Eckbert's suggestion she tells the story of her strange childhood to their friend Walther), is a long scene of pure melody, mostly very sparely accompanied. Indeed you realize as you listen that each of its lines is a melody, as though Berthe had often sung them to herself, polishing and perfecting them. Each adds a twist to the unfolding of the drama and brings closer the first of those 'explosions': in a casual remark the visitor, only a recent acquaintance, reveals that he knows more about Berthe's childhood than even she can remember, much to her bewilderment. In the theatre the interval at this point is a well-nigh unbearable interruption.

The almost wordless opening of the Second Act (in which Eckbert, fearful of Walther's mysterious omniscience, kills him) is another example of the richness hidden within the deceptive simplicity of Weir's music: the darkly beautiful lyricism is filled both with foreboding and with shadowy recollections of the music of German romanticism: forest murmurs, woodland horns. The nightmare that ensues (Eckbert is befriended by a stranger – but he has Walther's face; he revisits the scene of Berthe's narration; he meets Walther again in a shocking new form; he learns ... but no: we mustn't give the end away) has an amazingly swift economy. The invariable reaction after listening to *Blond Eckbert* is to want to hear it all over again, from the beginning.

The small cast is uniformly excellent, Jones properly blithe and bird-like (didn't we mention the bird? The entire opera is framed as a story told to a dog by a bird who plays a crucial role in that story; so does a dog, though not necessarily the same dog ...), Owens and Folwell in fine voice and grippingly dramatic, Ventris producing just the right effect of reedy strangeness for the enigmatic Walther. Edwards paces the opera well, and the very exposed lines of the smallish orchestra are finely played. The very clean recording is taken live from the ENO; there are a few very unobtrusive studio noises that detract not one whit from the opera's powerful magic.

Hugo Weisgall   American 1912

Weisgall Six Characters in Search of an Author.

Andrew Schroeder *bar* Accompanist
Philip Zawisza *bar* Stage Manager
Joslyn King *mez* Mezzo
Bruce Fowler *ten* Tenore buffo
Susan Foster *sop* Prompter
Michael Wadsworth *bass-bar* Basso cantante
Kevin Anderson *ten* Director
Dianne Pritchett *contr* Wardrobe Mistress
Elizabeth Futral *sop* Coloratura
Robert Orth *bass* Father
Elisabeth Byrne *sop* Step-daughter
Nancy Maultsby *mez* Mother
Gary Lehman *bar* Son
Victor Rooney *treb* Boy
Jenna Heffernan *sngr* Child
Paula LoVerne *contr* Madame Pace
Chorus and Orchestra of the Lyric Opera, Chicago / Lee Schaenen.
New World Ⓟ Ⓒ 80454-2 (two discs: 136 minutes: DDD). Text included. Recorded at performances in the Civic Theatre, Chicago on June 14th and 16th, 1990.

According to *Grove*, Hugo Weisgall is "perhaps America's most important composer of operas", and of his full-length ones *Six Characters* is his "most theatrically successful". It was first performed in 1959 by the New York City Opera, but after a revival the following year it was not heard again until the staging in Chicago of which this is a live recording. "Theatrically successful" therefore means not that it has been widely performed but that it works well on stage, and there is good evidence of that here: the audience is audibly absorbed by every word of the drama, laughing at the jokes, in suspense at the twists and turns of the plot, warmly applauding an aria in praise of opera singers. Pirandello's theatre director, his stage taken over by six characters from an unfinished play in search of a new author who will give the drama of their lives some meaning, has of course here become the director of an opera company, who are grimly and reluctantly beginning to rehearse 'Weisgall's *Temptation of St Anthony*'. "I know that some of you don't like it", he admits, "To tell the truth I hate this modern, tuneless stuff myself. But ... man cannot live by *Faust* alone." Clever: at a stroke Weisgall has not only one of the most gripping and cunningly plotted plays of the century on his side, but he can also mine a rich vein of operatic jokes.

One of the reviews in 1959 described *Six Characters* as "almost breathless in pace". It is; for an opera lasting not much over two hours very little of Pirandello has been omitted. Weisgall's word-setting is fast and declamatory, halting often but always very briefly for arias, ensembles and choruses. His style is chromatic but never atonal; he achieves this by concentrating at any given moment on motifs drawn from a fairly restricted range of pitches. Much of the musical interest lies in ingenious motivic working in the orchestra. In this very competent performance the orchestra sound on the small side and, no doubt in the interest of verbal clarity, they are pushed into the background by close focusing on the voices. But the vocal writing is angular and not very grateful (it must have been hell to learn) and it is often curiously insensitive to words or to situation.

It is characteristic of this opera that the mysterious arrival of the Six Characters is marked by an oddly effective invention in the woodwinds of the orchestra, but by little change in the vocal writing. A real sense of ample, lyrical line, or of the Six Characters' strangeness and separateness, is not achieved until the final act, where the earnest eloquence of some of the Father's music and a lovely (if brief) aria with chorus for the Step-daughter at last warm the opera into life. Until then you find yourself admiring Weisgall's stagecraft (or Pirandello's) more than his responsiveness to a great play.

Hugo Wolf   Austrian 1860-1903

Wolf Der Corregidor.
Werner Hollweg *ten* Corregidor
Doris Soffel *mez* Frasquita
Dietrich Fischer-Dieskau *bar* Tio Lucas
Helen Donath *sop* Donna Mercedes
Kurt Moll *bass* Juan Lopez
Victor von Halem *bass* Repela
Helmut Berger-Tuna *bass* Tonuelo, Nightwatchman
Peter Maus *ten* Pedro, Neighbour
Gabriele Schreckenbach *contr* Manuela
RIAS Chamber Chorus; Berlin Radio Symphony Orchestra / Gerd Albrecht.
Schwann Ⓟ Ⓘ 314010 (two discs: 131 minutes: DDD). Notes and text included. Recorded 1985.

Alarcón's story, *The Magistrate and the Miller's Wife*, is basically a very simple tale; in *El sombrero de tres picos* Falla managed to condense all its essential action and most of its atmosphere into a one-act ballet lasting less than 40 minutes. Wolf's poet, Rosa Mayreder, took four acts and six scenes over it, and when he received her unsolicited libretto, in 1890, he dismissed it with angry contempt as "the silliest stuff I have ever read". Five years later, his desire to write an opera had become so obsessive and overwhelming that he looked at her text again and this time pronounced it "a miracle". A better librettist, writing for Verdi, say, or Puccini, would have concentrated on the essence of the story, removed incidentals and subsidiary characters (the opera has a cast of 12 of whom only five are essential to the plot), and given the composer pretexts for satisfyingly ample musical structures. Mayreder kept in as much of Alarcón's picaresque detail as she could, and there is every evidence that it was this superfluity of detail that prompted Wolf's change of mind about her text. He wrote the opera piecemeal, as a miniaturist, exclaiming in his letters about the beauty or the wit of this or that element in his mosaic. It is significant that the last act, which is packed to the point of incomprehensibility with irrelevant incident and unnecessary dialogue, was Wolf's own favourite.

So we have an opera in which Act 1 is concluded by the desperate expedient of wheeling in a Bishop and his retinue (none of whom sings, or appears again, or has any relevance to the plot), in which several crucial events take place off-stage and have therefore to be narrated at cumbersome length, and in which the action continually stops to give every character, however minor, some dubious pretext for a song. The heroine, Frasquita, left alone after her husband's arrest and announcing her intention of waiting up for him all night, embarks upon a positive Lieder-recital that only the arrival of the Corregidor with evil designs on her virtue prevents from indeed lasting until dawn.

But the music is enchanting; and in a sense far removed from the practicalities of the stage it is by no means undramatic. The comfortable affection of the Miller and his wife is beautifully sketched (their duets express the love of two people who are too close to need to be demonstrative); his jealousy at her apparent betrayal is the pretext for a fine monologue, the nearest thing to an 'aria' the opera contains; the serene lyrical warmth of the music given to the Corregidor's wife, the tolerant peacemaker, is affecting; the succession of tiny but beautifully crafted numbers or of flexible dialogue over a melodious orchestral web follows a meandering rather than a purposeful course, but for the first three acts at least it is a pleasure to be carried along by it. It is like a second "Italian Song Book" (rather than a "Spanish", despite the assiduous local colour), finely orchestrated (a few patches of overscoring apart) and linked by a plot that one can take or leave, as one pleases.

And the performance could scarcely be bettered. Most of the singers realize that it is a Lieder-singer's subtlety that this music needs, and the two interpolated true Lieder do not, as a consequence, stick out like sore thumbs. Fischer-Dieskau is a genial, relaxed Miller, darkening powerfully in his scene of jealousy (just a touch of strain at the top of the voice). Soffel is in lovely voice, bringing out the tenderness and grace of Frasquita as well as her resourceful sparkishness. Nothing on earth could make the Corregidor himself formidable (his title is pronounced throughout with a soft 'g', by the way) but Hollweg sings his not very rewarding lines incisively, and there are admirable lesser contributions from the elegantly lyrical Donath, the cavernously dark von Halem, the elegant tenorino Maus (in two roles) and others. Gerd Albrecht draws excellent playing from an orchestra that have been wisely (for such an intimate *opera buffa* as this essentially is) scaled down from their usual strength, and the recording is admirably balanced.

With one single reservation, indeed, the thoroughly sympathetic recorded performance that this infuriating, entrancing opera has been needing for years is here. The reservation concerns a cut in that impossible Act 4: Wolf himself made it (it amounts to over 200 bars of music) but he composed a briefer replacement. Neither version makes much sense dramatically, but neither does the solution adopted here of omitting both. A pity, but don't let it put you off.

Riccardo Zandonai Italian 1883-1944

Zandonai Francesca da Rimini.
  Elena Filipova *sop* Francesca
  Frederic Kalt *ten* Paolo il Bello
  Philippe Rouillon *bar* Giovanni lo Sciancato
  Kenneth Riegel *ten* Malatestino dall'Occhio
  Hana Minutillo *contr* Samaritana
  Danilo Rigosa *bass* Ostasio
  Anita Bader *sop* Biancofiore
  Tünde Franko *sop* Garsenda
  Jolana Fogasova *mez* Altichiara
  Jaroslava Horská *contr* Donella
  Alexander Kravets *ten* Ser Toldo Berardengo
  David Cale Johnson *bass* Jester
  Cheyne Davidson *bar* Torchbearer
  Sofia Chamber Choir; Vienna Volksoper Chorus; Vienna Symphony Orchestra / Fabio Luisi.
  Koch Schwann Ⓟ Ⓒ 31368-2 (two discs: 126 minutes: DDD). Text and translation included.
  Recorded at a performance in the Festspielhaus, Bregenz on July 20th, 1994.

Francesca da Rimini, whose music fuses post-Puccinian Italian lyricism with voluptuously rich orchestral colour owing something to Wagner, rather more to Strauss and to Zandonai's French contemporaries, is surely ripe for rediscovery (we say *rediscovery* – the work is still intermittently in the Italian repertory and that of the New York Met – because it is an extreme rarity elsewhere, and this is currently the only available CD recording). Those who are familiar with the work will know that what stands in the way of more frequent performance is the peculiarly demanding title-role, associated in the past with such formidable singing actresses as Magda Olivero, Leyla Gencer and Raina Kabaivanska. Is Elena Filipova up to those demands and those comparisons? The answer is an emphatic 'Yes'; indeed on the basis of this performance it is astonishing that this appears to be her first operatic recording. The voice is a forceful *spinto* soprano, yet capable of caressing softness and seamless line; she responds to words and to the ripe richness of Zandonai's style with quite beautiful phrasing. As Paolo, Frederic Kalt is a robust tenor with a burnished gleam that only occasionally takes on a harsh edge; he too is stylish, but would be twice as impressive if he occasionally sang quietly. Of the other principals Rouillon, as Francesca's unfortunate husband, is a fine, grave baritone; as the evil Malatestino, Riegel is vividly characterful if rather too often over the top if not half-way down the other side.

The problem with *Francesca da Rimini* is that of the two fated, tragic lovers Paolo does not appear on-stage until the Second of the four acts, and that he and Francesca do not have an extended scene together until the Third. Zandonai's richness of palette and his curiously but attractively anachronistic evocations of the past are quite enough to keep one absorbed until doomed love bursts into flame, but this live recording is kind neither to the singers (who are often backwardly placed, their words unclear) nor to the orchestra: Zandonai's luscious textures are sometimes dense, his colours occasionally coarsened. But the performance is admirably paced and controlled: the drama of the piece is very strongly projected. Though not as voluptuous as any performance of this opera should be it has sufficient quality to swell the number of those longing to see it on stage; and in Filipova it has a star soprano fully worthy of its central role.

Alexander von Zemlinsky Austrian 1871-1942

Zemlinsky Eine florentinische Tragödie.
  Iris Vermillion *mez* Bianca
  Heinz Kruse *ten* Guido Bardi
  Albert Dohmen *bar* Simone

A. Mahler Die stille Stadt. Laue Sommernacht. Bei dir ist es traut. Licht in der Nacht. Waldeinsamkeit. Emtelied (orch. Colin and David Matthews).

Iris Vermillion *mez*
Royal Concertgebouw Orchestra / Riccardo Chailly.
Decca Entartete Musik Ⓕ ⓪ 455 112-2DH (71 minutes: DDD). Notes, texts and translations included. Recorded 1996.

Zemlinsky's *Florentine Tragedy* is a disturbing, shocking piece, but to make its fullest impact it also needs to sound ravishingly beautiful. As the wealthy merchant, Simone shows Count Bardi (his wife's lover, as he already suspects) a robe of silver damask so exquisitely wrought with roses "that they lack perfume only to cheat the wanton sense" or, later, describes to him another of Venetian cut velvet patterned with pomegranates each seed of which is a pearl, we should almost be able to see these marvels. Zemlinsky's sumptuous scoring at these points urgently needs, in short, an orchestra of the Royal Concertgebouw's stature, and in this reading they sound quite magnificent. But the score also needs a conductor of subtlety and shrewdness to point up the fact that there are two passages of serene lyricism which are placed in high relief by all this richness. They occur in a brief scene where Simone's wife, Bianca, left alone for a moment with Count Bardi, assures him of her eternal love and, later, after Simone has murdered his rival, when husband and wife stare at each other, her passion for him awakened by his unexpected brutal strength, he awakened to her beauty by the fact of her adultery.

Vermillion is very fine at both these points, her mezzo timbre (the role is properly for soprano) adding warmth to her finely drawn line. Kruse is admirable too, fining down his ringing tenor in that duet scene, and in the most demanding role, that of Simone, Dohmen is forceful and dangerous, with bass blackness and baritone urgency both at his command. But Chailly is the real star of the performance, pacing the opera so well that it seems over in no time, drawing richly complex but never muddy textures from his remarkable orchestra.

If Zemlinsky needs the Concertgebouw, the first thought on hearing the Alma Mahler songs is that what they have been needing all these years is orchestration. The Matthews brothers' scoring points up her kinship with Zemlinsky (her teacher) and allows her vocal lines to expand in a way that her piano versions can seem to inhibit. She might have written a fine opera, on a subject as gamey as those Zemlinsky himself sought out. But here again, exquisitely though Vermillion sings these songs, Chailly must take at least half the credit. Each song is taken faster than in most recordings with piano, and every one of them gains from it in impulsive urgency. In both Zemlinsky's opera and Alma Mahler's songs the recording leaves nothing to be desired: the colours are rich but beautifully clean.

Zemlinsky Der Geburtstag der Infantin.
Inga Nielsen *sop* Donna Clara, Infanta of Spain
Kenneth Riegel *ten* The Dwarf
Béatrice Haldas *sop* Ghita
Dieter Weller *bass* Major-Domo
Cheryl Studer *sop* First Maid
Olive Fredericks *sop* Second Maid
Marianne Hirsti *sop* Third Maid
Berlin Radio Symphony Orchestra / Gerd Albrecht.
Schwann Ⓕ ⓪ 314013 (76 minutes: DDD). Notes, text and translation included. Recorded 1986.

Eine Florentinische Tragödie is one of Zemlinsky's one-act Oscar Wilde opera; this is the other one. It was originally entitled *Der Zwerg* and was given its première in 1922 in Cologne under Klemperer; but when the Hamburg State Opera revived it in 1981 its impossibly stilted libretto was radically rewritten to bring it closer to Wilde's tale, and his title *The Birthday of the Infanta* was restored. The work was heard at the 1986 Edinburgh Festival; but curiously enough, although this recording was made immediately afterwards by the same conductor and cast (with the exception of one minor character), the chorus and orchestra of the Hamburg Opera were here replaced.

The story relates how the little Infanta is given, among her birthday presents, a hideously misshapen dwarf as a play-thing: he has just been captured in the forest during a boar-hunt and is totally ignorant, even of what he looks like. He falls desperately in love with the beautiful princess and mistakes her insincere sporting with him for mutual attraction, until he sees himself in a mirror and literally dies of shame. Zemlinsky's music succeeds in portraying both the dwarf's revolting exterior and the ardent emotions seething below it, contrasting them with the cold formality and frivolous heartlessness of the court: the orchestral writing, full of invention and subtlety, dominates the first part of the opera (despite several brief ensembles), and it is not until the scene between the Infanta and the dwarf, and his subsequent horrified self-discovery, that the voices are given real scope for lyric expansion.

The whole performance here is of a high standard (with particularly fine orchestral playing) but this is an opera which loses much by not being seen, and two particular weaknesses may be mentioned. One is that, despite constant mentions in the libretto of laughter, merriment, girls tittering, and so on, all but the three chief characters do nothing but sing the notes (without much sense of character either), and anyone not understanding German or following the printed libretto would never guess at the raillery going on: the other is that, in the cruelly high-lying part of the dwarf, Kenneth Riegel sings so vitally and engagingly that it is hard to envisage him as a deformed grotesque (but here Zemlinsky must also take the blame). Inga Nielsen, with her bright, pure, cool voice, is ideally cast as the spoilt, thoughtless Infanta; and Béatrice Haldas brings a warmer quality to her maid, the only one with any reservations about the cruel sport made of the wretched dwarf. The opera is recorded with admirable sound and sense of perspective.

Zemlinsky Kleider machen Leute.

Hermann Winkler *ten* Wenzel Strapinski
Edith Mathis *sop* Nettchen
Wicus Slabbert *bass* Melchior Böhni
Hans Franzen *bass* Adam Litumlei
Stefania Kaluza *contr* Frau Litumlei
Volker Vogel *ten* Polykarpus Federspiel
Ueli Hunziker *spkr* Master Tailor
Björn Jensson *ten* First apprentice, Servant
Ulrich Simon Eggimann *bar* Second apprentice
Rudolf Hartmann *bass* Magistrate
Peter Keller *ten* Elder son of Häberlein & Co
Ruth Rohner *sop* Mrs Häberlein
Jacob Will *bar* Younger son of Häberlein
Rainer Scholze *bass* Innkeeper
Renate Lenhart *sop* Innkeeper's wife
Kimberly Justus *sop* Cook
Sarianna Salminen *sop* Boy servant
Claudio Otelli *bar* Coachman
Ulrich Peter *spkr* Prologue
Zurich Opera House Chorus and Orchestra / Ralf Weikert.
Schwann Ⓟ Ⓓ 314069 (two discs: 98 minutes: DDD). Notes, text and translation included.
Recorded at a performance in the Zurich Opera House on July 29th, 1990.

Premièred at the Vienna Volksoper on December 1st, 1910, *Kleider machen Leute* is Zemlinsky's fourth opera. Leo Fell's libretto is based on Gottfried Keller's novella about the journeyman tailor who, on the basis of the one fine coat and hat he owns, is mistaken for a Count. He is eventually found out and rounds on the hypocrisy of those who were prepared to fawn on him just because of his supposed rank. In the process he wins the heart of the girl he thinks he has lost. It is not a tale brimming over with suspense or subtlety of characterization, and the happy ending seems under less threat even than that of *Hänsel und Gretel*. The booklet essay stretches a point when it speaks of a "tiptoeing on the crest between 'genuine' and 'false' romanticism". If anything the ambivalence is between comedy of manners and allegorical fairy-tale and the dominant tone is one of good-humoured charm.

As usual with Zemlinsky the drama culminates in a heart-aching self-confession, and as with *Der Kreidekreis* the music rather fails to deliver the transcendence demanded at this crunch-point (contrast, for instance, the concluding monologue of Salome, or even the heartbreaking lament of Zemlinsky's own *Der Zwerg*). Again, it is characteristic of Zemlinsky, as indeed of a sizeable proportion of neo-Wagnerian opera, that the splendour and subtlety of the orchestral colour should rather overface the vocal writing. Just one memorable Hänsel-ish or even Schwanda the bagpiper-ish tune, one feels, could have made all the difference.

That said, this is a consummately beautiful score, with some especially salty harmonies in the orchestral interludes, all duly relished by Ralf Weikert and his excellent orchestra. Edith Mathis adds a distinguished Nettchen to her extensive recorded repertoire; Hermann Winkler as her hapless but ultimately triumphant beloved is somewhat dry of voice, especially in the later stages, but he and his colleagues all sing with impressive dedication. Being a live recording there is a certain amount of dodgy synchronization, particularly when the village chorus are involved. Otherwise, though, it is an assured and remarkably consistent performance, with minimal distraction from audience or stage noise. And the recording has come out exceptionally cleanly and well balanced in the circumstances (again the chorus suffer a little). The absence from the booklet of a production history of the work, of track numbers within the printed libretto (which in any case is littered with misprints) and of sufficient tracks to provide for access even to separate scenes, is most regrettable. But how much poorer would we now be were it not for Schwann's enterprise in recording this opera.

Zemlinsky Der König Kandaules (cptd Beaumont).

James O'Neal *ten* König Kandaules
Monte Pederson *bar* Gyges
Nina Warren *sop* Nyssia

Klaus Häger *bass* Phedros
Peter Galliard *ten* Syphax
Mariusz Kwiecien *bar* Nicomedes
Kurt Gysen *bass* Pharnaces
Simon Yang *bass* Philebos
Ferdinand Seiler *ten* Sebas
Guido Jentjens *bar* Archelaos
Hamburg State Philharmonic Orchestra / Gerd Albrecht.
Capriccio Ⓕ Ⓓ 60 071/2 (two discs: 128 minutes: DDD). Recorded at performances in the
Staatsoper, Hamburg on October 18th and 25th, 1996. Notes, text and translation included.

This is an issue of outstanding importance. *Der König Kandaules* ("King Candaules"), based on a
play by André Gide, is Zemlinsky's last opera, written during the Nazis' rise to power and complete
in short score when he fled to America in 1938. He showed it to his pupil, Artur Bodanzky, then a
Principal Conductor at the Met, but Bodanzky seems to have warned him that the libretto would not
be acceptable – in one scene Kandaules tricks his wife into undressing in front of a fisherman he has
recently befriended, then into sleeping with him. Zemlinsky proposed another subject, but was so
short of money that he devoted the remaining few months of his life to hack work, and the
orchestration of *Der König Kandaules* was never completed. He left, however, a large number of
indications of scoring, and on the basis of that and the 846 bars that he had finished Antony
Beaumont has now prepared what we should perhaps call a 'performing edition'. It had its first
production in Hamburg in 1996 and this live recording was made at the same time.

Beaumont's orchestration sounds perfectly convincing, as convincing as his by now widely accepted
revision of the final scene of Busoni's *Doktor Faust*. When two excerpts from the score were
performed and recorded in 1994 (Capriccio) as a sort of progress report on his work, it already looked
as though a major work by Zemlinsky was about to be revealed. And that indeed is the case: a
marvellous and quite characteristic score, but in some ways a dismaying one. All the orchestral
richness and the voluptuously singing lines that one expects are there, but wedded to a plot that seems
all too accurately to reflect the disorder and disillusion of the times in which it was written.

Nyssia, the wife so chaste and beautiful that until now no one but Kandaules has seen her unveiled,
is portrayed in music of quite sumptuous allure, but her reaction to his betrayal is more Salome-like
than tragic: she orders the fisherman Gyges to kill her husband and take his place, in her bed as well
as on the throne. Gyges, the poor but honest peasant (and his music has a touch of nobility to it), is
a murderer himself: he killed his own wife because, as Kandaules would have agreed, she was his
property. And Kandaules the seeming altruist, whose greatest pleasure is to share his wealth with
others, is in fact simply boasting of his good fortune: even his wife's beauty is a sort of torment to
him if other men are not jealous of it. And in Zemlinsky's musical portrayal the more his baseness
becomes obvious the more glamorous and sympathetic he is.

The performance is a fine one, O'Neal lacking only the last touch of heroic vocal stature for
Kandaules, Warren only a little stretched by the Ariadne-like role of Nyssia, Pederson first-class (a
moment or two of suspect intonation aside) as Gyges. Albrecht is perfectly at home in this sort of
music, the orchestra's admirable richness of tone does not obscure detail, and the recording is
atmospheric (stage business audible) but clear. Zemlinsky's reputation has been growing year by year
recently. It can only be enhanced by this ravishing, richly complex, disturbing opera.

Zemlinsky Der Kreidekreis.

Renate Behle *sop* Tschang-Haitang
Gabriele Schreckenbach *mez* Mrs Tschang
Roland Hermann *bar* Ma
Siegfried Lorenz *bar* Tschao
Reiner Goldberg *ten* Emperor Pao
Uwe Peter *ten* Tong
Hans Helm *bar* Tschang-Ling
Gertrud Ottenthal *sop* Mrs Ma
Kaja Borris *mez* Midwife
Gidon Saks *bar* Soldier
Celina Lindsley *sop* A girl
Berlin Radio Symphony Orchestra / Stefan Soltesz.
Capriccio Ⓕ Ⓓ 60 016-2 (two discs: 124 minutes: DDD). Notes, text and translation included.
Recorded 1990.

Der Kreidekreis was completed in 1932 and successfully staged just before the blight of Nazi artistic
policy descended on German opera-houses. Characteristically it is full to the brim with gorgeous
harmonies and timbres. The story is essentially the same as that of Brecht's more famous *Caucasian
Chalk Circle*, and the action culminates in the same *coup de théâtre*, in which the genuine mother
(Tschang-Haitang) refuses to harm her son by dragging him away from the impostor, Mrs Ma. But as
the author, Klabund (pseudonym for Alfred Henschke) put it: "The old Chinese drama of justice and

morals was usable only as raw material ... [I attempted] to invent a Chinese fairy-tale ... as if someone were dreaming of China" – particularly someone, he might have added, with a mid-European early-twentieth-century penchant for decadent eroticism. The twist in the tale – that the former prostitute, Haitang had been impregnated when asleep by the now Emperor Pao – produces a happy ending of such extreme self-indulgence it seems almost pointless to take offence.

Curiously, at this climax of high sensuality, Zemlinsky's music doesn't entirely rise to the occasion. Yet everything has been so promising until then – from the opening train-like ostinato with its snakey saxophone and Ravel-crossed-with-Weill *chinoiseries*, all the way to the gorgeous interlude for the journey to Peking. Perhaps it should not be surprising that a composer so closely associated with Mahler and Richard Strauss should demonstrate such a refined mastery of orchestral colour. But the constant caressing of the ear, never cheaply or blatantly done, is still something of a marvel. Ultimately this may be nothing more than a very late example of Viennese *Gefühlskultur*, but if so it's a taste you'll be glad to acquire.

The hint of Weill is an interesting sign of the times. There is plenty of speech and melodrama (speech with orchestral accompaniment) and several of the main characters introduce themselves matter-of-factly in the manner of Weill's Chinese morality play, *Der Jasager* (of 1930). Zemlinsky's affection for the idiom of *The Threepenny Opera* and *Mahagonny* is constantly in evidence, and there is a dash of social comment for those who wish to read such things into the work. As so often, when one detects an influence, or an obvious parallel (such as the courtroom scene of *Peter Grimes* or the 'speaking orchestra' of Judith Weir's *The Consolations of Scholarship*) this throws into relief the comparatively unfocused quality of Zemlinsky's more permissive style. That, and the dubious indulgence of the final scenes, may continue to deny *Der Kreidekreis* a viable existence in the opera-house; but with so much superb music home listening is still a joy.

The performance is first-rate throughout. The cast is without weakness, the orchestral support is outstanding and the recording finds a happy medium between richness and clarity (in fact it relegates the orchestra a fraction more than one might wish, but in an opera where every word counts that's fair enough). The only serious drawback is that Renate Behle as Tschang-Haitang is heavier of voice than the supposedly older Mrs Ma of Gertrud Ottenthal. Don't let that put you off, though.

Zemlinsky Sarema.

Karin Clarke *sop* Sarema
Laslo Lukas *bar* Dscherikoff
Norbert Kleinhenn *ten* Asslan
Andreas Scheel *bar* Amul Beg
Yuri Zinovenko *bass* Prophet
Nick Herbosch *bass* Godunoff
Florian Simson *ten* Herald
Trier Theatre Chorus; Trier City Orchestra / István Dénes.
Koch Classics Ⓕ ① 36467-2 (two discs: 102 minutes: DDD). Notes, text and translation included. Recorded during performances at the City Theatre, Trier on July 2nd, 3rd and 4th, 1996.

Sarema (1895) was the 23-year-old Zemlinsky's first opera, but despite his later fame it was soon forgotten: this recording is of its first production this century. It is not, of course, a fully mature work, but it makes it quite easy to understand why Mahler admired the young Zemlinsky so much and why Schoenberg (who prepared the vocal score of *Sarema*) found no need for any other teacher. He seems already to know pretty well everything that an opera composer at this date would need to know. He is skilled at Wagnerian declamation and at underlaying it with resourceful thematic working and striking orchestral texture, but he knows better than to reject Brahmsian influence. He makes telling use of brief characterizing motifs, and can build them into longer, expressive melodies. With an eye on Verdi or perhaps even Meyerbeer he can end an act with a stirring ensemble with chorus, and as this performance makes clear he already writes grateful and eloquent vocal lines.

The plot is rather awkward, however, and Zemlinsky isn't always quite sure how to handle it. Sarema ("The Rose of the Caucasus", as the subtitle calls her) is a Circassian who has fallen in love with her captor, the Russian commander Dscherikoff. Her compatriot, Asslan comes to rescue her (he also is in love with her) and she is torn between love and patriotism. Although initially spurned by her own people she leads them in victorious battle, and pleads with them for Dscherikoff's life. Still filled with guilt, however (her own father had been blinded by a Russian bullet: "loaded, perhaps by my own child," he says, "who rewarded the marksman with a smile!"), she kills herself.

The little oriental motif that opens the Second Act, set in the Circassian camp, is a bit too close to conventional local colour, for all that it is immediately succeeded by a Wagnerian chord progression, and when Sarema appears in the camp the assembled tribesmen react with a well-made but rather decorous fugue in the manner of Saint-Saëns. Where Zemlinsky is particularly successful, however, is in sketching the growth of the central character: she approaches nobility even in the First Act, by the Second can withstand even an apparent passing reference to Brünnhilde's *Todesverkündigung* and is affecting in her dying avowal of love for Dscherikoff.

The performance is not quite as big-scaled as Zemlinsky's imagination at its finest, but it is much more than competent. Karin Clarke in particular, a slight touch of fragility aside (in fact it adds to her portrayal, somehow), is a most convincing Sarema, and Andreas Scheel as her implacable father is the best of a reliable supporting cast. The chorus are a little raw, the orchestra not quite large enough, but the recording has considerable theatrical pungency. Not a neglected masterpiece, but fascinating evidence of Zemlinsky on the very brink of maturity.

Zemlinsky Der Traumgörge.

Janis Martin *sop* Princess Gertraud
Josef Protschka *ten* Görge
Pamela Coburn *sop* Grete
Hartmut Welker *bar* Hans, Kaspar
Martin Blasius *bass* Minister
Pater Haage *ten* Innkeeper
Victor von Halem *bass* Miller
Heinz Kruse *ten* Zungl
Birgit Calm *sop* Innkeeper's wife
Gabriele Maria Ronge *sop* Marei
Hesse Radio Youth and Figural Choirs;
Frankfurt Radio Symphony Orchestra / Gerd Albrecht.
Capriccio Ⓟ Ⓓ 10 241/2 (two discs: 111 minutes: DDD). Notes, text and translation included.
Recorded at performances in the Alte Oper, Frankfurt in September 1987.

Der Traumgörge ("Görge the Dreamer") should have marked an auspicious stage in the development of Zemlinsky's reputation. It was his third opera, completed in 1906, its predecessor, *Es war einmal* ("Once upon a time") had been successfully staged by Mahler in Vienna. *Der Traumgörge* was to all intents and purposes commissioned by Mahler to follow this up, but the opera was already in rehearsal when he resigned his directorship. His successor, Weingartner, cancelled the première and the work remained unperformed, indeed in a limbo of non-existence (most lists of Zemlinsky's works omit all mention of it) for over 70 years, until a complete set of performing material was discovered in the archives of the Vienna State Opera. It was first performed in Nuremburg in 1980, 38 years after its composer's death.

It is still a youthful work (in Zemlinsky's catalogue it immediately follows that uneven but gorgeous orchestral fantasy, *Die Seejungfrau*) but a remarkably assured one. The manner will be familiar to anyone who knows the two later one-act operas, *Eine florentinische Tragödie* and *Der Zwerg* (though the subject-matter of *Der Traumgorge* is far gentler than either of those). The basic texture is an evanescent, richly embroidered orchestral web, in which colour and harmonic movement are often as important as melody. In a sense it is an instrumental drama, its emotions are signalled by the voices but made manifest in the orchestra, and it is of the essence of the curious plot that Zemlinsky chose that this should be so. An allegory of the artist's role in society, the libretto taken at face value is of startling daftness. Görge, a country pastor's son, lives wholly in the world of fairy-tales, his continual mooning about Snow White and Puss-in-boots loses him his level-headed fiancée and he goes out into the world in search of a fairy Princess. He finds her in the person of Gertraud, a beggar-woman, feared and reviled as a witch and an arsonist; he is improbably hailed as leader by a group of youthful revolutionaries, but abandons them when he learns of their violent ends; he returns home with his beggar-princess to found a school and raise a family.

It is not the role of Zemlinsky's music to give flesh to these pasteboard symbolic characters (which would scarcely be possible: the uncomprehending peasants who mock Görge and curse Gertraud have more 'reality' than they) nor to express the stilted sentiments they utter. The music is there to represent the archetypes that Görge and Gertraud and their relationships stand for: the visionary artist, the misunderstood idealist, the unrecognized builder and shaker at odds with those who see no need to build or to be shaken. In scenes of pure dialogue one instinctively sides with the villagers in their exasperation at Görge's gormlessness, but Zemlinsky is far more successful in the evanescent lyricism of the visionary set pieces: Görge's dream of his fairy Princess, her lulling of him to sleep, his recognition of Gertraud as predestined "Mother, Sister, Wife", the grandeur of her vision of Pentecostal fire and above all the exquisite tenderness of the calm evening epilogue: a musical equivalent, almost, of Samuel Palmer. It is an important document in Zemlinsky's development, and one can quite see why Mahler (and Schoenberg and Webern, as it happens) should have found its combination of harmonic subtlety and orchestral opulence so appealing.

How good to have the opera in such an excellent performance: it is just the sort of thing that Gerd Albrecht does well, and most of his soloists are admirable. Protschka's gently ardent Görge is particularly likeable, but Martin's hard and unalluring voice in a role that needs glamour, above all, is less impressive. A clear and uncluttered recording, too, though in an opera where 95 per cent of the musical interest lies in the orchestra there could have been a less forward placing of the voices. Do try it: for all the awkwardness of its libretto *Der Traumgörge* evokes a very particular *fin-de-siècle* romanticism (close to Mahler's own *Das klagende Lied* or to some parts of Schoenberg's *Gurrelieder*, though melodically more fluidly elusive than either) with impressive resourcefulness.

Bernd-Alois Zimmermann

German 1918-1970

B-A. Zimmermann Die Soldaten.

Mark Munkittrick *bass* Wesener
Nancy Shade *sop* Marie
Milagro Vargas *mez* Charlotte
Grace Hoffman *contr* Wesener's Mother
Michael Ebbecke *bar* Stolzius
Elsie Maurer *contr* Stolzius's Mother
Alois Treml *bass* Obrist
William Cochran *ten* Desportes
Guy Renard *ten* Pirzel
Karl-Friedrich Dürr *bar* Eisenhardt
Klaus Hirte *bar* Haudy
Raymond Wolansky *bar* Mary
Johannes Eidloth, Robert Wörle, Helmut Holzapfel *tens* Young Officers
Urszula Koszut *mez* Countess de la Roche
Jerrold van der Schaaf *ten* Young Count
Karl-Heinz Eichler *spkr* Countess's Servant
Jürgen Bolle *spkr* Cadet
Jörg Geiger *spkr* Drunken Officer
Peter Flottau, Hans Tübinger, Uwe Rohde *spkrs* Captains
Stuttgart Opera Chorus and State Orchestra / Bernhard Kontarsky.
Teldec Ⓟ Ⓒ 9031-72775-2 (two discs: 107 minutes: DDD). Text and translation included.
Recorded 1988/9.

The cruelty and stupidity of military men might seem an eminently proper subject for a modern opera. An opera in modern style combining such a topic with an element of romantic tragedy has less obvious appeal, and when it is based, not on a contemporary, tailor-made libretto, but on a drama as challenging and idiosyncratic as J. M. R. Lenz's *Die Soldaten* (1775), the task becomes still more formidable. Bernd Alois Zimmermann, himself a complex and ultimately tragic figure, tackled it in his first and only complete opera, and the result has been regularly performed in Germany, including a production at Stuttgart in the 1980s from which this studio recording derives.

Die Soldaten was begun in 1958, when Zimmermann was 40, and completed two years later, but it was not staged until 1965, after extensive revision. Lenz was admired by Büchner, the author of *Wozzeck*, and Zimmermann's music can be thought of as intensifying the expressionistic idiom of Berg's opera. Yet the greatness of *Wozzeck* stems from its unsparing portrayal of human tragedy, while the problem with *Die Soldaten* is its obsession with inhumanity. Berg achieves a perfect balance between forcefulness of expression and control of form: Zimmermann seems merely extravagant. Rightly convinced of the profound seriousness of his subject-matter, he failed to appreciate that economy and understatement can often be more effective transmitters of stark dramatic truth than sustained and extreme intensity. It may indeed be the case that only the sardonic detachment of a Weill or an Eisler could give *Die Soldaten*'s mix of themes convincing dramatic life in the later twentieth century. Like Aribert Reimann in a more recent ultra-expressionist opera, *Lear*, Zimmermann seems unable to stand back, and the music's ideas are overwhelmed by its emotionalism.

If the expressionist clamour of *Die Soldaten* were totally unrelieved, it would be an unbearable disaster. In Act 3 Zimmermann does at least attempt a contrasting gentleness, a lyricism that allows some sense of positive human values to emerge. His medium is, of all things, a trio for female voices, and it would serve its purpose far more effectively did it not become overheated so rapidly, leaving even singers as expert and dedicated as those in this performance straining and strident.

Die Soldaten is an extremely visual opera, requiring a split set for its two principal locations. Collage-technique is prominent, and the multi-media display of Act 4 scene 1, with its three cinema-screens, comes across as little more than chaotic babel when heard but not seen. The recording wisely makes no attempt at extravagant spatial effects, and the conductor achieves miracles of co-ordination and textural clarification, aided by singers who on the whole are as strong musically as they are dramatically. *Die Soldaten* cannot simply be dismissed as a period piece, a monument to the extravagant, idealistic 1960s. But it is a problem piece, with a challenging subject which the composer lacked the experience and judgement to convert into a monumental piece of music theatre.

Udo Zimmermann

German 1943

U. Zimmermann Weisse Rose.

Gabriele Fontana *sop* Sophie Scholl
Lutz-Michael Harder *ten* Hans Scholl
Instrumental Ensemble / Udo Zimmermann.
Orfeo Ⓟ Ⓒ C162871A (72 minutes: DDD). Notes, text and translation included. Recorded 1986.

Udo Zimmermann (no relation to and not to be confused with his namesake Bernd-Alois) is an East German composer whose stage works have been conspicuously successful, if frequency of performance is any measure of success: within two years of its première in Hamburg *Weisse Rose* ("White Rose") had been produced in over 30 cities.

"White Rose" was the name adopted by a resistance group in Nazi Germany. Its activities, centred on the University of Munich, were discovered and the members of the group executed in February 1943, just a few months before Zimmermann was born. The fate of the group, of two of its members in particular (the brother and sister, Hans and Sophie Scholl) has obviously exercised a strong fascination on the composer, since this is his second treatment of it. The first, a sort of 'opera-documentary', was produced in Dresden in 1967; the present work, which apparently shares no material, verbal or musical, with its predecessor, is a sequence of 16 dramatic but non-narrative scenes exploring the memories and the state of mind of the Scholls as they awaited execution.

It could be regarded as at best an impossible task, at worst almost an impertinence to set such poems to music: No. 7, for example, which expresses Sophie Scholl's pitiful terror at the darkness of her prison cell and her dread of every footstep that passes it. Zimmermann's solution, effectively, is not to set it to music at all: the soprano speaks the words in a terrified, breathless whisper, accompanied by a rapidly fluttering ostinato figure that gradually descends in pitch and increases in menacing volume as the piece proceeds. That is all: not so much a setting as the devising of a pair of musical gestures to match the text, and this is often Zimmermann's way. Except when the instruments erupt in explosive or sinister dramatic grimaces (often reminiscent of Weill) their role is very much an evocative and accompanimental one. The voices often rise from speech to recitative and plaintive *arioso* (often based, like the accompaniments, on ostinato figures), but these melodies too are used more as gestures (or as what a semiologist would call 'signs': for nostalgia, pity, anguish or whatever) than as musical material to be developed and transformed into a structure greater than its parts. The parts are always effective, sometimes touching or horrifying, and you can imagine *Weisse Rose* being a gripping experience in a simple and sympathetic staging. You find yourself ungratefully asking for more. No. 8, for example, consists of two lines of expressively spoken text ("They have cropped her hair. What have they done to her?") followed by a pattern of staccato chords that grow gradually quieter. A graphic and pathetic 'sign' for Hans Scholl's pity and revulsion at his sister's disfigurement, but not much more graphic and pathetic than the printed words themselves. Honourably, but in the ultimate resort, disappointingly Zimmermann has concluded that music can effectively assist the utterance of such texts but cannot add to them.

At all events, one can scarcely imagine them more vividly projected: Gabriele Fontana copes with the cruelly extended range of the soprano line with heroic eloquence, and her tenor partner is accomplished both as actor and singer. The instrumental contribution (under the composer's direction) is precise and pungent, as is the crisply forward recording.

Manufacturers and distributors

Entries are listed as follows: **Manufacturer** or **Label** – UK Distributor

Accent Complete Record Co.
Accord Discovery Records
Albany Select
Archiv Produktion PolyGram Record Operations
Argo PolyGram Record Operations
Arion Discovery Records
Arte Nova Classics BMG Conifer
Arts Complete Record Co.
Auvidis Harmonia Mundi
Bel Canto Society Parsifal Distribution
Berlin Classics Complete Record Co.
BIS Select
Calig Priory
Capriccio Target
CBC Records Kingdom
CBS Sony Music Entertainment
Chandos Chandos
Channel Classics Complete Record Co.
Le Chant du Monde Harmonia Mundi
Classics for Pleasure EMI
Claves Complete Record Co.
Collins Classics Complete Record Co.
Conifer Classics BMG Conifer
CPO Select
Danacord Discovery Records
Dante Parsifal Distribution
Da Capo (Marco Polo) Select
Decca PolyGram Record Operations
Delos Nimbus
Deutsche Harmonia Mundi BMG Conifer
DG PolyGram Record Operations
EMI EMI
Erato Warner Classics
Etcetera Koch International
Finlandia Warner Classics
Forlane Target
Hänssler Classic Select
Harmonia Mundi Harmonia Mundi
Hungaroton Target
Hyperion Select
IMG Records Carlton Home Entertainment
Koch Classics Koch International
Koch International Classics Koch International
Koch Schwann Koch International
L'Empreinte Digitale Harmonia Mundi
L'Oiseau-Lyre PolyGram Record Operations
Lyrita Nimbus
Marco Polo Select
Melodiya BMG Conifer

Melodram Parsifal Distribution
MGB Musiques Suisses Complete Record Co.
Multisonic Priory
Music and Arts Harmonia Mundi
MusicMasters Nimbus
Myto Parsifal Distribution
Naxos Select
New World Harmonia Mundi
Newport Classic DI Music
Nightingale Classics Koch International
Nimbus Nimbus
NMC Complete Record Co.
Nonesuch Warner Classics
NVC Arts Warner Vision
Ondine Complete Record Co.
Opera Rara Select
Opus 111 Harmonia Mundi
Orfeo Classical Passions
Pavane Kingdom
Pearl Harmonia Mundi
Philips PolyGram Record Operations
Pierre Verany Discovery Records
Preiser Harmonia Mundi
RCA BMG Conifer
Simax Chandos
Sonpact Seaford Music
Sony Classical Sony Music Entertainment
Supraphon Koch International
Tahra Records Priory
Telarc BMG Conifer
Teldec Warner Classics
TER Classics MCI Presents/Complete Record Co.
Testament Complete Record Co.
Unicorn-Kanchana Harmonia Mundi
Vanguard Classics Complete Record Co.
Virgin Classics EMI
Warner Vision Warner Vision
Wergo Harmonia Mundi

Some labels, mentioned in reviews in this guide, may only be available through national (UK) or international mail-order dealers. Information on such dealers can be found in *Gramophone*. Specialist retailers will also often be able to assist in cases of difficulties in obtaining recordings. For additional information on manufacturers and distributors, refer to the Label Distribution Directory published in *Gramophone*.

Record Company names and addresses

Unless otherwise indicated all the companies listed below are based in the UK; addresses for record companies from outside the UK are given, where available (telephone and fax numbers should be prefixed with the appropriate international dialing code).

Accent Records Eikstraat 31, 1673 Beert, *BELGIUM*.
Telephone 32 2 356 1878 fax 32 2 360 2718

Accord 3 Rue Vatimesnil, 92300 Levallois Perret, *FRANCE*.
Telephone 33 1 4149 4249 fax 33 1 4149 4200

Albany Records PO Box 12, Carnforth, Lancashire LA5 9PD.
Telephone 01524 735873 fax 01524 736448

Archiv Produktion 22 St Peter's Square, London W6 9NW.
Telephone 0181-910 5000 fax 0181-910 3132

Argo 22 St Peter's Square, London W6 9NW.
Telephone 0181-910 5000 fax 0181-910 3132

Disques Arion 36, Avenue Hoche, 75008 Paris, *FRANCE*.
Telephone 33 1 4563 7670 fax 33 1 4563 7954

Arte Nova Classics BMG Conifer UK, Bedford House, 69-79 Fulham High Street, London SW6 3JW.
Telephone 0171-384 7500 fax 0171-384 7922

Arts Mühlenweg 5, 65445 Oberding, *GERMANY*.
Telephone 49 81 2297270 fax 49 81 2297240

Auvidis *FRANCE* 47 Avenue Paul Vaillant-Couturier, 94250 Gentilly.
Telephone 33 1 4615 8800 fax 33 1 4740 3685
UK 19-21 Nile Street, London N1 7LL.
Telephone 0171-251 3809 fax 0171-253 3237

Bel Canto Society PO Box 6613, Edison, NJ 08837, *USA*.
Telephone 1 732 417 2109 fax 1 732 225 1562

Berlin Classics Edel, Wichmannstraße 4, 22607 Hamburg, *GERMANY*.
Telephone 49 40 890 850 fax 49 40 890 85605

Grammofon AB BIS Bragevägen 2, 18264 Djursholm, *SWEDEN*.
Telephone 46 8 755 4100 fax 46 8 755 7676

BMG Conifer UK Bedford House, 69-79 Fulham High Street, London SW6 3JW.
Telephone 0171-384 7500 fax 0171-384 7922

BMG UK Lyng Lane, West Bromwich, West Midlands B70 7ST.
Telephone 0121-500 5678 fax 0121-553 6880

Calig Musik und Video Steinerne Furt 68-72, Augsburg 86167, *GERMANY*.
Telephone 49 821 7004 787 fax 49 821 7004 785

Capriccio Delta Music, Sailerbachstraße 16, 83115 Neubeuern, *GERMANY*.
Telephone 49 8035 1047 fax 49 8035 1049

Carlton Home Entertainment The Waterfront, Elstree Road, Elstree, Hertfordshire WD6 3BS.
Telephone 0181-207 6207 fax 0181-207 5789

CBC Records PO Box 500, Station A, Toronto, Ontario M5W 1E6, *CANADA*.
Telephone 1 416 205 3498 fax 1 416 205 2376

CBS Records *see under* Sony Music Entertainment

Chandos Records Chandos House, Commerce Way, Colchester, Essex CO2 8HQ.
Telephone 01206 225200 fax 01206 225201

Channel Classics Records Waaldijk 76, 4171 CG Herwijnen, *THE NETHERLANDS*.
Telephone 31 41858 1800 fax 31 41858 2475

Le Chant du Monde 31 Rue Vandrezanne, 75013 Paris, *FRANCE*.
Telephone 33 1 5380 0222 fax 33 1 5380 0225

Classical Passions PO Box 7, Oswestry, Shropshire SY10 9WF.
Telephone 01691 670750 fax 01691 670747

Classics for Pleasure EMI House, 43 Brook Green, London W6 7EF.
Telephone 0171-605 5000 fax 0171-605 5050

Claves Records Trüelweg 14, 3600 Thun, *SWITZERLAND*.
Telephone 41 33 223 1649 fax 41 33 222 8003

Collins Classics Premier House, 10 Greycoat Place, London SW1P 1SB.
Telephone 0171-222 1921 fax 0171-222 1926

The Complete Record Co. 12 Pepys Court, 84 The Chase, London SW4 0NF.
Telephone 0171-498 9666 fax 0171-498 1828

Conifer Classics Bedford House, 69-79 Fulham High Street, London SW6 3JW.
Telephone 0171-384 7500 fax 0171-384 7922

CPO Lübeckerstraße 9, 49124 Georgsmarienhütte, *GERMANY*.
Telephone 49 5401 8510 fax 49 5401 851 299

Da Capo (Marco Polo) Christianshavns Torv 2, 1410 Copenhagen K, *DENMARK*.
Telephone 45 32 960 602 fax 45 32 962 602

Danacord Records Nørregade 22, 1165 Copenhagen, *DENMARK*.
Telephone 45 33 151716 fax 45 33 121514

Decca Classics 22 St Peter's Square, London W6 9NW.
Telephone 0181-910 5000 fax 0181-810 3132

Delos International Hollywood and Vine Plaza, 1645 North Vine Street, Suite 340, Hollywood, California CA90028, *USA*.
Telephone 1 213 962 2626 fax 1 213 962 2636

Deutsche Grammophon 22 St Peter's Square, London W6 9NW.
Telephone 0181-910 5000 fax 0181-810 3132

Deutsche Harmonia Mundi BMG Classics Music, Kastenbauerstraße 2, 81677 München, *GERMANY*.
Telephone 49 89 41360 fax 49 89 4136160

DI Music 13 Bank Square, Wilmslow, Cheshire SK9 1AN.
Telephone 01625 549862 fax 01625 536101

Discovery Records The Old Church Mission Room, King's Corner, Pewsey, Wiltshire SN9 5BS.
Telephone 01672 563931 fax 01672 563934

Dynamic Via Mura Delle Chiappe 39, 16136
Genoa, *ITALY.*
Telephone 39 10 272 2884 fax 39 10 213 937

EMI Records Customer Services Dept,
64 Baker Street, London W1M 1DJ.
Telephone 0171-467 2100 fax 0171-467 2229

EMI Sales & Distribution Centre, Hermes
Close, Tachbrook Park, Leamington Spa,
Warwickshire CV34 6RP.
Telephone 01926 888888

Erato *FRANCE* 50 Rue des Tournelles,
75003 Paris.
Telephone 33 1 4027 7000 fax 33 1 4804 9543
UK The Warner Building, 28 Kensington
Church Street, London W8 4EP.
Telephone 0171-938 0167 fax 0171-938 3986

Etcetera Voorstraat 5, 2964 AH
Groot-Amners, *THE NETHERLANDS.*
Telephone 31 184 662 799 fax 31 184 662 040

Finlandia Lansituulentie 1, 2101 Espoo,
FINLAND.
Telephone 358 9 435 01 308 fax 358 9 455 2352
UK The Warner Building, 28 Kensington
Church Street, London W8 4EP.
Telephone 0171-938 0167 fax 0171-938 3986

Forlane 15 Rue de l'Ancienne Mairie, 92100
Boulogne Billancourt, *FRANCE.*
Telephone 33 1 4825 0217 fax 33 1 4603 2547

Hänssler Classic Postfach 12 20, 73762
Neuhausen, *GERMANY.*
Telephone 49 7158 1770 fax 49 7158 177119

Harmonia Mundi *UK* 19-21 Nile Street,
London N1 7LL.
Telephone 0171-253 0865 fax 0171-253 3237
FRANCE Mas de Vert, 13200 Arles.
Telephone 33 4 9049 9049 fax 33 4 9049 9614
USA 2037 Granville Avenue, Los Angeles,
CA90025-6103.
Telephone 1 310 478 1311 fax 1 310 996 1389

Hungaroton Nagy Jenö U 12, Budapest 1126,
HUNGARY.
Telephone 36 1 202 3188 fax 36 1 202 3794

Hyperion Records PO Box 25, Eltham,
London SE9 1AX.
Telephone 0181-294 1166 fax 0181-294 1161

Kingdom Records 61 Collier Street,
London N1 9BE.
Telephone 0171-713 7788 fax 0171-713 0099

Koch International *UK* Charlotte House,
87 Little Ealing Lane, London
W5 4EH.
Telephone 0181-832 1800 fax 0181-832 1808
USA 2 Tri-Harbor Court, Port Washington,
New York, 11050-4617.
Telephone 1 516 484 1000 fax 516 484 4746

Koch Schwann Lochhamerstraße 9,
82152 München-Martinsried,
GERMANY.
Telephone 49 89 857 950 fax 49 89 857 95100

L'Empreinte Digitale Domaine de la Garde,
13510 Eguilles, *FRANCE.*
Telephone 33 4 4233 3322 fax 33 4 4233 3324

L'Oiseau-Lyre 22 St Peter's Square,
London W6 9NW.
Telephone 0181-910 5000 fax 0181-910 3132

Lyrita 99 Green Lane, Burnham, Slough,
Bucks SL1 8EG.
Telephone 01628 604208

Marco Polo Select, 34a Holmethorpe Avenue,
Holmethorpe Estate, Redhill, Surrey
RH1 2NN.
Telephone 01737 760020 fax 01737 766316

MCI Presents 76 Dean Street, London
W1V 5HA.
Telephone 0171-396 8899 fax 0171-396 8903

Melodiya BMG Conifer UK, Bedford House,
69-79 Fulham High Street, London SW6 3JW.
Telephone 0171-384 7500 fax 0171-384 7922

MGB Musiques Suisses Postfach 266,
8031 Zürich, *SWITZERLAND.*
Telephone 41 1 277 2071 fax 41 1 277 2335

Multisonic Zirovnická 2389, 10632 Praha 10
CZECH REPUBLIC.
Telephone 420 2 6718 2112 fax 420 2 74 9295

Music and Arts Programs of America
PO Box 771, Berkeley, California
CA94701, *USA.*
Telephone 1 510 525 4583 fax 1 510 524 2111

MusicMasters 1710 Highway 35, Ocean,
NJ 07712-9885, *USA.*
Telephone 1 908 531 3375 fax 1 908 531 1505

Naxos Select, 34a Holmethorpe Avenue,
Holmethorpe Estate, Redhill, Surrey
RH1 2NN.
Telephone 01737 760020 fax 01737 766316

New World Records 701 Seventh Avenue,
7th Floor, New York, NY 10036, *USA.*
Telephone 1 212 302 0460 fax 1 212 944 1922

Newport Classic 1 Willow Street, Newport,
RI 02840, *USA.*
Telephone 1 401 848 2442 fax 1 401 848 0060

Nightingale Classics Nussdorferstraße 38,
1090 Wien, *AUSTRIA.*
Telephone 43 1 310 4017 fax 43 1 310 4967

Nimbus Records Wyastone Leys, Monmouth,
Gwent NP5 3SR.
Telephone 01600 890682 fax 01600 890779

NMC Francis House, Francis Street, London
SW1P 1DE. Telephone/fax 0171-828 3432

Nonesuch *USA* 75 Rockefeller Plaza,
New York NY 10019, *USA.*
Telephone 1 212 484 7200
UK The Warner Building, 28 Kensington
Church Street, London W8 4EP.
Telephone 0171-938 0167 fax 0171-938 3986

Nuova Era Records Corso Marconi, 39,
Torino 10125, *ITALY.*
Telephone 39 11 669 8903 fax 39 11 650 5613

Ondine Fredrikinkatu 77 A 2, 00100 Helsinki,
FINLAND.
Telephone 358 9 4342 2210 fax 358 9 493 956

Opera Rara 134-146 Curtain Road,
London EC2A 3AR.
Telephone 0171-613 2858 fax 0171-613 2261

Opus 111 37 Rue Blomet, 75015 Paris,
FRANCE.
Telephone 33 1 4567 3344 fax 33 1 4567 3388

Orfeo International Music Augustenstraße 79,
8000 München 2, *GERMANY.*
Telephone 49 89 5421360 fax 49 89 54213621

Parsifal Distribution 21-27 Seagrave Road,
London SW6 1RP.
Telephone 0171-381 1170 fax 0171-381 1172

Pavane Records 17 Rue Ravenstein, 1000
Bruxelles, *BELGIUM.*
Telephone 32 2 513 0965 fax 32 2 514 2194

Pavilion Records Sparrows Green, Wadhurst, East Sussex TN5 6SJ.
Telephone 01892 783591 fax 01892 784156

Philips Classics 22 St Peter's Square, London W6 9NW.
Telephone 0181-910 5000 fax 0181-910 3132

Pierre Verany 36, Avenue Hoche, 75008 Paris, *FRANCE.*
Telephone 33 1 4563 7670 fax 33 1 4563 7954

PolyGram Classics and Jazz
22 St Peter's Square, London W6 9NW.
Telephone 0181-910 5000 fax 0181-910 3132

PolyGram Record Operations PO Box 36, Clyde Works, Grove Road, Romford, Essex RM6 4QR.
Telephone 0181-910 1799 fax 0181-910 1675

Preiser Fischerstiege 9, 1010 Wien, *AUSTRIA.*
Telephone 43 1 553 6228 fax 43 1 553 4405

Priory Records Unit 9b, Upper Wingbury Courtyard, Wingrave, Nr. Aylesbury, Bucks HP22 4LW.
Telephone 01296 682255 fax 01296 682275

RCA Bedford House, 69-79 Fulham High Street, London SW6 3JW.
Telephone 0171-384 7500 fax 0171-384 7922

Seaford Music 24 Pevensey Road, Eastbourne, East Sussex BN21 3HP.
Telephone 01323 732553 fax 01323 417455

Select Music and Video Distributors
34a Holmethorpe Avenue, Holmethorpe Estate, Redhill, Surrey RH1 2NN.
Telephone 01737 760020 fax 01737 766316

Simax Akersgten 7, 0158 Oslo, *NORWAY.*
Telephone 47 2241 2400 fax 47 2241 5552

Sony Music Entertainment 10 Great Marlborough Street, London W1V 2LP.
Telephone 0171-911 8200 fax 0171-911 8600

Sony Music Operations Rabans Lane, Aylesbury, Buckinghamshire HP19 3RT.
Telephone 01296 395151 fax 01296 395551

Supraphon Palackého 1, 11299 Praha 1, *CZECH REPUBLIC.*
Telephone 420 2 24948782 fax 420 2 24 24948728

Tahra 1 Allée Georges Bizet, 95870 Bezons, *FRANCE.*
Telephone 33 1 3961 2690 fax 33 1 3961 1908

Target Records 23 Gardner Industrial Estate, Kent House Lane, Beckenham, Kent BR3 1QZ.
Telephone 0181-778 4040 fax 0181-676 9949

Telarc International 23307 Commerce Park Road, Cleveland, Ohio OH 44122, *USA.*
Telephone 1 216 464 2313 fax 1 216 464 4108

Teldec Classics The Warner Building, 28 Kensington Church Street, London W8 4EP.
Telephone 0171-938 0167 fax 0171-938 3986

TER Classics 107 Kentish Town Road, London NW1 8PD.
Telephone 0171-485 9593 fax 0171-485 2282

Testament 14 Tootswood Road, Bromley, Kent BR2 0PD.
Telephone 0181-464 5947 fax 0181-464 5352

Unicorn-Kanchana Records PO Box 339, London W8 7TJ.
Telephone 0171-727 3881 fax 0171-243 1701

Vanguard Classics Wildenborch 5, 1112 XB Diemen, *THE NETHERLANDS.*
Telephone 31 20 6603 7700 fax 31 20 6603 701

Virgin Classics *UK* 64 Baker Street, London W1M 1DJ.
Telephone 0171-467 2100 fax 0171-467 2229
FRANCE Rue Camille Desmoulins, BP 49, 92133 Issy-les Moulineaux Cedex.
Telephone 33 1 4629 2020 fax 33 1 4629 2155

Warner Classics (UK) The Warner Building, 28 Kensington Church Street, London W8 4EP.
Telephone 0171-938 0167 fax 0171-938 3986

Warner Vision 35-38 Portman Square, London W1H 0EU.
Telephone 0171-467 2524 fax 0171- 467 2564

Wergo Postfach 3640, 55026 Mainz, *GERMANY.*
Telephone 49 6131 2468967 fax 49 6131 246212

G

M

	Saturday	Sunday	Monday	Tuesday
6.00				
7.00		On Air		
8.00				
9.00		Brian Kay's Sunday Morning	Masterworks	
10.00	Record Review			
11.00			Artist of the Week	
		Artist of the Week Encore	Sound Stories	
12.00	Private Passions	Music Matters	Composer of the Week	
1.00	The Radio 3 Lunchtime Concert	The Radio 3 Lunchtime Concert	The Radio 3 Lunchtime Concert	
2.00	Vintage Years		The BBC Orchestras	
3.00		Spirit of the Age		
4.00	Young Musicians' Strand	100 Great Singers Centurions	Opera Series	Voices (rpt)
5.00	Jazz Record Requests	The Year	Music Machine	
6.00	Jazz Series	Sunday Feature	In Tune	
7.00		Private Passions (rpt)		
8.00	Opera on 3	Sunday Play	Performance on 3	
9.00				
10.00	Speech Strand	Choirworks	Postscript	
			Voices	BBC Orchestras
11.00			Mixing it	Night Waves
	Jazz on 3	World Music		
12.00		Record Review *Building a Library (rpt)*	Jazz Notes	
			Composer of the Week	
1.00		Through the Night		

Wednesday	Thursday	Friday	
			6.00
	On Air		**7.00**
			8.00
			9.00
	Masterworks		**10.00**
	Artist of the Week		**11.00**
	Sound Stories		
	Composer of the Week		**12.00**
	The Radio 3 Lunchtime Concert		**1.00**
			2.00
The BBC Orchestras		The BBC Archive	**3.00**
Choral Evensong	The Piano/ Ensemble(rpt)	Music Restored (rpt)	**4.00**
	Music Machine		**5.00**
	In Tune		**6.00**
			7.00
	Performance on 3		**8.00**
			9.00
	Postscript		**10.00**
The Piano/Ensemble	Music Restored	Hear and Now	
Night Waves			**11.00**
Jazz Notes		Jazz Series (rpt)	**12.00**
Composer of the Week			
Through the Night			**1.00**

Gramophone

Other titles from **Gramophone Publications**

Gramophone Classical Good CD Guide 1998 In association with B & W Loudspeakers
The new *Gramophone Classical Good CD Guide* recommends the best classical recordings currently available.
The Guide is compiled by our panel of reviewers, recognized as the world's most knowledgeable writers on
classical music. This eleventh edition is the largest and most comprehensive to date, with thousands of reviews
and additional recommendations. **£13·99**

Gramophone Jazz Good CD Guide, 2nd Edition In association with B & W Loudspeakers
The *Gramophone Jazz Good CD Guide* is the essential companion for those interested in buying the best jazz
performances currently available on CD. The Guide recommends the most representative recordings by every jazz
artist of significance, with a hand-picked team of 23 international experts. **£12·99**

Gramophone Musicals Good CD Guide, 2nd Edition In association with Naim Audio
Uniquely arranged by composer, with an additional section devoted entirely to singers, the *Gramophone
Musicals Good CD Guide* explores the glorious heritage of music theatre. The *Guide* features biographies of
featured composers and lyricists together with some 400 CD reviews of shows, films and recitals. **£9·95**

Gramophone Film Music Good CD Guide, 3rd Edition In association with Arcam
The *Gramophone Film Music Good CD Guide* explores the rich musical heritage of film music from its earliest days
to the very latest box-office hits. The Guide offers a unique perspective on the increasing popularity of soundtrack
albums and is, as described by Film Review, "an essential purchase for the serious soundtrack collector". **£9·95**

Gramophone explorations 2 Perspectives on Contemporary Music
Published in association with Unknown Public, the creative music quarterly
The second volume of *Gramophone explorations* focuses on the exciting diversity of contemporary music.
Gramophone explorations 2 contains interviews, articles, features and suggestions for further listening, drawing
not only on the classical tradition but also covering areas such as jazz, improvisation, electroacoustic music and
the avant-garde. **£4·95**

Gramophone: The first 75 years Edited by Anthony Pollard
To celebrate the 75th anniversary of the famous magazine, *Gramophone*'s publisher, Anthony Pollard, has
produced an illustrated history describing *Gramophone*'s development set against the evolution of the record
industry as seen through the pages of the magazine. This limited edition, hardback publication is filled with
documents and photographs from *Gramophone*'s extensive archive. **£29·95**

International Opera Collector
Edited by Michael Oliver
IOC is the only publication for the collector of opera recordings, past and present. It contains a judicious mix of
contemporary and historical articles and provides a forum for debate on issues of interest to the opera aficionado.
£16·00 (UK annual subscription price) **£4·50** (single copy)

International Classical Record Collector
Edited by Tully Potter
ICRC is the quarterly music magazine that covers all aspects of collecting classical music recordings from the
past, from cylinders and 78s to analogue LPs and historic reissues on CDs.
£16·00 (UK annual subscription price) **£4·50** (single copy)

International Piano Quarterly
Edited by Harriet Smith
IPQ is the only magazine to cover all aspects of the classical piano on record, both historic and contemporary. It
contains a lively mixture of artist features, record reviews, in-depth articles on specific works or genres and
discographical information. **£16·00** (UK annual subscription price) **£4·50** (single copy)

Gramophone magazine
With contributions from the world's most respected critics and reviews of around 200 new classical CDs every
month, *Gramophone* is recognised as the best classical music magazine in the world. It is published monthly and
is available with a complementary CD. **£47·40** (UK annual subscription) **£3·95** (single copy)

These publications are available through newsagents, bookshops and record stores, or direct from the publishers.
Gramophone Publications Limited 135 Greenford Road, Sudbury Hill, Harrow, Middlesex HA1 3YD,
Great Britain **Telephone** +44 (0)181-422 4562 **Fax** +44 (0)181 869 8400 **E-mail** info@gramophone.co.uk